Passing the Time in Ballymenone

Publications of the American Folklore Society
New Series
General Editor, Marta Weigle
Volume 4

Passing the Time in Ballymenone

CULTURE AND HISTORY

OF AN ULSTER COMMUNITY

Henry H. Glassie

Photographs and Drawings
by the Author

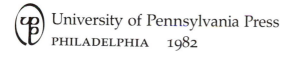 University of Pennsylvania Press
PHILADELPHIA   1982

First published 1982 in the United States by the
University of Pennsylvania Press, Philadelphia.

First published 1982 in Ireland and Britain by
The O'Brien Press Ltd., Dublin.

This work was published with the support
of the Haney Foundation.

Design by Dariel Mayer

Library of Congress Cataloging in Publication Data

Glassie, Henry H.
    Passing the time in Ballymenone.

    (Publications of the American Folklore Society)
    Includes bibliographical references and index.
    1. Ballymenone (Northern Ireland)—History.
2. Folklore—Northern Ireland—Ballymenone.
3. Folklore and history—Northern Ireland—
Ballymenone.   4. Ballymenone (Northern Ireland)—
Social life and customs.   I. Title.   II. Series.
DA995.B15C55   941.6'3   81-43515
ISBN 0-8122-7823-2   AACR2

Printed in the United States of America

for my father

Contents

Illustrations

PREFACE

Passing the Time in Ballymenone

Ballymenone is a small place of green hills, white homes, and brown bog, lying by Upper Lough Erne in the County Fermanagh, seven miles north and nine miles east of the border breaking Ireland.

Passing the time is what the people who live there say they are doing when they work by day—following the cows up the grassy damp slopes, sweeping their kitchens clean—and it is what they say they are doing when they fill the night's length with stories that hold the mind away from danger.

Passing the time is what they said I was doing when I worked beside them, sweaty on the meadows, asking too many questions about agricultural technology, and it is what they said I was doing when I recorded, again and again, every story they told.

Like theirs, my work passed the time, consoling me, testing me, and like theirs, my story made me think and tied me during its telling into a web of responsibility.

I owe my teachers, the people of Ballymenone, honesty and accuracy. I let their creations stand as they shaped them, but I accept more than their words and the works of their hands. I begin my tale with their categories, with night and day, ceiliing and farming, home, clay, moss, bog, talk, chat, and story, then push beyond, following their modes of reasoning to propose their world for contemplation within our own.

My responsibilities begin but do not end with my teachers. Ballymenone's people of the future will find here the texts they will need to understand their place, the texts they would have gathered themselves had they gotten the chance that I did.

To my colleagues in Ireland, North and South, I offer the startling richness of one small spot on their island, four square miles of undramatic landscape, and one man's effort to integrate the study of "material culture" and "oral literature," folklore and folklife.

Members of my own community of American scholars will find address to different problems within the traditions of folklore, history, anthropology, linguistics, geography, archaeology, art, architectural and literary history, but I cannot stop there. We must have some higher calling than destroying experience to consolidate our disciplines and advance our careers. At war with academic conventions, at peace with the gentle wisdom of old men, I have exploited the synthetic power of my discipline, folklore, to form a unified program for the study of human beings. Its base is the manifest reality of the individual, the society, and the world. Its thrust is that what we call folklore (or art or communication) is the central fact of what we call culture, and culture is the central fact of what we call history, and that people, as history's force, create the phenomena we study whatever name we give our discipline. We have one enterprise. We could call it historical ethnography or local history or folklore in context or the sociology of the creative act or the ecology of consciousness—the potential for flashy neologism seems boundless—but whatever its name, study is distorted and reality is mangled when disciplines harden into ideology, categories freeze into facts, and the sweet, terrible wholeness of life is dismembered for burial.

Rationally, study begins in division, in the acceptance of traditional economies, but if work is good, old categories will slip and shift, and then melt away as we find the place where social science joins the humanities, where art and culture and history, time and space, connect, where theoretical and empirical studies fuse.

No more prolegomena. No more anthologies. It is time to get on with our work. And we will know our work is good when we feel in it no roughness, no leaps between bogus "levels," no gaps between the particular and the universal, the real and the abstract, no disruptive jolts as we swing from fact to theory and back.

Good work is not the end of our task. Scholars are citizens, in debt to their society. Our study must push beyond things to meanings, and grope through meanings to values. Study must rise to perplex and stand to become part of a critical endeavor. We study others so their humanity will bring our own into awareness, so the future will be better than the past. The others I studied and choose to describe to you do not occupy some misty island from distant days. They live in a hard corner of the same world you and I inhabit. Money is scarce there, work is ceaseless. Their skies crack with storms and pound with bombs. Ulster. The sacred heart of their community has been split by political terror. Despite it all, they remain good people. We have much to learn from them.

Telling their story, my story, I must be responsible to readers with different interests and to people who helped me in different ways. Like Tristram Shandy, my aim is to write a good book. This is not an archive in book's clothing from which folklore items can be handily retrieved. My purpose is not to present forms for others to set in historic-geographic constructs, but to search through forms for meanings, which leads me to embed art in life's thickness. Still, I admire comparative research and, hoping others with different goals will find my work useful, I have set at the end a section entitled "Sources," where, chapter by chapter, major texts are given authors and dates, as well as comment and reference, so they can be connected to texts from other places.[1] This book is not an exercise, its strength is not orthodoxy or bibliography, but I have sprinkled numbers through it to refer you to the first section at the book's end, "Notes," where I set my findings in scholarly tradition and join my opinion to writings that have inspired me. But my debts to others are so great that I would not feel comfortable hiding them away at the back of the book. My major debts require voice here at the front.

My teachers in Ballymenone are real people. I would be unkind and ungrateful, and I would break with one of folklore's virtuous traditions, were I to murder them prematurely with anonymity or pseudonyms, so I will identify them properly and let them speak fully, returning to them some of the humanity they have given to me by serving as their historian. Many helped me, and you will meet them, but these must stand first: Michael Boyle, Ellen Cutler, Peter Flanagan, Hugh Nolan.

As a student and teacher in two of America's major folklore programs, I have been blessed with fine teachers and colleagues: MacEdward Leach, Tristram Coffin, Kenneth Goldstein, Don Yoder, Richard Dorson, Linda Dégh, Warren Roberts, Felix Oinas, Ilhan Başgöz, Dan Ben-Amos, John Szwed, Tom Burns, Barbara Kirshenblatt-Gimblett, Brian Sutton-Smith, Dell Hymes. Kenny Goldstein, my teacher and friend, wrote *A Guide for Field Workers in Folklore*. People have quibbled over its detail and extended its argument, but along with other books published at the same time by Roger Abrahams, Alan Dundes, and Edward Ives, it is a monument in the evolution of modern folklore study. First and last, what I think is best about my own work is that it answers the spirit of Kenny's guide.[2] Dick Dorson, my chairman at Indiana University, my friend today, helped keep my interest in history alive during a period when historical concern flagged in the discipline we share. This book, the presentation of a community's history by its own historians, expands easily into territory previously mapped in many of Dick Dorson's essays on the relation of folklore to history.[3] Linda Dégh, in *Folktales and Society*, struck the course that my book follows when I consider the connections between people, their stories, and culture.[4] Dan Ben-Amos' theories of genre have had a beneficial effect on modern folkloristic thinking, and one of my goals is to present, in Chapters 2 and 32, the full system of Ballymenone's native genres, responding to Dan's call for such work.[5] Dell Hymes, my neighbor and friend, is one of the great thinkers of our era. His influence on me is diverse, but most important his effort to create a social theory of language, his model of performance, has given me a way to describe storytelling in Ballymenone.[6]

Two anthropologists have drawn me into their studies of artifacts. James Deetz has shifted from American Indian pottery to Colonial American material culture without ever losing himself in things as things. To Jim, artifacts are evidence of social patterning and expressions of culture. My work is now happily intermixed with his. Together we are using old objects to discover our past.[7] Robert Plant Armstrong has not succumbed to the world of ease, but, contemplating the sculpture of the Yoruba people of West Africa, he has given us three wonderfully serious essays on the nature of art. Bob is also my dear friend, and his idea of the affecting presence, the work of immanent power, has moved me deeply.[8]

Two great geographers have taught me generously. Fred B. Kniffen, my first and best guide, directed me to the study of architecture and has, more than anyone, molded my intellectual life. His lucid writings, his concern for the people and their land, and his friendship will always carry me on.[9] When I was an undergraduate, Fred Kniffen introduced me to E. Estyn Evans, who has since played gracious host to me and my family in Belfast, where he listened to me talk about my work in Fermanagh and sent me back into the country excited. In his grand books on Ireland and in his superb geographic ethnography, *Mourne Country*, Estyn Evans has provided the largest frame within which I hope my book will become a contribution.[10]

By setting thanks to my friends here to the fore, I have given myself a way to avoid repetitive reference and state my program efficiently. In Ballymenone my task is to discover and record completely those rich and deep creations that correspond to Bob Armstrong's concept of affecting presence, then to site them within Dell Hymes' social model of performance, and then to site it within Estyn Evans' historical concept of geography. That is what makes my work folkloristic. I do not begin with floating wisps of fact which blow in our breath too easily, or with a preconceived, trim and bounded entity, subdivided by firm categories into which illustrative anecdotes can be crammed. I begin study with sturdy, fecund totalities created by the people themselves, whole statements, whole songs or houses or events, away from which life expands, toward which life orients in seeking maturity. I begin with texts, then weave contexts around them to make them meaningful, to make life comprehensible.

My debts run beyond my close friends. Irish scholars, some of them long dead, have eased my task.[11] One of the great delights that came in writing this book was reading the noble old historians Geoffrey Keating and the Four Masters. English historians and critics who have studied their past with purpose—W. G. Hoskins, E. P. Thompson, Christopher Hill, and Raymond Williams—have helped me keep my vision and hold to the hope of William Morris.[12] French thinkers have forced me to work with care and energy. By bearing down on his own projects so relentlessly, Claude Lévi-Strauss has driven me deeply into my own. If the method I use in this book to make its texts meaningful needs a name, structuralism is the best one.[13] Not only did Jean-Paul Sartre thrill me at an impressionable age, but his essays have continued to compel me into manhood, and if the guiding idea of this book needs a name, existential ethnography is as close as I can come.[14]

Help of other kinds has been crucial to my work. The John Simon Guggenheim Memorial Foundation provided funds for my first lengthy stay in Ballymenone. Subsequent trips became possible because I was named consultant to the Ulster-American Folk Park near Omagh in County Tyrone, and Eric Montgomery and Bob Oliver arranged trips to Northern Ireland for me. Grants from the National Endowment for the Humanities and the American Council of Learned Societies allowed me to pursue comparative research in a village in England, and, though mentioned only occasionally, that work helped refine my understanding of Ballymenone. Scholars in Ireland welcomed and directed me fruitfully: E. Estyn Evans, George Thompson, and Alan Gailey in Belfast; Seán Ó Súilleabháin, Caoimhín Ó Danachair, and Bo Almqvist in Dublin. Scholarly friends have kept me happy in my work: Roger Abrahams, Saki Bercovitch, Charles Bird, Ron Brunskill, Jan Brunvand, Bruce Buckley, Bob Cochran, Cece Conway, Lewis Dabney, James Marston Fitch, Allen Grimshaw, Bill Hansen, Lee Haring, Bernie Herman, Sandy Ives, John Kirk, Billy Lightfoot, Rusty Marshall, Jay Mechling, Elliott Oring, Barry Lee Pearson, Phil Peek, Jerry Pocius, Jules Prown, Ted Stebbins, John Vlach, Bill Wiggins, Bert Wilson, Terry Zug. Conversations with all of them over the years shaped thoughts that visited me as I wrote, and while I did, I talked constantly with my great friend Tom Burns, who was conducting a superb field study of urban black religion at the time. Our talks were always good; thanks especially to Tom. While I was serving as chairman of the Department of Folklore and Folklife at the University of Pennsylvania, Teresa Pyott lent me constant support and helped me steal the odd hour during which this book was written. I cannot transcribe music but wanted to include the melodies of certain songs. As usual, Kenny Goldstein came to my aid, helping me copy tapes that Julie Górka and Lore Silverberg used to transcribe the tunes you will find in the Sources. The fitful task of constructing a book out of a manuscript was made as smooth as it could be by Maurice English, the graceful and courageous editor of the University of Pennsylvania Press, and by the team the Press assembled: Malcolm Call, Dariel Mayer (who designed the book), Ingalill Hjelm, Lee Ann Draud, Warren Slesinger, Peggy Hoover (whose copyediting was sensitive and efficient), Marta Weigle (editor for the American Folklore Society who made several helpful suggestions), and John McGuigan. Knowledgeable editor and fine folklorist, John is my good friend who came with us once to Ballymenone and has returned since. Nanette Moloney McGuigan was more than the book's capable, embattled typist. She was its first critic, and, Irish herself, an enormous aid to its completion. Nanette put endless hours into a long manuscript, and, with John, she has been up the hill to P Flanagan's.

Friends in Ireland helped with important details. Séamas Ó Catháin not only secured copies of two texts for me from the marvelous archive at Belfield, where he serves as archivist, he conducted a seminar on place names over the breakfast table when he visited me in Philadelphia. Mr. P. J. O'Hare, editor of the *Fermanagh Herald*, encouraged me with an excellent review of my first book on Ballymenone, and he spent many hours searching through the files of his newspaper to help me with problems I had. Bryan Gallagher, headmaster of St. Aidan's High School, Derrylin, also took time to correspond with me, answering my questions.

Members of my family accompanied me on most of my trips to Fermanagh. Polly, Harry, and Lydia sat and listened, learned, and helped me continually by making me happy. Kathleen Foster not only sat with me by the hearths of Ballymenone, she gave my life joy and this book a careful reading, helping me to bring it nearer clarity at many points. It is nice to be, as I am, in love with an excellent writer and fine scholar, as Kathy is. My family, parents, and grandparents have always suffered my interests to expand freely. Once my father came with us to Ballymenone. For all those years, for being my friend, I dedicate my book to him. He nudged my youth softly toward an appreciation of history and beauty. He let me become myself while loving him.

Finally, this book is a matter of the simple relationship between the people of Ballymenone and myself.

I came up from the river bottom where I had been measuring the ruins of abandoned houses, getting a feel for the place, and above me, atop the muddy lane, a man swung his scythe beneath the gray sky. "That's bad weather," he said, when I stepped by him. Rainy winds blew across us. I agreed. "Aye, a bad summer," he said, "the worst," offering me a cigarette. We turned our backs on the wind from the west and made a tent of our jackets. I snapped matches through the wet until we were lit. We bent together against the wind, looking into a dripping dark hedge, talking. It was too wet to be at the hay, he said, so he was mowing the laneside to keep it tidy. Fire fizzled through damp paper and smoke whipped east. But the weeds can wait. He wrapped its blade in burlap and hooked his scythe over a tree's low limb. I followed him through a thorny gap, across a field, and down another into his warm kitchen, where he hung our sodden coats above the stove and got the kettle boiling. Creamy and sweet, hot tea and buttered bread and a stream of soft talk filled and warmed me. "You're rested now," he said, and I followed him back into the wind and to the hilltop, where he stood, shook my hand, and politely asked my name. I told him and asked his. "You will be home awhile now," he said, asking. I said I would. "Then you will come back to me," he said, wishing me God bless and bowing once more to swing the laneside free of weeds. Ballymenone is a place of endless wet and work, of great gentle hospitality, open and easy to enter.

An old country man and I were moving between pubs through a market throng in the town when a man of his generation grabbed his arm. It had been years since they had seen each other, and they laughed aloud to meet again. They stood close, touching, as the crowd bumped past, small men in caps and loose black suits. The man who had stopped us glanced through his round glasses at me, then spoke low, in rapid mumbles. "Do ye mind the time?" he began with a jab and a wink, and hurried chuckling through the tale of a time when they were lads, stacking hay on a bright sunny day. They had been taking a rest aloft when someone pointed up the road, gestured to a man below, and a hidden rifle was sent up. "Twas a lucky shot," he said, snorting a laugh and bobbing a nod. One shot and an English officer toppled from horseback, dead. "Ah, the poor creature," my companion said sadly, looking away. The lads scattered, never to be found, and, grown old, they stand now, while around them shoppers bustle and jostle happily down the street past freshly bombed-out homes. Echoes of explosions roll across the sheen of Lough Erne. Green-clad, well-armed young men from England prowl the back country lanes. Ballymenone is a place of ancient, constant tension, complex, impossible to know completely.

Shan Bullock, Fermanagh's novelist, wrote that he preferred the Catholics among his neighbors along Upper Lough Erne. They were gentler, wiser, more entertaining, more "lovable" than his fellow Protestants. Yet there was a reserve, some secret in them closed to him, and he could not get to know them well. Sean O'Faolain, writer from Cork, swept around Ireland to make a book out of his journey. In Ulster, his "great ambition" was meeting a real Orange Protestant, and he imagined such a man in Tyrone, north of Fermanagh, but O'Faolain was in a hurry and, though it did not stop him from generalizing about Protestant feelings, he got to know only his fellow Catholics during his trip through the North.[15]

Ballymenone is split, and no one could find both its sides equally easy to know, but I was lucky to be foreign enough to be removed from the local divisions, so I could meet everyone cordially, and yet I was not so alien as to be beyond welcome and intimate conversation. I have both Catholic and Protestant ancestors. Though raised a Protestant—and culturally still one I suppose—religion is not part of my life. I am not Irish, or even Irish-American; my ancestors are Irish, from both North and South, but they are English as well, and Scottish. Some in Ballymenone correctly recognized the Gaelic word for green within the Highland Scots name, Glassie. Between my second and third trips to Ballymenone, my great-uncle discovered that his family, my father's mother's family, the Cafferys, lived in Fermanagh near Enniskillen before joining the great sweep of early eighteenth-century migration from Ulster through Pennsylvania into the upland interior of the South. So, when a man I did not know met me in a pub in Enniskillen and asked me the usual question about my ancestry, I could say for the first time that some of my people came from his country. It was strange, I said, how I felt immediately comfortable in these low hills, made friends easily, and only later learned that some of my ancestors came from this very place. I would feel the same shock of comfort years later when I got to know the north Devon countryside that my mother's mother's people left early in the eighteenth century. My thought was that those first settlers sought familiar country, hilly and open, then turned it more familiar through work. I grew to feel at home in such surroundings, so when I returned to their home-land in Ulster and Devon, rolling green farmland like Pennsylvania and Virginia, I felt at once at ease. My drinking companion listened patiently to my story. Dogs, he said, are taken away and they always come back. Salmon return every year from the wide sea to the same mountain stream. If a fish can find its way home, he said, surely a man can.

He looked at me as if I were the most witless of fools, took a drink, and said, "Sure, a man can find his way home."

HENRY GLASSIE

PART ONE

A Territory of Wits

Upper Lough Erne

Cuilcagh and Benaughlin

The Arney River

Passing the Time in Ballymenone

Lumps on the Bog

Rooks on the Meadow

Summer

Winter

Cleenish Parish Church

Drumbargy

Gortdonaghy

Rossdoney

Sessiagh

Mrs. Cutler's

1

Crossing Drumbargy Brae

When I stood first on the road into Ballymenone, in July 1972, two problems pressed me forward. One was personal, mine, but by analogy yours as well. The other was traditional, ours, but by responsibility mine alone.

As a young professional I had published a paper that conformed to academic norms and dutifully cleared a patch of intellectual new ground, but it offended the man I wrote about and lost me a friend. Friends are worth more than books, but writing is my way to discover what I think. Unable to retreat from analytic writing, I turned from people to study their shadows on things, their projections into earth. Artifacts became my company. I could question aggressively, push, rip, criticize. Old houses remained placid and unconcerned. But artifacts gave me more than things to destroy and rebuild with words. They led me to history.[1]

From somber old barns and merry round pots, I learned how to expand history beyond the control of a prosperous, literate minority, and I learned a way to force the study of folklore past description. It is strange that in the name of science many folklorists have abandoned history for events they can observe, while many historians have abandoned folklore for facts they can count.[2] Without history, folklorists lack the means to explain what they see, and they are left to circle forever, refining and refining techniques of description. Without folklore, historians can find no alien mind in the constructs they build out of small facts, which become but mirrors, infinitely reflecting back to us our own worn visages.

Artifacts taught me that folklore and history are one subject, and they taught me much about the dead who left sad songs and broken houses as their legacy, but what I learned was too clear, too thin, fragmentary. I yearned for resistance, conversation, live guidance, a sense of the wholeness of another life so that I might better shape my own. So when I stood, in the midst of my coming, on the gray road into Ballymenone, my private goal was to study people, to probe and write and learn without harming anyone. There can be no questioning my wish to cause no pain, to atone for youthful misdeeds, but why study people? That is our problem.

A century ago William Morris understood.[3] If our experience is contained by the walls around us, we begin to mistake artifice for nature. Complacently, we accept preposterous conventions, dismiss our failings as life's fault, and lose the ability to separate the bad from the good. What is becomes what is right, and advancement becomes impossible.

Bravely we engineer programs out of abstractions, but since the abstractions were drawn from the smallness of our own experience, we are doomed merely to perfect our imperfections. Our need is for a sustained investigation of alternatives, a human science in service to morality.

This science will work by establishing a second center of experience distinct from our own. Around it facts will be built into a true portrait of another way of life so rich and complete it can stand on its own. If adequate the portrait will prove so powerful that we will come to respect the people it represents. We will not alter their arts. We will not meddle with their lives. If adequate it will challenge by its very integrity the validity of our own existence. Through comparison our culture will rise into awareness and disassemble; then we will draw an ellipse around two centers of equal power, and between those centers find a way to genuine improvement.

Scholars need energy to gather enough information to create full portraits. They need imagination to enter between facts, to feel what it is like to be, to think and act as another person. They need courage to face alternatives, comparing different experiences to help their fellows locate themselves.

For William Morris, alternatives lay backward in time. Studying old churches, finding them symbols of missing spirit, he learned respect for their creators and worked against the violence of restoration to protect and preserve them as they stood, unaltered, intact. He collected old manuscripts and incunabula, but he analyzed old books to make new books and studied the carved stone of ancient buildings and the taut line of skaldic verse to envision a new society. Looking backward, he laid the foundations of modern design and dreamed of a better society, but since his inspiration came from the past, his futuristic vision, so clear as to detect flaws in his own utopia, can be ignored, mocked as nostalgic by critics anxious to protect their portion while the world around them runs with blood.

Historical imagination seems to turn us from the future. The revolutionary act of preserving artifacts from the past that are better than those we produce is defused, diffused when preservation becomes a hobby for antiquarians. Old societies alienated from us by chronology become but academic curios, no challenge at all to the status quo. The outward search for alternatives can likewise die into thrills and souvenirs, but when the traveler is serious the quest through space leads through confrontation into culture, into fear, and it can prove trying, convincing, profoundly fruitful. The crucial experience for William Morris did not come while he was examining medieval artifacts or reading philosophical argument, but when he met real men in Iceland. From them he learned courage and took hope.

The reason to study people, to order experience into ethnography, is not to produce more entries for the central file or more trinkets for mi-lord's cabinet of curiosities. It is to stimulate thought, to assure us there are things we do not know, things we must know, things capable of unsettling the world we inhabit. The success of anthropology in the first half of our century proved that the great verities are beyond the grasp of middle-class intellectuals whose encloseted meditations can but spin endlessly into themselves. Only serious investigation of the human reality, in the highlands of New Guinea, the green hills of Ireland, the back alleys and boardrooms of our cities, can form the basis for rational and decent values.

Artifacts had carried me back, but I needed an outward venture to put things in their place, to let old houses do what they could and not more, to locate a new center of experience. My problem was to be scientific, compassionate, respectful; it was to create an ethnography strong enough to cause disquiet in my world, but gentle enough to cause no discomfort among the people I wrote about. There were other problems I did not have.

The landscape displayed no community. Before me, between tall hedges, a road lifted at a flat sky. Across the green, whitewashed houses scattered in no apparent pattern. The map folded in my rucksack had words on it but no clustering of dots to indicate a center of population, but I had to know the community. Our society, shifting (its critics say) from rugged individualism to frightened selfishness, needs information on how people form voluntary associations. Enacting our culture without a pause for thought, we study artists as individuals outside of their social scenes and delude ourselves into worthless theories of creativity. To help my profession and by extension my society, I wanted to study people as they grouped themselves through action, but I was not worried that I did not know where I was. Had there been a village with a name, I could have been misled, for I wanted to construct a community as the people who lived in it did, and there was no reason to assume their arena of action would match a territory on a map.[4] In no hurry, I was confident that one person would lead me to another. Connections would multiply and repeat. Eventually I would be able to drape the net of their social motion over a map of their place.

I knew nothing about the community and I had no hypothesis. Time for study is limited, not everything can be recorded, and erecting a proposal to test helps guide what to record. Before coming to Ireland, I had tortured myself through a meditation on hypotheses. Experience taught that they were not necessary, but I found sociological arguments to the contrary convincing. Study without hypotheses, and you might reach no conclusion. Or you might come to any conclusion with no means for its evaluation. But these are caveats inappropriately imported from natural to social science.[5] Culture is not a problem with a solution. There are no conclusions. Studying people involves refining understanding, not achieving final proof. Perhaps if you observe people as though they were planets or orchids, proceeding without hypotheses is foolhardy, but that was not my intention.

Ethnography is interaction, collaboration. What it demands is not hypotheses, which may unnaturally close study down, obscuring the integrity of the other, but the ability to converse intimately. It is vain to attempt ethnography without a knowledge of the language of daily life, and I expect much fancy theorizing about "unconscious mind" to be but compensation for an inability to ask and have answered a complicated question. English is the language of Northern Ireland. Using it, I would be able to find the community's wise speakers, and while scanning broadly to test their generalizations, I would let them guide me. They know.

They will not have the culture reduced to a formula, ready to hand over, but the community will include people who can turn interviews into conversations, who can present its significant texts. These will not take the shape of philosophical treatises, and they may not even be verbal. They will emerge as recurrent actions recognized to compress most richly the essence of right thinking. By recording them exactly I will have a base for study, created not by me but by them. I might interpret incorrectly, but the data will be inviolably right, and science will be served. The community's thinkers will point me to the key texts around which the rest of life will spread as context. I must be patient.

Years later I entered an English village. My Irish experience prepared me to attend to stories and farming practices. I heard stories, people farmed, but within a couple of months I was listening to bells. I had not planned to study call-change ringing—I had never heard of it—but once I settled in I found that was where the community had its intensity banked: in the ringing chamber, under the great bells of an ancient church tower.

What I would study did not worry me. People would direct me to one another. Among them I would locate teachers who could suggest texts to analyze. The community would appear, hypotheses would grow naturally out of experience. What did concern me was comparability.

Asking for comparability, I do not ask for the culture to be rolled flat and cut into bits to compare with other bits from other cultures, but that the culture as a whole must come out looking like a human product. Then it can be compared with others to scientific ends, and it can be compared with our own to keep us from drowning in vanity.

Of all the techniques devised within the academy to prevent comparison by making people seem less or more than human, errors traditional to two disciplines that have concerned themselves with people in small country places most concerned me when I was on the road to Ballymenone.

Historians often exalt leaders into angels, aflutter on wings of free will, then denegrate most people into plodding dumb beasts, brutes of conditions, followers who can do no more than take orders. Folklorists celebrate the individuals stewed into masses by conventional historians, but they disregard conditions to concentrate on exceptional moments, little instants of freedom and escape. While the historian sees peasants as oppressed, grease for the economic system, meat for the battlefield, the folklorist sees them as singers and dancers. Either way, country people seem weak or silly, hardly a challenge to us.

Human beings are defined neither by conditions nor by moments of escape. Wishing for frightening comparability, I want to see people as they are: free and stuck in the world. My interest is in the constant interplay of will and circumstance, so I care less about the rare celebration than about the daily round, and I care less about form than about content. I am concerned less with the structure of society than with the quality of social life, less with the economic system than with the nature of work, less with genres of literature than with the meaning in texts. I ask not how people fit into the plots of others but how they form their own lives, not what people do once in a while but what they do all the time.

My task was not to write another ethnography, but to write accurately and usefully about the workaday reality of other people. I wanted to know how people who share my world make it despite boredom and terror. Northern Ireland was a good choice.

Life's larger conditions loomed monstrous in Ulster. I could not possibly lapse into some vision of country people as jolly, colorful singers, nor would I be able to break them out of history, confining their culture in timeless circularity; they could not be portrayed as unaware, mere beasts. Journalists may repeat one another, describing the situation in Northern Ireland as an anachronistic religious squabble, but it is dreadfully part of our era. The political solution of partition was pioneered in Britain's first colony, and the variety of economic-cultural conflict that rages in Ireland will continue to erupt in small countries, once colonies, for the rest of our days.

I was in Northern Ireland to create an ethnography that would avoid common error by facing the commonplace. It did not matter where in Northern Ireland, as long as it lay near the Border and included both Catholics and Protestants, so I was in County Fermanagh because colleagues in Belfast and Dublin said they knew little about Fermanagh, and while my own problems guided me, I wished to contribute as well to the quite different native program of folklore research. And I was in this part of Fermanagh because it pleased me.

Green small hills swelled around me, split by tree-lined hedges, and before me rose a gray-blue road. There was nothing to be done, no excuse for delay. I let it take me up, then paused at its crest. To my right, a river glinted through the trees. My map called it Arney and indicated that after swinging south it would curve northeast to end like my road at Upper Lough Erne. An account written in 1700 called this area "wild," saying it was "scarce inhabited by any human creatures but ye O's and ye Mac's, who pillaged all that comes in their way, robbing the whole country," and concluded that "it was ye common Proverb of ye Northern part of ye Country to express a thing irrecoverably lost—'It's got beyond the Arnoy.'"[6] The Arney gleamed in flashes; the land could not have looked gentler, less wild, more inviting.

"A maze of woody islands" slipped past Arthur Young when he came to Fermanagh in 1776, rowing across Upper Lough Erne to describe this as a place of "wet tenacious clay," mostly under grazing, broken into small farms where people work "with spades they call loys" and subsist on potatoes, milk, and oat bread. After visiting Lough Erne about sixty years later, Mr. and Mrs. S. C. Hall wrote: "Both lakes are richly studded with islands, mostly wooded, and in many places so thickly clustered together as to present the appearance of a country accidentally flooded; . . . and it may be easily conceived that two sheets of water so enriched, and circled by shores finely undulating, to a great extent richly wooded, and backed on most points by mountains of considerable elevation, must possess the elements of beauty to a remarkable degree." At the end of the last century, Lough Erne's native novelist, Shan Bullock of Crom, wrote, "Our lake had the sinister look of a flood that had submerged a forest region; very often, indeed, it was a true flood, creeping up under everlasting rains to the foot of the hills, destroying crops and fuel, making roads impassable, leaving a precious deposit on meadow land that made the haycocks thicker when summer came again." Away from Lough Erne, through Fermanagh country like this, wrote Bullock, for miles "towards the Mountain were countless holdings, none of them more than forty acres in size, most of them much less, all of a pattern, cut into small fields by criss-cross hedges, and somewhere on each a small white house . . . hundreds, perhaps thousands, of holdings, each dependent and contributory, all pouring in rents, this half-year, next half-year, every half-year, as a matter of course and legalised custom, possibly after much struggling on the part of those paying, but with little effort on the part of those receiving other than was needed to sit at a desk in the agent's office and give receipts for money down." Since Shan Bullock's youth, the rampaging Lough has been tamed, the tenants have become proprietors, but the look of the land, soft, hushed, and dotted over with white houses, remains as he described.[7] Standing upon a gentle rise with the damp green around me, I could not imagine a loud noise disrupting the quiet that spread thickly and liquidly between the low rounded hills.

Surveys in our century have termed this land bad and poorly drained and described its people as mostly Catholic, unprosperous farmers dependent upon cattle of rough grade.[8] I stood, surrounded by lush small fields, trim hedges, a landscape under control, covered by the cool scent of distant water. Then I turned down to meet a ruined old house by the roadside. Camera, tape measure, and notebook appeared, detailed plans grew across paper. Then, damning myself for delay, for doing what I knew how to do, I pushed on.

To my left, a low ridge ascended. Above it poked the gable of a house. Light smoke played from its roof, and I forced myself through the first opening in the hedge, reclosing it with a dead branch, slipped up a wet field, scattering its cows, fumbled along the next hedge, scratched through, stumbled into a drain, mucked my way up another field, skirting its bull, tore through more thorn, and stood finally atop the hill in front of the house. In front of it too stood a compact, handsome man in a black suit holding a rosary in both hands before his breast. He said I looked tired and invited me in, quietly introducing himself and the small man who sat in a big chair by the fire. They were two old brothers, he said, who lived on their lone. He was Peter, his brother was Joseph, they were Flanagan, and he apologized for the accommodations, gracefully placing a stool for me at the hearth between them.

Long after, once we had ceased mistaking each other for representatives of different nationalities, Peter would say I had scared them. I was too tall and they could not identify my accent. People who emigrate from here to America go to the Bronx. They return with Yankee accents. I said I was American, but they guessed my speech for Scots. I told them why I was in Ireland, but they guessed I was a detective. We talked about the weather.

Even after I spotted two violin cases leaning in a corner and began a conversation about music, what I said made no sense. Mr. Flanagan said he liked all music, though really the old Irish music was the only kind that was any good. He asked what kind of music I liked, and in the midst of an endless answer that twisted and qualified itself into nothing, I mentioned "Soldier's Joy," by chance the only tune to appear both in the Southern Appalachian fiddling repertory I knew well and the local one I did not. That made a little sense.

Cordially, our conversation staggered forward through the topics of high prices and the cold, wet summer, "the worst season ever there was," said Joseph. Then at my second request, Peter rose slowly, formally, apologized for being out of practice, lifted the bow suavely and splashed it into the strings, sending a torrent of notes, a wild cascade, through the room. Music rushed, flowing, swirling, breaking to the edge, perhaps over, then it was quiet again. Joseph smiled softly. "You are satisfied now," Peter said. Backlit curls sparkled around his head. The shirt, buttoned neatly to his throat, gleamed white beneath his smile. My enthusiasm gushed, and though he would tell me later that my words seemed still to lack reason, they appeared sincere. The fiddle sang again, then the tin whistle. Tunes and time passed, the conversation cracked, and we were laughing. I was the plainest, best gentleman ever to come out of America. He was the greatest musician since Michael Coleman. We were shaking hands over the stones sunk in the clay before his doorway. They apologized for the poorness of the entertainment. I protested I had never been entertained so well and promised to return in two days, on Sunday, so we could get his music on tape and go out for some drinks. "God bless," they wished me, and Peter, called P, showed me the way across the pasture to the lane leading smoothly down from their place, Drumbargy, to the road I came in on, the Rossdoney Lane. I was off.

Soon I met Rose Murphy on another road, and Hugh Patrick Owens in

Peter Flanagan, July 1972

the bog, and Hugh Nolan, and he sent me to Ellen Cutler, and everyone told me to visit Michael Boyle in the hospital, for "Michael was very entertainin when he was at himself, so he was."

Half a year later, having come around the back way by the bog pass, I climbed an old carttrack up Drumbargy Brae and was stopped by the sweet smell of turfsmoke, a puff borne along the hill from the Flanagans' chimney. I pictured their hearth and turned, looking downhill to the flat brown bog, across to the green hills, their cows in gentle motion and houses glowing in low sharp light. I knew all their inhabitants and understood the community.

To the world, they live in Ireland, to Ireland they live in the North, to the North they live in Fermanagh. They use three kinds of spatial division smaller than the county to locate themselves more exactly.

Smallest and most important is the "townland," an official division entered on maps, in records, used by the post office and police for addresses. Townlands vary in size, containing two to fifteen households, and the terrain shoves them into odd shapes, but all are as small as they can be and still afford their inhabitants all the kinds of dirt necessary to life, and they are conceptually circular. Grassy upland rises in the middle of each, where houses are built, cows graze, and hay grows. Around the perimeter spreads bog, where turf is cut for fuel. Between bog and upland, a ring of moss ground bears gardens, and through the bog run drains to separate townlands from each other. Some townlands are grouped into unofficial, unmapped "districts," all are contained in parishes.

Cleenish is their parish, named for an island two miles north of the mouth of the Arney in Upper Lough Erne where Saint Sinell, student of Finnian of Clonard, established a monastery in the sixth century. They call their area the Lower End of the Parish. It is bounded on the south by the Arney, on the east by Lough Erne, on the north by the Back Road and the Chapel Road, on the west by the Swad Road. But boundaries are less important than centers. There are two large, predominantly Catholic centers— the district of Ballymenone on the east, the townland of Sessiagh on the west—oriented toward the Arney Cross with its chapel, school, store, and pair of public houses. Between and west of them are two smaller, predominantly Protestant centers, oriented toward the Bellanaleck Cross with its store, Orange Hall, and little Church of Ireland church, its tilting tower pinnacled in Georgian Gothic style. People shop at the store nearest them, and without any hint of religious-political commitment identify themselves when away from home as coming from about Arney or Bellanaleck.

The Lower End of the Parish is a place on the land and in the mind, but when I asked people about their kin and their movements, when I accompanied them working by day and socializing by night, I found that the constellation of households created by common action did not match a corner of the parish. People living on major routes formed associations along the road, while those living on smaller lanes followed the natural grain of the land along the Arney River. Ballymenone's center shifted southward

Fermanagh in Ireland

The Lower End of the Parish in Fermanagh

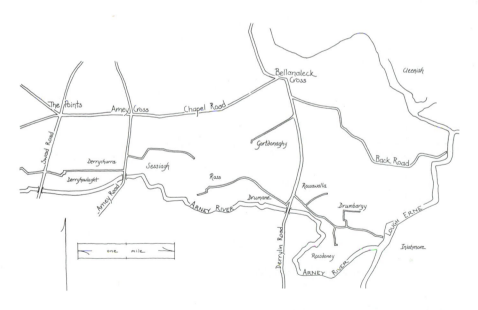

Townlands of the Community

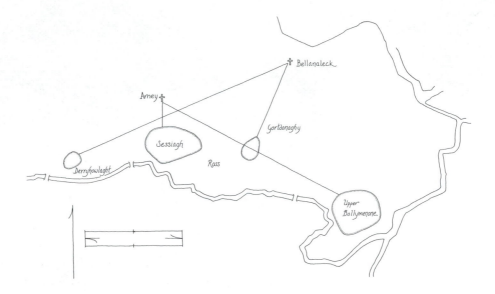

Centers of Population

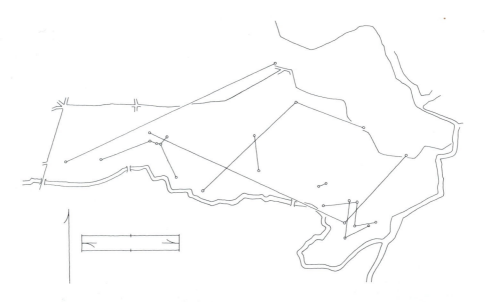

Kin. Connections among close relations.

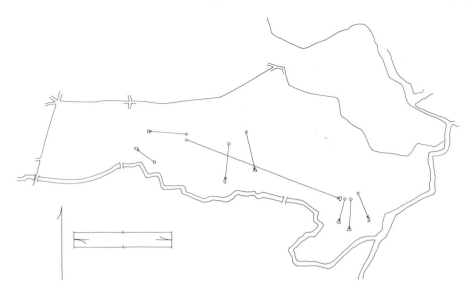

Movements. Movement of individuals from one home to another during the current generation.

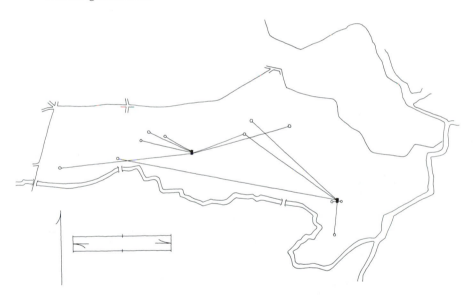

Work. The houses—in black—of two workers, one a tradesman, the other a farm laborer, and their clients.

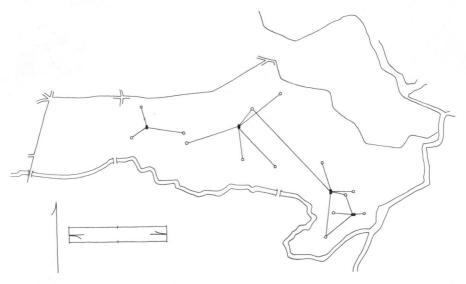

Ceiliing. Customary patterns of night-visiting to four houses.

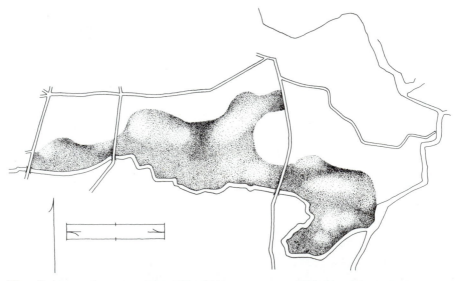

The Community. The shape of the community, "our district of the country," shaded to indicate topography.

Enumeration of the Community's Households

HOUSEHOLD	PROTESTANT	CATHOLIC	FARMING	FARM AND JOB	NON-FARMING
Couple with young children	4	5	3	5	1
Couple with young children and widowed mother		1	1		
Couple with grown, unmarried children		7	4	3	
Couple with married daughter, her husband and child		1		1	
Elderly man with daughter and grandchild		1		1	
Elderly couple with no children at home	2		2		
Elderly mother with middle-aged son		2		1	1
Elderly widow	1	1			
Middle-aged unmarried man		2	1	1	
Elderly unmarried brother and sister	1	5	4	2	
Elderly unmarried brothers		4	3	1	
Elderly unmarried man	1	4	4	1	
Total	9	33	24	14	2

into Upper Ballymenone, the townlands of Drumbargy and Rossdoney, and sent its ties westward, leaping road and bog, to Sessiagh.

Their community is a matter of constant negotiation, always shifting, sometimes radically. They call their place "the locality" or "our district of the country." It is real, but no permanent name can contain it precisely, so, playing free with their words, I will call it the District or use the folk name Ballymenone loosely.[9]

In 1972 (this book's present) the community had forty-two households. They are numbered easily, but the population is elusive because children who have left home often return for extended periods to help with the farmwork, and some do not leave again. The total 129 is about right. Religion is clear—thirty-three households are Catholic, nine are Protestant—but economics are not. Only two households gain no living from the land. Twenty-four depend primarily on farming. The others draw livelihood about equally from farmwork and jobs with the County Council or in factories and shops in towns, but occasional employment, generally of a family member other than the farm's "boss," and a decent system of subsidy, grant, and pension bring cash from beyond the fields into all homes.

Connections beyond the community do not melt away equally in every direction. Social affinities are strongest to Inishmore, east across a strip of the lake, and to the districts of Mackan, Montiagh, Derrylin, and Kinawley, running south-southwest to Swanlinbar beyond the Border. They call it "Swad" (early eighteenth-century sources spell it as they pronounce it, "Swadlinbar"[10]), and they get there for drinks and sport on Sunday nights when public houses are closed in the North and the best singers and musicians come out of their small rural communities along the Cavan-Fermanagh border to form a casual parliament of artists in the pubs of Swad. Commercially and administratively, Ballymenone is pulled five miles northward to "the Town," Enniskillen, county town of Fermanagh, set on an island between Upper and Lower Lough Erne. The population in 1971 was only 6,553, but the feel of the Town is thick and urban.[11] Its long main street, busy with shops and pubs, curves from the cattle mart on the east, across the bridge by the Orange Hall, past the Court House, Town Hall, churches, and cathedral, to exit over the western bridge between the gray stone Water Gate and the clean neoclassical bulk of the old barracks, sandbagged and bound by barbed wire.

Confidently, I lingered on the hillside, the fragrance of turfsmoke around me. Across the grass the red metal roof from which the smoke blew touched me with familiarity. I would spend the night, my last in Ireland, with P and Joe. The day before, a chat with Michael Boyle had been squeezed between visiting hours. He was up, dressed, ready to go home. The conversations we recorded, he said, had done him more good than the doctors' medications. That evening had been charmed by Mrs. Cutler, filled with wit and tasty food. Now I was on my way to see Hugh Nolan. I would turn, cross the brae through the trees, and descend Drumbargy Lane to make tea for him while he put on tape a few stories he had artfully worked into the conversation when the crowd gathered at his hearth a few nights past. I knew the community and had found its speakers. Tomorrow I would return to the States with twenty-four reels of tape, 2,192 photographs, 2,387 pages of notes, and my problems unsolved.

I had missed the center. During the next year I freed the folklorist within to write about Christmas mumming, a comical little play of death and resurrection performed from kitchen to kitchen when the year turned black. Once it had been a bright spot, a high point in the year. By discussing mumming and all it drew to it, the Great Days and Set Times, gay moments of festivity, I planned to cut away the exceptional and find the commonplace.[12] When 1973 ended and 1974 began, I was back in Ireland, the first draft of a book complete, with questions prepared to polish it off. Peter Flanagan had played Miss Funny, treasurer of the mumming squad. He was gentle and generous. We got the questions behind us. Michael Boyle had played the Doctor, the fullest, funniest role. He had been out of the hospital and worked at the hay, but he lay now, stilled, thin, the light gone from his eyes. "Is that me Yankee friend?" he asked, his hand on mine. My questions dissolved. We tried to smoke and talk as we had in the past. Soon Hugh Nolan would write me of his death on January 24, 1974.

March 1976: The book was out. I had sent copies ahead, but there had been no time for replies, and after a shallow, fretful sleep in a cold room in a small hotel in Enniskillen, I walked rapidly out of the Town. Changes met me. Tin had replaced thatch. The main road had been leveled and widened. Electricity had stalked on poles into Ballymenone. But there was no change in my welcome. "The book is great," P said, and when a neighbor interrupted our reunion with a request for a lock of plants, the book, wrapped in paper, was brought down to the kitchen and he was forced to take it and talk. "That's a quare book," he said, turning its pages, thinking about cabbage, leafing slowly from back to front until he came to the portrait that began it. "That man looks like Wee Joe," he said. "It is," P said impatiently, "it is ourselves." And then he revealed that I was the author and that the book told "the whole of the ould mummin."

"I love me book," Mrs. Cutler said when I entered her kitchen. All that "annoyed" her was people in the east of Ulster who call potato bread "fadge" when fadge is really soda bread. She had memorized passages out of it and recited them when we chanced to arrange ourselves into the book's scenes. Sitting in her big chair by the fire, she said, "She sits in her big chair by the fire. She has a lovely smile. . . . Do I, dear?" At that she would laugh, then smile. She does.

The book was not entirely harmless. I consigned its royalties to my teachers in the District (as I have again with this one; less is unimaginable), and some jealous talk rose among the neighbors who had overestimated

Enniskillen

Passing the Time in Ballymenone

the profits scholarly books bring. But my teachers were planning the next book before I was, and their letters keep me at it. One problem down: I had written and lost no friends.

Encouraged, its way cleared of distracting exceptions, my thought became direct. Common days break into light and dark. While the sun shines, they work. When night falls, they assemble in the kitchen and talk. The nighttime gathering of neighbors is called a ceili (pronounced kaylee). Its center is held by stories.

I had not come to Ireland to record stories, nor had I concentrated on them during my first visit, but the more I considered my experience and read through my notes, the more stories consolidated their centrality. It is not the folktale as a category of oral literature that claims such significance, but those stories adults who know one another tie into the conversation when they face the long night together. As I thought about stories, life began to arrange itself around them as context.

Context is not a difficult notion. But loose colloquial use can trick us into employing "context" to mean no more than situation. Then the power of the idea evaporates, and studying context we enlarge and complicate the object we describe but come little closer to understanding than we did when we folklorists recorded texts in isolation. Context is not in the eye of the beholder, but in the mind of the creator. Some of context is drawn in from the immediate situation, but more is drawn from memory. It is present, but invisible, inaudible. Contexts are mental associations woven around texts during performance to shape and complete them, to give them meaning.

Meaning is a difficult concept, for it means too much. Meaning begins in the correspondence of sensate form to invisible idea, logically links intention and response, then expands through private association to join all a thing is with all it can be in the minds of its creators and perceivers. Finally, meaning carries through the shared experience of form and idea to philosophical bedrock. Most crucially, meaning is that which joins people through things, transforming forms into values, values into forms. Understanding values is the purpose of study.

The tale in the ceili is central, situationally, contextually, philosophically. It emerges in the middle of the nighttime's conversations. It draws widely from life to make itself meaningful. Its meanings lead into confrontation with fundamental values.

When I went to Ireland next, in June 1977, I felt I had located the culture's key texts, and stories were our topic. I came to stories from ceilis, from their situation, rather than the other way around, and that was good, for I knew how they fit their scene, and I knew I was dealing with tales that were alive and throbbing with importance. They could lead me into the culture.[13] But I had happened on them as they were told and had returned to record only those I heard first in ceilis as part of a general program of interview. Though recording sessions usually led to new tales, I could have missed whole classes of narration. Fragments of repertories can be made meaningful, but since stories provide contexts for each other, only the entire repertory can be followed properly into culture, into the deep structure of values. So I asked questions about what stories are and how they are classified, and when I showed up again in August 1978, not only did I have the texts of 231 stories, mostly taken verbatim from tape, but many were the same story in different renditions by the same and different tellers, and I was confident I had the community's corpus of ceili tales. I did not know every story. Mr. Nolan told me six during that visit, and one was new to me—the origin myth of the bicycle. But all I heard confirmed the patterns emerging in my book's early chapters.

This book was blocked out and mostly written by the time of my latest trip to Ireland in December 1979. While Christmas came without mummers, and black winds broke over the hills, I sat quietly with Peter Flanagan, Ellen Cutler, and Hugh Nolan, asking them what they thought of the ideas in this book.

When the people of Ballymenone tell stories, they say what they know to discover what they think. My writing is the same. I learned why—though the enterprise of the folklorist should be to record, present, and analyze a community's complete works—that is not the discipline's norm. It takes too long and the result cannot fit into one volume. So I began with historical stories because they are rich and because Peter Flanagan said "the old history" would make the best topic for my next book. Tales of mystery and comedy are left to the future. More important, I learned that the reason I could concentrate on stories was that I had come to an understanding of the whole of daily life first. Once I tried to present stories as alone occupying the cultural center, I found it necessary to double my task and tell about the day as well as the night.

Day and night are different experiences. Each is a situation, each has a memory, a history. These connect into a culture that complexly traps people, forcing them into awareness, into courage, into action.

Night's stories remain one entrance to the culture. We begin on the road into Ballymenone by seeing how stories fit together into a system constructed by those who tell the tales.

2

Silence, Speech, Story, Song

"The tongue," said Peter Flanagan, man of words, "is the worst instrument attached to the human being. It's the most destructful on the soul.

"I don't know what the situation is with any other nationality, but the Holy Island is the worst now. There's alot of people that find alot of faults in even their neighbors. They criticize, reject and despise, dishonor.

"A man can keep to the rules of God and still they will sit and criticize him. They pass their own opinion.

"It's all due to ignorance. I suppose God will forgive them. But.

"That's the fault I find. The tongue is the worst instrument of the body. It's a real danger.

"It smashes the whole community up.

"And when word comes back to you it often puts you into despair. It often caused destruction. It often caused murder. It often caused hanging. It often caused imprisonment.

"It's all be the tongue."

It is a virtue to be "quiet." The quiet person avoids bad talk and attracts the adjectives of good weather: calm, mild, settled. Like calm days, calm people bring no trouble to those living around them. They are "harmless."

To be quiet is not to be silent. People sitting wordlessly cannot help but think. Thinking cannot help but make them sad, for the world is hard, life is short. As the mind drops into sadness, the soul is drawn toward despair, and despair pulls the body out of connection, snapping the bonds of obligation that bind people together, sucking the soul toward damnation. Silence is not harmless. It brings disengagement. As surely as the evil tongue, silence threatens the destruction of the self and the community.

"Quiet" is engaged, gently, harmlessly. But harmless is not "good," is not in itself a positive act. "Not everyone can be good," Peter Flanagan said, "but they don't have to be Hitler or Oliver Cromwell either." The common proverb is "If you can't do good, at least do no harm." It is not enough to be quiet, harmless. The goodness under quiet needs demonstration, and that comes when mild energy is made into a gift. Quiet work—weeding the spuds in the garden, drawing tea at the hearth—produces food, then food is given as a sign of goodness. The gift of food is called "entertainment."

Entertainment is also a name for speech—not all speech, but that which does the work of food: gathering personal energy into a gift to others which pleases them in the moment, then carries them on to further life.

"Talk" is not enough. Michael Boyle told of a man who would not converse with his bride. He sat in silence, gazing into the fire, and she complained to her father. When a friend asked how he liked his new son-in-law, he replied, "Ah, he's all right. He's all wrong. There's not a word on him but the cow, the calf, and the doughal."

Talk about cattle and dunghills and talk about the weather is necessary in an agricultural world, but alone it is not pleasing, not beneficial, not entertaining.

"That's the thing," Peter Flanagan continued, "when the mouth's open, you must give it a wee consideration what you're sayin. And if it's beneficial in any way or respect—that's great.

"Entertainment is the greatest thing."

Talk begins to entertain when it pushes past greetings and isolated comments, when it pulls people out of dangerous silence and brings everyone into conversation. Then it is "chat." Chat worth calling entertaining is informational or "witty," and when wit snaps dialogue forward it becomes "crack." Especially "entertainin chatty" people are called "great crack." They might sound like they "swallowed the dictionary," they might "blether" you to distraction, but they are always better than the man "that hasn't a word to throw at a dog." At their best, these are the men and women capable of pulsing chat through "turns," surprising shifts clearly tied to the group's topic but leading adventuresomely and interestingly into new areas, into engagement and excitement.

Cracking, turning chat ends in "bids," followed not by the topic's elaboration but by compliments to the speaker's wit: "Ah now, that's really good." A bid is not a "sayin," a conventional summary, a proverb. The wisdom of sayins is credited broadly, their wit is undermined by introductory clauses: "As they say . . . ," "As you have often heard it said . . . ," "They do have a sayin in this country, When you're down, down with ye." The bid is clever and condensed, like the sayin, but it is original, personal, risky, an offer of private capital like the bid in a card game or auction.

Bids end conversations by framing a thought precisely and poetically or by exaggerating the topic to a humorous limit no one else can reach. The bid's tendencies perfect themselves in verbal action beyond talk, in poems and stories. Neither are chat. Both are more beautiful, more richly entertaining, and both are the primary responsibility of one person at a time.

"Poems" scan, often freely, and rhyme, often lavishly. Poems are highest when riding "airs" as song. The melody of song is refined into music, the ultimate entertainment, wordless, incapable of harm, good. Music serves the ear and spirit as food serves the tongue and body.

Ballymenone's old mummers' play displayed the progress of entertainment. It began with a greeting to break the disjunction of silence, cracked through a comical poetry of conflict and exaggeration, and concluded in a tune to which men, disguised beyond personal identity, danced identically in wordless accord. Their play over, the mummers were repaid by the quiet audience with food and drink. Different kinds of entertainment had been traded.

The shape of Ballymenone's concept of sound can be imagined as a terraced sequence leading upward from silence to music and from separation to social accord. Silence, talk, chat, crack, story, poetry, song, music: with each step, entertainment increases, sound becomes more beautiful, and the intention of the creator of sound becomes more clearly to please the listener. Individual creations and whole events feel as though they shift from plateau to plateau along a flight of steps that lift people simultaneously toward aesthetic perfection and social union. Central and crucial to this rising sequence is the story.

"Stories" lie in concept between crack and poems. Hugh Nolan, master storyteller, will explain the nature of story. He thought it irrational to speak of stories in the abstract, as things apart from their tellers. He begins by describing those with whom stories originate:

"The way it is: the greatest stories, sure, they're all composed; they're all fiction.

"Somebody made them up.

"And isn't it a very smart person, man or woman, that can frame a tale? It's wonderful, you know.

"It's wonderful talent to be able to picture a long hot one and then fill it up, line by line. Oh now, it's wonderful.

"Well, do ye see, the way it is, it takes a person to be gifted in that line to do that. There's a gift attached to it, do ye see.

"Well, they're the same type of people as these authors that can compile a story there that you read out of a storybook or out of a newspaper, do ye see.

"These ones that can compile these short funny stories, they'd be the same type.

"Well, do ye see, an educated person with that gift, they could write away without ever—they'd be writin out of their head, do ye see—aye, whatever was in their head. But the other man that would tell these jokes and short stories, they mightn't have the education for to write, but they had the gift at the same time. The same gift. Aye.

"Well, it's very hard to explain how that gift comes about. But there's alot of people endowed with it, both educated people and uneducated people.

"And, whatever, it's surely a gift, because the uneducated man or wom-

an, if they're given to that, they could come out with the same discourse durin the tellin of this as what one of these writers would.

"And, they mightn't know themselves the meanin of the words that
they were usin, but they knew that they fitted in this tale that they were
tellin.

"You see, the way it is with alot of these ones—the George Armstrong,
John Brodison, or Hugh McGiveney type—they'd think of makin a poem
or makin up a story. Well, they'd take a lock, first and foremost, at a certain
group of words, and if it was a poem that they were goin to make, they'd
judge, could you put that into verse. Well then, it would be the same with a
story; they'd just judge, would this go well for the listener, would I be fit
for to make this that it would carry away the listener or that there'd be a
joke in it for them, do ye know. Aye."

The artist's gift, Mr. Nolan makes clear, is doubly one of words and
vision. Innately, artists have the uncanny ability to use words correctly,
even words they do not understand, and they begin the creative process by
selecting a group of words. The words are ordered "line by line" within the
"picture" being "framed." Deciding what to say and how to say it, artists
are guided by the intention to entertain, to amuse their listeners or carry
them away. Stories are composed by gifted people who give their gift to
others. People who use their talent to vaunt themselves are held in low
regard:

"Well, there was some men and their stories just—they weren't as humorous as the stories of other men, do ye see.

"They'd amuse some, but they wouldn't amuse others. But everybody
that would be listenin to one of these men, do ye know, they were all inclined for to enjoy it, do ye see.

"There bes a class of men and they go in for tellin stories, but there bes
a kind of blow—they make themselves very bright, do ye know, without
anyone waitin for to pass that judgment; you know what I mean? That they
come out *bright*. Och, they're always the winner in these stories.

"Anybody that was always talkin on their own, their own abilities or
their own smartness, do ye know, they were looked on—there was a word:
that man would be a *bum*. He was always braggin of himself, do ye know.

"He wasn't well thought of: the man that come out bright in all, in every
transaction. The man that would get into where he failed himself, that man
was thought the honestest man and the best company. Aye. There was give
and take in that man.

"He's the victim. He's the sufferer. He's the victim of the whole—the
man that'll risk criticism, he'll come out with the best story."

Composers of stories are "stars." They shine not through the deeds
they describe but through the story as an artful entity, a selection of words

and lines that entertain. Their flashes of brilliance become the stock of other tellers:

"Well, there was some people that could make up a story just as they went along. And there was other people, and it was on stories they heard they traded."

Not everyone can tell a story. Some, Mr. Nolan says, lose its wholeness:

"Oh now, I have came across alot of people that would not be able to rehearse a story that they heard.
"They'd go a wee bit, and—Och, I forget—and they'd drop it at that; they weren't fit for to mind the whole story."

Other tellers lose the flow of parts:

"Well, of course, the discourse in every story would be more or less different, do ye see. In tellin a story you often have to use words of your own, words of your own.
"When you're not just able for one sentence to follow another, do ye know, it leaves no good in a story.
"There wants to be a connecting link from one sentence to another, do ye see."

Stories are narratives. That is their wholeness. But narrative alone does not make a story. Even more deeply, stories are matters of "discourse," of "connecting links" and "line-by-line" ordering—of special diction.

For years our perceptions were so conditioned by literary convention that we had nothing better to call tales than prose. Recently noting similarities between spoken narrative and modern verse (much as critics have noted similarities between folk art and modern painting), we have begun to think of them as poetry.[1] The change is productive. Poetry has exalted connotations in our culture, and naming stories poetry (like naming patchwork quilts abstract art) fights nobly against the denegration of their creators. Some American Indian people do order their narratives into lines and stanzas, and setting any tale out on paper as though it were verse assaults the reader's complacency by forcing the story's words into visibility. I have benefited greatly from new thinking about the poetic of the tale, but as my transcriptions of Ballymenone's stories will show, they are neither prose nor poetry—or to set them more validly into the complex local scheme of speech, they are neither chat nor poems.

Stories begin and end in conversations. During their course they refer to their social situations by returning to the thick, uncadenced sound of chat. In other passages they crack free to arrange themselves in lines. Convolution and embedding yield to grammatical simplicity and aural clarity. Interruptions and clauses of the "do ye know" variety which maintain talk's hum are erased by dashes of silence. "Do ye know" is a way to punctuate chat, but within tales the tongue forms lines by flicking momentarily into stillness. Repeated words at their beginnings and strong words at their ends further define the integrity of lines. Tellers form habits of marking. Mr. Nolan is apt to end a line with a slight increase of volume, Mr. Boyle by an ascending tone, but in different performances the same teller will locate a different sound between tongue and ear, a different ratio between silence and noise, to suit the pitch of telling.

Two modes make stories.[2] One is full and flat in sound, complex in grammar; it is used to digress informationally, to orient the listener, and it approximates prose. The other is melodic, rhythmically broken, grammatically simple; it is used to advance the narration, to excite the listener, and it approximates poetry. Neither prose nor poetry, thought nor action, stories are both.

The dynamic of storytelling involves more than dramatic alternation from one mode to the other. Suppose you had a story on paper. The written texts of Lady Gregory would serve you better than many purporting to be transcriptions from tape, for she did not eliminate all the repetitive opening words of lines in an effort to make prose out of stories, and those words, though less important in performance than silence and tone, are the conspicuous clues to the poetry of the tale.[3] Reading the story and noting its repetitive patterning, you would be likely to discriminate between the story's modes too efficiently. As a poet will read against meter and rhyme, tellers will sometimes repeat the first words of sentences, streamline their grammar, form parallel constructions, then hurry the "lines" together without beat or shots of silence. At other times they will shatter lines into phrases, or even words, isolating them for power.

Words ornament tales. The words at lines' end often resonate in alliteration, assonance, or even rhyme. But more important in the decoration of a story are key words, deep in meaning, repeated precisely and peppered through the text, appearing in its prosy and poetic sections to unify the whole.

My transcriptions are not designed to make stories look like prose or poetry, but to make them look like they sound. To that end the most important device is leaving white space on the page to signal silence. The only odd mark I have found it necessary to add is a diamond (◊), indicating a smile in the voice, a chuckle in the throat, a laugh in the tale. Stories enter the mind through the ear, not the eye. Transcribing them, I thought more of music than verse, and I worked them over and over, without changing a word, until I felt no disharmony between eye and ear as I simultaneously read my transcription and listened to the tape.

Stories are narratives artfully ordered to do the serious work of entertainment, pleasing their listeners in the present, then carrying them into the future with something to think about.

When different kinds of entertainment meet, Ballymenone achieves its perfect social moment. And that is what a "ceili" is: the conjunction of proper quiet with proper noise, the exchange of wordless and wordy gifts. In ceilis, food and stories are given, taken, traded.[4]

Ceilis are composed of neighbors who come out of the night to sit together and, as Hugh Nolan says, "pass a lock of hours." Their topic is the neighbors. Talk begins with greetings—"How's Tommy?" "What news"—and expands as the "ceiliers" examine the community's health. Agricultural workers need one another. They have to know who needs their help and whose help they can count on when troubles arise. Cattle, weather, and the neighbors make important topics, but they are not interesting enough to hold attention for long.

"Talk about the neighbors" becomes entertaining when it is transformed by turns into an exploration of human nature. Danger. Most people "pass no remarks" on the weather or the people around them, but it is precisely the person passing remarks who sparks entertaining chat. The wrong remark can lead the chat into "ridicule," critical talk that smashes the community on which the ceili depends and which it exists in part to preserve. Chat cracks easily, too easily, into ridicule. Once ridicule was perfected in satiric poetry, but that was when the community was healthier. Now with some "big men" and many of the youth removed on the pursuit for happiness, the need to hold the farming community together has increased. Ridicule is shunned. Begun, it is cut off: "Ah, don't be talkin." If it becomes too engaging and gathers laughter around it, the ceiliers, realizing they have gone too far, will balance the chat by finding something kind to say about the absent, injured party.

To connect themselves and discover their minds, people must talk. Other people provide the most obvious, useful, interesting topic. So people enjoy speaking in celebration of others, but investigation into human nature cannot be confined by affirmation, and negativity cannot be allowed to escape through the community. The solution is to speak of the dead, making history the way to discuss the present. People from the past are made black holes of gossip, sucking energy into them. I was able to watch this as men died. One never mentioned in life became after death the very type of greed. Another became the model of the solid farmer.

Speaking harshly of the dead releases anger and leaves the living unremarked, but it makes the ceiliers uneasy. They struggle to find "the good word" to say about the person they have just condemned. The singer so bad "you would rather hear an ass bray in the bog" did know many songs. The personification of stupidity whose malaprops make comical memories was good-hearted for all that: "Ah, the creature."

Bad words are bad acts, evidence of bad faith. The ceiliers would prefer to explore humanity through approval, defining the wrong by describing the right. Compliments spray abundantly among people talking together, and the virtues of absent people are elaborated with zeal from talk to tale. And that is what the usual ceili tale is: a celebratory account of an action from the recent past by some individual who embodies a virtue it is important to consider.

The centrality of the ceili's story begins to become clear. It envisions the universal (human nature) through the particular (a real act of a known neighbor). It connects the immediate situation (tonight's ceili) to the culture (the values enacted by a neighbor). That connection is the stories' axis of meaning. On it they turn, gathering meaning to themselves and spinning it back through existence.

Conceptually, the central genre of ceili tale is the "exploit." Its issues are strength and courage. As the bard ends the epic in challenge to the living, and as the ancient Irish historians preserved the great deeds of heroes to prod and chide their descendants,[5] the ceiliers tell of a local man's victory in a brawl, or a local woman's long walk, to whip the fainthearted out of the torpor of self-pity and to celebrate the courage it takes to live their workaday reality. Michael Boyle tells an exploit:

"Well, there was a man lived in our country, William Quigley. He'd be an uncle of Paddy Quigley's.

"Well, he was a big, stout lump of a fearless man, and he was afraid of nothin.

"He wouldn't ask better than—any place he heared there was a *ghost* —someone'd tell him, So and such a one seen a ghost, such a place. Well now, says he, I must go till I see it.

"And he'd go away at night, in the middle of the night, to see would he *see* the ghost.

"And he *never* seen it.

"Aye ◊. That was the kind of him, you know.

"Well then, if he cut his hand—there's many's the one that cut their hand there—knock a lump of skin off it—he'd get a needle and a thread, and whatever kind of nerve he had, he could sew his hand with the needle and thread. He *often* done it.

"And *often* done it.

"Aye indeed.

"There was one time,
          he was doin somethin with the donkey and cart.

"The donkey bogged, you know, went down in the soft ground.

"And when he was gettin the donkey pulled up,
               some part of the cart,
               catched him be the shin,
          and tore a big lump of skin out of the shin,
               ah, that length.

"And he took a barber knife out of his pocket.

"And he cut off a lump of skin and threw it away.

"And got a needle and thread and put two or three stitches in it.

"And he hit it a rap of his fist,
          and he says:

Ye'll be the tidier out of that.

"Aye, he was a great character altogether, this Quigley, a very powerful man."

In that tale, Mr. Boyle used the story's modes in the most usual manner. He opened with an introduction to William Quigley that twisted and ran like chat, but when the narrative began, when time shifted from the general to the particular—"There was one time . . ."—he broke the story into lines set off by repetitive opening words and richly decorated. They echo internally: down, ground; part, cart; him, shin; skin, shin. They end in repetition—cart, cart; shin, shin—or they are bitten off alliteratively: cart, part, pocket, it, fist, that. And that sound rebounds into the lines at the story's end: hit, it, fist; tidier, out, that. Without its poetic, narrative section, it would be no story, but the prosy introduction is part of the story too. He stitched the tale's parts together with the repeated phrases "needle and thread" and "lump of skin."

When talk about the neighbors rises to chat by locating an idea personified in known individuals, it does not usually ascend again to story, but when it does, when a particular event is recounted, the story remains joined to the preceding conversation. Presenting Mr. Boyle's exploit, I chose to begin it where he began to talk about Quigley. I might have dropped the preamble on ghosts, beginning the story at "Well then, if he cut his hand . . ." (though we would have lost the hero's name), but I would have totally obscured the storyteller's art had I started at the narrative passage—"There was one time . . ."—or if I had eliminated the concluding comment, "Aye, he was a great character. . . ." Mr. Boyle used informational passages before and after the poetic, active passage to draw the tale out of the conversation and to reconnect it at the end, blending it into the chat of which it was part and making it more than a specific anecdote. It addresses generally the idea of courage. Many have hurt themselves. Quigley was especially powerful.

Information and action, word choice and order, all these make Mr. Boyle's text a "story." What distinguishes it as a special kind of story, an "exploit," is its topic. It tells of a courageous deed by a local individual. Mr. Boyle knew him and identifies him by his nephew, a man I know. William Quigley was a real man who lived in the ceiliers' neighborhood. He existed in the world they inhabit. His example is not beyond them. As a tale of bravery, Mr. Boyle's is an exploit. In its quoted conclusion—"Ye'll be the tidier out of that"—it urges us to other genres.

More common than tales of courage are tales of wit. "Wit" is not repartee but creative intelligence, exhibited in speech that is exciting, not dull; reasonable, not mad. Sitting together, bravely facing the long night ahead, it is wit that will get the ceiliers through, and they turn often to the subject of the "stars," men like themselves whose wit got them through. While they are remembered, their personalities discussed, their deeds related, tonight's ceiliers recreate the stars' creations, reusing their genius, working tales of two types smoothly into the chat and elevating it clearly into entertainment.

Stories that situate bids, recounting a particular, spontaneous display of wit, are also called "bids." They may conclude in a phrase memorable for its beauty, or (as in tales of the bards abounding in medieval Irish manuscripts[6]) in a brief poem extemporized on the spot to demolish another in swift, wicked satire. Or the bid may end in good humor, a punch line to life's joke. Usually humor takes the hyperbolic turn and sails to an exaggerative limit beyond recall. Here is a clear example from Hugh Nolan that rose while he was telling us about a man he knew:

"Well, Tommy Martin
        was a laborin man
                and he lived at Derrylin.
"And he wrought with the Fermanagh County Council.
"And he was very comical.
"And his bids was very—was full of humor.
"And he was very quick at makin up a *passage*.
"So. There was a clergyman lived convenient to Enniskillen: Canon Pratt. And he was a man that was fond of comin across men of Tommy's type. And he was told about Tommy. And he made up his mind to try and get in touch with him some time or another.
"So the County Council was doin a job from Reilly's Cross on up to where the Canon lived.
"So the Canon heard that Tommy was one of the workmen.
"And this mornin he come down for to have a chat with Tommy.
"And he inquired of the first man that he came across where Tommy *was*.
"And he directed him to where Tommy was workin on the job.
"So the Canon came down and
        spoke to Tommy and
        Tommy saluted him.
"And they had a chat about various things and
        after some time the Canon says to him:
                Tommy,
                do ye know much about Brian Boru?
"I know, says Tommy, a gooddeal about him.
"I was leavin out the milk
        the mornin they went away
                to the Battle of Clontarf ◊."

With Mr. Boyle's exploit, Mr. Nolan's bid instructs about story diction. Here are tendencies for the teller to play against: Large sections begin "Well" or "So." Lines start "And." Descriptive sections coalesce into paragraphs. Action breaks into lines. At the story's peak, lines fragment for attention. These fragments do not begin with the decisive tone of lines, bright with new capitals, but they are set off sharply by silence. They can hold steady in pitch; these I marshal leftward into file. Or they can descend in tone, in which case I let them drift to the right in transcriptions.

Mr. Nolan's story teaches, too, about its genre. Bids build to abrupt ends. Quickly Tommy Martin caught the Canon's historical reference and threw it out of reach. Nothing can follow the conversation in the tale, and the conversation surrounding the tale will return to its topic: the wit of the stars, the nature of creative mind.

The bid elaborates in tales of contest. Two poets meet. The first "makes a poem on" the second. The second tops it with another. The story ends. Or two men meet and the hyperbolic, humorous bid of the first is surpassed. Mr. Nolan and I were talking about John Brodison, one of the great stars of the last generation, when he told this story first:

"Oh many a good story John told.
"There was one time there was a terrible windstorm.
"It was—ah, it lasted the most of a day and a night, do ye know.
"The wind started, we'll say, tonight, about twelve or one o'clock, do ye see, and then blew on to mornin, and then it continued durin the followin *day*. It would be the followin evenin when it settled.
"So anyway, there was another man lived convenient to John. He was the name of McGrath. Oh, he was a great star.
"So a few days after this storm, the two met on the road, and of course generally in this time of year in Ireland when two people would meet there, they'd be talkin about the nice day it was at this time of year. That would be in the *winter* season. That bes a thing that nearly everyone talks about: the *good* day, that there'd be no rain or no wind; they'd be commentin on how nice a day that was for that time of *year*.
"So anyway their conversation was to that effect and then it came round about this storm that had passed.
"So John Brodison says:
"Well now, he says, it was as bad a storm as *I mind*.
"Ah now, there must've been alot of harm done
                    through this country.
"Now I was standin
          in the door, he says, at about seven o'clock
                    that night.
"And it had been blowin *all* the day
          and blowin from the night afore
          and it was still, it was still blowin.
"And there went a haystack by
                    and a man on the dass of it.
"Oh, says this McGrath man, I seen worse that night
          because I was comin down from Bellanaleck Cross
          and I met a byre comin from Arney
                    and the cows all loose through it.
"Aye ◇.

"Weren't they a pair of smart men that could go on that way?

"Do ye see: this McGrath man, he composed that while the other man was tellin him about what he seen, do ye see. He just composed that, do ye see. He had it ready when the other man was done. To beat him out.

"Beat him out, do ye see, that was the idea.

"Oh aye, surely.

"This was a wonderful place for witty bids and good yarns and bein able to compose a thing, do ye know."

Hugh Nolan related the encounter of Martin and Pratt as well as that of McGrath and Brodison. The stories feel different. The first sped from line to line, the second thickened in description. These differences do not lie in the tale as a preconceived entity, but rise during performance as the artist chooses to swing the story toward poetry or pull it back toward chat. It will never reach either extreme, will always alternate between modes, but the teller is free to please himself and his audience by stressing one or the other. Another telling of the Big Wind contest will make this clear. Immediately, Mr. Nolan signals the presence of story by breaking the first sentence into three phrases, gently descending in pitch, exactly as he had in recounting Tommy Martin's bid, then he proceeds efficiently, presenting a swift, lean rendition of the Big Wind, matching in feel his tale of the meeting of Martin and Pratt:

"Ah, there was a lot of comedians
    around our country
        in days gone by.
"There was two men lived at Bellanaleck.
"And they were great crack.
"One of them was John Brodison
"And the other man was John McGrath.
"There was one time
    and there was high wind.
"I mind the wind meself.
"The next day or so these two men was talkin.
"And this John Brodison says:
"Now it was a terrible storm.
"I was standin in the door about six o'clock
    yesterday evenin.
"And there went a haystack by
    and a man on the dass of it.
"Ah, says John McGrath,
"I was goin down from Bellanaleck Cross
    about eight o'clock.
"And I met a byre
    and the cows all loose through it ◊."

No simple explanation of variation will do. I was the audience for both tellings. The Big Wind achieved spareness the third time I recorded it, but Tommy Martin's bid was pared down in its first recording. Mr. Nolan identified the artist's gift and technique with verbal ability and said every story will differ in "discourse." Discourse names the teller's freedom. Shifting from mode to mode, the artist grants himself wide latitude while holding tightly to certain ideas. One is narrative sequence, plot. The other is quotation, the words preserving lost wit. Here is the end of yet another rendition of the story by Hugh Nolan:

"But these two men—it was at Cathcart's that they were talkin, do ye see. So this John Brodison says:
   "It was a terrible storm, he says.
   "I was standin at the door, he says, at about seven o'clock
            in the evenin.
   "And there went a haystack by
            and a man on the dass of it.
   "*Ah*, says John McGrath, he says:
   "I was goin down from the Cross, he says,
         and I met a byre, he says,
               comin down from Arney
         and the cows all loose in it ◇.
   "Aye ◇. That was a quare game you got listenin to that."

Stories vary in little detail. Only in the third telling do we learn where the event took place—Cathcart's store at the Bellanaleck Cross. Only in the second do we learn that both men lived near Bellanaleck. The first, though it contained the fullest account of the storm, lacked McGrath's given name. The whole event lies beyond any single text, but every text contains its essence. This is its truth, its existence as history. Tellers are obliged to preserve that truth while exploiting freedom in the realm of discourse to be entertaining.

Scholars attempt to control and understand the phenomenon of the story in different ways. Some attend to situational variation and reduce stories to momentary negotiations. Plots become conveniences for effecting social arrangements. Others reduce stories to narratives. Words become vehicles for presenting plots. This second way, customary to the folklorist, leads smoothly to historical research as translatable plot summaries, called types, are compared to trace their movement. But it is hard to get from tale types back to social reality. In the folklorist's familiar formula, the text is the revelation of plot in words. Asserted, it accrues social consequence. So a story is a plot, surrounded by words, set in a situation, followed by functions. Perhaps such a definition is useful in cross-cultural comparison, but it distorts the concept Hugh Nolan has been teaching.

Ballymenone's story texts record one person's attempt to coordinate multiple responsibilities to time, to the past event, the present situation, the future of the community. Social effect does not postdate texts, it organizes them. As entertainment, stories intend functions, they feed their listeners, nurturing them for future life together. As entertainment, stories are art. Their discourse is more than the transparent veil through which plot is read. Like so much of Irish literary art, from the dream visions of the bards to James Joyce's mythic nightmare, Ballymenone's stories are deeply things of words. By setting one person's choice of words in another's, they conjoin the best judgments of different speakers and exist to test and celebrate verbal dexterity. At the same time, by setting the past in the present they rise between fluid contingency and nonnegotiable facts, incorporating both and beckoning thought through them to truth. Stories preserve actions and quotations; their wholeness requires memory as well as verbal skill. While existing for themselves as confections of the speaker's craft, stories connect the transitory to the immutable through the fragile self.

The events in exploits and bids happened. Though true, they are never told by the people involved. That would be aggressive, self-aggrandizing, an attempt to make oneself seem "bright." They would call you a bum, so you act, and if the act shines with bravery or wit, others will form it into a tale and keep it alive. Tales of contest are implicit warning against assumed brightness. The underdog wins to prove brilliance is a matter of action, not status or self-esteem.

When bids pit a local person against an outsider, characters are subtly defined to embody the great world's power relations. Wit overturns strength. The local person, weaker and poorer, the ceilier's representative, proves intellectually superior and emerges victorious. In one story, a local farmer out-curses a rate collector, the petty functionary of an oppressive economic system. In another, a local farmer fools the police. Hugh Nolan identified Tommy Martin as a laborer, less than a landholder, who lived at Derrylin, six miles south of the District. In another bid, Martin identifies himself:

> "Well there was some time
>> this Tommy Martin
>>> he had been in the army.
> "And he
>> was a wee bit curious at one time:
>> the nerves give up,
>> and he was in the clinic at Omagh for a *while*.

"And like many other laborin men that used to get their pay on Saturday night, he got into a row, and he got jailed for a while.

"But when at one time the work became scarce and he seen that he'd have to sign on the dole.

"So he went in anyway, into the dole office. The dole man started questionin him, and he says, You're an ex-soldier, he says.

"I'm an ex-soldier, says Tommy,
    an ex-convict,
    and an ex-lunatic ◊ ."

Such a man should be less intelligent than an educated clergyman from the Town. But when Martin faces the Canon, not only does he get the last word, in the style of heroes in black tales from the southern United States,[7] but he reminds Pratt that men like him were present and doing their daily work, just as he is now, when Brian Boru, after uniting South and North, drove the invader from Ireland at the Battle of Clontarf on Good Friday in 1014. Conflict and hope hide just beneath the surface of bids in which local people best strangers, in which their potential for victory lies gently coiled in wit.

In contests between local people, the famed star loses. The pattern comes clear in a pair. In one, Master Maguire, a Catholic teacher, poet, and fervent nationalist from Kinawley, conquers the Methodist preacher, John Wesley, in a poetry match, but loses to an unknown farmer named Murphy in a second. The Big Wind is enriched if we know John Brodison was held in greater repute than John McGrath. Brodison stars in many of the District's tales, and McGrath makes his lone appearance to beat him.

Exploits and bids are left to others for telling.[8] The second genre of witty tale, the "pant," is composed and told by its protagonist. It is his sole possession until he abandons it, bequeathing it to other tellers, who present it in conversations after the fashion of the exploit and bid, always crediting an author. Like bids, pants are woven easily into the ceili's chat, normally to illustrate the inner light of a fallen star, and by extension the intelligence of the District's people, people like those drawn to the fire tonight. Their lack of education and poorness in the things of the world tell nothing about their good minds. This place of low hills and modest farmers was, said Hugh Nolan, "a territory of wits."

Pants risk ridicule. They expose the imaginative personality, and, as Michael Boyle notes, creativity brinks on insanity:

"All them brilliant men all be wild.
"Ah, there bes a kind of mad drop in them. Do you remark it?
"There bes a kind of mad drop on them."

Madness comes with the artist's gift. People will talk, using the word "curious," but if genius is channeled into entertainment, if the self is risked to help others, pulling them away from the perils of silence, then wild self-centered talk can be excused as natural to the artist's "way of goin on." There is, though, no excuse for fanning oneself into brightness. Yet the pant seems poised to do exactly that.

Pants are, in folkloristic parlance, tall tales. There seems a fitness between tales of gigantic cornstalks, monstrous mosquitoes, superabundant hunts, and the wide spaces of the New World where braggarts are venerated,[9] and it might not be expected that a people given to decorum and patience, moving upon a landscape of controlled, intimate spaces, would have for their prime fictive genre the tale of fierce exaggeration. Certainly collections of Irish folktales would not prepare you for that fact.[10] Yet Vivian Mercier begins his excellent survey, *The Irish Comic Tradition*, with fantasy, and, though he includes more, he keys on the tall tale's force: the release of worldly imagination.[11] Lies of extraordinary luck in the hunt may bring mountain riflemen, weekend fishermen, and Baron Munchausen to mind, but they find an early and complete development in the ancient Irish epic *Táin Bó Cúailnge*, which warps often into hyperbolic humor.[12] Twentieth-century Irish novelists—consider the distinct cases of Flann O'Brien and Samuel Beckett—often come at humor by extending reality past possibility,[13] and Ballymenone is not the only modern Irish rural place to contain its madness in comical exaggeration. Michael J. Murphy, playwright, novelist, and folklorist from Armagh, told me he won American contests for whoppers by mailing Irish tales across the ocean. His notebooks, deposited in the grand archive of the Department of Irish Folklore at the University College in Belfield, Dublin, contain the texts of many tall tales. Here is one, taken down in 1966 from Jerry Greene, age seventy-three, from Lisnaskea. It was entitled "A Lough Erne Pike," though I suspect in Lisnaskea, as in Ballymenone, tales, unlike songs, have no titles.

"A man out shooting wild-fowl saw a huge pike leaping in the Lough. He had powder but no shot and used haws (seed of hawthorn) instead: fired at the Pike and hit and it then swam off:

"'Two years later this hedge with a washing of clothes on it was seen coming down the lough: it was the pike: the haws had taken root . . . !

"'They'd tell that on the island when I was young.'"

Mr. Murphy, the Irish Folklore Commission's collector for Ulster, noted that the tale was known by another man, and through his rich notebooks tales of the sort are attached to an outstanding individual, Ned Noble, "The Lisnaskea Liar."[14] Lisnaskea is a town in Fermanagh, across Upper Lough Erne, seven miles east of Ballymenone.

John Brodison, Hugh McGiveney, and George Armstrong were the District's great perpetrators of pants. They were not alone, but they were the brightest in a brilliant generation; its lesser lights included James Quigley, James Maguire, John Williamson, John McGrath, Hugh Mackan, Francis Keenan, and Charlie Flynn. People today do not attribute that generation's excellence (it is the same one in which Yeats, Synge, Lady Gregory, A.E., Shaw, Hyde, O'Casey, and Joyce overlapped) to its being the last of the old order. It came naturally in the ebbing and flowing of blood. I asked Peter Flanagan and he said:

"I think like everything else, that generation comes up once in a while. It's not just a general thing that people would be born talented in one generation after another generation. That's my opinion.

"I think it's like that. It's like the good year comin in farmin. And there's more bad years than there is good ones. This country has seen alot of bad, and yet at that time a good one comes, and it's the same, I think, applies to men of talent and smartness. They come up once every hundred years or once in every fifty years.

"I think that's the story about these people."

John Brodison came from Leitrim, his wife from Cavan, and after moving within Fermanagh from below Lisgoole to Arney, they settled near Bellanaleck. "In them days," Hugh Nolan said, "lots of men came from west Cavan, Leitrim, and Sligo, and came North to work for farmers, and some to get jobs. There was more work, do ye see, here in the North." Brodison was "a fine, strong, hefty, ginger-haired man. You'd know by lookin at him that he was always thinkin. Between him and the wife, well, they done the wonders of the world." He died in the 1940s as "a pensioner, an old man." Hugh McGiveney was "quick as lightning from he was a young man." Poet, historian, comedian, he farmed a patch in Rossdoney and died in the 1920s. George Armstrong lived at the end of his life in a small house on the grounds of the rectory at Bellanaleck. He died in the hospital after being severely burned in the 1940s. To tell about George Armstrong, Hugh Nolan tells two of his pants. The first is an unelaborated Lucky Shot. During two other tellings, in which Mr. Nolan ascribed the tale to the Brodisons, the lone lucky shot ramifies preposterously to bag more game than geese. The first story passes quickly; it is but prologue to the second, one of the District's great tales:

"This George Armstrong, he lived in a little house in Gortdonaghy. His house was down at the foot of the hill. Missus Cutler's house, do ye see, would be away up on the top of the hill. Well, you'd have to come down towards the north to come where his house was.

"When he left it, a nephew got the farm, and that man built a house on the Arney Road and sold the farm to a neighbor. Before he left he built a temporary iron house.

"He was a wonderful storyteller, a wonderful storyteller of things that there was nothing *about*.

"He was tellin about:

there was one mornin he was sittin at the fire.

"He heared a flock of wild geese.

"And, do ye see, there was guns goin in this country in days gone by. They were *muzzle loaders*.

"Ye charged them with powder and shot, and you put in the powder first. And you put a piece of paper in after it, and you had a *ramrod*, and ye pushed that away down with the end of the ramrod.

"So then you put in the shot after, and a piece of paper on the top of it. And you pushed it down.

"So then there was a cap on the gun and when you pulled the trigger there came a spark out of the cap that set the powder afire and it blew the shot away out.

"Them was what they called muzzle loaders.

"Well, he minded this mornin that he had no shot.

"So he ran

and he put powder into the gun,

and he pushed it down with the ramrod,

and he left the ramrod in the gun,

and he ran to the fire,

and as the wild geese was crossin the house,

he fired.

"The ramrod went up,

and it stuck in three of their necks;

three of them fell down on the roof of the house,

dead.

"The ramrod stuck in their necks ◊.

"Aye ◊."

Without pausing to let the laughter die or frame a transition in words, Mr. Nolan goes right on:

"He was in Australia

in his young days.

"And he was doin the best, makin plenty of money.

"But there started a disease, they call it cholera. It's goin in foreign countries *still*, I think.

"So,

he was very bad with it,

and he thought he was goin to die.

"Finally he started to mend anyway, and he got in the latter end that he was able to get to his feet, and

get out.

"So he made up his mind that he'd get back to Ireland

if he could atall.

"He hadn't very much money. It wasn't hard in them days for to pay your fare on the *high seas*.

"But anyway, he started.

"And he discovered that the ship that he was travelin in:

that there was a cow's grass of land, he said,

of the best land ever he set his eyes on,

in the ship,

and there was a rood of the best turf bog
       that ever any man put a spade in.
   "So anyway, he made his way on anyway and I think it was in Derry he landed.
   "So he made his way to Enniskillen,
       and he got out on the platform,
       and there was a weighbridge on the platform,
       and he got up on the weighbridge,
       and he was three pound weight.
   "Aye ◇.
   "So he was seven mile from home at the time.
   "And he seen that was all for him, frail and all that he was—was to walk home; he had no way—there was postcars in them days, but, ah, you wanted to have a lock of shillins about you, you know, for to hire one of them.
   "So he started anyway.
   "So he come on, and at that time there was a railroad crossin on this Derrylin Road, down near the end of it; it's gone now; you wouldn't see hardly any track of it, only a bridge across the Sillees River.
   "So anyway the train was comin,
       and he just took a notion he'd count his money,
           he was sittin on the back of the ditch,
       and he searched his pockets,
           all he had: thruppence.
   "Train passed anyway,
       and he got to his feet again,
       and he come on,
           and finally,
               finally he made his way,
                   so he landed at the house.
   "There was no noise atall off his step;
       he was that light.
   "He came along without any noise and when he arrived at the door,
       the mother was doin something at the fire,
           and she never found him
               till he spoke.
   "So when she turned round and seen him,
       aw she nearly lost her life at the appearance of him.
   "There was a wee basket hangin to a purline that was in the kitchen,
       that she took down the basket,
       and she put him into the basket,
           and she put a white cloth over him,
           and she left him up at the fire.
   "So the rumor went out about the country that George was returned, that George was home.

"So there was alot of people arrived there the next day, for to see him and have a talk with him.

"And when they came in there was no sign of George about.

"So anyway some of them says:

"Well, we heard that George was home and we just came to see him.

"Oh, *here he is*, says the mother. He's home yesterday evenin.

"And some of them says to her, Where is he at the present time?

"Oh, he's not far away, says she.

"So she went and lifted up the wee basket,
        and took the cloth from over him ◊,
        and they looked in it ◊."

Mr. Nolan lets the laughter run loose for a moment, then controls it and resumes:

"That was all the chat you got out of George; he wasn't able to talk.

"It was pants like that you know, pants like that he used to tell."

Pants like that are what Mr. Nolan had in mind when he said the greatest stories are fiction and when he said the best stories make their heroes victims, sufferers. The star avoids seeming bright by darkening himself in the tale, and like the noble Samuel Beckett he helps his audience by witnessing to their deepest fears, then dismantling them by driving them to an extreme so extreme they squeeze a laugh out of terror. At the end of a later telling of George Armstrong's Return, Mr. Nolan concluded:

"It was pants like that that used to keep the community tellin, and every day you'd nearly hear a fresh one. And you'd like to come across them, do ye know, when you'd go down in that locality."

To that I said, "That's a funny story, but it's pathetic."

"Aye," Mr. Nolan replied. "Oh now, it was surely one of the trials of this life, mind you, when things turned out that way.

"But he made a joke out of it."

Making a joke of the trials of this life puts wit in service to courage, makes the self a gift to the community. It encourages people, keeping them "tellin," talking and alive.

Humor is a useful diversion from life's pain. Art, the District's people feel, should not reinforce unhappiness. For that reason they banned "Barbara Allen" from ceilis. "Life is sad enough," Peter Flanagan said, "without singin about it. I never liked a sorrowful song. Give me a song with some kick in it, a bit of sport." So the ceili's tales are funny, but they do not avoid reality, for that would be cowardly. Some pants like the Lucky Shot prick a laugh and pass on into the scholar's category called the tall tale, but in the District such stories gather, more through discourse than plot, a mood of melancholy which sets them away from tall tales told elsewhere. When John Brodison discovers an enormous potato in his garden, it becomes during his struggle to hoke it out and saw it into lengths less a celebration of abundance than an Irish countryman's nightmare, a palpable reminder of famine in the past, drudgery in the future. The District's most developed pants, with Armstrong's illness to illustrate, break beyond the tall tale. Crushing them back into academic categories would stifle their spirit and miss their point. Their fantasy does not spring free but screws downward into reality. Ballymenone's dark pants grew out of an international class of jocular tale, but they flourished among these hills, maturing in rich minds to burst into seriousness.

Between laughter and pain, stories open to reveal their importance. One of the three times Mr. Nolan described the star's gift, he ended at that point:

"Well, do ye see, the way of it is, *all* good stories and good novels, they're all fiction. They're composed be some brainy people.

"Sure, look at all the men and women that has gained a great name for themselves by bein able to compose and publish a book, do ye know.

"They're all fiction.

"There may be little things in them that alluded to certain times, but the most of it all, do ye see, is good talent—imaginin, do ye see.

"Oh, it's a terror.

"But even they're fiction, there bes a warnin. And there bes information in them too."

The warning in George Armstrong's pant concerns emigration, a profound Irish issue. The story jolts thought rather than directing reaction. It does not quite instruct people to stay home, does not quite reassure those who remain. Had he not been smitten with cholera, Armstrong might have gotten rich, for "he was doin the best, makin plenty of money" in Australia. But the story does say trading home for cash can bring failure, and it draws the mind through wit, past emigration, into confrontation with broader, deeper issues when it displays extremes of poverty and bodily decay. Having stayed in Ireland while others sought wealth abroad, having stayed on the farm while others profited in jobs, the ceiliers are not prosperous. Everyone gets sick, all fail, shriveling into death. Against that deepening darkness, the star shines as poorer, sicker than his companions. Reaching the bottom, he rises above it all, making life a joke.

The neighbors know more. George Armstrong's story is also a story about George Armstrong, a story about storytellers. It contains, in Mr. Nolan's words, information as well as warning. It describes the transformation of the star's power. In the beginning, his power is the worker's. He emigrates, prospers, cholera strikes, his body shrinks to near nothing. Death and life touch, merge. Then he is reborn in new power, the power of the aged, gifted artist. Read the tale closely. He arrives at home unseen, and comes to his mother's door without sound, like a breeze, a ghost, a new life. She keeps him, a tiny being unable to talk, in a basket, warm by the fire, covered by a white cloth, a corpse's shroud, an infant's sheet. The neighbors come to view him, standing over and peering down at his remains as though at a new baby. Armstrong ends his story there, but it is the ceiliers' now. They know he lived for many years, growing into a strapping teller of tales. They know the artist's life was born of the worker's death. He gives them heart. They may not succeed in the world of the body, where power is measured in health and wealth, but, withered and poor, they may succeed in the world of the mind, in the ceili tonight, where power is wit. There is life after death of the body in the will to make death a joke.

Pants are "jokes." The stories usually called pants are also called "phrases," "passages," "yarns," "rigamaroles," "blunders," "fibs," and "lies." This multiplicity of terms would confuse a person who believes order results from breaking reality into ever smaller and more isolated categories, into boxes, caskets to be buried in books and forgotten. Ballymenone's logic works more by association than by disjunction. Names are used less to kill a phenomenon as an instance of a class than to animate discussion and thought.

Names bridge without destroying generic distinctions. It is enough that each genre has a most common name and that only one genre could attract all its names, for genres are understood primarily in terms of intrinsic character. Names can slide. Hyperbolic bids like those of the Big Wind contest are also called pants. Marked sections of artful speech are called phrases and passages, and so are both bids and pants. Any comic tale can be called a joke or a yarn. Funny talk is called "joky," and "yarning" also names a kind of amusing chat through which the exaggerative impulse of the pant is released. Spinning, unwinding, "raveling on and on," yarning coils into "rigamaroles," confusions produced by comical complexity. When its subject is present, yarning can twist into good-natured teasing, but if it gathers a tinge, a smack of viciousness, it is called "codding." Just as the string of yarning is wound up in yarns, the word or deed or person that stinks with codding is called a cod: "c-o-d: big fish." Pants are called yarns, but never cods; their energy is benign.

Overlapping names connect certain acts, cumulatively demarcating a special region in the world of speaking. The District's people lack a name for it. Scholars paid to understand such things have none either, and we have tried. We have tried analogy, but the contradictory term, oral literature, includes too little and befuddles study, drawing us from act to item, then cajoling us to emphasize items in accordance with their resemblance to belles lettres. We have tried shoving antique critical dichotomies into speech, breaking it into the aesthetic versus the utilitarian, the expressive versus the instrumental, but the result, verbal art, includes too much. Any balanced, grammatical sentence might be verbal and art and not "verbal art."

Ballymenone's storytellers use terms which situationally signal a single kind of speech but conceptually indicate others, so names slip and expand to join genres of story to each other and to the whole range of pleasing, informational, and humorous talk. They do have a name for this sector of spoken experience: entertainment. But they do not restrict that word arbitrarily by medium to speech, or unnaturally by academic convention to literature. Intelligently, it embraces music, dance, and drama, food and drink, as well as stories and conversation. Anything given by one person to another to bring pleasure and benefit is entertainment. Unfortunately, we cannot appropriate Ballymenone's term because it names a realm of experience higher than what we call entertainment and broader than what we usually mean by art.

Some names build associations by revealing similarities beneath apparent difference, as when a story and a conversation are both labeled rigamaroles. Other names propose associations to destroy them. When one name links superficially similar but deeply different phenomena, the mind is attracted, confused, and led to fundamental principles. People are forced to clarify distinctions in their own thought. Blunders are mistakes, evidence of stupidity. Pants look like mistakes—call them blunders—but they are intentional mistakes, evidence of wit, the precise opposite of stupidity. If they are not mistakes, they must be lies. Call them fibs or lies and you raise an issue of profound importance.

The District's people are literate. They write shopping lists, read newspapers, and transfer songs on written "ballats," but they treat literacy as a marginal convenience and conduct all important exchanges with the body in motion, the other directly engaged. Their world is ordered orally. When the song is sung, the ballat is absent. Matters of history, genealogy, and land tenure, cooperative arrangements between farmers, rental agreements, sales at marts, the "fireside law" governing land use, routes across private property and access to water, and most profoundly, the rules of the church—all are held in the memory and expressed face on, intimately, in words. Words must be true. Life depends on them.

Ballymenone has no worse accusation than "liar." Death came quickly upon that word in the local mummers' play. The importance of the genre of the pant rises partially out of its location over the point where the lie is defined. Naming pants "lies" forces refinement of the concept of truth, clarifying the obligations people owe one another as inhabitants of a world made of words. Lies are crimes. They spill off the tongue to smash the community. Worse: lies are sins. They bring, as Peter Flanagan said, destruction upon the soul.

Pants cannot be lies. While I was figuring out the District's generic sys-

Sean South

(1)

It was on a dreary new years day as the shades of night came down a lorry load of Volunteers approached a Border town There were men from Dublin and from Cork Fermanagh and Tyrone But the leader was a Limrick man Sean South of Garryowne

(2)

And as they moved along the street up to the Barrick Door he saw the danger the would meet the fith that lay in store He were fithing for old Irelands cause the Gleam of Garryowne and the foremost of that Gallant man Sean South of Garryowne

(3)

But the Sergant hailed there Sarvint Round he fired them thro the Door

then the sten guns and the rifles soon a Vaim of Death begun and When that aufal night was Past two men lay cold as stone there was one from the Border and one from Garryowne

(4)

no more heal hear the seagul cry Or the murming Shannon tie for he fell beneath the northern sky O And Hankes by his side he gone to join theat Gallint Band aslanted tears and tall a marter for old Irelands Sean South of Garryowne Sean South of Garryowne

Song Ballat. In the District, a ballad is not a song but, as it was in Shakespeare's day (*The Winter's Tale*, act 4, sc. 4), a sheet of paper with a poem on it, and it is pronounced as it is in the Southern Appalachian region of the United States, where the meaning is the same, with a hard sound at the end: "ballat." This ballat of "Sean South," given to me by Mrs. Cutler, illustrates the local norm. Stanzas are not divided into lines, but break when the melody repeats. Spellings reveal that the text was written from memory or taken from dictation (the end of the last stanza is usually sung, "He has gone to join that gallant band of Plunkett, Pearse, and Tone / Another martyr for old Ireland, Sean South of Garryowen"). The ballat, then, is a written link in an oral chain of transmission.

tem, I asked Mr. Nolan if he would class a story he had just told as a pant, and when he said he would, I commented that I had also heard pants called lies, and he told me a bid, a story about stories, to explain the problem:

"Aye.
"There was someone at one time and he asked a clergyman was it a sin to tell *lies*.
"And the clergyman replied,
"It depended on the source of the lie
        that you told.
"If you told a lie that would injure your *neighbor*,
        that would be a sin.

"Or that would spread any kind of scandal or anything like that.
"But he said,
"The lie that no one would believe ◇
        ◇ there was no harm to tellin that lie ◇.
"Aye ◇.
"A thing that no one would believe ◇."

Then I defined a pant as a "harmless lie," and Mr. Nolan agreed. Pants differ radically from other lies in intention, in "source." The lie that is not a pant is inherently evil and brings harm to the neighbor. The lie that is a pant brings no harm to the self and helps the neighbor. The pant's good intention is displayed in clear incredibility. A pant is not a lie, precisely because, as Mr. Nolan said, "you'd know before it was fully told that it *was* a lie." Long before George Armstrong folds swaddled and shrouded into a basket at his mother's fire, his pant had revealed itself for fiction. The homeward ship contained, as it probably did in his mind, a stretch of Irish landscape, grassland and bog. His fortune had fallen to three pennies, his weight to three pounds.

First in good intention, which removes them from sin, second in unbelievable words, which removes them from crime, pants peel away from other lies. Then they break utterly free by being true. Today, when times have tensed a turn, pants are reports. Sometimes, like bids, they are set in the situation of their original telling, usually a scene of contest, but they are always presented as accurate accounts of what a real person really said. Their fiction is attributed and clearly, safely embedded in fact. They are true. In this they are like bids, and both genres of witty tale are like exploits, and all are history.

The exploit owes its centrality to its historicity. Bids and pants are, in effect, though the term is not used, exploits of the stars. The two other main classes of ceili tale comparably connect to the exploit. One is "the story of history." The other centers upon "the experience."

The "experience" relates an event of one's own life. I agree with folklorists who bring the personal narrative into the domain of the folktale,[15] for the autobiographical fragment provides a primary mode of traditional expression in individualistic societies. Like any folktale, it fuses the personal and the collective. Its events, though unique, happen, stick in memory, and achieve performance in accord with culture.

True tales of the self are told in Ballymenone. Hugh Nolan will tell of his trip to Scotland. Peter Flanagan will recount his victory in a musical competition. But such narratives are not common, not nearly so common as they are in my world, and when they do appear they come cautiously, apologetically, carefully shaded so they will not reflect on the brightness of the narrator.[16] Here is Ellen Cutler's account of a trip she took with her sons, Dick and John, to see the parade of the Black Preceptory in a Fermanagh town to the northeast:

Ellen Cutler, March 1976

"It was the Twelfth of August.

"Dick would be about twelve, so he's thirty-one now.

"Anyway, I had never been till the Twelfth of July or the Twelfth of August, well, from I come here. And that was in nineteen and thirty-seven when I come here.

"And I never had been till the Twelfth of July or the Twelfth of August because the *men* always went out and I just stayed home with the childer.

"But.

"This Twelfth of August, me husband says, Can't you go the day to Irvinestown and bring the childer with ye.

"Says I, I'm not a bit fussy about goin, I'd sooner be at home.

"So anyway, he made me go anyway and I brought the two boys with me and their uncle and we set sail on the *bus*.

"And goin down to Irvinestown the sun had got that *hot*
     it was actually crackin the windows in the bus.

"And we weren't right in Irvinestown—
       such a thunderstorm:
          thundered
          and lightnin
          and a cloudburst.

"And the steeple in Irvinestown Church was split in two with the lightnin.

"And with the cloudburst,
     the drums,
     and bicycles,
     and, in fact, *childer*,
        was swept down the streets.

"And I got the two childer in till an entry,
     must be belongin to an undertaker.

"And there was a gratin in it, and we were standin on the gratin, and the first thing I saw was my young boy, he was just lifted off it with the force of the water in under it, and we were just swept out onto the street.

"We were just actually *soakin*.

"So says I to them before we come home, That's my first Twelfth, says I, and surely it's my last.

"And when we come as far as Bellanaleck here on our way home, the road was that dry and nice, you could get down and roll on it.

"And when we come on up home then—there was a man the name of Tommy Murphy used to work here, and him and me husband were out rookin *hay* when we got home. And they said they never seen a drop of rain that day.

"So that ended me and the Twelfths, and I'm an old woman now and I'm sittin in the *corner*.

"Good for nothin, only scoldin ◊.

"My two boys is married and away from me and I have five grand-children *at the moment*; I don't know how many more there'll be.

"And the best of luck to them.

"Ah now."

Mrs. Cutler's remembrance was clearly, humorously, and dramatically told in the style of the local teller of tales. The event was of general importance, both the specific storm and the ongoing march of Protestant men to commemorate the defense of Derry in 1689, and it marked a turning point in her life, much as George Armstrong's pant marked one in his. Ellen Cutler was born Doherty in Enniskillen on June 26, 1902, and raised at Boho, eight miles northwest of the townland of Gortdonaghy, where she lives today. She married Billy Cutler at the age of thirty-six, and the Twelfth at Irvinestown was the one time she returned to the freedom of her youth. But she was forced into it and gained from it nothing but trouble. At once her account is a myth of the self, explaining why she sits now in the corner, a widow at her hearth in her house on the hilltop, and it testifies to the condition of women in her society.

Mrs. Cutler's text is well formed and important, but such are not called "stories" in Ballymenone. The personal narratives connected by name to entertainment mute pride. They do not display the ego but offer personal possessions for general use. They are either clearly fictional (pants to amuse, warn, and inform) or they are "experiences," in which case they are a variety of "ghost story" or "fairy story," or they recount glimpsing some facet of that "other world" important to all, toward which thinking about ghosts and fairies leads.

"Experiences of the other world" do not assert belief. They explore the nature of nature to discover what to believe, just as other stories explore the nature of humanity to discover what to value. Since the shape of reality is known to no one, anyone can gain a hint of its limit and bring that experience into story. This distinguishes experiences from other kinds of ceili tale—exploits, bids, pants, and stories of history—which are the preserve of special people. They are elderly. Notes Hugh Nolan, "A young fellow might give a witty bid, but he'll never get into makin up pants. It's not until a man gets up in years that he'll make up a story the like of John Brodison or George Armstrong or Hughie McGiveney."

Stories are signs of the power of the mature mind. Their tellers are old, and they are male.[17] "This old history," Mrs. Cutler said, "is men's work." When I asked the question of Michael Boyle, he expanded:

"No, they never went in much for tellin the yarns; it twas more the men. The women didn't go in for tellin stories; it twas more the men went in for that.

"Seemingly it was a man's job.

"There was some grand singin women in our country, but we had no storytellers or poets, no women poets.

"But there was some famous Irish women poets. Oh aye, there was. But I never knew any women poets now in our district.

"They did sing. There was some fine singers. There was a family in our country the name of Gunns, lived down about Bellanaleck, and there were three or four girls in it, and they were lovely singers. Beautiful. There was a couple of them used to sing together, and they were good now.

"They were. They were good singers.

"And there was a family at Arney. The schoolteacher that taught in the old school—not the present school at the chapel; the old school was on the other hand side. Oh, it's vanished longgo—there was a man taught in that school and he had a great family, a big family of boys and girls. A couple of girls in it was wonderful singers, beautiful. You would sit there listenin to them for a *week*.

"Of course, he was the choirmaster in the chapel, do ye see, he knew music, was a good singer himself. But these girls were better, I think, than ever he was. The boys of the family used to sing, but there was no attraction to them like the girls. The girls were great singers.

"But it was men now that done the storytellin."

Men, old men, rarely gifted old men tell stories. They are exceptional people but it would be wrong to think of them as marginal. Ballymenone's society is built of interlocking specialization, of composite excellence. Women and men give different kinds of entertainment to the ceili. The young give muscle, the old give knowledge to the maintenance of life. Old tellers of tale are not astray in a wilderness of nostalgia. Born in new power, they fill a crucial role in their community. They preserve its wisdom, settle its disputes, create its entertainment, speak its culture. Without them, local people would have no way to discover themselves, and their community would lie vulnerable to rot creeping from beyond.

Folklorists who come from societies in which creativity and wisdom are suspect—societies in which artists are dismissed as isolated cranks and old people are pitied as diseased young people—regularly display misunderstanding of the social organization of communities like Ballymenone in unsuccessful predictions of the deaths of arts known only to a few aged people. Generation after generation contains the last basket weaver and the last ballad singer.[18] When they were young, Hugh Nolan and Michael Boyle were not noted storytellers. They would not have performed for a visiting folklorist. Their elders, George Armstrong and Hugh McGiveney, would have told the tales, while the folklorist foretold the demise of the art and young Hugh and Mick cut turf and hay. But now they are the tellers. As never before, young men are wrenched out of the community, and drawn to jobs and films, but some still come to ceilis. They sit quietly after work, unable to tell tales, but they are listening, and some day they will.

"When you're young," said Tommy Lunny, Mrs. Cutler's neighbor, "you do laugh at what the old people say, but then the young get older." Young people rip ahead, assuming the world is as it appears. It is the task of the old to keep the argument open. Wise enough to know they do not know, they remain willing to consider evidence of the other world, the possibility that there is more to reality than meets the common eye.

Joe Flanagan, Peter's elder brother, is quiet and mild, no teller of tales. But he has experienced too much to take nature at face value, enough to make stories. Our conversation had been about fairies, and Joe had presented good evidence for and against their existence. Without committing himself, he summed things up and moved into a different dimension of the topic:

"So now, it's a droll—it's a curious world.

"This woman, she had a brother. He took sick and died. And then there was no one on the place, only her. Ah, she told me several old passages about things.

"She told me she was in Bundoran one night in the lodging house. There used to come a thing across the lough like a barrel. *Rollin.*

"So, says she, she was scared of course. So she was tellin the landlady the next mornin. Aw, says the landlady, You say a prayer for that person and you'll not find it more.

"And she did.

"That was that. She never found it more."

Joe pauses, lights his pipe. The company at the hearth remains quiet, attentive. He continues:

"Well, I heared me mother tellin about:
> he was workin in this house,
>> her father.

"Of course, he knew the woman of the house as well as I know you now.

"Well, he moved out of that house then, up to another house, up the lane further. And twas a shop down, and he used to get his tobacco in it.

"He was a workin man, you see, workin.

"So. He went this night anyway and he stopped be it. Might be one o'clock when he was comin by this house that he used to work in.

"And this woman had died.

"So there used to be wee outlets at houses longgo, porches they used to call them.

"So he was comin by,
> and he was comin forenent the door.

"The
> woman
>> was
>>> standin
>>>> with her
>>>>> back up to the door."

Joe stops, flicks a glance to me, and draws on the pipe:

"Wasn't that a tight one?
"The woman that he had worked with
     and he knew her as well as—"

Joe gestures at the reality around us, the hearth and tables and walls.

"But he went on by, and he says, the hair stood on his head.
"Well.
"There used to be ould ghost stories told longgo, but I think it's done away with now; there's not much of it now."

I ask Joe whether that is because people are not interested or because things like that no longer happen. With a laugh, he answers:

"They wouldn't think of things like that now. Gomelty's sake!
"You get in the car now, and that's that. Away with ye. Young people now wouldn't care about things like that."

He smiles. "What do you suppose that means?" I ask. "Do you suppose there never were any ghosts, or—" Swiftly Joe cuts me off:

"Oh now.
"I wouldn't rule that out.
"I'm afraid there was ghosts.
"I seen me goin up by a place
    when I was told there was a man
        and a ghost followed him.
"I used to, I used to go up the hill, every night.
"And of coorse I was thinkin of that too—that I'd meet the ghost.
"So I had to, I had to go by it, and I was in a heat.
"This man was comin out at me—this man lived here in this townland, and it was away up in Clontymullan.
"And he had a turf spade with him.
"And they say a ghost won't go near steel.
"So he had to hold this turf spade out to keep the ghost away from him.
"So he got home anyway.
"But I seen me goin up this way every night. And I never found a haet.
"And I stayed a night in the house me lone.
"That a man and woman went away to a weddin, and they told me they'd be back, but not aback, and twelve o'clock came, and, Ah, says I.
"I got up.
"I got a candle.
"Took a notion I'd go up and
    go to bed and
    lock the door.

"Put out the light,
    went up to the loft and
    kneeled down and
    said me prayers and
      went into bed.
"And they—him and her landed at seven o'clock next mornin."

Joe laughs. He had told us there were ghosts, then speaking slowly, lowly, with a hint of a quiver and quake, he had prepared us for a ghost. It never came. The topic remains open. Joe continues:

"So I had to stay on me lone.
"And there was always supposed to be a ghost in it, at it.
"So what was I to do if he hadda come?
"But I knew he wouldn't come near me."

I ask, "How would you protect yourself?"

"Prayer," Joe says.

Joe had prayed. Perhaps that is why no ghost came. It is a curious world. Joe Flanagan leads us into understanding stories of experience. Fairies join ghosts, both join witches, the Devil, and "tokens"—signs of death, falling rocks, mysterious lights, wandering wraiths, scampering rats, the lonesome cold howl of the banshee. All are agents of the other world, piercing normality to make fugitive contact with mortals.

Cumulatively, agents of the other world gesture at the whole of which the workaday world is but part, and provide a way for believing people to contemplate belief. Atheism is unspeakable. Doubts are contained in discussion of supernatural phenomena less than God.

Fairies, ghosts, and tokens provide subjects for contemplative study. They are not equal. More people credit ghosts than fairies, more credit tokens than ghosts. None is universally believed, so all are open to colloquy.[19] The goal is forming observations into propositions that can be tested in specific situations to determine what to believe and, more deeply, whether to believe. People have learned they can protect themselves from ghosts with steel and prayer, and Joe Flanagan told tales to support each idea, thus drawing the other world into consistency, toward comprehension.

"Experiences" are entries in an investigation. They provide confirmation, or negative evidence of the kind William Quigley collected in Mr. Boyle's exploit, or disconfirmation of the other world's agents.

Many of Fermanagh's little hills are topped by rings of trees, rooted in Iron Age earthworks.[20] Only some people believe these "forths" are the homes of fairies, but few will cut the trees or disturb the branches that fall within their dark, twisted circle. Tommy Lunny told me of a forth with a double ditch at the Battery down the Skea Road from the Arney Cross, of another at Mullinaman, across the Chapel Road from Sessiagh Bog. Within

Gortdonaghy Hill. Looking south from the Chapel Road at the long ascent of Gortdonaghy Hill, you see near its top a tight clump of trees, a ring about 120 feet in diameter: Tommy Lunny's forth. Typically, forths, like this one, are set just down from the top of the hill. The tall tree to the right of the forth marks the location of Mrs. Cutler's house.

Inside Tommy Lunny's Forth

the District, there is a forth on Crozier's Hill, another at Quigley's in Rossa-walla, and one on Tommy's own land. "When you are raised hearin about the forths from the old people," Mr. Lunny said, "you hear that it is bad luck to cut a stick or lift a stick in it. I don't know is there anything to it, but I never did cut a stick there. The cows go in it, and it is wet. But it is good land, the best. I wish all my fields were land so good." The forth called "Tommy Lunny's" rises atop Gortdonaghy Hill, next to Ellen Cutler's house. She offers a proposition. You must not cut the branches of a fairy forth or trouble will follow. She tells the story. Her husband needed skivers to pin open the carcass of a slaughtered pig. She warned him not to cut them from the forth. He did, going against the advice of his wife and the old wisdom of his community. The pig burst. Its hams brought little at market. By violating her injunction, Billy Cutler confirmed the existence of fairies. [21]

A conversation like Joe Flanagan's that includes positive and negative evidence, bundled into stories, can also include tales of disconfirmation, such as this from Hugh Nolan:

"Well then, there's alot of people and they imagine that they see ghosts. And if it was investigated it's just something ordinary that takes their eye, and that they be under the impression there's a ghost.

"You could see a thing that looks like a ghost, and then if it was investigated,
             it's no ghost atall.
"Now I was comin from a house
        away over there
             on the Back Road.
"And I was comin through Drumbargy.
"And I was walkin along the pad road.
"And I looked to me right.
"And I seen
        what I took to be
             a very stout little man
                  standin
             a distance away.
"So I come on for a wee piece and says I,
        to meself:
"It's a pity to go home without findin out
        is it really a man,
        or who would it be.
"So I turned back.
"And I went on down to where this figure was.
"And I found out what it was.
"There had been a sally runt—that's one of these plants in this country that there grows big long wattles out of, do ye know. There used to be in days gone by, the ould men used to be very anxious for to come across

some of them; they were great for makin creels, do ye know—big, strong wattles.

"Well, there had been some of them growin on this.

"And that day they had been cut, do ye know.

"And the wattles was cut off this,
    at the distance,
    and in the darkness,
    it was terrible like the shape of a wee stout man.

"So.

"That was what I found out when I investigated."

Discussion of the other world is restricted by rules of evidence. Good evidence comes from reliable sources. It can be gathered by one's own senses or received from others, but that other is never a vague friend of a friend. Joe tells only his own experiences, and those he was told directly by a woman he worked for who saw a ghost in barrel shape rolling on the waves off the Donegal resort, Bundoran, by a neighbor who fended off a ghost with a turf spade, by his mother, whose father saw the ghost of a woman he had worked for in the porch of her home.

Evidence of the other world appears too rarely for knowledge to be limited by personal experience. So most stories of fairies and ghosts will come from others, and when told they will relay the experience of another, a known other like the heroes of exploits and the stars of bids. The main difference is topic.

Opening the mind to strange possibilities, experiences open a possibility for fiction to stars who compose stories that sound like experiences but that are untrue, not evidence. Fictional tales of fairy and ghost, witch and devil (but not token) are like pants. They extend reality to trip pleasure, not in comedy but in a contained instant of fear as apt as humor to startle a laugh. Like pants, fictional experiences are now stories of stories. They turn from lies by lacking attribution or by clear attribution to a star like James Maguire, known to "walk and talk with ghosts."

Experiences—"ghost stories" and "fairy stories"—are true, true because they happened or true because, like pants, they are fictions set in fact. They tell the truth about the other world or about the little world of the community.

Truth seals the ceili's contract. Stories pull away safely from live neighbors, then push into emphatic relevance by siting themselves locally and using real local people, modest farming people, as their characters. Since stories are true, they treat the neighbors, the people in the tale and the people hearing the tale, decently. The community is affirmed, and stories of, by, and for the neighbors are history. Logically, the most important of the ceili's tales are those deepest in truth, unimpeachably true, the stories called "history." They are owned by the whole community, so—unlike pants —they lack authors. They were not learned as entities from individuals;

they were "gathered up" from every reliable source by certain learned old men called "historians."[22]

Truth is the issue and rationale of Ballymenone's generic system. Lies harm community, so fiction must be carefully framed. People fear falsehood. It destroys. They build their society on true words, so they are accustomed to saying what is so. They find truth easy to speak, and more deeply, truth, they believe, is natural to human beings. Hugh Nolan became a historian, a teller of factual tales, because he "enjoyed it." It is logical, Mr. Nolan said, for people to forget fiction; its remembering is a struggle of mind against soul, but truth is effortless, pleasing to recall:

"I'll tell ye the way it is. If it would be a true story, do ye see, you'd mind it far better. But these made-up things, do ye see, ye'd loss track of the work.

"A true story, it'll not go out of your head as quick as a story there's nothin about.

"Oh, that's the way with the human being."

Truth suits the soul. It puts the person in touch with a center within, brings calm joy to the remembering mind, and flows smoothly over the speaking tongue, unfolding to control the whole of the storyteller's creation. As knowledge moves, step-by-step away from the speaker, truth maintains its grip. Stories of the self (experiences), stories of known others (exploits, bids, pants), and stories of unknown others—all are true. Those most distant are most scrupulously preserved and named by the central idea: history. So they provide the deepest entry into the world of the story and the nighttime scene of the ceili, the "stories of history."

Some "stories of history" are like exploits. They relate the valiant actions of local individuals, but differ by being placed clearly in the larger context of Irish history, the Famine or the Days of the Landlords. The most important tales of individual heroism tell of time's beginning, when the Saints brought God's word to the locality and left in it indisputable signs of God's goodness. "Saints" comprise one great class of historical tale. "Battles" are the other, tales of political conflict displaying the problems of collective, rather than individual, action.

This book will include every story of history told today in the District. This chapter shows how these tales fit into a system of narration constructed by the neighbors as they gather in the common event of the ceili.

Ceilis unify in the truth the speaker receives and gives, and true stories give the ceiliers a way to conceive of their existence. Tales of Saints lay the world's sacred foundations. Experiences explore its dim rim. Exploits, bids, and pants preserve the human traits essential to survival: courage and wit. Battle tales symbolize the community, showing how brave, smart people group themselves for victory and defeat in a world that has limits known to no one and a center in constant flux.

In ceilis, in tales, neighbors raise and face the issues their scene demands. They must accept limitations without knowing what they are. They must be brave, gathering themselves for battle to fight boredom with wit, or their ceili will not happen. "Life," they say, "is just a little ceili." When it is dark and there is no work to be done, nothing to occupy the hand and brain, time opens enormously, and life's empty terror presses in on the mind. Nightly, repetitively, life is faced and conquered in the small pleasures of convivial company, tea, chat, and tales that describe and enact the virtues necessary to forming ceilis out of time, lives out of ceilis.

Ceilis are not planned. They happen. At night you sit to rest and perhaps a neighbor or two will lift the latch and join you at the hearth. Or perhaps you will rise to your feet after supper and go out along the black lanes to one of the local homes known as a "ceili house." If a "company" forms in a kitchen, and if strength remains to lift talk into chat, a ceili arises. Tea draws, chat turns, and the night gathers as a good one. In the past, special ceilis were prearranged to ascend swiftly to story and song. Our topic begins with Hugh Nolan describing a tournament of pants:

"It was the usual thing that used to happen by the fireside, the ceilis that used to be longgo: one man would tell somethin, then another man would tell something forenent that, and it would go on around, and that's what they'd spend their night at. And then there'd be a discussion on whose pant was the best one.

"Well, the people used to come along for to get a number of these stories, for to judge which of them would be the best to tell if they were in some company.

"They used to analyze it from beginning to end and judge for themselves which story was the best, do ye see.

"Someone would propose this round of storytellin. Then if there happened to come strangers along, the natives would be watchin to see what stories that these men would give.

"But that has died away altogether in this country. The younger generations are not interested in it—from the radio and television came along.

"There was another custom was in this country. They'd gather a lock of people into a house and they'd all be singers and every man or every woman that was there, they'd sing a song. That used to be counted a great kind of night."

Mr. Nolan pauses, and I comment that his description sounded unlike the ceilis I know, in which singing and storytelling are unusual, then I ask how these special ceilis were organized.

"Well, I'll tell you the way it used to go.

"You and I would meet on the road, maybe some night during the winter. And you had Saturday night left out for to go ceiliin, or you had Sunday night. Well, if you were around the locality together, couple of mile, you'd pick out where would be the best place to go for a night's singin.

Or where would be the best place to go for a night's storytellin. That was the way it used to be organized.

"So you'd arrange on goin to a certain place. A certain man, if he didn't live there, he used to ceili there. Then we'd tell a couple more, Francy Corrigan and Paddy McBrien, where we were goin, and they'd go *too*.

"And that was the way. Everyone would sing a song, or tell a story. That was the way that the custom was kept *alive*."

Understanding what he meant by a certain man and a certain place, I say, "So you'd make a special effort to get all the singers or storytellers to come for a special night," and Mr. Nolan answers:

"Oh, they would. And it all depended on the place that you were goin. If the place that you were goin to go, if it was celebrated for storytellin, well, you'd go for a night of that, and if it was celebrated for singin, it was the same thing. And then if there was a musician or a couple of them, you'd go to whatever house they'd be in."

Today, when the neighbors' night visit rises to entertainment, it may include a few stories, deemed to fit the chat, or even a song, produced on request, but the ceili is not a storytelling or singing session. Once, though, the ceili's spirit was purified in nights arranged to focus on one or the other of the highest forms of verbal art. Such were still ceilis; their stories were the ones you hear in ceilis today. When I asked, Mr. Nolan replied:

"Well, there'd be a certain class of stories chosen. There wouldn't be anything dirty or offensive, do ye know. It would be exploits and adventures, and pants. Good composers would be at it. And they would tell these short stories that would amuse adults and children."

Ceilis happen at home, in the kitchen by the hearth. If men do the telling, the company includes women and children, and the wild mind is tamed in stories to do no dishonor to the spirit of the domestic fire alight at life's center. Once, other events broke nearer the edge. Mr. Nolan:

"In days gone by, there used to be what they called *joins*. It would be a gatherin up—there'd be an announcement made round the neighborhood: Well, we're goin to a *night* in such a house, do ye know. And we're gatherin up a lock of bobs to get a drop of drink and maybe *tea* and *bread*. So men used to put in their bit. That happened every year for years and years.

"There was some one particular man took charge of the money. It was spent on the spree.

"Every man would give in a subscription, and when there'd be a bit of money all gathered up, some two would go to *Arney*, and they'd buy a go of—it was generally *whiskey* in them days. Whiskey was *cheap*. A lock of half-pints of whiskey.

"Ye'd get a half a pint of whiskey in them days for fourteen pence in the old money.

"You paid so much and I paid so much and Johnny Boyle paid so much and Francy Corrigan paid so much, and, well, it was generally men that was *drinkin*, men that was drinkin.

"So they'd get right boozed. And this man Bob Flynn, he used to start makin the wills of all the men round the country, drawin up their wills on the table.

"So now, he'd leave the land to such a one; he'd leave so much money to such a purpose, all to this.

"Oh, he used to make a whole go of wills, you know. Every man in the house, he made their will.

"He was a great man for makin a bit of a speech. Comical kind of man.

"He lived in a small house, the next place to Quigley's, in Drumbargy.

"I heared a man tellin about
       bein at one of these functions.

"And this Quigley, he was a very hot-tempered man.

"And he was great fire when he'd get drunk, you know.

"But this night Hugh McGiveney was in it.

"And Christie, as his name was, he got real drunk.

"So anyway, Hughie was sittin at the fire and he looked towards the dresser.

"And there was a wee pot just in the front of the dresser.

"So Hughie got up to his feet and
       he went down and
       he lifted up the pot and
       he looked into the pot and
       he looked under the pot and
             where the pot *was*,
       and he looked round the whole dresser.

"Some of them says to him: What are you lookin at Hughie?

"Well, he says, I seen the Devil goin into that pot.

"So man ◊, Christie was sittin in the corner,
       and Christie up to his feet,
       got aholt of the pot and he out
       and ◊ he broke the pot into bits agin the wall ◊.

"Well then, ah, it used to last until near mornin."

The join's company was all male, and its entertainment broke the ceili's bonds. Ceilis might include a story and a bottle of stout, but the norm is chat and tea. The men of the join took tea and bread, but they were drinking; what they wanted was plenty of yellow whiskey, and when right boozed their wit cracked narrative conventions.

At the beginning of our century, Lady Gregory understood that the drama of rural Irish art lay in words, not gestures, and she built the stately style of the Abbey Theater on that observation.[23] In Ballymenone, tales delivered in ceilis approach verbal purity. The teller sits still, his eyes in the fire, and his words come clearly, rarely aided by gestures. His texts emerge in measured precision, while the listener looks away, yielding him space, letting the story arrive as pure words upon the ear. In joins, the spirit of story was loosed into the world of action, of touch and gesture. The contract was forged not in intangible truth but in palpable coin. The gift was not symbolized in stories and food, but written out in mock wills. Experience was not fictionalized and confined in devil tales, it was acted out hilariously.

What the join drove to the edge, the "ball" elevated. The ball's pattern was the ceili's, heightened. Balls gathered the neighbors in a home for abundant food and drink and music, provided a bright night's pleasure, and worked on the community's behalf, for funds raised at balls were spent to benefit neighbors in need, to repair the roads or outfit the local fife-and-drum band. The ball's power continued after its entertainment ceased as people traveled improved lanes and the band marched, a symbol of local unity.

Ceilis casually draw neighbors into one home, but balls provided a formal mechanism for gathering the community together. Everyone in the neighborhood was offered a chance to subscribe to the ball by a treasurer who went from house to house collecting money to buy tea and sugar, drink, and a plenitude of rich and fancy food. The mummers used their impersonal disguise and stylized drama to enter every home, including homes of people who normally withdrew from communal activity. Once in, the mummers demanded engagement, coercing the shy and reluctant into participation. At the end of their play, Miss Funny, a man dressed into marginality, like neither a man nor a mummer, stepped out of the troupe's circle to waltz with the house's boss, accept donations, and invite everyone to the annual Mummers' Ball.

At balls people ate to enjoyment and danced to the fiddle. Interludes filled with song. Most memorable of all performers was the late Peter Cassidy of Arney. One of the District's great historians, Mr. Cassidy trained to be a teacher and worked as a postman. He was that type of old man, Peter Flanagan said, who kept bundles of notes tied up with string in his pockets. At balls he donned a long black coat and waltzed an enormous imaginary woman—"as big as a rook of hay," P said—whirling the floor while singing. His song was "Maxwell's Ball," sung to the tune of "The Garden Where the Praties Grow" and composed by Mickey McCourt, Hugh McGiveney, and at least one other man, probably Master Mick Maguire, about a ball on nearby Inishmore.

"I don't believe," Hugh Nolan said, "there's one in Inishmore or Montiagh or this country that has more than a verse of Maxwell's Ball.

"He was a man by the name of McCourt that made it. Mickey McCourt. He lived in Inishmore his lifetime. He was a shoemaker.

"There was alot of people in days gone by, and they were interested in puttin anything that happened, puttin it into *verses*."

Michael Boyle describes the song's origin, providing another and different instance of local wit, and recites the text:

"It's a song that was made on a *ball* that was in the island of Inishmore: Maxwell's Ball.

"The poet was kind of unknown, I think. There was three or four of them, I think, three or four of them at the composin of it. There was a fellow the name of McCourt. He lived in the island of Inishmore, do ye see, and he was at the composin of it: Mickey McCourt. He lived in the island of Inishmore. And he was another rare boy, this Mickey McCourt. He had alot of songs. He had alot of songs, and he had some of his own composition, but he had others then, do ye see, that he *picked up*. But at any rate that's not the story.

"This Maxwell's Ball, it was in a house the name of Maxwell's in Inishmore. And of course a gooddeal of the lads of our country went over to it. So anyway, there was a song made. And the song was made on a girl and a fellow, do ye see. And the girl she left the fellow durin the ball, do ye see. They were sweethearts, do ye see, and durin the ball she left him and went away with another fellow, so he was in a terrible state, of course.

"So anyway, didn't some of the lads make up a song about it anyway.

"The song run:

One night when I was courting,
*   I went unto a spree.*
With polished boots and fancy socks,
*   I was dressed up to a tee.*
With tommy cuffs and buttons,
*   and a collar white and tall,*
I went to meet my Nora
*   that night at Maxwell's Ball.*
They were there in all persuasions,
*   in numbers great and small.*
They hailed from Carna Cara
*   and from Tonyloman too,*
And from sweet old Montiagh's shores,
*   their numbers weren't few.*
They braved the dangers of the waves;
*   they came both one and all*
To patronize the gathering
*   that night at Maxwell's Ball.*
The ladies they were charming
*   and beautiful to view,*
And some were dressed in Blarney tweed,
*   and more in navy blue.*

While some, they wore tight jackets
  to make their waist look small,
Till I really thought they'd split in two
  that night at Maxwell's Ball ◇.
It was there I spied my Nora
  unto her I did say,
Just come into the dining room
  and we will have some tea.
Right willingly she came with me,
  she was ready at the call.
Oh, she et the dose, I paid for all
  that night at Maxwell's Ball.
But then my pleasures ended,
  and my heart felt sore and sad,
When I found me Nora had left me
  I went distracted mad.
I rambled up and down the room
  on Nora I did call,
Till I found her on her suitor's knee
  that night at Maxwell's Ball.
While some did laugh and more did chaff,
  while I sat in suspense,
Thinkin how I lost my Nora
  likewise my eighteen pence.
And everywhere I go, the boys do on me call:
Or did you get your Nora
  tonight at Maxwell's Ball?
But now the ball it's ended,
  and I have one word to say:
It's never go in for courting
  till the ladies takes the tea,
For if you do, I'll tell to you,
  they'll make you very small.
They'll set you runnin mad like me
  that night at Maxwell's Ball ◇.

"That's the poem now. That's the song the boys made up.

"Mickey McCourt and Hugh McGiveney, they both helped with it. But they bid to be clever boys because they were supposed to make up the song that night and sing it at the ball.

"They did. That's what I believe.

"There were a couple that was at the ball told me that.

"An old man that's dead and gone longgo, he told me that they composed it at the ball, made it up at the ball. That's what I heard.

"That was a true song. That all happened.

"My mother—God be good to her—she remembers it happenin. And I was talkin to fellows that was at it. I was talkin to old men—they were old men in my day—that was at the ball, that remembered it all.

"And I knew the men that made it. I knew the men that made it all right."

Elaborate in rhyme, rich with sound, "Maxwell's Ball" displays the District's taste in poetry. Add melody beneath, and an apex is reached. Talk struggles upward to chat, chat rises to stories, stories at the top of their arc swing through rhythm and echoing sound toward poetry. Song is speech at its decorated peak.

The ball was the decorated peak of social interaction. Visits become ceilis when they join pleasure to neighborly purpose, and the ball raised the ceili to its highest power. Its food was sweeter, more abundant, its words were music, its action was dancing, not sitting. Its social intent was plainer and broader. "Maxwell's Ball" describes people of "all persuasions" coming from Tonyloman (two miles northwest), Carna Cara (Hugh McGiveney's part of Rossdoney), and Montiagh (Master Maguire's district, three miles south), braving the waves to Inishmore, bringing money that would be used to strengthen the local community.

"Maxwell's Ball," composed at a ball to describe a ball, performed at a ball by a man pretending to be at a ball, marks and merges aesthetic and social high points. The song, traditionally satiric, employs the most intense and difficult kind of speech—poetry—to comment on the most intense and difficult of those social interactions which, like ceilis and balls, bring immediate joy and lead to long connection: courtship.

Balls and joins are gone. Ceilis endure. Though diminished and restrained, the old conjunction of pleasure and social purpose, of aesthetic and ethical values—the "entertaining," the "good"—is achieved anew when tea appears and talk cracks, when the neighbors bring a little happiness into the night while reaffirming the relations that make them more than people who chance to live near one another.

In ceilis, people are ceiliers, part of a company. Tomorrow they will be neighbors, people who work together and count on one another when troubles come. In other scenes they have other identities, other performances. Ceilis are not the only current occasion for art, nor are ceili tales the District's only stories.

Dinner is done. People rise from the table next to a wall of the kitchen and carry their chairs and cups of tea to the hearth so chat can continue to fill the evening without breaking. If neighbors enter the kitchen, the first and central space of the home, a ceili might develop, but if no one comes, the scene is one of the "fireside." Its participants are not ceiliers but members of the family. Its tellers of tales are not fraternal—the neighbors—but parental. Their stories are directed to children.

The parental teller might offer a ceili tale, but shade it for amusement or instruction. Stories of experience, which are evidence of reality's shape among adults, are told children to surprise, scare, and control them. Peter Flanagan and Ellen Cutler both said tales of fairies and ghosts were told children to keep them from wandering the roads after dark. I read that country folk believed wild horses lived beneath the surface of Lough Erne, but when I asked Mr. Nolan he explained:

"Och, I heard about it, but I don't believe ◊ that there's anything of the kind.

"I'll tell ye: longgo it used to be told to youngsters to keep them from goin too near the water.

"Their fathers and mothers and people that'd be in charge of them, they'd then, do ye see: Don't be goin near the River because there's wild horses in it and they'll come out and take you *away*. Do ye see.

"But there was nothing to it because nobody ever seen any of them that ever I was talkin to. There'd be otters and badgers and animals like that, but I never heard tell of wild horses in the Lough.

"They talked about it but there'd be nothing about it."

Two genres of tale told children are not told in ceilis. Fictional and didactic, they are not appropriate for adult conversation.

One is the "fireside tale," the wondrous long narrative folklorists call märchen. These are few in number. Both Peter Flanagan and Hugh Nolan remember "Willie the Wisp" from childhood. Hugh McGiveney named one of his cats Willie the Wisp. This tale in which a blacksmith after tricking the Devil is denied entrance to hell and sent wandering the world with a live coal, a hot unwanted soul, is bound in memory, in topic and childish delight, to the "fireside song" of "The Devil and the Farmer's Wife." Between rollicking choruses she reveals herself too tough, even for hell. The children of the next generation similarly remember one tale, "Huddon and Duddon and Donald O'Leary," in which a poor, clever farmer out-tricks his jealous, evil neighbors and prospers. Michael Boyle learned the story from Hugh Nolan, who learned it from the newspaper, and both told it to the children of Drumbargy and Rossdoney to teach them endurance and that strength and wit are rewarded.

The other genre of tale for children is the "example." Its characters are animals. "Fireside songs"—Terry Maguire's "The Frog's Courtship," and Peter Flanagan's "The Field Mouse's Birthday Ball"—also use animals to delight young listeners with fantasy. The example's moral conclusions are explicit. "Lesson" is another name for these tales telling of foxes and sour grapes, geese and golden eggs, owls condemned by other birds for calling a man's boot a man's boot.[24] Typical is Peter Flanagan's about a sick deer. When he told it once to my youngest daughter, he expanded with emotion while the deer failed and died for the want of food, but he was reluctant to put it on tape for me. It was, he said, "only an old readin out of a book." He was reluctant, not unwilling, and when years later I asked again, he turned to Polly, my eldest, and told her a spare version, its first line the story's title, the last, its moral:

"A deer that once was sick
 and lay down on the rich grass
 on a lawn close be the forest.
"So that she'd have good food to eat durin her illness.
"And all the wild beasts came on a visit to see her.
"And all assembled from all airts and parts.
"And durin the time that they were visitin the deer, they started to eat up all the grass
 round her.
"And be the time that she recovered out of her illness, she had nothing to eat, no food to eat.
"For want of a thought we may do harm even when we mean to be kind.
"And.
"I think that's the way it ended up. It's only a little lesson.
"That's the way it went."

What is only a lesson, only a reading out of a book, is not fit for adult conversation. Stories properly transfer authority. Adults tell their peers stories they learned from other adults, but they tell their children stories they learned from their parents or got from print. Properly set, they are important moral lessons. Children who hear about sick deer will grow into ceiliers obliged to visit and accept hospitality. They must learn to be aware of the repercussions of their own best intentions.

Fireside tales and examples are contained, named entities, asserted by dint of implicit authority. A parental figure has the right to instruct. But ceilis are made of equals, so their stories do not propose conclusions but raise problems. Ceili tales reverse tales for children: their moral is unformed and implicit, their authority is often explicit. The narrator entertains us and then leaves us to find the messages in his stories—their warnings and information—while reminding us that his stories are truth, not fiction, when he says he knew the people he tells about, the heroes of exploits, bids, pants, and experiences. Joe Flanagan argues that ghosts cannot be dismissed, because reasonable people, people he knows, have seen them. Hugh Nolan discounts water horses, because no one has seen one. Michael Boyle's account of "Maxwell's Ball" is believable—the event in the song and the origin of the song can be taken as true—because he talked to men who were there, it happened in his mother's day, and he knew the men who made the song.

Tales are not rammed into ceilis. They are welcomed, and the company maneuvers its conversation to receive them. Other situations are too quick and confused for talk to rise cordially and gracefully to art.

The neighborhood is the net of human association created by people as they move between the hearth where they are host and parent and the hearth where they are guest and neighbor. Beyond the neighborhood, surrounding the District, the neighbors' place is Fermanagh. Their points of interaction are not the hearths in homes but public spaces: the streets and shops of Enniskillen, the fourteen public houses of the little town of Swanlinbar. Here, identified as people from Arney or Bellanaleck, Sessiagh or Rossdoney, they act as part of "the crowd." Most of the others in the crowd are known by face or association, place, class, or political alignment, if not by name, but the crowd holds together more by rules of conduct than by culture. The crowd's people are not governed by the intense experience of neighborliness, so they are at once merged into a mass and broken into individuality.

Within the neighborhood, people are neighbors first, part of a cooperative enterprise. In the crowd, their roles simplify toward consumer or producer. As members of a congregation in a church beyond their parish, dealers at the cattle mart, shoppers in the Town, drinkers in the pubs, people take what is offered and return cash and decorum.

During ceilis, one man gives a story, one woman gives tea, but the situation would be misrepresented as one of performers versus audience. Roles shift gracefully and constantly through the evening; things begin and end in equality. In public places, roles near fixity. Mrs. Cutler went to Irvinestown to watch the Black Preceptory parade, to stand along the street as part of the crowd viewing and cheering as bands and men in black thundered by. Her neighbor, Bobbie Thornton, went to the same parade, not to watch, but to be seen, to be part of the crowd marching through the crowd, to assume the role of performer in a public political display.

The street is the crowd's place of extremes. Its art is very public, the march of uniformed men, or very private. People meeting briefly amid shopping have no time to "raise chat," so they pass with greetings or pause for repartee. This is the locus of the "joke." Quick, fictional, funny, sometimes ribald, starting abruptly, ending sharply with a punch line to match the example's moral, the joke will not fit the ceili, where stories stretch smoothly out of chat, ride on truth, remain interesting enough to tell again in familiar company, and are kept, as Hugh Nolan said, from becoming offensive.

The idea of the street is notched a degree nearer intimacy and a degree higher in art in the public house. The pub is a house. The home's open, central space is its "kitchen," lying between the grassland of the neighborhood and the familial rooms closed off each of its ends. Visitors enter the kitchen immediately and effortlessly. They rarely enter "the Room," the polite, impeccable parlor preserved at one end, and they never enter the utterly private bedroom at the other end. Conceptually, the "public house"—and so it is called more often than pub—is composed of the home's spaces. The big "shop," with its bar and supplies of food and drink, is entered like the farmhouse kitchen, straight from the street. Interior doors lead into the small, neat, domestically appointed "Room" and into the private quarters of the publican's family.

Within, drinkers arrange bodies and speech to define space. They can go into the Room, circle chairs around a heater, and with stout rather than tea form a "company" within "the crowd," a ceili in public. Turning their backs, they knot themselves tightly for neighborly exchange, planning commerce, trading stories and dirty jokes. Or they can break their company open into general participation, engaging in public performance, snapping "entertainment" toward the wider, wilder pleasures of "sport."

When the crowd surges toward unity and orients toward art, its beauty, as at balls, is formed in song and music. As in the street, art's public content is usually political, sometimes comic.

At last the noted singer, drinking in the company of his neighbors, yields to repetitive request. Song rises in his throat, attention is gripped, and he is encouraged. "Good man," they say. "There's the quare, grand air." Words of support knife between the stanzas. Voices join at the ends of lines, and the song is followed by applause and a flurry of compliments. "Good man, Flanagan." "That's the man can sing." The singer steps out of his company toward the shop's center, or his companions standing in support around him separate slightly to bring attention to him as he stands and sings again, encouraged. New drinks appear at his place along the bar. His voice strengthens, the shop quiets as ears cock to hear, and the men around the singer shush drunken conversations. Another song, he swings wider, answering requests, bringing singers from other communities and singers of less renown into performance. The night will be remembered as a good one, full of sport.

It begins after Mass, after dinner, after farm chores, as Fermanagh men pack into cars and glide on black bikes south through Kinawley, across the Border to Swad. Our dinner done, Peter Flanagan adjusts his necktie, rolls his flute in a brown paper bag, and inserts it in his breast pocket. When he arrives he is asked to play, but his fame is secure, and he will wait for the right moment, for a few drinks, for a knowledgeable audience. The Troubles in Ulster depress him, he says, he is not in a mood for music, and he has no wish to play unless those around him are capable of deep appreciation. The shop fills. Men in black crowd together. Smoke drifts and hangs, clamor rises.

Tommy Lunny joins us, saying there is music in the Room. Young men, freshly shaven and modishly dressed, press around the piano. A man of middle age and professional bearing talks with a woman in one corner. In another, two elderly women attired in bright pastels sit behind a low round table in close, quiet conversation with sweet aperitifs. The walls are newly papered in floral stripes, hung with hazy prints of rural landscapes. Chairs are stuffed and comfortable. In a voice high and clear, somewhere between an Irish tenor and hillbilly twang, the pianist, a young blond farmer from just north of the Border, responds to requests, switching happily between old country-and-western standards—"Folsom City Blues," "You Came Down from Heaven"—and new songs of resistance. Again and again, the men around him, their ages between eighteen and thirty-five, ask for "The Men Behind the Wire," a current hit often heard on the radio, anthem of the internees held without charge at Long Kesh near Belfast, where eerie light at night whips barbed wire into the eyes of motorists on the swift highway.

Peter Flanagan waits, a drink in his hand, a tin whistle in his pocket, at the edge of the crowd. Deferentially, without comment, the pianist's next choice is a traditional reel. At its end, Mr. Flanagan steps into the noise, draws the flute, and plays the tune again with beauty and power.

Light applause follows, but requests in the babble return to the young singer at the piano, and his song brings silence, then cheers:

> Twenty-six were won and six were lost.
> That's the price our freedom cost.
> So let us rise and sing today:
> Heroic men of the IRA.
>
> Sean South was murdered by a British gun,
> O'Hanlon died for the green and gold,
> James Crossan died from a brengun's stray,
> MacManus died for the IRA.
>
> So let us rally one and all,
> The young and old, the big and small.
> And we are free of England's reign;
> Support the men of the IRA.
>
> Stop when we've won back thirty-two,
> And thank brave men who are so few,
> And we are free of England's reign;
> Support the men of the IRA.

"Up the Provos," shouts a thin young man, coiffed like a cavalier, and talk thickens merrily in the smoke. Words are loud, happy, clattery, then behind them, across the Room, a new song begins:

> A great crowd had gathered outside of Kilmainham . . .

The voice is high, sprung. The singer, an older brother, sits stiffly, a drink held against his breast. Loud talk continues around the piano.

> Their heads all uncovered, they knelt on the ground . . .

Memory had stirred. The references in "Twenty-six Were Won" were recent. Sean South and Feargal O'Hanlon died in the raid on Brookeborough in Fermanagh, January 1, 1957. Each has his commemorative song. James Crossan was an innocent man shot down on the Border after a night's drinking here at Swad in the same year. "God rest you, God bless you, James Crossan of Bawn . . ." runs the chorus of his song. Patrick MacManus was blown up in 1958 while making a bomb in a house above Swad. The brother's song remembers and returns to the moment in 1916 that led to sorting Ireland's counties into six and twenty-six:

> For inside that grim prison lay a true Irish soldier,
> His life for his country about to lay down.

"Good man," they say. He pauses. "Go on. Go on." The circle at the piano opens toward him. His eyes are shut, his voice strains at its upper limit:

> The black flag was hoisted, the cruel deed was over,
> Gone was the man who loved Ireland so well . . .

By the stanza's last line, the voices in the Room have risen around his, drowning it more in shouts than in singing:

> When they murdered James Connolly, the Irish rebelled.

He is seated in his chair across the Room. "Good man." His back is straight, his neck is taut:

> God's curse on you England, you cruel-hearted monsters . . .

His face fixes near anguish. The Room is silent, but the song has fled, dissolved in emotion and alcohol, gone. For an instant there is no sound. "I'll sing no more," he says softly. "Good man," they say, circling back around the piano, closing noisily around another request for "The Men Behind the Wire." These men have friends behind the wire. Unsteadily, the older brother tips new stout into his glass and shakes it to his lips. The Room disassembles into many conversations. Again someone asks for "The Men Behind the Wire."

Lost in the crowd, P Flanagan elbows through younger, taller bodies and stands into the circle's center, turning to deepen history and preserve the breadth of the singer's repertory. Educator, entertainer, he says to the young men, "It took the boys in Fenian days to carry it on until the Men Behind the Wire came. Wasn't that right?"

The clatter continues around him. He stands, persistent: "The old fight had to be fought, and it had to be fought from the days of eighteen and sixty-seven, and indeed it went back further. Seventeen and ninety-eight, that was the first Rising. That's what you want to know: the background to everything. *Do ye see?*"

It is not quiet. Some young men have given him their ears, others talk on.

"Now I'll sing a song," Mr. Flanagan says, "and I'll bet you, yous never heard it. But it's patriotic too."

The crowd is nearly quiet. With deep force and a slow, sad air, Mr. Flanagan begins:

> The slave may bend in abject fear,
> And he may hug the chains that bind him,
> And the coward may run his base career,
> No flag of freedom find him.
> But while above us floats the flag,
> Of green and orange blended,
> No tyrant, nor no knave, its folds shall drag
> While our stout arms defend it.
>
> We ask for not but what's our own
> Of friend nor foreign foeman.
> We are one in love and blood and bone
> We yield nor we bend to no man.
> We fight the fight our fathers fought
> Beneath that same old standard,
> And they nobly died, as brave men ought,
> While leading freedom's vanguard.
>
> Gaze on that standard as it flies,
> By true man's hand supported,
> A prouder yet neath heaven's skies,
> A fairer never floated.
> It waved o'er O'Brien and O'Neill,
> O'er Sarsfield, Tone, and Emmet.
> It oft has braved the foeman's steel
> And foeman's blood begem it.
>
> No hireling, servile slaves are we
> To bend with mock submission
> To the alien's grinding, tyrant he,
> And despot's fierce ambition.
> But for our own, our suffering land,
> Ten thousand hearts are ready,
> For to strike a blow against alien wrong,
> Calm, patient, firm, and steady.
>
> And we'll shout it out to foe or friend,
> To those who hate or love us,
> While life remains we will defend
> The flag that floats above us.

Applause explodes. He had sung with raw power, enunciating the poem's words clearly, sneering at coward and tyrant, gesturing as he turned to the flag above. "That's one of the good old songs," he says, laughing as the young men congratulate him for manly singing.

Names in the good old song gesture backward past William Smith O'Brien, transported after the Rising of 1848, past Robert Emmet, whose speech from the dock in 1803 Mr. Flanagan has memorized, past Wolfe Tone, leader of the Rising of 1798, and Patrick Sarsfield, hero of the Battle of Limerick in 1690, to Hugh O'Neill, Earl of Tyrone, who led the Ulster confederacy against Elizabeth's generals into defeat at Kinsale on Christmas Eve 1601. The song came forward in melismatic minor and lofty rhetoric to achieve unity with "Twenty-six Were Won." Neither tells a tale; both refer to events in other songs and use the names of martyrs to call for steadfast defense.

Different songs overarched differences of age and taste to preserve aesthetic diversity while establishing immediate social unity. For an hour old dance tunes are traded. The piano proves capable of jigs and reels. Young men as well as old have tin whistles in their pockets. Music holds them together and caps the night.

Then, closing time, the proprietor sweeps empty glasses and black bottles onto a tray, and young men, men from the North willing to put their bodies on the line, stand straight and solemn while Peter Flanagan plays the national anthem, "The Soldier's Song."

With people moving past, laughing, jamming in the doorway, a quiet handsome young man who has known the terror of midnight roads, the engine's hum, the feel of a makeshift bomb in his palms, stands, looking at no one, and says softly, "When I hear the old men sing, I love Ireland more."

Outside in the dark street the crowd shifts and stirs awhile, then breaks slowly for home with good words for the night and promises to meet next Sunday. We tie Tommy's bike to the roof of the car, fill the interior with neighbors, and head north over cratered roads. Somewhere on a black country lane a soldier's swinging light will stop us. Headlights will die and the car will glide forward, so he will not be caught in their glare, a target. We will be searched, questioned in sharp English tones, and then in total darkness we will snake through a barricade of hideous armored cars, past camouflaged, frightened young men, tall West Indians and Lancashire farm lads with machine guns. In a couple of miles Joe will lower the kettle to the flame so we can have tea, bread, quiet chat, a little ceili.

In the ceili, makers of tea and chat create the community. In the street, cattle mart, and public house, they buy and sell, watch and march, listen and sing, and form the crowd, the population of their region, Fermanagh. And beyond that . . . you have seen them, a little lost, standing alone in wordless confusion, country people, dressed neatly, poorly, on the streets of big cities.

That is where the politicians and their agents, the false scholars, want them: weak, bewildered, and, above all, silent. The man who is a learned educator at the fireside, a sparkling wit in the ceili, a bold singer in the pub, becomes, in the gigantic milieu of the nation, silent, nearly nothing, a follower for a politician's doctrine, a statistic for a scientist's scheme, a member of the inarticulate masses.[25] The idea is evil. The politician, glib in his office, is but part of the masses at a football match, ignorant and lost in the green countryside or the back streets of his own city. But to support a frantic equation of power and wealth with intelligence and verbal skill, the false scholar contrives a pyramidal picture of society with kings and madmen at its peak, a silent majority at its spreading base. Then reality is ordered to trickle down from top to bottom, from power to weakness, wealth to poverty, intelligence to stupidity, invention to imitation, light to obscurity, texts to silence. Even scholars who strive to be democratic sometimes accept the ugly metaphor and propose to study things from the bottom up. Society is not peaked like a pyramid or layered like a cake. It is composed of communities simultaneously occupying space and time at the same human level. Some are composed of upper-class fox-hunters, some of middle-class scholars, some of poor farmers. All seem reasonable from within, strange from without, silent at a distance. The way to study people is not from the top down or the bottom up, but from the inside out, from the place where people are articulate to the place where they are not, from the place where they are in control of their destinies to the place where they are not.

Soldiers on the battlefield, artists in the studio: generously we study some people in terms of their own excellence. All people deserve comparable treatment. Decent, serious study begins on the inside, where people are articulate and powerful and in control. In Ballymenone that is at the hearth, at home, in the midst of a ceili where history is created.

The only way to preserve the fantasy of the inarticulate masses is never to listen to members of the masses when they are articulate. Stay home.

Tourists leave home, and some share their observations in travel literature. But always in a hurry, they never stay long enough to learn something new. Deadlines and profits beckon. Languid or angry, their shallow writings on Ireland, her farrow and pain, are constructed of quick encounters in street or pub where people talk too much, too cleverly, too dogmatically.

If the tourist to Northern Ireland calls himself folklorist, he meets people in public houses as singers of songs, Orange or Green, and if he follows them home and badgers them onto tape, whining with impatience, they have no way to treat him but as a child, so they sing him fireside songs, old ballads, and they tell him scary stories and fabulous märchen. Real adult fare would come only if the folklorist settled in and waited.

Unhurried, we sit in the kitchen. To one side is the bedroom, private and shut. What happens there is none of our business. Out the front door opens the public arena of commerce and momentary escape. Between burns the fire where the family connects to the community. From the middle of life, the hearth presents the ceili, the most intimate event in which the scholar from beyond can or should participate. Here is the natural entrance for the patient, serious traveler.

Hasty travelers may represent the rural Irish place as one of hilarity and anger, of pubs and parades, ballads, bulls, and blarney. But this is a culture of the hearth, of penetrating thought, deep faith, and courtly hospitality, a place of small fires and hard work, where people calmly, plainly tell one another the truth.

Truth is most beautifully and painfully compressed into "stories of history." We have learned how they fit into a literary system, how speech and situation define each other to create genres of artful action. It has been too abstract. We need to feel how stories unfold in real time. The date is August 29, 1972.

PART TWO

Saint Febor, Black Francis, and the Performance of History

Drumbargy Brae

Drumbargy Lane

The Performance of History   91

The Flanagans'

Phil Flanagan about 1920

Passing the Time in Ballymenone

Tommy Love

Joe Flanagan

Peter Flanagan

3

Ceili at Flanagans'

The house cattle should have been onto the hillsides early in April, but summer came lashing wet winds down the brown hedges and through bleak fields. Across the bog and over the hills, air lay bone cold. Some of the cows, they say, starved in their byres, dying on beds of sodden rushes, and into the minds of men waiting for the sun blew years when black frost shriveled the spuds in the ridges, years when turf lay on the spread through the summer, and winter closed down without food for the belly or fuel for the hearth. The bright, warm days expected in May and June never came. In running gray skies, in the dank sloughs of the gaps, summer broke, damp, chilled.

Now it is calm. Fat cattle move slowly in the blue harvest evening. Lush grasslands swell and fold in the haze. Some of last year's potatoes and turf and hay remain, heaped into pits on the moss ground, thatched in lumps on the bog, piled in haysheds, built into rotund pecks along the lanes. Old defenses against hard times, displays of industry cover the land.

A month ago summer ended in a blaze of sunshine and a frenzy of work. Hay was rooked, turf was clamped. Sun and warm winds drove out the wet. Once built into rounded conical rooks, and clamps the shape of ancient oratories, hay and turf are considered won. That is their word for victory in the cyclical war fought with the hand-tools they call weapons: the pitchfork and spade.

Now it is quiet, an interlude in work and worry. The main crop potatoes are not yet ready to dig, nor is it time to transplant winter cabbage, shear the corn, or drive the cattle onto the sweet aftergrass of the meadows. Work slows but does not stop. It is a time for gathering in the spoils of war, drawing turf and hay home, and it is time to hack back hedges with billhooks and cart broken turf to gardens built on barren land. Gently, the next campaign begins.

Turf and hay are won. For a month the new potatoes, the Epicures, have been boiled for dinner. It is a time, too, for mild extravagance. This year's potatoes are boiled in lavish numbers, fires built of this year's turf are unnecessarily hearty. Winter's word is bitter. In its depths, when winds pound at the walls of home, potatoes will be sparingly spent and the fire will be stretched with gathered sticks, but today victory expands in little luxuries.

Joe Flanagan turns from the sack of turf next to the open front door. Damp green and blue melt behind him. He cradles an armload. P lifts a violin from its case in the corner and settles on a stool by the hearth. Dinner is done, the hens are fed, empty teacups sit on the floor. Joe tongs live coals from the fire, lines them in front of the hearthstone, and sweeps the ashes off to his side with a besom of heather bound round with twine.

Half a century ago their father, Phil, moved his family into this house. When they were children in Cavan, above Kinawley, the household contained five girls, five boys, and Mrs. Flanagan's father, James Maguire, called James the League for his work in the Land League Agitation. They moved northeast to Kinawley, then Sessiagh, then here, Drumbargy. Two sisters went to America and married, two brothers, Phil and Frank, farm together near Lisbellaw in Fermanagh. Joe, born in April 1900, and Peter, his younger brother, remain.

Their father traveled throughout Ireland, and to Scotland and England as well. He was a tailor, professionally trained in Leeds, and Ned Cooney of Sessiagh, himself a tailor, recalls Phil Flanagan as a fine craftsman. He made the policemen's tunics and Billy Cutler's wedding suit. Phillie Flanagan is well remembered as "the neatest wee man," dapper, stout, an artist on the violin and flute. On the great wooden concert flute, P says, "he was Ireland's best. He had great volume. He could fill the flute, me father, and he had some right songs, so he had. When he was tailorin, he used always to sing. He was very fond of Moore's Melodies, and his father before him was a great singer of Moore's." Music filled their home. Mrs. Flanagan was a singer who knew the words to songs others forgot. Three of the boys formed the Flanagan Brothers' Band, with a big drum made out of an oil drum. One sister became a harpist. And Peter remembers his father rising in the morning with a tune in his head and playing it at the hearth before he had his morning tea.

Joe places a bog sod against the backstone, turf-side out, replaces the red coals, and leans dark brown turf in a semicircle over them. P in his work clothes, black suit and heavy shoes, holds the violin upright, facing him, and plucks the strings tuning it. Recently he sold his other fiddle to the father of a beginner, and this one lay in disrepair until the hay had been won. Now he has glued its cracks and strung it anew.

Music, P says, is his life. As a boy he blew the flute until his father good-naturedly ordered him out of the house: "Get away out of here with that old fidiog." Fidiog is good Irish. Their grandparents spoke it, their parents understood it, but Irish is known only in shreds to P and Joe and their neighbors. When his father brought the first violin into the house, P snuck off with it. He sat under a hedge by a forth so his strange sounds would be taken for fairy music, and twisted and twisted the pegs until all the strings snapped. His father understood, for music drove him too. Like so many great musicians, P learned less from teaching than from listening. He tried, listened, and played and became excellent, famous like his father. Martin Crudden, a great singer from Kinawley, one of the stars of Swad's public houses, tells the tale of a time when P, then a teenager, entered a contest, played "The Harvest Home," and won even though his competition included his teacher, the bandmaster from Kinawley.

P's young life centered on the fife-and-drum band—"For me," he says, "it was all band, band, band"—and playing the fiddle at balls and country-house dances. Now he wishes a quiet life. He likens himself to a local schoolmaster who burned in his youth for learning but abandoned his books as an old man to walk in solitary thought along the country lanes. But a quiet life is living: music maintains existence through action. "It keeps my hand in," he says, "the same as Paddy McBrien followin his cows." A contemporary of P's, Mr. McBrien "sloughs and plows" after the four cows pastured on the brae rising before his home. They graze slowly through the view framed by the Flanagans' front window.

Joe leans over the fire, fanning it with a square of cardboard. Wisps and white tails of smoke lift between the new turf. P touches the bow to the strings.

Comparing music and farmwork makes sense for P. They are his delight, intertwined in his mind. When icy winds whip winter around the house, the fiddle lies dead in its case, the spirit shrinks in pain. P considers not bothering with a big garden in the new year:

"Then the spring comes. It turns warm, and the land begins to turn green. The cuckoo calls, and things begin to stir, and I throw Larry off—that's what they call laziness in this country: Larry. I throw Larry off me back and take up the spade.

"I couldn't be happy seein the moss ground and no pretties in it. No, I don't feel one bit good unless that I'm workin when the spring comes in. And when things is goin well, I can take up the flute or the fiddle. If there weren't spuds in the ridges, I couldn't take down the flute or the fiddle. I could not now. Until I know things is goin well, I don't feel good atall. So I don't.

"But when the spuds peep, I take down the flute and I can play."

Ripped from his bow, winging and swift, "The Sligo Maid's Lament" keens through the kitchen and escapes over the green fields. Smoke curls, clouding around the turf, speeding up the wall beneath the chimney hood. Joe cracks a match, pulls its flame into his pipe, and sits back, listening.

The quiet life P wants is advanced with both spade and fiddle bow. But he speaks of his godfather, who got through life to the great age of ninety by playing music, and it is on music that P most depends to prevent things as they are from shadowing his mind and weakening his soul. "Music," he says, "carries me on."

Drifting, the tune subsides. Joe nods across the hearth in congratulation. With a frown, P brings the violin back to his knees for retuning. When they first bought a wireless, P gave up playing for two years and listened to the radio's "free music." The young people like it, he says, and that is natural, but it became repetitious to him, and since then the wireless has been left on the front table, next to the shaving mirror, beneath the window, in silence—except for occasional bursts of bad news—and P has played for himself the tunes he wished to hear.

Again the bow bites into the strings. The old Fermanagh fiddle style was developed in imitation of the flute's tone. Clear, melodic, flowing, it is simple and pure. P calls it "sweet." One of his brothers became accomplished in the style, but P was excited by the recordings of Michael Coleman, the Sligo master. P's sisters visited Coleman on his deathbed in New York. Phil Flanagan resembled Coleman, P said, in appearance and as a musician. Coleman's records thrilled P, inspired him to complexity. And answering the demands of his own psyche, P's style is, in his own word, "wild."

Driven hard, the notes pop, flutter, and break free, coiling into themselves, cracking outward, hurtling up to the roof. Under the roof, shadows deepen. The kitchen's corners lose their angle, thickening into darkness. Details fade from the dresser opposite the hearth. Its clocks and mugs and rows of platters and plates, the hay twister, the bottle of holy water, the pitcher with the song ballats rolled within, blur, merging with night. Day remains only at the doorway and in shards of gleam on the crockery. Joe rises and curtains the windows. The gas lamp on the front table is left unlit. Slowly the room withdraws to the circle around the hearth. The sky beyond pales and then darkens, pulling its stripe of gray light out over the threshold.

P is turned on his stool away from the hearth. Fire finds highlights in the curls of his hair, and the arm as it rams and dances the bow over the strings. His eyes are closed, he is not playing for us. Tunes do not come in neat pairs. Jigs and reels repeat, spilling into one another. He is finding the groove of this violin and giving his musical mind a stiff test. This is no special night. Our dinner was plain: cabbage, potatoes, salt. P is playing for himself. Joe and I smoke, chat, and relax while the room dims out of awareness and music colors to dominate our senses.

"The Heathery Breeze" fills the kitchen, gusting. For a moment the doorway is blocked, darkened, then it brightens behind Tommy Love, who enters dancing to P's reel. It cannot be easy to stepdance in thick rubber Wellingtons, but Tommy is light and trim and executes a flashy figure before folding with a laugh into a stuffed chair at the hearth. "Well men" is Tommy's greeting.

"How's Tommy?" Joe answers.

"The best" is Tommy's proper response. P keeps playing.

The kitchen of a ceili house like the Flanagans' affords no physical privacy. The door is open, literally. Visitors enter at any time without knock or invitation, so it is a right of the inhabitants to continue on course uninterrupted. While Tommy offers us cigarettes and I light us all, P's tune blows over our conversation.

Mr. Love often ceilis here. The house where he lives with his wife, son, and daughter lies over the hill and down a long lane, south toward the Arney River, but he has land on cutover bog, north of Drumbargy Brae, and his walk takes him along a disused carttrack in front of the Flanagans'. A few weeks ago I helped him rook the last of the hay he had next to the bog when a shower came on. Today he went there after dinner to look at his oats. Many fields of corn failed during the cold summer, but with a little sun his will be ready for shearing in early September. "A couple of good days," Tommy says with a grin, "and we can go away with it." He will stook the oats, clean them through a graip, then slash them for thatching straw.

The hay is won, the oats are standing, and Tommy in rubber boots, overalls, suit coat, and fedora sits loosely, deeply, in his chair, Joe's customary chair, letting the smoke drift. The tune ends.

"Good man, P," says Tommy, and requests "The Humors of Mackan." Shifting forward on his stool across from Tommy, P smiles slightly and his elbow bobs, whirling that reel off the strings.

Music ends and begins again quickly, encouraged by brief words of compliment. Between tunes we unify in comment on them, but while playing, P leaves the role of entertainer, performing only for his harsh inner critic, and our chat finds its own path through the smoke. Its route begins at music, for conversations commence rigorously in shared experience. Tommy evaluates P frankly as a "middling good fiddler." Were he bad, Tommy would have said nothing or that he was the best. Then the chat wanders on to find topics within the usual areas of concern: climate, agriculture, neighbors, politics.

Without a word of greeting, Tommy Lunny enters the kitchen, draws a chair from the back table to a place beside Tommy Love, and joins the conversation. Tommy Lunny, Mrs. Cutler's neighbor, our companion in Swanlinbar, has two farms, one in Gortdonaghy, where he lives with his brother, and another to the south. He runs a large herd, and for the last few days P has been helping him lift hay bales. He sits stiffly, hands on his knees, for though he will demonstrate suppleness by riding his bicycle great distances to chapel, pub, or football match, his legs pain him terribly. Tomorrow will bring long hours of work. It is best now to rest and sit still.

The company has grown and P turns to the hearth, tearing into "Bonnie Kate," driving it, presenting it directly to the ceiliers. Finished, he rests the violin upright on his knee, saying to Tommy Love, "Now give us a tune, Tommy."

It is the responsibility of the entertaining man who occupies the ceili's center to pull others into performance, and it is the responsibility of those others, though acknowledged as lesser talents, to take their turn. Singers without air, who can only talk a song through, and poor storytellers, who lose their tales in muddles, are expected to carry the ceili on for a while, diversifying the sport and giving the man who must do most of the work a rest. The obligation to entertain will return to him.

Tommy Love owns no violin and has not played for twenty years. In a public situation, P would not ask, and were he asked, Tommy would refuse. But this is a ceili, everyone knows everyone, they have worked together, the mood is tranquil, and Tommy demurs for but a minute: "Ah no, P. I wouldn't mind a tune, you see. Honestly."

"Tommy's not played much," P tells the rest of us, excusing him, providing him the option of refusal.

"Ah not atall," says Tommy Love. He is sitting back against the chair's arm, his knees crossed, and his position does not change to receive the fiddle P hands over the fire. He rests it against his chest, and holding the bow lightly ripples through an "Irish Washerwoman" that is tenuous and shaky, but good enough to reveal him as once accomplished.

A punch of the bow ends the jig. "Now," Tommy Love says loudly. He is immediately engulfed in a cloud of affirmation. "Good man, Tommy, good man yourself." Hearty wordy encouragement, called "goodmanning," expresses gratitude for the diversion. More deeply, it shows understanding of the great courage it takes to perform, risking oneself for one's fellows.

"Lovely, Tommy," says P, master of the ceili. "Ah, play another."

"No, no, no. I'll play no more." Resting the violin along his arm, chuckling fraternally, Tommy says, "Not atall. For God's sake. I'd rather hear P playin, that's in the habit of playin."

"Ah now," P says, folding his arms and rocking forward to rest his elbows on his knees, "I can't play to me likin on that fiddle atall."

"Well, do ye know, she's a good fiddle," says Tommy Love.

"It's a right fiddle, P," Tommy Lunny says.

"Ah, she is," P replies, "but she's a bit rough now."

Talk about the instrument carefully deflects conversation from playing itself. No comparisons or evaluations come forth, and Tommy Love is free to play again.

"Ah now, she's not a bad wee fiddle, all right," he says, beginning a slow air. His tone is thinner than P's, more fragile, and he attempts few complications, but he plays sensitively, almost lyrically, and the men at the hearth are moved when he is done.

The goodmanning is quieter, less robust, deeper. A gentle chorus of yes and aye continues as P asks, "And what's that now?"

"It's Mary of Argyle, P," Tommy Love answers.

"Oh aye," says P.

"You often heard it, didn't ye?"

"Well, I did. I heard it and I couldn't just name it at the same time."

"It's a quare nice song," Tommy Lunny says.

"Aye," Joe agrees.

"It's a nice song," says Tommy Love, looking down at the violin. "You often heard it."

"I did indeed," says Tommy Lunny. "Mick Mack's sister used to sing it." He sits without motion, the soles of his Wellingtons flat on the floor.

Under his breath P whistles a bit of the air. "Aye she used to sing it."

"Aye," Tommy Lunny says, while Tommy Love lilts the melody's first line. "Tommy was a right good singer."

"Aye," says P.

"Damn it, but P, he was a quare good singer," says Tommy Lunny of Tommy Love. Compliments are constant. Approval is often given face on, but the favored mode is indirect. Two people discuss a third in the third person's hearing, buttressing the ego of the third while bringing the speakers into wordy accord, renewing the bonds that join them all.

"Aye," P concurs, "he was. He was a quare right good singer."

"A right good—" Tommy Lunny begins, then starts again, "a nice fiddler."

"Oh aye, Tommy's not in practice," P says.

"Oh now, I can't play atall," interrupts Tommy Love. His comfortable position does not change, his face is relaxed and smiling.

"He could fiddle twice as well as that," P continues.

"Aye," Tommy Lunny agrees. "He played plenty at one time."

"I did."

"Och, he did of course, why not," says P. "He played at dances years ago." Tommy Love draws the bow gently over the strings, and P pulls the conversation back to the instrument to eliminate embarrassment. "That fiddle is not easy. That's only a raw kind of a fiddle, fixed up there. I fixed it up there meself; it's not easy playin."

"I'll tell ye what beats me," Tommy Love says, sliding his left hand along the fiddle's neck. "I don't know when I'm right on that."

"You could get a fiddle, Tommy," says Tommy Lunny.

"I must get a fiddle," declares Tommy Love, delighted, launching a creditable reel. Confidence rises, control returns. P's feet begin to tap, the black shoes dance, clacking in complex time, accompanying, answering, pushing Tommy's tune. The bowing strengthens, tightens, feet beat, the pace quickens, lifts, flies, and P shoves the stool back, stands, and dances. Heavy black shoes clatter elegantly on the cement floor, repaying Tommy's greeting, joining him in the music.

Happy laughter rings the hearth, rising with the smoke, fading with the fiddle's sound, as P pulls his stool back within the ceili's close semicircle and receives the fiddle from Tommy. Joe tumbles an armload of turf next to the hearth. The fire goes down, they say, when the sport is good.

Neighbors, old companions, they treat one another with courtly delicacy, taking every chance to establish agreement. The playing, the fiddle, the tune, the past—all are used to bring the ceili into the soft words, yes and aye, into oneness.

Joe begins rebuilding the fire while Tommy Love whistles a tune, its name forgotten, as a request for P, who sits erect and finds his way with strength and grace through "The Centenary March." Though P now plays for the compact company as much as for himself, the scene remains informal. This is not a performance in a public house where one must cry for an ear, or a feis, where P says you are "suffocated with music" and knowledgeable judges and other competitors comprise a critical audience. "The Harvest Home," "The Sunshine Hornpipe," "The Copper Plate" (Tommy Lunny's regular request), "The Pigeon on the Gate," "The Cottage in the Grove," "The Floggin Reel" for the second time, "The Sligo Maid's Lament" for the third—the tunes do not march in pairs, formally avoiding repetition, and the ceiliers feel free to listen or trip away in chat. We laugh over comical titles for nonexistent tunes—"The Creel of Dung," "The Cat's March to the Child's Porringer"—we agree on the fortunate change in the weather, we share pity for the two men who were blasted into scraps by a bomb in Enniskillen four days ago.

At a subtle nod from P, Joe leans forward and shifts the crook bearing the kettle a few links down the chain that hangs, furry with soot, from a pole high in the chimney. Flames lick up, reddening the kettle's bottom, flicking bits of color, pink and yellow, onto the boots and skin of the company. Beyond, the kitchen is lost into the widening night. We sit, knees touching, atop a clay ridge by a small fire.

Golden, molten, veined with the blue, flecked with emerald green, the fire burns, foaming, turning to hold the ceiliers' gaze. In the back of the kitchen, in shadow, Joe stands cutting slabs of bread from a loaf. Another tune ends. P rests the fiddle across his knees.

"You will give us a song, P," Tommy Love says.

In a public house P would wait, letting requests pile up before releasing the songs in his head. Then to amuse the crowd he would select "a comical" like "Pat Molloy" or one of Harry Lauder's. "I'm Looking for a Bonnie Wee Lass to Love Me" is his usual choice, and he swings it coquettishly through the shop, flirting with the text, taking liberties with the rhythm. More usually he pleases the clientele, old Fenians, young supporters of the IRA, with a "political" or "patriotic" song, an emotional commemorative piece—"The Manchester Martyrs"—or a rousing call to arms: "Come to Kinawley and there take your stand, in the struggle for freedom we'll join heart and hand, and an Irish Republic is all we demand. . . ." Charlie Farmer's "Kinawley" is P's favorite, for his boyhood passed near Kinawley, just north of Swad, near the Border, and he knew the song's author.

P's style for public houses is mannered, histrionic, designed to trap fugitive attention. Now, seated among men he knows well at his own hearth, he does not resist, but looks down into the fire. The song he chooses is politically charged but older, more narrative in structure, more austere in rhetoric, than the customary fare of the pub. Around him it is perfectly silent. Joe spreads butter thickly on the cuts of bread. Without lifting his eyes, P sings plainly, directly in a slow and regular waltz time:

> *In Dublin's town I was brought up,*
> *That city of great fame.*
> *My parents reared me tenderly,*
> *As many has done the same.*
> *For bein a bold United boy,*
> *They sent me across the main.*
> *And for seven long years, down New South Wales,*
> *To wear a convict's chain.*
>
> *I was hardly landed six months*
> *Upon Australian shores,*
> *Till I turned out a Fenian boy,*
> *As many has done before.*
> *There was MacNamara in yon green wood,*
> *And Captain Markey too,*
> *And they were the chiefs who associate*
> *With bold Jack Donohue.*
>
> *Oh, Donohue was out walking now*
> *One Sunday afternoon.*
> *And little was his notion*
> *That his death would be so soon.*
> *When a sergeant of the horse police*
> *Discharged his carabine*
> *And cried loudly to O'Donohue*
> *To fight or else resign.*
>
> *To resign to you, you cowardly dog,*
> *Is a thing I ne'er will do.*
> *I'd rather fight with all my might,*
> *Says bold Jack Donohue.*
> *I'd range these woods and valleys*
> *Like a wolf or a kangaroo,*
> *Now before I'd fight for government,*
> *Says bold Jack Donohue.*
>
> *Nine rounds this horseman fired,*
> *Now until one fatal ball*
> *Lodged in the breast of Donohue,*
> *Which caused him for to fall.*
> *And when he closed his mournful eyes*

To this world he bade adieu.
Oh, people all both great and small,
Pray for Jack Donohue.

Wavering gently at its end, the song stills the hearth. "That's good, P,"
Tommy Love says softly, echoed with a murmur of inbreathed ayes.

The kettle sings. Joe picks some coals from the fire with the slender
steel tongs and scrunches them into a bed.

"Have you that one, P?" asks Tommy Love, lilting the opening of a
hornpipe.

"Aye," says P, checking the tuning. At the back table Joe spoons a hil-
lock of black tea into a pot. P lifts the violin, rosy light flashes the length of
the bow, music arcs into darkness. Down on one knee, Joe tips boiling
water into the teapot, caps it, settles it on the bed of coals. "The Belfast
Hornpipe" fills the kitchen. It is one of P's virtuoso pieces for tin whistle.
He is not used to playing it on the violin, but he negotiates the tune's long
runs and complex cadence smoothly.

Steam waves from the teapot's stroop. The strings cease vibrating. Joe
pours new tea on top of the milk and sugar in the cups he had lined on the
back table, and while he hands each man a hot cup and they pass a plate of
bread around, P leaves the fiddle on the front table and rummages in a
cardboard box atop a table in a back corner of the kitchen. Above it from a
nail a fiddle bow and rosary hang. P releases a slim silver flute from its
brown paper shroud and stands at the ceili's margin, sailing magnificently
through "The Belfast Hornpipe." The tin whistle is his instrument, and its
notes erupt, ascending like a showering skyrocket, flaring into the black
vaults of the roof.

It is time, strong and intricate tempo, that marks P as unique and sets
him above the others of his generation. That is what I would be told years
later by Cathal McConnell, master fluter with the Boys of the Lough, who
began life in Bellanaleck and learned his instrument from P.[1] When I told P
that, he said he did not know. What you hear is not satiny smoothness, but
surprise, not athletic speed, but power, free genius, when his soul enters
music.

The ceiliers remove caps or hats, hanging them on a knee, setting them
on the floor, to squint through the steam for a hesitant first sip. With a shy,
pleased laugh, P lifts the bread from his cup, the cup from his stool, and
rejoins the ceili, bringing tea to his lips in two hands.

We sit, sip, surrounded by darkness. Topics rise, but none is snatched
up and converted into crack. The tea is good. Joe is the man can make
a right cup of tea. The harvest is a success. No hunger will come on the
cows the year. An old woman is remembered who served her workers gravy
like what young ducks would puddle in. So mean she wouldn't give you
the black of her nail, she is dismissed as not too bad after all: Ah, the creature. . . .

Like a living thing beaten out of copper, the fire breathes, boweled in black turf, pulsing into the silences that fill the gaps in conversation. The fire is the ceili's visual center, its spectacle. Fascinated, the ceiliers watch as it writhes, flowing over itself, twisting, glittering like the conglomerate deformed beasts in the borders of an ancient manuscript. The ceiliers' eyes will rise to sustain long, motionless contact, then descend to search the coals as they sparkle and glow through endless metamorphosis.

In childhood they were trained not to use gestures instead of words. It is bad manners to nod. Say, Yes. Postures hold for long periods, and if gestures accompany words, they aid the speaker more than the listener, who, turned away and watching the fire, must understand. They were trained to speak in complete sentences. It is bad manners to answer abruptly, Yes. Say, Yes, I do. The origin may lie in Irish syntax, but it is part of the etiquette of English speakers now. Words must present thoughts clearly. The idea beneath clarity is truth, the ceili's contract, the neighborhood's infixed law. The situation of clarity is darkness, the ceili's shadowed, nighttime scene. The hearth's low light prevents seeing. Speakers cannot rely on their bodies to make meanings clearer or subtler. They do not wave their hands about, do not say the strange words uh or um, do not endlessly interrupt themselves into verbal muddles. They form efficient lines of air, construct clean texts of speech. Words alone, clear and true and unmistakable, come out of the darkness into the ear while red fire rolls in the eye.

P flips the dregs of his tea through the silence toward the hearth and sits back, crossing his ankles. "Tell us this, Tommy: about Saint Febor that was in your own country." Both men watch the fire.

Three weeks ago I had met Tommy Love's brother, Packie, in a public house. I asked where he lived. He answered through reference to the story of Saint Febor, saying she thrust down into the rock the castle of bad men who hunted and killed her pet deer. Next to the early seventeenth-century Scottish castle of Monea dips the hummocky depression of an ancient crannog.[2] Monea rises on the upland near Boho, where Packie Love lives, where Tommy lived before moving eight miles southeast to his present home in Rossdoney. The legend of Saint Febor set Packie in space. As emblem for his locality, he quoted me a bit of an old poem:

> Green are the fields and the mountains are clear.
> Monea, where the Saint has caught her deer.

The Saint and her deer are commemorated in stained glass in Boho Chapel. The story seemed important, but the bar's jostle and racket set no scene for its telling. Two days ago, when our conversation turned to the Saints of the Fermanagh dawn, I asked P if he knew about her. "I have heard nothin about her atall," he responded. Now with Tommy Love, a native of Boho, at his hearth, P, curious about the history of his church and land, asks for the story. Tommy, still holding his empty cup, begins:

> "Saint Febor had a lamb, a pet lamb,
> and it was drowned in the Sillees."

Tommy pulls his gaze from the fire and meets P's look.

"Aye," P says.

Both men avert their eyes to the fire. Tommy goes on:

"She was comin toward Monea,

and it was drowned in the river there."

"Jumped out of her arms," P interjects, gesturing the lamb's leap along his line of sight into the fire.

"Aye, the very thing," agrees Tommy, continuing:

"It jumped out of her arms.

"And it was drowned in the Sillees, and she cursed it.

"She cursed the river, and that's why, as they say, it is good for drowning and bad for fishin."

"It is a twisted, a twisted old river," P adds, "the crookedest river in the world. And at Lisgoole you can see it: it curves the shape of an S."

"Aye," agrees Tommy. "And it runs against the hill."

"It does," says P. "Aye indeed, it runs against the hill there. And it runs a kind of westward but the Arney runs to the east."

"It's a dirty ould river, that," says Joe.

"A dirty river and a twisted river," Tommy synthesizes, summarizing. "And she put a curse on it."

"Aye."

Union.

"Boys do catch perch out of it," comments Tommy Lunny, sitting straight, his eyes in the fire. He is a man of practical notions.

"Aye," says Tommy Love, "but the Sillees is not a good river for fishin."

"No, not atall," Tommy Lunny agrees quickly.

"No, it is not," says P, reaching over the fire for the tongs, plucking out a coal to light my cigarette, then his own. "It is not now."

P rocks forward, addressing the fire. "Where does it rise?"

"That's just the thing, the very thing. That's what I was thinkin of askin you." Tommy Love holds the cigarette before his lips, his eyes deep in the fire. "Where does it rise?"

"Well, I would say at Derrygonnelly," offers P. "I would think that: that the Sillees River rises near Derrygonnelly. I would think that now. So I would." He does not move. His head is cocked, his eyes do not rise from the hearth. Turf sparkles. Words stream free in the darkness.

"There was a man leapt that river," says Joe.

"Aye," says P, "he was a highwayman."

"That was a quare leap," says Joe.

"Aye."

Joe draws on his cigarette, vacating the topic. His hands still clasped, smoke coiling around them, smoke rising through his vision, P dilates:

"Aye, he was a Black Francis Corrigan, they called him.

"He was a highwayman, and he stold the treasure of Lisgoole Abbey.

"And they were chasin him when he leapt his horse over that river."

"They said it was a great leap." Joe nods sharply.

The fire burns, blackness spreads.

"Aye," continues P:

"And he said they run a long race to it. It twas a very long race, and he came over Derryhowlaght Hill, toward Dreen, up that way.

"And he threw the gold from the horse.

"And he said that some man would be rich after him.

"But no one has found it."

"That would be in the bog," opines Tommy Lunny.

"In the bog," says P. "Aye, that is right. In the bog."

Smoke rises, P finishes. "It's in the bog yet, but no one has found it. That's the way."

We sit. Turf smolders. It is quiet. The folklorist wants to pursue Black Francis, but I relax into the group's mood, letting him gallop back into memory. For them the topic is drained of interest. Soon another will come to carry us along the long night.

In the midst of a ceili my scholarly interest lies in the event's construction. Later I will return and talk singly with the men to get the story, record the texts. Now my concern is more for scene than story. I do not want to be discourteous, and I want the ceili to find its natural shape. It is not that I do not participate, for I have come to be relied upon as a "chatty man" (alternatively, "a blether"), but I neither falsify myself as a storyteller, nor detain my comrades in topics that obsess me. I learn the ceili's pattern by watching and listening—patience is the field-worker's virtue, attentive passivity his key mode, innocence his productive attitude—and by participating in a manner appropriate to the situation and myself. I give little lectures on American nature and agriculture, history, society, and politics. American Indian ethnology is surefire material for ceilis.

Topic descends upon topic, the night falls forward, and after midnight Tommy Love leaves: "Well men, carry on with the good sport."

As he had with Tommy Lunny an hour before, and Tommy Love an hour before that, P walks out with me when I leave, after a last tea, into the night. Ceilis provide no chance for intimate conversation, so farewells are exchanged outside, one on one, in case the ceilier had a purpose other than passing the time for calling upon the house. And it is courteous to be sure the ceilier finds the best route out of the territory the householder knows best. The land is pocked with sloughs, netted with complicated routes through gaps in a maze of thorny hedges.

Night's deep gray encircles us enormously, broken only by amber light, muted on the curtain, flowing opulently from the front door. I envy the descriptive power of the palette of Whistler's nocturnes, watching the white house recede under gray washes. Pale mists rise in the hollows, trees hang, black from the sky. There is no sound. P leads me through a gap, down a meadow, and onto a pass through the bog. It is totally dark. Safe home, Henry, God bless. God bless, Peter. All the best. Safe home. God bless. Words continue at conversational pitch until I have walked them out of hearing, along the pass toward the road. The narrow lane, the trees walling it, the bog and fields beyond, the sky—all is one blackness. There is no light, utterly, no sound.

4

The Next Day

Last night's ceili peaked in music. Its first plateau downward was occupied by history.

History is a topic for conversation. To fit a ceili in Ballymenone a topic must first exist within the momentary experience of those who are inventing the remainder of their relationship in communication. The weather, for example. Individuals are connected by their experience of the climate. Weather has the good topic's second requirement. It is interesting enough to hold potential for expansion. These are farming people. Their climate is mutable and weird, their destinies depend on the rain in clouds and on the sun clouds hide. Talk about the weather turns easily into chat about the agricultural year, and that opens all of past and future time for consideration. Greetings have not been reduced to an environmentally alienated "Good day." They remain comments on real conditions: "There's a good day now." "Dull of a day." "The days are gettin short now." Response is attentive: "Aye, indeed. But it hasn't forgotten how to rain in old Ireland yet." "Well, it's not rainin, and that's the main thing." "Aye, but the nights are a grand length." Fleetingly joined in a common concern, people pass or stop to let the weather take them into farming, into memory or hope. The entertaining person is the one who leads out of the shared scene into something beyond.

History is beyond. But first it must meet the requirements of conversation in being both accessible and capable of expansion. Books can preserve the unmemorable, but the history that owes its existence to an oral dynamic, to limited memory, and to the intricacies of the social contract cannot be boring.

The two historical subjects connected by last night's ceili were interesting and expandable. Peter Flanagan knew that Saint Febor interested me as well as himself, and that Mr. Love would know her story. Joe Flanagan knew his brother could tell about Black Francis. It is likely that P's outlaw ballad, "Bold Jack Donohue," helped Joe decide to jump Corrigan into the chat. Surely P's choice of song was guided by one he and I had heard in a public house nine days before.

It was past closing time. Men stood barring the door so a beautiful young woman, Teresa Rooney, who came of the MacManus family in Knockninny, four miles south of the District, could glide without let through "The Wild Rapparee." Its pace, intensity, and melody are reminiscent of "Jack Donohue," its tale is close. A boastful man committed to the Irish cause is harried by horsemen in a wild setting and brought to death at the hands of the government. It closes like "Jack Donohue," asking the listener to pray for the outlaw.

> *How green are the fields that are washed by the Finn.*
> *How grand are the homes that those peelers live in.*
> *How fresh are the crops in the valleys to see,*
> *But the heath is the home of the wild rapparee.*
>
> *Ah, way out on the moors where the wind shrieks and howls,*
> *Sure, he'll find his lone home there amongst the wild fowl.*
> *No one there to welcome, no comrade has he.*
> *Ah, God help the poor outlaw, the wild rapparee.*
>
> *He has robbed many rich of their gold and their crown.*
> *He has outrode the soldiers who hunted him down.*
> *Alas, he has boasted, They'll never take me,*
> *Not a swordsman will capture the wild rapparee.*
>
> *There's a stone-covered grave on the wild mountainside.*
> *There's a plain wooden cross on which this is inscribed:*
> *Kneel down, dear stranger, say an Ave for me,*
> *I was sentenced to death being a wild rapparee.*

Immediately upon hearing it, Mr. Flanagan picked its melody out on the tin whistle. On the way home that night he declared, "I *must* have that song," and he told me about the rapparees, remnants of the army defeated in the Williamite War who took to the heaths, robbing the rich to give to the poor, rather than fleeing to the Continent or submitting to English law and religion.

During last night's ceili I sat in my usual place, on a low creepie stool, leaning on the brick wall the turf burned against. Opposite, across the fire, sat Tommy Love. Tommy Lunny sat to his left. P sat to my right. He knew I would like "Jack Donohue," having liked "The Wild Rapparee." He knew I would be interested in his extension of Joe's suggestion, so he saddled the chat for a while to the back of the local rapparee, Black Francis.

More than a millennium separates Black Francis and Saint Febor. Their connection is not temporal, but spatial. He leapt the river she cursed. The Sillees rises near Derrygonnelly between Monea and Boho and snakes down through the drumlins, flowing under Lisgoole Bridge, where it appears to writhe toward the hills before spilling into Lough Erne. It was the river they used to channel Mr. Love's story back into the flow of conversation, and it was the river Joe used to tie Tommy's story to P's. Wet land unifies. Its experience, its dirt and climate, join farmers in a commonality of concern. Land obliterates chronology, connecting modern men to the people of the past who marked it permanently. The Sillees River remains bad for fishing. Derryhowlaght Bog still holds its treasure. The past lives as the land. Geography was the natural way to bring different speakers and different stories into aesthetic and social union.

It would be wrong to approach communication among the ceiliers of Ballymenone with radically individualistic assumptions that turn the participants in social interaction into rival merchants in a market, or contestants in a sporting match, or attorneys in a court of law, or apes in combat. When people in Ballymenone create a ceili, they order their conduct so their communication will be pleasureful, purposeful, collective action, as much like prayer as play, more like courtship than war.

Carefully, the ceiliers select topics they hope will prove interesting. Generously, they expand topics into performance. Performance requires people to differentiate responsibilities. Some lead, others follow.

In instrumental music, leadership comes of talent. In singing, leadership is established by talent or knowledge. By knowing complete texts, whole poems, the unmusical singer gains a central place. In the performance of history, leadership is established by knowledge. The person who knows is obliged to share information, and so to lead.

Performing history begins when the role of leader is set up and not filled. A knowable unknown is demarcated by a request or by quiet. P asks Tommy about Saint Febor. Joe opens the matter of Black Francis, then leaves it empty for P. Once the role is accepted, the leader is abandoned, cut free from conversation, accompanied in isolation only by the facts. Their essence is presented swiftly. The lamb drowns. The horse leaps. He pauses. The followers can turn the topic back into chat by inserting a fact anyone can talk about. The river is dirty, they say, and the special status of the one who knows is eliminated. Or they can encourage the leader to maintain authority by quiet attention, or by repetition (Joe tells twice of Corrigan's leap), or by proposing a logical advance (P guesses that the lamb leapt from the Saint's arms; Tommy Lunny guesses that Corrigan scattered gold in the bog). "Goodmanning" is the follower's most usual way to encourage the leader. As people around the singer insert words between his stanzas to prove their attention is alive and active, the teller's audience helps him develop rhythm by filling pauses with brief comment: "Oh now," "Oh man," "Man dear," "That's a sight," "That's a terror," "Terror," "Oh aye," "I see," "I know," "Good man," "Go on." Encouraged, the leader surrenders power into the conversation or returns to enrich the facts. The second time the lamb drowns, Saint Febor was coming from Monea. The second time Corrigan leaps, it was at the end of a long race. With further encouragement, the story moves to its conclusion. Mr. Love can tell the cursing of the Sillees. Mr. Flanagan can tell the dispersal of the treasure of Lisgoole.

Ceilis ascend to performance through the interplay of roles. The change from leader to follower happens so swiftly in conversation that the effect is one of an equality of contribution. Distinctions are not the ceili's but life's.

Some people are quiet, others are chatty. But when roles stabilize, if only briefly, when a leader assumes the culture's expressive tasks and a follower goodmans him, when all the participants enact their responsibilities to one another, themselves, and the accuracy of received fact and text, performance happens in Ballymenone.

During performance, history issues from coordinating the need to inform with the wish to know, the need to lead with the wish to be entertained. Founded upon an ethic of social accord, compressed in emergent communication, history normally appears in ceilis in brief pieces. But it would presuppose a false homogeneity to think long tales lie unspoken in memory, revealing themselves in conversation as but abbreviated narrations or transitory references. Instead, there are different orders of information about the past. People will say they "know about" something—the arrival of Saint Patrick, the Battle of the Boyne—without "knowing its history." Such information about past people and events floats free, unorganized in vast quantity, waiting to be selected and attached to something about which people do "have the history." When you have the history, you can cluster facts into an account that may be informational, even sequential and causative, but is less than a "story." The "story of history" corresponds roughly to the folklorist's "historical legend," but unlike folklorists, the people of Ballymenone are not combative about their definitions.[1] As a story, it is entertaining, a full and artful narrative. As history, it is important and true. A person might know facts about hundreds of events, have the history of dozens, but there is a small, economical treasury of historical stories in Ballymenone. They recount events of continuing significance that took place in Ireland, generally within the locality. Only a few men "have them."

These historians are responsible for the local past. They have assembled the fullest narratives. So long as they have them, the community has them, even if most people do not. Historical references in conversations may be references to history known by the speaker, but usually they are not. Historians know history.

Appearing infrequently in fragments, Ballymenone's history is complicated by conversational requirements, by the social and aesthetic patterns of ceili and performance, by orders of historical comprehension and the highly specialized nature of deep historical knowledge. Having to gain a lifetime of understanding in a brief period, the visiting folklorist turns from listening to interviews.

With Black Francis on my mind, I walk south, the day after the ceili at Flanagans', out of Enniskillen, over Lisgoole Bridge, across Drumbargy Brae, and down to Mr. Nolan's. "Well, Henry," he says, his eyes beaming a welcome.

Hugh Nolan is acknowledged to be the great historian of Ballymenone. When questions about their own past arise—genealogy or land rights—people come to him, and in response to my queries about history they send me to him.

"In most districts," Mr. Nolan told me, "there is someone that knows the history." When he was young his pleasure came from listening to the old men and, being uncomfortable with writing, he "took a mental note" of all they said. He "gathered up" his district's past. A week ago I asked him if he had heard the history of Saint Febor. "I did," he answered, smoothly proceeding:

"Well, I'll tell ye.
"That was a woman, a very saintly woman.
"And she was a wonderful writer.
"She wasn't like me; she could spell ◇.
"Well, she had a whole—och, a library just, of books.
"And the way that she used to convey them (I suppose she was travelin on horseback herself):
      she had a deer.
"And she had these books in some kind of an article that she used to put them across the deer's back, do ye see.
"So the deer was the same as a *dog* as far as she was concerned.
"The deer used to follow her any place she went. All she had to do was go to this thing, take out a book, or books, if she wanted them.
"But anyway, comin some place about Boho, there was some party put a pack of hounds
      on this deer
      and hurt it.
"So the deer, for safety, took into the Sillees River to get away from the hounds, do ye see.
"And didn't the books all fall off his back
              into the water.
"So.
"She was that much annoyed and heartbroken about the books,
      she pronounced a curse on the river.
"And if you'd remark, there's no way you'd see it as well as from Lisgoole Bridge there—if you stood on the bridge and took observation of the river,
      the river is runnin against the hill.
"The river was running in another direction, for the *sea*
      at the time that this happened.
"And it turned its course,
    and it's comin now,
      and flowin into Lough Erne,
        convenient to Enniskillen.
"So that's the history of that, as far as I know."

Remembering Packie Love's account, I asked Mr. Nolan about the hunters' castle driven into the rock at Monea. He had not heard that episode. After a smoky pause he resumed:

"No, I never heard tell of that.

"There was a terrible deal of very rich literature lost because she was a wonderful writer, a wonderful writer.

"It was a rascally act to set the dogs on this deer, do ye see.

"Ah now."

The pause said the story was complete, that Mr. Nolan was ready for a different part of his store of knowledge to be preserved on tape.

As Packie and Tommy Love told it, Saint Febor took revenge on the river for the loss of her pet. In Mr. Nolan's rendition, the Sillees was cursed for destroying wonderful books. Though offended by the cruelty of men who upset the balance of the natural and the sacred, harrying a land, this land, where once a wild animal served a saint as dogs and donkeys do modern people, it was the loss of knowledge and literature that most concerned the historian Hugh Nolan. Against that loss with question, with thought and word, he has waged the war of a lifetime.

He sits quiet, powerful, and bent. The neighbors name him more than historian. He is a holy man. Until recently he rode his bicycle every Sunday to Mass in Enniskillen as well as in the Arney Chapel. He lives, they say, like an ancient monk. That wonderful poem from the Irish ninth century in which the scholarly monk compares his craft with that of Pangur, his cat, his quest for wisdom with his pet's for mice, gets Hugh Nolan just right.[2] He sits in his long black coat, tied with a sash, in his cell, dark and close, lit by one tiny window, alone with his cats and his brilliant mind. From his seat at the corner of the hearth long routes lead over the clay floor. The path along the front of the kitchen carries from the Room past the table with its brass candlestick and tin of tea and butter, to cross the path running between the dresser and the couch before the hearth, from the table at the back with its tins of food and bucket of clear water, past plates set out for the cats to the blue front door, which gives immediately onto Rossdoney Lane. In one direction lies water, in a neighbor's byre, in the other toward the Lough, sticks are heaped, split for kindling by his neighbors.

He represents the fourth generation of his family, and its end, in Rossdoney. His grandfather Hugh built this house of local brick. His father, James, inherited it. He had seven uncles. Only three married. He was born on the day after Christmas in 1896 and lived an only child. "I had no one, only meself."

He is, they also say, "a man of iron." He was a great worker in his youth, the strongest man of his size in his generation. When I touch his arm it is rock hard with muscle. He was entertaining. A lover of music, he would beat on the drum, and though no great singer, both Paddy McBrien and Peter Flanagan, men younger than Hugh, remember him singing songs of his own composition in a shy, charming style. There was a young woman. But he worked on. At age forty-one he sold his cattle and went to Scotland to seek his fortune as a farm laborer. After six months he came home

Hugh Nolan in 1922

for Christmas, intending to leave again, but World War II exploded and he remains, holy hermit, the District's great historian.

I am confident he will have the story of Black Francis, and he is anxious for me to record the knowledge he has accumulated. When he was my age he sat with the old men, men like Hugh McGiveney, his neighbor, and recorded the old history. I am an outsider. I use a machine rather than my mind. But the situation is not strange; it is natural and right for a younger man to gather and store the treasure from the past he holds in trust for an uncaring future.

There is time. I am here for more than information. We settle into each other's presence with the common topic of contemporary politics.

Often in times of trouble, he says, times like these, when men strike men down and blood rises in rage and fear, a plague breaks out to redouble the terror. He hopes it will not happen now in Ireland, but it could, and if it does, "there's no flyin in the face of God." We will have to accept and endure. As age hardens in the back bent from endless seasons of wheeling turf, he sums up life's pattern: you spend twenty years looking forward ambitiously, wanting to get out on your own, then twenty years working, adjusting to life as it is, then the rest of your time struggling against your sad understanding of the way things are. "There bes alot of troubles, but you have to learn to live with them."

A scrap of noonday gray is caught on the shaving mirror next to the cold candle beneath the small front window. Ash-colored light filters through the smoke down the chimney and over the bricks of the hearth. I ask if he would like to record before I make tea. I place the machine between us. The white cat returns to my knee, purring, while Mr. Nolan tamps his pipe with a finger and draws a small flame into the tobacco remains.

The low ceiling is black above us, the corners black beyond. A curve of dull silver outlines the side of his head. His eyes gleam. "Well, Hugh, I have just heard about Black Francis and wonder if you could tell me about him." The light in his eyes draws me in. I fix on his face. The kitchen disappears. He begins:

"He was the leader of a highway gang that was in Fermanagh in days gone by.

"The way it was, do ye see, after the Williamite War, there was alot of the Irish army went away to France.

"And they figured in alot of wars that France had with other European countries.

"And they were known as the *Irish Brigade*.

"But then there was a section of them that didn't leave this country, but they took to the hills.

"And they were called the rapparees.

"And what they followed up was:
　　they used to rob the rich,
　　and they used to give the money to poor people,
　　　　do ye know.

"So that went on for a length of time.

"And they were in every county in Ireland.

"But this was a part of them was in Fermanagh, and whether this man was O'Brien or not, I just can't remember, but I heard it anyway.

"But there was five of them.

"And there was one fellow,
　　he was Corrigan.

"And he was a terrible jump
　　or a terrible leap.

"It was supposed that it was Lisgoole Abbey that they were goin to rob this night for some ones that wasn't able to pay their rates, or meet their accounts. And they used to give the money to people like that, do ye see.

"So anyway, there was one of the gang and he insulted a girl that was in this house.

"And this Black Francis bid to have been clear, only for a laceratin that he gave this fellow
                    for interferin with this girl.

"He was chastisin this fellow for his bad manners, and for the crime it was for to interfere with a woman-person, do ye see.

"But anyway the word went to Enniskillen.

"And whatever kind of a post—whether it was military or whether it was the revenue men, I can't just tell ye which of the two it was—but they started out, and didn't they get the length of the place before the gang got away.

"Only this Corrigan fellow.

"And this Corrigan fellow leapt the Sillees River.

"So Black Francis and the other ones, they were arrested.

"And there was a death penalty for robbery in them days.

"So anyway these ones were tried, and they were found guilty, and they were executed at Enniskillen, where the technical school is—that was the jail in them days.

"So anyway, the executions took place outside in them days.

"And this Corrigan fellow, he dressed himself up as a woman.

"And he came along.

"And when Black Francis was brought out for to be hanged, whatever way Corrigan managed it, he attracted his attention.

"So he made a very long speech, Black Francis did, about seein his sweetheart, in the crowd, and that he hoped she'd be able for to protect herself.

"Aw, it was a terrible speech. He was a very clever fellow, you know. And it was all on this supposed lady that was in the Gaol Square, as they called it.

"And the lady was his companion:
                    Souple Corrigan.

"So anyway they were executed anyway and Souple Corrigan made his way to America."

Mr. Nolan stops and brings a match to his cold pipe. "When was that?" I ask.

"It was in the early part of the eighteenth century as far as I know.

"Well, do ye see, these men wouldn't be some of the men that fought in the Williamite *War*, but they'd be descendants of theirs, do ye see, that followed up the same trade as their fathers before them."

I wait for the pipe to cloud with smoke before asking for Souple Corrigan's given name. "I don't know what his first name was," Mr. Nolan responds. "I never heard his first name. All ever I heard for him was Souple Corrigan." Next, I ask about Corrigan scattering gold in the bog, but Mr. Nolan has "never heard about that," and I end my pursuit with the vague sort of statement that often begets further comment: "So Corrigan was the only escapee." And Mr. Nolan continues:

"Corrigan was the only survivor of the gang, and there was either five or six in it.
"And what they spent their time at before they were catched was:
"They robbed rich men
             and they gave the money to poor men
                                     widow women,
                                     and orphans;
             and people like that, that was in poverty.
"And only for this incident,
        at this place,
             and it's supposed to be *Lisgoole,*
                     they'd have got away thattime,
             only for the fellow insultin this *girl,*
             that this leader was givin him a chastisin
                 for his rudeness and *badness*
                     and all to this girl.
"And the forces arrived.
"And Corrigan made out and jumped the river
                     and got away.
"And the rest of them was brought to Enniskillen."

Another match snaps. Through the smoke billowing about his pipe, Mr. Nolan chuckles gently as once again I congratulate his memory and narrative powers.

Off the tongue of a master like Hugh Nolan, history aspires to song. As the story unfolds, he pulls away from conversation. Closing his eyes and fists, concentrating to avoid the fillers and false starts of chat, straining to push the story on in sharply marked, efficient sentences, he honors the attention of his listener and sets a project for the artist within, testing his memory and verbal skill.

History is more than tale. Respecting the facts he has collected and their cultural significance, Mr. Nolan retards the story to site it historically, providing a background for the rapparees, establishing their political motivation. And he interrupts himself, breaking the flow of words when uncertain of the truth. Black Francis' name might have been O'Brien. It may have been Lisgoole they robbed. It could have been the military or revenue men who captured them.

As with all historians worth the name, Hugh Nolan's desire to tell a good tale is not allowed to overcome his wish to present the facts clearly and accurately. Art is subordinate to truth. Performing "the old history" in Ballymenone is not employing a tale to flaunt the ego or amuse the audience. Accepting the role of leader, a person must create a balance among personal integrity, the needs of the follower, and the truth that lies beyond the scene. The performed text is an epitome, merging the self with the other, the artistic with the factual, the traditional with the momentary.

An interview is not a ceili. Some people cannot shift easily from format to format. Hugh Nolan can. The situation is not strange. This house was known as a ceili house when his parents were alive. It still is. Neighbors like Johnny and Packie Boyle, Tommy Love, Paddy McBrien, and James Boyle are drawn regularly to its hearth, for Hugh is an entertaining man. History is entertainment. He is accustomed to the role of conversational leader, of ceili master. Not everyone who ceilis at a house is close to the keeper of the hearth. I am not prevented from natural performance, from assuming correctly the role of follower, on the arbitrary grounds of being an American folklorist. My direct questions about details, about names, dates, and alternative versions, are inappropriate encouragement. They are necessary to me, but they verge on discourtesy, break with custom, and jar the teller. But when I offer an observation ("So Corrigan was the only escapee"), I properly echo the story; Mr. Nolan returns to analyze his tale, repeating its conceptual essence (robbing the rich to feed the poor) and repeating its narrative essence (Black Francis pauses to castigate his unmannerly companion while the soldiers arrive to capture him and Corrigan escapes). When I make a request with a reasonable expectation of its being filled and wait in attentive silence, confirming my interest with brief sounds (my tapes show me helping the rhythm, providing response and stimulus with "yes" and "ah" in the swift silence at the ends of lines), then I goodman in a way understandable enough to produce true performance. Mr. Nolan accepts me as follower. He becomes leader, his culture rises, creating itself, exposing itself through him. We join in performance.

Together we sit in the peace of accomplishment, in the smoke of turf and tobacco. The cat sleeps, the clock ticks, nothing happens. "Did you hear other stories of men like them?" I ask. Freed by my continuing interest to go another round with his own talent, he is off without pause:

"Och, I heard stories of men like them in different parts of Ireland.

"Some of them was rascals, do ye know, because there never bes any gang but there bes a ruffian in, do ye know, that does things that, well, shames the rest of them, do ye know.

"There was a novel,
        it was a Tyrone man composed it,
                he was the name of Carleton.

"It was Willy Reilly and His Dear Cooleen Bawn, that was the name of the novel.

"So the way it twas, this ould squire, he went out one evenin,
        with a few other men,
                and they lost their way.

"And there was one of these, rapparees they were called, came across them, and he was a rascal.

"And the like of these well-to-do men, they always had *money* on them, do ye see.

"And he was about for to shoot them, and take their money, when one of this squire's companions, he puts his two fingers into his mouth and he gave a terrible whistle.

"And there was another young man, he was the son of a landlord, and he heard it and he knew this fellow's whistle, and he replied.

"He could do the same. He replied.

"And it was no time till he landed at the spot
    where the lad was goin to shoot the squire
        and his companions.

"So him and his men chased the rapparee.

"So this ould squire, he brought the man and whoever he had along with him—he brought them home.

"And the squire had a very nice *daughter*.

"And didn't the young fellow take a likin to her.

"It was the same way with her: she took a likin to him.

"It turned out for to be a *courtship*.

"But then there was a lot of stumblin blocks.

"This man, he was a Catholic.

"And the squire was a Protestant, and the daughter was a Protestant.

"So it was against the law in them days for any ones of different religions, do ye see, for to *marry*.

"So they couldn't get married and they made up their minds for to leave the country.

"He knocked about for a long time
    before they came to this conclusion.

"And he even dressed himself up as a laborin man,
    and he came and he got a job with this squire
        for his gardens
            for to be near this girl.

"So finally, there was another ould lad used to come along (he was a wonderful companion of the squire's), and didn't he detect this man; he told the squire that he was no laborin man atall, because he knew be his hands that he had never wrought till he came there.

"So *anyway*, they found out—him and the girl found out—that it wouldn't be long till he'd be banished from out the place.

"So anyway, they made up their minds for to fly.

"So they started this night anyway.

"They weren't long gone till she was missed and the hunt went out after them.

"She had a whole lot of very valuable jewelry, and I suppose money as well, and she had give it to him for to keep, do ye see, for her. He had a better way of carryin it than what she had.

"But anyway they were followed be her father and a strong force of servants belongin to the father's place.

"And the girl was got back.

"And she was locked up in a room.

"And he was given up to the *authorities*.

"So this jury was got up.

"And to steal anything in them days, there was a death penalty attached to it.

"So anyway he had to stand his trial,
     and the charge against him was:
        carryin off an heiress
           (she was underage)
        and the stealin of these jewelries.

"So the case was left over to the assizes.

"But in the *meantime*, this rascal of a fellow that had met with this ould squire and his men out in the darkness, he was arrested, and he was arrested through another man that had belonged to his gang but that had left them, but that he was still on the *run*.

"But. The way it was: if you were on the run in them days and done somethin in the line of assistin the crown forces for to track out a criminal, you got your pardon.

"So this man, he was goin with a *girl*, and she was a maid belongin to this lady, the squire's daughter, and he knew the position they were in.

"And he made up his mind that he'd try and get his freedom, the way that he could be some assistance, especially because he knew that the other man that was in jail would be maybe hanged or transported.

"But anyway, he set himself for to track down this lad,
                  the rapparee,
     and get his pardon from the *crown*,
       that he'd be a free man for to do all he could in the crisis.

"So anyway this rapparee had a house that he used to call in;
       there was a lonely woman lived in the house.

"So this fellow that was on the run and wanted to get this lad taken, he started this night for this house.

"And he went in as a poor beggar man, went in prayin, do ye know, and beseechin her for to keep him for the night.

"So anyway, she fixed up a bed for him in the corner, and at some time in the night
        didn't this lad arrive.

"And before this man Reilly was arrested, the sheriff had been robbed of a very large sum of *money*. And it was this rapparee that had robbed him.

"So.

"He *come* in anyway, and he seen the man lyin in this corner, and he made a tear for to waken him up for to see who he *was*.

"So this woman wouldn't let him; she said he was a poor man that came in at nightfall, and that she had fixed up a *bed* for.

"So anyway, the robbin of the sheriff was one charge that was a-bringin against this Reilly fellow that had took away the heiress. And didn't the fellow—he raveled out the whole thing of robbin the sheriff, and that Reilly would be charged with it, all to this.

"So anyway after some time he went away.

"So the lad got up in the mornin and he started away,
   and he went to the sheriff,
   and he told him what information that he got the night before.

"So the *thing was*: gettin this rapparee arrested,
   and it was a very hard job.

"So this lad
   was sent with the military
     on the track of the rapparee.

"And he had an idea of where the rapparee was *hidin*.

"So the house was surrounded,
  but when they went inside,
   there was no rapparee.

"So the lad told them for to examine the roof outside.

"So they examined the roof,
  and he had made a hole in the roof,
   and he was lyin outside in that hole.

"So he was brought away anyway,
   and put into jail.

"It was in Sligo Gaol they were *all* lodged.

"So anyway, the trial come on.

"The rapparee's trial, I think, was first.

"And there was another ould fellow; he was a well-to-do ould rascal, but he had done alot of crimes, and he had been arrested, and he was on trial *too*.

"So they were both sentenced to be hanged
      on a certain day.

"And then Reilly's trial came along.

"And—och, everyone betted that he'd be hanged. He had the jewelry when he was arrested, and there was no chance for him.

"So *anyway*, the girl went to the assizes.

"And he had a very clever counselor.

"So she was called.

"So of course the charges was read out, do ye see, and most of them was the stealin of this jewelry.

"So anyway, when she was called to the witness box, she gave out that the jewelry wasn't stolen, she gave it to him for to keep safe.

"So that case fell through.

"So then all the case then that there was against him was: the carryin off of an heiress. Well, it wasn't punishable by death. So he got seven years transportation for that.

"So he was brought away anyway.

"*She* was brought back home, and this fellow's girl was her companion durin the time that the intended was in penal servitude.

"And the Cooleen Bawn, as she was styled, she never spoke to anyone, and it wasn't very long till the ould father—remorse set in on him for bringin the thing up atall or bein the cause of this man bein transported.

"He thought that the seven years would never come to an end.

"But finally he put in the seven years,
       and he come out,
           and they got *married*.

"But *then* the best of it all was: the hangin of these other two boys.

"There was a fellow, and he was catched—I think he was one of the rapparees too—he was catched and he was sentenced to be *hanged*.

"And on the mornin that his execution was to take place, didn't the hangman drop dead.

"So they were without a hangman.

"So there was a promise given that anyone in prison or anyone under sentence of death, that would take on the job of hangin, that they'd get free.

"So didn't this fellow take on the job for to get hangin this rapparee and this other ould lad that was sentenced to death.

"So it was at the trial of the Red Rapparee, *all* his crimes was all read out and he was found guilty, and the judge—it was before he passed the sentence, he was givin him—well, a laceratin, do ye see, for the life he had led and all to this, and he told him that it never was a sin to repent.

"So the lad answered him back and he says:
"*A grain of sorrow*, he says,
     or a *grain of repentance*, he says,
         never I'll shed, he says.
"And if I had the way of doin it, he says, at the present time,
"I'd give you a *pill*, he says, that'd turn the whites of your eyes up ◇.

"Ah, the judge told him he was a hardened, unreligious rascal; he was goin to die now on the scaffold, so he sentenced him to death.

"So then the other ould fellow was sentenced.

"This fellow that had took up the job of hangman, he thought every minute and hour till the day of the executions be comin on—they were both to be hangin the same day—till he'd get the hangin of them, because he had a wonderful hatred for both of them.

"So this rapparee was brought out first.

"So he hanged him anyway.

"Then this other ould lad was brought out, and when he was puttin the rope on his neck he says:

"*Your companion*, he says, the Red Rapparee, has gone *before ye*, but I told him to stand to one side ◇ and wait on ye, the whiles you'd both be goin down together ◇.

"So he hanged them both, and that was the ambition of his life ◇."

A soft laugh signals victory. Great, powerful hands rest fisted in his lap. Mr. Nolan is content. His task was not easy. He had to grapple the whole lumbering plot into order (Carleton strung it through 880 pages) and elevate his diction into story without abandoning our chat.

He began conversationally with a generalization illustrated both in the story he had told—the one I requested—and the one he was about to tell. Connections are set, the topic is known, we are engaged. At "There was a novel," the story broke into lines, rising, often becoming, as in the rapparee's retort to the judge, markedly rhythmic. But he never left speech for song. His syntax remained unbent, he pronounced -ing words without final g's like a talker, not a singer. He broke the bonds of steady song tone. Stories never swing as free as speech, they never climb crack's wild heights of verbal mimicry, but Mr. Nolan disturbed sound in animation, describing the man disguised as a beggar in a shivering, whimpering voice, letting the Red Rapparee rant in a growl.

Songs are full of names. Chat is not. Talk about the neighbors is made delicate and vague by omitting names, and that trait is transferred into tales where things are done by this man or that young fellow or the ould lad or the other ould lad. The story becomes hard to follow, just as conversations do when people are minimally identified.

Conversations hold to the subject. Shifts of topic are made carefully, overtly. Once begun, a song, though suggested in its scene, snaps free to obey its own rules, seeking excellence in flowing melody and perfectly repeated text. Stories are flexibly built into chat. Rapparees drove Willy Reilly into Hugh Nolan's mind. He began at our topic, highwaymen, and as he proceeded, selecting "bits here and there" out of William Carleton's long novel to compose his own story, he emphasized the action and character of the rapparees. Though it seemed anticlimactic to the marriage of Willy and the Cooleen, it was logical for him to conclude with the hanging scene, a wedding's opposite, for it brought his story back into our chat and made of it context for Black Francis.

Mr. Nolan did more than reorganize the last chapters of Carleton's novel so his story would end with hanging rather than marriage. He compressed sections, stressed others, eliminated the episodes of priest-hunting, and he diminished the role of Sir Robert Whitecraft, the Cooleen's wealthy, malevolent suitor, using him but twice, once to spy Reilly's white hands, later to be hanged with the Red Rapparee. William Carleton's novel, a passionate tract on religious tolerance, is also a rumpled, erratic adventure story, which Mr. Nolan smoothly recomposed so that it would reverberate thematically with his own first tale. Both begin in robbery, turn on relations with women, exploit disguise and escape, end in hanging. Like Willy Reilly, Black Francis is a Catholic, an honorable robber, whose respect for women brings him to trial. Like the Red Rapparee he is hanged after a speech. Black Francis merges with Reilly in innocence. Contrast with the Red Rapparee clarifies his character: he is noble, his motives are selfless and political. Together better than apart, the stories force the issue of justice to the fore. They recall a time when—the point is hit in each tale—the punishment was worse than the crime and robbers were hanged. They reflect upon a world in which wealth and power lie in the hands of a few squires who, backed by law, mistreat others, poor tenants, widows and orphans in the first tale, their own daughters and young Catholic men in the second. Joined, the stories define a need for action against authority, justifying the outlaw, the rebel, Black Francis.

Mr. Nolan suspended his story out of Carleton between chat and song. In that it is like all other stories in Ballymenone. In other ways it is unique. No other story is so confused by profusion of personnel, so stretched by subplots. Oral narratives in general compress personalities and roles. Their forms do not elaborate in simultaneity but string into episodic sequence. As Hugh Nolan proved, a gifted teller can keep a grip on novelistic complexities. It is the listener who cannot.

Those very complexities helped the story of Willy Reilly fit our conversation. Its manifold structure and believable content make it feel like history. In reality lives do intersect in large numbers and weird ways. In reality outlaws are hanged, people fall in love, Protestant squires are rich, and young men like Willy Reilly and Jack Donohue are transported. As the District's only tale invented out of a novel, Mr. Nolan's was the only one in the local oeuvre that was not history but still suited a historical conversation. Novels in Carleton's day were fake histories.

William Carleton was born in 1794, twenty miles to the northeast, in country like this. Athletic, a great dancer, "designed for a priest," Carleton left the Clogher Valley of County Tyrone for Dublin, left Catholicism for Protestantism, then filled books with the people he had been raised among. He was proud he knew them. He had suffered and gotten drunk with them, and the only merit he claimed as a writer was having been close to them. But they irritated him as unhelpful to progress. Sometimes his writings seem affectionate, sometimes mean. He defends their English as a language in transition, then pounces on their errors, exaggerating them in grotesque orthography. He admires their virtue, then castigates them as slaves of religion. The Irish are the most imaginative of people, he writes, too imaginative for their own good. These are not the confusions of a small mind, I believe, but the pains of a great heart.[3]

William Carleton is difficult to approach. The young William Butler Yeats edited Carleton and said he "was a great Irish historian. The history of a nation is not in parliaments and battle-fields," Yeats wrote, "but in what the people say to each other on fair-days and high days, and in how they farm, and quarrel, and go on pilgrimage. These things has Carleton recorded." Feeling in Carleton "no wistfulness" but a "clay-cold melancholy," Yeats named him "the great novelist of Ireland, by right of the most Celtic eyes that ever gazed from under the brows of storyteller." Then Yeats thought again and found Carleton's sketches portraying the people as farcical and silly, and he contrasted Carleton with Douglas Hyde, who knew the country people and their arts so well that Yeats could stand with Hyde in Galway, listening to the mowers sing Hyde's poems without knowing their author's name. For Yeats that was a hopeful sign of cultural unity and a compliment to Hyde's understanding.[4] It is a compliment to Carleton that his novel has entered the oral tradition of his region. He built into it matters of deep importance and real interest.

There should be nothing surprising in all this. Artists like William Butler Yeats, William Carleton, and Hugh Nolan are always on the lookout for good ideas. Yeats sought spiritual wisdom in East and West, among old philosophers, fashionable theosophists, and visionary peasants. He gained poetic guidance at once from William Blake and William Morris, Scots ballads and Irish sagas. Mr. Nolan's acclaimed fireside tale "Huddon and Duddon and Donald O'Leary" was expanded from a Christmas number of the *Fermanagh Herald*, where it had been reprinted out of a book edited by Yeats, who got the tale from a chapbook into which it had been swept out of the international tide of oral tradition; folklorists call it number 1535. And William Carleton constructed his novel of 1855, *Willy Reilly and His Dear Coleen Bawn*, around a popular ballad.[5]

So in the pleasant quiet following his tale, I make a little conversation: "There was a song made about that." Mr. Nolan agrees:

"There was. There was. A very long song.

"Well, their escape was referred to in the song, and then the trial at the assizes.

"I had wee bits of it. The ould fellow, her father, got up and he said that this villain had disgraced their family, and that he had stold his daughter's jewelry, he said.

"Oh wonderful: he had a wonderful charge against him.

"Then when she got up, she contradicted all the father said.

"And she asked Reilly in the dock for to return the jewels if he had them.

"And she said there was one ring among them, and she told him for to keep that ring and to wear it in memory of her where he'd be on his exile."

Events are often differently formed for presentation in song and story. Most of the District's great happenings are sung as well as spoken. In the context of Willy Reilly, tale and ballad, I ask Mr. Nolan if there was a song about Black Francis. "No," he replies, "I never heard tell of any song made about them. No, there was none that ever I heard tell of."

The clock on the dresser behind us says it is not long until time for the news. My questions cease. Neither of us is comfortable with them. I link the kettle down and begin making our tea. He moves his chair back to clear a path to the front table, where he unwraps the wireless and clicks it on. It crackles. To feed his own interest and fuel future chat, Mr. Nolan catches every newscast. With smoke and sweet tea, buttered bread, smoke and foul news, chat and smoke, the afternoon passes, and I leave him standing in the doorway, his shopping list in my pocket, his blessing on my ear, and climb the lane between chopped hedges under the mouse-colored bowl of the sky.

Paddy McBrien's cows move gently aside as I cross their pasture. I step through the paling, over the stones of the street, and enter the kitchen. P and Joe are sitting in the cool darkness, waiting. We have a project for the evening, making a tape to send their sisters in the Bronx. P has been practicing. The fiddle rests across his knees.

Peter Flanagan will not be called "historian" or "storyteller." He respects those roles and knows he did not listen hard enough to the old people when he was young. Music claimed him and he did not "work at memorizin the old history." An artist, he knows how good he would have to be at telling tales to satisfy himself, but his wit is keen, stories entered his mind and lodged there, and he uses his vast verbal abilities to deliver them excitingly. Wild in words as well as music, P does not restrain himself in the manner of a famed teller like Hugh Nolan. The voice runs free, flamboyant gestures carry him into the bodies of the tale's characters. That style can burn up tales in single renditions, so it is sometimes hard for Mr. Flanagan to repeat a story in the interview scene. The coolness of Ballymenone's performance norm, with its pristine ideal of clarity, allows multiple response and keeps stories alive for retelling.

Last night P wove a short version of the Black Francis tale into the ceili. Tonight, with the recorder still cluttering the hearth, the musical letter to Elizabeth and Rose Ann complete, I ask if he would be willing to tell it again, wondering if he got the whole story out. He does not want to, but will, for we have become close and he understands my work. Slowly he begins:

"His name in Irish, he was titled as Proinsias Dhu.

"That was the Irish style; it was Black Francis, he was Francis Corrigan in the English language.

"And he was known as a highwayman. In those days there was men and he was one of those highwaymen. His policy was: to rob the rich and serve the poor—give to the poor.

"And Lisgoole Abbey was started be monks, I understand, religious men, and he went this night and he robbed, he took a certain amount of stuff out of it in gold and silver.

"And the monks communicated with the military; in those days they were known as militiamen. The headman of them came out gallopin—it was all horse regiment thattime—and he came gallopin out.

"And Francis was goin toward Enniskillen, and he turned back.

"And they pursued after him: he's runnin and runnin from nearly Enniskillen on to Sillees River.

"And there was no bridge.

"And he leapt the twenty-foot river across.

"And says the headman of the regiment, he says:

"Corrigan, he says, that's a good jump.

"He says: the divil thank ye, he says,

      I had a long race for it ◊.

"So the chase continued.

"The headman of the army got across on a ford above

         and chased him on.

"And he came on

     as far as Derryhowlaght.

"And they were right on his heels there.

"And he took into the right there.

"And they went in after him

    on up towards a hill they call Druminiskill.

"And he was goin down the hill.

"And the horsemen was right on top of Derryhowlaght Hill;

     he threw the whole hoard of stuff into a hole.

"And he says, some man, he says, or woman, he says, will be rich some day.

"So it never was discovered from that day to this."

P stops, his story ended, and Joe provides its coda:

"Oh many times we heard of Souple Corrigan.

"They called him Souple Corrigan."

Granted space for speaking, Mr. Flanagan claimed it tentatively, filling it loosely with information, until the headman of the horsemen came galloping. Then with the horses he picked up speed, took command, and marshaled his lines with authority. Peaking with the exchange between Corrigan and the Captain, information tightened starkly into story.

The narrative sequence created in the open but apparently artificial situation of the interview was the same as that in the natural ceili, where Mr. Flanagan seemed to have less elbowroom: name, theft, chase, leap, race, treasure dropped, treasure remains. The difference is detail. P pried open the story with more facts. He gave the wild rapparee's name in Irish and set the same motive for him Hugh Nolan did: robbing the rich to give to the poor. He specified the military nature of the men pursuing him, the width of the Sillees, that it had no bridge, that the soldiers chased him over Derryhowlaght Hill. Knowing Lisgoole had been an abbey, he deduced that monks alarmed the army. Mr. Flanagan took what he knew and widened it without wildness or blarney into a fine, crisp text.

The teller of historical story has more than words. He has the facts, rich and right. Peter Flanagan will tell me history, then always say I should consult Hugh Nolan. Or Michael Boyle:

"He's the best historian around this side. He pursued old history from he was a cub, and he talked to alot of the old people around this district that knew that sort of thing.

"He gathered up the details that was carried down from generation to generation. And I think no man has a more clear recollection of what he heard than Michael Boyle."

5

Late Harvest

Arcing flatly eastward from the Derrylin Road, Drumbargy Brae slides into Lough Erne. A line of houses runs its crest. One near the middle is the Flanagans'. Between it and the Hillhead, above the Lough, tumbled rock walls remain from the boyhood home of Michael Boyle. To the south the land glides down to Rossdoney Lane, rising then to carry Hugh Mackan's house, where Michael and his mother lived after leaving their farm in Drumbargy. Mackan, Michael's mother's brother, died intestate. The old house is hollow, locked; its thatch begins to rot.

Michael Boyle, Hugh Nolan's great companion in youth, had his lungs wrecked in farm labor during cold wet weather. His home is now a bed in a hospital ward. "If you could go to the hospital," P tells me, "and inquire for Michael Boyle, a patient there, you could hear all the history of the District. He knows it from Ah to Zed."

He does. And he burns to have it recorded. It took me nearly two months to come to his bedside. It took but an instant for me to explain my mission and for him to join it. He wastes no time in small talk when I arrive. Our work must go on. He has been thinking of things to teach, rehearsing, waiting. My job is threading tape, pushing buttons, keeping quiet. His job is giving me, and through me the world, the history he has arduously assembled and precariously preserved.

He sits, drawn up in bed, at the end of a long excited account of a battle, his eyes ablaze, cigarette smoke rolling furiously about the bones of his face. In the ruined thin cage of his body, the soul smolders. Mr. Boyle is indeed the historian many have told me about. That and more: he is a man of tough, energetic intelligence. He sits, taut and angular, beneath the covers within the fluorescent glare of the ward.

Snapping with enthusiasm, his battle tale had carried over the still bodies of sleeping old men arranged in rows, and disintegrated through the hearing of staring old men, wavering at sleep's edge. But it brought to us one man, who stood a few feet off, listening with interest for the story to end.

It has, and he steps to the bed, engaging us in quick, earnest historical discussion. He introduces himself as Francis O'Reilly and says he comes from Derrylin, about eight miles south of the District.

Mr. O'Reilly opens the conversation with a question. It engenders misunderstanding. Mr. Boyle thinks he wants to know about—to tell about—Tom Russell, a leader of the United Irishmen in 1798, hanged after Emmet's aborted rising in 1803, and commemorated in Florence M. Wilson's poem "The Man from God-Knows-Where."[1] Instead his man is the The Mysterious Stranger.

Conversation begins, and they are trapped between the wish to agree, the need to hold to historical truth, the desire to tell the stories they know. Such a moment of confusion is rare among people who ceili together. Competition lies in the past, and people defer gracefully to one another's recognized expertise. These men are not familiar with each other. What the other knows is unknown. They agree when they can, affirming and building in litany off one another's words. They want to achieve a peaceful conclusion, enacting the ceili's yearning for union, but they refuse to sacrifice history to momentary accord. Truth lies deeper.

Their first task is establishing the identity of their subject. True stories commence in identification. William Quigley was an uncle of Paddy Quigley's. Tommy Martin was a laboring man, and he lived at Derrylin. George Armstrong lived in a little house in Gortdonaghy. Saint Febor was a very saintly woman and a wonderful writer. Black Francis was the leader of a highway gang in Fermanagh. Comparably, friendly conversation among strangers begins when each person has assembled enough information to locate the other in social and geographical systems and say happily, "Och, I know you." The other is known when situated exactly among the Malones of Ballydusk as Jim the Fiddler's sister's son. Traits of character as well as appearance are believed to pass in blood within families. Families and localities are known to have religious and political affinities. With "I know you," talk has found a base. It can loosen, deepen, continue. When the identity of a historical subject is known, irrelevant disagreement is eliminated, deep knowledge is balanced in readiness, and narration can proceed. All that remains is sorting out the roles in performance—a difficult, delicate undertaking, demanding courage and courtesy, wit and sensitivity.

So each man proposes a tale. But not until several points of agreement about past history and contemporary politics are found and fixed does Mr. O'Reilly yield to Mr. Boyle and withdraw into quiet participation, waiting to tell his story, which through positive response, narrative recapitulation, and logical anticipation he is encouraged to turn over and over, expanding and enriching it as it recurs.

The exchange the tape recorder hears occurs so swiftly that setting it out as a dramatic fragment, a playlet, seems best. The scene is late afternoon at the end of the season called harvest, in the hard, timeless light of the Erne Hospital. The characters are two elderly Irish countrymen and an

American folklorist, who are interested in history, and two nurses, who are not.

FRANCIS O'REILLY: Did you ever know what The Mysterious Stranger's name was?

MICHAEL BOYLE: Oh aye. The Man from God Knows Where. Russell.

O'REILLY: Was he?

BOYLE: Aye.

O'REILLY: Was he not Souple Corrigan?

BOYLE: Ah now, I don't think so.

O'REILLY: Yes.

BOYLE: I always heard he was Russell.

O'REILLY: He was Souple Corrigan.

BOYLE: Is that right?

O'REILLY: He was Souple Corrigan from your own country.

GLASSIE: Souple Corrigan?

O'REILLY: Well, that's my version of it anyway. Souple Corrigan. You see, he had another name of course. They'd call it a code name now, a coverup.

BOYLE: Well, I always thought The Man from God Knows Where was Russell.

GLASSIE: Well, maybe you-all are talkin about different people.

BOYLE: That was in Ninety-Eight.

O'REILLY: I know it was.
        When?

BOYLE: Wasn't that the Ninety-Eight?

NURSE (*wheeling a squeaking stainless steel dolly, laden with newspapers, candy, cigarettes, up to the bed*): Would you like a paper, Mister Boyle?

BOYLE: Give us The Times. Ninety-Eight.

O'REILLY: Ninety-Eight?

BOYLE (*giving the nurse coins for a paper and a pack of cigarettes*): Aye. Tom Russell was in Ninety-Eight. He came and organized the United Irishmen. There was a poem on it. There was a poem on The Man from God Knows Where.

O'REILLY: The Mysterious Stranger was far before that, was he not? At the time of the Priest Hunt.

BOYLE: No, no. He was not.

O'REILLY: Are you sure?

BOYLE (*passing cigarettes around*): I am, surely.

O'REILLY: Didn't they follow him from Enniskillen to that mountain under Cuilcagh to have a priest say Mass on Christmas Eve?

BOYLE: Oh, och aye. Well, they often done that of course.

O'REILLY: Well, there was snow, wasn't there?

BOYLE: Aye, snow.

O'REILLY: That's right.

BOYLE: Aye, that's right. Oh aye.

O'REILLY: Souple Corrigan was what they called a highwayman. The Mysterious Stranger was Souple Corrigan.

BOYLE: Yes.

Well, do you know what I heard about Souple Corrigan?

O'REILLY: Well, I know.

BOYLE: Souple Corrigan.

There was a highwayman, the name of Frank McHugh. Proinsias Dhu, they called him in Irish, and the English translation was Black Frank. You see.

O'REILLY: I know. I understand. He'd be Francis McHale in other words.

BOYLE: Aye, Francis McHugh.

Well, he was a highwayman.

Well, do ye see, the English made a highwayman of him . . .

O'REILLY: Well, that's what I was goin to say.

BOYLE: . . . made a highwayman of him.

They put the poor man out of his property.

O'REILLY: That's true. The Planters.

BOYLE: The Planters, they put him out of his home, out of his property, and they put someone else into it.

O'REILLY: He was one of the famous rapparees.

BOYLE: He was one of the rapparees. But the English christened him a highwayman, a *murderer*.

O'REILLY: Aw, they know how to do it too. They haven't changed their tactics a bit.

BOYLE: Well, he plundered, Proinsias Dhu plundered this English settlement. It was a monastery in olden times, Lisgoole Abbey.

O'REILLY: That was where part of the Four Masters was completed. At Lisgoole.

BOYLE: Aye, at Lisgoole Abbey. But the English put the monks out of it, do ye see, and occupied it themselves.

And this Proinsias Dhu plundered it.

But in the plunderin, he was captured.

And Souple Corrigan was along with him.

And Souple Corrigan leapt the river

they call the Sillees River.

It runs under the road there at Lisgoole yet.

And he jumped the river.

And that's how he got his name,

his nickname, Souple Corrigan ◊.

O'REILLY: Aye.

BOYLE: You see, the Yeomen was chasin him, the English was chasin him, do ye see, on horseback, and, damn it, he beat the horsemen and he jumped ◊ he jumped the Sillees River and then he was christened Souple. He was Ritchie Corrigan, Ritchie was his name, Richard, or Ritchie for a short name, and then he was christened, Souple Corrigan.

O'REILLY: Now he wasn't The Man from God Knows Where.

BOYLE: Och, no.

O'REILLY: But he was the man who went into the Cromwell Barrack in Enniskillen and spotted the whole thing and went out in front of them in the snow and saved the priest.

BOYLE: Yes.

O'REILLY: And the English army followed the tracks in the snow.

BOYLE: Yes.

O'REILLY: And they had a team of men ready for them.

BOYLE: Yes.

O'REILLY: And they pitched into them and put them back, as the word says,
and mowed them down,
and they carried on with their night Mass
of a Christmas Eve.

BOYLE: Yes.

O'REILLY: Isn't that true?

BOYLE: Aye, it is.

O'REILLY: That was in the days of the persecution and the huntin of the priests.

BOYLE: Aye.

GLASSIE: And what's the whole story of it?

O'REILLY: He went in and spied on them,
in the Cromwells,
in their own Barracks,
in their attire.

BOYLE: Yes.

O'REILLY: And he had his horse of course.
And he was stabled in a certain house.
And he was a singer, he could sing. He was clever.
He went in disguised as a poor man, but he had his horse in the yard, and some of Cromwell's spies was drinkin on Christmas Eve, and they let the whole thing slip. So that's the whole situation.

BOYLE: Aye.

O'REILLY: And he got out, he slipped out, as any ordinary person would do.
And he got in front of them.
They had two, as the word says. There was another man, I forget the name, along with him.
Oh, he was a fiddler, be Christ, the second man was a fiddler,

and they got them dancin and drunk, and they slipped the secret that they were goin out to get the priest.

But they didn't get.

BOYLE: Souple Corrigan saved the day.

GLASSIE: I see. Corrigan got to the priest and warned him.

O'REILLY: Yes.

And he had his army ready, his men ready for them.

It was on the side of Knockmullineny,
            on the side of Cuilcagh.

Amn't I right?

BOYLE: Aye, that's right.

O'REILLY: Och well, I'm always readin anyway. I have a book. It's only a small book, but it has the most coverage in it that ever was seen.

GLASSIE: It tells about Souple Corrigan, does it?

O'REILLY: No. I don't think so. But it goes away back and it gives a brief account of all the things that happened.

Wasn't this county the last county in Ireland that the Planters settled in, wasn't it?

BOYLE: It was. County Fermanagh.

O'REILLY: A most strategic county.

And it's still the most strategic one.

BOYLE: It is.

O'REILLY (*turning, moving back toward his own bed*): All the best.

BOYLE: All the best.

GLASSIE: Good-bye. Thanks.

BOYLE (*softly*): He's Francis Reilly. He's from Derrylin, up the Sandpit Road there; you know, by Ballyconnell at the Border. That's where he lives, up there.

However, what were we talking about?

GLASSIE: About Souple Corrigan, I guess.

BOYLE: Yes. Aye. Well.

Black Francis was hanged.

But Souple Corrigan was present the day he was executed.

I haven't the full details of it, but he was there anyway, and he was disguised as a girl. He was cryin for his true love, do ye see.

Do ye see: he was cryin about his *true love*.

The authorities; he was afraid they'd detect him, who he was.

And he was roarin and cryin.

And some of them asked what was wrong.

He says: that's my true love, he says, that yez are executin the day.

Of course, they passed no more remarks, but he was some kind of girl that was cryin about her intended *husband*. Aye.

Now unfortunately that's all I know about Souple Corrigan, that

	and that bit Mister Reilly related there about him gettin to Cuilcagh Mountain where the Mass was celebratin and savin the priest and the congregation.
GLASSIE:	Do you know when that was?
BOYLE:	Well, it would be sometime in the early part of the eighteenth century, like.
	Yes, it would.
	You see, Catholic Emancipation was passed in eighteen and twenty-nine. Well, that was some years previous to that, do ye see, that the priest-huntin was goin on.
NURSE:	You'll have to get up, Michael.
BOYLE:	I'll not get up. Me and this gentleman, we're havin a bit of a discussion here about history.
NURSE (*leaving in a little huff to find a superior*): Well!
BOYLE (*whispering conspiratorially, his eyes flashing*): We'll continue on as long as they'll let us.
	Well, where were we? Souple Corrigan.
	Them two instances about Souple Corrigan is about all I could relate to you.
NURSE:	If you don't come now, Michael, you'll get no dinner.
BOYLE:	All right, nurse. All right, all right.
NURSE:	The soup will be cold.

His long robe around him, Mr. Boyle is off to dinner. He will return quickly, having scooped new topics for recording out of his memory while eating. Our work will go on.

What happened was this: a simple encounter was driven through discord toward union.

Mr. O'Reilly approached us, wishing to make contact by telling a story relevant to our conversation about Fermanagh history. Politely, he had selected a tale connected not to his locality but to Mr. Boyle's. He could have been denied entrance. That would have been discourteous. Or he could have been allowed to tell his story. Mr. Boyle could have replied, "No, tell us about that," surrendering his control and launching Mr. O'Reilly into immediate leadership. That too would have been a dismissal, brinking on the unethical. We would have taken his information. He would have been repaid with another story. That did happen. There was a trade of Souple Corrigan tales, but it was slowed and confused in accord with an ethic of engagement.

During a fair exchange, story for story, information is withdrawn and transferred from mind to mind without affecting social relations. At the end, individuals, both a little richer, stand in isolation. Such an economy of storytelling will not account for things in Fermanagh. Through courteous challenge, parry, thrust, and the search for points of agreement, Michael Boyle and Francis O'Reilly were thrown into discord, into the need to clarify their separation so they could resolve, rather than covering to forget, their difference. They ended in unity, not in mere totality—in union, not in separate but equal independence. Each man got to tell his tale and hear the other's, but in delicate face-on grappling he also gained approval for his own story and learned the essence of the other's political and religious positions. Together they prepared the way for deeper future communication.

Engaged union is the social goal of communication in Ballymenone. Commonly in chat, more complexly in tales, most sublimely in music, most extravagantly in mumming, the same wish for positive accord rises through life. Look again at the transcript of the ceili at the Flanagans', noting how in the chat about fiddles and fiddling, then in the performance of the stories of Saint Febor and Black Francis, the men shifted thought and words into yes, aye, union. Though their encounter was more difficult, Mr. Boyle and Mr. O'Reilly did the same. Their words gathered the social world into engagement and toward oneness.

Social action in Ballymenone builds out of intense reciprocity. Of reciprocity there are different modes.

In most situations reciprocal action springs from an egalitarian supposition. People are assumed to have equal amounts to contribute. Since everyone brings culture and language to a conversation, all can "take their turn carryin the chat on." Men drinking together in a public house join in a tacit pact to stay together during the night so each can take his turn buying drinks for the company and accounts will stay even. When two men meet, a cigarette is offered. The person who accepts lights the other first, then himself (matches cost money, money is scarce), and as soon as possible he offers a cigarette and receives a light in return.

In the past, men passed a clay pipe back and forth or around the company, each man taking his turn as recipient and donor, filling the pipe afresh when it smoked out in his mouth. The egalitarian nature of such exchange was underscored in a story told me by Tommy and Peter Lunny one afternoon at their hearth. Once a rich man went to a blacksmith to have his horse shod. He had a big wooden pipe which he lit, puffed for a while, then passed to the smith, who took a puff and handed it back. When he received it, the rich man ostentatiously wiped the stem off with a handkerchief. Later the smith took out his clay pipe, filled it, and passed it to the rich man, who lit it, puffed it, passed it back. The smith put it on the anvil and in disgust smashed the end off with his iron hammer. On the streetcorners of American cities, men who stand around drinking wine from bottles wrapped in paper bags comparably count it a high discourtesy, a fighting insult, for a man to wipe the mouth of the bottle before tipping it to his lips. It is more than wine, more than a bowl of tobacco; it is a symbol of interpersonal unification.

Real differences of wealth are not allowed to intrude in normal sociability. Richer men buy no more drinks, give no more cigarettes. With hay to win or a roof to thatch, a farmer does not hire a laborer. He comes to his

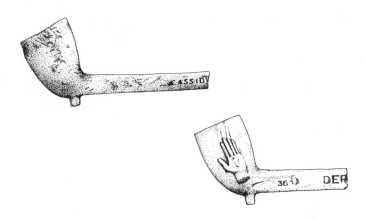

Clay Pipes. Tommy Lunny dug these up during farmwork. They are of the kind in use about 1910, made in Derry for a shopkeeper in Enniskillen named Andrew Cassidy. Dropped, they broke, Mr. Lunny said, "like an egg," and Mrs. Cutler said, "like a cup." Originally both would have been the same length, about three-quarters of an inch longer than the one at the top which measures now four inches. The lower pipe has the red hand of Ulster on one side, a heart on the other. Others had shamrocks. When Mr. Lunny gave these to me he was prompted to tell the story about the gentleman, the smith, and their pipes.

neighbor, decorously requesting his "help" with an elaborate description of his need. The laborer listens closely. He recounts the demands of his own work and typically firms no formal agreement. In accordance with his assessment of the farmer's needs, he may arrive early the next morning, or he may never come. Should he arrive, perhaps after repeated visits of request, he is assisted by the farmer who works by his side in the hot meadows, who has prepared the material, the straw and scollops, and helps him while he thatches. During the day the laborer is hospitably treated to big meals. Once the job is done, a little time lapses, and the farmer calls on the laborer to thank him profusely and accept tea at his hearth. At the end of their ceili, out on the street in the darkness, the farmer does not pay for service rendered but "gives" some money to his host. A standard rate, two pounds a day, is known to all. The money is not pay, but gift. The gift need not be cash—farm produce or the loan of tools will do. The American clock, a one-hundred-year-old Ingraham with an eagle on the bob that beats time on the Flanagans' back table was given P by a woman, a Protestant neighbor, he helped regularly. Money, spuds, clock: the gift, like work, is a donation to the social order.

Not all relations are symmetrical and egalitarian. Connections between some people exist apart from intimate sociability, such as those between a few prosperous farmers and their salaried workers. "Big men" pay, feed, and work beside their laborers. They act together, but they bank profit in separate accounts and use it to effect enterprise in distinctly separate social spheres. Within them, though there are differences of material well-being, interaction is based on a polite fiction of equality. Richer and poorer people alternate in buying drinks and talk not about working for pay but about "helping a neighbor." The rise among them of a cash economy has not blocked the neighborly way or eliminated the old ideal of cooperative work.

Class distinctions in a capitalist frame are not the only source of asymmetrical reciprocity. Special hierarchical rights and obligations shape the connection of cleric and congregation, parent and child, and an aristocratic set of responsibilities prevails when intimate associates moving within an egalitarian sphere do not have equal amounts to give to the maintenance of collective energy. Sheltered in his home, supported by his larder, the host provides for those who come to his hearth with Homeric generosity. The guest is assumed to be tired, hungry—"poor"—and the host has plenty, a place to rest, food to eat. His front door stands open to damp breezes, small hopping birds, and travelers, whose view into the dark interior swings to the fire. A chair will be swept to the center of the hearth, tea will be prepared, the traveler will be set back on his journey, rested, entertained, restored for contingency.

Special powers come to individuals in the moment, when yesterday's guest becomes today's host, and in the eternal design. A few people are thrust into permanent aristocracy by dint of genetic makeup or family tradition. The musician's talent is a "gift," as is the star's ability to compose stories and poems, as is the "intelligence" it takes to carry out hard tasks, telling tales, weaving willows into creels, driving automobiles, curing disease.

Everyone knows remedies for common ills. Whiskey punch will calm a savage cold. Scald some whiskey, pour boiling water on it, add a little sugar, and drink it as hot as you can. A clove of garlic boiled in a porringer of buttermilk will also tame a cold. If symptoms persist, eat a bowl of garlic-laced gruel. For a sore throat, drink a cup of milk into which red-hot tongs have been plunged, turning it a rusty color. Most medical knowledge, though, is left securely in the hands of specialists.

People "desperate with pain" will try anything, but little faith is given "quacks," the men who brewed magical potions in the past, the man who advertises electrical treatments in the newspapers today. "Doctors differ and patients die," they say, yet the doctors in the hospitals, though often arrogant, are sometimes right. People go to them quickly, easily. It costs, as is reasonable, nothing.

The local medical experts given confidence are the owners of "cures," common people (they have no special name or status) who have received within their families cherished secrets. Most people do not know how the cures work. They know they usually combine herbal concoctions with pre-scribed procedures, subtle prohibitions, and a "charm" in which the real power lies. More important, they know they work and who has them. The McConnells have the cure for whitla, the McBriens the cure for jaundice, the Corrigans of Drumbargy and the Nobles of Inishmore have cures for sprain. If a cow has the red water, a woman in Maguiresbridge has the cure. So long as you tell her whether the beast is calf, cow, or bullock, she can say a charm, even over the telephone, to prevent it from bleeding to death from blood passed in the urine. A man near Florencecourt has a dreadfully painful but efficacious cure for skin cancer, a plaster that sucks out strings of flesh and drives you momentarily mad, but leaves you well.[2]

These cures for specific diseases, preserved in certain family lines, are "right," emphatically "true." A woman I know suffered great pain. Gall-bladder was the diagnosis, and surgery was prescribed. She asked if she could go home for three last days "among the green hills of Bellanaleck." A friend got her the cure from a priest in the Republic. They do not allow cures in the hospital, so she went to her son's and "took the cure." She ate nothing all day, had a breakfast of tea and a biscuit the next day, then three times took a powder the chemist compounded according to directions, drank a tumbler of olive oil off at a draft, and was cured. She never had the operation and has passed along the paper with the cure written on it.

Medical knowledge, like historical knowledge, is possessed by very few people. Yet it is the possession of all. It must be shared.

The community demands individual wealth. Entertainment—talk and tea—is requested by the guest's sheer presence. Most requests are verbal, frontal, nearly aggressive. The musician is not fawningly adored. His talent is known, evaluated objectively, and demanded. "Give us a tune," they say. The framing is not interrogative, the request is plural. "You will play for us now, P," they say. He is obliged to return personal power to the group, to lead, to entertain. Similarly, the person with medical or historical knowl-edge, or the person with a car or an abundance of potatoes, is told to share. "You will give us a lock of pretties, P. Mine was killed by the frost."

The aristocrat of the moment must give. An unspecified but equivalent return may come. The man told to donate a long ride in a car will receive without comment a dozen eggs or half a day's help in the bog.

In other cases, the gift cannot be matched. The host of a known ceili house contributes more than he receives, both of words and food. He gives without thought of balanced reciprocity. The theory is that some day he or some one of his kin will be alone, cold and hungry, on the road. Someone will feed and care for him. The host's gift is made through people to hu-manity. It is his heroic duty to keep generosity alive in the world.

Aristocrats do expect immediate return. It will not equal their gift, but they expect it. The host hopes the guest will give attention and chat, wit or news, to the hearth. At least he demands, and demands assertively, that his gift be accepted. You cannot refuse a hospitable offer. If you do not want tea, you must ask not to be asked, because if the tea ceremony begins, if the kettle is lowered to the flame or the host says, "You will take tea," and you decline, he will push until you take something, and the offers will escalate embarrassingly. Refuse tea, and you will be made to drink the house's last bottle of stout. Refuse bread, and you will be made to eat cake. You must reciprocate in acceptance. A drink of tea is your acknowledgment of the host's unavoidable responsibility, his aristocratic role. You are in his debt.

The musician, talent's blooded aristocrat, demands recognition of the fortitude it takes to entertain and maintain aesthetic standards. His wit, strength, and duty must be acknowledged. He will not play unless certain of appreciation. That will come, and so will a few gratis drinks from beyond his company, but he wants more. When the flute comes to his lips, he wants the dancer's feet to answer. When song rises, he wants the crowd's good-manning. He demands engagement.

The speaker of stories asks more than the audience's dumb ear. He pushes the listener into verbal agreement, using the follower's brief comments to help him crack the tale's block into crystalline lines. Remember how Francis O'Reilly's story came only after numerous points of agreement were reached, how Mr. Boyle's repeated "yes" propelled him into efficient narration, how the tale's conclusion was social harmony: "Amn't I right?" "Aye, that's right."

Artistic performance in Ballymenone achieves engaged union on a base of aristocratic reciprocity. Artists are exceptional people, gifted and knowledgeable. They are obliged to lead. Others, in return, must follow actively.

When Michael Boyle, Peter Flanagan, Paddy McBrien, and their comrades came mumming at Christmastime in the past, they claimed the kitchen floor to present a rhymed drama that progressed from individual assertion to discordant argument, from argument to fight, from fight to death, from death to rebirth, from resurrection to a dance of agreement. Textually and situationally, the play displayed and resolved alienation. At the beginning, players and audience were radically separated. The family was seated at the warm hearth. Masked and unknown, the mummers stood in the cold, out on the street. At the end, distinctions between participants had been erased. A single human circle swung around the kitchen, from one side of the fire to the other. Gifts drew it. The householders had been given a play. The mummers had been given money and perhaps tea, for they were guests at the hearth. Action unified them. The householders had been asked to guess the mummers' identities and to request a song or a tune from them. The host danced with Miss Funny, his daughters tussled with the mummers during the guessing game, and his sons followed them out the door, joining the crowd that trooped from house to house, up the muddy lanes, through the chilly night.

The mummers' play was received as an entity, a text accompanied by a code of rules for performance. It was memorized, rehearsed, and presented in a stylized manner. The conversation around Souple Corrigan between Michael Boyle and Francis O'Reilly spattered surprisingly out of instantaneous interplay. Those two events, one traditional, the other emergent, differed in dynamic. Yet they were structured comparably. Each passed from assertion to engagement to accord. Both, in fact, fused the traditional and the emergent. Both were artistic performance, so both required the adoption of known roles that required the joint acceptance of a conclusion into which the roles were completely lost.

In Ballymenone, art's successful conclusion rests on two interlocked assumptions. One is a plain idea about social existence. The other is a complex theory of personal responsibility.

You know the people you meet. Strangers pass through—soldiers, tinkers, tourists—and people leave, but the people you encounter on the country lanes are known. You know their names and where they live; you know their religion, politics, and genealogy. Even most of the faces in the crowd, thronged along the streets in the Town, are familiar. The people you meet cannot be ignored, you will meet them again and again. And the time will come when you will need each other. Rain will swell the clouds with vicious blackness when your hay lies unwon on the meadows. The Arney will overflow its banks, flooding the bottoms, drenching your newmade rooks. Lightning will ignite the thatch, sending you shivering into the night. Famine and pestilence will again waste the land.

In the past, people worked cooperatively, "swappin," trading energy and tools. The unit for work in the bog, "a spade," consisted of three men. Though less usual today, cooperation comes with calamity. "Methals of men" will gather automatically to save drowned rooks or rebuild a burned house. Future disasters cannot be predicted. Engagement remains necessary.

You cannot luxuriate in the assumption that people with whom you disagree will not be seen again, that you can go through life seeing them but not engaging with them. You may need them. So disagreement is driven into the open and resolved, often violently. Tonight angry words will bloody fists. Tomorrow will bring cordial—stiff, restrained, but cordial—greetings. I was caught in such a situation when two men came through hot words to hard blows. My tradition of loyalty caused me to side with one of them and shut the other out of my life. After weeks of avoiding my new enemy, I discovered the two of them had worked together the next morning and had been interacting normally the whole time. Resolution of disagreement does not mean enemies become friends. It means they agree to overarch differences in their common predicament.

Ballymenone has no word for friend. "Friends" are blood relations. To comment on amicable associations you speak of the frequency of ceiliing. "She ceilis to it." "He is often and often in it." Though closest to the people you ceili with, the named social units are "friends" and "neighbors." You have no choice but to live in engagement with both, one because of blood, the other because of proximity.

Neighbors come first. "Your neighbor forenenst your friend" is Ballymenone's proverb that parallels in opposition another culture's "blood is thicker than water." Answering a neighbor's thanks for help, young Hugh Quigley said, "When times of trial come, sure, what good is your friend and them ten or a thousand miles away in London or the Bronx. It's your neighbor you rely on." You might dislike your neighbors, you may differ with them ideologically, but you are joined with them, like it or not, by the land, by an ethic of neighborliness rooted in clay and covered by clouds. You must be prepared to cooperate with them when disaster strikes. It will.

The neighborhood sets the norm of social experience. Within it the essence of the idea of personal responsibility is easily put: the self exists in connectivity. In Ballymenone, neither past and present nor individual and society are conceived oppositionally, antagonistically. What is easy to say is not easy to understand.

Talent is inherent. The special qualities of musician and storyteller, craftsman and witch, arrive as a "gift" in the blood from the ancestors. Knowledge is heritage. Cures are learned from parents and grandparents. History is learned from the community's elders. By blood or communication, the present is a gift from the past.

Excellence is not passively accomplished. Musicians wrestle with their inner abilities through years of obsessive practice. People given cures gather herbs on the wild mountainside and learn to mix and administer them correctly. Historians work to assemble the fullest, truest stories. Work makes the aristocrat a hero, solely responsible for the preservation and improvement of the talent and knowledge on which the entire community depends. But when the artist stands proudly before his audience, he stands humbly before the whole of the past. His excellence came in essence from others. So he has no need for false modesty, no call for inflated conceit. Others can evaluate his talent objectively. They can demand it, and it must be given, but not lightly. Only the farmer truly in need is given help. Only the ill are given cures. Only the appreciative are given music. The deserving recipient and capable donor connect through mutual respect in the moment to the past that connects them more deeply.

Excellence is individual. Young men play in "march bands," but mature artists do not play in ensembles. Standing alone, the fiddler must be able to "fill the air with music." But the role of entertainer requires him to bring others into performance, and the norms of performance require the active participation of the audience, their dancing and percussive whoops, their goodmanning, their verbal concurrence in tale-telling. There must be engagement.

Engagement signals the grateful, joint acceptance of the past's gifts. If the fiddler gets drunk and betrays his talent, if no one goodmans a song, if a historian distorts the truth to please his audience, lowering his art to propaganda or amusement, then irresponsibility toward the past evinces disrespect in the present. It is an insult. Performers must act conservatively toward tradition, avoiding whimsical variation, holding to transcendent truth. In the very different situations of ceili and interview, Peter Flanagan presented fundamentally the same story about Black Francis. Hugh Nolan told the story smoothly in an unencumbered and supportive scene. Michael Boyle's broken telling came amid contention and confusion. Still, their tales were ordered comparably. Black Francis is identified. He robs Lisgoole. He is captured. Corrigan escapes, leaping the Sillees River. Black Francis is hanged after making a speech to Corrigan, who stands in the crowd dressed as a woman.

Every story is made to fit circumstances, but if the truth abiding apart in a timeless realm of absolutes does not appear, unscathed and intact, during performance, the tale is falsehood. It lies on an axis of crime with theft and murder.

I found it hard to understand why the District's people class lying, theft, and murder together. To me murder is categorically a worse crime. Final, irreversible, the theft of life is not like the theft of property, and in my enormous, deracinated world, lying and theft are so common among all social classes as to be nearly a way of life, a feature of the environment. But in Ballymenone they consider the small lie a great evil; there is no worse instrument than the tongue, said Peter Flanagan. And they think the man who will steal will kill. The liar is a small murderer. I found it hard to understand why they spoke calmly about political killings and why they spoke with such frequency and fear about stealing, especially since it is so rare among them. Grocery vans drop bundles of goods and bottles of milk along the lanes to be picked up hours later. Farmers leave tools and bicycles propped casually against hedges. Outoffices are not locked.

When set into the social experience of the neighborhood, the question has this answer. Theft is the clearest instance—more concrete than lying, more frequent than murder—of the most terrible of crimes: an attack made by one member of a community upon another who is innocent.

Soldier, policeman, vociferous politician, the quiet young man with his handmade bomb (the "bad boy" who "plays in the game")—those who participate know their risk. Death is lamentable but expected. But a harmless person should be safe from harm. The death of "innocent people" is universally cited as the worst aspect of the current Trouble. Innocence should protect you, not from fate—bacteria, lightning, the car speeding in the night—but from those with whom your destiny is linked.

Neighbors cooperate. Cooperation requires accurate communication. The community is founded on truth. A lie is an act of contempt and withdrawal, a theft of honor from individuals and order from society.

In a neighborhood, compact and socially intense, all things have known owners. Theft is not the illicit appropriation of property, it is—like ridicule—

a direct attack made upon a known individual. In a scene of material scarcity, where all artifacts are in some measure tools, stealing removes the means to gain a livelihood and pursue the happy life. The thief is death's ally.

When the trigger is squeezed and a soldier is dropped, a creature is gone, but when an innocent person is prematurely stolen from the community, energy is robbed from the little commonwealth. All are harmed.

A false tale represented as true, a stolen bicycle, a pitchfork bloodied in the meadows—all are assaults through flesh upon the tissue of community, the system on which life depends. Communities are built of crime's negation: truth, not lies; gifts, not theft; love, not murder. And the community is the model for moral existence. "All mankind," they say, "is your neighbor." Crime is the opposite of the host's hospitality. It affronts humanity, denies life. When a tale is true, freely and affectionately given, it reverses crime. Like the gift of tea, it signals respect, affirms social order, contributes to human goodness. It is an emblem of life.

The teller who repeats a story's core while siting it gracefully in the conversational moment behaves responsibly toward his dead teachers and live listeners. They are not the only ones he owes respect. He must act responsibly toward himself, for if he is uncommitted to performance, if he speaks, as they say, "from the teeth out," he stops his talent from unifying him with his tradition, himself, and those around him. Disengaged, his act is inauthentic, unethical, less than art.

Artistic traditions do not persist because they exist. They persist because they serve social and personal purpose. An individual's expressive needs can be met in cultural convention. Alone in his dark home, Hugh Nolan tells about himself in his choice of stories rendering respect to women and affection toward young lovers. His Black Francis delays escape and suffers death to chastise a man who mistreated a woman. Willy Reilly and the Cooleen Bawn, lovers held unnaturally apart, appear in different guise in other of his tales.

Accepting tradition does not mean sacrificing the godlike soul. Constrained by tradition, by sonnets and landscapes, jigs and reels, the strong talent is not destroyed, it is aided. It is given resources, prevented from degenerating through self-indulgence into mere eccentricity, and it is submitted to public testing.

To honor the ancestors from which it came, a talent must be used, driven against truth and circumstance toward perfection. When the work of art is personally satisfying, situationally appropriate, and still embodies truth, perfection is reached, evaluation is possible. Artist and audience can know good from bad.

Bad fiddlers drop notes from complex melodies by playing too fast. They dull tone with insecure fingering and lose continuity in erratic, undanceable tempo. Bad singers begin with incomplete texts, forget words, mumble when uncertain, and obscure melody in agonized phrasing, overmuch "drizzening," quavering, or ornamentation. The good teller's tale arrives trim, clean, uncluttered with extraneous words, unmuddled by histrionics. In complete, flowing lines, not in crazy bursts, it presents the whole truth, achieving the teller's wish for beauty, answering the neighbors' need for clear, accurate communication.

Talent is tested. The self is risked and accomplished. Human power is restrained and focused to make the self a gift to the other, the past a gift to the future. Past and present, internal and external collapse into union. Art adheres to its own rules while the senses seek their pleasure and the social unit confirms itself. The beautiful tale—clear, complete, true—is the good tale, a moral presence.

Two problems confused my attempt to reduce the District's theory of responsibility to prose, causing words to spiral, coiling back over similar conclusions. Both rose out of a disharmony between my scholarly obligations and Ballymenone's thinking. The first is a matter of discourse. The second leads to cultural understanding.

Since the ceiliers know one another and can assume a deep unity of values, they present principles in efficient proverbs and discuss them by telling stories in which principles are subtly trapped. Having culture, they do not describe culture, but refer to it. Theirs is a poetic, open mode of discourse. Since I do not know what you know or believe to be true, I must close things down in prose, shoving principles to the fore.

The principles in Ballymenone's theory of responsibility interlock simultaneously like clock gears. Simultaneity is hard to capture in communicative modes fated to linearity. That is why structuralists excited by simultaneous phenomena—complex social connections and poetic meanings—so often resort to diagrams and lose their readers in elliptical, fantastic writing. The point hidden by sentences incapable of accommodating more than two or three relations is that, acting within a frame of aristocratic reciprocity to create engaged union, the historian owes respect simultaneously to the dead people in the tale, the dead people from whom the tale came, the dead people from whom his talent came, to his inviolable self and the others with whom he is speaking, to people beyond in his community, and to those in the future whose lives depend upon associations properly formed in performance.

My other difficulty came of the complexity of my scholarly task. I want to produce a particular description depicting a real community in its own terms, yet I want my writing to connect to general theory. Those goals are not at odds, but they do make things difficult. When I discuss my conclusions with my teachers in Ballymenone, they usually say that I am right but that I have come to my findings along an unnecessarily troublesome, roundabout route.

In recognition of the basic truth that human beings exist at once alone and in society, a realistic theory of artistic performance has to center on the individual at the moment when the personal and communal, the authentic and ethical, mesh. That is the folklorist's center. Something is not folklore merely because it is old in a community. The teller may not like the old story. He will give it to a wandering collector, but it will not gather his being into its performance; it will come forth as a relic, not as folklore. Something is not beyond folklore because it is new. The teller can take a tale from a book, and if he invests it with culturally derived power, it will ascend to folklore. The heart of folklore is gripped when the individual takes personal responsibility for the collective destiny.

The historian uses the best sources, written or oral, to create the truest stories about the past. When he performs them, in writing or speech, blending into them, communicating, he builds the future out of the past he holds within. The name for that act, whether the historian be middle-class professor or poor farmer, is folklore.

Since art can be created in isolation and cannot be created by traditions without the intervention of real people, folklorists begin study with an individual in a moment. But that is not Ballymenone's center. It lies between the fleeting vapor of the present and those set points in lost past time from which the capacity to act in the moment came. It lies not within the individual but between people. These are the implications:

The present is an unpredictable permutation of an unknowable past. Actions, while willed, are weirdly preconditioned. So you must act, facing what comes, living in all seasons, without any assurance of success. Problems do not always have solutions. Virtue is not always rewarded. One must endure.

The social unit is not the individual, it is the group formed by common problems and collective action. So individuals have the means to endure. If they fall, others will lift them. If they begin a dangerous fight, others will stop them. They have talent and knowledge, wit and courage, even if they do not have them in their lone selves. And if they do, if they are craftsmen, musicians, a bit curious, anointed with the mad drop, they are not shot into isolation. The community is compounded of diverse excellence.

A community conceived as a series of individuals and aspiring to equality must eliminate aristocracy in the name of democracy. The community conceived in egalitarian oneness exploits aristocracy for its own well-being. Its stories celebrate exceptional individuals: courageous characters and witty stars, saints, outlaws, heroes.

Artistic performance is the aristocratic enactment of communal will. It comes from, leads to—and is in itself—engaged union.

Coming to these first conclusions about storytelling in Ballymenone, we have strayed within the gravitational pull of the anthropological theory of functionalism. In an early manifestation, social rather than psychological, functionalism held that the little community was coherent and its institutions served like a body's organs to maintain that coherence.[3]

Troubles in that formula are not sufficient to eliminate functionalism from serious attention, but they are real. As part of the romantic heritage of anthropology, connecting functionalism to earlier and later schools of thought, the little community was projected as the opposite of a negative critique of modernity. By viewing it as socially and culturally cohesive, sacred, organic, and unified, rather than rationalistically fragmented into experiential and conceptual alienation, scholars praised the little community —and stripped it of history. All it could do was wait in a dream state for the diffusion of ideas from without to crack its stasis. Since its institutions functioned to preserve equilibrium, its potential for disorder was confined to little rituals of reversal and licensed moments of license, and its power was left to circle endlessly without direction or explanation. If the little community exists to maintain its existence, it and the theorist are locked in unproductive tautology. The little community may as well be swept away. Functionalism may as well go out of fashion.

Proposing social accord as the goal of art seems an endorsement of simple functionalism. Yet we can hold to that idea, I believe it is true, and to some of the virtues of the functionalist tradition without losing descriptive accuracy or theoretical power, if we step up to look with precision at the community created by art, and if we step away to observe the community's situation in the world.

The District's people live compactly. Through repeated contact and communication they build cultural consistency. They recognize themselves as bound by necessity into a community, and it is not wrong to find among them a Rousseauian oneness, reinforced institutionally. The mummers visited every house—Catholic, Protestant, rich, poor—and invited everyone to a ball. Their purpose, said mummer Peter Flanagan, was "to bring unity amongst them."

In reaching out to "all the neighbors round and about," mumming exemplified art's communitarian function. But it was an unusual performance, doomed to entombment in memory. The ceili's tale is today's work of art. An aesthetic and ethical unity, it is not socially degenerate art for art's sake (it is not solipsistic, inaccessible, autoerotic), nor is it infertile utilitarianism (it is not polemic on behalf of the social order). The tale approximates the radical romantic ideal, a fusion of the beautiful and the useful. It serves society. But the community it produces is not firm before its telling, not coterminous with the community on the land.

As common occasion, the ceili is a locus for art and a force for social cohesion. Old men tell stories, but people of all ages and both sexes are present in the kitchen. Women, young men, and the majority of old men who lack artistic pretension fill the role of follower, unifying with the teller and one another during performance. Visitors to the ceili house join its inhabitants through reciprocal action, taking tea, giving chat, and they connect ceili houses to each other by varying their routines of nighttime travel. People ceili most often with people they like, who may live some distance away, but they also ceili with "near neighbors."

Affection and proximity draw people through ceiliing, through stories, into a social net and into cultural congruence. But the net does not hold everyone. Its mesh is wide, irregular. Not everyone ceilis. Some opt out of sociability and pass the howling nights alone. A few prosperous people and some young people travel in cars to houses beyond the community for their ceilis. Most people, though, are tied together by ceili paths crossing the place where they live and work.

Their movements in the night are influenced by more than affection and proximity. Kinship draws people. So do religion and politics. They say it was not so in the past, when times were better and mummers announced Christmas, but now when bombs rattle the sash in their frames and armored cars screel along the back country lanes, most ceiliing joins people who share religious and political commitment.

The ceili is the night's way to connect people. Associations develop in daylight among neighbors who do not ceili together, who do not ceili at all, whose farms adjoin, whose strips of bog and moss ground run next to each other in the hollows between the hills. Neighbors join in need. That does not mean a patchwork spreads over all rural Ireland. Their place has boundaries.

It occupies a segment of the globe, bounded by water on east and south, by roads on north and west: the Lower End of the Parish. Within it agricultural cooperation and ceiliing are confined. But community is more than place; it is a proposition. Trading tools and help, people produce a daytime net that does not stretch to meet the boundaries of the geographical community, and when people come into agreement in the ceili's tale, they construct every night a new order of loyalty that affirms only some of the neighborhood's associations. Their community is a thing of their will, not someone else's government.

The map's community exists in the mind, but it is not the same as that created by day in work, and work's community is not the same as that built out of courteous nightly chat. The community suggested by tradition, refined by work, is separated by creed, torn by politics.

The anthropologists who developed functionalism could see but not explain the tribe's drive to equilibrium. To explain, they would have had to free the little community from the scientific convenience of self-containment and place it in world history. Then the commitment to balance might have been read not as tropism or conservatism, but as resistance to an imperialistic onslaught of which the anthropologist was an embarrassed, functioning part. Perhaps the little community's internal efforts were responsive political action. The mummers of Ballymenone did not visit every home in the Lower End of the Parish out of some innate impulse to preserve order. They were directed by their community's wise old leaders to restore order to a community that had been ripped to shreds by a violent civil war. They were successful. The mummers' period was peaceful, but they are gone, both mummers and peace. Mummers, now old, are storytellers, and they speak of saints and rebels.

Stories bring into union only those who choose to be engaged. The tale's community is drawn from among the neighbors, but it is less than the neighborhood, for it develops in the face of multiplex threats to personal happiness and local stability, oozing out of mindless chatter over slick conference tables in secret chambers, set beyond real space in an international web of political-economic intrigue.

By fragrant turf fires in lime-washed houses on low damp hills rolling out of Lough Erne, art is made by people who like one another. With increasing precision, the ceiliers are neighbors who share religious belief, political sentiment, and class affiliation. Conversation cannot help but bring up matters pressing in from beyond. Intimate associations come to embody ideologies, traditional arts incorporate political developments.

In everyday life—in her shopping, in his storytelling—people move between the traditional world, where face-to-face knowing is valued above ideology, and the modern world, where the real and experiential matter less than the abstract and conceptual. A shift in primary political orientation from fleshy neighbors to intangible ideology has no impact on the ethical nature of the artistic event. Its participants remain real neighbors, cooperating to produce social accord. But the event's functions and its social consequences are greatly altered. The ceili tightens: its community becomes not our place but "our side."

The transition from traditional to modern is not complete, nor can it be. Like the traditional world, the purely modern world is supernatural, a ghost of the imagination. Change is a matter not of going from one location to another but of adjusting priorities while getting through another day. Sometimes the shift is abrupt, and the world seems strangely new. In such an instant, Tommy Lunny's grandfather, hearing news of the Fenian Rising, rammed his spade in the ridge and left, saying, "When my country calls, I must go." Stiff in the dirt, abandoned, its shadow lengthening over work undone, his spade marked precisely the moment when international politics took precedence over farmlife, and the little community lost its hegemony over his mind. But usually matters drift in contradiction and unresolve while the hierarchy of value mutates slowly. Fragmentation waxes, unity wanes, but pure states are not inhabited by people, and the agricultural community stretches and tenses without splitting.

Real people change their minds constantly, maintaining sanity. The neighborhood, their place of daylight work and encounter, remains the primary community for most of them.

The Troubles have hurt, not killed, the neighborly ethic. The neighbors of "the other side" are no threat. It is those hooligans in Belfast, those foreign soldiers, those bloody politicians. Without concurring on solutions or the ultimate reasons for conflict, Protestants and Catholics will say the immediate cause is the Big Boys who live elsewhere and find it to their own benefit, profit, or prestige to keep the people fighting. Listen to the voices of Ballymenone:

"This old Trouble has nothin to do with religion. It's the Big People tryin to hold on to what they have. And the Little People want some of it too."

"It's the leaders now causin it all, do ye see. Oh aye, it's the rich people tryin to keep the good jobs for themselves.

"The Troubles don't touch the leaders, do ye see. It just hurts the people. The leaders do make wild speeches and the stupid people listen. And the leaders can keep arguin over words and arguin over words. It's the people gets killed."

"There's been Trouble this fifty years since they divided the country into six and twenty-six. And the Fenians will keep this Trouble up and just keep nibblin away until they have it all won.

"It's terrible. The Big Men in the IRA sit back with their drinks and their big cigars and send these poor lumps of cubs out to do the dirty work. Now."

"Sure, what does the British government care? Just send twenty or twenty thousand stupid lads over here to get killed."

"If there was an IRA man at the door and thousands more outside, I would say, Yous will have to shoot me. I will die for my wee country the same as yous are pretendin to do.

"I would never change. The Church of Ireland reared me, and I will die Church of Ireland."

"The Catholic people is not bad now; it's the politicians lead them into ignorance."

"The Troubles has gone on too long now. There has been too much destruction of property. There has been too much loss of innocent life.

"The IRA are good men. They try and not harm innocent people, but they set claymore mines and it could be innocent people goin over them the same time as the military.

"The IRA are doin what they think is necessary, and they are good men, but at the very same time, the thing can get out of control, do ye see.

"And every man's life is dear to himself. And dear to his family. Even the soldier: it is sad when the soldier is killed. The soldier could be innocent too, do ye see. He might just sign in the army there, and then he might be sent here, not knowin. It's the generals, do ye see, it's the generals and the leaders, the ones that know, they're to blame. Aye.

"No one wants to be taken away before their time. A man that's a sinner, even that man is made in God's image. He shouldn't be taken away.

"If people lived be the rules of religion, there would be no killin, and there would be no prejudice. And everyone would have a good job and a good house. But if people is kept down, they will rise. And as long as they keep stoppin you, and stickin their old guns in your face, and bayonets, well, this thing will go on, and it must go on."

"Och, one side is as bad as the other."

Despite the Troubles, because of their impossible complexity, neighborly accord prevails. Deep ideological differences are overarched in real contact. Formal conduct is framed that recognizes differences, then holds them apart while life goes on. Daylight dealings remain cordial. Though tightening, ceilis have not contracted into political purity. Loyalty to their own side does not compel people into disloyalty to their neighbors.

Political speeches, toasts on historic occasions, and children's rhymes may be framed as attacks:

> If I had a penny, I know what I'd do:
> I'd buy a rope,
> And hang the Pope,
> And let King Billy through.

> Up the long ladder,
> And down the short rope.
> God save King Billy,
> And the hell with the Pope.

> Here's to the Purple goose,
> And the Papish gander:
> To hell with the Pope,
> And, No Surrender.

Mature, sober arts do not attack but celebrate. Drinkers toast "Here's health," "Here's luck." Even angry drinkers usually toast "Up our side," not down theirs. Public displays are stark and strident, conceptually simplified, rhetorically heightened, but the stern march through the streets with banner and drum, and the pub's aching patriotic song, affirm more than defame. Their force is loyalty, not hostility.

At the hearth, where the mind has space to remain subtle, complex, and free, the will remains positive. The wish to affirm, to goodman, extends beyond the ceili's company. Investigations of human nature, particularized among the neighbors, living and dead, peak not in ridicule or mean-spirited mockery, but in celebratory stories, in exploits of the brave, bids and pants of the witty and wise. And in the ceili, that good spirit enters even the dread realm of political conflict, where it brings unity among the engaged without lowering to assault upon missing others.

Ceiliers want to say the good word about themselves, the neighbors, all mankind. When they turn to history, their stories tell their story, the record of their side's heroism. Protestants and Catholics do not have different versions of history. They have different histories. They begin at different points, follow different routes, embrace different personalities. Ask a Protestant about rapparees, and you will not get his side of the story, in which they are condemned as villains. He will say he knows about them but does not have their history, and saying, "That's their side," he will refer you politely to a Catholic who will have the history but not the story and will direct you to Hugh Nolan or Michael Boyle. Restrained by neighborliness, history is not so much a weapon for conflict between groups as a means to consolidate one group. Confined to truth, stories of history consolidate less by demanding loyalty than by presenting similarly committed people with facts they must preserve and consider together. The facts are not simple or sanguine. The rapparees were the rebels after the Williamite War, which confirmed Protestant domination of Ulster, English domination of Ireland. In the period 1690 to 1798, they were the heroes of the "Catholic" side. But many of them, Hugh Nolan stressed, were irreligious rogues. In Mr. Flanagan's telling, the noble Black Francis robbed monks, holy men of his own religion. The past is like the present. History offers it in preparation for an unknowable future.

The accord preceding a story is more than courtesy, more than a docile wish for peace. It is an exploration into the potential for community. A historical tale told before the achievement of political and religious agreement could be an affront, an attack, a crime against community. With political concord, no cheap discord will follow. The tale will be admissible, and disagreement will be confined to its content. That is why Francis O'Reilly and Michael Boyle struggled for agreement before telling their stories. Performance had to end in oneness. It had to prepare for future social—and political—action. So the tale could not begin unless it could connect them on levels deeper than conversation. At the bottom lies the bedrock of personality, where people join in ongoing affection, but that level cannot be reached without excavating through the strata of politics and religion. Once Mr. O'Reilly and Mr. Boyle had found their opinions similar, they could imagine an intensification of their relationship. They could become ceiliers together. And they could consider the tale in itself, accepting it as a frame for discourse and a whip for thought. Their scene was not street or public house, where too many people move too quickly and only clear rhetoric can cut through the confusion. Within the context of their agreement, the story did not descend to propaganda. It could exist in all of truth's ambiguity and complexity, taking on meaning.

Meaning is the center of our study. It carries us from sensate things—words, artifacts, behavior—into the invisible structure of values, into culture, into the human mind and heart. Meaning challenges scholars to study people as though they were human and to use study to challenge the world's ordering. But we have let our great traditions deflect us from our task.

Meaning submits to no conclusive tests. It expands, escaping final proof. A subject for discourse among intellectuals and not an exercise for technicians, meaning is not beyond science, but it is beyond the nightmare of methodologists who think science is a matter of measurement, demonstration, and proof, rather than disciplined understanding. Lost in the decadence of science for science's sake, technicians endlessly count, assemble, and reorder sensate phenomena without addressing values, without considering human beings in the fullness of their abilities to think, feel, love.

Even our noblest humanistic tradition, rising in critique, has blindered attention, causing us to consider some dimensions of meaning at the expense of others.

Things fall apart. Horrified by disintegration, appalled by art as it declined from serving the spirit to serving wealth, as it degenerated from expressing culture to expressing the ego, the great romantics of the nineteenth century searched the far past and remote present for evidence of unity. They discovered and proposed a unification of art and social life. Most exquisitely, John Ruskin, after painstaking study of the Gothic, demonstrated that art could—must—be evaluated as a moral as well as an aesthetic phenomenon. It was Ruskin that William Morris read as a college student, and Morris with whom William Butler Yeats dined as a young man. Like Bernard Shaw, Yeats was son to Morris. Yeats, Morris said, wrote his kind of poetry. Morris, Yeats said, was the happiest poet. The unity of being that Yeats called his religion came from Morris. Both took it from peasants and John Ruskin, and all took it from close study of old things, the carved churches and sinewy songs of the Middle Ages. Their hope for unity remains, diversified in paintings, some dreamily ethereal, others minutely realistic, in architecture, textiles, and books that strike us as fussily Victorian and shockingly modern, in essays of scholarship, criticism, and manifesto that seem sadly dated and frighteningly cogent, in a poetry bridging the medieval and modern to unite peasant and gentleman in a new social order.[4]

In the era between the Pre-Raphaelite dawn and the Celtic twilight, the second half of the last century, anthropology, sociology, and folklore came into impressionable maturity. The little thinkers in the shadow of the big ones could not think alone. They took evolution from scientists. From the romantics they took organic unity. The concern for the relation of art to life that so drove Morris and Yeats, making one the first great modern designer, the other the greatest modern poet, was built into the human sciences. In Ireland, Britain, and the nations of Europe, in distinct but connected and consonant traditions, the romantic ideal of a social art and an artful life became part of thought, and it remains fresh and blended in the writings of our day's great scientists and critics.

The anthropologists who formulated functionalism early in the twentieth century did not have to read the romantics, any more than scholars today have to read the existentialists. They needed only to mature in the glamour they cast over their age, an age they hated. Then when they encountered exotic people, they envisioned them as their own opposite, as something unified, and developed their own, new idea. Oriented for our use, brutally simplified, it was this: art builds community; symbols create, incarnate, and transform social order. It is an idea worth preserving and refining. In Ballymenone, art does not function to maintain equilibrium in a bounded community. It serves to create community anew in each performance. Ballymenone's people seek order not out of a timid, witless conservatism, but in a spirit of rebellion against the terrible, larger world.

The center holds. Recently linguists, and most cogently Dell Hymes, sharing social ideals with the great romantics and their existential heirs, have gone beyond solipsistic formalism to place the idea of performance in the middle of our thinking. In performance the artist presses inborn power beautifully through collective competence into personal action, as part of society, within life. By implication, folklore, like any art, is not a matter of individuals generating tales, or of traditions operating—diffusing, evolving, surviving—without human agents, according to law. Folklore results from an individual controlling the strength born within and nurtured in conflict and affection, using the vast power of the mind for society's good. Responsibility, the existentialists' word, is the key. Ballymenone's storytellers are responsible artists.

It is no falsification to find a fit between the hopes of the angry romantics and the intentions of Ballymenone's tellers. Their stories exist within two intersecting categories of action that compel the creative person into social responsibility. As a heightened kind of speech, the story lifts above the "silence" through which individuals sicken into themselves. Stories rise above "talk" where words are idle, unconnected, or potentially harmful. Stories rise above "chat," where words bring people into engagement, above "crack," where engagement becomes amusing. Aloft, stories seek the beauty and benign power of music. As "entertainment," stories are like food, gifts designed to please other people and carry them on. "Stories of history," since they are stories, are more than factual. They provide nourishment. Indirectly but truthfully, artistically but generously, historical narratives give their listeners "information" they must know and "warnings" they must heed as they endure the present and go to meet the future. Stories of history are at once beautiful and useful. As "stories" and "entertainment" they bring people into engagement and urge them to accord.

Folklore's tradition is at base romantic. It leads me to see art as social, action as meaningful, things as the enactment of values. It led me to Ballymenone and back again and again. For there people really do use stories to create unity. But my tradition does not lead me efficiently to meaning's other side, where unity is used to create stories.

The closer we look at the relation of art to social life as they interpenetrate functionally, as they emerge, merging in particular performance, the more exact our formulas become. We draw ever more detailed diagrams of the machine that grinds at once the beautiful and the good. What we miss is content. When the people of Ballymenone perform stories, they achieve union. And through the open, poetic nature of their art they propose explosion. Finding unity, they allow into existence words without bounds that force them to imagine, to think beyond art and society. They use stories to make the mind work against artistic conventions and to consolidate their group, and they use stories to escape unity, rattle order, defy the organic, and transform culture through ambiguity and paradox into personal philosophies and modes of historical action. Unlike the immediate social world of performance, the inner universe of content has no need to close into union. It expands, yielding space to the mind.

It is time to consider content. Having understood the dynamic of agreement, of reciprocity and responsibility within a violent political climate, it is time for us to look into content, examining the whole corpus of Ballymenone's stories of history.

When Tommy Love and Peter Flanagan joined across the hearth to reaffirm affection, each danced to the other's tune, each provided an example of one of the two main kinds of historical tale. Mr. Love's was sacred, Mr. Flanagan's political. Religion and politics are not separate cultural realms— all history is unified in concept and on the land—but stories of saints and stories of political strife are classed apart in Ballymenone. We can consider them sequentially while feeling toward the meanings history holds for people who gather at the ceili's fire while black night cracks with distant thunder that may be the report of a bomb blast.

PART THREE

Saints

6

Sacred Beginnings

Dark mountains loft on the west. Along them cuts the Border. From them rivers of rain and green hills fall, crest after crest, into Lough Erne. Half-drowned small hills rise through the reeds, disrupting placid waters. The island hills of Lough Erne, Hugh Nolan teaches, contain history:

"Well then.

"There is certain islands in Lough Erne, and there's a history to them.

"There's an island here beside us, Cleenish they call it; well, there was a monastery on that island.

"Well then, there's another island; it's further down; it's Inishkeen. There was a monastery on that island.

"And then there was another abbey in Derryvullan or Derrybrusk, and that would be in the other side of Lough Erne, along the Dublin Road.

"And there's a very celebrated island down below Enniskillen, Devenish they call it. There was an abbey on Devenish. And the round tower there remains.

"Well then, there's a demesne there as you go to Enniskillen; it's Lisgoole Demesne, and there was a monastery there

in days gone by.

"It's on this Derrylin Road. When you pass where that military camp was, you'd see piers and a big railin, do ye know, and gates openin into an avenue. That avenue leads to what is known as Lisgoole Abbey.

"It has been gone a long time.

"I'll tell you the time that Lisgoole Abbey went. It was after the Plantation of Ulster, do ye see. Any of these abbeys or monasteries that remained after the Danes, they were taken over and the monks was expelled, and some of them was killed, and some of them died. Their lands were taken over and given to some of these settlers, King James' settlers: Scotch gentry.

"Well then, it ceased for to be a religious place. But it bears the name to this day of Lisgoole Abbey.

"There was a graveyard at it.

The Round Tower on Devenish Island

"And there was a graveyard also in Inish*keen*, across the *Lough* a piece from that.

"And there was a graveyard in Cleenish.

"And most likely that there was a graveyard in Devenish too, if anyone was fit for to point it out."

The twelfth-century round tower stands down the slope from the rising crossing tower topping the remains of St. Mary's Abbey, dated 1449, next to the burying ground of the Maguires, chieftains of Fermanagh, by the ruins of the oratory called Saint Molaise's House after the sixth-century founder of Devenish. The round tower is visible far across the bright breadth of Lower Lough Erne. Like the name Lisgoole, it remains to remind. Local history is deep. Hugh Nolan made that point, but it was not his main one. That came at his conclusion, when he located ancient graveyards along the Lough between his home and Devenish Island. These places are not merely old. They are holy. Monasteries may be leveled and lost, but graveyards are indestructibly sacred places, carrying ancient blessings to join modern people with those buried beneath and those who sought wisdom, sanctifying mortification, and safety from mad Danes on Lough Erne's islands.

"Ireland, land of saints and scholars" is an encomium often repeated in the District. This very locality is especially saintly and scholarly, especially Irish. Men, as Peter Flanagan tells, came from afar to establish monasteries just here:

"There was a monastery on Cleenish Island there. They have the stones there yet, and aye the inscriptions on the headstones.

"It is a shame to tell you: I was on the Island workin often and often and yet I never was at where the monastery was.

"There was a Saint Sinell. This chapel down here was dedicated to him. And he traveled—I believe he was a Longford man, the monk or saint that he was: he was a Saint Sinell—he traveled down on foot from the County Longford, on down to Cleenish Island, and that was, I suppose, roughly the most of fifty miles, so it is.

"He traveled down here to Cleenish Island.

"It lasted for over a century, the monastery, till the invaders came in of course, the English, and I think they were responsible for demolishin it, or bringin it to destruction. I think that now."

Hugh Nolan tells of a man educated at Cleenish:

"There was many saints in this country.

"Saint Naile must have wrought here. Kinawley Chapel is dedicated to him. He was a Donegal man, like Saint Columcille.

"Well then, there was another saint. There's an order to this day called after him: The Knights of Saint Columbanus. I suppose you have heard of him.

"Well, Saint Columbanus, he was a young fellow that came from the Midlands somewhere; I just don't know what county he belonged to. But there was a monastery and school here on Cleenish Island in them days. And he came to it to learn. And that's where he got his education.

"And when he became a man, do ye see, he became a priest.

"And he was sent away to Europe to convert some of the—Europe, do ye see, they were all pagans in them days and they had no knowledge of Christianity at all. And that's where he spent his life. And he's buried, I believe, in whatever country he converted.

"So he was a youth that came from the Midlands, got the first of his education on Cleenish Island, and after that went to Rome, and then from Rome he was sent to some of these European countries that was pagan for to be converted.

"Do ye see, from the time that Saint Patrick converted the Irish to the Christian faith on till the arrival of the Danes, it was a terror what Irish men, both clerical and lay, that went out through all the world. Well, it was mostly Europe because America wasn't known of, nor Australia wasn't known of, and then for Africa, well, there was very little known about them either, but Europe was a place that was well known. But it was a heathen place, and it was Irish men took the faith to England and to all of Europe."

In these statements, examples of history less than story, meaning is plain. Ireland's special ancient virtue combined learning and sanctity. This place compressed those peaceful qualities powerfully, attracting, educating, sending saints abroad. When Europe was wild, this place was civilized, but its order was disrupted, first by the Danes, then by the English who pillaged and took the land. The ancient monastery of Lisgoole was made a landlord's demesne, an alien island. Reduced from sacred to secular service, Lisgoole lay open to attack from Black Francis, who plundered it as it had been plundered, repaying theft with theft.

As Hugh Nolan moved northward in his account, Devenish defined the limit, a bare seven miles away. When their land is proposed as sacred, special, it is not out of an ingathering of glory from all Ireland, or even the rich Lower Lough. Saints blessed, and cursed, the very land they work.

The Irish predawn, savage times of cattle raids and salmon leaps, heroic slaughter and sexual excess, of sun-pierced, rock-built, mounded tombs of love gods and warped warriors, are not part of local history. There is talk of "a time of giants." Both Peter Flanagan and Hugh Nolan tell stories of an Irish giant—P named him Phil McCool—who built the Giant's Causeway and hurled a rock at a Scottish giant which fell short to become the Isle of Man. But such are only readings out of schoolbooks, "folklore" heard on the radio, fireside amusement for children, of no deep importance.

History begins with Saint Patrick. Without endangered souls, people are not fully people. Christianity forms the historical base for existence. Though crucially important because, as Mr. Nolan said, he "converted the Irish to the Christian faith," Patrick is not a local responsibility.

The historian's scope is small. Space delimits his task. Hugh Nolan surrendered saints beyond Devenish to others. Peter Flanagan considered Saint Febor part of Tommy Love's country, not his own, just as Francis O'Reilly considered Souple Corrigan part of Michael Boyle's. Their homes in Boho, Derrylin, and Ballymenone precisely define the historian's responsibility. It lies inside a circle with a radius of seven miles.

If history expands too broadly, Hugh Nolan told me, it loses detail and sharpness and becomes inaccurate. While others write sweeping stories that generalize themselves unto falsehood, he said, local historians like himself preserve the "full particulars" of "the whole tale" and cleave to the truth. Were history false, he would lose the pleasure of its company.

This locality is rich in itself, and it is the pleasant job of its historians to preserve information about those who first wound the clock of history here: Saint Febor, Saint Sinell, Saint Naile. So Peter Flanagan, who had never heard of Saint Patrick being in Fermanagh, and Hugh Nolan who had, both told me to inquire among the people of Armagh and Down for the details before telling me what they knew about Saint Patrick.[1] Mr. Flanagan first:

"Well, I never heard much about Saint Patrick.

"Of course in the County Down he was supposed to be buried. In Saul. That's where he rests: Saul in the County Down, Downpatrick.

"And the first fire he lit here was supposed to be on the Hill of Slane, in the County Meath. That's where he lit the first fire.

"And the Druids at that time said, Extinguish the fire.

"He said that the fire he lit couldn't be quenched.

"Of course he meant, be the fire, the faith.

"Aye.

"And it was never known clearly where he came from.

"He was educated of course in Rome, Saint Patrick. He was sent be Pope Celestine in the year four thirty-two.

"He was sent over here as a shepherd first.

"He remained as a shepherd on the mountains down in the County Down. I think it's the Slemish Mountains they call them, in the County Down.

"And then we went back again.

"I don't know was he of Irish origin; I just can't tell you that.

"There has been a lot of explanations about Saint Patrick, but it is definitely known that he came from Rome in the year four thirty-two. That's right."

Having never seen a book on Saint Patrick,. and knowing he has not

South Fermanagh. The names on this map, the places in the local history, suggest the historian's scope, the community's larger region.

received the kind of history that would descend in the place of the Saint's work and burial, Mr. Flanagan speaks cautiously. He stands off from the story and does not invest his integrity in its presentation. Circumspect, his account exists as an intelligent man's perception of distant matters. Yet it is mythically potent. It establishes the origin of Ireland precisely in time and space: A.D. 432, the Hill of Slane in Meath. And during its one narrative moment, Saint Patrick confronts the Druids, the incompletely human incarnations of dark old order, vanquishes them without bloodshed, and begins history by lighting the unquenchable flame of faith.

Telling his history of Saint Patrick, Hugh Nolan, like Peter Flanagan, brings into order many of the facts he has heard. They are not strung out, but packed and linked into a statement broken into parallel halves. Only the first is local, his responsibility, so only it is stated firmly and formed as an artful narrative, a story, but both are introduced in a quick passage, followed by an informational setting for an action by Saint Patrick that, like lighting the fire on the Hill of Slane, holds continuing power. On Inishmore, the great island across a thin strip of Lough from Ballymenone, Patrick discovered an herb. From it sufferers gain relief, as they do at the well the Saint blessed eleven miles due west in the mountains on the Border, just north of the town where the Sport at Belcoo marks the Day of Our Lady on the fifteenth of August. It is the major warm-weather event for south Fermanagh's Catholic people.

At Belcoo, after Mass, the crowd flows happily around peddlers of food and raffle tickets, streaming along the street where bands march, bumping along the field where Gaelic footballers run and thump, breaking, eddying around platforms on which young dancers, embroidered over with ornament from the Book of Kells, bob and leap sternly for prizes. People meet, eat, laugh, and listen, while over the platforms, the Hoopla stand, the military post, twangy country-and-western music, march tunes, and endless Irish reels roll through the trees and out over the lake. By night, celebrants jam the pubs around the fiddlers and walk easily back and forth past the customs stop and the earnest young men selling pamphlets, crossing and recrossing the bridge connecting the public houses of Belcoo with those of Blacklion, Northern Ireland with the Republic, intending their drink-strengthened stroll as an eradication of the Border.

When, as Hugh Nolan tells us, Saint Patrick blessed Belcoo's well, he blessed too this "sport." The jovial event commemorates the Saint's presence in Fermanagh, just as, according to Peter Flanagan, the fires once lit on the hillsides amid the dancing and storytelling of Bonfire Night, the shortest night, June twenty-third, commemorated Saint Patrick's first and eternal flame.

In the beginning, Saint Patrick brought faith. His fire burned the night away. With the Christian dawn the soul's long sleep ended. It was roused and enlightened. The new human day did not end but incorporated ancient festivity. Mr. Nolan:

168   Passing the Time in Ballymenone

"Well, the principal story that ever I heard related,
　　it was when Saint Patrick came to Ireland.

"He landed down south
　　and he traveled on towards the north.

"And you'd think for to hear about Saint Patrick that he was just a lonely missioner that landed in this country, and he had nobody *along* with him.

"But he had a very big contingent.

"He had tradesmen of all classes.

"And there was a staff of women for to make vestments (that'd be the robes that the priest would be wearin while he would be sayin the Mass), and for to make all the linens in connection with the altars. He had them.

"And he had men then for makin the altar vessels and everything that was a-wantin.

"And then he had men for lookin after the horses and keepin them shod and keepin them *right*.

"But they traveled on anyway and finally they got as far as Inishmore.

"They come on right up from the south of Ireland and they were travelin through Inishmore on this occasion.

"And didn't the horse that he was ridin upset,
　　he slipped and he hurted his back,
　　and of course he wasn't able to get up.

"So there was some kind of an herb,
　　or something in the grass,
　　　　and Saint Patrick lifted it up,
　　　　and he rubbed it to the horse's back,
　　　　and the horse jumped up.

"Well for years and years after, there used to come people from all airts and parts where they'd get hurts,
　　　　or bruises,
　　　　or cuts or anything.

"And there was people, they were the name of Nobles.

"And they were Protestant farmers.

"And it was on *their* land that this herb was.

"And they were all the men that knew it or could point it out.

"So they used to point it out to these people.

"And they used to apply it.

"So I haven't heard any word now about it this long time, because the family died out, do ye know, and whether they bequeathed this knowledge they had to anyone else, I never heard.

"But they knew it, and they would point it out to you or me or any other person that was sufferin.

"The herb was known as dho. That was the name of it.

"So then there was other notable things that was, well, connected to the history of local saints, do ye know, like *wells* and things like that.

"There's a well, it's above Belcoo; it's between Belcoo and Garrison. And it was one of these places that was—ah, it was blessed be a saint.

"I believe Saint Patrick had some connection with it because, I'll tell ye, there was alot of places and they were noted for what they call, a day's outin. And maybe there'd be a dance and some terrible function, do ye see, at these places.

"Well, when Saint Patrick came along, he didn't discourage the sport or mirth that used to be at these places, but he made these places holy places, do ye see.

"And then afterward they were visited by pilgrims and people that was sufferin from illnesses and things like that.

"This sport, do ye see, went on elsewhere or convenient to the place that it used to be in ould times.

"On the fifteenth of August, there bes a big day at Belcoo.

"Well, in olden times that big day used to be at this well that I'm tellin you about. There used to be games and singin and dancin. So this is kept in memory of it."

The power of ancient Irish Christianity lay less in theology than in great individuals,[2] and that is how the District's people tell it. In Mr. Nolan's account, Saint Patrick traveled to Fermanagh, the fire bringer came to the Lough shore. Mr. Flanagan casts saints of the next century in the role Patrick played in Mr. Nolan's story. They pierce the interior, bringing cures for the body, hope for the soul. He tells first of Saint Naile, hero of his boyhood home, Kinawley.

"There's a cure in Saint Naile's Well.

"If you had any external ailments or warts or growths on your hand, if you'd rub a wee drop of the water to it, and cut the sign of the cross in the name of the Father, Son, and Holy Ghost, your wee warts or lumps or tumors or anything like that would diminish away.

"This is in Kinawley, and the water's risin crystal in under an ivy bush.

"You could go to Kinawley, if you weren't rushed, and you could search and search for quite a long time. Except that someone told you, you couldn't get it atall.

"Well, when I was there last it was invisible nearly, you know. With the growth in the graveyard, the well just disappeared, but if you got down to it, and it's only about the size of that kettle,
       it's as clear as crystal.

"It's just boilin up there.

"And it's supposed to cure any external warts or lumps of any kind that would come on your hands.

"Saint Naile, he said he'd leave the cure behind him.

"And he put his hand down like that and he cut the sign of the cross. The ould tradition says that. And up the spring riz. It says that.

"He says, There's my cure, he says, there for all time.

"The wee well. It's just in under a wee ledge like that. It's limestone rock, though it doesn't appear like high land or anything like that, but it's all limestone around Kinawley. And that's where the good springs comes from in this country, I suppose in your country as well.

"And they say he just cut the sign of the cross, like that, in his old age, when he was about to retire. Of course like every other one, he knew that his time was gettin short.

"And it was said this wee spring, fountain, just sprung up. And there it remained from that day till this.

"Saint Naile.

"That's what tradition tells anyway, that that's how the thing happened.

"And he had performed a few miraculous cures. He had conferred a cure on some invalided people.

"And when he was asked about when he would go,
     will there be cures after him.

"And he stooped down and he cut the sign of the cross. He says, There would, he says.

"And up the wee fountain sprung, and developed into a wee well and there it remains.

"And it's rather peculiar to look at. It's something brighter than water. It seems to be more crystallized or more brighter than ordinary water. Aye. You'd think that there was like lime or some colorin stuff through it, you know. It has a peculiar look off it."

Philip Flanagan is buried in the graveyard by the late medieval church at Kinawley. Headstones, some as old as the eighteenth century, bearing skulls and coffins and crossed bones, spill out of the ruins, behind the beaten screen of rock wall that carries the unglazed east window, and descend a gentle incline where a tree bows over Saint Naile's Well.[3] Once he had knelt quickly in the long wet grass to pray for the soul of his father, Peter Flanagan took me, his duty done, to see the well. It was dusk of a windy late November day, but a glow remained in the shadows beyond the well curb, and P commented that no matter the weather, wet or dry, the water level remains the same.

Saint Naile's Well is brighter and more consistent than other wells. It springs beneath limestone, anomalous on low land. Blessed, made by a holy man, it is not natural. Yet it is like natural features, for it is encountered as given, a part of the environment.

Saints and land connect. The Saints knew nature's secrets. Saint Febor's beast of burden was a wild deer of the forest. Saint Patrick knew which herb in an unknown locale would cure his horse. They controlled nature. A gesture from Saint Naile, and a crystal fountain gushed. A word from Saint Febor, and a river turned upon itself, writhing from the ocean back to the Lough. Faith was their power. Its concrete, living symbol is the very

Saint Naile's Well, Kinawley

land. The crooked Sillees remains bad for fishing, good for drowning. Saint Naile's Well, the herb Saint Patrick found, the well he blessed, hold benefit for modern people. Christianity was their great gift, but cures are their tangible, testable legacy. Physical and spiritual spheres turn in accord. Cures continue to bring relief from bodily pain and to remove warts, just as faith heals and purifies the sick and blemished soul.

Joe Flanagan said prayer would guard him from ghosts. Faith protects as well as repairs. So does holy earth. Clay from the grave of Saint Mogue near Bawnboy in Cavan was collected and thrust up in the thatch, Tommy Lunny told me, to prevent lightning from blasting the home. It was carried, Peter Flanagan will tell us, by emigrants on the voyage to America to be cast on wild seas to still them. The peculiar dirt over the dust of this older contemporary of Saint Naile's remains so charged that it can shield human beings from nature's violence. The Saint stands between God's storms and God's people.

"Saint Mogue, he was a wonderful saint, they say.

"Saint Mogue.

"He was in the Diocese of Kilmore. This is the Diocese of Clogher.

"Saint Mogue is buried on a wee island this side of Bawn.

"And all the emigrants ever went to America, even me sisters, they brought Saint Mogue's clay with them.

"It's a whitish color, more like chalk, or like putty, that nature. It's a wee crumby stuff.

"It's interestin that when they'd be goin to America longgo, they'd chip a wee bit of it, like that, into the sea. And the sea would be at its roughest and it would drive the waves back.

"I heared that now. I'm only just tellin as I heard. I wasn't an emigrant meself, nor had nothing to test it or anything, but I heard that about Saint Mogue's clay.

"It was always took be all the emigrants and specially when there was the ould sailin ship, when it twas more hazardous goin away
out on the ocean."

When P finishes Joe adds:

"There was an uncle and an aunt of ours, and they set out (that would be a brother and a sister of me father's) and it took them four months to go to America.

"A storm riz and blew them out of their course altogether, do ye know. They had to wait then for the storm to cease.

"They were ould sailin ships at the time."

The time was about 1880. Phil Flanagan's sister had decided "to go out," and as usual they held a party with plenty of food and drink for the neighbors all around. At the "hooley," her brother and a companion of his decided to go too. Money was scarce, but passage cost only four pounds, ten shillings, and a collection was taken among the company. They were never heard from again. Sixty years later, P and Joe's sisters left.

They took a pinch of Mogue's clay, of holy Irish dirt. Others took the three-leafed shamrock. Though Tommy Lunny said any time you look for it the shamrock can be found, many believe it appears first each year on Saint Patrick's Day in the middle of the season called "growth."[4] The shamrock's seeds made the voyage, but would not root in foreign soil.

On Rose Murphy's bedroom wall hangs a print of Saint Patrick driving the snakes from Ireland. While I sat at her fire with tea and biscuits, she read me a letter from her mother's brother, who left at eighteen, sustaining himself for the six-week voyage on oatcakes. The letter told of his golden wedding anniversary. He had married a girl from Cork, just as the Flanagan sisters married Irish men in New York, and the celebration drew their sons, all doctors and executives, and their daughters, all executives' wives, to their home in Kansas. Another of her mother's brothers, Charles Owens, also went to America, traveled, and became wealthy.

One of the great treasures owned by Hugh Patrick Owens, Rose Murphy's neighbor in Sessiagh, is the Book, a ledger kept by his family with entries beginning in 1835, recording births, marriages, deaths, dates of confession, agricultural arrangements, and recipes for cures. Through all runs a litany of emigration. A sample:

for the Cough: 4 ounces of hunney, 4 ounces of Shuger & Candy, one glafs and a half of punch viniger, 4 ounces of the Brown Shuger, one ounce of ginger, Some drops, one tumbler of flaxseed.

September the 13th, Confest, 1857.

The sow went to the hog, November 14th.

December the 19, 1869, Hugh Corrigan died. April 12, 1870, Hugh Owens went to America.

Thomas Owens went away, 22nd April, 1872. the name of the ship is the city of Agra.

January 24, 1873. I got the meadow from William muldoon.

May the 12, 1877, John Owens went to Queens Land.

Septebr the 12, 1878, John Owens went to America.

John Magvney went to Queens Land, 1879, May the 28.

Thomas Owens married, 27th January, 1896.

Cassie Owens born, 27th December, 1896. Maggie Ellen Owens born, 24th October, 1898. John Owens born, 27th June, 1900. Francis

Thomas Owens born, 14th August, 1904. Hugh Patrick Owens born, 27th March, 1907.

Francis Thomas Owens Went to America on Saturday 9th April, 1927
+ Johnny Owens Widdows also.

"There is no one in this country," James Owens said, "that doesn't have friends in America." That is not quite so, for Harry Crozier told me he was exceptional in having no relatives in the States. But most of my conversations with strangers begin at the question "And how long are you home?" assuming I am a "returned Yank," and proceed to accounts of relatives who are doing the best in America.

Today's emigrants are mostly young women, like the daughters of Hugh Patrick Owens and Paddy McBrien, who go to England in search of good work. One lovely and modish young woman who had not yet gone stood in the dark kitchen of her thatched house on the hillside, her curls permed into a sunburst, and told me she hated everything Irish. Her mother was out milking the cows. She gestured at the black kettle on the hearth and the buckets of water carried from a distant well and said she couldn't wait to leave.

Emigration is a great and complex fact of Irish history. The island of saints and scholars commenced in purity. God came upon the earth as man. Satan came upon the earth in the form of a serpent. As he created man in Ireland by breathing souls into bodies, so Patrick cleansed the land of slithering evil. Snakes are the opposite of human beings; their cold, limbless bodies cannot survive where the flames of faith burn. Ireland is the Holy Island, sad, hard to leave. Yet people do.

Stories of Saints tell the beginning. The only full-blown historical story taken from outside the locality is Hugh Nolan's of Saint Columcille, brought from beyond to raise within and at the beginning the issue of exile.

We were talking about Sligo. Mr. Nolan once visited, as we just had, the ruins of Sligo Abbey. Our talk carried Columcille into his mind, for the Saint's great battle was fought in Sligo. Mr. Nolan turned upon the ambiguity in the words "this country," normally meaning this District but also meaning Ireland, to collapse all places of sanctity and learning into one, and beginning cautiously he took control of the famous legend of Saint Columcille, whose home territory—Derry, Donegal, Durrow, Kells—sweeps around Fermanagh, and made it his own. To please Truth, himself, and the American ladies at his hearth, his story rises from apology toward poetry as he develops parallel constructions, decorates the text with incisive repetitive words, "book," "Ireland," and varies tone and pace, slowing, lowering to a terrified, passionate hush when Columcille receives his sentence of exile:

"Columcille.
"Well, do ye see, he was a native of Donegal.

"There's a place in Donegal they call Glencolumcille,
        and I think maybe that's where he's from.
"You see,
        he had to leave this country
                over a book.
"I don't know what's this man's name was,
        but he wrote this religious book.
"(I'm just not well up on this story.)
"And I think that Saint Columcille got the book
                for to read.
"And he took a copy of the book, do ye see.
"So when he was givin back the book, as far as I can remember, he wanted to keep the copy, do ye see, that he had wrote.
"So the man that owned the book, he wouldn't agree to that.
"And they wrangled and wrangled and wrangled for a long time about this.
"So finally the case was referred to the high king.
"There was a king in this country at that time.
"So the way he decided it was:
        that
                to every cow belongs her *calf*,
        and
                to every book belongs its *copy*.
"So he give judgment in favor of this man that owned the book.
"So then Saint Columcille, of course, naturally enough, he was vexed.
"And any man would be vexed
        about bein deprived of his own writins
                and what he considered to be his own.
"So anyway, he decided that he would put it to a battle,
        and whoever would win the battle that
                this copy of this book would be his.
"So anyway, both men prepared for the battle.
"And there was a day appointed.
"And a battle took place.
"And Saint Columcille's men won the battle.
"And he had to get the copy of the book.
"So whenever it was *over*
        he got sorry for what he done,
                for puttin it to that fellow.
"And he went to some holy *man*
        to get his advice on it.
"And what this man told him was that he'd have to do a little penance for the loss of what life was in the battle, that he'd have to try and convert as many as was killed in this battle.
"So anyway, his sentence was

that he'd have to leave Ireland
for all time
for to never return,
and that he'd have to go to some pagan land
and convert as many to Christianity
as was killed in the battle
that was over the book.

"So anyway, he started.

"And it was in Scotland he landed.

"And he wrought in Scotland till he died
in preachin and convertin.

"All the time that ever he came back to Ireland was—and he had to come back blindfolded because the penance that was left on him was that he'd never see Ireland more and that he'd have to *leave it*.

"So he came back blindfolded on an errand.

"And the errand was:

"There was at a *time* and there was a section of the Irish people used to go about in bands: they were the bards.

"There was an instrument, there are instruments to this day yet in places in Ireland: the harp.

"These ones played on harps and others sang and they went round from one town to another, and noted places like Arney and Derrylin and Enniskillen, and put in nights and amused the *people*.

"So there was some kind of a law that these people were all going to be banished out of the country.

"So Saint Columcille was informed about it in Scotland that that was comin to pass in Ireland.

"So he came back to Ireland blindfolded.

"And he made an appeal to the authorities
for not to banish these
because he was a lover of music
and stuff like that.

"So that was all the time he got back to Ireland
from he had to leave it.

"So he died in Scotland
at a very big age.

"He was a great, a great man, and wonderful for bringin people to the knowledge of God and Christianity.

"And then he had his own troubles too."

Stories mean in association. Providing contexts for each other, they reach through the mind to connect, narrowing into system, reducing toward principles. At the same time they reverberate, pushing beyond system to touch and embrace life.

Between stories, stories and life, Ireland is defined. Here the sacred became natural. This land, free of serpents, springs cures. Its dirt protects. Ireland is the Holy Island. Yet here men have been evil. Rascally hunters coursed a saint's pet. Invaders pillaged, stealing homes, reducing holy places to ruins. In stories, the law of man is bad. It hangs thieves, allows the rackrenting of widows and the persecution of priests. It causes men to turn informer on their comrades and to delight in their murder. It prevents Protestants and Catholics from marrying, punishes elopement, takes from a saint his holy book, threatens to banish the bards. Law joins crime in the negation of happy life.

Conflict between sacred origins and historical realities, between religion and politics, life and law, forces action. People cannot accept things as they are. Their place, once pure, decays in injustice and poverty. They despair, abandoning the soul Patrick gave them, or they emigrate, abandoning Patrick's land. Or they rebel.

Vexed at the loss of his book, Saint Columcille fights, and vexed at the loss of her books, Saint Febor destroys a castle and curses a river. The Planters take his home, so Black Francis robs Lisgoole. Deprived of his love, Willy Reilly steals her away. Violence is just.

But rebellion brings exile. Saint Columcille wins his battle and is banished. After robbing Lisgoole, Black Francis is sent into the final exile of death. His companion Souple Corrigan, the priest's savior, escapes, dropping stolen treasure in a bog, and emigrates to America. Reilly wins the Cooleen's love, wins at his trial, and is transported. The victor loses Ireland.

Ballymenone's tales of exile are not transformations of a single idea. Yet, standing apart, each in its own integrity, they align to echo through the mind. Saint Columbanus won the wealth of wisdom on Cleenish, then left to dispense it among the spiritually poor of the Continent. Thirteen hundred years later, George Armstrong was driven from his home two miles from Cleenish by poverty. He prospered in distant Australia, then cholera struck. His success led to deeper failure. It is worse for the body to shrivel in pain than it is to live without wealth. Saint Columcille's victory in battle led to greater loss. It is better to lose a book than it is to lose Ireland.

Columbanus and Columcille lie buried far from Ireland. Columcille and Armstrong returned, Armstrong permanently to become a storyteller, Columcille temporarily to save singers and musicians from exile. Each came home handicapped, Armstrong ill, Columcille blindfolded, to insure the continuation of entertainment in Ireland. They sympathized with the distress of the Holy Island. Its people should have art at least to carry them on. Art brings personal pleasure and social accord. It stands against law and argues for life.

New vitality is born of personal failing. Out of Armstrong's shrunken body, a star rises to pull others from the darkness of silence into engaged union. Saint Columcille errs, then brings as many into new life in Christianity as he had brought to death in battle. The story ends with the self in service to life: Columcille's mission, Armstrong's entertainment, the marriage of Willy and the Cooleen.

Saint and storyteller merge. All the key stories were told by Hugh Nolan. Like Columcille, Mr. Nolan left Ireland. Like Columcille and George Armstrong, he returned. Poorer not richer for having gone, Mr. Nolan abandoned the worker's ambitions and became a holy man, a great entertainer, his community's aristocratic servant.

The Saints comprise a distinct genre of historical tale. Their message is not clear, nor should it be. To be effective, stories connect, unifying meaningfully. The structure of values shifts into visibility. To be affective, connections remain intricate and imperfect, leaving space for people to discover new and personal meanings within and between. The enactment of values remains an individual responsibility.

Gray as standing stones or men at work in seaside fog, the Saints move in the mist between the explosion of creation and the small storms of our day. God's mediators, they partake of divine power and human weakness. They snap rivers from their courses, convert hordes of heathens, then act like anyone else. Saint Sinell and his student, Columbanus, needed earthly education. Saint Columcille loved music and like "any man" was enraged at the loss of "what he considered to be his own." Saint Naile "like every other one" felt death come.

The Saints stand too remote to serve as models for behavior. They resolve completely none of the dread arguments of brain and soul. But their lives were examples, gifts to their fellows, the ignorant and faithless, to us. As the first persons of our era, made like ourselves in God's image, yet closer to God, they incarnate propositions about existence. Purified and blessed, the earth holds solutions to earthly problems, but not all problems have solutions as death intrudes to prove. Even the saintly man makes mistakes. Though "wonderful," he has "his own troubles too." Life's troubles must be endured, but not without the comfort of religion, the delights of entertainment, the excitement of convivial sport, the right to act against nature and unnatural law. Dispossessed, one can fight. Victory may lead to loss, but personal failure balances in work for others. Work and faith give life purpose and hope but no guarantee of success or happiness. One must carry on.

7

Saints at War

"The closer you look at it," Hugh Nolan said, "the worse it looks. But you can't despair. You must carry on."

Bravely but sadly compressed, that is the key principle in Ballymenone's philosophy of existence. We reached this point studying stories. The District's people come to the same place more easily. They discuss their state, their position in the world, through stories, so we can listen and gain some understanding, but they present the essence of their vision in efficient proverbs that shock thought. Their state is endurance, carrying on despite conditions. That central idea is undergirded and enriched in other propositions. The first is the message the Saints brought.

"Any thinking man," Peter Flanagan said, "knows that God created the earth." Take heart: the world is not absurd, it was intended. Your courage is not in vain. God set cures in the earth. The Saints discovered and bequeathed them to you. Yet incurable illness smites. Saints sicken and die.

"God's ways," they say, "are not man's." It is not given to us to know God's plan, so "we must take what comes." That is what Johnny Boyle said of the bad weather and Annie Owens said of her brother's illness. The remoteness of divine design from human perception is acknowledged frequently in scenes of dashed wishes. "There's no flyin in the face of God." "A man must live in all seasons."

Not knowing God's will, but knowing things come of God's will, there is no alternative to enduring the day while holding to faith. But that is not enough, for "the body without faith is dead and also faith without good works is dead." Prayer is good work, but a person cannot spend every minute down on the two knees in praise of God. So prayer's spirit, the love of God, is expressed in helping and loving others. The Saints of story do not burn their eyes and beat their chests in isolated oratories. They are people of action's world. The faithful person is quiet and harmless but no help. One must rise, speak, give. The ceili's gift of tea and story is good work, implicit prayer. Peter Flanagan expands upon this idea:

"Well, when you don't put a thing in practice, then your belief is all in vain. It's not a bit use. When you go—it's no use in saying, I can do a job, and sayin that to me every day in the week—if you don't just go and put it into practice. And do it. And show that you can do it.

"Well, that's only just an illustration.

"Well, God made that clear in the Gospel. *Faith without good works*. It's no use in me standin up here or sayin I'm a Roman Catholic. Not a bit use in sayin that. Another person would be far better in the sight of God than me, if I don't put me faith into practice.

"You must put it into practice.

"The body without faith is dead, and also faith without good works is dead.

"So. Your whole belief without puttin it into practice—that's be prayers and other good works, lovin your neighbor like yourself. Well, I'm not that well up on religion, but: just go about and meet the good people and treat them as good people, and meet the bad people and not do anything to them.

"That's the way you want to go on *in life*.

"The same as you came out of America and me takin and turnin you out of that door on a cold night like last night. I had to try and do the best I could. The best I could, and if I had better, I'd do it.

"Well, it's the very same with God.

"God's watchin down from the bright throne above. And if I say I'm a Catholic and goin about and do bad to me neighbors, and not doin anyone any good, nor sayin prayer in praise and love of God and the Blessed Virgin Mary—

"He didn't put us in the world to do nothing. Absolutely nothing.

"He's there.

"And on the other hand, God didn't fill you with that great spiritual power that He's goin to just take you on your departure from the world, soul and body, up into the bright kingdom either.

"He left every human being on this earth with a—as far as I understand—He leaves you to your own free will. You're sittin on the fence when ye start off in the world. Ye can go that side, or ye can go that side. Ye can go forward; ye can go back. With the result: at the same time He has left you in that position, He has filled you with grace and courage to exercise in the right way.

"But He wants to *see* what are ye made of. As you have often heard the word used, What are ye made of? And what certain amount of belief do ye have? You can go your own way. You can have a good time.

"There was joy at the wedding at Cana. Ye can go about in the world. Ye can take a drink. Ye can enjoy yourself. Ye can listen to music. Music is not sin.

"Ye can participate, as far as I think, in any company. But if you go about doin the bad thing and usin bad language—

"Well, it doesn't make a man of any man. William Lunny's father, he said, One big feed, he says, at a weddin doesn't make a man of any man.

Well, the bad language and all that sort of thing, actin like some swank comin out of a royal palace, it doesn't get a man anywhere, as you know yourself.

"There's too many villains and bad people all around.

"We are persecuted with bad people.

"God help us.

"Faith without good works is dead."

The body without faith. Prehistoric people may have been noble, raucous old heroes, but they were hopeless. Without faith, they battled in dead bodies. History starts with Saint Patrick. To be alive, truly human, is to have received his message, to be burdened with soul, the obligation to act.

Faith without good works. One lives in work. Good work is defined when all the Bible's thundering negativity is reduced by the District's people to two positive commandments: "Love God before all things. Love your neighbor as yourself and in that you shall live."

Since God made the earth—"He's there"—one must be good to one's neighbor. The Saints were; they gave light to the soul, health to the body. But not everyone is. Some people are bad. Evil exists in the world. That, said Hugh Nolan, is because "the human race is a fallen race. So they find it easier to do the wrong thing than the right one."

Peter Flanagan said when he was a young man he was so filled with love for God that he thought others would be the same and the world of man would be ordered by a sense of duty held within each individual. That is naive, a childish and foolish position, he said, because while one person moves quietly and harmlessly within his or her faith, another is doing evil. While you are loving your neighbors, they, though blessed with strength and commanded to love, are allowed free will, and they may be lying to you, stealing from you, plotting your murder. "We are persecuted with bad people." There must be a law to confine them. But laws are made by men, and man's ways are not God's. Law can be wrong. Disharmony between the law of God and the law of man requires you to think. Sometimes you must say No. The result is rebellion at the personal level and war at the collective level. Levels merge in real individuals. Columcille's personal rebellion against the king's law erupted as war.

Over ancient gray ruins on Lough Erne's islands, low clouds roll, crossing the hills in silence. For a moment a field glows, turns gold, then dulls as its light passes to a field beyond. Resting amid steady work, the farmer sits to smoke while sun-chased shadows flow through his vision. The shovel is propped against the cart. The donkey in his traces does not move. Light rises, falls, smoke drifts, clouds explode: clattering like hell's wheels and chains unloosed, a helicopter drops, muck-green, from the sky to burst the ears and rattle the skull.

Hedges sprayed with pale blossoms wall the lane. Up it the farmer in black pedals slowly, a scythe over his shoulder, cresting, letting the bike glide gently down by children playing quietly with sticks at make-believe war, past a woman dressed smartly in spring pink, walking toward her day's chatty shopping to meet young men in drab olive uniforms, hung over with radio equipment, prowling forward, machine guns at the ready.

Fit for reverie, for endless days of slow work and long nights of sacred story, Fermanagh's is a landscape of warfare. The District's great class of historical story is called "Battles."

PART FOUR

Battles

8

The Ford

The Ford is a long thatched house at the end of a lane curving south from the road through Sessiagh. This was the home of the first of "the Owens of Sessiagh," the townland's dominant "clan," and it remains for them an emotional focus. In the days of Old John of the Ford, in the last century, it was the seat of a small commercial empire founded on butter-packing and brick-making. His descendant, James Owens, works the land prosperously today, sending milk out to Enniskillen. The eldest of his two sons will be the next in the long line of Owenses farming the Ford.

The Ford's center, its kitchen, gleams with clean glass, creamy enamel, and polished metal. Mrs. Owens, its creator, places in the sunlight before me a plate of sliced fresh fadge, rich with butter and jam, and a cup of sweet tea to fortify me for our journey. When I first met her she told me the house took its name from a ford across the Arney River, where once a battle of the Maguires took place. She invited me to return on a Wednesday, when shops in the Town close early and she would be free to guide me to the site.

The soda bread upon the plate was baked in the cooker that blocks the fireplace beneath a picture of Christ. She stokes the cooker with sticks as well as turf, for sticks burn cleaner, leaving less ash. On the wall behind a couch in the rear hangs a portrait of the slain Kennedy brothers. An aerial photograph of her farm hangs above the television. Like few of their neighbors, they have electricity from the main. Theirs, she says, is "a nice wee farm," fortunately removed from the madness in Belfast. Fermanagh, she tells me, is "quiet." A plate of the Madonna of Lourdes hangs between the front door and the front window, through which thick liquid daylight flows over the table and bread.

All is bright around us, alive with reflected sun. The walls are pink, the doors light blue, the ceiling white. Over our heads, under the high boarded ceiling, stretches a curved collar, faced with molded boards, stiffening the couple that has splayed the brick walls out of plumb. Stakes for a new house have been driven in the front yard. They need a bigger house, she says, to entertain their friends at Christmas.

Rested, refreshed, I follow her out the back door, across the haggard, past the outoffices and hayshed. A lane leads away eastward, behind the

The Ford

The Ford

The Penal Tree

byre, along the field of corn that will be cut for thatching, toward the bog where this year's turf, already won, waits to be drawn home. When we have crossed the level fields and come upon the Arney, it is flowing southward. We pause by a lone tree on the riverbank. "In the Penal Days, under Cromwell," she says, "the Irish people used to come across the River there and say their prayers under that tree. They would have their services under it. And on the side of it there's a place where the grass never grows. That's where the priest stood." She points to the spot.

A patch of bare dirt, strangely free of grass, lies beneath and to one side of the Penal Tree: sacred earth. Past it, the Arney sweeps east, widening around an island where a stream enters, carrying water off low hills to the north. In the past, the River ran so shallow here that stepping-stones provided a ford to a second island, since removed. It was here in the bright waters that the great battle happened. But Mrs. Owens knows none of its history. Though married into an old Sessiagh family, she comes from Belcoo. She suggests I ask Rose Murphy.

Rose and Joe Murphy live in the next farm, east along the Arney, the last before the bog separates Sessiagh from Ross. Their home is made of Sessiagh clay. Rose's great-grandfather walked the fields, selected the site, and laid out the house. Her father and his father dug the clay from the

Rose Murphy's Home

lower fields and burned it into brick; they burned lime out of local stone, cut trees off the land, and built the house.

Rose is a native of the country. She remembers the ford. A great dancer in her youth, she was among those who waded out to the island in the Arney on Sundays for dancing, fiddling, and singing. She knows a battle took place there years ago, but neither she nor her son, Joseph, has its history. Joe is a craftsman, famed for his handiness. He thatches many of the local homes—Ellen Cutler's, Hugh Patrick Owens', John Gilleece's. He has taught me about roofing and work in the bog. Now he tells me the island at the ford on James Owens' farm was removed as part of the Erne Drainage Scheme, when the Arney was dredged, deepening its channel to prevent seasonal flooding.

When I ask Peter Flanagan, he refuses to mislead me:

"I really can't talk on the Battle of the Ford. I cannot. I cannot. Honestly. I couldn't give you the date for it. I could not.

"There was a battle just there at that ford. There was a battle at Drumane too. There was surely.

"There was two battles.

"And there's a field they call the Bloody Meadow where the real battle did ensue in Sessiagh.

"They call it the Red Meadow.

"Them all had taken place at the one time, when they were crossin. There's a ford up there, they call it Point's Ford. And then Drumane, do ye see: that bridge is only erected about a hundred years. I think it was a wooden structure had been in it. And before that you had to wade across.

"There was two big battles took place there. There was.

"The Battle of Point's Ford and the Battle of Drumane.

"But I'll tell you who might relate a bit of it. That's Hugh Nolan. I think Hugh might be fit to relate it to you.

"And Michael Boyle. He was a native and his father before him. They were here for generations.

"The Owens of Sessiagh, they have been here for years. That James Owens at the Ford, Jimmy of the Ford they call him, he is not a historian. But Hugh Patrick Owens there in the Hollow, and James Owens that lives in the thatched house there, the first house on the road, the thatched house built on the slated house when you're comin into Sessiagh, they might know. Aye.

"But the real historian died there a few years ago. Indeed, he had all the old history about the battle. He had all the old stuff gathered up. He was educated for a schoolmaster, and he was a very clever man, the name of Cassidy.

"He could relate the Battle of the Ford and the Red Meadow and the Battle of Drumane, now.

"Had I seen him, I could have related a bit of it to ye, but I'm not goin to give you any false information on it, you see."

Peter Flanagan is not "a native of the District." His father came from Cavan, and P was raised three and a half miles south in Kinawley. So Mr. Flanagan defers to members of local families and compromises on the controversy over the Battle of the Ford by saying there were two battles. Here is the sort of dispute that can rise on a foundation of agreement. Catholics of the Lower End of the Parish concur that the battle was important, but people in Sessiagh locate it on the point of land James Owens farms, around which the Arney swings, while the people of Upper Ballymenone (Rossdoney and Drumbargy) pull history closer and site the battle near the bridge at Drumane, beneath which the Arney flows a mile and a quarter east of the Ford.

Sessiagh's great historian, the noted singer of "Maxwell's Ball," Peter Cassidy, called Barney, lived in a slated house on the Chapel Road by the bog. Over a low hill, in the Hollow, north across the Red Meadow from the Ford, lives Hugh Patrick Owens, keeper of the Book. When I ask him for the history of the battle, he begins by relating the origin of his "clan," narrating the descent of the Ford within the Owens of Sessiagh, making the story a myth of his kin and connecting himself with the site of the battle

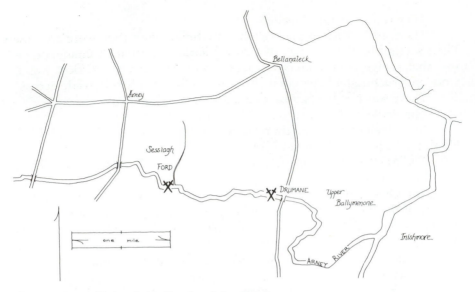

Competitive Sites of the Battle of the Ford

and the fight itself. His association with the locality is direct, personal, deep:

"Well, the man that owned the Ford first was a man the name of Peter Martin. The first of the Owenses that came to Sessiagh, he married Peter Martin's daughter.

"They came from the west of Ireland. That's where they came from. So they're here since.

"And that was away two hundred years ago.

"Old Morrissey was the first. John was next. Then came two sons: James and John. Phil was next. That's James' father, James of the Ford.

"Morris was my grandfather, the son of Old John, the grandson of Old Morrissey. And my grandfather was ninety-three or ninety-six when he died. His great-grandfather, John Owens, bought this farm, in fact bought all the land, you see. Old John bought houses for all five Owens families in this townland.

"Well, there was a fight. And that's the time, you see, that Old Morrissey came. He was belongin to the Connacht army. He was one of the invaders.

"And this girl was there that time. She was a lone girl, Miss Martin.

"And that's how he came to this country.

"The Maguires were the old Fermanagh chieftains. I just don't know who now the Connacht chieftain was.

"And they met at the Ford.

"The bottoms are called the Red Meadows still. The meadows were bloody, you see, and they christened them the Red Meadows.

"That's where the fight was fought after they crossed the Ford.

"Well, there's a dispute over it.

"Some maintains that it was at Drumane Bridge, that fight.

"But it wasn't. It was here.

"There was no bridge at Drumane thattime, and no ford, and no way for them to cross. Not atall. But there was stones here, wee steppin-stones they could cross on, you know.

"It was really at the Ford, definitely at the Ford. Surely.

"That was the proper place.

"Some took it on them to say that it was at Drumane, but the fight was here. That's why the meadows are called the Red Meadows."

When he finishes, his position firm, I ask when the fight took place. Mr. Owens answers:

"I don't know.

"Barney Cassidy is dead. He lived on the Chapel Road, but he was reared in Sessiagh. And he was a great hand at old folklore. Ah, he knew all the old history. But he's dead.

"But it's a long time. It must be up to two hundred years."

Hugh Patrick Owens' Home

Later, after tea, we walk his long lane, past depressions left from brick-making, to see the Red Meadows. While they open beyond us, he says he will get the battle's date from James Owens, who lives on the roadside, and when I see him next he has it.

"The Ford of Biscuits battle," Hugh Pat says, "took place in fifteen and ninety-six.

"Armies thattime carried biscuits with them and when they crossed the ford, they lost them, and that gave it the name, the Ford of Biscuits, though they call it really, the Ford."

James Owens, caretaker of the battle's date, lives with his sister Annie, next to Andy Owens, across the road from Phil Owens, past whose byre the lane descends to the Ford. Family photographs, a print of a rural scene, and religious pictures, the Madonna and Child, Christ of the Sacred Heart, Pope Paul, decorate the white kitchen walls. A mirror above a dark Victorian sideboard next to the cooker behind us reflects the crucifix hanging over the fireplace where the three of us sit. The tape recorder turns, and I ask about the battle. James Owens has been ill, but he has "mended right well, thank God," and answers swiftly:

"First of all. I heard why it was called the Ford of Biscuits, the battle that was fought there.
"They had a barrel of biscuits.
"And there came a *flood*.
"And it upended the *barrel*,
        and they lost their *biscuits*
            in the *flood*.
"At that battle then, whoever they were fightin now, they *fled*, and it's only about hardly half a mile from this ford to where the *battle* took *place*.
"And this meadow is called the *Red Meadow* from that day to this. And I used to hear tell of the Red Meadow before I knew what it *meant*, do ye see. People would tell you they were workin in the Red Meadow the day.
"Well it twas a battle. And that meadow was supposed to be red with *blood*,
        red with blood,
            and the battle was fought there.
"And that was, I think, in fifteen and ninety-five, I think, that the battle was fought.
"I suppose some of them showed you the meadow."

After recounting the trip Hugh Patrick Owens and I took to view the Red Meadow, I ask, "Do you know who was involved in this fight?" Properly, his answer echoes my question:

"No, I don't know who was involved in this fight.

"But this chap outside next door, he had to write a composition on that now that you are on.

"And he was writin it out anyway.

"And he came runnin in here.

"Can you tell me, he says, when that battle was fought, the Ford of Biscuits, he says, I have to write a composition on it.

"So I gave him the date.

"Well, he was tellin me after, do ye see, that he didn't know how he done; it would have to be taken away to see whether it would *pass* or not. But at the time that I asked him, Oh, he says, I have not got the result *yet*.

"And whether he succeeded in it or not, I don't know.

"But he'd be only like me: he'd be tryin to gather information from what he *heard* about it."

Quiet until now, Annie interjects, "That's all you can do," and James continues:

"Well, there's a bridge here and they call it the Old Arney Bridge.

"And they were talkin about cleanin this *River* up, do ye know.

"And this bridge is not right; there's a curve in the road like that, and the bridge is there.

"And this man came out to tell about: he says, We're *not* goin to remove the Old Arney Bridge, because it's too long there. It's the oldest bridge in the country, and we're not goin to remove it. And whatever way they are goin to fix the road, but I think they'll put on a new bridge, and they won't interfere with it, *owin* to its *age*.

"Isn't that funny now?

"It was that old, he said, do ye see. I suppose maybe he had the history of how *long* it would be *there*."

In fragments, history floats on conversation. You hear a bit—the date of a battle—and having been given it, save it without a plan for its use. A friend might ask for it, a schoolboy need it for a theme. The historical fact can be made into a useful gift in the social scene. But old history is not important in itself. It seems funny for a man to be thrilled by a bridge because it is old. Narrow and bent, it is inefficient for modern traffic and seems to stand in the way of the Erne Drainage Scheme. Undredged, the Arney would overflow its banks, destroying hay won on the bottoms. Perhaps the history that man knew invested the Old Arney Bridge with significance . . . perhaps. But age alone is nothing.

Old songs are not preserved because they are old. Nostalgia is not a disease, nor yet a need in the District. Songs are sung for their poetry and melody and meaning. Historical songs must refer far into the past. Peter Flanagan says a major purpose of song is "to keep the memory of great men, so people won't forget." But new songs can do that as well as old ones. Most songs descriptive of early events were written in later days in a spirit of commemoration. The District's main songs on the Rising of 1798 are the well-known "Rising of the Moon," written by John Keegan Casey about 1860, and "The Men of Ninety-Eight," composed by the local poet Charles Farmer about 1924. It is the event in the song, an event of continuing importance—not the song—that is old. Both event and song become new with every singing.

Old family homes are altered freely, radically, and often. Pebbledash is slathered over, tin replaces thatch, large metal casements punch out small wooden sash. James Owens' family will move easily from the Ford into their modern home, the first in the District designed by an architect from beyond, a man named O'Brien from Irvinestown. But the new home will rise only a few steps in front of the old one. Blood is fixed by touch in place. It is not the house, but the home place, the earth manipulated by generations of Owenses, that contains their power, claims their attention. House follows house as crop follows crop and generation follows generation on the old land: historic earth.

Loyal old furniture and utensils are consigned to the midden without worry. Things must be useful. Bridges, songs, houses, tools, land—like food and tales and good neighbors—should help to carry you on. When I once showed an interest in a piece of antique crockery, Mrs. Cutler rebuked me, "Aw, put it in a glass case and throw lumps of sugar at it."

Human interest, affection, and energy should be given to the living. Unconnected to modern use, history is unimportant. Most people are not historians, and for them the details of the battle—its issues and personages—do not matter. What matters is: some fight happened and from that day to this, the Ford of Biscuits and the Red Meadows, features of contemporary life, have had names.

It is not the date that matters, it is the place. Time passes, but land endures, demanding attention. For most people, history's purpose is to enrich the world they inhabit by explaining the origin of some feature on the landscape—a twisted river, a spot bare of grass, the name for a meadow—for that is the most obvious way the past forces itself on the present, and the past unalive in the present is not history.

History accumulates. Mrs. Owens knows the battle's place, but none of its history. Joe Flanagan knows only that some battle at a ford in the Arney gave a name to the Red Meadows. James Owens has the date and can explain both names of the battle site (the Ford of Biscuits and the Red Meadows), but he does not know who fought there. Historians know more. For the historian, history does not reduce phenomena to explanations. It is a way to think.

Michael Boyle, historian, turns history into story, opening truth to thought. Telling of the Ford, he is characteristically excited at first, running over with words, but he holds still long enough to provide an introduction setting his tale in its era. Then he takes off smoothly, pacing the story with repetition, enlivening its texture with detail, bringing gathered facts into

Hugh Mackan's, Michael Boyle's Last Home in Ballymenone

narrative. He does not abandon the common center established by people who are not historians; he swings from it. He does not neglect his toponymic responsibility. Like James Owens, he gives places names. Neither does he drift into antiquarian fascination. His story stays useful. Expanded, his tale expands history's potential for connection to the world around us:

"Well, you see, it was the time that the English occupied the country, occupied Ireland, do ye see.
    "Coorse, they occupy it *still* ◇,
        they occupy it still.
    "But, do ye see, the country was different thattime, do ye see. Do ye see: every county had its own chieftain, do ye see.
    "And the name of the chieftains of County Fermanagh, they were the Maguires, the Maguires of Fermanagh. They were the chieftains of Fermanagh for centuries.
    "And their possessions, their castle at Enniskillen was occupied by the English, do ye see. They were put out by the English. The English, do ye see, put them out of their home they lived in, and occupied it, do ye see. And occupied it.
    "So.
    "They laid·siege to it.

"The Maguires gathered up their clan, their men, their armies, and they laid siege to Enniskillen Castle to put the British out of it.

"But the English sent a force up from Dublin, do ye see, for to relieve them, for to relieve the garrison; the garrison was under stress, do ye see, and the fort was goin to fall,

Maguire's men was goin to *take* it.

"So this big force was comin—well, a lock of thousands was considered a big force—six or seven thousand men and so many horsemen, do ye see; it was enough to relieve the Enniskillen fort.

"But Maguire and his men didn't wait. They got the dispatch that the force was comin.

"And they didn't wait to let them come as far as Enniskillen.

"They marched out
and attackted them
at this ford.

"They marched out of Enniskillen, and they lay in ambush. The whole hills, the whole surroundin country at that time was all wood.

"It was all woodland, do ye see, with big trees.

"And they lay undercover
till they saw the force comin,
and they marched out and they attackted them
at this ford.

"And they defeated them at it.

"And they drowned their whole resource. They had a big resource, do ye see, alot of provisions and men and everything to relieve the fort, but Maguire's army defeated them. That's how that ford got its name:

"Béal Átha na mBrioscaí, the Ford of Biscuits.

"The English lost their whole supplies,
their whole stores,
in the river
there.

"They had to retreat and leave them behind them.

"And they were all lost
there.

"And it was christened the Ford of Biscuits,
Béal Átha na mBrioscaí in Irish, in Gaelic.

"But it really is the Ford of Biscuits in the English translation."

Since Michael Boyle is a Drumbargy man, I can assume he will locate the battle near his home. I ask, "Is that ford right at Drumane Bridge?"

"Yes, at the very bridge. Where the bridge is built is where the fight was. And the country right around there."

"I've heard too that it was at James Owens' in Sessiagh," I say.

"No. Aye, we used to be contradicted, but the teacher that taught me, he was a Master Corrigan, Richard Corrigan, he was a native of the District, he taught me in Rossdoney National School.

"Andrew Boyle lives in that ould school where I was taught and where all the men of my age and generation was taught.

"Well, this Master Corrigan, Richard Corrigan, was a great historian, a great teacher, and above all a great Irish historian.

"And he had an old history; I think it was written by a man named Murphy, Murphy's History of Ireland, and it was very ancient history, and he was trained in college in Waterford in the south of Ireland. And he got this old history out of Waterford College with him, and had it as a keepsake.

"And when he was in doubt about a point of Irish history he always consulted this old Murphy's History, and he went there for his information for his arguments.

"So accordin to Murphy's History it was where the present bridge stands that that was where the fight was, and that's Béal Átha na mBrioscaí.

"That's where the fight was. Aye.

"I mind Master Corrigan told us that. He taught us the history of that fight.

"The fight was where the present Drumane Bridge is,
        that's Béal Átha na mBrioscaí.

"Aye.

"Well another thing
        about Béal Átha na mBrioscaí.

"That's the River Arney that flows under the bridge; that's the River Arney at Béal Átha na mBrioscaí.

"Well then, do ye see, that's the division between two parishes, between Cleenish Parish, the parish that I live in, and the parish of Killesher.

"Well then, Killesher Parish and Kinawley Parish and Knockninny Parish, them three parishes, they're in County Fermanagh and they're in the Kilmore Diocese. Do ye see.

"And the history of that was—that Master Corrigan taught us after consultin his old History was—that at one time previous to that, two centuries before that, there was a battle between the Maguires of Fermanagh, and the chieftains of Cavan, they were the O'Rahillys, the O'Reillys. The O'Rahillys was the Gaelic name but O'Reilly was the English translation.

"Well, the O'Rahillys invaded Fermanagh
        as far as Drumane
        as far as the Arney River.

"And the Maguires made a stand there
        and drove them out,
        drove them back.

"But three parishes still remained, do ye see, in the Diocese of *Kilmore*.
"And still is.
"And always will be I suppose now."

Concluding energetically, Mr. Boyle stops for me to add, "And Kilmore is in Cavan. I see. So there was an earlier battle and it was at Drumane too."

"Yes, and it was fought at Drumane too. The Maguires made their stand at Drumane,
>
> and drove them back,
>
> > drove the O'Rahillys back.

"That was a main travel route, do ye see.

"There was no road thattime of course like what there would be now.

"It was more a track, do ye see. A track.

"There was no vehicles of the present day. It was principally horsemen and ould trucks that horses pulled, do ye see, coaches and one thing and another.

"They're buildin a new bridge there and makin a new road. It was a danger, there's no doubt about it. And then, do ye see, there was a point at the bridge and the bridge run that way and then there was a sharp elbow, and it was very dangerous.

"*Although* there was never many accidents, very serious ones, at it. But still it was a danger."

The scholar's art achieves its excellence in the dialectic of inward direction and outward reality. Follow the inner direction only, the theoretical or subjective, and nothing strange and new will be learned. Gather reality's facts without purpose, and they will lie in disorder. Inquiry out of curiosity can bring discovery. James Owens learns how the Red Meadows got their name. Peter Flanagan finds out who Saint Febor was. A few facts satisfy most needs. But the scholarly soul, like Michael Boyle's, rebounds from discovery to new curiosity. Careering between action and passivity, it is condemned to wander, never quite happy, assuming there is more to learn. During the quest, original motivations cannot be forgotten, but neither can they hinder. Inner commitments—political beliefs or theoretical persuasions—do not prevent scholars from searching openly, just as the facts do not stop them from making judgments and telling good tales.

As a folklorist whose trained interest was pricked by hearing frequent mention of the Ford, I came to knowledgeable men to get the story, but I would have been less than a scholar, a traitor to my teachers, had I collected texts without listening to what people had to say. Allowed to begin where he wished, Hugh Patrick Owens gave me his genealogy. Allowed to let their statements trail off where they would, James Owens and Michael Boyle both ended at bridges, crooked old stone-arched bridges, spanning the Arney two and a half miles apart. Letting them lead, I recovered more than the texts I wanted. I gained clues concerning their theory of history.

History's primary connections are made in space. Its secondary connections are categorical. As the Sillees River joins Saint Febor and Souple Corrigan, the Arney River joins old battles to new bridges. Categories strengthen connections. Mr. Boyle brought together events two centuries apart because they happened at the same spot, at Drumane in the Arney, and because both were battles.

In other traditions, historians link unconnected events because they occupy the same age. Here it is place. Space joins past events to each other, and it unifies past and present in two ways: progressively and mythically.

Land, river, ford, and bridge form an associational set. Progressively, the set is transformed through two channels to bring the past into the present. One is transportation: land to river to ford to old bridge to new bridge. People and goods traveling overland—once on horseback and wagons, now in cars and lorries, once on a track, now on a paved highway—are carried across the Arney ever more swiftly and easily along the same old route. The other is drainage: river to ford to deepened channel to better land. "There was places along all these rivers," Hugh Nolan said, "that was only swamps. Then the Erne was dredged and sunk and the fords was taken out to prevent summer floodin. And it was a great improvement in the meadows."

Mythic events, sacred or martial, mark the land abruptly, immutably. For all time three parishes in Fermanagh will be part of the Cavan Diocese of Kilmore, the Ford of Biscuits and the Red Meadows will have names, the crooked Sillees River will empty into Lough Erne, dirty and bad for fishing. For all time Saint Naile's bright well will contain a cure for external imperfections, and the flame of Slane will burn in the Holy Island.

People achieve connection to the progressive past retrogressively through action in the built environment. This past is served by continuing its direction, by forgetting songs bereft of use, by cutting hay on improved meadows, by building new houses and destroying old bridges to advance transportation and agriculture.

Connection to the live force of mythic events also comes of involvement in place. But it begins at birth, not in willed action. Anyone can claim responsibility for progress by acting, by cutting grass, but only those who grow like the grass, who have been here since a time before personal volition, can join myth. This past lies beyond human intention in the eternal design. It is served when people who are part of the environment, people like Master Corrigan and Michael Boyle—unlike Mrs. Owens and Mr. Flanagan—people who are "native," tell the inchoate tale of place. When Hugh Patrick Owens begins the story of the Ford with his own genealogy, he merges with the Arney and the battle as part of this locale. He is naturally responsible for his story. He is to be believed.

Simultaneously changing and unchangeable, history is place. Place joins those who make and mark the land with those who remake it, accepting its tasks. It joins saint to rebel, warrior to farmer, God to man. In place, the person is part of history. That is why the location of the battle is a crucial issue, demanding precise definition, and the date of the battle is let drift, why Mr. Boyle called the learned native Master Corrigan and Murphy's History to his aid when arguing for Drumane as the battle site, and why he pushes past numbers, back to place and story, toward another learned native when I ask, "Do you know when the Battle of the Ford took place?"

"It twas about fifteen and ninety-eight, ninety-seven or ninety-eight, some of them. That's the year that the fight took place, that Béal Átha na mBrioscaí got its name.

"The English came from the Pale. You see there was four or five counties down around Dublin, and the English settlement in Ireland thattime was driven very small and they occupied just these few counties.

"So this force was comin from the *Pale*. There was a song made about it, now, but I just wouldn't be able to mind the song. I had it and I lost it.

"It was made be Hugh McGiveney. Oh, he was a great wit.

"Well, I only remember just a few words of it. I might know a verse or so here and there.

"There was:

This did enrage
* and so engage*
*   the gentry of the Pale,*
They sent a force
* with a great resource*
*   their laws for to prevail.*
Of warlike stores
* for Lough Erne's shores*
*   but it never passed Drumane* ◊.

"That's part of it.

"And there was another bit that was earlier in it:

"There was a courier sent, do ye see, on horseback to notify Maguire that the force was comin, do ye see.

"And he said:

I saw the plumes
* of Duke's dragoons*
*   south of Belturbet town.*

"I don't remember any more of it. No. I'll tell ye, there was one time it appeared in the Fermanagh Herald here. And I cut it out to preserve it. And of course changin around from one place to another, it was lost. It was a pity."

The Castle Keep, scene of the siege, rises rebuilt on the foundations of the old home of the Maguires at the western end of Enniskillen. It is guarded now, screened by the Water Gate, a rock wall lifting to sprout a pair of early seventeenth-century Scots bartizan towers. Lough Erne flows

Enniskillen Castle and the Water Gate

The Water Gate, Carved on a Gravestone of 1798,
Saint Macartin's Cathedral, Enniskillen

slowly beneath the towers' eyeless gaze. Moving southward against the current—"up" as they say along the Upper Lough—you pass Inishkeen, then Cleenish Island, and the Lough is pressed between Inishmore and the shore at the mouth of the Arney. Just to the north, a road follows the River westward, leaving Rossdoney Quay to split Ballymenone and end in a mile and a quarter at the Derrylin Road. Rising from the Lough, the road skirts a pair of old houses sheltering carts and tools and meets its first inhabited house when it dips through the Hollow. With its face downhill, east toward the early sun, and its gable to the road, this is the house of the brothers Johnny and Packie Boyle. The Boyles' hayshed stands across the road, over the site of Hugh McGiveney's home.

Hugh McGiveney was a small farmer, a weaver of creels. He was an old man in the youth of Michael Boyle and Hugh Nolan, the major historian from whom they learned. He was a poet, one of the composers of "Maxwell's Ball" and author of the song that helped keep the Battle of the Ford of Biscuits roiling in memory. He was the creator of bids and pants, a great star. Mr. Boyle's memory is clear:

"Ah, I mind Hughie well.

"He was a small-sized man, and he had a kind of a crouch. He walked with a kind of a crouch, with his two hands behind his back.

"And he was a nice man, a nice discoursed man, you know. Aye, a great wit. In fact, he was the wit of the whole country, Old Hughie.

"Oh, he was a great man.

"He had an old donkey; he called it Fanny Ann.

"Fanny Ann.

"And he used to go to the bog for a load of turf, two creels, do ye see. Straddle and mats. There was a pin stickin up out of the straddle, do ye see, and a creel fixed on every pin. And he used to go off to the bog every day, him and Fanny Ann, for two creels of turf, a load of turf.

"I remember McGiveney.

"He used to go to all haystacks.

"They used to put hay in big ricks before the haysheds was built.

"He went to all haystacks, you know, and there used to be great bids with him. It was a great day at a hay stack longgo: There'd be a jar of porter and a good big feed, and then the ould boys would get a mug or two of porter to put them in humor.

"And it would be the greatest fun ever you seen
                              with these old boys.

"It would be great entertainment.

"He was a great man at dressin one of these big ricks of hay, do ye see, keepin it in order. A funny man.

"Ah he was a great lad, a great wit.

"Oh, he was a terrible wit.

"Oh, he made several poems, you know, about things. He was a great

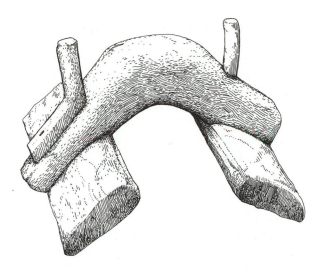

Straddle. The straddle was placed upon mats over the donkey's back, then creels for turf were hung on its pins. This disused straddle rests in a shed by Rossdoney Lane, about 200 yards from the site of Hugh McGiveney's house. It is 14 inches in length and 16 inches wide.

wit, do ye see, he made several bits of songs about things that happened.

"Ah, he was a great lad, Hughie McGiveney. He was a great wit, you know, terrible clever man, do ye see.

"We'll say that it was nowadays, that the same facilities was in education. If he had the same facilities in them days as there is today, he'd have been a counsel. Oh yes. He was as quick as lightnin in his answers, do ye see. He had two brothers in America. I never met them of course (they were gone before my day), but they turned out great men in the States.

"There was one of them a John McGiveney, another Owen. They turned out great, great men in the States.

"And of course, you see, he had only a small wee home there, a wee small bit of land. And they sent home the full of a hat of money to him, do ye see. There wasn't a great livin on that couple of cows' grass of land. He got piles of money from them, and they never came back to visit him, I think. But indeed, they didn't forget him anyway.

"He would have been a great man if he had of got the chances that there is now. He was terrible quick. He wouldn't have to mass a thing until he'd have the answer out, do ye see. Great bids in him, do ye see.

"He was a great character.

"Ah, he was a great star.

"He was a great star."

A bell rings the end of visiting hours. The three of us—Hugh Nolan, James Boyle, and I—rise to leave. Michael Boyle is upright in bed. He had greeted us with excitement—"Well, me bold men, me bold Nolan"—and entertained us with good crack. The trip was hard on Hugh Nolan, and a melancholy current flowed under the hilarity. "Well, didn't we have a great time, Hugh. Ah, we did. Great times now. And we never did one bit harm."

Old companions, they would not meet again.

The visitors are gone, the lights in the ward are cut off. Michael Boyle is left in the dark with his endless memory amid the rattling, whispering sleep of old men, and we are having a pint in the Town. Michael lies in our minds, but Hugh McGiveney is used in our chat to exemplify stardom. James Boyle, who lives next to the ruins of Michael Boyle's childhood home, just up Drumbargy Brae from the Hollow where Hugh McGiveney lived, says he remembers the old man working in the fields struck suddenly with an idea for a new composition and, leaving his work undone, running to the house to write it down. When once James recounted some of old Hughie's bids to the parish priest, he was told McGiveney's mind was "too active." That genius ran in his veins. It brought his brothers, the emigrants, financial success.

Had he, like them, like George Armstrong, gone out, he would have become wealthy, but he stayed, and confined, held by a small holding, he, like Armstrong, became a star. In a different time or place, the genius of such men would make them famed authors or prosperous lawyers. Cramped here, their minds spun, whirling out entertainment for their neighbors. Squeezed, their spirit erupted, blew out, and they died poor, remembered by few.

Hugh McGiveney's father, James Boyle says, was also a great wit, and he had a cousin, an actor, who graduated from the parish priest's plays to the professional stage in Dublin, England, and America. James and Hugh agree that such familial brilliance is fated to blaze extravagantly in an individual, then die. Mr. Nolan:

"Ah now, Hugh McGiveney was a wonderful, intelligent man. Well, he had brothers and they were the same. They went to America. They could make poems.

"It's a general rule that a race like that finally dies out altogether, because I've seen a couple of instances in this country. The people that was celebrated for some thing, they died out in the finish. Aye."

Though married, Hugh McGiveney had no children. Nothing remains of his house. Westward past its absence, Rossdoney Lane curves up between tree-crowned hedges. The whitewashed brick front of the next house sheers the road's verge, mirroring the sunlight of summer.

A cat blinks on the warm threshold. Within, in the small circle of light at the hearth, Hugh Nolan sits. There is a hush from the fire as it smolders,

Hugh Nolan's Home

a tick from the clock shelved among cups and mugs, platters and plates on the dresser behind him. Brilliant, he is the end of his line. The Room above, behind the fireplace, encloses immense silence, and his life is wrapped darkly around him in the kitchen where days pass like cool breezes, where he entertains the ceiliers who come up through the night. In dim stillness, he sits with his pipe and his cats and his splendid mind, waiting to give the history he has saved.

Twice Mr. Nolan recorded stories paralleling Mr. Boyle's, leading from the siege of Enniskillen to the victory at the Ford. Then he brought together a second about the youth of Red Hugh O'Donnell, Irish leader at the battle, to explain the campaign's background. Chronologically it comes first, and we begin with Hugh Nolan singing the wrath of Red Hugh:

"There was another piece about Hugh O'Donnell, but it was a different tale altogether.

"You see. The way it was with the Ulster chiefs at that time: the Crown had got into sort of terms with them, and bestowed titles on them, but at the same time, the English had no claim on the nine counties of Ulster. They were ruled be the Irish chiefs.

"But at the same time, they were tryin to work their way to influence—ah, to get control of the whole country.

"Well, Hugh O'Donnell, he was Irish be his father, and he was Scots be the mother. The mother was of the Scotch MacDonnells that had settled down on the east coast of Ulster.

"So.

"*His* idea was,

from he was a very young lad,

for to get the English all shifted

out of Ireland,

out of every part of Ireland.

"The more that his father was an English knight,

he didn't want to follow his father's footsteps atall,

if he could have got on with what he *intended*.

"And the English always had secret agents knockin about, that used to get in to talk with the people and find out the people's minds, and they discovered that this young O'Donnell was goin to be a real rebel and that his enemy was the English government, and the crowned head.

"So anyway, the government came to the conclusion that to catch this fellow when he was young, and keep him in prison for a while, and get him for to take up English ideas, and that'd put this rebel idea out of his *head*.

"So anyway, they put a ship on the ocean, pretendin that they were wine sellers that owned it.

"And they called at every Irish port and made sham sales. Course, they had stocks of wine and they sold it to the people.

"But anyway.

"They wrought on,

and wrought on,

and wrought on,

and wrought on,

till they got to the north of Done*gal*.

"That'd be the furthest point north.

"And the news went out about this company comin around with wines for sale.

"There were a whole lot of people went away to this place where they could be got,

and bought some of the wine and got into the ship,

and was examinin everything.

"And this young O'Donnell.

"The way it was in them days, the sons of these chiefs, they used to be sent to some place when they'd get into their *teens*,

for to be trained to *war*,

and to be good warriors,

and to be not altogether attached

to their own people at *home*.

"So there was other chiefs in Donegal at that time; they were Mac-

Sweeneys. And didn't O'Donnell's father send this lad of his to be trained with *them*

to warfare.

"So there was a contingent of them came for to see this ship,
and they had O'Donnell with them.

"And of course O'Donnell, he was a-watchin, the more that he was only gettin out of the boy into the man, he was a-watchin be these English agents.

"And of course there was some of them on this ship *too*, as long as she was at anchor.

"When they got O'Donnell on the ship, there was an *armed guard* occupyin portions of the ship, so they came out and O'Donnell was placed under arrest.

"And the ship set sail and started back
to Dublin.

"And he was lodged in Dublin Garrison.

"So.

"It caused great grief to the father and mother,
and great grief to all the locality where he was known.

"Of course, there was always people knowin he'd be taken out of Dublin Castle, no matter how long he was held in it.

"So he got out one night,
him and two other kinsmen;
they were two of the O'Neills
that was in bondage too.

"They took the mountains.

"There got up a terrible storm,
snow storm.

"So.

"They were followed,
and they were captured
and they were brought back again,
put into the castle,
and O'Donnell was put in chains.

"But anyway after some time, there was a change of lieutenants. The old Lord Lieutenant that had been in Ireland was changed back to England and there was another fellow *appointed*.

"And he was the divil for money.

"And the Irish knew that if he got a good bribe,
he'd let O'Donnell *out*.

"So anyway, there was a good deal of money gathered up. And there was an old fellow that used to go about rivers and places like that and he used to gather up—ah, there was wee valuable pebbles in them days in these rivers, and he used to gather them up, and he had a terrible go of them.

"He gave *all* to this collection that was for to get Hugh O'Donnell out.

"So anyway.

"Oh, they had a big amount of money anyway, so they presented it to the Lord Lieutenant.

"Oh, he was only too glad to get it.

"So the arrangements was made for O'Donnell's escape.

"And these ones went away.

"And the ould lad joined to count the money he had got.

"Man, he says, this is a great price for a bit of a rope, he says ◊.

"O'Donnell, do ye see, was to get down on a rope, get down on the wall, do ye see.

"There was a fellow came the whole way
>> from Ulster
>> to Dublin
>> to meet him.

"And he was there to accompany him
>> till he'd get across the border again
>> into Ulster.

"And it was of a Christmas Eve night.

"And it was one of the coldest and stormiest nights that had been for years before it.

"Well, O'Donnell got out *anyway*,
> and him and this lad took the mountains for it.

"So the way it was with the Lord Lieutenant, he had to report this escape, do ye see. *But then*, he delayed reportin till he was of the opinion that these boys was out of reach of being catched.

"So anyway, the storm was so bad that they nearly died.

"But there was a man. He had some job under the crown, but at the same time he was a great friend of the Irish people. And didn't he get O'Donnell and this friend of his; his men got them in an exhausted state and they were brought to this man's house.

"And his wife knew they were breakin the *law*,
>> be having these two boys in the *house*,
>> and that they'd have to notify the authorities
>>> about them bein *there*.

"But these messages had to be carried on foot in them days, and it'd be a very long time from you'd send a message till it would reach its destination.

"So she managed for to get this errand-carrier for to go all the rounds that he possibly *could*,
>> the way that he'd be a long time
>>> gettin to *Dublin*, do ye see,
>> that these boys would be gone out of the house
>>> before the government troops would *land* at it.

"So it was managed anyway.

"So in the long run, O'Donnell got across the border into Ulster
        without bein catched.
"So that was what led up
        to this Siege of Enniskillen.
"He vowed that he'd try and put the English out of the country,
        if he possibly could,
        no matter how long it was.
"So that's what brought about the Battle of the Biscuit Ford."

Mr. Nolan's is the story of power. Power is personal. Red Hugh O'Donnell held "this rebel idea" within, locked in his head, and he had the
strength to follow it despite his father's allegiance to the Crown and his
own English education, despite men who bound him in chains and nature
which hurled storms against him. Personal power is necessary but not
enough.

Saints can draw power from themselves, for the force within is God's.
In godlike isolation, Saint Febor and Saint Naile create natural phenomena.
But even the saints' power comes also from the world beyond. They leave
their native place for education, taking orders, learning from men how to
be holy. They depend on others for help. Hugh Nolan said Saint Patrick,
though pictured as a "lonely missioner," was the leader of "a very big contingent" containing "tradesmen of all classes." Saint Columcille waged his
personal fight with an army of men.

Then consider the secular leader, exemplified in Red Hugh. He was
sent from home to learn warfare. His inner commitment did not make him
a solitary rebel, but placed him foremost in an army. Even the wild rapparee, Black Francis, was no lone outlaw on the heath but the civil leader of
a gang. Power is social, political as well as personal. How one becomes a
leader is the question, and loyalty is the answer.

Loyalty courses through blood. Red Hugh's father was the Donegal
chief, his mother was of the MacDonnells, and they, Mr. Nolan said, "had a
clan in the County Down at the time." He was related, Mr. Nolan tells us
further, to the O'Neills of Tyrone. His kin ties stretched the breadth of Ulster, from far west to far east, and knotted him to the center of power in
Tyrone.

"There was always people knowin he'd be taken out of Dublin Castle,
no matter how long he was held in it." Imprisoned, O'Donnell could count
on his kin. Friends help. Old John of the Ford bought farms for all five
Owens families in Sessiagh. Hugh McGiveney's brothers sent him hatfuls
of money from America. The yoke is double, reversible. Friendship brings
loyalty; loyalty brings friendship. From Cú Chulainn to Columcille to Red
Hugh, fostering was Ireland's old way.[1] Families traded boys. Home ties
weakened, Mr. Nolan said, while war lore grew and the foster son or brother
firmed new relations through which unrelated families joined in a bond like
blood. Today affinities outside friendship are often named as though kin

were involved. Warmly regarded elders, though no relation, are called uncle and aunt. Adults address children they like, though not their own, as son, daughter, my child. There was no place in the social structure for an intrusive American folklorist, so people assuming I was home for a visit developed the fiction that I was a relation of Peter Flanagan's through his sisters in New York. Ellen Cutler asked my children to name her grandmother, and they call her Granny Cutler. There was no way to bring me comfortably into the community, to explain—and claim—my loyalty unless this were my home, these my relatives.

Marriage is the natural, sacred culmination of loyalty between unrelated people. In the great ballads of Scotland and England, as in the chivalric romances before them, the idea of loyalty is symbolized in the relations between lovers, between husbands and wives. Eochaidh Ó hEoghusa, ollamh, court poet to the Maguires, used bardic convention passionately in verse to conceptualize the relation of leader to man as marriage. An earlier poet had proclaimed Cú Chonnacht Maguire Ireland's husband. In his poetry, Ó hEoghusa is lover and wife to Hugh Maguire, Fermanagh's chief, Cú Chonnacht's son, cousin and brother in arms to Red Hugh O'Donnell. Maguire is killed in battle; "I am widowed," wails Ó hEoghusa.[2] In later years Souple Corrigan posed not as any woman but as the "true love," the betrothed of his leader, Black Francis.

Loyalty comes in friendship through blood, and it comes in neighborliness through the land. When Red Hugh was captured, grief smote not only his father and mother, the septs of Ulster's west and east, but as well "all the locality where he was known." By virtue of his wide connections through blood and fostering, the localities in which he was recognized were many. All Ulster was his community. So, Mr. Nolan told me, "whatever chieftain of the Maguires of Fermanagh that was on the go in that day" joined him. They were his neighbors, and so, as Mr. Boyle said, "the Maguires gathered up their clan, their men, their armies" for the fight. Since only Ulster was free of English dominion, truly Irish, then a man would come from the North to help O'Donnell escape, another would donate the water's jewels to the Lord Lieutenant's bribe, and a man in the South who was "a great friend to the Irish people" would be O'Donnell's friend too. Enraged in his rebel will, seething at the nexus of familial and neighborly force, Red Hugh embodied Irish history for his moment.

The District's connections are those of blood or place; loyalty comes of friendship or neighborliness. Deeply that dichotomy dissolves when loyalties unify in the native, the person who because of blood is rooted in place, as Hugh Patrick Owens is in Sessiagh, as Red Hugh O'Donnell was in Ulster. In place, the person is swept into history and charged with its tasks. Those tasks demand that loyalties fuse in the present, shaping responsibilities, directing reciprocal actions. Accepting the tasks of the historical place, one rises as hero and gathers strength as the individual mission is goodmanned and joined.

Hero and historian merge. Connected by blood and place to power, one man becomes the live force of collective will. Red Hugh O'Donnell declares himself leader. An army gathers behind him. Hugh Nolan declares himself historian. There is an idea in his head, courage in his heart. Old native of Ballymenone, he receives the community's knowledge and his neighbors' support in performance. Alone at the whispering hearth of his small house, Hugh Nolan takes aristocratic responsibility, gets power, and speaks for his people.

Typically, Mr. Nolan tells his land's story with less excitement and more detail than Mr. Boyle. Here is his first rendition of the battle tale:

"Well.

"I have heard a gooddeal about the Ford of Biscuits battle.

"Do ye see: at that time there was no town in Enniskillen. There was only a fort.

"Do you know, when you'd stand there in Henry Street, and look across the Lough, you see two things like round towers. Well, that was a fort on the edge of the lake, in the middle of the sixteenth century; that'd be somewhere in the fifteen-hundreds. Aye.

"Well, there was an English garrison.

"Do you see, the Plantation of Ulster, it took place in the early part of the seventeenth century. That would be very early, about sixteen hundred and nine.

"It twas after the Flight of the Earls. They were Irish gentry that had position and owned the property, the land like, in this country. So then they lost in the wars with the British, and they had to leave Ireland.

"And then, James the First was the king at that time. And he brought over a very large contingent. And he gave them the lands that these *earls* owned, do ye know. So that was what they called, the Plantation of Ulster.

"Well then, there was a garrison here at Enniskillen in days before that,
            while the O'Neills and the O'Donnells was in prominence.

"There was an English garrison here on the island of Enniskillen.

"So this garrison was attacked be Red Hugh O'Donnell;
            he was a Donegal chief.

"They were attacked.

"And nothing could get in or out
            because there was an army surrounded the castle.

"So finally, in the long run, there was a soldier got out.

"And he got into a boat.

"And he rowed the boat from Enniskillen to Belturbet
            up Lough Erne.

"Well, do ye see, the way it was at that time, the southern part of the country was in English hands, but the North wasn't, because these earls that I have told you about, they held Ulster.

"And it was only an odd place that the English could get in—like gettin in on this island in Lough Erne, *Enniskillen.*

"So he got to Belturbet anyway, and he got word sent to Dublin
        about this attack on Enniskillen *castle.*

"And it was ten weeks from the castle was attacked till the chief secretary got the word about it in Dublin.

"So anyway, when he heard the news, he formed a powerful great army, all over the other three *provinces.*

"There was Irish men on it too from Ulster, that started marchin for Enniskillen.

"So then O'Donnell then, he raised an army in the *North* here
        for to intercept the Lord Lieutenant's army.

"So they came on out through this country,
        O'Donnell's army.

"And they took up their positions
    along the *banks* of the Arney River,
       from Drumane *all* up to Arney.

"So they waited there for the arrival of their opponents.

"And there went a man on a horse on as far up as Belturbet
    for to see was there any sign of the Lord Lieutenant's army comin.

"And he came back,
    and there was a song about it,
    and his answer was put in *verse.*

"He told O'Donnell—there was a general the name of Duke, and he was leadin the Lord Lieutenant's forces, do ye see—so he told him:

I saw the plumes of Duke's dragoons,
south of Belturbet town.

"So anyway, they remained here through this country, and all along the banks of the Arney River.

"And finally the Lord Lieutenant's army arrived on the *other side.*

"That would be from Derryhowlaght down to Clontymullan, and all along there.

"And they wanted to get across the Arney River and get on to Enniskillen.

"So the other ones gave them battle there.

"And the battle,
    it was a runnin fight,
       along the banks of both sides.

"The English forces couldn't get across the River because it was all fords; there was no bridges, do ye see, in them days.

"It was *all fords.*

"Every ford that they came to, they were guarded, do ye see, and they couldn't get *across.*

"So there was one ford there in particular. It'd be a wee piece up from Drumane Bridge. Accordin to tradition, the battle finished up there.

"It's called the Biscuit Ford.

"The English had all sorts of food with them, do ye know, includin a terrible go of biscuits.

"So the battle finished up there.

"And the English was beaten back.

"And alot of the provisions that they had with them went into the River.

"So that's known to this day as the Biscuit Ford.

"Aye."

Lucid and full, Mr. Nolan's narrative leaves few questions. Still, I need to be sure of the fight's spatial and temporal coordinates in his mind, so I ask if the ford "above Drumane" is the one on James Owens' land, and he responds as a Rossdoney man should:

"No, that's not the ford. It's further down, between Sessiagh and Drumane, do ye know, along the River.

"It'd be in Mrs. MacManus' land. That woman that lives at the Bridge, it'd be in her land.

"The battle went on from that up to what they call now the Arney Bridge, do ye know.

"Do ye see, the way it was: it went along them whole banks, do ye see, on up past the Red Meadows.

"Aye, aye.

"It was a runnin fight, do ye see. It twas the same as you wanted to get across here to Inishmore, and that there was an army in front of ye. Well then, you'd go along the banks till you'd come to another ford, do ye see. So that's the way.

"So it took in that whole scope of the locality. Aye, from Drumane on up to Arney."

He stops and I ask the last question, "Do you know what the date was, Hugh?"

"It would be somewhere about the middle of the sixteenth century. Because it was about, I think it was about sixteen hundred and nine, the Flight of the Earls, and that finished up the native rule in Ulster. The English, they got top hold of it then, do ye see."

While he relaxes and cracks a light for his cold pipe, I disturb the air with flurries of compliment. A little smile sneaks into the shadows over his face. He accepts my goodmanning and ends my gabble appropriately with a concise recapitulation:

"Aye, well.

"How the thing started was: O'Donnell sieged Enniskillen.

"Enniskillen was a British garrison.

"He sieged the garrison and finally this soldier, British soldier—they weren't styled British in them days; it was English they were called—he got out and got to Belturbet

in a boat.

"And surely that was an ordeal.

"And he communicated with the chief secretary of the Lord Lieutenant. And they raised this army for to come to Enniskillen and put O'Donnell's men from *about it*.

"And in the meantime, O'Donnell raised his army here in Ulster and marched on out till he came to this country, and took up his positions along the banks of the Arney River.

"And the way it was: when the English forces, when they'd be beat back at one ford, do ye see, they'd run to *another*.

"Well then, the Irish was there *too*.

"So finally they were worn *out*.

"And there was a battle, or a scrimmage at this particular ford,

and there was alot of them killed,

and their whole provisions was all destroyed.

"And they had to retreat back.

"And that's what happened."

Mr. Nolan's synopsis is the sort of thing that often goes for legend in collections of folktale. It is oral, narrative, and historical, but it is a plot summary, not a story. There is no initial informational setting, no historical context: no mention of native rule or the Flight of the Earls or the Plantation of Ulster. It is generalized away from geographical precision and lacks the place-naming conclusion. Though broken and ordered efficiently, it displays little of the embellishment that testifies to an ego being invested in its presence in the world.

Leave aside matters of pace and tone (you should hear his voice drag and shudder with Red Hugh in the blizzard and sweep with the English army running the banks of the Arney) and look only at the text of Mr. Nolan's battle tale. It is most obviously enriched when he quotes Hugh McGiveney's song, but subtle decoration is constant. There is an internal repetition of sound (rowed the boat, all along, beaten back) alliterative end stops (one sequence ends: attacked, out, castle, out, boat, Belturbet), and even rhyme (a set of sentences ends: army, Arney, army). Overall the mood changes from strength to weakness, firmness to fluidity, will to fate, as predominant sounds shift from sharp and percussive at the start (attack, castle, Enniskillen, Belturbet) to flowing and hissing at the close (across, along, banks, Arney).

Like rain on lake waters, repeated words pelt over the surface, lending radiance and coherence to the tale. As the informational introduction breaks into narration, the story cracks with sudden power as these words appear rapidly in this order in the first three sentences: garrison, Enniskillen, garrison, Enniskillen, garrison, attacked, attacked. Place names are driven throughout—Enniskillen, Dublin, Belturbet, Arney—nailing the tale together and into the land. In one early section, lines conclude: Belturbet, Erne, Ulster, Fnniskillen, Dublin, castle, Dublin, provinces, Enniskillen. The four lines in the battle section ending "there" stop motion (Michael Boyle repeated the same word at the same place in his story), while repeated phrases slow the story for its conclusion, playing the desperate efforts of men off history's inevitable shape: along the banks, all along the banks, all along there, get across, along the banks, get across, all fords, all fords, get across, the battle finished up there, the battle finished up there.

Repetition of sound, of word, of phrase is the textual way narration is given sparkle and tempo. Unrepetitive, Mr. Nolan's précis is not poetic. It is not a story but a reference to a story. That does not leave it without worth. Streamlined and stripped to narrative line, it is the first step in a structural analysis of story form. Reduced to action, it clearly represents Mr. Nolan's conception of events.

The Ford of Biscuits is the District's first great battle tale. It tells how the English dispossessed the local chief of his home and how a hero who had vowed to free Ireland assumed his native responsibility. To aid his neighbor and kinsman, to avenge his loss, he sieged the stolen castle, then marched the men of Ulster out to defeat the British at the ford. Here in the little River Arney, glinting between the trees at the meadows' edge, forming the southern boundary of the people's home parish, the invaders were beaten back.

9

Mackan Hill

Drums thunder early on the Twelfth of July. At the far end of town by the cattle mart, marchers and musicians mill, assembling while people dressed to stand the rain and chilly winds begin to line the main streets. Up and down bands parade, banging a martial beat between the fronts of shops and homes. Against the steady cannonade, booming, pounding, the Lambeg drums rattle a battle call. Onward slowly, the big drums move, borne by a pair of men in hard hats, coats off, sleeves rolled to hot work, stepping forward, swiveling together to whack a rackety tattoo, whipping around them a wild storm of sound, as people nearby, frowning and laughing, cover their ears. Bands pass and cross, recede and arrive. A thumping din throbs, cracks, clapping to echo the hard damp streets and make of the town a drum.

In other towns this morning other bands are marching. By noon they will gather in some central place to drum up memory and pound out loyalty. For southwest Ulster it is Enniskillen this year, and they come from all Fermanagh, from Monaghan and Donegal too, and soon, smoothly, Lodge after Loyal Orange Lodge will step out in order, moving away from the Gaol Square where Black Francis was hanged, along Belmore Street, past the solemn monument to the Great War's dead, across the East Bridge beneath the banner strung from the Orange Hall: God Save Our Queen.

Leaders come first, broken out of the ranks, then men supporting the high banner that tells their place, the name and number of their Lodge. Banners billow and flap, portraying local heroes, the dead of two world wars, and Protestant martyrs who preferred death by fire to life under popery. "Civil and Religious Liberty," the banners proclaim, "No Surrender," "Temperance," "Fear God, Honour the King," "The Throne Is Established by Righteousness," "Soldiers of the Cross," "No Cross, No Crown." A crown sits upon a pillow, fluttering in the wet wind, a dark man kneels, unclothed and wide-eyed, before a queen on a throne, extending to him a black Bible: "The Secret of England's Greatness." Most often of all, King William of Orange, turned astride his white charger, rides through Boyne waters. "In Glorious and Immortal Memory": it is William's victory over James at the Boyne in 1690, the first of July by the old calendar, the twelfth by the new, they celebrate this day.

The Twelfth of July in Enniskillen

220   Passing the Time in Ballymenone

Behind each banner stride in file, in black suits and orange collarettes, the men of the Lodge, their jaws set, their eyes fixed firmly ahead, until they spy someone they know, and a smile breaks, but step does not. Onward. Between the Lodges come the bands, flashing through the black stream. The Young Loyalists strut behind their drum major, high-stepping to great applause. Pipe bands in Scots war regalia, kilts and tartans, sporrans swinging, wail "Scotland the Brave," "The Enniskillen Dragoon," and ironic Jacobite laments. Teenagers with accordions in sparkling white shirts march, mixing hymns and Orange tunes: "Onward Christian Soldiers," "We Guard Old Derry's Walls."

Lodge after Lodge peels out of the crowd and swings up the street. Among them step the District's men, the Bellanalack True Blues, L.O.L. 1567. Marching, drumming, cheered by the crowd, they pass the columned portico of the old Court House and the blank facade of the new Post Office, beneath pennants of red, white, and blue. Banners floating and snapping, they climb the curving main street and gain the Diamond. There the street opens to the Town Hall before rising again between the mirrors of reverberating storefronts, up the Church Brae where St. Macartin's Cathedral spires at the sky from its graveyard, and St. Michael's offers it portals carved with damnation and hope to the street running down, descending through shops and rain to carry the parade, black as a Bible, steady as time, across the West Bridge, above a narrow neck of Lough Erne. To the south the gray Water Gate looms at the foot of Enniskillen's tumbling hillside of chimneys and rooftops. Water slaps at rock.

East to west, from one bridge to the other, men have walked the length of the Town. The line of march follows the Brook toward the Quay and Portora Royal School, but turns and breaks apart on a wide hillside, ringing with the rhetoric of No Surrender. Drums cease, banners are reefed, feet take a rest. There are long speeches, neighbors to chat with, a series of staunch resolutions, then all sing "God Save the Queen" and filter back to the town their marching has once again claimed and won.

In the wet dusk on the West Bridge, people in pale raincoats hurry past men in black and bright uniforms who stand and drift, cupping match flames against the damp, shifting toward the bright, smoky pubs for a night of political talk and toasts and drink. A dreary rain falls. The headlights of cars blink on the bridge and along roads running west around the mountains. The northerly road reaches past the Lower Lough by Belleek at the Border to Ballyshannon where the River Erne enters Donegal Bay. The other, breaking south at the West Bridge, crosses the Border at Belcoo on its way to Sligo. South from the Sligo Road, along the Upper Lough, the Derrylin Road, aimed at Belturbet in Cavan, crosses the Sillees on Lisgoole Bridge, cuts the Bellanaleck Cross, squeezes through Drumane Bridge, and pulls up Derryhowlaght Hill, where Souple Corrigan outrode the crown's horsemen. Then it dips. When it rises again, the road lies over Mackan Hill.

Hushed, tense, they speak differently of Mackan Hill than any other event in their history. The voice is held back; now it races, confined and driven by the terrible relevance of the old Mackan Fight.

On an autumn evening, three months after the Lodges trooped through Enniskillen, I asked Michael Boyle to tell me the story. He glanced around us through the hospital's icy light, then turned his eyes into mine and began quietly, nearly whispering as though in the confidence of a secret:

"Well, that was a religious fight.

"And, do ye see, at that time the men that professed the Protestant faith, do ye see, *they were in control*.

"See, the Catholic people had no life atall—just *they were slaves, they were serfs*, do ye see.

"Do ye see: there was no life for them, they had no livin. They were even apprehended and molested goin to their place of worship on Sunday.

"So anyhow, the Twelfth of July was a great day of celebrations, do ye see, for the Protestants and the *Orangemen* as they are known as. It was a great day of celebrations, do ye see.

"And they were celebratin—wherever they celebrated the Twelfth, I don't know, somewhere anyways, at some meetin.

"But the next day
            they assembled.

"And there was some trouble up at a place at Derrylin they call Mullineny. There was some trouble up there, another religious fight.

"But it twasn't as serious as the Mackan Fight turned out to be. I don't know whether there was any life lost in it or what now, but the word came down to these Orangemen in Ballymenone.

"There was alot of Orangemen in Ballymenone, do ye see—
            very terribly Protestant populated.

"And there was word came down, it was passed down to them, to go up to assist their brethren in Derrylin at Mullineny.

"So they set out on horseback anyway, a good many of them (they were nearly all on horseback), for to go to Mullineny and assist their brethren up *there*.

"So when they were goin over Mackan Hill,
            when they had came as far as Mackan Hill,
            they said that when they'd be comin back,
            that they wouldn't leave a Catholic house,
                but they'd burn it to the ground.

"So anyway, the boys didn't let them get any further.

"They got out.

"And the Orangemen was all armed with *guns*. The weapon at the time was an ould *gun* they called the musket.

"She fired a *ball*—oh, *deadly*, a deadly weapon.

"But she wasn't modern like the present-day gun; she was loaded at the muzzle, do ye see. She wasn't a needle gun, a breech-loadin gun; she was loaded at the muzzle. There was a handful of powder brought down the muzzle of her and a lump of paper put down after that, and twas rammed down with a *ramrod*. And then this ball was put in. Oh, I saw the ould balls; I seen a few that was kept for a souvenir. It was dropped in then, and another lump of paper put down, and rammed tight to keep it in its place, and then there was what they called a nipple. She was a wee lad that length, do ye see, and the powder was packed into that. And when they were loadin, it was hit be the hand and the powder went into the nipple and there was what was called a cap put on the nipple, some kind of wee explosive cap, and then, do ye see, the hammer—when you pulled the trigger, the hammer fell on this cap and it exploded and put off the powder in the bore.

"Of course if that ball struck a man, it would go through him.

"It was death.

"But then, do ye see, you had to load again, and you had to load again.

"It was slow.

"But then it was the method used, do ye see, and them that was shootin against them had to do the same, do ye see.

"Well, these Orangemen were all armed with muskets, do ye see.

"Some of them had bayonets on them,
   well prepared,
   for the fight.

"But the poor Catholics, do ye see, had nothin, only pitchforks, pitchforks and every kind of weapons they could get their hands on.

"They sallied out
   and attacked the boys.

"So faith, the boys didn't wait too much till they took to their heels,
   and they run
   for all they were worth.

"And the Catholics followed them
   and prodded away at them,
   and knocked them down on the roads,
   and everything.

"But there was none of them killed outright,
  just that the chase went on,
  and there was a fellow,
  they called him Owney the Dummy,
  and he was workin at hay,
   with a Protestant farmer
   in a townland they called Clinulsen,
  and he heard the hullaloo,
  and he knew it was a fight,

and he started away out of the hayfield,
and he brought the pitchfork with him,
and any man he got lyin on the road,
he killed him *out*.

"There were three Orangemen killed in the fight anyway.

"One of them was the name of Mealey. He lived in a place there on the Back Road; he's a man the name of Foster lives in it now. He's a Jim Foster.

"Well then, there was another man the name of Robinson and he lived in a townland they called Gortdonaghy.

"Well this Robinson lived *there*
and he was *killed*.

"And there was another man named Scarlett and he lived in the townland of Gortdonaghy and he was killed also.

"There was three of them killed.

"But at any rate, that ended the fight;
they didn't burn the houses on Mackan Hill;
they run by them in the *slip*.

"They forgot all about it.

"But at any rate, of course, the Catholics was all arrested.

"I forget now the number of fellows that was arrested and lodged in Enniskillen Gaol, but there was a trial before the assizes, do ye see.

"The fight took place on the thirteenth of July, the day after the Twelfth.

"And there was a wholesale arrest, do ye see, connected with the fight, and a good many of them was sentenced to be hanged. At the assizes in Enniskillen. They were sentenced to be hanged.

"So there was a priest, he was a Father Ned McHugh, he was a parish priest in Knockninny.

"And he rode a horse to Dublin
to petition to the Lord Lieutenant of the time,
the English Lord Lieutenant,
to *reprieve* these men.

"There was a whole lot of them wasn't guilty.

"They were proved guilty, but they weren't guilty; do ye see: proved guilty on perjured evidence.

"So he rode a horse to Dublin.

"And he got the reprieve,
he got the reprieve,
the Lord Lieutenant reprieved them right enough.

"And Father Ned McHugh was comin with the reprieve.

"And it twas the day that was fixed for the execution.

"And he was *comin in the Dublin Road*.

"And he was *wavin it in his hand*,
the way that *it twould be seen*.

"But *still they wouldn't wait*.

"*They hanged one man.*

"They hanged one man, his name was MacManus.

"He was Ignatius MacManus, he was from a townland they call Corc-nacrea—Corcnacrea, it's in the Montiagh District; Corcnacrea, Mackan Post Office.

"Yes, he was hanged.

"They hanged him anyway, but then the priest was in. I don't know how many there was more, six or seven more, and the priest had came and they couldn't hang them.

"They couldn't hang them, but they transported them. They trans-ported away to Van Dieman's Land; that is what is known as Australia at the present time. They were transported there.

"And after some few years in transportation,
        they were released,
        and they got farms,
        big wild Australian farms,
        and *they done the best*.
"*They done the best.*
"*They done the best.*

"They got on the best, better than what they would've done in this country, in Ireland at the time.

"So, you see, of course they communicated on with relatives for a long time.

"But then of course they've all died out now, do ye see.

"That fight took place in eighteen hundred and twenty-nine, do ye see, eighteen hundred and twenty-nine.

"But there is still a distant relation of Ignatius MacManus, and he has a public house in Enniskillen. He owns a big bar there in Enniskillen, they call it the Central Bar. He's a stout strong block of a young red-haired fel-low, a nice fellow when you come to chat with him. He's a distant relation of Ignatius MacManus.

"Aye, and he has an uncle livin there yet; he has an uncle livin up there yet. He is a Eugene MacManus, in the townland of Corcnacrea, all right. He's livin there with a family. And the two of them is distant rela-tions of the man that was hanged for his part in the Mackan Fight: Ignatius MacManus.

"Ignatius MacManus had a son and I heard a story told about that too. He had a son that was watchin the execution, and he was only a small, very small wee fellow.

"And he never grew.

"He never grew any more.

"He was known as the Wee Man, as the Small Man for ever after—or the Wee Man as the ould people said.

"He was known as the Wee Man for ever after.

"He never grew after seein his father a-hangin."

Like his story of the Ford, but even more extremely, Mr. Boyle's Mackan Hill swings between modes. He will lay phrases tightly and daub them with do-ye-sees, jumping out of time to provide, as the do-ye-knows stress, circumstantial information. Then he runs with time, snapping lines through silence to advance narration.

Michael Boyle begins each battle tale informationally, pulling facts from the past to join it with the present. At the time of the Ford, he says, the English occupied Ireland. At the time of Mackan Hill, Protestants were in control. The facts call for action, and Mr. Boyle shifts swiftly, moving the story's people forward and moving his telling from prosy stability to poetic action: "So. They laid seige to it." "But the next day they all assembled." Mr. Nolan does the same. He provides the Ford's background, then: "So this garrison was attacked be Red Hugh O'Donnell."

Modulating from mode to mode and blending them, both men push the story on, then stop to explain, enhancing drama with shocking shifts of pace. Mr. Boyle sets the Orangemen on the road and brings the Catholics out to confront them, then nearing the climax, he kills motion with a long manual of arms. Telling George Armstrong's pant of the Lucky Shot, Mr. Nolan paused identically, inserting a full account of gun-loading between Armstrong's hearing the ducks and killing them. Both men used the muzzle-loading interlude to wrench tempo, holding us in long suspense while glossing the action. Comment comes in facts set away from narration rather than through subjective intervention. Truth, not opinion, stops us, makes us think. Armstrong's shot was the luckier for the weapon he used. The Protestant musket was "Oh, deadly, a deadly weapon." The Catholics, armed only with their agricultural "weapons," were the braver for fighting, the luckier for winning.

Between the level tone of information and the variable tone of action, stilling as men are murdered, ripping when Father McHugh gallops in with the reprieve, the story unfolds and its points are made. The first concerns the men of Mackan, their character and condition.

They are courageous, willing to face a "well-prepared" enemy. Still they do not act until their homes are threatened with burning. Mr. Boyle has moved from house to house, watching them decay behind him. Now he has none. Eviction, for him, is the prime justification for political violence. Black Francis turned robber because the English "put the poor man out of his property . . . out of his home, out of his property, and they put someone else into it." The siege of Enniskillen and the battle at the Ford came about because the English put the Maguires "out of their home they lived in, and occupied it." The victory at Mackan came when "they didn't burn the houses on Mackan Hill; they run by them in the slip." (Slip is the local term for coursing hares with greyhounds.) Brave men, fearful of losing their major possession, the men of Mackan—like Columcille, like "any man"—had no choice but fighting.

They were right to fight. They fought, yet remained innocent. It was a deficient, uninvolved laborer, Owney the Dummy, who did the killing, so it took "perjured evidence"—the unlawful, sinful lie—to convict them. A holy man argued their case before higher authority, and they were reprieved. Though not guilty, one of the men was hanged, exactly where Black Francis was, proving with his death the injustice of their situation.

The virtue in the men of Mackan and the evil surrounding them become yet clearer in the story's conclusions. Transported, they prospered. Like Hugh McGiveney, who had not much living on that couple of cows' grass of land, a little farm of six acres, the men of Mackan were held down in Ireland: they "had no life atall—just they were slaves, they were serfs . . . they had no livin." Like McGiveney's brothers, when they left Ireland "they done the best." They were brave, innocent, and inherently capable of success.

Real people are used in story to symbolize abstract principles. They are formed in words, set in action, to enable philosophical discourse. Exploits, bids, and pants prove local people, poor farming people, to be courageous and creative. Those virtues thrive in real people, but people do not live outside conditions. We have our own free will, said Peter Flanagan, and we are persecuted with bad people. In a benign setting, in the Nowhere across the sea, bravery and wit produce success. In Ireland, in reality, they produce only the ability to endure disappointment, to carry on through all seasons. Stories that celebrate the excellence of the District's people stand as intrinsic critique of the system that confines them. Defining the negative by discussing the positive is Ballymenone's naturally affirmative way to keep evil in focus.

What expands in utopia, in dream, shrinks in reality. That idea is diversely demonstrated. In America the McGiveney genius makes smart men rich. In Ballymenone it makes a poor man smart. Unable to become wealthy, old Hughie becomes a storyteller, poet, and historian who gets through life by playing in his mind and helps others get through by giving them entertainment. In far Australia, George Armstrong becomes wealthy. He succeeds personally but fails in his person, so he returns to become, like Hugh McGiveney, a poor star. At home his energy does not serve himself: it runs out to his comrades, lighting their way through darkness. While his father's brothers at arms did the best in Australia, Ignatius MacManus' son struggled at home. Though stunted, as Armstrong had shriveled, the Wee Man lived on, and his descendants made it. One is the proprietor of a public house, another leads a family on the old soil. Despite conditions, MacManus blood endured.

That is the story's second point: the material continuity of past and present. There is still a Mackan Hill. Orangemen march on the Twelfth. The slain man's house stands. MacManus blood runs. The implications are plain. As the past lives, it will live. As people are treated unjustly, they will justly rebel. Farmers with pitchforks, lads with bombs, will face death, bring death.

As history, a use of the past to discuss the present, Michael Boyle's Mackan Hill beams a clear message. There might seem no need to go further. But there are plenty of reasons for looking at other statements before concluding our examination of the story. Mr. Boyle's tale was full. He rolled along anticipating the questions I had. Still, as he wove the story he strove to maintain its beauty as a spoken piece, and some details might not have fit the moment. There may be more to Mackan Hill. In his tale, Mr. Boyle offered both cultural and personal points of view. We steal neither collective power nor individual integrity from him to say other tales will vary from his.

Variation is the folklorist's old test of authenticity. As ideas are transferred from person to person, as they are taught and learned, some become so deeply absorbed into the self that when they reappear in the world they bear the impress of their unique makers. And since their makers are striving to communicate, they shape their creations to suit unique situations. As a result, works of art display variety, much as individuals in a society display varieties of personality. This variation between things created by different people acting in different moments is one product of sincere involvement, one clue to authenticity. Intrinsic excellence is another. Quantitative variation is the folklorist's customary measure. Quality, excellence, signature, is the art historian's. Both signal authenticity. Tales of the same event narrated by Michael Boyle and Hugh Nolan differ because their tellers do. They have different biographies, personalities, attitudes. Their stories form beautifully because talented men commit themselves to their performance. Both variation and excellence mark art and enable its perpetuation.

Meeting different, yet fine versions of a manifestly single idea, different people are free to create personal places within a tradition, whether of storytelling or novel-writing, by synthesizing uniquely to suit their own taste and opinion. There will be more to Mackan Hill. Different people will know and emphasize differently. Without abandoning cultural coherence, stories will reveal different egos—thereby authenticating collective order—and they will convey different opinions.

With Michael Boyle's clear tale, we have but begun. Even he knows more. Our conversation had wandered to other matters, but he kept thinking. In a lull he brought us back:

"Well, we'll get back to Mackan Fight.
"There was a song on that. I know a verse of Mackan Fight.
"I heard it.

Twas on the thirteenth of July,
   in the year of twenty-nine,
      bein the time of these bloody No Surrenders.

"You see, No Surrender was the slogan of the Orangemen.

> They were cheerin loud and shrill,
>> till they came to Mackan Hill,
>>> for the face of a papish pretender.
> Our gallant sons of fame,
>> prefeciously they came,
>>> to confront these bloody tigers in battle.
> And with our pitchforks made of steel,
>> we forced them for to yield,
>>> though their bullets like hail did rattle.
> Through malice and through spleen,
>> they swore in nineteen,
>>> and all our loving brethren did suffer.
> The first of our bleeding swains
>> to fall from Montiagh plains
>>> was the gallant Ignatius MacManus,
> Who with faith and courage bold,
>> like a martyr he died on the gallows.
> Where his innocent blood did fall
>> it stained the flags and walls.
> They scrubbed but all in vain,
>> they never got it clean
>>> it remains there, a token of vengeance.

"That's some of it anyway."

The segment of song he remembered preserved names and dates for him, and it supported the second of his story's points, that of historical continuity through space. Not only does Ignatius MacManus' innocent blood continue to flow, but it left stains, marking for all time the walls and paving stones of the jail, a perpetual sign of injustice and cry for "vengeance." But the song itself, not politics, has become the concern of Michael Boyle, historian, and he continues:

"Aye, that's some of it anyway.

"It used to be sung about. There was a man in Inishmore Island had it. He's a James Lunny. He lives in Inishmore. It was him I heared singin it, and I only picked up them bits, do ye see, be listenin to him."

"Were there other songs on it?" I ask.

"There were several songs on it, but that's the only one ever I heard. Oh, there were several songs on it, all right. But that's the one Lunny used to sing.

"It twas composed by a man named—he was a Mick Maguire. Noble Mick, they used to call him. He lived in the Kinawley area. It was him composed that song. Aye, it twas.

"It was him composed that song.

"Mackan Fight."

The author of "Mackan Fight" was, like the author of the ballad of the Ford, one of south Fermanagh's stars. Hugh McGiveney was a Ballymenone man, Mick Maguire is associated with Kinawley and Montiagh, so less is known about him in the District, but on another occasion Mr. Boyle placed a story about him in a geographical frame:

"Mick Maguire, he was called the Yellow Master. He wasn't a native of our country, do ye see. He lived up the Kinawley way.

"He taught school at the place they call Graffy Kesh. Graffy's sticks, and of course there was an ould wooden bridge where there was a stream, do ye see, a wee river, and there was a wooden bridge over it, and this school was there.

"And of course there's a modern bridge at it now. This Graffy Road runs from the main Derrylin Road and goes out at Kinawley Chapel, a narrow road.

"There's a bridge at that school and that's where the Yellow Master taught.

"He was a great poet. The Noble Mick, they called him.

"The scholars used to go in the mornin,
    and rise him up out of his bed,
    and make his breakfast for him,
    and bring him to the school.
"And this day anyway they forgot to go for him.

"And the inspector came and he wasn't in school.

"And the school was closed
    and the inspector tossed him out,
        put him out.
"See, the school was closed and it shouldn't have been.

"The scholars forgot to go for him *that* day, do ye see, or didn't *go*.

"And he lost the school. He was dismissed.

"Of course, do ye see, the pay wasn't much anyway. See, they had to pay him themselves, so much a quarter. The teachers weren't paid thattime by the government; it was the scholars, do ye see."

When I asked Hugh Nolan about the song "Mackan Fight" he said he heard it from the same man Michael Boyle did:

"Ah, there was different songs made about it, but I don't know any. There's a man over here in Inishmore; he's a man the name of Lunny. He's a Jim Lunny and he had a song on that fight. It was handed down."

Like Mr. Boyle, though with less certainty, Mr. Nolan credited the song to Mick Maguire, but the Noble Mick was not the Yellow Master:

"There were several poets in that family. I knew where them ones lived, as you go to Kinawley from here. But they're all gone.

"They're all dead and gone.

"The man they called the Yellow Master, he was some of that race, but he was a different man from Mick Maguire. Aye, a different man. There was a couple or three generations of them Maguires that was gifted that way. But then in the finish up, there came one generation, and when he died that was that. That was the last of them."

The schoolmaster is a leader in the little community. Though trained outside and set apart by erudition, the master was a neighbor, a settler of small disputes, a writer of wills, entrusted with the delicate task of measuring roods of ground for rent. The old master was like the priest in Patrick Kavanagh's poem set in Cavan: he was "part of the place, as natural as stones in grazing fields." Stones do not belong in pastures, but they are of the same earth as the grass. They belong more than most things.[1]

Master Maguire in Kinawley and Master Corrigan in Rossdoney both came of local politically active families. They brought learning in from the outside and whaled it into their pupils, but they learned from within as well. Their role did not prevent them from knowing and telling the tale of their place or living the rooted life.

Mick Maguire was a teacher, Hugh McGiveney a small farmer, but both were poets. Deeply, they were the same, examples of the type of the artist and of the local man. Master Maguire was also distracted, peculiar, gifted, one of a race fated to blaze and burn out. Like his neighbors, he was underpaid and mistreated by higher authority. Maguire and McGiveney remain the subjects of bids in which their quick wit is kept forever fresh. Both are remembered as contributing, along with Mickey McCourt, the shoemaker, to the composition of "Maxwell's Ball." Poets can be craftsmen, farmers, or schoolteachers. Finally, all are unique people with troubles.

A learned native, Master Corrigan was the natural leader of his community's younger men. He organized their Gaelic football club and taught them their past. I complimented Mr. Boyle on his telling of Mackan Hill, and he turned to his master:

"Well, I'm doin the best I can. When I was younger in me life, I had a great memory, especially if it was told me or kind of drummed into me. This Master Corrigan used to drum the history into us.

"He used to say he was hard on his pupils; he kind of drummed away. And when he drummed a thing into ye, you never forgot it. You'd mind it longer than if you read it there in a book or a paper.

"Aye, he was a great man, Master Corrigan. There isn't the like of him today. Aw, he was the greatest."

"Did he teach you about the Mackan Fight?" I ask.

"Well, yes he did. But he wasn't supposed to teach it, do ye see, in the National School. It was more on the q.t. like; I used to often ceili with him and he taught us all he knew.
"Ah, this chat's better to me than me dinner."

Old masters make intense memories. A tear rose in the eye and ran down the cheek of one old man while he told me his heart broke when his teacher was stripped of his school for introducing politically charged subjects. His master, he said, cared for him, was teaching him Irish and pushing his English vocabulary. Then he was gone, and with him went the will to study. Schoolmasters were tough but dedicated. Revered like parent or priest, the master was special, a guide, but a member of the community for all that, an entertaining guest at a ceili. When I asked Mr. Nolan how history came to him, he described the teacher's teachings as a natural part of his learning:

"Well I'll tell ye.
"There was always people in Ireland that was takin note of what was happenin. They were called scribes. They wrote down every happenin, especially happenins of importance—the Takin of Hugh O'Donnell and the Siege of Enniskillen and the Battle of Kinsale. They had all these things in writins.
"Well, we were talkin about Lisgoole the last time you were here.
"Well, what prevailed when Ireland was fully conquered be the English: these four monks, they came to Lisgoole and they had gathered up all that ever had been written be these scribes or writers, and they put it all into the one book. And that's what preserved all that history of them happenins.
"It was the Four Masters. It was to their credit.
"Well then, the master that taught me, and the people of my day, at school, he was a man that, as he went along, he explained everything.
"What you couldn't understand, he used to explain it.
"Well some of that come be readin, be readin.
"But I'll tell you about books. You'll get the general history of a country, but you'll get no local history in them unless some local person, do ye see, that took an interest in it and was educated enough for to write a book on it.
"Well then, there was another means that brought alot of that: listenin to the old people talkin.
"Well, that's the way I got the grasp of it.

"That old history is a-talkin as long as I mind. I'd hear the old people talkin and I'd learn that and I'd put in the details along with what I was taught be the master, do ye see. Oh aye."

Irish history could not be taught in the classroom,[2] but the master slipped it in, raised it in ceilis, and sent it into the wider community as song.

In a bar one rowdy night, the battered chat reeled around through the smoke and black stout to the authorship of "Mackan Fight." Among the men present were natives of Kinawley, Peter Flanagan and Hugh MacManus. Like P, Mr. MacManus has left his boyhood home. He lives in Cavan now. They agreed quickly that the Yellow Master, though a poet, was not the song's maker. Mr. Flanagan said the author was Tom Forads, Forads being the nickname of a particular branch of Maguires, but Mr. MacManus disagreed, saying it was Tom's father, Frank Forads, who composed the song. Master Maguire, the poet, they said, lived from before 1850 to around 1900. Frank Forads died about 1872. Mr. MacManus' father knew him and said he could not write, so he dictated his poems to Neddy Anderson, schoolmaster and noted distiller of poteen. Though he agreed in the moment with Hugh MacManus' convincing argument, months later Peter Flanagan reattributed "Mackan Fight" to the Yellow Master, and years later he held the same view.

A valuable small book published as a souvenir of the centenary of St. Naile's, the new church at Kinawley, provides a chronicle of local education. It tells of the poet Mickey Maguire and quotes verse he wrote for the church's dedication in February 1876. Though "continuously in trouble with the inspector on the grounds of unpunctuality and lack of discipline," Maguire moved from a school conducted in an abandoned barn to a National School in 1856, and served as principal of the Old Kinawley School from its opening in 1862 until his retirement in 1879. Andrew Anderson became master, and in less than a decade he hired as assistant the son of a Donegal farmer called Seumas MacManus. It was the first teaching position for the young man, who in 1888 would return to become master of his home school before achieving fame as a poet and historian, novelist, folklorist, and husband of the nationalist poet Ethna Carbery. In his autobiography, MacManus says Master Anderson had released the word that the young master was a poet. Rumor ran to a poetry match held in a Kinawley kitchen. His opponent was Frank Maguire, greatest of the local poets, whose composition for the contest recounted a great rally in Enniskillen that drew men from all Fermanagh, including "Montiagh lads and Macken men that fought their way and won." Young Master MacManus' own poem was an elegy on the Old Master, the old poet and wit not known for punctuality, Mickey Maguire, who had died the week before.[3]

Frank Maguire, Seumas MacManus' opponent, is one candidate for the authorship of "Mackan Fight." Mick Maguire, his subject, is another.

Surely some Maguire, gnawed by the worm of poesy, who lived some-where about Kinawley or Montiagh around 1875, composed "Mackan Fight," among other pieces.

Peter Flanagan was the first to tell me about Mackan Hill. On our way to Swanlinbar for a Sunday night's sport, we passed a crossroads, called Hannah's Cross, and he said a "faction fight" had occurred there "in the year of twenty-nine." It began on Derryhowlaght Hill, he said, and surged down through the Cross and up Mackan Hill. Later, having heard frequent reference to the fight, I brought our conversation back to it. He described the action fully and promised to find a ballat of the song that had been writ-ten out for him.

That was two weeks ago. Another Sunday has come. P and Joe are back from chapel, our dinner is done. Time remains before our departure for music and drink in Swad, and we have settled to quiet before the muted sparkle on the hearthstone. P would prefer for me to forget Mackan Fight. It is not possible to avoid religious classification in Ulster. A joke making the rounds has a civil servant enter "atheist" on an application only to be told by the examining official that it is all very well for him to be an atheist but he must specify whether he is a Catholic atheist or a Protestant atheist. P is a Catholic. Protestant is all he can call me. Mackan Hill brought men like ourselves into violent confrontation. He can see no good coming into our relation from talk about the fight. But as an American I am not quite classifiable, and P wants to help.

I ask about the song. He has searched the house and found it for me. It is "too sectarian" for him to sing, he says, and not written out well, but he rises and rummages in the dresser at the kitchen's far end, while Joe, who had called the event "a quare foolish fight," begins its story:

"They were goin to fight at Derrylin first. And the fight was stopped at Derrylin, and they came on to Mackan.

"And it riz there."

P rejoins us at the hearth with papers in his hand. Looking down at them and remembering he told me the fight erupted during a Twelfth of July parade, he draws on his cigarette, frowns, and says:

"It states there that the fight was on the thirteenth. You can have a look at that yourself there. Just bring it to the door and give it a wee rough goin over. You see Mackan Fight at the top of it there."

With the ballat, I follow P to the open doorway, where we stand with our backs to the sky's cool light. "Is this the song that was written by Ma-guire?" I ask. P is standing by me, looking with me:

"Aye, it tis. But I'm afraid that the song is not just perfectly written down, you know. It was only a young girl that wrote it, a National or ele-mentary school girl.

"And the person gave it out, she was an old woman of course. She wouldn't have the genuine version of it, you know. But I was lookin at it yesterday, and it seems to me it's worded all right.

"It's long years now since I heard it sung. I hadn't much interest in singin at the time, but I remember a fellow singin it.

"I was tellin you about the poet Charlie Farmer. And this boy had all the songs that Charlie Farmer made, and amongst them he had this Mackan Fight. And of course if I had been a bit older I would have got the song from him; he had the real genuine way of it, you know."

Behind us the sky widens, lambent, clear, wet. Milky light runs over the papers in our hands. P continues:

"But whether that is right or not I do not know. There was one night I was down at Johnny Boyle's with his mother, and the talk came around about Mackan Fight, and, says I, there's not anyone has got Mackan Fight in this country.

"Aw, she says, I have it.

"Oh, says I, Missus Boyle have you got it?

"She says, I have.

"Well, says I, you'll give it out.

"Oh, she says, it's too late the night. She says, I'm not in form.

"So, she says, I'll have Patsy—that's the wee niece—she says, I'll give it out to Patsy, she says, and she'll write it.

"So there it is now. As I got it."

Having it, Mrs. Boyle could not withhold it after P's firm request, just as he had to pass it to me once I asked. It is written on four small sheets of lined paper, on the back of a grocery list for Cathcart's store in Bellanaleck, and it reads:

Written by Patsy Cornyn

Mackan Fight

I implore you, gentle mind,
My nation to refine,
To enlighten my feeble invocation.
My mind is deflustoraded
To see my friends degraded
And banished to the shades of obsturation.

How dismal was his cry,
Transcured with weeping eyes,
By means of that rapacious monster,
Who swore away our lives
From our children and wives;
We are convicted by Jibb, that bloody bulker.

On the 13th of July,
Of the year of twenty-nine,
Being the time of these bloody No Surrender,
They were cheering loud and shrill,
To they came to Mackan Hill,
For the face of a papish pretender.

Where they drew up their lines,
In square and rank and file,
The cry was for No Pope or No Surrender.
But with steadfast hope,
They who consmate the Pope
All his nuns and crucifix pretenders.

Our gallant lights are fame,
Propathing they came
To confront these bloody tigers in battle.
With our pitchforks made of steel
Who forced them for to yield
Though their bullets like hail did rattle.

Through bogs and quick did they run,
Who flung away their guns,
And mercy was the cry of these villains,
When they met the popes,
They soon changed their notes:
Quite different to the Boyne or William.

The first of our bleeding swains
That fell from Montiagh plains
Was that gallant Ignatius MacManus,
Who with faith and courage bold,
May the Lord receive his soul,
Like a martyr, he died on the gallows.

Where his innocent blood did fall,
It stained the flags and walls,
And it cried unto Heaven's bright mansion.
They strove but all in vain
They never could get it cleaned;
It remained there a token of vengeance.

Frank McBrien was tried the first,
Accused for a breach of trust,
And all our loving brethren had to suffer,
Who never should impart
The great secrets of our hearts
Or to any damned heretic discovered.

Now I will drop my quill
Upon Mullineny Hill,
Where the trumpet of Joshua was sounded,
Where McDonnell of great fame,
May glory shine on his name,
He was the hero that day that commanded thousands.

Its formal invocation and envoi, its lexical bravado, sound schoolmasterly and seem characteristic of the poet Maguire. Its aabccb rhyme scheme was used by many of the local poets.[4] Complete, contained, P defers to it. As a singer who believes in the truth of received poetry, he often quotes bits of song to sum up his own feelings, his affection for Ireland, his political position. As my friend, he would like the song to tell the story. But scanning the text, I find it less complete than his earlier account: "It doesn't tell the part about the sow, does it?"

At my shoulder, P replies, "No, it does not." He takes off his glasses.

"Yet," I say, "that seemed pretty important."

Together we return to the hearth, and while the tape recorder turns, he sits and patiently answers:

"Aye that's right.
"Well, it was supposed that riz the whole trouble:
    Mackan Fight.
"That the opposite side, the Protestant Orangemen, was goin by and they drew out a dagger and stuck this sow belongin to this man, just down the road, at Monaghan's.
"Of course, there wasn't any of his generation there at the time. It was a man the name of Howard. Howard was the owner of the place.
"And they stuck this sow.
"She was crossin the road.
"And that put up the blood, of course, and then
    the fight started there,
    but it calmed down, I think.
"But I think then they went on, and this wee meetin was goin to be held someplace around Derrylin.
"And they held the meetin and on their way home, the trouble started. But it didn't just develop proper till it came here to Mackan Hill, I think."

P pauses, tossing the butt of his cigarette into the fire. Joe is poised at the edge of his big armchair, the tongs loose in his hands. I ask no question, but encourage P into repetition and continuation by saying, "So the fight started at Peter Monaghan's."

"Aye, it was, well, the first origin of it anyway. That's where it started first; the trouble riz there. And this sow or pig was stuck.
"And then it riz the anger and indignation on both sides, I suppose.

And it started off there, and then they went on ahead and assembled at Derrylin, and when it was over then, of course, they started to shout party slogans, you see.

"That thing is goin on yet, of course: such as No Pope, and things like that, you see, and one thing brought on another till the fight on Mackan Hill there.

"Our side took a notion they'd oppose them.

"The fight started and there was *two men killed* just there on the Cross, here below this side of Mackan Hill.

"And that was that.

"The military or Yeomen came along and they arrested these two men who had done the wrong.

"And they were tried here in Enniskillen, and one of them was *hung*. He had got his reprieve. The Viceregal Lodge was in Dublin at the time, and there went an appeal to the Lord Lieutenant for his reprieve, and the *Lord Lieutenant granted* reprieve to him.

"Oh aye. He got reprieve but he was executed before the news came back that he got it. Of course there was no cars in them days or no way of quick conveyance or road transport, and it was horseback, I believe, that it was a priest that went (I'm not sure of that), and when he came back, he came gallopin in with his reprieve

but the execution was over.

"The body was brought up Lough Erne here on opposite—just where we turn for Kinawley—up the Lough, the remains was carried in a boat. His remains was carried up the Graffy Lane and brought to Kinawley Cemetery.

"He was Ignatius MacManus. He's buried in Kinawley.

"And there was another man, the name of Francis O'Brien, or McBrien. He was tried, but they couldn't just get genuine proof to ask the death sentence. He got so many years, what number of years I really do not know, but he got a *substantial* number of years of imprisonment. Yes.

"It started in the year twenty-nine. On the thirteenth."

Slowly, without flash, P's voice carried the event from its beginning at the farm where Rossdoney Lane comes upon the Derrylin Road, to its completion in MacManus' burial near Saint Naile's Well.

He stops, his gaze in the fire. Taking the tongs from Joe, he pinches out a coal to light our cigarettes, and I push him again: "You mentioned, when we were drivin by Hannah's Cross, about a Dummy."

"Yes. It twas supposed that there was a man the name of Dummy, and that he was deaf and dumb. And that it was him that stuck these two Protestant men. One of them was Mealey, I believe, and the other was Robinson. Was he Robinson?"

P's question swings the topic to Joe, who has been listening closely and answers, "He was Scarlett." P lets smoke rise from the cigarette sheltered in his palm, shifts in his seat, and agrees:

"Aye, Scarlett. Aye, Scarlett. There was three; there was three men anyway. I don't know was there three killed, but there was two anyway, Mealey and Scarlett. And Robinson was badly injured, but he recovered out of his injuries.

"But I think Mealey and Scarlett was killed. Scarlett lived in Gortdonaghy. Where Mealey lived, I just can't say, but I'd say that he was local in them days. There's no name of his around this District now."

P rests for another puff. Joe takes things in hand:

"He might have lived in Gortdonaghy. There was several farms in Gortdonaghy thattime, and I think he lived in one. Robinson lived down here in Tonyheig."

Through conventional repetition, I keep the topic alive: "So they were goin to a local Orange celebration." P accepts my offer, "Aye, a local Orange celebration, what they called District Meetings." And Joe adds:

"Well, in them days, they used to walk, do ye know. They used to get out and walk to such and such a place. They had appointed houses for Lodges for holdin their meetins."

A new subject has risen. P expands it:

"They had to walk, for there was no transport in them days. It was all walkin. Even there was a meeting in Enniskillen, they would walk maybe twenty mile to it. There was no such thing except donkeys to ride on.

"I don't think, even in twenty-nine, that there was many carts. I think it was donkeys' backs that the burden was on, the same as the elephant.

"Well then gradually, gettin up to eighteen and sixty, around that, the carts were pretty plentiful. Aye.

"But there was no carts, I believe, at that time in this part of the country.

"I don't think so now."

The comparability of affairs—the cry of No Pope and No Surrender—carries the past into the present, while the evolution of transportation estranges the past, separating us from the deaths on Mackan Hill. Times were different as well as the same. In that frame, I bring the topic around once more: "There were laws, weren't there, against Catholics having guns at the time?" Quickly P answers, clearing the stage for three personal anecdotes:

"Oh yes there was. They had no guns atall. They hadn't a gun. The Catholics had no firearms atall. No firearms.

"The Orangemen had guns, what they call flint guns. I saw the one that was at Mackan Fight.

"It was a descendant of the man that was killed that had it. I worked in William Dowler's. Billy Dowler they called him. That's where I saw it.

"And Billy was cleanin this gun.

"He says, That's a bit of a treasure.

"Says I, Is it? Says I, It seems to be an old gun ◊.

"So he says to me, he says, That's a keepsake.

"He says, That belonged, he says, to my uncle.

"He was killed, he says, at Mackan Fight.

"Well, the mountins on that gun was as bright as that there."

P lifts the tongs. The steel gleams.

"I believe it might be in Jack Armstrong's yet."

P turns the tongs. A liquid sheen flows down their shafts, while Joe agrees, "I'd suppose it's there yet," and P continues:

"I expect it is. Oh aye. I saw it some years after again.

"Madeline says, There's an ould thing, she says, and me father prized it very highly. She says, That ould gun, she says, and I wouldn't be *bothered* with it.

"So I seen the gun that was at Mackan Fight,
                    one of the guns.

"And the Catholics had only farm implements.

"It says in the song: With their pitchforks made of steel, they surely made them yield.

"It was old, what they called, forged forks—big thick rough grains in them, you know. They weren't made in the same shape as the modern ones. I saw one of them too.

"It was supposed to be used in Mackan Fight now. I saw it surely.

"An old man showed it to me and said it twas used in Mackan Fight.

"It twould be on Derryhowlaght Hill I saw it. It twas an old man of eighty.

"And he says, Did you ever, he says, see one of those. (He was a school-teacher's brother.)

"Says I, No Pat—his name was Pat MacManus—no, says I, I never saw one of them.

"Says I, I never saw one of them before, what is it?

"He says, That's a homemade pitchfork, he says, what they call a forged fork.

"He says, That has a bit of tradition behind it.

"Says I, What tradition has it?

"Well, he says, that was used, he says, at Mackan Fight.

"He says, On their retreat back, they came in here, he says, and they threw it in some particular place. And, he says, it lay there, he says, and me father condemned it altogether and was goin to do away with it, he says, and it twas mislaid, he says, and, he says, since we have grew up into manhood, we have left it aside, he says, and there it is, lyin there in that corner, he says, maybe this fifty years. And, he says, I forgot all about it, but, he says, I knew its origin.

"He says, There it tis now.

"So it was only about that width, more narrow than a modern pitchfork, and very big, rough grains on it, you know. Aye."

Its wrist gripped in his left fist, P's right hand extends, cupped beyond his knee. The middle fingers, held together for the grains of the forged fork, separate to emulate the upward-curving thin tines of a modern pitchfork.

A matter of fact, of memory as much as creativity, speaking history requires restraint. Truth is its own art. P's is a spontaneous personality, comfortable at the edge, accustomed to risk, expressed best in a musical style called wild. To tell of Mackan Hill, he bound himself tensely, and it felt good to abandon the far past for anecdotes into which his pent spirit could run. He sits up now, his hands on his knees, his eyes in the fire, receiving my thanks. Possessions—tea, historical information, song texts—must be shared. He is a generous man:

"But there was no call for the fight atall. It was just only at the same time that one crowd was suspicious of the other.

"I think that if both parties concerned had the normal proper wit and had confidence in each other, I think this Trouble wouldn't have started atall.

"Of course bigotry was at very high tension at that time, you know. I think they had been pretty troublesome times before and after that too, I understand.

"But I disagree with the whole fight, with the result that I didn't recognize the song so very much. I'm not so interested because, really, I'm teetotally against that sort of thing of people fightin in their own country.

"I wouldn't like to see anyone killed. I'd be more inclined to do a good turn than do a bad one. I don't like it. Really.

"I detest it now.

"I hate to recall it to you because it's a very grievous story to have to explain.

"I'm very sorry to have to give any quotations about it atall.

"But that's not holdin me back."

Peter Flanagan is a man of many deeply considered, fitfully pondered opinions. His position on Mackan Fight is not simple, but it is clear. It interests him enough to know its history, but not enough to memorize its song. Yet he has a large repertory of political and patriotic songs. When he told the story, though he was less strident than Michael Boyle, he gave the Catholics plenty of reason to fight. They were threatened by men who displayed their mettle in murdering a pig. Like Mr. Boyle, he underscored the difficulty of Catholic existence by contrasting musket with pitchfork, by making it plain that the hanged man had been reprieved and was not the slayer. The situation was intolerable. Their cause was just. Yet Mr. Flanagan opposes the fight. Not because he is against fighting for one's rights. A follower of the rebel Sinn Fein in his youth, he is a staunch Nationalist now. What he opposes is "people fightin in their own country." The fight that brings neighbors to violence is wrong.

Calling Mackan Fight "this Trouble," Mr. Flanagan obliterates differences between 1972 and 1829. The past joins the present along roads—of all, the roads P knows best—running from Ballymenone to Kinawley. Space absorbs time. So the men of Mackan are "our side," and Mr. Flanagan can strike a personal position on an event from the far past, exactly as he would on one reported in last night's news: "But I disagree with the whole fight. . . . I'm teetotally against that sort of thing."

Old history blends with news off the wireless, news of innocent people blown apart, of men interned without charge. Mackan Fight presents enduring propositions concerning existence: Innocence provides no protection from bigoted threats, persecution, prosecution, incarceration, execution. Courage will not necessarily bring victory, just as wit will not necessarily bring success. Victory may not even bring victory. Winners lose. Columcille is exiled; MacManus is hanged. Losers win. Transported men prosper.

The question smoked out of that confusion is, What can one do? The problem does not lie in innocent, brave, smart, capable people. It is a matter not of will but of circumstance. If circumstances are the product of political oppression, and rebellion seems the answer, but rebels lose, and when they win they lose worse, the course of action is anything but clear.

Politicians want people to mass into ideological consistency so they can be controlled. But helped to awareness by history of their own making, the people of the District's thirty-three Catholic households vary widely in attitude. Not all of them see cause for modern anger. Things are getting better. Citing excellent medical service and grants for capital improvement as examples, they describe life in "the wee North" as good and place all blame for the Trouble on young men of their own faith. Others, of whom there are more, point to a bitter past and to current inequities in hiring and housing, to gerrymandering that robs political power from areas of Catholic majority like south Fermanagh. Some of these feel action should be confined to the political sphere, while others feel the IRA must act. Act how?

Different people draw the line at different places. Property can be destroyed, but people cannot be killed. Yet when property is particularized, opinion clouds. Attacks on foreign-held property designed to undermine the material base of colonialism—attacks on property, even when, as is usual, no one is hurt, deprive people of jobs and therefore of money, food, life. Local people suffer or emigrate. The Lakeland Hotel near Bellanaleck, where people of both sides enjoyed a drink before a bomb lifted its roof and blew down its walls, had a British owner, but it employed Catholic people, including daughters from the local Owens and Quigley families.

Many will cede property to destruction. Something must be done. People can rebuild. The day after every bomb finds glaziers at work, masons mixing mortar, people getting on with life.

All balk at death. There is no joy in the white, cool faces of the young men who serve as death's agents. Still, some draw their line to make British soldiers fair targets. They are the "invader." A few less bring members of the police and Ulster Defense Regiment within the pale of rightful execution. They are "British tools"—but they were born here. A very few extend the dominion of death to include the Protestant elite. But no one considers their Protestant neighbors the enemy.

That is why it matters so where the dead of Mackan Hill lived. They lived right here. When Peter Flanagan cannot locate one man, a man Mr. Boyle sited precisely in Jim Foster's house on the Back Road, just across the bog from Drumbargy, he assures us "that he was local in them days." The dead were neighbors. One was the uncle of Billy Dowler, with whom P worked, of whose family P was fond. Larger conditions, dirt and rain and thundering storm, require neighbors to cooperate. They must stay engaged and in union despite ideological differences. Yet neighbor threatens neighbor. Visions rise of houses burned, of livestock destroyed, of eviction and famine. Neighbors are supposed to help build houses and help in the harvest of food, to join in preserving life. Then: neighbor murders neighbor. Deep evil is harrowed and scraped into view. The evil of politics, of distant leaders who care nothing for the little community's health, is alien no more. It has entered the neighborhood, come into the breast, and soured the clay with blood.

Mackan Fight was right and wrong, an exact and enduring symbol of the daily predicament. The political climate prevents the happy life: one must fight. The natural climate disrupts the happy life: one must cooperate. The problem of action is rammed into the forepart of the mind.

Mr. Flanagan sits, the fire of turf he won burns. Perhaps the matter of action—of what action is safe, what successful, what right—revolves in his mind, for after pulling smoke through the silence that followed his declaration, he begins another historical account in which Catholics act decisively and correctly:

"There was supposed to be another great fight, just in the town that we are goin to every Sunday.

"The landlord gave an order that the place of worship, the chapel in Swanlinbar, had to be tossed.

"I don't know what year it twas. I think after Mackan Fight. It might be in eighteen and sixty or sixty-five. Mackan Fight was in twenty-nine, eighteen and twenty-nine. I think it twas in the late eighteen-hundreds anyway.

"He gave an order:

the Swad Chapel had to be taken down,
and it had to be drawn away to build some castle.

"I didn't hear really what the stones or the buildin was goin to be converted into.

"But anyway, of course, the Catholics all opposed it.

"Why not?

"There and then.

"As the Protestants would, I suppose, if there was a church a-tossin.

"So them all assembled from all parts of Fermanagh, Cavan, Leitrim. They assembled all; it was the biggest gatherin ever there was.

"The Yeomen or the British army was goin to protect the men that was goin to take the chapel down.

"And they stayed about Swad for about a week. There was fifty or twenty thousand,
all prepared to fight.

"So the landlord reversed his decision about it. He said he'd call it off.

"There were troops comin from Enniskillen. Of course there was garrisons of troops here and there in Ireland, you know.

"And they were comin from all airts, so he gave the order that he'd extend the time to see and consider whether he'd toss it or not.

"So *nothin*, nothin happened, nothin ensued or nothin happened, and it was never tossed from that day till this."

P finishes, having provided an example of successful, just, and bloodless resistance to a threat that was patently wrong and came not from a neighbor but from a landlord. Joe carries on:

"So the mornin they were goin to toss it,
they got him dead in bed that mornin,
Lord Cole."

Five miles north of Swanlinbar, four miles due west of Mackan, back in the trees, Florence Court, seat of the Coles, spreads its symmetrical bulk. Its country Georgian facade, its bold hallway and rich plasterwork remain to be seen. The present inhabitants, upon whom the mansion descended as a surprise, have come from East Africa to inhabit a wing. Soon, after writing sentimentally about their Irish home,[5] they will make off with the best of the furnishings, abandoning to the public this sturdy stone monument to mid-eighteenth-century pretension. Here, according to Joe Flanagan, Lord Cole died in his sleep, turned black as a boot, while troops stood to defend his whimsical destruction of a holy place. P continues:

"He was an ancestor of this Cole here. Though this is not a real Cole that's here now. The last of the generation of Coles has died. This man was some relative; he was out of Kenya."

Joe adds, "He would be the grandfather of this Cole or great-grandfather."

P: "It was one of the Coles surely."

H.G.: "So he was one of the Coles of Florencecourt. And he owned all the way to Swad?"

Joe: "Oh, he did surely."

P: "He did indeed. It twas all the landlord's estate. They were liftin the rents, you see. There was a rackrent put on all the wee farms, you see."

Joe: "Their forefathers was all generals and big fellows in Cromwell's army. And every one of them got as much in this country as their eye could see."

P: "But then all the chapels was under government control, you see. And then Dan O'Connell, you know that song I sing about him. And he said that he'd pass a bill and tried and did, in fact, pass it, what they call Emancipation, so that the Catholics had their church free from the bonds of the British government.

"He fought and fought for two or three years and he got the Emancipation Act passed.

"And that's what freed,
          that's what freed the Church.

"And after that the government never interfered with the Catholic Church."

With quick efficiency, the confrontation at Swanlinbar is joined into a historical structure of religious and economic grievance. In Cromwell's day, when priests were hunted and Catholics celebrated Mass under trees in the fields, foreign lords took the land. "The priests had to go into caves, in the mountains," Joe Flanagan said, "and the people too. Their chapels was tossed. It was shockin." Profane landlords made monasteries into demesnes. Their descendants rackrented the natives. The men of Mackan were slaves and serfs, "they were even apprehended and molested goin to their place of worship on Sunday." Daniel O'Connell had to fight. His victory became law. But after Emancipation, the landlord still cramped people on their wee farms and threatened to destroy their chapel. Of course men assembled to protect it. "There and then."

And of course their valor was commemorated in song. People disagree on which Maguire composed "Mackan Fight," but they agree that, whoever he was, he wrote "The Swad Chapel Song" too. Yet in notes assembled by the Irish Folklore Commission and kept in the great archive of the Department of Irish Folklore at Belfield, Eamon Anderson, son of Master Anderson, attributed the song to a schoolteacher from Swanlinbar named Mary Byrne. The Swad Chapel poet was a master of the idiom. The song has the real scholarly style.

In a public house, P Flanagan met an Enniskillen man named Cunningham, a stout stonemason known "to have sight of songs." He asked P if he had "Swad Chapel." P said he did not, and asked him to rehearse a verse of it. He did, and promised to have his wife write the words out. She did, but the ballat has been lost.

"I never heard The Swad Chapel Song," Hugh Nolan said. "And I think that there's no one has it now. It'd be, do ye know, some of the last generation that had it.

"There was men at that stage in history and they'd have a song and they could sing it, but they mightn't be more than able to write their own name, do ye see.

"And that was the cause of alot of songs goin out of existence. Because the people that had them wasn't fit for to *write* them down, and then nobody else bothered about it.

"They'd listen to a person singin, and they'd enjoy the song, but the thought never occurred to them that it would be a good job to get that song wrote down, do ye see."

Often I heard mention of "The Swad Chapel Song," but I did not hear it until late in November, and when it came, it came like no other. Its singers brought their song out like a secret treasure. As they opened it, pure force rose slowly, expanding through the shop, filling it, agitating the crowd, gripping every man. Invisible cables snapped. Unmoored, the room drifted into isolation, moving under its own power.

Until then the night had been like many others, a Sunday for south Fermanagh men to cross the Border past the blasted customs hut for a drink in Swad. They came out of the cold, bursting through the frigid doorway to pack along the counter and around the shop, muffled in warm clothes. Huddles of men traded cigarettes and sent emissaries to the bar. Back they wove, balancing fistfuls of black drink through the crowd that thickened, shifting as one uneasy beast, blurring in the smoke and smell of warm wool and porter. Heat and patternless sound increased until the right request met the right mood within the men obliged to entertain. They took the lead. Night began to pulse. On the bar, amid the accumulation of undrunk drinks offered with a quick nod and winky smile, my tape recorder turned evenly. The microphone at the end of its long cord was passed around, up and down, as the courage to perform was pressed on new men, and the crowd pulled behind their leaders toward unity.

Things as usual begin with Peter Flanagan. Bowing at last to request, he slips the flute from his pocket and drives through "The Belfast Hornpipe," called "Burke's" by those around him. He laughs, plays again, and having wrung attention from the men at the middle of the counter, tells young Hugh Collins to play too. Standing at P's side, playing for him while he sits and pours his glass full and drinks it off, Hugh's fingers ripple the barrel of the flute for a couple of tunes before returning the instrument to P, who swings into the shop pushing the cheap tin whistle far past its capacity. High, fluttering sound circles the room and dies away. Goodmanning turns back into chat. The loudness of many conversations comes once more.

A drink passes. People stir in the smoke. Separately answering the demands of his company at the front of the shop, square by the door, Owney

McBrien, a sturdy, grand singer from Killesher, north of Kinawley, sings "The Derrylin Fair," composed by his brother-in-law, describing the fair's wily, wordy hawkers and cataloging its commodities: "Everything you call for, everything you want . . . everything from ould hats to women's underwear, from undershirts to corsets, sure, you'll get them in the Fair." Subdued but strong, his rollicking song had gathered listeners who mumbled a few words in unison, and now it brings a wish from a man whose request is always the same and so frequently made that he is nicknamed the song's title, "The Rocks of Bawn." With his elbows on the bar behind him and his eyes straight ahead, Owney sings out manfully, and when he is done the crowd breaks into applause, a higher and more general kind of goodmanning. He has assembled a following. Neatly dressed, he stands, a burly man in mid-life, topped with a natty fedora. While those nearby shush the talkers, Owney draws volume from his big chest and sings with slow power:

> When I was young and foolish, my age being twenty-four,
> I left Lough Erne's lovely banks and to Boston I sailed o'er,
> And there I met a lady gay of honor and renown,
> And from her shores I asked the way to famous New York town.
>
> What do you think young man, she says, along with me to stay,
> And let us talk of Ireland and Lough Erne another day.
> I have ranches down in Texas, I have horses by the score,
> And I'll lead you down to the Rio Grande, it's far from Erne's shore.
>
> Ah no, kind lady, pardon me, your wealth I do disdain.
> I'll go with you some other day, your fond love to maintain,
> For there is no night or lady bright is half so fair as you,
> But Erin's dells, its braes and glens to leave them I would rue.
>
> How could I leave Lough Erne's banks where my young Molly dwells?
> Your castles and your mansions are to me like prison cells.
> Were you ever on Lough Erne when the sun was setting low,
> And the purple and the heather and the hills a fiery glow?
>
> Your castles and your mansions are the best that e'er was owned,
> Your steers and donkeys in the ring are the best in San Antone,
> But I'd give them all had I my call and more I would bestow
> For to feast my eyes on Ireland and lovely Erne's shore.
>
> Ah, the fair of Enniskillen is the grandest fair of all,
> For the colleens are the sweetest and the boys they are straight and tall.
> So, I'll bid adieu to Texas too, for I'll see it never more,
> For I'm going back to Ireland and lovely Erne's shore.

Clapping cracks and splatters through the shop, swells and brings attention to Owney's corner, to song. Up the bar, Peter Flanagan steps out of his company. "Good man, Flanagan," says a man by him as P turns to the crowd, saying, "Now I'll sing a song. It's about General T. F. Bourke."

"Go on," they say, "good man." Noise persists as P's voice rises: "As you all may know, he commanded the Irish Regiment and he was captured and he was transported to Van Dieman's Land, with the result he dreamt—it's all about a dream now—he dreamt that he stood on the green fields of Erin, you see. And the air is a very familiar air to alot of people, namely O'Donnell Abu. O'Donnell Abu."

Small, in black, the curls around his head, the clatter around his ears, P turns in the center of the shop, rung by smoke, hard men, and racket. "I'm goin to sing now. It's concernin T. F. Bourke, the Fenian general imprisoned in Van Dieman's Land. The same as John Mitchel. And he dreamt this dream that I'm a-goin to sing about."

Around him the room spins, buzzing, blurring in loudness. Men stare and talk. "Go on, go on ahead," someone says.

"I will," says P softly to himself, then the voice rises and widens magnificently, the shop falls suddenly quiet:

Lonely and sadly one night in November,
I lay down me weary head for to repose
On my pallet of straw which I long do remember,
Overpowered by sleep I fell into a doze.

Tired from working hard, down in yon prison yard,
Night brought relief to my well-tortured frame,
Locked in my prison cell, surely an earthly hell,
And I fell asleep and began for to dream.

I dreamed that I stood on the green fields of Erin,
Premeditating on what was to be done.
Ah, surrounded by comrades, no enemy fearing.
On stand was the cry, every man to his gun.

I thought that I saw our brave noble commanders,
Mounted on chargers in gorgeous array,
Oh, with their green gilt with gold and their bright shining sabers,
On which stands the sunbeams of freedom that day.

On was the battle cry, Conquer this day or die,
Sons of Saint Patrick all fight for liberty,
Show neither fear nor dread, vanquish the foe ahead,
And cut down their horse, foot, and artillery.

On came the Saxons then, facing our bold Fenian men,
But soon they reeled back before our pike volunteers,
Whose cry was, Remember still Wexford and Vinegar Hill,
New Ross, Father Murphy, and his bold shelmaneers.

Bang, bang, the cannons flew, lines they were soon cut through.
Men upon both sides were dying or dead.
But our Fenian men on oath were bound to die or to hold their ground,
And back from the vengeance, the proud Saxons fled.

The green flag was floating high, beneath the azure sky,
When every man, he cried out, Go on gloriously.
Ah, come from your prison Bourke, Irish men have done their work.
Aye, and God, He is with us, aye, and old Ireland is free.

I dreamt as the night clouds were rapidly closing,
I saw lyin stretched on the crimson, gold plain,
Ah, beneath the moon's pale beams, death's sleep reposing,
And comrades I knew I would never see again.

While over the mountain track, homewards I hastened back,
With joy Mother fainted, now hollered, now screamed,
With the shock of which I awoke just when the day it broke.
I found myself an exile, and all was a dream.

Applause thunders. "Good man," they yell as P., laughing, returns to the bar. Emigration and exile, valiant defense of home, warfare and sacrifice, the topic becomes Irish heroes, Irish martyrs. Owney McBrien sings "Sean South." Hugh Collins sings "Kevin Barry." Feelings tighten, heighten, expand. All coax Eddie Kelly, a shy man from Derrylin, into song. Strained at the top of its pitch, his voice threads through "The Valley of Knockanure," an ambush of patriots near Tralee, and "Molly Bawn," a man's murder of his own true love. Good man, Eddie.

Again talk rises, disassembles, and it is only loud. The shop is lost in mere noise, then in the midst of the good times a young man, trembling with excitement, picks up the microphone from the tacky counter and nervously speaks:

"There's only one or two words I can say to you the night.
"Is:
"The people in Swadlinbar is enjoyin themselves and *Sean MacStiofain*
is dying in a hunger strike.

"He is tried by the British imperialists in the *Twenty-Six* counties. So we all can enjoy ourselves tonight while poor Sean MacStiofain is dyin on hunger strike. And we all give a good clap to Sean MacStiofain.
"I hope
        that he
                is brave.
"And that he will continue his hunger strike to show up the Irish government. What they are. And what *Jack Lynch is*. And what his party are."

For an instant it is quiet. No clapping sounds. It is not that the crowd at Swad is out of sympathy with MacStiofain, who was arrested in Dublin a week ago and convicted yesterday for being a leader of the Provisional IRA. The hunger strike has proved through the twentieth century an effective goad to revolt. In a land over which famine hangs in memory, food is precious. It brings the body joy and life. As a gift, food creates social existence and echoes powerfully from blessed sacrament. Pitiful death by self-denial, the last resort of the frustrated rebel, has often shaken drowsy minds into political anger in Ireland. No one disagrees with the speaker's sentiment. Even those opposed to the violent methods of the Provos are proud of their courage and offended by government actions against them. But the speaker's words were too direct. The way to discuss the present aloud in the pub is to offer images from the past and offer them in a way at once patriotic and entertaining. Public words should be referential and complex. More cannot be done; more contention would make life impossible. The young will learn. An indirect message is sufficient for the initiated, and it frees others to take the political statement as art if they wish. The right way to bring MacStiofain into thought would be to sing "The True Love." Peter Flanagan often sings that song here; it commemorates Thomas Ashe without even mentioning Ashe, who died after being brutally force-fed through a tube rammed down his throat at the end of a hunger strike in 1917. His funeral, greater even than Charles Stewart Parnell's, massed thousands in Dublin. The volley of rifle fire over his grave, Michael Collins said at the time, was the proper oration for a dead Fenian.[6] People know. News of the failed attempt to break MacStiofain from prison provides a major topic for talk tonight within the shop's tight knots of men. They need little to remind them, so out of the pocket of quiet a small voice angered near disgust asks, "Is that it all?"

"I say it is," the young man screams into microphone: *"As a member of the Republican movement, I am proud to be an IRA man. And I hope Jack Lynch will be brought down."*

Calmed by his own explosion, his denunciation of the government of the Republic, he lays the mike aside, lifts his drink, and returns into his company. The crowd chooses to ignore his speech or treat it as entertainment, and the tape recorder picks up a scatter of goodmanning before a wave of noise breaks, washing clear words beneath the clatter of bottles and torrent of babble, bobbing with laughter. Wheels turn, gathering racket. Across the room, Peter Flanagan lilts a reel. Closer by, a man at Owney's shoulder asks for a song. As he begins, noise recedes, leaving a hollow for his voice to hoist "The Standard of Sinn Fein." Heroic names from past times—1798, 1803, 1916—and references to other songs, "The Men of Easter Week" and Thomas Davis' "A Nation Once Again," roll history into the present as Owney's deep voice, sprung with intensity, swells through the shop:

> True, ardent fellow countrymen that back up Ireland's cause,
> We are out again for freedom with our backs up to the wall,

To mobilize our forces or our freedom to regain,
And high o'er our Republic float the standard of Sinn Fein.

We are out for independence and the struggle must go on
By every means within our reach till victory is won,
And never rest till Ireland is a nation once again,
And high o'er our Republic float the standard of Sinn Fein.

It was for this Lord Edward fought and for this young Emmet died.
For this Wolfe Tone has fought and bled and thousands too beside.
For this the Men of Easter Week their blood's poured out like rain
When they flung their banners to the breeze and the standard of Sinn Fein.

Now rally round it Irish men and wave it to the sky
No milk and water tie Home Rule, let Freedom be the cry.
Those noble souls that shed their blood, they have not died in vain,
For the flag they raised is flying still, tis the standard of Sinn Fein.

So Irish men of every belt, come let you all unite
Beneath the standard of the free, the orange, green, and the white.
We have got to guard and guide us on, our freedom to regain,
And we'll have old Ireland's forces neath the standard of Sinn Fein.

Old song of civil war days, rebel cry, it still serves, calling men to unity, placing them under historical obligation to continue the old fight. Owney sang with all his strength, enveloping the song, pressing his breath through the slow, emphatic minor air, the same he uses for his signal piece, "The Battleship Sinn Fein." Between lines and stanzas they called out encouragement—"Ah ho! Good man, good man, Owney"—and clapped long and loud at the end. Bottles of stout, silent return for entertainment, assemble at his place. Talk begins to flow but soon subsides as a far-off voice rises.

Across the shop, through the smoke, a big man is standing. His cheeks are shaved pink, his hair is glossy and black as a raven's wing. A glass of stout wrapped in a heavy fist is pressed against his chest. Deep eyes hold dead ahead. By the time he has pulled attention from the bar, he is singing of Saint Patrick. "Lovely," says P, directing our ears to him:

He has consecrated
>   *three hundred bishops,*
>   *drove the snakes and serpents from our saintly isle.*
And told the people
>   *that our church would suffer*
>   *great persecution till the end of time.*

The men of Owney's corner join in on the last line, saying, "Good man, good man, Pat," at its end. He is Pat McGovern, from Cavan near Swad, I am told in whispers, and his song marches forward. Lines and clauses are bitten off sharp. Suddenly, almost audibly, silence surrounds him. His body is straight, unmoving. His song tells that Saint Patrick predicted Satan's power would continue undiminished. Just as Satan tempted Judas "to sell our Savior for the love of gold," so has he tempted his earthly bailiff in Swanlinbar to destroy the people's temple. But they rally:

> Had you been there
> > on that Friday mornin
> > the twelfth of August or the night before.
> When Grania's sons
> > they were all assembled
> > from Lisnaskea to Ballinamore.

The song's last two lines pull the men together. With P Flanagan leading, they boom the words, not in chorus but in independent assertion, each man driving the song through him as he will. Excitedly, Charles Gilleece, one of Owney's company, shoves the next verse out ahead of the crowd. Waiting for him to finish, Pat McGovern repeats it in his martial cadence and marches on to the next, which all raise simultaneously, not melodiously but triumphantly:

> My stupid brain
> > cannot state their number,
> > one hundred thousand they exceeded far,
> All payin homage
> > to the star of Europe,
> > the saintly curate of Swanlinbar.

Now, Patrick McGovern, you gather wind from deep within and blast out the apostrophe the poet addressed to the men of Montiagh. Their inactivity and division dishonor their fathers, who assembled with pitchforks at Mackan, men who would fight before seeing their chapel tossed. This is what they had been waiting for. Answering Owney's call for solidarity beneath the standard of Sinn Fein, matching their ancestors' courage with their own bold singing, the crowd roars the memory of Mackan Hill. Song explodes. Good man, they scream to the singer, touching, moving among themselves, laughing with broken emotion. The smoke from their singing drifts away, a hush lowers. They had taken the song a level too high in feeling. Prematurely it ends, and the shop is quiet, tense. People are moving with no place to go, searching with nothing to see, then Owney is standing, commanding performance. He slows the pace to suit his power, deepens pitch, and hammering the beat smoothly into melody continues:

> The Swanlinbar boys
> > were all determined
> > to repulse the tyrant and make him yield.
> And their cheers raised

to the heavenly regions;
the men knew for to encouraged be.

The sound of Owney's last word still lingers when Pat McGovern picks up the melody and sings again the verse in which the poet's "stupid brain" finds the numbers of men uncountable. That is what so charges them, a hundred thousand and more acting as one, and as soon as Pat is done, Owney repeats the verse, and when he finishes, applause engulfs him. Mere sequence is lost: "The Swad Chapel Song" is not a ballad but an immense presence. Each man stands in his company, Owney at the front of the bar, Pat, half-turned across the shop. They are joined less in the moment than in the song, which seems to revolve in perfect completion above them. Each sings the last stanzas at once, separately, unlike in text or tempo, giving the song independently back to its town. When the final word arrives in Owney's mouth, Pat is long done, for Owney's pace is far slower. Applause rolls across the shop, breaks, rolls back.

"Good man, Owney. Good man."

"You done great work," P tells him, while others call, "More, more. Go on. Go on ahead."

"He'll sing it again," says Charles Gilleece. "He'll start it from the beginnin. You'll start it from the beginnin," he tells Owney.

P silences a man attempting to start a conversation, "You ungrateful man. This man's goin to sing."

"You'll start from the beginnin," P tells Owney.

"I will. Aye," Owney says mildly.

"You will start from the beginnin. Aye. Go on ahead."

"Will you tape it?" Owney asks me softly.

"Of course," I answer.

"You will start from the beginnin," a man at his elbow says.

"I will. Aye. I'll try it anyway."

"I'll help you with bits of it, all I know," the man encourages. "All I know."

"Don't help atall," Owney the great singer replies. "I'll sing it better on me own."

"You will indeed," the man agrees happily.

Owney plants his feet and sets out:

You gentle muses
pray excuse me
for my intrusion on learning's wing.
And inspire my genius
you bards and sages;
my country's praises I mean to sing.
Tradition teaches
without consultation,
and blessed Patrick was first and all,

To Pope Celestine,
    and prune our vineyard,
        called Inisillgie or the Virgin Shore.

Ah, like Saint Peter,
    when his Master told him
        to feed his lambs and these flocks to keep,
He arranged the deserts
    the hills and mountains
        and plowed the ocean for the straying sheep.

By this time Pat McGovern has joined the song. A word or two ahead he moves into the next stanza, while Owney at the other side of the shop goes on at his own speed:

He consecrated
    three hundred bishops,
        drove the snakes and serpents from our sainted isle,
And he told his people
    their church would suffer
        most persecution till the end of time.

It came to pass
    as the Saint predicted,
        for Satan's powers, as we are told,
They are now as strong as when
    he tempted Judas
        to sell our Savior for the love of gold.
The fallen angels,
    as yet impatient,
        they drove from heaven for creatin wars,
Has as lately tempted
    that ugly bailiff
        to seizin the temple in Swanlinbar.

Oh, had you been there
    on that Friday mornin,
        the twelfth of August or the night before,
When old Grania's sons
    they were well alarumed
        from Lisnaskea unto Ballinamore.
My boys prepare in
    a moment's warning
        ye shall be guided by the morning star.
For now is the time
    to repulse the tyrant
        and save our chapel in Swanlinbar.

Owney now swells his chest and blows the song out while the crowd joins in, enacting the song's power. As the men in the poem assemble for war, men in the shop assemble for song. Living and dead, soldiers and singers unite:

> From Leitrim mountains
>> they came uncounted,
>> from Cavan hills and Fermanagh gay,
> Sayin, Where is the offspring
>> of Martin Luther
>> that dare opposes our church today?
> Our valiant heroes
>> from famed Drum Reilly,
>> Drumlane, Knockninny, and Templeport,
> And the warlike chieftain
>> from Aughnacashelem,
>> the Leitrim pikemen he led to sport.
>
> As those Milesians
>> they were all assembled
>> in rank and order, in sept and clan,
> Sure, I heard one chieftain
>> say to another,
>> Where are our brothers from unfaithful land?
> Oh, Montiagh brave,
>> have you been divided?
>> You once won laurels, but now called slaves.
> For your sons of order
>> on the hills of Mackan
>> would lose their lives or their chapel save.

"Good man, Owney." Again, chastising the sons of the men of Mackan brings a general eruption of song. Excited, Charles Gilleece starts the next verse first. Owney keeps his pace:

> My stupid brain
>> cannot count the numbers,
>> one hundred thousand exceeding far;
> All payin homage
>> to the star of Europe
>> that saintly curate in Swanlinbar.
>
> I'll lay down my pen now
>> as the case is settled;
>> come fill your glasses with rum and gin.
> We will drink a health
>> unto friend Montgomery
>> to noble Maguire and Bennison.

I'll lay down my claim
    to the men of honor
      that ne'er was guilty of crime or wrong,
And the Swanlinbar boys
    cannot be forgotten;
      it's noble to call them old Grania's sons.

This time goodmanning is gentle, calm reigns. Little remains of the night, and that passes quickly.

Michael J. Murphy, the Irish Folklore Commission's collector for Ulster, told me he once heard "The Swad Chapel Song" in Blacklion, across the bridge from Belcoo. It began and a man left. Time passed, and he returned, only to find the song still going on. He asked where they were, was told they had only gotten as far as the chapel door, and he left, saying he would return in a while once the thing was over. No one left that night in Swanlinbar. The song is rarely sung. Its performance is special, precious, its idea is troubling and profound.

The clarity of conflict at Swanlinbar slaps thought into order and drives it down through history to first things and constant principles. When the Flanagan brothers spoke of Swad, their thought dropped from Lord Cole back to Cromwell's conquest and the subsequent black days of religious persecution and economic oppression. The situation cried for response, for Emancipation and Agitation, and at last for "the biggest gatherin ever there was," men from Fermanagh, Cavan, and Leitrim, "all prepared to fight" to defend the chapel at Swanlinbar. When the Swad Chapel poet wrote the song for later men to sing, he or she broke thought and set it sailing along two lines drawn in clear opposition: the antagonists at Swad accumulate all history into themselves and personify good and evil.

The courage of the Swanlinbar boys joins them through the men of Mackan to "those Milesians," Scythians who sailed from Spain to conquer the magical Tuatha De Danann and establish the ancient line of Irish kingship running for eighty-one monarchs from Heremon, son of Milesius, who ascended the throne in the Year of the World 2738, to Roderick, who surrendered Ireland to Henry II of England, two and a half millennia later, when "churches and religious houses were plundered and destroyed without mercy and distinction; murders, rapes, tyranny, and the most unconscionable oppressions . . . made the island a most deplorable scene of bloodshed and misery."[7] So it is told in *The History of Ireland*, compiled in the early seventeenth century by Geoffrey Keating, bard, priest, contemporary of the Four Masters. Keating was almost surely a source for the Swad Chapel poet. Thus validated in myth, ennobled, the Swanlinbar boys can be called Grania's sons, the men of Erin.

At the same time, guilty of neither crime nor wrong, innocent, the Swanlinbar boys are God's sheep, unsullied heirs to the church Saint Patrick established while cleansing the Virgin Shore of hissing snakes. In Ireland, Patrick is Peter, founder of the Church, shepherd to the flocks. God gave these lambs hills to graze, oceans to stray. He prepared the world for pastoral farmers and emigrants and sent them, in Celestine's charge to Patrick, the rule of religion.

Through the Milesians and their fathers at Mackan, out of their own courageous ability to unite for war, the Swanlinbar boys embody Ireland's political destiny. Through Patrick, Peter, and Christ, out of their own innocence, they are God's sheep. When they rally to defend His church, their cheers ring to heaven. Their victory is God's.

Lord Cole is the descendant of foreign warlords. He is the offspring of Martin Luther, who dared oppose the Church. Luther, Judas, Lucifer: he is the betrayer of Christ, a man of greed and pride, tool of the fallen angels who created war. His threat is Satan's.

At Swanlinbar, the native and good meet the alien and evil, the snaky, avaricious, haughty, profane, violent. Real people enact the endless struggle of God and Satan.

Persecution, Saint Patrick predicted, will not cease until the end of time. The eternal is the background and major dimension of the story. Its temporal foreground, its narrative, is simple. Hugh Nolan's summary of events is efficient:

"I mightn't be able to relate the whole story.
"The chapel was goin to be tossed.
"And the people all turned out—och, they turned out in hundreds on the day that it was goin to be tossed.
"And, ah, they couldn't get near it;
 there was that many people around it.
"And finally it fell through, and it wasn't tossed.
"Oh aye."

A simple tale, but connected with Mackan Fight it proves oppressed farmers can cooperate when threatened. The gathering of men in oneness, even more than their victory, is the center of energy. Whether the threat is heaven's, loosed in wind and water, or man's, displayed in shouts and mechanical weapons, people can lift their agricultural tools and work together to defend home and church. They can win. Despite political Troubles relentless as weather, and weather that seems willful war against man, life can be conducted.

The heroism commemorated in song and in story is reenacted in singing and telling as people assemble behind their leaders, encouraging them, taking heart from them, working together to preserve their own history, testing, proving anew their capacity for cooperation and victory. Within tradition, through art, they claim and gain and practice the virtue of old heroes.

Telling Mackan Hill, Peter Flanagan told about Swad Chapel. Singing

"The Swad Chapel Song," men recall Mackan. Tightly, those conflicts make context for each other. They reverberate to raise a single issue: If you are courageous, virtuous in heart, innocent, virtuous in soul, and wise enough to join with those who share your conditions, you can endure, unbeaten. That idea has pure presence in The Tossing of the Swad Chapel. The victors contained sacred power and became capable of mythic action. As god-like saints create permanent features on the land, so the Swanlinbar boys rise, and their chapel "was never tossed from that day to this." Saintlike, they had only to gather and stand forth in virtue. God killed Cole.

Mackan is muddier. The threat—neighbor to home, not lord to church —was less plainly evil. Response was less plainly correct. People brought death and died as a result. Maturer, less pure than the Swanlinbar boys, the men of Mackan make a story more complex, more challenging to the mind, more open to varying interpretation. The general meaning of Mackan Hill comes in relation to Swad Chapel. The particular meanings of individual tellings vary with their distance from Swanlinbar, the degree to which they incorporate the idea pristinely present in Swad Chapel: when they rebel against intolerable political conditions, modern men, local farmers, serve, like saints, as God's agents in the interminable war against evil; they are right.

Things look hopeless at Swad, then God reveals His support in sudden victory. In Hugh Patrick Owens' telling of Mackan Hill, God's support, and thus the virtue of the men, is comparably clear. Things look hopeless, then a priest prays:

"There was a fight at Mackan.

"It was a faction fight, what they call a faction fight. It was between Protestants and Catholics, you see.

"Well, they fought with billhooks and with scythes. There wasn't any guns. They had no guns.

"And a young priest was lookin out his window on Derryhowlaght. He was home, do ye see, and he was lookin out at the fight.

"And his mother says to him,
     the Catholics were losin and she says to him:
"For God's sake, Son, can you do nothin?
"He says, I was waitin for you to ask, he says.
"And he went into the Room, and he started prayin, and from that time on, the Catholics started winnin.
"And not another one was killed.
"Now, my father made a song on it. He made a song on that fight.
"But it's lost."

Hugh Patrick Owens is sitting forward, elbows pressed on the arms of his chair, a Windsor "made out of the hedge" by John James Lunny, Tommy's deceased elder brother. A cake of fadge bakes in an iron oven above the turf smolder. We sit in its sweet smell. Outside, his sons are rattling loads of hay into a shed. Mr. Owens holds his eyes on mine to tell me of his father, the poet, Thomas. He was raised by Old John of the Ford, keeper of the family ledger, and he blinded himself with books. One eye went, but he would not stop reading, the other snuffed. Before his death thirty years ago at the age of eighty-three, he would sit, sightless, in that chair and dictate the poems growing in his mind to one of the Murphys, who came from the back of the hill to ceili and write them down:

"Poetry makin was as easy as walkin for me father. He was well-educated. He'd sit in the corner there, makin them up.
"He could compose poems the best. Ah, he made a hat of them."

During bread-making, Mrs. Owens has been moving with quick grace between the hearth and the large table beneath the back window, listening as she worked. She leaves the kitchen now, while Mr. Owens, his eyes steady, recounts his father's career.

Without getting "tuppence for it," Thomas Owens served as Secretary of the Land League for the "Schoolands," an irregular strip of land running from Lough Erne to Benaughlin and including Rossdoney and Sessiagh. Rents paid through an agent named Bennison at Ballyconnell went to the Commissioners of Education. Before the Land League rallied the people, Hugh Pat tells me, landlords rackrented their tenants, raising the rates at their pleasure to drain all prosperity off the wee hills into their own purses. Then: "He got them united. And they agitated. They fought for the Three F's and they won. They won the greatest victory Ireland got for years and years." Rates were lowered and stabilized, land tenure was secured, and rate payment was made to lead to fee-simple possession. Now all the farms on the Schoolands are owned outright.

"Ah, but the landlords still wanted their rackrent. They wanted to penalize their poor tenants.
"And then they shot Lord Leitrim up here.
"Oh, he was a bad pill.
"He was the bully buck.
"He was above bein spoken to, and he wanted to be lord supreme. He wouldn't humble himself to sell to the tenants. Oh, no.
"Then they shot him in his bed at night. Lord Leitrim.
"And no one suffered for it, *no one*.
"And that scared them all,
        them all agreed to sell.
"Yes."

His eyes remain in mine. Smoke is drawn in and released, his gaze does not shift. "Yes," he repeats, unblinking.

Silence burns between our eyes, an anger so old, so terrible. Mrs. Owens waits for it to cool, then hands me an envelope. When her husband mentioned his father's poems, memory stirred. With a little searching, she has recovered a fraction of the lost works of Thomas Owens. One poem in the envelope is the melancholy soliloquy of an exile in Brooklyn recalling his lovely, lost home in Arney. The other two are on Mackan Hill. The first lacks a page and begins on the sheet numbered "two":

> The Mackin Heroes they knew no fear,
>   and they were Victorious front and rear.
> Their Friends flocked in from the Country round,
>   but when the yeo's were found,
> The Wemon removed the wounded and dead,
>   and the Armed Bullies Homeward fled.
> Four dead yoeman lay on Mackin Hill,
>   and the spot where they died is marked out still.
> Many more were wounded in the Fray,
>   their names are well known to the present day.
> The Mackin warriors received not a scratch,
>   for the Prince of darkness for the Almighty was not a match.
> A young Priest was near to the raging fight
>   and the Old people said it was He won the fight.
> He prayed to God, and God heard the prayer,
>   and His people won the Victory back then and there.
> Ignitus McManus did give his life
>   on the Scaffold in sight of his Son and Wife.
> For God and Ireland his life he gave,
>   he died a true man and a Hero brave.
> By his side two young Montgomerys did proudly stand
>   ready to die for faith and father-land.
> They were reprieved and transported to New South Wales
>   and their bones rest there.
> They lived and died true Irish men,
>   but the home of their Fathers they ne'er saw again.
> And Old Man Kerrin and his two brave Sons,
>   they faced the yoemen with their Guns.
> They were transported to the Australian Shore,
>   but one died on Sea on the Voyage o'er.
> The memory of Mackin will long cherished be
>   and those names be written in History.

Things peak in one of Thomas Owens' couplets when the idea set clearly in "The Swad Chapel Song" (but diffused tentatively, diminished to hope in "Mackan Fight") is carried onto the hazier landscape of Mackan Hill and planted forthrightly. The clash of Catholic and Protestant is the clash of the Almighty and the Prince of Darkness. God's soldiers, the Mackan heroes, escape without a scratch. They align with the Swanlinbar boys in cherished memory. The ground they hallowed is pointed out still, as the next of the poems, which exists complete, emphasizes:

A Tourist-Visit-to Arney and Macken

To Arney a Tourist did find his way;
    he came along to pass the day.
At the Points he alighted and made for Cassidy's Store
    and his well stocked Bar that stands next-door.
He praised Jim's Biscuits, they were a treat,
    washed down by good Old Whiskey neat.
Soda water, stout, or wine,
    Jim Cassidy's Drinks are all genuine.
In a splendid Car Jim drove him round,
    as to his charges, no fault he found.
He expressed a wish to see Macken Hill;
    Jim drove him round with his good will.
He was told the story of the true men bold
    and heard the tale that was oft times told:
How the men of Macken the Yeomen defied,
    how they fought and conquered and on the Scaffold died.
The Yeos were all armed with baynot and Gun,
    from they Scythe blades and pitchforks they cut and run.
The Tourist back to Arney came,
    tired and thirsty but he was game.
He was greately pleased with his day out,
    and refreshed himself with boiled stout.
He put up a drink for those stand in round,
    and left for Enniskillen safe and sound.
His praise of Arney seemed sincere,
    for the Heros of Mackin he raised a cheer.

Note:

The times are changed for the better too,
We are no longer trampled by the Tyrant crew.
We can hold up our heads and hold them high
And will hold them higher in the near bye and bye.

The scene is easily imagined. Alighting at the railroad station, now a home, the tourist walks the Station Road, then finds his way the mile east from the Five Points to the Arney Cross. He enters the public house built onto a store there, buys some drinks, and gets repaid with entertaining chat. The most important local event to tell him about is Mackan Fight. He listens, seems interested, and is taken to see the site. Perhaps forty years later I was comparably treated in the same pub, no longer a thatched house called Cassidy's, but a sleek modern bar, The Regal, owned by Tommy Gilleece.

It is momentarily fashionable to compare tourism and field research. Some tourists are amateur scientists, and some scholars are mere tourists, collectors of curios. Individual days of holiday travel and ethnographic study can look the same. But the two endeavors are radically differentiated by seriousness of purpose. The tourist left Arney for Enniskillen. So did I, but I came back again and again, to enjoy myself, have a drink or two, see the sights, certainly, but more to engage in the task of understanding reality as it is constructed by other people. As a tourist, I saw Mackan Hill as something out there, farmland green in the sun, the location of a past battle. As a scholar, I felt Mackan Hill lift within me as the major landmark in the historical topography of a foreign consciousness—human, like mine, and therefore penetrable, but so differently developed and environed as to be approached, explored, and mapped only with humility and fear. The field-worker is afoot in strange country on the most profoundly human of all quests. He is the confused, serious tourist of the interior landscape.

Thomas Owens' poems are among those other songs mentioned by Michael Boyle and Hugh Nolan. Unlike Maguire's "Mackan Fight," they were not generally accepted for singing. But they are more like Maguire's composition than they are different. Like his, and like Hugh McGiveney's song of the Ford, they are commemorative, built after the event out of remembrance. They preserve dates, names, details, and less tell than refer to the story. Though Owens' poems were not swept into oral tradition, they are authentic expressions, performances on paper. Compare their style and sentiment with those of other men, and you will find them deserving the name—depending on your tradition—of "folklore" or "art." They bear the stamp of their maker, and present collective values sensuously. From the dry silence of an old envelope, they speak for many who do not—the inarticulate, the shy, the dead.

Hugh Nolan lives to speak. Native and artist, he is doubly prepared, and when I ask about Mackan Hill the gates of memory swing back and history spills quickly into the narrative channel, racing, expanding into motionless pools of information, then rushing, surging once more. Like Mr. Boyle, Mr. Nolan interrupts marching men with technical and geographical description, shifting modes to make his telling something more than a factual narrative, something other than fiction, a textured "story of history"

"Well, that was a fight, unfortunately, like many other fights that took place in this country. It was between Catholics and Protestants.

"Well, the Twelfth of July, do ye see, they do celebrate the victory at the Boyne in this country, the Ulster Protestants; they're known as the Ulster Orangemen.

"Well, this was on the thirteenth of July.

"And they started a parade from about Bellanaleck.

"And they paraded on up the road, and they were usin terrible
    ah, terrible language towards the Catholics
        as they went along.

"And they didn't spare their own side either, any of them that they didn't like. Because there was an old man tellin me that where Peter Monaghan lives now (you know that house there where you turn for Enniskillen) there was a Protestant man lived in that house.

"And he had a sow with a litter of pigs.

"And in them days, a sow, when she'd be goin to pig, would be brought into the *house*.

"And she'd be let have her pigs in the corner there.

"And they'd be kept in the house for about a week before they'd be put to some outhouse.

"And a couple of times a day, the sow used to go out, do you know, and come back *in* again.

"Well this parade was comin along.

"And this poor old man,
    and his wife,
        their sow went out.

"And of course with the noise of these fellows comin along,
    didn't they forget about the sow.

"And there was one fellow,
    and he was walkin in front
    and he had a rifle.

"There was no rifles in them days; they weren't styled rifles, they were styled carbines.

"And there was a bayonet on the top of it.

"And the sow was on the road.

"On this side, if you remark it, there's a drinkin pool there, just at the foot of that brae, facin Crozier's gate.

"The sow was nosin about.

"And damn it, he run to the sow and he put the bayonet through her.

"Killed the sow on the poor old fellow.

"But they went on anyway.

"And the people away up the country, do ye see, heard the noise of them comin.

"And in them days, the Catholics, do ye see, they daren't have arms, but they did have weapons that they called pikes. The blacksmiths used to make them; ah, there was a lad and it was the shape of a fishin hook, do ye know; it was a blade, do ye see, kind of turned. And ye could run forward to a man and just give him the jab of it, do ye know.

"So anyway, the people all up the country, up be Mackan and round be Montiagh there,
    they all turned out with pikes
    for to meet these boys
    that was threatenin—

"Oh, they were threatenin to do everything that was rotten
        on the Catholics
            when they'd be comin back.
"So the two forces met, at a place they call Hannah's Cross. It's at the foot of Mackan Brae. Hannah's Cross it used to be called in days gone by. There was an old lady lived convenient to it; she was a Hannah Montgomery, and then this cross took its name from her.
"So the fight started *there*.
"And the Orangemen lost.
"The pikemen came in under them and they
        stabbed
            and whaled
                and finally the Orangemen retreated
                    on down the road.
"And some of these wounded fell here and there
        along the road
            and others of them got dragged away.
"But anyway this man that killed this man's sow at Peter Monaghan's there, he got home.
"And I'll tell you where he lived.
"You know where John Moore lives there, in Rossawalla; it's the next house to Peter Monaghan's; when you're goin to Enniskillen it's on the same side of the road.
"Aye. Well, there's a farm up there. Peter Monaghan has it now. And there was several people livin on it, do ye know. It was in small wee lots at that time.
"Well, this man lived up there.
"He was the name of Scarlett.
"Well.
"He was brought home anyway.
"And the mother had a feed of sowens. That used to be a great luxury in Ireland in them days. It was what we'd call oaten gruel *now*, do ye know—oaten meal, boiled, not thickened, but a nice drinkin, warm, do ye know, and there used to be sugar put on it—oh, it used to be great.
"So anyway, he took some of the sowens.
"And, savin your presence, I heared an old man sayin the sowens came out through the wounds.
"So it was wonderful direct punishment for what he done on the man goin up the road.
"So anyway there was a whole lot of Catholic fellows was arrested,
        and they were tried
            and they were sentenced to be *hanged*
                in Enniskillen.
"There was a jail in Enniskillen at that time, where the technical college is today. That was a jail in them days.
"So anyway, there was a petition sent to the Lord Lieutenant,

and they were granted a reprieve:
> *transportation* for life,
> *six or seven* fellows.

"So there was one man was hanged afore the messenger *landed*
> from *Dublin*
>> with the petition.

"So that's as far as I can give the details of the battle."

Mr. Nolan brings the pipe to his lips. Comforted by his generosity, thrilled by his intellect, I delight in collaborating with him in preserving his community's history. "Hugh Patrick Owens told me a priest was involved in Mackan Fight, Hugh, can you tell me about that?" He looks up from the fire, glances beyond his pipe, and patiently returns it to his lap, cradling its cool wood in his powerful hands.

"There was a priest, he prayed for the safety of the people durin the time that these ones was goin along the road,
> and before the fight took place.

"Because the way it was: every Catholic along the road thattime they weren't sure but they'd be killed, do ye see, for they'd be bound to be comin back. Aye indeed."

He pauses. His eyes close. The fire recedes into embers. As he told it, the pig's murder revealed only irrational passion, for its owner was a Protestant. The killer's oozing wounds were wonderful direct retribution, but that little circle of crime and punishment seemed not reason enough for bloody battle. Like Peter Flanagan and Michael Boyle, he put hot words in the marchers' mouths, words that feel the hotter for coming from mad killers of livestock, but the fight's cause, fear sparked by threat, appeared in need of emphasis, so Mr. Nolan hit that point again before falling silent. He is objective, not disinterested. He sits. I am used to waiting while he works in his inner archive. The fire at our feet darkens. A point of ruby shoots within, quivering. Soon I will bring new turf he will splash oil, a flame will leap, heating our faces for a furious moment. Oil makes the best of fires, they joke. The clock's tick increases. I say nothing. He speaks:

"Aye, that priest, he was a Father MacManus.
"He was a native of that locality and he happened to be home to see his people and this thing took place durin that time.
"He prayed fervently for the safety of the Catholics,
> for peace to come along
>> before things would go to the worse."

Again he stops and raises his pipe. Once it is going well, I ask when the fight took place. His answer and a new tale come quickly:

"That was in eighteen and twenty-nine, on the thirteenth of July, eighteen and twenty-nine.
"And there was another fight *before* that.

"And it was between Catholics and Protestants *too*.

"The way it started, there was some of the Catholics from Inishmore or that locality happened to be in Lisbellaw.

"And they were in some public house.

"And they came across a number of Protestants, do ye see.

"And of course the drink worked them on to arguments
and challenges.

"Finally they arranged that they would have a fight
between the two parties.

"And the Orangemen, or the Protestants, said that they'd come to Inishmore,
and that they'd have the fight in the island.

"So they did anyway.

"And, damn it, wasn't there one of the Protestant fellows killed.

"Aye indeed.

"So they rushed away back to Lisbellaw and to the surroundins and they gathered an awful, an awful armed party.

"And they came back.

"And the whole Catholics all cleared out of Inishmore over here to Rossdoney and to these townlands.

"And the Orangemen, or gunmen, they came to the shore there, just facin the Rossdoney Road, where it ends.

"And they fired across. They couldn't get across because all the vessels was brought across to the Rossdoney side.

"And there was a house on what they called in them days the Hill Head; it was just above the Lough a wee piece.

"And they fired at this house.

"And the house had been whitewashed.

"And when the firin was over, there wasn't a haet but the bare bricks. The whole whitewash was all cut off with bullets.

"So anyway after some time, they quit and went away.

"So the people got back to their homes again.

"So then, that was in eighteen and twenty-two. That was called the Inishmore Fight.

"And then in eighteen and twenty-nine then, the fight took place at Mackan.

"I heard about it. I often heared me father and old men about this country talkin about it."

Past events worth saving in story live simultaneously as autonomous works of art (texts), as situated communications (the foci of social interchange), and as cultural essences (nodes in a collective network of concept). Cultural essence matters most. It provides a reason to frame one event, and not thousands of others, as a story, a reason to preserve and ponder stories between rare performances, a reason that a story proves moving when it emerges in the social scene. Its containment of cultural essence guards a tale against death in isolation and sets it throbbing through endless metamorphosis. Alive, pulsing, it absorbs power and sends it back through the connections that bring stories meaning, while relating and interrelating meanings to force thought to values, making life meaningful.

Mackan Hill coils with the live force of "serfs" in rebellion against "bigotry." As Catholic farmers join for battle in the face of economic and religious threats, their story joins other local narratives—Swad Chapel by Peter Flanagan, the Inishmore Fight by Hugh Nolan—and places local events in a national context of liberation: Catholic Emancipation (religious freedom), the Land League Agitation (economic freedom). As connections stretch and tighten, the tensions within Mackan Fight increase.

Alone an account of courage, Mackan Hill tied to other stories becomes a tragedy, a great victory, and an "unfortunate," "quare foolish fight," a defeat. Like the Swanlinbar boys, Daniel O'Connell, and the Land League's leaders, the Mackan heroes were driven to action, and they were brave. But were they innocent? Swanlinbar and the Agitation brought death, but the dead were Satan's bailiff and one "bad pill." In Destiny's eyes, those deaths in elegant beds were right. No one suffered for them. At Mackan, two, three, or four men, local farmers, were murdered. Ignatius MacManus was hanged, his son was stunted, his comrades were banished. They were innocent by man's law. What of God's?

The Protestants who died in the Inishmore and Mackan fights were not innocent. Their threats brought the battles on. But they burned no houses. They took no lives. Their deaths were too dreadful atonement.

Mackan Hill becomes the tale of Catholic frustration. Genuinely oppressed and provoked, men have no heroic choice but to fight. Yet the foreign gentry who hold the land and prevent material success, governmental officials who administer the economy and institute intolerant, intolerable law, judges who condemn innocent men—the leaders are unavailable. They are somewhere else. Just vengeance, then, is meted out on men who do no real harm, who are not the cause but only the medium of trouble—men who are available: the neighbors.

Now: Cleverly young men rig a bomb to the ignition of a car owned by a military officer known for his hardness toward the Catholic populace. The night is cold. He lends his keys to two men so they can sit in the car's warmth, idling the engine to drive the heater while they wait out the night's length. The engine turns over. The explosion leaves only the rear axle on a street in Enniskillen. Nothing but scraps remain of two harmless men, one the son of a local postman. And bravely a young man steps into the path of a bus at Belcoo. His machine gun rips through steel and shatters the windshield. The driver, a Protestant military man, dodges. Death comes to a laborer, a Catholic father, riding the bus to work.

And then: Daniel O'Connell fought, and "after that the government never interfered with the Catholic Church," but his contemporaries and fellow Catholics fought on Mackan Hill and brought a worsening of local conditions. Families broke, the community weakened, shredding.

Upper Lough Erne. The view northward at Rossdoney Quay, Ballymenone on the left, Inishmore on the right.

Like John Ball, historic leader of the peasant revolt in William Morris' strong novel, or central figures out of a fiction by Sartre or Camus, the men of Mackan must act, whatever their actions bring. The universal dilemma of the free man trapped in unknowable circumstances is particularized with exquisite propriety for this District in the story of Mackan Fight. Acting manfully, the Mackan heroes fight not their enemies but men to whom they are interdependently bound by the ethic of neighborliness, men with whom they must cooperate if life's large battle is to be won. Their free and just actions damage their own chances for free and just existence. They die, shrink, suffer exile. More terribly, they win, and winning lose the kingdom of heaven.

Setting Mackan Hill by Swad Chapel sets both in the ultimate context: the world made by God. Now the cultural essence of Mackan Fight comes to view. When men rebel against evil, they become God's agents in His war with Satan. When men fight their neighbors, they break God's great commandment: "Love your neighbor as yourself and in that you shall live."

God, Peter Flanagan taught, wants to see what you are made of. Stand on the street before your doorway, watch smoke from the chimneys of many neighbors streak the cloudy sky. Feel within the fire of anger, kindled by unjust treatment. How, history asks, are you to live?

10

The Band

Sea-bound small island land, enveloped in one cool cloud, Ireland poses an environment for unity. Her story is division.

Ireland's epic, the *Táin Bó Cúailnge*, a tale of the eighth century set in the Iron Age, survives in three recensions in several manuscripts. No mere war between provinces, the *Tain* sets Ireland against Ulster and splits the men of Ulster, proving them treacherous when they should be loyal, loyal when supposed enemies. The climax comes not in the great battle of armies, or in the emblematic struggle of two bulls as they rage the whole of Ireland in one night until Donn Cuailnge scatters the gore of Finnbennach across the land to name it, but in the single combat of foster brothers. Cú Chulainn meets Fer Diad at the ford. For four days they fight. On the last the waters run red and the dread barbed gae bolga does its duty. Cú Chulainn lives to lament, "O Fer Diad, it is sad that I should see you thus, bloodstained yet drained of blood. . . . Our fostermother imposed on us a pact of friendship. . . . Alas! the friend to whom I served a drink of red blood has fallen. . . . Sad what befalls us, the fosterlings of Scáthach, you dead, I alive and strong. Valour is an angry combat." Cú Chulainn lived to kill his own son.[1]

When Geoffrey Keating began his *History*, half a millennium after the *Tain* was written into the Book of the Dun Cow, he first gave the names of his island: Inis alga, Eire, Inis fail, Scotia, Hibernia, Irin, Irlandia, Ogygia. Next and immediately he lists the seven ancient divisions that broke the noble isle, fatal, elder isle into two, three, four, and five parts. Late in his chronicling of kings, as Irish men divide, some to help, some to fight the Danes (latest in a long series of invaders, last before the love-entangled King of Leinster invited the English to invade), Keating pulls one of his lucid generalizations from the facts. "It was the misfortune of the Irish," he wrote, thinking on his own torn seventeenth century, "that they were never free from intestine divisions, which contributed to their ruin."[2]

Irish intestine divisions—South and North, Gael and Gall, green and orange, white and black, yes and no, Catholic and Protestant—were among the multitude of opposed pairs James Joyce hosted three centuries after Keating to propose and decompose the unity of mind in *Finnegans Wake*. As the lines in ancient art spiral forever, diverging and merging in geometric

containment, the *Wake* revolves through endless opposition and association: dichotomies resolve into unity, unities dissolve in dichotomy: time becomes space; space, time; life, death; flesh, stone; male, female; water,
earth—all becomes Ireland, the world, the fitful, cyclic dream of a Dublin
publican, father of two sons, called Humphrey C. Earwicker. Earwick is
Timeplace. Humphry was the Danish commander around whose threat
the Irish divided to inspire Keating's generalization. Keating was a source
for James Joyce as he was for the author of "The Swad Chapel Song."[3]

The *Tain*, Keating, the *Wake*—these are the great Irish myths—and
they raise the great Irish issue: the division in unity. Owned by neither
class nor tradition, that idea has driven ancient men and modern, monks
and warriors, saints and sinners, peasants and gentlemen, singers and
scholars. It is built into the silence of the island with its monuments to cor-
porate power and separate strength—New Grange, Tara, Dublin, clachans,
raths, farms. It is spoken aloud by the District's people.

Two men sit at the polished bar in the mirrored lounge of a public
house. The first is a tradesman, the second a banker, both are Protestant.
The first says that, though the second hates to hear it, the landlords treated
their tenants viciously in the past. "When they were buildin Castle Coole,"
he says, "they paid the poor workers sixpence a day. Sixpence and a bit of
barley and wheat." Castle Coole is a monstrous masterpiece designed by
James Wyatt in the coldest neoclassical mode for Lord Belmore and built of
imported stone east of Enniskillen in the 1790s.[4] "They made beer at Castle
Coole," the tradesman says, unwilling to release the topic or the eyes of his
drinking companion, "and they sold it to the workers. They didn't give it.
They *sold* it. It was an outrage." Many Protestants like himself, he says, are
Irish, lacking a drop of English blood. The landlords were, many of them,
Irish. They treated their countrymen terribly.

Two men sit in the shop of a country public house. Both are small,
tough men in tweed caps and black suits who own small, wet farms. Both
are Catholics. The first says the landlords treated their ancestors like slaves,
but then, "the Land League won Ireland's greatest victory." The second
agrees: "Aye, it was a great victory. They sent the landlords out in seventy-
nine. And then the Irish could tyrannize over themselves. Och, the Irish
acted as bad to other as what the English had."

The civil war of 1922 provides the dim, constant background of modern thought. Gunmen in trenchcoats walk the halls of memory, rapping at
the doors of midnight. Informers snivel out intelligence in the back rooms
of police stations. "The Irish," they often say, "is bad to the Irish."

The Mackan heroes were Irish. So were their Protestant neighbors
killed along the road. The Ford seems clearer, an Irish victory, and that is
how Michael Boyle told it, but Hugh Nolan emphasized that the English
gathered their army from the other three provinces of Ireland before marching into Ulster. His fight—like the *Tain*, the redundant battles in Keating, the
ceaseless mental war in the *Wake*—pitted the Irish against one another.

Consider the logic of error. Hugh Patrick Owens thought the Ford was a battle between Irish chiefs, Connacht and Fermanagh, much like the fight between the O'Reillys and Maguires that Mr. Boyle tied to his telling of the Ford. Hugh Nolan and Michael Boyle gave Black Francis a proper enemy, the foreign lords who took the Holy Island (once the Irish earls had fled, abandoning it), but Peter Flanagan assumed he robbed monks of his own religion.

If the facts are wrong, the structure of larger truth holds. In reality there is no pure disjunction of good and evil. Righteous courage is set off against ambiguous consequence. In real local events, the events in which one can participate, something prevents victory's perfection. That, the ineluctable melancholy of reality, provides the setting for the last of the District's histories: the battles of the band.

The band's battles were both set in verse by Hugh McGiveney and remembered in tales by Michael Boyle. The first bears strange cousinage to Mackan Fight. In it, Catholics, not Protestants, parade on the Derrylin Road, and a Protestant, not a Catholic, attacks the marchers with a farm implement, a four-pronged graip used to spread manure. In other respects, the tale is not upturned. It begins when a Protestant "neighbor" takes land from a Catholic, who naturally becomes angered. The Protestant starts the fight, and it is he, not a Catholic, who receives bodily harm. And it is the Catholics who are tried, convicted, exiled.

Things shift and hold firm. External differences rise within the community to assault the neighborly ethic. Result and warning stay in place.

"There's another poem of Hughie McGiveney's.
"Well, it was about a row the band got into.
"A row,
a political row,
a religious row too.
"There was a parish priest was in our parish
"And there was no land to the parochial house—there was no property there at the *time*.
"And he used to keep a horse. It was before the advent of the motorcar, do ye see, and he used to keep a horse.
"And there was a Protestant man, a neighbor.
"And he was a big land owner, that owned alot of land around where the parochial house was.
"And he used to set him two fields to graze the *horse*.
"But this year, whatever was up, he wouldn't give him the fields, do ye see.
"And there was another man that had a public house, down where Mister McKevitt is there, below the Arney Chapel.
"Well, there was a man the name of Carr. His name was Jack Carr and he was the proprietor of the pub; he had a pub thattime.
"And he took the piece of land that the parish priest used to have.

"And of course the parish priest was in bad humor and so were the parishioners.

"So that was a great tip thattime: if you had a spite against anyone: to get out the band and give them a *tune*, do ye see.

"Give them a tune.

"So the band rigged up this evenin, and they went up to play around Jack Carr's public house.

"He was, what they called, boycotted. None of the Catholics in the District would go into the public house, do ye see.

"So they went up with the band anyway,
     and on their way home
     they were passin a Protestant house.

"And he's a fellow the name of McHugh lives in it now. Phil McHugh. It's on the west side of the road; a nice wee slated house. He's a carpenter and there's a carpenter's workshop at the house.

"But this Price, he was a carpenter also. He was a Protestant man—oh, gettin on, not too young a man, but *fairly* young.

"So he was in great wrath at the band goin up to drum this Jack Carr. Jack Carr, do ye see, was a Protestant.

"So he came out.

"There was two or three men at the extreme tail end of the crowd that was followin the band.

"And what did he do, only come out with a graip; he come out with a graip and attackted these couple of men that were behind. There was two. There was a man named James Maguire, and a man named Nathaniel Corrigan.

"And he come out and attackted *them*.

"So of course they retaliated. They were fine big strong young men
     and they knocked him down,
          and they gave him a bit of a doin ◊.

"Gave him a right beatin anyway.

"So anyway then, with that the whole band heared the row and they went back anyway and, odds and ends, they gave him plenty anyway.

"And there was lumps of young lads, do ye see, and they fired stones through his windows and broke the windows of his house.

"So anyway he went to the police.

"And the police came and arrested the men the next day.

"And they were brought up here before the magistrate, do ye see, and one of them got a month in jail (Corrigan got a month), and Maguire got two weeks, a fortnight.

"They were brought up here to an old jail that was here in Sligo. Sligo Gaol.

"But anyhow, McGiveney made a song
     on the band
     and the evenin's proceedins.

"And the song run:

Carpenter Price with graip and vise—

"See a vise is a yoke that a carpenter uses there; do ye see: it tightens up, two jaws, and it tightens up to put articles of wood in, to be workin at.

"So anyway, the song run:

Carpenter Price with graip and vise,
His mind bein agitated-o,
With graip in hand to stop the band
On Frankie's Brae he capered-o.

"There was a wee brae goin up to the house, but it's gone now; the County Council removed it. But it was there thattime, and they called it Frankie's Brae. I don't know how it got its name, only it always had it anyway:

On Frankie's Brae he capered-o.
The band came up playin Busha's Buck.

"You see that Busha's Buck—ould Price's wife was the name of Busha:

The band came up playin Busha's Buck
And down with Carr the grabber-o.
Billy went out to have a bout,
But he went in a wiser man but sadder-o.
They knocked him down upon the ground,
Upon the dirty carsie-o,
And they broke three ribs all in his side,
While he did roar for mercy-o.
We'll now let him up, the Orange pup,
We'll kill him now, the mouldy fowl,
The scoundrel for wife beatin-o.

"He used to beat the wife, do ye see.

The scoundrel for wife beatin-o.
Billy got up,
        the door he shut.
And he made his way to Arney-o,
Where information he did swear
Before ould Sergeant Carney-o.

"He was a Sergeant Carney, was a sergeant of the police.

Before ould Sergeant Carney-o.
Oh make no noise, I'll arrest the boys,
I'll send them out of this Irish nation-o.
A warrant I'll get from some Orange pet,
From Bull or Orange Peggy-o.

"Bull was what they call an R.M.—a Resident Magistrate.

From Bull or Orange Peggy-o.
And then he swore a mighty oath,
He'd get them transportation-o.
Billy swore and Bull did roar;
The case it was high treason-o.
And Cromley then with voice and pen
With them he began to reason-o.

"Cromley was a magistrate too, do ye see, on the bench along with Bull. Bull was the chairman of the bench.

And Cromley then with voice and pen
With them he began to reason-o.
But they'd take no bail, but they sent to jail
Corrigan and Maguire-o.
The parting scene at Letterbreen
Set them all near crazy-o.
So we'll give three cheers for the League,
And down with Carr and Billy-o.

"So that's the bit of song that McGiveney composed.
"Well, that happened, do ye see.
"It wasn't that he made a ramas up out of nothin. That every word was the truth, do ye see; it all happened.
"Aye."

Like other conflicts—the Ford, Mackan Hill, Swad Chapel (though not, said Hugh Nolan, the Inishmore Fight)—Price Versus the Band is remembered both in song and story.

Separate artful reconstructions of single events complement one another. The memorized song preserves details and uses its art to prick interest in the story. The emergent story carries the whole event, start to finish, and expands during performance into explanation. Complete, the story frees the song to follow its own path to entertainment. Long ago Douglas Hyde remarked that the Irish had not mastered the ballad.[5] Their impulse is lyric, and Irish songs, unlike Lowland Scots and English songs, the noble ballads of Percy, Scott, and Child, do not tell clear stories.

The songs of Mackan and Swad do not tell what happened. They rely on separate knowledge preserved by historians. Hugh McGiveney's song on the band is not a full account. It begins with Billy Price's attack and dwells on the trial without geographic precision or provision of cause. It is allusive. That quality heightens and obscures its humor, so Mr. Boyle stops his recitation, storylike, for glossing. He could count on me to understand that making Orange Peggy a magistrate was both farcical and a clever comment on the partisan nature of the law. She lived in the nineteenth century on an island in Lower Lough Erne and is remembered for covering the bodies of her drowned husband and son with an orange cloth. Her portrait, it is said, hangs in the Orange Hall in Enniskillen. Hugh Nolan, who remembers her grandnephew, Billy Davis, drummer in parades on the Twelfth, called her "a wonderful loyal class of a woman." Other references were less obvious, so Mr. Boyle paused to explain as I do. The band was not really playing "Busha's Buck." There is no such tune. But there is a "Cromie's (Cromwell's) Buck," and since Busha was his wife's name and Price was a Protestant and a wife beater, the tune McGiveney made the band "beat" is subtly, doubly comic.

Stories of history are not comic. Serious, restrained artistry signals the presence of history in performance, distinguishing narrative truth from chat or narrative fiction, leaving a special place in the local literary structure for song.

The sensual sound of speech peaks in song. A fine tale like Mr. Nolan's Ford pulses out of chat and marks itself with alliteration, assonance, and rhyme. Story's sensuous tendencies are perfected in rhythmic, rhyming song. The first sound of "The Swad Chapel Song" comes again immediately: You, muses, excuse, intrusion. McGiveney's "Band Song" rhymes internally in the first and third lines and at the ends of the second and fourth lines of each stanza.[6]

On melody, in poetry, songs sail above stories, far above speech. In other ways, songs are conversational.

Clever chat becomes "crack" through the logical, free play of wit. Crack snaps with humorous figures of speech. The convention of attributing proverbs generally and bids particularly eases Wellerisms into talk. At last comprehending: "I see, said the blind man, You're a liar, says the dummy, Give him a kick in the arse, says the cripple." Starting a fire: "As the fox said when he pissed on the snow, That'll make a fire if it lights." Life's military context provides a matrix for metaphor. Not only are agricultural tools "weapons," but also the bachelors' home is "the barracks," chickens confined in overturned creels and babies in playpens are "in prison," the cock, "an old warrior," is not killed for dinner but "executed." Fanciful comparisons enliven chat. The hungry ceilier offered tea is "willing as a bride on her wedding night." Lighting a cigarette, the ceilier is told, "Throw back your lugs and pull like an ass." In a pointless hurry, a person fidgets "like a hen on a hot griddle." The hopeless task is "like lookin for holy water in an Orange Hall." Talk in Ballymenone sails easily to extremes. Things are the best and the worst; over a few nights you will hear the same woman call many plain, modest men "the best wee man that ever wore a hat" or a coat, and the company's chat cracks constantly with the spirit of exaggeration. The chilly draft in winter's kitchen is "a wind so cold that it'd clean corn." Hot bracing tea is "that strong a mouse could trot on it." A tall woman enters the chat. She is elevated to six foot eleven, then eleven foot six. The ceiliers give themselves a laugh.

Through unequal comparison, metaphor blends smoothly into exaggeration. Most characteristically, those tropes, the logics of association and extension, combine in hyperbolic analogies that amuse and contain potential for conversational expansion. A man is "strong as a horse." A naïve man is "that green, if he went out in the fields the cows would eat him." A stupid man is "ignorant as a crateload of arseholes goin to a fartin convention." An old man is "like the Glenfarn chimneys, hid in the thatch: you'd want a search warrant and a pair of nippers to find it." There are as many (though there are not) islands in Lough Erne or windows in Florencecourt Castle as there are days in the year.[7] A plump chicken, called big as a cow, is transformed during tricky banter into a monster, a chicken with horns, literally as big as a cow, "a real horny boy" coming up the hill to eat the ceiliers who have already eaten him.

Association and exaggeration, mental acrobatics and verbal fancy, make a dynamic vital to fiction, to bids and pants. But that impulse is purged from stories of history. Cleverness would confuse their clarity, undermine their truth. Metaphor leads to hyperbole and so to the lies that history shuns.

Song is licensed. It contains metaphor. The judge who sentenced the men of Mackan is a "bulker," a leech. Song is allowed exaggeration. The Swanlinbar boys exceeded one hundred thousand in song. In Peter Flanagan's telling, they numbered fifty or twenty thousand. Hugh Nolan's story has them turn out in hundreds. Michael Boyle stressed that Hugh McGiveney's song was true. Like a historical tale, it was not a ramas, foolishness: "it all happened." Still, the scene in the courtroom, the trial for "high treason," is let spin in the direction of the judicial proceedings that conclude Flann O'Brien's triple fiction, *At Swim-Two-Birds*.

Historical songs are not false, but they abandon literal truth for a rhetoric that takes the ear and shakes the mind. That rhetoric serves both to entertain and to drive messages home. The very force of association and exaggeration which makes songs enjoyable becomes, in the political sphere, stirring and strident. In song it can be said, as it cannot in story, that the curate at Swanlinbar is the star of Europe, that the fights at Swad and Mackan were worldly manifestations of the struggle of God and Satan. Compare Hugh Patrick Owens' telling of Mackan Fight with his father's poem. Songs shade fact into figure, coercing response. Stories dab pure, true colors next to each other; they hold back, leaving the listeners to do the mixing, creating their own messages, coming to their own conclusions.

Songs appear in public, among the crowd. Their rhetoric meets the needs of the public house where many preoccupied, imperfectly known individuals are called to attention by art. Then, depending on what they know or want to know or need to know, people in the crowd are amused and left alone, or they are grabbed, disrupted, and driven into engagement.

Stories appear in calm, intimate ceilis, among a familiar company. Austere and objective, what they lose aesthetically they gain philosophically. Stories are pleasing enough to the ear, moving enough to the heart, but complete—not partial—and literally true, they are gifts to the mind. They are offered to known others whose attention is won, those loyalty is assumed, whose need is for hard facts against which the brain can bend to direct life aright.

The thick ornamental surfaces and referential qualities that make songs engaging can obscure the truth and fragment reaction. Placid and entire, stories will not allow the mind to luxuriate in mere words or fall between the cracks in the narrative. Clear surfaces attract the mind's eye through them into the wholeness at the bottom of things.

Historical songs and stories fit different occasions, serve different ends. They rely on the experience of real people who shift between places and social groupings, moving from public excitement to hearthside education to unify historic events in the mind. When Michael Boyle brought the band's song into his comprehensive telling, he brought Hugh McGiveney's voice through his own, as he would in telling one of old Hughie's bids or pants. Between different voices, between clear, complete story and decorative, allusive song, the memory of the event is presented, a twofold unity.

The band's first fight is like Mackan Hill, a confrontation of Protestants and Catholics, Catholics and law, a battle tale, a battle song, but neither the event nor its artistic expression has gained insistent presence in Ballymenone's mind. In that way it is nothing like Mackan Fight.

I passed Phil McHugh's house daily, but other than the telling Mr. Boyle volunteered for the tape recorder, the only mention I heard of Price Versus the Band came during one of several sessions Hugh Nolan and I gave over to land tenure and genealogy. These were not merry interludes of folklore collecting, sparkling with story. They were, instead, times of the kind essential to serious ethnography, times of the kind that give field research the name work—good, but difficult times that come only after the folklorist's job has been explained so carefully that the subject has become a colleague willing to work hard in collaboration. As the tape recorder turned at his hearth, we went together over every farm in the District while Mr. Nolan raked his memory to give me the fullest possible historical account of its inhabitants. When we arrived at Phil McHugh's, Mr. Nolan told the story of the band's battle as part of its chronicle before pushing on to the house's more recent occupants. In his telling, note the characteristic geographic and social setting as well as his description of Billy Price as "bitter." That is the word locally applied to people whose political commitment interferes with their capacity to act in a courteous and cooperative—neighborly—manner.

"Aye, well then there was a man the name of Price lived in that house.

"And he was in a row with the band.

"The band, it used to be kept where John Moore lives now. They were a family the name of Dugans at that time.

"Well, they used to keep the band.

"But that was in the latter end, but at the time that this row took place, the band instruments was kept in Peter Keenan's father's. You know that long house up in the fields when you're comin up the road, a long iron-roofed house.

"Well, that's where the band was kept at the time that this row took place.

"They had been on parade and when they were comin back, this—ah, he was a bitter kind of a neighbor—he came out with a graip, out of his work and

he attacked some of the fellows of the band and
of course they gave battle and
he got the *worst of it*, you know.

"So then he summonsed them then, and there was two of them brought into court here and one of them got a month; he'd be an uncle of Francy Corrigan's here.

"And the other man, he was a brother of Terry Maguire's here, he got a *fortnight* in jail.

"Then this Price went away out of that. It was occupied then for a long time by a man. . . ."

Mr. Nolan remembers the big day—it was about 1902 and he was a lad—when the band went out to meet the men released from prison. Then, when Terry Maguire, Terry the Cat, Terry the Fluter, brother of one of the jailed men, was star of the band, and in the next generation when Peter Flanagan was star fluter, bands were central to the social life of young men. In P's day, the Lower End of the Parish had three Catholic bands—Sessiagh, Back Road, Rossdoney—and a Protestant band at Bellanaleck. There were others nearby: Protestant bands at Druminiskill and Florencecourt and between six and eleven Catholic bands (accounts vary) between Arney and the Border. Once or twice a week and on certain Great Days too—Patrick's, the Twelfth of July, the Twelfth of August, and the Fifteenth—bands swung along the country lanes. If they met on the road, they beat competitively against each other for hours. "Man dear!" Joe Flanagan said. "It was *great*.

"They had big flutes, wee flutes, and piccolos. They had the big drum and the wee drum. They were great bands, too, great.

"Oh man, you wouldn't be tired listenin to them. The Wearin of the Green. Old Folks at Home. The Harp Without the Crown. O'Donnell Abu. Napoleon's March. Oh man, they could play.

"But this old Troubles ruined that. Bigotry. It takes unity and peace in a country to do that. If a Catholic band went out now, they'd have to get a permit. And that left the people careless. They had no heart for goin out, you know. And now, surely, with the Trouble, it's worse.

"The old generation had a better interest in a band, you know; the young don't take an interest. And it's a bad thing in a way because a good band in a country is a great thing.

"If a good day comes on, boys-a-dear, it's a great thing to have a band turn out."

Bands are not gone. They give the Great Days rhythm. But they play infrequently, their importance has diminished, and, as Joe said, it is a bad thing.

For the men on parade and the people along the lanes, whose routine was broken by march tunes, the band was a diversion—and a social focus. Subscription house parties, "band balls," were held as an excuse for a hooley and a way to buy new instruments, so all the neighbors could feel they contributed directly to their local band. The instruments, "the band," were stored in different homes, whose owners were drawn into the band's activities. For a while it was Hugh Nolan's, and Hugh "was clean wild about the band," Joe Flanagan recalled. "He was dyin about music and would listen from mornin to night."

The band's members were mostly between the ages of eighteen and twenty-five, between adolescence and marriage. Young boys brought money to weekly practices to pay "the bandmaster," a teacher, exactly like scholars at school. They learned fingering, rhythms, and reading crotchets, so they could participate and through participation integrate with the neighborhood's older men. Fireside ties weakened, new solidarity formed. Cooperation, playing, marching, moving as one, became natural.

Money and music were exchanged between young and old, players and audience, to draw people together. Bands built and symbolized community, so it is no surprise that Joe laments their failure and the story of the breaking of the Old Ballymenone Band is memorable. This second and more important of the band's battles is also Michael Boyle's.

"Well this Old Ballymenone Band, do ye see, it was a good big band, quite a good flute band, do ye see.

"But then it lay in abeyance for a few years, do ye see. Some fellows left the country and the band lay up for a few years and no one was interested in it; the instruments were there, good instruments. And they were housed in a house down the road there—you might remark it, it's between Bellanaleck and Rossdoney. They're oil suppliers; a family of Moores lives in it; just on the roadside you see the oil tanks there and everything, oil storage tanks. Well, the band was there. It twas a family the name of Dugans were livin in it thattime. And that's where the instruments were, do ye see.

"And there was a big Sinn Fein meetin comin off in Enniskillen. It twas in nineteen hundred and seventeen. That was the year after the Rebellion, do ye see, in Easter Week.

"And our country, the Rossdoney end of Ballymenone, it was aligned, do ye see, with the rebels. It was all a rebel area. They were all Sinn Feiners.

"But the other end, the Back Road end, do ye see, they were all the opposite; they were opposed to the *whole* thing, do ye see.

"And the Rossdoney boys took a notion they'd get the band
        rigged up

and bring it to this meetin in Enniskillen.

"And didn't they ask some of the Back Road boys would they come with them, do ye see, and form the band up again.

"And wouldn't they give in to go.

"But what did they do?

"They gathered up one evenin, ten or eleven of them, and they came up and they took the instruments out of Dugan's without notifyin anyone in *Rossdoney*, do ye see, any of the *Rossdoney* boys.

"And they went in and they asked the man of the house, Dugan, about the instruments, and, ah, they said they were goin to take them out for a tune, that they were long enough lyin there.

"And, damn it, he handed them out the instruments, do ye see,
            and there was no Rossdoney men.

"And as soon as he done that, he regretted it.

"He says, There's something wrong, he says, I don't see any of the Rossdoney men here, and they *should* be here.

"But the instruments was gone,
            and that was that,
            and away they went;
            the Back Road men took them, do ye see.

"They brought them away to the Back Road.

"So then of course when the Rossdoney men heard it the next day, they were furious, do ye see, but there was no way of gettin them back. There was no good in goin for them, for they wouldn't give them to them, do ye see.

"So damn it anyway, they done a foolish thing of course—puttin the country to alot of expense—put themselves, Rossdoney, to alot of expense. They went away and they took legal proceedins against them, do ye see, for the recovery of the instruments.

"But it twas tried here in Enniskillen before the County Court judge. He dismissed the case.

"He dismissed it, do ye see, he wouldn't give judgment for Rossdoney.

"So then that was that.

"They appealed the case before the judge of assizes.

"And they were beaten again.

"And that heaped on extra costs.

"The Rossdoney men was payin the cost for years and years, do ye see, and had no instruments.

"But then there was an ould set of instruments lyin on, do ye see, that, well they thought was wore out, do ye see; they had got new ones. And didn't they rig up the old instruments and started a second band in Rossdoney, with the result that there was *two bands* goin for a few years.

"But then this Trouble came along.

"Nineteen and twenty:
            nineteen and twenty,
            the shootin and the trouble here, do ye see,

and both bands went into abeyance anyway.

"But anyway what happened the followin years, do ye see, the Republican IRA at a time,

> they gathered up one night,
> and they went down to the Back Road.

"They weren't admitted, do ye see, but they had to break in the doors.

"They broke in the two doors ◊ and they cleaned the whole instruments out ◊.

"They cleared the whole damned instruments away.

"And I don't know what they done with them,

> destroyed them I suppose.

"They cleared them away anyway ◊.

"And that ended the Ballymenone Band."

Once the Ballymenone Band helped unify the Catholic people of the Lower End of the Parish. It could mobilize swiftly to redress wrongs committed against them. That was a point in the story of Price and the Band. When the priest's land was taken, young men were ready to march, as they had been when Maguire's castle was taken and the homes on Mackan Hill or the Chapel at Swad were threatened. Then the band broke in two, one for the Back Road, one for Rossdoney.

Through conduits connecting Ballymenone with everywhere else, the world beyond intruded to provide means and a reason for a schism. World history became local. The potential for quick, unified action was lost.

The means for schism were legal. When the community's problem was taken into the courts of law, and the right of arbitration was surrendered to the British judicial system, the local problem was radicalized, publicized, magnified. Social and economic costs redoubled. But that is how things were done at the time.

True communities are built not of dewy affection or ideological purity but of engagement. The District's social intensity, positively displayed in an artistic tradition of engaged union, an economic tradition of cooperative work, in neighborliness, was negatively displayed in ridicule (the neighbors care what you do) and constant disputes over "mearns and passes," land boundaries and rights of access. The Monaghan poet, Patrick Kavanagh, ably describes the anger grown on thickly settled, overused land in his sad novel, *Tarry Flynn*. "Hating one's next-door neighbor," he muses, knowing the beauty and pain of damp little fields, "was an essential part of a small farmer's religion."[8]

At one time the District's wrath passed in hot talk and fistfights. The worst cases prompted men disguised in straw hoods and skirts to stone and sod homes, smashing windows, splintering doors on Hallow Eve. Old cases hardened into permanent "spite," silence, a scar on communal tissue, but hate remained a local matter, contained in the neighborhood. For a while, though, anger was formalized in lawsuits. "Ah, they were always fightin over rights of way and passes," Hugh Patrick Owens said. "The courts in Enniskillen were full of cases over rights of way and passes. A man wantin to get to a separate field would have to go through fields belongin to some other man. People would stop you goin through, and it would lead to a killing or at least a suit. But that has all died out now."

Soon, though not soon enough to save the Old Ballymenone Band, people came to recognize that "only the lawyer wins when people law other." Today they say lawyers are predators, preying on the problems of others for their own profit, and that people who use legal means to personal advancement are stupid. Those attitudes are codified artfully in story. Hugh Nolan will tell of lawyers as the Devil's solicitors and best clients. Peter Flanagan enjoys an anecdote about an old man who had an old cow he could not sell, so he cut a piece of her tail off and went to the police, wishing to sue a neighbor for malicious mischief. Suspicious, the police told him his suit would go better if he could find the bit of missing tail. When the case came before the magistrate, he produced the tail scrap and was fined for cruelty to animals. "So he had the ould cow with part of her tail gone and was out twenty pounds beside." Law makes fools of people.

Law and life exist at war. When law is immoral, the moral man will be an outlaw. That was Black Francis' inescapable conclusion. Then, making men outlaws, law makes them corpses or exiles. As Mackan Hill showed, Catholics cannot expect justice in the Empire's courtrooms. As the band's second battle shows, the community's problems are exacerbated, not solved, in litigation.

When the band split, law was the means, politics the reason. No community exists in isolation. Today the radio drops its daily burden of bad news into every country kitchen. Tonight's ceili will lift it, staggering under its weight, into the night. During discussions of bombs that blew buildings out of towns and bullets that tore lives from bodies, opinions will be reformulated, the community will be questioned and reconstructed. The violence following the Easter Rising of 1916 comparably entered and disturbed Ballymenone.

Joe Flanagan remembers the English army marching south on the Derrylin Road that bisects the District. They took all of a long June day to pass, and the dust from their boots darkened the sky. An officer on horseback leapt his great beast over a hedge, then back. A woman standing by Joe asked the horseman, "Well, boys, and where are yous goin the day?" To Dublin, he replied, "to crush Shine Fine at all costs." Sinn Fein survived and grew into the force of resistance to the scheme to slice six of Ulster's nine counties out of the Republic of Ireland. One was Fermanagh.

Some Catholics, sick of bloodshed, favored compromise. Others stood with de Valera's IRA and held out for a united Ireland. Civil war broke, Ballymenone split, its band ripped.

The party of compromise, the "Molly Maguires," was considered traitorous by the "rebels" of Sinn Fein. That was no abstract sentiment. When the band on the road beat "The Green Cockade" or men in the pub sang Charlie Farmer's song "You'll find lots of the blackguard in Molly Maguire," they were consolidating against their neighbors. The men of Upper Ballymenone, rebels all, could stand on Drumbargy Brae, look north across the tan bog to the white houses of Lower Ballymenone lining the Back Road, and think of their inhabitants, though Catholics like themselves, as enemies. These men, aligned on opposite sides in a war fought to determine what nation they would live in, met tensely at prayer in the chapel and at work in the bog with weapons in their hands.

When his story of the band's rupture was done, I asked Mr. Boyle to tell me more about the political persuasions of the men in the row.

"Well, do ye see, the Back Road men, they were called Molly Maguires. Hibernians, they were called, but they were originally the ould Molly Maguires, do ye see.

"They belonged to the ould Irish party, do ye see. The ould Irish party was led be John Redmond, do ye see. Then they belonged to it. And, do ye see, the Rossdoney ones joined up with the new Sinn Fein party. Aye.

"So that's how the split came in the Ballymenone Band.

"Aw, it *ruined our country*.

"It ruined that whole District for years and years.

"Do ye see, it was a terrible *spite*.

"Oh, it ruined it for years and years.

"And the first thing that united it was the football team,
        the Bellanaleck football team.

"See, there was a football team away back before my day, but then of course the fellows that played in it, they got old and some of them emigrated, do ye see, and with the result that the team died out for years and years.

"So a lock of us young fellows got our heads together and we took a notion we'd start *another* team.

"*So we did*.

"And took in fellows from both ends, do ye see, from the Rossdoney end and the Back Road end and all, and we got up a great football team.

"Well then the people all got out to the football matches, with the result that it was the first thing here *healed up that split*.

"*And it did*.

"And the football team's goin to the present day:
        a good wee team yet,
        the Bellanaleck Art MacMurroughs they're called.

"The first team that ever was formed in Ballymenone was called the Art MacMurroughs.

"And the man that formed it, that was the means of it bein formed, was the teacher that taught me and taught all the young fellows, Richard Corrigan. He was the first man to start football, the Gaelic games, in Ballymenone.

"Aye, indeed.

"And it was it brought the two sides together. It was ridiculous the way they were carryin on.

"Course, I suppose the anger was about the instruments bein taken and everything and,
> why,
> > there'd be two rival crowds
> > > at the chapel gate,
> > > > one standin here,
> > > > > and one standin there,
> > > > > > and them jeerin at other, you see.

"It was ridiculous.

"And then to make things worse, do ye see, it was a big Protestant community, and the Protestant population was laughin at them,
> was just *laughin* at them.

"Well, that was the first thing healed the split anyway that was caused by the band."

As Mr. Boyle pauses and cigarette smoke rolls over his bedclothes, I wonder aloud, "Was there a song about that?" His answer comes quickly:

"Yes. You know that old poet, Hugh McGiveney, he made a poem on it, and a song on the band. It had an air; there was an air of its own put to it. And the poem run:

> *Johnny dear and did you hear*
> > *the news that's goin around:*
> *Our band it has been stolen*
> > *away from holy Sinn Fein ground.*
> *It was stolen by John Redmond's men,*
> > *a pack that's low and mean,*
> *And the reason that they took it*
> > *was to murder poor Sinn Fein.*

> *They dragged it off to prison,*
> *But martyrs don't complain.*
> *They forcibly threatened, tortured it,*
> *And its only crime Sinn Fein.*
> *But we will liberate it,*
> *And it will sound again,*
> *And strike a blow for Ireland's rights,*
> > *and its own beloved Sinn Fein* ◇.

> *Ah now, Paddy, let me tell ye,*
> *The meanest thing that crawls,*
> *Who apes to be an Irishman,*
> > *brought up in a Saxon hall,*
> *He stole away I. M. Sullivan's band,*

Twas well worthy of its name.
But we will liberate it,
And it will sound again,
To strike a blow for Ireland's rights,
  and its own beloved Sinn Fein.

We have Mackan and ould Montiagh,
And faithful Inishmore,
The gallant Larkin and O'Brien,
They were loyal to the core.
We have Rossdoney and Drumbargy,
Rossawalla and Drumane,
Who swear they'll die or conquer
To rescue our band
  and restore it to Sinn Fein.

"Now wait'll I see now. There's another verse:

So now me boys take warnin:
When fillin up your ranks,
Don't get beat to your bandroom
By red slaves or cranks;
Don't put your trust in Redmond,
William Trimble or the D.I.,
And when life remains all in your veins,
Let Sinn Fein be your cry.

"That's the song.
"That was made be Hughie McGiveney of Rossdoney."

The oppositional associations trapped alive in the old song text reveal the depth of rancor of the era of war, murder, and civil war, 1916–1923. The band thieves, "low and mean," only ape Irishman, being raised in Saxon ways. They are "slaves," associated with the British government, the District Inspector, and the Protestant ascendancy. William Trimble was editor of Enniskillen's Protestant paper, *The Impartial Reporter*. A clever, most partial journalist, he is remembered in another of Charlie Farmer's songs: "Trimble and Trimble and Trimble's his name, and he trembles and trembles when he hears of Sinn Fein."

In plain opposition to those false Irish, the "faithful" men of Sinn Fein are heirs to "holy ground," all Ireland. Their loyalty joins them to old heroes, "gallant Larkin and O'Brien," two of the three men hanged in 1867 (the third, Allen, is probably lost within the adjective "gallant") for their part in smashing a police van in Manchester and releasing, over the corpse of Sergeant Brett, the Fenian leaders, Kelly and Deasy.[9] Several songs memorialize them as the Manchester Martyrs. Peter Flanagan knows three of them; here is the one he offers when the crowd wants a political piece:

"It's eighteen and sixty-seven. It was made on the Manchester Martyrs, Allen, Larkin, and O'Brien:"

It was in September, I well remember,
Three noble heroes from Manchester came.
It's on their intention, I am going to mention,
To free old Ireland from our trodden chains.

The police viewed them as if they knew them,
And for to subdue them, they did not fail.
Aw, they did surround them, with handcuffs bound them,
And they marched them off to their county jail.

When Allen heard of his men being taken,
To O'Brien and Larkin he quickly flew,
Sayin for every man to go to the van
And to smash it open and set them free.

My local friends now what happened after,
Those three young heroes as you may plainly see.
Now judge and jury has found them guilty
And they died three martyrs for their country.

It was on the scaffold they gazed around them.
Not a man from Erin could there be seen.
Aye, and for miles around them, they came in thousands
To see them die for the love of green.

The bolt was drawing, those three young heroes,
For God and Ireland stood heart in hand,
And the blood flowing down from the English scaffold,
And they died three martyrs for Ireland.

Their beds was made in the highest heaven,
And the holy angels around them sing.
And Saint Patrick met them with a crown of glory,
Sayin, Welcome martyrs from Ireland.

The band in Hugh McGiveney's song is a Fenian "martyr" held in prison. "We will liberate it," the song declares, and the logical action for the Rossdoney men is smashing the door and freeing it, Manchester style. That is what they did, and the song validated their violence by connecting it to a historical event known to all through song.

As in the dreaming mind of Joyce's Humphrey C. Earwicker—Here Comes Everybody, Haveth Childers Everywhere—the levels and categories thinkers create to destroy the world prove false. Community and nation merge. Distant events penetrate, local events expand, conventional distinctions between history and local history, history and myth, past and present, fade, become untenable. The band's thieves were Redmond's followers, the personified force of accommodation and compromise. The band's defenders were rebels, Fenians, agents of perpetual resistance, at one with the Manchester Martyrs, the Swanlinbar boys, and Red Hugh.

A small happening reorders the locality and the world. The sung catalog joins the people of Upper Ballymenone with adjacent townlands (Rossawalla and Drumane), nearby districts (Inishmore, Mackan, and Montiagh), and with old Fenian cause, in opposition to their traditional neighbors and fellow parishioners in Lower Ballymenone and politicians in Dublin. Politics, international in scale, split the neighborhood and revised the structure of cultural priority. The little community came to matter less than the nation. Ideology replaced neighborliness as the prime force of social organization. The experiential gave way to the conceptual, the real to the abstract, and the seemingly minor battle over band instruments becomes a major landmark on the evolutionary path to modern existence.

Both battles of the band speak of division. That of the first is Mackan Fight's. Ireland is Catholic and Protestant. Since that division remains, Mr. Boyle can join emotional song and calm tale into a single statement. Since he feels the division of the second battle, that which split the Catholic side, was wrong, "ridiculous," he disconnects his own statement in which the fight "ruined our country" from the song that joined the fight to past heroism. At the end of the first battle, things are left as they are, painful. At the end of the second, the wound is healed.

Hugh McGiveney's witty personification of the band instruments was apt, given the band's nearly human ability to effect social cohesion. That power was recognized by Master Corrigan when, in 1929, he brought Michael Boyle and the District's young men together in a football team. A farmer donated a field. The first was given by Terry Maguire, the fluter, and lay in Rossdoney by the Arney. Currently the field is one of Paddy Quigley's near the bog in Rossawalla. Others gave money. In exactly the way the band had, the football team integrated the youth, accepted the community's contributions, and provided a spectacle for all.

Football registered its importance in art. Charlie Farmer composed a song about his local team. Hugh Nolan tells tales of his. Once in the midst of a hot match Hughie McGiveney looked up, said, "Well, boys, it's milkin time," and walked off the field without waiting for a whistle. Another time, the Bellanaleck team was charging down the field. The goalkeeper for Mackan (it was the father of the craftsman, Hugh Patrick MacManus) tore down the goal and heaped it into a pile, and when the Bellanaleck forwards arrived, they found no goal, no way to score. The team was victorious. Though ceiliing patterns today bear evidence of the old split, and Catholic political opinion still varies from conservative to radical, no overt division cuts the District's Catholic people. As Mr. Boyle said, the football team put right what the band had disordered.

At the same time, for the same reasons, James Owens and Peter Cassidy, the historian, assembled Michael Boyle and his mates—Peter and Phil Flanagan, John, Jemmy, and Paddy McBrien, Benny and Paddy Quigley—and taught them the mummers' play. With the band and old football team, mumming had been a casualty of the 1916–1923 Troubles. Like the band and team, the mumming squad brought young men together to accept and repay the community's gift. There was a difference. The mummers visited every home in the District, Protestant as well as Catholic, and accepted donations to mount a Mummers' Ball to which all, Protestant and Catholic, were invited for dance and music, food and drink. But there were always separate bands for Catholics and Protestants. The Bellanaleck Art MacMurroughs (named for a rebellious and victorious medieval king of Leinster) played Gaelic football. Protestant boys play soccer.

Band and football team represent one side of the community to itself. Each is an entity within which differences dissolve as footballers cooperate on offense and defense, as drummers and fluters, percussion and melody, become one in music. That unity is presented to the rest of the world when band or team compete against those from beyond. Mumming squads did not compete. They met in parleys before the Christmas season, marked out territories, then performed within them displaying the whole divided community to itself. In the play, Saint Patrick and Prince George, Ireland and England, sacred and secular rule, fight over falsehood and money. Patrick is killed but, revived by a Doctor, the community's healing spirit, the Saint rises to fight again. New threats bring no new fight. Armed men in frightening straw hoods, devils and warriors—Beelzebub and Cromwell, Devil Doubt and Hector—stand in a circle of peace as music brings unity to the kitchen.

Symbolic differences among band, team, and mummers fit the scale of their intentions. Different hopes made different histories. Mumming is gone. Band and team play on. With mumming dead, the conflict of the Ford, Mackan Hill, and Price and the Band, England and Ireland, Protestant and Catholic, lives. With band and team alive, the conflict of the second band battle, that which subdivides sides, has died.

Mumming was planned to overarch all the District's distinctions, those of both band battles. It did help, but real change had occurred. Some wounds gaped too deep for healing.

When Mr. Boyle's metaphor is abandoned, the issue becomes clearer. The community, conceived as a unity, broke apart. Its leaders understood and developed solutions. That they succeeded in one instance and not in another provides us with a means for discovering a basic structure in the District's culture.

Culture is usually discussed today in terms of system. Through a fashion, and truly no more than a way of speaking, the concept of system represents a great advance over old notions that reduced culture to lists of discrete traits, institutions, or folklore genres. As convenient as it was unreal, rationalistic classification shattered experience, battering and flattening culture into comparability. System demands connection, and that sorts well with our understanding of culture, not as sets of things out in the world, but as ideas in a perpetual state of dismemberment and development in singular brains. Culture exists only in lone savage minds like H. C. Earwicker's, where perforce distinct things gain interrelation. System, however, implies a neatness not to be found in something so grotesquely complex and fluid as culture. Cultural order is a proposition to test, not a geometry to assert. And system seems to suggest efficiency, as though culture should function in lieu of will to provide people with smooth ways through life's difficulties.

Culture is not a policeman in the head. Culture does not determine; the ideas we call culture and describe as systemic do not so much act instead of thought as provide tasks for thought. Culture leads out of chaos into dilemma.

Here is a simple example from our District. When one human being comes into the shelter of another, they are not deranged by infinite possibility. One becomes host, the other guest. Their subsequent behavior could be described as though by accepting those roles all they had to do was follow the "rules" built into them and a smooth interaction would ensue. Not so easy. This culture's "rules" assume the host has plenty, the guest is tired and hungry. The host must give, the guest must take. The result is frequent discomfort. Sometimes the host's larder is empty and the guest's belly is full. Ellen Cutler, a perceptive observer of her own scene, commented, "I was always taught it was very bad manners to force a person. And I was always taught it was very bad manners to refuse. So what are you going to do?

Now let us take a hard example. The dilemma at the core of the District's culture will come into view when we consider neighborliness.

Neighborliness is the social organization of the agricultural economy. If we consider it alone as a system, closed and self-regulating, neighborliness can be described as a thing, formalized in principle, tricked out with anecdote, but it cannot be understood.

Understanding human products—stories, fields, acts of agricultural aid—requires compassionate spiritualization. Will must be located behind states of affairs, and variability must be read as the result of consciousness under control. Hugh Nolan's Ford and Peter Flanagan's Mackan Hill vary from Michael Boyle's tellings of those tales not because each failed to achieve the perfect model present in some heaven called culture, but because these men—neighbors, contemporaries, Catholics, Nationalists, bachelors, poor farmers—feel differently about the world.

Neighborliness is advocated by everyone, considered by all a high good. Yet not everyone is a good neighbor. If we think about neighborliness in ethnographic isolation, we are left with no explanation for that fact, save the trite, uninteresting observation that a gap lies between the real and ideal. The variable reality of neighborliness deserves a better explanation than behavioral deviation from cultural norm. Variation is not merely the product of idiosyncrasy, mental lapse, or, to use the Ballymenone way of saying it, evidence that "the human being is weak," inherently disposed to serving the luxurious self at the expense of the other.

Two congruent ways lead out of this cul-de-sac. One is a belief. If culture is a totalizing system, some relation must obtain between its neighborly and other parts. Through these connections, neighborliness could become so interlocked that it would have to be sacrificed in certain situations in order for the culture of which it is but part to be preserved. The second and less abstract tactic involves frontal encounters with the people's own modes of organization. In this District that means listening closely to the stories in which the culture is at once constructed, discussed, and presented.

Ask a question about inert principle, and you will be answered with a description of specific action. I asked Ellen Cutler, "What makes a good neighbor?" She replied, "I mind seein Tommy Lunny come up here in the middle of the night to help when the cow was goin to calve. Now that was a good neighbor."

It is not that principles are unknown, or that answers cannot be framed abstractly, but the natural, efficient path to concept leads not to pristine axioms surrounded by crowds of qualifying corollaries, but toward story. There was such a thing as "the Mummer's Rule," a known code, but when I asked about mumming, I was not given a list of the play's rules, I was told of particular performances in which the tradition's essence was properly enacted. Mrs. Cutler's account of neighborliness is exact. Though not a member of her religion, a man whose politics could not be more different from her own but who lives nearby came at a time inconvenient to himself to help in work on which her economic well-being depended without mention of repayment.

Mrs. Cutler's answer was not a "story," but it illustrates the kind of thinking from which stories grow. An action is described in which principles are embedded with precision. When such actions are strung into a narrative, sufficient margin is left for reality's ambiguity, and actions are related in such a way that their infixed principles are allowed to come into synthesis or conflict. The "examples" told children teach values. Adult stories do not teach values; they raise them.

Stories can be of culture and about culture without falsely resolving culture's tensions. Stories embody argument over important ideas and push toward the frontiers of culture to provide the outsider as well as the insider with a means for constructing the culture in its own terms. The outsider's task is learning what the insider already knows and having the courage to discriminate among an infinity of facts to key on those which give the text context. In the case of Mrs. Cutler's answer, I had to know about her beliefs and economy, and Tommy's, and where they both lived.

Historical stories, from the Ford to the Smashing of the Band, alive as they are with the issues of leadership, unity, and conflict, demand as surely as a theory of cultural system that we join neighborliness—cooperation among people who live together—to other aspects of life as it is.

In real life, not everyone is a good neighbor. Conversations in the District locate different causes for that fact. One is personality. Some people are "mean," inherently incapable of the generosity essential to neighborliness. Others are "backward" or "old-fashioned." Those words can be used to describe conservatism, but more often they are used to qualify people shy to the point of illness who work unsociably in isolation, hiding behind their hedges, walling themselves into the caverns of their homes and rejecting all invitations to participation.

Recent social disjunction, reducible to the intrusion of capitalism, provides another cause. Nonparticipants in the economy of neighborliness may become nonparticipants in the sociability of neighborliness. The "big man" for whom farming is business and the young man who has taken a job off the land may opt into noninvolvement. But the big man might help his neighbors with loans of tools and land, maintaining connection on the model of aristocratic reciprocity. His Catholic laborers credit Bobbie Thornton, a happily ambitious big Protestant farmer, with being a constant help to them. The young man "in a job" might use his vacation to help with the harvest, his car to help in emergencies, and remain firmly a part of his place. Economic difference does not compel cultural difference. Neighborliness is a matter of choice.

The key cause of unneighborly behavior, not statistically dominant —for that is economic withdrawal—but conceptually most important, is trapped in the cold and barren, wintery word "bitter." People are expected to dislike one another and hold opposed opinions about religion and politics, but it is "a bitter kind of neighbor" who lets anger become spite or who lets political commitment stand in the way of decent sociability. Personal bitterness harms the community, but people will fight (there's no use in talking) and their fights stay in the family. The frightening, constantly discussed cause of bitterness is political. Politically bitter, the person breaks out of connection with great numbers of neighbors and becomes the channel through which the political force of the world beyond enters the community to destroy its own political structure.

Neighborliness is a political concept. The District's political style was displayed perfectly in establishing the football team and reviving mumming. Generally, the community's leaders move outside the bonds of economic interdependence. Rector and priest, schoolmaster, elderly men and women, give advice rather than agricultural aid to the people they live among. Day-to-day this guidance filters through conversations on the road, in the shop, at the hearth. In times of crisis casual connections prove too weak and leadership must be exercised with force. The period following the civil war was such a time, and the community's natural leaders—a schoolmaster and a pair of learned extroverted older men—perceived its problems. Knowing how their community worked, in touch with its inherent power, they did not claim central roles for themselves. They did not command and exhort on the militaristic model of national politics. Instead, they plunged to the heart of neighborliness, gripped it firmly, and founded institutions on the model of the "methal," the emergency work force. A compression and direction of cooperative energy, the methal was the natural, old way to solve specific problems. The leaders got things started, then removed themselves entirely, leaving action wholly in the hands of teams of men who worked in anonymous unity, in uniforms and costumes, according to traditional rules, who symbolized community while bringing community into order.

The methal is the perfect opposite of the bitter neighbor. It groups men to work with purpose for others, consolidating community, while he withdraws into sullen aloneness to become the local agent of national politics.

Dynamically and functionally, the politics of community and nation are different, often incompatible, antagonistic. The community's business is the community. Its politics coax people into coexistence to defend the home place; the function is economic. Methals of men are gathered to save swamped hay. Football teams are established so future men will be able to assemble and save future hay. Politics serve the nation by demolishing local allegiance, so people will align with others they do not know behind leaders they have never seen who wish to use them as they use cattle. As citizens they become tied less to flesh and blood and clay than they are to abstractions, ideas of race and theories of governance, through which they are manipulated to the benefit of people who live in communities elsewhere.

The community's leaders leave action to the people. The nation's leaders are the actors. Blended into the masses, their followers are but measures of charisma, toys of whim, tools of profit.

A strong contrast shadows across the District's historical art. In the beginning, heroes could act alone as Saint Febor and Saint Naile did, but from Saint Patrick to Black Francis, and perfectly in Red Hugh, heroes were men with groups behind them. In the recent past—that which is continuous with the present—heroism is collective. Their stories describe the Mackan heroes, the Swanlinbar boys, and the Old Ballymenone Band moving swiftly, effectively, like a football team, without leaders. Not leaders but victims, fools, and wrongdoers are named in stories. Mackan Hill, Swad Chapel, and the Band Battles name the dead (Mealey, Scarlett, Robinson, MacManus, Cole), the imprisoned (McBrien, Corrigan, Maguire), the judges (Jebb, Bull, Cromley), the foolish wrongdoers (Owney the Dummy, Billy Price), the offended (Howard, Carr), and that Dugan who mistakenly surrendered the instruments to the Back Road men. Victorious men are lost unnamed into the names of their places: Fermanagh, Leitrim, Cavan, Swanlinbar, Montiagh, Mackan, Ballymenone, Inishmore, Rossdoney, the Back Road. The exceptions are the priests, McHugh and MacManus, the schoolmaster Corrigan, leaders properly removed from the central action of conflict.

Even national heroes who rise outside story and inside song are usually victims, martyrs, hanged like Black Francis and Ignatius MacManus: Robert Emmet, Allen, Larkin, O'Brien, and Kevin Barry. The modern hero who looms from among his comrades is exiled from them by imprisonment or death.

The association of heroism and death on the field of politics is well illustrated by the song "Sean South." South begins as hero, ends as martyr. His song is the most common piece in the contemporary south Fermanagh repertory. Here is the version sung with sweet force by Gabriel Coyle, son-in-law of John O'Prey, the Flanagans' next-door neighbor:

> It was on a dreary New Years' Eve as the shades of night fell down,
> A lorry load of volunteers approached a border town;
> There was men from Dublin and from Cork, Fermanagh, and Tyrone,
> But the leader was a Limerick man, Sean South of Garryowen.
>
> And as they marched along the street up to the barracks door,
> The sergeant spied their daring plan, he spied them through the door.
> Aye, with Sten guns, aye and from rifles too, a hail of death did fall,
> And when that awful night had passed, two men lay cold as stone,
> There was one from near the border and one from Garryowen.
>
> No more they will hear the sea gulls' cry o'er the murmuring Shannon tide,
> For they fell beneath that northern sky, brave Hanlon by his side.
> They have gone to join that gallant band of Plunkett, Pearse, and Tone.
> Another martyr for old Ireland, Sean South of Garryowen.

After the Rising of 1798, its Protestant leader, Wolfe Tone, slit his throat before he could be hanged. He had asked, as Kevin Barry would in 1920, to be shot like a soldier, not hanged like a dog. Catholic poets, Padraic Pearse and Joseph Plunkett, were among the Men of Easter Week shot in May 1916. Last in the hideously protracted series of executions by gunfire was that of Connolly, the socialist writer and organizer for the Industrial Workers of the World, and "when they murdered James Connolly, the Irish rebelled." One wave of rebellion broke immediately. The next great wave broke after the Civil Rights Movement was founded in 1967 and civil rights demonstrators were massacred in Londonderry in 1972. But the sea of pain that engulfs life today was anticipated in a period of violence from 1955 to 1961, during which the great event was "the Brookeborough Raid" on the first day of 1957. Then Sean South and young Feargal O'Hanlon (made rebel by stories of Connolly's execution in Dominic Behan's "The Patriot Game") both died. [10]

Ellen Cutler has clipped bits from newspapers telling of storms and weddings, the Royal Family, and local brawls. Most chronicle the terror surrounding her life. Among them, along with a handwritten ballat of "Sean South," are several describing the Brookeborough Raid. The Royal Ulster Constabulary's report, quoted in the *Impartial Reporter* for January 3, 1957, reads in part:

"At about 7 P.M. this evening the R.U.C. police barracks at Brookeborough was attacked by a party of armed men who reached the village in motor-lorries.

"They opened up machine gun fire on the station from a number of points and police returned it and the attackers made off in a lorry.

"The police went in pursuit and at Altawark between Brookeborough and Rosslea, they came upon an abandoned and blood-stained lorry.

"A search of the area was at once organized and in a disused house one dead man and one wounded man were found. The second man has since died.

"The identity of the men is so far unknown. . . .

"The legs of one of the dead men were almost severed with machine gun wounds, while the abdomen of the other was shattered by another burst.

"One of the two dead men was described as 'about 40, with ginger hair and long beard'; the other as clean-shaven and about 18."

At the time Sir Basil Brooke said, "Our chaps did a good job." Brooke, Lord Brookeborough, former Commandant of the Ulster Special Constabulary, was Prime Minister of Northern Ireland. He had advised his fellow Protestants to do as he had done and fire their Catholic laborers. Later, in another clipping, he would reminisce, "No doubt the attack on Brookeborough was meant as a kick in the seat of the pants for me, but the courage of the boys in the station in handling these people and teaching them a lesson changed it into a kick in the seat of the pants for them." [11]

Of national significance, the event was also a local one. Brookeborough lies in Fermanagh beyond Inishmore, over Lough Erne from Ballymenone. People remember. Mrs. Cutler used the raid to exemplify the tyranny of distant leaders and the evil both sides come to in bad times. She had just heard a newscast from Belfast:

"Och, it's sad seein wee childer out throwin rocks. They don't know any better. Their parents teach them.

"And it's the very same with the leaders. They send poor stupid lads out to do the work. Like that Brookeborough Raid.

"There was a lad the name of O'Hanlon. He was wounded. And some of his men took and left him in an old house or a byre. And he told alot of news when he was found. Gave them information about his side, you see. And then he asked for first aid and one of the boys of our side says, This is first aid enough for you, and hit him with the butt of a rifle.

"Now wasn't that terrible?

"And this other boy South, that was with them, he said that they would be killed if they had come back without carryin out their orders.

"And wasn't *that* terrible? Ah now.

"This South was a spy. He came all through the country into houses, sellin Old Moore's Almanac and old books and clothes and brushes. And many people seen him.

"A Sheridan boy over be Florencecourt put up a ladder to his hay, and went up it, and South jumped out, jumped off from the top of it. He recognized him. I heard him talkin about it down here. So I did.

"I never seen him, but I heard about it."

People remember Sean South, the man. He and O'Hanlon were not alone in the raid, but they are the ones who are remembered, the ones who are commemorated in song, because they died. As heroes they were members of a group of men, but death particularized them. It is death that most perfectly makes people into individuals, isolating them from society. The idea reverses. The individual who breaks out of the group is vulnerable— potentially, figuratively, actually dead. When the warrior rises through heroism into isolation he becomes a martyr. When the worker withdraws through bitterness into isolation he leaves the community of mutual aid. He gets no help when storms break. The hay rots, his cows stagger and fall and die. His source of food and cash is gone, and he totters on death's brink. His opposite, the good neighbor, the member of a methal, moves gracefully at the center of living. In communal engagement, unnamed, unparticular, he swells victoriously with life.

Mrs. Cutler often repeats for the pleasure of young people around her a rhyme from her childhood:

> *Sir Edward Carson had a cat,*
> *it sat upon the fender.*
> *And every time he fed the cat,*
> *it cried out, No Surrender.*

> *De Valera had a cat,*
> *he fed it on a plate,*
> *And every time he hit the cat,*
> *it shouted, Up Free State.*

Sir Edward Carson, whose portrait hangs above the mantel in Mrs. Cutler's Room, treats his cat better; he lets it sit unhit, on the bright fender by the warm hearth. But the rhyme's verses are more alike than different; George

Sir Edward Carson in Mrs. Cutler's Room

Bernard Shaw conflated them in his memory.[12] The men are the staunchest. Carson led the resistance to the Home Rule Bill of 1912, helping found and arm the Ulster Volunteers. Eamon de Valera, though sentenced to death after the Easter Rising of 1916, was reprieved and became the leader of Sinn Fein, risking life and victory in civil war. The men make a mirrored pair. So do their cats, who repeat party slogans when fed and symbolize the people who humbly and loyally surrender their human will to ideology.

Become a follower, the individual becomes a housecat, a kept beast. Shouting slogans, he leaves neighborliness for bitterness and loses membership in the human community. To be human is to own a soul and so to accept the divine commandment to live in neighborly love. The bitter neighbor is a man no more; he is the opposite, the opponent of men. The "true men" of Mackan fought "tigers" and were sentenced by a leech. In Hugh McGiveney's band songs, magistrates are "pets," Price is a "pup" and a "mouldy fowl," the roaring judge is fortuitously named Bull, and Redmond's followers only "ape" men. Alive as an animal, the follower is dead as a person.

Living the brutish death of the bad neighbor or dying the heroic death of the martyr, the follower abandons social existence and marks the limits of the conscious life most people lead as they ponder the interval between the community and an unknown beyond. To one side lies the beastly existence of bitterness, to the other, the angelic absence of martyrdom. Between lies the human state. Shifting there, few aspire to extremes. Ireland's armed rebels, the willing to die and perhaps dead of soul, number but a few hundred. The District has no one bitter in all seasons. Ever divided in mind, all maintain some degree of neighborly connection, preserving themselves as human.

Political tensions confuse their attempts to bring experience into conceptual order. They do not always succeed. Sometimes they collapse into bitterness. Some lie for weeks in bed, paralyzed by "nervous breakdowns." But usually they face the constant perplex, working against the potential for cultural destruction built into their culture with a daily etiquette that avoids political discussion.

The substance of neighborliness is economic, its topics are weather and cows. Around them people engage politely, without erasing conflict from their thought, to maintain some sense of community, but it is not what it was. Work's purpose has shifted from cooperation and endurance to enterprise and success; life's base has become the family farm, not the neighborhood. Still the old community lives in memory, in small acts, and the occasional methal.

At night things are different. Politics must appear in conversations, so work's single loose community breaks into several tight ceiliing communities. Within them, unchallenged by basic disagreement, the interpersonal intensity and cooperative style of the past continues to thrive. Work is no longer generated out of the idea of engaged union. Ceilis are.

Ceilis seem poised to effect the community's breakup. Yet that is not what they do. The ceili's tales reverse the rhetorical complexity and ideological simplicity of songs. Singing in public, men praise and lament heroes. Talking among themselves at the hearth, thinking through stories, they wonder. Mackan Hill provides the great example, but the Smashing of the Band will do as well. In song, the men who broke down the doors and cleared the instruments out were heroes like the Manchester Martyrs. In story, "they done a foolish thing" and "ruined our country."

Stories in ceilis do not confirm the ideological unity of the people present. They use social unity to raise the truth that confines ideology and calls doctrine into question. Is an event right when it brings death to the neighbors? No answer comes. People return to daylight encounter, unwilling to sacrifice community to anger.

The community can be defended against the divisive onslaught of national politics. Discussing the band's second battle, Mr. Boyle made this point: when social wounds are produced solely by politics, they can be healed. Conflicts can be resolved by resort to the old values remembered in accounts of cooperative work and enacted nightly in ceilis. But—and this is the great exception revealed by the failure of mumming, the stories of Mackan Fight and Price and the Band—when the political and religious intermingle, conflicts prove unresolvable.

Neighborliness is a religious concept. Not alone for reasons of personal peace and economic stability do people get along despite their dreadful, wider scene. The District's statement of the essence of Christianity is

"Love your neighbor as yourself and you shall live. That's what our Lord taught. That's the first commandment." To be Christian, to live in this world as a human being, to live in the next at all, you must love your neighbor. There is no release from that command. It is absolute.

When people place the nation above the community and flail through a bitter spell, they not only risk death by isolation, they deny God and risk damnation, an eternity of torture.

God created the world. Faith is the base of social existence.[13] The great historian, Marc Bloch, wrote that modern scholars who are unable to free themselves from skepticism find it impossible to understand the motives of medieval men,[14] and the scholar who cannot believe that others believe contorts into baroque explanations for reality when facing communities like Ballymenone. It is not fear of police that prevents theft, not social pressure that makes conversations truthful, not expectation of return that prompts generosity, not the specter of hanging that keeps people from killing their neighbors. The District's people are honest, generous beyond reciprocity, committed to peace despite war, because "He's there." Their faith defends their minds from bitterness and drives them to good works. Without them, faith is dead, so people help their neighbors, even their backward or bitter neighbors, and need no worldly repayment. God is watching. Christianity restrains the wild force of politics.

To hear it said in the news media, the Ulster Troubles are an archaic religious war. I understand why journalists, anxious to meet deadlines, use the facile labels they do, for I too have heard Catholics describe the persecution they suffer within the British Empire, and I have heard Protestants express fear for the loss of religiously based civil liberties in a united Ireland. I have also heard Protestants say local Catholics are being used by politicians in the South driven by selfish ambition and a regressive racist notion of Irish destiny, and I have heard Catholics say local Protestants are being used by rich industrialists who fear the nationalization of enterprise one Ireland might bring. I have heard people of both sides blame the British soldiers, saying their interruptions and rudeness, their violent presence, is the real cause: they keep the IRA stirred up and through their own discourteous, if not illegal, actions preserve sympathy for the terrorists, while making everyone's life miserable. I have listened as a staunch Loyalist told me he hated the English people; sometimes pompous, usually crude, they are always unmannerly, overtalkative, and shallow. He could accept a separate Northern Ireland, he said, but the last thing he wanted was to be part of England, and what he really wanted was the unification of Ireland as a separate dominion in the Empire. Another Loyal Protestant said of the British Prime Minister, "Och, what does she want, only to be rubbin butter to the fat sow's arse—and down with the poor. They should tie a sack over her head and throw her in a drain. She doesn't care a haet about the poor people sufferin here in Northern Ireland." I have listened as a member of the Provisional IRA, with deaths notched on his soul, told me that the Protestant paramilitary radicals, members of the UVF and UDA, were his brothers. Their common enemy was the British army and American capitalism. In the new Ireland, for which he was game to die, Protestants, by dint of industry, would run the business and disproportionately influence the government, but British soldiers would no longer prowl the streets and all truly Irish traditions would flourish. The Orange Lodges would still troop proudly on the Twelfth, he said, and Catholics would be left to their green farms and ancient, sacred culture. I heard too much. I came to Ireland with experience in the American civil rights movement, but my experience did not apply. In Northern Ireland the disadvantaged occupy the mythic center; the "minority" hold the cultural power, while the "majority" hold the political power and struggle for identity. Though I came with a tradition that teaches problems have solutions, I listened, and slowly, as complexity mounted complexity, begetting complexity, as right and wrong lost focus, all explanations became too muddled for acceptance, and I adopted the view from Ballymenone. The Troubles might die down. They have in the past. But there is no solution for them. I do not know, for no one does, but I feel that religion is not the cause, that religion is being used by politicians to obscure the economic issues at the root of things, and I believe that were it not for religion the situation would be unimaginably worse.

I do not know Belfast, but I know Ballymenone. People there are not religious fanatics. They have not the terrified ersatz faith of zealots who, protesting too much, praise their own sanctity while cluttering their speech with unnecessary references to God. The District's people hold a faith so deep, so sure and serene, that it rarely comes to their lips. They do not quote scripture in vain or discuss doctrine. All are, after all, Catholics, some Roman Catholics, others Church of Ireland. Religious difference, they believe, is a matter more of birth than persuasion, and all forms of religion are valid.

A "joke" Peter Flanagan learned from his father, who used to tell such "wee bits" at wakes "to relieve the great burden of remorse," underscores the foolishness of religious wrangling:

"Now troth, there was some funny tales told in this country some years ago.

"But like that: I heard hundreds of them; I just forgot them. I'd want to get down to that work again and think of them.

"It was like one I heard me father and—he was—ah, God, the two of them's dead now—and they were tellin. I was only quite young. Well, I wasn't that young, I was fourteen, but at the same time I hadn't much sense for yarns. I don't know; I was stupid.

"And they were tellin funny yarns the whole night and they were keepin the whole house in laughter.

"And both men had close relationships. They were nearly from the same country, you know. And they were funny.

"And I mind one they were tellin
        about the
                Catholic and the Jew
                        that was discussin about religion.

"And the two of them come as far as they said:

"Well, I have more saints now in my *side* than what *you* have.

"I'll bet you, says the Jew, he says, we have more saints, he says, on our side, he says, than what you have, he says to Paddy.

"The two of them had beards.

"Well, says one to another, now, he says, we'll start to mention, he says, saints.

"He says, And every saint, he says, that I mention, he says, I'll pull a hair out of *your* beard ◊ and, he says, every saint, he says, that you mention, he says, you can pull a hair out of *my* beard ◊.

"So that was the agreement between them.

"And of course, I couldn't at the very same time just mention the whole saints, but they started anyway:

"*Saint* Peter.

"*Saint* Paul.

"*Saint* Michael.

"*Saint* James.

"And the chins started to get a bit sore, of course. Got nippy with other.

"And the Jew put over his hand
        and he says, the Twelve Apostles, says he.

"And Paddy put over his hand, and he took the whole beard, and he says, the *Dublin Fusiliers* ◊."

As it had in the house of dying, where petty piety and sectarian differences prove fatuous, P's joke brought great laughter to the hearth. Not only does the joke display unconcern with the details of religion (nothing in it would suggest a difference between Judaism and Catholicism), but it sets up the widest possible Irish distinction, Jew and Catholic, and reveals its final insignificance as P, a wholly devout man, makes one of his own religion and nation, named for the first Saint, seem silliest. What interests people is not scrambled doctrinal surface but the pure sacred essence to which anyone can connect to become good.

A Protestant farmer: "We will only be here a lock of years. What difference does it make what religion you are? We won't be asked on the Last Day what religion you are, but only what kind of life you led."

A Catholic farmer: "It's like a mountain. And the Catholics are goin up the one side. And the Protestants are goin up the other. But they are both headin for the same place."

The top of the mountain, salvation, is death's conquest. Economically, neighborliness is a way to make a living. Socially, neighborliness is the way to peaceful life. Religiously, neighborliness is the way to eternal life.

Bad people, they feel, are bad not because of religion but because they betray their religion. Religion is not the community's problem; it provides the base and frame and force of neighborly existence.

Since politics are held in check by sacredly founded communal life, the community's forces for disorder, other than madness, should always be held in control. Yet they break free and death follows. That happens when national politics exploits religion, undermining the community's natural base for resistance.

Housefronts buckle, armored cars whirl the lanes, walls fall, lights circle in silence, slate and glass clatter onto the street, wounds gush. The air breaks with bombs, breathes with terror. In the babble of oratory and the rattle of gunfire, as decent people try to make sense of their wee lives, national politics seeks for order and validation in a more profound cultural stratum, in sacred bedrock. So long as the world of politics turns free of religion, life is not sweet, but the hierarchy of values holds: religion prevents total explosion and consoles the pained soul. But when old channels between the social and sacred are flooded with words, and deep Christian concepts are pumped out for rhetorical use, then conflicts, finally matters of capital distribution, begin to be accepted as religious.

Then the martyr to political cause becomes a martyr to sacred cause. Martyrs: the banners of Orange Lodges depict Protestant martyrs, and the pub's songs make rebels saints. Ignatius MacManus was a "martyr," so was the old band. Sean South was "another martyr for old Ireland." His song quoted that which preceded his as south Fermanagh's favorite, "Kevin Barry." They remain linked in performance. When "Kevin Barry" ends in a prayer, as it does not in calm scenes, varieties of martyrdom merge. Peter Flanagan's rendition, sung on an emotional night in loose unison with Joe Hynes from Enniskillen, follows:

> In Mountjoy, one Monday morning, high upon the gallows tree,
> Kevin Barry gave his young life for the cause of liberty.
> Just a lad of eighteen summers, there was no one can deny,
> As he marched to death that morning, Kevin held his head on high.
>
> Shoot me like a soldier, do not hang me like a dog,
> For I fought to free Ireland on that still September morn,
> All around that little bakery where we fought the Black and Tan.
> Shoot me like a soldier, for I fought to free our land.
>
> Calmly standing to attention as he bade his last farewell
> To his brokenhearted mother whose grief no one can tell.
> For the cause he proudly cherished, this sad parting had to be.
> Then to death went softly smiling that old Ireland might be free.

Another martyr for old Ireland, another murder for the crown.
Brutal laws do crush the Irish, but cannot keep their spirits down.
Lads like Barry are no cowards from the foes they will not fly,
For their bravery all has been Ireland's cause to free our land.

Mother of Christ, Star of the Sea,
Pray for the Wanderer,
Pray for me.

Sprung high, P Flanagan's closing song-prayer seems to come out of clear air, from nowhere and from everywhere. Pilgrim's prayer for rebels, martyr's prayer for other exiles, it suggests an identity of singer and hero, Mary and Kevin's mother, Kevin and Christ. Only a suggestion, but there is no question about the Manchester Martyrs. Dead, they are met with a crown of glory by Saint Patrick. When he recorded "The Manchester Martyrs" again, years later, Peter Flanagan substituted a different last stanza in which Patrick purifies and sanctifies Ireland:

You holy hills, I consecrate thee;
No poisonous serpents can there be seen,
And that is why they are banished from it.
It's the coat of honor, the shamrock green.

Men who fight to preserve the holy island are welcomed by the Saint who made it holy, and "holy angels around them sing" while men below sing around them, sanctifying their sacrifice.

The spirit of Swanlinbar lifts to purify war. In "The Swad Chapel Song," Saint Patrick "drove the snakes and serpents from our sainted isle," making Ireland heaven's prelude. Ireland's defenders become God's warriors, then angels. Their enemies, the judge and jury who found them guilty, their executioners, become Death's minions, Satan's agents. Conflict clears, life clouds.

When in times of terror political strife enters deep sacred realms, God's commandment to neighborliness no longer contains conflict, and a dilemma locks, systematically, at culture's center. Then religion tells you murder is sin, rebels are damned. And religion tells you murder is just response to evil, that rebels are gathered into eternal glory. At once you are instructed to love and fight your neighbor. Not clearly, but with precision, culture frames the dilemma and offers no solution.

They say that if you do not adjust to the Trouble, to bloodshed constant as rain, you will go mad. And they say if you do adjust, you are mad. Blood is not rain.

You feel it first at the base of your spine, then it blows out of the silence in the center of your skull, exploding through your ears to rattle the windows and crack the beams above. "Thunder," says P. "Aye," says Joe. Black silence reassembles. "I would say now that was thunder over the Lough,"

P says. "Aye," says Joe, and I say, "Yes," knowing as well as they that the radio tomorrow will tell us who the thunder, so cunningly man-made, swept away.

They speak of the Trouble as a climate. Like the weather, it was here before they were born and will continue after they are gone. Like sun and rain, it is beyond full comprehension, out of control, God's will, something to endure.

So what are you going to do? All you can do, Hugh Nolan said, is not think about it, for the closer you look, the worse it looks. But as a human being you are doomed to memory, looking and knowing. What you cannot do is brood, for that brings paralysis, and you must carry on. There is work to be done. The hay is to mow, and now to rook. Then black clouds roll swollen over wind-bent trees at the ridgecrests. Men gather with pitchforks in the breathless dark light, moving swiftly across the meadows.

If some days drift noiselessly over lone work, others burst with thunder. Your neighbors need you, and you need them. It is not possible to forget. Workaday existence raises the neighborly issue, and however we think about it, we come to the same conclusion.

As a valid section of Ballymenone's culture, neighborliness integrates the economic, social, political, and religious spheres, which are separated in old-fashioned ethnography. Making a living requires cooperation. Cooperation is founded on sacred commandment. In times of extreme trouble, cooperation must be politically organized. If the sacred and the political align, the result is a cooperative institution, a methal. If they are opposed, the result is a dilemma. At the heart of neighborliness, its political-religious and religious-social gears bind, grinding in opposition, and culture is not, as it is in the methal, a way to solve problems, but a problem to solve.

That culture, a collective structuring of mentality, is the profound context for historical stories. If instead of shifting focus from context to text we do the reverse, beginning at stories and weaving contexts around them, drawing germane experience to the things the people themselves create, then we have a slower but less abstract, more generous, better way to understand their thinking.

The District's people class their stories of history into Saints and Battles. Saints come first, displaying their power in dazzling feats and bringing God's message, which makes people human, obliging them to be good. To be good, people praise God through loving their neighbors. Even saints find that hard. They must be taught to praise God. They become enraged and bring death in war.

Battle tales use politics to describe by extremes the human condition. Life is threatened. If people cooperate, they will win, saving the home, but victory can bring greater loss because conflict is the normal state of social existence. The problem is discriminating between conflicts that can be resolved and conflicts that must be endured, like the weather. Battles display the varieties of conflict. The Ford's, pitting native against alien, and fraternal conflict, exhibited in the Smashing of the Band, can be resolved through victory or peaceful cooperation. But the conflict among natives, that which comes of the community's inbuilt divisions, has no end. That is why Mackan Fight is so crucial, why it has produced more art than any other, why its kind of conflict thrust more than one event into memory, and we have the Inishmore Fight, Swad Chapel, and Price and the Band, as well as Mackan Hill, from which to learn about religious hostility.

Religious difference comes with human birth. People are expected to be loyal to natal faith. "A person," they say, "should follow his father and be what he was born." Religion creates the one, natural, unalterable division in the community. Then, through sacred commandment, religion overarches that division in love. But when religion becomes a reason for threat, a reason for conflict, it cannot stay fear and anger; people fight, risking death and damnation. Perfectly, stories of religious faction fights symbolize all the community's reasons for division, all its forces of destruction, and describe its reality. To be a community, it must have unity. To be real, it will be divided. Existence, everyone's life, forms between unity and separation, society and self.

Stories and culture merge, closing down around the same point. People are abandoned to the counsel of their own souls and forced to be free. Perhaps differently in every moment and situation, individuals must resolve in instantaneous action a problem vibrating without resolution in their heads. They meet their neighbors on the road and hear stories at night, and, caught between community and conflict, unity and division, feeling simultaneously the pull of peace and war, people have no choice but to choose. So opinions on historic fights vary, and the ways people pick through existence are their own.

Abraded by culture, people make endless decisions through which their lives become human. When they decide for peace, as the people of Ballymenone usually do, it is not to culture's credit but their own. They are good people.

11

Saints at Work

Our need is to conceive of another life. We study others not to chain them into our schemes but to free them so their lives will form coherently as something different from our own, yet like enough, complex enough that they feel wholly and disarmingly human.

Properly, we have entered the world of Ballymenone through texts created by the people who must live there. You have now read the District's stories of history. There are not many of them, they are not frequently told. Their tellers do not personify their community's norm. They are older, most are poorer, brighter than the average. No one can encompass all a community's factions; the District's historians are male, Catholic, most are unmarried. Yet, the historians' stories have plunged us far into the community's culture and opened to us its hierarchy of values.

At top, in the bright, confusing surface of things, the person confronts the power within, using it, pleasing and testing it. The pleasure of engagement with self is the aesthetic. At base, in the mists beneath, the person encounters the eternal and unseen, the sacred. Between, he or she arranges the self in relation to other human beings. No mere conventions of philosophy, the aesthetic, sacred, and social are absolute dimensions of existence. These varieties of universal experience are formulated variously in cultures where they do not exist only as independently established institutions. They interact hierarchically as values.

Values gain existence in action, in deeds and words. I will state the case plainly for stories. The story, as Hugh Nolan taught, must be beautiful and true: clear, smooth, complete, and radiant in diction. Well told, the story appears at once as an aesthetic presence and a gift to society. Its beauty engages, its clear truth enables engagement to become union. The tale's performance enacts the ethical ideal while raising the issues of conflict and sanctity. Conflict describes social reality. Sanctity contains conflict in God's word. Sacred commandment forms the base; it brings the social world into order and compels aesthetic endeavor to generosity and clarity, limiting, not eliminating, the realm in which personal delight is discovered. Life makes sense.

Rare, the possessions of few people, historical stories are not marginal or oblique. They hit dead center, providing an exact, confined, insistent experience that can be applied widely and generally through life. Still, knowing Ballymenone, I sense a thinness, an incompleteness. The culture in tales is like an armature, a tight, stable, inner structure, lacking body. If stories speak of the relation of a person to the self, the other, and God, of culture's aesthetic, ethical, and sacred dimensions, they tell too little of man's relation to the natural environment, culture's ecological dimension, and in that connection lies an entire history but barely hinted at in historical tales. The armature discovered in stories lacks the clay of common experience which gives life richness and conviction. Stories may be right, but proof of their rightness escapes them. Life's reason emerges in molded clay, in daily work.

Let us return to the beginning. The Saints came upon the world when it was still in transition, still cooling. The Sillees still ran for the sea when Saint Febor's wild deer bore her sacred books across the hills. Saint Patrick brought fire to the Virgin Shore and discovered an herb upon an island in the Lough. Saints' cures, Patrick's dho, Mogue's clay, Naile's crystal fountain, bring benefit out of the land to man, prefiguring the agricultural work of forty generations of south Fermanagh people. Solutions to worldly problems rest in the earth, and from earth comes a way to learn the truth of God's message. The cure is conceptually central.

"There is some herb in the fields to cure everything. God made it so. There is even a cure for cancer. That's God's law." Peter Flanagan finds such optimism reasonable, a logical consequence of creation. "What is amazin," he says, "is how these ideas came to people." Like wandering Bloom in James Joyce's great novel, Mr. Flanagan wonders how human beings came to match diseases and cures. It is apparent to him that modern science is but an extension of "the old science," but the origins of medical science are puzzling.

There is a theory to account for specific family cures. They came to ancient people from God and have been preserved within lineages. God's word rang in the head of Saint Patrick, who plucked the dho on Inishmore and placed it in the secret care of a family, the Nobles. The cure is administered with a "charm," a prayer, a reciprocating expression of gratitude to God. The cure works because God works through it. When a pale place on the first joint of your finger grows into a "beeldin," it may be "whitla" or "whittle." If untreated, the finger will have to be amputated, so you go to that member of the McConnell family who is curator of the recipe. Herbs will be gathered on the mountain and boiled down in the kitchen. Odd odors will waft across the Derrylin Road. God will be thanked. You will be cured.

Cures known generally pose a riddle. Peter Flanagan entertains different solutions. Perhaps they descended through the generations from ancient people who heard God's voice whisper like far thunder. They might have been discovered by scientific investigation, but experimentation is dangerous. Bloom muses punnishly, "The first person that picked an herb to cure himself had a bit of pluck."[1] Poisonous plants grow in the field: deadly nightshade, fox's tongue, laburnum. A carrotlike root in the marshes kills cows. Poisonous plants, says Joe Flanagan, are enticing to the eye and sweet to the tongue. "The laburnum bush has peas on it that are tempting. He is a lovely bush, an ornamental bush." It does not seem reasonable that people could have experimented randomly, for so many would have died in the process. Still, cures may have been discovered through courageous research, but if they were, all scientists were doing was stumbling across the laws God built into the world.

Revealed or discovered, God's forces stay God's forces. The diseases He sends are countered in cures He provides. Pusey, a plant with a purple flower, grows in the meadow in early summer. A tea made of it and taken every day for a couple of months will cure tuberculosis. Shooting stars leave "a transparent globular stuff like frog spawn" on the ground. Of different degrees of transparency and different colors and sizes, often big as a football, these fragments of star, found mostly in wet years on the hillsides, are applied to burns. Relief is immediate. A creeper grows on the moss ground. Called "the tormenter" and "the gardener's bane" because it spreads its grip and chokes the plants, this weed has a small root that can be boiled down in milk to provide an essence that cures kidney trouble. In the sand and lime plaster of old houses, the house leek roots. Its leaves are placed in the bottom of a "tinnie" or "porringer," a tin cup, boiling water is poured over them, and the liquid is applied to sore eyes.

The idea that all diseases have cures is easily turned around. "There's not a plant in the field," Joe Flanagan said, "but has some cure in it." Working in the bog, sitting in turfsmoke at the hearth, people breathe in the fumes of the broken and burned compressed herbs of which turf is composed, and their health is improved by unknown antidotes. Sickly children are fed goat's milk because goats search out and eat herbs cows avoid.

The cure is an expandable concept. The world was made for humankind. "God made everything useful," Peter Flanagan said, "even the worm turns the soil. And it is useful for fishin." A tea substitute can be brewed from the pignut, "a hard little plant to find." The red berries that ripen in harvest on the briar can be boiled, strained, and made into jelly. Wild mushrooms gathered in August are peeled and cooked in butter. "I had an aunt," Ellen Cutler said, "that would look anywhere for watercress. We wouldn't eat it, but she did. *Watercress*." Flutes can be made from sections of the field scout, a tall, light, hollow plant. With finger holes burned in by a hot nail, it makes a better homemade flute than a bicycle pump, because the field scout tapers naturally.[2]

Even nature's troubles contain benefit. The tormenter that battles man for control of the moss ground, and the house leek that cracks plaster, both contain cures. Thief of produce, the rabbit becomes a good winter dinner when skinned and roasted with an onion. Nettles, growing as the ghosts of old homes, raise stinging welts to bare skin, and "to nettle" is used like "to hackle" as a verb of annoyance. Yet, "you pull them and boil them just the same as you would cabbage. It's for the measles. To bring them out. These days they would laugh at that, but the old people all made nettle tea for children for the measles. Pull them and strip them and boil them, and, sure, the water would be green, but what odds? The cure would be in it." And, Mrs. Cutler continued, "you can eat nettles like cabbage. Boil them and strain them. They're lovely. I've heard tell of people boilin them for cabbage, and I've eat them. They don't have one bit jaggers on them. They're lovely." Essence of nettle-root tea made a horrible-tasting spring tonic to thin the blood and purify the body.

Rushes spring and spread on poorly drained hillside fields, taking space from good grass, diminishing productivity, and symbolizing sloppy husbandry. Though a nuisance and embarrassing, rushes point, men say, to good soil beneath. They can be rotted, "steeped," in a pond to spread as a poor sort of fertilizer for broken ground. They are cut for cattle bedding and, champed into the byre manure, they stretch it to make the best "top dressin" for the meadows. Rushes can be cut and thrown into sloughy gaps to firm the earth. In the past they made "rush candles" by peeling "big fat bulrushes" and steeping them in oil. Today rushes are used to thatch potato pits, haystacks, temporary buildings, "rittilins," and, pulled through a graip to remove their heads and clinging grasses, they are used to thatch homes. Rushes are slow to work because they are short, and a roof of rush will last only a couple of years. Still, John Gilleece said, "they are as good as bad straw."

From noisome nettles, a tea to cure measles; from rushes, a roof; from the bad comes some good. "God made it so."

God is most often evoked as cause in extreme situations. Knowing that the seemingly useless, even harmful thing—a worm, a pignut, a clump of rushes—was devised to serve humankind, people learn hope. The worst earthly contingency, illness, is part of God's plan. It drags us toward despair to make us struggle consciously toward life.

At his hearth in the dark Hugh Nolan said, "There's a sayin in this country: Hunger will break stone walls. It's terrible to see a beast hungry, for they don't understand. The people can reason, but the brute can't." Without reason, the cow feels a wrench of pain in the viscera. People recognize the pain as hunger, and hunger as conquerable. "I've been watchin the weather since I was eight," Mr. Nolan said, "and there was no year so bad that some man didn't get his crop in." There is reason to hope. For people, hunger is more than pain; it is a creative principle, a goad to thought, a metaphoric appeal to action. "The hungry eye sees far," Mrs. Cutler said. Reason condemns people to remembering and planning, carrying on with purposive action. Pain stimulates thought. The eye sees farther, then real and figurative hunger is conquered in work.

But if pain is too great, it is we who are conquered. Unable to rise to neighborly commandment, we lie still when backs are needed on storm-threatened meadows and sit in silence when words are needed to keep the ceili alive. Ill, we cannot even help ourselves, and despair opens beneath to suck our souls into damnation. Then plants are boiled, seasoned, and served, leaves and roots from little plants are mixed and boiled, a prayer is said, and we are brought back to health and involvement, renewed in hopeful action. The hungry soul is fed.

"We must live in hope," Mrs. Cutler said, "or die in despair," and hope is no lie to the self. "Between heaven and wantin," she said, "I'll get what I need."

Saint's gift, the cure is an aid to salvation and a figura for salvation. Hunger is transitory, illness can be cured. Despair, the sensation of hopelessness, the breath of nothingness, the egotistical thought that God has forsaken you which leads straight to hell, can be overcome in the knowledge that God made the world for you. Little plants in the fields hold cures for your pain.

The first proposition of the District's philosophy, that God created the world, that He's there, is suggested in story but proved in cures. Worried I had carried analysis too far, I asked Peter Flanagan if cures prove God's existence. He did not pause:

"Oh, it proves there's a God, surely. Aye. Aye. It certifies.

"Sure that's the thing. That's the thing. And outside of any saint's cure, you're not goin to get a cure. It certifies surely to anyone that has any Christianable faith about them and has any belief in God. When you get a cure like that, there's nothin—it's past contradiction.

"Isn't it?

"There's Saint Naile's Well, and it's supposed if you had any sore or anything—several hundreds, I think cured.

"Rub it on just, in the name of the Father, Son, and Holy Ghost.

"It would cure it.

"There never had been any improvements carried out in olden times. And all the shrines now, as you know yourself, the shrines of Bernadette and all these shrines has all been modernized. All very attractive. But it hasn't happened in Kinawley. And I believe it is the greatest shrine of them all: the well, Saint Naile's Well. Because if you had any sore, such as boil or any skin disease, you could rub on to it in the name of the Father, Son, and Holy Ghost. It twas a permanent cure.

"It proves to you that there's a God. It entails both. It takes in the both.

"It'd prove there's a God on high. And with the intercession of the saint's power, it's supplyin it to you: spiritual strength. And to wipe out and relieve you that ailment that's givin you very much trouble.

"Aye, it's a great thing to know it. It tis, surely.

"And it's a great thing, as you say, that surely certifies past all doubt there's a God on high."

By joining radical need with radical uselessness into a logic of hope, the cure demarcates existence. It refers beyond to eternity and closes down around life's center, where the disease is common hunger, the cure is common food. Here the talk is less of God, but the logic holds tightly. The world is a gift. Paradise is lost. The gift requires work. The saint's cure demands preservation and preparation and prayer. The born musician plays beautifully only after hours of struggling practice. God's land does not yield without the water of sweat.

Life's center, work, is a prayer and a mode of becoming. The spade bites the dirt, muscles grapple with creation, God is thanked. The hay is "saved," a project is completed, and the individual comes into human existence in the formation of a philosophy of hopeful action that guides the body through work into health, the mind through hardship into wisdom, the spirit through pleasure into happiness, the soul through faith into salvation.

The Saint's message asserted in story is proved while solutions are worked out of the soil. We gain enrichment and conviction as we shift from night to day, reading the texts created out of common work.

PART FIVE

Working the Land

William Lunny

James McGovern

John Drumm Thatching

Gabriel Dorsey Rooking

Spade

Potato Pit

Turf Clamps

Hay Peck

Lane

Gap

Cattle on the Upland

The Croziers'

Fresh Fadge in the Oven at Mrs. Cutler's Hearth

Rear Window of the Flanagans' Kitchen

12

Plans and Snags

God's blessing, Mr. McGovern calls it. Heat rises, wavering over the grass, and only a few rooks remain at the field's far edge. Smoking, we sit in the shadows of the hayshed, squinting through the slight sting of hay-scraps and sweat, scanning the steamy green field. He has other meadows scattered east and south. Their rooks will be snatched by a buck rake, scooted home by a tractor. But these were built on the wet bottoms. A buck rake would mishandle them, leaving won hay behind, dragging sodden hay in to rot holes in the cattle's winter feed, so we have gone to each one, unroped it, and rebuilt it over the cart's brackers. The last damp wisps have been separated by hand and spread to dry further, and at slight command the ass has shifted his shoulders, tightening chains, turning wheels, drawing the cart, a mobile mound, toward the shed.

"It's a wonder," Mr. McGovern says, "the way he walks away with a load." Work's rhythm is built into his hide. Each tall, pale load sways slowly into place at the mouth of the shed, then he stops, standing stock-still, while every matted swatch is pitched out. Head down, hooves planted, he does not move. The clammy hay is piled along the shed's tin sides to bake dry, the rest is layered neatly to the roof. Then he feels no weight and drifts, grazing, the gleaming cart behind him, while we sit, resting. The field shines, sliding flatly in the sun, across to the dun hillocks of the last hay rooks. "This good weather," Mr. McGovern says, "is God's blessing."

James McGovern came to Sessiagh from "up in the State." He rented this farm until he could buy it. Constant work has hung iron gates in his gaps, metalled the street, and replaced the old sod house with a new one of block. "When I was a young man," he says, "I would never have guessed that I'd be as good as I am today. I don't mind admittin I've worked for my day's wages." James McGovern is seventy-two. His life has passed in hard work. He has provided a bright, comfortable home for his daughter and her daughter. Behind us the shed is packed full. Before us the field planes emptily under a wide, clear sky. Victory is assured. But "you can't have it the two ways," he says. A pipe and a plug of tobacco are all his delight, and our smoke is done. Again the cart goes out light, comes back heavy, and we pause. There is no cause to rush. He looks across the field. "It's grand weather, mister, so it is." The day blazes green fire, blue smoke. "But there was no worse weather than what we had the year. It was the hand of God strikin man for what evil has been done in Belfast."

Northern Ireland's death toll, the papers report, has just passed five hundred.

The old historians, the Four Masters and Geoffrey Keating, recorded ancient instances of political wickedness bringing wild weather and famine to the land.[1] Mr. McGovern's theory bears antique authority, and he is not the only one in the District who connects bad people and bad weather to explain the cold, wet spring of 1972 as, to use Keating's phrase, "the vengeance of heaven."

Cause and effect, bombs and thunder, blend into one context of hardship. Hugh Nolan said famine accompanies war and when people do great wrong, "God will scourge them, and there's not a haet can be done about it. God will keep it up until He decides to stop it. This Trouble will go on until God stops it. And we must carry on."

To Hugh Patrick Owens, James McGovern's neighbor, "all these bloody satellites" provide the immediate cause of bad weather, but immediate causes—climatic mechanics, satellites, civil war—are as nothing beside the ultimate cause. For Mr. Owens and many others, the bad spring seemed to fulfill one of the last prophecies of the end of the world attributed to Saint Columcille.[2] A time would come, the Saint foretold, when ships would go upon the sea without sails, and ships would sail in the sky. They do. A time would come when the milk of ten townlands could be churned in one churn. "People didn't believe it," Mr. Owens said, "then came the creameries." The Last Day nears. "In that time you will not be able to tell the difference between the summer and the winter except be the leaves of the trees and the hedges." This year "it was colder on the longest day than it was on the shortest," and before the tardy sun arrived, this, many said, was that summer.

Cold summer winds and "wars and rumors of wars" sweep Ulster, all, said William Lunny, fulfilling old prophecies of the End. Mrs. Cutler heard the old people tell it:

"There was prophecies that there was to go carts on the road and no horses in them. And sure there's cars on the road.

"There was to go ships in the air.

"And sure the airplane's goin in it.

"And before the end of the world there was to be no difference between the summer and the winter,

only in the hedge and the tree.

"That's all the difference there was to be.

"And sure, Lord bless us, that July there, after the Twelfth of July, it twas more like winter nor summer here.

"It was."

Weather is not mere climate, an absurdity. It is the revelation of God's power in rain and sun. His warning echoes through prophecy. Doom rolls in the clouds and shrinks through the hedge.

Weather is the great condition of human existence. The most obvious of conditions, it stands for them all. Its explanation is profound but simple. As James McGovern said, the weather is God's blessing or curse. Storms and sickness, rushes and sun, interminable warfare—all are God's plan, never to be wholly understood, ever to be endured.

In some cultures first things command attention, posing puzzles to the mind. Myths concern gods bringing a soft and unsettled crazy world into order, and starting the flow of historical time. Ballymenone's stories of Saints fill that need. The Saints put the finishing touches on creation and told men God's law. But art directs attention less to Saints than to Battles. The topic is less prime order than it is the ways people operate within that order to build and destroy human associations. So it is in the whole culture. The first principle is crucial but not a question. God made the world. The question concerns free will more than God's plan, culture more than conditions. How do people create within creation? The world is in order. It is the ordeal of people to adapt. While they do, arranging and adjusting the superstructure of moral action upon firm sacred foundations, the human issues of culture and history cry in their minds. At work on the world, in the world, they learn their way.

"This is the way I look at life," said William Lunny, Rossdoney's lone Protestant farmer. "This was all here when we came here and it will all be here when we're gone." He pitched another shovelful of turf mould onto his garden and said, "In this trade you must look to the future." Plans must be made. But, says Hugh Nolan, "No matter what the business is, there's always some little difficulty attached. You can't have it complete. There's always some snag." No plan achieves perfection. Still, says Paddy McBrien, "We must hope, even if we despair the day. We must take advantage and look ahead to the good day." Life's key principle, stated by Tommy Love, like Mr. Lunny, Mr. McBrien, and Mr. Nolan, a Rossdoney farmer, is: "No matter the weather, you must carry on."

Endowed with reason and soul, wit and will, human beings are sentenced to freedom. And they are confined in God's plan, His creation, His scheme of apocalypse, which they cannot entirely understand. Their lot is to carry on, planning, having plans wrecked, planning anew, formulating between plans and snags, a "way of goin on."

"Every man and woman, all the children," said Tommy Lunny, "have their own way of goin on. Bless them every one." Out of inherent traits and life's chances, between blood and encounter, people develop personal patterns, odd patterns perhaps, but acceptable in their own integrity. Wrongdoing is condemned but unusual life-styles are excused, dismissed with the comment, "Ah, but that's their way of goin on." One's way is more than a personality, it carries an aura and a memory, a sense of fortune—and the collective pattern, "the Fermanagh way of goin on," is not exactly a culture. It cannot be reduced to a structure of consciousness, does not reside set in the mind. Even less can it be reduced to a fatalistic or scientistic formula, a program of conditions beyond will. The Fermanagh way of goin on is an existential pattern, a principled coordination of local tradition and local conditions, built out of history for the future.

Ballymenone's thinking combines analogy and abstraction into a dynamic of mind close to what Claude Lévi-Strauss calls the science of the concrete and Gregory Bateson calls abduction.[3] The District's people derive principles from experience. Facts and acts are dismembered and associated abstractly within, so, though extracted from common occasions, they can be applied in novel situations. New things form around old ideas. When expressed, abstractions are lost within real actions, and when described they emerge through potent particulars, in terms of gods and farmers at war and work. For the people Lévi-Strauss studies, the matrix of thought is the timeless world of nature; for the District's people it is the historical, cultivated world. Human action upon the land provides the great experience from which ideas are taken and the realm in which ideas most easily gain statement. Plans for work yield a convincing theory of will, a testable philosophy of human action. Weather provides the blatant contingency, the most frequent snag. Intentions contrived in the freedom of a clear head are immediately constrained, caged by conditions beyond control. People carry on.

Since God made the world for human beings, and the ancestors have gone before, working solutions out of the earth, people do not strike their course without maps. They are probably right when their schemes work, but they may not be wrong when they fail, for conditions are ever beyond, maps are always incomplete. People are free and alone, but they have the hope of the cure, and struggling to present God's gifts of soul and reason to God's gifts of good weather and useful dirt, striving to touch God's blessing incarnate in climate and feel the mystic ease of fit between their will and God's, people drive between plans and snags, wanting and heaven, finding a way.

Their way becomes a philosophy in their creation of the world. It is the shape of their creation, not God's, which stands at issue.

As the old scientists read the wondrous world as the product of divine planning, our task is to read the world for evidence of the existence of man. We accept it as intended, as made by people not beasts, and draw spirit from materials, allowing time to rise from place and spin away so we can enter mind anew through the world made by the people who live in it. Their creation, their manipulation of the God-given environment, breaks into four parts: home, clay, moss, bog.

13

Home

The hearth is on center. Directions within the home are set by motion around the fire. You are going "down" when the hearth's open mouth is behind you, and "up" when it is toward you, and you go up toward the back wall, down toward the door through the front wall. Beyond the home you go "down" to the north and east and "up" to the south and west. Like a swirling swastika, space spins, its four directions extend, then curve, spiraling down or up, merging to embrace half the world, returning, turning through the house to center precisely on the hearth.

In days gone by, Peter Flanagan learned from his father, the fire burned in the middle of the floor. People had no chairs and sat on the earth, completely encircling the dancing flame. Now the fire has been pushed to one side, next to a wall from which a chimney hangs to draw some smoke into the sky. Though located midway on the wall so its chimney will emerge at the roof's crest, the hearth is no longer in the center of its space. But the hearth burns still in the center of the mind, and its space, the kitchen, occupies the middle of the house.

"All the old houses," Peter Flanagan said, "was built on the same plan or the same model." His exemplifies the type. The kitchen opens through its center, lofting fully to the roof, expanding suavely from front to back. Windows break above tables through the front and back walls. At the center of one end wall, the fire smolders and smokes on an "open hearth." Below, across the kitchen, an open "dresser" displays crockery. At the end of the front wall by the dresser, one door opens outward to the world. Low-ceiled rooms flank the kitchen. Generally, as befits their multifunctional nature, these get no name save "room," so a house will be said to have a "kitchen" and so many "rooms," usually three or four. The space below the kitchen is broken. Below, to the front, is a small bedroom—too small P says. It holds little more than his bed—mine when I sleep there, waking to watch new light dapple through lace curtains and bring into relief the still life of rosary and old calendars on the wall. Above, behind, is a yet smaller room attendant on the kitchen. The Flanagans use it for storage. Across the wide kitchen, behind the hearth's wall, is the room some call the parlor but most call, with the emphasis of an initial capital, the Room.

The Flanagans' Home

The East Front

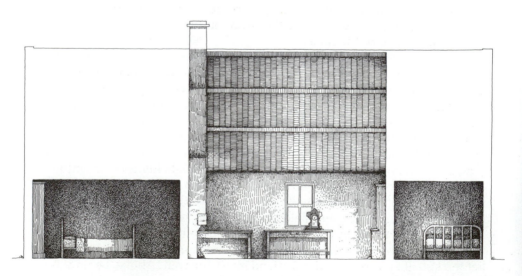

Longitudinal Section

The Hearth Wall

The Dresser Wall

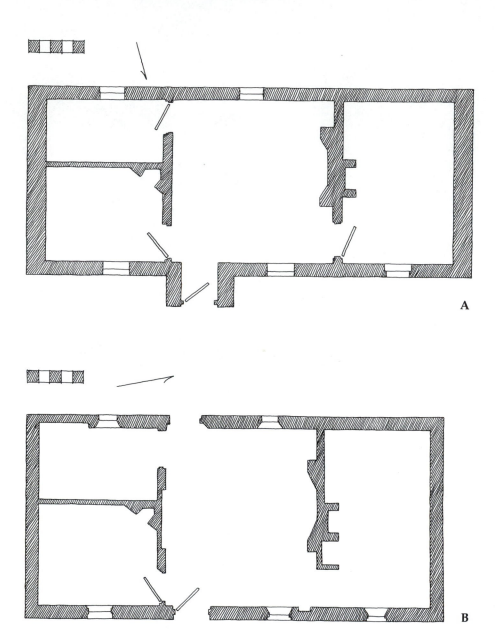

Plans of the Local House Type. **A**. Abandoned house in Drumbargy, associated with the name Balfour, once inhabited by Johnny Boyle. It has stone end walls with brick gables and front wall. **B**. Abandoned house in Sessiagh, associated with the name Browning. It is built of brick. House B is unusual, but not unique, in having a rear door; still, both the houses, along with the Flanagans', the Murphys', and the Cutlers', exemplify the dominant local form. Scales in feet.

Behind the Room in many houses, though not the Flanagans', hides a second bedroom.

Knowing that all the old houses conceal a single plan, that none will surprise and disorient the visitor, people gain a symbol of community.[1] Factions are not separately housed. Rich and poor, Protestants and Catholics, build and inhabit identical homes. They are not truly identical—they differ in size and quality of appointment—but differences of well-being and ideology are not allowed to influence basic shape. Form ignores division.

Rose Murphy's house lies just across the bog from Ellen Cutler's. It was built of brick at the end of the nineteenth century. Mrs. Cutler's was built of stone long before, I would guess between 1790 and 1840. Neither time nor materials separate them. Both stand atop rises, facing east, beneath bright whitewash and thatch. Joe Murphy thatches them both. The Murphys' has always been the seat of a small holding worked by Catholic tradesmen. The Cutlers' has long been the center of a large Protestant farming operation; its Room once held the meetings of the local Orange Lodge. The houses differ in size; Joe Murphy calls his house "small" and Mrs. Cutler's "big," but their plans are the same. The kitchen fills the middle, a hearth on the center of one wall, a dresser opposite, stationed between the doors into the home's lower end. Far to that end of the front wall, one door, "the hole the mason left," breaks through to the outside. Above it, for those departing, are emblems of luck, a Saint Brigid's cross at Rose Murphy's, a tinfoil-wrapped donkey's shoe at Ellen Cutler's. On the back wall, offset to the dresser's side, and so directly in the line of sight of everyone entering, a calendar portraying Christ hangs at the Murphys' and an embroidered "Lead Me and Guide Me" at Mrs. Cutler's. Below the kitchen is the unheated room to the front where each of the women sleeps. Behind there is a small room for storage. Rose Murphy calls it a "lie-by" and keeps wood and water in it. Ellen Cutler calls it a "pantry." It stores plates in a glass press and holds water, a sink for washing, and a gas burner. At the upper ends of both houses, the Room's fireplace is sealed off and family photos stand on exhibit. A bedroom is partitioned behind the Room. Here Joe Murphy sleeps beneath a print of the crucifixion. At Mrs. Cutler's this small room is vacant, though she and her husband and their two sons slept there when Billy's cousin, John McMullen, lived with them and slept in the little bedroom below.

These houses present similar facades, one-story and sparkling white, three windows, one door. Each has a solid block "porch" with an iron window recently built around the door, and old byres built off their ends. They open immediately, providing visitors identical experiences. The District's old houses do not materialize the community's differences but express oneness. All aspire to a single architectural model of appearance and use.

Architecture is to be used. It is shelter, shedding wet, blocking winds,

Rose Murphy

The Murphy Family about 1935. Rose is standing to the right. To her right
stands her father, then her mother. Joe stands at the left.

The Hearth of the Murphys' Home

East Front

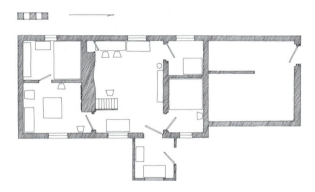

Plan. From left to right: Room to the front with a closed fireplace, a dining table in the center, a press against the end wall. Bedroom behind. Kitchen, entered through a porch, with a table at the front and rear, a couch at the rear toward the hearth, a dresser across from the hearth. Bedroom to the front. Lie-by behind. Byre off the right end. Scale in feet.

The House from the Northeast

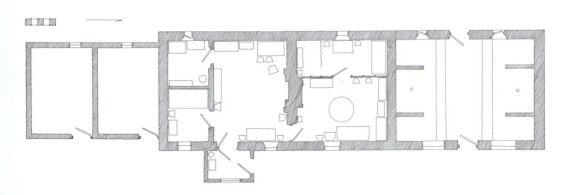

Plan. There is a brick stable off the left, a stone byre off the right. Within the house, from left to right: Bedroom to the front. Pantry behind. Kitchen, entered through a porch, with a table at the front and rear, a sofa at the rear toward the hearth, a dresser across from the hearth. Room to the front with closed fireplace, dining table in the center, press and bureau against the end wall. Bedroom behind. Mrs. Cutler's house is unusual in having no rear window in the kitchen. Scale in feet.

The Dresser Wall of Mrs. Cutler's Home

Ellen Cutler

The Cutler Family about 1963. From right to left: Billy Cutler, Mrs. Cutler, Dick and John, their sons, John McMullen, Mr. Cutler's cousin.

enabling people within to carry on, eating, talking, sleeping without thinking about the building around them. The house is a means to other ends, a stage for social play, a machine to prolong existence. Hollow, every house is a tool.

Architecture is to be seen. It is an arrangement of volumes and voids, colors and textures. Both sculpture and painting, an end in itself, every house is a work of art.

Precious designers, envious of artists, may abandon the architectural center, masking interiors behind fantastic facades, tickling the eye while deceiving the body, but the District's old architects—men like Rose Murphy's great-grandfather—designed organically, unifying tool and art: the home's interior unfolds out of use onto its facade. Noting the door's location, its relation to windows, one for each room, the visitor knows the house's plan. He knows one shift of the hip will carry him over the threshold onto the kitchen floor. There is a minimum of hindrance, no steps up or down, the floor lies at ground level. Welcomingly ajar to help control the chimney's draft, the front door will swing back toward the dresser's wall, blocking the bedroom door. Nothing will stand between the entrance and the fire. It is bad manners for the guest to knock and bad manners for the host to stop a visitor in the doorway. Quick greetings will pass while the guest walks upward toward warmth and light to join the host seated at the hearth. A chair will be drawn to its front, greetings will permute into chat.

The kitchen is not a private place. It is gracefully vulnerable, open and occupied. People from without pierce quickly to its very center, where a fire burns, ready to boil water for tea. People within must pass through the kitchen as they move from space to space, and as they do, they orient themselves by the hearth, gauging every movement as carrying them up or down. When motion stops, people are usually in the kitchen, at the hearth. There they sit, ready to give talk and aid, ready for encounter to eventuate in union. While life passes through the center of the house, seeking order at its midmost point, other volumes are sealed off.

In some houses the small front bedroom contains a fireplace, built athwart a corner and sending a flue up the back of the dresser's wall to sprout at the ridge, a second chimney that defines on the exterior the partition within. But a fire warms its throat only in times of illness. Only illness—of mind, if not body—would carry a person into a room during daylight. Entering a room, like "walkin the road on your lone," is a sign of trouble within. Of a terrible happening, it will be said, "It put me in that much despair, I could go up into the room." People should stay in the kitchen, in company, where they can be watched and helped, lured from brooding. So bedrooms cramp too small for more than sleeping, and, not worth heating for a few hours' slumber, they confine a hollowness, an unseductive chilled stillness through the day. Their doors stand shut, often tied from the outside to prevent them bumping in drafts. Not until late at night will the bedroom's door be opened to release its dead, cold breath

Bedroom Fireplace. Mrs. Keenan's.
For scale, the opening measures
30 by 21 inches.

into the kitchen. On the worst nights, sheets will be brought out and held above the fire to dry them. Hot-water bottles or heated bricks or potlids wrapped in cloth will go first to bed, then bodies. Icy air will lie across the face, but if the sheets are dry so the cold that penetrates will leave, and if you know enough to lie still beneath mounds of blankets, coats, and old clothes, not shifting positions once a pocket of a feeling like warmth is found, sleep will come and then another day, spent like every other in company, constantly in full view of other people, safe.

Across the kitchen the door to the Room is also closed tight. "Now that's a room we don't use much," Mrs. Thornton explained. "We use it at Christmas time and sometimes when company is coming, but then only if we know well ahead of time because it is cold, and it takes a while to build a fire and take the chill off." I was told the Room was used for important visitors, and when still strangers my family and I were occasionally fed in the Room, but normally we were, like the most important visitors, the rector and priest, entertained, even first times, in the kitchen. I was told the Room was used at Christmas, but when I was there at Christmas time, I found most people celebrating in the kitchen, for it is more "homely," and Christmas is a holiday for home and family. The mantelpiece in the Room framed no fire, the air lay thin and frigid between big dark furniture and sheets of glass, cool mirrors and the fronts of china cabinets.

The Room is used ceremonially. When the family gathers to mark an event in its history, another Christmas or a wedding, the solemn furniture

Mrs. Cutler's

The Thorntons'

that stands in decorous idleness for months will work to serve rich meals. Christmas brings a fat goose. Then the certificates framed on the walls— the school prizes, military citations, and elevations of rank in fraternal or- ders—will remind everyone of past familial success. Photographs of an- cestors and children, emigrants and the home's inhabitants in youth, will widen attendance past time, space, and flesh. Mirrors will create portraits of the living next to those of the dead, who stare an endless blessing down on the few major occasions that open the Room to life. Between those lav- ish, familial events the Room is working. Its wardrobes and presses store clothing and bedclothes. Butter is kept on its shrouded round table, taking advantage of the cool atmosphere to stay fresh. But more than an occa- sional ceremonial space and a steady storage area, the Room is a work of art, no more to be used in normal times than a painting; the idea of using the Room casually creates the revulsion of Duchamp's project to use the Mona Lisa for an ironing board. The objects in the Room—large, heavy fur- niture, a spray of fragile figures, old Staffordshire horsemen, glass dogs and cats, porcelain ladies in eighteenth-century dress, propped photos of brides, grooms, young men in uniforms—are arranged to be lovely, not to be shifted at whim.

Closed off from the kitchen, the Room remains quiet, tidy, and cool. Constant smoke, spats of staining soot, muddy boots tramping in and out, in and out, the endless moving of pots and kettles and chairs and brooms, the hum of chat and aromas of cooking make a kitchen. The Room is left in order. It must be specially prepared to receive company, but the kitchen is always ready, willing to be momentarily dirtied and disarranged. The kitch- en depends on the Room to prove that the homemaker is tasteful and capa- ble of keeping a clean house. The Room depends on the kitchen to stay open so that life can flow through, messing it up during meals and ceilis, to accomplish its own order.

Open, the kitchen lies between the familial privacy of closed rooms and the whole world. Barriers are thin, permeable. Lacking electricity, de- pendent for heat and light on small flames, the house is entered by nature's conditions. It is cold in winter, dark at night. Seasons and days turn through live bodies within. Lacking plumbing, the house frequently sends its peo- ple outside. Outside? Early on I was told a funny story about a city man who came to a wedding reception in a local home and, having to relieve himself, asked a boy in whispers where he should go. Outside, he was told. He said he knew, but being a city man he expected a privy, and asked, Where outside? The boy replied, "Well, anywhere between this and Binn Rock"—Benaughlin rises on the southwestern horizon, five and a half miles distant. The door, open on good days, unlocked at night, offers no resistance, swinging often to let people out and in. Visitors do not pause at the threshold, so the community extends smoothly from grassy fields to every fire, incorporating all kitchens within its territory. The community is precisely the space linking hearths.

Around the hearth, the kitchen expands. Rooms are ceiled, squeezed, subdivided, but the kitchen widens through the center of the home to command its full height and depth. What is central is primary. It may or may not be so evolutionarily, but it is in experience and concept: though central, the kitchen is the home's first place. It is entered before all other rooms, and other spaces are planned dependently around it. Rooms extend from each of its sides, then along that axis in both directions, "byres" for cows and "stables" for horses and asses continue upward and downward trajectories, stringing off both gables of old homes. The "house" is all these joined volumes; all are governed by the hearth: at Mrs. Cutler's the byre as well as the Room is "above" the fire, the stable as well as the pantry is "below." When the house shelters both people and beasts, its front presents several doors. The one nearest the middle is a batten door, beaded at the edges and centers of its vertical boards, with a latch high on its face above the central one of its three internal battens, and it shines with green or brownish-orange enamel. Here green and orange colors lack political associations, tell nothing of political opinion within. The "ochre" varies through gold from light to dark and comes out a warm tan; along with green and light blue, ochre indicates the dwelling's entrance, distinct from the doors of red on byre and stable. When shelters for animals are not attached, the

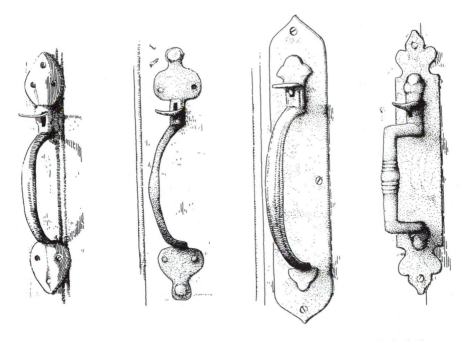

Latches. Mrs. Cutler's, brass. Mrs. Keenan's, wrought iron. Dick Cutler's, brass. The Balfour-Boyle house, cast iron.

home's door is often red, just as latches can be iron as well as brass, for red is the cheapest paint, and not everyone has the same money.

Out the front door, along the house, runs the "street," a paved section of earth, providing a transition between muddy lanes and the floor of the kitchen. Behind the house opens the "haggard," a transitional area between fields and house. Once safe in the haggard, hay and turf are "home." Across the street, around the haggard, or dropped separately along the house's axis, other buildings stand, "outhouses" or "outoffices": the dairy, the hay-shed and turfshed (often built combined), the cartshed and small houses for calves, fowl, and the broken, disused, future-useful odds and ends South-ern Montaineers call plunder and people in the District "ould trumfery." These buildings, the major ones usually strung in rows to face the south or east, parallel or perpendicular to the house, comprise the "home place." From the hearth, through buildings of whitewashed stone and brick, of red wood and metal, the home place stretches, breaks apart, and spreads into small, squarish fields of the greenest green.

The District's small compass contains three traditions of siting. On ridges like Drumbargy Brae, houses line the crest, each fronting the sunrise with its blank back to prevailing winds from the west. On domes in the terrain as in Sessiagh, houses circle the peak, down the slope from the top, parallel to the rise and looking downhill, no matter what winds pound their faces. Gortdonaghy provides another example of the dome's pattern and suggests the history of settlement. At the top springs a ring of trees, an ancient rath, and next to it stands the townland's oldest house, Mrs. Cut-ler's. Down the hill on all sides rise houses of intermediate age. Then at the base of the hill on cutover bog lie the newest homes. Material evidence alone indicates that townlands were formed first upon the hilltops, then grew downhill as population expanded. On ridge and dome, houses are sited with reference to nature, to sun, wind, and slope. Along the road-sides, houses align with the run of man-made roads, but since major roads wind between the hills, the houses of the roadsides, like those on the domes, usually back the rise of the land. All these patterns—ridge, dome, road—are broken, generally in the interests of environmental efficiency, to bring the front of the home into the warmth. Bobbie Thornton told me that in the past it was believed one should not build to the south or east of a house. New construction would keep natural warmth and light out of the old kitchen. Mr. Thornton scoffed at the superstition but said that when his house was erected its builder set it to the sunny side of the old one. His wife had twins. Mother and children died suddenly of diptheria, and peo-ple said it was because the new house was built just south of the old one, which faced east. Not all houses face the warmth, but if they do not, they still face the downhill view or the action on the road. Every house is oriented so its open door and front windows will admit the most interest-ing spectacle for those within. Mind's pleasure matters more than body's comfort.

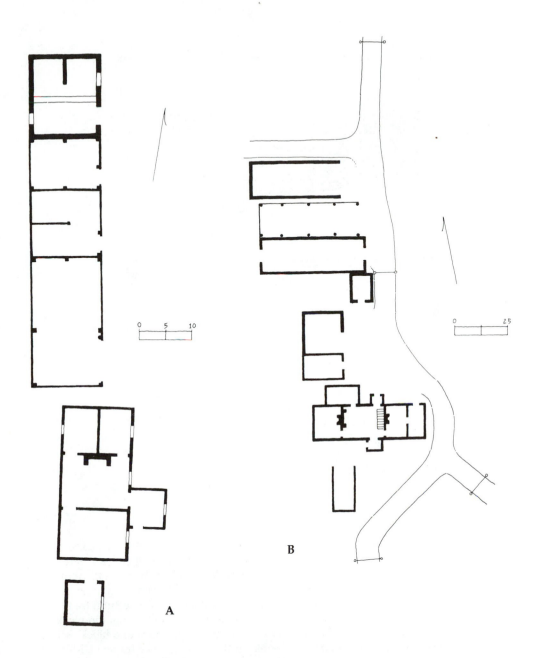

Farm Plans. **A**. Laborer's home on Gortdonaghy Farm, including dairy, dwelling, hayshed, and byres. **B**. Billy Dowler's farm, including hayshed, dwelling, byres, hayshed, and silage shed. In A, the outoffices string along the axis of the house. In B, the outoffices string in a line behind the house. Scales in feet.

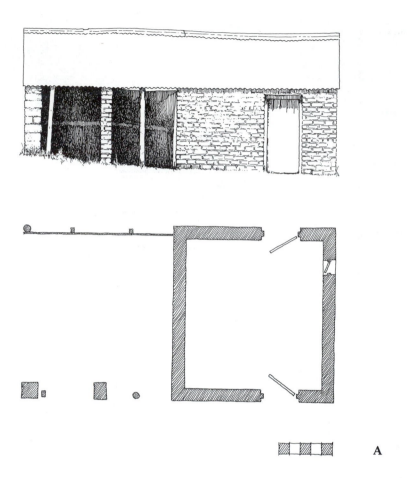

Outoffices. **A.** Mrs. Keenan's brick turfhouse and hayshed. **B.** Crucked turfhouse and hayshed abandoned in Derryhowlaght. **C.** Phil Owens' byre. **D.** Owen Cleary's byre. **E.** Byre on Hugh Corrigan's farm in the Point of Rossdoney. **F.** Disused byre on Ross Lane. **G.** Bobbie Thornton's stable. These buildings illustrate basic principles of the local architectural tradition. First, continuity through continual rebuilding. C is brick, rebuilt in block; D is frame, rebuilt in block; F is stone, repaired with brick and block. Second, continuity through addition. The bay at the right of B is a framed addition to the original crucked building; the original stone section of G has had sheds in stone, in brick, in wood, and in block added to the right end and the rear for calves and chickens. Third, continuity through adaptive reuse. E was a stone house with brick gables that has been converted into a byre; the right-hand section of stable G was partitioned in block to house pigs and store potatoes. Fourth, the separability of form and materials: forms are translated

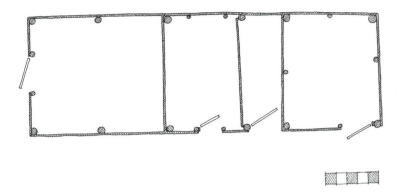

B

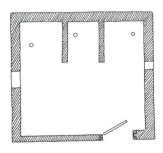

C

from material to material without change, and comparable forms are built in different materials. The left-hand segment of stone byre F is like the brick stable built off the left end of Mrs. Cutler's house. Fifth, forms result from conceptual manipulation. There are two basic types of byre in the District, a tripartite type and a single-cell type. These are combined and divided to create the plans for real buildings. The right-hand section of byre F is a tripartite form like Mrs. Cutler's byre with a runway separating a pair of "settles" (platforms on which cows stand) behind each of which normally runs a manure gutter called a "groop." The left-hand section of byre D consists of two-thirds of the tripartite form; it has the runway to the side, one settle, and one groop. The right-hand section of byre D is a single-cell form, rendered in isolation in byre C, composing the right-hand section of stable G, doubled in Mrs. Cutler's stable, and in the left-hand section and rear ell of byre F. Scales in feet.

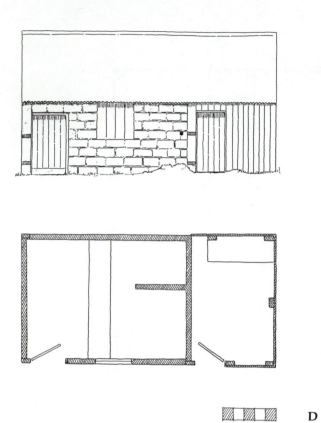

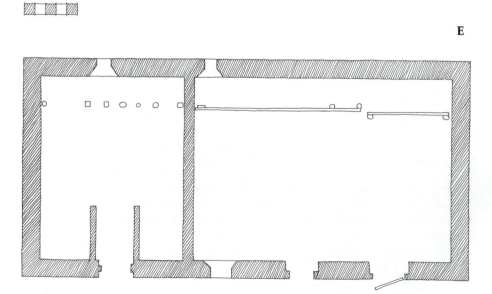

D

E

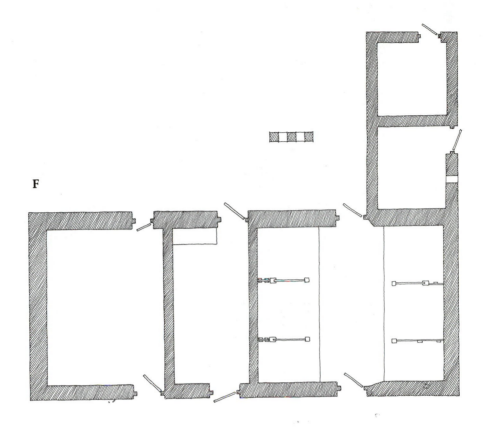

F

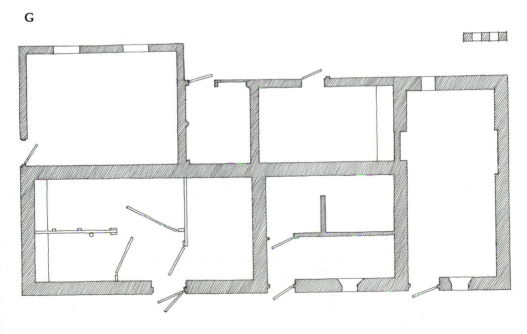

G

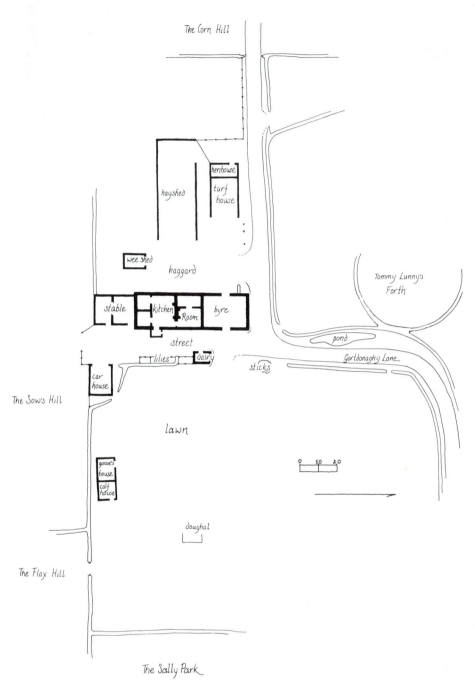

The Corn Hill

henhouse

hayshed

turf
house

wee shed

haggard

Tommy Lunny's
Forth

stable   kitchen   Room   byre

street

pond

lilies   dairy

sticks

Gortdonaghy Lane

car
house

The Sow's Hill

lawn

0   10   20

goose's
house

calf
house

doughal

The Flax Hill

The Sally Park

Plan of Mrs. Cutler's Farm. The space covered is roughly the top of
Gortdonaghy Hill. All the names are hers. Scale in feet.

Visually, conceptually, and socially, the kitchen is poised to join its people to the world beyond, which expands away from the red fleck of the hearth, drifting from light to dark, heat to cold, dry to damp, familiar to unknown, controlled to uncontrolled. The hearth is the center of the dwelling, the dwelling of the house, the house of the home place; then fields roll, broken by hedged ditches, to merge with other farms. Edges are lost in fields scattered beyond. The home's mode of organization extends in space as fields join, gathering the warm homes of the upland into the center of each townland, before fading toward cold, wet, unoccupied peripheries. The community is comparably a thing of centers, not margins. No name precisely stakes its limits, but certain centers—Sessiagh on the west, Upper Ballymenone on the east—clearly define its existence.

Look on the build of the earth. Little hills hump into the light, tipped often with clumped circles of trees, spreading above the earthen walls of Iron Age farmsteads, now the forths of fairies. Tops of hills stand out clearly, but their sides decline slowly, sliding under water, into shadowed hollows, blending with the flat plains of bog. Tops and centers are sharp, but borders fade, becoming lost into the land. The District's way of ordering space seems to be drawn from natural terrain and then applied by analogy in other domains. What feels natural at the level of the townland, where centers are hilltops, and seems a logical consequence of topography in those ancient days when each hill bore one circular steading at its crest, becomes arbitrary, convenient, and conventional at the level of the farm in days when many houses scatter across every hill. But the hearth remains on center. People have come out of the dampness onto the hilltops, lit fires, and built homes around them that face the sun and back the rise of the land. Square shapes assemble around the hearth, forming concentric rings. Between rooms and fields, street and haggard, stable and byre, the kitchen is set at dead center. The first ring outward is primarily domestic: rooms to each side, haggard behind, street to the front. The next ring is mixed industrial: stable and byre to the sides, hayshed, turfshed, and other outoffices to the rear and front. Then fields, then moss, then bog, then the world—in ever-enlarging circles, all space spreads from the home's fire. A cross laid over this circle makes four directions into two, pointed toward infinity, intersecting at the center, the hearth, where damp turf gathered from the dark borders burns bright, where distant news becomes familiar through chat, where the private meets the public, and where connections are forged between the family and the community, people and beasts, work and entertainment. The universe comes to, spreads from, and gains unity at the little fire on the hill.

The one becomes the all at the center. This way to create order is not restricted to space. It is applied in the still more arbitrary realm of time. The year is organized around centers more than beginnings, ends, and edges.

The instant separating this year from next is noted, not celebrated. Bells echo through Enniskillen on December's last night, but New Year's is only one of the twelve days of Christmas in the countryside, and a year is

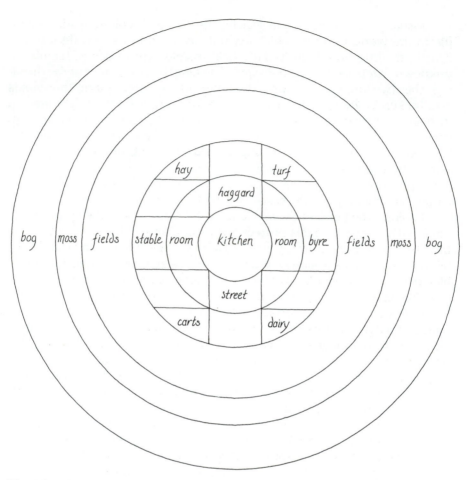

The Idea of the Farm's Plan. A schematic diagram of farm-planning, based on
Mrs. Cutler's.

marked for remembrance on a day near its middle, the Twelfth of July for
Protestants, the Fifteenth of August for Catholics. Without fretting about
contradictions, the District's people use two calendars. The new one consists of a subdivided unit, the year begun on the first of January. The old
year's first day is either Saint Brigid's Day, February 1, or May Day, or both
or neither. This spring can be compared with last spring, whatever day began the year, and a year's beginning and existence as a unit matter less than
that a year is composed of four seasons: spring or growth (February, March,
April), summer (May, June, July), autumn or harvest (August, September,
October), winter (November, December, January).[2] As the four directions
become two, up and down, in motion, the year while turning breaks into
halves at May Day, the dawn of flowers, and Hallow Eve, the night of the

The Old Year. Ballymenone's seasons and Great Days. In the center is a grave-stone of the early eighteenth century from Kinawley.

dead. Each season is marked by a major festival. The old year is revolved against the new one, so only one of the four seasons has its festival at a terminus. Hallow Eve ends harvest, but like May Day, Hallow Eve Night is set at the midpoint of one half of the year begun on Saint Brigid's Day. The seasons' other Great Days are all central, coming in the middle of their middle months: Christmas at Midwinter, Patrick's Day in the center of spring, Bonfire Night at Midsummer.

The Great Days rise out of time like hills off the land, signaling centers, letting boundaries drift from attention. In space, this pattern comes clearest when applied at a scale too large for centers to coincide with real hills as they do in townland and community. The region of south Fermanagh is most easily defined by its incorporation of certain districts: Kinawley, Montiagh, Mackan, Derrylin, Ballymenone. Those districts are not subdivisions of a geographical whole but independent foci within it. Their borders do not meet. Many places are not in any district, but they are still in "south Fermanagh."

Ballymenone's way to create order is not to demarcate a whole, then cut it into parts. Still rationalistic after all these years, we worry about consistency, exceptions, and contradictions, defining things by their surfaces and boundaries, and become happy when everything fits. We name culture a system, describe it as a closed entity, breaking it down into parts that interlock into a unit like a machine. They describe culture in epiphanies, by spotlighting key occurrences suffused with cultural essence. They craft centers with care, leave edges ragged, letting the whole take care of itself. We consider history a unit broken into periods, and geography a unit broken into regions. A year is an entity to be sliced ever more minutely into seasons, weeks, seconds. For them history is a cluster of powerful events, space is a collection of landmarks, the year is a set of Set Times marked by big meals and coming together. Vaingloriously we create orders, then orders of orders. Lacking trust in order itself, we define reality as that which fits the scheme we alone know. They cede orders of orders to the nature of things, to an endless reality that cannot be completely known, to the infinity of space and time. So they remain open to wonder and wonder's presence within: the urge to create. They do not shirk. Ordering what it is theirs to order, they arrange centers with precision, sympathetically enacting within them the dynamic of the universe.

In garden, at hearth, in story, their small creations match creation, not through redundant, fearful diagrams of the cosmos contained between beginnings and ends, but during the formation of middle moments which surrender ultimates, first and last things, to concentrate on the integral power of centers. Their responsibility is not the shape of the whole, but the force of wholeness: continuity.

Continuity works through human plans that begin in the middle, then open outward to stretch in every direction, infinitely. From the Great Days, time spreads both ways, backward and forward, to form seasons; seasons become years, years are lost in time. From the hearth, the house expands to form the farm, farms become community. While communities then lose themselves in ceaseless space, this community ties back to particular hearths, weaving itself uniquely around real fires.

The hearth is a point in the continuous whole, the family's midpoint in space. The hearth is the crucible of continuity; here, at the center of space, people work to unify time, keeping a fire alight that consumes the intervals between the generations, between the Great Days and every day and night, filling all gaps with man-made heat, melting moments into the endless whole of time.

At night, coals are raked and banked, opened to new blaze each morning to burn every day away. A house is sad—they say it looks lonesome—without a fire. When its hearth grows cold, the heart of the house ceases to beat, the couples will fall, the walls crumble, thatch will mound in on the floor. Open doors and smoke trailing from kitchen chimneys are constant signs of life within, welcomes to life without.

Unstoppably, time flows through the hearth, urged on by people who keep the fire going. Someone is always there to tend it, for it burns in harmony with its people. A cold hearth is a symptom of despair. Fire dies with the spirit and lives to join people during meals and ceilis.

In the past the fire was allowed to die only once a year, on May Day, when symbols of life—eggs hung on bushes, flowers strewn on the street—protected the home's life-force. Travel from the hearth is a danger. People leaving are sprinkled with holy water, as are cattle about to be driven to market. On their way out of the house, their last view is of crosses, horseshoes, an eternal flame beneath the Sacred Heart. At one time, the breaking points of the year, when people left one temporal space for another, were comparably guarded. On the eve of Saint Brigid's Day, crosses were woven of rushes and hung for the year's duration above the door for luck, and a few remain over byre doors, on the dresser near the door at Hugh Nolan's, over the bedroom door at Hugh Patrick Owens', by the entrance at Rose Murphy's and Bob Lamb's.[3] Flowers sifted into the breeze at the old year's other entrance—May Day, the first day of summer—also meant, Peter Flanagan said, luck and life. When the hearth was let cool, these flowers stood in the place of light and heat. Luck, they say, is "full and plenty," the farmer's success through which life continues. Like flowers, fires hold high color and glow with living. Like Saint Brigid's crosses, fires protect the seams

Mrs. Cutler's Kitchen

in space and time, stitching them safely. The hearth's fire is discussed as alive, as giving cheer when bright, as dying sadly. The perfect opposite of death's dark cold, the hearth's fire vaguely yet profoundly associates with the idea of life in Ballymenone. It is tended with care, nurtured from day to day.

Like Patrick's flame, the hearth's is eternal. Each of the day's many fires is built round the coals of the old one. They say the fire never dies, and it hardly ever does. On the hottest days of summer the hearth may cool for a few hours, but if a ceilier calls, a small fire is immediately built. Heat and light are not needed. The hearth must be ready to offer its gifts of tea and spectacle. Neighborly life is forged fire.

A turf fire demands constant attention. It cannot be started then left, for it falls apart easily and fills and clogs with ash. Again and again it must be tonged into order, swept clean, rebuilt. The fire sets a constant task and becomes the kitchen's metronome.

Cooking is not an occasional task, but a continual one. People eat many small meals during the day: breakfast, then dinner at noon, supper at five, a tea in midafternoon, another in the evening, and, should a ceili develop, one or two or three more as the night wears on.[4] Though called teas, they are made of more than hot liquid. There is bread at least, but that is only a "dry tea," lacking grease, and teas usually bring butter, a dab of jam, and ideally, though rarely, an egg or a bit of bacon. Most meals include no meat; protein comes in tea's cream, bread's butter. Only dinner and supper require boiling potatoes and cabbage and setting the table, for most meals pass at the hearth with plates balanced on knees. Still all the day's five or more meals mean breaking bread and butter out of hiding, boiling water in a kettle, drawing it in a teapot or drawer, disordering, then reordering the kitchen.

Cooking means cleaning. The kitchen is not allowed to become "tossicated," in need of "retting out." The pot or big kettle hanging perpetually above the flame holds water for washing. After every use pans are scrubbed, dishes and cups are washed and replaced. In one long and elegant motion, the farmer drains his mug of tea, swishes it clean, sets it back to shine amid the others on the dresser, and is off to the fields. Sweeping is endless. People are willing to toss trash toward the hearth because it will be swept soon. They are content to rest plates of food and live cigarettes directly on the floor because it has just been swept. The kitchen cannot become "clatty" and cluttered with dirty dishes, for it cannot be closed from view. It stands wholly open to every visitor, and its furniture will be rearranged, its floor swept, as soon as he leaves.

Since it serves many purposes, the kitchen cannot be arranged for any one of them. In the "council houses" people inhabit when they leave the District, separate areas are permanently arranged for cooking, eating, and talking. An old bachelor like Hugh Nolan simplifies the kitchen, emphasizing its use for ceiliing, eliminating its convenience as a space for cooking

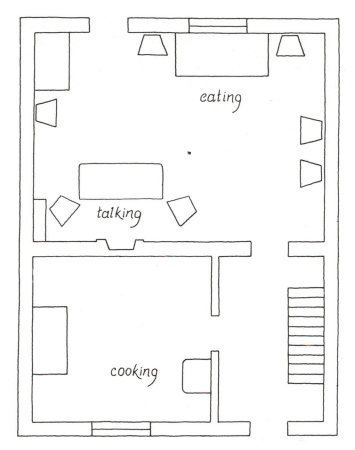

Council House. Sketch plan of the ground floor of a house from a County terrace in Derrygonnelly inhabited by a man born in the District, his wife, and their children.

and eating, by setting a couch before the hearth. But most kitchens remain open and poised for multiple tasks. Everything in its place: utensils and chairs are shoved to the walls where they are not used, but await use.

Windows break through the wall above internal work spaces, over the front table and back table and the sink in the pantry, dancing sunlight into the kitchen. At night when windows are closely curtained, a lamp lit on the front table before the window maintains a source of light in the daytime's sunniest spot. By night and day, the hearth opens onto "a cheery blaze," a window inward, a "companion" Mrs. Cutler calls it, something to watch while working. At least some work can be done sitting. The only piece of furniture that intrudes upon the kitchen floor is the only one shifted off axis, between down and up: the chair of the fire tender, set at the upper corner of the hearth, stolid, turned to be convenient for work at the fire and to command the interesting view out the front window and door. It comforts the one who must stay within to keep the house alive. Usually it is big and upholstered, soft like Mrs. Cutler's and Joe Flanagan's. The old form was a kind of Windsor. Comparable chairs, low-backed and sprung with turned spindles, like those of England and America, were commercially available. Hugh Nolan's, with its arms sweeping around him, is such a one, but chairs of an old and distinctively Irish type were crafted locally, and since they were, they were often gifts, prepared by young men for their elders, such as the one Tommy Lunny's brother made for Hugh Patrick Owens' father, or by old men for children, such as the little one made for Mrs. Thornton's mother by her great-grandfather.

Steel tongs for building the fire, and a besom or brush to clean it, lean by the big chair from which the hearth's "crooks" can be reached. In some houses a "crane crook," set to swivel heavy pots from the floor over the fire, stands to one side. It would seem to be most convenient for the crane to be hung at the hearth's upper corner, at the fire tender's spot, and many are, but that pattern is overridden by another which directs the crane to be hung at the left so that when it turns it will move outward in the ancient Celtic manner, following the arc of the sun. In other houses a pole high in the chimney drops chains to the fire. In both cases rows of black iron claws dangle to hold pots, kettles, and pans for cooking and washing.

The fire keeper's chair does not move. All others do. The smallest and most mobile of seats is a four-legged stool used for milking in many byres and set by some hearths to receive chilled visitors in need of getting down close to the fire. So small that it moves across the floor with you as your body shifts, it gains the name "creepie." The kitchen's other chairs come in sets. The old type, Empire made plain, was employed through the nineteenth century by local carpenters.[5] Chairs on this model, varying in severity, were painted, often in colors to match the kitchen's trim. Newer chairs of varnished oak are streamlined Victorian, made after Eastlake's impact, somewhere else. Alone the shapes of these chairs suggest moments of prosperity, points of convergence with the outside world, around 1840 and 1900, and indicate, along with the old Windsor form, a long run for the aesthetic of plainness.

While the cook works alone, chairs stand back. Her path is clear from the hearth to the upper spaces where food is stored, to the back table where it is prepared, to the front table where it is served, to the supplies of fuel in a sack by the front door or out the door in the porch. And the visitor's path is clear to the hearth.

Every encounter requires chairs to move. For dinner they assemble around the front table. Though usually larger than the back table, it is no more formal. Square of leg, stiffened by tenoned stretchers, with a drawer punctured in its apron, the table was usually made by the same carpenter who made the kitchen's chairs and dresser and the press and mantel in the Room, who helped build the house, framing its doors and windows. In the

The Local Windsor Chair. Made for Thomas Owens by John James Lunny. Its
left arm and left front leg, which would rest
nearest the fire, are replacements.

Creepie. Mrs. Cutler's milking stool.
See also the photograph of the
Flanagans' new hearth.

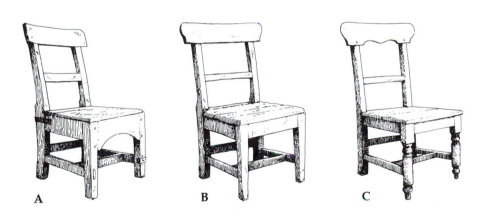

A

B

C

Kitchen Chairs. **A.** Owen Cleary. **B.** and **C.** Maguire of Drumane. All are
painted. From the ground to the seat, A measures 15 inches, B and C measure 16 inches. The height of the back and the front width of the seat in all
the chairs is between 17 and 17½ inches.

past, tables were hinged, Hugh Nolan told me, pointing to the spot where one once hung on the back wall of his kitchen, so they could be lifted out of the way after use. Those are gone, but tables are still pushed to the wall. People leave them quickly, taking cups of tea and their chairs to the hearth to sit around the fire for dinner's long conversational conclusion—less a conclusion than a fading away, a beginning, as some replace their chairs by the wall and leave for outside work, some start cleaning, others linger to ceili through additional teas. Children are taught that if you lift a chair once, lift it twice. Chairs are shifted to the table for dinner, to the hearth for teas and ceilis, then they are not left standing. They return to the wall, awaiting their next use, whatever it might be. Once furniture circled the walls, away from the fire. Though the flame has been drawn to a wall, chairs and tables are still shoved to the peripheries, and the kitchen's middle remains open. All routes are clear to the hearth.

Fire centers space, brings common life into time's flow, and burns away categorical disjunction. By day it unifies the work of men and women, blending outside work and inside work into food consumed by people seated in a semicircle around the front window or the hearth. By night it attracts people out of darkness, serves up tea, and sets the scene for the formation of society.

The community builds itself at the hearth so the rules it devises for its own regulation are "fireside law." When children join adults to grow within the family, they are instructed and entertained through "fireside stories" and "fireside songs." While adults make ceilis out of "fireside chat," children are not exiled, prisoned in rooms; they sit silently, practicing patience, watching the fire, poking at it with tongs, learning life's way as participant observers, so when special occasions yield the kitchen to children, their games circle the fire, symbolically repeating the ceili. Peter Flanagan remembered one. A sally rod is lit. Once well burning, it is passed from child to child. Each must keep it twirling a circle in the dark while repeating the same rhyme:

> Jack now, me man,
>   if you die in me hand,
>   the straddle and mat shall go over your back.
> Through a rock, through a reel, through an old spinnin wheel,
> Through a miller's hopper,
> Through a bag of pepper,
> Through a sheep shank, shinbone.
> Riddle me that and I'll let ye alone.
> Here.

"It would go on round and round and round. It would be all in a circle, you see, in the house, and this'd go on around and round and round and round. And if it happened to die just in some unfortunate person's hand, they were ill-fated, and ye'd have to get out there and they would put that table and dresser and every haet on top of your back.

"You called that Stick Jack. And then when it could be comin near a dyin point, ye'd hurry up and shove it on to the next. And then the person that was at the extreme of goin out, ye'd refuse it. You'd let the person that said the last rhyme hold it, so they were the victim.

"That was a childer's rhyme, and of course, childer's pastime, you know."

Like the ceili's invisible baton, the burning stick went from person to person, making each perform in turn. When the fire died the whole burden of the kitchen was heaped on an "ill-fated" individual. So it will be in the ceilis of maturity. The fire decays, one person must rebuild it. The chat darkens or cools, one person is obliged to brighten it or fan it to heat, and if words fail you and black silence presses in, freezing you, leaving you incapable of helping to lift things back into motion, that is how you feel: as though the kitchen had collapsed over you, burying you beneath fallen furniture—a foretaste of the tomb's bitter cool.

The fire must be kept burning. Making food and society, fire makes life possible and worth it. So each person stays alert, ready to offer new fuel or hot tea, "bright" wit or a "hot" story, an old rhyme, an old riddle, ready to take responsibility for the kitchen's dynamic.

Continuity names the kitchen's dynamic. Here in the middle of the home place on the hillside, diverse activities blend into organic order. The word "organic" can be loosely used, but I intend it specifically to mean the way that distinct categories of thought, conduct, and purpose submit to an embracing unity of experience. Cooking and washing and talking, working and entertaining, are brought together in the kitchen through action. Connections are made in time as time flows through the kitchen's space to force connections among concepts. For Ballymenone it is best to describe organic order in terms of its dynamic: continuity. The continuities of thought and action (which are shaped by the individual's sacred obligation to generosity, and which are the reality of life in the kitchen) glitter in the constant flame on the hearth and reflect across the kitchen from the dresser.

A shelf divides the dresser into halves. Below, behind curtains or doors, pans, irons, big pots, little machines, and bags of spud spray hide from view. At the top, dressers hold great platters, "sideplates." Next come plates. Last, a row of cups and mugs and bowls cross above the counter of "the shelf," where more platters, big bowls, pitchers, teapots, and tin boxes stand. The dresser's sections are so distinct that in the poorest homes the upper half can appear alone as a hanging dresser. The upper half calls the eye; its expansive display is a thing to behold. Mrs. Cutler's "dresser of delph" is famous in the District. "I've taken *such* good care of it, and I *hate* to think of it after me." Fearing the next generation will not understand, she said, "Sometimes I feel like takin an axe and breakin it all up."

Mrs. Cutler's Dresser

Imagine it smashed and years of dark earth heaped over. The archaeologist bringing its remains to light would learn that most of it was English manufacture, that some was made at the Fermanagh pottery at Belleek. Shards sieved from the dirt, reassembled in the lab, would take shape as transfer-printed platters and plates, as plates, mugs, and bowls decorated by sponging through stencils the colors of the land that dominate the kitchen's decor, from its bright front door to the furniture and woodwork within: green and tan. Some would bear on their bottoms the extravagantly Irish Belleek mark, compounded of harp, wolfhound, round tower, and shamrock, while others, though unmarked, would strike the analyst correctly as examples of the same ware. Our archaeologist would learn that the scraps in every dresser deposit span time widely, ranging from early nineteenth-century English blue willow platters, through late nineteenth-century pale English china and Belleek, green, white, and gold, to John Gilleece's Batman mug and Mrs. Cutler's plate commemorative of the Queen's Jubilee of 1977.

From all this the archaeologist might infer that the people of the place were primarily subjects of the English commercial empire, though they were served as well by native craft. The Belleek Factory, founded in 1858, famed for delicate fantastic porcelain made for export, also met local need and taste with a hearty, serviceable ware.[6] If iron in rusted clumps could tell him what I was told by the people who used it when it still formed utensils, he would come to a similar conclusion. Major cast objects, "pot ovens" and the three-legged and banded, potbellied cauldrons called "pots," were made in England, while attendant pieces, "breadsticks," "crows," "pothooks," and the cranes, trammels, and hooks collectively called "crooks," were forged by local smiths. The archaeologist would be only lucky to hit the right reason for the diversity of age among the shards.

Old delph is preserved for display, to be beautiful, to become a memory. "Delph is not to use," Mrs. Cutler explained. "No. It is for passin on to people that won't use it." At the end of our very first meeting, feeling I understood, she gave me a blue willow plate. It hangs on our kitchen wall. I see it and think of her. She sees the delph on her dresser and thinks of others. That broad, cobalt-blue, willow pattern platter at the top descended from her grandmother's mother.

Standing before the dresser, confounded by the idea that things that can be used must be used, that useful things cannot be art, you would see it as an open toolbox. Letting its order and glow enter your mind, hearing people compliment its loveliness, you would be persuaded that it is an exhibit, an untouchable work of art. Neither is quite the case. Stay awhile. Though most of the crockery put daily to use hides in the pantry, you will see some of the dresser's sideplates break out for service at dinner, and other of its pieces constantly at work. At the upper end of a row of unusable Belleek mugs stands the one and only cup Mrs. Cutler uses for all the day's many teas. The resplendent dresser is a work of art, but it gracefully

Belleek Mugs

Belleek Marks

incorporates utility too. The ratio of display to use, art to tool, varies greatly from dresser to dresser, but all stand through time as beautiful.

Experiencing the dresser visually, you would join the homemaker in one dimension of her delight. The dresser's beauty is its gift to the visitor, but its more important dimensions abide invisibly. One is social association. The Belleek plate that seems pretty to you and to her also means a wedding to her, a gift, a lost friend. And her deepest pleasure comes in action. The dresser is not put into order and then surrendered to dust and films of smoke. Like the fire, it endures by mutating through constant intervention. Regularly disassembled, taken apart, and rebuilt, the dresser becomes a simple externalization of the mind, a tangible demonstration of its mechanics, a proof of its health. Mrs. Cutler says it makes her "happy as money" to take down the pieces of delph, wash them and their shelves, and set them up again in neat, gleaming rows. Her greatest delight comes in involvement with herself and with others as she manipulates each plate or cup through sudsy water and clear air and back into place, perhaps a new place in the wholeness of the dresser.

The dresser's pieces of decorative delph are called "ornaments." That word connects them to the kitchen's other "ornaments," which, broken from the wooden frame of the dresser, purify the idea in delph conspicuously. Glass and pottery people and beasts, little statues stand atop dresser and mantel, on hanging shelves and windowsills. When cottage-shaped teapots, cow-shaped creamers, brass candlesticks, and pictorial tea cannisters stand among them, and when plates hang among the framed pictures on the walls, they come to exist ornamentally; yet they gesture through the possibility of their use toward the dresser and through the dresser to utility itself. Modern painters struggle desperately to pretend their works have no use beyond art (though they bring food, shelter, and status in the leisure class). Their vanity is precisely reversed by one venerable European tradition within which works of art are forced to grow directly out of common work, as ornamental flower gardens grow out of agricultural technology, and made to suggest utility in form. Across the Continent, in Toft's England, among Germans in Pennsylvania, plates were flowered in paint, slip, and sgraffito.[7] In isolation they look like plates to eat from, so curators name them craft. In place on rack or wall, on display, they are for one culture precisely what painted canvases are for another. Manifestly there for art's sake, the ornaments glistening around Ballymenone's kitchen walls, plates as well as pictures, feel no need to tell frantic lies about the separation of art from workaday life.

The ornaments display clear patterns of content. Family pictures stay mostly in family rooms, while the community's kitchen raises the community's issues. Most obviously, ornaments in the kitchen (and in the Room to a lesser degree) reflect the community's deep division.

British leaders fill Protestant homes. In the kitchen at Bob Armstrong's and Ellen Cutler's, tins commemorating the coronation depict the Queen and the Duke. Plates on the Thorntons' kitchen mantel show Philip and Queen Elizabeth reviewing gaudy troops. Winston Churchill's portrait hangs above the door into their kitchen, a horse brass of Edward VII is affixed next to the door leading into Mr. Thornton's office, and in their Room, as in Mrs. Cutler's, a print of King William III hangs proudly. There are also portraits of George V and Queen Mary in Mrs. Cutler's Room, and a brass medallion of King William centered on the lintel crossing her kitchen's hearth.

Irish leaders of either side are lacking—totally in Catholic homes. No portrait of Sarsfield balances William, no portrait of de Valera matches Mrs. Cutler's of Sir Edward Carson. Catholic homes are filled with religious stat-

A

B

Ornamental Plates. **A.** Mr. Thornton found this Belleek plate from the Knock-ninny Hotel on a farm he bought, and it hangs on the wall of his dining room. **B.** Souvenir plate from the wall of Mrs. Cutler's kitchen, memento of a trip to Bundoran.

ues and portraits on paper and plate, which are absent from Protestant ones: Christ, Mary, Patrick, Brigid, Saint Martin de Porres. As in Protestant homes, leaders are foreign. There are portraits of popes, Paul at James and Annie Owens', John at Hugh Patrick Owens', Pius in a bedroom at the McBriens'. John Kennedy's picture hangs at the Ford, at the Carsons' and Monaghans'. At the Loves', heart-shaped plates of John and Jacqueline Kennedy flank a plate of Christ above the center of the kitchen's hearth.

Less obvious but more abundant imagery bridges division. Ornaments refer constantly to Ireland, and lest the idea of Loyalty mislead you about loyalties, you should know that these are more common in Protestant than in Catholic homes. An old engraving of Devenish Island hangs in the Thorntons' parlor. On the back wall of the kitchen at Mrs. Cutler's hangs a shamrock-shaped plate with raised letters spelling out "Ireland." A plate above the door into her Room circles clockwise with Irish tourist scenes, a plate from Connemara is on display within, and next to her front door hangs a small plate showing a sort of an ass laden with creels of turf, saying, "from Ireland." A miniature brass pot of the kind that hangs above Mrs. Cutler's fire stands on a back window ledge in the kitchen at Bob Armstrong's, "Ireland" written across its belly.

Still less obviously and more abundantly, houses are filled with rural emblems. Split by religion, connected by Ireland, these people are powerfully joined by their farming life. The romantic American folklorist cannot surpass, can only occasionally reach, the level of affection the people of Ballymenone feel for their land and their way. They exhibit it all around them. Most patently reflexive are aerial photographs of their own farms, purchased from a flying huckster, framed on the kitchen wall at the Ford, the Cutlers', and Thorntons'. On their kitchen wall the McBriens have a photo from a calendar of a lovely thatched house at Derrylin. (Imagine an oil painting of a typical brick rancher on prominent display in the main room of a suburban American home.) Within Mrs. Cutler's thatched house there is a print of a thatched house on the back wall of the kitchen, and next to it on a shelf is "a glass wee man with an ass and cart"—like the one her husband used to transport milk down the long lane of Gortdonaghy to the creamery. Misty chromolithographs of rural scenes, more English than Irish in feel, but matching still in predominant green and blue hues the landscapes framed by the windows, are hung in house after house. Throughout the District, images from the countryside enter the kitchen and come to the dresser: the pictures on the delph are of birds and flowers.

Final unity in the District's kitchens emerges on small plates bearing a simple verse asking, "Bless this little kitchen, Lord . . . ," and found often on the walls of both Protestant and Catholic homes.

Other ornaments make other connections. Links between the family's generations appear in the kitchen's display. Teenage daughters account for the photos of Elvis Presley at James McGovern's and of Brian Coll and the Buckaroos, a local country-and-western band, at the Loves'. Plates or

Blue Willow plate.

Belleek platter.

plaques with poems to mother and father, as at the Loves' and McBriens', came as gifts from fond children. The family's spirit steals subtly from the rooms into kitchen to raise a powerful idea.

And again the idea of the gift carries us far into the District's thought. If the ornaments themselves sometimes seem trivial, triviality is lost in the associations they contain. Many were gifts from beloved children. Their presence in the kitchen brings absent children to the mind's hearth.

There are toys among the ornaments. A dippy duck bobs on the windowsill of Mrs. Cutler's kitchen, a doll in a kilt stands on a shelf at the rear. "I am just a child," she said of it, "and I always wanted to go to Scotland." Toys have not been stripped of delight for adults denied them in youth. I spent some hilarious hours one afternoon with two unjaded, aged men playing in wonder with a mechanical hopping chicken. But funny toys become ornaments in the adult world, mostly because, like Mrs. Cutler's "wee Scotch Doll," they were the fetching, natural gifts from children to old people.

Gifts from children are contributions to the space of their raising. Whatever their content, many ornaments remember special occasions. I asked Mrs. Cutler what the photo of a puppy above the door into her pantry meant. She said she did not know; it was a Mother's Day gift. Reciprocating, children give to those who give to them. The gift is received with joy— "I'm the divil for ornaments," Mrs. Cutler said—and then absorbed into the memory-filled decor of the space through which life flows.

Other gifts arrive after trips. Since people do not travel far, the souvenirs they retrieve record places nearby, Derrygonnelly, Bundoran, Knock: Ireland. If they were richer and went farther, ornaments would look different, but the sentiment would remain the same. Souvenirs are given through people who stay home to the home itself. While I was gone, they say, I thought of you. My mind did not abandon our home. The gift compensates for the loss of company. Become an ornament, it becomes company, a continual memento of the one who remembered the one whose responsibility was staying home to keep the home alive.

Absence need not be long—intensity will do—and some gifts come of occasions like that perfectly caught by the poet John Montague at the end of his pained hymn to the new highway through County Tyrone, when the farmer, "mad drunk after a cattle mart," struggles home, a bravely unsightly domestic ornament in tow.[8] The home is to be repaid for his venturing, his joy. Like a big soft chair—and the bright wit of the ceili's stars—ornaments give some comfort to those who do not leave.

Judge the kitchen's ornaments on their inherent, particular merit and you will miss the point. Find them lacking as art, and all you have uncovered is an economic fact. These are not wealthy people, and if only rich people can own art, then art is reduced to commodity, and—to put it plainly—all is lost. No, what individual ornaments appear to be is the least significant thing about them. Their meaning lies less in their manifest content than in their magical capacity to bring events and human beings to life in the mind. (And so it is in pretentious modern paintings, which would be junk if the mind could not assemble art history around them.) The art of ornaments does not lie in them, as part of their fabric. They become art in mind and manipulation. They exist to clean and to order.

Ornaments take a shine. Brass pans on the walls, repoussé with ships, little brass souvenirs on shelves, join the mantel's candlesticks, the fender and tools of the hearth, the knobs of the dresser drawers, the latches of the doors, all brass, in one buffed, golden splash. Porcelain figures of saints, glass creatures, small mirrors and plates on the walls, delph on the dresser, glass panes in the windows—all shine, gleaming the kitchen into a symphony of cleanness.

Ornaments are mobile. Once gifts, they become gifts again, passed on, flowing into the kitchen then out to link distant homes. Mrs. Cutler gave both of her sons old pieces of family delph upon their marriages. To Dick, her eldest, she gave her cherished Staffordshire figure of King William on horseback. Kathy and all my children own ornaments that once decorated Mrs. Cutler's house. Mrs. McBrien gave Lydia, my youngest, a painted plaster statue of a fairy straight off a shelf in her Room.

Proud kitchens like Mary McBrien's and Ellen Cutler's are never at rest. Ornaments descend to be cleaned and shift constantly from place to place. The places they fill, centrally between every opening, centrally above every opening, do not change, but they do, wandering to sweep a band of variable brightness around the kitchen at eye level and above. This whole array, not its elements, is the homemaker's creation, her glittering and orderly artwork. As the painter arranges dabs of paint on canvas, the homemaker arranges bits of brightness and color within the home to make an object of beauty.

The ornamental idea that fills the Room and circles the upper half of the kitchen, sparkling, comes to a blaze, across from the fire, among the dresser's delph. Apparently for use, primarily for art, neat, clean, ordered, the dresser is the Room's ambassador in the kitchen, a delight to the eye, a bank of familial memory, a victory for the homemaker over the forces of filth.

The dresser, like the house, is at once a thing of appearance and use. Above on the shelves, as above in the Room, it is clean and not for using. Below, behind closed doors, the dresser rests tools between moments of use, as below, behind closed doors, the house rests people between moments of work. In the middle, on the dresser's "shelf" and in the home's kitchen, delight and utility fuse in action.

Items on the shelf answer the needs of the hearth: a tin of tea, a small teapot, soap and big bowls for washing. Conveniently, the dresser provides from its middle the tools and materials needed most often during the day's endless intermixed sequence.

Cooking flows into washing. Classed together on the shelf, tea and soap, teapot and bowl form a set. The vessels hold water in which dry matter dissolves into gifts. The offering of tea to tongue and stomach matches the gift of clean ornaments to the eye and mind. And as tea is fed guests, soapy water is fed the ancestors.

Art, as the wise anthropologist Robert Plant Armstrong argues, demands curating as well as creating.[9] The valued object requires care. In one culture fabulously expensive monuments are erected to house works of art, and specialists wait upon them, dressing them with chemicals, surrounding them with proper light and air, to keep them from decay. In another culture works of art are kept in shrines and fed the blood of black cocks. Ballymenone's ornaments, gifts from absent friends, are lofted above harm on wall and shelf. Exposed, they demand care. They thirst for soapy water and regularly digest the sacrifice of human energy, which they store and beam back in brightness, creating, like museums, like shrines, stirring environments for people.

Like turf, tea and soap are eaten into life's stream running between dresser and hearth, through the kitchen.

Rising on opposite walls, dresser and hearth match, limiting, unifying the kitchen. The dresser reaches out of its delph, embracing the kitchen's upper half, closing its ring in ornaments on the mantel. Pairs of things, of colored tin boxes, candlesticks, dogs or cats, mirror each other atop mantel and dresser in the center of each of the kitchen's side walls. The dresser's lower half, jammed with iron pots, extends both ways at once, opening like pothooks past useful tables in front and rear, beneath which tools and fuel are often stored, to close on the iron pots low on the hearth. The dresser's narrow middle plane spins evenly through the mid-layer of the kitchen's conceptual stratigraphy. Its drawer holds silverware for the tops of tables. The bright platters propped on its shelf are the ones used for dinner. Here again are the tea and soap the hearth wants for its ceaseless cooking, washing, and entertainment.

Time's flow through the hearth echoes from the dresser. At the center of the shelf of cups and mugs a little round clock ticks. It is not alone. There are usually others on that shelf, perhaps one on a table, one centered on the mantel, almost surely a fine one in the Room. One of them keeps time so people can keep appointments, especially with the outside world that enters through the wireless. Others run, but nonchalantly off on their own courses, behind or ahead of the big world's time. A few are silent. The long-case "grandfather clock" in Mrs. Cutler's Room, crafted early in the nineteenth century in Enniskillen, stands noiselessly now, though once its vigorous striking rang to the road. Clocks join the kitchen's several pictorial calendars, one of which is turned to the current month, while others remember months and years gone by. Released beyond concern for their contradictory messages, all these clocks and calendars refer both to the time and to time itself. Happily unsynchronized in their numbers, tocking, and bongs, they make mere time yield to continuity, all time.

Now time and space converge. The kitchen's order repeats the year's. Entry is offset, and structure remains obscure until you have entered and joined in ongoing motion. Then you find one major composition at the center of each of the four walls, one bright event at the center of each quadrant once the circle is squared. The hearth sparkles on one side, the dresser gleams on the other, and windows with tables beneath pierce to light in front and rear. All is oriented by the perpetual fire, the sun on the hearth. The day turns between tables, dresser, and hearth, as the year turns through the Great Days.

The Great Day is marked by lavish meals and extravagant sociability, trips away, and the wide ingathering of friends. The hearth's daily motion is the Great Day's made calm. Through small meals and gentle ceilis, the hearth's necessity sets reality's pace. It is not broken but exaggerated on the Great Days. On the little days, people carry on, working to maintain the center.

The center is undying fire: the sun, Saint Patrick's flame, the hearth. Around spin days and years, away spreads space, and through the center, through its heart, matter and energy are consumed in the creation of warmth, light: life. Time seeks centers in space, then burns through them, setting the midpoint in motion. The center becomes its own force, the undying fire of life making life.

Life gives us little things to work on, or it gives us emptiness. It is that simple, a matter of choice, courage. Life can be lived as meaningful or not. I elect to accept the world as a creation, not an accidental congeries—a creation not of heartless gods but of people who blessed it with mind and set us, their fellows, the task of teasing meaning from it. Ballymenone's modest homes stand around me as wondrous revelations of their creators' minds. I take mind to be logical. Let us call this logic continuity.

We will understand it more easily if I crack it unnaturally. One aspect is continuity of concept: organic order, the growth of reason through an incompleteness, complexity, and interpenetration of category. The other is continuity of space and time through centers.

Some people seek order through classification, breaking the world's unity into pure, exclusive segments. Over here we have art and there work, here church, there state. Boundaries are firm, sharp. Spaces within are endlessly subdivisible. That is an order more of maps than of travel, an order that depicts and does not experience. It is not alien to Ballymenone. The dresser's top is composed of platters, then plates, then cups. The ceili's story breaks into exploits, bids, pants, and history. But no obsessive wish for purity attends. Little ornaments, eggcups and souvenirs, scatter through the delph, bills and shopping lists are rolled in the bowls, the shelf for cups includes some for use, some for appearance, and clocks too. Genres of story, while clear at their centers, merge at their borders, and names overlap to suggest wholeness. Not parts, wholeness is the thrust. So the concept of neighborliness blends the sacred with the secular; it unifies the social, economic, political, and religious spheres that it is a proud purpose of science and law in another culture to separate. So the house, its kitchen and furnishings, less break experience into categories than suggest categories to break into wholeness. Space and time, day and year, day and night, work and entertainment, tool and art, male and female, adult and child, family and community, inside and outside, flowers of the field and flowers of delph—all is brought into association at the hearth, in the kitchen, in the home.

The result is not the chaos predicted by misanthropic planners from another frightened and decentered world. Order does not come from codified programs but from people who effect conceptual continuity out of time's continuity at centers under their control—the hearth, for example, where perpetual fire joins cleaning to cooking to talking to social stability to life, to all. From, through, centers of human control, infinity expands.

If we look back on stories with continuity in mind, we find them organically ordered. They do not fit the categories we accept as given, they attack them. Historical stories are neither prose nor poetry, science nor literature, ornaments nor tools. Like dressers, stories are assembled and reassembled out of received elements to be beautiful on the surface, meaningful in association, useful in the darkness beneath, to be gifts to guests, delights to their curators and creators, symbols of life, and so, part of wholeness, irreducible to any single abstract notion.

Stories are centers in wholeness. They flow out of ceilis that flow out of daily action at the hearth.

Before a ceili, the house's people sit at the fire in conversation. After it, they are the same. Between, people enter without invitation or forewarning. The company grows, diminishes, shifts through the evening with a minimum of ceremony to mark changes or disrupt the chat circling the hearth. Greetings are brief and made on the move, people join conversations raised before their arrival and leave without waiting for resolution. Like the fire, like the world, the chat was going before their coming, will be going after their leaving. Life, they say, is just a little ceili. The ceili is just a little life.

To leave, people stand and move down toward the door. If they say nothing, they might be asked, "Are you away?" A negative answer might be accompanied by a conventional explanation. "No, I'm just off for a short one" or "I'm only goin to wet a stone" or "baptize a stone" or "lose a button" or "take a pump" or "show my arse to the hedge." But "I am not" is usually enough. If the answer is "Aye," a few words might follow from the hearth, "All right, then" or "All the best" or "Safe home," or the host might come onto the street, beneath the wheeling stars, to join the ceilier for a piece of his ceaseless journey, as the ceilier had joined the household for a piece of its ceaseless chat. For a moment their wee lives meshed. Another night, and they will be together again with the same topics to discuss. Nothing starts or stops, exactly. Things go on.

Night comes out of day, tales come out of conversation. They are clearly connected to the ceiliers' topic and so smoothly connected that, though their middles stand out clearly, their beginnings and ends are easily lost. The folktale from which John Synge built *In the Shadow of the Glen* had a prologue he did not give in the text he quotes in *The Aran Islands*. An observer less sensitive than Synge might not have recognized the rambling preamble for part of the story and might not have commented—as Synge did—on its absence.[10] Lacking a tape recorder for playing speech back, and back, any folklorist might miss the conversational openings through which the good teller in Ballymenone shifts from chat to story, for stories begin without elaborate formulas and do not find the pace that makes them art, or the temporal specificity that makes them narratives, until they have begun.

With a word they open and another they close, but only silence clearly ends them, for stories conclude as they begin without ornament for framing. As they lift gradually out of chat, so they descend, often helped by a laugh or a compliment that prompts the teller to repeat with diminished intensity some part of his story, a punch line perhaps, lowering his pitch from tale's height to chat's plane, easing the story into the stream of talk. Even songs that wing away from conversations on melody are brought down at the end. Their last words are drawn out, shaded into silence, or they are spoken, not sung. In content as well as dynamic, the ends of tales, like their beginnings, connect with the ceili's flow. Concluding words seek the topic of the tale's preamble, the conversational thread on which for a moment the tale formed a bright bead.

Ceilis are framed, not made, by greetings. The presence of a visitor or two at the hearth is not enough. The ceili is heightened above practicality. Some visits are only requests for help, but ceilis are delightful in themselves, as well as means to other ends. The ceili is not boring, but some visits are: chat never cracks, tea never steams. Only once you are happily in the middle of a ceili can you know it is happening and recollect to the greetings with which it began and project its farewells.

Stories develop more within individual command, they are more predictable than ceilis, yet their unfolding is comparable. Unlike songs, stories are not memorized with openings and closings intact. The teller has the core actions and pertinent facts of many stored in his memory. He finds the conversation moving toward one of them. The first word is tentative. Ceiliers greet, "Well, men." The teller starts, "Well, Saint Columcille." The visit may rise to ceili, the ceili to tale, but the situation is not entirely in one person's control. After a wary sentence or two, the teller may reevaluate his environment and abandon his developing plan, letting his knowledge appear as but a small contribution to the ongoing chat. We might learn something about the Saint, but not hear his story. It is not until a story is happening, and its narrative core is being swung into lines, that it can reach backward to claim its first word and the informational preamble that urged it into existence. Not until then can it look forward to a conclusion enabling its reintegration into conversation. Opening outward from the center of its becoming, the story invents its text.

A text, like a season, like a ceili or a lifetime, is a segment of eternity. It exists at once as a whole and as part of a larger whole. That duality is not fought but stressed in tales—and seasons and homes—that unfold from thick, lit centers to signal independence while expanding through thin, dim borders into their environments. Beginnings, ends, and boundaries do not so much reinforce an entity's isolation as fade to the minimum to let it bleed into connection. Like a season or a townland, the story rises to centers of conceptual complexity held firmly under human control, then spreads, descending to blend with the wholeness that lies beyond will.

Ballymenone's great texts are the stories of history its men tell and the hillside homes its women make. Reading them by the same light, we have come to comparable conclusions. Both display continuity in organic order and an emphasis on centers that gives forms integrity without stealing connectedness from them. Rarer and less complex creations will reveal similar organization. The mummers' play was a "diversion," a comic thrill, and it was a serious attempt at social maintenance. Its climactic action blazed centrally between balanced processions that joined players to audience, family to community, the warm kitchen to winter's chilled darkness, stylized art to life as it flows. Further investigation and other comparisons will deepen and refine the idea, but continuity of thought, time, and space will remain fundamental to the power of Ballymenone's culture.

If we leave it there, we will have peeked into consciousness and found it consistent, logical. And we will be lost in the anthropologist's delusion. It will feel as though logic works in the mind despite people. While human beings retreat into passive compliance, the mind grinds efficiently, ordering stories and houses alike, because it is inherently, biologically logical. It probably is, and saying it is provides a healthy antidote against sick, vicious ideas that once held some minds, especially those cased in poor or dark bodies, to be less than logical, not rational. Yet the good idea leads to the less harmful but still false notion that culture, collective mentality, is a function of logic and not of will.

History is necessary. The timeless portrait of a culture gives it shape but no direction. It gives people no capacity for intention or decision, no way to create their own destiny. Synchrony petrifies them in an inhuman state, thrall to the scholar's model of consistency. History frees them, proves them capable of change—not that mere change disruptive to the decorum of proper ethnographies, or that fragmentary change banished from serious consideration beneath the self-congratulatory rubrics "acculturation" and "modernization," but real change, intended, directed change: history, the record of logical shift, of culture in time. As anthropology has proved people logical, it is history's duty to prove them willful.

So far our examination of the District's homes has yielded a cultural picture, consistent and nearly devoid of history. It has been an essential, necessary first step. Professional historians customarily barbarize local history. Without pausing to consider it in its own integrity, they sweep through, thieving anecdotes to meet their own needs. First the local picture must be complete, the culture established in its own terms, then when it begins to throb into time it will set its own beat, striking its own course, providing an independent history against which others can be compared to test their validity, with which they can be linked to forge a history worth knowing.

Written descriptions of Irish homes carry us easily back through the seventeenth century.[11] Fynes Moryson, fellow of Cambridge, came to Ireland in 1600. He puts Irish people "in a poor house of clay, or in a cabin made of the boughs of trees and covered with turf, for such are the dwellings of the very lords among them. And in such places they make a fire in the midst of the room, and round about it they sleep upon the ground. . . . And this manner of lodging not only the mere Irish lords and their followers use, but even some of the English-Irish lords and their followers."

The Plantation surveyors of Ulster in 1609 note in Fermanagh that one English settler "has contrived an Irish house into three rooms and built a wattled chimney in it," and another, Thomas Flowerdew, "has built an Irish house with a chimney at the end made of wattles, contrived into two rooms, and a frame for a timber house of birch, most part to be set up in a Dane's Fort." One English officer built "a good timber house after the English fashion," while the younger brothers of the dead rebel Hugh Maguire "built a great coppled house, in which they dwelt."

Pynnar's Survey, a decade later, found at Knockninny "a Town, consisting of forty Houses of Timber Work, and Mud-wall," and in Fermanagh other houses, thatched with walls of timber, limestone, and "Cage-Work."

Two books called the Irish Hudibras jingle and bounce the past to us. The first, written in 1689, parodies Aeneas' descent to Hades in order to herald the arrival of "England's Augustus," William of Orange, who will free Ireland from the priests and bring a "Golden Age of Liberty." Early on, it gives a "Description of an *Irish* Cabbin" as a setting for a humorous wake:

> *Built without either Brick or Stone,*
> *Or Couples to lay Roof upon:*
> *With Wattlets unto Wattles ty'd,*
> *(Fixt in the ground on either side)*
> *Did like a shaded Arbour show,*
> *With Seats of Sods, and Roof of Straw.*
> *The Floor beneath with Rushes laid, stead*

Of Tapestry; no Bed nor Bedstead;
No Pots, nor Bolts, nor Hinges in door,
No Chimney, Kitchin, Hall, or Windor;
But narrow Dormants stopt with Hay
All night, and open in the day.
On either side there was a door
Extent from Roof unto the floor. . . .
Betwixt the doors there was a spot
I'th' middle, to hang o're the pot. . . .
I'th' presence was no stool, but one
Old Creel, for Nees to sit upon:
For all the rest, as they did come,
Made stools and Cushions of their Bum. . . .
In this so rich and stately Cabbin . . .
. . . in one end the parted Brother
Was laid to rest, the Cows in t'other.

The author of the second Irish Hudibras plundered the first, broad-
ened its humor, and extended its account of Irish life at the end of the seventeenth century. In his second canto he describes the home of Gillo, the
native Lord, a hero in defeat at Aughrim:

In spacious plain, within a wood
And bog, the house of Gillo stood;
A house well built, and with much strength,
Almost two hundred foot in length,
A house with mountains fortify'd,
Which in the clouds their heads did hide.
At one of th' ends he kept his cows,
At th' other end he kept his spouse
On bed of straw, without least grumble,
Nay, with delight did often tumble;
Without partition, or a screen,
Or spreading curtain drawn between;
Without concern expos'd they lay,
Because it was their country way;
And when occasion did require,
In midst of house a mighty fire
Of black dry'd earth and swinging blocks
Was made, enough to roast an ox;
From whence arose such clouds of smoak,
As either me or you choak:
But Gillo and his train inur'd
To smoak, the same with ease endur'd;
For sitting low, on rushes spread,

The smoak still hover'd over head;
And did more good than real harm,
Because it kept the long house warm,
And never made their heads to ake;
Therefore no chimney he wou'd make. . . .
And if perhaps you do admire,
That this great house did ne'er take fire,
Where sparks, as thick as stars in sky,
About the house did often fly,
And reached the sapless wither'd thatch,
Which like dry spunge the fire would catch,
And where no chimney was erected,
Where sparks and flames may be directed;
St. Bridget's *cross hung over door,*
Which did the house from fire secure,
As Gillo *thought, O powerful charm!*
To keep a house from taking harm:
And tho' the dogs and servants slept,
By Bridget's *care the house was kept.*
Directly under Bridget's *cross*
Was firmly nail'd the shoe of horse
On threshold, that the house might be
From witches, thieves, and devils free:
For Patrick *o'er the iron did pray,*
And made it holy, as they say;
And banish'd from the hills and bogs
All sorts of serpents, toads and frogs,
By cross and iron: You may guess,
What faith this Gillo *did profess. . . .*
But let his faith be good or bad,
He in this house great plenty had
Of burnt oat-bread, and butter found
With garlick mixt in boggy ground. . . .
And this they count the bravest meat
That hungry mortal e'er did eat.

In 1699, a scurrilous little pamphlet, designed to "give such a Description of Ireland, as should make my Reader laugh at its Inhabitants," does provide some information on early housing, while grasping for comedy: "Their *Dwellings* or *Cabans,* I should more exactly describe if I durst have adventured oftner into them; or could have staid long enough to have Survey'd them at my being there; which I did once *Essay,* but found it as hazardous almost, as *Orpheus* his descent into *Hell,* where there might be indeed a greater *Fire,* but not more *Smoak.* . . . As for the outward *Structure,* an *English Cow house* hath more *Architecture* far. . . . The *Walls* are made of meer *Mud*, mixed with a little wet *Straw*, the Covering is *Thatch*; the Floor *Earth*. . . . They seldom have any *Partitions* or several Rooms, but sleep in common with their *Swine* and *Poultrey*: and for second or third *Story* you may look long enough e're you find any. *Windows* would discover their *Poverty* and *Sluttery* too much, and a *Chimney* is reckoned as *superfluous* as a *Steeple* at a new fangled *Conventicle*. . . ."

Such documents are suggestive. They indicate change, provide early instances of later practice, demonstrate the mixing of native and English culture in Ireland, and reveal the radical openness and organic ordering of the ancient house with its beasts tethered at one end and its fire in the middle where people sleep as well as eat together. They also raise all manner of difficulty. Never complete, they force us to argue over their accuracy, representativeness, and relevance to our District. But the extreme skeptic who would foolishly dismiss them from consideration is still not excused from the responsibility of history, for the District's houses themselves are documents, and to use them in writing history we need do no more than observe carefully and ask a few reasonable questions.

The cultural portrait you have read was not built from memories. It states the case for 1972, but it does not tell the whole story. Its sources were houses of the old type, inhabited in the old way. Our picture provides a baseline from which to measure, describe, and explain recent developments. Always in process, unstoppably changing, houses record the logical will, the cultural history of the District's people.

The old house exhibited organic order—conceptual continuity—most clearly in the multiple use of a few large spaces, kitchens for cooking and talking, Rooms for sleeping and eating. In time, spaces fragment and constrict, and functions simplify.

In the past a "settle bed" provided a seat by day and a bed by night in the kitchen. Few remain; they are used only for sitting, and the settle's place has been taken in most kitchens by a plain "couch" or a "sofa," usually Victorian in contour, reclining on fat little legs. The fire tender might nap there in daytime, and old bachelors still sleep by the hearth, but night's rest for most passes outside the kitchen.

Set along the back wall toward the hearth's end, in full view from the doorway, the settle bed was like the fire's glow, a sign of hospitality, for it was mostly used by travelers. With its bed gone, the kitchen's generosity diminishes. It remains an open stage for a ceili, a place for an evening's rest, but it offers no overnight accommodation to the visitor.

The smallest house contains but two spaces, kitchen and Room. Such stand as fragments, references to the whole form. They await addition to bring them to completion, and recently the O'Preys built onto their home, fulfilling the type. Or these small houses drop from completeness as lone old men seal off and abandon the lower end, then dismantle it to create the fragmentary kitchen-plus-Room form, revealed on its exterior by an arrangement of a door at the end, two windows to one side. Formally sim-

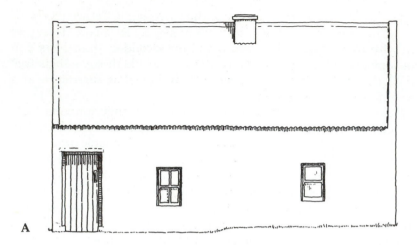

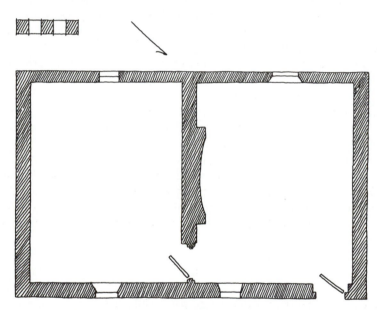

The Two-room House. **A**. Facade of Hugh Nolan's. **B**. Unoccupied house in Sessiagh used as an outoffice, once inhabited by the Flanagan family. Scale in feet.

plified, these houses are functionally complicated. With the bedroom and small storage room of the lower house missing, the kitchen absorbs the responsibility of storing water in covered buckets and fuel in sacks and heaps, and the Room or kitchen adds sleep to its tasks.

In some full houses, the Room is not broken but contains a bed or two as well as formal furniture for sitting and dining. This, the ancient duality of the parlor, a place for nighttime sleeping and daytime withdrawing, split when a second bedroom was contrived behind the Room. Old, associated activities were driven apart, given separate compartments. A change in form bespeaks a change in mind. The new bedroom materialized a shift in logic, a rise in the desire for categorical clarity, for boundaries. Change was not brought on by new prosperity, for the house was not enlarged, its spaces were subdivided. Many new houses, like Rose Murphy's, were constructed with the space above the kitchen sundered into Room and second bedroom, even if it left both feeling small, and older houses were partitioned about the same time, around 1890. I suspect that happened at Mrs. Cutler's, for the partition is wooden and does not reach the ceiling. I know that happened at Mrs. Keenan's, because I found it in ruins and could pick at its history with a penknife.

Categorical separation was accompanied by social separation, an increase in the wish for privacy. Upper beds were now shielded from the kitchen's public space by two walls, not one, and from the lower bedroom by three, not two. At the same time, the Room's purposes clarified. Like the kitchen, it was no longer for sleeping.

The next step led upward, and floors as well as walls drove between the most public and most private parts of the house. After adding laterally to their home, completing its plan, the O'Preys added vertically during the 1970s, launching bedrooms over other spaces. Francy Corrigan's, once a one-story thatched house of the old kind, now presents a grand two-storied facade to Rossdoney Lane. When bedrooms are pushed upstairs, as they are at Bobbie Thornton's, not only do bedrooms multiply, separating sleepers, and not only is rest broken from the working house below, but the rooms beneath are functionally purified. To one side of the Thorntons' kitchen is the parlor, to the other is not a bedroom but "a dining room." First sleeping was taken from the Room, then ceremonial eating, leaving it a parlor only.

The kitchen remains central, but behind the Thorntons'—and the McBriens' and the Loves'—another appears. The unity of the old kitchen divides. One of its traditional purposes grows, expanding through the home's center, making it a place to eat by day, ceili by night, while the other is relocated in a new, dependent volume, a special place for cooking and washing. Now furniture shifts. The dinner table moves to the old kitchen's rear to be near the table for food preparation, removed into the new kitchen, and the sofa moves to the front wall or a spot before the hearth, expressing the old kitchen's new primary commitment to entertainment. Things have not passed through change into confusion. New order grows clearly from old order. At the same time, the second kitchen, like the second bedroom, represents a new way of thinking.

The arrival of a separate kitchen for work marks a major evolutionary development. The wealthiest homes of the Middle Ages separated kitchens from the high lofty halls of eating and entertainment, scenes for bloody ballads. When second kitchens enter the English yeoman's house in the late sixteenth century or the District's homes in the mid-twentieth, they are welcomed by the mind's wish for separation. The old kitchen blends washing and storytelling, cooking and eating and news. The new arrangement drives work into a separate back space so it will not intrude upon sociability. If the household has wealth enough to afford servants, the second kitchen sets them away, out of sight with smoke and black pots, and suggests a hardening of class distinctions. Walls separate cooks and diners, those who labor from those who enjoy. When wealth is less, as it usually is, the new kitchen requires designating some member of the household as servant. Gender distinctions harden. In either case, masonry walls symbolize the separation of dirty work from clean pleasure, and associate some people with one, some with the other.

The District's people use two calendars, and they use two modes of architectural order, one of integration, one of disjunction. Most homes lack second kitchens, and in those that have them, women learn the housewife's dance, swinging between her space and their space, conducting her business while trying to stay in touch with the life spinning away from her in the old kitchen. Through houses increasingly arranged to express order by separation, she moves to reintegrate existence in constant action. But direction seems set. Yearly the old calendar falls further into disuse, and in architecture multiple use yields to functional purity, the logic of action yields to the logic of plans.

Change within the house parallels change in the whole home place. As Hugh Nolan taught during his story of Mackan Fight, sows once farrowed in the kitchen. At Mrs. Keenan's, chickens roosted in the lower room Mrs. Cutler uses as a pantry; daily a file of fowl paraded past her dresser. Now working beasts have been exiled, leaving the dwelling to people and the occasional luxurious cat. Many older homes have stables, byres, or henhouses built onto them, as part of "the house." Since thick walls rise between and no doors cut through, no sound or smell indicates the proximity of beasts when you sit at the hearth. The mind must sense them, though, for byres have been torn from the ends of some houses and rebuilt, still in line along the axis of the house, but far enough away for clear air to intervene and provide a barrier for the eye and mind between people and beasts, between the farm's domestic and industrial segments. Houses of the past half-century have been built without byres attached, and newer outoffices are not only out, they are behind, so the home's rearward trajectory extends

A

B

C

Farm-planning. **A**. John Gilleece's. The dwelling and byre are sheltered beneath one roof. You enter his kitchen through the porch and you enter his byre through the door to the right. **B**. The Ford. The house and byre are separated but they remain in line. **C**. The Croziers'. The byre is located behind the house.

through the new kitchen to the buildings behind, linking cooking in the kitchen to toil in the haggard, separating living from making a living.

The old house spreads its unity to view. Working spaces press into the same plane as living spaces and merge the dwelling into one long white string. The working parts of the new house break away and move to the rear, hiding or rising behind to provide a backdrop for the independent dwelling thrust clearly to the fore. The organic mixture of domesticity and industry that formed the interior and facade of the old house was displayed frankly before it, along the street, in a zone that incorporated working dependencies, dairy and cartsheds, as well as a strip of "lawn" and patches of flowers. The space before the new house is cleared of references to work; its grass, shrubs, and flowers are only decorative and domestic. No thoughts of farmwork enter your mind as you cross the lawn and enter the kitchen from which cooking has been removed. Above, rooms for rest lie on a plane above work, and the home's central space, stripped of necessary tasks, surrounds you with a clean welcome. Efficiently, the new house breaks the old organic order of work into the categories of labor and leisure.

The old house is open, its center expands to incorporate life. History closes it down.

Like a medieval hall or a church, the old kitchen lifted to the peaked underside of its roof. Only a few still do. Helpfully, that great space gathered errant smoke into a cloud above the head, but it blackened and grew beards of cobweb to wag in the drafts. It was impossible to clean. Soon after she married and moved into Billy Cutler's house, Ellen had the kitch-

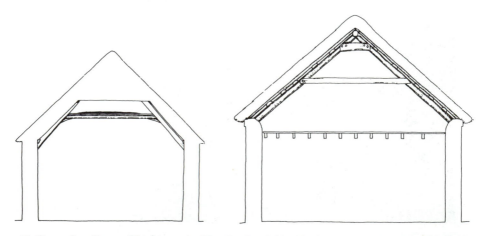

Ceiling the Open Kitchen. **A**. The Ford. Molded boards cover the curved collar and case the couple, and boards form a ceiling over the kitchen. **B**. Mrs. Keenan's. Joists inserted parallel to the ridge carry the floor of a loft above the kitchen. Newspapers glued to the walls above suggest the change was made by 1936.

en ceiled. Some houses, like the Ford or Rose Murphy's, were ceiled high at the level of the "tie" that joined the principal rafters of the roof's "couple," while others were ceiled from the tops of the walls, providing in a few a useful space above, reached via stairs ascending from the kitchen. Apparently the Croziers', certainly Mrs. Keenan's, underwent that change. It left the kitchen low, but as Mrs. Boyle said of Mrs. Keenan's, "the brides weren't hard to please."

When Paddy McBrien built his house, the mason suggested leaving the kitchen open to the roof, but that would make "a rum lookin shop," Mr. McBrien said, and ceiled it over. New kitchens begin closed, old ones are closed down. Most often, the space above is not used; the ceiling is not a bedroom's floor but a smooth clean surface over the kitchen's sociable arena.

The traditional wish for smooth surfaces and straight lines, for clean artificial planes, nears perfection as houses are modernized. Exterior walls are cemented to eradicate the shadowy textures of whitewashed masonry. Inside, ceilings are drawn to screen the roof, openings are rebuilt to plumb lines, and walls are sheetrocked into straightness and papered.

The original hood above the hearth was a wattled "rod brace," Tommy and P Lunny told me. Their house had one but it is gone, as it is from all

1972   1979

Change in Decor. The door from the Room into the kitchen at Mrs. Cutler's.

The Open Hearth at Hugh Nolan's

The Closed-Down Hearth at the McBriens'

others, replaced by a masonry chimney corbeled off engaged pilasters. That change in materials (cued by cleanliness and permanence) mirrored from the chimney to the floor. Old clay chimneys were rough in texture and demanded attention. Chips of clay cracked off exposing rods to sparks. Old clay floors are uneven. Wetness craters them, and a bucket of clay must be kept handy to rebuild the surface. Fine old floors were boarded in rooms, bricked in the kitchen. Today smooth, permanent "good concrete floors," covered with slick "lino," sleek ceilings and plastered, papered chimney breasts spread most kitchens with surfaces distinctly unlike the bumpy, mutable clay of lane and field.

Beneath the chimney, the fire burns on an "open hearth." No box cramps the flame lit against the wall between the wide shallow jambs that rise to support the hood that funnels some smoke out of the house. Open hearths are not yet a thing of memory alone, but in most houses within the last thirty years they have been "closed down." Bricks or blocks have been laid between the old jambs to create a trim little firebox. Some, too small for cooking, serve solely to warm and light the social scene, while others remain large enough to hold pots above their flames. Mrs. Cutler's son, John, did the work for her, removing the old crane crook, now built into a fence, inserting a straightened strip of "cart shoein" to crook pots from, and narrowing the hearth with concrete block. Once she told me the hearth was closed to improve its draft. The old hearth, she said, "would pull the hat off ye," and the new one draws more efficiently. Another time she told me the change was only a matter of fashion. The closed hearth looks tidier. James and Annie Owens had one of Hugh Pat Owens' sons close their open hearth because they got "tired of lookin at all that soot." Closed hearths like ceiled kitchens look better, neater, cleaner, and the next step is enclosing the fire entirely, encasing it in a "cooker." Late in the 1970s, while the Flanagans called in a mason to close down their wide open hearth, Mrs. Cutler filled hers with a cooker, a great gleaming steel box of a stove within which fire burns and from which smoke leaves obediently through a pipe. The cooker need not eliminate the fire. It can be set, as it is at James and Annie Owens', Hugh Patrick Owens', or the McBriens', on the dresser's wall, across from the hearth, but especially when the house has but one chimney, the logical place is the old one. The cooker encloses the fire, and the kitchen closes down around its traditional wish for cleanliness and becomes new.

A blazing center of attention, the hearth is the example people use to discuss change in the kitchen, but its history, like its culture, reflects off the dresser. The useful, lower halves of the oldest dressers like Mrs. Cutler's bring beauty to them in curvaceous vasiform splats, pierced by hearts at Hugh Nolan's and John Gilleece's. Skirts of soft curtains hang in their openings. Newer dressers like the Flanagans' (the Lunnys' big kitchen holds one of each type) are composed of straight lines. More directly utilitarian, they stand severely; below they close tightly and completely with flat, hard

The Flanagans' Hearth, 1979

Mrs. Cutler's Cooker, 1978

doors. Old or new, their upper halves spread open, exposing delph to sight and smoke, but the newer pieces that come to fill their slot in the decor display the wish for cleanliness and permanence through doors that protect their contents, eliminating the need for constant washing. At James McGovern's and Hugh Mackan's, where Michael Boyle lived, the dresser has been replaced by a "glass press." Crockery remains on view, clocks still tick, but all is sealed from touch and smut by panes of glass. Then sight as well as touch is eliminated when the dresser's location is usurped by a bureau at Bob Armstrong's or a "sideboard" at the Croziers' and William Lunny's. Once the dresser merged the spirit of the Room with the needs of the kitchen. Now it gives way to an assembly brought from the Room, a sideboard with a mirror above it, dark below and bright above like the dresser, and still bearing a clock at the middle, but lacking any reference to the kitchenness of the home's social center.

Closed, cleaner, more fragile and formal, the old kitchen displays new intentions in its furnishings, its ceiling, and its walls. In the past the lower walls were painted a dark color, and the bright ornamental upper half was whitewashed—often. A decorative border ran between, a stream of stenciled shamrocks at Denis Gilroy's, a pinked horizon of points at Mrs. Keenan's. But clean kitchens can be papered like rooms. The old style is to stop the repetitive medallions or flowers of pale patterned paper with a tape a foot or two from the floor, so the wall below, which is apt to get dirty, can be frequently whitewashed, but some kitchens are now treated exactly like rooms and papered down to an enameled baseboard.

The change from whitewash to paper alters the look of the kitchen. Patterns run the wall, cross the linoleum floor, and spill over the cloth of shelf, table, and dresser. Plain to patterned, yet there is no change in basic concept, for no single idea unifies the decor. Each pattern strikes its own course, beats its own rhythm, and finds its own dominant hue. The whole chatters in happy cacophony. Unification does not lie within the design that filters into the world, blending with its multitude of patterns. Order comes of human action.

Order is created by the active eye of the beholder and the active hand of the homemaker, so action cannot stop. Things exist in a state of continual reworking. Most outoffices once were built of wooden posts sunk in the ground and channeled on their faces to receive horizontal lath on which boards were nailed vertically. Slowly stone and brick and block grew between the posts and replaced the posts, and wooden buildings permuted to masonry without change in form or disruption in use. Houses are constantly rebuilt. Scholars accustomed to traditions in which rebuilding is rare or neatly periodic become frustrated by the impossibility of assigning dates to Irish houses. New houses contain early stone corners; homes expand and shrink and shift over old sites, continually absorbing diverse materials into their walls. The roof is frequently repaired and rethatched, and inside it is the same. Kitchens once regularly whitewashed are regularly papered and repapered. The chimney is reamed out with a bush controlled by ropes above and below, and the hearth needs new color over its plaster, a broad black band of paint or tar where the smoke runs up, and white-wash or paint, pale green, cream, or scarlet and white to simulate brick, at the sides. Mrs. Cutler painted the smoky center of her hearth black and the sides green, her favorite color, with brave big dots of pink like the red ber-ries among the green holly leaves that circle her kitchen at Christmas with the colors of blood and growth.

The house does not pause. It is cleaned constantly, its ornaments move, move again; hearth and woodwork want paint often, and the kitchen must be repapered every couple of years. People do not wait for a change at the hearth to paste the walls with paper, but paper is less risk, less vulnerable when the smoky fire is contained in a closed hearth, or better still, wholly enclosed in a cooker.

Enclosing, covering, containing was the old way to cleanliness. Tester beds, box beds, cupboards, cabinets, wardrobes, presses, chests, boxes of all sorts fill the ancient house.[12] Tiny rooms placed in larger rooms pro-tected their contents against the dirt and the wafts of smoke and dusty drafts the house necessarily also contained. The major piece of furniture in the open kitchen is the open dresser, its shelves bearing delph that must be constantly washed. In the closed Room, the major piece is the closed press in which textiles are protected behind solid, paneled doors. Things that must be clean are wrapped in second skins in the open old homes of Bally-menone. Cloth that can be removed and washed, or paper that can be fre-quently replaced, covers tables, sills, shelves, and mantels. Clocks run, still housed in the boxes in which they arrived. Between playing, radios and musical instruments are boxed or wrapped in bags. Eating utensils hide in drawers. Food keeps in boxes. Recently boxes have grown and gathered more within their walls. Cookers confine fires, sideboards contain china. Al-most no kitchen has reached the limit of enclosure, more fulfill the old pat-tern than the new, and most have come to momentary rest at a halfway point. Hearth and dresser remain wholly open at Hugh Nolan's and Rose Murphy's. The closed-down hearth and glass press that mark midway stand at the McBriens' and Hugh Patrick Owens'. Steps farther are taken in the cooker and glass press at the Ford and the Loves', and the closed hearth and sideboard at the Thorntons' and James and Annie Owens'. The old drive to cleanliness through containment continues.

Closing means separation. The physical closet symbolizes conceptual closure and cleanliness. In the act of classification, we talk of putting ideas in boxes. Discontinuities in space—boxes—bring discontinuities in time, signaling discontinuity of concept. The second kitchen removes women's work from the sociable fireside, breaking the endless thread of time spun from diverse fibers at the home's single center, disturbing the family's unity, unweaving the conceptual fabric of work into its pleasurable and necessary strands. Once separate, things are ready for storage. Perfectly separate from

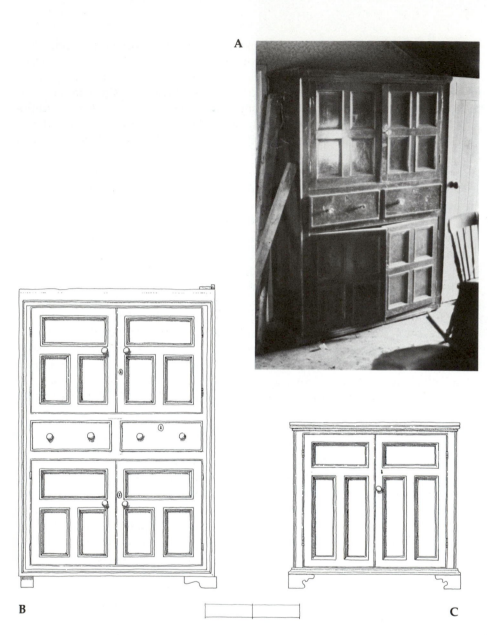

Presses. **A**. Billy Stinson. **B**. Rose Murphy. **C**. Mrs. Keenan. A and B are precisely the same size, each door measuring 21 by 26½ inches. B is missing one bracket foot and the cornice which is still in place on A. Both the tall (A, B) and low (C) forms are called presses. B and C were both, unlike A, painted, and both were placed in the same location: at the front of the end wall in the Room so that they would be seen immediately upon opening the door from the kitchen. Scale in feet.

The Half-Door. This house on the Back Road, which was destroyed late in the 1970s, displays the half-door and small windows once common on the District's houses. See the drawings of Mrs. Cutler's Kitchen.

society, the individual is put in a casket. Separate from sociability, the woman is put in a new kitchen; her tools, her cups and her fire, are closed in boxes.

Boxes have doors. Opening them, we bring spaces into connection but with the same act recognize separation and break time's flow. Open a door to poke at the fire, open another to retrieve a pot, and the reality of invisible categories registers in experience. Increasingly the kitchen boxes its parts. Then the whole house closes, making the kitchen a box within it as the rooms had always been. Doors must be opened to get to the boxes that must be opened to get to life.

Old kitchens stand open. Some had "half-doors" hung before their front doors. When closed, they remained open to light. The bright rectangle framed over the half-door, like that of the dresser's top half and those above the working tables, joined the ornaments circling the upper walls to provide delight to the eye within. From without, the half-door gave immediate visual access to the home while better unriddling the question about when a door is not a door, being a door that, when closed to low, scamping creatures, remains open to people. Half-doors are almost gone, and most houses never had them, but even when shut against wind and rain, front doors provide the thinnest division between exterior and interior: one swing destroys separation. Then a second door appears, and the kitchen retreats along a twisted route, removing itself from direct contact with the world's climate and people.

Block porches reach out and around the kitchen's door, embracing and protecting it. During the past quarter-century, porches have risen in front of most older houses, Rose Murphy's and Ellen Cutler's for example, to keep bad weather at bay. Now winds pounding the front must break through two doors, and since the porch's door pierces its side, winds have no straight shot at the kitchen. On cold days the porch door is opened then closed before the door into the kitchen is opened. Weather stays behind. So does dirt. "I don't know how they lived here before the porch was built," Mrs. Cutler said. "The wind comes off the street and it blows the ashes of the hearth all around." Billy Cutler built her a porch where fuel is set out of the kitchen, caked boots can be kicked clean or left to stand, and a bowl for washing rests on a chair.

Since porches encroach on the street, houses on the roadside cannot have them, and an abbreviated speer-wall is built inside, parallel to the dresser's wall. When curtained, it works like an intruded porch to keep the kitchen warmer.

Cleanliness and environmental efficiency also provide the rationale for the most complete way to close the kitchen, a "hall" framed across the front of the house. Most twentieth-century houses have been built with halls, and they have been built into several older houses instead of porches. As with the second bedroom, the house does not expand, it fragments internally: the hall steals space from the kitchen. While its purpose is protecting the tidy kitchen, even more than the porch the hall rises to seek privacy as well. Now people within can move from room to room without disturbing the kitchen, and people from without do not pass through the doorway to the hearth. They enter facing a small window trained through the hall's wall, then turn, turn again, and break through another door to enter the kitchen.

The old house has two wishes, comfort and generosity. It holds them in balance between closed rooms and open kitchens, and symbolizes their easy coexistence on hearth and dresser. The new house tips to comfort. To be generous, a house has to be less than comfortable, open to winds and dirt as well as guests. When you get your house clean at last, the last thing you want is a surprise visitor fresh from mucking the byre, so you stop people in vestibules and invite them to come when you want them, fretting while they stand on your carpets with drooling drinks in tipsy hands and cigarettes snowing ash. The open house of constant fire, the truly generous house, must welcome all people at all times, though that means winter enters with them and cleaning must follow. But that is right, for the kitchen was cleaned for them to use, and closed rooms contain the permanent displays of neatness.

Generosity is the basic value and ordering principle of the open old kitchen. Early travelers commented constantly and sniffily on the dirtiness of Irish houses without connecting what they took to be disorder with generosity.[13] In 1779, Arthur Young wrote that "the cottages of the irish, which are called cabbins, are the most miserable looking hovels that can well be conceived: they generally consist of only one room," and that "the furniture of the cabbins is as bad as the architecture; in very many, consisting only of a pot for boiling their potatoes, a bit of a table, and one or two broken stools; beds are not found universally, the family lying on straw, equally partook of by cows, calves and pigs." Yet, he did note, "I was in the cabbins of dairymen and farmers, not small ones, whose cabbins were not at all better, or better furnished than those of the poorest labourer: before, therefore, we can attribute it to absolute poverty, we must take into account the customs and inclinations of the people. . . ." Wisely the Irish put their money into their farms, he argued, and not their homes, but Young, the economist, did not consider social custom. Another visitor, in 1805, who was able to see virtue in the Irish country people, their wit and love of music and literature, came close to understanding when he wrote: "Their hospitality, when their circumstances are not too wretched to display it, is remarkably great. The neighbour or the stranger finds every man's door open, and to walk in without ceremony at meal-time, and to partake of his bowl of potatoes, is always sure to give pleasure to every one of the house, and the pig is turned out to make room for the gentleman. If the visitor can relate a lively tale, or play upon any instrument, all the family is in smiles, and the young will begin a merry dance, whilst the old will smoke one after another out of the same pipe, and entertain each other with stories." That was the spirit the old house sheltered.

As the house becomes new by ordering itself around its old wish for comfort, it releases generosity. More and more, the kitchen takes on the appearance of a room—ceiled, papered, lacking in smoke—and once defended by a hall, the kitchen becomes less accessible to visitors than the master bedroom of the old house. The new kitchen is cleaner and warmer, Mrs. McBrien told me, but people do not come much any more.

Serving better those who occupy it, the house serves worse those who do not. Shifting toward comfort, the house shifts away from hospitality and reveals a change in values: the personal matters more, the communal less.

Space breaks, purposes simplify and enclose themselves in boxes. The house seeks internal order through division, then writes new order onto its facade. The balanced, organically ordered front of the old dwelling set its door off-center, revealing to every visitor the plan inside. The newest houses pull the door to dead center, making it the middle element of a bilaterally symmetrical design. Each half mirrors the other, so visitors cannot know what lies behind. Motion is interrupted: people must pause on the threshold and await directions to the hearth. Hosts try to patch that break in old etiquette by leaving the front door and hall door open so the house, and not the

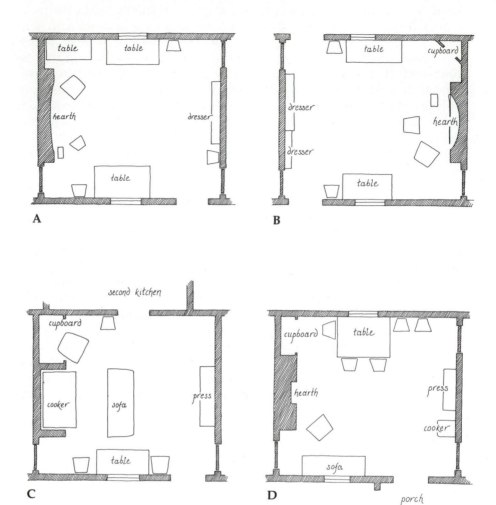

Change in the Kitchen. These diagrammatic plans are based on real kitchens.
A. Open kitchen with open hearth and dresser; P and Joe Flanagan. **B**. Open
kitchen with open hearth and dressers; Tommy and P Lunny. **C**. Open
kitchen with second kitchen, cooker and press; Tommy Love. **D**. Kitchen
closed by a porch, closed-down hearth, cooker and press; Hugh Patrick

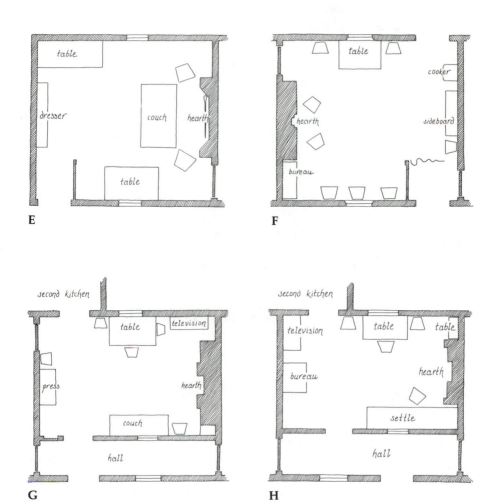

Owens. **E**. Speer-wall vestibule, open hearth and dresser; Hugh Nolan.
F. Speer-wall vestibule, closed-down hearth and sideboard; James and Annie
Owens. **G**. Kitchen closed by a hall with second kitchen, closed-down hearth
and press; John O'Prey. **H**. Kitchen closed by a hall with second kitchen,
closed-down hearth and bureau; Bob Armstrong.

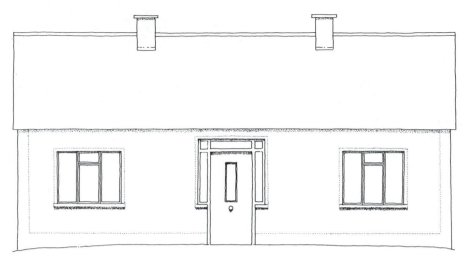

The Symmetrical Facade. The Kennedys' home, built on the site of an old house in 1959.

householder, can point the route inward, but the symmetrical facade, like the hallway and second kitchen, marks a major change.

It was not hard to reorder the facade symmetrically. The old house front is pierced by the Room's window, then the kitchen window, then the door, then the bedroom's window. The central door of the newest house is sidelit, so its facade contains the same quantities arranged to read: window, half-window, door, half-window, window. It was not hard to do, required no new materials or talent, but why was it done?

Before going to Ireland, I completed a study of old houses in a small area in Virginia. I went looking for the architectural personality of a section of geography, for cultural pattern. I found history. The problem houses pressed on me was the meaning of a revolution recorded in their timber walls, a revolution precisely parallel to the one in Ballymenone.[14]

When I pondered those houses as empty, as spaces to use, I discovered the old house was open, one step led from outside into the main room, while the new house was closed, one step led into an unheated, unlit corridor through which, then out of which, more steps carried the body into inhabited rooms. This hallway made environmental sense, sucking cool air through hot houses, a breath of relief in torrid summers, but as soon as the hallway appeared it was blocked, its breezes were stifled by additions, second kitchens, tucked around the rear of the home. The environmental rationale was lost, and I interpreted the shift from open to closed as a cry for privacy. The new hallway inserted a social lock between the people of the house and others.

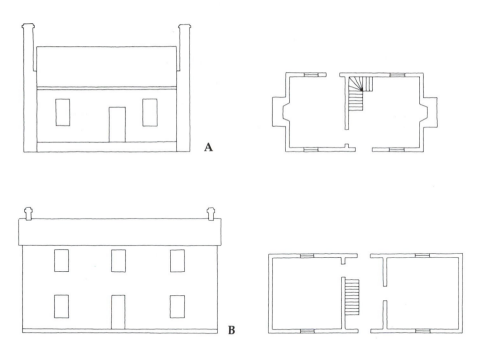

Architectural Change in Middle Virginia. **A**. The hall-and-parlor house, dominant in the eighteenth century. **B**. The I house, dominant in the nineteenth century. The change from A to B, largely effected between 1760 and 1820, shifted the facade from balanced to symmetrical and the plan from open to closed.

When I considered the house as a thing to see, a piece of wooden sculpture rising off red clay among old oaks and black pines, I saw its facade shift from organic balance to bilateral symmetry and interpreted that change as evincing a wish for order. The symmetrical facade masks the interior, gives no information, and composes its elements placidly, abstractly, according to geometry, not use.

Linking interior and exterior, I found the new house of old Virginia coupling fear and courage. The retreat from experience revealed in its plan was covered by the valiant assertion into the world of an impeccably orderly facade. My argument ran: sensing disorder abroad on the land, hearing the far tread of foul beasts, the Virginians stepped away, hid, but did not comply by turning the glass on chaos. They replaced the order that seemed suddenly absent from the world with a brave new one of their own devising. They classed internal affairs into boxes, then drew on the face of their own box a simple diagram of a world in control. Symmetry needs nothing beyond it, nothing out there. Alone it is complete; its parts repeat, mirroring themselves into totality. Easily perfectible, contained entirely within itself, bilateral symmetry is the simplest way to create balance, the simplest proof of control, a certain, fearful emblem of order.

Virginia's period of architectural change—1760 to 1820—was indeed a time of massive strangeness, a time for fear and courage. Houses closed and became symmetrical while the American world transformed, shifting from dependent colonial status through violence into independence.

We can know more about the era during which the District's houses changed from open to closed, balanced to symmetrical, since it lies within living memory. I talked to those who were there. It can be located precisely. I had to guess the ages of Virginia's houses and dated many too early, but I know the first house of the new type was built in the District in 1900 and the last one of the old type was built in 1948. In Virginia there is little beyond the texts of the houses and the conventional facts of the historian, thin or only obliquely germane, from which to construct the mood of the period. Think how impossible it would be to assemble the District's opinion out of census data and newspaper accounts from distant places. Even meeting the District's people in public, watching their parades, hearing their songs, you would miss the essence and complexity of their thought, which appears only in gentle fireside scenes. But I have been there and have transcribed their statements, so you already know about the period of architectural change.

Houses changed during the era of the band's battles. Just when Billy Price attacked the Old Ballymenone Band on its way back from boycotting a Protestant pub, the first house of the new type was built in the predominantly Catholic area by a Protestant policeman. It makes sense to think of it as broken by a hallway from its community.

Conflict was the topic and the reality when the community's people began curtaining themselves behind new walls and masks of composure. Though the sectarian conflict of the band's first battle ran back to Mackan, the conflict of the second battle was new, and taken with other historical stories it asserts division as much as unity to be the community's nature. Like the second bedroom before it, the halls of its time, the second kitchen of the future, the second band battle split old units in the quest for conceptual cleanliness. National politics provided the tool to smash the band. A "martyr," it was sacrificed to ideological purity during the attempt to secure a clear, stable position in the confusion following the Easter Rising.

The Rising cannot be the cause of the District's architectural change, any more than the American Revolution can be the cause of the comparable change in Virginia's housing. Since houses began to change before war broke, it would be more reasonable to posit them as war's cause than the reverse; but neither is cause, both are results, symptoms of a change in logic registered in houses before politics because houses are closer to people, more important than politics. A change in the hearts and minds of men changed houses and made the subsequent political revolution possible.

Ireland's history runs with continual conflict, punctuated by risings:

1594, 1641, 1689, 1798, 1803, 1848, 1867. That of Easter Week 1916 worked. When they shot James Connolly, strapped in a chair—as when the embattled farmers fired the shot heard round the world—the people rose, but no evil or heroism would have sufficed had they not been ready, psychically set for action.

We have been told of another event that transpired in the time of architectural change, the Land League Agitation. Begun before change in houses, it drives nearer cause. Ideology touches few. Those it grips, it arms and sends from Sir Edward Carson's speeches into the Volunteers, from the Gaelic League into the Post Office. But land gets to every farmer, homes to every person. In 1880, a year after the Land League was founded, Fermanagh's first public rally was held—in Sessiagh. Land touched and galvanized the people and gave them victory in successive land acts in 1881, 1891, 1896, and 1903.[15] Then when the world cracked open politically, between 1912 and 1923, events were not taken as more odd rumor from distant Dublin and met with apathy. They were faced consciously with fear and courage, the need and will to act.

Seeking order through separation and containment—through analysis—a new mentality forms new houses, socially closed and visually symmetrical. Houses make palpable the thinking essential to new ideology, testing it, finding it good, and so stand as heralds, announcing in advance the violent, conspicuous events historians arrange into our past. The event need not be open war, as it was in America and Ireland. The industrial revolution followed closed, symmetrical houses in England. The birth of the spinning jenny was as dependent as armed revolution upon a logic of division and functional purity.

Joined by house form to places beyond, our little Irish district points us behind the revolutions of the English world, industrialization and the American war for independence, to find the real cause that predates the housing change and bears the relation to them that the Agitation does to Easter Week. And there are the Enclosures breaking sacred villages into commercial towns and productive farms, there are the Commonwealth's new property laws and Parliament's legal destruction of community in the name of profit and efficiency, there are the land-based, dug-in-the-dirt issues it took industrialization and colonial war to unravel to their conclusions.[16] Ask for a deeper cause, and I can do more but not better than report the shock I felt when I met an armillary sphere in an exhibition of medieval artifacts. Here is a globe of brazen rings, the transits of planets, the band of the ecliptic engraved with zodiacal signs, all circling the pearl of the earth set on a rod and wheeling its own equator and meridian bands out to the spherical limits, extending its axis to become the axis of a universe that holds at dead center our planet, the apple of God's eye. Reduce the pearl to a cooling rock, a mote of dust, set it spinning into insignificance in the swarm of an infinite universe, and people will crumble in fear or rise to take God's place, creating order out of themselves, a religion of personal soul, an art of the eye, a philosophy of the mind, an economy of acquisition, a politics of conquest and consolidation—the materialistic, reductive, man-centered universe of the Renaissance.

The democratic symbol and intimate vehicle of the new mentality was a Renaissance house form. Its facade was placidly, rationally, exactly symmetrical. Its interior was divided by a hallway. When architectural historians confine study to architecture, as though it were a valid self-contained realm of experience, all they can say of a new form is that it represents a change in fashion, another in a whimsical succession. If all fashions were accepted at an equal rate, fashion might be an explanation, but since they are not, it is not. The question is which fashion and when, so we can ask why.

Confronted with a novelty, people do not simply adopt it. Instead, they accept actively, dismembering the novelty, taking from it what they want when they want it, then discarding the residue. Though the closed and symmetrical Renaissance house form hit England well before any George took the throne, though its origins are Italian, not English and its distribution is international, scholars call the form Georgian, accidentally revealing a deep ideological bias: what but an inbuilt, conservative theory of active leaders and passive masses would name art styles after monarchs incapable of making anything so useful as a house or a chair? But the Renaissance form did spread rapidly through English-speaking regions while endless wars ripped through the reign of the Georges, and when it rose from rarity to dominance on Virginia's landscape times were right, strained and hopeful. Then country carpenters did not copy the Georgian houses of an isolated elite, but robbed what they wanted and designed their own new houses, split by hallways, masked by symmetry. Had they been looking for fashion instead of devices of closure and images of order, they would have embraced the next fashions, but they did not. The romantic revivals, Greek, Gothic, Tuscan, swept past, leaving only enough behind—a column, a gable, a bracket—to prove the carpenter knew the fashion but rejected it. His basic house form was set, and it endured unshaken into the twentieth century.

The Renaissance house had sprung in Fermanagh by the middle of the eighteenth century. Florence Court, built between 1758 and 1768, stands still. A grand hallway opens through its center behind a rigid, emphatically symmetrical composition of stone. Enniskillen's streets are packed with Georgian houses. Dark corridors within end in dainty side-lit, fan-lit doors on stuccoed facades, scored and quoined like ashlar, smooth and bright. These were familiar sights to country people drawn to the Town's fairs and marts and pubs. If you argue that the District's people got through the whole of the nineteenth century without emulating Georgian houses because they did not see or understand, they left plenty of refutation. Large sash prove they saw and liked one aspect of the Town's houses. Old windows had been tiny, immobile panes of glass or "wee toady" holes shut-

Florence Court

Model of Florence Court

tered by wicker. These were replaced in the nineteenth century by sliding glass sash admitting vastly more light. The arrangement of the dresser and the dresser's wall—door, dresser, door—proved they could achieve bilateral symmetry when they wanted it, but if it appears they did not understand how the idea could be applied to facades, disconfirmation arrives in a marvelous piece of sculpture Bobbie Thornton owns, a ceramic model of Florence Court made by a laborer in the brick industry during the last century.[17] That it is not a good likeness makes it all the more useful, for it proves a local man could extract the concept of symmetry from a real house and realize it perfectly in familiar materials. No. The District's people were capable, but they let the hallway and side-lit door wait in old houses until they wanted them. Times changed, and antiquated Georgian ideas came to answer their needs and suit their minds.[18]

Were people logical machines, no real change would come, and were they brutish products of conditions, they would be blown through ceaseless revolution into madness, but since they develop between logic and conditions, they invent sanely to meet the times. It was a time of hope. The Land League promised to secure rights of ownership. Ireland's "greatest victory" meant houses could be improved and passed between the generations as pieces of delph had been.[19] It was a time of tension, rebellion, war, then civil war. While the political climate grew gusty, then cracked in a storm of blood, people sought secure shelter. First Protestants broke away, but when things finally calmed, all sides had suffered schism and Ireland lay split. The new border made permanent the old tensions of Mackan Fight. The failure of mumming proved the community could no longer absorb its factions into unity. Life would continue forever unhealed. New ideals of social separation and geometric order replaced the old ideals of social integration and organic order. The house of new ideals, the Georgianized Protestant home, was adopted by Catholics, and the whole community came to express its new, wounded balance in a new form.

The new house is a landmark of cultural evolution. In different times and places, from Italy in the Renaissance to rural Turkey today, closed, symmetrical houses rise to speak a new mind.[20] Closure was accomplished in many ways. The houses of southeastern England and New England brought their second kitchens around back, so the chimney could squat centrally behind a vestibule blocking entrance to the home. In northwestern England, Lowland Scotland, and through the Potomac River drainage, a stairway, not a chimneystack, rose behind the door to insert a lobby between insiders and outsiders. In the Highlands of Scotland a small bedroom was partitioned in the middle to draw a lateral hallway across the house front. In the west of England and the southern United States, a transverse hallway did the job. And with internal closure comes frontal symmetry. The District's new house is another. When it rebalances itself to emphasize comfort over generosity, personal aspirations over communal participation, it marks with houses all over the West a revolution, an evolutionary moment second in significance only to the Neolithic. The Neolithic revolution placed man above the environment. Earth, plants, and animals were brought under control as pots, crops, and beasts of protein and burden. Neolithic myths concern the relation of man and nature. The next revolution, ours, broke the sacred grip of community and set the self above others. Man-made objects were ordered to class people. New myths, urbane novels or the fireside stories of rural districts, concern the relation of man to man.

All times are times of change. Conditions are always wild and mutable, people are always free and creative. Diaries kept by fretful, reclusive individuals make every era look revolutionary, but times of deep cultural reorganization are rare. Since houses can reveal the common mind and stand into efficient comparability, they let us separate genuine revolutions from the ceaseless flux.[21] Though always changing, evolving, the District's houses display one radical logical shift, providing an instance, fully comprehensible in local terms, of a massive revolutionary change in the culture of the West.

That argument may seem right to the intellect, but it feels wrong, or incomplete, to the whole person. It is the archaeologist's sadness to have to study people through material remains, chipped flint, burnt clay, but it would be the ethnographer's madness to try to comprehend the complexity of culture through one kind of expression. Ballymenone's houses certainly display a shift from open to closed, from organic to analytic ordering. From a great distance that change seems revolutionary, but close up what looked sharp feels dull.[22]

New order grows from old. Its force is old force, though narrowed, directed, purified in response to conditions. Cleanliness had always been effected by containment, by boxing. Now more is contained. Order had always been created through centers. Now centers are further clarified by sharp boundaries. Symmetry had always been implied. Now it is overt, insistent. When the world was inhabited by trusted people, implications sufficed. Now with less sure, with less fixed in nature, the latent is driven to the surface.

The change is real, new forms mark it, but since the new order had always existed, implicitly, comfortably within old order, what looks from the outside like revolution, feels from the inside like logical growth.

Since it does, since change feels gradual—the product of will, not coercion—the revolution recorded in forms can be fought by action within them. Papered and protected, the kitchen still admits ceilis that flow through them into the organic hearts of tale. Just as they live in one community by day and another by night, just as they use two calendars, the District's people can hold at once two ways to be reasonable. Look at houses only, and you will find their logic one of separation. Look at stories only, and you will find their logic one of continuity. It is not that people are con-

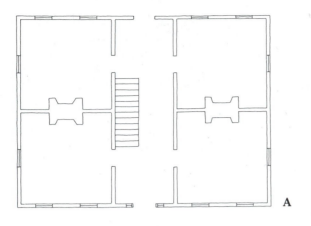

A

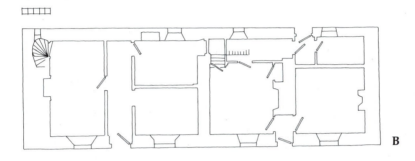

B

Varieties of Symmetry and Closure in Domestic Architecture. **A**. The Georgian idea: symmetrical on plan and in all elevations, with five openings across the facade, central stair hall, chimneys pulled to internal partitions in the double-pile arrangement. **B**. House in Clanfield, Oxfordshire, England. When this early stone house was extended and converted into a pair of cottages, the result was two houses, each with the usual British window-door-window facade, and each supplying an example of one of the two most usual modes of closure in Britain: the house to the left has a transverse hallway (compare it with F); the house to the right has a vestibule in front of the chimney (compare it with C). **C**. Vestibule in front of the chimney; framed house of the Cape Cod type, east of Old Saybrook, Middlesex County, Connecticut, U.S.A. **D**. Vestibule in front of the stairway, framed house, St. Catherine Island, St. Mary's County, Maryland, U.S.A. **E**. Lateral hallway in front of a small bedroom, connecting kitchen and parlor; crucked stone house, Drumdewan, Dull, near Aberfeldy, Perthshire, Scotland. **F**. Transverse hallway; log house, south of Collierstown, Rockbridge County, Virginia, U.S.A. Late additions to C, D, and F were removed to facilitate comparison. These houses, like all the others pictured in this book, were measured during the period of the book's creation, 1972–81. Scales in feet.

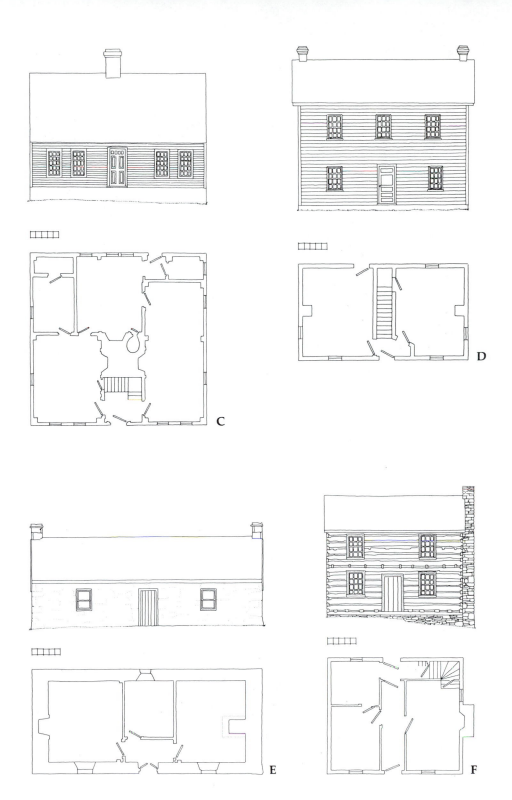

C

D

E

F

Tommy Love's Home

fused, caught in contradiction, but that, being human, they are capable of graceful inconsistency, shifting to apply different modes of organization in different spheres of activity.

But deeply those modes are one, the way of one mind responding to different conditions. When times are smooth and people are at peace, relaxed by a familiar hearth, the mind forms organic centers in the continuous flow. When times are rough and people feel pressured, tense in the public gaze, the mind cracks centers into isolation, boxes them, and thrusts them forward behind composed, symmetrical masks.

Look broadly across the land, and you will discover again what you have through close observation at the hearth. Though the first of the new houses was built in 1900, only eight more have joined it. Ten remain unaltered, wholly open. The rest are houses of an old type, not always old themselves, closed by porch, hall, or internal vestibule. Most houses exist at an evolutionary midstage. All the open houses are owned by Catholics. Catholics have less money and they are numerically dominant, but more to the point, all but one of the open houses stand far from the main roads. Tommy Love added a room to his, completing the traditional plan. It is a beautiful house, thatched and bright white with painted quoins and gleaming yellow sash, set amid beds of flowers. He is proud of his home, and he is a good craftsman. He built the byre behind it. When I asked why he added no porch, he said he did not have to because his house was far from the road, and it is. A hill shields it from the routes of common travel. It does not need to be protected from strange visitors. Only neighbors would find their way to Mr. Love's at Rossdoney's southern limit, just as only neighbors would cross the fields to the Flanagans' or Lunnys', so their homes, unconnected by paved roads to the world beyond, remain unclosed by porch or hall and spring open within to the rafters as all homes did when everyone who came could be trusted to bring with them, within them, the neighborly ethic.

The diverse wholeness of the community's architecture would be broken by an analyst from afar. Classing houses into new and old types, the student would repeat divisions known to the people who live in them, who see and discuss the differences between old and new plans. If the analyst thinks the old house is a "folk" or "vernacular" type and the new one is inauthentic, an alien imposition, the people would not agree, and they would be right. As surely as the old house, the new one is a local product. It belongs, and the District's people are right to see both types as creations of the same mind differently conditioned.

The old house bridged the community's divisions with a single form, and the new house does the same. The Thorntons' was built of brick in 1900 and houses the family of a prosperous Protestant farmer. The Mc-Briens' was built of block in 1944 and houses the family of a small Catholic farmer. Differences of age and material, religion and economy, are minor beside similarities. There are differences of size and form. Mr. Thornton added a porch to the front, hanging on its side the old but solid front door, and his house encloses bedrooms under its gable-lit eaves. The McBriens' bedrooms are on the same level as the kitchen. But both houses exemplify the same type, the new type. The door is central, and the central kitchen is trapped between a front hall and a second kitchen at the rear. Though closed down, the hearth in each remains a warm, generous center where I was entertained wonderfully well.

The symmetrical faces of their homes do not invite the mind in through the eye. They block the body. But they do not repeat the community's divisions. If the community seems no longer to unfold from its sacred midpoint, then order must be built up out of separate units. Order becomes an individual responsibility, a matter of honor. Honorably, the new house compensates, staying the hand of chaos by bringing the old order of the interior, of the box and dresser's wall, right to the surface. The house stands in isolated composure and sends its signal of truce across a hurt, confused community to other houses standing, too, restrained and noble, above a landscape of battle.

The symmetrical facade interrupts the visitor's experience but it projects an indisputable sign of rationality to the stranger on the road. The hallway behind the facade disrupts the entrance of a neighbor but it provides a convenient location for strangers, for potential enemies to meet and negotiate through formal etiquette. In the hall, strangers eliminate or af-

View from the South

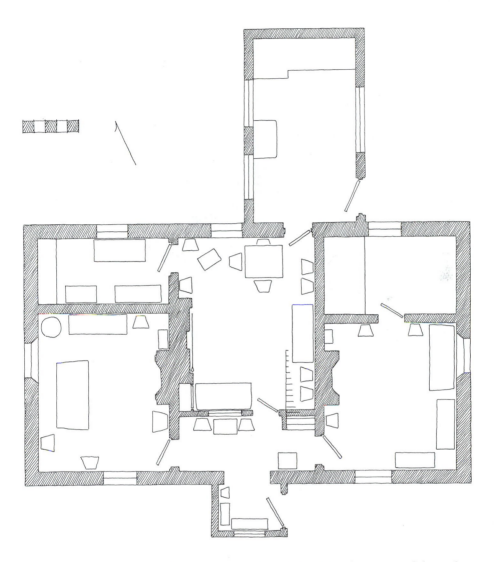

Plan. From left to right: Parlor to the front. Office behind. Kitchen, entered through porch and hall with a second kitchen behind, closed-down hearth, couch in the front, table and television in the rear, sideboard across from the hearth beneath the stair. Dining room to the front. Bedroom behind. Scale in feet.

The McBriens' Home.

View from the North.

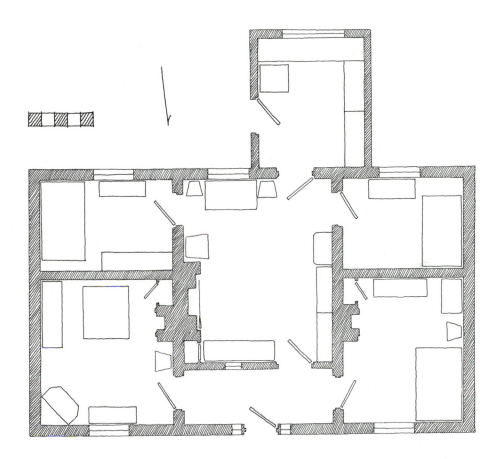

Plan. From left to right: Room to the front. Bedroom behind. Kitchen, entered
through a hall with a second kitchen behind, closed-down hearth, couch in
the front, table in the rear, press across from the hearth. Master bedroom to
the front. Bedroom behind. Scale in feet.

firm differences so that behavior can be framed to enable life to be conducted sanely.

The old house of Ballymenone was organically ordered on the sacred, experiential ideal of neighborliness. It fit a place where people were known and assumed to share basic values. It stood forth frankly, vulnerably, generously. The new house was rationally ordered on the secular, conceptual ideal of honor. It fit a world of strangers and danger. It closed itself around comfort and presented an image of order and decorum. Evolution from one house type to another displayed the response made by good people to changing conditions.

Change is natural. The people of Ballymenone are not thrashing around, struggling to find the way from their place to yours. They are on their own course, creating, adapting, creating anew. Though they see time as continuous and read the new as evolved from the old, they do not mistake change for progress. Evolution is not beyond evaluation.

While discussing buildings I had recorded with Hugh Nolan and Tommy and P Lunny, I learned about the evolution of framing. When the walls of houses were built of sod, they could not support the roof, so posts were set down into the earth within the walls, their tops chiseled to receive the roof's couples. Tommy Lunny aptly called such jointed cruck-framing, "buildin on knees." No houses of the sort remain, though wooden outoffices bear plenty of evidence of the practice, and one fine example of a crucked hayshed stands in the nettles behind the ruins of a house in Derryhowlaght near Bobbie Thornton's. At the time of Land League, houses were rebuilt in permanent materials, mostly brick, and that was a great improvement because the sod house, like the rod brace and clay floor, demanded constant attention. But brick walls presented a problem: whether to treat them like sod or stone. Some early brick homes, laid up in random bond, were crucked like sod-wall houses, others were roofed like houses of stone with "couples," the top half of the cruck, its A-frame, set upon the wall heads. The trouble was that the couple, untied at its feet, splayed beneath the weight of thatch and shoved the side walls out of plumb. Thick stone walls and well-bonded brick walls bent and bore their load, but the thin brick walls of small new houses collapsed, destroyed by the burden of the roof, and that was no improvement. So masons began building internal lateral walls fully to the ridge, making them into solid masonry crucks from which sawn purlin carried the roof across rooms and kitchen without couples to interrupt. Newer houses like the Flanagans', brick and lacking couples, represented an improvement, more permanent than sod, more stable than the coupled house. In the case of framing, evolution led, and led rapidly—probably between 1880 and 1910—to clear betterment. [23]

Other changes tell more complicated tales. Inside, the mind focuses on the hearth. The cooker is a great gain—and a great loss. Boxing the flame, it deprives the kitchen of the flicker and glow that glimmered light onto the ornaments and provided the homemaker with something to watch. She is

Roof-framing.

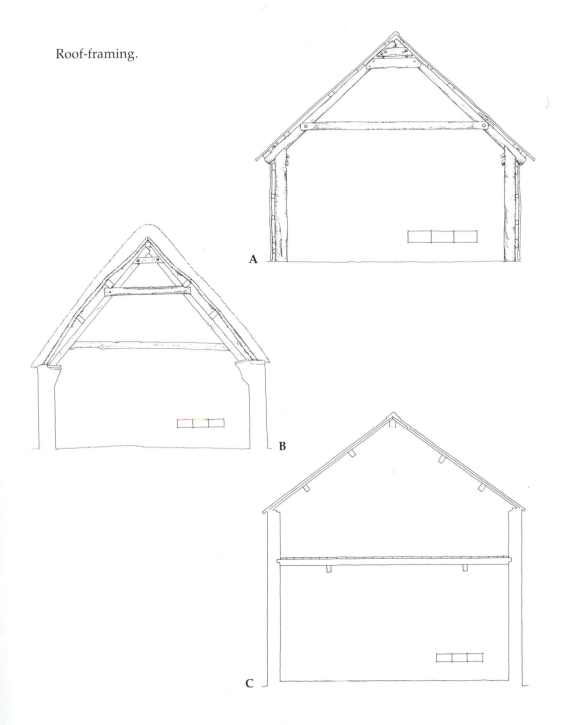

A. Jointed cruck. Turfhouse and hayshed abandoned in Derryhowlaght. Its plan is
found as B among the outoffices. B. Coupled. John Gilleece's byre.
C. Purlined. Billy Dowler's house. Scales in feet.

lonely without her constant companion. Food cooked in a stove tastes dry, bland, unsavory. There is something special about food cooked in an iron pot above a turf fire. That is what the old people say, and I know they are right. The most delicious chicken I have ever tasted was baked with carrots and onions over the Flanagans' turf coals and served up as a Hallow Eve feast. Young people raised with cookers do not know what they are missing; for them the change is only good. But their elders remember, so their opinion is complex. After explaining the virtues of the new cooker—how tidy it is, how convenient—the old woman smiles, stands, walks halfway across the kitchen, then with her fists balled tight, spins: "Ah, fuck the ould cooker."

Outside, the people of Ballymenone use thatch for thinking, classing houses into thatched, slated, and iron-roofed.[24] Only three in ten of the local homes are still thatched, yet thatch makes better insulation, Tommy Love told me, because being thicker, it is warmer in winter and cooler in summer than slate or iron, and the frost cannot penetrate it. More useful, thatch is also more beautiful. We stood at the head of the lane descending to the deep green hollow where his house sparkles and glows. A slope, rich with rooks of hay, rose behind it while Mr. Love said of the roof he had just thatched, "When it is new with straw, it shines like gold. The sun glints off it, and it is lovely. It is lovely right enough."

But weather steals its luster. Rain follows the rooks and magpies that burrow into the straw, and it must be renewed, "darned," often. New straw is "stappled" into the "hollows" annually, and its ridge, its "riggin," must be rebuilt every few years to keep it at work and looking good. Within a decade a whole new coat must be supplied. Dark, dead thatch is pulled out, and vertical "beds," a cubit wide, are laid on, right to left, and pinned down with "scollops" of willow, "sally" or "willie," that are hidden by successive layers except at the eaves, the "easin," in most houses and the riggin in all, where exposed stretcher scollops define the top and bottom of the roof's smoothly combed and beaten face.

Roofing "straw" determines how quickly the job can be done and how often it must be done. Lough reeds, "quilrods" and "risp," are long (thus quick to work) and "lasty," but they rot into the "scras," the strips of sod rolled over the rafters to which the straw is pinned. Both Tommy Love and thatcher Johnny Drumm said flax had the longest life expectancy, approaching a quarter of a century, but its color was too "dull," so it was rarely used. Wheat is long and might last fifteen years, but the ground is too wet to grow wheat. Oats and rye are preferred. Rye, "wet straw," is "lastier." Joe Murphy said it could live for twenty years, but it is not used more often than oats, "corn," even though a roof of oat straw has to be recoated every six to twelve years.

Oatmeal porridge and oaten bread were staples in the past, so people know how to handle oats. Harry Crozier said most of the land is too rank even for oats, but with care they can be grown on cutover bog. "The old

Bob Lamb Helping John Drumm

John Drumm

New Riggin on Bob Lamb's Roof by John Drumm

Joe Murphy

Roof by Joe Murphy

Scollops Prepared by John Gilleece

Roof by Harry Crozier

420   Passing the Time in Ballymenone

people wouldn't let you into the corn with a scythe," said Hugh Patrick Owens. "It wasn't tidy enough." Today some cut oats with a scythe, especially if they are standing and short, but others still shear them with a hook, bowing to cut the corn as near the ground as possible to get straw of the greatest length to lash for thatching. It is hard work, but worth it, for it leaves the ground clean and oats are reckoned to make the brightest, loveliest roof.

The trouble with thatch is that it demands constant work, hard work in the cold wet weather of the year's slack times. Iron is permanent and easy to maintain, but it is not lovely. Mrs. Cutler was "annoyed" when dairying regulations required removing the thatch from her byre, and she was "heart broke" when in 1977 it became necessary to cover the rest of the house with iron.

Iron provides poor insulation and binds people into the cash economy. Thatch could be grown and worked without monetary cost, but iron must be purchased. That change comes to the fireside as well. One reason hearths were closed down was to burn coal. If those who hate the smell of coal smoke and keep their hearths open seem only sentimental, it is a hard fact that coal burns money. If turf is burned on the grate of a closed hearth, it does not have to be built carefully and watched closely as it does on an open hearth, so time is saved, but it burns too quickly, so closed hearths mean someone must work more in the bog to win more turf or someone

Mrs. Cutler's in 1979

must labor somewhere to buy coal. Since most people burn turf in closed hearths, they do not need more cash, but they do if they want a cooker, and if cookers are fired by gas, not turf, local people become tangled in international economic affairs, subject to the bottomless greed of energy moguls. Much is lost, much is gained, and the major gain is familial continuity. Young people who want to be modern and have no feeling for the old way's virtues will stay home and accept custody of the old house if it is clean within and covered with a nice iron roof.

No wonder thatch claims their attention. Roofing alters so swiftly that one need not step away to note and gauge change, and it is so fraught with meaning that it registers massive evolutionary shifts with clarity. The new iron roof represents the trade of beauty and economy for permanence and ease, the trade of self-sufficiency for dependence in a cash economy. But the trade is necessary because the community has weakened. No one will come to help thatch any more. Unless like Harry Crozier or Tommy Love or Joe Murphy you do it for yourself, it will not be done. Iron is necessary. Cash becomes necessary. Life becomes easier, the land less lovely. Iron fits the new age. It is a sign of rational adjustment. That does not make it good. You have to live in all seasons, but you do not have to like it.

Hugh Nolan said it best.

It is March 1976, and I am on the road again, moving swiftly in well-known territory. Beneath me soft earth bounces, the carttrack. To my left spreads the brown expanse of the bog, hummocky, pocked, empty now before men have come to cut it for fuel. To my right, Drumbargy Brae slides down under hedges into P's garden. A long turf lump, roped and rush-thatched, rises at its edge. Cabbages stand in the black ridges. Paddy's garden comes next, then the patch where Tommy shears oats, and the narrow path up the hill will slice between the trees, running for the crest. The wet grass is familiar about my boots, and the tilt of the brae, its faded winter green, dark spiky trees, white tips of gables, Flanagans', O'Preys', the cool pale sky—all is familiar. Then I am standing. As though commanded to stillness by a voiceless noise, I stand stunned by strangeness: poles.

Poles bear wires along the spine of Drumbargy Brae. Letters during my months of absence brought news of the new bridge taking the Derrylin Road across the Arney at Drumane, but no mention of electricity. Wires swag black, stilted into the sky.

Slowed with my sack of gifts of stout and cake and cigarettes, I climb the old track into the trees. My eyes run along the wires. It was politically smart, I think, to bring electricity at last into this not remote but mostly Catholic and angry corner of Ulster. "Ugly but good," my field notes say, for here I learned how little one needs electric lights but how grand a thing is a hot bath in winter. And yet, new things to own create division. The wires, I note, do not connect to the Flanagans'. And there is something about hardship . . . the hard life grinds the mind sharp, honing wits that dull with ease. Yeats was right to say that country people, because they live hard up against life as poets struggle to do, become artful and wise. And yet the old order gives way, and that is good. People deserve comfort. I must hold to William Morris' old hopeful assertion: things once changed can change again. Perhaps.

The darkness of the trees contains then releases me, and I descend Drumbargy Lane, alive with thoughts without order, then turn toward Hugh Nolan's where, too, the wires do not reach. Bent over a stick, he grants me a sun of a smile. "A hundred welcomes to you, Henry."

I bring in an armload of sticks and build them into a snappy blaze while our topic skips quickly past the weather into the topic the land demands. "It's a forest of poles at the present time," Mr. Nolan tells me.

Our words gather around the issue of change. Prices are on the rise. He recalls when pretties were threepence a stone. Now they cost one pound, twenty. Five years ago a thatcher asked two pounds a day but now demands fifteen. People cannot afford to have their houses thatched. John Gilleece has given up and thatched his own with rushes. The birds have torn up the riggin at Mrs. Cutler's, the roof has to be renewed, and she fears she will have to be content with iron, though she hates the thought. A nice tea room in Bellanaleck is the only new thatched building. "It's all metal roofs now," Mr. Nolan says, and cites galvanized iron gates hung on concrete posts as another sign of change along Rossdoney Lane.

"Hugh," I say, "you have lived through the greatest change in history." I am thinking of the change from communal self-sufficiency to individualistic dependence. "Tell me what it has meant." A clear eye gleams within the shadows of his cap, then loses itself in darkness as he looks down into the fire to frame his answer. Boxes are piled along the kitchen's rear wall. The clock ticks on the dresser behind us. The kitchen is low, lacking light. A black bottle stands in his great fists.

"Aye," he agrees. He has lived through history's period of greatest change. "There has been a great change in transportation." He was "eyewitness" to the first automobile in Enniskillen, an open car with four people in it wearing goggles and long white coats, and people ran into the street to see. Before that, he says, people walked or rode on horses. "The ass and cart, it was a great improvement in its day. Then came the car, and now there's the helicopter." He sits still for a moment. "And there has been a great change in communication." Once news traveled by word of mouth, then, he says, the newspapers came, next the wireless, and now with television the diffusion of news is instantaneous. "All these changes"—his hand sweeps across the table with its candlestick and out of the darkness to include the poles rammed into the hillsides—"have brought a great improvement to the people. All do have the electricity now. And that is a great thing." He pauses again, lifting his eyes into mine:

"But the greatest change in my lifetime has been that people has lost all respect for authority, civil or divine.

"Today there is neither law nor order.

"And that is the greatest change."

Together we look into the fire. A small red and gold flame runs and bobs, licking softly from the black sticks. He sips his stout. I sip mine. He illustrates. In days gone by they would auction meadows, and men in need of hay would come to bid for the right of mowing and winning. He remembers an auction over Rossawalla Hill when the men got drunk and bid so competitively that a fight broke out. Mouths and knuckles were bloodied, but no one was hurt badly, and the next day men worked together as though nothing had happened. Today the wireless told him of an auction in France where similar anger unholstered revolvers and a man was killed. That is the difference. Nothing controls the beast in man. Northern Ireland is but a specific instance of the way of the modern world, he says. People, unbound, go to extremes. They hold no order within them, nothing to prevent their quest for freedom from passing the limits of law. In the past the self was restrained by the sacred rule of neighborliness. Today nothing contains the ego.

Better than the shapes of old houses, Mr. Nolan connects the rise of comfort to the decline in social order. He has explained the need for closed, symmetrical homes and sits back in silence again.

Again it is quiet. The fire pops, flares, glows on. His cats sleep and he sums it up:

"Aye, the two things happen at the one time.

"Things get better.

"And they get worse."

14

Clay

White houses spring amid green fields and along gray lanes. Hands assembled them out of the land's rocks and trees and mud to stand as shelter and art, as exhibits of logic in service to will. For understanding, we crack them apart, treating logic and will, culture and history as separate, but these are one: culture, collective logic, is the result of history; history, collective will, is culture in time. Separating, boxing them academically, is folly, certain to prevent understanding. Like the house builder, old breaker of stones and splitter of trees, we must destroy, but not to leave the world in disarray, shattered into millions of little cards, sealed in hermetic typologies. In the spirit of the builder, we break reality apart to rebuild it into a better environment. He makes houses out of smashed scraps of nature. We make meaning out of ruined houses, moving from pattern to change, logic to will, culture to history to create a new useful totality.

Step out onto the street. The whole blue world sings with meaning. We could read it by the hearth's small light, using it to test the cultural and historical patterns we discovered in homes. That would seem rigorous, but there is nothing to worry about, no need for hobbling hypotheses. Since the things we study were made by human beings, they are meaningful. So let us keep old discoveries in mind, alert for ways to improve them, but face new things directly, for we will learn more if we come upon them afresh.

Beyond the home place, three kinds of soil define the common problem and potential of the people of the District: clay, moss, bog.

Out of the bogs, through the moss, roll low hills of slick, sticky "clay," heaving to form the "upland," then descending to the "bottoms" by the Lough and River. Over the hills, moving usually east off the ocean, flying clouds carry constant dampness to the earth: "mist," "mizzle," "drizzle," "showers," and "spittin," "bucketin," "lashin," "teemin" rain, crashing "like bullock storcs with their horns down": 230 rain days out of the 365, about forty-five inches of rain each year.[1]

A blanket of "till" covers the clay. The ideal till, they say, would be like Tyrone's: loose, deep, and gravelly to let the water sift through. But Fermanagh's till is shallow sod that traps water at the surface, then breaks to let the clay "rise" into soggy sloughs. Agricultural engineers agree with the

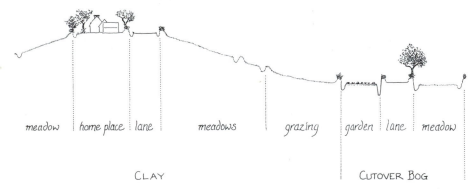

meadow   home place   lane   meadows   grazing   garden   lane   meadow

CLAY   CUTOVER BOG

Land Use. A schematic diagram based on Drumbargy and Rossdoney, looking west.

local farmers. Their wet, rank land is bad for tillage, for "croppin," but it is good for grass. Grass feeds cows, Shorthorns and Friesians for milk, White-heads for beef, and cows are the mainstay of the economy.

When a gentle snow powders the upland or late light rakes it, old ridges are revealed, running downhill. During World War II, cropping was compulsory and stimulated by subsidy. You got eight pounds for an acre of potatoes, and spuds were so plentiful they were fed to the pigs and mashed and boiled for the cattle. Before the war, upland fields had been worked for generations to yield potatoes, wheat, rye, and oats. "People used to crop alot," Tommy Love said, "but there's not a plow in this country now."

An old iron plow is built into a fence on reclaimed bog in Sessiagh, another, an English-made "Irish Gem," stands forlornly in a field in Der-ryhowlaght, and iron-shod, socketed wooden plows remain in the mem-ory. In the past, a man with a winged plow and a pair of horses would come to break the sod, opening the fields, forming "the drill and furrow," then closing them, plowing to grow the crops for twenty farms.[2] "You would love to see the horses work," Peter Flanagan told me. "They were steady and wonderfully surefooted." But finicky, opulent beasts, horses demand care and rob grass from profitable cows. Three cows can subsist on one horse's feed, and land here is precious. Most farms have between twelve and sixteen acres. Thirty acres makes a good farm, one hundred a big one. So small farmers use asses for traction, as donkeys eat modestly and require little attention, and for big farmers, Tommy Lunny said, "Ulster is the home of the tractor." Tractors on today's large farms do not pull plows, they work for the cows, baling hay, cutting and drawing silage.

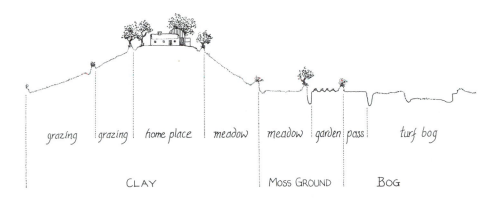

grazing   grazing   home place   meadow   meadow   garden   pass   turf bog

CLAY   MOSS GROUND   BOG

"In days past," Hugh Nolan said, "every farmer, let him be large or small, he would have a certain amount of oats. He would thrash them, clean them, and bring them to the mill. There was no house in the wintertime that wouldn't have a certain amount of oatmeal. But, do ye see, the way it is now, it's all foreign production. There is only about one out of every twenty that has the spuds.

"The cattle is the whole go.

"All the land has gone to grass."

The land of grass is a rebuke to some, the lack of plows and cropping a sign of modern laziness. But with horses gone and tractors expensive, the upland would have to be ripped open with hand tools. Mrs. Cutler remembers men turning six acres on her farm with spades. "Lord bless us, at that time they were out from daylight to darktime. It was slavery." Sharp memories buttress the logic of grass. So do economic developments. With the coming of the creameries and the expansion of the subsidy-supported market for beef, the hills and bottoms were most profitably ceded to grass.

Some land has been reseeded to increase its yield, but, they say, it does not need it. The natural grass grows abundantly, luxuriantly. But nature cannot work alone; human intervention is necessary. First, people must discover the land's properties. This is no land for wheat, not even for oats. Its crop is grass. Then they must push nature, prodding, maximizing its inherent potential. So they divide the clay into fields, into pastures ("grazin") and "meadows"; some of the grass will be grazed off, some will grow into hay. Since farms are small, cattle cannot be released to wide ranges.

Fields are broken small and hedged tight to control the cows. From grazin to grazin, the cattle are driven to eat all of each field's grass, even that in odd corners, and they are kept from the meadows until the hay has been drawn home, assuring them feed for the winter. Then gaps are opened and they are let on to the "aftergrass" of the meadows before being driven again. From November to March, the milk cows, the "house cattle," are brought to the byre while others remain on the grazin. They are cold out there, but hay is knotted in "wops" and carried to them, because they stay healthier in the fresh air. In the past when all cattle wintered in the byre, they failed, lost their hair, and brought little money in the spring marts. Smitten by "crippin," a form of arthritis, they weakened and could not stand, and even healthy cattle had to be lifted from hunger to their feet in the spring, so most now roam the chilly pastures, and the dairy cows stay fat in their byres. This improvement in cows is owed to improvement in the fields.

Fields are not rotated or often changed. "It just runs from father to son," said Hugh Nolan, "that such a field was meadow, and such a field was grazin. In days gone by, there was hardly any treatment to the grazin. If there was any manure, it was put on the meadow. Now artificial manure, bag stuff they call it, is put on the whole land to increase the grass." In the days of sickly cows, manure was scant, but now it is rich and plentiful enough to be spread with the mould dug out of the drains onto the meadows, and artificial fertilizer is applied to all fields. The result is more grass. Tallied in rooks, Peter Flanagan estimates the increase to approach tenfold. More grass.means more and healthier cattle.

Farms are measured both in acres and in an old unit, "a cow's grass of land." Hugh Nolan explains:

"Well, a cow's grass was counted be the old people, three Irish acres.
"Well, the Irish acre was bigger than the English acre or the statute acre.
"Well, three of them was supposed for to graze a cow and have a lock of hay for her and have a little crop."

The old unit's name tells implicitly—and correctly—that the economy has long depended on cattle. Though once there was more cropping, this region was never so much agricultural as pastoral; it fits in Europe's highland zone, where settlement is dispersed and man's worth since prehistoric days of epic cattle theft has been measured in cows.[3] The unit's size bespeaks progress. William Lunny has kept twenty-two cows successfully on thirteen acres, and one cow per acre, as on Hugh Patrick Owens' farm, is the norm for an efficient operation today—three times what it was in the past.

The upland was improved by manuring at the same time that the bottoms were improved by the Erne Drainage Scheme. At best lowland hay was considered inferior to upland, and as many as three times a year in the past the Arney would flood over its banks, ruining the hay crop of the bottoms. The great geographer E. Estyn Evans told me it was once said that for part of the year Lough Erne was in Fermanagh and for part of the year Fermanagh was in Lough Erne. Low spots like the Hollow below Hugh Nolan's, where Hugh McGiveney lived, were so regularly flooded that men became adept at walking on stilts to get from place to place. There were two meadows of about three acres in Rossdoney that lay under water in the rainiest part of harvest and winter, yet, Peter Flanagan said, when the water drained off, it left the ground exceptionally dry, "too dry for crop, but it was perfect for meadow. Oh, it was grand. But the other bottoms now along the Arney was too marshy and too rishy, and they wouldn't cover atall. For them the Erne Drainage was a great improvement."

The green fields surrounding the white houses of Ballymenone contain history. Once they were cropped with spades and loys during long days of heavy toil, but now they have been given over to grass, and the farmer's life is easier. Once the fields along the bottoms were flooded regularly, but now the Arney has been dredged, and the lowland hay is better. Once the grass of the upland fields was sparse, and it took three acres to support a cow, but now the grass has been thickened with fertilizers, and the cattle are healthier and more numerous. The farmer gains milk and money. Life improves, and improvement comes of change, but change need not come from, or lead to, violent disruption. Progress can serve to purify culture. The house improves, changes radically, by focusing on its old wish for comfort, then driving forward. On the clay, improvement takes the same course. Once the land's infixed idea is grasped—this place is good for cows—it is extended, and the act of extension leads through cyclical maintenance to progress. This real, economic experience holds a cultural principle. Its premise is acceptance: you must take what comes. Once when Hugh Patrick Owens was coming back from the beach at Bundoran in an open wagonette the heavens burst. Umbrellas shot up, and rain cascaded off them onto a man who sat awhile, becoming drenched to the skin, then stood up in the storm above the umbrellas saying, "I'll just take it the way God sent it." That bid is amusing, worth remembering and retelling, because you do not have to take what comes sitting down.

Acceptance is not passive. They talk about "come day, go day, God send Sunday" people who let reality wash over them while their gardens smother under weeds and their kitchens accumulate filth. I found people in Ulster beyond south Fermanagh who stereotyped the area as a lazy one. Possibly they misunderstood its pastoral, plowless tradition. Probably they allowed their prejudices to connect the dominant local religion with a lack of industry. In fact, the recent land-use survey of Northern Ireland showed south Fermanagh to be the wettest area with the worst soil, at Ulster's bottom in milk yield and acres in tillage, and yet at the top in percentage of improved, manhandled land, not a place of success perhaps, but surely not a place of laziness.[4]

Within the District, I found the traits most often ridiculed to be meanness (working only for yourself) and laziness (not even working for yourself). Such ridicule projected concern and set ideals by negativity more than it described reality, for, while I met mean people and saw that some worked more than others, I met no one who was lazy. Gardens chastised as weedy were trim and bore an abundance of vegetables. Fields decried as gone to rushes supported fat cattle. It is a man from the past who is resurrected anecdotally to serve as the personification of sloth. He shuffles through memory in the ruins of a clatty mud cabin with one wicker window and the ribs poking through the thatch. Demented, he sits by the cold hearth drinking reboiled tea, taking it as it comes, to reveal how not to be.

James McGovern said, "You can't have it the two ways," and Peter Flanagan said, "You can't grow the two crops, pretties *and* weeds." Work is a constant state of being. Inside, it is the hearth, its incessant glow, the endless sequence of cooking and washing, while outside, it is grass that hums life's drone. No day—not Christmas, not the Twelfth or Fifteenth—is made wholly of rest. Every day the cows must be milked and the cattle of the hillsides must be tended like fires, for they can fall into drains and slough to their bellies in the bottoms, and they grow wild, lean, and skittish if human beings do not visit them constantly, talking to them while driving them to better grass. And hay in its season joins hearth and cattle to keep people in continual action.[5]

Cut as soon as wet weather permits, hay lies in a "swathe." If rain prevents raking it into long, narrow "rees," it must be lifted wet and turned to keep new grass from growing through the matted cover of the swathe, binding it to the ground and rotting the hay. Today they use pitchforks, but in the past the hay was "tedded" by lifting an armload and shaking it into "cushocks," hay free of the clots in which rot can take hold. Once rolled and raked into rees, it was "lapped," lifted, and bent over the arm, "arching the lap," but that was worse for the back than it was good for the hay, and now while it lies it is given two or three shakings of the pitchfork to keep it loose so air can circulate to dry the hay drawn into long strips across the meadow.

Under clear July skies the hay is spread with a rake into the "broad band," where it cannot stay. If rain comes on, the hay must be "lapped and left in rows like little buns"; the image is Mr. Nolan's. If the weather holds, the hay is "rooked." The broad bands are marked into rectangles, then raked and forked into rings. One "lock of hay" is pitched to the center, then another, and "bit be bit, bit be bit," the rook rises "round and round," as the pitchfork picks little wisps and big, dips then lifts, while rakes pat down and comb away locks to be scooped up on the fork's swing to the ring and back

Rooking Hay. In July 1972 Paddy McBrien was in the hospital. His hay on mead-ows in Drumbargy was rooked by Paddy Farmer, Gabriel Dorsey, Thomas McBrien, and Jerry McBrien. Thomas, who lives in County Down but was

home for his holiday, and Jerry are Paddy McBrien's sons. Mr. Farmer and Mr. Dorsey are both married to daughters of Paddy McBrien. Paddy Farmer set the pace and dressed each rook. Thomas McBrien and his son Kenneth

twisted hay rope to bind the rooks. Jerry McBrien's fiancée brought drinks to the workers. Mrs. Farmer and Mrs. McBrien brought tea in the late afternoon, then stayed to help with the work.

to the rook rising amid the rhythmic bobbing and heaving, tamping and combing of its builders.

Some men feel only "built rooks" turn the rain effectively. A man or boy clambers to the top of the truncated cylinder of half-made rook to tramp it down, receive locks from the forks, shake them loose, arrange them across each other, and build the rook's "head." Built rooks demand cooperation, so people working alone must content themselves with "fork rooks" built from the ground, which will work, they say, if you are careful to keep "the heart full and the head narrow."

Nearing completion, rooks are raked around their waists to keep their sides vertical, then "dressed." Loose locks are pulled from the base, arranged in a neat ring around the rook and tossed on the head, then "combed" down so that in concept, though not appearance, the thatched head is "sharp" and "swift," and the rook tapers inward from its shoulders so the rain, the endless rain, will run off. Finally the rook is bound into shape with hay ropes, spun on the thumb in the old days, on homemade "twisters" today. A stumpy tail is twisted out of the rook's base, the rope is woven in and tossed over to be tied on the other side. Crossing, a pair of ropes hold the rook until time for its release.

Rooked, hay is "won" but work is not done. In rows up the meadows, rooks stand between a fortnight and a month while the winds dry them. During that time the ropes will have to be tightened to keep the heads of the rooks from being blown off, and the odd rook may have to be dressed again, but the hay will dry, "God willing," to be unbuilt and rebuilt into round "pecks" or haysheds. With plans in mind, clouds in the sky, hay on the ground, work is ceaseless.

Acceptance is not passive and not irrational. The environment is inherently useful, and the human task is to discover through work the logic of its construction. Plants hold cures. Thick clay, poor till, and rainy skies create a situation poised for pastoral success. As surely as God set cures in plants and grass in clay, He set reason in people, so they hunger and from pain argue through memory and foresight into the improvement of their lot. The old tradition was to crop the upland, and the government required the tradition's continuation and expansion, but these people are not fools, coerced by the old ways and compelled by law into proving their fortitude by bullying wheat out of weak soil. The work was "slavery," and no one will do it today. But that change during which a tradition lapsed was not revolutionary. It was a return to the essence of God's gift, a recentering, a concentration upon the land's immanent logic: grass grows cows.

Comforting ourselves with the thought that there is no alternative to anxiety but stagnation, we happily dichotomize culture into modern or traditional, scientific or mythic, rational or superstitious, hot or cool, progressive or static, revolutionary or cyclical. Ballymenone does not fit.

Revolution is not the District's way. People do not feel obliged to overturn for the sake of overturning. Dirt, like a cure or a talent, is a gift from

God through the ancestors. Reasonable people in the past divided the grasslands into fields, and there is no reason to level the sod walls and rethink the land's planning from abstract principles onward. A century or so ago, the old people told them, the fields were smaller, having been subdivided through inheritance. Now, people feel, they are the right size, the size they were before the land was pressured by overpopulation, when, it was calculated, every rood of land had to support one person. Mechanization and the Common Market, they say, will increase the size, decreasing the number of fields, while farms expand and decline in number. This expansion of a few large farms, accompanied by the emptying of small houses, and the flattening of walls and consolidation of fields for the convenience of machines, is the greatest of all the changes occurring today on the land. Angrily the small farmer looks on that change and the future it presages as fitting with the Troubles into the greedy plot of the Big Boys. "The big farmer wants the small farmer's land and his work," said Paddy McBrien, the billhook in his hands, "and wants to leave the wee man, like myself, with nothin, just nothin." Still, in those days people will adjust and the fields will be the right size "for the times that are in it," times of mechanization and capital expansion. Not revolutionary, the District's way is not static either. Its cycles tip, spiraling within reality's close confines, from God's gift toward a limitless and unknown but endurable future.

Founded upon the sacred, environed by uncertainty, acceptance is active and rational. The responsibility of the individual swept along in the gradual spin is to examine shifting states of affairs, conserving the best and extending it logically, willfully progressing.

This simultaneous conserving and extending is the historical force of continuity, the way change is created by the mind that favors connection. The new kitchen conserves the old idea of cleanliness and extends it into bright, tidy boxes. New farms of grass purify the ancient pastoral pattern.

Clay and grass, cows and hay, provide a general and crucial experience from which ideas are drawn and formed abstractly to use in other realms. That is how culture shapes into consistency. The idea that can be proved true again and again on clay is applied in novel, rare, or fleeting scenes where ideas cannot be tested. So we can locate the structure of thought at the base of the pastoral economy and find it at work not only in daylight, in the praxis of grass, but as well at night in the ceili.

In the meadows one man is "boss." He begins each rook, and once it is rising properly he pushes on to start the next, then yields that to others while he returns to the first to build its head and dress and complete it. A dozen must rise in a day. In a ceili, the known but unspoken master gets things moving, then abandons leadership to draw others into the chat. After their contribution has been made, he takes control again, bringing their topic to its peak and perfection. Ballymenone's aristocratic idea, necessary on the meadows, is a generous convention at the hearth.

Between leaders and followers things flow steadily, smoothly. Rooks rise across the meadows, topics rise out of talk. Once "riz," chat is tended like a growing thing, fed tea and words to keep it aloft and rising, circling, "comin round" to various topics. Talk by the roadside can die quickly into farewells. Banter in bars can be jerked through aggressive jocularity. But the ceili's chat must be "carried on" like work in the fields, for life comes of its continuity. The ceiliers who sit for hours together tonight will work together tomorrow. They bring topics up again. And again. Repetition is risked to make sure every topic has been completed, that nothing of interest remains unsaid. As chat circles, as speakers are encouraged to say again what they have said, as new speakers repeat what has been said before, people seek centers, topics of rich potential lying beneath the surface of words.

Once such a center is found it is extended to its limit along one of two trajectories.

Humor begins with mimicry, the accurate, comic imitation of the gestures and verbal habits of others. It rises to bids, then shoots into stories, "yarns"—note the name—unraveled from the wound-up balls of the brain. Their humor is hyperbole, common ideas whipped to uncommon extremes, the comic perfection of the idea of extension.

Information rattles through questions, requests, and goodmanning to establish one person as expert, then he aims the chat into tale. History is the great topic, and the informational trajectory carries "stories of history" at the top of its arc. This is where Saint Febor came in.

Ballymenone's storytellers isolate the concept of extension in their comical pants, and they codify their wish for conservation in their deep concern for historical truth. Then they meld these ideas in chat, for both of their common lines of conversational entertainment accept the topic as given, conserve its essence, then extend it logically and beautifully into tales. The story begins here, in our reality, but its momentum is governed only by reason as it breaks free of situation to grope for the mind's limits or to dwell in the salient past. Stories, like the sizes and uses of fields, are received, accepted, then husbanded efficiently and actively reworked, pushed to make life possible.

Work in the fields hits a center—grass-covered clay—then drives through it, carrying its inbuilt potential to an extreme: the land is all grass, cattle are the whole go. Work in the ceili hits a center, a rich topic, then rides it out to the limit. Analogy with organic growth, with the way tall, branching trees spring of small round seeds, is obvious, but we are talking about thoughts, not plants, so I will name this dynamic of mind "conservative extension." It is not revolutionary because it comes of old centers and carefully conserves their energy. It is not static because it drives through them for all they are worth, wringing out of them every drop of value, unraveling them to the end of every implication. Time's shape is not the line of progress or the circle of stasis, but the spiral, at once driving forward and rotating around primary points.

Daily enacting the principle of conservative extension at the hearth and in the fields, people put into play a fundamental philosophical tenet they use most deeply in the construction of their own wee lives. Just as they are given topics to discuss, food to prepare, dirt to farm, people are given existence. Actively and rationally accepting existence, one reels between internal capacity and external constraint. Within, universal reason blends with the soul's hope and those traits borne in the blood. Outside, unpredictable uncontrollables—storms, bomb blasts, visits from friends and bacteria—thwart, threaten, and comfort the poor pilgrim on his way. Accepting existence, one must take what comes and (people are not brutes) understand. Understanding, one says, "There's no use in complainin," and endures the bad, no matter how dreadful, conserves the good, no matter how slight, and extends it maximally, "doin the best."

Doing the best is the right answer. Close acquaintances greet with questions. "How's Tommy?" He can reply, "Not so bad," but what he usually says is, "The best," which means the same thing. A drunken head rises from the counter, sticky with stout, totters above a heap of shoulders and coat. Bobbing, it wobbles, turns down the bar, saying, "Ah, the best. I'm doin the best," before slumping once more, having failed to disrupt the conversations around it. A woman seated at her warm hearth with a cup of creamy tea and photos of her lovely grandchildren completes the narrative of her unhappy life of hard work: "So here I am in me corner and nothing to show for it, but sure, I done the best." A lean man in black and Wellingtons stands on the hillside among his few tight acres of grass. Cattle move gently around him in brilliant sunshine. "I'm doin the best, so I am," he says. That phrase, constantly repeated, is their way, once you understand it, of speaking the courage of existence, getting the idea of conservative extension into words.

My notion is not that their philosophy was invented in farmwork. I am not speaking of ultimate origins, and farmwork could not exist as it does without the hope and terror imported from religion onto the clay. But in Ballymenone, ideas are most cogently formed in work. They must be. Storytelling is too free, life's major decisions too rare, to provide theories with convincing tests. In farming, an idea like conservative extension is tried harshly, continually. Life depends on its success. There is no way to fake success, for life is made of work, and work works or it does not. In farming, the philosophy applied in other domains is proved—proved repetitively—to be correct. The grass increases, cattle fatten, life improves, the culture is right.

Back to the dirt. We have more to learn.

The sod that blankets the clay inhibits cropping, severely limiting agricultural possibilities, and yet, like nettles and rushes, it is diversely useful.

Squares of "ordinary bog sod" are set at the backstone of the hearth to contain and prolong the burning turf's heat. "Scra," the tough, thin light sod lying over virgin bog, was cut in strips, rolled on sticks, and unrolled over the rafters—three lengths stretching from one easin over the riggin to the other—so that new thatch could be stitched through with a thatching needle and pinned to it. Upland sod, "sod with a kind of a grip in it that wouldn't moulder away," was cut with spades, laid like bricks, mortared with a mixture of bruised clay and chopped rushes, to form houses, both dwellings and outoffices.[6] Sod houses were raised from the ground without foundations, but they were finished buildings, as Hugh Nolan tells us:

"When a sod-wall house would be completed and thatched, it was as nice a little buildin as you could see.

"And they used to plaster powerful well, inside and outside, with sand and lime.

"And they were nearly all what they call hip gables. They were thatched round and round. The gable quit at the square, do ye see. And they were thatched both ends instead of toppin the gables. Well, that was the way these sod buildins was finished off.

"And they were very nice and warm. They were the warmest house goin. But then, they had to be kept well thatched and well plastered.

"Oh now, they were very compact."

Sod houses are gone with plows and rod braces, but the grasslands are still broken by walls, "ditches," built of upland sod. Removing a line of sod for ditch-building establishes the course of a "sheugh," the drain lying along the ditch to suck water out of sodden fields and push it downward to River and Lough, away to the ocean. With typical lucidity Mr. Nolan explains:

"The land was kept dry be the drains havin to be made. Because there bes alot of water held up where ye have a drain full up even with the fields, do ye see. There's no land but there's a certain amount of water in. And that drain has to be cleared to run for to keep the land right.

"There would be one what they used to call the *main drain*. That'd be the leadin drain that'd be carryin the water maybe away to the River or maybe to Lough Erne. And then there would be contributaries runnin, carryin the water to this drain, supplyin this drain with water, if things were kept right, do ye see. Well then, where that wouldn't be observed the land used to get terrible *wet*, and it used to go to rushes,
terrible to rushes.

"So, to *keep land right*, even that you had stock on it, you'd want to keep the land drained in parts of this country.

"Keep the drains open.

"Let the water flow."

Sod ditches were raised on the grazin sides of drains to keep the cattle out of them, to divide the fields, and establish boundaries, "mearns," be-

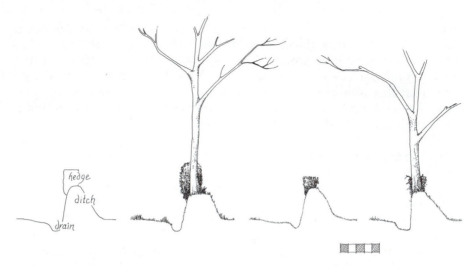

Ditches. Sections through ditches in Rossdoney. Scale in feet.

tween farms. In the days of "the old people," the parents of today's elders, there was no "plantation" on the ditches, and they had to be rebuilt often, melting as they did in the rain. Now they are set with "quick," thorn hedges, the roots of which hold the ditches firm.[7] One result is a permanence of field shape, unfamiliar to the person used to rail and wire fencing. Another is that ditches alive with twisted hedges accept wildflowers and trees, birds and small creatures, to become contained strips of wilderness and valuable resources.

Running over civilized land, carrying bands of nature through every endeavor, hedges are a pleasure, a joy to observe and contemplate. People know the snore of the sleeping hedgehog, the calls of many birds, and natural history makes a fine topic for a ceili. Their observations come of curiosity, a direct delight taken in nature's ways. It is a wonder, they say, how oil on the heron's legs attracts salmon fry, or how an owl can be evicted from the hedge and killed by a squadron of small birds. But "nature's way of goin on" is God's, and close observation produces a Whitmanesque hammer for infidels.

Ballymenone's wish to conserve the best in things as they are is a wish to preserve God's imperiled creation, and a deep idea, an implicit prayer, runs beneath the little couplet with which Mrs. Cutler liberates spiders— "If you want to live and thrive, let a spider walk alive"—as it does under the plain attitudes that turn most men in disgust from blood sports and cause them to feel that, though rabbits were a pest in the garden, it was wrong of the government to eradicate them. Things should not be changed any more than necessary. Still, the hierarchy is intact. Rabbits, birds, and fish can be used. Nature is driven back, beaten into the hedges. And observation is not wholly disinterested. Animal habits mark the seasons. When the birds called "the seven sleepers"—most conspicuously the cuckoo, corncrake, and swallow—return, summer has come. Harvest begins with the salmon running the Arney past Drumane, and it is ending when, during the second moon in October, the badger wins the grasses to sustain his winter's nap in the hedge. Successful farming requires correctly gauging the seasons' turning.

Hedges are elongated forests. Fields are not relinquished to trees, so hedges supply willow for creels and scollops and "clayveen" bird traps,[8] wood for ashplant and blackthorn walking sticks, for Windsor chairs, for the couples and ribs and rafters of homes, and for the "firin" that cuts winter cold. Though it does not last like the good black turf, ash wood makes a hearty blaze. Partially decayed sally wood burns long and hot, and "greesha," the ash of hawthorn sticks, is especially good for baking.

Thick hedges take space from grass, but they are an inefficient use of limited land only for people who think of nature as an enemy and have no need for a ready source of wood. For most farmers, the hedged, forested ditches are right. They make good mearns, their near permanence is something to accept and actively curate. Free times, the bright late days of harvest and winter, when men used to gather to thresh outdoors, fill now with paring down the sides of drains with "hoes" and hacking the hedges back with billhooks, "facin" them to thicken their growth. Some lines of hedge are allowed to grow up into windbreaks and cattle shelters, but most are cut back severely, for the cattle will not go near them. Wild, thorny hedges are wasteful, as they prevent the grass along them from being eaten.

Angling, converging, the many hedges give the landscape a wooded look. This is not Ireland's picturesque, rocky and barren West. Nor is it the manicured "too well hedged" Tyrone of the poet Montague's boyhood.[9] Still, most hedges are faced, trim, sharp, clean. A sloppy, "rough" hedge tokens laziness. A neat, smooth hedge expresses industry, and more. It contains simply a cultural principle. The neat hedge works best and looks best. The useful is the beautiful, the tool is sculpture. Efficiently husbanding the old land, like efficiently husbanding the old tale, is at once an eco-

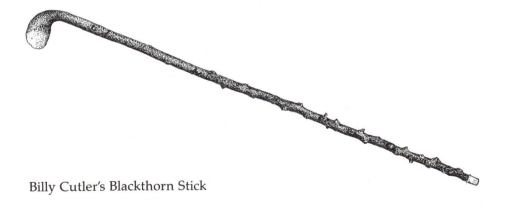

Billy Cutler's Blackthorn Stick

nomic and aesthetic act. Its proper product, field or tale or thatched roof, displays a "smooth" appearance.

Smooth meadows, trim hedges, trees in line, crisp white houses arrayed on green fields: this landscape of farmwork is a work of art. No part of it has gone untouched. Will has intervened everywhere. Rocks have been broken and assembled. Earth has been moved and molded. Shaped with spades, shaved with scythes and billhooks and cattle, the land is an enormous piece of sculpture, continually presenting a collective idea of beauty. People hide trash discreetly under thornbushes, bury ruined machinery in holes near the bog, mow the weeds along the lanes, and honor the Maker by clearing the stage for the play of light. It is light, Mrs. Thornton said, light shifting beneath fast clouds across velvety fields, that keeps people's minds usefully on the climate and makes them appreciate their countryside's beauty.

Sometimes my prospect was low. The drab colors of frozen bog and leafless trees, of muck and rusted iron, dominated my vision. Then I would feel the hills rise, and oblique light, cut by low-sailing clouds, would flash across the braes, mottling the green from black to gold, and I would understand why the worst I ever heard anyone say about their place was, "It is lovely in good weather." There's no use in complaining. A land this handsome must be the best. Many have traveled and seen. Nowhere is as beautiful as Ireland, and no spot in Ireland is as good. Everywhere else is too hilly or too flat, too wild or too calm, and they can look upon their home with the wonder of a tourist, hanging pictures of rural scenes within, standing without to watch light's play.

One music-filled night at Swanlinbar, the fine singer from Kinawley, Martin Crudden, encouraged to perform, presented a brand-new song:

> Good people all, on you I call, and this song I will sing to you.
> Twas written with a loving hand, each word is fond and true.
> It's all about Fermanagh, and the first thing I will do
> Is take you to the Hangin Rocks near the village of Belcoo.
>
> There's lovely Devenish Island with its tower so tall and grand,
> Its lovely lapping waters and its stretch of deep brown sand.
> The lovely hills of Knockninny have a beauty rich and rare
> Where as a child I roamed for miles without worry or without care.
>
> When tourists visit our country, sure, the first place that they seek
> Is our world famous pottery and its china that's unique.
> For we that are familiar, sure, there's no need for to speak,
> For when you mention pottery you can only mean Belleek.
>
> Of all Fermanagh's beauty spots, I can only mention some,
> And one of them must surely be the castle down at Crom.
> There's lovely Enniskillen and likewise dear Lisnaskea,
> And when you visit Fermanagh all these places you can see.

And if you come along with me, it is proudly we will march,
By the winding roads through Florencecourt to the lovely Marble Arch.
And it will be my pleasure for to show you all these and more
When you come to visit Fermanagh on Lough Erne's lovely shore.

Response surpassed goodmanning. The musicians present, Peter Flanagan and the great fluter, John Joe Maguire, rushed to Mr. Crudden, turned him out of the crowd, huddled around him, and quietly, directly, effusively congratulated him for having a major new song.

That night I was told the song was written to win a contest for an original poem, set to an original tune, to be used to attract visitors to Fermanagh. Whether or not a tourist ever heard it, the Fermanagh men who gathered in Swad requested it constantly from Mr. Crudden from that day, August 20, 1972, onward, and within a few years I no longer heard mention of its chamber-of-commerce purpose. The song was composed, I was told, to answer a challenge, to prove that the muse was not dead, that new songs in the old style (and note the internal rhyming, the glistening sound) with new airs (and its melody ripples and flows) could be composed. I first heard it was written by Master Gallagher from Derrylin in about 1968 and was set to music by the fiddler John MacManus of Knockninny. Later I would hear it was composed around 1974 by a singer and schoolteacher, Valerie Brown, who had married into the great musical family of MacManus of Knockninny.

The act of attribution holds high significance among Fermanagh's singers. It is a way to claim a song, to pull it tightly into the tradition through which poet, singer, and audience gain unity. The act of performance, in which a song is taken over so totally that distinctions between singer and song evaporate, is the most powerful way for a song to be claimed for the tradition, but crediting a work to a local poet who shares the land with singers and audience is an effort in the same direction, a means of folding a song into the culture while celebrating the culture as excellent. People present songs as well as stories as products of the local genius, ascribing them to specific poets, perhaps different poets. They argue courteously over the authorship of "Mackan Fight," emphasizing that its learned composer was one of them, and most credit "The Fermanagh Song" to Bryan Gallagher, headmaster of St. Aidan's High School, Derrylin, so in 1981 I wrote, inquiring, and Mr. Gallagher generously responded saying that the song "has been attributed to many people in the locality and many have claimed authorship of the words and music. The only thing I know for certain is that I did not compose either. There was a competition in this year's 'Feis Fearmanach' for any Fermanagh ballad. One of our pupils sang this one. The adjudicator described it as 'of doubtful musical merit,' by which he meant, as he told me later, that the music was not original. However, the song has, as you state, entered the local musical tradition."

Performed, attributed, quickly taken to the hearts of Fermanagh people, "The Fermanagh Song" shows plainly the affection the people have for their place. Its historical allusions are rich: Belcoo, Devenish, Enniskillen, Castle Crom, Florencecourt, Belleek (Saint Patrick, Saint Molaise, the Siege, the Plantation, landlords, industrialization). The song's key word—appearing six times in twenty lines— is "lovely."

Early in our friendship, Hugh Nolan, who went to Scotland but returned, strung two stories together to introduce me to his place. The first is a bid of Hugh McGiveney's:

"Well, there was a very comical man lived in this townland, very witty, you know. And there has been people that moved away and then they came back.

"And funny enough: there was people that got dogs from other localities, and didn't the dogs go back to their own country.

"So. This comical man said, I don't know what there is in this country, he says, but it seems always the same to me: when people are taken away, they come back.

"Aye ◊.

"Well.

"And there was a man that lived at Mackan, and he lived there his whole life.

"He had never been out.

"And one sunny day, a neighbor came upon him.

"And he was just standin, lookin out on the fields just, and he says:

"It's a lovely country, he says, a lovely country altogether.

"He was like a visitor that had never been here, do ye see, never been here before,

and he *lived here his whole life.*

"Well, Ireland is lovely. And there'd be nobody leavin atall if there was a way to make a pound here, the same as what there is in America or Australia, or, nearer by, England or Scotland."

I agreed with him and he with me. "It is a lovely country," he said, "and there's no place you'd see it better than from Missus Cutler's, that thatched house up on the hill." Like a beacon, Ellen Cutler's long white house atop Gortdonaghy Hill shines over the District. From her street you watch the neatly broken land glide, green and misty, east to the silvered strips of Upper Lough Erne. To the south and southwest the hard dark rocks of Knockninny, Benaughlin, and Cuilcagh erupt from gentle hills. I took her on a drive once, touted to tourists as beautiful, through the forests along the wide Lower Lough. She thought the place was ugly, the trip silly. As we drove, her interest was aroused not at all by unchecked wilderness but by the rooks on the meadows, the clamps on the bogs, and she was glad, "be it ever so humble," to be home. While we were recuperating with tea and buttered fadge, she pointed through her front door at the bright

The View from Mrs. Cutler's, Knockninny on the Horizon

green and blue, and said, "A person, and him hungry, could go out that door and take the view in and not need a prettie. It's that good. It fills you."

Her connection of view and food was precise. Food's "value" is to "carry you on." To carry you on, food must be "strong" (it must fill and sustain, generating energy for work) and it must be "good" (it must appeal to the taste). They call food "necessary," and they call food "entertainment," and they say other entertainments—interesting chat, beautiful music—are as necessary as food. Pleasure is necessary.

Were pleasure only escape, sleep or hilarious balance for reality's grind, its rarity would make life unbearably bad, but pleasure also comes in the smoke between rooks, the chat pulled from talk about cattle and climate, the taste of common food. Food called "the best" is not luxurious. People talk about food constantly and have sharply developed senses of what they like. What they like is what they have, done well. They like the potato boiled until it splits its skin "laughin," so flaky and "sparklin with flour" that add a little salt and you have the whole meal. They like cabbage boiled into smoothness. "Ah now," Mrs. Cutler said, "there is nothin as good as a nice cabbage, when it is white with green runnin through it, and it is boiled right. There is nothin I like so well. Oh, it's lovely. I don't even want bacon to it. I *love* a good cabbage, so I do. Oh, lovely."

In "The Fermanagh Song," in Mr. Nolan's story, and outside Mrs. Cutler's door the land is "lovely." Praising cabbage, she brought that word through taste into the fullness of personal involvement: lovely land, lovely cabbage—things to love. "Lovely" is the District's way to say aesthetic. The lovely thing can appeal to the eye or the ear, the tongue, nose, or fingertips, to produce pleasure, the sensual excitement that names experiences as diverse as a view over the land, a rippling fiddle tune, and a potato, "lovely."

"It is a great principle to be satisfied," they say, and what the District's people love, what enters the heart through all the senses and stirs into delight within, is common excellence, their own plain world in its lovely moments: a green field full of golden rooks, a dresser of bright delph, a plate of smooth cabbage. Suddenly life expands out of a workaday center, filling and feeding the spirit, quickening the mind, carrying you on. This is good. For an instant more is unnecessary.

In Ballymenone, good food satisfies in a single unadorned course. There is no need for relishes and desserts. Stories are good in their completeness, clarity, and flow. They have no need for ornate rhetorical figures.

Music's "beautification" is its "ornamentation," quavers and grace notes, but the tune is well played when entire and smooth with no "gaps" or dropped notes, no "squeals," no "rough spots" in the tempo. Ornamentation is not essential to good music. When compared with the famous styles of the western regions of Ireland, Fermanagh's style of singing and playing the violin is plain, direct, melodically clear, and gracefully flowing.

"Ornaments" glitter high on the kitchen's walls and fill the Room, but the home of a "house-proud" woman need not be rich. A house called "the best" can be, like good people, "poor but clean." Poverty is only a condition, but cleanliness expresses the soul, so cleanliness forms the prime rationale for architectural change, for dropped ceilings, closed hearths, halls and porches. And ornaments but mirror and restate the household's central wish for cleanliness and order and friendship.

Ornamentation is peripheral.[10] It comes to dominance in the rarely used Room and on the rare day, when the Christmas kitchen is festooned with balloons and red-berried holly, or the Hallow Eve dinner concludes with a sweet currant "brack," but the District's deep idea of art is not caught in decorative detail. Ornament does not intrude upon utility. Furniture is not carved or painted over with flowers. Forms stand plain under polish or glossy paint. At home, amid the merry conflict of patterned paper and cloth, curtains and lino, women may wear floral housedresses, matching the flowers pictured on delph and cut in the vases of sunny windowsills, but the public clothing of women and all the dress of men, though modishly cut and draped, is solid in color. Women in general wear dresses and skirted suits—blue, green, shades of purple, clean pastels. Men (mostly Protestant) wear subdued, dark tweed jackets or (mostly Catholic) suits, blue and deep purple when young, black and blue when older. The look is crisp, neat, unfussy. Black shoes shine. The lazy man who polished only the toes of his shoes, saying no one would notice the heels, became an object for ridicule. White collars sparkle. That whiteness, a flash set off by a dark coat, calls us into Ballymenone's idea of art.

White sheets flap on the line as the homemaker's flag, a sign of victory over dirt, an emblem of accomplished plans. Some modern houses fade under pebble dash and rough-cast cement, just as their people fade from view behind partitions, but proudly most houses deny the earthy tones of their materials, and crack away from the natural hues that environ them, asserting their presence as pure human products in whiteness. Every few years a new coat of whitewash restores them. Whitewash is useful protection for the walls, often composed of soft brick, but it beautifies as well, covering dark and irregular colors, unifying form, and presenting to the world a smooth, brilliant appearance. Once there were kilns at Enniskillen, Derrylin, and Swad, and one remains in the weeds on the road into Ross, and when limestone was burned down locally, lumps of "roach" lime were found among the "slack." These were tipped into a tub, boiling water was poured over them, and they exploded with a deafening pop to make the whitest of whitewash to brush across the house's facade. "In them days," Mr. Nolan said, "you could see a well-whitewashed house for ten miles. It used to shine that well of a good day, a well-whitewashed house."

White, the word, does not carry positive power. It is used for any light color. Winter's dead tan fields seen not here but elsewhere are called white. Colored cloth, bleached from washing, and pale-brown turf are called white. What I see as whiteness is the radical statement of their wish for brightness. Not hue, but luminosity, radiance signals beauty. The white wall below, the golden thatch above, both when fresh are "bright."

Beauty is bright. Good weather is dry, unclouded, so the lovely day is bright with sun, the lovely night is alive with stars. The beautiful woman and witty man are "stars." They shine amid darkness.

Beauty is smooth. Things are not. They are "rough," imperfect, and incomplete. The meal that leaves you unsatisfied, the behavior that hurts people, the roof of rushes darned with exposed scollops, the ragged tale or tune, the cold windy wet day—all are "rough." Ballymenone's people call themselves rough. Somewhere else people are smooth and fat, mannerly, educated, rich with "money like hay." But within prevailing, overwhelming roughness, smoothness remains the District's goal. Within a rough climate, they fight, and when things are smooth, when fields and hedges and homes are smooth, they win. Inherently their food is "rough country feed," but the good cook makes it smooth. They follow "an ould rough country way of goin on," but their etiquette is courtly, their diction precise, their art is sleek. Like cleanliness in a world of dirt, smoothness in the context of inescapable roughness is difficult and courageous, wholly willed and transcendentally artificial. The very boiled cabbage, the very white house, the very neat hedge: the completely controlled landscape is a great victory.

When things "go smooth" they are unfolding according to plan. When things are smooth they perfectly materialize the phantoms of hope that preexisted them in the mind. A project completed, the linked and flowing tale, the trimly faced hedge, presents silently to its maker a proof of capacity, and it offers aloud a comprehensible idea, a pleasurable sensation, a useful form.

Rough and smooth are common experiences. Tommy Love showed me roughness: when it rains and the cattle trample the gaps into sloughs and the sun breaks to dry them, the ground hardens, jagged and rugged, "rough," unpleasant to walk over. Peter Flanagan showed me smoothness: when cabbage is boiled completely it has no tough seams, no lumps, it is "smooth," comfortable to eat when you have no teeth. From common experience comes a way to put thoughts into words. Within the person, smoothness is the force of reason, roughness is the failing that prevents perfection. Beyond, smoothness is that which aids the actualization of reason, roughness is that which thwarts. Plans and snags: the idea deepens beneath the common proverb, forcing it to convey the District's particular philosophy of active, rational acceptance. Hugh Nolan:

"The world is not a happy place. But people are not here to be happy.
"You have to take the rough with the smooth.
"You will think your degree is bad until you see someone and their degree is worse. It's a great principle to be satisfied. Well, do ye see, the person that's always complainin—that's a poor way to be. If that got in on a person, it could do alot of harm.
"The best way to do is to take everything that comes."

Things could be worse. One must be satisfied. Things, being bad, could get worse, so one must struggle. Struggling, one creates art of the order of Mrs. Cutler's house and Mr. Nolan's stories. If they lack, it is not because of their creators but because of their conditions. In rebellion against the rough, dull, dirty realities that confine them, they bravely, generously aspire to perfection, doing the best.

Within the struggle to do the best is sprung the District's idea of art, its theory of good human creation. Not dull with dreariness, with drivel and dirt, but bright, things attract attention. Not rough with fragmentation and failure, but smooth, they invite consideration of their unity. Not dirty with detail and noisy with confusion, but clean, they pull attention through their wholeness into their purpose. Once captured, attention is not allowed to dally at ornamental surfaces. Decoration withdraws, surrounding form or abandoning it, revealing it to be no more than shape. Attention falls through and is sucked into action.

The kitchen is clean and sparkling, but empty without its content. Its content is human action. People enter, crowding within to cook and eat and tell their stories. The stories are smooth and clear, but empty without their content. Their content is human action. People move through stories to serve other people, making them think. Thinking, one must act. Unavoidably, action is life's center, the force of its continuity. When action is human, it comes of purpose. The right purpose blends the "lovely" and the "necessary," the beautiful and the useful. What is beautiful and useful is "good." It delights the senses, helps the body, fills the mind.

Food that both pleases and nurtures is the common, tangible embodiment of goodness. It is produced out of the cooperative work of men and women who accept and energetically extend God's gifts of dirt and plants and life, who act responsibly toward their fellows, giving them the ability to carry on, happily and healthily. A story's goodness is formed on the model in food: it is a gift, received, reassembled in the intimate kitchen to fill the moment with pleasure and sustain life beyond.

Action's great product, the collaboration of God and man, is the land. The beautiful earth is empty without its content. Fill it with workers to keep it smooth and clean, then it is lovely, then like houses and food and tales it is useful, beautiful, good, worth loving. It may be ornamented. Little islands of flowers are arranged before some houses, and like the ornaments within these may contain messages. The house with a portrait of William of Orange in the Room probably has orange lilies and sweet williams planted along the street, but most flowers, like most ornaments, are only "beautification." As the fancy dessert rises from common cooking, flowers bloom from the application of agricultural knowledge and experience to the task of creating for pleasure's sake. But this is not a land of sweet cakes and flowers, of frills and escape. Here human action makes not gardens of ornament but gardens of sustenance. Efficiently, energy and reason are directed to grow potatoes and onions, rhubarb and garlic, broad beans, turnips, beetroot, carrots, lettuce, and lovely cabbage.

15

Moss

When the season called growth begins on Saint Brigid's Day the weather is cold. "February snow and blow, bring the ditches full of snow," they say, but the air is dry, the ground is soft, and the horticultural year starts in the month of snow. Then the "ridge-and-furrow" is built on the "lea," the fresh, green, uncut ground.

If the land tilts, ridges are cut to run downward to carry the water away. But almost all gardens are formed on "the moss ground," the beach of the bog at the base of the hills, and it is level. When flat land was furrowed with plows, the ridges ran the long way on the plot, because, as Peter Flanagan noted, "You couldn't have them too long, as the word says," to save the space and time a team of horses took to turn. The ridges of modern gardens run the short way, for plows are gone and the gardener's tool is the spade.[1]

"The spade is the weapon for the moss ground." Its shape has shifted within memory. The blade, "the iron," has become wider and shorter and carries less "lift": the angle of its profile is less acute. Like everything else, they say, the price has risen (from three shillings to two pounds), while the quality has declined, but "what odds," said Tommy Lunny, "it makes for more jobs." The new spade has clearly developed from the old one, and its manufacturer still provides the one tool, the long-faced Fermanagh spade, that works this dirt, so it is occasionally given the name of the old factory in Clones and called "a MacMahon." It took a heavier tool, the "loy" or "loya," to break the upland, ripping the scras and root-twisty "keeb," but the loy is more usual in Cavan and Leitrim, and the Fermanagh spade is right for Fermanagh moss.

Two kinds of earth compose the moss ground. The best is the black, the broken turf tossed back in the bogholes after cutting. The "flow" is lighter in color, and while not so rich, it is loose, good for growing seed potatoes, and resistant to frost. Frost is the terror of the gardens lying low in cool hollows under the hills around the bog.

Sod covers the moss, and it must be broken to build the ridge-and-furrow. The first step is "strikin the line." One peg is driven in at a corner and another, bound to it by twine, is pulled out, pounded in, and bent back, tightening the cord. A straight line is "nicked" with the spade a quarter of an inch outside the taut string. A gauge of sally rod, varying slightly in length from man to man, from three feet, nine inches, to four feet flat, is laid at right angles to this line, and a new line is struck with pegged twine and nicked parallel to the first. Then the spade is driven downward and in through the nicked line. After every pair of strokes, the spade is levered up, "coping" the sod, turning it up along one line, then the other. The sods, their length determined by the length of the spade blade, do not meet when bent up. A long open "heart" is left between them, down the center of the ridge. Behind, along the ridges, with the vanished nicked line at their centers, the furrows open. The cut sods are not broken free, but left "hinged," so they can be swung back into the furrows until time for planting. Shallots are set and onions sown in February, when the lea sod is broken, but most garden work lies a month into the future.

"The moss land is better than the upland for growin," Bob Armstrong explained. "It has no rocks. The trouble is: it is low. Often it is cutover bog and it has to be drained well. The water is down in the furrow, you see, and then the ridge: the ridge is built up to keep the crop out of the dampness." While conquering wetness, raised ridges offer their crops accessibly. Pat McGowan, who has moss ground taken from Mrs. Cutler, remarked, "The ridges are right for this country, with all the rain, and they are easy to work and keep wed. They are neat." Neat as a faced hedge, turned impeccably along twine-struck lines, the ridge-and-furrow is fastidiously rational. Laurence Sterne (Irish like so many of the innovators of English literature) twice has Tristram Shandy come out of his rigamarole to use the straight line of "cabbage planters" to symbolize direct narration, the Christian path, the moral and reasonable journey.[2]

On the first day of March, some "for luck" turn a sod over, testing the soil, maintaining their connection to it, and staying in action during a slack time. The weather then is normally too cold for work, but winter is over and men are anxious to move. About two weeks later "the warm side of the stone turns up," and on Saint Patrick's Day, in the center of spring, or during "Patrick's Week" that follows, some "for luck" put in a few potatoes, but unless the climate is strangely benign, most planting is detained until the last week of March and the first weeks of April.

When "byre manure" was scarce, time in March was spent "scaldin" or "stovin" the moss ground. A couple of creels of "fums," the pale, reddish, "white" quick-burning turf from the "flow bog," were carried to the garden and lit. The ground at the time was dry and grayish, "white." Turf coals were set every three yards along the ridges, and soil was heaped up around them to make conical hills, likened to chimneys. Allowed to smoke for two to three weeks, the ridges emitted a heavy odor some found enticing, others repellent. Then the little volcanoes were leveled, the ash was spread down the ridges, and the potato sets were dibbled into the warm

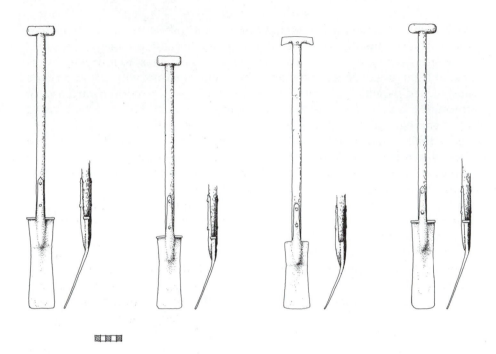

Spades. From left to right, these spades belong to Hugh Patrick Owens, John Gilleece, Peter Flanagan, Joe Murphy. Scale in inches.

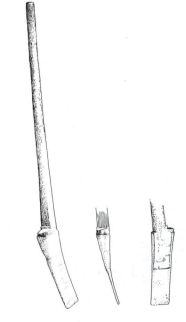

Loy. Bob Lamb's. For comparison, it measures 57 inches overall, while the longest of the spades illustrated measures 53 inches. Its blade, its "iron," measures 14 by 3½ inches, while the longest of the spade irons is 17 by 4¾ inches.

earth. "They would grow quickly," Peter Flanagan said, "when they found the heat." If stoved too often, the black moss turned red and its usefulness for cropping was wrecked, though it remained good for meadow.

Now, planting begins when byre manure is spread along the heart of the ridge. Artificial bag stuff, of course, cannot be used, as it would give food a bad taste and cause serious illness. Once the manure is laid on, the cut sods are coped again, "mould" is dug out of the furrows, and the heart is filled. Potatoes are planted in the lea and in the "awalea," the same ground's second season. In the past, corn would be sown into the ground in the third year, its stubble being used to fertilize the soil, and the ground would alternate between spuds and corn from then on. Now, potatoes are the crop in most ground in all years; the old pattern is simplified, extended.

Potatoes must be "blind set" in stiff ground. A dibble carved from the handle of an old graip or a "steeveen," a pointed stick with a peg spur to push against, is thrust in at an angle so rain will not enter the poked hole to rot the small seed potatoes, "set in the round," or the "cuts," the eye-bearing halves, thirds, or quarters of large potatoes. In loose ground these "sets" can be pressed in directly. They might be ordered in ranks, three abreast, down the ridges, but usually they are "diamonded." Five forming a square with one at its center are set in at one end of the ridge, then in triangular groups of three they march for its length, looking smart and leaving the right room for their growth.

Ideally, potatoes have been set out by May Day, when summer comes in, but the season for planting runs beneath erratic skies from the middle of March until the end of May. Some like to plant near Good Friday, but most scatter their planting throughout the season to insure some success, and "you are not counted late, puttin in the spuds," Hugh Nolan said, "till the twenty-second of May." The date you plant is a matter of risk: the earlier the potatoes go in, the better their flavor, the higher the likelihood of their murder by "the black frost."

As it is on the meadows until the hay is rooked, work in the garden is relentless until the spuds are "moulded." When they first "peep," shooting green above the black, the mould of the furrow is dug, loosened with spade or graip, scooped up, and spilled over the shoots, covering them. The mould is loose, shoots pierce it easily, and when they peep again, they are moulded again. The third time they peep they are "given the shovelins." The side of the ridge, its "broo," is nicked and tipped into the furrow, tossed up to thin it, and shoveled on top of the peeping spuds. Then all that must be done is spray them with "bluestone" to prevent blight (new thatching straw is dipped into a bluestone solution to preserve it), and keep them weeded and clean by cutting along the broo with a spade or hoe. If ground is "let out" to grass periodically, it will not become cluttered with weeds, but used every year, as most ground must be, it will grow up

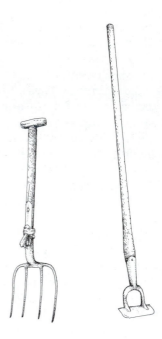

Gardener's Tools. Peter Flanagan's graip.
William Lunny's hoe.

in a shallow rooting creeper called chickweed. "He's a harmless weed, except when the pretties are small," Peter Flanagan said, "then he can stop their growth," so they must be defended against him.

There are two classes of potato, "early" and "maincrop." The Elephant and American Rose served in the past as early potatoes, but the Epicure reigns today. The early or "new potatoes," the "eight-weekers," should be ready to dig by the middle of July, and surely they will be boiled for dinner before summer ends on July's last day. They are dug not at once but piecemeal as needed, for they continue to grow. Many varieties have made the main crop: the Scarry Blue, the White Flake, and the Kerr's Pink, the Sharp's Express, Arn Victory and Arn Banner, the Flounder, the Up-to-Date, British Queen, Gladstone, and Champion—the last making as well a memory for Tommy Lunny: "The Champion was a Scotch prettie came here in eighteen and forty-seven. After the Famine. It was the best spud in the world, the real John L. Sullivan. It was a yellow spud like flour. Oh, it was tasty with milk, but it's gone." A potato of French origin, the Arn Banner, gives the greatest yield, as much as twenty-three tons an acre, they say, twice that of any other, but it is a big, soft, watery spud, no good for eating at all, so it is fed to cattle or sold to restaurants. The usual maincrop potato is smaller and lower in yield, but firmer and tastier. Farmers, in Mrs. Cutler's words, "put in bits and pieces to see what'd do best," and gardens normally have four varieties, early Epicures and Kerr's (Carr's, Care's) Pinks, the Arn (Arran, Aran, Erin) Victory, and Sharp's Express for the maincrop. In a good year, maincrop spuds are ready for digging by the last day of August, but they are generally dug in October, harvest's last month, and they must be dug before "the white frosts" of winter kill them.

To dig the maincrop, you start at the lower right corner of a plot. That is where a thatcher begins a new roof, and just as he works upward along the beds, the man "hoking" potatoes works backward along the ridges, cutting smoothly into the broo from the side and shaking the spuds onto the leveled ground behind. Thrice moulded, usually of three varieties, the maincrop potatoes are sorted into three groups, the largest for eating, the small and thick with eyes for seed, and the very tiny ones. "Them will be fed to the fowl," Paddy McBrien commented. "Nothin will be wasted." Peter Flanagan, whose chickens roost beneath thatch at the end of their house and feed on table scraps and meal, scatters "the wee lads like marbles" beside his garden because "you wouldn't want the curse of the crows upon us." Clouding the gardens black at harvest, crows too must eat.

Potatoes for eating and for seed are built as they are dug into "heaps" or "pits," two at once. A flat space is trampled over broken ridges. As one would do to build a house, a "track" is made, firm and level, so potatoes will not roll away or get pressed into the soil while they are heaped as steeply as possible into the hipped shape of a roof and "rished." Butts down, heads crossing, rushes are arranged vertically over the spuds, but since crows will peck through them, a cut mass of matted, curly chickweed, useful in its uselessness, is laid over the rished pit until it can be covered with a three-inch layer of deep brown mould. If the weather stays warm, the potatoes might "heat," so the pit's ridge is left unmoulded to let the air in. To keep crows out, the slit is hidden by chickweed, weighted by dead hedge branches. Once winter has gotten its grip, another three inches of mould is tamped over the pit, and its top is "pointed" to keep the frost out. Protected from mice with snap traps or open cans containing a mixture of meal and cement that sets lethally in little stomachs, the moulded pits lie on the moss ground like sunken houses, carrying seed potatoes into the spring and providing a starchy staple for the winter table.

Winter's three months—November, December, and January—cover the land with chilled stillness. In summer they say winter is not cold, in winter they say the cold will not last, but it holds in low blank skies and wind-bent bare trees, in ice-scummed sloughs and clammy bedclothes. The house enlarges emptily around sharp air, and people pull their knees to heat, passing the time with hot tea and quiet talk. Hushed, blood thickens, life slows, but it cannot stop. Cows shift in the byre and move on the hillsides. Fuel and food must be shouldered up to the kitchen, and in winter's midst men go down to the moss ground where the old ridge-and-furrow, though broken, remains visible. They dig the furrows anew, rebuilding the ridges. Then when spring breaks, the ridges are divided and the ground is leveled, leaving narrow "bones" standing along the centers of old ridges. Manure is laid equidistantly between the bones, and the

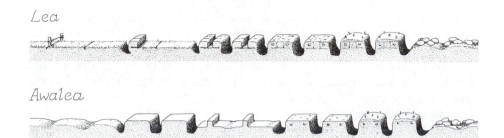

Lea

Awalea

Forming the Ridge-and-Furrow

ridge-and-furrow forms anew. The spade is driven, deep to its "lugs," turning the soil to prevent "squitch grass" from rising to strangle the spuds. The bone is used as a guide. Marking the course of the new furrow, it is dug away as soil is turned to each side and ridges rise over the manure laid on the line of last year's furrow. The spuds are set, the cycle continues.

The rhythm of potatoes concentrates work in two periods: from the middle of March to early May, and from late September to the end of October. Early potatoes make work in July. Planting the purple-topped turnip pushes garden work forward, for turnips cannot be sown until their flying enemies have vanished around the middle of May. Harvesting corn pushes work backward into September. Still, it might seem that the year could be imagined as a sequence of periods: winter, garden, turf, hay, garden, winter. But cabbage will not allow it. "I do have cabbage the whole year round," Peter Flanagan proclaimed.

The main cabbage, once the only cabbage, is the Flat Dutch or Drumhead. Its pattern matches the spuds. Plants sown in July and dormant in winter are dibbled into the ridges when the potatoes are set, and often among them. If frost gets to their roots, they will die, so Tommy Lunny advised, "Try a lock of them in all the months, in March, in April, in May; see how they do." Twice moulded, they can be "bladed" by June, stripped to supply leaves for boiling and to consolidate the heads, which will have grown so large by harvest that a "share," one quarter, will make a meal for a family. In the best year, they are ready with the maincrop spuds by late August, but like potatoes they are usually harvested and built into pits in October.

Grown in numbers large enough, the Flat Dutch will provide a year's supply of cabbage, but it cannot answer a deep wish of the District. Just as they like them clean, smooth, and bright, people like things "fresh."[3] They drink fresh milk. If refrigerated past its natural turning point, milk may not taste bad, but it is not fresh, so even people who own refrigerators often do not keep milk in them. Milk and butter are kept cool in dairies and unheated rooms. People like cheese and are amused by its mild aphrodisiacal qualities, but they rarely eat it and do not store their milk in the form of cheese. It is the same with meat. Tinned meat causes cancer. People had cancer in the past—they called it "the evil" just as they called arthritis "the pains"—but it is four times as common today, because, they believe, people eat tinned meat. The trouble is not the preservatives injected into the meat but the fact that, though it does not taste bad, it is rotten. Oatcakes cooked on "breadsticks" or "irons" before the fire will last, and people like Rose Murphy's uncle took them along on voyages to new lands, but today's homemade bread is "fadge," soda bread, baked daily, eaten fresh. Oatcakes are gone, along with the meat once smoked in the chimney. Even black currant and rhubarb jams that can last for months are eaten "in season," within a week after they are made. The desire for fresh food and antipathy to preservation parallels the absence of antiquarian spirit. Old homes and utensils and songs are preserved only if, like food, they maintain their freshness, their live ability to carry you on healthily. It is a happy fact, then, that varieties of cabbage have been developed to provide every meal through the year with fresh, green vegetables.

October's Flat Dutch is followed by the Harvest Savoy, too tough to eat until it has endured a frost, and good until February when it shoots into seed. By then the Curly is at its best, and as Peter Flanagan said, "there is somethin in a Curly makes you love him." The Curly is ready for eating by Christmas and lasts into May, overlapping with the Winter Savoy. Dozing until roused by spring's first sun, the Winter Savoy is good in April and May. By June, the "twelve month" cabbage, the "early cabbage," the Infield or Flower of Spring or Main's Number One, matures, enduring for the season of early potatoes until the Flat Dutch again offers itself. And there is the Greyhound which, though rarely ready in the promised six weeks, can be set in spring for summer or harvest to fill the gaps. "He's an emergency cabbage," Peter Flanagan explained. "You put in the Greyhound when the others fail. Or to get cabbage at the odd time."

Like cleanliness in a kitchen trampled with mud, freshness in a world turning stale requires constant work. Fresh cabbage puts the spade in the fist often, and at times when gardens would seem to demand the least and meadows the most. Once coaxed to sprout the length of your hand, cabbages must be transplanted, "set" in rows of two or three across the ridges, "dropped" thick or thin depending upon the variety's root. Patterns of planting and transplanting vary widely from farmer to farmer, but this sequence will give you some idea of the way of work. In June and July the Harvest Savoy, sown in March, is transplanted from bed to ridge with plenty of manure. In late July or early August the Curly and twelve-month cabbages are sown. The Curly will be transplanted in rank ground with room aplenty for his large root, perhaps twice, in October and between April and May. The twelve-month cabbage, Infield most often, is set in March or with the Winter Savoy in October. Generally cabbage has to be planted in fresh lea ground to prevent "finger and toe" from destroying its roots. To survive the winter, the twelve-month cabbage is planted in lea ridges in the upland, in "the worst ground you have," not along the hedges, where frost hits hardest, but out in an exposed spot where dirt must be kept built up around the stalks. And in the coldest weather the garden must be patroled to defend it against the hares driven by scarcity from their covert in the hedge to slit the stalks, suck out the juice, and kill the winter cabbage.

Before rabbits were eradicated, guarding the cabbage was a worse problem, though not insurmountable, as Michael Boyle tells us:

"At a time there was a terrible plague of rabbits in the country—ah, they destroyed all the vegetables.

"So John Brodison had a wee cabbage bed anyway,
            and his was safe.

"And someone asked him how did he manage to keep his cabbage bed safe from rabbits.

"I had no bother, he says.

"I went down to the quarry, he says,
        and I riz a wee cart of stones,
        and I put the stones around them, says he,
        and I went to Cathcart's shop there,
            and I bought a pound of pepper,
        and I dusted the stones, he says, with the pepper,
        and the rabbits came and they started to sneeze,
            the pepper got into their noses
            and they started to sneeze,
        and they knocked their brains out ◊
            agin the stones, sneezin ◊.

"Aye.

"Aye: they knocked their brains out agin the stones.

"Aye, he was one star. He was one star, this Brodison."

It takes a bright person to work the land, extending its potential into agricultural success or a pant's wild humor.

In Ballymenone a specific thing calls attention to its cultural importance when it claims a general term. "Work" is not any labor, but the specific work of farming. It contrasts with the "job." Farming is made of multiple jobs, tasks that blend into difficulty and constant action, so the man who has spent his life at one task, at carpentry or medicine, has had a "job," a simple task broken by periods of leisure, and he can be said never to have "worked." Though "corn" can mean wheat, rye, barley, or oats, the word is also used with clarity to mean oats only. Oats are central to thought. The good person is not said to have a heart of gold, but "the heart of corn." Oats are more than golden. They once provided nutrition through porridge and bread, they still provide shelter through roofing straw: beautiful, useful oats, stooked on the field, bright icon of successful work.

"Plant" can mean any growing green thing, bigger than grass, smaller than trees, but it can also mean cabbages only. Cabbage is more than the main vegetable, it is the ideal plant, fresh in every season. And cows: not only is "cattle" used to mean cows, but "beast," the most general term, means cow. Cows are not the subject of peripheral chores, they are the center of the economy, mainspring of the farmer's hopes.

Work, corn, plants, and beasts are ever present. A farmer is a worker forever. When corn is not growing, it is turning the rain. Plants oblige the farmer to work in every month. Beasts make him work every day.

Men's work in the fields matches women's work at the hearth. It is continuous.

Ordering things around centers, homes around hearths, townlands around hilltops, seems sometimes a convention, sometimes a necessity. There is no reason built in time for the calendar to open its seasons from midpoints, but the agricultural year must unfold that way. People plant from March 17 to May 22, but mostly in April. They harvest from the end of August to the first of November, but mostly from the middle of September to the third week in October. The weather is too variable to allow a ritualized schedule. Plans are made. Ideals are held. But artificial constructs are gracefully abandoned to circumstance. The schedule smears. Of necessity, beginnings are tentative, endings trail off, dying into time's flow.

Describing the important job of cleaning the drains, Hugh Nolan shows that while work might be conceived as an annual cycle, broken into seasons, it is a ceaseless reality:

"Where you had a drain for a mearn, that drain, it wanted to be cleaned every year. The two broos wanted to be nicely pared with the spade.

"Well, in days gone by, there was weapons, there was scythe blades that the tang was straightened. Well, there was a long piece of wood and the end of it was bored with a fine auger and this tang was driven into it. Well then there would be a ring then on the end of this stick for to keep it from splittin. So when you had your blade on, and this ring properly fixed, you had a great handy weapon; a scythe-knife, it was generally known as.

"Well then, what that was used for was: if you couldn't stand in a drain with an overabundance of water in it, you stood on the broo, and you took and you cut the grass on the bottom of the drain with this lad. You cut it into nice wee sods.

"And then when you had your drain all cut, ye had your sods divided that two men, one on each broo, could pull one half of the sods up on the one broo, and the other half on the other broo.

"And then often, do ye see, they'd rise a sod ditch on the side that the cattle was on. But then to make a drain complete, both broos were pared down.

"The way it is now, any man that his drains gets what you'd call outlandish—*bad*—there's men now in this country and they have this machinery for the purpose of cleanin the drains.

"But in the past, it was spades and the scythe-knife. There would be weeks put in at it. Well, it used to be a job in the early spring when cattle would go to the grass. And then of a good harvest then, there was alot of it. But the way it was generally: when a job like it would become necessary, no matter what time in the year, it had to be done.

"It had to be done, do ye see.

"If your cattle went into some other man's land, do ye see, and the mearn yours, or the half of the mearn yours, the drain had to be cleared. Even that it was in the *hay season*, do ye see."

Work is organically ordered. Wild weather prevents its cycles from cracking into exclusive periods, and no season, no day, can be filled with work of but one kind. Continual, simultaneous sequences of cattle and hay, cabbages and potatoes, corn and turf, make each moment a matter of coordinating demands and expectations in different realms with climatic conditions. Nothing is set, nothing complete. All is mobile, multifunctional, fleetingly balanced for change.[4]

Men do not wear special work clothes but transplant cabbages wearing caps, old jackets, and ties, ready for the unforeseen, the chance encounter with a cleric or a woman, the sudden trip to the shop, the call for help from a neighbor. In the garden, as in the kitchen, things are lifted, shifted, kept in motion. As they say again and again, "They made it round to go around."

The environment and force of organic order is time, unbroken, unstoppable, ceaseless. While things are planned and replanned, built and rebuilt, nothing else stops. "You are always on the go." Work has no end. And yet they say, "Happiness is the main thing" and "If you're not happy, you're not right." That is a sturdy word in Ballymenone's lexicon, "right." It means far more than correct. "I'm rightly," the happy person answers the greeting "How's Tommy?" The person who has "failed" but "mended" well is complimented, "You're right then." The right day is sunny, the right house is solid, the right young man is supple and smart and helpful. As the connoisseur says the old piece is "right" when it is wholly original and true to its period, the District's people are "right" when they are complete, natural, in good health, in perfect tune with conditions. To be right, you must be happy. To be alive you must be working. Happiness then must be defined so it can be discovered in work, and work must be ordered to incorporate happiness.

Happiness results when work produces objects of delight, when the gleaming dresser and trim ridge-and-furrow grow out of necessary toil. "In the towns, they used to style the countryman a hoker," Mr. Nolan said, "but the country man has to have alot of skill." When that skill reflects back from bright and smooth, clean and fresh creations, a smile widens in the worker's breast.

Happiness is to be found more in permanent flow than in fragile product, more in kitchens than in Rooms, more in gardening than in gardens, more in motion than in stasis.[5] That idea is founded upon the District's concept of time. People seem to describe time contradictorily, because they are free to adopt either of two points of view, one from afar, one from within. These two perspectives, each with its summary proverb, pose a paradox escaped in action when similar conclusions are drawn from different premises.

A man of middle age, earnest in his drink, sat next to me in a public house in the Town. We had left small talk behind us, several whiskies past, and his eyes bore upon me within one of those eerie moments when all seems crystalline. "I don't know if there was ever an Adam and Eve," he said, "or a Moses in the bulrushes. All I know is I'm alive. I'm alive, surely. But I don't know why." His jaw was firm, his eyes startlingly clear. "Life is only a shadow. We're only passin through." He did not blink, but snapped his fingers, crack, saying, "We're nothing to eternity."

His was the radical statement of a basic concept. Tough Hugh Patrick Owens put it this way: "We are alive a short time, and dead a long time." You live once and for an instant. The individual life is "wee"—small, dear, minor. People who risk that flicker of existence in political strife are "wasting their wee lives altogether."

The brevity of existence is condensed in the common proverb "Life is just a little ceili." A ceili is a visit. We are visitors here, temporarily occupying this warm, lit space. But a ceili is pleasant. Our visit, though brief, need not be painful. We deserve health and happiness, comfort and learning, the music and sport and right to rebel granted in tales of the Saints. Normally people say "Well, as they say, life is just a little ceili" to explain the pleasure they take in work. That is what a small farmer said to me to summarize his argument for handwork. He owns little land, and to keep himself happy he keeps it meticulously. His garden and orchard are trim, his hedges hacked clean. A big farmer whose rapid expansion—more land, more cows—means ignoring the land's request for a garden and letting the hedges grow wild, justified his enterprise, his constant motion, not on economic grounds but out of the traditional observation that life is brief, unique, and one must do what brings pleasure: Life is just a little ceili.

Swinging the philosophical eye from the edge of the cosmos into the skullcase, time looms enormous and the key proverb is "The man made time made plenty." The District's usual complaint is not the modern wail of limited time, but exactly the reverse. Time opens vastly before us. With nothing to do, we will quiet into boredom. Bored, we contemplate the way things are. Contemplation must lead to unhappiness, and unhappiness leads to despair. In despair, we are unable to work, and we begin to collapse through inaction into damnation. A great virtue of work, then, is that it keeps us in action, holding our minds away from the sadness of reality. It "passes the time."

Passing the time is basic to the District's way. Activities have value if, like work in daytime or ceiliing at night, they pass the time. But events that pass the time are not joyously complete. Far from ecstasy, they are not "good times." I once called an evening filled with drink and humorous chat a good time, only to be reproached by my companion, one of the District's hardworking small farmers, "Och no, that's not a good time. A good time would be to be shet of the bog and the cows and my old tit, and me in Monte Carlo, with a blonde on every arm and me pockets bulgin with money. That'd be a good time." The truly good time is as inaccessible as the truly smooth existence.

Life's center flows with time being passed. On the inactive side of the center lie the misery of "boredom" and the necessity of "rest." Rest is one "consolation." To Ellen Cutler her lovely view is "consolation" for her lonely setting. To Peter Flanagan music is "consolation" for his hard life. To the worker rest is "consolation." But people rest to work, rather than working to rest, so the best rest is filled with "entertainment," with food and chat to carry you on, enabling you to work again. Entertainment turns rest into time-passing action.

At the side of life's center opposite rest, the force of entertainment accelerates into "sport." Conversation rises to song. Tea gives way to stout. With a lock of shillings in his pocket, a man enters the pub and declares, "I didn't come for a drink. I came for a drunk." He will be let down if the drink does not make him "feel different." Many of the District's people do not drink. Those who do, do infrequently, but when they do, when some Sunday night turns into a wee spree, their goal is not seeing how much they can hold without showing it—a waste of rare silver—but coming as close as they can to a "good time" through the violent alteration of routine. Meet them only in the public house, I say again, and you misunderstand them, for people rarely drink at home, but the pub's night is a useful break. Its "sport" will contain music, garrulous chat, and—"Drink's in, wit's out," they say—a loss of inhibitions.

Passing the time is surrounded by danger. To one side is the rest that lengthens toward despair, so people often say, "A change is as good as a rest." It feels good to shift within organic order, varying within the flow. That shift, a gift to the mind, is as useful to happiness as rest, the gift to the body. To the other side, sport can break frail limits into "fight." With a smile, Hugh Patrick Owens recalls:

"In days gone by, there was a fair and a pub, a public house, at Arney Bridge.

"And there had to be a fight at the end of the fair. If I had an ashplant,

I'd go over and tap you, and they'd all be into it. Ah, there were some good ones. They were rough long ago. People are more civilized now. In a sense.

"The fair was had one day every month. It was away in the evening, four or five in the evening, that the sport would have to rise. Everyone carried his stick. They had to be ready for it: you couldn't go without it."

Sticks are no longer carried as sidearms, but "a drop of the creature" can still grease the way for hard words and blows.

"Sport" can lead to harm to others and ultimately to the self, ripped by violence out of the tissue of communal reciprocity. Rest can lead to harm to the self and ultimately to the community from which one withdraws in despair. The middle path, "safe as houses," seems to lead into the gentle action of passing the time, but it is not that easy. One complexity comes clear in the consideration of the District's basic classification of action's atmosphere.

States of affairs—climatic, political, social—are described as "calm" or "wild." Since that dichotomy parallels the smooth and the rough, the calm should be favored over the wild. Now, these dichotomies are no phantasm of structural analysis. The people of Ballymenone do order the world in contrastive pairs—"open" hearths and "closed," "bright" days and "dull"—but the terms in antinomy are not conceived as equal and opposite forces yearning for gray mediation. Instead, one contains and confines the other which strives within it, against its dominion. Things are open, people try to close them. They are dull, people try to make them bright. Things are rough. Though fated to failure, the human will struggles to make them smooth. When things are wild, the wish is for calm, but when things are calm (as they are too often), a little wildness is savored.[6] People speak with approval of the great winds that break the weather's routine and provide the mind with food to chew. They speak with approval of the daring exploits of the "bad boys" whose antics befuddle without eliminating political authority, and of the wild sprees, slashing ashplants and smashed glasses of porter, that disrupt but cannot overturn the prevailing calm of social existence. "Ah, there were some good ones."[7] Simply, when the world is in order, the little community relishes its differences, but when it is not, the community fears itself. That is why the old community allows great personal freedom, and the modern world requires conformity, closed, symmetrical homes.

Picture the yin and yang emblem and you have the whole structure: a field of rough black enclosing a white dot of smoothness and undulating against a white field of calm in which a black speck of wildness is trapped. Set your vision in motion, letting the dots strain to expand, and you will see why, just as they value the smooth, people with a wink of admiration forgive the wild moment. Its disruption is temporary. Calm can get boring, and boredom is death.

Ballymenone's classification of externalities into calm and wild fits its basic classification of personality types. People are "quiet and harmless" or they are "chatty," "entertainin," and "full of sport." The saintly, calm, and harmless person, like settled weather, is overtly preferred, for, as Mrs. Boyle put it, "all are wrong that do harm to others." The entertaining person might blether you into boredom or escalate the "jovial times" to the point of battle. Troubles whip like autumn winds around the entertaining man. People criticize, but they are attracted. They might prefer to be known as harmless, but they would rather spend time with the person who provides "diversion," so they travel the hills of night to his fire, making his home their "ceili house," for they need the star's light in their darkness. Sport, the bright spot in the dark norm, is useful to the maintenance of a happy life. Saint Patrick blessed The Sport at Belcoo.

Mothers chastise and praise children with the same word, "bold." "That's the bold bad cub." "That's the bold wee cutty." The ambivalence over boldness, caught by John Synge and extended in his extravaganza *Playboy of the Western World*, is one reason meekness is praised more than desired. Sometimes it is good to be bold and full of wildness. The other reason is that boldness, "manly courage," is required even in making the daily round. The gardener in the midst of necessary work must be bold. He must risk himself against rain and opinion. Meadow and grazin encircle the home, but the moss ground lies down by the bog, split into roods, half and quarter roods, and roods are small. "Well, a rood," Mr. Nolan explained, "would be forty perches, and an Irish perch is seven yards and a statute perch is five and a half yards. It was generally statute measure that was used in *this* country. Sometimes it was Irish measure, Irish Plantation Measure, but generally it was statute, Statute Measure." Two systems of measurement confuse them no more than two calendars (machines, not people, need simple consistency). However measured, roods of ground are small, so a man's garden might lie far from his home, disconnected from his fields, and surely it will lie, side-by-side, with the gardens of others, exposed to the hard scrutiny of all the neighbors. The garden is a version of the self exhibited for all to examine and judge, and the neighbors do judge, and harshly.

At the end of June in 1975, Peter Flanagan awoke to see the ground silvered with frost. Frost is death on the moss. If you know frost is coming you can light fires at the edge of the garden so the north wind will blow smoke through the night across the fragile plants. If you rise before daybreak you can call a neighbor, and the two of you can walk the furrows with a hayrope stretched between you, raking across every stalk, shaking frosty waters out of them. If an overcast day follows a frost, disaster is averted, but a sunny day usually breaks, and Mr. Flanagan saw the sun burning through the mist and knew its warmth would kill his crop. He put the potatoes in late in one of his gardens, that by the Heathery Bog. They would be protected by earth. But in the other, lying in the shadows under

Drumbargy Brae, the vulnerable shoots had been murdered. He thought about it, then went to work. "All the neighbors round said I might as well be sittin in the corner or walkin the road. But I wrought on." July came. The potatoes remained "dead," but he kept working and became so embarrassed that when a man would rattle along the bog pass on a tractor, P would hide in the tiny rush-thatched "hut" he had built to shelter his onions, his bicycle, his graip and spade. Then he would emerge and work quickly, moulding and weeding, until another would pass, driving him into hiding once more. It seemed futile, but by the time for harvest in October, "I had a great crop, so I did."

The work that life requires demands courage. To be is to be bold. From daylight to dark, the courage learned in work is carried into entertainment. The gardener becomes singer, as Peter Flanagan describes:

"Now music is just dyin out. It is a lack of interest causes that, and a lack of hearin music: that's the disadvantage. There's not many will sing.

"It takes courage to do that because the man that's a good singer, the neighbors do talk about him.

"And the man that's afraid, he's very bad in pronunciation, singin. I think they might be afraid, that they were doubtful that way, that they would come to a word and they'd think that it wasn't proper, and they would a kind of swallow it or not pronounce it just right. And then they don't give out the song right."

When P stands out of the crowd to sing, his enunciation is exact, his voice is loud and firm. Bravely he "gives" the song clearly, completely,

Peter Flanagan's Hut. Plan, section, and elevation of the framed and wattled, thatched "hut" Mr. Flanagan built in September 1972 next to his garden. The central rear post in its frame is a living tree. Scale in feet.

"right." Common ceilis as well as rare nights of sport demand valor. Most people sit, intent on the fire, avoiding those around them, whistling under the breath quietly to themselves, waiting for the bold speaker—an Ellen Cutler or a Hugh Nolan—to take control, risking error and ridicule to entertain them. Hearing Mr. Nolan describe how courage fades as awareness grows, we learn that the success of every night's ceili, like every day's work, comes of courage.

"I'll tell you the way it is. A person might be able for to converse well enough and say things right, but there bes a dread on them that they will make mistakes, do ye see. It's a thing that accompanies old age. A person gets—they haven't, well, the courage they had in years gone by, do ye see, to speak right out and then say, Ah, what odds, what way. They haven't the courage to make that remark.

"And then, there's many a thing a body'll say there and if it came back to them again, well, a young person would say, Ah, what odds about it.

"But then, when a person gets real old, they'll say, Aw, look what I said.

"You worry more. That's about the size of it.

"But you have to meet everything as it comes."

Happiness at life's center does not stem from certain safety. It comes from knowing that the worst perils in life are avoided in chat and work. It comes from knowing work will be balanced and relieved by periods of rest and entertainment. And more, it comes from controlling time's flow so daily endeavor will "pass the time." Work is slowed and opened to incorporate gentle pleasures from the adjacent, congruent realms of rest and sport. Work is constant, and constantly interrupted to sit and smoke, to stand and chat, to take in the many small meals that carry you on. While not so disparaged as the lazy man, his opposite, "the rusher," is considered little better off. The man frantically at work in every instant is avoiding crucial social duties and firing himself headlong into heart trouble, mental disorder, a "nervous breakdown." One renowned local rusher, a model by negativity, careered wildly, nearly unspeakably, into a gruesomely botched attempt at suicide. Sometimes one must rush. Black frost clutches the baby spuds. Storms roll over the lying hay. But normal weather is calm, so work is slowed and expanded. People have neither hobbies nor a need for more free time than night thrusts upon them.

In 1841 the "peasantry" of Fermanagh were described as a "fine race . . . active, yet not overstrained or industrious. Whether from habit or a natural propensity, the people do not rise to a late hour in the morning and the cows are not milked until noon."[8] Small farmers still rise late and linger through long conversations over breakfast. They were up late the night before, doing the serious work of reaffirming social relations in tea and talk; they own little land, their way is pastoral, and if they rose at dawn's crack, the day in most seasons would provide them with too little to do. When their friends go to America, they become rich, they say, because America is so boring there is nothing to do but work. If they had nothing else to do at home, they might become rich too, but reality crowds with neighbors and confines them on small farms which they whip to the limit. If extra time opens during the long days of summer or the short ones of winter, they work it full, rebuilding the ridge-and-furrow in the dead cold, rooking hay as long as grass remains. Though motion is slow, everyone produces more than enough. Bogs are humpy with thatched turf lumps, old and in decay. The edges of fields are mounded with old hay pecks turning gray. There are many reasons for superabundance. Generosity and memories of bad years provide the chief ones, but another runs in the momentum of work. While evenly paced, it does not stop at some artificial level of sufficiency, but continues until the time has been passed.

In the midst of unremitting work, shifting gracefully from task to task, unrushed, pausing briefly, carrying on, the man in the fields like the woman at the hearth finds neither pain nor pleasure, purely. His work passes the time, and he is not exactly unhappy while at it. What's the use in complaining?

Then the sky darkens and the spade is propped in the byre. The cows are milked and the kitchen darkens. Chairs are scraped to the hearth, and the farmer, his cracked hands around a mug of tea, unrolls his story into the ashes. The purpose of a story, they say, is to pass the time.

The company is the same, the stories are old. Again men meet, in revulsion, affection, desperation, surrounded by time. One asks the other if he remembers a story suggested by their conversation. The other says, No. Vladimir asks, "Shall I tell it to you?" Estragon answers, "No." So promising "it'll pass the time," Vladimir tells it, demanding that Estragon respond. When strangers intrude, then leave, having provided a bit of sport, Vladimir says, "That passed the time." Estragon replies, "It would have passed in any case." Vladimir understands: "Yes, but not so rapidly." They have become used to the muck, capable of entertaining themselves despite it, while waiting for Mr. Godot.

Samuel Beckett was born in Dublin and educated in Enniskillen, and if he is our world's man, a Nobel prize winning author and denizen of art's city, Paris, he is, too, a man of Ireland inextricably.[9] In his great trilogy of novels he slowly strips man of society and sense, exploring human minima to the conclusion that I, with no reason at all, will go on. Then his works struggle courageously to assemble society around man and invest him with reason. Man, in *How It Is*, drags his sack through the muck of experience, remembering "time past vast tracts of time . . . scraps of an enormous tale . . . murmured to this mud." Within the "monster silences vast tracts of time perfect nothingness," he tells himself to "reread the ancient's notes pass the time" and crawls forward, learning to communicate through pain, while forming an idea of society and history. Earlier, in *Mercier and Camier*,

Samuel Beckett had given man a companion, a friend for adventuring, the only one who could love the likes of himself, but he held that novel back when his idea found perfection in the play *Waiting for Godot*. Drama allows simultaneity, the existence of two on the stage.

Vivian Mercier's witticism that *Godot* is a play in which nothing happens twice obscures all that does happen. If Godot does not come, his messenger does, and he assures the waiting men that Mr. Godot does not beat him, feeds him fairly well, lets him sleep on the soft hay in the loft, and has a white beard. Given a hint of the kind Ballymenone's people find in cures, Vladimir and Estragon hold together, despite boredom, repeating old stories. They may not be joyous. They do not progress. But the world beyond them revealed in successive visits from its representatives, a gentleman and his servant, has decayed to babble and silence, violence and weakness, madness. The true horror of Beckett's great play is not the petty boredom of waiting. It is that these men are better off than most people. They have each other, they have signs of Godot's reality and goodness. They resist suicide and stay with each other, maintaining their sense of justice and decency and outrage, while the world of gentlemen and servants becomes foul and falls apart. If the universal message of *Waiting for Godot* concerns the absurdity of waiting, then its particularly Irish message is deeper: it is a play about friends passing the time.

Old stories and plain daily work pass the time.

Achieving continuity through the construction of organic, useful, and beautiful centers, accepting, conserving, and bravely extending the given, "passing the time" as a concept seems to have grown out of the farming surface of the Christian world of places like Ballymenone. The ridge-and-furrow, smooth to save space and look good, to stay dry and productive, calls the body to work all the year round and shares daily attention with the cows. It risks public exposure while providing its maker intellectual delight when his project is brought to successful completion. What a victory Peter Flanagan won over both frost and opinion with his fine crop of spuds.

Daylight work seems nearly to have determined the idea of passing the time. At night, when constraints are slacker, things could be different. But the evening yawns. Yet another night, swollen with time, gapes ahead monstrously. The ceiliers meet its challenge with ideas proved effective in the dirt: topics are conserved and extended into bright, smooth tales that defeat boredom, pull the soul from the void, and push life ahead.

A tale is a piece of conversational flow, just as the planting season is a segment of endless action on the evergreen, black moss ground—preceded by turning a ritual sod on March first, coping the lea in February, rebuilding the ridge-and-furrow in winter—followed by summer weeding, autumn harvest, winter rebuilding, spring coping. . . . Like a garden, the story is organically ordered within continuity. It is partial, joining tea (as herding joins digging) to pass the time. It is complex, combining the artful, the useful, and the brave.

Meeting the night's dark threat, people work together building ceilis out of visits, stories out of ceilis. Their attentive goodmanning witnesses to the performer's difficulties while encouraging him to overcome his natural and proper reticence to sacrifice himself to keep them engaged, safe, and passing the time. For a long time I misunderstood. I thought of time as a series of periods and of action that passed the time as filling those periods like water poured into so many cups standing in a row. But the good meal or tale elevates time so that it momentarily pleases you, then carries you on. It is like a wave on an endless ocean that lifts and rides you over the trough that inevitably follows.

Comfortably at home in the cages our tradition provides us, we cunningly misrepresent reality. The captains of management, conniving to maintain control of the wealth, have convinced us that gala vacations, weary evenings, empty weekends, childhood, and retirement are fair recompense for maturity's half-century of weekdays. Gratefully we break existence into unpleasant labor and futile leisure. Artists, anxious to join their patrons in an idle elite, have convinced us that their work is not work, their rules are not ours, their creations float above our ken. Happily we separate art from our lives. Then, confronting art in other times and places, we exalt it into isolation or trivialize it into recreation—not creation but recreation. Consider the stories of Ballymenone. They less break time than pulse it forward. They are less moments of disjunction, reversal, and escape than instants of electrical convergence fusing the past vividly into the present, the artful usefully into the commonplace, the transcendent mystically into the real, the personal generously into the collective.

At the peak of an evening, at the nexus of force, the story emerges. We may think about it economically. The story is husbanded like fields of grass; it is set, tended, raised, prepared, and consumed like cabbage. We may think about it aesthetically. It challenges its creator and moves its audiences. We may think about it socially. As emblems of excellence and counters of reciprocity, stories define and refine the relationships among people. In all these ways, tales are like food. Both entertain, both are gifts, both conjoin the aesthetic with the economic through the social.

Food and stories wrap human energy as a lovely gift to the social order. Art and toil blend to serve society. That conclusion does not seem exactly false. The thought that "entertainment" is an ethical matter is right as far as it goes, but confined by the puny convention of measuring reality by man, it is not the deepest way to think about what happens when one person gives a spud from the moss ground or tea or a tale to another. That way is pointed by analogy with Holy Communion.

Tea is not wine, not blood. Ceilis are not heresy. The people of Ballymenone are not authors of intricate, mechanical analogy. Meanings in their arts pop open and echo, rebounding obliquely, expanding through vague, deep, endless reference. These people are not cloistered philosophers busy in the contrivance of scholastic systems of correspondence. They are farm people doing their best, and their culture is not a completed program but, as they say, a "way," a direction through chaos. As they strive on their way, it is logical for them to orient their struggle for goodness toward that instant when, not over or around, but straight through a simple act and common substance, an individual makes mystical connection at once with God and other human beings.

Dimly, the central act of the social world—eating and speaking together—aligns with sacred mystery. Impossibly, entertainment strains to the transcendence of Holy Communion. Receiving a gift of tea or tale, you are doubly joined to other people, to the ancestors from whom the gift came and to those who receive it with you. But follow either of those connections to its end, the one back through time, the other outward through space, and you will find not the limits of the community but the limitless universe.

The gift of entertainment is made out of an individual's work. At one remove, it comes from those who created the stories and first broke the land. But ultimately the talent out of which tales are composed and the environment from which food is wrested were gifts from God. Though muffled, impure, and weak when compared with the priest's sacrament, the host's tea and tale have the same source.

Right there I felt my analysis going too far, so I asked Peter Flanagan. I told him how I saw farmwork and entertainment as being the same, how both seemed secular aspirations to sacred goodness, and I asked whether he thought his gift of music was like the priest's of the Eucharist. He sat straight on his small stool, his head cocked to the side, looking down at the cigarette, its thin pale smoke rising from his curled palm. Outside, the winds of a winter morning battered at our hill. The tape recorder turned at his feet by the fire. He thought a moment, then answered, beginning slowly, speeding up as the topic opened:

"Aye, the very same thing.

"Well, it's another bracket altogether, you see, it's not that high a standard. But ye try to do the best.

"Aye surely, that man that gives music, he does the best he can. That's his motivation and intention. It twouldn't be really just to learn music or to go out and get drinks that a man would play. It would not, now.

"Aye, the person that you give your tradition to that you got from your parents, well, you could save them people by that music in the early stages of life from goin astray and adoptin the wrong way of life. It engaged their mind and kept them out of injurious work.

"Aye, he's a child of God surely, the person who does that. Even that ye haven't the real good faith. Doin good works, that's the principal thing in religion. If ye accomplish that, and if ye carry on that to the end of your lifetime, there's no danger. I don't mind what persuasion a person is, that's what God wants.

"That's the same as a prayer: doin a good work, if you're fit to do it. Goin about idle, walkin about: the person that's not doin good, he's always doin evil. He has time for contemplatin and thinkin of something—his mind is not engaged on profitable work. With the result that he can be led into temptation. Well, the person that's not employin or doin nothing, he can turn very quick, and the evil thought can come to him.

"And there never has come any time in the world with as many temptations to cause destruction to the soul as the present world.

"We have a strong inclination to evil, owin to our First Parents. It wants to be in accordance with the laws of God what you speak or what you do. For the good of your country and the good of your neighbors.

"The same as work: it wants to be beneficial, either spiritual or corporal, your talk."

Beneficial talk, like music and bread, is a gift. The social connections built out of gifts cannot produce the mystical oneness of the community of Communion, but neither are they the product of credit and debt or mere reciprocity. The ethical is framed on the sacred. Neighborliness is a commandment. Giving to the other is a sacred obligation. It is not surprising, then, that asymmetries of reciprocity are allowed to continue, that some people give night after night, that the talented person is told to give, recipients are forced to receive, and thanks are slight. While saying, "I don't want to push you past your pleasure," the host will also say, "I would rather you kicked me in the teeth than not take tea with me," and the guest says, "I will take anything I can get, only strokes and abuse," and the host when thanked replies, "Thanks? What for? There's no thanks to it."

In my society, underpinned by avarice at worst, affection at best, the ledger must be kept carefully balanced, and thanks are profuse. About when I was beginning to notice that my fellow ceiliers were less extravagant than I with words of gratitude, Hugh Nolan noticed my pattern and told me no thanks were necessary for his vast generosity. He said it was as though I were walking to town and a man in a car came by. He would pick me up of course, and leave me at my destination. If I thanked him, he would reply, "There's no thanks to it. The car was goin there anyway." We are together on this journey, you and I, and of course we will help each other all we can. One need not be thanked for fulfilling a religious duty.

Through the simple gift in the middle of a ceili, goodness flows from God and outward to the neighbors, and "all mankind is your neighbor." Assembling the gift, a twisted, corroded conduit for the original spirit, an individual abandons social isolation and gains infinite connectivity. Connected, the self is absorbed into the gift, sucked backward through the ancestors, shoved outward through the fellowship of the ceili, pulsed backward and outward into the unknowable from which power returns to locate the giver, delicately, centrally, in right relation to the All.

Right relation is not achieved by sitting placidly on a hill humming like an idiot. Rains of ice lash the roods of golden corn. Machine-gun fire cackles through the streets. Vile winds shriek from open wounds. The Saint's old prophecy of doom is frozen in thorn. You have to stand, for man is fallen, and move bravely against black gales of dirt and decay. God's gift must be accepted. The poet must control the tongue of flame licking in his skull. The farmer must nurse green shoots out of gray seeds under sunless skies. The fire tender must keep the flame dancing. God's gifts must be passed on. The artist must give, and in giving demand not silent adoration but the live force of engaged union. The host must give, and in giving demand not repayment but social order. In action, taking and transferring God's goodness, people find pace, a sweet spot in momentum. Balanced in universal motion, they are passing the time and happy enough.

Happiness, like smoothness, cleanliness, and freshness, is an endless struggle against the nature of things, overwhelmingly rough, dirty, stale, and sad. When people see magpies flying they say, "One for sorrow, two for joy," then comment that you usually see only one on the wing. The world is not a happy place; its inhabitants exist in decay. From the Old Woman of Beare, ebbing to brave Peig Sayers, Irish literature is full of laments for aging. [10] "It is sad to grow old," said handsome Tommy Love, and Hugh Nolan, who has endured, replied, "They will say to you that you're gettin older, but all people is gettin older. With every tick of the clock, Tommy. Even that new baby in Francy Corrigan's, it's gettin older. And there's not a haet can be done about it. So it's better not to think about it atall, but just live life as it comes. That's the way." Live life as it is and sorrow will wash over the mind and extinguish the spirit. But meet it head on, taking it as it comes, and time passed is a victory.

To be alone is the saddest sad. Reversing the logic that names the specific with the general term, farming with "work," cabbage with "plants," the word "lonesome" expands to cover every kind of sadness. The child in a crowd with a broken toy as surely as an old woman despondent at the hearth of an empty house is "lonesome." The opposite of lonesome is "heartsome." The heartsome person is hopeful, happy, "right"—in balanced connection with other people and, therefore, with God.

Passing the time in entertainment is more than momentary distraction, it is heartsome, not lonesome, an epitome of connectivity. The ceili is a model of how to be: happy and in society. Saying life is a little ceili is not a joyous conclusion, but neither is it melancholy. It is both accurate and encouraging enough to give the quick visitor a reason to continue while waiting.

If we follow the ceili back into daylight, we will find the garden off center. There the worker finds delight, most completely in the bright green of growing plants, flourishing as evidence of his responsible acceptance of God's gifts and proper participation in God's design. His efforts yield food given to others in affirmation of social relations and in fulfillment of divine commandment. But while he works, he is alone, removed with his spade from the sort of interchange that makes nights into ceilis. He is potentially sad, lonesome. When he is happier, when the best patterns of day and night match, his work is collective as well as productive and responsible. Closer to the ceili's model is work beyond the moss on the spongy, bumpy, brown bog.

16

Bog

"Three men is the way for the bog," said Joe Murphy. Hugh Nolan put it like this: "To work in comfort in the bog, you wanted to have three men, one cuttin, one liftin, one wheelin. I cut. I lifted. I wheeled." These men formed a unit called "a full spade." Their agreement, termed "swappin," arranged for each man's bog to be cut in turn by its owner with the help of two neighbors. [1]

Where bog has been cut it is pocked with "hollows," dipping to end at the sheer "face" from which turf was shaved last year. Atop this small cliff runs the "bank" to be pared away in layers, providing a year's fuel. If heather grows over the bank's "head," men burn it off before they "open the bog," removing its coat of sod and as much as three feet of "mould" with spades, "strippin the bank" to reveal the slick surface beneath. The "strippins" are tossed over the edge into the deepest part of the hollow, the "boghole" sour with still, brown water. If the strippins float, a trench must be cut to a drain, or water must be "teemed out" with buckets to dry the hole. The exposed turf bank is now smoothed with a shovel. Cutting begins.

The cutter, they say, has the easiest job, but it takes the most skill. He moves along the bank, right to left as you face him from the hollow, jabbing his spade "underfoot." The "turf spade" has a "wing," so its jabs in series articulate with each other and with the open bank face to create brick-shaped slices of turf. The cutter has to move quickly not to retard his companions, but he must cut well, leaning out over his spade, cutting straight down so the turf will fall into the lifter's hands without leaving their "heels" behind. In groups of five or six, the lifter pulls turf from the wall and sets them in three rows in a barrow. Barrows come in pairs, supplied at five pounds the pair at their place of manufacture, the town of Lisnaskea across the Upper Lough. As soon as one barrow is filled, the wheeler pulls it to the level "spread ground" and dumps the turf in rows while the lifter is filling the other.

When the end of a bank for the width of its stripping is reached, a "floor" has been cut, its depth determined by the blade of the spade. The new surface is cleaned with a long-handled shovel. Its cleanings, bits of broken turf called "offalls," are saved by some men to burn, but most throw them into the hollow, and cutting the next floor begins.

Joe Murphy's Turf Spade

Uncut "flow bog" has a few top flows of "white," "fum" turf, then six floors of "brown turf," then five or six floors of "black." The darker and harder the turf, the better. "The fums blaze to please you," but black turf burns longest and hottest. The last two or three floors of the best turf lie beneath the level of the hollow's bottom, so a "bridge" is "nicked" the breadth of your hand and left standing as a bulwark to hold the water back. Behind the bridge, turf is excavated until the cutter "bottoms the hole" on clay or until the turf crumble, no longer holding together. Next year's bog-hole results.

Depending on the weather and the household's needs, cutting lasts from three days to a week. After the turf have been "out" for three or four days they can be spread in a single layer across the paths left for wheeling, "the barrow rows," to expose them all to wind and sun.

The turf "lie on the spread" until ready for "clamping," ten days in good weather. I clamped with Hugh Patrick Owens. When our task was done and we were rewarding ourselves at night, he filled the public house with compliments for me: "He's the man can clamp the turf. Aye, he's the man can clamp as fast as you'd walk." Actually, he left me to do the simple jobs with Michael, his son, and he "built the bottoms" of every clamp, establishing forms and setting the pace like a boss on the meadow or a star at the hearth.

The three of us moved through the lying turf, Mr. Owens working away from the bank, along the spread's edge, laying out three clamps in a row, returning and laying out three more. He would work on one until we

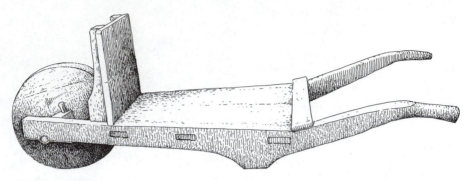

Turf Barrow. Joe Murphy's. For scale, the wheel measures 17 inches in diameter. Stand between the handles, your back to the wheel, stoop, lift, and walk away, pulling the barrow, laden with wet turf, behind you.

finished ours, and when we appeared, he would move off to start the next. We set the tempo between us, and I fell effortlessly into our rhythm, moving forward, letting the clamps rise on clear ground behind us.

We took our main meals in the house, but Mrs. Owens brought our tea down to the bog, and we paused for sandwiches, buttered fadge, biscuits, and hot liquid, and then went on through the turf, remembering to "stagger the corners" after the manner of a mason's quoins, keeping the clamps level, building them "the same as you would a wall." When the Angelus toned from Arney Chapel, we stood in wordless isolation, the dull colors of the bog around us, then Mr. Owens moved and we followed, reuniting. He built one corner first, setting two turf side-by-side and another athwart them. Next he assembled the adjacent corner of the clamp's end with three more and reversed himself to lay two courses of the long side begun with the first pair, working clockwise around, like a builder of rooks, until the bottom was "closed." From the corner, he built in both directions, enacting the logic that plans houses and stories and seasons from their centers outward. As we came up, bent and ready, he moved off, and we, like the ceili's followers, built on his foundation, "breakin the joints" by placing one turf on two and some on the diamond, so each could "take a grip," and channels would be left for ventilation. The point of clamping is to dry the turf.

We paused for a smoke in the shelter of a new clamp. A cold wet wind was blowing and, as he would say that night, "there was not a bush between us and heaven." Out of focus beyond him, the fairy forth of Mullinaman encircled its hilltop, and we sat, motionless, huddled, chilled. "Clamping," he said, "is not as hard work as cuttin them, but it's tedious." Our cigarettes finished, we rose cold and began again. When he selected the well-formed turf for building, a small pile of misshapen bits accumulated that we used to fill the bottom's center. "There must be no waste. You don't want to leave any tails behind." At its base, the clamp was three turf wide. On the third course, we turned one in the center on edge. By the fifth, its width was two. One topped it, the clamp battering to stay loose and open, yet sturdy.

Dried in clamps, turf is "won." All that remains is drawing them home to the turfshed or building them into rope-bound, reed-thatched "lumps" in the bog. Some call the squarish lumps "wee stacks," in memory of the enormous rectangular stacks of the past, reserving the term "lump" for those round on plan, while others call them all lumps, shapes and names being not more than matters of personal preference. In lump or shed, turf must be "built" so it will not "fall" into clods or mould, so it will supply the hearth with heat for a year.

Work on the bog teaches time's lesson in two ways. Poised in the nothingness of the present, you look to the unknowable future, planning out of experience, knowing you must surrender plans while adjusting to circumstance. And you look to the past to learn that you are a minute part of history, obliged to adapt to its evolutionary power. On the bog, as on the clay and moss, either orientation drops you into time and instructs you to be flexible, taking what comes.

In the future as planned, turf will be cut in a week in May, spread in three days, clamped in ten, and brought home within a month. But you may find yourself directed by the climate to cut as early as April or as late as

Hugh Patrick Owens and His Son, Michael, Clamping Turf

How to Build a Clamp

Lump. A turf lump on Sessiagh bog, the forth of Mullinaman in the distance.

June. "You can cut turf in mixed weather," Hugh Nolan said, "but you want dry weather for the winnin of them." If the weather is a bit bad when the clamps are disassembled, the unwon, wet turf are lumped on the bog while the dry are drawn home. If the weather is worse you may have to clamp twice, removing won turf and rebuilding the damp into clamps, and if it is the worst, the turf might lie on the spread through the summer, never to be clamped, never to be won. It is then that people plunder antique lumps and gather sticks from the hedge and burn whins and gorse and stalks of kale and pads of manure, turned to dry on both sides, and—as the saying is—"the bottom boards of the bed."[2] A sense of the desperation cold brings on a land unprepared can be gathered from a letter Mrs. Cutler wrote me during the bitter winter of 1979: "Well, dear, we had a terrible snow storm since. The 9th Jan it snowed 8 inches that night and off and on till the weekend. And talk of frost, it was dreadful. I couldn't go out on the street. And talk of the cold, I near died. But there came a thaw on the 16th Jan. I hope there comes no more snow or frost this year. Of course the snow storm is all over far worse than here, but there was a few old people burned to death trying to keep themselves warm. God help us all."

But summer brings sunny days, and if the weather is very good, turf can be "won on the spread" without clamping. "In a bad season, the turf mightn't be dried atall. But if the season was good and if they were a good quality—that'd be the hard black turf—then in a week or ten days you could bring them home or put them in lumps. But," Mr. Nolan goes on, "what would happen if it was too dry, and you got a wonderful break in the weather, they would crumble, and all would go to loss." Exceptionally good weather is no better than exceptionally bad. The best is the norm. Plans are formed out of common experience, and people follow the middle way out of the realities of work, between common proverbial summaries: "Something is better than nothing" and "Too much of anything is worth nothing at all."

We have seen that opposed forces in Ballymenone are conceived as an unresolvable structuring of a subordinate within a dominant. Smoothness will ever be contained by roughness, joy by sorrow. Now, in the middle of the bog, we have come upon the most abstract formulation of Ballymenone's essential idea that one must plan but something will go wrong so one must go on. The planned is subordinate to the circumstantial, will is contained by forces beyond human control. No synthetic middle term provides the answer. Culture proposes but does not dispose, and mediation is left up to the individual acting in the moment. The happiness people seek in action, through the accomplishment of plans, will never be perfect, and life will remain less than smooth, clean, joyous.

Ballymenone's dual view of time collapses in action. With too much and too little, they pass the time, trying to make life a ceili while out there forces gather to wreck their design. Hopes inevitably held are inevitably checked by the physical environment and by vague, distant circumstances rolling as the force of history. Begun before our involuntary arrival, things are conditioned by remote international events and will continue long after our pitiful departure.

The bog formed as the Deluge receded. William Lunny, who told us that this was all here before us and will remain when we are gone, explains the bog's origin. "You see, the bogs came the time of Noah's Flood. The trees and vegetation fell. And when the water dried up, slowly the bog was formed in the bottoms. Now, that's what I've always heard." Begun in primeval times at God's command, bogs bear evidence of continual human occupancy. Bob Lamb dug down to the stumps of great oaks strung in a perfect line, indicating to him that the trees beneath were planted by men. Peter Flanagan was told that turf cutters in Cavan came upon a soft spot in the bog and found a preserved man, his flesh and eyes intact, the track of his clothes in the soil. Six floors down in the turf, Mr. Flanagan unearthed the horns of an ancient cow, stretching four feet from tip to tip. Another time he found a great wheel of cheeselike butter that lay around until the rats ate it, and once cutting with James Boyle he discovered a platform deep within the turf. P guessed it had been "a quay in ancient days when the bog was a lake and the people had no way of travelin, only the canoe. The roads was bad and this was a dock for the ferry for gettin from Drumbargy across there." The bog is interesting.[3] Hugh Nolan, his wonderful mind always at work, developed this explanation for their discovery:

"Now I was under the impression that there had been some kind of an entertainment at this spot and that this platform was put up. And it never was taken down.

"Well then, it was a field that run along a bog and my opinion about it was: that one year after another that this sunk away down into the soil. That's all I could make of it. But you could ask P or James.

"When they came down to this row, do ye see, the ends of these planks was protruding from in under the bank, so they had to take and cut lengths off them for to get out the flow of bog in under, do ye see.

"So then, I think that they bid to hoke back for a piece, because I seen lumps of them planks that they had discovered put across drains over there.

"Well, do ye see, nearly in all bog you'll find *bog oak*.

"Well, when they'd be clifted up, do ye know, well, they made the best firin, and, ah, you could use them for buildin purposes, but you couldn't drive a nail in them; you'd have to bore, do ye know, you'd have to bore with a gimlet or an auger, do ye see.

"But I'll tell ye what the opinion is about that bog oak, that has been discovered in the bogs. That them was trees that fell in the time of Noah's Flood. That's what it's *supposed* to be, you see, and that they were buried—

that they went down into the ground. And the soil grew over them. And it was only when there was drainin or there was turf a-cuttin that they were discovered.

"Well that's the conclusion that I have come to, and others as well as me: that them trees fell the time of the Flood."

The bog is a place of change. It holds strange and secret reminders of an ancient past that whisper of time's enormity, the smallness of the present, and it records clearly the changes occurring in our days. Bogs can be "cut out," scooped down to the clay. The Rossdoney Bog at the southern foot of Drumbargy Brae is gone, so Rossdoney men cut turf on scattered roods in Rossawalla and Sessiagh, drawing the community out, bringing men from different townlands together for work. If "cutover bog" is carefully drained, they say it will "rise" and given time will yield fuel once more. Today Paddy McBrien cuts turf exactly where Hugh Nolan cut the bog out half a century ago. Cutover bog can also be reclaimed by draining, so men who once owned roods of bog now own roods of "reclaim" on which corn and hay will grow. It is encouraging that used land remains productive, that the buried wood that interrupts cutting is useful. Strips of "bog deal," steeped in oil burned like rush candles in the past, and bits of buried platform make "footsticks" over drains in Drumbargy today. It is encouraging that the bog seems inexhaustible and that there is bog aplenty. Uncut flow bog remains in the townland of Ross. But work in the bog is more than a matter of a man, a turf spade, and damp earth. "Turf-cuttin," Peter Flanagan said, "is a three-man job": it is a matter of social organization, of assembling a full spade, and it is in the social world that the greatest changes have taken place.

"When I was a young man," Mr. Nolan said, "you wouldn't see one, but you'd see a hundred and twenty-five carts bein pulled, full of the turf." We sat at his hearth in the dark, smoking. He and James Boyle were teaching me, and Mr. Boyle added:

"Aye. At one time you would look down the bog by the Back Road there, and you'd see the bog full of men in white shirts, some cuttin, some loadin, some spreadin. And some early ones might be clampin. Or even drawin the turf home."

"Aye," Mr. Nolan agreed. "And now there's not a man on the bog."

"Not a one," said Mr. Boyle as Mr. Nolan continued:

"No, the bogs are not a-usin in this country at the present time. They have cut off cuttin turf. And the young men have got off it altogether. They don't fancy learnin anything about it."

"No they don't," Mr. Boyle agreed. "No, there's not a man on the bog."

There are men on the bog, men who still cut turf, and others joined them as fuel costs rose during the years of inflation following that conversation in 1972. But Mr. Nolan and Mr. Boyle were not wrong. They used the District's conventional mode of extension to describe the present situation in accordance with the local evolutionary theory of history. The past is viewed from the present, its relevance determined by current reality. The past is antecedent. It has passed, but it is not dead, for the future will be its creation. The momentum of the past sweeps over and swallows the present, forming the future as its extreme, nearly hyperbolic projection, then the future rebounds to define the present and wash it into the past. In the blur of the past receding and the future arriving, what is becomes lost between what was and will be, and the past perfects its shape in the future. Seated at his open hearth, Mr. Nolan looks beyond it to comment that open hearths are a thing of the past, that all have electricity now. Though most fields are bound by hedged ditches, there is enough new wire fencing for him to see into the future and say, "It is all wire fences at the present time." Once everyone cut turf, now only some do, the historical trajectory is set. The past becomes the future becomes the present, and "there's not a man on the bog."

What has gone is not turf-cutting but its social scene. Work is action between labor and art. The "laborer" owns no land. The labor he does for others consists of "jobs" for pay. He gains neither permanent benefit nor total involvement from his efforts; his work is not "work." In labor, work's pleasures decrease. In art, they increase. Solitary work is made enjoyable by complications, challenges to hand or mind met in technological virtuosity and displayed in "lovely" forms. The impulse to pleasure within work is most obviously pushed toward art by concentration on "ornament," when the farmer becomes a flower gardener or the brick maker becomes a sculptor. Collective work is made pleasant by its incorporation of the spirit John Synge named, too enthusiastically, "festival."[4] When the pleasure of collective work is purified toward art, what remains is chat and sociability: life's little ceili full of stories. Men still cut turf, they wheel and lift and spread and clamp, but they work in isolation. One man is the way for the bog today. Some pleasure remains for him in the completion of his project, but that scene of the dark bog sparkling with the white shirts of men has gone, and turf-cutting has slipped toward labor.

From the hearth at the center where turf burns, to the bog at the edge where it is cut, Ballymenone's people have struggled to form their place smoothly. Their work's pleasure lies less in "beautification," in carving or painting or stitching or planting flowers around forms, than in the chatty sociability that surrounds the making of "necessary" things, food or rooks or clamps, with happiness. Newly alone in a clean second kitchen or an empty bog, the worker loses the basic pleasure that lightened unavoidable toil.

Twice while the tape recorder ran, Hugh Nolan wound discussions of other matters into clear expositions of the collective work of the past. From them we learn exactly what has been lost. His first statement begins with a description of mearns, the boundaries separating farms and townlands, then swings through a happy, rhythmic passage to arrive at a classification of the cooperative work that eliminated boundaries between people:

"Well, in this part of Fermanagh, it was generally drain mearns. There was some places and there was hedges, whitethorn hedges, but in the low parts of the country it was generally *drains* like what you'd see in *Holland*.

"Well, often cattle, especially big cattle and *horses* often went into *drains*. And there used to be an *awful* job in pullin them *out*.

"Well, there was plenty of men in them days, do ye know, workin on the land, and livin about the *country*—not like *now*.

"There was none of these public works, do ye know. And the way that it'd be done, well, maybe there'd be a house and there'd be two men about it, maybe the father and the son or maybe two brothers. And nearly every house in the country there was a *man* that devoted his whole time to his large farm or little farm or whatever he had, do ye see.

"Well, when a beast would go into a drain, the rout used to go round, do ye know: Such a *man has a cow in the drain*.

"*Where?*

"Oh, in such a *field*.

"*Well*, there'd be no time till there maybe would be ten or fifteen men in that field.

"Younger people used to think it great value, do ye know.

"They got there,
     and they got a rope,
     and they pulled, do ye know,
     and often ◊ maybe the rope broke ◊,
     and maybe four or five men would fall on top of other ◊.

"It was a bit of *sport*, do ye know.

"So then, do ye see, changes came along then. And nearly every man got a job of some kind or other. Some would be workin in quarries and some in garages and some in factories, you see. So it wound up that there wouldn't be a man about the country from eight o'clock in the mornin till six in the evenin, do ye see.

"So to leave things safe for *cattle* nearly all the farmers have put wire palins along the drains with this thorny wire. Do ye see, the way it used to be, how they used to slip into drains: well there'd be maybe long, soft grass growin on the broo of the drain, do ye see. The cattle was very fond of that. And they'd go. And they'd put their feet on the side of the drain, and they'd eat away *down into the drain*, do ye see, and then maybe go headlong in the drain, do ye see. And then the wire then keeps them away from *that*, do ye see.

"And that's all the way now that a man could rest content that his cattle was safe, because, as far as *gatherin* a crowd of men nowadays,
     you couldn't do it.

"Because they're all engaged,
          all engaged.
"And in days gone by, they used to what was styled *swappin*.
"I went to *you*
          the *day*.
"And then I had something the morrow and you came to *me*.
"And then I went back to you then the next day and so on. That the work was got done. *Two* men's work would be goin on at a time.
"That was the way.
"And then there was the methal.
"It used to apply to where there'd be a man that wasn't in good form. Or that some one of his family was sick.
"And that he wasn't able to work himself, nor he wasn't able to get workin with the trouble that was in the house.
"Well then, on a certain day then, *all* the men of the locality would all turn out, and maybe they'd put in a whole field of spuds. Or put in a field of oats or *some* thing like that, do ye know.
"And if it was in the hay season, they done for a day, and if he had his hay raised up, it'd be all put up, do ye see. That was the way. *Groups* like that, that's what they were called: methals. The whole men in the locality went out for a day to one particular man, or to a widow-woman. Aye.
"It was a common thing to happen in this part of Fermanagh.
"I seen often nine and ten men in one field, workin for some man, as I was tellin you, that wasn't able for to do it himself. Or that there was some trouble about the house that he couldn't get it done."

When he stopped, I asked with the naiveté necessary to the ethnographer whether the men of methal expected pay. Nearly aghast, Mr. Nolan replied, "Oh no. No pay. It was a voluntary act. Oh aye." Helping a neighbor in trouble is a sacred responsibility. That is one thing that has gone: the confidence that, if things go awry, you will not have to meet them alone. The other is the "bit of sport" that brought "great value" into the workaday round. Mr. Nolan's second statement grew out of a conversation we were having about architecture. Immediately he sees homes less as shelter than as social environments. (His house was and is a ceili house.) Then he pivots on the notion of the hard life of the poor to swing from the evening's ceili to aspects of ceiliing that lived in the group work of the past but have died out of the solitary work of the present.

"Well then, in old times in this country—well, I didn't hear it told, but I seen it in print—in some houses, in the kitchen, they used to have the fire in the center of it.
"Well then, when the ceiliers would come in then, of a winter's night, they could all sit in a ring around the fire.
"They could play cards and them sittin at the fire. Tell stories and sing,

and I suppose if they took a notion of dancin, there was room enough for them to dance around the fire, do ye see.

"I never seen it, nor I never heard any of the old people talkin about seein it, but they was in existence, especially with the poorer classes.

"Well, the poorer classes, do ye see, was always counted the jolliest.

"Well, you could associate more with them than with the Big Bucks in all ages, do ye see.

"Well, do ye see the way it is, the poorer and plainer people, they get made to this hardship. And it's their life. It's their life, do ye see.

"They get made to it.

"But of course at the present time, the younger generation now in this country wouldn't go in as much for *hardship* as what their ancestors. They wouldn't go in for the system of working that they had. Nor, they wouldn't have the same patience.

"They wouldn't have the same patience. If they can't get the job done quick, it's goin to be an encumbrance to them, do ye see.

"Well then, I suppose how that has come about: there has came through many types of machinery, that young men has got away from the old system of the spade and the scythe and the shearin hook and all these weapons that you lost plenty of sweat.

"When I first mind the harvest, the meadows were all mowed with scythes. In my early days, when I got out on the road, it was all scythes: three men, one after another, mowin away from mornin to night.

"Well then, the mowin machines came then and no one would go out with a scythe. A man would cut his hay and look at his neighbor and see that he could do in an hour what took him two days. And you couldn't get a man to do it.

"And I'll tell ye, longgo when the turf was a-cuttin—you see, there's very little turf now a-cuttin in the old way—well, there'd be men in the bog. And they'd be workin hard. And dinner time would come. And when dinner'd be over, maybe all that was in the bog workin, they'd gather together, and there'd be a smoke and a ceili and the wait of an hour before they'd resume again.

"And then there was another custom: if there was two men workin beside other they could chat from one job to the other and work away, do ye see. Aye.

"But, do ye see, that has all ceased now. Because when you're on a job, well, ye'll get so long of a break for lunch and the like of that, and when that's over maybe there'd never be a word spoke, do ye see, when they'd be takin their lunch."

Adroitly Mr. Nolan built his explanation of contemporary life on this sequence: hardship rejected, impatience embraced, silence. When I locate his statement in the context of commentary by his peers, it deepens and solidifies as a key text in one generation's critique of modern existence.

People express, stress, and exemplify differently, but within their words a certain logic holds. These old storytellers watched the birth of the world you and I accept as given. Let us face their critique, entering it through conventional complaints.

Modern life is "too easy." Life in the past was hard. In getting made to its hardships, people learned to accept interminable work and ultimate failure. They could not rationally defer gratification until their work was done, for it never ended. They could not sacrifice a few miserable years for some future heaven on earth, for it would never come. They could indulge themselves in neither variety of modern temporal madness, neither nostalgia, living in the past, nor the more insidious illness of preoccupation, living in the future, spending today planning for tomorrow and tomorrow planning for the next day, longing, as Yeats said, for the tomb. "The Divil take the morrow": they had to stay awake for the moment, and to make the moment tolerable they had to bring pleasure into work, pausing for a smoke in the bog, moving at a pace that would not exhaust them. When three men went out to mow in the past, swinging their scythes in unison through the hay, they put the oldest man in the lead to establish a rhythm all could follow, swath after swath, "like the beat of a drum." In such a world, said Michael Boyle, "they were poor, but they had comfort and sport"—the security of community and the moments of pleasure Mr. Nolan described in his first statement.

Modern people are not responsible for an organic ordering of endless jobs. They have one job, and it can be finished. Because they finish their tasks, modern people are left with idle time. So one man will call them lazy. Another will blame the Troubles on their leisure: "If people would only tend to their cows and hay and crop, they wouldn't have time to go around killin each other." They seem to have adopted the pattern of the luxurious politician: "The politicians make millions suffer for the few. That comes from life being too easy. If they had more hardship, they'd think more about other people and not go around incitin people to killin other." And another man will see modern people as vulnerable to "communism," by which is meant not an economic system but a foreign slime seeping into society to dissolve personal freedom. Idle people in the past were apt to be "washin Old Nip's shirt," doing the Devil's work,[5] and today's people having not been toughened and shocked into consciousness by failure are weak in the face of temptation. Clanking machines bear their burden: they have it "too easy."

Modern life is "too fast." Since people with jobs can finish their tasks, they rush to do so, becoming impatient. Just as outsiders might mistake for lazy the man they see working slowly, not realizing he will be keeping that pace up for hours and hours, outsiders might mistake at a glance Fermanagh's people for impatient. My memory is of a traveling man trying to set up the diminutive stage for a Punch and Judy show at the Sport at Belcoo while the crowd milled and mocked, shoving and throwing things at him.

He took what seemed to me an intolerably long time, yet when he was ready at last, the crowd was still there. Their way to wait, their mode of acceptance, is not docile. They chatter and shift, staying in motion while nothing much happens again. In other places people might look more patient, queuing quiescently, but their patience runs out more quickly.

When the District's people act hastily, they are told, "Take your time." In such situations, Mrs. Cutler often recites a rhyme:

> Patience is a virtue,
> Find it if you can;
> Seldom in a woman,
> Never in a man.

With such lines people upbraid themselves for the times they chafed in the shackles of "the old system of the spade and the scythe and the shearin hook," but they know that their patience, bravely maintained amid hardship, is a virtue. It brings no harm and keeps them on the right path. Unwilling to be restrained, modern people adopt the frenzied, sick mode of the rusher. Their rewards are comfort and lonesome lives. Michael Boyle, Hugh Nolan, Tommy Love—all of them independently decried auto travel, comparing it unfavorably with the slow motion of bicycle and cart. Speeding by in the cars they have labored so long to own, people have no time to enjoy the beauty of the countryside and no time to stop for a roadside chat. They miss little pleasures and fail to fulfill social responsibilities. They do not pass the time; time passes them. Roaring machines set their pace: they go "too fast."

Modern life is too . . . no local word capsules the conclusion of Ballymenone's critique and no imported word—alienated or individualistic—gets it quite right. Modern people have jobs that take them away during the day. While they are at labor, too few men are left at home on the land. Crowds cannot be gathered, so people work alone, without security or camaraderie. Since modern people do not labor among the people they live among, the social fabric stretches, becomes threadbare, and at night when they could get together, they do not. They are either "away on the car" to consume prepackaged pleasures, or they sit at home "starin at the wall, doin nothing for themselves." As a result, said Peter Flanagan, "people have got to be dummies altogether." Accepting alien fashion, they neglect "the old national culture," which Mr. Flanagan exampled with the fiddling of Michael Coleman, the poetry of Thomas Moore, Charles Kickham, James Clarence Mangan, and William Butler Yeats, and which he said is the necessary foundation for a sane life. "And they don't ceili. Ah, they just sit there without a word bein passed."

As the 1970s wore on, patterns became clearer. "There used to be ceiliin in this country," Joe Flanagan said in 1977, "but that's all passed now. The young people don't stay here at all. They get cars and they're away, off to sprees." Experience of the new world's machines increased. In 1979, Mrs. Cutler's son gave her a television. I asked her if she liked it and she said she liked the bagpipe music. She got up, flicked the channels, found no bagpipe music, turned it off, and sat down again, speaking from the surprised depths of an important new discovery: "Do you know about that thing: when it goes on, the chattin stops. I think it's silly." In the same year, Mr. Nolan said:

"Sure, chattin as they used to call it, it has nearly went out of existence with television and radios and all these things. The people's continually listenin. They're not talkin atall. Continually listenin.

"They may have a few words with other. But they're listenin to something on the radio or on the television.

"Aye, indeed."

Mr. Nolan continued to observe and learn, but years before he had said it precisely when he ended his description of modern labor with the pathetic image of men on the job sitting through their brief lunch break in silence.

Silence is the key idea. It betokens at once stupidity and cowardice. Unchallenged by adversity, having it too easy, modern people have let their minds wither, and they have lost the courage it takes, and the generosity it takes, to reach out through conversation to help their fellows and establish through words a community founded on mutual aid. I have heard old men say it is a shame they do not speak their "own native tongue," but it is not the loss of Irish, three generations past, that most concerns them, it is the loss of rich, articulate English. Modern people stumble around in the language, repeating over and over the same dirty words—"effin this and effin that"—without clearly expressing themselves. Some blame this trait on emulating British soldiers (remember the foul mouth of the English private who knocked Stephen down in Nighttown), and the Troubles are kept boiling by blaming the English for the general decay of modern life, for alienation of all sorts, including that which separates people from their capacity to speak. But whatever its source, it is a fact, and they see it as symptomatic of laziness, stupidity, and selfishness. Modern people do not "take the time" to speak efficiently. Words are the force of community. What has been lost is the spirit of neighborliness that depended on cooperation and chat, daily in the bog, nightly at the hearth.

Their life of hardship jolted people into awareness. It directed them to find pleasure in the moment. Most important, it conditioned them to accept God's commandment to neighborliness. Now that cooperative work and ceilis are things of the past (not actually but in accordance with their hyperbolic evolutionary view), it is not surprising that they hold the great fear of theft I found so confusing. The rise of silence and decline of the neighborly way are evidence of the loosening of the rule of religion. Unconnected, out of control, people might do worse than retreat into isolation behind partitions and symmetrical facades. They might become aggressive. While bombs eviscerate little towns, the people of the countryside wait, watching for an increase in instances of theft to mark the next stage in the evolution of their community's decay.

The old people's critique is not a description. It does not portray things as they are, but identifies negative tendencies in reality, pulls them out, and joins them into an instrument used to gauge evolutionary change. Their critique is not an indictment of anyone, nor is it nostalgic. They wish to live well and must be able to judge change to do so, and they find unconsidered adherence to the old ways as foolish as the witless acceptance of fashion. During our architectural discussion, lolling as it did in days agone, Mr. Nolan felt it necessary to clarify his own position and chide my fascination tenderly before continuing our topic. He did so appropriately, indirectly, with a little story:

"Well, do ye know that public house at Arney. Tommy Gilleece's.

"When Tommy came to that place first, it was a long thatched house.

"So, there was some man, he was some type of traveler.

"And he often passed through different towns
         without takin a drink
              till he'd come to this place: *Arney*.

"And it was the old-fashioned make of the house
              that he fancied.

"He liked to have it to say that it was in a place like that he took his drink.

"So anyway, Tommy got tired of the shape of the old house;
         didn't he build this present one.

"You know, it's down from the Cross; when you're goin to Sessiagh, you pass by.

"So he made it modern.

"So damn it,
         the next time this man come back,
              he wouldn't go in.

"His favorite had disappeared.

"So he went on.

"Well, do ye see, there's some people is attached to these old fashions and old ways of doing things and old buildings and all to this. And they just can't get on to the *modern*.

"That's the way with alot of people.

"Curiosity, do ye see, brings them into that mood.

"But, you see, the way it is now, style has went to such a pitch in this country, and I suppose it's the same in every country, if you haven't a lovely kitchen or a cooker or a range or somethin like that, do ye see: you're behind the times.

"But then, everybody can't get that."

In the near past lived men who refused to use machinery. Mechanical mowers, they felt, destroyed the meadows, and the scythe was the only weapon for the hay. But today they say, laughing, "You never heard a cow ask was the hay cut be the scythe or the mowin machine." The purpose of criticizing modernity is not to retard progress—that would be impossible—but to hold some measure against change to bring it into the mind. While, in Peter Flanagan's phrase, "Ireland is becomin modern in the eleventh hour," it is inherently no more reasonable to adopt the new than cleave to the old. What is stupid is doing anything without awareness. Paddy McBrien presented a sensible prescription for the future: "Young people should be taught the old ways and the new ways, then they would be prepared, no matter what snags they met."

Carried along in history, people use their land to take a fix on their course, balancing loss against gain. The bog's lesson is loss. Work devolves to labor as the community declines, and the community's decline is evidence of people having "lost respect for authority, civil or divine." But the bog lies beneath the hills, and the turf cutter is also a herdsman who knows that the dynamo sucking men off the land to use as its fuel also produces the artificial fertilizer that allows the small farmer to endure, enabling the neighborly way to survive in ceilis in the dark. With their carrying capacity tripled, grassy fields bespeak gain.

Even setting bog against clay in tension is too simple, for the bog's loss echoes from the upland. Hay is cut alone, and if rooking remains a collective and happy experience, broken by teas, filled with playful chat, some men, lacking large families, must work alone, contenting themselves with fork rooks, and the jolly work of stacking is gone.

For food, a drop of drink and a scatter of crack, crowds used to assemble to raise safely won hay into great rectangular stacks. They took four men at least. One on the top "buildin," one on a ladder, and two below, passing the hay up and circling the stack to make sure there were no "bulges" or "hollows." But groups can no longer be gathered, so like the great stacks of turf, six feet wide and sixty long, haystacks are gone, and hay is built into smaller round pecks that two men can handle, or, more often, it is piled into haysheds, for one man can do that alone.

Technological advancement is but compensation for social disintegration. People take jobs. Wire fencing, iron roofs, and metal "wagon roof" haysheds and turfsheds rise to make up for the loss of cooperative capacity. They require cash. More people take jobs. "As you have often heard it said, it was made round to go around."

Artifacts are historical mementos. The gardener turning up the rusted lock of a Tower musket or an old clay pipe, or the turf cutter encountering a platform buried in the bog, reinvent the idea of archaeology and place themselves in history. While making artifacts, transforming nature into tools, people teach themselves one theory of history: evolution. Another theory is learned in story, but men at work heaping hay into sheds, and women at work assembling spuds into dinner, recall past experience through the fingers to evaluate the present and locate themselves in time. From the kitchen, let us take the example of boxty.[6]

Every woman has a slightly different recipe for "boxty bread." The culture's homogeneity leaves room for personal diversity. But Ellen Cutler's is representative. First, peel thinly half a dozen of the biggest potatoes you have. Grate them, not your knuckles, on a can lid in which holes have been punched with a nail. Wring the gratings "oh, so tight until not one taste of water is left" in a strong cloth and mix them with salt and boiled mashed potatoes. Mary McBrien said to add the marzipanlike substance skimmed off the water, and to use equal parts of grated and mashed potatoes. Mrs. Cutler uses a bit more than one mashed potato for every two she grates. Next mix the potatoes with flour, about half as much as there is potato, until the whole becomes "nice and dry," then form it into puck-shaped, circular "hurleys," five inches across and one in depth. To cook they need more water than a saucepan will hold, so fill the big black pot, get the water "mad boilin," and slip the hurleys in, remembering to put a plate in first to prevent them from sticking to the bottom. Keep the hurleys moving with a spoon, and in half an hour they will be white clear through and ready for eating. Boxty is eaten "hot out of the pot" with butter and sugar, or the hurleys are split in two or sliced in strips and fried the next day in "drippins." There are also "boxty cakes," baked rather than boiled, and "boxty pancakes." For them Meta Rooney adds water and mashed potato to the "gratins," while Ellen Cutler uses only grated potatoes, but both women add flour, "a lock of salt, and a wee taste of soda" to make a pancake that you butter while hot. "You'd do yourself harm eatin it," Mrs. Cutler said, "it was that good!"

Boxty is a focus of attention. No other food gets talked about so much. Like thatch, it is conceptually rich.

Boxty is the most radical alteration of the most common food, the most unpotato a potato can be. It represents like a lump of won turf a complete conquest of nature, a total victory of will.

Boxty is both useful and lovely. It is the very type of "strong" food. Mrs. Cutler said, "It was dear bought, but it was worth it. Boxty was a great feed. They were one thing you could fast from early mornin to dark night on." Peter Flanagan used similar words: "Boxty bread was a strong food. You'd eat it of a mornin and wouldn't need food again all day." He supported his assertion by telling of a local woman who always fed her sons boxty before their long day's labor in a factory. At the same time, boxty is delicious. "They're alot of work," Mrs. Cutler said. "They are too much work. But, the Lord, they were lovely." Boxty is so tasty that it became a special, ceremonial food, eaten on Hallow Eve and on Boxing Day. From that happy high point in the Christmas season, Mr. Flanagan feels the food took its name.

Boxty is hard work. "It's not as hard as makin butter," Mrs. Owens said, "but it's quare and hard." So boxty represents the hardship the young wish to escape. In sympathy with weary Odysseus, an oar over his shoulder, a young woman told me her plan was to leave Ireland and search until she found a man who had never heard of boxty. Then she would marry and settle down. To older people the work was worth it. Boxty embodied the local idea of goodness, turning a common substance through complex work into something to please others and carry them on. And the hard work was collective. "Och, there's an awful lot of work at boxty," said Mrs. Cutler, "you'd want help at it." In the past women gathered to make boxty, finding consolation for their work in the pleasure of chatty company. Now, alone in the kitchen, the cook finds the work too hard, and boxty is a thing of the past. It is not, actually, for I have eaten it often and can attest to its rich flavor, but boxty, the cooperative product, is going and therefore gone.

Once again we have entered the kitchen, which is cleaner than ever before but somehow a little empty. In the kitchen and in the fields, in the interdependent realms of men and women, the aspiration to smoothness, to a controlled, willed existence, has created progress in personal comfort (there are machines to mow the hay and cook the food) and regress in social comfort (groups no longer collect to cut the hay or grate the spuds). Homes are clean and closed.

And what is the verdict? There is none in the culture. Decisions are left to individuals. The young have known the old way only in decline. Few of them are ambivalent. Things are better, though not good enough. Lurid magazines and American films have dazzled them with gaudy images. Many leave, young women especially, seeking smoother places. Others stay, mostly young men with an eye on the family farm and a head full of plans for improvement. They are often respectful of the old ways but do not pine for the past. Neither do their elders.

Laments for old times are left to outsiders who need the strength and imagination of country people to save them from the decadence of their own society and who fear the political and economic aspirations of the poor. Wishing to unite the dream of noble and beggar, William Butler Yeats could early declare that a nation's art must be rooted in its folklore and at the end command his fellow poets to sing the peasantry. Yet when the peasant turned real and sought his own creature comfort, the great poet grew resentful. Leader of Ireland's next generation of poets, a man who had learned his trade and tasted the sour clay of farmlife, Patrick Kavanagh understood that only a person with a good roof and a warm car from which to view the heathery bogs can mourn without irony the passing of the old way.[7] The old people of Ballymenone knew that way too well to lament its demise. And they knew it too well to rejoice at its death. Their virtue was forged in the smithy of hardship. They hold no conclusion and alter their opinions of both past and present in accord with the moment's perspective.

Near boredom in the bog, a man straightens above another clamp to stretch his stiff back and survey the wide plain of turf still lying on the spread. Lonesome, he feels the loss of community, and in its loss reads with terror the dissolution of God's control over human affairs. There is no one there to tell him to pause, no one to smoke with, none to help. He bends again and when, hours later, he returns home, its dull metal roof takes his eye. The thatch he tore off last year came of his own mind and hand. It asked no cash. In harmony with God's construction of the earth he planted the corn, sheared, lashed, and laid it into a smooth bright face. The iron roof needs no tending, but it is not lovely; he did not make it, does not deeply understand it. Yes, it tells him he is a success, but its language is alien, its smile remote. Like the tractor in the tin shed and the gas-fired cooker, it nags him to accumulate capital. To stay on the land now, most young men go off the land for most of their lives, adding a job in the town or one on the road to the endless stream of jobs on the farm. To get it done, farmwork must be simplified. It becomes inherently less interesting, and, impatient to get it done, the farmer rushes, pressured and unhappy.

Seated at his hearth, Mr. Owens passes me a cigarette. We settle, a good dinner and long day of clamping behind us, while he tells me that men in the past would work all day, cutting hay with a scythe for a shilling and food. They ate well, whole sideplates of spuds, food so strong it caused nosebleeds, but their wives and children got nothing, seasons came in the year with no work to be had, and the rent on a house was a shilling a week. "When I was a young man, you'd get one and six or two shillings, maybe half a crown for a day's work. And you'd work from seven in the mornin till seven in the evenin."

On the day he married, Hugh Patrick Owens had two shillings to his name. He felt dry and went to Arney for a drink, but a neighbor stood it for him and he returned with his wealth intact. The next morning he carted a crate of turf to town. "You had to get up early to get the trade," and a crate, a cartload, brought only four bob, but he worked on, "cadging" the turf he cut, and purchased an adjacent farm of nine acres to bring his holding to thirty acres. He has thirty cows, ten for milking, and a car parked on the street. His children have prospered in the larger world. One son is the manager of a supermarket in Larne. Two daughters and a son are doing well in London. Another daughter has a good job in Enniskillen. His youngest son, Michael, is a success in school, and T. P., who is twenty-nine, has taken over the farm. "I'm beaten and broken, I'm hangin it up." At sixty-five, Mr. Owens has just retired. He has hawked turf, milked cows, and poured his life into the damp black dirt to gain his portion. We sit in his clean, thatched house, smoking, while Mr. Owens, a compact, powerful man who played left forward for the Bellanaleck football team for twenty-five years, tells me with characteristic steely realism:

"Things are much better now.

"Now you won't get rich. But you won't starve. At one time you would. Oh aye, you would.

"And we have Hitler to thank for that. It has nothin to do with this

War. But Hitler was a kind man that didn't want people to work so hard. He got the wheels of industry goin and they have never cooled. He wanted everyone to have a car and a good life. Because he started it then, there has been a great change and a great improvement.

"When people talk about the good old days, it is because they have forgotten that they never had a cigarette then or a ride in a car.

"Aye, life is much easier now."

PART SIX

Patterns of Historical Action

17

The Man Who Would Not
Carry Hay

At work on the bog, discovering a relic within it, noting its wide emptiness, the turf cutter locates himself in history.

Seeing history, recognizing change is only a matter of staying alert. While he sharpened scollops for John Drumm to use in thatching his roof, Bob Lamb told me of the time he and Peter Flanagan were hired to cut scras for a man planning to extend his thatched house. To transport the sod from the bog, they borrowed an ass and cart from Gabriel Dorsey, a young man with whom I had rooked hay. When Gabey came where they were working, cutting the scras in ten-foot lengths, double the width of a spade blade, P told him to stop and watch because he would be the only man of his generation to see that work carried on. Thatchers today rework old roofs. Though he has thatched hundreds, Joe Murphy told me he had never begun one. Bob and P were cutting the last scras for thatching. Later I brought my son, Harry, to climb the ladder and sit on Bob's rooftop while Mr. Drumm thatched and across the road Mr. McGovern worked the meadow with ass and cart, its wheels flashing in the sun. I told Harry the same thing: to watch closely, for some day he might be the only man alive to remember such a scene.

As it happens, change is noted. Then it is shot to its limit in the mind, so its course can be traced in the present. Work's impulse to conservative extension is exaggerated in the freer realm of conversation where the passing becomes passed: "There's not a man on the bog." William Lunny, who cycles to Enniskillen and even Sligo and was amused by my un-American habit of walking everywhere, told me a "yarn" to underscore the laziness of modern people and poke a little fun at his own generation's hyperbolic formulations. Its punch line repeats a conventional complaint. A young husband comes home from his job to find his wife proudly teaching their toddler to walk. He asks what she is doing and, when told, replies, "Sure, that's a waste of time. Nobody walks any more."

Change is the normal state of human affairs. History, like the weather, is an inescapable condition. It must be watched so life can be adjusted to its power.

Whether their plans will be wrecked by climatic or historical forces, people propose them with equal caution. Catholics usually say, "God willing" or "please God"; the Latin "D.V." is rare. Protestants say, "All bein well." But no one speaks of the future without attaching to their hopeful assertions clauses admitting final impotence. "We will meet the morrow, God willing." "The hay will be saved be Sunday, all bein well." When orientation is retrospective, God is thanked for success, and failures are written off to His unfathomable will. As much as the weather, history is God's to know, ours to endure.

But history is not exactly like the weather. Winds blow straight from heaven. History's forces are transferred by human agents. Hugh Patrick Owens said Rose Murphy once told a neighbor how glad she was her parents got the old-age pension. "We should thank God," she said. "Don't thank God atall," he replied:

Bless the goose that grew the quill
That signed the Old Age Pension Bill.

That bid locates cause precisely. History's agents are people, but normally so removed from us that they are lost as individuals, merged into a power nearly as imponderable as God's. It is not Parliament, much less one of its obscure particular members, that deserves thanks, but the body of a goose nonchalantly oozing feathers through its skin.

History's causes are weirdly remote, so though its course is apparent, the individual's role within it is not. War is waged against God's environment with the farmer's weapons, and certainly the human climate of history need not be received meekly. It is observed, clarified through exaggeration, evaluated, and exposed for rebellion. The rebel's opponents are, like himself, members of a fallen race, not to be trusted without question, so he cannot resist his own will. Even the Saint rebels against regal verdict, follows his own feelings, and brings death upon his fellows and exile upon himself. Like the farmer and saint, the rebel has no assurance and no option save action.

One mode of historical action parallels the farmer's conserving and extending. The human scene is read after the manner of the climate, and a rebellion is framed that alters old patterns, cleans them up, and urges progress forward. James Owens told me the story of such an event. We were having a cup of tea and talking about the house that sheltered us, when he said:

"The brick that built this house was made down there below. And the only transport they had was a creel on your back. Carried them up on a creel.

"Now you imagine all the brick that's in this house—to carry them in a *creel* on your *back*.

"They had no other way.

"And they used to carry the hay in on their back.

"There would be a man out in the field and that was his job: tyin up. He tied up the load for ye, *put it on your back*, do ye see, and away you went. Of course there might be five or six of them at this now.

"Well, there was only one horse cart in this country.

"It was down at the Ford there.

"And this man went this day to put in hay.

"He says, I'm goin to carry no hay and a horse standin up in the stable doin nothin.

"*Strike*. He went on *strike*; he went on strike.

"And they put the horse in the cart and they drew in the hay.

"Well, that ended the carryin of the hay.

"Imagine a horse standin up in a stable, and a cart, and carryin the hay on your back. Now didn't they do foolish things?"

Annie, his sister, who had been sitting with us and listening, commented in the silence that followed: "Well, they had no proper gaps." And Mr. Owens continued:

"They had no gaps. What you went in through was only the width of a cow, do ye see. And they had it ditched in and they didn't want the bother of levelin this down.

"That ended the carryin; wouldn't do it for you now."

There should be more stories like James Owens'. That there are not reveals the remove of history. Evolution from creel to cart to tractor is caused by people. Sometimes they are, like the man who would not carry hay, local people. Usually they are not, and the climate history kicks up is more circumstance than creation for Ballymenone.

Since human creation is structured subordinately within circumstance, history envelops the individual whose task is to reason out of hunger. Evolutionary history—that which combines with the environment to shape economic enterprise and condition individual comfort—set around the people of the past a constant ring of difficulty.

The people of the present erect two eras of hardship out of the past and talk about them often to contemplate the role of people, real people like themselves, in history. One is the Days of the Landlords. The other is the Famine. Matters for chat, occasions for story, both help shape through memory patterns of modern action.

18

The Days of the Landlords

The dread Famine, sweeping a quarter of Ireland's population into death or exile, was the crucial event of modern history, but its message is not complex. People speak more frequently of the Days of the Landlords. As usual, I will rely on Hugh Nolan to provide us with a full, clear account of that era. Twice he told me its history. Though his accounts rose from different topics—building materials first, place names later—he began both at the ruins of a manse on Drumbargy Brae, just above the cutover bog that lies across Rossdoney Lane from his front door. Then he carried both of them from the Plantation through the administrative organization of the landlord's estate, into the geography of the demesne that included the District, arcing in a southwesterly strip from Lough Erne to Benaughlin. Only his first account reached the conclusion of the Land League's victory, and that follows, but since—remarkably—his two descriptions were structured identically, I take the liberty of patching in a few sentences from the second, amplifying without distorting his statement:

"There used to be old mansions, do ye know, that had decayed and that had fallen, and they were generally all built with stone. Well, them stones wouldn't want so much dressin. And then there was people had them old ruins on their land. And they could get a house built handy.

"I mind there was a mansion
      up in Drumbargy
         in days gone by.

"And it was a gentleman's residence. It was just beside John Carson's. I saw the ruins of it. Well, it wasn't standin when I seen it, but the stones it was built with was all there.

"And I mind John Carson's uncles, they got an office-house built out of the ruins of this. It was a whole stone *buildin*.

"It was just beside Missus Carson's. When you was goin forward to Missus Carson's *house*, this mansion was on your *right*, just where the plantation is *now*.

"I'll tell you who he was. He must have been a Frenchman.

"And I'll tell you what he was. He was a clergyman, a Church of Ireland clergyman. And he was what they called a middleman.

"After the Plantation of Ulster, the lands was given be the king to the gentry, to English and Scotch settlers.

"And they'd be what they called *landlords*.

"Well, some of them didn't come to Ireland atall to live. But these what they called the middlemen, *they* took the land from the landlords at a rent, do ye see. And then they set it then in small farms and in large farms to *tenants*, do ye see. That'd be the common people.

"Well, there was alot of them middlemen. They were livin here and there through the country. This man lived in Drumbargy. This man, he was LaDew. He was a William LaDew. That's a French name. Well then there was another of these middlemen and he lived in Tonyheig. He was the name of Acheson. And different other places there was men of that type.

"Well, this LaDew, he owned Drumbargy and Rossdoney, and whether he owned any more possessions elsewhere, I can't tell ye. But he had this taken from whoever the landlord was at that time. The landlord might have been in London or some other place. And he lived in this house, up on the top of the hill.

"So after some time, them men went out of existence, and the houses was unoccupied and finally they fell and *disappeared*.

"And the middlemen faded away and it was back in the landlords' hands again, and then there was *agents* appointed then for to collect the rents. And there was another position in connection with it: the bailia. There was a man that would be in every district that used to watch the tenants, do ye see, and not let them be abusin the land or doin any harm.

"The bailia—or bailiff—they weren't liked at all. They were hated; they were hated.

"He was under the agent. The agent was under the landlord, and the bailia was under the agent.

"I just don't know whether these type of men was on all the estates or not, but they were on the Schoolands anyway. Do ye see: after some time it was the Commissioners of Education bought this estate that Rossdoney's on, and Drumbargy, and it was known from that as the Schoolands.

"There has been changes all down the ages. And whoever that the landlord was that this LaDew had the land taken from, maybe his family became extinct, and that it was taken over be the Commissioners of Education.

"Well then, there was a man lived up at Ballyconnell. He was—aw, he was a gentleman. He was the agent. And then these other boys was a-*watch-in* for him, and if you cut a tree or done anything like that, do ye see, it went to the agent and from him to the landlord and it could be the cause of you bein evicted. Aye.

"At one time there lived a bailiff in that house beside Andy Boyle's, the Keenans', and there was a bailiff there for a while.

"And there was a bailiff at a cross on the Swad Road.

"Do ye see, the course that this demesne took, it started here on the shores of Lough Erne, and it took a vein with it nearly up to Swanlinbar.

"Sometimes it was very narrow and sometimes it widened out, do ye see. It took a kind of a bend and Sessiagh and Derrychurra was a part of this estate. And how them two townlands got to be part of the Schoolands is what I don't know, for I never heard, nor—of course, I suppose, if I had been interested enough in it when the old people was all livin, they might have been able to give some explanation about it, but I came to the conclusion that it was a *purchase*, that the Commissioners of Education, *or* whoever owned the Schoolands before they got it, that them townlands was a purchase that they made.

"Well, then there was other demesnes then on both sides of it owned be landlords. The Schoolands would lie between Cole's demesne and Kinawley. Lord Enniskillen owned Clontymullan and on up towards the Hangin Rock; that was all Cole's demesne.

"And there was some of these demesnes and they were just owned be men that raised, well, be *good pull* and be industry that had got to be landowners, do ye see. But it was the Commissioners of Education that owned this at the time that the Land Acts came along that the landlords were all disqualified or paid off. The Agitation started and finally the government took the land over. And the people got what they called Tenant Right. They got to be owners of whatever land they possessed. They could sell it or keep it or will it or do what they liked.

"Well, there was some of them estates remained in the hands of the landlords for some time after the Agitation. And then they got what they called *bought out*—bought out be the government, do ye see.

"There had to be acts passed, do ye see, in Parliament, do ye see, for to take the land from these and compensate them, do ye see.

"So the government compensated these owners and then they fixed a rate then on the land for takin it away. So the people was payin that on till whatever the government had gave for the land. When they got it back, do ye see, the land was rent free.

"How that happened was: there started what they called the Land League in Ireland. And that was a movement against the landlords. Their points was that the rents was too *high* and that the conditions wasn't suitable to the people and so on. And that Agitation went on and went on and finally the government took it over and set it out.

"It was a campaign, do ye know, a campaign for to relieve the farmin class.

"It was considered a wonderful victory."

Honestly admitting, "I have a fairly good knowledge of history," Mr. Nolan has given us a clean account. It carries attitudes as well as facts, but, as is so characteristic of his work, it strains toward an objective ideal. To be

Auchenleck Memorial. A memento of the Days of the Landlords, the
Auchenleck Memorial of 1680 remains in Cleenish Parish Church,
Bellanaleck.

fair he overcompensates, remarking that some landlords attained position by industry. He restrains opinion, submerging his own feelings about the bailiffs and the agent, Bennison, just beneath the surface of words. He labels speculations as his own and uncertain: perhaps LaDew owned more than Drumbargy and Rossdoney; perhaps Sessiagh and Derrychurra were absorbed by purchase into the Schoolands.[1] His statement is passive, disengaged. Acts are passed, campaigns conducted, bailiffs hated nearly without human agency. At once that expresses Mr. Nolan's vision of history rolling beyond control and reveals his scholarly wish to present the facts without cluttering emotion. The facts are enough. Response is not dictated.

More typical of the District's feelings about the Days of the Landlords are those of Hugh Patrick Owens of Sessiagh. His account is less complete, less cool, less broken from our days, but it remains historically set and informative:

"The land through here was what they called the School Lands. It run from Lough Erne to Binn Mountain. And the agent was a man the name of Bennison; he collected the money at Ballyconnell, up in County Cavan.

"Do ye see: the land was all owned by landlords.

"See, they all had big estates for themselves. They had big crops. And they'd come by and if you wanted to save your wee harvest, they could order you away to theirs, leavin yours to rot. That's the way it went on for hundreds of years.

"At that time, you could make no will. When you died your family could be out on the road in a week.

"And the landlords are bound to rackrent.

"So, they fought the landlords for ages. They formed up the Land League and they called big meetins. And they marched here and there and agitated, the same as they are doin at the present time, to show the government they were all in favor of this thing. They had bands and banners and they made speeches.

"Now, that's the way they done it: they organized and held big meetins.

"And they got rid of the landlords. The government bought them out, you see, and gave you a tenant rate on the land. And then you'd pay rent to the government. And the government gave them a big reduction. The rent was half or less than half of what it was before. And they couldn't be evicted.

"You got a receivable order, do ye see, and you went to the bank in Enniskillen in May and November and you paid your half a year's rent.

"Before that you could be evicted any time. And they did it. They did it.

"And there was no reason to improve your property. You couldn't own it or sell it. You had no deed.

"It was the first great victory ever they got was to get rid of the landlords.

"Before that, the landlord came and if he seen a decent cake of bread on your table, you could be out on the road Monday mornin.

"Oh aye."

Mr. Owens' statement is not so much history as historical commentary. It alternates between situation and response. The situation was bad: the oppressive environment created by the landlords after the Plantation of Ulster, beginning in 1609. The response was rebellion: the successful campaign of the Land League, beginning in 1879. Sadly, nothing in oppressive situations fates them to eradication through rebellion. Situation and response are linked, not by moral historical law, but by frail, fleshy human beings. The Land League's Agitation was a peasant revolt that worked. Since its mode is comparable to the Civil Rights Movement out of which the current Troubles boiled, it is a ripe topic for discussion, and the historical link between situation and response can be explored by examining the character of the inhabitants of the Days of the Landlords.

Landlordism was a system, but as Hugh Nolan emphasized, it was a system dependent on individuals. Even if the landlords were absent, the middlemen, agents, and bailiffs were not. They lived right here. And they were Christians. William LaDew (Michael Boyle gave him the name Gladeau) was a clergyman. Since they were Christians, Peter Flanagan said, they had received a divine commandment to treat their fellows well. Yet they did not; Lord Cole rackrented the tenants and threatened to toss the Swad Chapel. So they could be opposed, fought, and justly murdered.

Often we cease thinking by erecting superorganic explanations, making culture a determinant of conduct and people pawns of history. While recognizing that individuals and groups have their own ways of goin on, the District's people do not believe culture overpowers reason in such a way as to excuse evil. The most firmly committed among them will debate whether the courageous acts of patriotic men condemn them to eternal hellfire, and most believe they do.

Snug in Tommy Gilleece's bright pub at Arney, Ned Cooney and Peter Flanagan were talking about the Days of the Landlords when Mr. Cooney said his father and P's were worked beyond bearing and treated "like slaves out of Africa." That comparison stung, because another man in another pub had just told me the tale of one of his ancestors who shipped on a slaver, sailing between Africa and America, but, horrified by the system his work supported, he jumped ship in a foreign port at great peril to himself. Carrying cultural relativism past the breaking point, the historian might find it convenient to describe the slaveholder as only the normal practitioner of accepted tradition. But one Southern farmer freeing his slaves (and more than one did) proved it was possible to say No. Holding slaves was saying Yes. It was cultural, and it was immoral. Culture does not determine. The landlords cannot be excused. Their humanity made them conscious. Their Christianity made them culpable.

The landlords were responsible. So were the people encased in their economy. The tenants were obliged to rebel. But it is not that simple. The less obvious complication arose from divisiveness stimulated by the ruling elite. Here is Peter Flanagan's explanation:

"There were tenants that sided with the landlords. They weren't much liked in this country. Ah, they were not.

"They got backhand or castle money, as the word was.

"There was the Lord Lieutenant's office in Dublin at that time, and they would pay these people to follow the landlord. Then you and I, we would disagree, and there would rise anger between us and the tenants that got this backhand money.

"That's a trouble that is still with us at the present time. The rich men don't want to loss their good jobs, or their power, and they keep the poor class of people split apart and fightin.

"That's the way, now."

The chief reason for the long absence of political resistance was not intrigue or unawareness but finite energy. It took all one's strength to war with the climate and pull through another day. Everyday heroism is the point of the one story used to illustrate life in the Days of the Landlords. Diverse and abundant conversation surrounds that era, but thought funnels through one tale, often cited, widely known.

The shape of my education in Ballymenone should be clear. My teachers have chosen roles that suit their personalities and interlock to provide a comprehensive understanding. For full, balanced, historical accounts, we go to Hugh Nolan. Hugh Patrick Owens supplies the tough comment. Peter Flanagan reveals the moral issue. Michael Boyle has the story.

Like his comrade Hugh Nolan, Michael Boyle passed the time of youth listening to old people tell of days gone by. One of them was the woman whose trek to Ballyconnell gives the District its tale of life under the landlords:

"There was old men about, and the people didn't get information enough off them, do ye see. People could have learned far more of the olden days from the older people.

"Now, I remember an old woman in our country.

"She was the name of Timoney. She'd be some friend of Jimmy, the present Jimmy Tumblety's. She lived where Tommy Love's livin; that's where she lived.

"And she had a wee farm. Her husband had it. Her husband died when she had three of a family, two girls and a boy.

"And her husband died when her family was small, do ye see.

"She had to go out the best she could. As well as doin the wee bit of housework, she had to go out to the field and labor with the spade, tryin to earn a little money, put in a crop to try to rear the wee family.

"And the rate of that land in Rossdoney had to be paid to a man, that Bennison, John Joe Bennison of Ballyconnell.

"You had to go beside Ballyconnell Town, and you had a big lot of hours to walk; there was no other way of goin thattime.

"She had the rate ready for to go to Bennison's this day,
>   and she out to Bennison's
>   and when she arrived at Bennison's,
>   she was late.

"Her name was sent down to Enniskillen to the Crown Solicitor to serve her with the Provost; well then, he could bring her to court.

"The clerk at Bennison's office told her, says he:

"If you could get to Enniskillen
>   before three o'clock the day
>   you'd save the costs;
>   they wouldn't put the costs on.

"So she set out from Ballyconnell,
>   and she walked down to Enniskillen
>   after walkin from Rossdoney to Ballyconnell.

"She set out and she walked from Ballyconnell to Enniskillen
>   and she was there before three o'clock
>   and she saved the costs.

"And when she had it all paid, she had one shillin in her pocket.

"One shillin.

"And she bought a quarter stone of oatmeal,
>   and a pound of sugar with the shillin.

"And she walked home to Rossdoney,
>   and she made a noggin of what they call gruel.

"It's great stuff, gruel, a great reviver. It's made out of oatmeal. It twasn't made as thick as porridge; it's made nice and thin. It's the same as sowens, only it's tastier than sowens, and she sweetened it well with sugar.

"And she took a great feed of that and went to bed,
>   and got up the next mornin
>   and went out on a hill
>   with the spade
>   and dug lea
>   the whole day
>   after the whole walk.

"Didn't that old woman live to be ninety. I remember *her*. I *remember* her, and was talkin to her often.

"And she was only a small woman. I remember her. I think I can see her yet: she wore a wee white cap over her head always, and Irish lace trimmed round it, and tied with a nice wee bow here, and she wore what they call a shawl-handkerchief over her shoulders.

"She lived to be over ninety years of age. I remember the time she died. I was often talkin to her. She remembered the tail end of the Famine, the famine that was in Ireland in forty-six. She remembered that. Them times were terrible.

"Her father was a shoemaker, and I used to remember her sayin she'd have to go to Enniskillen a couple of times a week to buy leather for him and, well, stuff, nails and spriggs for the boots; for he was the shoemaker. They called him Mickey the Warrior. Mickey the Warrior was the name they had on him.

"And, aye, she used to say she saw people lyin along the road just exhausted with pure hunger. Aye. Oh, I remember her sayin she remembered the tail of the Famine.

"She was married to this man, Timoney. Her name was McGiveney. She was some friend of that Hugh McGiveney. She was."

Normally, Mr. Boyle's delivery is excited and quick, but he slowed this telling, wearying his voice, dragging, making it ache in sympathy with Mrs. Timoney's ordeal. With no exaggeration, her tale presents the extreme case. She personifies the fortitude of all the poor in those hard times, compacting their strength in her body, expanding heroically, yet without fancy, to tell the plight of them all. She endured both the Famine and the Days of the Landlords. She was a small person with a small holding, she was mother and father, homemaker and farmer and tenant. She had to take time from her great responsibilities to walk forty miles in one day to pay her rent. Her reward was a shilling. Her consolation was a bowl of gruel. But with characteristic appreciation for simple, accessible delights, Mr. Boyle says gruel is great. It gave her a small pleasure, then carried her into another day's hard work. She endured. No other tale is needed. Hers tells it all.

I heard about her first when Hugh Nolan told me the original owner of Tommy Love's house was a man named McGiveney, a relative of the McGiveneys of the Hollow, the family of the great star. On his death the farm descended to his daughter, who married a grand-uncle of the postman Jimmy Timoney, whose farm mearns William Lunny's in Rossdoney. Years passed before I asked Mr. Nolan if he knew the story. His answer came quickly:

"I seen that woman meself. I *knew her*.
"And the way the story went:
"The people had to go to Ballyconnell to pay their rate.
"And she was a poor widow-woman.
"And she had just the rate gathered up.
"And she had to go some business to Town, to Enniskillen first.
"So she came to Enniskillen here and she done whatever business she had to transact.

"And she got, I think,
    a bowl of soup.

"She couldn't afford to get any more because she'd have to break in the rate.

"And she started out of Enniskillen,
    and she walked to Ballyconnell,
        and walked back to Rossdoney again.

"It was a terror.

"Well that would be in the beginnin of the nineteenth century.

"Oh, I seen the woman. I seen the woman.

"At this time that she done this Remarkable Walk, her husband was dead. And she had two little girls, and they were only *children*.

"Well, when I came to know her, she was livin with the son-in-law and a single daughter.

"It was in the house where Tommy Love lived."

The tale of Mrs. Timoney's Remarkable Walk describes the oppressive situation and celebrates the courage it took to live through it. At the same time, calmly the story holds motive for response. Perhaps it was used to rouse men of the past into action. It keeps them awake today.

A rainy Twelfth of August had chilled the men of the Black Preceptory as they marched through Enniskillen, and once their pipes and drums had stilled, they abandoned the wet streets, retreating into the warm interiors of public houses. In one of them I sit by the wall, late in day's drinking with an old man from the District who had come to Town to "take a deck" at the parade. Across the shop, men in black suits and bowlers and collarettes crowd loudly at the bar. They are not the same as the Orangemen, he tells me, for these gentlemen, "lookin so fine in their gloves and hard hats," represent the Protestant minority that really owns Ulster, while the members of the Orange Lodges who tramped these streets a month ago are only, like himself, members of "the three-fifths," the real working majority.

As we drain yet another stout into ourselves and they thicken happily along the counter, old pains and past history rise. He turns deep, sad eyes from them back into my face, saying mildly, evenly, "I'd like to take a gun and shoot the bloody shit out of every one of them."

With a cheery nod, a man returning to the table next to ours deposits two black bottles of stout before us. They stand. His eyes hold steady and he goes on:

"They are the Planters. And this is our country. They came into it, drivin us into the hills and the hollows, lettin us live as we could. In the hills and in the valleys. On the bad land.

"They depressed us. It was depressin.

"The landlords racked us.

"There was an old woman and she had only twelve acres of flooded land. And her rate was eight pounds. Eight pounds.

"And she had one pair of shoes, a middlin pair of shoes, and she would throw them over her shoulder and walk all the way to Ballyconnell and pay her eight pounds.

"And if there was anything left, if there was a penny or a ha'penny, she'd buy a loaf and carry it home.

"That was all she got: one loaf of bread, two times a year.

"It makes your blood boil, so it does.

"There was no Republican thoughts them days, do ye see, and the greatest victory for Ireland was getting the Tenant Right.

"But things are not improved. Oh no. When they say things are the best, I say they are not, and it's still depressin."

He points to a man at the bar. The spirit is high, the body unsure.

"If that man goes out of here drunk, he will go on. But let one of our side show a drop of drink on him, and he'll be taken down the street. Oh aye. He'll be taken to the depot.

"It's depressin. And that's what they're fightin for now.

"For too long they have been walked on.

"But now they are standin up."

His eyes move off, then lower to the table. He tilts his bottle, and stout rises slowly under its head. A laugh cracks among the clink and chatter within the mirrored blue smoke at the bar. He lifts his glass in a thick hard hand and says, not loudly but not quietly either, "Up our side." The men in black at the bar continue, and he carries his full glass to the next table, leans over it, and repays the drink's donor, a distant relative, with a joke about Pat, Mike, and sexual numbskullery.

Mrs. Timoney's story is complete. It begins, ends, and in the renditions by Mr. Boyle and Mr. Nolan presents a specific event. But it spurs no catharsis, contains no resolution. It slices a piece out of time. Days like the one within the tale stretch behind and ahead, so the telling on the night of the Black Preceptory's parade could be framed generally. The story records past hardship—life would be bad enough without the landlords making it worse—and records it with such clarity that it calls for action beyond story. Eventually the Land League would conclude Mrs. Timoney's tale. In the meantime, she works on, walks on, without help. But there is another on the stage: Black Francis.

Black Francis and Mrs. Timoney were never, in my hearing, linked in performance. But they live in the same generic frame, stories of history. Though they represent extremes—she of situation, he of response—they were real people. They did not occupy the same moment. Black Francis was hanged in the eighteenth century. Mrs. Timoney lived into the twentieth. But they lived in the same era. His land, like hers, had been taken by the Planters. Her response was to endure, his was to help "poor widow-women" like her.

Black Francis rides and plunders to express the hunger of the dispossessed. He is a leader of men bound to him with a bond like betrothal. He robs landlords to give money to peasants unable to meet their tenant rates. As a leader, dedicated to socioeconomic justice, Black Francis is a political being, a forerunner of the Land League's organizers.

Black Francis stands against the landlords. They were gentlemen in name, he was a gentleman in deed. They exploited the weak, he protected them. Their goal was profit, his was justice. Whatever he was in his own day, Black Francis exists in today's history to expose the evil in a legal system. By saying No, he shows the landlords were saying Yes, were guilty. By saying No, he shows that others can too, that the personages of history are not beasts lacking will, but human beings.

Ballymenone's repertory of historical tale is parsimonious and precise. The grievance of the tenants is compressed into one story about one woman. One man embodies the limit of redress possible during the period of preparation before victory. Black Francis and Mrs. Timoney fit together to reveal the pattern of action in the Days of the Landlords. There were other choices. One was collaboration. Some tenants took castle money. Another was escape. Leaping the Sillees and abandoning his treasure, Souple Corrigan made his way to America to become one of millions of emigrants. Those who stayed and acted properly, those who posed legitimate models for the District's people, found themselves shocked into awareness between the poles represented by Mrs. Timoney and Black Francis: endurance and rebellion.

God made the world. Patiently one must endure. Endurance means living in all seasons and work without end, but in even the worst situations work brings consolation, the bowl of gruel, the bit of crack. The farmer passes the time.

Men rule the world. Impatiently one must rebel. Rebellion means responsible action on behalf of those who share your predicament, but until victory is won, rebellion will carry beyond law into death. The hero becomes outlaw becomes martyr.

The border drawn across Ireland means the era begun with the Plantation has not ended in Ulster. Contemporary conditions, though vastly improved—"Aye, life is much easier now," Mr. Owens said—remain for some comparable to those of the Days of the Landlords: "It's still depressin." Alive today with extreme cases out of the past argued in one story on each side, people hold no option for unawareness. They cannot plead ignorance and are forced by conscience and the will to survive to formulate a life between rebellion and endurance, between pulling the self through and sacrificing it to the common good.

19

The Famine

The Days of the Landlords and the Famine are not sequential periods but distinct historical foci within a single era of hardship. We will be taken far toward an understanding of the Famine's force in the modern mind by learning its history from Hugh Nolan. I recorded nothing else quite like this. "History," not "story," it proceeds without lingering on specific events or people, yet its pace and clarity, its verbal precision and overall order, mark it as a performance, a story in style if not in structure. Our attention is trapped as he works slowly to create, uniquely, an artful unit compassing great sweeps of time:

"You see:
"In days gone by,
       but it's a very long time since,
    there was no such crop in Ireland as spuds.
"The spuds was imported.
"It was one of Queen Elizabeth's generals, at the time that they were a-conquerin Ireland. To the best of my opinion, it was. He brought the spuds, he brought the spuds to Ireland.
"And the first place they were grew, I think, was in County Cork.
"Well, before that, it was wheat, oats, and barley that was the crops that used to be put in. There might be vegetables too, but there was no such thing as spuds.
"So, these crops, they gave great employment. They were all put in with spades and loyas. And then there was a big job then
      at the cuttin of them
      and the gatherin of them
      and the lashin and the thrashin of them
        and till they had it ready for the mills.
"Well then, there was a lot of mills in Ireland at that time.
"And they were all workin, with a fairly big staff.
"Well, there was no such thing as tea
        in them days.
"*But*, if you were travelin *there*,

there was what they called along the roadsides:

there was *inns*.

"That was places where you could get a meal.

"Well there was at one time in Ireland that you could get a wonderful great meal of *milk*, and either wheaten bread or oaten bread. There used to be oaten bread made. There was irons for bakin in them days. The women used to wet the oatmeal and make it into the shape of a cake, do ye know.

"And these irons went round the fire.

"And this bread baked hard.

"And you wanted to have good teeth.

"But it was lovely with butter.

"Well, in them days you could get a wonderful great meal of sweet milk,

either wheaten bread or oaten bread,

well buttered,

for tuppence,

if you were travelin.

"Well, the pretties was introduced. And it was discovered that one man could put in durin the spring as much spuds as would do his household till thattime twelvemonth. And if he had extras they could be give to cattle and pigs.

"Well, the *oat*—

the *corncrop*—

and the *wheatcrop*,

and the *barley*,

it died out.

"And it caused a wonderful lot of emigration. Because these men that was workin in these mills had to quit, do ye see, when there was nothin for them to do, do ye see. So these men had to emigrate to foreign countries.

"So then, the prettie crop, it got very common.

"And there was two famines.

"There's not so much talked about the first famine. The first famine, I think, was about the year of seventeen and forty. It was a failure in the potato crop. Because they were livin principally on the potatoes.

"There were some used to have a lock of oats. And they'd take their breakfast of porridge. And then they'd have the dinner of spuds. And then before they'd go to bed at night, they'd have another feed of spuds. And they had plenty of sweet milk of coorse then at the same time.

"But these two years, the potato crop was a total failure.

"And they had nothing to eat.

"And alot of them died.

"Well then in eighteen and forty-six then came the second part of the famine.

"And it was a *worse*—a worse famine. Because the population of Ireland had riz at that time to eight million.

"So.

"Aw, they died in scores.

"Britain was blamed.

"They had wheat and meal and other things that they could let out and didn't.

"So anyway, between *death and emigration*, when the Famine was over, it was down to about four million.

"So it has never riz since.

"So there was relief works was started here and there durin the time of the Famine. But then, do ye see, the men wasn't able to work because they had nothin to eat.

"So it was a terrible calamity.

"And the result of it is to be felt to this day.

"Emigration: any of them that was able to leave the country, they went out of it. And then emigration started wholesale. And as soon as young men grew up, they were away. That's how there's so many Irish in America. In Australia. These countries that took in emigrants."

Mr. Nolan stops, snaps a match, and pulls its flame into his pipe. He tied cause and effect neatly together, making emigration his theme. In some times the potato led to fewer jobs, in others to starvation, but in all times the potato produced emigration. Deftly he connected the present to the Elizabethan conquest of Ireland, thus tying in the Plantation, which followed the Flight of the Earls at the end of that conquest, locating the Famine within the Days of the Landlords and politicizing the whole of recent Irish history. I sit in silent admiration of the way he wove one crisply patterned web of political, military, social, and economic strands. He lets smoke drift from his lips and, lifting his eyes from the fire to catch mine, begins again:

"So now, if you were talkin to a more intelligent person than me, people that had read more, they could tell ye more about it, but that's a rough outline of it.

"The cause of the Famine was: the failure in the potato crop. And then there was no foreign stuff comin in, do ye see.

"And then:

death and misery.

"Do ye see: at the present time, with exception of a meal in the day, it's all foreign produce that the people's usin. Foreign wheat and all the necessaries of life is comin from abroad; only just one meal in the day of spuds is as much as any person now will relish, do ye see. And not very many of them. Well, in them days I'm tellin you about before this famine two men could sit down at a big side dish of spuds and not leave one of them on it. They used to eat them to *butter* and *milk*.

"Men got oatmeal gruel for roadwork, durin the Famine. And there was fish and there'd be meat too. But it wasn't easy for the poor to have money to buy it.

"They were stricken the both ways. They were stricken for the want of gettin the food. And then they hadn't enough money to buy whatever kind of stuff was goin.

"There wasn't much in this country except fish that you could get handy. Well, I suppose anyone that had pork, they could kill a pig. But then you can't eat bacon its lone. You want something along with it. It's an accompaniment to some other class of food. You wouldn't just start and eat away—it twouldn't be any good to ye.

"So it was the introduction of the potato crop that caused this misery. "Ah now."

Memory of the Famine remains on the land in the empty ruins and masonry mounds of abandoned homes. Famine opened the floodgates of emigration, and neither Ireland nor this small place in Fermanagh has regained the strength of its population. Emigration weakened the community before war broke it. In 1841, before the Famine, the population of Fermanagh was 156,481. By 1851 it had fallen by a quarter to 116,047. In 1971 it lay at 49,960.[1]

Through the Famine, history comes home to the gut, spins fears for the brain, and provides a terrible past to the farmer's future. As he works the dirt, looking ahead without certainty, the Famine contains the extreme of his anxiety. It is not some delicate, preposterous economic system that depends upon his success. People, history proves, can starve to death.

A meal is a victory. A bowl of gruel saved Mrs. Timoney and the stonebreakers of Famine times. Today's dinner, cabbages and spuds again, might seem unenticing to people with no memory of want, but it will do for people raised among men and women who remembered when local people, Hugh Nolan said, "were often in that state that they'd have to tackle raw vegetables to appease the hunger," when a woman walked all the way from Tyrone to buy Rossdoney's last head of cabbage, when emaciated travelers lay along the roadside, exhausted and dying.

Bluestone spray protects the spuds from mould, but the black frost still descends on the moss, rains beat down on the meadows, money is scarce, and the Famine persists in the minds of the older people. So they take delight in simple food. "The old rough country feed is best," P Flanagan proclaimed, "it really is. Fadge bread. Pretties. A little bacon and cabbage. It's the best." So they shop frequently and spend cautiously, buying only what they need, buying today exactly what they bought yesterday, keeping the larder full and their modest treasure banked in a hidden box. So they ration themselves to be sure that many of last year's potatoes remain when this year's are ready for the pot, and they grow diverse varieties of cabbage, fresh all year round. So they take five or six small meals daily, assuring themselves of plenty and passing the time in preparation and eating, rather than stuffing consumption into a few large meals, luxurious of food and economical of time. "I wouldn't be happy," Mrs. Cutler said, "without me wee picks and bits all the day long."

And so food is often served to the mind in song and story. Peter Flanagan's fireside song for children, "The Field Mouse's Birthday Ball," and his comical song, "The Irish Jubilee," both set food at the center of sociability, at the height of rare celebration. Food is festive—and necessary. The sick deer in Mr. Flanagan's example starves. Fed, Mrs. Timoney makes it into another day of toil. The loss of food accompanies defeat. English men drowned with their "resource" at the Ford of Biscuits, trying vainly to get victuals to their starving comrades in Enniskillen. In Mr. Nolan's telling of Mackan Fight, sowens spilled from Scarlett's wounds. Mrs. Timoney's opposite, he could not receive his oaten reward, and life left him. Food creates personal and social health. Bread, tea, and smoke enter the body as words leave to establish lasting bonds. The jilted suitor at Maxwell's Ball thought buying food for a woman would join her to him in love. Essential to life— entertainment—given and taken as secular communion, food steams with meaning, hunger cries with power, and a source of sustenance is the topic of the District's lone tale of the Famine. It is Michael Boyle's:

"There was a man named McBrien.
"He lived somewhere in Rossdoney, in the Point of Rossdoney as they call it.
"And he had a *wife*
    and five children,
        five young children.
"And they hadn't a haet; there was no food,
    there was no food,
        and they were in a starvin condition.
"And he said he'd *fish*;
    he'd try and fish in the Arney River,
        that run along his land,
        that was convenient to his land.
"He said he'd *fish*,
    try and fish to see would he get a few fish to eat
        that'd keep them from dyin.
"So he did; he went out this day,
    and he caught seven fish.
"Well he went every day,
    well for a good many days.
"And he caught seven fish every day.
"And one of the children died anyway.
"And he caught six then.
"And he caught *six every day*.
"The number went down to six.
"Aye, I heard that too, about the time of the Famine. That happened in Rossdoney, the townland of Rossdoney, along the Arney River there.
"Now that happened; it was told anyway.
"It came down from the Famine days."

That is one of the great stories of Ballymenone. Note first its craft. Mr. Boyle pared its informational prologue down to two lines, one to place the protagonist within a local family, another to site him on the land. McBrien is "known." Next he created three sentences beginning "And." All are slowed, opened, and charged with power by repetitive phrases, "five children" in the first, "no food" in the second. Though similar in rhythm, the sentences of this first triad grow in length, so the last incorporates a pair of repetitions, "he'd fish" and "his land." One by one, the next three sentences grow shorter to flow into the following section in which he presents the heart of the story in three short, sharp lines. The first and second triads match. All their sentences are constructed on the same pattern, a quick statement—"And they hadn't a haet," "He said he'd fish"—expanded in the clauses that follow. The first and third triads match in having their sentences begin with "And," but they differ in mode of emphasis. Expansive, repetitive phrases are built into the first. A two-line summary is set outside and after the single-sentence lines of the last triad. This summary joins the preceding section by beginning with "And," while its second line echoes to the first line of the midsection by omitting any conventional opening word (it begins with no And, Well, or So). As a pair, the summary lines parallel the two-line preamble, rounding the tale and preparing for Mr. Boyle's coda, in which he frames the story as an entity by repeating the geographical information of his introduction, and draws it back toward conversation by raising the issue of the story's veracity.

Plot gives stories their conspicuous order, but narrative structure is only one way to shape a tale. Mr. Boyle built his story of units, roughly analogous to the stanzas in a poem. During the narrative, units consist of sentences in this order: 2, 3, 3, 3, 2. But he swept that symmetry aside as sentences expanded, contracted, and held steady. In lines per sentence, the sequence is: 1, 1, 3, 3, 4, 3, 2, 2, 1, 1, 1, 1, 1. Spreading, the story appears less a sequence than a stream, but the stream is pulsed, the pulses transcribing a rising, falling, flattening curve. The whole scheme might be pictured like this: ascending: 2 (1, 1), 3 (3, 3, 4); descending: 3 (3, 2, 2): planing 3 (1, 1, 1) 2 (1, 1). But that is not what you hear. It is the storyteller's art to suggest, then obliterate, structure in a sound that swells and rolls like the ocean's waves.

Individual words as well as overall rhythm mark the well-made story. Although pace and pricks of silence most exactly demarcate the story's lines, words—conventional words at beginnings and strong, repeated, rhyming and echoing words at ends—further define the story's parts and blend them into the sweep of the whole. Mr. Boyle's tale had twenty-seven ending words. Only ten are used once. Of the last twelve ending words, five are "day," two of them coupling in rhyme with "anyway." Important words are embedded within as well as set out at edges. Repetition irritates the eye and is avoided in undergraduate writing. But repetition pleases the ear, so the oral writer exploits it (think of William Faulkner or Flann O'Brien), and the repeated key word is a prime decorative feature of spoken narration. Feel the word "fish" jump in the text. Mr. Boyle avoided pronouns, synonyms, or forms that would distinguish verbs from nouns, so the one word, "fish," can appear seven times, four times internally, three times at the ends of lines. That repetition, unifying the story and removing it from the norms of prose, poetry, and casual speech, seems still more emphatic in performance because the practiced teller, like Michael Boyle, pronounces the key words identically. They are not swallowed or altered but hit with the precision of a smith at work on iron.

An analogy is inescapable. At the height of Irish art in metal and manuscript, in the eighth and ninth centuries, the embracing design first perceived dissolves, surrendering to pulse and flow as the eye follows lines swinging, twisting out of geometry into endless motion, encountering in its course minute impeccably repeated motifs studded over the surface. But the eye is not trapped to flutter in mere decoration. Ornament contains and converges with meaning, writhing around, penetrating sacred texts, housing holy relics, springing from mathematics to reference as a graceful line swells into a bird's head or repetitive embedded jewels become staring, eternal eyes. The trapped eye is led in. The mind follows.

The decoration of Mr. Boyle's story does more than please the listener. His repetitive, rhythmic passages are the opposite of the hey-nonny-nonny-whack-fol-de-rol choruses of old English song. They lead toward rather than away from meaning. Extract them, and you have the tale's essence: five children, no food, he'd fish, his land, and he caught seven fish every day, and one of the children died anyway, and he caught six every day.

The word that pops out like jeweled eyes on gold, like crosses amid the coil, is a crucial one, fish, set into the text at the very middle: twice in the last sentence of the first triad, three times in the first sentence of the second, once at the end of that section's second sentence, and once within the first line of the third triad. As with the swirl of old art that runs circling into and spiraling out of centers, repetitions thrust the story forward along its narrative track, pull attention back to its center, and ram the story's message into awareness.

The folklorist's fascination with surface structure has often made craft of tales. But the good story is crafted for purpose. It uses its appeal to the senses to gain entrance to the mind. It is art.

To be art, a thing must move the senses and the intellect. It will have form and meaning. Meaning is not to prove but to approach.

The search for meaning leads through form, through text into context. Particular surroundings can affect an artist's capacity to create. Different company influenced different tellings by Peter Flanagan of the tale of Black Francis. Mr. Boyle told his story of the Famine to me alone in a hospital ward, but most of our environment had nothing to do with his telling. Relevant were the facts that I was attentive and quiet (he was free to take the time he wanted), that I was, while familiar, an outsider still (he was constrained to explain as well as present, exactly as he would to a young man of his locality), and that a tape recorder rested on his bed (he wished to form a good statement for posterity). What matters is not what chances to surround performance in the world, but what effectively surrounds performance in the mind and influences the creation of texts. That is context.

A text is an incomplete entity. Context molds and finishes it and brings it to life. Some of context is drawn into the text from the situation during its performance as the tale is shaped to dance to its goodmanning and to relate to the conversation from which it grew and which it must rejoin at its end. But the more important dimensions of context cannot be inferred from observing the story's situations. These are the meanings in words, the ideas words convey, the values under ideas, the multitudes of invisible association that echo oddly through the mind, conditioning the emergent product, surrounding and saturating it with meaning, making of it a living thing.

Learning what the artists know, learning their history and culture and environment, is one way to reconstruct invisible associations, to pump blood into dry texts. After reading Franz Boas' ethnography, our reading of Kwakiutl myth is constricted and enriched. We follow Erwin Panofsky into the comprehension of an altarpiece as he teaches us about the artistic, scientific, and religious traditions of its creator.[2] Mr. Boyle's story is deepened if we know that, though the District's people live along the Arney, fish do not and did not form a major part of their diet, and a fish, or any lone piece of meat, is not considered a sufficient meal. Salmon run the Arney quickly and only at certain times. At the time of the Famine the landlord's "water bailia" patroled the River to prevent people from fishing. Mr. McBrien was doubly blessed. He caught fish consistently and was not caught himself. He was not extravagantly blessed. He got fish, not a miraculous abundance of really good food, potatoes and cabbage.

Facts that the ethnographer records hold and deepen texts. Another way to meaning is to treat stories not as isolated but as interlocked, effectively making stories into contexts for each other, as Hugh Nolan did with the tales of Black Francis and Willy Reilly. That is how Claude Lévi-Strauss started the static texts of Indian myths into motion, forcing them through transformations to resonate with each other, vibrating into meaning and deep unity.

William Butler Yeats accomplished more than an unrivaled number of great poems. He arranged his poems carefully into books, rewrote them, reworked their ideas in other works in other media, and set his poems into conversation, lacing his images into phantasmagoria, his thoughts into philosophy. At the end of his oeuvre, at the end of his life, dictating changes from his deathbed, Yeats set "Under Ben Bulben," in which again the fairy host rides, the vision gyres, in which again he contemplates the virtues of violence, affirms the Pre-Raphaelite critique, and espouses a nationalism founded on the distinct excellence of saints, peasants, and aristocrats. Yeats aligned his epitaph so it could enhance his earlier works, so they could enhance it, so meaning could erupt between as well as within texts.

The student of the stories in which a people work together through their deepest thoughts can, as the student of Yeats must, interpret discrete works in each other's light. When stories are juxtaposed and allowed to tremble into meaning, they cohere as expressions aloud of silent philosophies, and the culture's hidden essences rise into view as forms break through meanings into values.

Let us stand Mr. McBrien alongside Mrs. Timoney. Each is the hero of the one story told in Ballymenone to commemorate different foci within a single historical period. They were neighbors, living near each other in the south of the townland of Rossdoney at the same time. Both worked small farms of low sodden land, both were heads of families, responsible for the well-being of small children. In their stories both are taken down to the limit, but not beyond. Things could have been worse. Mrs. Timoney and her family could have been evicted. Families were. Mr. McBrien and his family could have starved to death. Families did. Instead, each is given food, a source of life. Both endure, and the Timoney and McBrien names survive to the present in Rossdoney.

Together the stories say: in the worst situations there will be enough to enable survival—not more than enough, but enough. But there is a difference. Mrs. Timoney's great hardship was caused by men, so she can be paired with the rebel Black Francis. The Famine was closed to rebellion. Though exacerbated in the realm of men, though Britain could have helped, its cause lay beyond control. No rebel can help Mr. McBrien.

Differences of cause provide reason to focus separately on the Days of the Landlords and the Famine within the historical period begun with the Plantation. Human beings created the hard conditions of the landlords' era. Against them men fought and won Ireland's greatest victory, that of the Land League. As those conditions persist, men will continue to fight, confident of final triumph. The Famine was not caused by men, and it has led only to the endless defeat of emigration. Knowing both victory and defeat, people must learn to distinguish among causes while shaping within hardship a life between rebellion and endurance. Sometimes taking the rough with the smooth is the best that can be done. But nothing comes to those who wait. If the District's stories of hard times are not about eviction and death, neither are they joyous tales of gifts of riches. Endurance takes work. Mrs. Timoney had to walk, and "walk" is her story's key word. Everyone can walk. She did a lot of what anyone can do in order to survive. Mr. McBrien had to fish. The key word in his tale is both his obligation and his reward. People must work. Having worked, they work more.

There is mystery in McBrien's fish. Mrs. Timoney's hardship was caused by men. She alone saved herself. Mr. McBrien's hardship was not caused by men, and his work could not bring him success. Those fish appearing in exactly the right numbers were a gift, and no conclusion is possible within Ballymenone's cultural frame except this: if you stay in action, holding to hope, God will provide.

In the worst situations, people who do not despair, who keep working, are provided the minimum for survival. She gets her bowl of gruel. He gets his daily fish. The pattern repeats the cure. God sends disease, testing mankind, and He gives people, through saints and nature, cures. If you work to discover, preserve, and extend God's gift, His curse will be balanced by His blessing.

Work through this life of hardship, and victory will be yours. God's covenant is in the earth.

PART SEVEN

Enough and a Little Bit More

20

Butter

The land, God's gift, is enough. It provides oats for gruel, fish, food for the belly. It can be wrought into shelter. Rock dug out of it, and bricks molded from its clay, form the walls of today's older homes. Sod made walls in the past, and Tommy and Peter Lunny told me how still simpler houses were once built of clay. Their floors were sunk so the walls could be low. Then mud was "soured," mixed with scraps of straw, and the house was built "round and round," layer by layer, letting each course dry before the next was beaten onto it. Since rain could melt a "mud-wall" house, it had to be thickly plastered with a concoction of lime burned from local stone, sand dredged from the Arney's bottom, and cow manure. Like sod walls, mud walls were weak, so jointed crucks were built within them, tamped down into the earth. Oak was used because of its resistance to damp. Said Tommy:

Keep me wet.
Keep me dry.
Oak am I.

The simplest house, thrown up in times of emergency, say when a dwelling burned, was the "bog cabin," laid up of unmortared sod or built on knees and sided with planks, on a rood of bog.

The roof of every house was covered with scra peeled off the bog, and thatched with upland rushes, loughside reed, or corn sprung from the moss. Rose Murphy, whose father, grandfather, and great-grandfather were all house builders, whose son is a thatcher, a builder of new block porches, and a paperer of new kitchens, said of the people of her youth:

"They had clay for brick. They had their own trees. They cut the trees and made their roof.

"They had their own thatch and thatched it. It didn't cost a thousand pounds either.

"They lived, didn't they? They lived."

They broke the land's rocks and clay, its grasses and trees, and assembled them into shelter. They brought in chunks of dried peat bog and lit them. They took plants from the edge of the bog to boil over the fire and eat. The upland grasses fed the cattle to give milk, butter, the bulk of their protein. The earth gave life. In the worst of times, they took fish from its water and they were enough. In better times, the land provided "enough and a little bit more."

That "little bit more," they say, is for the neighbors. Not everyone has the same. In the past, only some farmers had wells, but all had the right of access to them. There is a "springwell" in front of Hugh Patrick Owens' house, and another on the adjacent farm. Some people used to walk half a mile to use them. Today only some farmers have water mains, but their neighbors enter their byres freely to fill buckets for cooking and washing. Supplies less crucial than water are also shared. Mrs. Cutler's farm has plum trees in the haggard and two apple orchards, "Johnny's Orchard" in the corner of the field called "the Sow's Hill," and another that came with a farm of eight acres Billy Cutler bought from Ziah Hare, a Boer War veteran. They bear Bramleys for cooking, Sheep's Snouts, Pippins, and Beauty of Bath for eating. Her neighbor on the Derrylin Road, Bob Armstrong, has a big Bramley tree, and "they get enough from it to do them the whole twelvemonth." West across the bog, Rose and Joe Murphy have plum trees. And small gifts of fruit circulate among them.

These gifts bind people together. Of her neighbors down Gortdonaghy Hill to the north, Ellen Cutler said:

"The Lunnys are good neighbors. They're the best now.

"Tommy's mother often sent up a lump of butter, nice and sweet and good.

"And I seen John James, Tommy's brother, he's dead now, comin up the lane with a whole cart of pretties and puttin them in the shed at the back.

"For some reason, there was none here. The crop was bad. And they brought many's the prettie here for us.

"And you daren't offer them anything.

"Billy and Johnny gave them a big hedge for firin, and they never forgot.

"Tommy does come by and borrow the ladder to thatch his pecks of hay. And he always stops by to see is there any wee thing I need. Ah, they're the best.

"Tommy's father used to come to ceili with Billy. Billy had a pipe and they'd sit at the fire there, passin it back and forth."

This flow of gifts carries us to life's sacred foundations where neighborliness is an obligation, generosity is a holy act, where nothing is wholly owned. Earth is God's gift to all mankind. People care for it, cajole its crops to bloom, but they could not reach their goal of "full and plenty" alone. So Peter Flanagan advises, "Grow enough to do you and a little bit more for the neighbors." His gardens bear a superabundance of cabbage, and his neighbors in need feel free to ask him frontally for his surplus. And so the idea of using the land for personal gain twitches uncomfortably in the mind.

The activities necessary to life can be extended into profit. The moss ground can be forced to yield produce for table, neighbors—and sale. Hugh Patrick Owens worked long hard hours, taking from the bog in such abundance that he developed a clientele in Enniskillen and accumulated cash sufficient to annexing Lipton McCaffrey's small farm. More land means more cows. Cabbage and turf can bring money, but cattle are the District's traditional measure of wealth and base for profit.

In the past, men could not easily follow cows to advancement. Today farms are passed on to one person, a son-in-law or a son, not necessarily the oldest, but the one who is most interested. In the past, land was scarce and made scarcer by partible inheritance. Tommy Lunny tells of a farmer who owned a small farm split by a road. He left one son the land on one side, another son the land on the other, and gave his third son the road. The road, leading to the city and foreign ports, was the only route an ambitious younger son could take. Farms were small, they carried few cows on sparse grass, and, as Hugh Nolan tells us, the profit to be made from cattle was slight:

"In them days cattle wasn't of such value. There was lots of cows around every house, but it was principally to supply milk and butter for the men that were at the brick-making and the turf-cuttin.

"I'll tell you what used to be: there used to be a fair on the tenth of every month in Enniskillen. Cattle wasn't very valuable, except the poor men had them. But the prices were small.

"Generally the calf that'd be born in the springtime, that calf would be sold before Christmas to have money for the season. And the price of that calf would be three, four, rarely five pounds.

"Before the creamery, all the milk they had to spare, they would thicken it and churn it. And any butter was left that was worthwhile, they would store it, salted, in a butt. That was made be the cooper. It was wooden and had wooden hoops, do ye see. And the churn, it was made be the cooper.

"It was as good a trade as what the motor mechanic would be today.

"And then the creameries started then, and that put an end to the whole business.

"Well, every Tuesday you would carry your butt of butter to Enniskillen. And there would be butter buyers, do ye see, in Enniskillen that would buy it by the pound.

"If ye couldn't fill a butt, your butter would be sold in the shops for a very low figure.

"Do ye see: the best lookin cow walkin, and her at the calf, would get you twelve, maybe fourteen pounds, and the neighbors would say you did well. And very few occasions there would be a twenty-pound cow. If you heard of a cow bringin twenty pounds and you at the fair that day, you'd be goin to see her. Oh aye. For a twenty-pound cow was a wonder.

"They would call that a Twenty-Pound Cow."

From Mr. Nolan we learn that the small profit arising from the sale of cattle became a gift. It was "for the season," for buying presents for the children, for standing drinks in the pubs during the Twelve Days, for buying the delicacies, the fruit and jorum of whiskey that would dress up the goose dinner served on Christmas Day to the wider family and to lonely neighbors gathered out of the cold into the family. We learn, too, that before the creameries the only vehicle for getting ahead was butter.

Just as the best eggs, deepest in taste and color, come from "free range" chickens who wander, and not from cooped up "deep litter" fowl, the best butter comes from cows who graze the sunny upland of summer. "When the cows were out on the grass," Mrs. Cutler explained, "they gave richer, more yellow butter. When they were tied up in the house and fed on hay and an odd lock of meal, the butter was paler." The cattle released into nature's care fared best, but a role remained for man because cattle on the grazin had to be kept from the cabbage, turnips, and mangolds spread for the sows on the hills, and from the onions that grew wild, or the butter would "tack off." It might look, even taste, all right, but it smelled bad.

People milked in the fields in the old days, but the current practice of herding the cows home nightly to the byre and milking them in steady surroundings to familiar songs has held through the lives of today's people.

In hot weather, milk was ready for churning in a day. In cold weather, it took two. The milk was strained into a crock placed outdoors in warm weather, in the pantry in cool weather, waiting for the milk to "thicken." Milk for bread-making can be hastened toward thickening by "souring" it in a pan by the fire, but for butter you have to wait patiently for nature. Once the milk thickened, boiling water was poured into the churn, then out, to heat it, and the milk was poured in. It stood for half an hour, and, said Mrs. Cutler:

"Then you churn it. In hot weather it might come in less than an hour. But in cold weather you might churn for hours and hours.

"I've seen many's the time I'd churn and churn until my arm ached and the tears was streamin down my face.

"If it didn't come atall, the old people said that the butter was stold. That some old woman that had a spite against you had come into the house and said, under her breath, Come all to me. Come all to me.

"There was nothin to do then, only give it up.

"If the butter was long in comin, you'd put a drop of hot water in the churn, scaldin it, but you daren't put too much. Too much hot water would ruin it. You can tell when the butter's come because it'll join all into one lump."

At that point, you wash your hands carefully and pick the lump out in handfuls, placing them into a bowl filled with cold spring water. There the lump is patted and patted, rejoined, and washed by emptying its water out and pouring on new until, after four or so times, no milk comes with the water. Then mix in salt at two teaspoonfuls per pound. It must be mixed thoroughly. "If you just threw a lock of salt in, it wouldn't save, but if it's properly salted, it twill last for weeks. That's in the mixin. And then it can be just put on a plate in the Room, or put in the dairy in hot weather." Once salted, the butter is patted to remove every drop of water by pinching a bit into one hand and slapping it with the other, or by setting it into a "trencher" and patting it round with a "spade." When the last water is gone, the butter is formed into pound or half-pound rectangular blocks and decorated with a "butter print" or marked by pressing the scored face of the spade down one way, then the other, "dicin it" to make it "look lovelier."

Butter was usually churned three times a week, and that made enough, Mrs. Cutler said, "for us and the neighbors round about. We'd always give it away." Theirs was one of the largest farms. Billy and his cousin Johnny McMullen, who lived with them, milked ten cows in the byre, and a "tank," a night's milking, yielded about a pound.

Since the flow of milk into butter was uneven from farm to farm and from time to time, butter was passed around among the neighbors as the most common counter of reciprocity, the most frequent material gift to community. It took hard work and gave an essential pleasure.

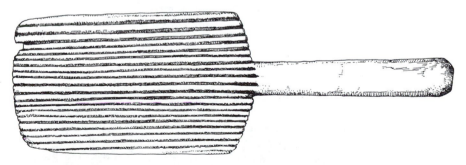

Butter Spade. Mrs. Cutler's. When the grooves "close" from use, you "open" them with a nail. The terms are the same as for plowing a field. It measures 8½ inches.

Since butter could be preserved, it was the major farm product people could sell. After the creameries came, the tank was sent out (once a bit of cream had been clandestinely skimmed off for churning) in cans on mats on the backs of donkeys and later in carts. Money came directly from milk. Today's milk goes out to the creamery in Fivemiletown and the cheese factory in Lisnaskea, but beef cattle are the main source of cash. In the past, though, butter was the marketable product, and in the context of its function as a gift, its potential as profit, butter sits strangely in the system of contemporary tale. Butter enabled one person by using God's gift of the land to get ahead of another, selling without what should be given within, to break the routine of endurance. It is as though thinking about butter forces open a door into a vestibule from which yet another door opens into another world.

As population declines, Big Men accumulate land to graze increasing numbers of cattle. When the land was strained, people emigrated or carried on within the pattern of large and small farms that grew out of the Plantation. Yet one local family prospered, a Catholic family with a modest holding. They did so through the butter trade. And with the Wee Woman.

Annie Owens introduces a common historical topic: "The Owenses of the Ford, they were the better-off people of that time. They were in the butter business. That's how they were so well off." Her brother, James, echoes her and continues:

"That's how they were so well off.
"That Wee Woman.
"It was found throwin stones accidentally, and throwin stones the way childer will, they lifted it and remarked it.
"Wasn't that funny?
"Well, wasn't that funny how that come there?
"That's the whole mystery: how did it come there?
"But it was supposed to bring them good luck anyway."

"They went to different little towns," Annie explains, "and bought butter and salted it, and put it in butts and sold it then like. That was it."

And James Owens concludes, "The Wee Woman brought them good luck now."

The Wee Woman is protected by Hugh Patrick Owens in a tiny, carved wooden barrel. It appears to be cast with great precision, yet it looks like slate. When Mr. Owens handed it to me, I found it astonishingly light. "The hand of man never made it," he said. "No, no natural hand made that." Months later, when they showed it to my children, T.P., Mr. Owens' son, said, "It surely was made. But it's a wonder people in the past knew how to make it. Being made, it's no less the wonder." Hugh Patrick Owens tells the wonderful tale:

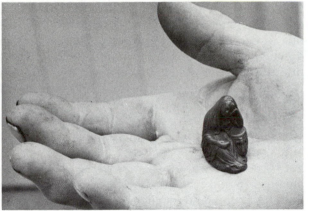

The Wee Woman

"It appertains to butter-makin.

"John Owens of the Ford, he was in the butter business. He used to buy butter by the ton.

"And the boys, the sons of John, were throwin stones at a tree. And one of the lads picked up a stone, and the other noticed that it was odd. They cleaned it off. And it was the Wee Woman.

"The Wee Woman is seated, you see. And she has a butter spade in the one hand and a water jug for wettin the butter, and it is a butter firkin she's restin on.

"It's harder than flint.

"And they found the Wee Woman at the Ford when they were startin the butter business.

"Tom Owens, an uncle of my father's, he found the Wee Woman.

"You see: the Wee Woman was found in a potato field, this side of the Ford.

"The two boys were weedin potatoes, this time of year.

"After great-great-grandfather was married, he was after startin this butter-packin, over a hundred and fifty years ago.

"The Wee Woman was lifted like a stone to throw at a tree. And when the old man saw it, he said, That depicts what we are at. And from that day until they quit the butter-packin, the money rolled in.

"He died a wealthy man in them times.

"It brought luck to them. Aye. It brought luck to them certainly."

When the Lord Cole heard about the Wee Woman, he rode over from Florence Court to see it. He did not dismount, and "they wouldn't give it into his hand, only just let him look at it." Though Hugh Pat said that "it wouldn't be sold for no amount of stoned fields" and that "it never must go out of the name of Owenses," it was once sold into the MacManus family. But an Owens who had prospered in Australia "went to a table and threw down gold sovereigns until it was sold back." It was he who had the "wee firkin" made to house the Wee Woman in which Mr. Owens keeps it now. He cherishes it, along with the Book, though it has never brought him luck, for its luck is specific to the butter business.

Getting through requires work. Getting beyond requires more. Exploits tell of local strength. Bids and pants tell of local wit. Battle tales tell of local courage and cooperative capacity. These people are poor, but that is not because they are weak, stupid, cowardly, and divisive. Their inherent qualities should make them rich. Since they do not, it is something other than hard work and intelligence that makes people rich.

Achieving wealth requires "luck" or evil. No one ever said the source of the Owens' luck was anything but benign. Evil, though, lay beneath other attempts to profit through the dairy. Mrs. Cutler told us of old women who stole butter with a charm.

When the old year broke into halves at the arrival of winter and summer, and the farm's rent was due, time's fabric weakened, and matters of life and death shadowed through its weave. On Hallow Eve Night the spirits of the dead rise and go on the earth, girls at the hearth play at divining the identities of future mates, and in the past boys dressed in suits of white straw and caroused over the hills in the company of the dead, attacking the homes of men who kept their daughters from the cohort of bachelors. Into the girls' kitchens the "strawboys" broke, demanding a dance, a pantomime of procreation, and stealing food, life's resource, from the home. At the opposite point in the year, May Day, when life's flowers lay on the street, the home's product was kept indoors. Fastidious and generous custom was suspended, the ashes from the hearth were not thrown out, and nothing was given or lent. It was believed the person who managed to borrow something on May Day would never repay it and would have stolen the farm's luck for a year.[1]

Peter Flanagan said not many people held the old belief when he was a boy, though people remained leery of anyone who came to the door with a request on May Day, and there was one old woman, well remembered in the District, who regularly tried to borrow a cup of milk in hopes she would take with it a whole year's milk. On May Day, for one day, everyone withdrew from normal reciprocity—everyone but the woman willing to risk the name "witch," willing to enter through mysterious theft a permanent state of disconnection from neighborly giving. She would trade community for easy profit.

What witches do is steal. What they steal is the natural product of Fermanagh's lush, damp grasslands, the flower of the clay: butter. They steal milk that can be churned into golden butter to build community or sold to bring comfort to the home, or they steal soft butter from the churn. How witches contrive their theft is through "the black art." Hugh Nolan explains, and as I encourage him, he spins a story:

"It was supposed there was people and they had what they called the black art.

"And I don't know how the black art run, but it was something in the line of witchery, that they could take the milk of cows there. It was supposed that they used to go out before day in the mornin with something *white* in the shape of a *rope* and trail it along the grass.

"And that when the cows would go in to be milked, they'd give no milk atall.

"It was a common topic in days gone by. And whether it was genuine or not, you wouldn't *know*, because cows could loss their milk for the want of grass. They want water and many a thing, do ye see. That's what they used to say was the cause of it. Aye, that it was the black art.

"And these people with the black art, if they had cows, their cows would have the milk that ever was lost."

I ask, in a pause, if the people with the black art used a charm, and Mr. Nolan answers quickly:

"Oh aye. It was supposed that it was the charm, that the draggin of the rope was only—ah, it was just an accompaniment, but that they had the charm of words that took the milk.

"Well, there was a man told me
    about
        that place where Missus Cutler lives.
"In days gone by, I think, there was ten cows kept on it.
"And there was another man lived beside them,
    and he had only a small farm,
        three cows in place.
"It's all in Cutlers' now; Cutlers' ones, they got that farm after he left.
"But this man told me that while he was in the country that he used to supply more milk
    to the creamery
        off his three cows
            than the McMullens
(they were McMullens that lived where Missus Cutler's livin),
    that he had more milk
        than they had off *ten* cows.
"So it was supposed that he had this black art.
"That was the way while he was in the country."

When he stops, I comment that mysteries demand explanation. The comment is proper, and he lifts the topic once more:

"Well, this man told me that anyway.

"It was a known fact that the McMullens' milk went down altogether from he came to the country and that his *increased*."

Again I enter words of interest and Mr. Nolan continues:

"There used to be a story about
    persons that used to change into the shapes of animals
        for to take the milk from cows.

"There was a story told about the same person and the supply of milk that the cows was givin was gettin *very* small.

"So they took a notion that they'd watch the fields at *night* for to see was there anyone comin milkin the cows because it was a thing was often done: people that'd have no milk of their own, they used to go out and milk *neighbors'* cows.

"But this night anyway there was a couple of men watchin
    and one of them had a gun anyway
    and there came something in the shape of a *hare* along
    and she started suckin a cow.

"So of coorse, he wouldn't fire at her when she was in that vicinity because he could shoot the cow, you see.

"But anyway when she moved away, or when the cow moved away from her, he fired,
    and he *struck* her.

"And she made off anyway.

"But in the next day or so, there was some lady goin about with a gunshot wound
    in the locality.

"*That* was told anyway. But I wouldn't credit it."

Hugh Nolan is a true historian. Like the monk who transcribed the *Tain* into the Book of Leinster, then wrote that "some things in it are the deceptions of demons, others poetic figments . . . intended for the delectation of foolish men," but who recorded the whole text nonetheless, like Geoffrey Keating, who reported stories he knew to be false because the historian's responsibility is not to do the job of the intelligent reader but to preserve and rationally order the wealth of the past, Mr. Nolan provides a complete account of a tale he does not credit.[2] When finished, he answered in response to a question that he supposed people with the black art learned it from books, though he knew little about it. Peter Flanagan was the one who explained witchcraft to me, reporting and interpreting in his characteristically personal fashion:

"There was witchcraft in this country.

"There was a belief about witches longgo in this country that they sold their soul to the Devil.

"They were gettin their power from some evil source.

"Aye.

"Whether that's right or not, I don't know now."

I ask if there was a special way for a soul to be sold, and he answers:

"Well, I don't know what form they would do it. I can't say what way they would go about it, or how anyone would have that inclination to do so, if they had any belief in the hereafter or anything like that.

"I wonder why they do it. Even though that they would be poor or anything, it's the life hereafter you have to look to more than the present life you're livin.

"We must firmly believe from when you come into the world until the day you leave it, or the night you leave it. Uphold your beliefs. That sort of life wouldn't be in conformity with the rules of God, I mean.

"Well that would be the belief that we'd have, and of course the Catholic church as well, and of course the Protestant church too.

"I don't see why. I never could get down now to believin that, I really think that it's just a gift, the same as these boys that put you to sleep, these hypnotizers. They're much the same. I always thought that it was really the same that these people had got. That they had that gift that they could read your horoscope or read your future.

"Then the people that wasn't able to do it formed that opinion about them. That they hadn't the art of forecastin or foretellin the fortune or the future to anybody. They could have came, I mean, to wrong conclusions about them.

"Them people, they just had got that special gift from God to do that.

"If a person came and forecast to me or foretold me future, I wouldn't come to that bad conclusion and say that she was an evil person, I would not, let it be he or she. I'd appreciate it, for I'd think it was a gift they had got. They were born into the world with that talent."

"There's certain people with them gifts," Joe interjects, and P concludes:

"It's just like a musical talent."

Musician, son of a musician, Peter Flanagan speaks for the gifted. The ability to foretell the future, like the ability to make a wooden fiddle sing, is a gift from God. He knows how people without talent willfully misunderstand the gifted and speak of them critically. "Musicians," he admits, "have an odd way of goin on. They are curious."

Peter Flanagan's faith is so firm he finds it impossible to believe that people could trade their eternal souls for worldly gain. To make his point, though, he had to abandon the word "witch" and illustrate his argument with an instance of the benign transference of natural power: the seer gives a forecast to the less blessed as the homemaker gives a pound of butter to the less fortunate. The witch who steals butter is either evilly misusing a gift from God or properly using a gift from an evil source.

Calmly Mrs. Cutler mentioned the witch's theft while describing the hard job of churning, and the workaday world broke open. Mr. Nolan said the theft was accomplished through the black art, and Mr. Flanagan said the black art was a gift from Satan.[3] The idea of easy profit leads to the Devil's door. Hugh Nolan tells a wonderful tale about a man hungry for wealth making Faust's pact:

"There was a man,
    he lived there just,
        on this side of the parochial house.
"John Maguire, he's livin there now. It's when you're goin up the Arney Road there, the house is on your right-hand side. There's television aerial that you'd see there, apparatus. He's John Maguire that lives there now.

"But there was a man lived there before him, he was James Quigley.
"And he was great, great rant.
"I heared him tellin about
    there was some man and
        he was gettin it very tight for money.
"And he tried all ways of makin money, but it was a failure.
"But he heared of such a thing as sellin yourself to the Divil
        for a length of time.
"But you'd have to go with him when this time would expire.
"But durin the period between you'd made the bargain
    with him,
    and between the time that you'd have to die,
    you'd have plenty of everything,
        plenty of money,
            and everything that you wished for.
"He'd supply it.
"So anyway, this man he got in contact with him anyway,
    and he sold himself to him for a number of years.
"So he got terrible rich.
"Everything went well with him.
"But anyway, the time expired.
"So he used to *meet* with him
    on different occasions, do you know.
"And Ould Nick, as they called him, used to tell him everytime how long that it had to go now, till he'd have to be goin *with* him.
"But anyway in the middle of his whole riches he got downhearted.
"And he started to worry.
"So,

he didn't know how he'd get rid of him,
　　or how he'd get the bargain broke.
"So it was givin him terrible trouble.
"And he put things before the Ould Nick that he didn't think that he'd *do*
　　　in the line of,
　　　　　ah, supplyin money to houses of worship,
　　　　　and things like that, do ye know.
"Everything was a failure.
"So *anyway* in the long run,
　　he got totally downhearted.
"And the wife noticed him,
　　she got afraid that, well,
　　that he was gettin near his death or
　　that he was goin to loss his senses.
"So she got around him anyway. She never had knew anything about
this bargain that he had made with the *Playboy*
　　　　　　till that.
"So she sifted on
　　and sifted on
　　　　and sifted on at him,
　　till she got him to tell her,
　　　　　　to tell her all.
"So.
"Oh now, he says, I have no hope, he says,
　　but he says, that he *has me.*
"No, she says.
　　He hasn't ye *yet,* she says.
"So when they started the bargain first, there was one time that the
Divil came along and he had a wee drum with him and a pile of sticks.
"And he gave the man the wee drum.
"And he says,
　　Anytime ye want me, he says,
　　　　give a roll on this drum.
"So anyway that was the way he used to notify him when he wanted
to get anything *done.*
"So says the wife to him,
　　He hasn't ye *yet.*
"Aw now, says he, how do *you* know;
　　I know his decision.
"There's one thing, says she, that ◇
　　if you ◇
　　put it before him, she says,
　　he'll not give into it, or he'll not do it.
"And what is that, says the man.

"Well, says she, ◊ the next time, she says, when he comes along
    tell him
    that you want him
    to do *one* thing,
  and it's the last thing that ever you'll ask him to do,
  and that if he does it, you're willin to go with him.
"And what is it, says the man.
"*Ask him*, says she, *to make all lawyers honest men.*
"He *up to his feet and he got the drum*
        and he *rolled.*
"Oh aye ◊.
"Aw now, there *never was a roll of a drum heard as far in the world.*
"So it was no time till the lad appeared.
"What do ye want now, he says.
"Well, he says, I *want* ye to do a thing, he says, and it's the last thing,
he says, that ever I'll ask ye to do,
    and if ye do it, he says,
    I'm willin to go with ye, he says.
"*What* is it, says he.
"I want ye, he says, to make all lawyers honest men.
"HA!
"Oh, now, he says,
   there's *women*, he says,
    at the back of this, he says.
"It's a thing, he says, I'll never do, because if I did I wouldn't be long
before I wouldn't have a coal on me hearth.
"Give me that drum, he says,
   because, he says,
    I'm *finished* with you ◊.
"So he got rid of him.
"That was the last of him."

How Mr. Nolan's voice twisted and ran, grumbled with the Devil, sniveled with the downhearted man, softened, and burst. Happily we relax, chuckling. Smoke lifts. I ask if James Quigley invented the tale. Still smiling, Mr. Nolan responds:

"Well, I suppose it could happen that he did because he was a wonderful composer.

"But of course, do ye see, there was such a thing as people sellin themselves. That was often the cause of many a suicide, do ye know. Aye."

I ask, "Did you hear of people actually doin it?"

"Well now, I never did. I never heard of anyone in my knowin that ever done it, or that ever happened to be so unfortunate, but it has been, well, the opinion of alot, do ye know, that suicides often comes from people that has gave themselves up.

"But I never knew, thank God, someone that it happened to."

Three nights later I asked Michael Boyle, who had told me several of James Quigley's hilarious pants, whether he knew that tale, and he told me his own:

"I heard tell of a story like that, but it didn't take place of course in our country. No, it didn't take place in our country. It happened in another district of the country.

"It happened, I think,
    away out beyond Inishmore,
    in Killarover, that district of the country.
"About this man and he was very poor for a long time, a good part of his life.

"And he was very *poor*.
"And all of a sudden he got rich,
    got up powerfully in the world,
    got an awful amount of land,
        and had alot of horses.
"And he had a stallion or an *entire* horse, do ye see.
"And they're very determined animals, do ye see, one of them.
"So there was eight men workin anyhow, and this night he got terrible ill,
    and he wanted the clergy,
        the *priest*.
"So anyhow this fellow that used to be workin with this stallion horse
        he went
        and he got up and run.
"And there was what they call a blood, a *race* mare at it.
"And he put the saddle and bridle—it twas in the olden days before bicycles or motorcars—he put the saddle and bridle on the race mare.
        and got on her.
"And there was a big yard, you know, and a gate on it, and when he was goin out through the doorway, there was a big barrel blazin in the gateway—a *barrel*, something like a big round lump blazin in the gateway.
"So he put the mare at it, and she refused to cross it.
"She wouldn't go *at it*.
"So he put her at it again,
    and she wouldn't go at it.
"And he put her at it a *third time*, and she refused.
"So he jumped off the mare's back and he went to where the stallion

was in the stable, and he put the saddle and bridle on the stallion and jumped on him and he *out*
>> on the stallion.

"And when the stallion came to the blazin *ball,*
>> *he made a lep* over it,
>>> a lep on top of it.

"But the barrel hurtled on before him.

"And that's the way the stallion galloped after it the whole way to the priest's house.

"And when he went there, woke up the priest, he told the priest what had happened to him.

"Oh well, he says, the horse that brought you here has to bring me there.

"So the priest got up on the stallion, and the fellow walked beside him and led the stallion be the head.

"And when they got to the house, the man was very near death.

"But the man died anyway while the priest was in the house.

"And he had to leave the priest back at his dwellin, at the parochial house, on the stallion's back.

"And when he came home after leavin the priest back, the man was dead.

"And the next mornin when he opened the stable door to feed the stallion, the stallion was dead."

In measured quiet lines, each rising at its end, Mr. Boyle's story ended. His eyes burn into mine. It seems very quiet. "What was the explanation for it all?" I ask.

"Well, you see, he had sold himself to the Devil. And that was supposed to be the Devil that was in the barrel, for to delay the boy that the priest wouldn't get *to him,* do ye see, delay the messenger, that he couldn't reach the priest.

"And the mare wasn't fit to pass it. It took the good horse with the determination to *pass* this object that was blazin. That was the explanation."

And I say, "So the priest got back in time to save the man's soul," and Mr. Boyle continues:

"Yes. He got back in time to save the man's soul.
"And the horse was dead in the mornin.
"He'd worn himself out fightin the Devil in the dark.
"Well, that didn't happen in our country. I think it was out beyond the Lough, beyond Inishmore, about the Lisnaskea area, around there. That's, I think, where it happened.

"I heard that story told, that it happened. It's supposed to be a true story.

"It happened all right."

Mr. Nolan's tale was fictional and comic, Mr. Boyle's was historical and serious, but both men believe people really did sell their souls for wealth, and their stories are structured similarly.

Here is a man who is poor and who, rather than working the land, enduring in that modest estate called doing the best, wishes to rise without working. He does, and having risen, falls into the despair that leads to suicide and hellfire. But at last, prodded by his wife's nagging or his body's pains, he reaches out to others and they help him. Connected, his soul is saved. In Mr. Nolan's tale his innocent wife saves him by knowing the need the Devil has for dishonest people who profit from the troubles of others. In Mr. Boyle's, a laborer (a humble, persistent worker who risks himself to help another), a horse (the determined power of nature, complete and unaltered), and a priest (the man who transfers God's blessing) combine to pull him at the last instant from perdition.

Accepting the gift of existence on the land, you gain a life of hard work and the obligation to love your neighbor. In the worst times, you will be aided by a mysterious Will that dispenses fish in minimum numbers. In normal times, you will carry on, passing the time, consoled by good food and talk. To prosper, you need an additional gift. Accepting it does not require abandoning life's old center of work and love. It can be conserved and extended. Though aided by the Wee Woman, made by no natural hand, the Owens family of the Ford worked hard at butter-packing and generously shared their wealth with other members of the Owens clan, their neighbors in Sessiagh. But to prosper without toil, free from the obligation to love, you need a gift that is not from nature, not from God. The most driven of men abandon Christian precepts, coil in greed, and sell their souls to the Devil. The less courageous, less evil man remembers that fairies know where pots of gold are buried. He has been raised with stories suggesting that fairies are real. He walks wintry lanes above which, crowning hilltops like clumps of antlers, fairy forths remind him of secret riches, and while skeptical, he stays on the lookout.

In one long, smooth statement, Peter Flanagan introduces us efficiently to the world of fairy, building within two tales, told in the low, slow, quiet, surprising style of the "experience," at once informing me and entertaining my children, who sat wide-eyed and silent at his hearth.

"It was a fairy tale told that if you could get ahold of a fairy,
    that he would tell you where there was a crock of gold.
"Supposed to be gold buried here in Ireland at all these forths.
"They're on the top of every hill.

"They were supposed to be made at the invasion of the Danes.

"The Danes invaded Ireland, you see—away back—well, a thousand years ago. I can't give you the particular date.

"And these are fortifications built.

"The Danes are the first stranger invaded Ireland—used to come in canoes, and it was for plunder they came, the Danish people.

"And the Irish had to *all* collect, *on* the hilltops, and build these fortifications round, round as an *o*, or as round as that ovenlid there. And all get inside of it and they were all on the watch out.

"I was here on this hillside in my fortifications, and if they saw the Danes comin, they'd blow their bugles, and it passed on from one to the other, from one end of Ireland to another, whenever the Danes invaded.

"So there was a king. He was Brian Boru. He raged war against them, and twas ten hundred and fourteen, that's the date he banished the last of the Danes. In ten hundred and fourteen, at Clontarf, here in the south of Ireland. And that ended them. So.

"And there's supposed to be money buried at these forths, and that's where the fairies are supposed to *be*.

"There was witch*craft* in Ireland *too*, in them days.

"And these witches were supposed to say to the people, if you shoot me, I'll watch this crock of gold till the day of judgment, till the end of time.

"And they're supposed to be watchin, and the Good People knows where these crocks of gold is, and if you could catch one of these fairies—some calls them leprechauns, that's another name—well, they'd tell you where the crock of gold was.

"But.

"A man made a great effort up here to catch one of them. He walked out of this clump of bushes, and he spoke up to him, and he told him that he was goin to tell him where the crock of gold was.

"He wanted to do him a favor,
    but the man couldn't understand him,
        so he made a grab at the fairy.
"And the fairy just leaped up above him,
        and lit just on a branch.
"And that was that.

"He couldn't get him.

"It was the nearest fairy tale that ever I heard. And I saw the man.

"I saw the man. Yes.

"He spoke calmly to the fairy. He says, Wait, he says, till I catch you. So he went to make a grab at him . . ."

P lurches to one knee, grabs through the air, then stands, his head to one side, looking up at the fairy safe on the branch above him:

". . . like that, on the ground.

"But he had wings on him and he went up in the branches.

"And that was that.

"And if he had of taken him calmly, the fairy said that he'd tell him where the crock of gold was.

"But then, he scared the fairy, the way the fairy disappeared into thin air.

"That was that."

P returns to the hearth and sits, his arms folded, his elbows on his knees, and, having enchanted his audience, continues:

"He was an old beardy man. I saw him. He's not so very long dead now. That's that."

He lifts the tongs from next to Joe's knee, picks a turfcoal from the hearth, relights his cigarette. Silence surrounds him. The children watch as he exhales. Smoke drifts away and he says:

"And then fairies used to take away children, the same as your children here. If they fancied a child, they might—if they got it outside—they might lift it
        and away with it.
"An old man was tellin me that there was a very nice child, in his country. But now that might be over a hundred years ago.
"And it twas taken away.
"The mother was in a terrible state about it.
"But,
        years rolled on,
                and she died,
                the father died,
                the parents died.
"And.
"They had a son; he was married,
        and one night he was awakened at the window,
                the window of his house.
"He says, Who's that?
"He says, Is me father, he says, inside,
                or me mother,
        mentionin them by their name.
"No. Who are ye?
"So he gave his name. And this young man—what relation he would be in the next generation—he says:
"And where are ye?
"He says, I'm with the fairies.
"He says, How long are ye with them?
"He says, They brought me away with them, he says, last week.
"And he says, "I'll be comin by, he says, on a horse, he says, here. I'll be on the second horse.

"He says, If you're out and throw an iron hoop around me, he says, I'll get free, he says,
                    I'll get home.
"So they talked it over and they counted the time. They'd heard of him bein taken away.
"And him and the wife talked the next day, and it was somethin over a hundred years he was away,
                    over a hundred years with the fairies.
"So, on that *particular* night, he says, I'll go out, and I'll take a hoop of a churn, he says, or the shoein of a cart, he says, and I'll try, he says.
"But he says, If you miss me, he says, I'll never get back.
"So he went out, and he heared the tatter of the hooves comin, in the middle of the night, somethin around two or half past two in the night.
"And he had his hoop ready.
"And he threw it like that."

P's arm flings.

"And he missed.
"He missed him.
"The horse was travelin at an awful rate. There was six or eight horses.
"And *down below* the next mornin, there was the shape of a person got
                    lyin on the grass,
                    on top of the grass.
"And he was just
                    in dust.
"He fell off the horse as he went down, and the grass never grew on it since.
"And a man showed me the *spot*. Really. Whether that was right or not, I do not know, but he showed me this particular spot and the grass was—it was as bare as that floor.
"That was in Tiravally, a townland called Tiravally up there. I don't know if there is anyone now could show you the spot, at the present time, or whether the ould tradition is carried on or not, or whether it was kept alive, I do not really know. But that's what the old man told me. He was up to a hundred years of age."

Beautiful lights follow their movement, and fairies make the world's loveliest music. They serve rich food in their bright houses. When Mr. Flanagan had finished and was smoking again, Polly, my eldest, asked him what the fairies did with the children they took, and he replied, "They say they have the greatest time in the world with the fairies. I heard tell of one comin back and said that she would not come back. And only think: a hundred years is only like a day in fairy land." He snaps his fingers. "Or maybe a thousand years is only like a day."
Gold is hidden in the forths, but disaster follows the plundering of a

forth. Witches protect the gold and will keep it from people who shoot them when they steal. Fairies know where the gold is buried, and they will show the spot to men. Yet no local story tells of anyone receiving that gold. All report near misses. Both Mr. Flanagan and Mrs. Cutler tell the story of a man, an uncle of that Billy Dowler who preserved the musket from Mackan Fight, who met a fairy who promised to show him where gold was buried on the Round Hill, a ghost-haunted rise below Gortdonaghy Hill, but he grew frightened, afraid to perform the tasks the fairy set. He hid in his house, and the fairy walked in and struck him deaf.

Fairies seem to promise wealth, but they will not give it without work. They will not give it at all. What fairies do is fool and harm people who annoy them, destroying the pigs of men who cut sticks from their forths, leveling the houses of those who build across their routes of travel. What they do is steal young women to be their brides and steal handsome children, leaving quarrelsome, terrible "elves" in their places. Mrs. Cutler heard of one just north of Bellanaleck. Mr. Flanagan saw one when he was mumming up in the mountains.[4]

All agree fairies are the angels who followed Lucifer into defeat in the "War of Heaven." They were not hurled into hell but set on earth, on the ocean, and in the whirlwind. Not good enough for heaven, not bad enough for hell, fairies are fallen angels wandering eternally between.[5]

God gives eternal joy. Satan gives eternal suffering. God gives a world that must be worked in pain to yield. Satan gives a world of easy riches. Fairies, Satan's minions, promise wealth and steal life. A cross cut with the hand in the air, accompanied by a prayer, will protect you from fairies, as it will from devils and ghosts.

Butter, gift and profit, connects the world of work to "the other world" and connects the District's different classes of story, those that are true with those that are fiction through those that might be true. The witch who steals butter belongs to accounts of things as they were, to "history," and she belongs to investigations of how things are, to "experiences," for there were witches, without question, and there may or may not be powers that transform women into hares, powers that provide supernatural explanation for why cows do not give milk or butter will not come. There may or may not be fairies, but it is true that people have acted as though they existed, that reputable aged men have seen them, that one struck Mr. Dowler deaf with the back of his hand. It is true that some women tried to steal butter with charms.

Though gone, witches were. People saw them. They lived in Fermanagh and remain in history to embody the opposite of human good.[6]

The good person gives. The witch steals. The good person accepts the terms of a compact with God, written into the land, and becomes bound to generosity. God's gift of grass is made into butter and given to the community, within which life is nurtured. The witch accepts the terms of a compact with Satan and acts out of greed. The milk of others is stolen, and the witch breaks out of community into isolation, becoming the worst of neighbors, a lone, aggressive thief of life.

Holy Communion is the model of goodness. The black art is its opposite. Daily action falls between the priest giving red wine, the witch taking white milk. People move toward one when they do the good neighborly deed, and they move toward the other when they act out of self-interest. Neither priest nor witch, having chosen to submit to the discipline of neither extreme, God's or Satan's, people travel a mixed reality, using talk about the neighbors and concepts personified in stories to triangulate their troublesome course.

On the priest's side of their route, the secular limit is marked by Black Francis. His man, Souple Corrigan, protected a priest, thus aiding in the celebration of Christmas Mass. Black Francis gave to the poor, aligning himself with ancient saints who gave cures to the ill and recent saints who minister to the needy, like the popular Saint Martin de Porres, whose medal jingles with the District's pocket change, whose picture hangs on bedroom walls. The rebellion of Black Francis, though politically sanctioned, places him among outlaws from Robin Hood to Jesse James, whose civil disobedience in ballad and legend reverses our period's norm of taking from the poor to give to the rich.[7] In robbing the profiteers—the landlord and banker and lawyer—the outlaw rides to expose the dissonance in a system shifting, slipping, swinging between a social theory based on the community and one based on the self, between the Christian ethic founded on Communion and the capitalist ethic with its mainspring of greed. Once the terms of conflict are clarified, Black Francis must act on the side of the priest, not the witch, and his action entails the Christian extreme: self-sacrifice.

The opposite of the outlaw is the man of law, the lawyer who does not "work," who is idle and does the Devil's work of exacerbating the community's discord for his own profit. Black Francis' opposite is the landlord who legally mistreats the poor, living off their work. At his worst, the landlord is tempted by Satan, the creator of war, to destroy the temple, the one true defense against strife. With the landlord, within the Devil's dominion, stand the man who sells his soul so he will not have to work, who springs away from his neighbors, stealing from them energy needed for cooperative endeavor, and the woman who sells her soul and leaves the community through theft, prospering off the work of others.

Endurance is the middle way, personified in Mrs. Timoney and Mr. McBrien. But the very acts that enable survival in hard times bring profit in good times, carrying people through work's momentum in the direction of the witch. She is a projection, proposed out of fears within to mark the acceptable limit of success.

The witch's motives are spite and greed. Greed is wrong, sin. It brings harm to the self. No local person of recent memory fares worse in conversation than the man who sold his hay to make a few shillings, then watched his cows die in hunger as icy weather held into the summer. He is not beyond understanding, however.

Old "pishrogues" or "pisterogues," superstitions held with more amusement than conviction, cluster around worries, around death, travel, and money.[8] Bubbles on tea mean money. Sparks popping from the fire mean money—catch them. An itchy left palm means money coming:

> *Rub it to wood,*
> *It's sure to come good.*
> *Rub it to your ass,*
> *It's sure to come to pass.*

People like money. What they fear is money that brings harm, that comes from or leads to "spite." They do not want their flow of milk to increase at the expense of another's. They will not accept the easy life of the landlord if it means holding others near slavery. People who struggle to rise above their neighbors will be shot down with ridicule. The man who gets ahead breaks away from his community and breaks neighborly commandment. Leaving his fellows, he leaves God, and if he prospers it may be because he has leagued with Satan. So it is useful to have a Wee Woman on whom to blame success, and it is pleasant to fancy the purely lucky gain. It is pleasant to imagine money flying from the fire or finding the treasure Souple Corrigan left in the bog or meeting a friendly fairy, and big nights out often involve games of chance and varieties of lottery.

Profit is not wrong. The land's bounty is evidence of God's goodness, and success in extending it into profit can be read as a sign of His support. The Wee Woman blocks the witch, and people can map their way to happiness across a spectrum of possibility constructed out of local personalities who stand between God and Satan: saint, priest, Black Francis, Mr. McBrien, Mrs. Timoney, the Owens family of the Ford, lawyers, the landlord's functionaries, Lord Cole, the man who sells his soul, the witch. While some young men follow Black Francis, riding the roads at night to harass an alien presence, and others leave the District's society while staying on its land, becoming agents for an external power after the style of the bailiff, most people, secure they will do no worse than Mr. McBrien, form a comfortable place for themselves. They are free to do all they can so long as they negate the witch's traits of spite and greed by remaining "harmless" and generous, "good," so long as they uphold neighborliness: so long as they, as they would say, "fear God and harm no man."

Anxiety over profit focused logically in the dairy. Milk was neither processed nor marketed in a neighborly way. The "tradesman"—the thatcher, carpenter, cooper, mechanic—is paid in cash, and well. Paddy McBrien paid the mason who built his house a pound a day at a time he was making a pound a week as a farm laborer. But the tradesman's product remains within the community, and it continues to benefit from his work. Things are traded, cash flows, but internal balance remains. But butter and milk are sold beyond to be consumed by unknown persons, while some members of the community accumulate cash and internal balance unsettles.

Irish farms like those composing the District are classed by historical geographers as dispersed, in contrast to the nucleated villages surrounded by unfenced openfields that once characterized areas of low-lying thick soil such as the English Midlands. The District's farms, though, do not meet the dispersed ideal materialized in upland Britain or the United States.

In Braunton, a village in Devon where one of England's last openfields remains to be seen, and where I spent some happy months feeling the fit between a compact material form and a collective social ideal, the farmers I knew called the dispersed holdings of the Devon moorlands "ring-fence farms." The name is apt, designating a situation where a single unbroken fence can be imagined to encircle all a farm's activities. The Irish landscape, as E. Estyn Evans has taught us, is marked by old symbols of cooperation, enormous dolmens and clustered clachans, as well as by separate farms.[9] Tiny hamlets once dotted our District. Many houses that stand alone today had others, within aged memory, built onto their gables or right next to them. It is not only this fact from the near past (nor even the small size of the holdings which brings the houses, especially in leafless winter, close together) that pulls the District's farms away from the ring-fenced extreme of the isolated, self-sufficient James River plantation or Western ranch and back in the direction of an agricultural village like Braunton, with its rising spire, packed habitations, and open Great Field, ribboned with unfenced strips. In iconic support for Hugh Nolan's argument about the decline of cooperation, the District's dwellings have parted onto independent sites, but as mute testimony to the survival of the neighborly way, the landscape has not been reorganized in accord with the capitalistic emblem of the American family farm. Just as the District's ethic lies between the individualistic and the communal (and moral options for personal success are both open and constrained), its landscape projects an image between dispersed and nucleated.

The houses of Ballymenone are set separately among their dependent outoffices, and their inhabitants cannot imagine living in town "like two asses starin over a hedge at other." Hedged fields encircle the home place, but other land is broken from the farm's ring. Ballymenone contains no truly communal spaces, though the District's people know of a "coor meadow" just south of the Arney and a "coor pasture" northward by Lough Erne, where several farmers hold and work the land together. But the District's farms have not been rationalized into unity. Wills have given men fields scattered away from the home place. And at perhaps a long walk from home, past the houses of others, the moss ground and bog are split into small patches, where people work near one another, and often cooperatively, just as they would on the long, narrow strips of an openfield like Braunton's. The moss ground is rarely fenced, the bog never, and the man putting in extra cabbage or cutting extra turf will be closely watched. But cattle are tended near home, and their product is won and processed indoors. The byres where cows are milked, the small dairies where milk and butter are kept, are built onto the dwelling or set hard by. Butter was churned in the kitchen. Cans of milk were carted out by the farm's "boss." Only milk holds potential for secret profit, and only butter leads the mind toward both evil and success.

21

Brick

When cattle needed wide "scope" on scarce unimproved land and brought little cash with their sale, when butter was the dairy's main marketable product, the land gave people another way to make that "little bit more": "slapbrick."

Brick-making followed turf-cutting's mode. It called for many hands, demanded specialization and "swappin." Like bog, soapy blue-green brick clay lay only in some places, which had to be shared. "Not everyone," Hugh Patrick Owens said, "had brick clay on their farm, so they all had to have their kilns in the same area." Turf-cutting was the District's most neighborly enterprise, and brick-making approximated its pattern, so slapbrick, though made for sale, involved no anxiety. No Wee Woman helped, no witch hindered, no mystery attended. Bricks were made openly and cooperatively. Slapbrick offered people a wide, clear route to profit.

Hugh Nolan, who, according to Peter Flanagan, once wrote a long song on the brick-making trade, begins:

"At one time the brick-makin was the industry of the country. It was all the material they had for buildin, do ye see.

"In later years the factory brick, it came along and it knocked out the slapbrick altogether.

"And later then the blocks come along.

"I don't think there was any slapbrick made in this country since the decade between nineteen and twenty and nineteen and thirty. It was inside of that decade that the last slapbrick was made in this country. No. I'm wrong now. There was a few cases where men wanted some brick for their own use. Aye, there was a man the name of Monaghan and his father made a kiln of brick in nineteen and thirty-nine. That would be the last brick that was made about this country. That was for his own use, do ye see, but as an industry the last of it would be in the twenties.

"The men that used to work at it are all dead and gone.

"Do ye see: brick clay was all through the country. And it was a big industry in Sessiagh, Rossdoney, them townlands in the vicinity of the Arney River.

"Them all had small farms that was in the brick industry. The larger ones didn't do so much of it unless they wanted to build something for themselves. They didn't adopt it for a livin.

"But the small farmers: it was principally be that they lived."

Though the men who made the brick are "all dead and gone," many who did the work are still alive. Paddy McBrien is one, Hugh Patrick Owens another. Though passed, "the brickin" lives. Odd formations rumple the grassy land. Old men talk, and depressions become the oval holes from which brick clay was dug, and hummocky lumps form into the staple-shaped ditched "stands" of old kilns. They talk so often that complete descriptions of the brick-making process can be provided by men like Joe Murphy who, at forty-four years old, never witnessed the work. Slapbrick lives in memory.[1]

Some memories sleep and do not stir until disturbed by the outlandish interviewer. Others are a vital, though invisible, part of daily life, as capable of exerting influence in a given situation as a fleshy audience. As a once important economic endeavor and the very model of how profit can be gained while communal connection is maintained, brick-making, though

United Creameries, Enniskillen. The stack was built of slapbrick made in the District which is called "Arney brick" in the Town. This is the first major landmark you meet when entering Enniskillen on the road from Ballymenone. It is a hard reminder of the old local industry.

gone, remains a power in the culture of today's storytellers. Most of them found it a way to make money, all of them find it useful to contemplate and interesting to discuss. It belongs with historical stories of landlords, famine, and witchcraft, so I will let Michael Boyle, who worked at the trade, recount the process. His statement is useful for its fullness, and more for the way he orders and emphasizes.

On an evening late in November 1972, Mr. Boyle is sitting up in bed in a suit and tie. The color is high in his cheeks, his mood is lithe and springy. I click the tape recorder on, and once some questions lingering from our last visit have found answers, he proposes a new topic, gives me a cigarette, I light us both, and he is off, leaving me to puff behind without need to prompt or question:

"The brick-makin. Well, do ye see, it was a heavy job.

"Did ye see any of the brick ponds around the country? They were in a ring. They were in a kind of a semicircle, do ye see, and there was water in them. They were from about—ah, they would be anything up to ten foot, ten foot across and ten foot deep.

"Oh, it would be ten feet deep, I'm sure.

"And first they had to dig off the top, what they called strippin. It was dug off with a spade. It was stripped the same as the bog, as the turf bog.

"Well then that was dug off first, and it was thrown to one side and carted away out of the road, the way that it wouldn't interfere with the *industry*.

"Well then you struck the proper clay for makin the brick. It was a blue—a sort of blue nature and there was seams of sand here and there through it, do ye see.

"Well there was water, do ye see, down in this brickhole and the clay was dug with a spade down into this water. They dug: they started at one end and they come on around in a circle. They took a bench about four foot wide. Four to five foot wide the bench was, and all in a semicircle.

"And they dug it down into this water and then when that finished, and they had no water, two men, well generally two—if there were three, well then, all the better, but generally two, it was a job just for two—they got in. And they used to take off their pants. Well, they usually wore like football togs, just knickers. And take off their boots and socks (and their legs were bare from there on down). And the worst ould shirt you could get, ould flannel bag, you put that on, and you got in, do ye see, with a shovel. But the shovel, do ye see, the top was cut off, the broad was cut off half way. And a short shaft, the shaft would only be about half the length of an ordinary shovel for shovelin land: just take a regular shovel and cut it off yourself.

"And then you got down into this brickhole, into this clay.

"And you turned it.

"You champed it up into grout, do ye see. It was fairly soft, but *not too soft*—middlin tough, you know.

"And there was a way of turnin it. You shoved it in like that, do ye see, and just turned it over nicely."

Mr. Boyle rams the short shovel into the pudding of clay and gracefully, slowly turns his wrists, revolving a shaft of air above the bedclothes. His memory is banked in specific gestures and words. Repeating the motions of work, his body releases its remembrance into his mind, and as he repeats the industry's technical terms, associations form within and a full, textured memory spreads outward from points of detail. For most men this phase of the process is unpleasant to recall. The cut-off pants and old shirt were an indignity, as was working in a muddy hole, up to your hips, "all over muck." No joy comes in remembering the long toil of paring clay from the walls of the hole, peeling it off, Peter Flanagan said, "like the leaves of a book," and turning, softening, mixing it in the murk at the pit's bottom. Hugh Patrick Owens called this "souring" and said it finally ended when you could throw shovelfuls across the hole and instead of landing in a "pancake" the clay was thin enough to "run," leaving a trail of "tails" back to you. Mr. Boyle turns his fists nicely, saying:

"Take your time at it. It was a job you couldn't rush—you wanted to take your time at it. You started here at this end and you went on round your circuit till ye came to the finish up, and then you turned then and came back again. And you turned it again. You gave it two turns, and every time ye turned a shovelful, you champed it down, if there was any lumps in it, do ye see, to break them up. And then you came on till you finished and it was all grouted, do ye see. And ye left it there for two days.

"That was, what they call, it was in the *sour*.

"It lay two days in the sour.

"And then if it was very warm weather, it would bake; it would get a kind of a crust on it. Well then, if it was very warm weather, you'd get branches of *trees*, black sallies, they used to grow in the bogs. And you'd throw those branches on top to keep the sun off it. Well, some people used to cut rushes, you know, and throw it in, but rushes wasn't the thing because they'd get into the clay, you see, work into the clay and stick in it. But these big black sallies, there were alot of leaves in them and they weren't heavy, and there was no bother throwin them in and there was no bother throwin them out. They were light.

"After two days then, they started operations.

"There was five men at the work.

"And whatever job you took up, that was yours for the day.

"There was one man, what they called, *throwin out*.

"The man throwin out, he got back again in the brickhole, do ye see, with his half shovel, the half cut off it and the short shaft. He wanted to be a strong man, good muscles, do ye see, and active. He shot it in that way with a kind of a . . ."

Mr. Boyle jabs his fists in a line.

"It was a knack, you know, shootin in the shovel. And he gathered and he slinged it away up over his shoulder and out on the bank. And the bank was ten feet high. Oh, that was a hard job. But then when he got used to the job, he wouldn't swap with any of them.

"He was called the thrower-out.

"Well then, there was the wheeler.

"The table that the brick was made on was situated about—it could be roughly between ten and fifteen yards from the bank where this clay was thrown out.

"Well then, there was a man with a barrow.

"And he was the wheeler.

"*Box barrow*, you know, and he had one of these shovels too. And there was a knack in liftin. You couldn't just shovel it the same as you were liftin a shovel full of mud. There was a knack in liftin. And he shoveled it into the barrow, but he had to throw it over his shoulder on top of other, you see: light it into the barrow, and as long as you lit the shovelfuls on top of other, they spread out.

"And before you filled your barrow atall, ye had to, what they called, sand it. There was sand left to the one side. Generally horses carted it. And you went and you got a handful of sand, do ye see, and ye dusted the barrow and the sides, and then the clay didn't stick to it, do ye see.

"And when you went to the spot where the table was, you went on with your barrow and you tipped it up. And the sand kept it from stickin, and it tipped out in a nice wee load at the table.

"That was two men of the staff.

"Well then, there was, what they called, the upstriker.

"He was generally a lump of a young lad, not fully a man; a teenager could be *it*. It wasn't a heavy job.

"Well, he cut the clay down to the ground. There was the way of his two hands."

Mr. Boyle puts the tips of his thumbs together between our faces. The palms are flat, the fingers extended together. Then he scoops his hands, rolling them downward, and, spreading his elbows, he pulls them up, cupped, while saying:

"Well, that was the position he had of his hands. He cut the clay down, and he cut it down to the ground, and when he hit the ground, he lifted it up nicely that way and he dumped it down on the table.

"Well, that was *three* men.

"Well then, there was the molder.

"He was generally an aged man. Well, he could be any age, but generally the men ever I seen at it, they were middle-aged men, gettin on to middle age. And their job was:

"The mold, it was nine inches long. And it was three inches broad. And it was two inches *deep*. And there was no *bottom*. It was made of boards, do ye see, and they were nailed up. And there were two lugs about the length of a man's thumb, and they were out at both ends.

"We'll say, there's the table."

He points, and descriptions others have given enter my mind. The up-striker's lump of clay sits at one end of the table. The wheeler has returned with his barrow to the bank for more. At an earlier time he would have driven a horse hauling a "slipe." The molder's end of the table with the open frame of the mold upon it is kept clear by boards tacked to its top. Next to him stands a bucket of water into which the mold is dropped, out of which it is retrieved to slap full while a second is carried, wobbling with wet clay, to the beds beyond, where the "green brick" will dry. Paddy McBrien, whose family was active in the industry, remembers his grandfather molding. Since his hands were always in clay, someone had to put the pipe in his mouth and light it for him while he worked.

". . . there's the table. The mold was there, situated on the table. And the clay was up. And the molder's job was to lift the clay in his two hands and he had to put it into the mold with a good crack to make it travel.

"And when he put it into the mold, he had to hit it with his two fists."

Mr. Boyle's fists pound down together, knuckles foremost.

"And when he had the mold properly filled, he would run his two thumbs over it that way, do ye see, to level it off."

He pushes his thumbs, their tips together, away from his chest.

"Well, that was *four* men employed.

"Four men employed.

"Well then, the next man then, he was offbearer. There was a knack in catchin it. He was at the edge of the table . . ."

"How ye doin, Michael?" A man in a bathrobe with a wistful face has appeared at our bedside. His greeting is returned, we are introduced, and the tape recorder turns, gathering up the "car smash" that put him in the hospital and Michael Boyle's efforts to buck him up:

"Well, how're you goin on, Bob?"

"Not too bad now."

"Ah, you're rightly."

"I was near killed."

"Well, no bones broken."

"No, no bones broken."

"Well, you're not so bad. Anytime a man's two legs and his two arms and his neck's not broken, he's all right." Gaily, Mr. Boyle bats the chat away from complaint into light laughter and works in a topically relevant narrative:

"I had an accident meself once,

and I barely escaped with me life.
"I was comin down the road with a horse and cart.
"This fellow overtook me with a lorry.
"And he struck the cart.
"And he driv me and horse and cart down the road for ten perch.
"And he driv me down the road.
"And he driv me past a big *tree*.
"And if I had've struck the tree,
    I wouldn't be talkin to yous the night."

Michael Boyle's reputation as an entertaining man draws people to his bed. His role requires him to give bracing repartee and time-passing tale. He carries his accident into court, where the lorry driver, though cracking the shafts of Mr. Boyle's cart and stripping the fender and running board off an oncoming car, was fined but two pounds. "He was breakin the law, but he had some excuse that the brakes on the lorry failed. And I didn't ask any compensation. I didn't go hard on him."

Mr. Boyle dispenses his entertainment swiftly, for the bells ending visiting hours have brutally terminated our talks in the past, and he has borne the treasure of his memory to the brink of death more than once. Earlier this year, he lay still as the pumps of his lungs sagged. He has improved each time I have seen him, maintaining our chats about history do him more good than the doctor's medications, and feeling fit, he is anxious to record on tape the facts fragilely assembled in his head. Our visitor is gently dismissed:

"Well, you're lucky to be alive."
"A miracle I came out of it."
"I say, you're lucky to be alive."
"Aye, indeed."
"Well, there's none of us but has rough times and narrow escapes."
"Aye. Well, all the best."
"All the best," I echo, while Mr. Boyle's "Good luck" carries him on.
"Civil old boy," he comments, turning back to me:

"But at any rate, aye, we've came to the offbearer. His job is catchin the brick in the mold like that . . ."

Mr. Boyle's hands frame a square of air horizontally, they slide away from me and tip quickly to the vertical, thumb knuckles up.

". . . and give it a quick pull to him, and he had to hold it that way on its side to not let the brick fall out of it, do ye see. He had to be an active good man there. He had to run about fifteen yards like that to lay the brick on, what they called, the bed.

"The beds were all leveled out. It was ordinary land, do ye see, but it had to be very level. It had to be very *dead* level. If it wasn't level, you'd put in a shovel or two of sand, do ye see, to have it perfectly level, because if it was uneven, the soft brick would crack and break.

"And then there was a knack in what they called *strippin* the brick. If you pulled the mold wrong, you put what they called a lock-tight on the brick and that spoiled it. Ye had to lift the brick up with a straight *chuck*. Pick it up straight. And then you had a complete, nice brick, nine by three by two, do ye see.

"Well then, that'd be left there on the beds.

"Well then, the day's work for them five men was four thousand and a half. Four thousand and five hundred brick, that was a day's work. And there was an odd staff of men, if they worked late, they might put out five, but it was very seldom that five was put out.

"Well then, half a thousand was what they called a cast. The way it was measured was: it twas twenty brick that way and twenty-five that way. And that was the cast. And when the half thousand was out, the table was moved, do ye see. The table was moved; it was gettin too close.

"Every cast, they moved the table, and then the business started again. And the cast was a half thousand.

"At any rate, that was the day's work: four and a half thousand.

"It was heavy work.

"Oh, it took good men. And it took men who knew how. They wanted to have the know-how and have the strength as well.

"So then, if the weather was good, about in two days, them brick were, what they called, edged: they were slipped up on edge.

"You went in your bare feet. And you didn't want to have the feet too big either. I remember, it was more a job for a youngster. But the youngsters wanted to be careful. The brick had got tough, of course, but they weren't dry yet. You wanted to be careful; you could happen to crack them. And you put them up on their edge. And then, if the weather was good, they lay a couple of days on their edge.

"And after that they were put into hacks, what they called hacks."

Mr. Boyle glances up from the invisible brick edged across his bed and spots a nicely dressed couple standing silently by him. "Hello Tommy. And Missus Boyle. How're ye doin?" He introduces his visitors as members of "the Boyle clan," and though they do not live in the District and I do not know them, they know me as the one who "bes in Flanagans' and Cutlers'."

Mr. Boyle tells them we are talking about brick-making and tells me that Tommy, like himself and his father, worked at it too. Quickly, he starts again, "I have the brick made anyway. But we haven't them burned." I interrupt him to say I can come back and he ought to enjoy his friends' company, but he protests, "Sure, these ones, they're as happy as Larry. They have the family of theirs out makin thousands of pounds." He turns from me and says, "Me and you were born in the wrong year, Tommy."

Laughing, Tommy agrees, "Aye, we were born too soon."

"Well," Michael continues, "if in our time we'd have got the chances that these boys is gettin now, what'd we not have done?

"I don't know now what we wouldn't have done.

"Aye, we'd have built a town,

                aye,

        or tossed one."

His clever pace and sly tone, the look of roguish delight in his eyes, pricks us all to laughter. Then they stand placidly, patiently, and he says:

"But at any rate, we had the brick on their edge, I think.

"Well then after about, och four or five days, or maybe a week, if the weather was good, they were put in what they called hacks.

"They were put in what they called hacks.

"The hacks was four brick high. They were built four brick high in big long rows, one brick wide—four or five brick high, it doesn't make much odds anyway."

Hugh Nolan had told me the hacks were seven bricks high, laid the long way, and the joints were "bricked," one brick on top of two for stability.

"And they were covered first with cabbage leaves. The rain had to be kept off them, do ye see. And they were covered first with cabbage leaves, big green leaves, and on top that went rushes. Rushes was cut and spread nice and finely over the cabbage leaves and then there had to be something put on top of that, a bit of clay or stones, to keep the wind from blowin it off.

"And then they lay in the hacks. Well, they could lie in, if ye hadn't the time or if ye had to go and win the hay or something. You see, they were always made in the summertime when the hay and turf and everything—it was a busy time, do ye see.

"Well, they lay in the hacks, well, maybe, they would lie for two weeks. If the weather was good, they'd dry the quicker. When they were a white color, that was the time that they were proper dry. When they were white, they were ready for stackin then.

"Well then, they put them in stacks. And the stack was built in an arch. First, a brick was left down, and another on top of that and you built them up about that high. And you kind of kept them slanted. And you built them up four or five foot high.

"And then, you see, you put on the first row. You put on the next row a wee bit in, and the next row a wee bit further in, and on and on, and you *met them*. You met the arch, five foot off the ground. And then you started and made nice rows on the top of that, big long rows.

"And they had to *thatched*.

"And they used to sow what they called rye.

"They used to thatch the houses with it.

"And every man that made brick had a plot of this rye, do ye see. And about every three rows you put it in, and you put a row of brick on top of it, so it wouldn't fall off, and when ye reached the top, you topped it out with one brick just.

"Well then, you cut what they call scollops. And you made hay ropes. And ye run the scollop into the stack, in between the brick, in the wee crevice. And ye platted the rope round the scollops and you went on around in a ring till ye had your stack very finely thatched and roped. And then it was safe from wind and storm."

In Mr. Nolan's account, the brick stacks, battered like gigantic turf clamps, tapering to their single capping row, had been thatched with rushes, rushes along the foundation and over the top, covered with grass that took a bond. They were thatched, he said, like hay stacks or straw stacks. Then they were roped around—he specified three times—and across by the most careful workers, after the manner of turf lumps. Mr. Mc-Brien said reed could also be used for thatching brick stacks. We follow Mr. Boyle as he describes the purpose of the opening created by corbeling the courses of brick:

"You see, the stack was arched to help them dryin. Any wind came, went in through the arch and went up through them, do ye see, and helped to leave them ready for burnin.

"So then, they lay there in the stacks for a while until ye got the time, generally in the harvest time, and the hay was won and the turf was won and you burned them *then*."

Stacked and well-thatched, the brick could be left over the winter. Paddy McBrien's family burned them twice a year. But harvest was the usual time, according to Mr. Boyle:

"You burned them then.

"They were drawn to the kiln.

"I'm sure you've seen the stands of a few old kilns.

"There's a farm belongin to a man the name of Monaghan along the Rossdoney Road there. He made brick. There's the stand of an old kiln there.

"Well, the McBriens made brick. But the stand of their kiln's been drawn away.

"Well then, the kiln was arched the same as the stack, only that there was more arches in it. Generally there was a five-arch kiln. And the stack would have only one arch. There was five arches in the kiln, and they were built up about four foot. They were gathered to, do ye see, till you went up this four foot and then they were *closed*, do ye see. The arch was closed.

"And then they were all burnt.

"The day of the buildin, the day of the puttin them into the kiln was called the *crowdin*. They were crowded then, do ye see. That used to be a great day longgo. That we used to draw them in on the horses. There would be three or four horses, and there'd be a man drawin with every horse. Well then, there'd be a man out in the field and he'd be takin off this thatch and burnin it up carefully and puttin it to the one side and helpin the boys to build the *carts*.

"And they come in then, and—oh, it twas a big day's work; it took nine or ten men to be at it.

"And then a man would come in and he'd start on his lone and he'd pick two brick.

"We'll say I was here and you were there—generally the brick passed through about three or four hands. I was in the cart, we'll say, and I pitched two brick. And you catched them in your two hands. And you pitched them on to the next man. And the next man catched them and he pitched on to the next man, and the next man catched them and he pitched them on, till they went to the man, what they called, the crowder.

"And he was down, the same as he was buildin on a wall, only he had no mortar, do ye see."

Hugh Nolan had told me, "There was certain men that had the idea of crowdin, but it wasn't general knowledge. There was many men at the crowdin of the kiln, but it was only three or four men in the locality that had the knowledge of the crowdin of the kiln." They began by laying three pairs side-by-side and a pair across them to begin the second course. Then the next side was begun, two bricks high, two feet to thirty inches away from the first, and the first row was continued for the length of an Irish perch of seven yards. Two rows of brick raised the parallel walls higher. Then, said Hugh Patrick Owens, who worked at crowdin, "you sprung from the fourth and closed at the seventh": the fifth course overhung the one below it, the sixth overhung that, until at the seventh course the bricks touched and a corbeled arch of the kind that vaults the tombs of prehistoric chiefs, roofs the cells of ancient saints, and supports the chimney breasts of local homes, resulted. "The whole trade in it," Mr. Nolan commented, "was gettin the brick met at the top of the arch." Then other arches were raised contiguously, and brick was coursed the length of the kiln to the height of twenty-five rows. Each arch would contain, Mr. Owens said, four thousand bricks. A kiln, according to Mr. McBrien, would have three to six arches. The number was usually four, Mr. Nolan said. Mr. and Mrs. Boyle wait. Michael goes on:

"Well, there was a knack in pitchin. You weren't supposed to sling. You shot like that, do ye see . . ."

His hands form around the missing brick and swing forward together, smartly.

". . . to keep the nose up, the way they were easy catched. Mind ye: they were hard; they were hard on the hands. But if ye slung them like that . . ."

He tosses his hands across his body.

". . . it wouldn't do because they'd separate and one might fall. You wouldn't have so far to pitch them. We'll say you wouldn't have more nor two yards to pitch.

"And then, when the kiln was crowded, generally the height of the kiln was twenty-five brick, from the ground up. That included the arch and all. Twenty-five brick when she was crowded—they used to call the kiln *she*, like a ship—when she was crowded, the first thing they done after the crowdin was: the whole top of her was all covered with turf. *Turf*, do ye see, the ordinary turf that used to be cut in the bog. But it had to be light, light in nature. They wouldn't do, the heavy black turf. They weren't so good. It was a blaze they wanted, you see, so they used the fums.

"When the kiln was all covered with turf, well then there was a mound of clay built up, dug with spades, and sods and clay and *mud* of all descriptions, built up, do ye see, around the whole kiln, only the front where the arches were: they were left open. It was built up after the crowdin till ye went about two foot from the top, and that might be left.

"And then the front of it then was plastered with clay. The whole front of it was plastered. Ye went away and ye dug a load of clay and ye mixed it. Ye threw a bucket of water on it and champed it up like you're mixin mortar for buildin with two shovels. And then a couple of fellows would slap it up against the front of the kiln with shovels. That was to keep in the *heat*. And they rubbed the shovels over it—oh, plastered it very nicely.

"So then, they were complete then.

"Then they lit the fires then and let them burn until they had plenty of coals. And throw a bucket of coals in every arch. And then they got the blaze goin.

"And they burned the kiln in the front for about three days. And then the fire was shoved back. They had a big long shovel with a big long shaft in it. Christ, it was a hot job. There used to be terrible heat about it. The coals was crushed and crushed; they were crushed away to the back.

"And then they used to stand and, what they called, they'd feed them. They used to feed old turf to the back. And that was a nice job doin that. You see, it was only an odd man was an expert at it. Ye fired the turf and ye had it hit the center of the arch back there, and it hopped until it went to the far back stone. It wasn't just a kind of a shot in, ye know."

As Peter Flanagan had demonstrated for me, feeding involved a low sidearm, wrist-flicking pitch. The turf had to sail on a hop the length of the arch and hit the backstone built of old brick. The Boyles wait, listen, talk:

"And about three days more—or less—it took to finish.

"Well then, when the kiln got real hot and the blaze got up into her, the turf on top took *fire*.

"And as long as they burned, there had to be a mixture of what they called *yardin*—it was lumps of clay champed up fine, and it was brought up and thrown on top of the ashes of the turf on the top.

"And as long as she burned off, that was called strippin.

"And as long as she stripped, she had to be yarded.

"Till she was burned.

"And when the whole turf was burned off, your kiln of brick was burned.

"Well then, there was a couple of foot, we've heard before, that was left. Well then as long as she burned, that mound had to be made up to the *very* top.

"So when the kiln of brick was burned, she was covered on top with this yardin and banked up all round: she was complete.

"Well then, she had to be left there for two or three days."

Mr. and Mrs. Boyle make a motion of departure, "Well, we'll be goin."

"All right then, Michael says. "I don't know but I'll not be long till I'm out."

"All the best," they wish, leaving.

"All the best. Thanks for callin on me, Tommy, Missus. So any rate, she had to be left there of course a good while, after she'd what they call, cool. She'd cool down. You know, you daren't go near her to strip her to take any brick out of her because she was mad of fire. She'd burn the hands off ye.

"So she was left there a week and perhaps more, maybe a fortnight, until ye got a sale. And if ye got a sale, ye didn't wait too long, remember. Money wasn't too plentiful thattime. No.

"So then, do ye see, when ye got a sale, you took a notion you'd strip her to see what way your brick were: were they burned right or were they lookin well. And then when you got a sale, you stripped her and took her down in benches. And most of them was drawn to Enniskillen on horses and carts.

"Well, prior to my time, they used to locate alot of the kilns near the water edge, near the bank of the Arney River. You can see alot of stands of old kilns along the banks of the Arney River, in the townlands of Rossdoney and Derryhowlaght and Drumbrughas; them three townlands they built their whole kilns near the banks of the water.

"Well that time they were cotted. They were cotted to Enniskillen in cots. A big cot held two thousand.

"And it was a rough job. It took strong men to do that and they wanted to know how too.

"These big cots, do ye see, they were pulled with two big oars, a man at each oar. And then there was a man in the end with a wee bit of a short stick; it twas made like an oar, and he was, what they called, *steerin*. And his job was: he was sittin, lookin over his shoulder, to keep her straight in case she'd go to the shore. Well then, the two men, they sat with their backs to the front. Two big strong men, and the way that they had to pull the oars: they'd dip them down into the water and give them a shot every time they dipped in, and they sent the cot further on. And that man, what they called the steerer, he was sittin in the tail end, and he was paddlin about with this short stick. It was a kind of a flat affair. And he kept the cot straight.

"So they cotted that. I don't mind how many hours it took them to go with a cot of brick from the Rossdoney shore till they landed in Enniskillen.

"They landed in Enniskillen. There was a big contractor, the name of James Harvey. And he built alot of Enniskillen. He built half of Enniskillen. And he bought the weight of the brick along our banks, the Rossdoney banks."

Mr. Boyle receives a cigarette and lights us up without pausing:

"And he had a big yard. And they cotted them to this yard. And they had what they called a hand barrow. It was two handles on this end and two handles on that end, and you filled it, you see: put so many bricks on it. A man got into the two handles on that end and a man got into the two handles on this end and they lifted together and they walked out of the cot into this yard of Harvey's. And they had to count them. They put so many brick on a barrow, I think fifty on the barrow. And a brick was seven pound. They were seven pound weight. Seven pound! And I think it was fifty brick they carried on the barrow. And so many barrows then, they had to carry in. And Harvey, the contractor, always sent his man there for to watch the count to see that he was gettin the right measure, gettin the right count, to see that they weren't doin him in.

"So then, when the cot was empty, so of course they were hungry. Naturally. And naturally, they were all big feeders. Of course. Food: they wanted it. So then they went away and they bought a big loaf; it was a four-pound loaf. I never mind a four-pound loaf; it was always a three-pound loaf in my day. It was a four-pound loaf. Oh, I think it would fill a cart nearly when it was cut down ◊. So they away and they got a four-pound loaf. And they bought—there was three of them, and they bought three pound of beef
     and tea
     and sugar
     and butter.

"And there was a woman lived in Enniskillen convenient to Harvey's yard. And I'll tell ye the kind of a restaurant she kept. You brought her in the food and she boiled the kettle and made the tea. You supplied the food and she cooked it.

"So, the loaf cut up, and they sat down. And they got a couple of big mugs of good strong tea, you know, and they fairly left by the food all right. Well, they wanted it.

"Well, they were goin to rest for a while in this house. And they pulled their chairs up to the fire. And they were all pipe smokers of course. And there was tobacco they called black twist. Black twist. Oh, it was terrible strong. Me nor you, we wouldn't be able to smoke it.

"Well, they all smoked it. Do ye see, it was in a big roll and they got two ounces of it for sixpence at the time. It was cut with a knife, and they teased it, you know, and stuck it in these big pipes, generally clay pipes. And they lit them and they took a good smoke and then they went out and they drunk two or three pints of porter apiece.

"Every man bought a drink. There was three of them. And that man, three pints and them was drunk. And the next man, three pints and them was drunk. The next man, three pints and them was drunk. So then, they headed for home.

"Well then, they often contacted storms comin home. And the stream, do ye see: when they were goin to Enniskillen, the stream of the Lough was with them, but when they were comin back, the stream was against them. But they had an empty cot, of course. There was no weight. No, they had no weight in the cot. But then often there was parts of the Lough, outside Enniskillen and on up—very stormy. It could get stormy very quick. It could get rough. Oh, often and often, they had to lie in to beat the storm. Now, a good waterman, as they were, will pull in somewhere and tie the cot. And often, well it was: walk home or go to some house, and if they knew them, they'd keep them for the night. And if they couldn't get anyone to keep them, they'd have to walk home in the middle of the night, because there was no other way, and go back the next day and bring the cot home.

"Well, them men now carried on the whole winter at that. Except an awful day that they couldn't venture out."

The bell. The signal to end visitors' hours clangs through the ward, and Mr. Boyle has gotten brick-making on tape. Victory. While a man drifts from a bed nearby to greet us and receive his portion of wit and anecdote (the story will exemplify the bad manners of the man who leaves the company he is drinking with in a public house), Mr. Boyle concludes his account:

"See, money was scarce; it was very scarce in Ireland thattime. And there was very little employment for the men, especially the laborin class men. There was no employment for them atall in the winter, except for a man that had a wee bit of a trade or something.

"Well, how's Billy?"

Conforming to academic tradition, scholars who care about tales generally do not care about technology, and scholars who care about technology do not care about tales, and scholars who profess an interest in culture often disregard both. Yet the people of Ballymenone, and many like them, present their culture to themselves, and so to others, most richly in the stories they build out of words and the artifacts they build out of earth. No hobbyhorse will be ridden to truth. Imaginative literature and stolid objects couple to express collective mentality as dark and light make a day.

At night, when the body rests at the hearth, the mind sails, seeking the limits. Pleasure depends upon its excess. Good tales are built out of exceptions to define reality by extremes. During daylight, the body moves and the mind bears down on its tasks, directing the hand through familiar routines. Life depends upon its success. Good work rises from repetition to define reality at its center.

History stores experience. Working by extremes, its stories place Mr. McBrien and Mrs. Timoney on one side to endure the worst, and the Owens family on the other to do better than the best, gaining wealth through supernatural agency. But a wide space is left between where normal life transpires. There stand the brick men. Pushing them to the fore, Mr. Boyle's account deserves close attention.

Stories posit the normal by the abnormal. They must be reduced or reversed to find the commonplace. You are unlikely to be a Saint Patrick or a Black Francis or a man in the midst of a famine. You should not be a witch stealing from your neighbors or a landlord racking them. What you can and should be is one of the brick makers—not necessarily as they were, but as Mr. Boyle portrayed them.

The brick men were heroic. They did rough, heavy, dirty, hot work. They were strong diggers and rowers and lifters. Two of them could walk away with a hand barrow bearing three hundred and fifty pounds. They were active and agile, racing through the day with soft brick for the beds. They faced storms and walked miles through the thunder when the waters of the Lough kicked up.[2] Michael Boyle used local convention when he used their hearty intake to signify health. A big appetite means robust constitution. They ate four-pound loaves such as we have not seen. They smoked tobacco too strong for the likes of us. They were individuals of great stamina and physical strength. Yet they did everything cooperatively: two men to dig, five to mold, a crowd to crowd, three to cot, two to carry, three to drink. In every gesture—digging, wheeling, upstriking, molding, offbearing, stripping, pitching—the hands worked together as a unit, efficiently, symbolically: all is multiple but unified.

The brick men were strong and they were smart. Twice Mr. Boyle said it in nearly identical words: "It took strong men to do that and they wanted to know how too." You had to be more than industrious and strong. It took a "knack," he said, to shoot the shovel, to lift, mold, catch, strip, edge, pitch, crowd, feed, cot. Things were not merely done, they were done "nicely," "carefully," "perfectly," "properly," "finely," with finesse. Well-molded brick, well-thatched stacks, well-arched and plastered stacks—all display pride, a touch of artistry, as well as efficiency.

Mr. Boyle's account meets his standards. He avoided abstractions and utilized exact repetition for the sake of clarity (reread his description of clay-champing, brick-pitching, cotting, drinking in the pub). He ordered his thoughts with discipline (remember how he marched the five men through their work and kept the process in neat sequence within its temporal frame). Clear communication is both an aesthetic act and a neigh-

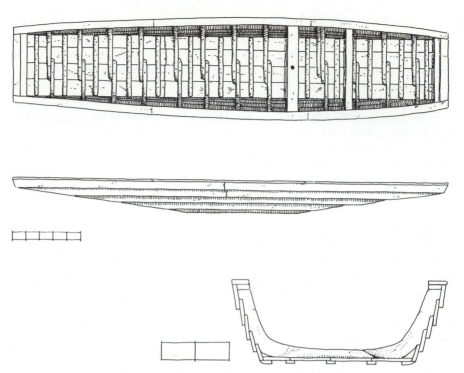

Cot. View from the top and side and a section through a boat, beached and
rotting on Trasna Island, which is locally said to be the last cot on Upper
Lough Erne. In August 1978, six years after I measured this one, I saw one in
use on the wide Lower Lough, ferrying cattle between the mainland and an
island. This one, owned by Terence Leroy, was powered by one sail, and,
fitted with high rails on the sides, it was also used to transport cattle. It is of
oak with a long-boarded bottom, framed by pairs of overlapping knees, most
of them on twenty-seven-inch centers, between which planks are pinned and
stapled. See note 2 to this chapter. Scales in feet.

borly, ethical, ultimately moral act; self-control is an obligation of the good
man. Mr. Boyle's art lay mainly in his strength and efficiency, yet while he
strove for full clarity, he wished to be entertaining too, most obviously when
he exaggerated the size of the four-pound loaf, borrowing an idea from a
pant by John Brodison, who once dug a spud out of upland ridges so large
it rolled downhill and blocked the Derrylin Road. It had to be cut in lengths
with a crosscut saw and carted away. Mr. Boyle built his statement on the
model in slapbrick. He got it done, nicely.

And he built his account on the model in stories. Telling about brick-
making clearly, completely, interestingly, Mr. Boyle enacted at once the role
of the day's good worker and the night's good talker. The people in his ac-

count fulfilled the ideals in stories. They were strong like the heroes of exploits, smart and artful like the stars of bids and pants, bold and cooperative like the Swanlinbar boys and the men of Mackan. Yet they were average men in average times.

Brick-making lives in memory as an intense instance of the old way working well. It brought great virtues—strength, intelligence, neighborliness—to bear on a difficult problem: turning soft, damp clay into hard, dry building material. The problem was solved. Brick-making embodies a specific version of the culture's formula for success.

Naturally, the land sprouts grass and bears bog and seams of sandy blue clay. Men cut these substances free of the earth with iron-bladed weapons: scythes, spades, shovels. They form the material into rectangular units, strips of grass and blocks of bog and blue clay. Then they spread them: the hay lies on the broad band, the turf on the spread, the brick on their beds. Next men build them into intermediate forms: hay rooks, turf clamps, brick hacks. The wind of the wet land is used to dry them, then separate constructions are brought into architectural unity in hay stacks or pecks or sheds, turf stacks or lumps, and brick stacks. Freed units spread on a single plane are twice rebuilt into larger compositions, much as individuals, without surrendering responsibility for their lone souls, are joined into communities, communities into the neighborhood of "all mankind." And as individuals are taken from the raw state, heated and dried into social utility, as vegetables are cooked, so wild substances are tamed and transformed, literally, from the natural, wet, and useless into the artificial, dry, and useful. Dry, potentially useful, they are "won," then in the last stage wetness is utterly obliterated in burning, and the useful is used. Hay is consumed to make protein. Turf is burned to make heat. Brick is burned to make money. Energy is consumed by life.

A pyre of victory, turf glows on the hearthstone, while the winds of winter rise, the kiln cools, and the cattle feed, fat in their byres. Once their dinner of cabbage and potatoes is done, people leave the table beneath the window embracing the gray-green fields and return to the hearth for a cup of creamy tea, a taste of tobacco, some chat about cows and climate. With this scene people give themselves a quiet symbol of their mastery over their damp environment and proof of their culture's validity. Land into shelter and food and pleasure: God's gift has been transformed into enough and a little bit more.

The little bit more symbolized in slapbrick does not extend to wealth. No Wee Woman adds her luck. No tales are told of empires built of clay. As Michael Boyle emphasized time and time again, lack of wealth is not due to lack of hard work or know-how. It is only that when industry and intelligence are constrained by community and set in normal times, and normal times are made of storms and the greedy plots of the rich, then great virtues bring comfort, not wealth. The brick men did not make money like hay, they made hay. Mr. Boyle ended his account of brick-making—just as he ended his tales of Mrs. Timoney and Mr. McBrien—at food, the work-er's desert. But the brick makers' reward, their bread and butter and beef, sugar and tea, their hours of rest, pipes of tobacco and pints of porter, were better by far than a bowl of gruel or a solitary fish.

Brick-making was ample to producing comfort for the family—and gifts for the neighbors. The best older homes, like Mrs. Cutler's, are built of stone. Those of intermediate age, the Croziers' or the Keenans', which was once the bailiff's residence, are laid up of brick. But brick was also given gratis to poorer people so their habitations could be more permanent than clay or sod and snugger than timber. Generosity is added to the brick men's virtues. Hugh Nolan provides the coda:

"How they used to know the brick was burned was: there used to come a burnin drop. It'd appear between two brick, and then they'd know they had fired enough. Some that wasn't experienced, they'd give it too much fire, and the brick would come out shaly, and they'd fall apart.

"Well, there was no kiln that was crowded or burned, but there was the soft brick. It could come out in any part of the kiln where the fire wasn't right. You could give it too much fire, do ye see, or you could give it not enough.

"When they used to be testin the brick, the buyers would hit them to-gether. And real good brick had the sound of two bottles there that you'd strike. And the soft brick, it made a deaf sound.

"And if they had a kind of a dull noise, they was called rejects. There was many little houses put up with rejects.

"They used sand and lime for the plaster.

"Do ye see: at every holdin there was a cot, a wooden affair. And it was manned by three men. There was two men with big heavy oars, pullin. And there was a man standin in the back to keep it straight.

"Well, they used to go out with these cots, and they had an apparatus for puttin down in the water. It had a scoop like what you'd see in the shop there, only larger.

"Well then, it went down then, and a man with a windlass brought the bucket back up and tumbled it into the cot.

"There's no cots left. Well, there might be some on Lower Lough Erne, but there's not many there now. Aye, there might be some of them cots to be had yet. And what they were used for was: conveyin cattle, horses and everything from the mainland to the islands.

"Well, there was no such thing as sand pits like now. And they got their sand in these cots, do ye see.

"Well, they wanted lime. There was no cement, do ye see. So they got stones and built a kiln. And they heaved stones into it. It was a round af-fair. And they'd fill it to the very top. And there was a place at the bottom where they'd put the fire.

"Well them stones burned and burned and burned and burned and burned and burned.

"They had to be limestone because there was slaty stone in this country too. And the fire crumbled them away until they come out lime. White lime. When that lime cooled, it come out in a pile at the bottom.

"Well, you'd mix the lime with sand for buildin, for mortar. It used to be melted down with warm water. And then the house would be whitewashed inside and outside, and they made the whitewash out of lime.

"You see, there was some of the lime, it used to come down in lumps, and some of it come out fine. Well, they used the fine for buildin purposes and the lumpy stuff made the best whitewash.

"Well. When a man's kiln of brick was opened, there was always some of these rejects.

"And the rejects was lyin all over. They were very handy then. Them brick was there at no cost. The soft, reject brick was left lyin around; it was there for the takin.

"And as long as you kept the house whitewashed, that house was *good*. The soft brick wanted whitewash, you see. And any place the brick would decay, you'd plaster with sand and lime. After a certain number of years, the sand and lime would die. It wasn't like cement, do ye see. Cement will live for years and years. But this sand and lime, it'd die and the wall would have to be reworked.

"Well, lime was a shillin the bag and sand was got in the River. And the brick was just lyin around.

"For the roofin, they went out through the lands and cut a straight tree and made ribs out of that. And a tie went across to hold the sides together. And then they'd thatch it then.

"Oh, things was done very cheap in them days.

"Everybody lived in an economizin way."

In remembered days, strong, smart workers actively accepted God's gift and cooperatively produced enough to live on, and a little bit more to console the self and give away to bind the community together. It was a hard life.

PART EIGHT

A Place on The Holy Land

22

Humanity

Humanity is our issue. The scholar's duty is questioning the shape of his or her own world, logically rebelling against its impulse to consolidate. Scholars who study people serve their own society by arguing with its definition of humanity. As a culture tightens around its vision of what it is to be human, its thinkers battle to keep things loose, driving forward, believing there is more to learn. Some scholars work by internal critique, feeling their society's pains like hypochondriacs, asking whether its own humanity is fully achieved, whether its treatment of others is humane. Others work by affirmation, by celebrating human excellence. Affirmation is the way of Ballymenone's thinkers, and it is the tradition of my discipline, folklore. Like history and anthropology, folklore is a romantic science that questions the status quo, seeking to disarrange and improve it through description and analysis of the qualities of people who might be forgotten or misunderstood, ignored, even mistreated. They must be brought to life, given a human presence so complete that its intrinsic order will challenge the norms of the society that provides the scholar a good living. That is the scholar's job, the way he earns his keep.

Academic disciplines provide refuge and exercise for technicians, but for the scholar the discipline is a way to become an intellectual.[1] The discipline trained the mind that no single profession can contain, and it remains the locus of a problem of wide importance. The problem of history is progress. Were the dead once people? The problem of anthropology is race. Are dark people human? The problem of folklore is class. Are the inhabitants of all economic estates people?

Yes, of course. But the answer comes too easily. If we believed our words, how could we support progress on the assumption that we are better than the people of the past, how could we support imperialistic schemes on the assumption that we have much to give and little to learn from societies we are pleased to call underdeveloped, how could we support an economic system that unequally distributes wealth on the assumption that some are more deserving than others? The slow, awkward answers to those questions will wind around to the idea of superiority. Some people (those most like ourselves, it will be found on reflection) are better than others. Those others—dead, dark, poor—are human, surely, in their bodies. They might be superior in strength like beasts. They have souls. They might be morally superior like angels. But we have named our species Homo sapiens. The real question is, Do they think well? Are they fully human?

Good thinking, our tradition holds, comes of diverse experience and leads to complex expression. During the Renaissance, when our tradition found its pace, people were sent out to explore unknown territories, expanding our knowledge, and monuments were sent up to embody complexity. Travel and technology signal our superiority. How, then, is our culture to be challenged by people who do not travel and have not produced a Santa Maria del Fiore or a hydrogen bomb? In our culture, primitive people (we still call them that) serve as a fascinating survival of an earlier stage of our development, and peasants at once fossilize our past and illustrate the colorful degradation of our achievement. While they languish in ignorance with the people of past times, conducting outré rites and perpetrating barbaric mimicry, evolution sweeps them yearning in our direction. Not so fast.

To be human even in body is to possess a brain capable of vast complexity. It follows that a people who do not control great material resources will accomplish complexity in a spiritual medium. Myth is one such. From Malinowski and Benedict to Lévi-Strauss, anthropological arguments have swung from myth as social charter to myth as imaginative negation and come to the conclusion that myth is a mode of thought, functioning as scholarship, as science and art do in our world. If the analogy is suggestive, a question remains. If myth is their technology, their realm of complexity, what is their travel?

Isolation is relative. For all people, there are others. Most have contact with outsiders, and all develop internal diversity—clans, clubs, moieties, castes, factions, classes—to complicate action and stimulate thought. Still, savage experience seems limited when compared with that of the explorer, the reader, the cosmopolitan junketeer. The capacity to think may be great, but with little to process through the mythic mill, the flowing savage remains potent, but like a child, incomplete, less than wholly human. In his grand discourse on totem and myth, however, Claude Lévi-Strauss has demonstrated nature to be an enormous resource for thinking. Just as we think by comparing people—biographically, psychologically, historically, ethnologically—the maker of myth thinks by comparing nature and culture, endlessly exploring through metamorphosis the interrelation of the human and nonhuman dimensions of the world.

The anthropological liberation of the savage mind leaves the agricultural consciousness, the worker's mind, bound. The celebration of the savage mind is accomplished by separating thought from action, art from life—by breaking, once again, the mind from the body. When that split is projected into the whole human world, some (the savages and philosophers) contemplate, while others (the savages and the artists) express, but the workers work and do not think. The savage becomes a leisured intellectual, a real person like ourselves, and the humanity of the worker remains in question.

If we consider Ballymenone's people as tellers of myths and as naturalists, twice we will come to the same conclusion. Work is a way to think.

The District's narratives of the beginning tell how the Saints altered the land, discovered its properties, and lit the eternal flame. The Saints are important for humanizing and localizing the sacred. Their message is profound, but not complex. The mythic corpus of Ballymenone is not expansive, nor is it rich enough to operate as a philosophical system. It will not bear comparison with the Zuni or ancient Greek, but it does not have to, for it exists not in isolation but as a part of life. Stories propose ideas that are refined and widened in workaday experience, then proposed anew in stories. Only when they are linked to daily work, to the creation of the landscape, can stories lead us or their people to philosophy.

The District's people are casual naturalists. They know the uncultivated world well enough to cross in thought the barriers separating the natural and the cultural. Heather flourishes beyond tamed spaces, and the young woman running out of control is "wild as heather, Jesus, she'd drink Lough Erne." Young males are "cubs," manly men are "bucks," rakes are "rams." People can be "cold as a frog" or "wicked as a wasp." Unmannerly people leave company abruptly, "away like a hare off a stump" or "like snow off a ditch." Farmers imagine the "broc," the badger, to be sort of a farmer. By the light of the big moon at the end of the harvest, "the broc's moon," he pulls grass out of the hedge and makes "the broc's fodder" by spreading it on the stubble of the cornfields, where it is "won" to provision him through the winter.

There is unity between the followers of the old way and the beasts of the fields who have been comparably overwhelmed by progress. Farmers hold sympathy for the rabbits eradicated by induced disease and miss the wild bees that once nested in the thick "sole" of the grass of the meadows but have not survived the artificial fertilizer and the earlier cutting silage requires. Surveying the bog once filled with men at work, Hugh Nolan said, "Even the wild geese that nested in the bog have gone."

Ballymenone's view of nature is not complete and contained. It will not measure up to that of the professional biologist or the inhabitant of jungle or savannah who uses the habits of birds and beasts, the traits of nature, as an independent realm for thought, and study of nature within the District is mostly channeled for human service. People observe the behavior of "Reynard" to protect their fowl, and of the salmon so they can be netted or gigged. The bees they miss provided sweetening for tea, the rabbits they miss were a source of food, as Peter Flanagan tells:

"There's some grand hares still, but we wouldn't eat them in this country now.

"Have you heard tell of maximitosis? I don't know is it in your country.

"The hares is immune from it, they say. But after that—the lanes was filled with the rabbits dyin—we never cared about eatin the rabbit or the hare in this country. They were a great food on till its introduction away back about fifty. Nineteen and fifty.

"The rabbit was a very nice wee animal."

Observing nature, people have learned that bright stars are a sign of frost, that a jay on the wing or a "weather goll," a fragment of rainbow far to the north or east, presages bad weather, that stormy winters mean good summers, mild winters bad ones, that wind from the east travels overland bringing sickness. James Owens had a neighbor who had a goat who knew bad weather, and if the goat came in he would not go out, even if the skies seemed clear. Cold stays in the steel of the hearthside tongs, and if the air feels warm when the tongs do not, good weather is only passing. These are farmers, and as they often remark, "It all depends on the weather." When they look over the land and proclaim it lovely, what appeals to them is not nature, but reflections of their work, their presence, their cooperation with divine purpose, their husbanding of His gift, His light dancing on their smooth fields. Banished to the mountains, imprisoned in hedges and forths, nature is conceptually and actually subservient to farming.

Ballymenone's people do not accomplish their humanity, their fullness of mind, by contemplating nature like a savage or romantic poet. They do not paint landscapes, they create them in the round. They act. If the savage mind expands by imagining transformations between the natural and the cultural, the consciousness of Ballymenone rises during alchemical toil, while the natural is literally transformed into the cultural, while food is cooked and bricks are burned. Outsiders, who will not attend to the work at life's center, lock country people in grim fatalism, painting their faces with the heavy masks of Millet, or they set them dancing to forgotten tunes like jolly, loose-jointed puppets.

Look around. Your environment is feeble with meaning. How was this book made, its paper formed? What is the composition of its ink? Where did the trees that became your chair grow? Who was the man who framed your roof or butchered your beef, and how did he go about his work? Our cultural environment is like the District's natural environment. We know it well enough to get by, to make it into metaphor, to use it as an argument for the correctness of our civilization, but we do not know it well enough to use as a way to consciousness. It is not big enough to travel in.

In Ballymenone, things are different. There technology is travel. Suppose you lived in the District and wanted a new home. When Paddy Mc-Brien did, he went to his neighbor, the mason, and described the house in his mind, designed "on the track" of one in which he had lived in Drumbargy. The mason's wife sketched the plan. The mason suggested an additional door to ease internal flow, Paddy agreed, and the house was built down the hill in Rossdoney. They staked it out together, and Mr. Moore laid it up, while Mr. McBrien brought in the material, mixing the mortar, cutting the timber himself from land near the Arney. Tonight he sits in an object formed within his control. Nothing alien, his surroundings disassemble in his memory from object into process, from process into plan. His home came of his mind's work. If it works as shelter, his plan was correct: he is "right." At home, the mind and body hold healthily together.

Some mystery pricks thought. One reason for the importance of the windows that expand in size with each renovation is that rock-hard, water-clear glass is bought, not made by local people. Pots and crooks and tongs were a comparable focus in the past. Metal was the major technological mystery. In ancient days the smith was a magician, and in the days of the old people his mundane product was counterposed to otherworldly mystery.[2] Joe Flanagan told us that "a ghost won't go near steel," that a turf spade, like a prayer, will protect you, and people in the past stuck steel pins in their clothes when traveling dark, haunted routes. Steel tongs were placed across the cradles of infants to prevent them from being stolen by fairies. In Peter Flanagan's story an iron hoop was used in the attempt to retrieve a man from fairy land. But too much mystery dulls the mind, releasing sensations of powerlessness through the frame. "Wisdom" said the saintly A.E., "is the right relation of our own being to That in which we live, and move, and have our being."[3] Without knowledge of the world we inhabit, we stagnate in environmental alienation, allowing the mind to follow the body into inaction, yielding the right to be wise.

There was little mystery and much to contemplate in the old home. It rose complexly out of specialization and expertise, while remaining accessible to all thoughtful people. Brick, plaster, whitewash, lumber for roofing and furniture, thatch, turf, bread, butter, cabbage, spuds, fish for dinner, cures for illness, poteen for a spree—all was processed by these people out of this earth.

Precisely through the creation of the land, they taught themselves to think about themselves. Work gave them the thickest, most serious way to form and test their thought. Add religion beneath work, making God's gifts and commandments its foundation, then crown it with pleasure, the fluttering notes of the fiddle and the hilarity of the free-spinning yarn, and you are ready to confront their culture.

Now dismember that culture, label its parts, pack them into familiar categories. Science seems to have been served. Our culture has been preserved. The false scholar has plundered reality to contribute more coin to our treasury of knowledge, without threatening the norms of his discipline, much less the values of his society. The status quo holds.

Instead, face that culture, trying to construct it as its people do, compassionately entering their subjective. Then we risk confusion, contradiction, and repetition, to come at truth and offer our culture the challenges it needs to advance.

At the center of the District's life, earth is cut, molded, and made anew. Through working the land, its people locate themselves.

23

Society

Work sets people among other people.

The District's community is not coterminous with a physical feature, be it natural like an island or cultural like an English village. Nor does it coincide with any division of church or state. It is larger than a townland. It is contained within Cleenish Parish and the Barony of Clanawley, and it once lay in the Schoolands. But it is smaller than these, and its shape is discovered through the net of neighborliness. The hearths on the hillsides are connected by people who walk the lanes at night and who work together in the meadows, on the moss and bog filling the dips between the drumlins, and those arrangements exist in constant flux. Blue clay coursed beneath the sod along the Arney, and the common problem of processing and marketing brick realigned the District's people. During the era of conflict, 1879–1923, political opinion followed the social channels deepened by the brick men. Patterns of work and therefore ceiliing and therefore political commitment reordered social affinities, and with them the shape of community, so that Upper Ballymenone, once oriented northward toward Lower Ballymenone, has shifted in our century to become more closely allied with Sessiagh on the west.

The District's society is not built up of smaller formal organizations. It depends less on clubs than on temporary ad hoc groupings—the "methal of men" who gather to crowd the brick. There is an Orange Hall at Bellanaleck, and there was a Hibernian Hall near the Arney Chapel. Men belong to marching bands and football teams. People meet in church and chapel and in the pubs at Arney. They frequent certain pubs in Enniskillen and Swanlinbar. But these associations, fracturing as they do along religious and political lines, do not overturn the community rooted in work on the land.

Kin is not a major organizational force.[1] Its basic discriminations between name, clan, friend, and family are unelaborated. People "of the one name" sense a hazy connection, for names, they believe, often derived from traits borne in the blood. The "clan" owes its connection to descent from a single ancestor. Before mass emigration, the clans—the Owenses of Sessiagh, the Boyles of Ballymenone—held power, but now the clan is a nearly jocular recognition of consanguineous relation among some people "of the one name," and it entails no social obligation. "Friends" are relatives, but friendship is not strong enough to carry precise definition or specific responsibility. Friends are cousins, but degrees of cousinage are usually unnamed. One group of friends consists of those close enough to describe by specific relation: "Johnny is me father's own sister's son." Another group is made up of those vaguely classed as "some friend to me." Usually people speak of their friends as friends of their father or mother, and whether their mother's friends are also their own is a matter of unimpassioned disagreement. "Family" is husband, wife, and children, the force of the household, the hearth's blood. Households do not branch today to siblings of the home's couple, or to uncles, aunts, or cousins of theirs. Three of the District's households extend to grandchildren, but only one of those shelters two couples beneath one roof. In much of Ireland, it seems, the family defines itself tightly, confining the household to parents and children, to avoid the tensions engendered by two women working at one hearth. That holds for the District, but more often people speak of the need for one man to own the house, direct the farmwork, and sit at the lower corner of the hearth as "boss." Memories of the bad days of the landlords, of farms not possessed, not wholly subject to the householder's will, prompt men to say, "I couldn't live happy hearin my footstep on the floor of another man's house." Normally, young couples who stay in the District buy or rent a new house, then move into the old one after the death of the last of their parents. If the boss retires and if the new boss is married and if he and his wife move into the old home, the retired boss and his wife move out. Since children who marry leave and unmarried children stay, households often consist of siblings, the offspring of dead parents, the family's remains. Ten households are composed of unmarried siblings, seven of lone bachelors who have inherited the farm and will bequeath it to nephews or nieces, who may live elsewhere, preserving the home within the family defined by their parents. If there is no next generation in Ireland, old people often sell the farm to an ambitious local farmer of their own side who agrees to let them "live out the rest of their days at home." Since many inherit or purchase farms or fields apart from their own houses, their motions and connections swing outward across the land.

The family provides an emotional focus. Siblings bond through love for their parents, embodying the idea of tradition, forging connections in the present to conserve the energy of the past. People sing sentimentally about their mothers, speak reverentially about their fathers, and honor their parents with visits to the old home or grave. Young emigrants return for holidays. When Joe Flanagan and I took a day's outing in the car, what he wished to see was the weed-grown rock ruin of his father's birthplace in Cavan. But the District's population has been and remains too mobile for kin to be used in creating social order.

Everyone has come from somewhere else, the general pattern of motion being downward, from the south and west. The Flanagans came from near Swanlinbar. Tommy Love and Ellen Cutler came from Boho. James McGovern, John O'Prey, and Bobbie Thornton's father came from up in the Republic. Hugh Nolan's great-grandfather was a weaver from Glenawley on the Cavan-Fermanagh border. Michael Boyle said the local Boyle clan sprung of two brothers, a smith and a horse trader, who came from Dundalk. Even the local Owens clan, so closely identified with the land that people feel they named it (Ballymenone meaning Place of the Owenses), came ultimately from Connacht.

People leave. Siblings and children are expected to go, and most do. Further, many never marry. About four out of every ten houses are run by unmarried people who can expect no children to help them. Experience in families is too uncertain for kin to form community, and logically kin cannot be the community's base, for people marry within their religion. Their connections through blood cannot join them to all they live among.

The fundamental contract is established between those who stay, those who live near one another—the neighbors. But a neighbor is more than one who lives nearby. Neighbors are those with whom you work, those who can be trusted to help. And the proper behavior of a relative is framed on the model of the good neighbor. Friends should help in times of need. "Your neighbor forenenst your friend."

Community is not a thing of territory or law or blood. It is not predestined. People atomized beyond communal bonds dismiss those who are not by saying they had no choice but to be buckled into a tight little society. It is not our fault that we lack community and live lives of quiet desperation, nor theirs that they have community and live in confidence, if not joy. Yet these people cannot count on their families for help, and they have no name for their place. "Our district of the country" shifts, forming and re-forming itself through endless negotiation during ceili and work. Here is a challenge: community is the product not of tradition but of personal responsibility, yours to build or destroy.

And if the destruction of community seems necessary to the construction of a self, to personal creativity, consider Ballymenone's old way. Religion, as Peter Flanagan said, radically isolates the individual through the concept of free will. There is no excuse, no external determinant or theory of an uncontrollable subconscious, to blame for moral failure. Though inherently weak, owing to original sin, the individual is at last alone with his or her own soul, forced into self-awareness and made personally responsible: individual. At the same time, religion binds people into communities, obliging them to neighborly acts, compelling them into engagement and union, co-opting aristocracy by demanding that people use inherent talents, gifts from the past, to benefit others. The creative are made to create.

The rule of neighborliness does not eliminate awareness or creativity, but it blocks the fulfillment of material desires, curtails competitive aggression, and checks acquisitive quests in quick, sharp ridicule.[2] Neighbors tolerate eccentric ways of going on, and they praise creativity, but they react immediately and harshly to those who withdraw or try to get ahead, who become self-centered. They shower foul words on the lazy, the bitter, the vain. They make the silent man talk. They make the singer sing.

The sacred chains shackling communities were not snapped to allow people to become creative individuals. They were already creative individuals. Change was necessary to free the aspects of the personality that the old community did stifle: aggression and avarice, the witch's traits. That some artists soared to new heights is true. James Joyce flew by the nets of home and religion to sail above, beyond, answering deep needs within, but Joyce—as he knew, said—was one face of the same coin that carried Hitler on its underside.[3] In isolation, some achieve new extremes of self-expression, great art, power, fabulous wealth, but others become vulnerable. Unprotected by community, alone, they become lost in an immense world, adrift in an atmosphere that is kind to the body, confusing to the mind.

Aggrieved by what seem excesses of individualism, people from beyond enter the little community to celebrate its collective spirit and its flexible drive to survive.[4] People within share the concern for cooperation and endurance, telling tales of the men of Mackan and Mrs. Timoney. But they tell, too, of warriors and rebels, artists and "great characters," whose individual excesses shaped and validated and transcended the collective order. People in the community look upon the past as a time of saints and scholars and upon the present as a time of silence.[5]

Ballymenone's people espouse the ideal of neighborliness and remain ready to do the neighborly deed, but they live apart and work mostly for themselves. They live between collective and individualistic urges, allowing both—and this is the key to their social theory—forcing both to unfold in action. In the year of the Easter Rising, A.E. described the Irish mind as attracted simultaneously to aristocracy and democracy.[6] The ancient individualistic spirit, he thought, was Ireland's problem, but many of his countrymen, born in penury, held the opposite opinion. The Agitation brought them some comfort. They deserved more. So times improved but emigration did not cease, and those who remained built nicer houses and labored to accumulate capital. But memories of successful cooperative endeavor beset them. They continue to meet on the lanes and work together on their hills. Though cash is now usually involved, people speak as though it were not, and in their daily experience the people of Ballymenone strive to better their lot without abandoning the communal ideal.

The community is not gone, but it is neighborly, not homogeneous. It does not eliminate its diverse personalities or several divisions. This community divides itself by possession of land and cattle.[7] Laborers own neither. The breaking point between large and small farmers is about thirty acres, about ten cows in the old days, thirty today. But the division is inexact. Religion refines the hierarchy only slightly. The few laborers include both Catholics and Protestants. The majority of the small farmers are Catholics, but most men are small farmers and Catholics. Large farmers are about equally divided between Catholics and Protestants. What gives status precision is not acreage but the manner of working the land. Big farmers did not make brick for cash. They do not cut turf or garden the moss ground, but purchase fuel and vegetables. They do not keep their hedges faced, for they have land enough to surrender wild ditches into unloveliness and cows enough to pass the time without handwork. Big farmers fertilize some of their meadows heavily and cut them early, when the grass is short and soft, for silage to be used in self-feeding sheds that accommodate large herds. Their other meadows are baled. Small farmers win hay in the old way, more wasteful of time, but more flexibly adapted to climate and terrain and less wasteful of hay.

Cattle consume the big farmer as he withdraws to the farmstead, away from the cooperative spaces where people made brick, cut turf, and weed spuds. It is a matter of orientation and aspiration as much as possession. Even the laborer may choose to work for a big farmer, tending his cows for a regular wage, or he may exploit his rights to bog and moss, winning fuel and growing vegetables for sale, while working for various neighbors, "helping" them when the season demands. The small farmer maximizes limited possessions through careful husbandry, trimming hedges to save space and present a clean face to his neighbors. He joins them for work in the public spaces between the farms.

Working, the District's people discover and create their community and their place in its divisions, its social hierarchy and its roles apportioned by age and gender.

Life's course is not fragmented by ritual. Moments of sacred and secular education mark a child's passage forward, but a sequence of tasks is more useful for fixing one's place in the mortal arc. There is a time—generally eight years—before work for play. In a tin cannister on her mantel, Mrs. Cutler has preserved her eldest son's first pair of long pants and the first piece of turf he won. Describing brick-making, Mr. Boyle was careful to assign jobs by age: youngsters edged the brick, teenagers upstruck, men in their prime dug, older men molded. Then at the end of life's day there is a time after work when wisdom and entertainment, rather than muscle, are contributed to the community's well-being.

The daily routine fuses at the hearth. Outside work delivers the land's yield. Inside work processes it through fire. These tasks are identified with men and women. Men cut furrows, hay, corn, trees, turf, hedges, clay to keep the land clean and its produce rolling toward the fire. Women keep the hearth clean, and cook to keep outdoor work rolling on. Their separate responsibilities are segments of the hearth's endless motion, less set roles than tendencies. Practice varies widely from couple to couple (itself an indication of open conception), but it is not unusual for a married man to make tea and sweep the hearth or for his wife to help in rooking hay. The

Kennedy Children

house and its environs, haggard and street, lie between the female domain of the interior and the male realm of the fields. Women ornament the kitchen's walls, but there is no rule for the exterior. Doris Crozier painted the decorative green trim around the windows of her home "for a whim." Tommy Love painted the yellow and black quoins on his. Flower-gardening is considered a feminine art, yet some married men pass the time tending flowers along the street. Milking is a man's job, but when the cows come home, women will be found working beside their husbands and sons in the byre.

Beginning a task, people become responsible for its completion and learn their place in life. Their place is not isolated but integral: the farm's tasks blend into its unity of "work." That parts make wholes may seem an uninspiring observation, but the whole of life in Ballymenone is not the construct of a privileged analyst, unavailable to its actors. They understand.

Brick-making was an assembly-line operation. Clay flowed from hand to hand. Tasks were distributed by skill and strength. But the workers on that line did not do their jobs in isolation. Michael Boyle performed only the youthful tasks, yet he comprehended the entire process from mining to marketing. Control and intellectual pleasure were not stolen from the laborer by a designer or administrator. Design and production, thought and action, remained unified.

Farmwork is segmented by gender, but home and work place do not lie apart. Women come to the fields bringing tea. In houses with one kitchen, men rest by the hearth, where meals are made. As an actor in a play will know his part and the whole plot, women who have never gardened can recite the complicated formulas for planting, transplanting, and tending cabbage, and men who have never cooked can give out complete recipes. All its actors understand the whole of the hearth's cycle. Thus, in exceptional times, women can do, as Mrs. Timoney did, the most masculine work, coping lea with a spade. And so many houses are occupied by bachelors that it cannot be called exceptional for a man to serve as cook and fire tender. "Butter to butter is no kitchen": though common, houses run by unmarried people of the same sex are not considered normal, and men may not do women's work well. Hugh Nolan, sturdy old wheeler of turf, is amused by his own inability to keep house and laughs when conversations distract from duty to let the fire die: "It bes a general rule in a house where there's no woman: that the fire will go down." With a smile of real admiration, he praises other bachelors for "wearin the apron" well. Cleaning and cooking and shopping are difficult tasks. The expert shopper gets a weekly trip to town, a day to balance the boss's night in the pub, a regular chance to dress up, get out, and expand association and experience.

Working, one learns not only one's position in the social scheme, but as well the configuration of the whole, how diverse occupations make a community, how a series of responsibilities make a life, how the interlocking unity of the hearth makes life possible. Here is another challenge: effi-

cient subdivision need not produce compartmentalization, departmental-
ization, alienation, that ignorance which breeds hopelessness in the self
and hostility toward the other. It can produce knowledgeable interdependence, a complexity that brings pleasure into necessary work and prods
rather than stifling thought.

24

Space

At work among others, people locate themselves in space.

Geographers and folklorists trace the course of people and ideas across the planet's surface, watching as they coalesce into regions. Listening closely to language in use, or examining the text of the play Michael Boyle, Paddy McBrien, and P Flanagan mummed in the Cutlers' kitchen, attentive scholars would have no trouble setting these people into western Ulster. An impressive scholarly tradition has divided Ireland into architectural regions.[1]

Fifty-three houses, eleven of them unoccupied, stand in the District. One of them reveals affinities to the east and south of Ireland, ultimately to southeastern England, and by cousinage to New England. Its front door is set at the upper end of the kitchen's front wall, so that it gives straight upon the hearth, which is protected from drafts by a short jamb wall. Five other houses resemble the characteristic houses of Ireland's north and west. Of these, most prominent is the Ford, and it is interesting to remember Hugh Patrick Owens telling us that the Ford's people came from Connacht. The overall proportions of these houses of the northwestern type are elongated, a narrowness emphasized in three of them, which, unlike any houses of the local type, were extended by additional rooms on the ends. Their hearths are narrower with deeper, straight-sided jambs. They have a back door in line with the front door. But most critically, they differ from the usual houses of the locality by having the Room set below, not above, the hearth. The remainder of the District's houses exemplify the local type, nine in its closed symmetrical incarnation, thirty-eight in its old form, three of which remain in its partial, kitchen-plus-Room, state.

Only extensive archaeology could tell for sure, but I expect the local house type derives from an English model; certainly its form is suggestively like the old hall houses of England, of which the Wealden house is the most famous example.[2] In the Irish world, the local house form exists between southeast and northwest. Its plan and proportions are like the southeastern house, but the relation of front door and hearth is like the northwestern house. It is open, not closed by a lobby before the fire.

Roof shape has been used to classify Irish house types, the hipped roof

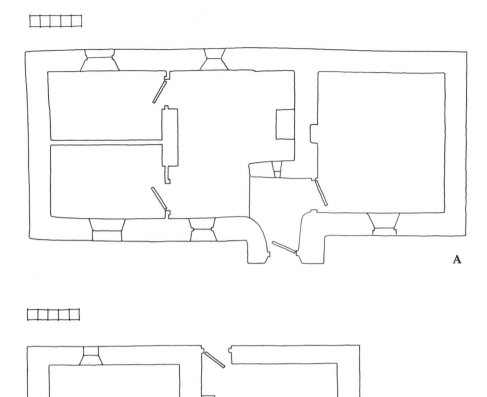

The Basic Irish House Types. **A.** Example of the dominant type of the south and east; near Clohamon, County Wexford. **B.** Example of the dominant type of the north and west; St. John's Point, County Donegal. In both these houses, the kitchen is the first space you enter, and a dresser is positioned opposite the hearth. If you reverse the locations of the front door and window of A, the southeastern type, you have the Ballymenone type. If you remove the parlor from the end below the hearth of B, the northwestern type, and relocate it behind—above—the hearth at the other end of the house you will have the basic two rooms of the Ballymenone type. That is, the relation of kitchen to parlor in Ballymenone is like the southeastern type, while the relation of door to hearth in Ballymenone is like the northwestern type. Scales in feet.

signaling the southeast, the gable roof, the northwest. Again the local architectural idea seems mixed, hybrid. The District's only house of the southeastern type, the abandoned Owen Cleary house, has a gable roof. One of the northwestern houses, the abandoned Billy Stinson house, had a hipped roof before it was destroyed late in the 1970s. While most houses of the local type have gable roofs, a few in Sessiagh, such as Hugh Patrick Owens' and John Gilleece's, have hipped roofs.

Knowing only these facts about houses, the geographer could locate the District culturally between the southeast and northwest, the English Pale and Irish Gaeltacht. At the same time, the scholar would see this architectural configuration in its own integrity as an emblem of this community's personality.[3]

The scholar's perspective is not unavailable to the District's people. They see their houses as materializations of their community's way. And they not only recognize themselves as set in a community, they have their own idea of their region, a place of belonging larger than the face-to-face scene, yet smaller than Ireland. The traits they use to distinguish their region differ from the scholar's. They see them not as imported from without but as growing from within. They call their region "Fermanagh," but it does not exactly match the county's borders. It is that section of the Irish whole where certain natural conditions have led logically to certain cultural practices. They define it by contrast.

Their region contrasts with Down and Wexford on the eastern coast where, they say, black frost never bites and the spuds can be set in February. "Up" to the west and southwest, toward the border with Cavan and Donegal, mountains rise to shape comparative images of wildness and hardship. Seasons are later. The "mountain people" are cutting their hay when Fermanagh people have theirs won. Justly, Fermanagh men believe, the mountain people, having less grazin, are given higher subsidies for cattle. Hugh Patrick MacManus, a craftsman who lives just south of the District but weaves its creels and thatches some of its houses (the Ford is one), told me that Fermanagh baskets are rounded but mountain baskets are flat-bottomed to clear the jagged outcroppings of rock.[4]

To the north of Fermanagh spreads fat Tyrone, where people have to sow seed for grass, and farmers, rationally less pastoral, crop more on their broad fields, blanketed with ideal till. To the south, grass grows even more luxuriantly. "In Roscommon," Joe Flanagan said, "you throw down a stick the night and it's covered with grass be mornin."

Rougher than the east, where no frost threatens the garden, but smoother than the mountainous west, where the heavy loy must be used to cope the stony lea and hay must be piled around poles to keep it from blowing away, grassy Fermanagh is perfect, people believe, for their cattle economy.

The District is blessed with abundant fuel. Turf, like grass, is useful to the formation of regional awareness.

Local Example of the Southeastern Type

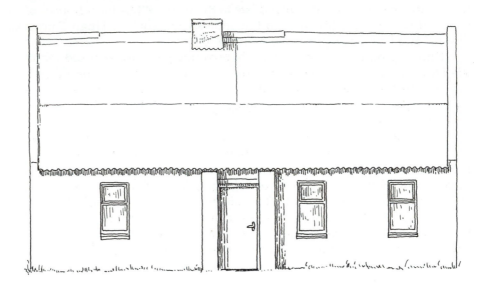

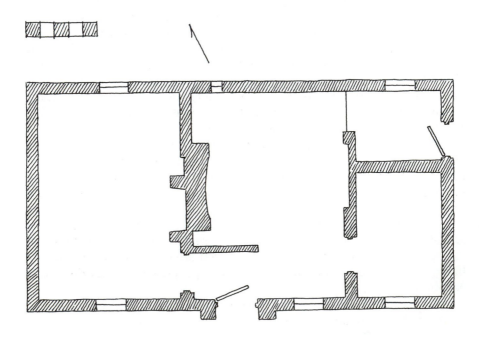

Plan, front elevation, and hearth of Owen Cleary's brick house. Originally,
the jamb wall protecting the hearth would have been taller. Scale in feet.

Local Example of the Northwestern Type

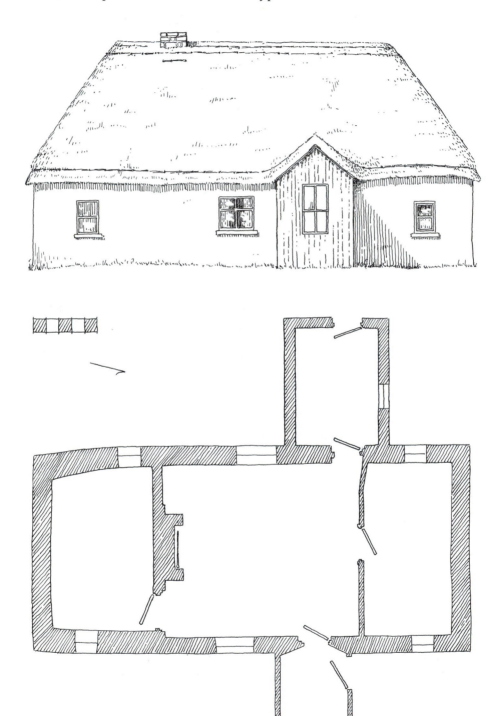

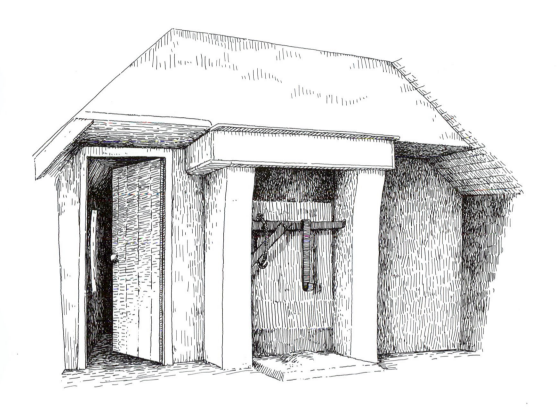

Plan, front elevation, and hearth of Billy Stinson's brick house. When this
house burned late in the 1970s, Alan Gailey discovered it to have been crucked.
Scale in feet.

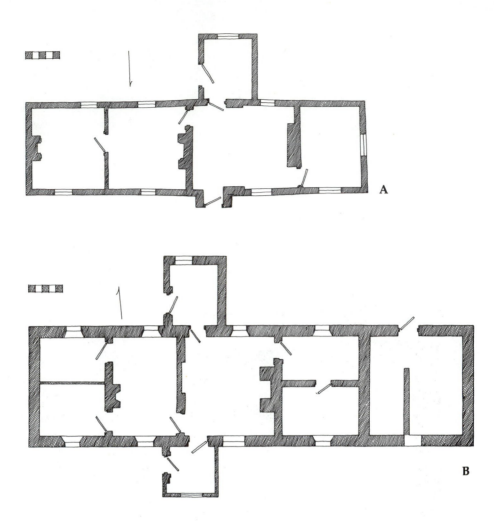

Plans of Local Houses of the Northwestern Type. **A**. The Ford, built of
brick. **B**. Maguire of Drumane, built of stone with brick partitions. The front
porch and back dairy are of block, and there is a byre off the right end. The
middle two spaces of this house—the kitchen with front and rear door in
line, and the Room below the hearth—provide a clear instance of the northwestern type, analogous to the hall-and-parlor houses of England and Virginia. Note the narrow fireplace with deep, straight-sided jambs. It is like
that in the Stinson house and provides a local marker of the northwestern
type, contrasting with the wide hearth with shallow, splayed or rounded
jambs found in Owen Cleary's house of the southeastern type and the
houses of the usual Ballymenone type. Scales in feet.

Johnny Boyle told us one afternoon at Hugh Nolan's that mountain weather is so harsh that an intermediate construction, called "foots," has to be inserted between spreading and clamping to win the turf. Mr. Nolan had never heard of that practice, but he said he knew turf were so scarce in the mountains that people had to burn sods:

"They'd spread them and clamp them, and when they'd dry, bring them to a turf house. I seen them burnin and they made the best of a dull fire.

"I seen it. I seen them burnin.

"I seen these clamps up in this bog and I was sure that it was turf, you know. So when I inquired, I was told they were the mountain sods that was just cut the same as you'd cut turf. And then dried.

"They made the best of a dull fire—not much of a blaze on them."

In other directions, turf was so scarce that fuels used in Fermanagh in only the worst emergencies were burned as a matter of course, and techniques unnecessary in Fermanagh had to be used to win turf. Mr. Nolan:

"In some places they breasted the turf. But it wouldn't be done be the natives of this country. But we'll say that there came a man from Cavan or some other county, do ye know, and that they were cuttin turf here in Fermanagh. Well they'd breast the turf.

"They'd strip their bank, the same as if you were goin to cut it in the ordinary *way*. And then they have some kind of an instrument, the type of a hay knife. And they'd take and they'd cut across the floor about the breadth of a turf, do ye know, all along until they'd go to the end of the floor. And then a man'd take a spade and he'd run it in; he'd cut the size of turf, do ye know, and he'd take and he'd fire them out to another man. And he'd put them in a barrow. And there'd be another man would come along, take away the barrow, bring in an empty one.

"And that went on, till he went down six or seven turf. And then he'd go again. And he'd start at the top. And it wasn't an ordinary turf spade that they had for doin it, but there was some name on it that I forget. It was a different kind of spade.

"I'll tell ye what I heard about them turf: that they wanted to be a kind of a firm turf, do ye know. The real soft black turf, they mightn't stand it. But, you see, the mountain turf would stand it. The mountain turf is a hard turf that wouldn't go like the turf in the bogs about here."

Peter Flanagan told me that in Monaghan they used offalls to make "mud turf" by throwing them into a boghole, letting them sour, then spreading the mud on a bank, three inches deep, where it was scored with a finger so it cracked as it dried into trim pieces. I asked Mr. Nolan about mud turf.

Example of the Ballymenone Type

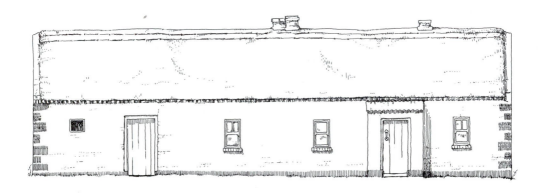

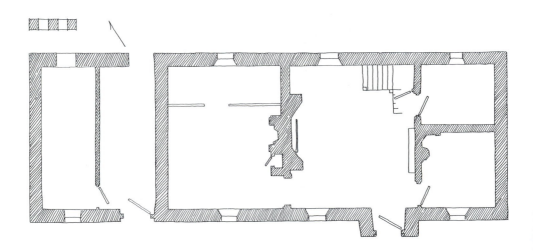

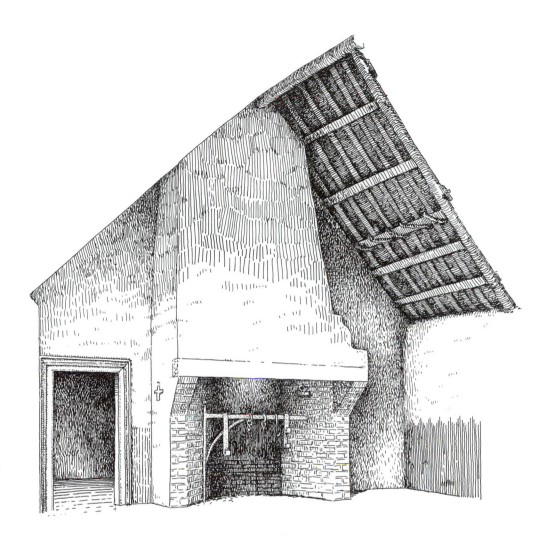

Plan, front elevation, and hearth of Mrs. Keenan's brick house, formerly
the bailiff's residence. There is a byre off the left end. Once there was
another byre or a stable off the right end. The rear wall of this house and the
partition through the Room had collapsed, but enough evidence remained
for accurate reconstruction. I drew the plan with the stair rising from the
kitchen to reach the loft, but I drew the hearth as it would have appeared
before the loft was inserted over the kitchen. Scale in feet.

Creel. Peter Flanagan's. Upturned and in use as a chicken prison.

"The mud turf wasn't common.

"That would be made out of the strippins of a bog. A bog that had been cut out, you could take and make mud turf.

"But ye'd want good weather at it. Because a bad season you never could get them for to dry out.

"Och, it was a tedious—*coorse*, when there was plenty of help in the country, they'd tackle anything in that line, but it was a tedious job.

"I never seen it a-doin.

"I made an offer for to do it meself at one time, and I seen that it was goin to loss. I hadn't the right method and I threw it there.

"But I think it's the strippins or the shovelins of the floors, do ye see, when you're cuttin, do ye see, when they're threw back, they turn into, ah, they turn into a soil—you couldn't make turf out of them. But if you got this job done, they'd be great for the back of a fire. It's the ould shovelins off the turf floor that composes these hollows.

"Well then, I suppose you could make them out of another class of a bog too, but it's just a thing I couldn't give ye very straight information about because it never has been done in my knowin. I heard tell of it bein done, and I had a piece of waste bog up one time, and I took a notion I'd *try* it.

"But I seen that it was goin to be a loss of time and I chucked it then.

Hay Knife. Hay knives are used for cutting hay out of pecks and stacks. This one lies in Mrs. Keenan's loft. Its blade is 17½ inches long. Mr. Nolan clarified his description of the alien implement used to breast turf by likening it to this familiar tool.

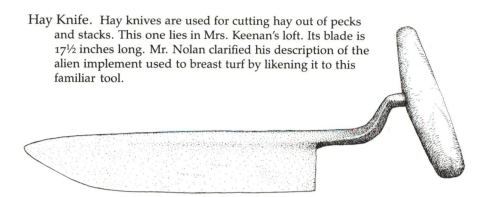

"My opinion about it is—I'm not right sure—but I think that the way it is: that you'd want to have this cut and in a pile and sour it with water, do ye know.

"Mix it up and mix it up and mix it up.

"And then when it'll get a kind of firm, cut it out like in small wee sods. I think that'd be the proper way.

"I think that'd be the proper way, as far as I can know, but I'm not real sure about that.

"They never practiced it around here."

Curious and knowledgeable about the ways of other places as well as past times, geographers as well as historians, the District's people are capable of objectifying their own ways, borrowing other ways, seeing their logic, and siting themselves.[5] Fermanagh is their place. They are made to its hardship. It is right for them. God made it so.

25

Time

At work among others on the land, people find themselves in time.

Earth's time is inevitable, unknowable. People tune themselves to its beat, moving between land and sky. Land is constant; clear plans unfold from its inherent properties. Sky is erratic, running, cracking to wreck the plans best laid.

The land was made for humankind. Its utility is infixed. Scarce and hard won through long Agitation, land is rarely sold, but it is often "set" on "the eleven-month take," rented so it returns to its owner one month out of the twelve, two months out of a "term" of two years, or five months out of five years. Rental remains impermanent. The owner can take the land back or strike a new bargain in accordance with changes in prices and the wishes of the renter. At bargaining time—anytime, though usually January—responsibilities are apportioned. Normally the owner keeps gates repaired, the renter keeps hedges clean and drains free. Land so "taken" is called "conacre."[1] The assumption is that the renter will use it for the one season embraced by the eleven-month period and use it only as it was meant to be used. Cows might be grazed on "conacre meadow," but normally the man who takes conacre meadow has the right only to win its hay. He cannot change its ditches or cut their wood for lumber or firing. He cannot plow it and crop it. Turf will be cut from bog: "If you took conacre bog, you'd have the right to cut turf for one season," Mr. Nolan explained. "If you wanted to cut again, you'd have to renew the take." The rood has reverted to its owner, insuring that the land's inbuilt potential has not been denied or distorted.

What it will be, the land is. Before its sod coat is stripped, bog is "turf bog," fuel, and blue clay is "brick clay," building material. With its grasses pale and stunted by winter, this field is already a meadow, that one is grazin. When work begins, the land entails its conclusion. Joe Murphy strips the bog bank, jabs his turf spade at the smooth brown surface, and says, "There they are"—"they": the earth is already split, won, fuel. When hay lies on the broad band in one continuous strip, they speak of it as so many "lyin rooks." Unwon on the ground, it is won in the mind.

Breaking into the land, people are trapped in its tempo, caught up like dancers, and carried to accomplishment. Dancer and dance: as though human beings were a part of nature—and they are—mediators between land and sky, they become the land's agents, its means for converting its potential to actuality, its water to fire. Beginning to act, they are compelled to further action. Their being becomes action in time.

Every variety of dirt contains its own clock, which will neither stop nor adjust its movement to those held in other soil. At work at brick-making, Mr. Boyle said, you were also at work in the bog and on the meadows. Set in one cycle, you are set in several, unsynchronized. And there are always the cows, always the hearth.

Beneath Fermanagh skies, you have not the luxury of pausing to get things in mental order before getting them into physical order. Nor can you break your predicament down, simplifying the field of design to solve one problem as though others did not exist. All is moving, interdependent, too complicated for the planner who thinks beyond time, contrives to perfection within a circumscribed reality, then jubilantly announces progress while the rest of the world falls apart. Time is. Living in all seasons, patiently, one must plan while acting. Plan is action.

Action is history. Every gesture has precedent and consequence. As the hand grips the spade, slaps brick, or grates spuds, historical time flows through the fingers and writes its narrative into the land.

Some professional historians feel the land, its fields, houses, and buried broken crockery, cannot serve truly as documents. Artifacts, even spoken texts, are suspect. Only the written word is meaningful and useful, and the historian's story retains its dreary elitist bias, since few of the past's people wrote and most of them were tied to an upper-class minority. And history erupts as a chronicle of anguish, since it is not a happy, balanced person who burns his nights out blackening pages in solitude, creating the documents historians use to compose the past as a series of crises met by prosperous men. Yet beyond, around us, spreads the vast and democratic handmade history book of the landscape.

The old inhabitant takes a step and it echoes historically. Hugh Nolan has lived eighty years in the little house fronting Rossdoney Lane. Imagine what he feels as he walks the Lane's mile, and what the historian who has entered his thought could learn from that small stretch of land.

As on the road to Kirk-Alloway, things by the way prompt memories of specific events. Historically set, they teach general principles too.

There are fewer houses. When Mr. Nolan carried his memory across the land to teach me its population, he discovered that the number of occupied houses in Rossdoney and Drumbargy had declined in his lifetime from thirty-four to fifteen. Hugh Patrick Owens said the number of families in Sessiagh had decreased from over twenty to thirteen since his father's day: "The old houses have fallen down and disappeared; the land has been sold. They were startin to dwindle out in my time, but my father minded them all." Famine and emigration have cut the population.

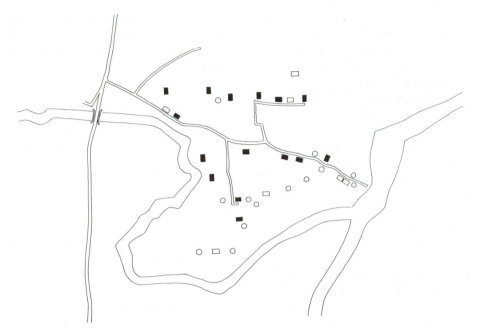

Population Decline. This map of Upper Ballymenone has blackened rectangles
for occupied houses, empty rectangles for vacant houses, houses in ruins, or
houses converted into outoffices, and it has empty circles for houses that Mr.
Nolan remembers but of which no trace remains. Note the contraction of
habitation from the ends of lanes and the back country to the paved roads.
The length of the main road running east to west, Rossdoney Lane, is 1¼
miles.

Houses are sited separately. Once, Bob Lamb said, Arney looked like a
village. Mr. Nolan described a cluster of four houses on the Hill Head, east
of the Hollow in Rossdoney, where now only two empty houses, built in a
line, serve as cartsheds: "It was," he said, "a sort of a little village at one
time." There was a house next to Tommy Love's and two next to Johnny
Boyle's. Three were clumped in the Point of Rossdoney, where but one remains, an empty "office-house." Hugh Corrigan's farm absorbed two farms,
one of which had once consisted of five farms. "So that's the history now,"
Mr. Nolan said. "Most of the Rossdoney farms were divided but finally
they all wore back into one farm. There was alot of little farms, and they've
all been gathered up into the one big farm." From a landscape crowded
with hamlets and little farms, to a landscape of separate homes and big
farms, the depopulated land shifts to provide privacy and enable individual success.

Houses have been sucked out of the back country, down to Rossdoney
Lane, and along it toward its intersection with the main Derrylin Road.
Paddy McBrien's, the most recently built, is aligned near the Lane, and

Francy Corrigan's, the most completely rebuilt, is perched on its verge. Houses at the ends of larger lanes crumble, abandoned, and over the hills vacant houses and the ruins and tracks of others have been left, along with the minor lanes that joined them, to nature's breezes, beasts, and weeds. The number of roads has decreased, and those remaining have been surfaced for auto travel. People with cars get out more easily, and—more to the point, since many have no car—police, soldiers, and salesmen get in easily. Things are reordered for the convenience of the automobile that carries people away, that must be bought with cash and fed on fuel from overseas.

The compass turns. Once a network of lanes and paths tied scattered habitations into the community's own center. Now houses are pulled to the thoroughfares and pointed at the larger world.[2]

This pattern of reorientation, of the concentration of power beyond the locale, as though a monstrous, distant magnet were drawing energy to it, is revealed in other buildings along Mr. Nolan's mile. Once there were two "sheebins," shops that sold spirits and provisions, in Rossdoney. Now the nearest place to buy a drink is at the Arney Cross, and the nearest place to

Francy Corrigan's Home. This house represents a radical rebuilding of a single-story thatched house, and it provides an example of the complete new form: symmetrical with a lateral hallway inside, two stories, and aligned with the road. The small building is the old cooperage, since razed.

A Place on the Holy Land   605

buy necessities—candles, batteries, bacon—has withdrawn to Bellanaleck. Once there was a carpenter and a tailor in Drumbargy, a basket maker and a shoemaker in Rossdoney. Jim Love has opened an auto repair shop at the head of the lane descending to his father's house, but the establishments of tradesmen have comparably retreated. Long disused, the Corrigan's cooperage has just been razed. The fair has vanished from Drumbargy, as it has from Arney. Livestock are traded in Enniskillen or Derrylin. The creamery at Bellanaleck is out of operation. Milk must be sent farther. The old school on the Laneside where Hugh Nolan and Michael Boyle studied, about which, said Paddy McBrien, Hugh once wrote a fine poem, is now Andy Boyle's home. The new school at the main road end of the Lane is vacant— soon it too will be converted into a home—and children must go to school in Arney. No trace remains of the church once said to stand in the Point of Rossdoney. Of such details are great historical principles built. Like so many places, this one has turned itself inside-out, trading the rich sense of locality which the poet, Patrick Kavanagh, called parochialism[3] for dependence within an international cash economy.

That convulsion is felt by the individual as a loss of control. New comfort consoles but does not precisely compensate. When Mr. Nolan was a child, the houses he played among were all composed of local materials. All were thatched. Now of the fifteen inhabited houses that enter his mind as he walks Upper Ballymenone, only three are thatched, and one of those —John Carson's at the far end of the lane through Drumbargy—burned before Christmas in 1972. The others are roofed with alien, purchased material. Haysheds are made of mysterious metal, wire fences are strung where ditches have been breached. Men are drawn from the land to pay for the convenience of the loss of cooperation, and in their moving they surrender the power of mind and hand over nature. Their destiny slips from their grip.

With loss, gain: the mansion of the middleman, LaDew, is gone, its masonry rebuilt into the outoffices of Catholic farmers, and one ruined house along Rossdoney Lane is that of the despised bailiff, in later days Mrs. Keenan's, a home for a Catholic family. The farms of Ballymenone were once rented, now they are owned. Ireland's greatest victory has left its material reminders on Mr. Nolan's landscape.

In the midst of it all holds the stability of dirt, of grasses that spring unbidden to fatten cattle, of bog that, cut over, rises again into usefulness. Then memory intervenes, and the upland grasses sing with progress, the bog laments the loss of community, the land incarnates values.

Near the mouth of Rossdoney Lane, on either of its sides, grassy dimples and bumps mark the old stands of brick kilns, mementos. With the passing of slapbrick and its replacement by block for building, people lost a way to turn earth into cash. They also lost a way to bring pleasure into work. Mr. Nolan remembers:

"A day's crowdin was always a fair amount of sport. It was a great pastime for young lads.

"You and I would be drawin the bricks from the stack to the kiln, and they delighted in the pitchin of the brick, two at a time."

"It was a great time," said Paddy McBrien. Tea was plentiful. Chickens were rolled in brick clay and roasted while the brick cooked. Men brought fiddles and fifes, and nights were brightened and broken with song. "It was a great entertainment," Peter Flanagan said. "They'd put up a canopy in front of the arches and they would play fiddles and dance and sing. Everyone would take a turn, singin some wee song. Hugh Nolan would take his turn, singin songs of his own composition. It was a great time now."

It was not. Hugh Patrick Owens and his brother, John, burned five arches of the District's last brick in 1929. When Old John of the Ford made bricks they brought eighteen shillings a thousand. Paddy McBrien said the price rose to six pounds at the industry's peak. The buyer from Enniskillen gave the Owens brothers fifty shillings. At 200 to 250 brick per cartload, that meant four or five trips with the ass and cart to Town—"Four or five trips for fifty bob," Mr. Owens repeated in anger.

The ruined stands of five kilns, owned by different farmers, scatter over his property between his home and Sessiagh Lane. As we walked through them, Hugh Patrick Owens said, tight with emotion:

"My flesh crawls whenever I walk where they made the brick. I've tried to explain it to my children, but they can't understand.

"There's no work now so cruel.

"That was brutal, slavish work. And it was blood money came from it."

When the Owens brothers dug and soured, molded, crowded, and burned, brick-making had become labor, stripped of the little pleasure that came of cooperative involvement. We stood where he had sweated in muted fury, and I was reminded of Tommy Love saying work in the bog was not so bad when many hands moved together and kept the pace even. Michael Boyle stressed the collective nature of brick-making, but the Owens brothers, at the end of the tradition, wrought alone. No friends helped in sunshine or brought fiddles up through the darkness to entertain the workers while they kept the kiln burning. Days thickened into dullness with mucky hoking. Nights were long, silent, hot. Past, slapbrick remains a memory that—and he used the same words every one of the several times he described the industry to me—makes his flesh crawl. Hugh Pat Owens has stayed, storing his bad memories of souring brick, barefoot in short pants, of "casting" as much turf as would do a family for half a year into the maws of the kiln, but his brother, once the work was done, emigrated. Hugh Nolan, who generalized brick-making as a great pastime for young men, also generalized it as a cause for their leaving:

"Young people got tired of brick-makin. It was hard work. And they took a notion to emigrate.

"And all these small pieces of land was sold. And some one man come to own it all."

Shapes along the lanes shake memories from their sleep in the head. As a memory, inescapable because of the forms it molded into the earth, brick-making is all of these: a proof of cultural capacity, of mastery over nature, a way to make money untroubling to the neighborly ethic, a happy gathering of people, a brutal brand of slavish toil. Land is history is meaning.

Motion is essential to simplified history. Mobile people have little trouble accepting the idea of progress necessary to the sacrifices politicians demand, or the idea of decline, carped by the oversensitive soul. During their migration upward or downward, surrounded by the meaningless artifacts of their temporary place, people can be tricked into believing that it is all getting better and that only bad attitudes, laziness, fear itself, some crisis of confidence, holds them back, or that it is all getting worse and days once gold have dimmed from brass to tin. In either case—and this is what matters—the individual is relieved of responsibility and allowed to drift without a need to know the past or build the future.

People long in one place, moving through an environment vibrant with meaning, know real change and hear around them the clamorous product of their own involvement in history. Such a man, Hugh Nolan, knows that things get better, and they get worse.

The land they have helped build teaches them history, and history sets them in life without answers or relief from seeking answers. One challenge this obscure patch of land, dented with old brick ponds, offers is to the historian. Knowing modern people are mobile, knowing history undergirds law and order, can the historian compensate for the deracination necessary to modern life by giving people a portable new past of paper as rich as their stationary old one of dirt, a past that is not mere prelude to present power, but a stimulus to the imagination, that builds within people an understanding of their situation, a need for direct involvement in the creation of their own destinies?

26

Life

Space becomes time as people turn earth into landscape and claim it with names.

The scope of the mind's Fermanagh is swept by the names in "The Fermanagh Song." Belcoo, Belleek, Devenish, Enniskillen, Lisnaskea, Crom, Knockninny, and Florencecourt draw a loop within which lies Ballymenone. Its upper half, the District's eastern center, is made up of Rossdoney and Drumbargy. Hugh Nolan teaches:

"Rossdoney. This part around here, we called it Carna Cara.

"Well, I'll tell you my opinion about it: it was just a name that was. It never was on any legal document, if you know what I mean.

"This whole townland, it was on all legal documents, it was Rossdoney.

"But I'd think it was a home-manufactured name, that: Carna Cara.

"Well, Rossdoney, it's the name for a point, as far as I have heard. This townland, it runs into a point, at the very far end of it.

"The river comes on down from Drumane Bridge, and all of a sudden, it gives a sharp turn.

"And it's said to be how the name of Rossdoney come about. And some would go on to say, but I never heard it told for a *fact*, that there was a church in this townland, in days gone by.

"But I wouldn't just sanction it because it's only hearsay.

"But the point, it has something to do—there's two words—it's *Rossdoney*, do ye see—some of them two has some connection with a point. So that's as much as I can tell you about it.

"But for bein able to give you any information about this place of worship bein in this townland, I couldn't because I have never heard at what time in history it was in existence, nor I have never heard in what part of the townland it was.

"It has never been explained to the people. They just know that this townland has such a name and that townland has such a name. And they have *got* no particulars of how that they got their names.

"Well, as far as Drumbargy is concerned, I have heard more about *it* than I did about Rossdoney.

"In days of old, there used to be a fair in Drumbargy.

"And I suppose it was one of these fairs that lasted maybe for a lock of days. There's places, you know, and there bes fairs and they don't be over in *one* day; they might last for a couple of days.

"And then there bes all kinds of games and trick-of-the-loops, and, aye, then, be general rule, the way it was always in Ireland, when the fairs was in existence, there'd be clothes dealers and there'd be different sorts of people that'd come along for to make sales, do ye see.

"So the way that *it* got its name, as far as I can relate, it got the name of Hill of Bargains: Drumbargy."

Peter Flanagan protested he knew little about the land's names. Yet he had "heard Michael Boyle at it, right enough," and wishing to please me created out of his memory and linguistic agility this response to my question about place names:

"Drumbargy, Michael said, was the Land of Bargains.

"It's Irish: Drum. Drum: noisy bargain. Drum is noisy.

"And Rossdoney is the Land of Stones, the valley of the stones.

"Rossdoney. It's supposed to be the stoniest land in under the ground. So it is. Real rock.

"I was at the layin of that watermain there and even the biggest digger that came to it was hardly fit for to remove the stones that was in that watermain—real rock. Real blue stone."

Michael Boyle is the expert:

"Rossdoney and where I lived in Drumbargy, it was all called Ballymenone, do ye see, it twas kind of an ould Irish name for it.

"Drumbargy. Drumbargy's Irish. Ye see: drum's a hill and bargy's bargains: the Hill of Bargains.

"There was supposed to be a cattle fair in it long ago.

"That's what I heard.

"Well then, Rossdoney. Rossdoney, do ye see, is a point; it runs out into a point. Well, it appears ross is a point and doney's Sunday in Irish.

"Doney's the Irish word for Sunday. And ross for a point. Well that was Sunday Point. There was a house of worship there in olden days, in the Point of Rossdoney. It was before the Penal Days, in earlier times. I think that was it.

"Well, in Rossdoney there's Carna Cara. That's over there where Hugh Nolan lives. He lives in Carna Cara. It was only a kind of a byname. There was four or five houses; there was Corrigan's and Nolan's and the McGiveney houses and another house the name of Flynn's. Them five houses. They were called Carna Cara.

"Well then do ye know the brae above it, it was called the Battery. It's on past Nolan's on the county road. When you go past Nolan's, down into the Hollow, it goes up that way; it's up the Lough Shore, overlookin the Lough. They used to call that the Battery.

"So I asked someone how did it get the name of the Battery, some of the older men. And they told me there was some kind of battery of guns on it in ancient times, do ye see, for defendin.

"Well then, there's another townland, Sessiagh. Well, Sessiagh: sé is the Irish for six, do ye see: Sessiagh.

"Well, it's the sixth townland from the mouth of the Arney River up.

"Well, Rossdoney's first. Drumbargy's two. Rossawalla is three. Drumane's four. And Ross is five. And Sessiagh's six."

Sessiagh is the District's western center. Hugh Patrick Owens said it took its name from the six holdings of its original settlers. Carousing with Mr. Owens in Enniskillen one night, I first heard Sessiagh's more intimate name when a barmaid welcomed her visitors from The Holy Land.

Sacred bedrock: the people's place of work is The Holy Land.

Less deeply, more exactly, the name is historical, political. "Sessiagh is The Holy Land," Mr. Owens explained: "No Protestant ever got a foothold here." After I had spent a day lifting bales with Mr. Owens' neighbor, John Gilleece, he told me:

"Now you can say you've helped with hay grown on The Holy Land.

"You see, Sessiagh's called The Holy Land. Because there's no Protestants here. And if one tried he wouldn't last long.

"No, he would not."

In the fall of 1972, at the beginning of the lane into Sessiagh someone painted IRA in large letters on the road surface with an arrow pointing into The Holy Land.

Though held in seriousness, Sessiagh's name also prompts laughter. Says Hugh Nolan:

"I just never heard how Sessiagh got its name, but there was at one time and somebody christened it The Holy Land.

"So there was a comedian, Lord have mercy on him, John Brodison. He lived down at Bellanaleck.

"And he was asked why Sessiagh was called The Holy Land.

"Ah, he says, dirty gaps,
    and the Divil never could get through them.

"Aye ◊.

"John Brodison. He was a Cavan man. He came to Fermanagh to work, and he settled down in it, and first he lived away down below Lisgoole.

"When I started goin to Enniskillen first he was livin down there. And then awhile at Arney and finally he came to Bellanaleck in the latter end."

In John Brodison's bid, untidy narrow gaps (remember James Owens' story of the hay carrier) protect the people of Sessiagh. Their place of hardship offers no entrance to Satan.

Humor and seriousness converge in the depths. These people are comfortable with life's sacred essence. Their Saints make mistakes. The Devil is mocked as well as feared; the idea of selling yourself to him spins into both comic and frightening tales. Their religion is not tottering in need of constant propping or a facade of desperate sobriety. It is firm as earth, pervasive as air. Yet what is, and surely is, contains mystery in its vastness. Laughter echoes from the unknown.

Helpful to normal life is the storied idea that saints, people close to God, walked this land. Naile, Febor, Mogue, Patrick—all stood here. On Inishmore, in Hugh Nolan's story, Saint Patrick discovered the dho. On Inishmore, in Michael Boyle's, he stopped:

"Hughie McGiveney used to tell a yarn, used to say—this whole district of the country was Ballymenone, and Saint Patrick, he says, never came to Ballymenone when he was preachin the gospel in Ireland.

"He came to Inishmore, he says,
    and he shook his staff over into Ballymenone . . ."

Abruptly Mr. Boyle sits up in bed, shaking his fist above his shoulder, his eyebrows arched, the eyes piercing the distance. Now he drops his tone near a growl and draws his voice slowly over the words, like a weight dragged across gravel:

"He came to the shore,
        over at Inishmore,
    and he shook the staff,
        over at Ballymenone.
"He says,
    Aw, Ballymenone,
        you are there, he says,
    I'll not bother callin to see you atall.
    I know you're there."

Laughing, relaxing, bringing his eyes back to mine, he concludes:

"Well, he never was in Ballymenone, he said.
"He came to Inishmore, he says,
    and he shook his staff over into Ballymenone ◊."

Saint Patrick brought Ireland hope. "I suppose," said Mr. Boyle, "he traversed the whole country." Yet in jest, Patrick does not think Ballymenone worth a visit. And yet he knew Ballymenone was there.

Their place is blessed. It is The Holy Land. God made it a fit habitation for cattle-raising men. But it is no paradise. Comic tales of their historic place point them back to work. Hugh Nolan's telling of John Brodison's bid removes Satan from the land, but Michael Boyle's telling of Hugh McGiveney's pant removes Saint Patrick. With a laugh to banish doubt, they leave the Devil on the other side of the hedge, they leave the Saint beyond a ribbon of Lough, then they bear down on the damp earth that yields them little more than enough. They hold their place in affection; it is their neighborly corner, smoother than the mountains where the wild winds howl, but rougher by far than fabled lands of running water and fat purses that lure youth to them. Set in place, they are set in a time when things are getting better and worse and little is certain. God made the world, but experience of that world does not lead to final and perfect knowledge. Life gives pain, teaches courage, the will to endure without knowing, and in their culture's most poignant structuring of the subordinate within the dominant, a person's progress toward knowledge is contained by the body's inevitable decay. Death consumes wisdom.

As they go to death, their humanity obliges them to smooth the rough and brighten the dull. They will lose. The joy they want will be surrounded by sorrow, the comfort they seek will be surrounded by hardship. But hardship teaches them strength, intelligence, and generosity, the virtues they use to create a world as human as possible, a place of clean kitchens and bright ornaments, smooth fields and clear stories, accomplished plans. Finally conditions will prove the winner, so they cannot look too closely at existence, but must fight to pass the time, doing the best, working, creating a life of the valorous will while keeping the eye on consolations, those pinpricks of light that shine through darkness to prove that, as surely as hardship contains ease, God contains hardship.[1] Beyond the world in which people struggle for freshness and know decay, there is another of eternal freshness, joy, smoothness, brightness—a world of Eternal Will. Their role is to carry on. Their danger is despair.

Despair is the background of existence for people positioned between Patrick's hopeful promise and the world's lesson of failure. Hugh Nolan catches the idea often in terse comment, but Peter Flanagan explained it best to me one night.

It was my first visit since my book about them was published, and my notebook filled with comparisons between what I had written and what I now saw. I complain to myself that I had cleansed the countryside: "It's brown, dirty, scruffy, poor. I was not wrong about the people. P is heroic. But he's more the hero because of the tattered context I left undescribed. I'd extended my bright view to the scene as though they—the people—illuminated it." Often my notes worry around this confusion: my scholarly interests keep intruding, getting in the way of friendships deepened beyond the needs of gathering information, and I resent them. Yet those very interests carried me over an ocean and twined my life with theirs, and I need them. I have not invented them to suit my ideas. Rather, they have helped me invent myself by living daily many of the values I have come to honor and obey. Generously, they have taught me. I have come back again.

My ambivalence did not slow me and, as the wintry dawn broke, I burrowed, chilled, into the clothes of the familiar swaybacked bed—"a good spring bed," P calls it—in the low room off the Flanagans' kitchen, filling page after page with all that had happened, without any plan for future use. I have to remember correctly.

Our reunion had been giddy. P and I burst with uncaused laughter, teasing each other about our mutual marginality, trading jumbled confusions of compliment. Each told the other he was handsome and talented. "Boys-a-boys," P said, "the book is great. You'd want to be a professor to read the like of that, and I'm not much for the readin. But I've read wee bits, and it is really reality. Me sittin on the wee stool. Man dear!" We made up for the months apart, rejoining our present with talk about happy times in the past until P told me I was tired and, after warming the sheets above the fire, tucked me in.

This night, days later, is calmer. No work calls. It is too early for gardening, and tomorrow men will move over the land, silently, slowly, tipping cartloads of manure onto the meadows, slashing billhooks along the hedges, waiting for spring. So we huddle in the cold dark house, I in my spot on the wee stool against the backstone with the fire at my side, and P less than an arm's length away. We pass cigarettes back and forth, toast bread on the points of knives, and let the night melt into dawn. As it rolls over us, our voices soften, our topics deepen.

We talk of music, and P says modern music is no good. It "splits your skull" with loudness, repeats its lyrics into meaninglessness, and loses the stories of its songs under excessive accompaniment. The old Irish fiddling is best, he says. It teaches your left hand to "hop," and once it has learned lightness, you can play any kind of music on the violin. We talk of progress, and he says it is a mixed benefit. "That television: for some it is an education, but for others it is just really destruction." We talk of the old way, and P names its essence "trust," an interdependence of "charity" and "confidence," based on "Our Lord's commandment to love your neighbor as yourself without regard to color or creed." He illustrates his principle with a local man who failed in isolation because he could not ask help from neighbors to whom he had denied help in the past, and with a woman, a Protestant widow, who was helped by her Catholic neighbors, though all she had for repayment was an ass and cart to lend. P tells me he has four hens laying. They supply more than his needs. Charitably he gives eggs to his neighbors. They can be confident about food for tomorrow, he can be confident they will help him in times of need, all can be confident that the social world, founded on trust, remains in order. While he teaches me, I remember that when I visited Hugh Nolan yesterday I found James Boyle and Francy Corrigan cutting firewood for him. Hugh can count on help his neighbors cannot imagine withholding. I tell P that, and he says Hugh was once wonderfully strong and it is sad he has become so frail. People age, he says, and that is terribly sad. At last we speak, when the night is spent, of despair. With so much unknown and life so hard, P says, the soul is tempted to despair.

So much is unknown. Yesterday Hugh Nolan told me of a man from Inishmore who was driving home at night about thirty years ago and had an accident on the viaduct over Upper Lough Erne. The men who helped him joined him in the car, and when they were coming along a country lane (Mr. Nolan was specific, of course, about location), a man recently dead stepped out of the infinite darkness into the glare of the headlights. No matter which way the car turned, he stayed in front of them, until at an intersection the driver twisted the wheel sharply and they escaped. Mr. Nolan heard the story often, often told it, and once told it accidentally in the company of a brother of one of the men in the car. He said it was true. It does not seem possible, yet who knows? "We can't figure out the whys of man-made things," Hugh said. We could not make, much less fly, an airplane, so how can we expect to understand God's ways? Skeptical by nature, Mr. Nolan said that when he was a young man he thought he would live to know it all, but now he is resigned to living without knowing. "We must die knowin we don't know."

Life is so hard. "It's a world of troubles at the present time," Mr. Nolan said, "and not a solution for them." He also said, "All has misfortunes, and we can take some comfort in bein alive." Taking some comfort is brave, necessary, and realistic. "There always is some consolation for hardship," P tells me, using his house as example. It is smoky, cold, dark. In the towns they have more comfort. They have electricity and central heat—and the racket of lorries and cars. "In me own wee house I have the consolation of quiet." He can get up in the morning, he says, and stand out on the street, letting the music of a thousand birds fill his ears. I feel the perfect silence around us, no electric hum, no creaking pipes or mumbling voices or distant whining engines, and I think back to our first meeting. My most exact and vital memory is of P tossing breadcrumbs toward the dresser for a tiny round brown bird on long thin legs who had hopped in over the threshold. Early this morning, while we sat with breakfast tea, a hen, a Blue Andalusian, paused in the doorway, gray with the gray house before her, the gray of the day behind. She stood in motionless tension, one foot set forward on the concrete floor, her head poised before a pale, colorless sky while her comb gathered and transmitted pure ruby light. I was stunned. A tiny point of brilliant red glowed within overwhelming grayness. I felt a flash of understanding: a scarlet speck on a field of gray, the hearth's glow in the dark interior, a moment of pleasure amid ceaseless work, hope within hardship. It is your choice to concentrate on the bright spark or lose yourself in darkness. P's life is so hard, but he loves the growing plants. His fingers are gentle around them when he lifts their leaves to the sun. In

Peter Flanagan, June 1977

town he would lose touch with God's goodness, pressing itself in birdsong and green shoots through the cracks of the hard world.

He would lose, too, he tells me, his "liberty." People like himself need space to develop their own way of goin on, for "musicians is curious." Were he jammed into the shove and hustle of the town, his spirit would be crushed. In the country, but not in the towns, P says, the old saying "Many men, many minds" holds true. Mr. Nolan talked similarly. When he was in the hospital recently, they treated him well but "scorched" him with steady heat, making it hard to readjust to the drafts in his house. They want him to move to a home for the aged. But, no, he told me as I draped another overcoat over his shoulders and busied with our tea at the hearth, there he would have to live by their rules and would lose the "freedom" that is his consolation. It is hard sometimes to rise. It is a long walk on an uneven floor between jagged furniture from the hearth to the dresser. But he knows the route. In these surroundings he has learned to do battle with the night's empty length. He has neighbors to help him, and he refuses to be taken away.

Life is uncertain and hard, but if people lose God into the vastness of the unknown, if they lose the will to discover consolation amid pain, the bright flash against darkness, they will still into inaction. They despair. Above all things, P tells me, it is your personal responsibility to prevent that happening. "You can't let yourself think that God doesn't love you. Then you are lost." When lost, he explains, you lose connection with law, by which he means God's law, cosmic order. All laws—physical, spiritual, social—fuse into one Law. When people lose touch with its center, God's particular love for them, Law disassembles into laws, laws proliferate, become intricate, trivial, and thought staggers into disorder as people, forgetting their relation to God, lose their connection to nature and their fellow creatures. They fall into despair, a state of hopelessness in which they are useful neither to God, themselves, or their neighbors. Hardship, P says, tempts us to despair. But we must be brave. We cannot contemplate suicide, but must endure. If you work to endure, P tells me, with the house black around us and the record of past struggles eaten into his memory, "God will reward your courage. Even if you are a bad sinner. Despair is the worst, the very worst.

"Life is hard but it must be lived. We must carry on. God knows life's hardships. He understands the temptation to despair, but He knows the gallant effort to keep going.

"We must carry on."

PART NINE

The Topography
of Past Time

27

Ballymenone's Terrain

Think of the past as space expanding infinitely beyond our vision. It is not a record of progress or regress, stasis or change; uncharted, it simply, smugly, vastly is. Then we choose a prospect. The higher it is, the wider and hazier our view. Now we map what we see, marking some features, ignoring others, altering an unknown territory, absurd in its unity, into a finite collection of landmarks made meaningful through their connections. History is not the past, but a map of the past drawn from a particular point of view to be useful to the modern traveler.

Serious study of a community's history does not begin with a raid to snatch scraps to add color or flesh or nobility to the history of another community. It begins when the observer adopts the local prospect, then brings the local landmarks into visibility, giving the creations of the community's people—the artifacts in which their past is entombed, the texts in which their past lives—complete presence. Whole artifacts are drawn and measured. Whole statements are recorded and left, beginning where their authors chose to begin them, proceeding in the words and order their authors chose, ending as they wished them to end. Even that is but a step in the right direction, for historical meanings lie between as well as within things. Relationships must be established so we will understand whole systems of historical thought. These systems will yield more than new facts for old schemes, they will help us see our own schemes for artifice, force us to envision their improvement, and allow us to imagine a truly global history. Then we render to the people of communities like Ballymenone the degree of freedom they already have. Their freedom, their reality, is not to be found in the subservient roles they fill in the histories of other places but in the way they construct their history, drawing their own map of past time.

Ballymenone's is a relief map. Over it runs a highway. The facts used to build it were selected from certain realms of experience, those which have left artifactual evidence on the real landscape people walk. One realm is economic, consisting of the technologies people have used to convert the natural earth into fields and homes and food and money. The other is social, consisting of the ways people have organized themselves to accomplish economic ends. Unlike academicians who disjoin these realms into the disciplines of economics and sociology, losing, despite statistical sophistication, the ability to understand how things happen, the District's thinkers connect them in the history of work. As Mr. Nolan showed clearly when he answered my question about change, facts from the interdependent economic and social realms are arranged in progressive sequence.

The District's people do not place themselves at historical climax. They are on the highway, not at its end. They look backward, but the far past, fascinating to antiquarians, does not charm them. They look backward only so far as that view helps them look forward. The beginning of the highway is lost over the curve of the earth, but they see enough of the past to gauge its direction, then they purify its momentum in prediction and locate themselves in the future's past. It is as though they were walking slowly forward, looking backward while the road receded rapidly beneath them. Hugh Nolan can say open hearths are gone, though his is not, that there is not a man on the bog, though some are. Reality is not in the present but between the past and the future.

The highway is smooth and straight, linear and progressive, but socio-economic development is complex, open to differing, contradictory evaluation. Some see it as good, others as bad, but none is unaware. The landscape beyond which they cannot exist is insistent, conspicuous, complexly informational; it blurs in motion: they are in time, inevitably, unavoidably on the road.

Though many historians would be satisfied by a map laced with roads converging on the present, the highway is not the only feature on Ballymenone's map. Hills rise across it. These are the artful, mythic compressions of great past events. At the historical landscape's rim, blocking whatever lies beyond, loom the low misty hills of the Saints. Between them and us lift the hills of Battle from which national political noise echoes onto the local landscape. At the top, each carries one prime event, while down their slopes occur lesser events, matching in concept those of the peaks. Between the hills of heroic battle and the highway of workaday existence rise small hills, monuments to individuals who endured or rebelled against socioeconomic conditions.

A vast bog of fact spreads between the hills and the highway. This is history known but not organized, neither laid into the highway's surface nor built up the sides of the hills. A context for both road and hills, it is a resource to be cut as needed and used to enrich the interpretation of progress or the artistic representation of heroic events.

Standing separately above the bog of fact, the hills beam their individual messages directly, perpetually to the present. They are not scattered at random; the map is man-made, and the order of their standing unifies, simplifying but deepening, their meaning.

Releasing the metaphor, we find there are three kinds of historical information in the District. There is history known but not ordered. There are socioeconomic facts linked by the idea of progress. There are heroic events, sacred, political, and socioeconomic, formed into works of art. The connective logic of these, the stories of history, remains our question.

When faced with the problem of arranging the historical stories for this book, I turned naturally to chronology, put the chapter on Saints first, and let the Battles follow in temporal sequence. My decision was not alien to Ballymenone's historical logic.

I was first told about each battle in chronological order. That most distant in time, the Ford, was least difficult to talk about and easiest to bring up in conversation with a stranger, while the most recent, the Smashing of the Band, remains intimate knowledge, embarrassing, and unlikely to hold much interest for an outsider. By the time Michael Boyle told me the story, he knew I knew his community well.

The storytellers know the chronology of their tales. They know Saints come first. Saint Patrick arrived, according to Peter Flanagan, in 432. When I asked him when the Saints came to Fermanagh, he replied:

"It was in the followin years after Saint Patrick that Saint Naile came. In the fifth century or around that.
"Saint Mogue was back in them years too. He was."

Answers to my redundant requests for dates varied in detail but did not change the sequence of events. Hugh Nolan said the Battle of the Ford took place in the middle of the sixteenth century. James Owens dated it 1595, Hugh Patrick Owens 1596, Michael Boyle 1597 or 1598. Peter Flanagan set Black Francis in the seventeenth century. Hugh Nolan and Michael Boyle put him in the early eighteenth. With Maguire's song and the annual parade of the Lodges on the Twelfth to remind them, everyone had Mackan Fight to the day, July 13, 1829. Battles of less local significance were located in relation to the major ones. The fight of the O'Reillys and Maguires took place at Drumane two centuries before the Ford. The Inishmore Fight came before, the Tossing of the Swad Chapel after, Mackan Fight. Hugh Nolan said the Inishmore Fight occurred in 1822. Peter Flanagan dated the confrontation in Swanlinbar to 1860 or 1865. The band's battles broke within memory. Hugh Nolan said the first took place in 1902 or 1903, Michael Boyle said the second happened in 1917.

Historical stories are fixed in time by more than numbers and sequence. When told, they are joined to facts beyond them, to history known but unordered. Peter Flanagan and Hugh Nolan placed Black Francis among the rapparees who rode the heath after defeat in the Williamite War, though neither told a tale of William's victory; that is a matter for the other side, commemorated in parades, not tales. Michael Boyle and Francis O'Reilly put Black Francis in the Penal Days, the time of the Priest-Hunting after Cromwell's conquest. Cromwell has left stories aplenty in Ireland, but not here.[1] Peter and Joseph Flanagan set the Tossing of the Swad Chapel in the context of Catholic Emancipation and the Days of the Landlords that followed upon the Cromwellian era.

Hugh Nolan told me no tale of the Plantation of Ulster, but he knew its date, 1609, and understood fully its importance for his community's past, so when he used that event to situate others, the Ford before, the Days of the Landlords after, he both deepened his discrete statements and established a neat causative chain: Elizabethan Conquest, Siege of Enniskillen, the Ford, Kinsale, Flight of the Earls, Plantation of Ulster, Days of the Landlords, the Land League's victory.

Within their stories the tellers place details to relate them to the socioeconomic sequence. Mr. Nolan used changes in transportation to illustrate the proposition of improvement, and modes of transportation mentioned in the tales both set them in the past and relate them via progress to the present. At the time of the early fight at Drumane, said Michael Boyle, there were no good roads, only tracks men traveled on horseback, and there were no bridges over the Arney at the time of the second battle there, according to Peter Flanagan, Hugh Patrick Owens, and Hugh Nolan. Peter Flanagan said Mackan Fight took place before carts became common, around 1860. He was right. The Scotch cart was introduced into northeastern Ulster after 1810, and south Fermanagh's first was made at Florencecourt about 1845.[2] So in 1829 men had to ride donkeys or walk: "they had to walk, for there was no transport in them days." Mrs. Timoney had to walk, Mr. Boyle said, "there was no other way of goin thattime." Michael Boyle set the band's first battle—as he had the tale of the man saved from the Devil and his account of brick-making—"before the advent of the motorcar." Mr. Nolan was there when the men were released from prison. Later he saw Fermanagh's first automobile.

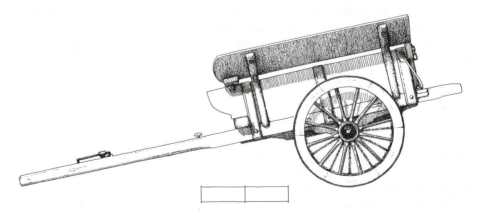

Cart. This disused donkey cart, found in a shed that was once a home on Rossdoney Lane, illustrates the local type. As usual, the shafts, wheels, and undercarriage are deep pink and the box is royal blue. The hayboards or "brackers" are in place. Scale in feet.

People think through artifacts to locate themselves in time's flow and build artifacts into their stories to site them on time's map. Oats were once the District's staple. People before the Famine in Mr. Nolan's account ate hard oaten bread: "It was lovely with butter." Mrs. Timoney receives oaten gruel: "It's great stuff, gruel, a great reviver." The wounded Scarlett is fed oaten sowens in Mr. Nolan's Mackan Fight: "Oh, it used to be great." In days past, Mr. Nolan told us, every farmer had oatmeal, cropped and milled in Fermanagh, but now the land has gone to grass. The wild, wooded landscape of Mr. Boyle's Ford contrasts with the smooth, cleared grassland of the present. The weapons of Mackan Hill, muzzle loaders and forged forks, so carefully described by Peter Flanagan, Michael Boyle, and Hugh Nolan, contrast with the horrible machines of war screaming daily through their gentle hills.

The hills of historical tale align with the highway of progress on Ballymenone's map of the past. If temporal sequence is allowed to connect the District's stories of history, how does the narrative run, and what is its meaning?

28

A Chronicle

It is written in the Chronicle of Prosper that in the year 431, Palladius, ordained by Pope Celestine, was sent to the Irish who believed in Christ to be their first bishop. He came and built three wooden churches before returning once more to Rome. In the next year, according to the Annals of the Kingdom of Ireland compiled by the Four Masters, Patrick came into Ireland with a great family of men and women, with bishops and priests among their number, a scribe and a psalmist and a bell-ringer, three smiths, three artificers, three embroiderers, one man to steer his boat, and others to cook and brew and drive his chariot. In his own *Confessio*, Patrick, born in Britain, a citizen of Rome, tells that he "came to the Irish heathens to preach the Good News and to put up with insults from unbelievers." He built seven hundred churches, ordained seven hundred bishops and three thousand priests, and he lit the Paschal flame on the Hill of Slane, doubly fixing the theme of Irish history.[1] He cast into darkness the whole of pagan prehistory. Its people did not struggle and hope within the confines of commandment and thus hold no lesson for later men. He purified the land of poisonous serpents, stone idols, specters, and demons, and established upon it his church, thus charging the men of days to come with its defense against attack from without and corruption from within.

His word became their duty, and some thirty years after the death of Patrick, around the year 520, Saint Finnian reorganized the Patrician church at Clonard in Meath, making it a monastery, a place to save and teach the sacred word. There Finnian taught Sinell, Molaise, and Columcille.[2]

When he had learned, Sinell traveled to Cleenish Island in Upper Lough Erne, where he built his monastery. When he was its abbot, Columbanus, born around 543 in Leinster, came to study with him before journeying to found monasteries across wild Europe as far to the east as Italy.

When he had learned, Molaise traveled to the northwest with his friend Mogue until at a sign from God, a bending of trees, they parted. Molaise went north to establish a monastery upon Devenish Island, isle of the ox, isle of the learned men, in Lower Lough Erne. Mogue went south to the place called Magh Sleacht, where Patrick had cursed and blasted

Cromm Cruiach, an idol of rock, rung by a dozen more, that once drank human blood, as it is told in ancient verse:

He was their God,
The withered Cromm. . . .
Milk and corn
They would ask from him speedily
In return for one-third of their healthy issue,
Great was the horror and scare of him. . . .
There was worshipping of stones
Until the coming of good Patrick of Macha.

There, where blood ran and stones stood in the hills of Cavan, Mogue made his place, and there is his grave, from which clay is plucked to calm terrible seas.

Saint Patrick prophesied the birth of Molaise and the birth of Columcille.[3] By the time he was a man of twenty-five, in the year 546, Columcille had established his monastery at Derry. It was Columcille who founded Durrow and Kells, famed for the two most beautiful of books, and Columcille who sent Naile, like himself a Donegal man of noble birth, into Fermanagh to build Cill Naile, Kinawley, where the healing well shines silver. When, in 564, Molaise died, Naile succeeded him at Devenish.

From Finnian—not Finnian of Clonard, but Finnian of Moville—Columcille borrowed a book, a text of Jerome's second translation of the Psalter, a text newly come from Rome and more accurate than the one known in Ireland. Wishing to preserve and spread the pure word, Columcille copied the book, writing swiftly through the long nights by a light burning from his hand. Finnian knew outrage. He took his wrath to Diarmait mac Cerbaill, High King of Ireland. Now this Diarmait was great-grandson to Niall of the Nine Hostages, and Columcille was great-great-grandson to Niall, warrior and king, who ruled Ireland for twenty-seven years and died in a raid across the seas in 427. Diarmait decided against Columcille, as the old historian writes, "using the familiar proverb, that 'the cow and the calf ought always to go together.'" So it was among cattlemen, but the Dove of the Cell was first named Wolf. From both sides, royal blood flooded his veins. Anger came upon him and he rallied his kinsmen. In 561, at Cúl Dreimne in Sligo, Columcille's army destroyed Diarmait's, and that, wrote the author of an old Irish triad, was one of the three worst acts of a saint. In anguish, Columcille went to the mate of his soul, Molaise of Devenish, and asked of him guidance. His penance was never to let his eye come upon Ireland again. His atonement was to bring as many to life in faith as died in bloody battle. Two years after the battle, at the age of forty-two, he sailed. Columcille was a member of the bardic order. Far from home, he wrote:

> *There is a grey eye*
> *That looks back at Ireland.*
> *Never will it see again*
> *The men of Ireland or her women.*

And again he wrote:

> *I ever long for the land of Ireland,*
> *   where I had power,*
> *An exile now in the midst of strangers,*
> *   sad and tearful.*

Columcille woes his battle, his journey, and envies the abbot of Durrow, who hears the blackbird among the Irish elms and the cuckoo at summer's coming:

> *I have loved the land of Ireland*
> *   —I cry for parting. . . .*

Become the first exile from *insula sanctorum*, Columcille became for Scotland what Patrick was for Ireland. Around 683, Adamnan, his kinsman and successor, wrote the life of Columcille, telling how he faced the Druids and how he drove the snakes from Iona, his sacred isle. He crowned kings, raised the dead, turned water to wine. He brought love with his counsel, death with his word. God sent him fish in the sea. With miracle and with prophecy, Columcille led the people of Scotland into Patrick's church.

One time only, Columcille returned to Ireland, and he came blindfolded, followed by a great retinue, to attend the convention of Druim Ceat in 575 and preserve the bards from banishment. On the ninth of June, 597, the Saint lay down and died. After his death, books by his hand that neither water nor fire could ruin brought rains to end droughts and fair winds for sea travel.

Columcille foretold ravages from the north, and four centuries sent Vikings to split the surf with slender ships and rip gold from holy shrines to hammer into rings for their women.[4] With war axes they came and did to death the mild monks of Iona, for they would not surrender the relics of Saint Columcille. In 795 and 802, in 806 and 825, and again in 986, Northmen plundered Iona, and blood ran to the girdles of men. Enfeebled, the mission retreated to Ireland where, too, heathens from the north harried the shores, and rove even into the interior, laying waste the holy places of Lough Erne. In 875 the Saint's relics were brought away to keep them from foreigners. In 1090 they were carried to Kells, and within eight years, Sitic Mac Meic Aeda, acting under the direction of the chieftain, Cathbarr O'Donnell, fashioned a shrine of wood and metal around the cut-down fragment of book, calf to Finnian's cow, that sent Columcille into exile. Cathach, battler, it was named, and when the O'Donnells, kinsmen of Columcille, went to war, the Cathach was borne before them, talisman of victory.[5]

Those battles of Cathach and O'Donnell were but forays of warriors, wild matters of honor and cattle-greed, until the times of the Tudors. The Norman invasion from the south was stopped at the Fermanagh border, and English dominion contracted into the Pale around Dublin, leaving unconquered Ulster to its own small wars. Subtly the Maguires, chiefs of Fermanagh, shifted allegiance between the great O'Donnells of Donegal and the O'Neills of Tyrone as they rampaged and conspired at liberty beyond English control. Then in the gluttonous new spirit that demanded land and capital to feed it, the English thrust into the Midlands, Henry VIII had himself proclaimed King of Ireland, and Ulster was brought into engagement.

Appeasement was the first response. With the Maguires last to concur, Ulster's chiefs yielded their territory, receiving it back, regranted with the title of Earl. For the first time the northwest shoulder of Ireland became part of the English realm, but the sons of the earls balked. His father had agreed to raise his son an English gentleman, but Red Hugh O'Donnell, fostered among the MacSweeneys, nurtured rebellion in his breast.

In fear and dread that Red Hugh was the Irish hero prophesied by Columcille, the English did, at Michaelmas in 1587, outfit a ship and send it laden with Spanish wine and a secret cargo of soldiery from Dublin to Donegal, where O'Donnell was enticed on board and, though not yet fifteen years of age, was taken and held in Dublin Castle. After three years and three months, he escaped, but by treachery he was taken once more and bound down in iron chains. "There came a great gloom over the Irish," wrote Lughaidh Ó Clérigh in the old life of Red Hugh. "There were many princesses and great ladies and noble white-breasted maidens sorrowing on his account. There were many high-born nobles clapping their hands and weeping in secret for him." Then the English Lord Deputy, William Fitzwilliam, well bribed by Hugh O'Neill, looked another way, and on Twelfth Night 1592, Red Hugh O'Donnell and Henry and Art O'Neill let themselves down on a rope through a privy high on the castle wall, slipped through the city's gates, climbed the palisade, and made the Wicklow Mountains. Henry lost the others in a great storm of snow and escaped alone to Ulster. Art, who had waxed corpulent and fat of thigh in prison, slowed their progress as they bore through "a violent downpour of rain and slippery slime of snow." At last they were discovered by friends from Glenmalure, seeming "not to be human beings at all, but sods of earth of like size covered up by the snow." There Art died, but Red Hugh kept a sup of beer upon his stomach and recovered in a house hid deep in the wood until a courier from Hugh O'Neill, who could speak the English language, ventured south and led him north to O'Neill at Dungannon, who sent him then into Fermanagh, where Hugh Maguire had a boat convey him along Lough Erne to Donegal. Until the spring he lay, the great toes of his two frost-pierced feet cut off, reminders eternally of his hatred of the English. On May 3, 1592, his old father stepped aside and Red Hugh was proclaimed The O'Donnell.[6]

Red Hugh O'Donnell's sister was one of the four wives of Hugh O'Neill. O'Neill's mother was Maguire. One of the four wives of Red Hugh's grandfather was Maguire. Hugh Maguire's mother was O'Donnell. The cousins, Hugh Maguire and Red Hugh O'Donnell, were both husbands to daughters of Hugh O'Neill. Kin thickened, and with nationalistic purpose in the context of militant colonialism, and religious purpose in the international context of Reformation and Counter-Reformation, Donegal, Fermanagh, and Tyrone confederated to defend Patrick's land and Patrick's church.[7]

Though knighted Sir Hugh in Dublin, young Maguire was first in the field, the alpha of rebellion. By October 1593, Enniskillen lay under siege. Home of champions and poets, smiths and "slender-lipped, satin-clad maidens," Tadhg Dall Ó Huiginn had proclaimed it in praise-poem, "white-walled rampart amongst the blue hillocks . . . fairy castle of surpassing treasure . . . splendid dwelling of the lion of the Erne . . . Enniskillen of the overhanging oaks." By February 1594, Enniskillen had fallen. By early August of that year, the English garrison at Enniskillen had diminished from thirty to fifteen men, reduced to eating cats and rats. Around it lay the armies of Maguire and O'Donnell, three thousand strong. O'Neill, eldest, most powerful, most ambivalent and subtle of Ulster chiefs, sent his brother to their aid. Sir Henry Duke, with six hundred foot, forty-six horse, and supplies to revictual and relieve the exhausted garrison, was marching north from Cavan.

A century later, south Fermanagh remained wild and wooded, and it was said that "a squirrel might have hopped from tree to tree the whole way from Florence Court to Belturbet." Imagine, then, the men of dauntless Red Hugh, second to Columcille greatest of all O'Donnells, marching south, the pipes wailing and the sun flashing between black-green trees, glancing off armor and blades and the cumdach of the Cathach, hanging upon the breast of its hereditary keeper. Sealed inside ride the remains of the book copied in haste a thousand years before, cunningly bound in bronze and silver half a millennium past, and often repaired on return from battle. God promised Columcille victory before Cúl Dreimne. Duke's troops array on the south side of the River Arney, shifting along the bank, running, turning, and when they find fords for crossing, fifty-six die, sixty-nine lie wounded, their sodden stores drift in the water, their blood soaks into the soil, giving the Ford of Biscuits and the Red Meadows names.

When Ulster came to be held within the British fist, and all Ireland lay within Europe, new ideas of man's estate and the writing of history arose, and men young at the time of the battle at the Ford put its tale upon paper. At the beginning of the seventeenth century, Sir James Perrott, illegitimate son of Sir John Perrott, illegitimate son of Henry VIII and Lord Deputy of Ireland from 1584 to 1588, who reduced Ulster to counties and authored the plot to imprison Red Hugh O'Donnell, set out to chronicle "the last, worst, most men-devowringe and treasure-consuminge rebellion" England had known: the rising of Ulster's chiefs. Writing history, says Perrott, leads both to private fantasy and to public profit, but he sets public service first and, having read the state papers and interviewed the principals, embarks upon the troublesome task of making "words masters of matters." In October 1593, he writes, the English army crossed a ford at Belleek into Fermanagh, "where nyne dayes were spent in burning and wastinge of the contrie" and a garrison was established upon an island in the Lough near Enniskillen:

"This garison (as they hoped) would suffice, both for the guarde of the contrie and to keepe the enimie occupied (if he grew to noe other state of strength then he was at that time). But this computation fell not out right, for it was not well waied that Mac Gwyer stoode not aloane in that action. . . . Odonell made Mac Gwyers quarell to be his, accountinge Mac Gwyer and Orurcke to be as two hedges to his contrie, which hedges beinge broaken downe, his owne contrie was to lie open to reformation. More then this, the Erle of Tyrone soe nearely lynked in aliance to Odonell, did advertise by his letters that he doubted Odonell. A matter sumwhat strange, he should be soe conjoyned to Odonell, and yet geive such notice of hym; but he was wonderous subtle, and did this only to indeare hymself to the State, and to put suspition from hymselfe, whilst he might better effect his owne purposes. . . .

"Magwyer recollected his forces, united them with such ayde as he could gette from Odonell and out of Conought with some secret supplies from Tyrone, grew soe strong that the weake garison of the English growinge feobler by sicknes and want of provision was inforced to keepe cloase, and could not goe farre abroad to forage, or seake victualles, for supplie wherof the Lord Deputy sent some forces under the conduct of Sir Henry Duke and Sir Edward Herbert, men experienenced in the service of that State thoe not soe well experienced in those partes, and in this expedition had eivell successe, for beinge incountred by the rebells whoe by this time had gathered a good strength together, they were defeated, some of the English cullers taken, the victualls and other provision surprised, and the cheife leaders made to retrayle, not without some difficultie and anger. This did much animate the traytors and raysed theyr hopes together with the deminution of our mens reputation. . . . This was the first defeature that the English had received synce the Lord Grayes goverment. But shortely we shall see, that where the weale publicke is not well cared for, first private mens estates doe perish and then the generall wellfare runnes to ruine."

On August 10, 1636, a year before the death of Sir James Perrott, Brother Michael O'Clery, Franciscan antiquarian from Louvain, born in Donegal and chief of the Four Masters, completed the four-year task of synchronizing and synthesizing the old Irish annals, from the Deluge, forty days before which "Ceasair came to Ireland with fifty girls and three men," down to the Age of Christ 1616, the death at Rome of Hugh O'Neill, styled Earl of Tyrone. The Four Masters labored, wrote O'Clery, so that people "might possess knowledge and information as to how their ancestors spent their time and life," and they wrote because, were the task neglected in the present, it could not be done in the future. The old books would be scattered and lost. Ireland would have no history. Under the year 1594 the Four Masters write:

"A great hosting was made by the Lord Justice; and he proceeded unperceived through the adjacent territories without any delay, until he arrived at Enniskillen; and he encamped around, and laid siege to the fortress; and the army proceeded to destroy its wall with the proper engines, and they never ceased until they finally took it. And the Lord Justice left warders in the castle, and then returned to his house.

"When Maguire heard that the Lord Justice had returned back, he assembled the greatest number of forces that he was able, and beleaguered the same castle, and dispatched messengers to O'Donnell (Hugh Roe), requesting him to come to his assistance. This request was promptly responded to by him, for he went to join him with his forces; and they laid siege to the fortress from the beginning of June to the middle of August . . . , until the warders of the castle had consumed almost all their provisions. . . .

"When the Lord Justice, Sir William Fitzwilliam, had received intelligence that the warders of Enniskillen were in want of stores and provisions, he ordered a great number of the men of Meath, and of the gentlemen of the Reillys and the Binghams of Connaught, under the conduct of George Oge Bingham, to convey provisions to Enniskillen. These chieftains, having afterwards met together, went to Cavan, O'Reilly's town, for provisions; and they proceeded through Fermanagh, keeping Lough Erne on the right, until they arrived within about four miles of the town.

"When Maguire (Hugh) received intelligence that these forces were marching towards the town with the aforesaid provisions, he set out with his own forces and the forces left him by O'Donnell, together with Cormac, the son of the Baron, i.e. the brother of the Earl O'Neill; and they halted at a certain narrow pass, to which they thought they would come to them. The ambuscade was successful, for they came on, without noticing any thing, until they fell in with Maguire's people at the mouth of a certain ford. A fierce and vehement conflict, and a spirited and hard-contested battle, was fought between both parties, till at length Maguire and his forces routed the others by dint of fighting, and a strages of heads was left to him; and the rout was followed up a great way from that place. A countless number of nobles and plebeians fell in this conflict. Many steeds, weapons, and other spoils, were left behind in that place, besides the steeds and horses that were loaded with provisions, on their way to Enniskillen. . . . The name of the ford at which this great victory was gained was changed to Bel-atha-na-mBriosgadh, from the number of biscuits and small cakes left there to the victors on that day."

"First defeature," "great victory," and greater followed. Enniskillen was recaptured in May 1595. Ulster's chiefs galloped the length of Ireland. Then: Hugh Maguire, dead in a raid at Cork in 1600; Hugh O'Donnell, dead of poison in Spain after defeat at Kinsale, in 1602; Hugh O'Neill, down on his knees surrendering at Mellifont in 1603. Four years later O'Neill took flight with the other earls, and in the autumn of 1609 intransigent, truculent Ulster was surveyed to plant it with new men.

"Having heretofore been the Nursery of all Rebellion," the North was broken into portions of three sizes—2,000, 1,500, and 1,000 acres apiece— for distribution among English and Scottish "undertakers," "servitors" who aided in the conquest of Ulster, and native Irish undertakers, who agreed to swear an oath of loyalty, conform in religion, and conduct their agriculture in the proper English manner. Fermanagh, "MacGwyer's country," was the next to last county surveyed. Within it, Clanawley was the next to last barony surveyed. Ballymenone lies in Clanawley. The commissioners of the survey found Clanawley to contain 75,469 acres, only 6,000 of which were arable. These were divided into four portions, two great and two small, three for servitors, one to be severed into thirty-acre tathes for the natives. Clanawley was one of two Fermanagh baronies granted in part to Irish undertakers, so most of the barony, being poor land, remained in native hands. A survey conducted a decade later discovered Clanawley less improved than other places. No buildings had risen on two of the portions, and by then the servitor upon the third, Sir John Davies—poet, historian, former Attorney General of Ireland—had returned home to England, having served as first member for Fermanagh in the Irish Parliament.[8] Already our area had become the exception it remains, an Irish reservation. At the end of the nineteenth century, only 179 speakers of Irish lived in Clanawley, but that was more than in any other Fermanagh barony. John Mogey's sociological survey, published in 1947, found Area 2 within Fermanagh, including our District west of Inishmore, to stand distinct in Northern Ireland: 71 percent Catholic, 80 percent farming, with the majority of farms between ten and fifty acres, 55 percent of them lacking married couples, almost all without electricity or running water. The Land Utilization Survey of Northern Ireland, begun in 1936, published in 1963, placed our area in Fermanagh's Region 2A, typified by poorly drained thick clay and small, unprosperous farms.[9] In 1972, I found it as I have described it, 83 percent Catholic, 60 percent male, only 4.5 percent nonfarming, still lacking electricity, poor in the things of the world, rich in humanity.

"The County of Fermanagh, Mack Gueres country, rejoice; many undertakers, all incorporated in mind as one, with their followers there, seek and desire to settle themselves. Woe to the woolfe and the woodkerne! The islands in Loughearne shall have habitations, a fortified corporation, market towns, and many new erected manors shall now so beautify her desolation that her inaccessible woods, with spaces tractable, shall no longer nourish devourers, but, by the sweet society of loving neighbourhood, shall entertain humanity even in the best fashion." Such was the spirit of the new Plantation. "Art thou a tradesman, a smith, a weaver, a mason, or a carpenter? Go thither, thou shalt be there in estimation, and quickly enriched by thy endeavors. Art thou a husbandman, whose worth is not past ten or twenty pounds? Go thither, those new manormakers will make thee a copyholder; thou shalt whistle sweetly, and feed thy whole family, if they be six, for sixpence the day." In Scotland and in England poor men heard and came. Within a generation most of Ulster was owned by Planters, and the defeated natives, so loving their land, said Sir Arthur Chichester, would prefer "to become tenants to any man rather than be removed from the place of their birth and education."[10]

Wars in the days of Oliver and William served to consolidate the conditions of Plantation. For the many there were distant landlords, present bailiffs, clandestine Mass, and endurance within the cycle of work. For the few: rebellion.

Cú Chonnacht Maguire, father of the "arch-rebel" Hugh, reestablished the ancient monastery at Lisgoole as a Franciscan House. It was there that Michael O'Clery, chief of the Four Masters, helped compile a late text of The Book of Conquests. Sir Arthur Chichester, King James' Lord Deputy and brother-in-law to Sir James Perrott, thought the site fit for a new county town. Sir John Davies, who had written glowingly of the beauties of Lough Erne and would write vigorously to advocate the eradication of such native Irish customs as fostering, accepted Lisgoole as seat for his portion in Clanawley. "Upon the Abby Lands," reports Pynnar's Survey of 1618–1619, "there is built a fair Stone House but no Bawne." Here transpired the last strike of Black Francis. The lady whose honor Francis defended during the raid pleaded for his life, saying he was a gentleman who had harmed no one, "a man of mercy who robbed the rich to feed the poor," but the earnest protestations of the happily named Miss Cue, daughter of the house, proved to no avail, and in faint echo of Cú Chulainn, who like Achilles chose the short and heroic life, Francis mounted the gallows saying, "I have run too fast to run long," and was hanged at Enniskillen in 1782.[11]

The obligation to rebel, the Saint's implicit command, remained. Its response divided into two issues around which emotion eddied to surge through the nineteenth century, flooding into our own times: Catholic Emancipation and Home Rule.[12]

In 1798, Daniel O'Connell was an affluent, thoroughly educated new lawyer who, horrified by the loss of life during the Revolution in France, where he had studied, stood against the Rising of the United Irishmen. By 1823 he had begun to move, the Liberator, orator and spearhead of the Catholic Association. Within the next year, when it seemed likely that a bill for Catholic Emancipation might be passed into law, excited men broke into battle on Upper Lough Erne. Unarmed Catholics retreated by cot from Inishmore. Angry Protestants plundered their homes and fired across the narrow stretch of lake. In 1829, three months to the day after the Emancipation Act gained royal assent, Protestants marching on July thirteenth (since the Twelfth had fallen on Sunday) confronted their Catholic neighbors on the Derrylin Road through Mackan. Four men, all Protestants, were killed: Mealey, Price, Robinson, and Scarlett. The trial began on Saint Patrick's Day 1830, Judge Jebb presiding, and all but one of the nineteen Catholic defendants were sentenced to death. All but one, Ignatius Mac-Manus, were saved from hanging when the Lord Lieutenant commuted their sentences to transportation for life to Botany Bay.

After the Famine swept Ireland, hopes for political independence rose slowly, gathered strength, and formed into two movements, one of them constitutional, the other rebellious, that drove forward side-by-side through the century, though the force of the desire for self-government oscillated from one to the other. The first to take shape was rebellious. The Irish Republican Brotherhood, founded in 1858 and energized in part by veterans of the American Civil War, arranged and led the Fenian Rising of 1867, made memorable by the execution of three Irish men in Manchester, but the insurrection diffused into minor skirmishes, confused plans, and failure.

In the next year, the bell ringing from the new chapel at Swanlinbar annoyed a lady of the town, who asked the landlord, Hamilton, to level the chapel to the ground. Though free now to worship as they pleased, most Catholic people did not own their farms. The land beneath the chapel was not theirs, and on August 12, 1868, the landlord's crowbar brigade came to toss the temple. But word had spread, thousands had assembled. When Dan Boylan, leader of the Leitrim pikemen, arrived, the road was thronged for two and a half miles behind him with men and women armed with farming weapons. Fearing the worst, landed gentlemen intervened, and the chapel was left to stand, a symbol of resistance.

The failure of the Fenian Rising did not kill the will to resist. But power shifted from the rebels to the constitutionalists, and they had a leader, a Chief to match the Liberator of the earlier nineteenth century, second in the succession of uncrowned kings. Charles Stewart Parnell was born in the famine year of 1846; Daniel O'Connell died in Italy in the famine year of 1847. Elegant, Protestant, Parnell rose to prominence when in 1876, as the new M.P. for Meath, he interrupted a speech on the floor of the House of Commons to assert that the men hanged at Manchester could not be called murderers but would forever remain, in Irish minds, martyrs. Within three years Parnell had become leader of the constitutional movement, and Michael Davitt, a Fenian recently released from Dartmoor, a socialist of peasant stock and a man Parnell's age, had founded the Land League in Mayo. Charles Stewart Parnell was the League's first president. The next year he was speaking to promote the League in Belleek and Enniskillen, and in 1881 the first major concession on the land had been secured, the Tenant Right, which did little more than legally confirm old custom. The Land League pushed on to ownership. Parnell pushed on for political independence, and by 1886 he had allied with the Liberal Gladstone, who offered Parliament, as he had promised, the first Home Rule bill, which would have provided Ireland control over internal affairs, while leaving the island within the Empire. Reaction was immediate in the Protestant northeast. Pulled in opposite directions by the movement for Home Rule and by resistance from those who wished to preserve the old Union, Ireland began to break, tensions rose, and the stage was set for the first battle of the Ballymenone Band.

Home Rule was defeated. Four years later Parnell's love for Mrs. O'Shea was public. Gladstone abandoned him, the bishops vilified him, his old colleagues turned against him. Parnell's party split. In a year Ireland's uncrowned king was dead. The next year, 1892, Gladstone would offer a second Home Rule bill for defeat, but soon he would be dead, and the constitutional movement, though loosely reunited around John Redmond in 1900, would never regain its former momentum. A third Home Rule bill was offered in 1912. The composition of Parliament insured its passage, but enactment was suspended by World War I, and political force had swung back to the rebels. Sir Edward Carson, a Dublin lawyer, formed and armed the Ulster Volunteer Force. In open defiance of English law he declared, "We will not have Home Rule." In response, men in the South, inspired by Douglas Hyde's Gaelic League and Arthur Griffith's Sinn Fein, armed, and the new Irish Republican Brotherhood seized the Post Office at Dublin, Easter 1916. Pearse and Connolly proclaimed the Irish Republic. Then they were captured, imprisoned, and shot. The Irish rebelled, and Eamon de Valera survived to lead Sinn Fein.

With war in Europe over, in 1919 the Free State held its first assembly, and in London the Home Rule bill was amended to exclude Ulster's counties with Protestant majorities. Ireland shuttered with riflefire and rumbled with the march of British troops. A treaty, signed in 1921 between the Free State and England, was ratified the next year by the Dáil Éireann. Ireland broke in civil war. Murder reigned, and rebel leaders were executed until in 1923 de Valera's followers laid down their arms. It had been a time of horror, reflected in the great terror-shot verse of William Butler Yeats and in the smashing of the Old Ballymenone Band.

Through history's turbulent caprice, the North again lay alone. Once the part of Ireland beyond English dominion, Ulster, reduced by one third, became Ireland's only province within the British Empire. A new border was promised, and sections of south Fermanagh with Catholic majorities were to be ceded to the Free State.[13] But Protestant leaders objected, threatened armed resistance, and because a new border would reduce the Catholics remaining in Northern Ireland to a weak minority, enthusiasm ran low among Catholics; the idea of the New Border drifted, placating for the moment, while twisted things settled into new order and weary people recovered. Then new men took up the old cause, raided Brookeborough, marched in Derry, and the Trouble goes on.

Linked into chronicle, the District's stories of history become an origin myth for the Troubles, pressing rebellion upon the listener. Too much is wrong with the chronicle.

It gives some satisfaction, because we have been taught to select facts from the past to arrange into temporal sequence while watching for signs of the arrival of the present. It is useful because it joins local events to national and international events, through which Ballymenone's past meshes with our own. While rigorously local, the District's history is not isolated, not merely local: it leads to Ireland and beyond to connect with the key occurrences of Irish history: from Sinell and Naile and Mogue to Patrick and the coming of Christianity; from Columbanus and Columcille to the eastward spread of Irish faith; from the Ford to Kinsale, the English conquest of Ireland, and the Plantation; from Black Francis and Mrs. Timoney to the era of the landlords, the Penal Days, and the Land League Agitation; from Mackan Hill and Swad Chapel to Catholic Emancipation; from Mr. McBrien to Famine and Emigration; from the first band battle to the Home Rule campaign; from the band's second battle to Easter Week, Civil War, independence, partition, ongoing Trouble. Without leaving the locality, the District's history brings home the major events of Irish history, providing a means for people to site themselves in their own place, while simultaneously feeling a connection to all Ireland. All the District's events are local. None is only local. Ballymenone's history is the history of Ireland.

The chronicle is useful, too, because it raises the issue of the accuracy of oral history.[14] The District's historians err in minor detail, but when their words are compared with those frozen in ink by other historians, they are—simply—right whenever it matters.

Still, too much is wrong with the chronicle, and we are left the task of considering its failings in two areas: culture and history.

29

Culture

Saints and Battles, sanctification and armed resistance, the idea in the chronicle was caught in "The Swad Chapel Song," and it appears in a song Peter Flanagan sings, "Green-Robed Inisfail":

Far, far away from Erin's home some of our brave sons roam,
Across the broad Atlantic foam, three thousand miles from home.
No matter where they chance to stray they love each green and vale
Where the Shannon's purple tide rolls free through green-robed Inisfail.

No wonder they would love their land, the land Saint Patrick blessed.
Ah, a lovely land and God's command, the Eden of the West.
Where peace had reigned triumphantly till the English o'er came,
And tore our Irish homesteads through green-robed Inisfail.

When Donal sailed away from the lovely western shore
Unto the olive groves of Spain for to return no more,
He is gone, he is gone, our heroes cried, his loss we will bewail.
He is gone, he's gone, he'll never return through green-robed Inisfail.

When Allen, Larkin, and O'Brien stood the gallows tree
Far from their homes and friends and their mother country,
It was in that dark and dreary cell in a cold Manchester jail,
They roared, May God save Ireland and green-robed Inisfail.

Dear land you have raised another son, the best that was ever seen
Who fought his way and rowed the troops of England's Virgin Queen,
Who fought for peace and liberty, it was dauntless Hugh O'Neill,
Who tore their flags, their Orange flags, through green-robed Inisfail.

Dear land you have suffered sorely through centuries it is true,
But thanks to God, those tyrants could not our sons subdue.
On many a well-contested plain, where the bullets flew like hail,
Our gallant sons, they nobly fought for green-robed Inisfail.

God makes, Patrick blesses, the new Eden. Peace reigns until the English invade and destroy Irish homes. Men rebel and go to exile or execution. Another comes, but his place is broken out of time. O'Neill tramples Orange flags that will not fly in Ireland until long after his defeat at Kinsale in 1601 and death in 1616. This anachronism emphasizes, like the contemporary dress in medieval paintings of sacred and historical subjects, less a particular event than the timelessness of things, the continuity of blessing and rebellion, victory and defeat, the idea in Ireland's name, Inisfail.[1] That such a song can be read as a distillation of the District's story reveals one major problem.

In today's terms, the chronicle feels "Catholic." But the District is predominantly, not exclusively, a Catholic place. I got as close to Protestants as I did to Catholics, I met everyone, but no one directed me to a Protestant historian. All the District's noted historians are Catholic men.

Protestants say they are not interested in history, and Catholics say that is because they cannot be: Irish history is filled with the mistreatment of Catholics and with Protestants who were, like modern Catholics, nationalists. Similarly, Catholics argue that Protestants cannot be interested in poetry because so much of Irish poetry takes history for its subject, and so many of Ireland's great poets were Protestants who sympathized with the nationalist cause.

Catholic men, I concluded, were guided by their nationalistic elders into accepting responsibility for maintaining an alternative history, while Protestant men became content with history as found. Alternative history is the creation of people who feel removed from power; it is the imagination's parallel to armed resistance. The older generation of Protestant men, I was told, those who survived from the days before Ulster's independence was secure, did tell historical tales, but they are gone, and their sons have surrendered history into the keeping of distant professionals who can be counted on to support the political system that supports them. Local history has become the possession of Catholic men, but it would be anachronistic to call it a Catholic history.

The Saints were not Catholics opposing Protestants, but Christians opposing pagans. Irish nationalism has been as much a Protestant as a Catholic hope. Tom Russell, the Man from God-Knows-Where who caused the confusion between Mr. O'Reilly and Mr. Boyle, was a Protestant who rose with the Protestant Wolfe Tone in 1798 and died with the Protestant Robert Emmet in 1803. Uncrowned King and fallen Chief, Charles Stewart Parnell, who broke up Stephen's first Christmas dinner and was remembered in glossy ivy and sentimental verse in the committee room, was Protestant. Protestant men from Fermanagh died among the rebels in the Easter Rising of 1916.[2] The leaders of the intertwined antiquarian and artistic movements of the earlier and later nineteenth century, founded on folklore and inspirational to nationalism, were largely Protestant: Ferguson, Davis, Croker, Petrie, Wilde, A.E., Lady Gregory, Synge, Yeats, Hyde. In the 1830s, Samuel Ferguson, Ulster Protestant gentleman, could declare a love for Ireland, then haughtily denegrate the Catholic people, but soon his study and translation of Irish poetry led him to respect for the Catholic heart and to the idea of a distinct nation founded on the virtues of the Irish people, Catholic and Protestant. In the 1870s, Douglas Hyde, prosperous son of a Roscommon rector, let his interest in language carry him into Irish, and through it into serious collecting, translating, and presentation of accurate folklore texts. In 1937 he was elected first President of Ireland.[3]

Today, in even so small an area as our District, the identity of Catholic with the Nationalist cause, and Protestant with the Unionist cause, remains imperfect, and projecting a cleansed distinction into the past prevents understanding all that the people share.

They share conditions. Fermanagh's population fell by a quarter and Clanawley's by nearly one-third during the decade of the Famine.[4] Blight smote the potato harvest of 1845. That winter disease accompanied hunger, and the wet warm summer of 1846 nourished the fungus spreading through the potatoes to kill them. The fields lay barren, and the government, of course, could not feed the starving, because that would disturb the system of free enterprise upon which economic strength depends. The next year was no better. Protestant as well as Catholic people stumbled feverish and famined along the roads into death or emigration. Thirty years passed, the crop failed again, and the Land League rose. When Fermanagh's first meeting was held in Sessiagh in 1880, one-quarter of those in attendance were Protestants, and when Parnell came to speak in Fermanagh, three months later in November, Protestants were full participants in the movement. It was rolling, unchecked by sectarian difference. Then, with Tenant Right won and the three F's—fair rents, fixity of tenure, and free sale—secured, the Land League was declared illegal, and in 1882 the people divided in confusion. Catholic economic expectations became tied to nationalistic purpose. The way was open for the landlords to convince their less prosperous co-religionists to identify their economic interests with defense of the Union. Solidarity among the working majority was lost. Increasingly through the years of Home Rule campaigns and the bloody first quarter of our century, political power broke along religious rather than economic lines. But even if political-religious alignment had achieved perfection, ending history there would miss the point.

The point is culture, the collective patterns of thought developed out of conditions, out of wet clay and winds alive with political terror. The District's people, though differently persuaded, follow one way. I would prefer to assert cultural unity, citing quantifiable house forms for support, but I fear some will read my writing through lenses of preconception and feel my argument is running in a "Catholic" direction when I describe culture's base as sacred, and in a "Protestant" direction when I stress the importance of work. My answer must be better than to say, that is not how I see it. My view does not take in bitter, broken Belfast, and though it may extend to other parts of rural Northern Ireland, it is focused tightly on one small spot, where I see Protestants enacting a deep sacred obligation when they give butter to their neighbors, where I see Catholics working industriously through long, hard days. I must offer some plain talk about Irish culture and culture itself.

No modern nation is ethnically or historically pure. All lie at crossroads of international exchange; all lie in the midst of complex histories of migration and diffusion. Though set at Europe's western rim, Ireland is no exception; her culture is the product of synthetic development.[5] Ireland's has been a history of invasion: the followers of Partholon, the Nemedians, Fir Bolgs, Tuatha De Danann, and Milesians—Celts, Christians, Danes, Normans, English, Scots, American films, the European Common Market. But the situation has been too marginal, the population too dispersed and shot with integrity. The Romans never came, and sly indomitable Ireland conquered her conquerors. Saint Patrick grew so fascinated with local pagan tradition that he was troubled into prayer and assured by his guardian angel that it was not wrong to listen to the ancient tales. Less than a hundred years after the Norman invasion, it became necessary for King Edward to issue an order to purge the Anglo-Irish of Irish custom and language, but two centuries later, though all but one of the members of the Parliament in Dublin were of Norman or English extraction, only one of them understood the English language. The descendants of the Plantation adjusted rationally, adopting Irish modes of housing and farming, and if their language spread, the Irish conquered it to produce—Yeats, Joyce, Beckett—the world's greatest modern literature. The interplay of native and stranger on the limited stage of the green isle has been the creation, not the undoing, of the Irish culture.

The Union Jack is flying, the Queen's portrait hangs in the kitchen. An easy reading of those images would lead one to think they were being used to effect identity with England. That is what Rudyard Kipling thought and put in verse, engendering angry response from A.E., who proclaimed pride in his Ulster Protestant heritage, then wrote, "The mass of Irish Unionists are much more in love with Ireland than with England. They think Irish Nationalists are mistaken, and they fight with them, and they use hard words, and all the time they believe Irishmen of any party are better in the sight of God than Englishmen. They think Ireland is the best country in the world to live in. . . ." Through our century other observers have spoken comparably. In an address, "The Personality of Ulster," delivered early in the current time of Trouble, E. Estyn Evans said serious study has revealed that "in many aspects of material culture as well as in speech and gestures, in folk beliefs and attitudes, in their dry satirical humour, the people of Ulster share a common tradition. . . . The planter has unconsciously absorbed much of the Irishness he rejects: witness the scorn the most fervent Orangeman will pour on the Englishman who fails to get his tongue round Magherafelt or Ahoghill. . . . One can only speculate on the amount of native blood absorbed in earlier times by the planters, or the extent to which for various reasons there were changes of religious adherence. It may be stated that what distinguishes the people of Ireland in general, including Ulster, is the high percentage of people with blood-group O, and the frequency of the combination of dark hair and light eyes. . . . It seems profitless to pursue the question of so-called racial differences." Beside such giants,[6] my work is dwarfish, but I never heard Unionists in private call themselves British. Irish is what they are. The planters have been in Ireland as long as people of British stock have been in the United States. It is too late to call them interlopers.

There are shamrocks among the regal portraits in the country kitchens. Unionists danced jigs and reels in youth, requested rebel songs from the mummers, even sang them in private, for "there is no harm in a song but what harm people put into it." But it is hard for them to identify with their place publicly. Recently, and it saddens them, the tradition they share has been claimed as exclusive property by those they call "Fenians" when angry, "the other side" when not. Today it is a nationalistic political act to enjoy openly the music which thirty years ago everyone liked. Mrs. Cutler, who plays the old reels with great spirit on the "mouth organ," wanted a Claddagh ring, but no one would give her one, because it had come to symbolize not Ireland but Catholic Ireland.[7] Being an outsider, I could give it to her. A young person of her side could not have, because Protestants have given Irish emblems away with music—and history. All that remains for them to symbolize their connection to Ireland is not Irish: Scots tartans and bagpipe music, the Union Jack, King William and Queen Elizabeth—in context these are signs not of British loyalty but of Protestant Irish loyalty.

Green robe and Orange sash: symbols in conflict do not necessarily symbolize a split in culture. Culture must contain conflicts to remain useful in strange situations, to allow for psychological difference, to enable change. The Fermanagh mind is not destroyed, it is formed in conflict.

Sometimes it seems from the language we use that the ethnographer enters a community, as though into a room through a door, and discovers the folk bearing traditions and carrying culture. These burdens were given to them and eventually they will pass them on. All we have to do is gain their attention, then maintain rapport for long enough to untie their sacks and read out their contents. Plunder enough burdens, a statistical configuration results, their culture is ours.

Things are little like that. Come to some strange place, we find people inviolably unique, all in motion, preoccupied beyond us. We watch, and with time discover pattern in the motion. To turn motion into action, pattern into intention, granting people their humanity, we interrupt to ask why they do as they do. Most will say they do what they do because that is how you do what they are doing. Then they will go on. Stupid question. Stop them again. Press them, and they will describe how things go wrong but not how they go right. It is not that they do not know what is right; but they know in what is called their unconscious. That is a bad word for a good idea. People know what they are doing. Their actions prove it. They dibble sets in the moss ridges and have food for the winter. They give their surplus to their neighbors and have help in time of need. They speak grammatically and repress harmful ideas and live peacefully among other creatures. What they cannot do easily is translate rightness into a language distinct from normal action. They display knowledge by acting correctly rather than by describing action.

They leave us a task: articulating the principles of right action. It is we, not they, who need to be able to do that. To accomplish our task we coordinate the commonplace with the exceptional.

We watch and listen. The commonplace takes pattern. Then we form an account of the mind that planned what we observe. We begin as they do in the innate wish for order, but proceed differently. They grew in experience, developing through imitation and admonition. We use rigor to make up for lost time, creating an account that holds to completeness while aspiring to simplicity. We improve our account while we watch, watch while we improve it, improve while we watch. The process has no end, but fortunately we are studying people, not wolves or stones, so we have other ways to get at our goal: describing another mind so it is strong enough to stand up against our own.

Every community has its few. It has artists who compress their culture's essences into beautiful forms. It has philosophers who objectify their culture for contemplation. Scholars, differently bent, treat the reality of exceptional people differently. Some build the normal out of the exceptional, making John Milton Mr. English Puritan, while others wrench the exceptional from the cultural, dismissing Milton as Unreliable Guide or Transcendent Genius.[8] Wonderful are the ways the academy has contrived to obscure simple truths. All people are alone. All people are members of societies. All thought is at once personal and collective, all art is novel and traditional.

While feelings drawn from broad contact and thoughtful participation are being shaped into rigorous accounts, we learn which works of art most perfectly and independently incarnate collective values, and we locate those thinkers who have cracked convention into principle. These are the people of sharp vision and refined memory who take command of faltering interviews. It would be wrong to represent them as average or marginal. These are the ones, the Ellen Cutlers and Hugh Nolans, who are both exceptional and central. Their less articulate neighbors have granted them power to speak. When they do, it is less important for us to fret about untangling the idiosyncratic from the conventional than it is for us to be able to feel when the personal and the collective mesh, fuse. Then people seize the power they have received from their birth into aloneness and their growth into social being; they take culture out of themselves and mold it for presence in the world.

Discovering these epitomes of connection does not end our task. The works of art in which the community presents itself to itself sublimely

(Mrs. Cutler's home, Mr. Nolan's tale of the Ford) and the statements its thinkers construct for us (Mr. Boyle on bricks, Mr. Flanagan on despair) await analysis and integration. They make our job easier, however, and if we persist in seeing art as some strange reflection of reality, rather than as reality itself, or as something apart from life, we make things hard on ourselves. In art and articulate statement, cultural analysis is already begun, and it has been begun by those who know the culture best. Observing the commonplace, our task is constructing the logic implicit in action. Confronting art and listening to the community's thinkers, our task is extending from the logic inherent in things of power, in texts charged with meaning. Coordinating these ways to learn, we begin to meet our responsibility. I choose to let exceptional texts stand on their own, then to build contexts around them out of common experience. Other ways might be tried, but the exceptional and the commonplace will be aligned and merged if the outsider is to get any understanding of the insider's logic, of culture.

Culture is not owned equally. Some have thought harder than others and sought wisdom with more energy. Only Michael Boyle and Hugh Nolan have "the full particulars" of the District's history. Some have developed richer modes of expression. Few can match Peter Flanagan's vocabulary, none can match his musical skill. These are matters of flair and raising. There are also differential tendencies of knowledge and expression breaking along the lines of sex, age, and religion.

Differences of role could produce different acts sprung of different ideas. The work of women could be founded on principles distinct from those underlying the work of men. The work of young men could be founded on principles different from those under the stories of old men. The houses of Protestants could be ordered on principles different from those in Catholic music. Since that is possible, it is not possible to enter culture through one door. We can move into the mind through stories, but we cannot be sure that the storyteller's mind is harmonious with the worker's mind until we enter it too.

Once consideration of the performance and content of stories had carried us to the culture's sacred base, we could not be certain that the culture in stories was the culture, so we left "Catholic" stories and started again by examining "Protestant" work. At that point there were two possibilities: work would reveal a pattern of thought unlike that in tales; work would enrich the mind revealed by tales. We found the latter. Phenomena customarily isolated merged in the world of Ballymenone and differently expressed cultural unity.

Does art imitate life or does life imitate art? The question is wrong. Out of both art and common experience people develop principles of rightness. They use these principles in different situations, so the ideas that produce aesthetic action in the realm of art produce ethical action in the social realm. Beneath the beautiful and the good abides the right. Diverse things in the world seem to reflect each other, because they are the source of the principles used to construct the coherence that lies under them and causes them to exist. The force of coherence is thought. Coherence itself is cultural mind.

When the young man pulls profit from the grasslands and the old man gathers stories out of the hearth's ashes, both employ the principle of conservative extension to effect survival. When young men join paramilitary units, and old men join in the pub for heroic song, they rebel against political givens. When women serve tea and men tell tales, they submit to the generous, artful idea of entertainment and create the social order through gifts. When women talk about boxty and men talk about thatch, they speak of the rise of comfort and the loss of social order. When Protestants arrange lovely kitchens and Catholics arrange lovely stories, they organically conjoin the beautiful and useful, the personal and traditional, into clean, smooth, bright works of art.

Though it is presumptuous of a foreigner to say, Ireland appears remarkably homogeneous from an American perspective, and I feel Irish scholars have talked too much about diversity at the surface, too little about the coherence beneath, too much about what foot people dig with and too little about the common soil they turn, too much about what language they speak and too little about what they say and how and why they say it, too much about the name of their religion and too little about the beliefs they hold.[9]

Ballymenone's people of different sides avoid generalizing about each other. They would prefer to smother bad thoughts with silence; still, Catholics will say Protestants are "too confined," too lacking in sport, and Protestants will say Catholics are too talkative, precious, and given to drink. But what each most consistently condemns in the other (letting condemnation expand in the large world while restricting it carefully to individuals within the community) is bitterness, the political commitment that blocks the neighborly way. Profoundly, Protestants and Catholics cleave to the same essentials. Not perhaps in their several places of worship, but in their places of work and ceili they profess an identical belief in God and an identical belief in the rightness, the social goodness and artful clarity, that belief necessarily entails.

Above the unity of mind, the surface is cracked. Consider the most complete break. Only two dates from the far past are generally known and charged with power. One is 432. The other is 1690. Both alone, as arrangements of mere number, hold meaning. Each has an attendant work of art: the tale of Saint Patrick's arrival; depictions on sashes and banners, in delph and framed prints, of King William of Orange astride his white horse in Boyne waters. Today, one means this, Ireland, is a Catholic land, and the other means this, Ulster, is a Protestant land. The people of Ballymenone live simultaneously in Ireland and Ulster, in two countries, and they are unavoidably Catholic or Protestant.

In the large world of politics, of votes and programs, matters are too

King William III. **A**. Print on the wall of Mrs. Cutler's Room. **B**. Detail from Billy Cutler's Orange sash.

complex to align in peace or war. Earnestly sought solutions escape. In the local culture, conflict is perfect. Opposed images contain identical messages. A hero arrives from across the sea. He is victorious in the Boyne Valley, in the River or on the Hill of Slane, and secures the land for his followers, charging them with its preservation. No surrender is their obligation.

Catholics must not surrender Ireland. Protestants must not surrender Ulster. In such a situation, knowing victory, the erection of the Free State and of Northern Ireland, and knowing defeat, the partition of Ireland and the dissolution of Union, people must develop a culture compounded of rebellion and endurance: rebellion because it would be irresponsible to deny the hero's commandment to defend; endurance because the alternatives are death and damnation. Politics provides the loudest instance of the hardship within which people struggle to create the smooth, happy life. Like bad weather or aging, they cannot think about it too much, and they cannot forget it.

In one situation, people construct one culture under symbols locked in impeccable conflict. Their way becomes one of tension, of patient endurance between obligation and failure. They carry on, the Troubles go on.

That was the conclusion, or lack of conclusion, to the District's chronicle. Old Catholic men told the stories it linked, so it can be said to represent a generation, a gender, a religion. Doubly, it is further reduced from statistical democracy. A special kind of person, the historian, chose a special kind of history, the story, to present, so the chronicle represents a certain personality, reflective and orderly, and relies on a certain source, the oral work of art. It is exceptional in the extreme, aristocratic, but that does not make it marginal.

The wider thought ranges, past stories to work, past old men to everyone, the more central the District's stories of history appear. They develop a key cultural proposition in terms of notable persons and events from the "Catholic" past, but that proposition is rooted deeper than history and branches wider than politics or particular Christian denominations. The first obligation placed upon people was not Patrick's or William's but God's. It charged them to live right, to defend faith, home, and neighbor. But people are weak and trapped in life's hardship. Perfect victory eludes them, and their minds form between obligation and failure.

When old Catholic men tell the District's story, they speak for themselves, their generation, their side, but most deeply, they speak for their community, authentically. The principles they use, though they use them best, are everyone's: they speak the culture. The problem with the chronicle is not its "Catholic" inflection. Its failings—one small, one overwhelming—lie in its nature as history.

30

History

From the prospect of Ballymenone, more than a millennium and a half of the past opens to view. No map of that terrain could be complete, yet I felt obliged to sketch it. Though limited by Ballymenone's selection of landmarks, my task would have proved beyond doing, even crudely, had I not resolved silently a host of fascinating arguments and accepted questionable—not false, but questionable—sources as accurate.

I took as essentially true the old lives of saints, though their authors were not bound by the rules of modern biography. They wrote as historians do today, selecting and arranging in accord with the thinking of their own era. It was not theirs to know that scholars a thousand years into the future would care more about sequence than significance, more about the details of a man's childhood than the miracles of his maturity. Modern scholars guided by modern goals must read old words critically, but we need not be cynical. There is nothing unscientific in imagining that people fifteen centuries ago could do things we cannot do, just as we can do things they could not. But there were things they could not do. Saint Molaise could not die in 563, 564, 570, and 571. Saint Patrick could not have first come to Ireland in 432, 456, and 462, nor could he have died in 457, 461, and 493. Yet you will find a good scholar to uphold all these dates. By not discussing such confusions, by sidestepping the question of whether there was one Patrick, or two or three, I got the chronicle written and produced problems of the sort the Cathach flushes into the open.

The District's stories of Saints make a loose web. Its stories of Battles are more tightly interwoven. I stitched the two together with Columcille's book. It was deposited in the Royal Irish Academy in 1842 and remains to be inspected. Though it bears signs of hasty copying and is arguably the oldest surviving Irish manuscript, some scholars judge it too young to be by Columcille's hand. Others accept it as his. Most remain skeptical but admit it is old enough to be his book. The fact is, no one knows.[1] When it was enshrined at Kells, it was believed to be Columcille's, and the O'Donnells carried the cumdach of the Cathach into battle often in the Middle Ages. Records attest that they bore it before them to war in the sixteenth century, but there is no evidence that it went with Red Hugh to the Siege of Enniskillen. There is no evidence it did not either, but it was probably not at the Ford, for though his men fought in the battle, Red Hugh himself was not there, much to his chagrin, said his first biographer.[2] He was off receiving Scots recruits to his cause, and by carrying the Cathach to the Ford, I was writing fiction, not history.

History resists being closed into neat and final tale. Claude Lévi-Strauss says history is our myth, and he is right, because history is used in literate societies as myth is in nonliterate ones to provide a distinct but relevant realm within which to explore the validity of the current regime.[3] As "nature" and primeval time serve the nonliterate philosopher, so "human nature" and historical time serve the literate one. The territory of the past exists to be dismembered, ordered, disordered, transformed, ordered anew. The historian's delight is endlessly arguing, while feeling no need for arbitrary restraint or the construction of inviolable conclusions. Drives toward order will produce not final order but the ceaseless expansion of mind: not death, but life is the goal.

The past cannot be studied. It has vanished, leaving scars, tracks, stains. These are what the historian studies, evaluating them as sources of evidence. Advances in critical technique at once bring new sources into view and old ones into review. If technique were perfected and facts were finally and firmly separated from fiction, the historian's job would remain undone. Once found, facts have to be strung into narratives to depict the past, but the past is too large: every string of facts refers implicitly to the enormity of its context and so to its own incompleteness. The particular myth cries for transformation, since it can contain but a shred of the whole of mythology, and every historical chronicle proposes itself for destruction since it is inevitably fragmentary.

Even if time stopped, the vastness of the past would make each string of facts unsatisfactory. But time has not, and history is a fact of history. Times change, and responsible historians restring facts in accordance with their society's needs. When Adamnan wrote of Columcille, his church had suffered defeat at Whitby, and he chose facts to give his comrades the steel of pious resistance. When Geoffrey Keating traveled Ireland consulting manuscripts and arranging his findings into his great *General History*, the earls had fled and Ireland was conquered. When Douglas Hyde brought the old histories into new order in his *Literary History of Ireland*, he wrote out of fear for the death of the Irish culture and language, while the Home Rule bills were going down in defeat. Historians in a prince's retinue and historians appalled by his tyranny can tell different tales without resort to lies. They must, if they are to be both historians and citizens.

Today, power shifts, expands. The formerly disenfranchised—the colonial, subject, oppressed, disdained—claim power, and power requests historical presence. Descendants of slaves march and burn the cities; they vote, get jobs, and demand places in the history books. The past has to be reconstructed.

So new sources are gathered. Neglected documents are opened. Artifacts and oral testimonies are given serious attention. New problems arise. What do birth certificates and census reports, wills and probate inventories mean? How do artifacts convey meaning? To what degree is oral history reliable? As truth rises from new sources, it is correlated with the chronicle developed at the behest of old power, and history widens to explain the shifting shape of our world.

History enlarges and improves unstoppably, while historians insure that it stays true and useful. This book can be absorbed into history's evolution, and I wrote my chronicle to help that happen. Another historian could dip color from it to use in painting history's big picture, making it a little more democratic, giving a few more people the feeling that they belong in the world of Western power. But that is not my goal. I do not believe that the academic history of the West, founded as it is on the needs of an elite regional minority, can be directed through revision to satisfaction. It will never expand to true global democracy, nor will it alone provide a base for a full theory of history. I believe a history useful to all humankind will come only if we first submit to the rigor of treating the world's many histories as independent cultural constructions. Histories of places like Ballymenone or Washington or Ponape must first be viewed in their own terms. And that is the overwhelming problem of the chronicle I wrote. It does not display but obscures the integrity of Ballymenone's history.

There is one past but many histories. We think of one of them—our own—as "history" and the others as "folk histories," but they are either all histories or all folk histories. All involve collecting facts about the past and arranging them artfully to explore the problems of the present. Academic historians create a history appropriate to their needs, and the no less serious historians of places like Ballymenone do the same: they create one that suits theirs.

Facts are always facts. They can be wrong. The most critical opinion would hold the District's historians wrong about the date of the Ford and modern academic historians wrong about its location, for they are as imprecise about its position in space as the District's historians are about its position in time. But both are right in general, if wrong in detail. Neither of their accounts can be absolutely factual, for the whole truth has gone with the past. But no historian wants to work with bad data, and all agree the willful use of untruth is something other than history—propaganda, art, stupidity, but not history. It is snide to make "belief" the basis of "legend," to speak of historians like Hugh Nolan as though they believed untrue things and used verbal trickery to convince their audiences to believe them too, and then to talk about our historians as though they were on a noble quest for truth. They do the same thing. Whether they teach at Oxford or wheel turf in Ballymenone, historians get the facts as accurately as they can get them, but since the past has passed, they cannot get all the facts, or get them all right. When they string facts into narratives, they will create something other than the factual past, if only by dint of omission and the dynamic of presentation, but they do not do so to fool people but to help them by driving at a truth larger than that trapped in factual scraps. Note how the District's historians violate the aesthetic of smoothness to hold to truth and keep it alive in the world, how Mr. Flanagan is reluctant to talk about what he does not know about, even though the situation demands performance, how Mr. Nolan carefully labels uncertainties and speculations, how Mr. Boyle sunders ramas from happening. "The job of the historian," Hugh Nolan said, "is keepin the truth." Truth makes history, because the will to truth makes historians. Their joy is finding, holding, manipulating truth.

Manipulating truth is essential to the formation of mind. Though any action can come of right thinking and incarnate culture, acts are unequal in their power of cultural display. The observer is attracted to instances of complex integration, to moments of communication. Logically the outsider focuses on times, such as storytelling or hay-rooking, when several minds bring diverse thoughts into play, making a multitude of interrelated decisions to form a unitary event. But during the event's blinding intensity, the actors are too involved to do more than create it properly, so it is useful for them to engage in acts which come out of right thinking and lead to objects they can contemplate. These provide the actors with convincing proofs of existence and cultural validity. In Ballymenone, as in other Western communities, perhaps all, these objects result from engagement with truth and fall into two classes: work's objects (artifacts) and thought's objects (history).

Artifacts result from human intervention in the real environment, physical, palpable, true. The environment is manipulated into things, into dinners or houses. Once these things reside in the environment apart from the self, the maker steps back, sees, and gains convincing proof of her or his existence. The actor becomes observer of the actor. "I think therefore I am" is empty. "I make therefore I am" is convincing. That thing of my manufacture stands on its own to prove that I do too. The artifact does more than stand. It becomes useful. Another takes it up. It is eaten. It shelters. I make a gift. You accept. Therefore, we are. The artifact becomes proof of social existence. We use it, and it works. Having eaten, we are pleased, filled, sustained. Sheltered, we can get on with our storytelling. By working, the artifact proves not only that we exist but also that we are competent. The ideas we share enable our survival. They are right. We are right. The artifact proves the validity of I, we, our culture.

History is intangible, a phantom of the mind, yet it is distanced from the dream of the self. History is a variety of imaginative literature, yet it shuns fancy for fact. As in making things, in thinking history, the real, the true is manipulated, arranged, made useful, accepted, made proof. Like artifacts, history depends on the individual for existence, but like the artifact, it is drawn from the world beyond the self, then pushed back into that world for objective evaluation.

History lives in performance and beyond. Ballymenone's historians not only tell history, they "rehearse" it, turning it over in thought to keep it fresh. It tests their reason: is the memory working, has it enough information, is the mind in order? The historian and his reader or listener can break history from the moment of narration to check it against all they know. It tests their contract: is the historian lying, does the reader share his point of view, is the social world, framed on truth, in order? Any story, including the historical one, can be beautiful or ugly, but the concept of fiction allows the beautiful to be not so. The fictional tale does not lie beyond evaluation, but it lies beyond proof. If a house leaks, it is either sculpture or a bad house. If a story is untrue, it is either not history or it is bad history. As the house endures in its climate, submitting to repair and improvement, history endures in a climate of critical memory to be rebuilt and patched endlessly toward unreachable perfection. In its striving, culture is tested. Are we preserving that which ought to be preserved? We look back to look forward. Are we on the right way?

That striving, a constant reconstruction by the light of truth, maintains culture in a healthy state of becoming. Truth is exactly that with which we engage to gauge life's course. Facts and principles are proved true by endurance. We hold to them to judge the self, preserve the society, and find the eternal in the transitory.

If people are stripped of the ability to manipulate truth, to make their own things and their own history, they may continue to act properly, but they lose the capacity to learn for themselves about their own rightness. They stagnate or surrender. If truth is located beyond the mind's grasp, if it is something that exists but cannot be touched, then culture cannot be advanced or defended. Made consumers, spectators, restrained from voluntary action, people become slaves, willing or not, happily or not, of powers that want their bodies. Those who steal from people their right to make artifacts (in order to sell junk to them) and those who steal their right to make their own history (in order to destroy their will to cultural resistance)—these can be condemned, for they steal from people the right to know that they know, the right to become human. Having observed, the observer learns and has no choice but to become an advocate not of a particular culture but of the human right to cultural construction.

History is a prime mode of cultural construction. That is how the history of Ballymenone, or anywhere else, is best addressed: as a way people organize reality to investigate truth to survive in their own terms.

History is culture. Culture is pattern in mind. Suppose we enter a community in search of its history, and let us say history is like an alphabet. One person tells us MSTQLKACE, another tells us DMKLRSTOABFWGN, and an-

Historical Knowledge

THE CHRONICLE		FLANAGAN	NOLAN	BOYLE
A.	St. Patrick in Ireland	✔	✔	
B.	St. Patrick in Fermanagh		✔	✔
C.	St. Naile	✔		
D	St. Febor		✔	
E.	St. Sinell	✔		
F.	St. Columbanus		✔	
G.	St. Columcille		✔	
H.	Viking Raids			
I.	The Cathach and the O'Donnells			
J.	Battle of O'Reilly and Maguire			✔
K.	Ford of Biscuits Battle	✔	✔	✔
L.	The Plantation of Ulster	✔	✔	
M.	Black Francis	✔	✔	✔
N.	Mrs. Timoney's Remarkable Walk		✔	✔
O.	The Famine		✔	
P.	McBrien and the Gift of Fish			✔
Q.	O'Connell and Catholic Emancipation	✔		
R.	Inishmore Fight		✔	
S.	Mackan Fight	✔	✔	✔
T.	Swad Chapel	✔	✔	
U.	The Fenian Rising			
V.	Parnell and Home Rule			
W.	The First Band Battle		✔	✔
X.	The Second Band Battle			✔
Y.	The Partition of Northern Ireland			
Z.	The Civil Rights Movement			

To the left are listed in sequence the major topics of the chronicle. Checks to the right credit the authors of the statements it links, suggesting the shape of historical knowledge in Ballymenone. Some topics are more well known than others, and no individual knows all of Ballymenone's own history. It is larger than the knowledge of any one person, but it cannot expand to include events (H, I, U, V, Y, Z) left untold by any of Ballymenone's historians.

other tells us JKMNPSWXB. That is exactly what we have in Ballymenone when the three people are Peter Flanagan, Hugh Nolan, and Michael Boyle and the letters designate stories or major historical statements, ranging from the Arrival of Saint Patrick to the Smashing of the Band. Out of these texts we can construct three sequences: A–G (Saints), J–T (from the first battle at the Ford through the Days of the Landlords and the Famine to Swad Chapel), WX (the band's battles). To fill in and write my chronicle, I imported facts from histories preserved in other places. That was wrong.

It is the analyst's duty to construct hidden relationships within a community's knowledge, but what a community does not know cannot exist within its culture, is no part of its own history. Again the Cathach illustrates error. I used it to insert alien letters between G and J. In December 1979, I told my story to Mr. Nolan, how Columcille's book became a talisman of victory for the medieval O'Donnells. He found it interesting but said he had never heard it before. "I lost track of the book," he said, "after Columcille sailed for Scotland." Plugging a gap in culture with ideas not part of that culture falsifies its shape, because culture has no gaps. Ballymenone's story is not flawed. Its alphabet—ABCDEFGJKLMNOPQRSTWX—is complete.

Scholars need courage and restraint. We must be courageous enough to extend and link the people's own ideas to reveal their fullness of mind. We must restrain from adding foreign ideas that, while seeming to make the culture more orderly, only serve to obscure and destroy the culture's own order.

If we scrape away the details I added to the already complete corpus of Ballymenone's historical narrative, it shrinks but strengthens, deepens, and recenters in the District's culture.

Ballymenone's historians drew into their corpus only two stories from other places. Each was a necessary addition, forming the first in sequences that interlock to propose the culture's essence.

Peter Flanagan told of Saint Patrick's coming to Ireland. Then he and others told of the arrival of Patrick or Patrick's word in Fermanagh. The saint's proposition lies in the cure. God made the world. He exists. People must love their neighbors. They must be good.

Hugh Nolan told the story of Saint Columcille. Columcille indeed connects the stories of Saints and Battles—not through the thin thread of chronology, but through potent concept. The Saint's is the first battle tale. Its structure repeats in the stories of the Ford, Black Francis, Mackan Hill, and both battles of the band. People are dispossessed or threatened with dispossession. Justly they rebel. They win. Victory is followed by exile, imprisonment, or death. The key tale, the swing tale in the chronicle, is the Ford. Enniskillen is taken. Ulster's chiefs confederate, rise and win at the Ford. Kinsale follows. The earls fly. Ireland is lost; plantation, oppression, famine, emigration, endless conflict follow. The warrior's proposition abides in battle. Mistreated people must fight. If they cooperate they will win, though victory may ask sacrifice. People must be brave.

People answer the command of both saints and warriors; they are good and they are brave. They are virtuous, but virtue swallows virtue. Though they love their neighbors, disobedient men assault them, leaving them no choice but courage, no choice but breaking God's rule and fighting their neighbors, so the victory of their bravery is contained by the defeat of their goodness. Gain is contained by loss, joy by sorrow, ease by hardship, light by dark. Ballymenone's historical tales retell the Christian myth of the origin of human existence, of exile from the garden. Paradise is lost: life is contained by death.

We must, like Mrs. Timoney and Mr. McBrien, carry on, digging in pain, finding consolation in our daily gruel. Cures in roots in dirt assure us there is an end to pain, a life beyond death.

31

The Idea of Place

Summer sun glimmers along Rossdoney Lane. In the dark we sit with Mr. Nolan, telling him of our travel. We have come from Sligo, where we went to see the ruins of the thirteenth-century abbey. There our attention was caught by a monument, erected in 1624 in high English Renaissance style to Sir Donough O'Connor, *famosissimus miles*, Lord of Sligo, who died in 1609, and his wife Elinora Butler, Countess of Desmond.[1] Old O'Connor leads to talk of the wars of his era. Mr. Nolan mentions the nearby battle of the Ford and offers to tell the story to Kathy and Polly, who have not heard it. Their enthusiastic response is quick and cheery. "All right then," he says and rises, shoves his chair back from the hearth, then shoves it forward to get past into the Room. The kitchen's little window gleams. He returns with bottles of beer for himself, Kathy, and me, a soda for Polly. I fetch the puller from the dresser and pop all the caps. He settles, lifts his beer toward us, saying, "All the best," takes a swig, then, waiting to be sure the tape recorder is working, he begins:

"Well, do ye see, in them days, all the part of Ireland that was free from English rule was the province of Ulster.

"That's the nine counties.

"That would be includin the North of Ireland and three of the counties of the Republic:

> Donegal, Derry,
> > Antrim, Down,
> > > Armagh, Monaghan,
> > > > Tyrone, Fermanagh, and Cavan.

"That was the Ulster of them days.

"And England wasn't more than a figurehead in Ulster, but they had the rest of Ireland; they were masters of it.

"So they gave some of the Ulster men, they gave them titles like Red Hugh O'Donnell's father, he was Sir Hugh O'Donnell. Well, that was an English title. He was the Earl of Donegal. Do ye see: he was appointed be the Irish clans, but then do ye see, the English king or the English queen, whichever would be on the throne at that time, do ye see, they gave him and the other Ulster chiefs, they gave him this title, the English title do ye see, that was Earl, but the Irish title was The O'Donnell or The Maguire or The O'Neill.

"Well.

"Hugh O'Donnell, his aim was, from he became a man, was for to clear the English out of Ireland *al*together.

"And above all, he wanted for to hold Ulster in Irish hands. Do ye know what I mean? To not let the English army get control of it like the way that they had control of the rest of the country.

"But the English managed for to get a garrison on the island of Enniskillen, a garrison, a barracks put up there, and put a number of troops into.

"So there was a number of English troops in Enniskillen.

"And Hugh O'Donnell gathered up an army of Ulstermen.

"There was Fermanagh men,

> Tyrone men,
> Donegal men,
> and men from the County Down,
>> in this army of O'Donnell's.

"O'Donnell's mother, do ye see, she was MacDonnell. She was a Scot. And then they had a clan in County Down at that time. And they used to fight side-be-side with the Northern chiefs, with the O'Neills and O'Donnells.

"But anyway, he besieged Enniskillen.

"So there was for ten weeks and none of this garrison could get out.

"They were marooned on the island

> be Irish troops.

"And there was a soldier managed for to get out one night,

> an English soldier.

"And he made his way be boat,

> from Enniskillen to Belturbet.

"And be the time he got to Belturbet, it was ten weeks from the siege started in Enniskillen,

> and they hadn't heard it in Dublin,
> and he got word conveyed to the Lord Lieutenant.

"So there and then the Lord Lieutenant raised an army.

"And he brought all the Irish chiefs through what's now the Republic of Ireland. They had swore allegiance to the Queen, do ye see.

"So anyway, he got them and their supporters into the army.

"Well, this army it was gathered from all over, from the Pale—there was a portion of the present Republic was known in them days as the Pale; it was peopled at the time of the Norman invasion; it was peopled by English—so they and the rest of these chiefs of the South and West, they had joined the Lord Lieutenant's army.

"And their intention was to come on to Enniskillen.

"But Hugh O'Donnell and O'Neill (it wasn't the great Hugh O'Neill, but a brother of his that was in the swim this time) they had couriers all over, watchin the movements of the Lord Lieutenant's army.

"And they knew that they were headin for Enniskillen.

"So O'Donnell and his men started from Enniskillen for to meet them.

"So O'Donnell's army got as far as the Arney.

"And the other ones was comin along, and it was the ould Arney Road. That would be the road that comes up by where Tommy Gilleece lived. That was the way to Enniskillen in them days, and there was no road here.

"They were travelin that road, do ye see, for to get on to Cavan and on to Dublin if possible.

"Hugh O'Donnell had left a force at Enniskillen, and he gathered up this army from Tyrone and Fermanagh and Donegal, do ye see:

> every man, do ye see,
>> turned out, do ye see,
>>> for to stop the Lord Lieutenant's army.

"So, accordin to tradition, they met at Arney Bridge.

"That would be on that road, some distance from Arney *Cross*.

"So of course they couldn't get by O'Donnell's men.

"The Lord Lieutenant's men were stopped.

"And of course when you'd be tryin for to get across any stream, you'll always run along the banks till you come to a narrow spot if you wanted to jump it, do ye see.

"Well, when they were stopped,
> at Arney Bridge,
>> they took to the banks.

"The Lord Lieutenant's men took the south bank of the Ȧrney River, and O'Donnell's men kept on the *other* side.

"So they tried in a couple of places, but they couldn't get over, and they came to this ford at Drumane.

"And the Lord Lieutenant's army, they mustered up,
> and made to come across the ford.

"But the other ones *beat* them back.

"And what made things worse, they had their supplies with them,
> and all was lost in the River,
> and alot of their soldiers killed.

"So they got that bad a beatin,
> that they had to turn back
>> for Cavan again.

"And that was the battle of the Biscuit Ford."

He stops, and while we thank him, he raises his bottle with a smile. "Oh now," he says modestly, taking a little sip. "Then what happened at Enniskillen?" I ask, and he answers:

"Then, do ye see, the garrison was put out of Enniskillen, do ye see.

"The garrison was rooted out of Enniskillen, do ye see.

"The fort that the English had put up, it fell into the hands of the Maguires, do ye see.

"So that's as far as I can give any information on the Battle of the Biscuit Ford.

"That's what brought it about.

"And that's how it ended."

Again our thanks and compliments begin to flurry, but he stops us saying:

"Well, I'll tell you now.

"There's more that flashed in my memory since when you joined to talk.

"There was a battle before that.

"He was governor that was in Connacht,
        an English governor.

"And he was the name of Clifford,
        he was Conyers Clifford.

"And he made an attempt at one time for to invade Donegal.

"And O'Donnell gathered up his army.
        and they met convenient to Ballyshannon.

"And the battle took place there.

"And there was a man the name of O'Connor,
        he was killed in that battle.

"And his body was recovered from the river,
        be a Franciscan monk.

"There was Franciscans in Donegal at that time.

"And this monk went into the river and took out that man's body.

"And that must be the man that's buried in Sligo Abbey.

"Well, that's apt to be the man.

"His body was taken out of the River Erne be a Franciscan monk.

"That battle took place somewhere on the River between Ballyshannon and Bundoran. The River Erne."

Listening to Mr. Nolan, we are reminded of essential features of historical tales forgotten when they are blended into chronology. They are not links in a chain, subdivisions of an ordered entity, but intense foci, centers selected out of history beyond which the past expands to uncontrolled, unknowable wholeness. These centers, hills above the bog of fact, flames flickering here and there in darkness, are characterized by economy and geographical precision.

Economy is spatial and conceptual. The District's historians focus on happenings in their locality, their community and its region, the Fermanagh of the mind, lying between the Lough and the mountains—Inishmore where Patrick stood and Belcoo where he blessed the well—between Enniskillen and towns on the Cavan border: Belturbet, Bawnboy, Ballyconnell, and Swanlinbar. Beyond this area, history is released into the care of others, into darkness, so local men enter it tentatively. Peter Flanagan's story of Saint Patrick, belonging as it did to Down and Meath, was offered humbly and compressed to the minimum of narration: two lines. Though Hugh Nolan told Saint Columcille's tale with force and feeling, it is not from his region, and he interrupted himself to apologize, as he did in no other telling, "I'm just not well up on this story." When Mr. Nolan wandered away from the Ford, leaving Maguire's Fermanagh for O'Connor's Sligo, he became uncertain and made mistakes. Conyers Clifford, Governor of Connacht, did attempt to invade Donegal and was defeated at Ballyshannon, but it was after not before the Ford, in 1597. Donough O'Connor was involved, for he had leagued with the English, had been defeated earlier by Red Hugh, and was wounded in the battle of Ballyshannon, but he did not die in the Erne. He lived to surrender his last castle to Red Hugh in 1599, when Clifford's head was displayed before him, and, knighted in 1604, he died in happy possession of his estate in the year of the Plantation. The man killed in the Erne was Murrough O'Brien, Baron of Inchi-

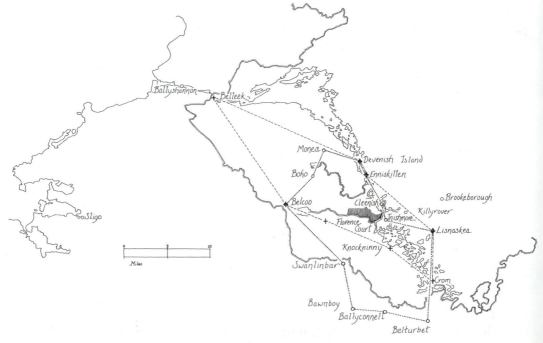

The South Fermanagh Region. The conceptual "South Fermanagh" is stretched along the western shores of Lough Erne. The circles linked by dots are the places farthest from Ballymenone that figure in the District's own history. The crosses linked by dashes are the places mentioned in "The Fermanagh Song."

quin, who was shot in the armpit, the crevice in his armor, and drowned in the river while leading the English and Irish armies into Donegal. His body was retrieved by a monk and interred in the Cistercian monastery of Assaroe, then after a dispute, removed to a Franciscan monastery in Donegal.[2] These small confusions, a date wrong by four years, a shot by a yard (for O'Connor was riding next to O'Brien when he was killed), are the kind of error expected in oral history, but the District's historians do not make them at home. In his own locality, Mr. Nolan gets even small facts right; it is true it was not Hugh O'Neill but his brother who led Tyrone to Enniskillen.

The historian's responsibility is confined to his own place. Even there he does not form every great happening into a tale. His wish is not for completeness. He tries not to control the whole of the past but to form out of it centers rich in concept, powerful in their meanings for modern people.

Stories of history are economically few. The historian's mind ranges widely, but most of history lies unordered, awaiting use in discussion or arrangement in the mind around stories. The District's people know much about the Days of the Landlords and talk of them often, but they construct from those times only two tales, one of endurance, one of rebellion, around which other knowledge spreads contextually, fading from relevance into irrelevance. The Irish past flames with endless battles, but local historians not only confine themselves to fights that took place in their place, they reduce the number of battles, investing their energy in those that display all the varieties of conflict and form the core of their District's history. The Ford tells of conflict between native and foreigner. Mackan tells of conflict between the community's sides. The second band battle tells of conflict within sides. Those tales are isolated into importance by place and concept, not chronology, by message more than chains of cause and effect. Other tales serve as clarification. The Saints show why one must not fight and yet must fight. Wider military history is subservient to these key tales—Ulster's Nine Years' War leading to Kinsale is but context for the Ford, the Easter Rising is but context for the band—and other local battle tales are positioned dependently around them. In performance, Michael Boyle placed the earlier fight at Drumane after the Ford, just as Mr. Nolan placed Red Hugh's fight at Ballyshannon after the Ford, though he thought it had happened before. Mr. Nolan placed the earlier Inishmore Fight after Mackan Hill. Peter Flanagan made the Tossing of the Swad Chapel an appendage to Mackan Hill. So powerful are these connections, not of time, but of concept, that, though James Owens does not know about Mackan Fight, when I asked him about it, he was led to Swanlinbar:

"Well I don't know much about that fight.
"But wasn't it Owen Cleary's grandfather was at that fight?"

Annie is seated by him and says, "Transported, I think so." Mr. Owens continues:

"Aye, transported to Van Dieman's Land.

"Well, Owen would be a first cousin of mine. But he's dead.

"Oh aye, but he's dead.

"Ah, there was a fellow here, he used to work with the parish priest. He had a great recitation on that now, and I do forget it, on Mackan Fight, wherever he got the history of it.

"And then at Florencecourt one time and they were goin to toss Swanlinbar Chapel.

"And there was a man there the name of Lord *Cole*.

"He lived up there where you see the mountains,
   he was goin to lead them,
     this mornin,
       to toss the chapel.

"And he wasn't turnin up, and they went to call him,
    and he was dead in bed.

"He was dead: he was black as your shoe.

"Do ye see now: the Almighty wasn't in favor of it.

"There is a monument there in Enniskillen yet, you know, Lord Cole's monument, out at the far end. That's the man was goin to toss the chapel.

"The IRA, they were goin to blow that up, and they were *caught*.

"Oh aye, they were caught. Some of the workmen left the gate open and they were *caught*. O Lord bless us, that would have been a powerful explosion: the *height* of it, do ye see. It would have done harm."

Annie comments, "Harm to innocent people," and James agrees:

"It would have done harm to innocent people, do ye see. All them bricks and mortar and the *height* of that. Look at the length it was goin to go.

"It might have done harm surely.

"And there was a song about the Swad Chapel too.

"A cousin of mine, Missus Cox, and many a night she sang that song for us. And that was their favorite song. He'd come in from the pub and he'd have a few in, and it was the Swanlinbar Chapel Song he'd want to hear.

"I don't know now who made it, but I just forget the words of it at the present time.

"Och, longgo, you know, the ould people here used to tell lots of Irish history, but you weren't interested in it when you were young. When you were young you weren't interested. No, no.

"It was only afterwards that you just might mind some of the things that you heard about it."

The few young men who were interested in history, who sat with the old people and listened with care, learned the complete stories of their place, and when they tell them, nothing is more obvious than that they set them primarily in space, only secondarily in time. Hugh Nolan's tale of the Ford, in both of its renditions, 1972 and 1977, sparkles with place names. He needs strong words to mark the ends of lines, and in his 1977 version lines stop: Republic, Derry, Down, Monaghan, Cavan, Ulster, Enniskillen, Down, Enniskillen, Belturbet, Enniskillen, Dublin, Enniskillen, Arney, Arney Bridge, Arney Cross, Drumane, Biscuit Ford—closing down around the place of battle, nearly providing a synopsis of the story. He sets the battle in space with great precision. The armies meet at Arney Bridge, run the banks eastward, and fight at Drumane. He sets the battle generally in time, in the days when the present situation was reversed and only Ulster lay beyond English dominion. Dates are not part of the story. As Hugh Patrick Owens demonstrated in his story of the Ford, tales can be told with little idea of their location in time. What interested Mr. Owens was where the battle took place, not when it took place. Even when the date is known, it follows the action. Michael Boyle dropped the date of Mackan Hill into the coda of his story. But usually dates follow the tale, because that is when I asked for them. Stories open with general settings, then proceed to location and action, leaving dates unspoken. Michael Boyle set his tale of the Ford generally in time, a time when the English occupied Ireland, then when he had finished I requested a date, and he said the battle took place around 1597 or 1598, only three or four years off the mark. Hugh Nolan set his tale of Mackan Hill conceptually, saying it was a fight like many others. When the story ended, I asked for a date and he answered correctly, 1829. Ballymenone's historians upturn the norms of academic historians and set events vaguely in time but precisely in place.

In the introduction to his superb translation of the *Tain*, Thomas Kinsella remarks on the importance of place names in the epic, noting that bits of narration seem to have been included only to name places, that place was a preoccupation of ancient and medieval Irish literature. The *Tain* is less an event of time than an event of concept and space, an essay on honor, a story out of Ireland. The poets of Kinsella's generation, ours, have learned and worked to speak with power and beauty the old Irish idea. Kinsella, a master of verse of love and fear, takes a walk in the country, and out of the fields, the flowers, the gleam of light on the waters of a ford, all of a violent past forms in his mind, Cú Chulainn and Fer Diad, Christ, Norman and Cromwellian conquest, "tireless rebellion." Monuments and names and land push the tortured story of brothers slaying brothers through his head into poetry. Seamus Heaney sees "a landscape fossilized," named to bring Planters and Vikings to life. In *Field Work* on Devenish he feels the Saints and hears the army's helicopter. Richard Murphy's long and excellent poem, "The Battle of Aughrim," tells of history that cannot be plowed out of fields in which "the past is happening today." John Montague named his sad, strong book of poems on Ulster for the Tyrone townland of his people, harsh land, strewn with meaning, with memories of Kinsale and rapparees: "All around, shards of a lost tradition. . . . The whole landscape a manuscript."[3]

Irish history has had its great chroniclers, but as daters of things, the Irish are Europeans. The native tradition of the *Tain* lives today in the words of poets and geographers, in the writings of men like John Montague and E. Estyn Evans, for whom the land is history. In the prime work of our days, the epic of consciousness *Finnegans Wake*, time is absorbed into place, and place into mind. The land becomes history, and history becomes thought as people cross space in awareness.

Setting history into their place, Ballymenone's historians make their place a gift to the mind. History makes the locality rich. Its names become cracks through which to peek into excitement. Its meadows and the fords of its little river become great tales. History is a consolation to the one who does not travel, a way to make the small place enormous, complete, inhabitable, worth defending.

Stories set in place bring history into the present. Dates alienate. They are a means to kill the past and bury it in irrelevance. So dates are avoided, and stories are given conceptual or spatial introductions, designed to connect them to the present. At the time of the Ford, the English occupied the country. They still do. At the time of Mackan Hill, Protestants and Catholics fought. They still do. The tale's spatial precision makes it tangible, real. The date, 1594, lies far from us, remote and unapproachable, nearly unimaginable, but the Ford is right here. Though she knew nothing of the battle's history, Mrs. Owens thought it important to take me to stand on the spot where men had died. I first heard of Mackan Hill when P Flanagan and I were driving past the site. Years before, the Tourist to Arney, in Thomas Owens' poem, had been taken to see Mackan Hill. In place you are in history, and the past presses heavily upon you, involving you in its preservation and continuation.

In the noble native tradition, history in Ballymenone is part of the durable idea of place. Place is space rich enough to provide travel for the mind while the body sits still, space so full of the past that it forces people to become responsible for its future. History is the essence of the idea of place. There are two local histories.

One history is evolutionary. It is not broken, but flows smoothly through you as you work. The landscape is its record. The bailiff's ruined house, the grassy dips of brick ponds, the bog's buried timber and empty expanse, metal roofs and haysheds, paved roads, poles: the landscape is written with evolution. Facts drawn from visible, tangible remains become values within, and the land beyond teaches the progress of comfort, the decline of community, and commands the individual to understand and adjust.

Ballymenone's other history is not evolutionary, and its nature is destroyed when it is chronicled. It is ordered like the old year, like the community, and consists of a set of separate works of art that rise out of wholeness with powerful messages for the mind. Like the Great Days, they form as centers in time's flow, moments of intensity when common action is exaggerated into visibility. Like hearths, they are bright points of perpetual light in the wideness of space. Stories of history are set in time, but not lost in time; they break above to stand as moral presences, eternally rattling the head with complexity.

Facing the whole of the past, the District's historians use two ideas to create useful order. They link some events by sequence, others by typology, so the person who is in place, located, understands two histories. One is a matter of continuity, of endless growth and decay. The other is a matter of centers, of immortal and moral issues. Everyone is a part of the first and obliged to adapt to its power as to a climate, the sun and storm of every day. The other preserves great personages in deathless life. It is the possession of the stars of the night, but it too is built into place and waits for those who dare to be heroic, breaking the grip of the inevitable, springing free of mortality. Both histories surround people, echoing, screaming from the land they walk daily, demanding that they choose their path and find their way consciously. Inescapably inscribed in the land, history is intrinsic to the idea of place that forces people to be human.

PART TEN

Stars

32

The Star's Nature

"There was some great poets in this country," Joe Flanagan says, sitting up in his big chair, the hands on his knees, the cap on his head.

"There was men livin beside us here. They were not far away anyway.

"And they were poets.

"Only just rough country men. You wouldn't think they knew anything."

Peter in bright white shirt and black work shoes is sitting on the middle chair before the hearth, leaning forward, watching smoke leave his after dinner cigarette. "Aye," P says, not changing his position or lifting his gaze, "that man that I do sing a bit of his song. He was a right good poet.

"Charlie Farmer.

"It twas him made that song, The Men of Ninety-Eight. And he was only a wee unsignified-lookin poor wee fellow with a wee chubby beard. And he lived all alone.

"And that was one of the songs that he made."

P kills the last of the cigarette's heat in a pinch and pitches it into the fire, clasps his hands, and sings quietly. Words and melody come clearly, but without force, as though P were withdrawing himself from the song, letting Charlie Farmer's work stand wholly on its own. His singing makes us think not of P but of the poet, Farmer:

A hundred years has passed and gone since Irish men they stood
On the green hillside of Erin and for freedom shed their blood.
The Irish race is called upon for to commemorate
Those brave United Irishmen who died in Ninety-Eight.

Then: hurray for the flag, the dear old flag of green.
And hurray for the men who beneath its folds is seen.
Hurray for those heroes we now commemorate:
Those brave United Irishmen who died in Ninety-Eight.

Tyrannical oppression reigned supreme throughout our land,
And trampled on the people's rights till they could no longer stand.

Our gallant soldiers up they sprung against Saxon's crown and hate,
And swore they'd save their land or die, the men of Ninety-Eight.

(*Chorus of the second stanza*)

The standard of the green unfurled while cheers does blend the air
That waved now proudly over the men of Wexford and Kildare.
And Father Murphy blessed our arms and bravely led us on.
We'll ne'er forget old Suchatharoon. Hurray for Father John.

(*Chorus*)

"There's another verse. Wait'll I see. Oh aye:"

They fought and died for Ireland, oh how they died in vain.
Are we content to live as slaves beneath a tyrant's chain?
Ah no, my boys, while Irish blood through Irish veins does flow,
We're ever ready at the call to strike another blow.

Then: hurray for the flag, the dear old flag of green.
And hurray for the men who beneath its folds is seen.
Hurray for those heroes we now commemorate:
Those brave United Irishmen, who died in Ninety-Eight.

P sits back, his arms folded, his eyes in the fire, memories in his mind. "Charlie Farmer of Tiravally made that song. He's dead since forty." Slowly P stands and walks to search in the dresser. Joe tells me:

"Well, there was a fellow, he had all the songs of the day. He died here not long ago. He was a powerful singer." Joe nods in emphasis. "Joe Neal they called him.

"And I often heard him singin the whole night at sprees.

"You wouldn't be tired listenin to him.

"He didn't make any songs himself, but he was well educated, you know, and he learned all these songs. He pursued that.

"And he had all Charlie Farmer's songs."

P has come back to us and waited for Joe to pause. He hands me a written text of "The Men of Ninety-Eight," saying, "And there it is. Cathal McConnell wrote it out." I hand it back to P, and he reads it over, singing parts nearly silently to himself. Joe fills his pipe, cracks a match, and lights up. P takes his glasses off, releases the ballat into one hand, closes the other into a fist on his hip, and turns on his chair to tell me:

"Oh, he made a lot of songs. That one is commemoratin the men of Ninety-Eight for their gallantry. He was very intelligent, and he saw the trouble his country was in and he composed these songs so people wouldn't forget."

The paper with the song's words, handwritten, has been passed back to me. "Were all his songs patriotic?" I ask.

"Oh no they weren't," P replies. "Oh no, indeed. He didn't make all patriotic songs. Aye, surely. No doubt about that.
"He made several songs. But unfortunately, I haven't them.
"He made several songs. It twas him made that Kinawley."

Peter Flanagan does have "Kinawley," a song of great local importance. A young Catholic woman sang it to taunt Ellen Cutler when they occupied the same hospital ward, and Mrs. Cutler remembers a bit of one verse:

Come until Kinawley and there you will see,
The green, white, and gold hangin from a tree.

Hugh Nolan has heard it often and knows part of a parody composed by "the opposition" to lampoon a noted Kinawley comedian:

Come to Kinawley and there you will see
Black John Maguire down on one knee.

On the snowy Sunday night of November 12, 1972, a celebration was held at St. Naile's Hall in Kinawley to welcome home internees released from Long Kesh and to award ribbons to four local men who had been interned fifty years before on the prison ship *Argenta* in Belfast Lough. Only one of the old men was present, and two of those who accepted ribbons for their brothers were Ballymenone farmers, Denis Gilroy and Hugh Corrigan. A small tricolor made by an internee was raffled, a large one hung above the stage, where a band played dilute country-and-western music, and men spoke, the priest gently and historically, the internees quietly and earnestly, the politicians cleverly and forcefully, promising that Protestants would not be mistreated in the new united Ireland as Catholics had been in Northern Ireland, promising that victory would some day be won. "Up the Provos," a boy in the crowd yells. One of the internees, bearded, well dressed, and calm, announces that the father has said the dance can go on for another half an hour. The band bursts into a rockabilly upbeat version of "The Men Behind the Wire." On one side of the hall, the crowd of young women breaks into jitterbugging couples while, across the floor, men young and old smoke, and around the walls, older couples wait for a waltz. The signs posted in the pubs of Swad inviting people to the big night read, "Come to Kinawley."

The song is often requested in Swanlinbar, but Martin Crudden, Kinawley's chief among singers, fears it will die out, because only Peter Flanagan has it, knows it all.

Once when the young Kinawley men around him asked for his song, P taught before singing, "Well, this song was writ on the Insurrection, the

Nineteen and Sixteen Rebellion. And it was composed by the late Charles Farmer of Tiravally, Mackan. A very humble man. He was a man lived without publicity or the like of that." Here is the full text:

> Come to Kinawley, that historic place,
> That once has been the pride and the home of our race,
> Before the invader, he dared show his face
> In our sanctified home in Kinawley.
>
> Come to Kinawley and there take your stand
> In the struggle for freedom we'll join heart in hand.
> An Irish Republic is all we demand
> And we'll have nothing less in Kinawley.
>
> Our own saintly curate, we'll greet with a smile.
> He loves every inch of our beautiful isle.
> He talks with his people the same as a child,
> And he's loved by us all in Kinawley.
>
> (Chorus of the second stanza)
>
> Our priest and our people together they'll stand
> With their backs to the wall, and they'll fight for our land.
> In liberty's cause they will join in the band,
> And they'll drive out the foes from Kinawley.
>
> (Chorus)
>
> Come to Kinawley and there you will see
> The flag of a nation, it floats from a tree.
> Stand under its folds if you want to be free,
> And shout up Sinn Fein in Kinawley.
>
> (Chorus)
>
> Come to Kinawley and pray at the shrine
> As of holy Saint Naile, it's in olden time,
> Before the Normans and Saxons committed the crime
> For to plunder our old homes in Kinawley.
>
> (Chorus)
>
> While begging from England we were but old fools.
> While trusting their statesmen, they made us ould tools,
> But now we are out for to kill British rule,
> And to bury their corpse in Kinawley.
>
> Come to Kinawley and there take your stand
> In the struggle for freedom, we'll join heart in hand.

And an Irish Republic is all we demand
And we'll have nothing less in Kinawley.

The song was composed to draw people to a big Sinn Fein rally at Kinawley during the period of conflict after the Easter Rising. A tricolor, green, white, and gold, was hung in a tree across from the Kinawley Barracks where the Union Jack flew. People streamed the roads to the meeting, Martin Crudden said, and when the police asked an old man named McHugh where he was going he replied, "I'm just goin to a hockey match." The saintly curate was "the Fenian Priest," Father Patrick McPhillips. Cubs went barefoot when P was a boy. Though he was a member of the Kinawley Band, P was told he could not march in an upcoming meeting, for he owned no shoes. Father McPhillips understood his sadness. He took P to the shop, lifted him up on the counter, bought him a pair of shoes, gave him two shillings, and P marched proudly in the band, youngest of all its twenty-seven fluters.

In its song the tiny Border town of Kinawley is sanctified and historic, place of Saint Naile, home of heroes. The martial tune is stirring, akin to "The Battle Hymn of the Republic," though taken, P says, from an old sentimental song, "Erin, I Adore." When he answers requests for "Kinawley," P often omits stanzas, usually those about the saintly curate and Naile's shrine, because "with the chorus in between it makes a very long song."

Joe and I sit with P. Knowing I know "Kinawley," that my memory can open around the place name to support his argument on the quality of the wee poet, P continues, telling me of another of Farmer's songs dealing with the same era, when Sinn Fein and Molly Maguire faced off, the countryside tore, the Old Ballymenone Band broke:

"And he made another song. On Molly Maguire. Do ye see: Molly Maguire it's not—it's a great society in America. That's the Hibernians. Well, the Hibernians were followers of John Redmond and they wanted compromise. It twas sectarian here in this country throughout a number of years back, you know, but not so much now. I think the Nineteen and Sixteen Rebellion dissolved it altogether and cooled it down.

"But the Molly Maguires and Fenians was two parties here was very much opposed to other. And it twas alot of rows and trouble when they were at their height, especially goin into the fairs. It's marts now to substitute for the old fairs in this country, but at the time of the ould fairs in Ireland, och, there was bloodshed with these two parties.

"And he made this song on Molly Maguire.

"And it's a very good one too.

"So it is.

"I just haven't it now.

"It started off. Do you mind the first of it?"

Joe's nature is quiet, not silent. He says little, but attends closely and helps when he can. "I don't," he says quietly. P wrinkles his brow and recites a fragment:

> *While going to Swad on the day of the fair,*
> *You'll find lots of the blackguard in Molly Maguire.*
> *Love, friendship, and unity is what they do preach*
> *About lovin their society and the great A O H.*
> *But poor ould Rory—*

"I think it was Rory Somethin was the founder of Molly Maguire. He was Rory Somethin now. I must get some man that can go deeper into history than me. He was the founder of the Molly Maguires. And that's what Charlie, do ye see, said in the song:

> *Poor old Rory, the rod you did spare*
> *In training this damsel called Molly Maguire.*

"He faulted the founder of it, you see. He faulted the founder of it for not givin her more of the rod, keeping her under subjection and puttin her on the right road, and not havin her out raisin sectarian trouble."

P laughs and hands me a cigarette. While I light us and Joe smiles, P goes on, telling me about Cardinal Logue (who denounced Parnell and warned against the militant Sinn Fein; in the 1919–22 period, he spoke out eloquently against Irish men fighting Irish men):

"And then there was a cardinal in this country at the time too. At Armagh. It was Cardinal Logue. Charlie put in the song that she talked about lovin her country and God, till the great Cardinal Logue had to give her the rod ◇. He had to bring her under subjection.

"And of course that was the way: they used to go into Swad there and rise rows and get innocent men to fight with other, and *kill other*. That's what he meant be goin to Swad on the day of the fair. That was faction fightin, you see. It was throughout all Ireland at the time.

> *When goin to Swad on the day of the fair,*
> *You'd find of the blackguard in Molly Maguire.*

"Ah, they were holy terrors."

P pauses for a puff. Joe and I smoke with him, waiting. He continues:

"And then he made another one—political too. He made one about the fight here on the Border.
"He started it off:"

> *The great League of Nations is now in despair,*
> *And war it is looming again in the air,*

And an order has came from Belfast to prepare
For a bloody campaign on the Border.

We thought when the rule of the Kaiser had ceased
That Europe was in for the blessings of peace,
But a hero named Cooper has taken his place,
And he threatens to march on the Border.

The law and the treaty, this hero defies
In a speech that he made on the Twelfth of July.
He shouts, No surrender, we'll conquer or die
In a bloody campaign on the Border.

His army composed of the A B and C,
Old men and cubs not the height of you knee.
It would be well worth your while for to go there and see
This rebel brigade on the Border.

I would advise Mister Cooper at home for to stop,
For to stay at his desk or remain in the shop,
For some of these snipers this hero might pop,
And the battle would be lost at the Border.

When he goes to the Border to make his attack
I would venture to say he would never come back,
Except his remains be sent home in a sack
To be buried away from the Border.

Charlie Farmer's "Bloody Campaign on the Border" satirized the staunch Protestant resistance to the idea of redrawing Northern Ireland's border to exclude south Fermanagh. Mr. Cooper, said P, was the Crown Solicitor of the period and a shopkeeper in Enniskillen, and Charlie Farmer wrote the song after reading an editorial supporting the B Specials, old men and young deputized as special forces to assist the army in their defense of Ulster. A young man in a pub told me Farmer was the more remarkable because he could not read, could not even sign his own name, but P replied that was not so. He remembers Farmer "puttin on the wee glasses with the wee bright rims and readin the paper as well as any professor." He always read the *Impartial Reporter* because he liked the strident style of the Unionist editorials. They inspired him to satire, to writing one song on the paper's editor, Mr. Trimble, and another on Mr. Cooper. The compliment was returned, P said, for "when Cooper heard the song sung be one of his own side, he found it very amusin, so he did."

P enjoys singing Farmer's song for its rollicking tune, a cousin of "The Limerick Rake," and he often lilts the air between the stanzas when he performs, but he is uncertain of the text, for he learned it by overhearing a man named Johnny Leonard sing it, so he usually omits stanzas, especially the third and sixth, and one night he inserted a new one before the last two which I remember running:

> When off to the Border our hero does go
> Like another Napoleon he'll make a great show,
> But there's a few things Mister Cooper don't know
> About the enemy he'll meet at the Border.

Every time we recorded the song, P left that out, and when I finally asked him for it directly, he tried to reconstruct it and came up with:

> When he goes to the Border for to meet his foe,
> Another Napoleon for the call as you know.
> And as he's so anxious to meet with his foe
> He'll ne'er get away from the Border.

Songs, P says, "get you on the hop." They come into your head in the heat of performance, then vanish, perhaps forever. Songs are fragile. P works to preserve them, to preserve within them the memory of men of excellence. Songs commemorate famous heroes like the Men of Ninety-Eight, and they commemorate the surprising and unsung heroes who compose poems. Another time P told me, "Charlie Farmer was the modestest wee man, as quiet as our Joe. To look at him you wouldn't think he had a word." Now, his gentle singing of old song done, and sitting with Joe at the hearth, P praises quiet men, saying of Charlie Farmer:

"Oh he was a great poet.
"Ah, he was."

Joe agrees, "He was a very smart wee man. You'd think to look at him that he knew nothin atall."

"Aye," says P. "He made another one. He was an old fellow, he was the name of Willie Oliver. And he lived on his lone.

"And there was two girls went to America. And they came back again of course. And them days there was all country-house dances, you see.

"And Willie took a notion he'd give this party
        for these two returned Yankees,
            they were the name of McCaffrey.

"And he made this song. He called it a Harvest Home; that's what he titled this dance, a Harvest Home.

"And he said in it (to show that it was a wonderful night):

> You have heard of sprees in Dublin,
> And you have heard of sprees in Cork,
> But we had girls here
> From the city of New York.

"And then he talked about what a big feed it was:

And when the table was cleared up,
You could hear them rift and moan.
And there never was such fun before
As at Oliver's Harvest Home.

"It went on like that; it was good."

Joe smiles, "Ah, that was a great song."
"It twas," P agrees. "And it had an ould swing of an air. It's nearly like the air of The Garden Where the Praties Grow. That's the air of it." P whistles the tune. "That was a great wee song. It's sung regularly in this country over the radio."
With a great smile, P sits upright and lilts the tune merrily.
"It's a toppin ould air," he declares. "You know, you sung it with a good rift. You want to get into it, you know. You could get another that could sing it in a different form and not have any humor in it, do ye see. It all depends on who's singin an entertainin or what you might call a funny song, well, you want to sing it with a bit of jollification. Put a bit of humor into it.
"Now this Joe Neal, he could get at Oliver's Harvest Home. And he'd swing the head this way and that way, you know. Well, you'd be delighted to hear him singin it.
"Aye surely.
"It has good rhymes and an air with a bit of a swing to it.
"He was William Oliver. The poor creature. He had a notion of these two girls, you see. And he threw them this party."
With a winking glance at me, P says, "He wasn't too lovable."
"He was a nice man," Joe says.
"He was nice in nature," P catches himself. "He had good qualities.
"But as a singer he was Ireland's worst. He was a kind of chain singer, and, ah the creature, you wouldn't be bothered listenin to him. You'd go outside in the snow and sleet till you'd be frozen to death before you'd listen to him.
"Och, you'd rather hear a bull roarin in the bog."
"That was a great song," Joe says.
"Aye, he was a wonderful poet. Charlie Farmer," P continues:
"And then he put good grammar into it."
"He did," Joe says.
"Now, however the dickens it came, I don't know," P goes on, "how he got his education. Of course education was at its highest standard in the nineteenth century, higher than what it is now. Indeed, far better scholars. But he was a person like every other country person that didn't get a chance.
"And you see in that song that he put great grammar into it.

"And he made another one then on sports that was up here. And he was an agey old man. And he was the name of Greene. And poor John, he got out with the cubs, the young fellows. There was a donkey race. There was a donkey race anyway, and John got in as a competitor in the race; he competed with his ass in it. And he galloped round with the cubs. And you know donkeys is very stubborn animals, and John fell off, and tumbled here and tumbled there, and he was the greatest laugh. It was the most entertainin part of the sports, I think, to see this old man ridin the ass and rollin off ◊ and him bawlin and the cubs shoutin at him ◊."

Joe laughs with us and adds, "He was contrary and cross," and P keeps it going:

"He was contrary and cross. He was wicked. He was the name of John Greene.

"And he said in one part of it:

Above all—

"There is a town up in Longford they call Skibbereen—is it in Cork or in Longford?"

Joe helps, "Skibbereen is in Cork."

P agrees, "It's in Cork, I think too.

"Aye, Cork, and he said:

Above all the jockeys,
From this Skibbereen,
There's none of them can ride an ass
Like you, my brave John Greene ◊.

"It went on like that. It was full of humor.

"He was the best.

"And there was another—there was old barracks, they have been done away with, here up the road, up above the wee bridge. The police was there for years and years: Mackan Barrack.

"And there was a policeman, and he was a great lady's man. He was the name of Reilly. And he was, coorse, very fond of women, goin round all parts of the country and tryin to get in with this. And he was a kind of an agey fellow too. Whether he was successful, I just can't tell you about that part of it.

"But he made the song on Reilly anyway.

"And he said:"

There's a thousand girls in Ireland,
And I'll put the figure mildly—
There's ten thousand girls in Ireland . . .

"A million," says Joe, with a little smile.

"Ah, there was two million, of coorse, but he put the figure mildly. He didn't want to exceed the number. It was a modest calculation:"

There's ten thousand girls in Ireland,
And I'll put the figure mildly.
And as far as I can understand,
There's not enough for Reilly.

P's laughter joins us closely. We smile around the hearth. It has near-ly darkened. Joe walks toward the door's brightness, pauses to look upon the sunny fields of early August while daylight burns away his profile, then stoops to the black sack of turf by the door. P brings the topic to its conclusion:

"Well them was two funny songs—three funny songs.

"He made several funny songs. He made old sentimental songs and political songs. Just that was the way. But he had no harm in any song. It twasn't to vex any party."

Good chat is not idle talk. It develops out of the group's topic, moving much like a story from the general to the specific, from proposition to ac-tion and example. Joe said there were fine local poets, and P used Charlie Farmer to illustrate, extending logically from the center Joe established. When the neighbors are the topic, extension takes negative or positive turns to become entertaining. The negative heads toward satire of the kind Farm-er set in verse. On that track, P became amused by his own hyperbolic de-negration of Willie Oliver as Ireland's worst singer. But ridicule is usually shunned or stopped; chat is celebratory, and that way leads gracefully to artistic presentation, to telling an exploit or bid or pant or singing a song that reflects well on the individual caught in conversation.

When talk about the neighbors extends into entertainment, it clarifies individuals into types to make them useful to thinking. Amid P's little flurry of ridicule, Oliver is no longer a man but the type of the bad singer. In Farmer's song, he becomes all old men who spend lavishly, vainly to gain the affection of young women. During conversation, Charlie Farmer came to exemplify the star.

Like Hugh McGiveney, Farmer was poor. Poets are poor because they are local farmers. Michael Boyle said of McGiveney, "He would have been a great man if he had of got the chances that there is now." Peter Flanagan said of Charlie Farmer, "But he was a person like every other country person that didn't get a chance." Poets are also poor because they are too brilliant to attend closely to their work. Master Maguire, credited with both "Mackan Fight" and "Swad Chapel," overslept and was fired. Hugh McGiveney, au-thor of the song on the Ford and both songs on the band, would leave his work, said James Boyle, and run to the house when inspiration struck. Of Farmer, P said, "He'd get an idea and sit down behind a bush and write out his songs, forgettin about his work altogether."

Stars are so brilliant they burn out, leaving no one behind them. That is what Hugh Nolan and James Boyle said of Hugh McGiveney, and what

Mr. Nolan said of the race of Master Maguire. Michael Boyle was telling me about James Quigley, who like George Armstrong had emigrated to Australia but returned to become one of the great local composers of pants; he told Hugh Nolan the tale of the man who sold his soul to the Devil. I asked Mr. Boyle if Quigley had a family:

"No, he had no family. Och, he married late on in life, and then he had no family.

"He lived a long time after he was married and was very comfortable and very happy. He was.

"But he had no family.

"No, Quigley had no family. That man McGiveney, he married late on in life too, do ye see, and he had no family. A gooddeal of them stars had no family.

"John Brodison had a family, and when they got up, they went away, some of them to the States, and more of them to England, and well, they were no good atall. There was no yarn in them like the old fellow. They wouldn't hear of that; they wouldn't be bothered listenin to their father tell yarns.

"Hugh McGiveney's father, now he was witty. He was very, very witty. And old Hughie was a star too, do ye see.

"But Brodison's family never took a bit of interest in it. They never took a bit of interest in it.

"No."

To complete the star's portrait, then, I have a logical question for P: "Did Charlie Farmer have a family?" He answers:

"He was a lone man. He had a sister. She went to America when he was young. And he remained on. And I think he got into poor circumstances. He had a small wee farm. She came back, and she redeemed the place for him.

"He was an easy-goin person that never had any ambition, you know, for workin or risin to great heights or anything like that, you know.

"He still held on.

"And of course age got in on him.

"And he had a big red cow. And he was bringin her, you know, what they call, to the bull.

"And she was a pet cow. And the poor fellow was walkin that way, just in front of her with the halter, and the cow was comin behind, and what did she do, only rise up behind him and put him down. And that was that. They had to get the doctor.

"He never riz.

"He was brought home then, and he lay in bed and he went to hospital, and that was the end of poor Charlie.

"That's what happened poor Charlie.

"And there was far worse poets in this country that has been recognized very much and got great publicity and all. He never—he had no ambition. At that time of course there was no wireless and no television. In fact there was no—music and song in these later years, it has been revived up terribly in this country. If Charlie Farmer had been alive now he'd have featured amongst the greatest of our Irish poets. That's namely, Thomas Moore and James Clarence Mangan, and all of them; you've heard tell of them all. Ethna Carbery. Charles Kickham that sings, I live beside the Anner. Well, Charlie Farmer was as good as any of them. Oh, he went very deep into—very deep-meanin songs.

"He composed, in fact—ah, I didn't hear the half of them. I believe he had a stack of songs and then the people that got his wee place at his death, they didn't know the treasure, nor the value; they burned stacks and stacks and stacks of his good poetry.

"Well, he has died now without any recognition."

Poor, unrecognized, but brilliant—that is the lot of local stars. They are not ambitious workers or successful parents.[1] They serve their communities by providing consolation, the witty bid, the hilarious pant, the fine poem that carries their fellows on.

The star stands at the center. Any consideration of a work of art, a story or song, in Ballymenone leads you to an exceptional individual. Individuals lead through conversation to the human type he or she exemplifies, and artistic personalities lead from genre to genre, from bid to pant, from story to song, from item to culture. The District's culture is not something apart from the particular individuals who are the force of its coherence, the reason for its existence.

Charlie Farmer draws us into the star's nature and urges us into the nature of song. From songs we are led into yet another of the District's histories. Charlie Farmer composed songs about local people and he composed patriotic songs.

Songs about local people fit the ceili. They depend, like chat, upon local knowledge, and so remain in the community spreading from hearth to hearth. When I asked Michael Boyle about "Oliver's Harvest Home," he said, "I heard tell of it. It took place in the Florencecourt area. But I don't have it. That'd be away out of my area." Florencecourt is four and a half miles from his home in Drumbargy. Days later we were talking about local poets, and Mr. Boyle said:

"I'll tell ye, there was another great poet. They called him Charlie Farmer. He was from Kinawley, up that country. P could tell ye more about him.

"He made a bit of a rhyme one time on a policeman that was stationed in the ould barracks at Mackan. He was the name of Reilly, and he was a great man for runnin after the ladies. But he summonsed this Charlie Farmer for somethin, ah, some wee simple event, you know, and Charlie Farmer made a bit of a poem about him:

> There's ten thousand girls in Ireland,
> To put the question mildly,
> But if there was ten thousand more,
> There's not enough for Reilly ◊.

"A bit of a rhyme, do ye see.

"I only seen him occasionally. He was a small-size man, a small-size man. Oh, I seen *Charlie*. But I never heard him sing like, or I never heard much of his poetry, only wee bits here and there, but he made alot of songs, do ye see. Oh aye, he did. P might know more of them because he lived convenient to him, do ye see, and he might be fit to have some of them."

Local songs, like most stories, grow out of talk about the neighbors, but usually they take the negative turn, balancing the celebratory force of exploits, bids, and pants, absorbing and releasing the wish to ridicule. Charlie Farmer's local songs were satirical, as was the District's most famous local song, "Maxwell's Ball." Not all were satirical, but since most were, another of the District's local songs, though not intended maliciously, brought bad feelings and did not gain the singing it deserved. Michael Boyle tells us:

"Well, there was another song composed in our District. I mightn't have it right, but I think I have a gooddeal of it right.

"It was made on a pair of lovers in our country.

"Aye, the boy's name was McHugh, and the girl's name was Barclay. And they were natives of the country. And they were goin together—they were married afterwards, but they were married in the States; they didn't get married in Ireland.

"So I think he was killed in the First World War with the American army, as far as I heard.

"But however, I'll make an offer to tell you all I know of it anyway.

"Well, the start of it is—

"Well, our whole district of the country was called Ballymenone. Well, this lady was called the Star of Ballymenone. She was a fine-lookin girl.

"But anyway:

> As I rambled out one evenin,
>   it being in the summertime,
> To view the pleasant Arney brooks
>   that do like silver shine,
> As I walked along the Arney Road,
>   I thought the country grand,
> With long brick hacks and big turf stacks,
>   all through The Holy Land.

Tonyloman looked so gay
  with its hills of shamrock green,
And many breeds of wild fowl
  fly up from Inishkeen.
The wild goose and the mighty swan
  and other birds are known;
It was a glorious sight to see their flight
  over the hills of Ballymenone.
As I followed on the wild birds' flight
  right to Lough Erne's shore,
And to the strand of an island,
  they call it Inishmore,
While walking down long Polly's Brae,
  a young couple there did roam,
And the fair one's name was Maggie,
  the Star of Ballymenone.
They both were of an equal stamp;
  she held tight by the hand.
No wonder why his darting eye
  might well entice
    the Star of Ballymenone.
This couple fair, they did compare
  about a song to sing:
I will my Jim, she did begin,
  with heart so keen,
    the Maids That Wore the Green.
And she says, My Jim, I must go home.
He gave consent and home he went
  with the Star of Ballymenone.
To all entrusted true lovers,
  this couple I'll recommend.
My advice to you, young Jim McHugh,
  is never for to roam,
But for your bride, take by your side,
  she's the Star of Ballymenone.

"That's the song.

"Well the composer was unknown. It never was known right who made it. Because I think it caused a kind of a wee bit of bad humor like. I think it did, as far as I heard. So the composer was kind of unknown; it never was known who made it anyway.

"There's not too much about it, but as far as I used to hear like—I didn't know the people atall. I know friends of theirs all right. I know friends of theirs to the present day, but I didn't know them. Well, they were gone away to the States before my time.

"But it's a lovely thing. I think that's it all. I might've dropped out wee bits in it, here and there, but that's the song, that's The Star of Ballymenone."

Hugh McGiveney was Ballymenone's poet, standing as Charlie Farmer and Master Maguire did at different times in the Kinawley district. "The Star of Ballymenone" sounds like his work, and it illustrates the pattern of local song. Made on traditional models, such songs can escape their communities, but they make most sense where they are set, where people know the meaning of The Holy Land and that Polly's Brae is a rise on the Back Road named for an old woman, where people feel that long brick hacks and big turf stacks are as much a part of the land's loveliness as wildfowl and silvery waters, where people know the people in the song. The local song opens through the ceilier's mind just as references to the neighbors in chat do.

Local songs fit ceilis because of their subjects and their tone. Satirical songs extend chat's humorous, ridiculing impulse. Other "sentimental songs" make art out of the ceili's affectionate mood, speaking aloud the love of person to person and person to land. "The Star of Ballymenone" is both a song about young lovers and a hymn to place. Ceiliers gather out of the neighborhood and around the hearth because they like one another, and when moved to song, their songs often express affection for mother and Ireland and tell of the love between man and woman. "Love songs," sentimental songs at their highest pitch, do not fit comfortably in the loud, rowdy scene of the pub, but they rise naturally, like melancholy "slow airs" on the violin, late in ceilis. Ceilis are like courtship, they are about love, and love songs perfect the emotion the ceiliers feel. Two songs of Peter Flanagan's often appear late on good nights. One is the popular "If I Was a Blackbird," which he learned from a recording by Delia Murphy; the other he calls simply "Love Song." He believes correctly that it is a very old song; he learned it from an old man, long dead, named Tommy Williamson from Tempo:

Here is a health unto all true lovers,
A health to my love where e'er he be.
This very night I'll be with my darling
For many's a long mile he is from me.

It was when he came to his true love's window,
He kneelèd low down upon a stone,
And through the pane he whispered slowly,
Are you asleep, love, are you alone?

She raised her head from her snow-white pillow,
And snowy, snowy was her milk-white breast,
Saying, who is that at my bedroom window,
Disturbing me from my long night's rest?

I am your lover, do not discover,
But rise up darling and let me in,
For I am tired of my long night's journey,
And likewise, love, I'm wet to the skin.

It was slowly, slowly she did put on her,
And twice as slowly she let me in.
It twas in our arms we embraced each other
Until that long night, love, was nearly in.

When that long night, it was nearly ended,
And the early cocks, they began to crow,
We kissed, shook hands, and alas we parted,
Sayin, Goodbye, darling, I must be goin.

Farewell, love, I can stay no longer.
The burning rocks I have to cross.
And it's o'er the hills I will roll in splendor,
From the arms of you, my love.

His singing is soft and sweet. A gentleness settles over the men drawn close to the fire. Soon, after a last tea, a token from Joe, they will part through the mists of graying night, reaching home while the sky pearls before dawn.

The pub's crowd is dispersed in smoke and rackety broken chat. When it shifts toward unity, its topic is politics. Patriotic songs fit the public house. Charlie Farmer is widely known not for his local songs sung in ceilis but for his "political" or "patriotic" songs. They are as dependent for vitality upon knowledge beyond their texts as local songs, but it is a knowledge all have, if unequally, knowledge about Ireland, not some small spot within Ireland. The public Ireland is made of its history of war. Each of Charlie Farmer's well-known songs is an example of one of the major kinds of bellicose song: songs to rally, songs to commemorate.

"Kinawley" is the great rallying song of south Fermanagh. You will remember that the heart of "The Swad Chapel Song" beat in its description of the gathering of men from Cavan, Leitrim, and Fermanagh, reenacted by its gathering of singers in the Border town of Swanlinbar, three and a half miles southwest of Kinawley. There are "Protestant" as well as "Catholic" songs to rally men. Peter Flanagan remembers one from the era of the third Home Rule bill which a Protestant neighbor of his in Kinawley, Johnny Crawford, used to sing to him as a good-natured taunt:

Rise, rise up you Ulster sons,
Raise your flag and shoulder your guns,
Once more I hear the enemy comes
With a Home Rule bill in the mornin.

Seven years has passed and gone,
And sixty more since the sun has shone,
Since our Loyal fathers freedom won
On the banks of the Boyne one morning.

Let John Dillon he beware,
Joe Devlin and Redmond take the chair,
For they'll not catch us in a Home Rule snare,
For we'll march to the Boyne in the morning.

Rallying songs harken back, they commemorate. "Swad Chapel" remembers Saint Patrick and Mackan. "Kinawley" remembers Saint Naile and the Norman Conquest. "The Home Rule Bill" remembers William's victory at the Boyne. And then rallying songs become commemorative. Johnny Crawford sang his song to Peter Flanagan long after the issue was settled, and Northern Ireland was erected, when he and P were good neighbors and P could tease him back by singing "Kevin Barry." The young men in the pub who request "Kinawley" from Peter Flanagan were not born when Kinawley's big Sinn Fein rally took place.

Whether composed at the time of the event, like "Kevin Barry," or years later, like Charlie Farmer's "Men of Ninety-Eight," written around 1924, most political songs are commemorative. Their power is not antiquarian or narrative. The goal is to bring the past into the present, making commemorative songs into rallying songs. "The Rising of the Moon" is the District's other major song on the Rising of 1798. Here is Joe Flanagan's version:

Tell me, tell me Sean O'Farrell, tell me why you hurry so.
Hush, nabostle, hush and listen, for your cheeks are all aglow.
I bear orders from the captain, get you ready quick and soon,
For your pikes must be together at the rising of the moon.
At the rising of the moon, at the rising of the moon.
For your pikes must be together at the rising of the moon.

Oh, then tell me Sean O'Farrell where the gatherin is to be.
In that old spot by the river right well known to you and me.
One word more: for signal-token whistle up the marching tune,
With your pike upon your shoulder at the rising of the moon.
At the rising of the moon, at the rising of the moon.
With your pike upon your shoulder at the rising of the moon.

Out from many a mud-wall cabin eyes were watchin through that night,
Many a manly heart was throbbing for the blessed morning light.
Murmurs passed along the valleys like the banshee's lonely croon,
And a thousand blades were flashing at the rising of the moon.
At the rising of the moon, at the rising of the moon,
And a thousand blades were flashing at the rising of the moon.

There by the singin river that dark mass of men was seen.
High above their shining weapons hung their own beloved green.
Death to every foe and traitor, forward strike the marching tune.
And hurray my boys for freedom, it's the rising of the moon.
At the rising of the moon, at the rising of the moon,
Hurray my boys for freedom, at the rising of the moon.

Well, they fought for poor old Ireland and full bitter was their fate.
Their glorious pride and sorrow fills the name of Ninety-Eight.
Yet thank God and still are beating hearts in manhood's burning noon,
Who will follow in their footsteps at the rising of the moon.
At the rising of the moon, at the rising of the moon,
Who will follow in their footsteps at the rising of the moon.

No story is told, a known story is evoked, and the song's point lies in its last stanza, in which modern men are charged with the continuation of the old fight. South Fermanagh's commemorative songs cluster around certain periods of conflict: the Williamite War ("The Sash," "The Battle of Limerick"), the Ninety-Eight Rising ("Boolavogue," "The Rising of the Moon," "The Men of Ninety-Eight"), the Fenian Rising ("T. F. Bourke," "The Manchester Martyrs," "God Save Ireland," "Erin's Lovely Lee"), the Sixteen Rising and its aftermath ("The Men of Easter Week," "The Day Was Gone, the Battle Ended," "James Connolly," "Kevin Barry," "The True Love," "The Upton Ambush"), the recent Troubles ("James Crossan," "Sean South"). None tell the whole story, all require a context of historical knowledge in the listener's mind. Some approach true ballads, but descriptive narrative songs are rare in any scene (their place is taken by stories), and they arrive most easily amid the ceili's quiet. "The Wild Colonial Boy" and "The Boston Burglar," called "the two brothers" because of their similar tunes and tales, are the most obvious ballads, but both are too well known to bother singing. I never heard either of them, but during gentle ceilis Peter Flanagan did sing "Bold Jack Donohue" and "Aherlow":

Ah, my name is Patrick Sheehan, and my years are thirty-four.
Tipperary is my native place, not far from Galtymore.
I came of honest parents, but now they're lying low.
And many a pleasant day I spent in the Glens of Aherlow.

Bereft of home and kith and kin and plenty all around,
I starved within my cabin, and I slept upon the ground.
Aye, and cruel as my lot was, I ne'er did hardship know,
Till I joined the English army far away from Aherlow.

Rise up there, says the corporal, you lazy Irish hound,
Why don't you see, you sleepy dog, the call of arms sound.

Alas, I had been dreaming of days long, long ago.
Till I awoke before Sebastapool and not in Aherlow.

I groped to find my musket, how dark I thought the night.
O blessed God, it was not dark, it was the broad daylight.
And when I found that I was blind and me tears began to flow,
And I longed for even a pauper's grave in the Glens of Aherlow.

O blessed Virgin Mary, I might end the mournful tale.
A poor blind prisoner here I am in Dublin's dreary jail.
Struck blind within the trenches, where I never feared the foe,
And never will I see again my home, sweet Aherlow.

The good ballad particularizes wide experience—here the poor man made a common soldier and ruined—so ballads spread easily from culture to culture, and P's song, composed by the Fenian poet and novelist Charles Kickham, is sung in North America and Australia. But to Peter Flanagan the meaning of "Aherlow" is peculiarly Irish. He knows that it and "The Heights of Alma" deal with the Crimean War, but the song reminds him of the Boer War, when, P said, though the Boers "was really just farmers tryin to make a livin," Irish men were seduced to enlist and die with the rumor that the Boers were boars, wildmen, and savages, and if they won in Africa, Ireland would be next in their march. It is the very same today, he said. Politicians tell Catholics lies about Protestants, Protestants lies about Catholics, "to keep the people split apart and fightin."

Like "Bold Jack Donohue," "Aherlow" is a political song, but its message is subtle. The pub's noisy, fractured situation requires political clarity. Its songs vary widely in degree of narration, but they always draw the past into the present to drive the old cause into the future. Charlie Farmer's "Men of Ninety-Eight" contains a minimum of tale. At the other end of the commemorative song's spectrum of narration lies "Ballinamore," its title, a place name like "Kinawley" and "Aherlow," reminding us again of the way history is a feature of geography. Martin Crudden's mother knew the men killed near Ballinamore in Leitrim, south of Swanlinbar. Peter Flanagan says, then sings:

"They were six boys that were shot up here in the Nineteen and Sixteen Rising.

"And they were betrayed and they were shot up here in County Leitrim. And here's the way the song goes:"

Young men of this brave Irish nation,
Who has followed the tricolor fold,
Come and join in sincere lamentation
For the loss of the brave and the bold.
It's all of a sorrowful story,

It's equal to bloodshed and tears,
While is wrapped in the emblem of glory,
The names of our brave volunteers.

It twas of an evening in springtime,
When all nature in charm did enfold,
Those heroes came down from the mountain,
Their numbers bein thirteen we're told.
Bein out for a day's recreation,
Of dangers they were not afraid,
And for their dear love of their country,
They were followed and beastly betrayed.

Here's to Byrne, Baxter, the O'Reillys,
Seamus Wrynne and young Sean Connolly,
Who gave up their lifeblood and homesteads,
Who died that their land might be free.

They came in their fast-traveling lorries,
With many a tall armored car,
With their maxim guns, lewis and rifles,
And other equipment of war.
They rushed to the hillsides for shelter,
But these guns poured their merciless rain,
They shot them like partridge in clover,
But six of our bravest were slain.

(Chorus of third stanza)

Six hearts that was true to old Ireland,
Lying cold on the bleak mountain side.
Borne high on the shoulders of comrades,
Whose grief now those boys could not hide.
And it's loved, respected, and honored,
Forgotten they never shall be.
While the night star shines over Glassdrummin,
And the Shannon rolls on to the sea.

(Chorus)

There's a parish in Aughanasheelin,
There's a cemetery on the hillside.
And there in a Republican corner,
Those heroes are laid side-by-side.
If you pass on a fine summer's evening,
The children is kneeling in prayer.
And if you ask them the reason,
They'll tell you that the dust of their loved ones lies there.

Here's to Byrne, Baxter, the O'Reillys,
Seamus Wrynne and young Sean Connolly.
That their souls may be shining in glory,
For now and for eternity.

The song forms around live memory, not dead event. And it is the same in the most popular Protestant song, "The Sash," which does not describe King William's victories but merely lists them in the chorus sung when men march to remember the Boyne. The facts of past battles matter far less that their effect on living men, the emotions that stir within on the Twelfth when silken banners fly and hollow drums rattle. "The Sash" recalls their pleasure and pride; it commemorates their commemoration more than it commemorates old war. Ellen Cutler often sings the chorus and plays the happy swinging air on her harmonica. She gave me a handwritten text; with her sung chorus inserted as the second verse, it reads:

The Sash My Father Wore

Here am I a loyal Orange man, just come across the sea.
For singing and for dancing, I hope that I'll please thee.
I can sing and dance with any man, as I did in days of yore,
And on the Twelfth, I love to wear the sash my father wore.

It was ould but it was beautiful and the colours they were fine.
Twas worn at Derry, Aughrim, Enniskillen, and the Boyne.
Sure my father wore it as a boy in the bygone days of yore,
And it's on the Twelfth I love to wear the Sash me father wore.

It's now I'm goin to leave you, good luck to you I say.
And when I'm on the ocean for me I hope you'll pray.
I'm going to my native land, to a place they call Dromore,
Where on the Twelfth I always wear the sash my father wore.

(Chorus of second stanza)

When ever I come back again, my brethren here to see,
I hope in fine old Orange style, they'll always welcome me.
My favourite line, Boyne Water, will please me more and more,
And make my Orange heart feel glad with the sash my father wore.

Commemorative political songs occupy the center in the public house. Two other kinds of song are sung on big nights out. Each orients toward the political midpoint. The sentimental spirit that peaks in the ceili's love songs forms in the pub within "songs of exile." Their idea is love for Ireland expressed from the emigrant's comparative vantage point. The penultimate stanza in Peter Flanagan's "Glen Swilly" captures the mood:

God bless you dark old Donegal, my own dear fatherland.
In dreams I oftimes see your fields and towering mountains grand.
Alas, three thousand miles does lie between yourself and me.
Ah, a poor forlorn exile cast away from Glen Swilly.

But "sorrowful" songs of exile do not usually stop at lament; they raise the political issue. Peter Flanagan:

Farewell my old acquaintance, my friends both one and all,
My lot is in America, to either rise or fall.
From my cabin I'm evicted and likewise compelled to go
From that lovely land called Erin where the green shamrocks grow.

Hurray my boys the sails is spread and the wind is blowing fair.
Full steam for Castle Garden, in a few days we'll be there.
For to seek for bread and labor as we are compelled to go
From that lovely land called Erin where the green shamrocks grow.

I owe the landlord two years' rent and I wished I owed him more.
One day a cowardly bailiff stuck a notice on my door.
My old and wearied mother, it grieved her heart full sore,
For to leave the house my father built, twas sixty years or more.

(Chorus of second stanza)

Farewell my old acquaintance, with whom I used to sport,
Where we'd sing and dance on a Sunday night where the girls used to resort.
For there's one I leave behind me, and she grieves my heart full sore,
For to leave her in old Ireland. Will I ever see her more?

Hurray my boys the sails are spread and the wind's yet blowing fair,
Full steam for Castle Garden, in a few days we'll be there.
For to seek for bread and labor as we are compelled to go
From that lovely land called Erin where the green shamrocks grow.

"Castle Garden" diminishes love song into a passing reference to the girl left behind, it undercuts any joy implied by the chorus with a slow, sad melody, and it sets the song in the Days of the Landlords to deepen its meaning. The most widely known song of exile, which has been translated into Irish, "Skibbereen," joins the Days of the Landlords to the Famine, and to the Young Ireland Rising of 1848 and a Fenian future, thus connecting emigration forcefully to political action among those who remain. Here is its singing by John O'Prey, the Flanagans' neighbor, the one song he sings:

Oh, it's father dear, I often hear you speak of Erin's isle,
Her lofty green, her valley scenes of mountains wide and high.

They say it is a lovely place wherein a prince might dwell.
Oh, why did you abandon it? The reason to me tell.

Oh, my son, I love my country with energy and pride.
Till a blight came over our crops, and our sheep and cattle died.
The rents and taxes were so high that them we could not redeem,
And them's the cruel reasons why we left old Skibbereen.

It's well I do remember that bleak December day.
When the landlord and the sheriff came to drive us all away.
They sent our roof on fire with their damning yellow spleen,
And when it fell the crash was heard all over Skibbereen.

When you were a boy of two years old and feeble was your frame,
We could not leave you with your friends, you bore your father's name.
We wrapped you up in our old frieze coat by the dead of a night unseen,
And we bid a sigh and said good-bye to dear old Skibbereen.

So it's well I do remember the year of forty-eight,
When we'd arise with Erin's boys to battle for the Fenian.
We were hunted as outlaws and traitors to the Queen,
And them's the best of reasons why we left old Skibbereen.

So it's father dear the day is near when vengeance loud will call,
When we will rise with Erin's boys, to rally one and all.
I'll be the man to lead the van beneath the flag of green.
Ah, it's right loud and high we'll raise the cry: Revenge for Skibbereen.

The issues of exile and war, the public content of sentimental and pa-triotic songs, connect in the pub to keep the idea of rebellion fresh in the minds of drinking men. The idea in "Skibbereen" was strung through the performance of separate songs to build the mood on the night of "The Swad Chapel Song." Owney McBrien sang of an emigrant spurning the New World's wealth for Lough Erne's beauty. Next P Flanagan sang of a Fenian general exiled and imprisoned, dreaming of victory. Then com-memorative songs of Irish martyrs by Owney McBrien, Hugh Collins, and Eddie Kelly led to Mr. McBrien's rallying song, "The Standard of Sinn Fein." The way was cleared for the excited hosting of singers and the shades of old warriors, the unsullied triumph at Swanlinbar.

Patriotic songs bring together men who remember when men in the past came together and worked for the common good, defending the homeland which many have been forced to leave, forlorn exiles. Like the ceili's battle tales, patriotic songs bring into focus the cooperative dimen-sion of daily existence, the virtues of neighborliness. Humor in the ceili cir-cles the dark side of neighborliness, searching for failings to ridicule in sa-tirical song. In the pub, the "comical song" is only "jollification." But funny songs are not void of bite. Like songs of exile, "comicals" belong to the class called "sentimental," and they too can point to the political center, and through it to sadness and anger. "Nancy Morgan," one of Peter Flanagan's comicals, is a silly enough stage-Irish ditty, but it tells of emigration to "the north of Americay." After being "knocked about like snuff at a wake upon the great salt ocean" and losing his wife, the protagonist submits to native custom and goes off to the wood to cut sticks, where he is caught and "well-hugged by a big Brazilian monkey." Scratched and torn, he wrenches free, only to meet a snake from which he escapes by climbing a tree where he sits through the night "like a Pilgrim on a monument," resolving to return:

> I said I would not be payin rent for their accommodation,
> So homeward, sure, I started, for I'd learned navigation.
> So take my advice and you'll have luck, and never go abroad, sir,
> For it's better to fight with a devil at home than a devil you do not know, sir.

A gentleman out walking for health in "The Turfman from Ardee," another of Mr. Flanagan's comicals, "meets a jolly sporting lad" with a "fagged and worn" ancient ass, and during their great conversation, the turfman gives him his feelings:

> Ah, you may talk about your countrymen, and how they are oppressed.
> They say they are goin to Parliament to get their wrongs redressed.
> We are led by human politics, aye, as you may plainly see.
> Aye, and we are led by human humbug, says the Turfman from Ardee.

And here is Peter Flanagan's "Pat Molloy":

> Pat Molloy, an Irish boy, he came from County Clare.
> He thought he'd go to London to see the wonders there.
> And Pat bid all his friends good-bye and he kissed his colleen dear.
> He left the sod, he did begob, and he never shed a tear.
>
> When Pat went to this country, it filled him with surprise.
> The looks of this big city fairly dazzled Paddy's eyes.
> Pat was goin on quite early, meditating to himself,
> When he met with a ragged cockaney with a donkey selling delph.
>
> This ill-bred ragged cockaney could not let Paddy pass,
> Sayin, Why don't you speak to your brother, pointing over to the ass.
> Ah, begob, says Pat, I didn't think I had a brother here,
> But I will go over and whisper into the donkey's ear.
>
> In whispering to the donkey, what do you think did Paddy do?
> He dropped in a chew of tobacco, he did, begob, it's true.
> The animal he went mad, crack-crazy, straight and square.
> Upset the little cart and broke all the earthenware.

This ill-bred ragged cockaney ran to get poor Pat in charge,
Sayin, You little Irish vagabond, you should not be at large.
Get off with you, says Paddy, looking at him with a smile.
Do you think you'll make an ass of me when I come from Erin's isle.

It was up before the magistrate poor Pat had to go next day,
And for to prove his innocence, he didn't know what to say.
Come here now, says the magistrate, we want no nonsense here.
And tell us every word you whispered into the donkey's ear.

I told the ass, says Paddy, he had got the wrong address.
Noble Old Ireland was no longer in distress.
We got rid of all the landlords and the country to ourselves we had,
And when this animal heard the news, bejeepers, he went mad.

The magistrate sat laughing and they all hung down their heads.
They could not keep from laughing, when they heard what Paddy said.
Well done, well done, said the magistrate, what a clever chap you are.
And for your clever answer, we'll dismiss you from the bar.

Ireland's "greatest victory" is registered in comical song. Laughing or angry, the crowd in the pub gathers around political memory into responsibility for the continuation of their nation's history. They lift their drinks and toast, "Up our side," and their songs are toasts, gestures made by drinking men through the past to each other, through each other to the past. The chorus of "Ballinamore"—"Here's to Byrne, Baxter . . ."—the last stanza of "The Swad Chapel Song," and the last stanza of Peter Flanagan's "Battle of Limerick," recounting Patrick Sarsfield's victory in 1690, when the enemy cannon were taken, planted, and exploded, form overtly as toasts:

"This is a song of Patrick Sarsfield. He stopped King William at a place called Ballyneety, outside Dublin. He was meetin King William at the Battle of the Boyne. And it goes as follows:"

The night fell dark on Limerick town, and all the land was still,
As for the foe in ambush, we laid beside the hill.
Long, impatiently we waited to rush upon our prey,
With gallant Sarsfield at our head, before the break of day.

From Dublin came the foeman with deadly warlike store,
Pontoons and carts of powder and thundering balls galore.
And little were they thinking that there was work to bale
When we came with our commander bold from dark Slieve Felim's vale.

Give the word, the word is Sarsfield, and Sarsfield is the man.
Here I am, our general cried, as down on them we ran.
Oh God, He cleared the firmament, the moon and stars gave light,
And for the Battle of the Boyne we took revenge that night.

When the convoy all was scattered, we took their mighty store,
Pontoons and carts of powder and cannons by the score,
And hastily with eager hands, we piled them up on high,
Lay down the fuse, applied the match, and blew them to the sky.

How pleasant laughed our general as fast he rode away,
And many's a health was drunk to him in Limerick town next day.
Here's another health to Sarsfield, who in that mighty hour
Destroyed the foe's artillery by Ballyneety's tower.

The mood in the pub rises, men move toward one another and ask for a song to bring them into unity. Most often P answers with a song he calls "O'Donnell Abu" because of the resemblance of its melody, "Scotland the Brave," to that of the old song of Red Hugh, and which he also calls "An Irishman's Toast":

Ireland's the land of the harp and the shamrock.
Now Ireland's the land of the true and the good.
Ireland's the land of the true Irish patriots
Who shed for their country, the last drop of blood.

Here's to the lake, to the vale and the green moss,
The harp and the shamrock, the green flag and cross.
And here's to the heroes old Ireland can boast,
May their names never die; it's an Irishman's toast.

Brave Dan O'Connell was a true Irish patriot.
For Ireland he fought hard, for justice and right.
No foes could alarm him, no brags could deceive him,
May his soul shine above where all is good and bright.

(Chorus of second stanza)

Green be the memory of the Manchester Martyrs,
The noble young Allen, poor Larkin and O'Brien.
Though the scaffold was their doom, sure, it was for Ireland's freedom.
May their souls shine above where all is good and bright.

(Chorus)

Long may it grow there, the dear little shamrock,
And green o'er the graves where our loved ones do lie,
Grow there to show unto friend and to foeman
How Irishmen can live and how Irishmen can die.

(Chorus)

Let Erin remember she has men to defend her,
With hearts just as true as the brave ones of yore,

Whose deeds we will cherish until memory do perish,
Let the toast go around for old Ireland once more.

Here's to the lake, to the vale and the green moss,
The harp and the shamrock, the green flag and cross,
Aye, and here's to the heroes old Ireland can boast,
May their names never die. It's an Irishman's toast.

The public political song is a commemorative toast. Up our side, it says. With great spirit, Ellen Cutler plays the tune on her mouth organ, then sings a toast for her side:

Drink me boys and don't be dry,
And drink your health to Willie,
For on the twelfth day of July
We'll hoist our Orange Lily.

Orange lily and green shamrock, opposite colors on the color wheel, cultivated and native plants, symbols of King William and Saint Patrick, of 1690 and 432: in public, conflict clarifies and the issue is the nation, the only issue that can join all who are present. Exiles and buffoons are Irish types, not real local people. Heroes are great, distant individuals—William and Sarsfield—not local men joined anonymously in their community's defense under the name of their place. The usual song of the pub, memorized intact and nationwide in distribution, does not directly body forth the little community's culture but refers to another dimension within each person: his or her existence as a citizen.

Firesides on the hillsides and bright pubs in the towns connect. The pub's repertory is narrow and focused on great national themes, but any song can be sung in a ceili. From the public house, the nation's songs are brought into the community, and through the pub the community's songs are sent back into the nation. If some local songs do not travel well, all songs are written by members of little communities, and some escape to spread across the globe. Charlie Farmer composed songs for his community and for all Ireland. Everyone is at once part of a nation and a community. The man who marches in file in uniform through the town's crowded streets today was a man in company at the hearth last night, a man at work in the bog yesterday, so all these histories are real to him: the clear, heroic national history of the public house and parade; the complex, paradoxical, local history of the ceili's stories of history; the evolutionary history of daily work, engraved in the land. In his mind, these different histories cross, connect, and war to make him form his own opinion and strike his own course as a free man, confined by conditions beyond him.

The community is compounded of different personalities. It has introspective poets who compose in private, and it has people who move boldly in public scenes to perform. In our District those different roles are filled by different people. The poet is quiet, reserved, withdrawn. The singer must be assertive, pushy, willing to make mistakes while others are watching. Art and life depend upon their cooperation. Peter Flanagan, singer, describes Charlie Farmer, poet:

"Well, poor Farmer, he was void of an air. The creature hadn't an air. He could make the song all right. And there was a fellow beside him, he was McCaffrey, John McCaffrey. He was only young of course. Farmer was maybe in his fifties. And he would put the airs to his songs.

"Well, I was very sorry when Charlie Farmer died, because I was gettin to like him at the time. Me and him was pretty great.

"So the poor fellow passed out of it. And this younger man that used to put the airs to his songs, he got married and him and the woman went away to Scotland, some part of Scotland. With the result I never could contact him. But anyway and everyway, not many years ago I met him, and he was a dead old man.

"He used to sing these songs of Farmer's in the country house dances, all little dances. They used to run an annual dance there in Kinawley for the upkeep of the parish school. He used to sing them whole songs, and that's the only way that I got in contact with them songs, Kinawley and the other few bits.

"Well, I was very pleased to meet Johnny McCaffrey, and I thought that he was the man that I knew thirty years before. But, I met him and shook hands with him and chatted on. I suppose you can sing, says I, some of Farmer's songs. No, I wouldn't mind, he says, one of them. He was old, he was, well seventy-five, and then he went away, and he died shortly after. All was lost.

"All was lost except the ones that I know. But he made, I suppose, a good deal of songs more than that."

Charlie Farmer had enough idea of his poem's melody that he could pass it to John McCaffrey, who improved it, then performed the song on public occasions. Peter Flanagan worked with John McCaffrey. His style of singing, high and nasal, was not pleasing to P, who prefers a more natural pitch and a fuller sound. The singers P most admired were Mickey Shannon, from whom he learned "Green-Robed Inisfail," Tommy Williamson, from whom he learned "Love Song," and Joe Neal. Neal was a soldier in the 1920 period, a laborer of no fixed address around Kinawley, and it was Neal, a noted public performer, who spread Charlie Farmer's songs. P's mention of Farmer brought Neal to Joe's mind, then P remembered Neal singing "Oliver's Harvest Home" with humor and swing. Farmer's "Men of Ninety-Eight" is widely known in south Fermanagh as "a Joe Neal song."

Others were drawn to Farmer's work. Eamon Anderson, son of Andrew, the schoolmaster who succeeded Master Maguire at Kinawley, a journalist and folklorist whose notes are preserved in the archives at Cultra and Belfield, wrote down the words of some of Farmer's songs.[2] Young P Flanagan was attracted to their airs and loved the feel of their words in his mouth. Only later, P says, did he discover their meanings out of his own memory, and now he keeps Charlie Farmer alive.

Poets are not public performers. Their creations would die if others did not take responsibility for them, as Martin Crudden did for "The Fermanagh Song" and as Peter Cassidy did for "Maxwell's Ball," composed by Mickey McCourt, Master Maguire, and Hugh McGiveney.

Stars must not try to make themselves look bright. A common proverb runs, "Self-praise is no recommendation," and Peter Flanagan expands on that idea: "Let a man be brilliant and show his intelligence, his neighbors will talk about him and try to bring him down." Vanity is ridiculed; the trait poets select for satire is the pride that prevents people from seeing and living their own limitations: the dandy at Maxwell's Ball who thought he had Nora won, the old policeman who thinks he is a ladies' man, the old man who thinks girls will like him if he throws them a party, the old man who thinks he can compete with the lads in a donkey race, the shopkeeper who thinks he is another Napoleon.

The satirist knows the stupidity of pride. To avoid seeming bright, the star does not push his own compositions. He offers them quietly. They attract others who take them over, performing them energetically, advocating them without reserve because they are not their own.

The star is childless, so he forms a special bond with a younger man, as Charlie Farmer did with John McCaffrey, who performs the poet's compositions in his lifetime, then carries them on after his death. Hugh McGiveney's singer was the great musician Terry Maguire, as Michael Boyle recalled when I asked him about McGiveney's poems:

"He just made them, you know, for a bit of sport for himself.

"He was that kind of man, do ye see: think of a story and make it, you know. Oh, he could make them very quick.

"Oh, he was a great character, this Hughie McGiveney.

"His songs used to be sung at wee sprees.

"Well, Terry Maguire, that fluter, he picked the weight of them up. He used to sing them like afterwards. When McGiveney was dead, he used to sing them at sprees, you know.

"They were very interested, the people. They were very amusin; they made a laugh, do ye see, a great laugh for people."

I ask, "So you heard them from both Hugh McGiveney and Terry Maguire?" He answers:

"Yes, I heard both of them, do ye see. I heard both singin them.

"It was great that someone could do a thing like that in the country."

Hugh McGiveney and Terry Maguire are gone. Michael Boyle saved their songs. Now he is gone. Hugh Nolan is the last to remember McGiveney's art:

"Hugh McGiveney he made that song about the Ford of Biscuits:

I see the plumes of Duke's Dragoons
Before Belturbet town.

"Ah now, he made up another few songs, but I'll tell ye: he never wrote them down, and then when he died, the songs were lost, you know. Aye, they were lost.
"Ah, he was a great artist."

Hugh Nolan was a poet. Paddy McBrien, who said his poems were fine, remembers Hugh in an instant of inspiration ripping open a brown paper bag and writing a poem on it. Peter Flanagan remembers that Hugh wrote a song satirizing a Major Lee of the B Specials who was bedeviled by the local lads, but all P retains of it is a shred of the chorus: "Isn't it a caution to see how they torture Major Lee." I heard that he had composed poems on the old Rossdoney School and on the brick-making industry, but when I asked Mr. Nolan if he wrote poetry, he replied:

"Och I did. But they never was up to much, do ye know.
"They were only ramases just.
"Oh aye, there was a time I could make up rhymes.
"They were just about happenins about. I never kept any of them in writing. And I didn't rehearse them.
"Och, they were just a kind of ramas. They amused young people, do ye see. You'll not be able for to gather them up.
"They're all gone."

None of the young people amused by Mr. Nolan's verse took responsibility for it. No one became his singer. His poems are gone. Since preservation is not the poet's task, he gains from the retention or loss of his works a sense of his own ability. More than modesty causes Mr. Nolan to dismiss his own poetry as unimportant.

Hugh Nolan is not a poet. He is a historian. His job is preserving the facts of history and the arts of others, the bids and pants of Hugh McGiveney, John Brodison, George Armstrong, Master Maguire, James Quigley, James Maguire, Francis Keenan, Charlie Flynn, John McGrath—and John O'Prey. When I asked Mr. O'Prey if he remembered any of the pants he composed, he said, no, he couldn't mind them at all. It was his job to create them, but not to save them. Someone else had to do the work of remembering, and that was Hugh Nolan.

John O'Prey, his wife, their daughter, Mary, her husband, Gabriel Coyle, and their son, have a bright, warm home in Drumbargy. John, sometimes called Sean, hails from Swanlinbar and has worked for years on the Fermanagh roads while managing their farm, which Mrs. O'Prey inherited from an aunt. Mary is a nurse. Gabriel comes from Lurgan and has a job in a factory near Enniskillen. Mr. O'Prey and Mr. Coyle both sing at home, but not in public. They generate their own electricity, and their home is in a constant state of improvement, expansion, and modernization. They live next door to the Flanagans, and P often helps with work on their farm. Both P and Joe remember that Mr. O'Prey was once a great wit who invented hilarious stories detailing violent adventures that never happened. Joe called them "blunders." P called them "rigamaroles" and "phrases" and "pants." Michael Boyle, Hugh Nolan said, once said of John and his brother that "they were fine fellows that there was no harm in. And what they put their time in at was: tellin some thing that they done that they never done, and tellin about some place that they were in that they were never in." People know John, a hard worker and admirer of the old Irish music, a strong quiet man, and they remember his stories, but only Hugh Nolan has them. He told me five, and a sixth which I guessed was his but turned out to be by his brother. Twice he linked these two into a single performance. They are Mr. O'Prey's signal pair:

"There was one time,
    he said,
        there was something came over him.
"Aw, he had never been in the North at the time; he was doin at home.
"And he was in dread of alot of people
        around him.
"And he was ◊ thinkin that if he could manage for to get a gun,
    and shoot these people that he was dreadin,
    that he'd be all right *after*.
"So he fixed up a place along the roadside
    that he'd leave the gun on
    that he'd have nothin to do
        only pull the trigger ◊
        when he'd find anyone comin ◊.
"And he was just goin to shoot
    all that he would face.
"But *anyway*, he had this prepared, and all he wanted was to get a permit from the Guards,
    for to get a gun.
"But *anyway*, the Guards had heared;
    they had got a whiff of what this lad was about.
"When he went there, they'd give him no permit,
    wouldn't let him get a gun.
"So he *lost*,
    he lost all control over himself, he said,

he was that angry at the way that he was handled.

"And now:

"He started kickin and beatin everyone that he met
            along the road.

"So that went on,
        no matter where he was,
            church or town,
            it made no odds,
                he started into the people.

"Well, he got plenty of abuse himself, but he'd start in the next place that he went.

"So anyway, he was gettin worse at it.

"He often would be standin in a crowd and maybe a man would take out the pipe and tobaccy, and he'd start to cut the tobaccy and fill the pipe, and he'd run up to him, and he'd draw the foot, he'd ◊ give him a kick and he'd put the tobaccy in all directions.

"But anyway, the people all in general got tired of him.

"And they all turned out
            and tackled him.

"So.

"There used to gather crowds in the evenins,
        and one party used to stand on the road,
        and there was another party went into a field,
        and the party in the road used to get ahold of *him*,
        and they used to kick him across to the party in the *field*,
        and the party in the field kicked him back again.

"So that went for—ah, it went on for about six weeks, or two months.

"So.

"The hay came in,
        and a lot of work,
        and the people quit comin,
        and ◊ he was lyin there in the field
        and nobody botherin about him.

"But then in the long run he took a notion to get up and go home.

"So he went home anyway, and he thought that, if he got a bath, it'd help.

"He took off all his clothes, he said, and when he took them off, he looked like that he was a darky.

"He was *all* black,
        all black from head to foot.

"So, he went to bed and ◊ he stuck in bed for eighteen months.

"He never got up.

"So when he got up,
        he came here to the North,
            and he never fought anymore ◊."

We have a good laugh together at the hearth. It was not the first time I heard that story, nor would it be the last, but it captures perfectly something about life in the country and always brings laughter in its wake. As we quiet down, I ask, "Did he make it all up?" Mr. Nolan's answer is swift, extraordinarily emphatic, "He *did make it all up.*" I could see Mr. O'Prey composing his story to answer redundant questions about why he moved to Northern Ireland, and ask, "To explain why he came to the North?" With a broad smile Mr. Nolan shoves past his answer into a second story:

"Aye, indeed. Aye, indeed. Oh aye.

"But the scene that the old man had that he was workin with to get him into the *car* the first time!

"This man, aw he was a well-to-do man, only he was badly gone on drink.

"And he used to take bouts of drinkin, and he used to let things go to loss.

"He went out to work anyway, but he had never been in a car before.

"He had seen cars in the distance, and he was terribly afraid of them.

"But he never was in one.

"But anyway, this man was goin someplace and he told him that he'd have to go with him.

"So he objected.

"So anyway, the man got aholt of him, and he opened the door of the car, and put him in, and closed the door, and they started off.

"And they didn't go very far,
            till the car left the road,
                        and she went up on the hedge.

"So anyway.

"The man had a gooddeal of drink in him, and he had fell asleep.

"And there was John in the car,
            and she was up on the hedge,   ˙
            and he had to get out,
            and try and get the car home again.

"So he got out anyway, and he pulled the car down off the hedge.

"And he got in the car, and he got aholt of the man that was at the wheel, and he pulled him away, across to the back seat.

"And he got in at the wheel
            and he driv the car home,
                        and put her into the garage.

"So the woman says to him:

"It's not long before you started that story, you told that you never had been in a car in your life till that day. How can you make the people believe that you driv a car home and driv it into the garage?

"Because, he says, that I had to do it.

"So anyway, the man didn't render out for a while, but he gathered himself up, and he went off of drink for a day or two, and he took a look at everything around. And, ah, the old cattle had failed. And there was pigs and they had went astray.

"Things was in a bad way.

"He got a kind of angry with himself for the way he was carryin on, and he says to John:

"He says, There's a man, he says, lives away up in the mountain, but he wasn't out of the house this twenty years. And if he could be got here, he'd regulate them pigs for us.

"And how, says John, are you goin to get him here?

"You take that car, he says, and go way up on the mountain, he says, and bring him down.

"I'll do nothin of the kind, says John. I know nothin about a car.

"Well, he says, the day, he says, that I went up on the hedge, he says, you took the car, and you drove it home, and you put it into the garage as well as I could do if I were sober.

"And take it out now, and go up. I'll direct you to where he lives.

"So anyway,
     he took out the car,
        and he started,
          and he turned up the mountains.

"And there was a whole lot of ould men and women out workin in wee pits around in the mountains.

"And there were big caves here and there.

"*Ah*, there was some of them, when he started up with the car, there was some of them run into these caves, and they were never seen more,
        nor heard tell of.

"Well, he went on, went on, till where this ould fellow lived.

"And he was sittin in the corner.

"He stopped at the door,
      and he went in,
      and he told the ould fellow that he had come for him,
      and what he was a-wantin to do.

"The ould fellow joined to roar and cry,
      and he wouldn't get into a thing like that,
      because he would be killed,
      because anyone ever went in was killed.

"So anyway, John got tired,
    and he run and got aholt of him.

"Hauled the man down to the door,
      and pulled him out,
      and opened the door of the car,
      and shoved him in,
      and closed the door,
      and run around,

and got to the wheel,
and started away.

"And twas the same when they were comin back: the old men and women runnin for all they were worth, and you'd see them disappearin into these caves.

"But anyway, when he got down to where the boss lived, the boss had plenty of drink, and he gave the ould lad a couple of good gorges of whiskey and stout, and anyway they got the pigs regulated.

"They never missed a meal, he said. And they were about twelve stone at the time that this ould man regulated them.

"Ah, they were done powerful well after. They were the best pork went to that market."

Authors of comical tales give their hardworking neighbors a laugh, a bit of diversion, and more. Their humor does not rise out of nothing, it erupts surprisingly out of the depths of the culture. Each of Mr. O'Prey's stories locates a point of power also located in the historical consciousness, then drives it to a wild extreme, prompting repetitive laughter in which the shape of existence is not dismissed, lightened, or obscured, but recognized.

Mr. O'Prey's kicking story turns to comedy the essential concept in battle tales. A man feels he has been mistreated by the authorities, deprived of a right, so he kicks his neighbors. The idea is the same as Mackan Fight. Once he is part of the world's kicking, parties align to kick him from the field to the road like a football. They kick him black as an African. He exemplifies the local man, a thing for political factions to kick around until they get on to more serious economic matters. During battle, he becomes a man of another race, alien, as though a slave, wounded, so he emigrates, leaving the place where he belongs, but no longer belongs, to try to improve his lot. He is the type of the Irish countryman, beaten in his political climate. But if we return to the beginning, we find the police mistreated him by denying him a permit to buy a gun to shoot his neighbors at random. The base of his tale is fear, the fear that comes of the inevitable tension of life passed within the narrow confines of a rural neighborhood. Social existence is painful. Life in a community that is fated to division, that is obliged to absorb ridicule as well as celebration, spite as well as love, will always be rough, never smooth. In a fantasy gloriously dark and comic in the mode of Samuel Beckett, Mr. O'Prey retells the battle tale, exposing the shocking impossibility of living within the community's rule of neighborliness, God's commandment to love.

Mr. O'Prey's second story grapples with the landscape's evolutionary history, the issue of modernization. The automobile symbolizes the fast, easy, noisy, mechanical, mobile modern world. It terrifies the countryman, but he is dragged into it. Once within, he finds it off course, stalled, and he takes command, guiding it smoothly home. Mrs. O'Prey asks John how he could do it. His answer, "Because that I had to do it"—not, "Because, I wanted to do it"—exactly states the feelings of the person forced to adjust. Having learned, he still wants nothing to do with it, saying he does not understand, but he accepts his direction, and Mr. Nolan describes him getting into the car with slow words and a sad air, a tone of wearied resignation. John drives to a remote rural area. Mountains to Fermanagh men symbolize the hard, old way. People there work mysteriously in pits and run into caves when the car roars through, terrified as John had been shortly before. The old man he is fetching, a smart, if backward, old country man who knows how to castrate pigs, is frightened, just as John had been, and refuses to get in, but as his boss had done, John wearies of protest and drags him into the car. The old man adjusts, does his job, receives his drink, and the pigs bring cash at market.

John O'Prey's tale describes the momentum of accommodation, how country men must adapt, learning to operate new machines, fighting, adjusting, then advancing the force of a material history that is not to their liking, not of their devising, but of which they are inescapably a part. His story accurately describes the diffusion of modern ideas from drunken, idle bosses through their hardworking, capable laborers to country people in the most remote areas. It tells the result. Country men lose control over their destiny but gain a gorge of booze, a little pleasure, while the bosses who depend on their skill and energy profit in the market.

Hugh Nolan linked John O'Prey's pants to pull the key concerns out of their community's two histories. The first raises the idea in historical stories: the tension of neighborly life. Between conflict and exile, endurance and rebellion, obligation and failure, one must choose and act. The second brings up the idea in evolutionary, socioeconomic history: unstoppably things get better and they get worse: one must adapt and carry on.

At base, in the thought of real people and the culture of their community, Ballymenone's two histories are one. Each tells of the defeats that accompany victory. Saints and warriors win in battle, then lose land or life. Farmers advance and retreat at once, gaining comfort, tobacco, drink, and clean homes, while losing the confidence that comes from meeting God's neighborly command. History tells of the loss of community through war, death, exile, or economic success.

History in its vastness opens wide to accommodate different personalities. We follow Peter Flanagan when we see the victory at Mackan as not worth the damage it did to the community. We follow Hugh Nolan when we see modern comforts as unable to compensate for the loss of law and order. But Hugh Patrick Owens feels the men of Mackan, like the Swanlinbar boys, were God's soldiers, never "guilty of crime or wrong," and he feels modern comforts fully make up for all that was lost when we escaped the bad old days of hardship.

Culture arranges around issues and becomes coherent because people argue over the same issues, not because they hold the same opinion. Individuals are left to judge for themselves, while their stories remind them of the mature truth that victory is always accompanied by defeat. If that seems a pessimistic or masochistic conclusion, then their stories also remind the District's people that defeat is accompanied by victory. In fiction and history, beaten men ascend to new success. George Armstrong emigrates, cholera strikes, he shrivels to a speechless, three-pound thing, enshrouded in a basket, a womb, a tomb, then he rises to become a great star. John O'Prey is kicked black into immobility, he lies twice nine months in bed, then rises to emigrate and prosper. Columcille is exiled but achieves new power and fame in Scotland. The men of Mackan are transported but do the best in Australia. Willy Reilly is transported but returns to marry the Cooleen. The stories people tell themselves boil down to the culture's essence: between winning and losing, nothing is certain; one must carry on, living in all seasons.

The community's artists create stories out of imagination, and they select facts from the past and order them into narratives, to bring life into awareness. Humor and history raise the same issues because they are the issues. Hugh McGiveney invented a funny tale of a saint, a pant of Saint Patrick. His song on the band's second battle, in which flutes and drums are portrayed as an imprisoned Fenian martyr, was a parody of patriotic song, a comic turn on the nationalistic public history. James Maguire composed humorous stories out of the frightening idea of meeting a ghost. James Quigley made a comical tale out of the horrible idea of trading your eternal soul for worldly wealth.

Fiction and truth, comedy and tragedy, blend toward the same conclusion. In a funny story, a man's clever, innocent wife saves him from the Devil. In a serious story, a man's hardworking laborer saves him from the Devil, much as John O'Prey saved his boss from his own failings. The conclusion is: endurance, carrying on without knowing, is man's lot, but endurance pays off. In the worst of times, Mrs. Timoney and Mr. McBrien work, eat, and survive. Despite the climate, despite endless war and endless change, people endure. In theory, life is impossibly difficult. Storms break. The community shatters. In fact, life is possible and people survive because they are brave, strong, smart, and generous, or because they are fortunate to live among others who are.

Finally, all is a matter of individuals. The community's wise, gallant artists make life possible. Stars rise above their own failings as parents and workers to help those around them, whose failures are less, whose abilities are slighter.

Ballymenone's artists accept a dual task. They create and preserve. It is the historian's obligation to preserve the facts and the works of art of the past. Both are essential to the community's health. When the historian, Hugh Nolan or Michael Boyle, performs a song or a comic tale, he does not present it as his own, but repeats it, making his art the clear and correct perpetuation of the art of another. His stories shift from the first person to the third, becoming stories of storytelling. His songs are reports of poetic genius. History, at last, is not the absent past, nor even the present place. It is a special kind of human conduct. History is an individual acting responsibly at once toward the dead and the living by telling the truth.

The historian mediates between death and life by selecting a few of the multitudinous facts from the past and arranging them for other people to see or hear. Selection and arrangement are guided by the historians' reading of society's needs: what should people know about the past so they can live in the future? Two modes of relation between distant facts and present needs dominate the scholar's moral endeavor. One is typological: scholars describe and clarify another reality in order to refine and improve their own world through comparison. The other is sequential: scholars explain their world by an account of its development. In anthropology, the typological need is met in ethnography, in descriptions of time passed in other places, while cultural evolution answers the sequential need. In history, detailed accounts locked within brief periods, keying on major events and usually stressing political and military happenings, provide typological understanding, while sweeping narratives of the long duration, usually stressing economics and seeking mechanistic formulation, provide sequential understanding.[3] The problem is coordinating and unifying those approaches to enlightenment. In my tradition, the solution is to let types melt into time by setting ethnographies into evolutionary patterns and viewing history's major events as flashes, symptoms at the surface of slow, massive, deep change.

Ballymenone's historians teach typological history through stories of Saints and Battles. They teach sequential history through the evolution of work. But when Ballymenone's histories merge, they do not flow into time. Time is eliminated, and history forms as a statement of the eternal human condition. One endures between loss and gain, preserving the soul.

Lines of conflict are drawn between histories that are fundamentally sequential, temporal, and secular and histories that are fundamentally typological, spatial, and sacred.[4] In one tradition, the individual fades into time. Cultural difference and historical development explain human beings in terms of varying, particular conditions. People are made responsible for conditions, but they are removed from ultimate accountability for themselves. In another tradition, conditions repeat, recur, collapse into space around people, and human beings are explained in terms of will. People are removed from responsibility for conditions and made accountable for themselves. Those distinct styles of explaining human affairs—one essentially temporal and secular, the other essentially spatial and sacred—provide the fundamental dynamics of the cultures we classify as progressive versus conservative, or modern versus folk. Though separated for analysis, though purified into warring ideologies, these ways to account for the world cross and mix in real minds, confusing people in their quest for life. Those who wish to aid their fellows are left to decide what must be preserved and what created to help carry them on.

The star has the courage to decide. The District's great creator is the poet. Its preserver is the historian. The roles are clearly distinct, but as they were in ancient Ireland, they are usually filled by the same person. Poets are not public singers, but they are historians.[5] Hugh McGiveney was not a famous singer, but he was a poet, a maker of quick bids and giddy pants, and he was Ballymenone's great historian in the generation before Michael Boyle and Hugh Nolan. Master Maguire is remembered as a poet and the author of witty bids, but it can be inferred from his occupation and the references in his songs that he was a historian too.

The roles of poet and historian connect. I asked Mr. Nolan and he said, "Aye, them jobs go together." The exceptionally bright man receives the community's history. He makes out of it difficult stories to perform within his district, and he composes out of it songs for the public place which others sing. This division keeps his role clean, for songs can extend away from the fullness of truth the historian must preserve into sentimental or patriotic excitement, humorous or political rhetoric, metaphor, hyperbole. The poet must be modest—he cannot perform his own works in public—but as a historian he receives others' works of art, which he can celebrate without restraint and perform with full force, while others treat his works with comparable affection and care, for works of art, even if fictional, are history: they are true when used as examples of the genius of the stars.

The star's genius is double. It is a genius of wild imagination. He invents bids, pants, and poems to provide his community consolation, the ability to carry on. And it is a genius of memory. He preserves the past to give his community the truth, the ability to carry on correctly.

Genius is wrapped in poverty. Unsuccessful in the material world, unrecognized by the world at large, but glowing bright within, the star is the extreme personification of the community: poor, apparently dull, brilliant.

The star is the community's memory and the community's creative force, its mind, the center through which local time pulses into continuity. When the community holds intact, the next generation remembers what the star preserved and what he created. Michael Boyle and Hugh Nolan remember Hugh McGiveney. Peter Flanagan remembers Charlie Farmer. But if the community weakens, no one remembers and continuity is lost. No young men have gathered around Michael, Hugh, and P. They have no sons or singers. That is where I came in.

"Hugh Nolan," Peter Flanagan said, "is the very same nature as Charlie Farmer. He'd let the house fall on him and sit under a bush writin a poem." With this book nearly done, our first conversation about Charlie Farmer seven and a half years in the past, I had one last question for P to finish the portrait of the star, the man on whom his community and my book depend for existence: was Farmer, the poet, also a historian?

"It's a pity Charlie Farmer wasn't in a district where there was singers. I wasn't just a native of it at that time. A house was wantin, and we happened to go temporarily to this house beside Charlie Farmer. But he was on the way *out*.

"And he had quit composin. And he had quit everything you might say. The poor wee fellow.

"You wouldn't think—if you seen him and he was a very unsignified lookin type of person. The modestest wee fellow and he had a wee beard comin down just like a wee nib of a pen, you know.

"He was the nice tiny wee fellow.

"And every word you'd ask him, he'd say,

"Aye.

"That's a good day, Charlie.

"Aye.

"You would think that he knew nothing—that type of person.

"But if he got into talk he could use the best grammar ever you heard. And I don't know where he got his education. Really. Sure, I was stupid and, of course, when you're young like that you don't look at the full details of history.

"It was a great sorrow, and often I would cry about the loss of his songs.

"He was a historian as well as a poet. He was both."

I comment, "Those things seem to be connected," and P agrees, "Aye, I think that too." Then I mention Hugh McGiveney, saying he did both of those jobs.

"Yes he did. He done both. He'd make a poem or he would make up a bit of a rhyme there like Bobby Burns. Bobby Burns could do that too. Aye. You could pass by, and Bobby Burns could make a poem.

"Like the solicitor that was a-burryin.

"Well, this solicitor died. And there was four solicitors carryin him on their shoulders. They were the bearers in under.

"Came on up to the corner of this street, the business corner of a town.

"I think Burns was a native of Dumfries.

"So.

"Well, said some of the boys to Burns (coorse they knew Burns) what could we do? Says one of them to him, Could you make a bit of a rhyme, he says, on them boys there, he says to Burns.

"Aye, he says, I think I could.

"Bent down his head for a few minutes, then he raised it up at the coffin.

"He says: *One rogue above*, says he:

Four in under.
His body's to earth,
His soul's on its journey,
And the Divil's at law,
And he wants an attorney ◊.

"Aye, Well, I heard that told.

"There was a rogue in the coffin above.

"And there was four in under. That was five rogues ◊.

"One rogue above, says he, four in under.

"His body's to earth, his soul's on its journey,

"And the Divil's at the law and he wants an attorney."

A wide smile remains on his face. "McGiveney," I say, "could make up a quick rhyme and so could Master Maguire; could Charlie Farmer do that too?"

"He could. He could make a wee poem all right. If he thought, at the very same time, if there was any offense in it or anything like that, he would hold it to himself. He might tell it to Johnny McCaffrey, for he was his right-hand man. I heard Johnny McCaffrey at these wee bits he made on people round, but he wouldn't go into the full details. He wouldn't be offensive or anything. It twould be in a kind of humorous way. He was very reserved and he always was.

"If it was a person far away, well, he might be a wee bit offensive. It might cause, you know, a wee bit of displeasure on the person it was made on. That was the way of Charlie."

We pause for a trade of cigarettes and fire, and repetitiously, I ask, "Did he tell these stories of history too?"

"Yes. But now as I have just told you, I never was in conversation with Charlie Farmer. I was just a young lad. And you could go in to Charlie Farmer and he'd sit there and he'd never let on. The fact of it is: you would come to the conclusion that he was a kind of simpleton, that he hadn't just the proper wit. You'd say to yourself, Well, he's a bit odd, and there's not a bit use in me startin a conversation with him. And even if ye did start a conversation, ye'd get no satisfaction from him. He'd only say, Aye.

"That was the type of man he was. You'd want to be with him for a while, and he got to know you and knew your ways and that you liked his ways."

Charlie Farmer was poor, modest, seemingly stupid, actually brilliant, a man like many country people. He was a man of memory and imagination, a historian and a poet like Hugh Nolan. "Those jobs go together," I say to P, "yet the job of the historian is to preserve the truth."

"Oh yes. Aye," P replies.

"Yet," I say, "the poet makes things up. It is as though the person were using different parts of the personality at different times."

"That's right," says P. Hugh Nolan had given me the same answer to the same question. "A historian can't use his imagination," I comment, and P answers quickly:

"No, he cannot. That's surely a fact. Charlie Farmer could do both. He was a good patriotic writer and a good sentimental or sport writer. He was a terror, and there's no doubt about that. You'd have to laugh at him.

"It's a pity. All the funny people's gone.

"He made great songs, Charlie Farmer.

"But there wasn't a singer in the townland where Charlie Farmer lived. And even if you're not a singer out in public. There's plenty of people, you know, are very good singers but wouldn't sing out in public.

"Well, if you even had them people in your district where Charlie Farmer was, for example, there wouldn't be a song of Charlie Farmer's but it would be alive today.

"Wherein, there wasn't a singer in this townland where Farmer lived, only this boy, McCaffrey. And there was plenty of young fellows. But they were deaf to music as a stone. Well then, the man that can't sing or hasn't much music in him, hasn't much interest in learnin a song or takin it up or knowin the value of it. There was only that one man that took a great interest in Charlie Farmer, and some of his script is down in Belfast, that was Eddie Anderson.

"Eddie Anderson was the man that knew the value of Charlie Farmer.

"He could see that day comin.

"And he done the same thing you're doin, gettin these songs down. You're doin a great thing. No one knows the value of men like you. It brings great honor and credit to a nation. There's alot into what you're doin.

"But you haven't a man in ten square miles around here, and I could extend it further, that knows the value of a man like Charlie Farmer.

"Well, it won't be very long before it will be extinct or gone completely, that no one will ever get a grip of it. No.

"It's regrettable that it hadn't been saved or preserved and kept alive. Now there's no one in Tiravally now or three miles round, or five miles, that would know one haet about Charlie Farmer, that he existed atall. That's the way.

"You want plenty of men like you. It's a pity there's not more. There's no one has the wee remnants of Charlie Farmer except meself. Unfortunately, I didn't see him early enough in life.

"In the present generation, if you're not fit to get a grasp on his poetry, it will die out. He made many, many songs. He made that one on the Border. And he made one on Trimble, the Reporter editor. And he made one about Willie Oliver, and one on the Molly Maguires, the A O H, that's the Ancient Order of Hibernians. And he made another on a policeman named Reilly. And he made that one on John Greene and the donkey race.

"He made some very funny songs. There's no doubt about it. Farmer was the last word in poetry. He was. He was a wonderful man."

Joe Flanagan, August 1978

Peter Flanagan, December 1979

Ellen Cutler, Her Son, Dick, and His Son, December 1979

Hugh Nolan, December 1979

33

Quiet

The man who gave us a ride out of town said Wee Joe Flanagan was dead. He left us at the foot of Drumbargy Lane. Night was at its blackest, and winter's winds, ripped off the Atlantic, broken over mountains to the west, pounded at the hill, snapped the hedges, cracked the trees east. We sloughed the mucky gap, made the crest, and found a faint light across the hill. Tiny fire sent enormous shadows into the black roof. P was alone, small by the hearth. It was the stream of life, he said, blood. On Friday, P got Hugh Quigley to call the hospital; they came and took Joe away. The doctor had said the hospital lacked room and promised to bring a specialist to see Joe at home. "Well, how's the patient?" the doctor asked when they arrived. "He's easy, Doctor," P replied. "The patient is restin at peace. He's dead."

We had not known Joe was ill. P had not known we were coming. "A gift from heaven," he said when we came to his hearth. We touched, spoke, got through the night, drinking the whiskey we brought, frying up a good tea, not searching for happy topics, but working through the grief, remembering Joe, all the times his shy wit shot little sunbeams into the chat—"He was as quiet with me as he was with you," P said—all the times he had patiently borne and generously fed the loud men around him. We remember the Sport at Belcoo a couple of years ago when Joe and Kathy had gone off together, leaving P and me to sing and drink too much with the other wild men in the pub. "He didn't like the Sport so well the year," P said. "He missed bein with yous. Ah, the creature." Joe made memories, and we got the night behind us. P warmed the sheets and lit us to bed through wavering monstrous shadows. All night black wind pounded at the hill, cold, pounded at the house.

Late, I stood the blast a moment, looking down on the land. The small place around me was immense with meaning. It had grown into a challenge. Simple equations of human excellence with wealth or power or education or liberation from sacred communal tradition—equations essential to the maintenance of my culture—do not hold. At one time, twenty years ago, seven homes stood along the half-mile crest of Drumbargy Brae. All were inhabited by hardworking people, small farmers and laborers. In one house lived John O'Prey, author of imaginative fiction, in the next lived

Peter Flanagan, the great musician, in another lived the brilliant historian Michael Boyle. At the foot of the hill, in the part of Rossdoney called Carna Cara, five houses stood. In one lived the old poet and historian Hugh McGiveney, in another lived the poet and historian Hugh Nolan. This little community of poor farming people contained an astonishing proportion of extraordinary individuals.

I stood in the cold near P's house, between the O'Preys' home and the ruins of Michael Boyle's, and remembered my first night in Drumbargy, the miraculous quiet, the pure darkness and wide sky of stars. Now the wind carried the bumping putter of start-o-matic lights. Pale spots shine on the hills. Electricity has come, bringing mechanical racket, replacing quiet fires with eerie babbling television sets, erecting arclights on poles to trick cattle into grazing all night to increase their yield. Comfort and cash, but the great change is not modernization. It is death.

In Ballymenone I learned not to look at the bad but to think of the good and never forget. I learned to mistake bomb blasts for thunder, smoke for mist, while not forgetting that the bones of plain people fuel the fires that burn the world. I did not learn a lament for old ways, but a lament for old people, a futile hatred of death.

The terror that tightens my chest every time I return is not for iron roofs or cookers or poles, it is for the meaning in ruined houses and gardens once trim, now gone to weeds: death. During my Christmastime visit, six years before, Joe was so ill he sat in dull silence while P and I acted silly. The doctor told him he had lived too long. I left fearing I would not see him again, but he brought himself through, and when I came next, his smile was bright, the old gentle light glowed in his eyes. I felt he had won, but he was dead on Sunday, December 9, 1979, and was buried on Monday at Arney. He lived seventy-nine years. I missed seeing him again by only a week.

I stood in the cold wind remembering how unprepared I had been for Michael Boyle's death. Though I saw him in January 1974, less than a month before he died, and he had failed and I knew, still I could not picture the world without him. Death took a man, but it took with him generations of men and women whose existence had been reduced to a memory he alone held, delicately. It was all their deaths that shocked me. Gone. And Packie Boyle, Ned and Pat Cooney, gone. Death is more vicious, more enormous when life is a matter of perishable brain, not written record. Bob Armstrong, Peter Lunny, Denis Gilroy, Hugh Corrigan—gone. I am the hopeless historian, astronomer of a darkening universe. It is not merely the cheap, mean, unjust side of life I fight, but death itself. Mary McBrien is dead, and Paddy has left the house he built for them. The Croziers sold their farm, and their lovely house decays, green slime streaks the whitewash, thatch moulders and drips on the kitchen floor. James Boyle is in the hospital. Tommy Love has moved to Enniskillen to work as a gardener. He is doing the best. Though "terribly invalided," P says, Hugh Patrick Owens still takes his drink in Arney. William Lunny, James McGovern, John

O'Prey, James and Annie, the Owenses of the Ford, they all carry on. I called the hospital before we went out to Ballymenone, and Ellen Cutler had been released, allowed to come home.

She had written me regularly, giving me the news, giving me the devil for not writing more often:

"Well dear, I can't tell you how glad I was to get your letter. It is snowing and raining and wind, and it is bitterly cold as I try to scribble this note. Glad to see by your letter yous are all well and in good health. Poor Hugh Nolan is in hospital. I was told he was very ill. He is not expected to do any good. The hospital is a grand place to be this bad weather. It is a dreadful bad day as I sit at the window thinking what I will write next. Kinawley barracks was blown up Sunday night, but there was no one hurt, but lots of damage done for miles and miles around. The IRA said they were responsible for it. Or where is it going to end? I still love *you* the best. Don't tell *Kathy*. . . ."

"Well dear, I hope yous are all well and in good form, not like me. I have to go back into hospital in three weeks' time. I don't know what they are going to do to me, that is if I live that long, and I do hope to hear from some of *yous* before that.

"From your old sweetheart, all my love,
"Ellen."

Late in the summer, Nellie, Dick Cutler's wife, had written: "Just a few lines to let you know that Granny Cutler has been in hospital since July. . . . She got me to write this letter for her. Any night I got to hospital to see her, she always asks have I written to you. There has been alot of wet weather in Ireland. The summer hasn't been very good atall this year. I think Granny will be in hospital for a very long time. I hope she will be alright again, but it is hard to tell. . . ."

She met us at the door and summoned a warm smile for us, but she had lost weight and her face showed suffering. "Every night, I ask the Lord why he does not bring me home. Why am I left here in such pain?" A white cloth covered the front table where her minister had just given her the rites of the church. Next summer, Eileen, John Cutler's wife, would write:

"Just a few lines hoping this finds you all well as we are the best here. It is with regret that I am writing to let you know that Granny Cutler passed away on the 12th July after a spell of eight weeks in the hospital. She hadn't really been that well since Christmas. She had asked me to write to you before she went in to hospital, but we didn't get down to it, for she took a bad turn and then she wasn't that well in hospital. . . . Anytime you visit Ireland, we will arrange for somewhere for you to stay. Dick and the family will be moving up to the hill, so you will always be able to visit up there. We had a bad summer. It is a hard time on the farmers. . . ."

She had said she hoped to live to see her next birthday, June twenty-sixth. She did, and died at seventy-eight. I wept for Ellen Cutler, as I had for Michael Boyle.

Young Hugh Quigley visited Joe in the hospital. "His day had come," Hughie said. "Aye," P said, "he knew what was comin." And Hughie said, "He was content." In tears, in rage, not at Hughie but at life, P said, "No. No. He battled to the end." When the men from the ambulance were carrying Joe out, his last words were, "Yous will bring me home." His fear was not death but living away from home. This dark house, small fire, big chair were his, and he would not fade numbly among muttering old men in the ward of a hospital. Peter promised to bring him home.

In eight days, Hugh Nolan will be eighty-three. We sit with him in the hospital. He has a clean bed and a drawer in a washstand that holds everything he owns. For years he resisted his doctor's pleas, refusing to leave his little house, but, wonderful rational old man, he thought about it, realized he could be burned up, that he could be robbed, that he might die alone, so when the doctor began the old argument again last March, he quietly said that he would go.

A television flickers and drones at the end of the ward. Crisp white nurses swish through on squeaky shoes bearing stainless-steel trays with coils of clear plastic tubing, chromium clamps, little boxes of gauze, thin long needles, vials of pale fluid. A green tree glowing with red lights stands upon the polished floor between the rows of metal beds. We talk about history. History had been his consolation. His life's delight, he says, has been "keepin the truth" and "tellin the whole tale." We reminisce about Joe Flanagan, who is rising slowly from death to become the timeless type of the quiet wee man. Once, Mr. Nolan says, the band master taught the lads to read by note, then left them to practice. Joe listened and said, "Boys, we've gone off it." They paid no attention to him, but when the master returned and heard them playing, it turned out Wee Joe had been the only one who was right. Another time Joe and Steve O'Prey, John's brother, entertained the company all night with one fine song after another. When he was told it had been a great ceili, Wee Joe replied, "No, it was not. But it was the best it could be when the men can sing weren't there."

A hundred times I had risen from his hearth, a hundred times he came with me to the door and wished me God's blessing, watching as I walked Rossdoney Lane away from him. Now he swung the metal walker before him through the corridors to the lobby of the hospital. We stood. Gray rain streaked the glass. Good old man, he never had the bad taste to become intimate, but I looked and said, "I love you, Hugh."

"I know," he said.

Notes and Sources

Notes

PREFACE

1. A great achievement of the folklorist's discipline has been the creation of master collections and indexes through which particular texts can be connected to international patterns. Of greatest use for my book are guides to tale types and elements: Antti Aarne and Stith Thompson, *The Types of the Folktale: A Classification and Bibliography*, F.F. Communications 184 (Helsinki: Suomalainen Tiedeakatemia, 1961); Stith Thompson, *Motif-Index of Folk Literature*, 6 vols. (Bloomington: Indiana University Press, 1955–58). And these regional indexes: Seán Ó Súilleabháin and Reidar Th. Christiansen, *The Types of the Irish Folktale*, F.F. Communications 188 (Helsinki: Suomalainen Tiedeakatemia, 1967); Ernest W. Baughman, *Type and Motif-Index of the Folktales of England and North America*, Indiana University Folklore Series 20 (The Hague: Mouton, 1966). For narrative song: Francis James Child, *The English and Scottish Popular Ballads*, 5 vols. (New York: Cooper Square, 1965; reprint of 1882–98 ed.); G. Malcolm Laws, *American Balladry from British Broadsides: A Guide for Students and Collectors of Traditional Song*, A.F.S. Bibliographical and Special Series 8 (Philadelphia: American Folklore Society, 1957). Numbers lifted from those works and assigned to a text lead to cross-cultural comparison, undercutting false nationalism and hinting toward global history, but the act of abstracting from a real text to a numbered type pulls the mind away from the social situations and cultural contexts through which meaning is discovered, and meaning is my book's task.

2. Kenneth S. Goldstein's *A Guide for Field Workers in Folklore* (Hatboro: Folklore Associates, 1964) has been recently extended by two others from American folklorists: Edward D. Ives, *The Tape-Recorded Interview: A Manual for Field Workers in Folklore and Oral History* (Knoxville: University of Tennessee Press, 1980); and Robert A. Georges and Michael Owen Jones, *People Studying People: The Human Element in Fieldwork* (Berkeley: University of California Press, 1980). In Ireland, Michael J. Murphy has written an account of his field experiences in *Tyrone Folk Quest* (Belfast: Blackstaff Press, 1973), combining sensitivity and useful advice with graceful prose. Among the multitude of guides produced in adjacent social-scientific disciplines, I have found only one to be a necessary addition to those written by folklorists: John Collier, Jr., *Visual Anthropology: Photography as a Research Method*, Studies in Anthropological Method (New York: Holt, Rinehart & Winston, 1967). I use the camera extensively and find helpful Collier's idea that the camera—like the tape recorder—can be used to gather data to study and need not be reduced to a way to collect decorations for an argument. The year of the publication of Goldstein's crucial *Guide* also saw the publication of major works by Abrahams, Dundes, and Ives,

making 1964 a watershed in folklore history. Roger Abrahams' *Deep Down in the Jungle: Negro Narrative Folklore from the Streets of Philadelphia* (Hatboro: Folklore Associates, 1964) not only opened new genres and areas to folkloristic investigation, but combined collection with analysis, placing obligations upon future collectors to analyze, future analysts to collect. Alan Dundes, *The Morphology of North American Indian Folktales*, F.F. Communications 195 (Helsinki: Suomalainen Tiedeakatemia, 1964), pushed the formal analysis of narrative line, well begun in historic-geographic typology, to new depths, revitalizing Vladimir Propp's *Morphology of the Folktale*, trans. Laurence Scott, rev. Louis A. Wagner, A.F.S. Bibliographical and Special Series 9; Indiana University Research Center in Anthropology, Folklore, and Linguistics 10 (Austin: University of Texas Press, 1968; 1st ed. 1958, completed 1928). Propp's ideas, often applied, were significantly extended by Claude Brémond, "Morphology of the French Folktale," *Semiotica* 2, no. 3 (1970): 247–76. Dundes' study prodded folklorists toward the different variety of structural analysis being practiced by Claude Lévi-Strauss. The two varieties are ably described and linked by A. Julien Greimas in his contribution to Pierre Maranda and Elli Köngäs Maranda, eds., *Structural Analysis of Oral Tradition*, Publications in Folklore and Folklife 3 (Philadelphia: University of Pennsylvania Press, 1971). Edward D. Ives, *Larry Gorman: The Man Who Made the Songs* (Bloomington: Indiana University Press, 1964), brought full biographical treatment to an author of folksongs. Though most books on folksongs had been compilations of texts, singers had been spotlighted before. Collectors had published accounts of their travels, adding color to their texts, notably W. Roy Mackenzie, *The Quest of the Ballad* (Princeton: Princeton University Press, 1919), and John A. Lomax, *Adventures of a Ballad Hunter* (New York: Macmillan, 1947). John A. and Alan Lomax had written *Negro Folk Songs as Sung by Lead Belly* (New York: Macmillan, 1936), Jean Thomas had described *Ballad Makin' in the Mountains of Kentucky* (New York: Henry Holt, 1939), and Byron Arnold had arranged *Folksongs of Alabama* (University: University of Alabama Press, 1950) by singer rather than arbitrary song category, as Edith Fowke would do in *Traditional Singers and Songs from Ontario* (Hatboro: Folklore Associates, 1965). But Ives' *Larry Gorman* was the first to treat a singer properly as an artist, as one might Chaucer or Burns. Since then Ives has added two other magnificent, full-length studies: *Lawrence Doyle, the Farmer Poet of Prince Edward Island: A Study in Local Songmaking*, U.M. Studies 92 (Orono: University of Maine Press, 1971); *Joe Scott: The Woodsman-Songmaker* (Urbana: University of Illinois Press, 1978). His lead has been profitably followed, most importantly by Roger D. Abrahams, ed., *A Singer and Her Songs: Almeda Riddle's Book of Ballads* (Baton Rouge: Louisiana State University Press, 1970), and in Ireland by Robin Morton, *Come Day, Go Day, God Send Sunday: The Songs and Life Story, Told in His Own Words, of John Maguire, Traditional Singer and Farmer from Co. Fermanagh* (London: Routledge & Kegan Paul, 1973)—a book especially important for us since Maguire lived not far from Ballymenone. Folktales have been comparably handled. Most have appeared in collections, classed by scholarly custom, though some have been ordered naturally by teller, such as A. L. Kroeber's *Yurok Myths* (Berkeley: University of California Press, 1976) and the fine work of Edward S. Hall, Jr., *The Eskimo Storyteller: Folktales from Noatak, Alaska* (Knoxville: University of Tennessee Press, 1975). Irish collectors of stories have often attended to their sources and given us collections arranged by teller, such as Kevin Danaher's *Folktales of the Irish Countryside* (Cork: Mercier Press, 1967) and books consisting of the repertories of narrators, a great case being Douglas Hyde's last major work, *Mayo*

Stories Told by Thomas Casey, Irish Texts Society 36 (Dublin: Educational Company of Ireland, 1939). Juha Pentikäinen analyzes a woman, her life and art, with care in *Oral Repertoire and World View: An Anthropological Study of Marina Takalo's Life History*, F.F. Communications 219 (Helsinki: Suomalainen Tiedeakatemia, 1978). Folkloristic studies of individuals have the virtues and limitations of conventional biographic, monographic studies of great artists. They make the individual and his or her art live, while slighting the social realities of artistic creation. It is my goal in this book to study not the total repertory of an individual but the total repertory of all the individuals who compose a living community of artists. Doing so, I am guided by the new spirit that rose out of folklore dissertations prepared by Goldstein, Abrahams, Dundes, and Ives, two at Pennsylvania, two at Indiana, which were all published as books in 1964. Remarkably, in the same year, Alan Merriam published *The Anthropology of Music* (Evanston: Northwestern University Press, 1964), a major essay on the connections of anthropology and art, an area where folklore and anthropology overlap into one endeavor. And in that year Dell Hymes published two major papers in anthropological linguistics (see note 6, below), another major area of disciplinary conjunction, and those papers form the theoretical base for the dominant concept of current American folklore in which the concerns of Goldstein, Abrahams, Dundes, and Ives are unified: performance.

3. Richard M. Dorson has written on all the varieties of the relation of folklore to history. His *The British Folklorists: A History* (Chicago: University of Chicago Press, 1968) is a major history of my discipline, valuable for its information on early Irish folktale scholarship. In *America in Legend: Folklore from the Colonial Period to the Present* (New York: Pantheon, 1973), Dorson relates folklore to the nation's chronicle. Papers in *American Folklore and the Historian* (Chicago: University of Chicago Press, 1971), esp. chaps. 6–9, and *Folklore: Selected Essays* (Bloomington: Indiana University Press, 1972), chaps. 7–8, describe well the relationship between professional history and folk history. Dorson edited a special issue of the *Journal of the Folklore Institute*, 8, nos. 2/3 (1971), on "Folklore and Traditional History," and he organized a panel on oral history and folklore to which he contributed "The Oral Historian and the Folklorist" and I contributed "A Folkloristic Thought on the Promise of Oral History," in Peter D. Olch and Forrest C. Pogue, eds., *Selections from the Fifth and Sixth National Colloquia on Oral History* (New York: Oral History Association, 1972), pp. 40–62. In editing *Folklore and Folklife: An Introduction* (Chicago: University of Chicago Press, 1972), Dorson provides us with a statement of the norms of the discipline in transition. Inta Carpenter assembled a selection from his vast bibliography in Linda Dégh, Henry Glassie, and Felix J. Oinas, eds., *Folklore Today: A Festschrift for Richard M. Dorson* (Bloomington: Indiana University, 1976), pp. 525–37. Two major works of high relevance to the problems of folklore and history, though not written by folklorists, are: Jan Vansina, *Oral Tradition: A Study in Historical Methodology*, trans. H. M. Wright (Chicago: Aldine, 1965); and W. G. Hoskins, *Local History in England* (London: Longmans, 1959), with its attendant guide by Hoskins, *Fieldwork in Local History* (London: Faber & Faber, 1967).

4. Linda Dégh, *Folktales and Society: Story-Telling in a Hungarian Peasant Community*, trans. Emily M. Schossberger (Bloomington: Indiana University Press, 1969; 1st pub. 1962). Dégh devotes the second half of her *Studies in East European Folk Narrative*, A.F.S. Bibliographical and Special Series 30; Indiana University Folklore Monograph Series 25 (Bloomington: Folklore Institute, 1978), to papers on the tellers, their art and community. The first half consists of comparative studies, so

her book breaks the field into parts and suggests its development. Other studies of the folktale admirable for their attention to personality, milieu, and culture include: Richard M. Dorson, *Negro Folktales in Michigan* (Cambridge: Harvard University Press, 1956); Melville J. and Frances S. Herskovits, *Dahomean Narrative: A Cross-Cultural Analysis* (Evanston: Northwestern University Press, 1966; completed 1958); Melville Jacobs, *The Content and Style of an Oral Literature: Clackamas Chinook Myths* (Chicago: University of Chicago Press, 1959); Daniel J. Crowley, *I Could Talk Old-Story Good: Creativity in Bahamian Folklore*, Folklore Studies 17 (Berkeley: University of California Press, 1966); Ruth Finnegan, *Limba Stories and Storytelling* (Oxford: Oxford University Press, 1967); Jerome R. Mintz, *Legends of the Hasidim: An Introduction to Hasidic Culture and Oral Tradition in the New World* (Chicago: University of Chicago Press, 1968); and Peter Seitel, *See So That We May See: Performances and Interpretations of Traditional Tales from Tanzania* (Bloomington: Indiana University Press, 1980). Leonard Roberts' *Up Cutshin and Down Greasy: Folkways of a Kentucky Mountain Family* (Lexington: University of Kentucky Press, 1959) sets a family's stories and songs within its life and so sheds tangential light upon his major collections of tales from the same region: *South from Hell-fer-Sartin* (Berea: Council of the Southern Mountains, 1964; 1st pub. 1955); and *Old Greasybeard: Tales from the Cumberland Gap* (Hatboro: Folklore Associates, 1969).

5. In the terms developed by Dan Ben-Amos in the concluding essay in his *Folklore Genres*, A.F.S. Bibliographical and Special Series 26 (Austin: University of Texas Press, 1976; 1st pub. 1969, 1971), I have ordered the works of art in this book according to ethnic genres rather than analytical categories. Ben-Amos has amplified his argument in "The Concepts of Genre in Folklore," in Juha Pentikäinen and Tuula Juurikka, eds., *Folk Narrative Research*, Studia Fennica 20 (Helsinki: Finnish Literary Society, 1976), pp. 30–43, and exemplified his approach in "Folklore in African Society," *Research in African Literatures* 6, no. 2 (1975): 165–98; and "Generic Distinctions in the Aggadah," in Frank Talmage, ed., *Studies in Jewish Folklore* (Cambridge: Association for Jewish Studies, 1980), pp. 45–71. His thinking on genre and the writings by Hymes cited in note 6, below, are essential to understanding the paper in which Ben-Amos defines folklore as "artistic communication in small groups." The rich implications of his essay are more important than its problems, and it stands as a signal piece for post-1964 scholarship: "Toward a Definition of Folklore in Context," the first paper in the landmark volume edited by Américo Paredes and Richard Bauman, *Toward New Perspectives in Folklore*, A.F.S. Bibliographical and Special Series 23 (Austin: University of Texas Press, 1972), pp. 3–15.

6. The key text is Dell Hymes, *Foundations in Sociolinguistics: An Ethnographic Approach* (Philadelphia: University of Pennsylvania Press, 1974). To understand the rise of performance theory in folklore, you will also want to read the original versions of Hymes' papers. Though his idea began to see publication in 1961, a pair of papers published in 1964 provide the classic source: "Directions in (Ethno-) Linguistic Theory," in A. Kimball Romney and Roy Goodwin D'Andrade, eds., *Transcultural Studies in Cognition*, American Anthropologist, 66, no. 3, 2 (Menasha: American Anthropological Association, 1964), pp. 6–56; "Introduction: Toward Ethnographies of Communication," in John J. Gumperz and Dell Hymes, eds., *The Ethnography of Communication*, American Anthropologist, 66, no. 6, 2 (Menasha: American Anthropological Association, 1964), pp. 1–34. Two of Hymes' later papers oriented to folklorists must be read: "Breakthrough into Performance," in Dan Ben-Amos and Kenneth S. Goldstein, eds., *Folklore Performance and Communication* (The Hague:

Mouton, 1975), pp. 11–74; and "Folklore's Nature and the Sun's Myth," *Journal of American Folklore* 88, no. 350 (1975): 345–69. Hymes' power is more than a matter of historical understanding and the ability to formulate wide concerns into logical theoretical formulas; it is a matter of purpose and commitment. To understand his thought, the introduction to his *Reinventing Anthropology* (New York: Pantheon, 1973), entitled, "The Use of Anthropology: Critical, Political, Personal," is essential, as are the essays he brings together in *Language in Education: Ethnolinguistic Essays*, Language and Ethnography Series (Washington: Center for Applied Linguistics, 1980). A major influence on Hymes is Kenneth Burke, and especially the forewords and first essay of Burke's *The Philosophy of Literary Form: Studies in Symbolic Action* (Berkeley: University of California Press, 1973; 1st ed. 1941). I have also found Burke stimulating, especially his *A Grammar of Motives* (Berkeley: University of California Press, 1969; 1st ed. 1945). The ethnopoetic dimension of Hymes' contribution will be cited below in Chapter 2, note 1; a sense of his impact and of the utility of his sociolinguistic concept for folklore can be found in the unusually valuable anthology edited by Richard Bauman and Joel Sherzer, *Explorations in the Ethnography of Speaking* (Cambridge: Cambridge University Press, 1974), and in Richard Bauman's *Verbal Art as Performance* (Rowley: Newbury House, 1978).

7. James Deetz, *The Dynamics of Stylistic Change in Arikara Ceramics*, Illinois Studies in Anthropology 4 (Urbana: University of Illinois Press, 1965); *Invitation to Archaeology* (Garden City: Natural History Books, 1967); *In Small Things Forgotten: The Archeology of Early American Life* (Garden City: Anchor Books, 1977). Deetz has also edited an anthology containing major theoretical essays on artifactual analysis: *Man's Imprint from the Past: Readings in the Methods of Archaeology* (Boston: Little, Brown, 1971).

8. Robert Plant Armstrong, *The Affecting Presence: An Essay in Humanistic Anthropology* (Urbana: University of Illinois Press, 1971); *Wellspring: On the Myth and Source of Culture* (Berkeley: University of California Press, 1975); *The Powers of Presence: Consciousness, Myth, and Affecting Presence* (Philadelphia: University of Pennsylvania Press, 1981). I reviewed Armstrong's brave, exciting venture as "Source for a New Anthropology," *Book Forum* 2, no. 1 (1976): 70–77.

9. Fred Kniffen's early and continuing interest in American Indian culture and geography should not be forgotten; a fine example is *Pomo Geography*, U.C. Publications in American Archaeology and Ethnology 36, 6 (Berkeley: University of California Press, 1939). Kniffen wrote the seminal paper on American house form, "Louisiana House Types," *Annals of the Association of American Geographers* 26 (1936): 179–93, then he gave us the clearest statement of the rationale for the geographic study of material culture, "Folk Housing: Key to Diffusion," *Annals of the Association of American Geographers* 55, no. 4 (1965): 549–77. He has written an eloquent bridge between folklore and geography, another crucial area of academic connection: "American Cultural Geography and Folklife," in Don Yoder, ed., *American Folklife* (Austin: University of Texas Press, 1976), pp. 51–70. Once he let me co-author a paper with him, "Building in Wood in the Eastern United States: A Time-Place Perspective," *The Geographical Review* 56, no. 1 (1966): 40–66. Gene Wilhelm prepared a list of Kniffen's publications and commented on them in *Pioneer America* 5, no. 1 (1973): 16–22.

10. As revealed in the bibliography published in one of the festschrifts for him, E. Estyn Evans is an archaeologist, geographer, historian, and folklorist who, though the master of Irish geography, has written about other places as well: R. H. Bu-

chanan, Emrys Jones, and Desmond McCourt, eds., *Man and His Habitat: Essays Presented to Emyr Estyn Evans* (London: Routledge & Kegan Paul, 1971), pp. 264–76. Evans' books on Irish folk culture are the basic works on the subject: *Irish Heritage: The Landscape, The People, and Their Work* (Dundalk: W. Tempest, Dundalgan Press, 1963; 1st pub. 1942); *Irish Folk Ways* (New York: Devin-Adair, 1957). He has written a magnificent, sweeping essay on Ireland, *The Personality of Ireland: Habitat, Heritage and History* (Cambridge: Cambridge University Press, 1973), and a superb local study, *Mourne Country: Landscape and Life in South Down* (Dundalk: W. Tempest, Dundalgan Press, 1967; 1st pub. 1951). This last work in particular inspired me, but with my early training in cultural anthropology I drifted in the field naturally in the direction of my American ethnographic predecessors in Ireland: Conrad Arensberg, *The Irish Countryman* (Garden City: Natural History Press, 1968; 1st pub. 1937); Conrad M. Arensberg and Solon T. Kimball, *Family and Community in Ireland* (Cambridge: Harvard University Press, 1968; 1st ed. 1940); John C. Messenger, *Inis Beag: Isle of Ireland*, Case Studies in Cultural Anthropology (New York: Holt, Rinehart & Winston, 1969). Robin Fox had not yet published his admirable *The Tory Islanders: A People of the Celtic Fringe* (Cambridge: Cambridge University Press, 1978). In a sense my work is suspended between, merging aspects of an Irish geographical tradition with an American anthropological tradition, but it is fundamentally folkloristic, for I begin at texts, at forms created by the people themselves, and move through them to the culture and the environment, and swing from the culture and the environment back to the texts, while feeling toward the meanings in works of art and attempting to gain some understanding of the world as viewed from Ballymenone.

11. Neither Irish nor a historian, I needed help while writing and was fortunate that scholars had worked to prepare many of the aids I required. Seán Ó Súilleabháin's *A Handbook of Irish Folklore* (Hatboro: Folklore Associates, 1963; 1st pub. 1942) is essential. The old historians proved invaluable. Geoffrey Keating's wonderful history, written in Irish between 1620 and 1634, has been Englished several times. A good scholarly translation is that of David Comyn and Patrick S. Dinneen, Irish Texts Society 4, 8, 9, 15 (London: David Nutt for the Irish Texts Society, 1902, 1908, 1908, 1914). In the introduction to the first volume (pp. viii–ix), Comyn calls O'Connor's translation of 1724 "unsatisfactory." Still I used Dermod O'Connor, trans., *Keating's General History of Ireland* (Dublin: James Duffy, 1861), because it was almost certainly the version that influenced the men and masters of Fermanagh during their construction of their own history. John O'Donovan, trans. and ed., *Annals of the Kingdom of Ireland by the Four Masters from the Earliest Period to the Year 1616*, 7 vols. (Dublin: Hodges, Smith, 1854), written in Irish between 1632 and 1636 and edited by a great nineteenth-century scholar, is both basic for study and great reading (hereafter referred to as the *Four Masters*). An understanding of political and military history is necessary for anyone studying in Northern Ireland, and Robert Kee's *The Green Flag: A History of Irish Nationalism* (London: Weidenfeld & Nicolson, 1972) proved constantly helpful. So did Henry Boylan's *A Dictionary of Irish Biography* (Dublin: Gill & Macmillan, 1978). No one in Ballymenone speaks Irish, but their English and mine are not identical, and I was helped to understanding many words that were new to me by reference to Patrick S. Dinneen's *Irish-English Dictionary* (Dublin: Educational Company of Ireland for the Irish Texts Society, 1970; 1st pub. 1927). Fermanagh is blessed with an excellent local history, Peadar Livingstone's *The Fermanagh Story* (Enniskillen: Cumann Seanchais Chlochair, 1969). There is a fine

guide to the County's monuments in Alistair Rowan, *North West Ulster: The Counties of Londonderry, Donegal, Fermanagh, and Tyrone*, Buildings of Ireland (Harmondsworth: Penguin, 1979), which includes a good essay on "Vernacular Housing" by Alan Gailey. The County's Town has a fine history: William C. Trimble, *The History of Enniskillen*, 3 vols. (Enniskillen: W. Trimble, 1919–21). And it has a good guide: Hugh Dixon, *Ulster Architectural Heritage Society List of Historic Buildings, Groups of Buildings, Areas of Architectural Importance in the Town of Enniskillen* (Belfast: Ulster Architectural Heritage Society, 1973).

12. W. G. Hoskins stands in England much as E. Estyn Evans does in Ireland. He has written works grand in scale; *The Making of the English Landscape* (Harmondsworth: Penguin, 1970; 1st pub. 1955) is a vast, inspirational volume. And he has written fine local studies, of which I like best *The Midland Peasant: The Economic and Social History of a Leicestershire Village* (London: Macmillan, 1965; 1st pub. 1957). His work on his native county, *Devon* (London: Collins, 1954) and *Old Devon* (London: Pan, 1966), probably best illustrates his idea of local history; as Hoskins defines it, local history is close to what we all should be doing. E. P. Thompson and Christopher Hill move me because of their willingness to study past people in their own terms rather than as accidental vehicles of historical development, and because of the clarity and decency of their commitment: E. P. Thompson, *The Making of the English Working Class* (New York: Vintage, 1963); *Whigs and Hunters: The Origin of the Black Act* (New York: Pantheon, 1975); Christopher Hill, *The English Revolution, 1640: An Essay* (London: Lawrence & Wishart, 1976; 1st pub. 1940); *The World Turned Upside Down: Radical Ideas During the English Revolution* (New York: Viking, 1972); *God's Englishman: Oliver Cromwell and the English Revolution* (New York: Harper & Row, 1972); *Change and Continuity in Seventeenth-Century England* (Cambridge: Harvard University Press, 1975). Among Raymond Williams' many fine books, the ones that most impressed me as I wrote were *The Country and the City* (New York: Oxford University Press, 1973) and *Marxism and Literature* (Oxford: Oxford University Press, 1977).

13. Claude Lévi-Strauss' mode of narrative analysis, which turns form into meaning, is best understood by reading without haste or worry through the volumes of the *Mythologiques*, but he has given the reader overt direction in chaps. 11 and 12 of *Structural Anthropology*, trans. Claire Jacobson and Brooke Grundfest Schoepf (Garden City: Doubleday, 1963), and in the "Overture" to *The Raw and the Cooked: Introduction to a Science of Mythology*, vol. 1, trans. John and Doreen Weightman (New York: Harper & Row, 1969; 1st pub. 1964). It is not only method but style and purpose that make Lévi-Strauss compelling. His key work, I think, is *The Savage Mind* (Chicago: University of Chicago Press, 1966; 1st pub. 1962), which is best read before the *Mythologiques* and after these books in sequence: *Tristes Tropiques*, trans. John and Doreen Weightman (New York: Atheneum, 1975; 1st pub. 1955), then *Totemism*, trans. Rodney Needham (Boston: Beacon, 1963; 1st pub. 1962).

14. Jean-Paul Sartre's works form a sometimes vague matrix for my own thinking which is not properly existential or Sartrean. The great works are: *Being and Nothingness: An Essay on Phenomenological Ontology*, trans. Hazel E. Barnes (New York: Philosophical Library, 1965; 1st pub. 1943); and *Critique of Dialectic Reason*, trans. Alan Sheridan-Smith (London: NLB, 1976; 1st pub. 1960), which lacks the prefatory essay separately published as *Search for a Method*, trans. Hazel E. Barnes (New York: Alfred A. Knopf, 1963). In addition, of particular importance for me are: *What Is Literature?* trans. Bernard Frechtman (New York: Philosophical Library,

1949; 1st pub. 1947); and *Between Existentialism and Marxism*, trans. John Mathews (New York: William Morrow, 1976; 1st pub. 1972), secs. 1 and 5. I reread Albert Camus' *The Rebel*, trans. Anthony Bower (London: Hamish Hamilton, 1953; 1st pub. 1951) while I wrote and was reminded of how, long ago, he like Sartre influenced me deeply before I was capable of resistance.

15. Shan F. Bullock, *After Sixty Years* (London: Sampson Low & Marston, n.d.; 1st pub. 1931), pp. 32–34, 126–28, 133. Sean O'Faolain, *An Irish Journey* (London: Longmans, Green, 1940), pp. 241–42; though he never met an Orangeman, I have, and I think O'Faolain was right to view the Northern Troubles as more economic than religious and to see the deepest rift as cutting between people and leaders, not between Catholics and Protestants.

1 Crossing Drumbargy Brae

1. My thinking has developed through the study of artifacts. Its record is a series of works oriented to different audiences, all of which contain fitful argument and elaborate bibliography surrounding many of the ideas I assert simply in this book: "William Houck, Maker of Pounded Ash Adirondack Pack-Baskets," *Keystone Folklore Quarterly* 12, no. 1 (1967): 23–34, reprinted in *Studies in Traditional American Crafts* 3 (1980): 3–34, a folkloristic study of a man and his craft; "The Types of the Southern Mountain Cabin," in Jan H. Brunvand, *The Study of American Folklore* (New York: W. W. Norton, 1968; reprinted 1978), pp. 391–420, a folkloristic classification and annotation of architectural forms; *Pattern in the Material Folk Culture of the Eastern United States*, Monographs in Folklore and Folklife 1 (Philadelphia: University of Pennsylvania Press, 1969; reprinted 1980), an essay on regionalism designed to connect folklore and cultural geography; "Folk Art," in Dorson, *Folklore and Folklife*, pp. 253–80, a folkloristic definition of traditional art; "Structure and Function, Folklore and the Artifact," *Semiotica* 7, no. 4 (1973): 313–51, an attempt to integrate structural and functional modes of folkloristic and anthropological analysis; "The Variation of Concepts Within Tradition: Barn Building in Otsego County, New York," in H. J. Walker and W. G. Haag, eds., *Man and Cultural Heritage: Papers in Honor of Fred B. Kniffen*, Geoscience and Man 5 (Baton Rouge: Louisiana State University School of Geoscience, 1974), pp. 177–234, a culturogeographic survey of technology in one locality; *Folk Housing in Middle Virginia: A Structural Analysis of Historic Artifacts* (Knoxville: University of Tennessee Press, 1976; reprinted 1979), an application of structural method to artifacts designed to display the utility of material culture and structuralism for writing history; "Archaeology and Folklore: Common Anxieties, Common Hopes," in Leland Ferguson, ed., *Historical Archaeology and the Importance of Material Things*, Special Publications 2 (Columbia: Society for Historical Archaeology, 1977), pp. 23–35, a comparison of recent developments in folklore and archaeology designed to draw their practitioners together; "Meaningful Things and Appropriate Myths: The Artifact's Place in American Studies," *Prospects* 3 (1977): 1–49, an essay on the need for artifactual study in history addressed to the humanistic scholar; "Folkloristic Study of the American Artifact: Objects and Objectives," in Richard M. Dorson, ed., *Handbook of American Folklore* (New York: McGraw-Hill, in press), rationale of the folkloristic study of the artifact. Though those works were written to describe and interpret artifacts, composing them I was led to the general principles I use in studying verbal as well as material art, so they can lead you from this book to others and toward the objects, methods, and goals I consider of greatest importance.

2. Historians who believe they can conduct their research without attending to developments in social science, and social scientists who believe they can study human beings synchronically, ahistorically, will be taken far toward an end to their delusions by reading chaps. 2–5 of Fernand Braudel, *On History*, trans. Sarah Matthews (Chicago: University of Chicago Press, 1980). Serious contemplation of the world will make historians of sociologists, sociologists of historians, amateurs and intellectuals of both.

3. The crucial essays are those William Morris collected in *Hopes and Fears for Art* (London: Ellis & White, 1882) and in *Signs of Change* (London: Reeves & Turner, 1888). Many of them had been and would be printed separately: *The Decorative Arts, Their Relation to Modern Life and Progress* (London: Ellis & White, 1878), later titled "The Lesser Arts"; *The Art of the People* (Chicago: Ralph Fletcher Seymour, 1902); *The Aims of Art* (London: Commonweal, 1887); *Useful Work Versus Useless Toil*, Socialist Platform 2 (London: Socialist League, 1885). They were brought together in *The Collected Works* (London: Longmans, 1910–15), vols. 22 and 23, and some have been anthologized—at an early date in *William Morris: Poet, Artist, Socialist*, Social Science Library 5 (New York: Humboldt, 1891), and in these accessible modern paperbacks: A. L. Morton, ed., *Political Writings of William Morris* (London: Lawrence & Wishart, 1973); and Asa Briggs, ed., *Willlliam Morris: Selected Writings and Designs* (Harmondsworth: Penguin, 1962). His ideas formed with near perfection in *A Dream of John Ball* (London: Reeves & Turner, 1888) and *News from Nowhere* (London: Reeves & Turner, 1891), both of which blend a gentle sense of beauty with manly hope and mature irony. From his relation to old artifacts, his wish to preserve them unruined and to create fresh and better things out of them, we can get a good sense of Morris' idea of historical responsibility: his letters on the Society for the Protection of Ancient Buildings in chap. 23 of Briggs' anthology; *A Note by William Morris on His Aims in Founding the Kelmscott Press* (Hammersmith: Kelmscott Press, 1898); *Some Hints on Pattern-designing* (London: Longmans, 1899); *Art and Its Producers, and The Arts and Crafts of Today* (London: Longmans, 1901). His designs accompany his essays and match his novels in their power to express his ideas. A contemporary defense of the movement of which Morris was the central figure can be found in Walter Hamilton's *The Aesthetic Movement in England* (London: Reeves & Turner, 1882). Appraisals of Morris' design by men who knew him include Walter Crane, *William Morris to Whistler: Papers and Addresses on Art and Crafts and the Commonweal* (London: G. Bell, 1911), chaps. 1–5, and H. Halliday Sparling, *The Kelmscott Press and William Morris Master-Craftsman* (London: Macmillan, 1924), while historical assessments for later days can be found in Nikolaus Pevsner, *Pioneers of Modern Design: From William Morris to Walter Gropius* (Harmondsworth: Penguin, 1977; 1st ed. 1936), and Ray Watkinson, *William Morris as Designer* (New York: Reinhold, 1967). Morris' enduring relevance has invited much biographical study. The major early work is J. W. Mackail, *The Life of William Morris*, 2 vols. (London: Longmans, Green, 1899). The major work for our day is E. P. Thompson, *William Morris: Romantic to Revolutionary* (New York: Pantheon, 1977; 1st ed. 1955). Thompson offers comments on how Morris' great historical imagination was directed to the future (pp. 28, 56, 235–36, 641–67, 739, 778, 809), and he stresses the impact of Iceland on Morris (pp. 175–88). Morris' own monument to Iceland was editing and translating the sagas with Eiríkr Magnússon, which carried after his death into the six volumes of *The Saga Library* (London: Bernard Quaritch, 1891–1905).

4. In the first chapter of *Reconstructing Historical Communities* (Cambridge: Cambridge University Press, 1977), Alan Macfarlane provides a clear statement of the

difficulties of defining a community. My experience in Ballymenone had this conclusion: the people there have created a community and it can be mapped, but they have created no documents of any kind, neither written nor artifactual, that would enable a future historian to reconstruct their community precisely.

5. Good arguments in behalf of the need for hypotheses can be found in Robert K. Merton, *On Theoretical Sociology: Five Essays, Old and New* (New York: Free Press, 1967), pp. 147–49; and in Robert Brown, *Explanation in Social Science* (Chicago: Aldine, 1963), p. 171. Only the chimera of synchrony allows the preservation of a connection between prediction and proof in human affairs. Hypotheses help scholars order their own thought, and predictions are of great use in refining understanding, but they cannot "prove" anything. A prediction can come true when the reason for the prediction was unstated or falsely formulated, in which case the method is magic, not science. What matters is not the prediction but the structure of explanation beneath the prediction, and that can hold true even if the prediction does not come true, because the future is not to know: people are willful, they do not exist outside of irreversible time, and they can change radically between the time the hypothesis was created and the time it is tested.

6. Eileen McCracken, "The Woodlands of Ulster in the Early Seventeenth Century," *Ulster Journal of Archaeology*, 3d series, 10 (1947): 17. In her *The Irish Woods Since Tudor Times: Distribution and Exploitation*, Institute of Irish Studies (Newton-Abbot: David & Charles, 1971), p. 55, she isolates the Lough Erne basin as one of the major early woodlands of Ulster. Howard T. Masterson, "Land Use Patterns and Farming Practice in County Fermanagh, 1609–1845," *Clogher Record* 8, no. 1 (1969): 56–88, shows the shores of Lough Erne as wooded in the seventeenth century (p. 60) and argues (p. 66) that the greatest visual effect of the Plantation was clearing the forests.

7. Arthur Young, *A Tour in Ireland; With General Observations on the Present State of That Kingdom: Made in the Years 1776, 1777, and 1778. And Brought Down to the End of 1779* (London: T. Cadell & J. Dodsley, 1780), 1:166–75, esp. 170. Mr. and Mrs. S. C. Hall, *Ireland: Its Scenery, Character, &c.* (London: Hall, Virtue, [1850]; 1st pub. 1841–43), 3:182. Bullock, *After Sixty Years*, pp. 2–3, 96, 46–47.

8. Leslie Symons, ed., *Land Use in Northern Ireland: The General Report of the Survey Compiled in the Department of Geography, the Queen's University of Belfast* (London: University of London Press, 1963), esp. pp. 238–39. John M. Mogey, *Rural Life in Northern Ireland: Five Regional Studies Made for the Northern Ireland Council of Social Service* (London: Oxford University Press, 1947), chap. 3. "The Diocesan Census of 1975" of Clogher gives the population of Cleenish Parish, in which lies Ballymenone, as 1,494 Catholics, 450 others (*Clogher Record*, 1977, p. 297).

9. Ballymenone? In the year 1512, Donnell O'Neill attacked Gill-Patrick Maguire. It was one of those numberless forays that brought a little pleasure into the lives of Ulster's old warrior-princes. O'Neill of Tyrone broke deeply into Maguire's Fermanagh, seizing spoils, "but was afterwards defeated, and stripped of those spoils. Many of his party . . . were slain and drowned between the townland of Bun-abhann and Inis-mor." So it is told by the *Four Masters* (5:1318–19). Their editor, the great antiquarian John O'Donovan, says in a footnote that Bun-abhann means the river's mouth, and the place is "now Bunowen, the name of a level district at the mouth of the River Arney, in the baroney of Clanawley, on the west side of Lough Erne in the county of Fermanagh." Nearly twenty years before his publication of the *Four Masters*, O'Donovan was serving with the Ordnance Survey, col-

lecting local traditions to help place accurate lines and names on the map of Ireland, and he wrote from Fermanagh on February 27, 1835, that the place of battle was called Baile-Bun-Abhann and that the name "is yet retained in Munone, a level district west of Upper Lough Erne, where the Arney River falls into the lake. The peasants of Fermanagh frequently pronounce M for B, as in this instance of Munone for Bunone, and Lismelaw for Lisbelaw." He then asks, "Does the name Ballybunone or Ballymanone or Bunone or Manone appear on the Maps of Fermanagh anywhere in the district around the Arney River?" Later, commenting upon a negative reply, O'Donovan says, "The name exists in the Country, but not as a Townland or Parish name, but as a natural division." Quoted from Michael O'Flanagan, ed., *Letters Containing Information Relative to the Antiquities of the County Fermanagh Collected During the Progress of the Ordnance Survey in 1834–35* (Bray: Privately printed, 1928), pp. 86–87. As in 1512 and 1835, Ballymenone lies west of the Lough at the Arney's mouth across from Inishmore. It remains "a natural division," entered on no map.

10. Charles S. King, ed., *Henry's Upper Lough Erne in 1739* (Dublin: William McGee, 1892), p. 49, Swadlinbar; he describes the Arney on pp. 52–53. In "On Barbarous Denominations in Ireland" (1728), Jonathan Swift recommends the elimination of the Irish language and the unpronounceable name of Irish places, then comes for an example upon a "famous town, where the worst iron in the kingdom is made, and it is called *'Swandlingbar,'*" the name being the "witty conceit of four gentlemen, who ruined themselves with this iron project. *Sw.* stands for Swift, *And.* for Sanders, *Ling*, for Darling, and *Bar* for Barry." *The Works of Jonathan Swift, DD., Dean of St. Patrick's, Dublin* (Edinburgh: Archibald Constable, 1814), 7:362. Peter Flanagan told me (10/29/72) Swanlinbar was named by and for three gentlemen: Swann, Lynn, and Barr.

11. The population of Enniskillen comes from *The Ulster Year Book: The Official Handbook of Northern Ireland: 1972* (Belfast: Her Majesty's Stationery Office, 1972), p. 7 (table).

12. My earlier book on the people of Ballymenone is *All Silver and No Brass: An Irish Christmas Mumming* (Bloomington: Indiana University Press; Dublin: Dolmen Press, 1976). It usefully accompanies this one, expanding on some ideas within it, introducing others, and I will draw its topic, mumming, into my argument to bring the books together. Alan Gailey's *Irish Folk Drama* (Cork: Mercier Press, 1969) excellently surveys mumming for all of Ireland.

13. Douglas Hyde recommended listening. The first time a story is told, he said, sit and smoke, then after it is over, ask if you can write it down: *Beside the Fire: A Collection of Irish Gaelic Folk Stories* (London: David Nutt, 1890), pp. xlvi–xlvii. Though I owned a machine capable of recording the tale without slowing the teller, that was still my practice: to hear the story initially in company, in a ceili, then to return. Like Hyde, I wanted first to hear the story, to get it in my mind unconfused by the intrusions of recording. I had other motives too. I wanted to hear live stories, stories enjoyed by their tellers and audiences, and I returned to record them so I could avoid the difficulties that have undermined attempts to analyze narrative content. Record a few isolated stories, and you will find them too easy to interpret; they will lead you anywhere or nowhere, and usually they will lead you back to your own scholastic preoccupations. But entire repertories are too sturdy to maul, so complex that their elements interlock, containing and directing quests for meaning. I hope to follow this book, in which all of Ballymenone's historical stories appear, with another that will include all the tales the District's tellers call experiences, ex-

ploits, bids, and pants, so that someone whose interests are different from mine, psychoanalytic perhaps, would have one community's entire repertory of live tales available for contemplation.

2 Silence, Speech, Story, Song

1. The first reason to think of spoken tales as verse is to improve transcriptions, as Dennis Tedlock discusses in "On the Translation of Style in Oral Narrative," in Paredes and Bauman, eds., *Toward New Perspectives in Folklore*, pp. 114–33. The idea is exemplified in the journal *Alcheringa* and Tedlock's superb *Finding the Center: Narrative Poetry of the Zuni Indians from Performances in the Zuni by Andrew Peynetsa and Walter Sanchez* (New York: Dial, 1972). As is proper, modern collections are being presented with increasing frequency in some variety of Tedlock's scheme, Seitel's fine *See So That We May See*, for instance. Because the stories of Ballymenone differ from those of the American Indians, my own modification is extreme. I base my transcriptions on prose rather than poetry, treating the lines as though they were tiny paragraphs, so they can flow easily into the long, thick, uncadenced sections. Dell Hymes has extended the idea into a variety of analysis of prosody. His thoughts are stated clearly and inspirationally in "Discovering Oral Performance and Measured Verse in American Indian Narrative," *New Literary History* 8 (1976/77): 431–57, and applied in "Verse Analysis of a Wasco Text: Hiram Smith's 'At' Unaqa'," *International Journal of American Linguistics* 46, no. 2 (1980): 65–77. For its length, Irish literature resists trim classification into poetry and prose. Few of the ancient tales are, in Hyde's words, "pure prose," for they contain (like Icelandic sagas) sections in verse, and reading them one discovers "prose" patches so heightened as to invite the words rhythmically to the lips. They were spoken aloud and must have veered from throat to ear in sounds that sometimes neared common speech and other times became—as Hyde guessed—song. Their variable spirit is softened but not lost in the performance of the modern rural storyteller. Conversely, some early poems consisted of lists versified to aid the memory, which are "hardly poetry," according to Myles Dillon, and other early poems lacked the metrical rigor of most bardic verse and seem to have grown out of decorated prose: Douglas Hyde, *A Literary History of Ireland from Earliest Times to the Present Day* (London: Ernest Benn, 1967; 1st pub. 1899), pp. 398–401; Myles Dillon and Nora K. Chadwick, *The Celtic Realms* (New York: New American Library, 1967), pp. 226–55; Kuno Meyer, *Miscellanea Hibernica*, U.I. Studies in Language and Literature 2, 4 (Urbana: University of Illinois, 1917), pp. 18–27. The mixing of prose and poetry remains a feature of Irish literature. In *Joysprick: An Introduction to the Language of James Joyce* (New York: Harcourt Brace Jovanovich, 1975), Anthony Burgess classes writers of prose into two types which parallel the two types of reader described by Roland Barthes, *The Pleasure of the Text*, trans. Richard Miller (New York: Hill & Wang, 1975). Joyce fulfills the second of Burgess' types in his concern for words, his creation of a prose that is poetic, musical. The Joyce whose late prose often breaks into song was born of Irish speech, so he both completes and influences the love for sound found in other modern Irish writers. Sean O'Casey's autobiographies, like Joyce's or Kavanagh's, are more than trouble for those who need a clear division between fiction and fact, between the genres of the novel and the autobiography; freed by Joyce, shaped by the spoken word, the prose of O'Casey's autobiographies is effortlessly repetitious and rhythmic, full of quotations from verse, and occasionally it forms on

the page as poetry—in the second chapter of the first volume, *I Knock at the Door* (New York: Macmillan, 1949; 1st pub. 1939), for example. The problem comes clearly into the open in anthologies of Irish poetry by Irish writers who extract the verses from ancient "prose" and more: in the notes to *A Book of Irish Verse Selected from Modern Writers* (London: Methuen, 1895), William Butler Yeats provides the prose introduction to Ferguson's translation of "Deirdre's Lament," given on pp. 99–102. Seán O'Faoláin leaves together the prose and poetry of O'Keefe's translation of "Sweeney the Mad," in *The Silver Branch: A Collection of the Best Old Irish Lyrics, Variously Translated* (New York: Viking, 1938), pp. 106–18, then comments, "I am very doubtful about including this . . . ; the whole thing is more like fiction than poetry, but as will be seen, poetry is so dramatic in Ireland that it is hard to say where lyric ends and something else, that is not lyric, begins" (p. 149). Padraic Colum includes a little set of graceful proverbial phrases, not poetry but not prose either, in *An Anthology of Irish Verse: The Poetry of Ireland from Mythological Times to the Present* (New York: Liveright, 1948), p. 45. Freest and best is John Montague's *The Book of Irish Verse: An Anthology of Irish Poetry from the Sixth Century to the Present* (New York: Macmillan, 1976), in which he presents modern prose reworkings of old poems by James Stephens and Flann O'Brien (pp. 79–80, 83–84) and prose settings or bridges for ancient verse translated by himself and Thomas Kinsella (pp. 77–78, 84–86); most adventuresomely—but correctly—he includes a piece of prose by Samuel Beckett from *Watt* (p. 296). Irish speakers of art, old bards, modern novelists, and country tale tellers, unite in the confusion they provide to people who feel a need to keep prose and poetry separate.

2. Our objects, modes, and purposes differ, but there is a consonance between my conclusions and those reported by William Labov, "The Transformation of Experience in Narrative Syntax," chapter 9 in his *Language in the Inner City: Studies in the Black English Vernacular*, Conduct and Communication 3 (Philadelphia: University of Pennsylvania Press, 1972), for he investigates dimensions of narrative beyond the sequencing of events. Melville Jacobs provides an excellent account of aspects of tales other than plot—"gross architecture"—in "Areal Spread of Indian Oral Genre Features in the Northwest States," *Journal of the Folklore Institute* 9, no. 1 (1972): 10–17.

3. In *Lady Gregory: A Literary Portrait* (London: Secker & Warburg, 1966; 1st pub. 1961), Elizabeth Coxhead not only provides a fine introduction to Lady Gregory, but also argues in her behalf, contending correctly that Lady Gregory has been underestimated and deserves more attention as an artist. The same can be said and should be done for Lady Gregory as a folklorist. She was not a modern folklorist, but viewed in the light of note 2 to my Preface, she remarkably foreshadows later developments. In *Poets and Dreamers: Studies and Translations from the Irish* (Dublin: Hodges, Figgis, 1903) Lady Gregory fully anticipates biographical studies of traditional artists, such as those of Ives, in her search for Raftery (chap. 1); she correctly treats recent creations as genuine folklore in "Boer Ballads in Ireland"; and she leaves a collection of tales intact rather than rearranging them by arbitrary scholastic class in "Workhouse Dreams." In *A Book of Saints and Wonders* (Dundrum: Dun Emer Press, 1906) Lady Gregory gracefully encounters the Catholicism of her informants as some of her fellow Protestants could not; see Coxhead's comments on p. 119 and Lennox Robinson's in his edition of *Lady Gregory's Journals, 1916–1930* (New York: Macmillan, 1947), p. 12. Not all the selections in *Saints and Wonders* are folk stories, nor does Lady Gregory present them as such, but in some the clarity

and repetitive opening words give one the feel of a real narrator beyond the text; for example, "She Remembers the Poor" (pp. 12–13) and "He Is Waked by Angels" (p. 70). The texts in *The Kiltartan Wonder Book* (Dublin: Maunsel, [1910]) are cleansed for the reader's eye, but not rewritten. "I have not changed a word in these stories as they were told," but in a note at the end Lady Gregory is constrained to admit to slight collation, "because folk-lorists in these days are expected to be as exact as workers in any other science" (p. 105). Lady Gregory's great folklore book is *Visions and Beliefs in the West of Ireland*, Coole edition 1 (New York: Oxford University Press, 1970; 1st pub. 1920), in which she does not pluck the beliefs out and rearrange them into academic formulas, but leaves them in the words that clothed them when she heard them. Said Yeats in the second of his appended essays, "She was not guided by any theory of mine, but recorded what came, writing it out at each day's end and in the country dialect" (p. 311). She wrote, "When I began to gather these stories, I cared less for the evidence given in them than for the beautiful rhythmic sentences in which they were told. I had no theories, no case to prove, I but 'held up a clean mirror to tradition'" (p. 15). The result was a collection of texts as good as any published before the arrival of recording machines; I think especially fine ones can be found on pp. 34–35, 45–47, 107–9, 126, 208–9, 243, 293. The result was also a book that looks like another collection, but which, when read straight through, stands as a monument to a way of thinking. Lady Gregory's modesty and clear vision—"patience, reverence, and a good memory" are her terms—made her a great folklorist. Unshackled by convention, her interest expanded naturally in the field. I did not come to emphasize historical stories in this book to compensate for a failing in my discipline. I was led to them by the people of Ballymenone. But it is true that folklorists have emphasized imaginative and mystical literature over historical literature, that historical legends have been neglected, and the most important anticipation of my work in Ireland is Lady Gregory's *The Kiltartan History Book* (London: T. Fisher Unwin, 1926; 1st ed. 1909). In her notes to the expanded second edition, Lady Gregory says she came naturally to historical stories from collecting supernatural ones, that she could have called her book "Myths in the Making," that the passion for Irish history is owed to its being shut out of the schools, and she does not apologize for including new songs like "Kevin Barry" in her book of stories.

4. On ceilis: For a century—say 1865 to 1965—while fashions in analysis changed, the steady progress of folklore was directed by the goal set for Ireland in Hyde's preface to *Beside the Fire*: the collection and presentation of accurate texts. Now that victory is won. Professional folklorists have books that oblige them and tools that enable them to record texts well. So we can turn back to draw value from the tradition Hyde dismissed, that of "the novelists Carleton and Lover." They wrote in a genre called the sketch, the sentimentally manipulated, highly colored vignette based on reality. Our trouble with the sketch is its degree of manipulation: some are like short stories, others like ethnographic anecdotes. William Carleton's first published sketch, "The Lough Derg Pilgrim," was written in 1829, and with "some offensive passages . . . expunged" it remained in the many editions of his *Traits and Stories of the Irish Peasantry*, first published in separate numbers in 1842. In the introduction to the ninth edition (1869) he calls that sketch "a perfect transcript," and in his *Autobiography* he likens it to "a coloured photograph," absolutely true and authentic. The virtue of the sketch is that its author is more interested in life than in lore, so he reports tales which folklorists ignore because of the academic concerns of the moment, and he describes the tellers and their situations. Though Hyde cor-

rectly castigates others for not identifying their sources, he gives his readers little feel for his sources, little sense of their personalities or scenes. To gain some feel for early days, we have to learn to read through the flippant or pathetic surfaces of the sketch and find the truth its author observed. William Carleton, who attributed "extraordinary powers of . . . observation" to himself as a gift from God, began to present his *Traits and Stories* as tales told in a nighttime gathering of neighbors. That frame cramped him. The ethnographic information he wished to present did not suit stories told at a hearth, so he abandoned the frame at p. 144 of the first volume. How much easier it became for him to tell his own tale can be seen by comparing the information he provides on wakes and funerals before and after that point (pp. 105–13, 220–35). But the frame itself is information; it is a "kailyee," which he defines as "a friendly evening visit": *Traits and Stories of the Irish Peasantry* (London: William Trigg, 1869), 1:9–13, 48, 53; 2:77. For his ideas on the sketch: *Traits and Stories*, 1:xi, xvi, 237–70; 2:363; and Patrick Kavanagh, ed., *The Autobiography of William Carleton*, Fitzroy edition (London: MacGibbon & Kee, 1968; 1st ed. 1898), pp. 91–92, 96, 106–7, 128–29. Later observers in Carleton's native Tyrone provide accounts that tally with his. Rose Shaw describes the "kailyee" or "ceilidh" in *Carleton's Country* (Dublin: Talbot Press, 1930), pp. 21, 39–46, 56–57. Though they have the arranged look of her photographs, her sketches do show people chatting about the neighbors and entertaining visitors with story and song. Michael J. Murphy describes a "ceili" well in *Tyrone Folk Quest* (pp. 30–35) and tells more in "The Late Patrick McCullagh of Curraghinalt, Co. Tyrone," *Ulster Folklife* 7 (1961): 34–35. Introducing his fine collection *Now You're Talking . . . Folk Tales from the North of Ireland* (Belfast: Blackstaff Press, 1975), p. vii, Murphy, a native of Armagh, says stories are told in "ordinary dwelling houses which we know in Ulster as 'céilí-houses.'" Reminiscence touches the spirit of the sketch, turns its sentiment from humor to nostalgia, but preserves its veiled accuracy. Lynn Doyle recalls fully the pattern and content, the tea and mysterious tales of the "kailyie" of County Down, "a gathering of neighbours in friendly chat round a hearthside," in *An Ulster Childhood* (London: Duckworth, 1927; 1st pub. 1921), pp. 54–55, 143–51. Crossing Ulster, from east to west, we come upon Seumas MacManus in Donegal, a latter-day writer of sketches. Like Carleton, Ulster son of Catholic country people, who worked as a schoolmaster before achieving fame as a writer beyond his home, MacManus recalls in his autobiography, *The Rocky Road to Dublin* (New York: Devin-Adair, 1947), that nightvisiting in Donegal was called "rambling," but that when he went to Fermanagh he found the same activity called "céilidhing" (pp. 66–67, 229). Fermanagh's novelist, Shan F. Bullock, presents an excellent instance of "kaleying" in his autobiographical *By Thrasna River: The Story of a Townland* (London: Ward, Lock & Bowden, 1895), pp. 191–209. He and a friend begin an evening visit. As "ordinary *kaleyers*" they come up the lane, lift the latch "without any ceremony," and walk into the kitchen, "clean . . . full of the rosy turf blaze glittering on the shining tins on the dresser," where they are welcomed, and conversation moves from "the weather, local news, current politics" into richer topics and music. Robert Harbinson, evacuated from Belfast to Fermanagh during World War II, wrote a gentle reminiscence, *Song of Erne* (London: Faber & Faber, 1960), in which he defines the "ceili (pronounced kaylee)" as "an evening gathering" (p. 9) and describes ceilis full of songs, stories, and tea, attended by both Protestants and Catholics (pp. 131, 179, 190–95). The idea in the sketch and reminiscence is made rigorous in ethnography. The "cuaird" of Clare described by Arensberg, *Irish Countryman*, pp. 118–35, is comparable to the ceili of

Fermanagh, though more formalized as to time and participation. The "ceildhiing" in Rosemary Harris' fine ethnography of "Ballybeg" in western Ulster, *Prejudice and Tolerance in Ulster: A Study of Neighbours and "Strangers" in a Border Community*, Studies in Sociology (Manchester: Manchester University Press, 1972), pp. 105–7, compares closely with the District's informal practice. Hugh Brody, describing a composite parish in the West, defines the "ceilidh" as a party held "in a cottage . . . open to all the neighbours . . . based on singing, dancing, and storytelling" to which he connects ceilidhs thrown to repay workers and "nightwalking," casual visiting that corresponds to Ballymenone's current idea of the ceili: *Inishkillane: Change and Decline in the West of Ireland* (New York: Schocken, 1974), pp. 24–30.

5. The great West African epic *Sunjatta* ends with the bard upbraiding today's little men: D. T. Niane, *Sundiatta: An Epic of Old Mali*, trans. G. D. Pickett (London: Longman, 1965), p. 84; Gordon Innes, *Sunjatta: Three Mandinka Versions* (London: School of Oriental and African Studies, University of London, 1974), p. 99. In Milesian times, says Keating, *History of Ireland*, pp. 164–66, every nobleman retained antiquaries to preserve the family's deeds for transmission to future generations to inspire and shame them into courage.

6. Robin Flower tells of impromptu competitive poetry among the bards in *The Irish Tradition* (Oxford: Oxford University Press, 1978; 1st pub. 1947), pp. 96–98.

7. Formally, Ballymenone's tales of contest compare with many Afro-American stories, both animal tales in which rabbits outfox foxes and tales in the John cycle, in which a slave masters his master, many good examples of which can be found in Richard M. Dorson's *American Negro Folktales* (Greenwich: Fawcett, 1967), parts 1 and 2; see also Dorson's comments on pp. 18, 66–67, 124–25, 300–301.

8. Since folklorists usually push past stories of recent local characters searching for ancient international tales, and anthropologists look around them to examine the society stories build, though scholars often comment that such tales are common, texts of the stories—the things that interest the people themselves—are not common in the literature. Arthur J. Pollock, "A Folklore Collector in County Down," *Ulster Folklife* 1 (1955), says that in addition to supernatural tales, he heard "a host of humorous anecdotes concerned with local people," then gives one that conforms to the District's idea of the bid (pp. 14–15). A "joke" from Gortin in Tyrone, quite like a bid from Ballymenone, is given by K. M. Harris, "Extracts from the Committee's Collection (3)," *Ulster Folklife* 6 (1960): 30. Lawrence Millman visiting Inishbofin met Michael Jack Burke, who told him stories of imaginative local characters, two of which are patterned like bids: *Our Like Will Not Be There Again: Notes from the West of Ireland* (Boston: Little, Brown, 1977), pp. 190, 192. The best texts can be heard on a recording by Dáithí Connaughton and Manus O Boyle, *Geordie Hanna Sings* (Dublin: Eagrán, 1978), side A, band 2, where Hanna, the great singer from Derrytresk, County Tyrone, tells about a colorful man he knew and in describing him narrates two stories that would be called bids in Ballymenone. They sound a little strange, because the collector, properly wishing to keep his own voice off the record, does not respond with the little laugh the teller needs to help him pace his presentation, and Hanna hurries over the key comic lines to provide more orientation. As a result, the record preserves at once good stories and an artificial situation that highlights the need for an active listener. When the local man turns author, he extends into print the traditional interest in local characters, the fascination with personal eccentricity and excellence that typifies the little community which seems homogeneous, even bland, from without, but diverse and exciting from within. A

good example from Fermanagh is William K. Parke, *Glimpses of Old Derrygonnelly* (Monaghan: R. & S., 1978), "Local Characters," pp. 61–62, in which known people are profiled and then stories about them are told which would be called bids in Ballymenone. Benedict Kiely, the superb writer from Tyrone, displays a constant interest in the characters of his locality, expressing in fine literature the idea in bids and exploits: the author's concern for his place, its history and people, his simultaneous interest in the collective and the personal, the general and the particular. In his funny, affectionate story of a bumpy spin out of Omagh, planned so that the father of the narrator can use the land to teach his family about history and himself, the father twice recalls one Martin Murphy, and in remembering him tells two of his bids. The style differs, but the impulse of the father, the narrator, and Kiely are akin to that of the District's teller: "A Journey to the Seven Streams," in *The State of Ireland: A Novella and Seventeen Stories* (Boston: David R. Godine, 1980), p. 94. The oral performance of stories can show through literary reworkings. In the chapter "His Father," in *Rocky Road to Dublin*, the Donegal novelist Seumas MacManus links bids and exploits through reminiscence about a particular personality, much as a teller would at a hearth, and in *Heavy Hangs the Golden Grain* (New York: Macmillan, 1952), p. 16, MacManus retells a pair of bids he once told Douglas Hyde. See also note 10, below.

9. Mody C. Boatright, *Folk Laughter on the American Frontier* (New York: Macmillan, 1949), sees the tall tale as "one of America's few indigenous art forms," a response to the enormity of the land (pp. 85–95). In *Jonathan Draws the Long Bow* (Cambridge: Harvard University Press, 1946), chap. 4, Richard M. Dorson argues that the tall tale is especially but not uniquely American. Two important American collections begin with reference to European precedents for the wild American spirit—Rabelais, Munchausen—then go on, quite correctly, to set the stories in their local scene: Percy Mackaye, *Tall Tales of the Kentucky Mountains* (New York: George H. Doran, 1926), p. 9; Vance Randolph, *We Always Lie to Strangers: Tall Tales from the Ozarks* (New York: Columbia University Press, 1951), p. 5. A century ago Samuel S. Cox wrote that expansive exaggerative humor, while an American trait, comedy's parallel to manifest destiny, is a composite heritage, owing much to Norse and Celtic sources: *Why We Laugh* (New York: Harper, 1880), chap. 4, esp. pp. 83–84, 95–96, and 426–28, where he speaks of Irish hyperbole. Gustav Henningsen begins "The Art of Perpendicular Lying: Concerning a Commercial Collecting of Norwegian Sailors' Tall Tales" (trans. Warren E. Roberts), *Journal of the Folklore Institute* 2, no. 2 (1965): 180–219, by saying that, though some Americans think of the tall tale as peculiarly American, it is both ancient and common in Europe; then he goes on to provide a good survey of the tall tale in Scandinavia. Gerald Thomas introduces a French collection, first published in 1579, with good generalizations on the nature of the genre and its neglect by folklorists in *The Tall Tale and Philippe d'Alcripe: An Analysis of the Tall Tale Genre with Particular Reference to Philippe d'Alcripe's La Nouvelle Fabrique des Excellents Traits de Vérité, together with an Annotated Translation of the Work* (St. John's: Department of Folklore, Memorial University of Newfoundland, 1977). The great Old World case is, of course, Rudolph Eric Raspe (and unknown others), *The Surprising Adventures of Baron Munchausen* (Mount Vernon: Peter Pauper, 1944; reprint of 5th ed.; 1st ed. 1785). In that edition at pp. 23–25 we find the deer shot with a cherry stone, Aarne-Thompson type 1889C, localized in Fermanagh; see note 14, below. At pp. 104–5 the Baron, who lived from 1720 to 1794, shoots partridge with a ramrod, Aarne-Thompson type 1894, usually extended into type 1890D, the Lucky Shot, which Hugh Nolan tells in this chapter. On p. 33, the Baron

sews his horse back together with laurel, which is Aarne-Thompson type 1889D, but since the wrong feature was hit upon for classification, that story has pulled away from the folktales that developed around motif X1241.1(e), which are drawn as an afterthought to type 1911A, under which Ó Súilleabháin and Christiansen (*Types of the Irish Folktale*, p. 326) speak of "an Irish by-form" about a horse thought dead that is skinned but revives and gets a new skin sewed on. In his *Handbook of Irish Folklore*, Ó Súilleabháin makes it no. 18 in his list of humorous stories (p. 641). A text of that tale from Sligo is given in Séamas Ó Catháin, *The Bedside Book of Irish Folklore* (Cork: Mercier Press, 1980), pp. 40–41, a book containing many good observations on folklore-collecting in Ireland. A version of that type, common in America, was told by Hugh Nolan; see note 10, below. From the days of Hardin Taliaferro's *Fisher's River (North Carolina) Scenes and Characters* (New York: Harper, 1854), organized around stories by and about great characters, including spinners of yarns and tellers of big hunting stories like Uncle Davy Lane and Oliver Stanley, who Taliaferro knew in Surry County in the 1820–29 period, American writers—Mackaye (pp. 12–19) and Dorson (pp. 5–8, 226–29)—have recognized that tall tales generally exist in attachment to extravagant personalities, to Munchausens. Such is also the case in Ballymenone. Two fine studies of such individuals: William Hugh Jansen, *Abraham "Oregon" Smith: Pioneer, Folk Hero and Tale-Teller*, International Folklore (New York: Arno Press, 1977); C. Richard K. Lunt, "Jones Tracy: Tall-Tale Hero from Mount Desert Island," *Northeast Folklore* 10 (1968): 5–74, which includes good comment on the active tall-tale hero (pp. 58–62). The depth of the exaggerative idea is suggested by the popularity of visual hyperbole, presented in Roger L. Welsch's fine book *Tall-Tale Postcards: A Pictorial History* (New York: A. S. Barnes, 1976). American cards, like American stories, emphasize male pursuits: hunting, fishing, and farming.

10. The finest collection of all, Sean O'Sullivan's *Folktales of Ireland*, Folktales of the World (Chicago: University of Chicago Press, 1966)—which includes an excellent survey of Irish folktale scholarship by Richard Dorson—presents a text of "The Great Liar," based on Aarne-Thompson type 852 and incorporating other tall tales, including an enormous potato (type 1960D: motif X1435.1), which, though much less elaborated, is similar to one told me by both Hugh Nolan and Michael Boyle and listed in the Sources. O'Sullivan's note to the tale (p. 286) suggests the popularity of the tall-tale idea in Ireland, but O'Sullivan, with nearly forty years of experience as archivist of the Irish Folklore Commission, unrivaled in his knowledge of the Irish folktale, writes, "Tales of lying (known as tall stories, especially in America) had only small vogue in this country, and were occasionally told as in-tales in longer narratives": Seán Ó Súilleabháin, *Storytelling in Irish Tradition* (Cork: Mercier Press for Cultural Relations Committee of Ireland, 1973), p. 23. The great IFC collection and Ó Súilleabháin's own fine books lean to the Irish-speaking West, so the importance of the tall tale in Ballymenone may have regional as well as local implications. Indeed, Michael J. Murphy, the IFC full-time collector for Ulster, introducing *Now You're Talking*, says the North is "rich in short, snappy humorous tales" (p. vii), and while most of those he gives correspond to what people in the District call bids, he does provide a text of the same type Ó Súilleabháin does, and he gives three other tall tales (pp. 136–37), all comparable to ones told in Ballymenone. Murphy collected tall tales in Fermanagh (see note 14, below), and some Fermanagh texts have been published. While telling about his life and songs in *Come Day, Go Day*, John Maguire, who lived south of the District, told two anecdotes (pp. 35–36,

55–56) comparable to the District's, the second of which shapes as a bid, and he gives a comic hyperbolic recitation (pp. 75–76), the only "lie" he ever heard. But north of the District, Paddy Tunney, singer from the shores of Lower Lough Erne, emphasizes tall tales among the stories he retells in *The Stone Fiddle: My Way to Traditional Song* (Dublin: Gilbert Dalton, 1979). They feel like Ballymenone's, and only twenty-five miles separate the areas. Two of his tales, like many in Ballymenone, suggest tales of other genres, then grow tall, one out of water horses (p. 3), which becomes the Irish (and American) version of type 1911A (see note 9, above), which Hugh Nolan told me: 11/8/72t, 6/16/77t (see the preamble to the Sources for explanations of modes of recording). Another of Tunney's tales (pp. 82–85) grows out of a butter-stealing tale like that Hugh Nolan tells in Chapter 20. Another (p. 88) is closely comparable to a tall tale Michael Boyle tells in Chapter 15. Yet another (pp. 102–3), told by Ned Noble (a variant of Aarne-Thompson type 660, discussed as a tall tale by Jansen, *Abraham "Oregon" Smith*, pp. 236–43), though unlike any particular story I heard in Ballymenone, matches the free spirit of the District's pants more closely than any other single published text. From Donegal, the next county west in Ulster, buried in the extravagant prose of the story "Barney Roddy's Penance," in Seumas MacManus, *Through the Turf Smoke: The Love, Lore, and Laughter of Old Ireland* (New York: Doubleday and McClure, 1899), pp. 89–111, lies a report of a man famed for "spinning yarns" and "lies" out of reality into humorous fiction. The story "The Counsellor" in the same volume (pp. 167–88) introduces a narrator who tells comic tales in the darkness of his home in a somber manner, then lets him string together several anecdotes in which Daniel O'Connell displays his wit. There are also reports from beyond Ulster. Samuel Lover, linked by Hyde to Carleton (note 4, above), though less analytic, less deep, and less close to the people than Carleton, was another writer of sketches. In the introduction to his *Legends and Stories of Ireland* (Dublin: W. F. Wakeman, 1834; 1st pub. 1831), Lover tells the learned doctors to lay his book down, for mirth is his intention, but don't do it. Readers who dismiss him as only a player of stage-Irish pranks will miss the observations he provides, especially in his earliest stories "given in the manner of the peasantry." In one sketch, "Paddy the Sport" (pp. 205–34), Lover tells of a character "much given to lying and tobacco, and an admirable hand at filling a game-bag or emptying a whiskey-flask; and if game was scarce in the stubbles, Paddy was sure to create plenty of another sort . . . by the marvellous stories he had ever at his command." Huntsman, good guide and shot, "professed story-teller, and a notorious liar," Paddy tells Lover stories of fairies, ghosts, and spirits. "Such were the marvellous yarns that Paddy was constantly spinning. Indeed he had a pride, I think, in being equally expert at 'the long bow' as at the rifle." There follows an exchange with the Squire in which Paddy's exaggerative turns of speech top his master, then Paddy tells a fabulous story of a forester's battle with a pipe-smoking fox, an elaborated version of Aarne-Thompson type 67** (another version of which Murphy gives in *Now You're Talking*, pp. 136–37). Gaudily clothed in the style of the period, Lover's sketch provides an early report from Ireland of a Munchausen. There are later reports from southern Ireland. George A. Little's *Malachi Horan Remembers* (Dublin: M. H. Gill, 1943) is a lovely book, and as Seán Ó Súilleabháin notes in his brief introduction, it is folkloristically important. Little lets Horan talk. Though asked about customs in general, Horan turns constantly to affectionate, reminiscent stories of local individuals, many comparable in form to exploits and bids. One character was Davy Brian, renowned for "telling lies" in competitions, and the tale Horan repeats, ending it, "Ah, Davy was a great man to skin a lie," is a version of the same tale Lover heard from Paddy the Sport a century before, in which a fox throws his hunter's breeches into the fire; see pp. 67–69, 101–29, esp. pp. 108–10. From Horan's Dublin we drop to the far west of Cork to meet another marvelous man in another superb book, *The Tailor and Ansty* (New York: Devin-Adair, 1964; 1st pub. 1942) by Eric Cross. The Tailor is the only man in all of literature who could keep up with Ellen Cutler, and he says things and tells stories more like those I heard in Ballymenone than any other person in print. Cross is not questing for Gaelic relics, so Mr. Buckley, the Tailor, often sails into hyperbole (pp. 46–55, 171–72) and once inserts into the conversation a version of the international tale, Aarne-Thompson 113A, The King of the Cats Is Dead, which is common in Ireland (Ó Súilleabháin and Christiansen, *Types of the Irish Folktale*, pp. 45–46) as well as England (Baughman, *Index of England and North America*, pp. 3–4, 83–84) and which Hugh Nolan told me (10/27/72t, 6/11/77t), calling it a pant. The Tailor tells other tall tales (pp. 79–80, 118–23), the first of which is the skinned horse, type 1911A, which Hugh Nolan also told; see above in this note. The Tailor remembers an old friend, Jerry Cokely, and tells about him (pp. 94–101), weaving in stories of his just as Hugh Nolan and Michael Boyle do when telling about Hugh McGiveney or John Brodison. Cokely sounds like the District's stars. Most of the stories about him resemble bids (the Tailor tells two other bids, pp. 176–77) and one of his stories (p. 98) is a tall tale, conceivably related to Aarne-Thompson type 1529, which Michael Boyle told about John Brodison (11/25/72t). Though he lived in the far southwest, on the verge of Kerry, the Tailor sounds familiar to me and suggests that the rarity of the tall tale in Irish collections might tell as much about the interests of the collectors as about the interests of the tellers.

11. Vivian Mercier, *The Irish Comic Tradition* (Oxford: Oxford University Press, 1962), chap. 2.

12. The passage in the *Tain* that most conspicuously contains the exaggerative spirit comes among the boyhood deeds of Cú Chulainn, from his extravagant bountiful hunt to his extreme reaction to an array of naked women. It has been variously translated from different recensions. Lady Gregory provides it in *Cuchulain of Muirthemne: The Story of the Men of the Red Branch of Ulster* (London: John Murray, 1902), pp. 18–20. In comparison to later translations, Lady Gregory's seems blunted and veiled. Shown naked women, Cú Chulainn buries his face in a cushion rather than plunging his head in a cauldron that explodes with the heat. But hers was a landmark of English prose in Ireland, the best Irish book of its time, Yeats said in his preface, written in English as beautiful as that of William Morris and a dialect as true as that of Robert Burns. Cecile O'Rahilly has given us good scholarly translations: *Táin Bó Cuailnge: Recension I* (Dublin: Dublin Institute for Advanced Studies, 1976), pp. 146–48; *Táin Bó Cúalnge from the Book of Leinster* (Dublin: Dublin Institute for Advanced Studies, 1970), pp. 169–71. The great translation for our days is Thomas Kinsella, *The Tain*, Dolmen Editions 9 (Dublin: Dolmen Press, 1969), pp. 90–92. Kinsella's translation is a major work of art. Perfectly illustrated, beautifully designed, *The Tain* is one of the finest books of modern times.

13. Flann O'Brien's most famous novel, *At Swim-Two-Birds* (New York: Pantheon, 1939), brims and bubbles with licensed imagination, and like his best novel, *The Third Policeman* (New York: Walker, 1967), it is structured fantastically. Two of his lesser works come still closer to the tall-tale mode: *The Dalkey Archive* (New York: Macmillan, 1965) and *The Hard Life: An Exegesis of Squalor* (London: MacGibbon &

Kee, 1961). Anne Clissman has written an excellent study of Brian O'Nolan (Myles na gCopaleen), whose hard lot it is to be Ireland's second-best modern novelist: *Flann O'Brien: A Critical Introduction to His Writings: The Story-Teller's Book-Web* (Dublin: Gill & Macmillan, 1975), correctly stressing the profound, often religious, ideas beneath his wild humor. *At Swim-Two-Birds* (in which textual interconnections and nonlinear structures are strung into narrative) and *The Poor Mouth*, translated from the Irish by Patrick C. Power (New York: Viking, 1974; 1st pub. 1941), with its comic-pathetic picture of Gaelic life, lampooning the works listed in note 16, below, and its hilarious spoof on folklore-collecting, should be required reading for all folklorists. Samuel Beckett's fantasy does not soar to the edge but carves into the marrow. Follow him through the great trilogy *Molloy, Malone Dies,* and *The Unnamable* (1951–53), down into the perfection of the grim comic mood of Ballymenone's best pants.

14. "A Lough Erne Pike" is quoted from Murphy's notebook IFC, vol. 1697 (1966), p. 34, with the permission of Bo Almqvist, head of the Department of Irish Folklore, University College, Belfield, Dublin. More information on Fermanagh tall tales can be found in that book (pp. 32–34, 183–85) and in IFC 1711 (1966): 192. People did hunt pike with guns on Lough Erne, hence this localization of Aarne-Thompson type 1889C. See note 9, above. I will have frequent occasion in the notes that follow to refer to manuscripts of the Irish Folklore Commission in the archive at Belfield, and they will appear in this form: IFC 1697 (1966): 34. That provides the number of the manuscript, the date of collection, and the page in the manuscript. Mr. Murphy told me he had not collected along the Arney or around Bellanaleck, but remained near the shore of the Upper Lough, where he heard plenty of "lies." Ó Súilleabháin lists this tale of the pike no. 17 among the humorous stories in *Handbook of Irish Folklore*, p. 641.

15. See "The Personal Narrative as Folklore" by Sandra K. D. Stahl in the issue she edited on stories of personal experience, *Journal of the Folklore Institute* 14, nos. 1–2 (1977): 9–30; and her paper "The Oral Personal Narrative in Its Generic Context," *Fabula* 18 (1977): 18–39, with the comment in *Fabula* 21 (1980): 82–87. Stahl has also written clearly on "The Local Character Anecdote," *Genre* 8, no. 4 (1975): 283–302. The classic statement on the memorat, the tale that is at once personal and traditional, can be found in C. W. von Sydow, *Selected Papers on Folklore: Published on the Occasion of His 70th Birthday* (Copenhagen: Rosenkilde & Bagger, 1948), pp. 73–74. From his idea, conservative argument unfolds gracefully to bring personal narratives of traditional experiences—meetings with ghosts, remembrances of baby's first step, epics of struggles with demonic editors over precious manuscripts—within the realm of the folktale.

16. Asserting the rarity of tales of the self in Ballymenone (other than accounts of supernatural encounters, which use the self to record a segment of everyone's external reality), I come into conflict with a notion of Irish country people that could be drawn from these deservedly famous autobiographies: Maurice O'Sullivan, *Twenty Years A-Growing*, trans. Moya Llewelyn Davies and George Thomson (New York: Viking Press, 1933); Tomás Ó Crohan, *The Islandman*, trans. Robin Flower (New York: Scribner's, 1935); Peig Sayers, *Peig: The Autobiography of Peig Sayers of the Great Blasket Island*, trans. Bryan MacMahon (Syracuse: Syracuse University Press, 1974; written 1935). All those books are built out of memories of small personal events. Their authors do occasionally generalize about their culture, Ó Crohan particularly, and they do use themselves to tell stories of others. That impulse is

strongest in Peig Sayers, and it is carried further in Peig Sayers, *An Old Woman's Reflections*, trans. Seamus Ennis (London: Oxford University Press, 1962; 1st pub. 1939), where she often removes herself from the center of her tales. Perhaps it was the island (the authors were all neighbors on the Great Blasket), perhaps it was the attention they received from hordes of visitors in love with their language, but I have surrounded this note with others (esp. notes 4, 8, 10, and 19) in which I cite works by authors of different kinds, describing different places, including Kerry, whose accounts of country life sound familiar to me (I know about nowhere in Ireland except Ballymenone), yet the moving autobiographies of the Blasket authors feel alien. The reason is their interest in the minor happenings of their private lives. It is not that the District's people have led no lives, or that they are undeveloped as individuals. Rather, they express their individuality in artistic performance (in which they are like the Blasket writers) and in formulating highly personal opinions on endless topics of general concern (and in this they are unlike the Blasket writers, who remember their actions but do not sustain arguments over the great issues). People in Ballymenone would not be left alone long enough to write a book, and their stories have to be interesting to their neighbors, who share (and would be bored by) their common experiences, so the District's people and the Blasket writers present the self differently. In their books, the Blasket writers show little interest in history; they avoid controversial opinion, and foreground the biographical facts. In their conversations, the District's people show great interest in history and in the symbol-rich doings of other people; they suppress and forget autobiographical detail, and they push to the fore their personal philosophies. Recently folklorists have revived and refined the anthropological idea of the life history; Jeff Todd Titon sets the life history among other kinds of autobiographical narrative in "The Life Story," *Journal of American Folklore* 93, no. 369 (1980): 276–92. But the District's people caution us: not everyone has a life history. For some, the full and true statement of the self would be not an autobiography but a philosophical treatise. The autobiography may be the construction of an individual—a Peig Sayers, a Sun Chief, a Honeyboy Edwards—who has shifted attention from his or her community to a world of unknown others, while people who remain oriented toward their own community focus on the way their ideas mesh or conflict with those held by the others with whom they create a society. Some societies, then, would be misrepresented by a set of life histories. Their reality would appear as a developing interstructuring of thought—a culture with a history.

17. In Ireland, storytellers are predominantly, but not exclusively, male: Jeremiah Curtin, *Tales of the Fairies and the Ghost World: Collected from Oral Tradition in South-West Munster* (New York: Benjamin Blom, 1971; 1st pub. 1895), p. 144; J. H. Delargy, "Irish Folklore," *Saorstát Eireann: Irish Free State Official Handbook* (Dublin: Talbot Press, 1932), p. 266; Ó Súilleabháin, *Storytelling in Irish Tradition*, p. 11; Murphy, *Now You're Talking*, p. viii.

18. In 1845, William Carleton wrote that "the belief in ghosts is fast disappearing, and that in fairies is already almost gone": *Tales and Sketches Illustrating the Character, Usages, Traditions, Sports and Pastimes of the Irish Peasantry* (Dublin: James Duffy, 1849), p. 60; published in 1845 as *Tales and Stories of the Irish Peasantry*, not to be confused with the less analytic *Traits and Stories*. Writing in 1849, with memories of the Famine fresh in his mind, Sir William Wilde opined that poverty, emigration, modernization, and political activism will kill traditions of the kind described by Carleton and Croker within twenty years: *Irish Popular Superstitions*, Irish Folklore

Series (Totowa: Rowman & Littlefield, 1973; 1st pub. 1852), pp. 11–27, 72–87, esp. p. 17. Forty years later, Jeremiah Curtin, collecting in Croker's area, wrote that the "old-time ideas" are "well preserved" only among people over fifty, and the minds of the rising generation are turned in another direction: *Tales of Fairies and the Ghost World*, p. 107. Thirty years pass, the old people die, and T. G. F. Paterson's experiences collecting fairy stories prompt him to say in his fine collection *Country Cracks: Old Tales from the County of Armagh* (Dundalk: W. Tempest, Dundalgan Press, 1945), p. 15, that the old stories will die with the old people, for the young are interested only in the cinema and dance hall. A generation after Paterson, 130 years after Carleton, their generalizations seem still to apply.

19. The folklorist's practice of isolating tales out of conversations, rather than letting them follow from happening to happening, topic to topic, has prevented understanding the nature of the experience story and its role in investigating reality's shape. There are important exceptions to that rule. T. Crofton Croker (see below, Chapter 29, note 3, and Dorson's *British Folklorists*, pp. 44–52) wrote the first major work on the folktale in English based on fieldwork. It is more than a collection of fairy stories. In three of his sketches, "The Little Shoe," "Fairies or No Fairies," and "Seeing Is Believing," he leaves tales in the situations of their telling, where they are used to explore the truth and where tales of disconfirmation as well as confirmation are entered into evidence: *Fairy Legends and Traditions of the South of Ireland*, Family Library 48 (London: John Murray, 1834; which omits ten of the less accurate and less valuable tales and many of the notes of the 1st edition of 1825), pp. 65–71, 95–96; and the edition by Thomas Wright, the antiquarian to whom Croker bequeathed his "secret wishes" concerning his "favourite book" (London: William Tegg, 1862), pp. 67–72, 85–90, 108–9. Jeremiah Curtin constructed the first half of his *Tales of Fairies and the Ghost World*, pp. 1–107, out of five sessions in one house, west of Dingle. At the beginning he comments on the variety of belief and disbelief, but the tales he reports did not appear in events like ceilis. They were given to an American visitor in an interview format. So truth is not the theme, but tales of fairies still lead to tales of ghosts and other mysteries, and even to comedy; one story recounts people who mistook other people for ghosts (pp. 54–57). Other visitors provide comparable reports. The American Clifton Johnson relates a session around a hearth on Achill in which a story on a fairy changeling leads to telling another "queer experience," then to another tale disconfirming a gruesome mystery, then to one of a local disaster: *The Isle of the Shamrock* (New York: Macmillan, 1901), pp. 202–6. Robin Flower describes an evening during which doubt sparks one fairy story then others, each lighting off the last to brighten the night and illuminate the topic: *The Western Island: Or the Great Blasket* (New York: Oxford University Press, 1945), pp. 130–38. Robert Gibbings, a Cork man traveling up the western coast, describes an evening's conversation in *Lovely Is the Lee* (New York: E. P. Dutton, 1945), chap. 10, in which fairy stories refute disbelief and carry into other stories of the world's strangeness, including a version of Aarne-Thompson type 113A (see note 10, above). Later Gibbings describes another night visit on Inishbofin that held no tales but has the feel of a ceili (pp. 130–32). In *Tyrone Folk Quest*, p. 86, Michael Murphy presents fairy stories as an argument over their existence. Seumas MacManus offers fictionally, but with a feeling for accuracy, a conversation over fairies in *A Lad of the O'Friels* (New York: Devin-Adair, 1945), chaps. 9 and 10, in which he connects disbelief in fairies to disbelief in God (p. 68), refers to experiences of fairies as both "stories" and "passages" (p. 73), and gives a fine in-

stance of the obligation to truth (p. 77) when Billy Brogan is pressed to tell of his own "quare" experience with the fairies. He blushes, admitting he had not earlier told it correctly, for he had put himself into the tale "just for divarsion," but "the seriousness of the occasion" (a ceili that turned to the topic of the reality of the fairies after Allingham's famous poem had been read from *The Nation*) would make that "sacrilege," so Billy reports the story accurately as the experience of another. The story itself, stripped of the context that makes it valuable, is reworked in Mac-Manus' *Heavy Hangs the Golden Grain*, pp. 41–43. An early version of the story is given by Croker, *Fairy Legends* (1834), pp. 22–27; (1862), pp. 17–22. William Allingham was from Ballyshannon; his poem "The Fairies: A Child's Song," in *Poems* (Boston: Ticknor & Fields, 1861), pp. 30–32, feels gauzy and tastes sweet, but like the stories of his region it characterizes the fairies, then recounts a theft. The issue of the experience is truth, doubt, and faith; William Butler Yeats begins *The Celtic Twilight* (Dublin: Maunsel, 1905; 1st ed. 1893, 2d ed. 1902), pp. 8–11 (see also pp. 141–42) on that note, and in *Visions and Beliefs*, Lady Gregory lets some statements stand as whole texts, rather than isolating items for classification, so we can gain some sense of how fairies, ghosts, and witches form a single investigation of truth (pp. 192–93, 210–11, 217–21). In a good paper, Linda-May Ballard, "Ulster Oral Narrative: The Stress on Authenticity," *Ulster Folklife* 26 (1980): 35–40, discusses mysterious tales (Mrs. Cutler told a version of the changeling tale she quotes—it is motif F321.1.4.9—set near Bellanaleck: 8/4/72d, 8/7/72t) as defenses of debatable truths. The larger theoretical frame of the experience story, its relation to belief, disbelief, argument, and action, has been established in a series of papers written or co-authored by Linda Dégh: with Andrew Vázsonyi, "Legend and Belief," in Ben-Amos, ed., *Folklore Genres*, chap. 6; "The 'Belief Legend' in Modern Society: Form, Function, and Relationship to Other Genres," in Wayland Hand, ed., *American Folk Legend: A Symposium* (Berkeley: University of California Press, 1971), pp. 55–68; with Andrew Vázsonyi, *The Dialectics of the Legend*, Folklore Preprint Series (Bloomington: Folklore Publications Group, 1973). A version of that paper—"radically cut" but "clarified" she said—appears as "The Crack on the Red Goblet: Or Truth and Modern Legend," in Richard M. Dorson, ed., *Folklore in the Modern World* (The Hague: Mouton, 1978), pp. 253–72.

20. J. Gilsenan, "Ring Forts in County Fermanagh," *Clogher Record* 6, no. 3 (1968): 574–77, maps Fermanagh's forths, most of them atop drumlins, dates most of them to the seventh and eighth centuries, and numbers them at over five hundred. They are discussed by V. Bruce Proudfoot, "The People of the Forths," *Ulster Folklife* 1 (1955): 19–26. F. H. A. Aalen, *Man and the Landscape in Ireland* (London: Academic Press, 1978), pp. 81–87, explains the raths clearly.

21. The experience story is often framed to enable investigation by conforming to the structure of belief established by Alan Dundes, "Brown County Superstitions," *Midwest Folklore* 11 (1961): 25–56.

22. Ballymenone's "historian" fills the role of "seanchaí" as outlined by J. H. Delargy, "The Gaelic Story-Teller: With Some Notes on Gaelic Folk-Tales," *Proceedings of the British Academy*, 1945, pp. 177–221. Late in his affectionate account of the Irish rural life cycle, *Yourself and the Neighbours* (New York: Devin-Adair, 1945; 1st pub. 1914), pp. 84–91, Seumas MacManus describes adopting the role of "shanachie." No longer an able worker, "because you were too old and the world was too new," you became a storyteller who amused children and adults alike. Since "every

single word of every single tale, as both yourself and your audience well knew, was real truth," your stories were important, and your word became law "as much because of the honour due to age, as to the superiority of wisdom that must accompany it. All questions of genealogy, chronology, and history are referred to you for settlement." So it is among the historians of Ballymenone. These older men know the "old history," the neighbors' genealogies, and the community's folk law. They tell the tales of their locality and settle its small disputes.

23. Lady Gregory told interviewers about the origins of the Abbey's style during her trip to America in 1911; quoted in E. H. Mikhail, *Lady Gregory: Interviews and Recollections* (London: Macmillan, 1977), pp. 50, 65, and see p. 75. The storyteller that Padriac Colum recalls from his youth told his tales in the evening by the dim light of a peat fire. "He was free to make all sorts of rhymes and chimes in the language he used. . . . His audience was small, no more than a score of people, and so he could be intimate in voice and manner. He had few gestures, this particular story-teller. . . ." *Story Telling New and Old* (New York: Macmillan, 1968; 1st pub. 1927), pp. 2–3. And John Messenger's good description of storytelling, *Inis Beag*, p. 116, fits the most famous tellers in the District, who also use few gestures—a blessing for this book, because written transcriptions can grasp truly the heart of performance.

24. Seumas MacManus from Donegal also calls märchen "fireside tales," and he calls the moral fables featuring animal actors, which his mother told him at the fireside, "parables": *Rocky Road to Dublin*, pp. 107, 285. He retells one of her parables in *Heavy Hangs the Golden Grain*, p. 84. Shan Bullock's mother told him The Goose That Laid the Golden Egg (*After Sixty Years*, p. 60), which Peter Flanagan told Polly, my daughter: 8/6/72r.

25. See Raymond Williams' definition in *Keywords: A Vocabulary of Culture and Society* (New York: Oxford University Press, 1976), pp. 158–63.

3 Ceili at Flanagans'

1. The greatest compliment I received on *All Silver and No Brass* came in a letter, March 23, 1976, from Mary McConnell, wife of the folklorist Alex, called Sandy, and mother of the great musician. A year later I met Cathal McConnell when he was touring through Philadelphia. We reminisced about Peter Flanagan, and Cathal played a perfect imitation of Mr. Flanagan on the tin whistle, illustrating how P's highly personal style is based on a complex idea of tempo that is lost if one tries to play too fast. Some sense of P's style can be gained from Cathal's masterful performance of a tune he learned from P that P learned from his father, which Cathal calls "Peter Flanagan's" and in which he employs some of P's characteristic phrasing: *Cathal McConnell: On Lough Erne's Shore*, FF-058 (Chicago: Flying Fish Records, 1978), side 1, band 6. Robin Morton writes in his notes to the record: "Outside the family an early influence was Peter Flanagan, a neighbor who played the whistle and fiddle. Cathal still speaks of him with great respect, 'Without him I wouldn't be the musician I am today!'" Michael MacConnell celebrated P as one who carried the old music on when it was not, as it is now, fashionable, in the special supplement on traditional music in the *Irish Times*, August 22, 1977. I am grateful to Mick Moloney for getting me a clipping of that brief sketch.

2. The scene is perfectly portrayed in E. Estyn Evans and Brian S. Turner, *Ire-*

land's Eye: The Photographs of Robert John Welch (Belfast: Blackstaff Press, 1977), p. 160. For Castle Monea, built 1618–19 by Malcolm Hámilton, see: Irish Castles and Castellated Houses (Dundalk: W. Tempest, Dundalgan Press, 1977), pp. 138–40.

4 The Next Day

1. Robert Georges discusses complications in the conventional definition of the legend (which differs in no way from the idea of history: a story about the past believed to be true by the author and his audience) in "The General Concept of Legend: Some Assumptions to Be Reexamined and Reassessed," in Hand, ed., *American Folk Legend*, pp. 1–19. Stith Thompson, *The Folktale* (New York: Holt, Rinehart & Winston, 1946), pp. 8–9, distinguishes legends from other kinds of folktale, but raises problems with his rhetoric by saying the legend "*purports* to be an account of an *extraordinary* happening *believed* to have *actually* occurred." The italics are mine. They suggest areas of investigation beyond texts which folklorists have largely neglected (though see the papers written or co-authored by Linda Dégh listed above at the end of note 19 to Chapter 2), but, more important, they suggest that legends, unlike history, are somehow false. What we call legends in other societies are precisely what we call histories in our own. Richard Dorson distinguishes the historical legend from other genres and criticizes authors who distort the nature of legends to make them into something else in "Defining the American Folk Legend," *American Folklore and the Historian*, chap. 9. In "Legends and Tall Tales," *Selected Essays*, chap. 6, Dorson says legends are believed to be true, but that they float from place to place and drift to the fabulous. That is an apt characterization of some traditions, but not Ballymenone's. The District's "stories of history" are anchored in space and severely restrained to remain true; they are matters not of "belief" but of the investigation of truth through facts. Sean O'Sullivan offers a clear definition in *Legends from Ireland* (London: B. T. Batsford, 1977), p. 12. Historical legends are set among other legends, legends among other tales, in scholastic schemes by Hermann Bausinger, *Formen der "Volkspoesie"* (Berlin: Erich Schmidt, 1968), pp. 170–223; Heda Jason, "Concerning the 'Historical' and the 'Local' Legends and Their Relatives," in Paredes and Bauman, eds., *Toward New Pespectives in Folklore*, pp. 134–44; and Linda Dégh, "Folk Narrative," in Dorson, ed., *Folklore and Folklife*, pp. 53–81, esp. p. 76. The problem in our definition of the historical legend rises out of our need to see the history of other people as inferior to our own.

2. Gerard Murphy places the poem, "The Scholar and His Cat," first in *Early Irish Lyrics: Eighth to Twelfth Century* (Oxford: Oxford University Press, 1970; 1st pub. 1956), pp. 2–3. Robin Flower sets it at the beginning of chapter 2 and discusses it engagingly in *The Irish Tradition*. Kuno Meyer translates it in *Selections from Ancient Irish Poetry* (London: Constable, 1911), pp. 81–82, as does O'Faoláin in *The Silver Branch*, pp. 40–41.

3. For Carleton, his life and opinions, see *Traits and Stories*, the autobiography in the general introduction, dated 1854, pp. viii–xvii, comments at 1:ii–iv, xviii–xxiii, 271; 2:8, 238, 275, 374; and *The Autobiography*, esp. chaps. 1, 3, 9, and his account of his conversion (pp. 92, 180), which he gives little space, and that largely to protest that he never became estranged from the Catholic people. His statements become especially moving in the light of the emphasis he places in *Willy Reilly* (note 5, below) to Reilly's staunch resistance to conversion. Reilly is an imaginative projection, Carleton's opposite: an aristocrat who left neither his place nor his faith.

The complexity of Carleton's opinion is discovered in several rich passages in his less "coloured" *Tales and Sketches*, pp. 177–78, 365–93. Benedict Kiely, the fine novelist from Tyrone, has written an excellent biography: *Poor Scholar: A Study of the Works and Days of William Carleton (1794–1869)* (Dublin: Talbot Press, 1972; 1st pub. 1947), in which see esp. pp. 6, 72–77, 103.

4. Early opinion: William Butler Yeats, *Stories from Carleton: With an Introduction*, The Camelot Series (London: Walter Scott, [1889]), pp. xvi–xvii. Later opinion: *The Trembling of the Veil* (1922), book 2, sec. 6, in *The Autobiography of William Butler Yeats* (New York: Macmillan, 1969), pp. 131–32.

5. *Willy Reilly and His Dear Coleen Bawn: A Tale Founded upon Fact*, 3 vols. (London: Hope & Co., 1855) begins with a preface in which William Carleton says the facts of the mid-eighteenth-century event "became celebrated, and were made the burthen of many a rude ballad throughout Ireland." One survived which, though "humble," is vigorous and expressive of "a kind of inartistic skill." It describes the terrible Penal Days, the heroism of "a young and handsome Catholic," and stands as "a triumph over the persecutors." When Carleton found it, the ballad was "in a wretched state of disorder" owing to "the inaccuracy of memory and ignorance," so he "restored" it to vindicate the honor and character of its "rustic bard" and provides a full text (pp. viii–xii). The song, sung in England and North America as well as Ireland, is: Laws, *American Balladry from British Broadsides*, M10. That is the song Hugh Nolan remembered. If Carleton rewrote it considerably—as he suggests—then it is his text that is in tradition; that written down in Holt County, Missouri, in 1874, and printed in H. M. Belden, *Ballads and Songs Collected by the Missouri Folk-Lore Society* (Columbia: University of Missouri, 1955; 1st pub. 1940), pp. 289–90, resembles Carleton's version, as does the slightly battered text from Australia, John Meredith and Hugh Anderson, *Folk Songs of Australia, and the Men and Women Who Sang Them* (Sydney: Ure Smith, 1979; 1st pub. 1967), pp. 31–32. A text nearly the same as Carleton's, except for the reversal of two stanzas, was published by Samuel Lover (whose wit Carleton praised, *Traits and Stories*, 1:iv) only five years after *Willy Reilly* without any mention of a connection to Carleton: *The Songs of Ireland* (New York: Dick & Fitzgerald, 1860), pp. 349–51, and Lover's text is the source for P. J. Kenedy, *The Universal Irish Song Book: A Complete Collection of the Songs and Ballads of Ireland* (New York: P. J. Kenedy, 1884), pp. 90–91. At the beginning of our century, P. W. Joyce noted that the song was sung all over Ireland, and he recalled singing it in his youth. His text, *Old Irish Folk Music and Songs* (Dublin: Hodges, Figgis, 1909), pp. 230–32, differs, he says, from Carleton's, but it does not differ significantly. And the modern text from Fermanagh, given by Tunney, *Stone Fiddle*, pp. 40–42, certainly comes ultimately from Carleton, as does the text in the great Sam Henry collection of Ulster folksong: Gale Huntingdon, ed., "Sam Henry's 'Songs of the People' as Published in the Northern Constitution, Coleraine, Northern Ireland, Between 1923 and 1939," pp. 101–3 (no. 234)—an unpublished manuscript owned by Kenneth S. Goldstein, which Kenny generously lent to me. Travelers remember the old song. Near Bundoran in Donegal, Richard Hayward points out Ballymacward Castle, built in 1739 by the ffolliott family, home of the "Colleen Bawn" about whom, he says, you can learn in Carleton's novel or in "the old ballad": *In Praise of Ulster* (Belfast: William Mullan, 1946; 1st ed. 1938), p. 312. During his *Rambles in the West of Ireland* (Cork: Mercier Press, 1979; 1st pub. 1907), p. 10, William Bulfin stops in Sligo at a tangled old demesne, the Folliard estate, where "the scene of 'Willie Reilly' is laid," to recall that he has followed the old song

around the world and heard it sung by the hearthside in Leinster and out under paraiso trees of the South American Pampas. Shan Bullock (*After Sixty Years*, pp. 70, 140) remembers the song as popular during the late nineteenth century by Upper Lough Erne, and before he wrote his novel Carleton had a man sorrowing over the death of his wife start to sing her favorite song, "Willy Reilly," and then break down: *Traits and Stories*, 2:58. The song's later popularity, as comparisons among texts prove, stemmed from Carleton, and Carleton's novel, based on an early song, was also popular. MacManus lists it among the few books owned in his rural Donegal community (*A Lad of the O'Friels*, p. 7), and Lee Haring reminded me that O'Casey's *Juno and the Paycock* ends with Boyle not answering Joxer's drunken question, "D'jever rade Willie . . . Reilly . . . and his own . . . Colleen . . . Bawn? It's a darlin' story, a daarlin' story!": Sean O'Casey, *Selected Plays* (New York: George Braziller, 1956), p. 157. I compare Mr. Nolan's story with Carleton's in the Sources.

5 Late Harvest

1. Texts of "The Man from God-Knows-Where" can be found in these popular books, publications of the kind that help keep memories fresh: Daniel D. O'Keeffe, *The First Book of Irish Ballads* (Cork: Mercier Press, 1965; 1st pub. 1955), pp. 74–77; *Songs and Recitations of Ireland: Book No. 4, The Tara Brooch* (Cork: C.F.N., 1972), pp. 13–15.

2. Patrick Logan, "Folk Medicine of the Cavan-Leitrim Area," *Ulster Folklife* 9 (1963): 89, mentions tying a string around a sprain as part of the cure, and a red thread figures in the local treatment. Beatrice Maloney, "Traditional Herbal Cures in County Cavan, Part 1," *Ulster Folklife* 18 (1972): 68, comments on family cures. Anthony D. Buckley describes attitudes toward medicine and the varieties of curer-patient relations and mentions plasters for skin cancer: "Unofficial Healing in Ulster," *Ulster Folklife* 26 (1980): 15–34, esp. 23. Robert Harbinson recalls his response to Fermanagh "charms" in *Song of Erne*, pp. 176–79. Alex McConnell of Bellanaleck describes local cures in these manuscripts: IFC 1403 (1955): 42–47, and his notebook, April 1958, in the archive of the Ulster Folk and Transport Museum (my pagination), pp. 25–33.

3. The classic statement of social functionalism is A. R. Radcliffe-Brown, "On the Concept of Function in Social Science," *American Anthropologist* 37 (1935): 394–402. The great critique and reformulation is Robert Merton, *On Theoretical Sociology*, pp. 73–138. Major folkloristic applications and discussions: William R. Bascom, "Four Functions of Folklore," in Alan Dundes, ed., *The Study of Folklore* (Englewood Cliffs: Prentice-Hall, 1965), pp. 279–98; Elliott Oring, "Three Functions of Folklore: Traditional Functionalism as Explanation in Folkloristics," *Journal of American Folklore* 89, no. 351 (1976): 67–80; Thomas A. Burns, "Folkloristics: A Conception of Theory," *Western Folklore* 36, no. 2 (1977): 109–34, esp. 122–27.

4. The prime text is John Ruskin's "The Nature of Gothic" in *The Stones of Venice* (London: Smith, Elder, 1851–53), 2:151–231, which William Morris printed as a separate Kelmscott volume in 1892. Ruskin provided much of the base for Morris' argument, *Hopes and Fears for Art* (see above, Chapter 1, note 3), that the study of the art of the past must move one to discontent, and for Morris' appeal for an organic, cooperative art in a new society: *Gothic Architecture: A Lecture for the Arts and Crafts Exhibition* (Hammersmith: Kelmscott Press, 1893). Morris had trouble with Ireland, certainly because of nationalism, which he thought sorted ill with so-

cialism, and probably because of religion, of which he had little and Ireland plenty, but he supported the Land League and the movement for Irish independence (Thompson, *William Morris*, pp. 268, 283, 340, 496–97), and he befriended the young Yeats, who recounts his early contact with Morris in *The Trembling of the Veil*. Writing a quarter of a century after Morris' death, Yeats says he no longer holds his poetry high, but would rather live like Morris than any other man: *The Autobiography*, pp. 85–88, and Denis Donoghue, ed., *W. B. Yeats: Memoirs* (New York: Macmillan, 1972), pp. 20–21, 24. Allan Wade's collection, *The Letters of W. B. Yeats* (London: Rupert Hart-Davis, 1954), shows his early correspondence from London, 1887–92, to be full of Morris, reporting dinners and the important support Morris gave his *Oisin*, as well as Morris' approval of Hyde's work in folklore (p. 94). In 1927, Yeats wrote May Morris, calling her father "still my chief of men." Later letters reveal him continuing to read Morris (pp. 759, 776, 816), as well as citing Morris as one of the main reasons he cannot hate the English (p. 872); repeated in *Letters on Poetry from W. B. Yeats to Dorothy Wellesley* (London: Oxford University Press, 1964), p. 111. Yeats' major statements on Morris are "The Happiest of the Poets" and "A General Introduction for My Work," in *Essays and Introductions* (New York: Macmillan, 1961). Morris' impact on Yeats was direct and indirect. Early in Yeats' relation with Douglas Hyde, Hyde was reading Morris, imitating his verse, and attending his lectures: Dominic Daly, *The Young Douglas Hyde: The Dawn of the Irish Revolution and Renaissance, 1874–1893* (Dublin: Irish University Press, 1974), pp. 74–75, 77, 123, 141, 150. When Yeats met Synge, Synge was leaning to socialism and reading Morris: Andrew Carpenter, ed., *My Uncle John: Edward Stephens's Life of J. M. Synge* (London: Oxford University Press, 1974), pp. 104–5. When Yeats went out collecting folklore with Lady Gregory, she was in the midst of "the longest friendship" of her life, with the anti-imperialist and poet, Morris' friend, Wilfred Scawen Blunt: Colin Smythe, ed., *Seventy Years: Being the Autobiography of Lady Gregory* (New York: Macmillan, 1974), esp. pp. 203–12, 284–85, 306–22. Blunt, like Yeats, Hyde, A.E., and her husband, worked to liberalize her politics. Another route from Morris to Yeats led through the Yeats sisters, whose press was inspired and assisted from Kelmscott: Liam Miller, *The Dun Emer, Later the Cuala Press*, New Yeats Papers 7 (Dublin: Dolmen Press, 1973), chap. 1. John Masefield, *Some Memories of W. B. Yeats* (New York: Macmillan, 1940), pp. 8, 11, recalled Yeats' admiration for Morris and that the central feature of the decor of his study was the Kelmscott Chaucer (which Lady Gregory gave him for his fortieth birthday). In his essay *William Morris and W. B. Yeats* (Dublin: Dolmen Press, 1962), Peter Faulkner assesses Morris' influence as primarily a matter of personality: Morris' realization of a unified life, more than any particulars of poetry or politics, inspired Yeats. And it was mostly the fire, the great personal "vitality," of James Joyce that caused Yeats to liken him to Morris. But the young Joyce was a man of his age. He had read and admired Ruskin, he called his own politics those of "a socialistic artist," and he adopted the critical Pre-Raphaelite stance toward the Renaissance and materialistic modernity: Richard Ellmann, *James Joyce* (New York: Oxford University Press, 1972; 1st pub. 1959), pp. 102–9; Stanislaus Joyce, *My Brother's Keeper: James Joyce's Early Years*, ed. Richard Ellmann (New York: Viking, 1958), pp. 89, 169–70, 179–81, 195; Richard Ellmann, *The Consciousness of Joyce* (New York: Oxford University Press, 1977), pp. 1, 75, 78, and chap. 3; Joyce's essay on the Renaissance in Louis Berrone, *James Joyce in Padua* (New York: Random House, 1977), pp. 13–23. Ruskin, Morris, Yeats, Joyce: literature's most modern voice rises out of the romantic quest for unity and discovers a center that holds in the dynamic nature of universal consciousness. *Finnegans Wake* anticipates *The Savage Mind*.

6 Sacred Beginnings

1. Indeed, introducing his collection of tales from Armagh, T. G. F. Paterson writes that tales of Saint Patrick are popular there, and, Armagh man himself, he remarks, "It took a really brave man to light that famous fire on the Hill of Slane": *Country Cracks*, pp. 11–13, and 26–28, 59–60, 83–87, 102. Paterson was born in Canada in 1888 but spent his life thinking and writing about the Ulster countryside to which his Scottish forebears moved in the seventeenth century. E. Estyn Evans and Paterson's nephew remember him at the beginning of the volume of his writings, which Evans edited: *Harvest Home: The Last Sheaf: A Selection from the Writings of T. G. F. Paterson* (Dundalk: W. Tempest, Dundalgan Press for the Armagh County Museum, 1975). There is a major entry for Saint Patrick in vol. 12, "Folk-Life," of the typescript Paterson left to the Armagh County Museum, p. 228.

2. John T. McNeill, *The Celtic Churches: A History, A.D. 200 to 1200* (Chicago: University of Chicago Press, 1974), p. 223.

3. Early gravestones of the kind that stand at Kinawley are also found in east Fermanagh and are illustrated by Helen Hickey, *Images of Stone: Figure Sculpture of the Lough Erne Basin* (Belfast: Blackstaff Press, 1976), pp. 96–103. I illustrate one of the Kinawley gravestones in the center of the figure "The Old Year" in Chapter 13.

4. The great papers on the historical and botanical shamrock were published by Nathaniel Colgan in 1892 and 1896. In them he concludes that the shamrock as symbol dates to the seventeenth century and that the shamrock is not one but several plants. His work is summarized by Robert Lloyd Praeger, *The Way That I Went: An Irishman in Ireland* (Dublin: Allen Figgis, 1969), pp. 264–69; and Jeanne Sheehy, *The Rediscovery of Ireland's Past: The Celtic Revival, 1830–1930* (London: Thames & Hudson, 1980), pp. 9–12. John O'Donoghue recalls the difficulty of finding the shamrock on Saint Patrick's Day in *In Kerry Long Ago* (London: B. T. Batsford, 1960), pp. 86–88.

8 The Ford

1. Fostering was common in ancient Ireland: Kenneth Hurlstone Jackson, *The Oldest Irish Tradition: A Window on the Iron Age* (Cambridge: Cambridge University Press, 1964), pp. 10–11; Dillon and Chadwick, *Celtic Realms*, pp. 100–101; Gearóid MacNiocaill, *Ireland Before the Vikings*, Gill History of Ireland 1 (Dublin: Gill & Macmillan, 1972), pp. 58–59. It continued into the eighteenth century: Edward MacLysaght, *Irish Life in the Seventeenth Century* (Shannon: Irish University Press, 1969; 1st pub. 1939), pp. 81–84. John Davies, an English lawyer who settled in Fermanagh long enough to serve as the county's first representative to the Irish Parliament, discussed fostering astutely in *A Discovery of the True Cause Why Ireland Was Never Brought Under Obedience of the Crown of England*, published in 1612 and included in *Historical Tracts: By Sir John Davies, Attorney General, and Speaker of the House of Commons in Ireland* (Dublin: William Porter, 1787). Irish political resistance, he argues (pp. 126–39), depends on the maintenance of Irish customs with fostering prominent among them. Fostering, he says, is more prevalent in Ireland than in

any other country, and it serves to expand allegiances beyond family and clan to create parties and factions, so it must be eliminated if civilization is to flourish and English rule is to be consolidated in Ireland.

2. James Carney, *The Irish Bardic Poet: A Study in the Relationship of Poet and Patron as Exemplified in the Persons of the Poet, Eochaidh Ó hEoghusa (O'Hussey) and His Various Patrons, Mainly Members of the Maguire Family of Fermanagh*, New Dolmen Chapbooks 4 (Dublin: Dolmen Press, 1967), esp. pp. 12–13, 16–18, 28. Carney's important essay is reprinted in Joseph Duffy, ed., *Clogher Record Album* (Monaghan: Cumann Seanchais Chlochair, 1975), pp. 187–211. The poem to Hugh Maguire's father is the first one in David Greene, ed., *Duanaire Mhéig Uidhir: The Poembook of Cú Chonnacht Mág Uidhir, Lord of Fermanagh, 1566–1589* (Dublin: Dublin Institute for Advanced Studies, 1972).

9 Mackan Hill

1. I quote from Patrick Kavanagh's fine poem "Why Sorrow?" in Peter Kavanagh, ed., *The Complete Poems of Patrick Kavanagh* (New York: Peter Kavanagh Hand Press, 1972), p. 169. T. Crofton Croker provides a lengthy portrait of the schoolmaster in *Researches in the South of Ireland, Illustrative of the Scenery, Architectural Remains, and the Manners and Superstitions of the Peasantry* (London: John Murray, 1824), pp. 326–44, esp. pp. 328–29, 335: "In an evening assembly of village statesmen he holds the most distinguished place, from his historical information, pompous eloquence, and classical erudition. His principles verge very closely indeed upon the broadest republicanism. . . . He praises the Milesians . . . , abuses 'the Saxon strangers'. . . : before congenial spirits he talks downright treason. . . . Our schoolmaster is a poet too, and consecrates his powers to the diffusion of patriotic aspirations—songs, treasonable, amatory, and laudatory on his 'Green Erin.'" The master, Croker says, is a nobleman, naturally bent to learning and classical imagery, who because of his religion has been reduced to poverty. He sits ragged within his "miserable habitation, of sods cemented with mud," crowded round by his disciples, to whom he gives high-flown poetry to sing. Many of his songs are printed as broadsides, and among the four hundred Croker purchased in 1821, fully one-third "were of a rebellious tendency." William Carleton gives the master's traits in his famous and influential sketch "The Hedge School," *Traits and Stories*, 1:271–324: he is expected to be slightly deranged, a severe disciplinarian and pompous pedant, possessed of a titanic Latinate vocabulary and deep knowledge of the classics and mathematics. He won his post through competitive poetic competition and conspired in rebellious movements. His duties included service as "parish scribe" and surveyor at conacre time. See also vol. 2, p. 69; *Autobiography*, p. 116. Those traits endured. Kevin Danaher sketches the master compatibly in *Irish Country People* (Cork: Mercier Press, 1966), pp. 55–60. With Danaher, Tunney (*Stone Fiddle*, chap. 21) stresses the master's pretentious poetry. Ronald H. Buchanan introduces his article "Folklore of an Irish Townland," *Ulster Folklife* 2 (1956): 43–55, with a good argument for the study of traditions as part of a local system rather than as isolated survivals, then includes a great master among the "characters" from the past about whom stories are told today. John O'Donoghue recalls his first master in *In a Quiet Land* (London: Country Book Club, 1959), pp. 67–68: a man who knew Greek and Latin, who fell into silent philosophical studies and

wandered, a creaking dandy, reciting Goldsmith to himself, a man who, except for the occasional fit of rage, was "like any ordinary man minding his cattle and sheep in the peaceful countryside."

2. Hopeful writers at the beginning of the twentieth century deplored the absence of Irish history from Irish schools: Sir Horace Plunkett, *Ireland in the New Century* (New York: E. P. Dutton, 1905), pp. 122–23, 152–53; Robert Lynd, *Home Life in Ireland* (London: Mills & Boon, 1909), pp. 95–97: "I myself, who was brought up in a district rich in history and in heroic tales, was never allowed to know at school a single human fact suggesting that this country around me and I had any relation to each other." Certainly a continuing policy of deemphasizing Irish history in the schools, and educating Protestant and Catholic children in separate classrooms, is designed perfectly to continue the tradition of violence.

3. Liam Gaffney, ed., *Kinawley Through the Ages: Souvenir of the Centenary of St. Naile's Church, 1876–1976* (Cavan: Kinawley Parish Council, [1976]), pp. 29–30, 66. MacManus, *Rocky Road to Dublin*, chap. 21, "Kinawley." Alex McConnell of Bellanaleck, IFC 1403 (1955): 93, credits the song to the hedge schoolmaster, the Yellow Master. In his Notebook in the Ulster Folk and Transport Museum of April 1958 (which I will refer to as "Ulster Notebook") Eamon Anderson of Kinawley, the son of Master Anderson, writes: "Perhaps in no district in the country was there as many Poets and rhymers as in this. There were Old Master Maguire and Frank Maguire in days gone by and Charlie Farmer and John Maguire of later times. The poets of days gone by here were almost as good as Thomas Moore. The old Master could hardly talk only in verse" (p. 47).

4. The rhyme scheme of Maguire's "Mackan Fight" is like that of Hugh McGiveney's song on the Battle of the Ford. The stanzas could be written out as couplets with internal rhyme in each line, and the local ballat writers' practice of treating each stanza as one long line, ending only when the tune repeats, has merit, despite our conventions which make it seem strange. Often in comparably patterned songs, the "internal" rhymes are less exact than they are in "Mackan Hill"; they echo in assonance or alliteration, and Gerard Murphy's term for them, "halfrime," gets the idea best; see the first of his essays in *Glimpses of Gaelic Ireland: Two Lectures* (Dublin: C. J. Fallon, 1948), which excellently introduces his subject, "Irish Folk-Poetry," arguing that Irish poetry grows out of conversational patterns, heightening them to concentrate on rhymes that (like the ancient art on paper and metal) prefer similarity to symmetry, and seeking cadences that end on strongly marked sounds to produce a verse perfectly merging sound and sense. In Ballymenone those traits, while most refined in song, characterize stories as well. Austin Clarke tells of A.E. reminding his fellow poets of Larminie's idea that "Gaelic assonance could be used in English to modulate rhyme." He describes experiments with "partial rhyming and muting" and the creation of a variety of "submerged rhymes" within his own verse and that of his contemporaries in Ireland composing in English in *Poetry in Modern Ireland*, Irish Life and Culture 2 (Cork: Cultural Relations Committee, revised ed.; 1st pub. 1951), pp. 42–47. It is a common but accurate generalization that the elaboration of rhyme into a pattern like "Mackan Hill," with the stanzas usually presented as internally decorated couplets, the decoration hardening from assonance into rhyme, was carried into Irish folksongs in English from the conventions of Gaelic verse: Thomas MacDonagh, *Literature in Ireland: Studies Irish and Anglo-Irish*, New Era Library (Dublin: Talbot Press, [1916]), pp. 54–55; Donn Byrne, *Ireland: The Rock Whence I Was Hewn* (Boston: Little, Brown, 1929), pp. 39–44;

Joyce, *Old Irish Folk Music and Songs*, p. 173; Breandán Breathnach, *Folk Music and Dances of Ireland* (Dublin: Talbot Press, 1971), p. 30; Seán O Baoill, "Irish Traditional Music," in Michael Longley, ed., *Causeway: The Arts in Ulster* (Belfast: Arts Council of Northern Ireland, 1971), pp. 122–24; Seán O Boyle, *The Irish Song Tradition* (Dublin: Gilbert Dalton, 1976), pp. 14–15, 24–25; Georges-Denis Zimmermann, *Songs of Irish Rebellion: Political Street Ballads and Rebel Songs, 1780–1900* (Hatboro: Folklore Associates, 1967), pp. 105–8. A good example of an Irish country poet, working in English, who thinks of assonance as rhyme can be found in W. R. LeFanu, *Seventy Years of Irish Life: Being Anecdotes and Reminiscences* (New York: Macmillan, 1894), pp. 89–94. A nice fictionalized sketch of an Ulster country poet is given by W. R. Megaw in "Peter, the Poet" in *Carragloon: Tales of Our Townland* (Belfast: Quota Press, 1935), pp. 176–89.

5. The Countess of Enniskillen, *Florence Court—My Irish Home* (Monaghan: Water Gate Press, 1972).

6. Ashe's funeral: Kee, *The Green Flag*, p. 608.

7. Keating, *History of Ireland*, p. 540; he treats the coming of the Milesians on pp. 95–153. A modern consideration of Milesian fact, history, and myth: Thomas F. O'Rahilly, *Early Irish History and Mythology* (Dublin: Dublin Institute for Advanced Studies, 1976; 1st pub. 1946), pp. 161–70, 419–43. Keating surely influenced the Swad Chapel poet. Though everyone told me it was one of the Kinawley Maguires, Eamon Anderson credited the song to a local schoolteacher named Mary Byrne: Michael Murphy, IFC 1695 (1965): 75, 80. That Keating's influence might have been direct is suggested by the use of a relatively unusual name for Ireland—"Inisillgie" as sung—which is given third in Keating's list on the first page of his history: "Inis alga." Seumas MacManus, who taught with Eamon Anderson's father at Kinawley, writes that Keating was one of the few books read by country people in those days, and he recalls Keating's permanent impact on him in *Rocky Road to Dublin*, pp. 147, 149. MacManus lists Keating, along with Columcille's Prophecies, the Seven Champions of Christendom, and Carleton's *Willy Reilly*, among the "great library of thirteen and a half books" in the Donegal community fictionalized in *A Lad of the O'Friels*, pp. 6–7.

10 The Band

1. O'Rahilly, *Táin Bó Cúalnge from the Book of Leinster*, pp. 232–33. See above, Chapter 2, note 12.

2. Keating, *History of Ireland*, p. 473; he recounts the *Tain*, pp. 198–225. Keating's importance for the development of Irish consciousness and art—myth—is properly emphasized by Russell K. Alspach, *Irish Poetry from the English Invasion to 1798* (Philadelphia: University of Pennsylvania Press, 1960).

3. Critics from beyond typically undervalue Joyce's Irish sources. Correctly they stress the role of Vico and Bruno in the construction of *Finnegans Wake* (New York: Viking, 1959; 1st pub. 1939), but they less often consider how its structure could have been derived from the Book of Kells, though Mary and Padraic Colum say Joyce often turned to that great work of art for inspiration: *Our Friend James Joyce* (Garden City: Doubleday, 1958), pp. 122–23. Keating is not listed by James S. Atherton, *The Books at the Wake: A Study of Literary Allusions in James Joyce's Finnegans Wake* (New York: Viking, 1960); see esp. pp. 89–90. Still, I feel his presence in the Wake when Kate, the Earwickers' servant, becomes the teller of forkings (stories

scooped up for kings, fortunes), p. 221, since Kate is Cait in Irish (Cathleen ni Houli-han: Ireland herself), Keating is Céitinn in Irish, and ceitre is four in Irish, which makes the Four Masters one (Kate: Ireland), and sets Keating among them, proba-bly as the most obscure of the four (who is missing from the list of them on p. 14 but is included on p. 398), Fearfeasa. In Irish Keating's book is *Forus Feasa ar Erinn*. At other points (pp. 298, 384–85), Keating is almost certainly the historian who works alone while the other four work together, for that is how it was in the early seventeenth century. Keating, mysteriously, like the man in the mackintosh (Joyce himself?: the author), drifts among the other writers, unnamed though more fa-mous than those who are named, personifying the fifth of Ireland's provinces: Ire-land has four provinces just as she has four masters, yet there was a fifth central but vanished province, and there is a fifth missing master. The historian of the *Wake* is M.L., and Keating worked in the South (Munster, Leinster) while the Four Masters worked in the North. Keating was a priest, banished, set to wandering for his de-nunciation of infidelity, so he is probably the clergyman, M.G. (Munster's or Mug's Geoffrey, Geoffrey of Monmouth reversed, the historian of the South opposed to those of Britain and Ulster), to whom infidelity is confessed (p. 520). Keating was too important to go unmentioned among the catalogs of Irish historians, too impor-tant to go unnamed unless on purpose. As a wanderer, he, unlike O'Clery, chief of the Four Masters who is named four times in the *Wake*, goes nameless to symbolize the fifth quarter, the free and individual, poetic source of history. His book is pres-ent, evoked by the words starting with the letter *f* that flock fearfully in the histor-ical passages (e.g., pp. 228, 254, 260). Scholars abbreviate his book FF, so it comes up as "fishy fable" (p. 245), and as the framer of memories of wranglers, F⅂ (p. 266). Neither Keating nor Humphry, the Dane who fought at Inis Catha (cata is battle in Irish: Kate: Ireland: Battle Island, chronicled by four masters and by one, ceitre and Céitinn), is included in *A Census of Finnegans Wake* (London: Faber & Faber, 1967) by Adaline Glasheen, though the central figure of the *Wake* is a Dub-liner of Danish descent to whom Kate-Keating is servant. As a divisive stranger in Dublin, Brian Boru's opposite, Humphry, provides a perfect first name for a hero whose next names are Chimpden (monkey cave) and Earwicker: inhabitant of e'er place (time-place, every place), Eire dweller, air dweller (ear would be pronounced air, launching the hero into the air or melting him into melody, and Joyce called his book music, just as he called it myth). William York Tindall, *A Reader's Guide to Fin-negans Wake* (New York: Farrar, Straus & Giroux, 1972), p. 65, convincingly makes Earwick mean Timeplace. The inhabitant of Timeplace, of All, is God. But Earwick is also earwig, a conventional Irish disguise of the Devil. The name proposes and resolves oppositions. In *James Joyce: His Way of Interpreting the Modern World* (New York: Scribner's, 1950), pp. 57, 77–79, 102, Tindall takes seriously Joyce's descrip-tion of his work as "monomyth," "the great myth of everyday life." H.C.E. person-ifies the force of myth, disintegrating, reintegrating, universalizing the particular, particularizing the universal. As Earwicker, he inhabits Timeplace, Everything, All. As Chimpden Earwicker he is cave dweller, air dweller, beast and angel, the human being broken, then unified, evolving. As Humphrey Chimpden Earwicker he is his-torical, primeval, and eternal, stranger and native, Irishman, leader and warrior, the simultaneous power of oneness and division: all-encompassing fragile egg, cleaving: Devil, sordid old publican, God.

4. The Earl of Belmore, *The History of Two Ulster Manors of Finagh in the County of Tyrone, and Coole, Otherwise Manor Atkinson, in the County of Fermanagh, and of*

Their Owners (London: Longmans, Green, 1881), pp. 263–65, tells of building Castle Coole, 1788–98. E. McParland's guide, *Castle Coole: County Fermanagh* (Belfast: National Trust, [c. 1975]) describes the house, as does Rowan's *North West Ulster*, pp. 176–79.

5. Hyde, *A Literary History of Ireland*, pp. 549, 605. Hugh Shields, "Old British Ballads in Ireland," *Folk Life* 10 (1972): 68–103, argues comparably that Irish song is traditionally lyric, that there was a lack of native Irish balladry, though British ballads were adopted and even translated into Irish. He reaches a pair of consistent conclusions. First, since Irish stories are narratives, narrative British songs are often transformed into partially spoken, storylike cantefables in Ireland. Second, the ballads accepted most vigorously in Ireland were those most lyric in form, ballads that told their tale through questions and answers, such as Child 46, which is especially common in Ireland and of which Shields provides a Donegal text. His conclusions gain support in *Now You're Talking*, pp. 49–51, where Michael J. Murphy gives a version of that ballad from Louth presented as a story told mostly in verse. And I recorded a remarkably similar story version of Child 46 from Michael Boyle (11/25/72t), which he said was not a song, though it consisted largely of a recitation of the ballad's stanzas with descriptive bridges. Patrick Kennedy, the great early collector from Wexford, noted that the most common of all the tales in his experience owed its popularity to the rhymes it contained: *Legendary Fictions of the Irish Celts* (London: Macmillan, 1866), pp. 53–54. He reasoned that the repetitions lengthened the tale, shortening the night, but his conclusion fits with Ó Súilleabháin's (*Handbook of Irish Folklore*, pp. 654–55; and *Storytelling in Irish Tradition*, p. 49) that the cantefable is especially popular in Ireland. Stories with rhymes, ballads becoming stories, drift toward a center where prose and poetry, narrative and lyric, merge. Near that center, Irish traditional tales and modern novels swing.

6. Hugh McGiveney's first song of the band uses the same rhyme scheme as his Battle of the Ford (see above, Chapter 9, note 4), which is comparable to that of "Mackan Fight" and "Swad Chapel," though Swad Chapel shifts nearer the old Gaelic idea by using assonance more than rhyme, thus softening the pattern. Indeed, D. K. Wilgus used a version of the conventional invocation employed by the Swad Chapel poet as his example of the use of the Gaelic idea in English: "Irish Traditional Narrative Songs in English: 1800–1916," in Daniel J. Casey and Robert E. Rhodes, eds., *Views of the Irish Peasantry* (Hamden: Archon Books, 1977), p. 121. The song Wilgus uses, "The Star of Slane," had been used by John Hand, *Irish Street Ballads*, Carraig Chapbooks 5 (Blackrock: Carraig Books, 1976, [c. 1873]), pp. 15–17, to illustrate the learned style of the schoolmasterly bard. Since Colm O Lochlainn ordered the songs in *Irish Street Ballads* (Dublin: Three Candles, 1962; 1st pub. 1939) alphabetically by first word, you will find three songs that open something like "Swad Chapel" and "The Star of Slane" together (pp. 192–97). The softness of the half-rimes in "Swad Chapel" (in contrast to the fuller rhymes of McGiveney's songs) could suggest a number of different ways to arrange the verse on the page. I was directed by performance. Michael Boyle recited McGiveney's band song so that every other line contained internal decoration, while he recited "Mackan Fight" in short end-rhyming lines. The singers at Swad phrased their song as I put it on the page, echoing from the end of the second line to the middle of the third, which ends in a rhyme with the sixth: "Ah, like Saint Peter / when his Master told *him* / to feed his *lambs* and these flocks to *keep* / He arranged the deserts / the hills and *mountains* / and plowed the *ocean* for the straying *sheep*." Poets who employed the

pattern of rhyme so popular in south Fermanagh song—which Samuel Lover called "ingenious" and "peculiarly Irish"—set it out on the page in different ways. The great case is "The Groves of Blarney," written by Honest Dick Milliken of Cork around 1798. It is a parody of the song "Castle Hyde," satirizing schoolmasterly verse, its assonance, classical allusions, and praise of place. Milliken's song, which P. W. Joyce termed "vile caricature" and "buffoonery," appealed, he said, to the "depraved sense" of other writers. Father Prout (the name of a real priest adopted by the poet F. S. Mahony) translated "The Groves" into Greek, Latin, and Italian as part of a playful spoof on antiquarianism. He added his own parody, "The Town of Passage," and wrote his famous "Bells of Shandon," as he said, "to the tune of the 'Groves.'" (Peter Flanagan likened the Swad Chapel tune to that of Father Prout's "Bells of Shandon.") In "The Bells of Shandon," Mahony did not mock, but employed the pattern for its musicality. The pattern is ancient—Sigerson finds it in the *Tain*—but witty and clever verse by Milliken and Mahony surely reinforced and popularized the old Gaelic pattern (or close family of patterns) found in so many Irish songs in English. Milliken and Mahony seem to have written their verses out in short end-rhyming lines. Another parodist, John Barham, imitated Milliken with long, internally rhyming couplets: T. Crofton Croker, *Popular Songs of Ireland* (London: Henry Colburn, 1839), pp. 89–93, 124–25, 141–49; Lover, *Songs of Ireland*, pp. 79–84, 150–52; Francis S. Mahony, *The Reliques of Father Prout* (London: Bell & Daldy, 1870; 1st pub. 1859 from essays of 1834–36), pp. 53–62, 158–60; Joyce, *Old Irish Folk Music and Songs*, pp. 200–205; George Sigerson, *Bards of the Gael and Gall: Examples of the Poetic Literature of Erinn* (London: T. Fisher Unwin, 1897), p. 14.

7. It is conventional to say that Lough Erne has as many islands as the year has days: Mr. and Mrs. Hall, *Ireland*, 3:179; Bullock, *After Sixty Years*, p. 3; Sheila St. Clair, *Folklore of the Ulster People* (Cork: Mercier Press, 1971), p. 48; Mary Rogers, *Prospect of Erne: A Study of the Islands and Shores of Lough Erne, Co. Fermanagh* (Enniskillen: Water Gate Press, 1971), p. 21; Kiely, *State of Ireland*, p. 279; Anderson, Ulster Notebook, pp. 35, 72. And it is said of Strangford Lough: Praeger, *Way That I Went*, p. 119; Murphy, IFC 1220 (1951): 347. And it is said of Lough Corrib: Richard Hayward, *The Corrib Country* (Dundalk: W. Tempest, Dundalgan Press, 1968; 1st pub. 1943), pp. 3–4. George McQuillan, whose family runs the boat service on Lough Erne and who knows its islands, opined, probably correctly, that the confusion arose when a conventional exaggerative simile was taken as literally true after its translation from Irish into English. Palaces made grand by windows as numerous as days in the year are found in the folktales of Seumas MacManus: *Through Turf Smoke*, p. 250; *The Well o' the World's End* (New York: Devin-Adair, 1949; 1st pub. 1939), p. 64, and in the South, as Oliver St. John Gogarty reports in *As I Was Going Down Sackville Street* (New York: Reynal & Hitchcock, 1937), p. 55.

8. Patrick Kavanagh, *Tarry Flynn* (London: Pilot Press, 1948), p. 176, and chap. 8 in general. Kavanagh is the greatest writer to speak for the south Ulster region, of which our District is part. His autobiographical *The Green Fool* (London: Martin Brian & O'Keefe, 1971; 1st pub. 1938) is a fine reminiscence in which he discusses, among other matters, neighbors going to law over trespass (p. 12), march bands, and Sinn Fein-Hibernian factionalism (pp. 136–43). Kavanagh dismisses *The Green Fool* too harshly as "stage-Irish" and praises his own *Tarry Flynn* as "not only the best but the only *authentic* account of life as it was lived in Ireland this century," in *Self-Portrait* (Dublin: Dolmen Press, 1975; 1st pub. 1964), pp. 7–8. In *Clay Is the Word: Patrick Kavanagh, 1904–1967* (Dublin: Dolmen Press, 1973), Alan Warner pro-

vides an introduction to the poet, discussing *The Green Fool* and *Tarry Flynn* in chap. 2. He gives Kavanagh's idea of literature in contrast to journalism (p. 78): literature is written from the inside, journalism from the outside. In that formula, the ethnographer, someone like myself, is a journalist vainly trying to write literature. Peter Kavanagh, his brother, provides us with *Garden of the Golden Apples: A Bibliography of Patrick Kavanagh* (New York: Peter Kavanagh Hand Press, 1972) and *Sacred Keeper: A Biography of Patrick Kavanagh* (The Curragh: Goldsmith Press, 1978), in which he, too, is hard on *The Green Fool*—"permeated with the lie of Mother Ireland"—but describes his brother's difficulty in writing the more mature *Tarry Flynn*, which he (Peter) "never really liked" and he (Patrick) did not enjoy writing, though it was "terribly funny and true in most places": pp. 59, 127–28, 159–60, 174–78, 242, 339.

9. Manchester Martyrs: Kee, *Green Flag*, chap. 19; Paul Rose, *The Manchester Martyrs: The Story of a Fenian Tragedy* (London: Lawrence & Wishart, 1970). Rose gives six ballads on the topic (pp. 129–35); two, "The Smashing of the Van" and "God Save Ireland," are known to Peter Flanagan, but the song he usually sings is not included among them.

10. Dominic Behan, *Ireland Sings* (London: Essex House, 1973), pp. 101, 152. G. Desmond Greaves, *The Life and Times of James Connolly* (London: Lawrence & Wishart, 1961).

11. I quote from Mrs. Cutler's clippings from the *Impartial Reporter*, January 3, 1957, p. 5; December 18, 1958, p. 9. W. H. Van Voris has prepared an excellent history of political developments in Northern Ireland during the years 1968–72, including the Civil Rights Movement and Bloody Sunday, based on transcripts of tape-recorded statements: *Violence in Ulster: An Oral Documentary* (Amherst: University of Massachusetts Press, 1975). The first person he quotes is Sir Basil Brooke, Lord Brookeborough (pp. 3–11).

12. W. R. Rodgers, ed., *Irish Literary Portraits* (New York: Taplinger, 1973), p. 133.

13. Religion is not one category of culture in Ballymenone, but culture's base. Early in *The Irish Countryman* (p. 32), Arensberg states that one key Irish paradox is that the love of political liberty goes hand in hand with profound religious devotion. He does not consider religion deeply in his book, nor does he explore the paradox he adroitly proposes. Normally, I argue, the paradox is not a paradox, because faith is a deeper value than political aspiration and therefore holds loyalty and rebellion in check. But in times of Trouble, the hierarchy crumbles, political and religious values are held as equal, and a real dilemma, a conceptual bind, results. In his ethnography *Inis Beag* (pp. 58–62, 88–97, 107–13), John Messenger correctly stresses religion. Inis Beag and Ballymenone are in some ways similar. A man told Messenger (p. 91) that different religions are like separate canoes heading for the same harbor, a seafarer's way to state the opinion the Fermanagh hillman does when he likens different religions to people ascending opposite sides of the same mountain. Inis Beag and Ballymenone also differ. The anticlericalism Messenger finds would be inappropriate in a tense situation where opposed ideologies shape religious loyalty. Priest and minister have little need to pressure people, religion wells within, and people do not criticize their religious leaders who are gentle, helpful men. Messenger's assertion that religion is essential to the formation of personality holds as well for Ballymenone, but where the primary trait of that personality in Inis Beag is, according to Messenger, "sexual puritanism" (p. 107), in Ballymenone it is

the will to endure bravely and generously. Not that "sexual puritanism" is absent from Ballymenone, but it is far less stringent than it apparently is in Inis Beag. Some older men express fear of women—"Ah, God, they'd eat ye"—but others speak warmly of women and love, and women, generally direct in sexual matters, often take, as Kavanagh says (*Green Fool*, p. 100), the bawdy turn in chat. In Ballymenone as in Inis Beag (p. 115), dirty jokes are not common, but unlike Inis Beag, there is no childish confusion of excremental with sexual functions. Elimination is not funny or interesting; it is dealt with frankly, as frankly as in the rural American South, much more frankly than in bourgeois urban America: people go together to the fields to continue casual conversations while answering natural calls. Ballymenone is generally more liberal than Inis Beag. Unwed mothers are not reviled but pitied, then accepted calmly as simple fact. As with the people described by Fox (*Tory Islanders*, p. 160), women prefer an illegitimate child to an unsuitable marriage, but, unlike Tory, having a child out of wedlock does greatly decrease a woman's desirability, which rich offers by her father to poor young men cannot overcome. Two of the papers by K. H. Connell in *Irish Peasant Society: Four Historical Essays* (Oxford: Oxford University Press, 1968), "Illegitimacy Before the Famine" and "Catholicism and Marriage in the Century After the Famine," provide important background for puritanism and chastity, with their concomitant late marriage, lifelong celibacy, and low proportion of illegitimacy—a general Irish syndrome in which Ballymenone shares. The attitudes toward illegitimacy in Ballymenone are much freer than those described as general in earlier times. Though, as Connell states (p. 55), the unwed mother is unlikely to marry if she does not marry her child's father, her shame is not transferred to the child (p. 62). Connell sees Irish sexual restraint as the product of Catholicism (see esp. pp. 119–22), and that seems true for Ballymenone, even among Protestants. Again religion is proposed as basic to the formation of the personality, but again I see sexual restraint as part of a larger, deeper pattern of self-control, courage, and kindness. Since differences of description arise from differences in scholars as well as differences in observed reality, I must state my belief that what is essential to human beings is not sex drive but the will to create. To state things coarsely: in rural Ireland, a culture founded upon religion directs that will to art and politics, leaving people sexually docile, while in America, a culture founded upon the economy directs that drive to sex, leaving people docile in art and politics.

14. Marc Bloch's comment on skepticism preventing understanding of the medieval mind comes within his discussion of the sacred role of political leaders in the important chapter "Modes of Feeling and Thought," *Feudal Society*, trans. L. A. Manyon (Chicago: University of Chicago Press, 1968; 1st pub. 1940), 1:84. He offers comparable comment on the connection between politics and religion in *Land and Work in Mediaeval Europe*, trans. J. E. Anderson (New York: Harper & Row, 1969; 1st pub. 1966), pp. 24–30. Bloch outlines the scholarly philosophy from which he argues in *The Historian's Craft*, trans. Peter Putnam (New York: Random House, 1953). That book has helped shape my ideas both of history and the scholar's task; see esp. chap. 4 where he says the scholar invites experience that upsets his cherished theories (p. 138), that he is obliged to select and order (p. 144), not to judge but to understand other people (pp. 139–40), to see people not as fragmented but as complex, whole, and human (pp. 150–56). On p. 86, Bloch writes that it is criminal of the scholar to allow his erudition to run in neutral gear; it is vain to treasure methods as ends in themselves.

11 Saints at Work

1. James Joyce, *Ulysses* (New York: Random House, 1934; 1st pub. 1922), pp. 83, 172.

2. I do not mean to contradict Evans' generalization (*Irish Folk Ways*, p. 11) that wild sources of food are rarely used, for they make up almost no part of the Ballymenone diet, but they are often discussed, and it is their importance in the mind I stress: there is a source of nutrition available in nature which, though not used, could be used if things get worse; nature is inherently hopeful.

12 Plans and Snags

1. The first entry in the Annals of Connacht, the year 1224, connects a good king with good weather, and a terrible storm and disease with his death (pp. 2–3), and other instances of connections between troubled politics, storms, and famine follow: A. Martin Freeman, ed., *The Annals of Connacht* (Dublin: Dublin Institute for Advanced Studies, 1934), pp. 64–65, 252–53, 282–83. The *Four Masters* provides examples of good rulers and good weather, bad rulers and bad weather (1:91, 94, 97), as does Keating's *History of Ireland*, pp. 84, 231, 273 (quoted). For discussions of the idea: Hyde, *Literary History of Ireland*, p. 28; Alwyn Rees and Brinley Rees, *Celtic Heritage: Ancient Tradition in Ireland and Wales* (London: Thames & Hudson, 1978; 1st pub. 1961), pp. 129–30.

2. The frightening poems on the future attributed to Columcille were and remain available in cheap popular books. *The Prophecies of St. Malachy and St. Columbkille* (Gerards Cross: Colin Smyth, 1970) incorporates the popular book of 1855 (pp. 109–42). Columcille's prophecies are mostly extrapolations from a negative view of human affairs, influenced by Isaiah 24:1–27:13, warnings predicting the decay of society and religion, telling of an awful time of famine and storm, poverty and unjust law, when greedy people will mistreat one another, babbling in a foreign tongue, when "a roof-tree shall not remain on the raths" and a "fraudulent system of trade" will ruin human life. Or his prophecies predict invasion, resistance by an Irish leader named Hugh, and defeat. The author of the Columcille poems foretells that the natural state and order of the seasons will be upset, but his predictions are not those of the countryside, the signs of the world's end found in Ballymenone, in Tadhg MacLochlainn, *Ballinasloe: A Story of a Community over the Past 200 Years* (Galway: Galway Printing Co., 1971), pp. 215–17, in Cross' *Tailor and Ansty*, pp. 99, 112–14, and in the writings of Joyce: John Garvin, *James Joyce's Disunited Kingdom and the Irish Dimension* (Dublin: Gill & Macmillan, 1976), pp. 94, 150, 192–94.

3. Lévi-Strauss' major statement is *The Savage Mind*. Gregory Bateson's consonant idea is presented in *Mind and Nature: A Necessary Unity* (New York: E. P. Dutton, 1979), pp. 142–44.

13 Home

1. My approach to architectural study runs through *Folk Housing in Middle Virginia*, which contains a bibliography on artifactual analysis. I think the most useful works are: Kniffen, "Folk Housing: Key to Diffusion," *Annals of the Association of American Geographers* 55 (1965); Christian Norberg-Schulz, *Intentions in Architecture*

(Cambridge: M.I.T. Press, 1968), and *Existence, Space and Architecture* (New York: Praeger, 1971); James Marston Fitch, *American Building: The Environmental Forces That Shape It*, 2d ed. (Boston: Houghton Mifflin, 1972; 1st ed. 1948); Gaston Bachelard, *The Poetics of Space*, trans. Maria Jolas (Boston: Beacon, 1969; 1st. pub. 1958); Amos Rapoport, *House Form and Culture*, Foundations of Cultural Geography (Englewood Cliffs: Prentice-Hall, 1969). In this chapter I improve upon my earlier studies of housing by moving from the outside to the inside, from form to use, from house to home. That shift entails a change of emphasis from male house builders to female homemakers. For Irish house forms, see below, Chapter 24, notes 1 and 3. For comparison, good descriptions of Irish home interiors can be found in these works: Mr. and Mrs. Hall, *Ireland*, 3:290–99; Carleton, *Traits and Stories*, 1:9, 277–79, 294, 411–12; 2:15, 75–76, 224; Wilde, *Irish Popular Superstitions*, pp. 91–92; Lynd, *Home Life in Ireland*, pp. 15–19; Evans, *Irish Heritage*, chap. 8; *Irish Folk Ways*, chap. 5; *Mourne Country*, pp. 198–200; Flower, *Great Blasket*, pp. 42–47; Ó Crohan, *Islandman*, pp. 32–39, 236; O'Donoghue, *In a Quiet Land*, pp. 16–21; Cross, *Tailor and Ansty*, pp. 20–27, 35–37; Leo Ward, *God in an Irish Kitchen* (New York: Sheed & Ward, 1939), pp. 4–6, 61, 71, 73, 75–78, 81–83, 144–45, 155–57, 176–79 (his theme is the hospitality of the house, pp. 45–46); Michael J. Murphy, *Mountain Year: Life on an Irish Mountain Side* (Dublin: Dolmen Press, 1964), pp. 9–11, 51; Harris, *Prejudice and Tolerance in Ulster*, pp. 24–42. Fermanagh: Shan F. Bullock, *After Sixty Years*, pp. 98–100, 166–68, and his novel *The Loughsiders* (New York: Dial Press, n.d.; 1st pub. 1924), pp. 28–29, 70–71, 145; Harbinson, *Song of Erne*, pp. 79, 95–96, 119–27. Irish country furniture has been too little studied, but see: K. M. Harris, "Extracts from the Committee's Collection (4)," *Ulster Folklife* 7 (1961): 25; Alan Gailey, "Kitchen Furniture," *Ulster Folklife* 12 (1966): 18–34; F. H. A. Aalen, "Furnishings of Traditional Houses in the Wicklow Hills," *Ulster Folklife* 13 (1967): 61–68; Timothy P. O'Neill, *Life and Tradition in Rural Ireland* (London: J. M. Dent, 1977), chap. 2. These manuscripts contain some description of south Fermanagh furniture: McConnell, IFC 1664 (1957): 114; Murphy, IFC 1711 (1966): 3–5, 69–70.

2. Caoimhín Ó Danachair draws the old calendar in "The Quarter Days in Irish Tradition," *Arv* 15 (1959): 47–55, and he assembles good information on the holidays beginning with Saint Brighid's Day in Kevin Danaher, *The Year in Ireland* (Cork: Mercier Press, 1972). Other accounts of the year, its Great Days and Set Times, can be found in Jeanne Cooper Foster, *Ulster Folklore* (Belfast: H. R. Carter, 1951), chap. 2; Evans, *Mourne Country*, pp. 205–7; Seán Ó Súilleabháin, *Irish Folk Custom and Belief*, Irish Life and Culture 15 (Dublin: Cultural Relations Committee of Ireland, [c. 1972]), pp. 61–75, and *Handbook of Irish Folklore*, pp. 322–54, 664–67. Ronald H. Buchanan provides an excellent analytic survey in "Calendar Customs," *Ulster Folklife* 8 (1962): 15–34; 9 (1963): 61–78. The antiquity of the old year appears in Dillon and Chadwick, *Celtic Realms*, p. 108, and the Rees brothers speculate ingeniously on the ancient year's meaning in *Celtic Heritage*, chap. 3.

3. The Saint Brigid's cross that I illustrated from Owen Cleary's byre in *All Silver and No Brass* (p. 111) displays the local type. For that, other forms, and associated customs, see Danaher, *Year in Ireland*, pp. 13–37; T. G. F. Paterson, "Brigid's Crosses in County Armagh," *Ulster Journal of Archaeology*, 3d series, 8 (1945): 43–48; John C. O'Sullivan, "St. Brigid's Crosses," *Folk Life* 11 (1973): 60–81.

4. When ecological differences are eliminated, John Messenger's good description of diet (*Inis Beag*, pp. 41–43, 73) tallies closely with Ballymenone's. Here too five small meals a day is the norm.

5. The most common locally made chair, a merger of the Empire style of around 1835 with the medieval slat-back form, is closely comparable to the usual traditional chair of the southern United States, the mule-ear settin' chair: *Pattern in the Material Folk Culture of the Eastern United States*, pp. 228–34. All the elements in the formula—the old slat-back, the new Empire chair, and the curved back synthesis (the mule-eared analogy to the Irish form)—from one southern region, interesting because of its German accent, appear in Lonn Taylor and David B. Warren, *Texas Furniture: The Cabinetmakers and Their Work, 1840–1880* (Austin: University of Texas Press, 1975), pp. 143–51, 156–59. Robert F. Trent has written a fine study of how new chair forms arise out of the synthesis of old, familiar ideas with new, alien ideas in *Hearts and Crowns: Folk Chairs of the Connecticut Coast, 1720–1840* (New Haven: New Haven Colony Historical Society, 1977), esp. pp. 60–90.

6. Belleek pottery made for farmhouse use has not attracted writers like the fragile ornamental ware, but it is mentioned as having been made with the same transfer designs from 1860 to 1920, and the typical mugs and bowls are illustrated from a 1904 catalog by Richard K. Degenhardt, *Belleek: The Complete Collector's Guide and Illustrated Reference* (Huntington: Portfolio Press, 1978), pp. 32, 187. Michael Gordon calls attention to working Belleek in a review, "Spatterware and Sponge," *Maine Antiques Digest*, January 1980, 22c. "Delph" is not delft, but all ceramic pieces put on display.

7. The wonderful slipware of Thomas Toft (d. 1698) and his school is presented by G. W. and F. A. Rhead, *Staffordshire Pots and Potters* (New York: Dodd, Mead, 1907), chaps. 10, 11; L. M. Solon, *The Art of the Old English Potter* (New York: John Francis, 1906), chap. 3; W. B. Honey, *English Pottery and Porcelain* (London: Adam & Charles Black, 1947), chap. 2. Decorative pottery from the other end of Europe—of much later date but representing a comparable evolutionary moment, when prosperity led to the efflorescence of a peasant tradition, prior to its destruction by an imposed aesthetic order—is described by György Domanovszky, *Hungarian Pottery*, Hungarian Folk Art 1 (Budapest: Corvina Press, 1968). In Pennsylvania that phase—when the old tradition, at once excited and threatened, burst into elaborate pottery—came chronologically between England and Hungary; its best record remains Edwin Atlee Barber, *Tulip Ware of the Pennsylvania-German Potters* (Philadelphia: Pennsylvania Museum and School of Industrial Art, 1903).

8. John Montague, "Hymn to the New Omagh Road," *The Rough Field* (Dublin: Dolmen Press, 1972), p. 63.

9. Armstrong, *Powers of Presence*, chap. 1.

10. At the end of the story that formed the basis for his play *In the Shadow of the Glen* (1904), Synge comments that the teller "speaks in the first person, with minute details to show that he was actually present at the scenes that he described," and he says the story was preceded by a "long account" to situate it: J. M. Synge, *The Aran Islands* (Dublin: Maunsel, 1907), pp. 33–36. William Fay of the Abbey commented that they later found three other versions of the story in different parts of Ireland, testifying to its folk nature: E. H. Mikhail, ed., *J. M. Synge: Interviews and Recollections* (London: Macmillan, 1977), pp. 27–28. Michael J. Murphy, "Four Folktales About Woman," *Ulster Folklife* 13 (1967), comments on the tale in tradition (p. 1) and provides a text (pp. 7–8). It is a version of the international tale, Aarne-Thompson type 1350.

11. Fynes Moryson, *A Description of Ireland* (1600–1603; 1st pub. 1606) reprinted in Henry Morley, ed., *Ireland Under Elizabeth and James the First* (London: George Rout-

ledge, 1890), p. 430. Edward M. Hinton, *Ireland Through Tudor Eyes* (Philadelphia: University of Pennsylvania Press, 1935), pp. 74–81, sets Moryson among other observers. The surveyors are quoted by George Hill, *Plantation Papers: Containing a Summary Sketch of the Great Ulster Plantation in the Year 1610* (Belfast: The Northern Whig, 1889), pp. 159, 171, 172. Pynnar's *Survey of Ulster* is printed in Walter Harris, ed., *Hibernica: Or, Some Antient Pieces Relating to Ireland* (Dublin: John Milliken, 1770); I quote from pp. 156–66. *The Irish Hudibras, or Fingallian Prince, Taken from the Sixth Book of Virgil's Aeneaids, and Adapted to the Present Times* (London: Richard Baldwin, 1689) describes houses (p. 31: turff from bog and blocks make a fire that wou'd roast an Oxe; and pp. 32–34, quoted in part), and the author, apparently James Farewell, comes to his Williamite point on pp. 132–34. The second is William Moffet's *The Irish Hudibras: Hesperi-neso-graphica: Or, A Description of the Western Isle* (London: J. Reason, 1755; 1st pub. 1724); I quote from pp. 5–8. *A Trip to Ireland, Being a Description of the Country, People and Manners: As Also Some Select Observations on Dublin* (1699), reprinted in *Five Travel Scripts Commonly Attributed to Edward Ward*, Facsimile Text Society, Series 1, Language and Literature 7 (New York: Columbia University Press for the Society, 1933), p. 5. I am indebted to Robert St. George for getting me this text. Philip Robinson surveys the early records efficiently in "Vernacular Housing in Ulster in the Seventeenth Century," *Ulster Folklife* 25 (1979): 1–28. And see Caoimhín Ó Danachair, "Representations of Houses on Some Irish Maps of c. 1600," in Geraint Jenkins, ed., *Studies in Folk Life: Essays in Honour of Iorwerth C. Peate* (London: Routledge & Kegan Paul, 1969), pp. 91–103.

12. Eric Mercer's excellent history, *Furniture: 700–1700*, Social History of the Decorative Arts (New York: Meredith, 1969), esp. chap. 2, shows much early furniture to consist of immobile, boxlike, multiple-purpose forms. In his masterful survey, *Oak Furniture: The British Tradition* (Woodbridge: Antique Collectors' Club, 1980), Victor Chinnery provides antecedents for Ballymenone's dressers (pp. 340–47), and illustrates a medieval prototype for the local press (p. 415). He places the distinctive Irish Windsor (which he prefers not to call a Windsor but to consider the ancestor of the Windsor) among the primitive comb-back chairs, developed out of stools like the District's creepies (pp. 75–78).

13. Young, *A Tour in Ireland*, 2:2–26. He speaks of the poor quality of upper-class houses (p. 77). John Carr, *The Stranger in Ireland: Or, A Tour in the Southern and Western Parts of That Country in the Year 1805* (Philadelphia: T. & G. Palmer, 1806), p. 159. He comments on music and literature (p. 135) and houses (pp. 94–96). Observation and opinion comparable to Carr's can be found in Thomas Cromwell, *Excursions Through Ireland* (London: Grieg & Youngman, 1820), 1:9–18; 2:88–89. T. Crofton Croker, of Cork, *Researches in the South of Ireland* (1824), blames the dirty smoking cabins on the "indolence and obstinacy in the lower order of Irish" more than on the policies of the landlords (pp. 102–3), then later he praises the "hovels" as scenes of great hospitality, where a traveler who lifts the latch "is welcomed to the best seat the cabin affords" and given the largest of the family's potatoes (pp. 226–27). Croker sets one of his tales, "The Lucky Guest," which he learned from the artist Maclise, in a rural house, saying, "The kitchen of some country houses in Ireland presents in no ways a bad modern translation of the ancient feudal hall," where the master sits, surrounded by kin, and "the benighted traveller, even the passing beggar, are received with a hearty welcome, and each contributes planxty, song, or superstitious tale, towards the evening's amusement": *Fairy Legends and Traditions of the South of Ireland: The New Series* (London: John Murray, 1828), 1:203; (1834), p. 274; (1862),

p. 295. A visitor eighty years later, Clifton Johnson, whose numerous American travel books are rich with folkloristic observations, did not like Ireland. His many and useful descriptions of home interiors emphasize a dirtiness his characteristically good photographs belie, but he does say the hospitality, the "sympathetic kindness," of the people made up for the unpleasant environment, dirty within, wet and unkempt without: *Isle of the Shamrock* (1901), pp. 47–51, 83, 94 (quoted), 97, 98–100, 112–14, 117–19, 166, 189–90, 227–28.

14. *Folk Housing in Middle Virginia* produced the conclusions I compare with those from the District, and it contains argument surrounding the shift from the balanced, socially open hall-and-parlor house to the symmetrical, closed I house. The basic volumes of the early Virginia hall-and-parlor house are closely akin to those in the old homes of Ballymenone: a large hall-kitchen where daily life transpires; a smaller, removed parlor-room used ceremonially and for sleeping. This pair of rooms—open and dirty, closed and clean—is fundamental to western European architecture. Jan Harold Brunvand, for instance, illustrates a Romanian house with two rooms—"hearth room" and "clean room"—in "Traditional House Decoration in Romania: Survey and Bibliography," *East European Quarterly* 14, no. 3 (1980): 295. Examples from England are found throughout M. W. Barley's superb *The English Farmhouse and Cottage* (London: Routledge & Kegan Paul, 1961), see esp. pp. 45–47, 123–25. Barley summarizes the data well in *The House and Home: A Review of 900 Years of House Planning and Furnishing in Britain* (Greenwich: New York Graphic Society, 1963), pp. 18–26, 40–42. For varieties of the hall-and-parlor concept in England: R. W. Brunskill, *Illustrated Handbook of Vernacular Architecture* (New York: Universe Books, 1971), pp. 100–103. The basic idea—hall and parlor, plus chamber and service—is shared by English, Anglo-American, and Irish houses. As I discovered in Virginia and then more richly in Fermanagh, and as I believe to be the case throughout the European tradition (see note 20, below), the fundamental change in architectural history entails pulling the hall away from contact with the external world, protecting it with some kind of vestibule, simplifying its use through the creation of a separate kitchen that draws its work off and leaves it a center for entertainment. Around the newly polite hall, specialized rooms—a parlor lacking beds, a dining room—assemble, while over it chambers split and multiply. The vestibule (porch, hallway, lobby) sets barriers between insiders and outsiders; the fragmentation of internal space (second kitchen, second bedroom, third, fourth) erects barriers between the insiders: privacy increases. Then the home is curtained by a symmetrical exterior that gives no hint about the location of the dwelling's inhabitants. Since the old facade grew out of the plan, the plan out of human activity, it revealed rather than hid the people of the interior. That model of change awaits improvement and use in different localities. Houses provide the major quantifiable, datable evidence on the change in culture from experiential to conceptual modes of order, and on the change in society from a neighborly to a familial base—the change from the "medieval" to the "modern" world.

15. William Carleton, *Traits and Stories*, 2:339, 382–88, predicted that the oppressive system of the landlords would generate a revolution if rents were not lowered and stabilized. They were not. The succession of laws that marked the Land League's victory is narrated by Elizabeth R. Tooker, *Readjustments of Agricultural Tenure in Ireland* (Chapel Hill: University of North Carolina Press, 1938), pp. 42–89; analyzed by Samuel Clark, *Social Origins of the Irish Land War* (Princeton: Princeton University Press, 1979), chap. 9; summarized by J. C. Beckett, *The Making of Modern*

Ireland, 1603–1923 (New York: Alfred A. Knopf, 1973), pp. 384–94, 405–10; Edmund Curtis, *A History of Ireland* (London: Methuen, 1961; 1st pub. 1936), pp. 378–82, 388–90; and T. W. Freeman, *Ireland: A General and Regional Geography* (London: Methuen, 1972; 1st pub. 1950), pp. 175–79. The local situation is ably set forth by Livingstone, *The Fermanagh Story*, pp. 258–62.

16. The enclosures, outlined in W. E. Tate, *The Enclosure Movement* (New York: Walker, 1967), led to the replacement of the openfield village by a landscape of independent farms—an event so powerful in its effect on the course of British civilization that it has been and remains crucial to value-charged arguments over the human condition. The folklorist George Laurence Gomme attempted to treat the village and its history in terms of both the scientific-evolutionary (progressive-capitalist) and organic-romantic (critical-socialist) paradigms of his age in *The Village Community*, Contemporary Science Series (New York: Scribner & Welford, 1890). Normally those traditions have been kept apart to avoid the paradox of simultaneous progress and regress. Neatly separated, these traditions extend easily into radically positive or radically negative views of historical development. In one tradition, the enclosures symbolize benefit. M. E. Seebohm correctly views the period of the change from village to independent farm as one of agricultural progress and increasing prosperity in *The Evolution of the English Farm* (London: George Allen & Unwin, 1952; 1st ed. 1927). The extreme formulation of that view produces the attitude toward the past that Herbert Butterfield calls *The Whig Interpretation of History* (New York: W. W. Norton, 1965; 1st pub. 1931), which is necessary to the political equation of advancement with the decline of the sacred and cooperative (symbolized by the village) and the rise of the secular and competitive (symbolized by the separate farm). The opposite tradition begins in conceptualization of the lost sacred community. A great historian's formula is that of Marc Bloch in *Feudal Society*, vol. 1, chap. 5. The classic anthropological statement is Robert Redfield, *The Little Community: Viewpoints for the Study of a Human Whole* (Chicago: University of Chicago Press, 1955). When the organic, sacredly based community is viewed positively and set into time, the enclosures symbolize social disintegration and decay. The great text is Oliver Goldsmith's *The Deserted Village: A Poem* (London: W. Griffin, 1770). Goldsmith based Auburn on Lissoy near his birthplace in County Longford, and some details—the schoolmaster, the chest that serves as a bed by night, the rood that must support its man—sound Irish, but its feel is English and his elegy for a bold peasantry, his castigation of luxury, and his acceptance of the role of sad historian make his poem an expression of transnational melancholy. Raymond Williams cautions us against the misty backward view, against nostalgia like Goldsmith's, in *The Country and the City* (chaps. 2, 3, 4, 9, and 10 esp.), saying it characterizes every generation, but in his dedicatory preface to Sir Joshua Reynolds, Goldsmith says his elegy is more than poetic imagination. Something happened. Personality and politics cause people to evaluate that something differently, but there was a massive cultural upheaval, the complexity of which is covered only partially by the period and events of the enclosures. Humanism, Protestantism, and capitalism provide the wider frame, but the enclosures, which rooted up collective forms to free enterprise and stimulate profit, do provide an apt symbol for the change that was necessary for the Cromwellian revolution and reform of property laws, progressive in their day, as Christopher Hill argues in *The English Revolution*. In English America, most swiftly in Virginia, more slowly in Massachusetts, enclosing was part of the process of westward settlement and a necessary prelude to social, architectural, and

political revolution. In Ireland the process of enclosure preceded the Land League's Agitation and the housing change. Irish enclosure is described well by Aalen, *Man and the Landscape in Ireland*, pp. 161–92. And as Christopher Hill presents ably in *The World Turned Upside Down*, new prosperity, coupled to a loosening of sacred rule, opened a wide spectrum of possibility to the individual. The old cosmic order was materialized in an armillary sphere—a sacred scientific, "secular" device—included in an exhibition at the Cloisters, illustrated in Timothy B. Husband and Jane Hayward, *The Secular Spirit: Life and Art at the End of the Middle Ages* (New York: E. P. Dutton and Metropolitan Museum of Art, 1975), p. 180. The failure of that image, essential to economic restraint and the development of a consciousness committed to continuity and unworried about orders of orders, is recounted by Alexandre Koyré, *From the Closed World to the Infinite Universe* (Baltimore: Johns Hopkins University Press, 1968). When the universe was closed, man's world could expand away from him into enchantment. As the universe expanded, man's need to analyze, explore, map, claim, and fence—enclose—the world increased.

17. The sculpture of Florence Court is a ceramic architectural watchstand, surely inspired by the Staffordshire pottery that flourished from 1820 to 1900. A few pieces of Staffordshire sculpture survive in the District, and many pieces in the Staffordshire repertory were designed for an Irish market, such as portrait figures of King William III, Daniel O'Connell, William Smith O'Brien, and Charles Stewart Parnell, and some were also the subjects of Irish songs like Master McGrath and Heenan and Sayers. I have found no prototype for the Florence Court sculpture, but ceramic watchstands and pottery models of houses where notable events, such as murder, occurred are not rare, and they likely helped our unknown sculptor create his work: Anthony Oliver, *The Victorian Staffordshire Figure: A Guide for Collectors* (London: Heinemann, 1971), pp. 30, 38, 54, 114, 134; John Hall, *Staffordshire Portrait Figures* (New York: World, 1972), pp. 21, 36; H. A. B. Turner, *A Collector's Guide to Staffordshire Pottery Figures* (London: MacGibbon & Kee, 1971), pp. 187–89.

18. As early as the Cromwellian period, then compulsively through the eighteenth century, Irish big houses presented symmetrical facades. Hugh Dixon, *An Introduction to Ulster Architecture* (Belfast: Ulster Architectural Heritage Society, 1975), pp. vi–vii, 37, 39–42, 47 (Castle Coole), 50, illustrates Northern symmetrical house fronts from 1667 to 1804. Maurice Craig, *Classic Irish Houses of the Middle Size* (New York: Architectural Book Publishing Co., 1977), shows symmetrical houses throughout and illustrates a plan from a pattern book, published in Dublin in 1757, recommending a lateral hallway for a smaller house (p. 43). The entry halls of Irish Georgian houses can, but usually do not, cut through the house from front to rear; rather, they form a lobby across the front. So these eighteenth-century houses contain the "hall" and facade necessary to the local development of a new house type around 1900.

19. W. G. Hoskins' paper "The Rebuilding of Rural England, 1570–1640," in *Provincial England: Essays in Social and Economic History* (London: Macmillan, 1965), pp. 131–48, is a landmark in the social historical literature. In it he argues that during the period leading up to the English Revolution (see note 16, above), newly prosperous freeholders with a "security of tenure" rebuilt their houses in permanent materials and altered them in line with ideas that arose in fifteenth-century Italy so that large internal spaces were subdivided and functionally simplified, halls were ceiled to provide bedrooms, and privacy came to dominate the idea of domestic design (see note 14, above). The change I describe for Ballymenone in this chap-

ter is an Irish "rebuilding," during which people newly prosperous and secure in their possession of land and home, rebuilt in permanent materials and subdivided large spaces to provide privacy, prior to a major political-military upheaval. Samuel Clark, *Social Origins of the Irish Land War*, p. 162, writes that the "popular explanation" for the poverty of Irish houses before the Land League's Agitation was that people did not improve because they were insecure as tenants. The truth, he says, echoing Arthur Young's comments in *A Tour in Ireland* (1779), 2:26, is that money was put into livestock, not houses. But Hoskins points out that English yeomen first put cash into livestock, then when they became more prosperous and secure they turned to improving their homes. The historians cited by Clark, who consider the traditional explanation of insecurity untrue, are the historians Hoskins chastises at the beginning of his essay who "have yet to learn to look over hedges and to treat visual evidence as of equal value to documentary." The visual evidence of Ballymenone's houses reveals a dramatic change in the 1880–1910 period, written in masonry walls and in subdivided privacy-seeking, improved, comfort-seeking interiors. That is, the houses support the "popular explanation" outlined during the Land League period by M. F. Sullivan, *Ireland of To-Day: The Causes and Aims of the Irish Agitation* (Philadelphia: J. C. McCurdy, 1881), pp. 141–50. Writing during the time of architectural change, Robert Lynd, *Home Life in Ireland* (1909), pp. 14–15, accepted the old argument that landlordism blocked the will to improve the home and said that homes have indeed been much improved since the land acts. And looking back, a modern scholar of the Irish house and land finds the old argument valid: Caoimhín Ó Danachair, "Change in the Irish Landscape," *Ulster Folklife* 8 (1962): 65–71. It is of the greatest importance for the development of a scientific social history that the Irish phenomena are closely analogous to those described by Hoskins for the England of three centuries earlier, and to those I described for the Virginia of a century and a half earlier—in all three cases the architectural change came after economic change and before political change.

20. The beginnings of English architectural change, stimulated from Renaissance Italy, are well described by W. G. Hoskins in the paper cited in note 19, above. The new idea achieved fulfillment in the symmetrical, double-pile, corridor-split "Georgian" form which rose to dominance in England, 1690–1760, and provides the source and parallel to Virginia's new house type of 1760 and Ballymenone's of 1900. Tom Carter has written a fine paper, "Folk Design in Utah Architecture: 1849–90," in Hal Cannon, ed., *Utah Folk Art: A Catalog of Material Culture* (Provo: Brigham Young University Press, 1980), pp. 35–59, in which he stresses symmetry and illustrates varieties of closure in domestic design in the Rocky Mountain West. While at work on traditional housing in Denmark, Carter wrote, October 14, 1980, of the comparable change there: "The asymmetrical-symmetrical shift happens dramatically, though quite late in the countryside—about 1840–1880. Straightening out the house facade is in evidence on the estates c. 1750. The symmetrical facade accompanies the so-called 'peasant revolution' of the late 18th century and early 19th century land reforms, i.e. enclosures, instituted by lords and government to stimulate the economy. Villages start breaking up by 1800 and a farming middle class arises. As farmers begin to consolidate their new economic position, they covet the symbols of their urban middle class counterparts. By 1880, all the farmhouses look the same. They are not direct copies of upper class houses, but combine some of the features of the old with urban style. Before the facade gets a facelift, the interior was changing. The older farmhouse had only a few rooms, open

from front to back. By the late eighteenth century, there is a growing tendency to compartmentalize; older rooms are divided up into smaller areas with separate functions." That is, housing in Denmark changed, 1770–1850, in a way quite like that of England, 1570–1760 (the change occurred at different times in different places in England), Virginia, 1760–1820, and Ballymenone, 1880–1930. In a fine dissertation, Ayse Zekiye Celebioglu describes the change from open, asymmetrical houses to closed, symmetrical houses occurring today in Turkey: "Elimination of an Indigenous House Form in Reference to Liquidation of a Peasant Community in a Rural Anatolian Town" (Ph.D. diss., University of Pennsylvania, 1978). Throughout the West, new synthetic types were developed. Among the earliest was the "saltbox" form of New England, created in southeastern England just before 1600, in which the most common southeastern English house was changed by moving its service area from the end to the rear, beneath a long shed roof, so that it could gain access to the central chimney and become a second kitchen, and so that the facade, formerly asymmetrical like the old Irish houses—window, window, door, window—could become symmetrical. The usual early East Anglian type is described by P. Eden, "Smaller Post-medieval Houses in Eastern England," in Lionel Munby, ed., *East Anglian Studies* (Cambridge: W. Heffer, 1968), pp. 71–93. His class-J (asymmetrical) is statistically dominant and provides, I believe, the prototype for the usual southeastern Irish type (see below, Chapter 24, note 1). His class-L removes service to a rear wing, but his paper shows the symmetrical front and rear kitchen to be less common in the Old World than the New, as my own fieldwork in England and New England confirms, and that makes sense, for the situation, socially and environmentally, in the New World was more frightening and more liberating: opting for the newer, more closed and symmetrical form follows logically. One of the early books on English vernacular houses did illustrate a perfect antecedent for the New England saltbox house: Ralph Nevill, *Old Cottage and Domestic Architecture of South-West Surrey, and Notes on the Early History of the Division* (Guildford: Billings, 1889), pp. 12–14 and facing p. 58. So there was no excuse for later American scholars to describe the saltbox as an evolutionary innovation in the New World. The usual asymmetrical southeastern English form and the saltbox type are both described by Harry Forrester, *The Timber-Framed Houses of Essex: A Short Review of Their Types and Details, 14th to 18th Centuries* (Chelmsford: Tindal Press, 1959), pp. 14–20. The New England saltbox house: J. Frederick Kelly, *The Early Domestic Architecture of Connecticut* (New York: Dover, 1963; 1st pub. 1924), pp. 6–19; Anthony N. B. Garvan, *Architecture and Town Planning in Colonial Connecticut* (New Haven: Yale University Press, 1951), chap. 5; and Abbott Lowell Cummings' excellent study, *The Framed Houses of Massachusetts Bay, 1625–1725* (Cambridge: Harvard University Press, 1979), esp. chaps. 1 and 2. The East Anglia–New England idea is completed in the "Cape Cod" house of one or two stories that raises a symmetrical roof to cover the saltbox interior; examples are found in Ernest Allen Connally, "The Cape Cod House: An Introductory Study," *Journal of the Society of Architectural Historians* 19, no. 2 (1960): 47–56. These English–New England houses are of particular relevance for Ireland, since the southeastern Irish house type (of which there is one example in the District—Owen Cleary's illustrated in Chapter 24) fits within their family. The direct transfer of the southeastern Irish house type from the Old World to the New is described in John J. Mannion's good book, *Irish Settlements in Eastern Canada: A Study of Cultural Transfer and Adaptation* (Toronto: University of Toronto Press, 1974), chap. 7. In all these houses, the chimney forms a lobby inside the front door. The northwestern English house that positions a stairway in the center to block entry and form a vestibule is illustrated in R. W. Brunskill, *Vernacular Architecture of the Lake Counties* (London: Faber & Faber, 1974), pp. 70–71. A comparable house from Lowland Scotland: Barley, *House and Home*, p. 53. The older, generally open and asymmetrical Scottish houses are excellently described by Alexander Fenton, *The Northern Isles: Orkney and Shetland* (Edinburgh: John Donald, 1978), chaps. 17, 20. The new Highland house type, symmetrical and closed by a vestibule, is described by I. F. Grant, *Highland Folk Ways* (London: Routledge & Kegan Paul, 1961), pp. 153–54; and Colin Sinclair, *The Thatched Houses of the Old Highlands* (Edinburgh: Oliver & Boyd, 1953), pp. 67, 71. Highland houses close with a short lateral hallway comparable to Ballymenone's, running in front of a small interior room. The transverse hallway dominant in western Britain and the southern United States is best illustrated in the scholarship on Welsh houses, which also shift from open to closed and symmetrical: Iorwerth C. Peate, *The Welsh House: A Study in Folk Culture* (London: Honorable Society of Cymmrodorion, 1940), chap. 5; Sir Cyril Fox and Lord Raglan, *Monmouthshire Houses* (Cardiff: National Museum of Wales, 1954), vol. 3, esp. pp. 129–35, and compare the plans on p. 130 (group A) and 132 (group 5) with the plans in *Folk Housing in Middle Virginia*. Later Welsh houses with hallways are described in this superb study: S. R. Jones and J. T. Smith, "The Houses of Breconshire," *Brycheiniog* 9 (1963): 35–67; 10 (1964): 100–114; 11 (1965): 89–114; 12 (1966/67): 56–65. I describe the comparable symmetrical, central-hallway, one-room-deep, I houses of British Pennsylvania in "Eighteenth-Century Cultural Process in Delaware Valley Folk Building," *Winterthur Portfolio* 7 (1972): 29–57. In addition to *Folk Housing in Middle Virginia*, in which chap. 6 is most important here, examples from the American South can be found in Henry Chandlee Forman, *The Architecture of the Old South: The Medieval Style, 1585–1850* (Cambridge: Harvard University Press, 1948): on pp. 74–75 he illustrates houses open and closed by both stair and hallway, and on pp. 88–89 he illustrates the usual plans, the hall-and-parlor type and the later house closed by a hallway. Marcus Whiffen, *The Eighteenth-Century Houses of Williamsburg* (Williamsburg: Colonial Williamsburg, 1960), describes the formal repertory well in chap. 4 and provides examples of houses with transverse hallways in part 2: see pp. 90–93 and 101–3 for the two basic plans, single- and double-pile, pp. 113–15 for the usual I house, and pp. 134–39 for the common fragmentary variant. Howard Wight Marshall describes well the range of domestic forms, dominated by the I house concept, in one western section of the South in *Folk Architecture in Little Dixie: A Regional Culture in Missouri* (Columbia: University of Missouri Press, 1981), chap. 3.

21. Because authors of public statements always see their eras as times of transition, if you read editorials and manifestos in sequence all periods look alike and collapse, depending upon the authors you choose to read, into time's flow as examples of progress or decay. And if the historian returns to a period he or she thinks is pivotal, there will always be some contemporary writer available to support the thesis. Evolutionary history, then, must be written out of works into which the historical consciousness projects unconsciously. Objects like houses that display long stretches of basic stability beneath a surface of minor variability, and then exhibit abrupt moments of deep reorganization, provide one class of valuable text for the historian. Imaginative literature provides another. We have no texts of stories recorded before the period of architectural transformation from our District, though we do know it was—in south Fermanagh (as in all Ireland)—a period of extreme

artistic creativity, and we know that the era before architectural change contained a spirit of wicked satire which people today, feeling the fragility of community, avoid. The literature published at the time of housing change, the tense era of the land war and Home Rule campaigns that antedated the period of war, is suggestive. Take one example. James Stephens' *The Crock of Gold* (New York: Macmillan, 1926) was published in 1913, before the Rising. The reader is struck primarily by its tone and allegorical layers. The literary historian might read it for Stephens' oriental mood, reminiscent of Yeats and A.E., for its qualities of synthesis which Joyce so admired that he thought Stephens could finish *Finnegans Wake*, and for its influence on Flann O'Brien's *At Swim-Two-Birds*. But the social historian would discover that here, three years before the Easter Rising, is a tale that tells of the ancient powers of Ireland, slumbering warriors, hidden fairies, forgotten gods, rising and hosting to break a gentle old philosopher, a saintly scholar—Ireland—out of prison. Stephens' novel is a poetic, prophetic reading of the turbulent mood around him. "All is silent," Stephens writes in one poem, thinking through the black streets, yet he says the silence and the darkness crawl and glide and frown with terrifying life, waiting. In another poem, a cold, gray, glum old man says were he young he would make the old man "get up and run about." Those poems were gathered before the Rising in a volume titled *Insurrections* (Dublin: Maunsel, 1909).

22. In the terms Robert Plant Armstrong develops in *Wellspring*, the old conceptual order of Ballymenone—centered continuity—lies between the syndetic and synthetic, and houses display a shift toward the synthetic. I stressed that shift in *Folk Housing in Middle Virginia*, as did James Deetz, *In Small Things Forgotten*. I am not refuting our argument, but asserting that, bound to one kind of evidence, artifactual, it is incomplete. And so it must be. As William Butler Yeats reminds us in *A Vision* (London: Macmillan, 1962; 1st pub. 1925), pp. 67–89, pure ideas are supernatural fantasy, all reality is impure. Cultures do not change from syndetic to synthetic; all cultures mix the syndetic and synthetic, and their history consists of shifts of emphasis. So, as Jim Deetz and I describe it, there really was a shift to the synthetic "Georgian mind-set," but I would put it like this. The mind is innately syndetic and synthetic; it seeks order through both association and disjunction. In time, different cultures evolve to favor one or the other mode. The Yoruba people of West Africa, according to Bob Armstrong, emphasize the syndetic in their art and life, at the base of their thought. After 1760, according to Deetz and Glassie, Americans came to emphasize the synthetic. Before 1900 the people of Ballymenone accomplished balance in a synthetic centering and a syndetic continuity. Times changed, grew painful, and the synthetic dimension of the culture enlarged and took over architectural design, but the syndetic remains, diminished yet alive in intimate sociability, and should times change again and people feel less pressured, there is no reason syndesis should not expand, emerge again as an equal force, and bring the mind back into balance.

23. C. F. Innocent described crucked building in England in *The Development of English Building Construction* (Newton Abbot: David & Charles, 1971; 1st pub. 1916), chaps. 4 and 5. Modern scholars have extended understanding, such as F. W. B. Charles, *Medieval Cruck-Building and Its Derivatives: A Study of Timber-Framed Construction Based on Buildings in Worcestershire*, S.M.A. Monograph Series 2 (London: Society for Medieval Archaeology, 1967). Richard Harris provides a good summary in *Discovering Timber-framed Buildings* (Aylesbury: Shire, 1978), chaps. 6 and 7, where he illustrates faced-pegged jointed crucks like those of Fermanagh (p. 77)

and notes that they characterize the southwestern counties, Dorset, Somerset, and Devon. That variety of cruck-building is also typically Scottish. Sinclair, *Thatched Houses*, illustrates it (pp. 68–69), and in the archive of the National Museum of Antiquities in Edinburgh, to which Alexander Fenton gave me generous access, there are photos of a byre from West Ross identical in its jointed cruck-framing to buildings in the District. The change from the cruck frame to masonry partitions carrying purlins was probably independently effected in various areas. It certainly took place in northwestern England. Brunskill, *Vernacular Architecture of the Lake Counties*, pp. 103–10, describes early crucked building, including jointed crucks, which evolved into trusses borne on the front and rear masonry walls that were replaced in the eighteenth century by purlins carried by the gables and internal walls. Once, following Innocent (*Development of English Building Construction*, p. 39), scholars believed Ireland lacked crucks. Then Desmond McCourt, "Cruck Trusses in North-West Ireland," *Gwerin* 3, no. 4 (1961): 165–85, provided a full description of Irish practice and noted the resemblance of Irish and Scottish framing. More followed: Alan Gailey, "Two Cruck Truss Houses Near Lurgan," *Ulster Folklife* 8 (1962): 57–64; Alan Gailey, "Notes on Three Cruck-Truss Houses," *Ulster Folklife* 10 (1964): 88–94 (in which, pp. 90–91, he related the native cruck tradition to the usual Irish coupled roof truss); Desmond McCourt, "Some Cruck-framed Buildings in Donegal and Derry," *Ulster Folklife* 11 (1965): 39–50 (which he opened with the idea that the later coupled truss evolved from crucks); E. Estyn Evans, "Some Cruck Roof-trusses in Ulster," *Ulster Folklife* 12 (1966): 35–40. In that paper, Evans reported the first cruck from Fermanagh, and in the same year Michael J. Murphy described cruck-building in his notes from south Fermanagh: IFC 1711 (1966): 49, 187. Evans also commented that there must be examples in Tyrone, though none has been reported. When Alan Gailey visited me in Philadelphia in November 1980, he said there are still no known crucks from Tyrone, so it is worth adding that I photographed the ruins of a crucked house near Newtownstewart in June 1972. Desmond McCourt derives the coupled roof from the crucked truss, describes an intermediate corbeled variety of couple (also known in our District), and relates Irish jointed crucks to western Scotland, arguing—correctly, I think—that connections predate Plantation in "The Cruck Truss in Ireland and Its West-European Connections," *Folk-Liv* 28–29 (1964–65): 64–78. Alan Gailey, "The Ulster Tradition," *Folk Life* 2 (1964): 34–35, shows that the coupled and purlined systems, sequential in Ballymenone, belonged at any early date to different subregions of Ulster, the border between which cuts through Enniskillen. In sum, in terms of the typology efficiently presented by Desmond McCourt, "Roof Timbering Techniques in Ulster: A Classification," *Folk Life* 10 (1972): 118–30, the District's roofing varieties are: the jointed open cruck truss, locally called "building on knees" and once the norm for erecting modest structures, which is especially common in north Derry and Down but has been reported from elsewhere in Fermanagh; the collar beam couple truss, which McCourt—like Hugh Nolan—says probably developed directly from the crucked truss, and which is typical of northwest Ulster (he notes a group from Tyrone and Donegal with wall corbels to support the couples, and there are instances of that variation from the District; I illustrate one from John Gilleece's byre); purlins without trusses, typical of east central Ulster and associated with weavers' houses. McCourt says the purlin roof could have developed in two ways, one of them the way I was told it developed by men from the District: discovering that internal masonry walls could perform the tasks of crucks.

24. Irish scollop-thatching like that of the District has often been described. T. Hennell compares Irish work during his good account of English thatching, *Change in the Farm* (Cambridge: Cambridge University Press, 1934), pp. 115, 149–67, 174. Irish descriptions: Evans, *Irish Heritage*, pp. 63–65, and *Irish Folk Ways*, pp. 50–58; J. M. Mogey, "Thatch," *Ulster Journal of Archaeology*, 3d series, 3, no. 2 (1940): 134–37. Ronald H. Buchanan, "Thatch and Thatching in North-East Ireland," *Gwerin* 1, no. 3 (1957): 123–42, describes the process well, relates it to British tradition, and mentions Fermanagh (p. 137) as one area where thatch is still common, one in four houses being thatched. Locally, the number was three in ten when I arrived in 1972, and had declined to one in five when I visited last in 1979. In "Stapple Thatch," *Ulster Folklife* 3 (1957): 19–28, Buchanan describes a northeastern variety distinct from the usual scollop-thatching of Fermanagh, and the distributional patterns for different kinds of thatching are set out by Alan Gailey, "The Thatched Houses of Ulster: The First Ulster Folk Museum Questionnaire," *Ulster Folklife* 7 (1961): 13–14. South Fermanagh thatching: McConnell, IFC 1079 (1946): 272–73; Anderson, Ulster Notebook, p. 15.

14 Clay

1. The words in quotation marks represent the local concept of the grades of increasing severity of rainfall. Storcs are young large cattle. Statistics on rain: Symons, ed., *Land Use in Northern Ireland*, pp. 79, 82, 234. Evaluation of Fermanagh's grasslands, their unsuitability as arable, come at pp. 71, 102, 116, 119 (compulsory tillage), 131.

2. The detailed descriptions of plowing given me by Peter Flanagan (10/25/72d) and Hugh Nolan (11/8/72t) agree closely with that Alexander Fenton provides in *Scottish Country Life* (Edinburgh: John Donald, 1976), pp. 112, 117, 119–21. Plows from Down comparable to that Tommy Lunny described to me (8/29/72r) are illustrated by George Thompson in Wilfred Seaby, "The Ulster Drill Plough," *Gwerin* 2, no. 2 (1958): 85–86. A. T. Lucas provides a characteristically thorough historical survey, "Irish Ploughing Practices," *Tools and Tillage* 2, no. 1 (1972): 52–62; 2, no. 2 (1973): 67–83; 2, no. 3 (1974): 149–60; 2, no. 4 (1975): 195–210.

3. A classic statement of the highland-lowland division is Sir Cyril Fox, *The Personality of Britain: Its Influence on Inhabitant and Invader in Prehistoric and Early Historic Times* (Cardiff: National Museum of Wales, 1952; 1st ed. 1932), esp. pp. 86–91. The dispersed, pastoral tradition is ancient in Ireland, but its history is not simple. It dominated in two periods, the Iron Age days of the raths (see above, Chapter 2, note 20) and the era following the enclosures of the seventeenth to the early nineteenth centuries, our days. But there were clustered habitations—clachans—and openfields along with the raths, true villages were planted in the Middle Ages, and remnants of clachans survive to the present (see below, Chapter 20, note 9): E. Estyn Evans, *The Personality of Ireland*, pp. 53–62, and "Archaeology and Folklife," *Béaloideas* 39–41 (1971–73): 127–39, esp. 132–36; A. R. Orme, *Ireland*, The World's Landscapes 4 (London: Longman, 1970), pp. 93–99, 106–9, 128–29, 133–35, 149–50, 167–91; and F. H. A. Aalen, who presents the age and complexity of the dispersed, pastoral pattern particularly well in *Man and the Landscape in Ireland*, pp. 8, 59, 65–71, 85, 94–95, 161–92, 207–8, 220–25.

4. The District's region is compared in Symons, ed., *Land Use in Northern Ireland*, pp. 54, 71, 116, 119, 128, 129, 131, 141, 167. Alan Gailey in "The Disap-

pearance of the Horse from the Ulster Farm," *Folk Life* 4 (1966): 55, generalizes on the basis of the number of horses that Fermanagh is especially resistant to change. Alternately it could be said that environment and economic conditions make the retention of "conservative" practices logical responses to modern conditions in Fermanagh.

5. G. B. Adams provides a superb summary of Ulster practices in "The Work and Words of Haymaking," *Ulster Folklife* 12 (1966): 66–91; 13 (1967): 29–53. Evans, of course, describes the work well: *Irish Heritage*, pp. 95–99; *Irish Folk Ways*, pp. 151–57. Alan Gailey describes the devices for making hay ropes: "Ropes and Rope Twisters," *Ulster Folklife* 8 (1962): 72–82.

6. Caoimhín Ó Danachair describes sod and clay techniques first in "Materials and Methods in Irish Traditional Building," *Journal of the Royal Society of Antiquaries of Ireland*, 87 (1957): 61–74, esp. 62–64. E. Estyn Evans surveys "Sod and Turf Houses in Ireland," in Jenkins, ed., *Studies in Folk Life*, pp. 79–90, and adds more in "Folk Housing in the British Isles in Materials Other Than Timber," in Walker and Haag, eds., *Man and Cultural Heritage*, pp. 53–64. Alex McConnell of Bellanaleck describes local sod houses in his manuscript, IFC 1076 (1946): 134.

7. On hedged ditches: E. Estyn Evans, "Fields, Fences, and Gates," *Ulster Folklife* 2 (1956): 14–21; Philip Robinson, "The Spread of Hedged Enclosures in Ulster," *Ulster Folklife* 23 (1977): 57–69.

8. R. A. Gailey, "Traps and Snares," *Ulster Folklife* 7 (1961): 74–75, depicts a "clavin" exactly like the bird trap Peter Flanagan described then built for me, which he called a "clayveen." Timothy O'Neill illustrates a trap of the same kind from Westmeath, *Life and Tradition in Rural Ireland*, p. 95 (top).

9. John Montague, "What a View," *Tides* (Chicago: Swallow Press, 1971), p. 55.

10. In his brief but insightful essay, "Ireland," in H. J. Hansen, ed., *European Folk Art in Europe and the Americas* (New York: McGraw-Hill, 1968), pp. 77–80, A. T. Lucas states that Ireland is exceptional in Europe for its lack of ornamental folk art.

15 Moss

1. Alan Gailey and Alexander Fenton, eds., *The Spade in Northern and Atlantic Europe* (Belfast: Ulster Folk Museum and Institute of Irish Studies, 1970), includes Caoimhín Ó Danachair's "The Use of the Spade in Ireland," pp. 49–56, and Alan Gailey's "The Typology of the Irish Spade," pp. 35–48, which sets the spade of the Fermanagh type, illustrated by an example from Leitrim, into geographic context (with Ballymenone near the center of distributional intensity), pp. 40–43, and, again with a Leitrim example, Gailey describes the loy, pp. 37–40. There is a good bibliography on spades and the ridges they form—generally called "lazy beds" in the literature, a term unknown in Ballymenone—in Caoimhín Ó Danachair, "The Spade in Ireland," *Béaloideas* 31 (1963): 98–114. He notes that the loy is known in Ulster only at the fringes in Fermanagh, Monaghan, and Cavan (p. 102). The map in Gailey's paper (p. 36) supports that contention, but it places Ballymenone well north of the northern limits of the loy, and while loys are rarely used today, they are well remembered as commonly in use when the upland was cropped a generation ago. Alan Gailey describes manufacturing spades in "A Family Spade-making Business in County Tyrone," *Folk Life* 10 (1972): 26–46, and he describes the implements and making ridges with a loy in a good paper, "Spade Tillage in South-West Ulster and North Connacht," *Tools and Tillage*, 1, no. 4 (1971): 225–36. Evans describes

the tools and work in *Irish Heritage*, pp. 91–94, 113–19, and in *Irish Folk Ways*, pp. 127–47. There is a film of the work, "Digging and Potato Setting and Sowing Oats: Fermanagh/Cavan" (April 1971), in the archive of the Ulster Folk and Transport Museum. John Maguire in Morton's *Come Day, Go Day* (pp. 27–31) gives a good account of the Fermanagh spade, gardening, and the group work of the "mechal." Alex McConnell of Bellanaleck describes the local tools—spade and loy—in IFC 1456 (1956): 223–26. Eamon Anderson of Kinawley describes scalding the ground in K. M. Harris, "Extracts from the Committee's Collection," *Ulster Folklife* 4 (1958): 41.

2. Laurence Sterne, *The Life and Opinions of Tristram Shandy, Gentleman* (New York: Heritage Press, 1935; 1st pub. 1760), p. 324.

3. In his clear, popular introduction, *The Pleasant Land of Ireland* (Cork: Mercier Press, 1970), pp. 40–41, Kevin Danaher says the wish for freshness (which requires the constant cooking of small quantities of food and the daily baking of bread) characterizes Irish traditional culture.

4. E. Estyn Evans speaks with wonderful insight in *The Personality of Ireland* (pp. 29–30, 37–38) when he tells of the effect of the environment upon the mind and when he evokes the intimacy of the drumlin country of south Fermanagh, where continually changing light and weather produce a "sense of uncertainty"—a willingness to gamble, an ability to drop plans, shift alertly, and carry on.

5. Shan Bullock says in his novel *The Loughsiders* that the people of the country around Upper Lough Erne are "given more to the joys of labour than of beauty" (p. 219). Work is one of the themes that unites the superb stories of south Fermanagh farmlife in Shan F. Bullock's *Irish Pastorals* (New York: McClure, Phillips, 1901). In them, spring promises "long days of fierce unresting labour" (p. 226) and angrily the digger of spuds condemns his life of "hokin' for rotten praties wi' a spade" (pp. 191–92): "It's not men we are at all—but danged fools an' slaves." Wet weather holds, floods the land, depresses the people, but at last the sun breaks, bringing work. "It was great—great to be out once more" (pp. 146–50). Work drives the women of "The Reapers" to competitive strife, but that work filled life, and usually work was slowed with rest and tea and crack (pp. 85–86, 97–101) and Bullock tells of "sweetening toil with laughter and talk" (p. 125). Work is hard, but it is harder still to sit with nothing to do. When the sun shines, people are out among one another, and Bullock speaks of haymaking as "a very feast of work, a mad riot of sweet toil" (p. 96). Six years earlier, Bullock published *By Thrasna River*. In chapters 6 and 14 he described work, a hard but collective activity broken by rest and play. Had all Bullock's fiction been like *Thrasna River*, he would be another minor novelist of country life, for the book's tone and plot stand away from its people. Many writers get the details of rural life accurately, they catch turns of phrase, fetching vignettes. Bullock does that, but in *Irish Pastorals* and *The Loughsiders* he does more. He steps into the lives of the people and constructs his plots out of their concerns. *Thrasna River* sketches themes and personalities he brings to tough maturity in *Irish Pastorals*, but in the later book he raises brave ideas he could not have touched earlier and which few have attempted, complex paradoxes of life in close places: the shy, thwarted passion of country men (chaps. 1–3), the confused deep affection and strange envy among co-workers of the same sex (chaps. 3 and 5), the gentle beauty and bitter pain of long marriages (chaps. 2 and 7), the anger and pride felt by poor people when a local man writes them into stage-Irish stereotypes (chap. 4), the revulsion and allure of home that makes some emigrate and some

stay (chap. 6). *Irish Pastorals* and *The Loughsiders* (which I describe below, Chapter 23, note 2) get into fiction important truths about south Fermanagh farming life, and they show that Shan Bullock is—whether or not literary critics attend to him—one of Ireland's best writers, one of the best novelists ever to write on rural existence.

7. Writers of sketches recorded the old blackthorn fights. Lover, *Legends and Stories* (1834), p. 52, called the stick "a usual appendage of the Hibernians," and Carleton, *Traits and Stories*, 1:181, wrote, "It has been long laid down as a universal principle, that self-preservation is the first law of nature. An Irishman, however, has nothing to do with this . . . commend him to a fair, dance, funeral, or wedding, or to any other sport where there is a likelihood of getting his head or bones broken, and if he survive, he will remember you with a kindness peculiar to himself, to the last day of his life." See further pp. 132–39, 182–235 in that volume.

8. Quoted from Livingstone, *The Fermanagh Story*, p. 179.

9. Samuel Beckett teaches that when people are viewed from the outside, as objects behaving, they seem crazy, as Mr. Knott does in *Watt* (New York: Grove Press, 1959; 1st pub. 1953, written 1942–44), or pitiful, hopeless, and absurd, as in *Imagination Dead Imagine* (London: Calder & Boyars, 1965) and *The Lost Ones* (New York: Grove Press, 1972). From the inside the view may be bleak, but the ring of the self never squeezes so tightly as to eliminate the will to endure, and his great trilogy ends in *The Unnamable* (New York: Grove Press, 1970; 1st pub. 1958, written 1949–50) at the triumph of the minimum. The discovery of the other by that reduced self is chronicled magnificently in *How It Is* (New York: Grove Press, 1964; 1st pub. 1961, written 1959); I quote from pp. 27, 80–81. *Mercier and Camier* (New York: Grove Press, 1974; 1st pub. 1970, written 1945) is caught between internal and external perspectives, so he left it unpublished when its idea achieved perfection in *Waiting for Godot* (New York: Grove Press, 1954; written 1947–49), where Beckett's brilliant solution is to have the actors say what they are thinking, leaving what they say unsaid to produce a simultaneity of internal perspective, a social scene constituted from the inside; I quote from p. 9 and facing p. 31. Beckett's great play speaks to the universal nature of communication, of making connections in time, and it describes better than any other work the texture of Irish rural life—hardly a delightful life, but, being the construction of equals, far better than lives led by outsiders that are formed in terms of dominance and submission. The courageous internal perspective maintained in isolation in the trilogy, extended into interplay in the great dramas, perseveres in Beckett's newest works, sensitive in their recall: *That Time* (London: Faber & Faber, 1976), *Company* (New York: Grove Press, 1980). I was helped to think about Beckett by the chronology provided by Hugh Kenner, *A Reader's Guide to Samuel Beckett* (New York: Farrar, Straus & Giroux, 1973). Vivian Mercier remembers his comment in *Beckett/Beckett* (New York: Oxford University Press, 1977), pp. xi, 74. He discusses Beckett's interest in Irish tradition (pp. 22–25, 42) and says that in the first production of *Godot*, Pozzo was dressed as an English gentleman and Lucky like an Irish peasant, so Marxist interpretations of the play are possible. Unquestionably. Pozzo was the nickname of John Maynard Keynes.

10. The frequent translation and publication of the ninth-century poem "The Lament of the Old Woman of Beare" reveals the continuing power of its tough, sad sentiment in Irish culture: Murphy, *Early Irish Lyrics*, pp. 74–83; James Carney, *Medieval Irish Lyrics: Selected and Translated* (Berkeley: University of California Press, 1967), pp. 28–41; John Montague, *The Book of Irish Verse*, pp. 71–75—his fine trans-

lation appears as well in *Tides*, pp. 19–22, and *A Fair House: Versions of Irish Poetry* (Dublin: Cuala Press, 1972), pp. 17–22; E. A. Sharp and J. Matthay, eds., *Lyra Celtica: An Anthology of Representative Celtic Poetry* (Edinburgh: John Grant, 1924; 1st ed. 1896), pp. 378–80; Meyer, *Selections from Ancient Irish Poetry*, pp. 88–91; Lady Gregory, *The Kiltartan Poetry Book: Prose Translations from the Irish* (New York: G. P. Putnam's Sons, 1919), pp. 68–71; Lennox Robinson, ed., *A Golden Treasury of Irish Verse* (New York: Macmillan, 1925), pp. 118–21; O'Faoláin, *Silver Branch*, pp. 101–5; Colum, *An Anthology of Irish Verse*, pp. 126–28; Dillon and Chadwick, *Celtic Realms*, pp. 257–58; Frank O'Connor, *The Little Monasteries: Translations from Irish Poetry, Mainly of the Seventh to the Twelfth Centuries* (Dublin: Dolmen Press, 1976; 1st pub. 1963), pp. 32–37. Peig Sayers expresses sadness eloquently in *An Old Woman's Reflections*, pp. 1, 128–29, and *Peig*, pp. 173–88, 210–12.

16 Bog

1. Work in the bog is a matter of cooperation and technology, toil and pleasure. Those dimensions come together in accounts of turf-cutting by Harbinson, *Song of Erne*, pp. 220–25, and O'Donoghue, *In a Quiet Land*, pp. 120–31, where he describes a "mihul" gathering to perform necessary labor, breaking for tea and chatting at work. Croker, *Researches in the South of Ireland*, p. 232, describes a "Mihill" assembling to cut turf in 1820. John Montague's superb poem "Almost a Song" grows naturally out of the work and camaraderie of the bog: "slicing . . . spreading, footing, castling and clamping," the "ritual skills," the "stretch & smoke," the "idle talk of neighbours and weather": *A Slow Dance* (Dublin: Dolmen Press, 1975), p. 25. Other accounts of work in the bog: Mr. and Mrs. Hall, *Ireland*, 2:263–68; A.T. Lucas, "Notes on the History of Turf as Fuel to 1700 A.D.," *Ulster Folklife* 15/16 (1970): 172–202; J. M. Mogey, "A Glossary of Turf Terms," *Ulster Journal of Archaeology*, 3d series, 2 (1939): 119–21; Evans, *Irish Heritage*, chap. 15; *Irish Folk Ways*, chap. 14; *Mourne Country*, pp. 136–38; Harry Percival Swan, *Romantic Inishowen: Ireland's Wonderful Peninsula* (Dublin: Hodges, Figgis, 1948), pp. 113–15; Flor Crowley, *In West Cork Long Ago* (Cork: Mercier Press, 1979), pp. 89–93. John C. O'Sullivan, "Slanes: Irish Peat Spades," in Gailey and Fenton, *The Spade*, pp. 221–42, shows turf spades (the term slane is not locally used) of the Fermanagh kind as his strap-socket type, though the local tools, such as Joe Murphy's, which I illustrate, often have a cow's-horn handle like those of his open-socket slanes. Reasonably his examples from Donegal and north Fermanagh most closely resemble the local type. Early photos of turf work in Fermanagh are included in the Green Collection in the archive of the Ulster Folk and Transport Museum: nos. 267, 350, 574.

2. On emergency fuels in Ireland: A. T. Lucas, "Furze: A Survey and History of Its Uses in Ireland," *Béaloideas* 26 (1958): 41–55; Caoimhín Ó Danachair, "Animal Droppings as Fuel," *Folk Life* 6 (1968): 117–20.

3. "A man who cannot find happiness and content in a turf-bog is a hard case. A turf-bog is a history of the world from the time of Noah," says the narrator of Kavanagh's *Green Fool*, p. 98. Seamus Heaney's "Bogland," *Door into the Dark* (London: Faber & Faber, 1972; 1st pub. 1969), pp. 55–56, moves through the wonder of bog discoveries—the bones of an elk, bog butter, tree trunks—into the Irish mind, driving downward, not outward, but deeper downward into the "wet centre." Approaching the vortex that swallowed Joyce into the *Wake*, Heaney in *North* (London: Faber & Faber, 1975), pp. 31–45, follows "Bogland" with a series of tactile

meditations on the leathery people pickled in foreign bog; the downward spins into the outward, place becomes local history, local history becomes all history, everywhere, and the Irish heaves toward the universal without abandoning the profound, common experience of the turf cutter.

4. Synge, *The Aran Islands*, p. 115: "Like all work that is done in common on the island, the thatching is regarded as a sort of festival. From the moment a roof is taken in hand there is a whirl of laughter and talk till it is ended, and, as the man whose house is being covered is a host instead of an employer, he lays himself out to please the men who work with him." Synge caught a happy, restful moment amid group work in his photograph of haymakers in Wicklow: Lilo Stephens, ed., *My Wallet of Photographs: The Collected Photographs of J. M. Synge*, Dolmen Editions 13 (Dublin: Dolmen Press, 1971), no. 8.

5. Washing Old Nip's shirt is what children who play with the hearth's crooks are said to be doing, not only by Ellen Cutler in Fermanagh, but also in Armagh, according to Michael J. Murphy in his fine book *At Slieve Gullion's Foot* (Dundalk: W. Tempest, Dundalgan Press, 1975; 1st pub. 1941), p. 24; in Monaghan, Peter Kavanagh, *Irish Mythology: A Dictionary* (New York: Peter Kavanagh Hand Press, 1958–59), p. 113; and *In Kerry Long Ago*, p. 71, according to John O'Donoghue. The child who meddles with crooks is using tools incorrectly and unusefully, and he is disengaged from the social scene around him, away on his own mental course, providing a doubly perfect model of idleness.

6. In 1846, William Carleton published a rich description of boxty, stressing the cooperative nature of its preparation, and its festive use: *Tales and Sketches*, p. 145. For recipes: Theodora Fitzgibbon, *A Taste of Ireland: Irish Traditional Food* (London: Pan Books, 1968), p. 12, called traditional in northern counties such as Donegal and Cavan; Carla Blake, *The Irish Cook-Book* (Cork: Mercier Press, 1971), p. 97; K. M. Harris, "The Schools' Collection," *Ulster Folklife* 3 (1957): 9, from Armagh; Harris, "Extracts (3)," *Ulster Folklife* 6 (1960): 20–21, from Tyrone with rhymes from Derry, Armagh, and Tyrone. Manuscript sources for south Fermanagh: Murphy, IFC 1695 (1965): 176; Murphy, IFC 1697 (1966): 108; Anderson, Ulster Notebook, p. 28.

7. Yeats' great early statement on the need for folk art comes in the Morrisian coda to *The Celtic Twilight*, pp. 232–34. If his opinions staggered in midlife, in poems like "Upon a House Shaken by the Land Agitation" and "Lines Written in Dejection," and in thoughts worse than these, he was centered again at death "Under Ben Bulben." Kavanagh's tough poem is "The Great Hunger" (1942), *Complete Poems*, pp. 79–104. The shift of his mood is revealed by comparing "Ploughman" (1930), pp. 1–2, in which the plow is a brush to paint the meadow and work is a prayer, to "Stony Grey Soil" (1940), pp. 73–74, in which the plow digs into the flesh and love shrivels and dies. But Kavanagh was too big a man to hold simple opinions. Struggling to escape stereotypes, first that of peasant bard, then that of gallivanting Dublin poet (creator of wordy art for posh American scholars to analyze), Kavanagh shook and shifted and prevented his feelings from stabilizing. Like Carleton, whom he admired with Moore and Joyce as the best of Irish writers, he seems a different man in different writings, for he was capable of taking both internal and external views of Irish country life. He attacked outsiders who sentimentalized rural existence, most powerfully in "The Great Hunger," where he drags the viewer near the dull, loveless side of farming life, and angrily in an essay, "Twenty-Three Tons of Accumulated Folk Lore: Is It of Any Use?" *The Irish Times*, April 18, 1939, which Peter Kavanagh sent me, in which the poet calls folklore "culturally

useless" and collections of folklore neatly indexed "rubbish" that place a dead hand upon the artist. Yet Kavanagh could be sentimental himself, especially but not exclusively in his early writings (see above, Chapter 10, note 8, and below, Chapter 25, note 3). And once he brought his warring feelings peacefully together in an important sketch, "Three Glimpses of Life," *Collected Pruse* (London: Martin Brian & O'Keefe, 1973; 1st pub. 1967), pp. 99–104.

18 The Days of the Landlords

1. Samuel Clark comments that middlemen were especially common on college lands and that their number declined by half between 1840 and 1878 (*Social Origins of the Irish Land War*, pp. 35–36, 113). Mr. Nolan's account provides local examples of these generalizations. Elsewhere (p. 234) Clark says that Land League chapters were not based on estates, but the Land League for the Schoolands, described by Mr. Owens and Mr. Nolan, is apparently an example to the contrary. For the Land League, see above, Chapter 13, note 15.

19 The Famine

1. Population statistics from Livingstone, *The Fermanagh Story*, p. 196 (his chap. 18 recounts the Famine in the county); *Ulster Year Book: 1972*, p. 8. Cecil Woodham-Smith summarizes the decline for Ireland in *The Great Hunger* (London: Hamish Hamilton, 1962), pp. 411–13.

2. My examples are not idle. Boas and Panofsky provide models for the person who does not want to become lost in texts or contexts but wishes to understand their meaningful interpenetration. Franz Boas' important contribution to folklore is outlined by Melville Jacobs, "Folklore," in Walter Goldschmidt, ed., *The Anthropology of Franz Boas*, A.A.A. Memoir 89 (Menasha: American Anthropological Association, 1959), pp. 119–38. Boas published several volumes of Kwakiutl texts; they are listed by Jacobs. Helen Codere edited a volume of Boas' *Kwakiutl Ethnography* (Chicago: University of Chicago Press, 1966), which surrounds the tales with background, and Boas related stories to culture in *Kwakiutl Culture as Reflected in Mythology*, A.F.S. Memoirs 28 (New York: American Folk-Lore Society, 1935). Erwin Panofsky wrote a model study of the relation of culture to art in *Gothic Art and Scholasticism* (New York: World, 1957) and of culture to individual creativity in *The Life and Art of Albrecht Dürer* (Princeton: Princeton University Press, 1971), and he prepared a general statement, *Meaning in the Visual Arts* (Garden City: Doubleday, 1955). It is odd that some today seem to view the "contextual" variety of folklore study as social scientific and the "textual" variety as humanistic. Not only is that division harmful, it is also fake. Panofsky the contextualist titled the first chapter of his general work "The History of Art as a Humanistic Discipline," and if my own approach seems to grow from my anthropological training, conditioned by Boas' followers, I feel it arises as much from lectures I heard as an undergraduate by John G. Allee on Chaucer and Irving Ribner on Shakespeare. Anyone serious about the meanings in texts will be interested in contexts. Anyone serious about studying culture will record texts. Anyone serious about studying people will be both social scientist and humanist.

20 Butter

1. E. Estyn Evans emphasizes the importance of the May and November holidays that broke the old year in half in "Peasant Beliefs in Nineteenth-Century Ireland," in Casey and Rhodes, eds., *Views of the Irish Peasantry*, pp. 37–56, esp. pp. 48, 52–54, as does Ó Catháin, *Bedside Book of Irish Folklore*, pp. 17–21, 118–24. In *Researches in the South of Ireland*, Croker gives his own findings of 1812–21 historical depth by quoting a sixteenth-century Irish account of people who refuse the woman "that commeth to fetch fire from them on May-day," fearing "the same woman will, the next summer, steale away all their butter. If they finde an hare amongst their heards of cattel on the said May-day, they kill her, for they suppose shee is some old trot, that would filch away their butter" (p. 95). Lady Wilde wrote on May Day customs, saying the primroses scattered at the threshold protected the farm's milk and that borrowers were refused then: *Ancient Legends, Mystic Charms and Superstitions of Ireland: With Sketches of the Irish Past* (London: Chatto & Windus, 1902; 1st ed. 1887), pp. 104–7; *Ancient Cures, Charms, and Usages of Ireland: Contributions to Irish Lore* (London: Ward & Downey, 1890), pp. 53, 99–108. Earlier her husband, Sir William, Oscar's father, described the same set of customs in *Irish Popular Superstitions*, pp. 52–61. Mary Carbery records May Day customs in her warm remembrance of prosperous farming life in nineteenth-century County Limerick, *The Farm by Lough Gur: The Story of Mary Fogarty (Sissy O'Brien)* (London: Longmans, Green, 1937), pp. 157–66. Rose Shaw tells of refusing a borrower on May Day in *Carleton's Country*, p. 22. Folklorist Michael J. Murphy makes much of the custom in his novel *Mountainy Crack: Tales of Slieve Gullioners* (Belfast: Blackstaff Press, 1976), pp. 65–68. Ronald H. Buchanan discusses it well in "Calendar Customs, I," *Ulster Folklife* 8 (1962): 28–30. Daniel Deeney associates comparable customs with "New Year's Day" in *Peasant Lore from Gaelic Ireland* (London: David Nutt, 1900), pp. 49–50. In the West of Ireland and in the North—Fermanagh especially—strawboys came to weddings and their leader danced with the bride: O'Donoghue, *In Kerry Long Ago*, pp. 41–68; Ó Súilleabháin, *Irish Folk Belief and Custom*, pp. 45–46; Richard Hilliard, "Biddies and Straw Boys," *Ulster Folklife* 8 (1962): 102; Alan Gailey, "Straw Costume in Irish Folk Custom," *Folk Life* 6 (1968): 90–92. Boys dressed in straw processed in some localities at Saint Brigid's and May Day. In our District they came on another of the Quarter Days, Hallow Eve, and they came violently. At a wedding the strawboys' captain demanded a last dance for the bachelors from the new bride. On Hallow Eve bachelors in straw dresses disrupted the home, unhinging the gates, dismantling the cart, and stuffing up the chimneys of the man whose eligible daughters had not been released to courtship or the man against whom the strawboys' leader held personal spite.

2. O'Rahilly, *Táin Bó Cúalnge from the Book of Leinster*, p. 272. Critics whose idea of history has narrowed bloodlessly to the arrangement of mere fact (in order to avoid deep truth) may fault Keating for his inclusion of myth, but Keating writes constantly (pp. 61, 63, 178, 190–92, 280–81, 342, 362, 364) that he knows the stories he tells are untrue but that his work would suffer more from their omission than it does from their inclusion.

3. Douglas Hyde's *Legends of Saints and Sinners* (Dublin: Gresham, n.d.; 1st pub. 1915) is of great importance because in most earlier collections, Kennedy's *Legendary Fictions* for instance, modern oral traditions of the Saints had been mixed by the editor with early written sources, while Hyde's are "actual folk survivals," and

Hyde estimates one-quarter to one-fifth of Irish stories deal with Christian topics. In his introduction (pp. ix–xii) Hyde says it is characteristic of Ireland that neither the Devil nor witches are important in the Gaelic tradition. Stories of old women who steal milk and turn into hares are, he says, quite common (see note 1, above, and the citations in the Sources for this chapter under the Black Art of Butter Theft), but stories of sabbaths or appointments with the Devil are wholly lacking. William Butler Yeats, commenting on Lady Gregory's *Visions and Beliefs*, p. 348, says Irish witches have no dealings with the Devil: "I have never come across a case of a 'compact' nor has Lady Gregory, nor have I read of one." Lady Wilde had reported two stories from the West linking the sale of a soul to witchcraft and butter theft: *Ancient Legends*, pp. 41–42; *Ancient Cures*, pp. 77–79. The extreme popularity of "Willie the Wisp," Aarne-Thompson type 330 (Ó Súilleabháin, *Storytelling in Irish Tradition*, pp. 17–18, 42; Ó Súilleabháin and Christiansen, *Types of the Irish Folktale*, pp. 81–84) suggests at least a wide interest in compacts with the Devil, and Seán Ó Súilleabháin tells us in "The Devil in Irish Folk Narrative," in Fritz Harkort, Karel C. Peeters, and Robert Wildhaber, eds., *Volksüberlieferung: Festschrift für Kurt Ranke zur Vollendung des 60. Lebensjahres* (Göttingen: Otto Schwartz, 1968), pp. 275–86, of the Devil's great popularity in legends as well as märchen. St. John Seymour, *Irish Witchcraft and Demonology* (New York: Causeway, 1973; 1st pub. 1913), pp. 3–15, writes that witchcraft was known in Ireland in English areas and in Ulster because of Scottish settlement. Protestants, he says, tell stories of witchcraft, while among Catholics the concern for the mysterious was trapped in other kinds of tale. In Ballymenone, Catholics tell of witchcraft, Protestants of fairies, ideas of the "other world" link the community's factions, and though the connection of Satan and witchcraft may be of English, not Irish, origin, the black art and the Devil's compact are joined and important in Ballymenone's system of story.

4. Ballymenone's tales of missed treasure and stolen people are like stories told all over Ireland (see the references to Mr. Flanagan's stories in the Sources), but their particular character is refined through comparison. In other places, though not here, people have prospered from fairy gifts. In other places, though not here, a person, usually a young woman who has been stolen away, is successfully retrieved when she rides past with the fairy troop. Prospering from fairy gifts (stories mostly swinging around motif F244.2, fairy reveals treasure in exchange for freedom): Carleton, *Tales and Sketches*, p. 77; Mr. and Mrs. Hall, *Ireland*, 3:31–38; D. R. McAnally, *Irish Wonders: Popular Tales as Told by the People* (Boston: Houghton Mifflin, 1888), pp. 144–45; Lady Gregory, *Visions and Beliefs*, p. 167. Successful retrieval, the precise reverse of Peter Flanagan's tale (motif F322.2, rescue of wife from fairyland): Kennedy, *Legendary Fictions*, pp. 111–13; Synge, *The Aran Islands*, pp. 154–56; Lynd, *Home Life in Ireland*, pp. 62–66; Shaw, *Carleton's Country*, pp. 57–59; Gibbings, *Lovely Is the Lee*, pp. 202–3.

5. Ballymenone joins all Ireland in saying fairies are fallen angels (motif F251.6). Synge calls it "the Catholic theory" (*The Aran Islands*, p. 10). Croker wrote that it is "a common mediaeval notion," "pretty general all over Europe," that the fairies "were a part of the angels who fell with Lucifer, but whose criminality was so much less than the others that they were visited with less punishment, and were allowed to inhabit the earth" (*Fairy Legends* [1862], p. 22). Wilhelm Grimm comments in his essay in Croker's *Fairy Legends: Second Series* (1828), 2:14, 64–70, that the Irish idea is especially common in Scotland and Denmark. Thomas Keightley followed Croker in *The Fairy Mythology, Illustrative of the Romance and Superstition of*

Various Countries (London: H. G. Bohn, 1850; 1st ed. 1828), retelling his tales, but Keightley was, as he reports (p. vii), Croker's friend, and because he was Irish himself his statement carries its own validity when he asserts that the Irish popular belief holds fairies to be fallen angels (p. 363). Carleton refers his reader to the works of his "learned and admirable countryman, Thomas Keightley," then gives his own understanding of the Irish "general opinion" that fairies were angels of the third class who followed neither God nor Satan but "stood timidly aloof" and were hurled out of heaven to await their fate on the Last Day: *Tales and Sketches*, p. 72. Fairies are fallen angels: Wilde, *Irish Popular Superstitions*, p. 125; Lady Wilde, *Ancient Legends*, pp. 37–39, 89, 206–7; Patrick Kennedy, *The Fireside Stories of Ireland* (Dublin: M'Glashan & Gill, 1870), p. 131; Curtin, *Tales of Fairies and the Ghost World*, pp. 42–43; W. B. Yeats, *Fairy and Folk Tales of the Irish Peasantry* (New York: Macmillan, 1973; 1st pub. 1888), p. 11; Lady Gregory, *Visions and Beliefs*, pp. 212, 216–17, 223–25, 238, 240; Reidar Th. Christiansen, "Some Notes on the Fairies and the Fairy Faith," *Béaloideas* 39–41 (1971–73): 95–111; O'Sullivan, *Legends from Ireland*, pp. 44–45; Elizabeth Andrews, *Ulster Folklore* (London: Elliot Stock, 1913), pp. vii, 11; examples from across the North, west to east: Harry Percival Swan, *Romantic Stories and Legends of Donegal* (Letterkenny: W. J. Barr, 1969), p. 89; MacManus, *Heavy Hangs the Golden Grain*, pp. 20, 41–43; Fermanagh: Murphy, IFC 1220 (1951): 347, and IFC 1696 (1965): 297; Murphy, *At Slieve Gullion's Foot*, p. 72; Paterson, *Country Cracks*, p. 103; Francis McPolin, "Fairy Lore in the Hilltown District, Co. Down," *Ulster Folklife* 9 (1963): 87.

6. Richard P. Jenkins, "Witches and Fairies: Supernatural Aggression and Deviance Among the Irish Peasantry," *Ulster Folklife* 23 (1977): 33–56, argues, correctly I think, that stories of supernatural aggression are used to clarify ambiguities in daily life (p. 49). Using data drawn from sundry times and places, he creates a scholastic scheme worth refining through ethnography in real communities. Thinking about the District, I feel he is correct in motive: both retaliation (more generally, anger, spite) and profit (greed) are mentioned as causes, though the latter is locally emphasized. The first half of his conclusion (pp. 51–52) that witchcraft symbolizes deviance from norms (more properly, ideals) seems true, but from there on things run obliquely. So his model does what models should: it illuminates specific instances which, in turn, improve it. Following Brody, *Inishkillane*, p. 20, Jenkins dichotomizes men's work as discontinuous, women's as continuous. That may well be true in some places, but it is wrong or it radically overclarifies the contrast for Ballymenone, so Jenkins' focus upon women as agents and the family (male-female relations) as the problematic field do not follow. When women steal milk from the churn, they steal from other women. When milk is stolen from cattle, men as well as women act as thieves; the one sure local instance, as told by Hugh Nolan, put a man in the role of robber. So, woman to woman, man to man, household to household: Ballymenone's problematic is neighborliness. The District's fairies stole young women, but they also stole young men, and Peter Flanagan's story in this chapter tells of a male relative trying to save another male, rather than the more usual situation in which a husband attempts to retrieve his wife (see note 4, above). Ballymenone's tales suggest these modifications. First, while retaining the conjunction of witches and fairies, the predominant greed motive joins witchcraft to fairy treasure more than fairy theft: Peter Flanagan made that connection when he told us that witches who steal butter protect crocks of gold to prevent attacks upon them by people seeking to retaliate for their theft. And the greed motive carries past fairies

to other tales of profit and retaliation, to landlords and rapparees. Second, Ballymenone shifts the relationship that produces guilt and requires clarification from man-woman (familial) relations to neighbor-neighbor (communal) relations, and that suits Ballymenone, where kin is not the major force of social organization (see note 9, below, and below, Chapter 23, note 1). Jenkins' formulation seems correct, but to fit all Irish communities, it should modulate to a more general level to account for any social relation that can become saturated with guilt and confusion.

7. The traits of the noble robber were isolated by the early commentators on the legend of Robin Hood as it artistically unfolded in verse and prose. See especially William J. Thoms, *Early English Prose Romances* (London: Nattali & Bond, 1858; 1st pub. 1828), 2:65–137; Child, *English and Scottish Popular Ballads*, 3:39–89. For our times, the best discussion of the social bandit, of which the noble robber is one variety, comes in works by Eric Hobsbawm—in the second chapter of *Primitive Rebels: Studies in Archaic Forms of Social Movement in the 19th and 20th Centuries* (New York: W. W. Norton, 1965; 1st pub. 1959), which is excellently elaborated in *Bandits* (New York: Pantheon, 1981; 1st pub. 1969); see especially the second chapter: the social bandit arrives during a time of upheaval, before a peasant revolution; he conforms to rural moral norms, acting chivalrously toward women, fighting fairly, robbing the oppressors, while trying not to bring death. Hobsbawm does not treat Ireland and gives but little attention to the extension of Irish social banditry into Australia. If he had, he might have had to qualify a bit more his generally valid assertion concerning the nonideological nature of the social outlaw (the rapparees continued to resist after defeat by William, the Australian bushrangers continued to resist after failed Irish risings), but if he had, he would have provided support for his interesting—and I think correct—suggestion in a footnote (p. 163) that there is a connection between the idea of the social bandit and the current reality of the IRA. There is a book on the rapparees: Terence O'Hanlon's *The Highwayman in Irish History* (Dublin: M. H. Gill, 1932), a collection of sketches that appeared in *Our Boys*, but it is not analytical, it does not tell of Fermanagh's rapparees, and it includes no stories closely analogous to those about Black Francis.

8. Spellings are diverse in the literature—pisthrogue (Carleton), pishlogue (Deeney), pisthrug or pistrug (Murphy), pistrog or piseog (Kavanagh), pishrogue (Evans), pisterogue (McConnell), pishogue, pishrogue, or pistrug (Ó Catháin)—and pronunciations are diverse in the District—pishrogue, pisterogue, pistherahog— but the meaning is steady: the pishrogue is a doubted superstition. These on money, all told to me by Ellen Cutler, are all known elsewhere in Ireland. John O'Donoghue, *In a Quiet Land*, p. 33, mentions sparks flying. Molly Bloom, *Ulysses*, p. 755, bubbles on tea. Lady Wilde, *Ancient Legends*, p. 206, says an itchy palm means money, and in *Ancient Cures*, p. 64, she connects the left hand with curses. The "rub it to wood" rhyme appears in Maggi Kerr Peirce, *Keep the Kettle Boiling* (Probably New Bedford, Mass.: Privately published, [c. 1978]), p. 54, a good collection of children's folklore from Belfast, c. 1931–45.

9. I was led to Braunton by W. G. Hoskins, who lists it among the three remaining openfield villages in England: *Making of the English Landscape*, pp. 48, 178; *Devon*, p. 347. We spent a happy summer there in 1978. Roy Millward and Adrian Robinson describe Braunton's Great Field in *North Devon and Cornwall* (London: Macmillan, 1971), pp. 73–79. A. H. Slee, a Brauntonian, describes it in his fine small book, important for its emphasis on colorful local characters: *Victorian Days in a Devon Village* (Braunton: S. J. H. Slee, 1966), pp. 6–7. For Irish separate farms and

clustered settlement: Evans, *Personality of Ireland*, pp. 37–41, 52–62. Evans has also prepared and introduced the book he discusses in his appendix—a rich source of information on compact clachans and rundale arrangements—as a separate volume: Lord George Hill, *Facts from Gweedore* (Belfast: Queen's University Institute of Irish Studies, 1971; reprint of 1887, 1st pub. 1845). V. B. Proudfoot describes "Clachans in Ireland" well in *Gwerin* 2, no. 3 (1959): 110–22. Robin Fox presents clearly and richly the retention of the clachan and rundale (Irish openfield) idea in *The Tory Islanders*, pp. xi, 91–126. And two papers in festschrifts for Evans provide fine summaries of clachans in the evolution of the Irish landscape: Desmond Mc-Court, "The Dynamic Quality of Irish Rural Settlement," in Buchanan, Jones, and McCourt, eds., *Man and His Habitat*, pp. 126–64; R. H. Buchanan, "Rural Settlement in Ireland," in Nicholas Stephens and Robin E. Glasscock, eds., *Irish Geographical Studies in Honour of E. Estyn Evans* (Belfast: Queen's University Department of Geography, 1970), pp. 146–61. The separate farm, though present from ancient days, has become increasingly dominant in Ireland in general (see above, Chapter 14, note 3) and the District in particular. Livingstone, *The Fermanagh Story*, p. 184, suggests rundale had passed by the early nineteenth century. The contemporary landscape is balanced between the nucleated and the radically dispersed. The local family farm is not a ring-fence farm, so the landscape's dynamic, its pattern of work, springs between the isolated and the cooperative. Basically the family works for itself, but (with decreasing frequency) farms are connected by arrangements usually called swapping, sometimes called joining, rarely called cooring. But beneath separation lies a sense of intertwined destiny that can bring people swiftly into totally cooperative methals. Arensberg and Kimball, *Family and Community in Ireland*, distinguish three grades of cooperation in Clare (pp. 59–75, 254–57). These—family work, cooring, and the "meitheal"—compare with those of Ballymenone. The big difference is that in Clare kin cooperate, whereas in Ballymenone neighbors traditionally cooperate and the shift to kin-based methals is recent and incomplete. Ballymenone is not anomalous. Jonathan Bell, "Relations of Mutual Help Between Ulster Farmers," *Ulster Folklife* 24 (1978): 48–58, esp. 49, reports a questionnaire which indicated that neighbors, not kin, most often make up cooperative units. Eileen Kane describes a mixing of neighbors and kin in group work in Donegal, indicating that tools are more often borrowed from neighbors, though kin forms a deeper emotional base: "Man and Kin in Donegal: A Study of Kinship Functions in a Rural Irish and an Irish-American Community," *Ethnology* 7 (1968): 245–58, esp. 250–53. The best description is given by Rosemary Harris, *Prejudice and Tolerance in Ulster*, pp. 69–105, 145, 184–86. In "Ballybeg" in western Ulster the "swopping group" was normally based on kin, especially in religiously homogeneous neighborhoods, but cooperative arrangements also spread to neighbors, even neighbors of the opposite religion, particularly in mixed neighborhoods. The egalitarian pattern of her hill district corresponds closely with that among Ballymenone's small farmers.

21 Brick

1. Brick-making in Ballymenone resembles fishing on Tory Island as described by Robin Fox: though the activity is past, it lives so strongly in the memory that describing it is an anthropological as well as a historical task (*The Tory Islanders*, p. 137).

2. On the Lough Erne cot: J. M. Mogey, "Wooden Canoes," *Ulster Journal of Archaeology*, 3d series, 9 (1946): 69–76; Francis Fitzpatrick, "A Lough Erne Cot," *Clogher Record* 1, no. 3 (1955): 118–20; Murphy, IFC 1696 (1965): 3–6, 165–67, and IFC 1697 (1966): 29; Mary Rogers, "The Navigation of Lough Erne in the 18th, 19th, and 20th Centuries," *Clogher Record* 6, no. 3 (1966): 608–9; Mary Rogers, "The Navigation of Lough Erne," *Ulster Folklife* 12 (1966): 97–103; Michael McCaughan, "The Lough Erne Cot," *Ulster Folk Museum Year Book, 1969/70*, pp. 5–8; Michael Mc-Caughan, "Irish Vernacular Boats and Their European Connections," *Ulster Folklife* 24 (1978): 6–7. Those papers support Hugh Nolan's theory that the cot evolved from the dugout log canoe, a couple of which were found in the mud along the Lough shore by Ballymenone, Mr. Nolan told me, during the work of the Erne Drainage Scheme. I discuss such boats, including Irish ones, in "The Nature of the New World Artifact: The Instance of the Dugout Canoe," in Walter Escher, Theo Gantner, and Hans Trümpy, eds., *Festschrift für Robert Wildhaber* (Basel: G. Krebs, 1973), pp. 153–70.

22 Humanity

1. Every scholar must read Jean-Paul Sartre's essay "A Plea for Intellectuals," in *Between Existentialism and Marxism*, pp. 228–85.

2. The ancient power of the smith is described by Lloyd Laing in *Celtic Britain* (New York: Scribner's, 1979), pp. 44–48, and the Rees brothers in *Celtic Heritage*, pp. 252–53. Lady Gregory tells of the power of the smith and his safety from strange forces in *Visions and Beliefs*, chap. 15. Seán MacGiollarnáth, *Conamara*, Irish Life and Culture 4 (Dublin: Cultural Relations Committee, 1963; 1st pub. 1954), p. 54, says the smith's trade is traditionally "sacred." Iron or steel as protection against supernatural powers (motifs E434.5, F384.3, G272.1, G272.11): Ó Súilleab-háin, *Handbook of Irish Folklore*, pp. 391–92, also pp. 64–66; Kavanagh, *Irish Mythology*, p. 27; O'Donoghue, *In a Quiet Land*, p. 27, and *In Kerry Long Ago*, p. 196; Synge, *The Aran Islands*, p. 47; Foster, *Ulster Folklore*, pp. 14, 46–48, 90–91; Murphy, *At Slieve Gullion's Foot*, pp. 63, 74, 75; McPolin, "Fairy Lore," *Ulster Folklife* 9 (1963): 81; Henry Mackle, "Fairies and Leprechauns," *Ulster Folklife* 10 (1964): 53.

3. Monk Gibbon, ed., *The Living Torch: A.E.* (London: Macmillan, 1937), p. 354.

23 Society

1. The necessary deemphasis of kin in the District's society pulls it away from other Irish communities in the anthropological literature, but similarities remain. The ideas of name and blood described by Elliot Leyton, *The One Blood: Kinship and Class in an Irish Village*, Newfoundland Social and Economic Studies 15 (St. John's: Institute of Social and Economic Research, Memorial University of Newfoundland, 1975), pp. 20, 41, compare with those of Ballymenone. The "clan" of Ballymenone is not the tribelike clan of Scotland. Edward MacLysaght, *Irish Families: Their Names, Arms, and Origins* (New York: Crown, 1972; 1st ed. 1957), pp. 10–11, would prefer to call such groups septs, but the local idea is close to that of the "clann," well described by Fox in *The Tory Islanders*, pp. 32–36, 68–70. Local membership in clans is restricted to people who bear the name, both husbands and wives, so descent is reckoned only through the male line. Ballymenone's idea of friendship compares to

that described by Evans in *Mourne Country*, p. 130; Fox, *The Tory Islanders*, p. 65; Arensberg and Kimball, *Family and Community in Ireland*, chap. 5; and Kane, "Man and Kin in Donegal," *Ethnology* 7 (1968): 246. The "family" is the "numerically small and genealogically simple" household described by Leyton (pp. 25–31) and analyzed by Harris in *Prejudice and Tolerance in Ulster* (pp. 59–65), though the social affinities and moral obligations Leyton outlines (pp. 43–44, 51), which are comparable to those of Arensberg and Kimball (chap. 4), differ. In Ballymenone the family is emotionally central and the home place is physically central, but one's closest associates beyond the home are not kin, and social-economic obligations are constructed more on connections among neighbors than connections among relatives.

2. Shan Bullock built his novel of life by Upper Lough Erne, *The Loughsiders*, out of a crucial local concept. Around the central figure, Richard, he arranges people whose faith commits them to a philosophy of endurance, of making the best of a bad deal, of keeping the mind focused on small consolations (pp. 9–10, 124–27, 150–55, 171, 196–97, 202). But Richard doubts God. He is willing to be unpopular, he schemes and cunningly manipulates those around him to advance, gaining a better farm, achieving success in the culture's material terms by exploiting his understanding of the culture's spirit.

3. Willard Potts, ed., *Portraits of the Artist in Exile: Recollections of James Joyce by Europeans* (Seattle: University of Washington Press, 1979), pp. 270–71.

4. Robin Fox eloquently states my feelings about Ballymenone when he tells of the collective spirit and the flexible will to survive he found among *The Tory Islanders*, pp. xiii, 154, 187–93.

5. The Tailor of Garrynapeaka, Cork, states the feelings of old men from Ballymenone when he laments the passing of scholars, poets, and witty characters, their replacement by weak and foolish puppets: "The more education they have they less they know": Cross, *Tailor and Ansty*, pp. 70–76, 86–87, 113–14, 143–45, 210.

6. A.E., *The National Being: Some Thoughts on an Irish Polity* (New York: Macmillan, 1930; 1st pub. 1916), esp. pp. 20–29, 36, 124–31, 165–66.

7. The hierarchical divisions among farmers—classes would be the wrong word—described for the nineteenth century by Clark, *Social Origins of the Irish Land War*, pp. 38–40, remain about right for the District. Arensberg and Kimball, *Family and Community in Ireland*, pp. 3–30, divide large and small farmers in a way that resembles Ballymenone, though the primary criterion—family labor versus hired labor—is not the same. In the District, small farmers, often lacking family, hire laborers, and big farmers may depend primarily on family help—and machinery. The distinction is the way the land is worked. The "wealth strata" of an Ulster Protestant community laid out by Leyton, *The One Blood*, pp. 23–24, based on capital, not land, are wholly different.

24 Space

1. G. B. Adams, ed., *Ulster Dialects: An Introductory Symposium* (Holywood: Ulster Folk Museum, 1964), opens the topic of dialect well. I have found constant similarities between meanings of words in Ballymenone and those given by Michael Traynor, *The English Dialect of Donegal: A Glossary* (Dublin: Royal Irish Academy, 1953), suggesting a western-southern Ulster dialect region, reinforced by simi-

larities among terms used by writers from Tyrone (Carleton, O'Brien, Kiely, Montague), Fermanagh (Bullock), Donegal (MacManus), and Monaghan (Kavanagh). I treat the regional nature of Ballymenone's mumming in *All Silver and No Brass*, pp. 68–75. Alan Gailey surveys the geography of mumming and includes my book in "Mummers' and Christmas Rhymers' Plays in Ireland: The Problem of Distribution," *Ulster Folklife* 24 (1978): 59–68. The basic Irish house types: Åke Campbell, "Irish Fields and Houses: A Study of Rural Culture," *Béaloideas* 5, no. 1 (1935): 57–74; Åke Campbell,"Notes on the Irish House," *Folk-Liv* 1 (1937): 205–34; 2 (1938): 173–96; E. Estyn Evans, "Donegal Survivals," *Antiquity* 13, no. 50 (1939): 207–22; E. Estyn Evans, "The Irish Peasant House," *Ulster Journal of Archaeology*, 3d series, 3 (1940): 165–69; E. Estyn Evans, "The Ulster Farmhouse," *Ulster Folklife* 1 (1955): 27–31; Evans, *Irish Heritage*, chap. 7, and *Irish Folk Ways*, chap. 4; Alan Gailey, "Vernacular Dwellings in Ireland," *Revue Roumaine D'Histoire de l'Art* 13 (1976): 137–55; Caoimhín Ó Danachair, "Three House Types," *Ulster Folklife* 2 (1956): 23–26; Caoimhín Ó Danachair, "The Combined Byre-and-Dwelling in Ireland," *Folk Life* 2 (1964): 58–75; Danaher, *Pleasant Land of Ireland*, pp. 23–52; Caoimhín Ó Danachair, "Traditional Forms of the Dwelling House in Ireland," *Journal of the Royal Society of Antiquaries of Ireland* 102 (1972): 77–96; Kevin Danaher, *Ireland's Vernacular Architecture* (Cork: Mercier Press for the Cultural Relations Committee of Ireland, 1975), pp. 11–12, 15–43; O'Neill, *Life and Tradition in Rural Ireland*, chap. 1; Aalen, *Man and the Landscape in Ireland*, pp. 249–58. See below, note 3, and see above, Chapter 13, note 20, for the English prototype of the southeastern Irish house. A good summary of geographic patterning in Ireland, including an excellent bibliography: Alan Gailey and Caoimhín Ó Danachair (and G. B. Adams), "Ethnological Mapping in Ireland," *Ethnologia Europaea* 9, no. 1 (1976): 14–34.

2. For the Wealden and other English houses that provide possible antecedents for the local house type: Martin S. Briggs, *The English Farmhouse* (London: B. T. Batsford, 1953), chaps. 3, 4; Barley, *English Farmhouse and Cottage*, pp. 26–31, 81; R. T. Mason, *Framed Buildings of the Weald* (Horsham: Coach Publishing, 1969), chap. 2.

3. The "local" house type that conforms to neither the northwestern nor the southeastern type is not only local. Driving around, I found that it extends northward into Fermanagh and as far south as Galway, where scholars have often absorbed it into the gable-chimney, northwestern type. The trouble is that it cannot always be distinguished from the exterior, since the key is whether the Room is above or below the hearth. E. Estyn Evans illustrates comparable hybrid forms from the neighboring county in "Gleanings from County Cavan," *Ulster Folklife* 26 (1980): 4–5. Alan Gailey has been the scholar whose meticulous, perceptive work has most consistently discovered problems in the conventional dichotomy and who has provided excellent information on houses of the Ballymenone type. He illustrated a comparable house from the Arans in "Aspects of Change in a Rural Community," *Ulster Folklife* 5 (1959): 32–33. In "Vernacular Dwellings," *Revue Roumaine* 13 (1976): 138–40, he gives plans from earlier papers that do not fit their authors' arguments on the basic types and describes hybrid forms. And Gailey has written two papers on the Fermanagh region that show the local type and situate it geographically: "Vernacular Housing," in Rowan, *North West Ulster*, and, most important, "Vernacular Dwellings of Clogher Diocese," *Clogher Record* 9, no. 2 (1977): 187–231, esp. pp. 193–206, where he speaks of the diversity of types and the development of intermixed forms in Fermanagh. Since the "local" type is not exclusively

local, different modes of interpretation—loosely, emic and etic—lie open. Houses are meaningful in terms of the local culture, and they hold scholarly significance in terms of large historic-geographic constructs. As with houses, tales: a story might have an international distribution, but once performed, once knotted into the local web of conception, then its meaning depends on the culture of which it is a part, and its wider distribution—insofar as it is unknown by its tellers and audience, its builders and users—has no bearing on its interpretation. But that wider distribution is useful to the scholar who wishes to see the local culture as part of large historical patterning. Comparably, there are two equally logical ideas of region, which prove confusing if they are not kept apart. One (emic) is the concept of place, larger than the community but smaller than the nation, which is developed by people who live within a region. The other (etic) is derived by the scholar through mapping comparable quantifiable traits.

4. The local "creel" has a rounded bottom. There were flat-bottomed baskets, called "pordogs," which Hugh Nolan described to me in great detail (11/22/72t), but they were not used like creels, which were mostly employed for carrying turf on the back with a "gad" around the chest or in pairs on straddles on donkeys. Pordogs had trapdoor bottoms and were used to transport manure to the fields. Joe Flanagan said (6/9/77r) they were trouble. One hung on each side of the donkey, and their triggers had to be released simultaneously to drop their loads; if one stuck and the other did not, the sudden shift of weight could send the light pordog hurtling over the donkey's back. The result was a mess.

5. Mr. Nolan's account of breasting and mud turf provides a perfect view from the inside of the process of diffusion. Strangers came and breasted the turf. Had it spread to the natives or continued among settled immigrants, we would have an instance of diffusion by dint of migration. Mr. Nolan heard of the alien practice of making mud turf. He tried it. Had it worked, and had his neighbors learned the procedure from him, the result would have been an example of the movement of ideas from place to place, not dependent on the movement of people. Since the strangers' technique was not adopted, and since the alien idea did not work, and since local people have traveled and learned about other places, their own mode of winning turf becomes a symbol of their place, reinforcing their feelings of belonging. Mud (or hand) turf and breasting are described in the references given above, Chapter 16, note 1.

25 Time

1. On conacre: Symons, ed., *Land Use in Northern Ireland*, chap. 11; Evans, *Mourne Country*, p. 127.

2. The great change is from inward to outward orientation. People are pulled away, population declines, energy withdraws, and the small country place becomes marginal, even to its inhabitants. In their hasty book *Gola: The Life and Last Days of an Island Community* (Cork: Mercier Press, 1969), F. H. A. Aalen and Hugh Brody present the extreme case from an island off Donegal; see pp. xiii–xiv for the thesis. There is a tendency to blame industrialization for the change, but there is nothing in industry that demands the reorganization of the little community. At fault is the economic theory that uses industry, or any other mode of production, so that it benefits a small minority and maintains an unjust distribution of material wealth. With more depth and feeling, Robin Fox describes the shift (from a self-sufficient

community turned in upon itself to a dependent one turned outward toward distant power) on another Donegal island in *The Tory Islanders*, pp. 28–30. Hugh Brody's loosely argued *Inishkillane* (esp. chap. 3) presents the case bleakly for the far western mainland. R. H. Buchanan recounts rural depopulation in Ulster, concentrating on County Down, in "The Drift from the Land," *Ulster Folklife* 6 (1960): 43–61.

3. Patrick Kavanagh's fine statement on the parochial (the authentically local) in opposition to the provincial (the timidly imitative) is "The Parish and the Universe," *Collected Pruse*, pp. 281–83, which he exemplifies in "Shirley's Monaghan" (pp. 62–65, in the same volume) and sometimes sadly, sometimes bravely, in his grand verse, "Spraying the Potatoes," "Common Beauty," "The One," and "Shancoduff," for example: *Complete Poems*, pp. 72–73, 205–6, 291–92, 346–47. It was the parochial, not the provincial, in William Carleton that Kavanagh admired: "Preface" to *The Autobiography of William Carleton*, p. 10; "Extracts from Ten Lectures Delivered at University College Dublin in 1956," in Peter Kavanagh, ed., *November Haggard: Uncollected Prose and Verse of Patrick Kavanagh* (New York: Peter Kavanagh Hand Press, 1971), pp. 68–71. Carleton was probably the source for Kavanagh's idea: *Traits and Stories*, 1:182.

26 Life

1. "If any man of them in that country were to open his eyes, if the fog in which they lived lifted, they would be unable to endure the futility of it all. Their courage was the courage of the blind." So Patrick Kavanagh writes in *Tarry Flynn*, p. 176. Yet Tarry opened his eyes, saw through the fog, found the world around him "lovely," and fell in love with "common things." Tarry is unusual, not unique. The person who lives in comfort and defines power as knowledge, not action, may speak demeaningly of the countryman's closed view, not realizing that for many a blinkered vision is necessary to enduring another day, while others have long ago and simply discovered out of hard experience the fundamental truths that the prosperous intellectual discovers only through great mental exertion, and then they have chosen—valiantly, consciously, as Hugh Nolan said—to avert the eyes, to avoid harmful brooding, and to train the attention upon bright little things, "the sunlight coming through the privet hedge," that so thrilled Tarry Flynn. Tarry was not deluded. His concentration on beauty—like his neighbors' blind courage—was necessary to carrying on. It is a luxury to focus steadily on one's own little problems. Only people with few and intermittent troubles can afford to concentrate on their worries and call sordid description of misery "realistic," while dismissing descriptions of life's little joys as "sentimental" or "romantic."

27 Ballymenone's Terrain

1. Seán Ó Súilleabháin, "Oliver Cromwell in Irish Oral Tradition," in Dégh, Glassie, and Oinas, eds., *Folklore Today*, pp. 473–83.

2. Ivor Herring, "The Scottish Cart in Ireland and Its Contemporaries, *Circa* 1800," *Ulster Journal of Archaeology*, 3d series, 7 (1944): 42–46; Eamon Anderson, Ulster Notebook, pp. 13–14, reprinted in Harris, "Extracts," *Ulster Folklife* 4 (1958): 48; G. B. Thompson, *Primitive Land Transport of Ulster*, B.M.A.G. Transport Handbook 2 (Belfast: Belfast Museum and Art Gallery, 1958), text facing fig. 3, fig. 6, plate ix.

28 A Chronicle

1. On Patrick: *Four Masters*, 1:128–31, 134–43, 154–57; Keating, *History of Ireland*, pp. 330–48. St. Patrick's *Confessio*, quoted from Joseph Duffy, *Patrick in His Own Words* (Dublin: Veritas, 1975), p. 28. In his chapter "Behind the Legend," p. 74, Duffy repeats that Jocelin's *Life* represents Patrick's legend at its height. My copy is J. C. O'Haloran, *The Life and Acts of Saint Patrick, the Archbishop, Primate and Apostle of Ireland, Now First Translated from the Original Latin of Jocelin, the Cistercian Monk of Furnes, Who Flourished in the Early Part of the Twelfth Century: With the Elucidations of David Rothe, Bishop of Ossory* (Philadelphia: Atkinson & Alexander, 1823), in which these chapters bear on my treatment: chap. 24 (how he was preceded by Palladius, but "to Patrick the *Lord* vouchsafed the conversion of Ireland"); chap. 27 (in which the Saint curses a river into sterility); chap. 39 (how he banished the Prince of Darkness by lighting a fire, of which a Magician said, "Unless yonder Fire be this night extinguished, he who lighted it, will, together with his Followers, reign over the whole island"); chap. 46 (how Darkness was ended by the Preacher of Eternal Light); chap. 169 (of his driving of poisonous serpents into the sea out of Ireland). The translator comments that the miraculous acts may not be "strictly true," but that Jocelin was not a liar, and the stories "can neither mislead our opinion, nor confound our judgments" (p. 244). David Rothe elucidates in the seventeenth century that, as it says in Scripture, holy men have power over wild beasts, and Ireland's lack of snakes is likely owed to Patrick's power (pp. 255–56). Eleanor Duckett opens her popular account, *The Wandering Saints of the Early Middle Ages* (New York: W. W. Norton, 1964), pp. 15–16, with examples of Irish saints who, like Saint Febor, were served by wild beasts. In his account of Ireland composed late in the twelfth century, Giraldus Cambrensis wrote that Ireland had no poisonous reptiles or toads or scorpions or dragons, and that "some indulge in the pleasant conjecture that St. Patrick and other saints of the land purged the island of all harmful animals," though it is more likely that "the island was naturally without these as well as other things." Giraldus did not lack in a sense of the marvelous (he told of a fish with gold teeth, a bearded woman, and a man who was part ox), but he said it was not Patrick but "some hidden force of the land itself" that repulsed poisonous beasts. John O'Meara, trans., *The First Version of the Topography of Ireland by Giraldus Cambrensis* (Dundalk: Dundalgen Press, 1951), pp. 31–32. Keating, who called Giraldus "an inexhaustible fund of falsehood" and took it as his own duty to refute him, makes the banishment of the snakes a symbolic matter; *History of Ireland*, pp. xvii, 106. Saint Patrick is of such importance and is yet so mysterious that writings about him display the extreme difficulties of setting the early saints into history, and so also display the changes in fashion among historians. Muirchu, who wrote the first formal life of Saint Patrick at the end of the seventh century (about when Adamnan wrote his great biography of Columcille; see below, note 3), said that he attempted to steer the boat of his brain into the "dangerous and deep ocean of sacred story," though his skill was small, his authorities uncertain, his memory treacherous, and his intelligence worn out, because earlier writers "never attained to one sure track of history, on account of the extreme difficulty of the task of story-telling, and because of conflicting opinions, and the very many surmises of very many persons." Bravely he tries to bring the truth of Patrick's life into order, and he tells fully in book 1, chaps. 15–17, the story of the Paschal flame. Muirchu's *Life* is given in Newport J. D. White, ed., *St. Patrick: His Writings and Life* (New York: Macmillan, 1920);

I quote from the preface, p. 72. In another age, rationalistic and critical, the historian J. B. Bury faced the fragmentary material on Patrick and after "methodical examination" he cast the facts "into the literary shape of a biography." History, he said, was both science and art. His art was too conjectural to end disagreement, but he did focus it. His work remains important for relating Patrick to the larger picture of the late Roman Empire, and he provides in his lengthy Appendix A a useful survey of the early writings on Saint Patrick. See J. B. Bury, *The Life of St. Patrick and His Place in History* (London: Macmillan, 1905); I quote from his preface, pp. vii–viii. Bury tells the tale of the Paschal flame on pp. 101, 104–13, 262, 302–3. The vexed question of Patrick—of what is so and what is wonderful, and of the issues that exercise the historian—has been ably ordered for our own days by James Carney in *The Problem of St. Patrick* (Dublin: Dublin Institute for Advanced Studies, 1973). He outlines the different opinions excellently in chap. 1, makes important comments on the nature of tradition and history (p. 93), and tells of Patrick lighting the Paschal flame on the Hill of Slane (pp. 24–25).

2. On Finnian, Sinell, and Columbanus, Molaise, Mogue, and Naile: *Four Masters*, 1:186–87, 202–3; John Healy, *Insula Sanctorum et Doctorum: Or, Ireland's Ancient Schools and Scholars* (Dublin: M. H. Gill, 1912; 1st pub. 1890), chaps. 9, 16, esp. p. 372; Máire and Liam de Paor, *Early Christian Ireland*, Ancient Peoples and Places 8 (London: Thames & Hudson, 1978; 1st pub. 1958), chap. 3; McNeill, *Celtic Churches*, pp. 74–75, 158; J. E. Canon McKenna, *Devenish: Its History, Antiquities, and Traditions* (Enniskillen: Fermanagh Herald, 1931), pp. 16–24, 90–91; Rogers, *Prospect of Erne*, pp. 42–43, 47–49, 102–5; Livingstone, *The Fermanagh Story*, chap. 2. On Cromm, Patrick, and Mogue: Jocelin, *Life and Acts of Saint Patrick*, chaps. 55–56; *Four Masters*, 1:42–43; Keating, *History of Ireland*, p. 152; Bury, *Life of St. Patrick*, pp. 123–25. I quote in part the poem translated by Douglas Hyde, *Literary History of Ireland*, pp. 84–89.

3. Columcille: Prophecies of his birth: Jocelin, *Life and Acts of Saint Patrick*, chap. 88; Whitley Stokes, *Lives of Saints from the Book of Lismore* (Oxford: Oxford University Press, 1890), pp. 171–72. The "Life of Colomb Cille" from the Book of Lismore stresses his noble lineage, his humility, his miracles, and says he went to Scotland to preach because he had been all over Ireland, sowing faith and founding monasteries, and it was time for him to go on pilgrimage (p. 178). The tale of the disputed book is not given in Adamnan's great *Life*, the text of which is described, set, and provided in Latin and English, by Alan Orr Anderson and Marjorie Ogilvie Anderson, *Adomnan's Life of Columba* (London: Thomas Nelson, 1961). They provide a biographical outline of the Saint (pp. 66–90), discuss the historicity of the battle, which Adamnan does mention as antedating the mission to Scotland (pp. 71–74), and comment that if Adamnan knew the story, he deliberately suppressed it. Adamnan does write a marvelous biography, and I pulled details from Wentworth Huyshe's translation, *The Life of Saint Columba by Saint Adamnan* (London: George Routledge, [c. 1918]), pp. 5, 7, 11, 13, 27, 77, 121, 124, 139, 167, 175–77, 224, 236. Book and battle, "the causes of his exile to Alba," are recounted fully in Manus O'Donnell's *Life*, written in 1532, which is the fulfillment of the legend of Columcille, standing for him as Jocelin does for Patrick. See A. O'Kelleher and G. Schoepperle, eds., *Beatha Colaim Chille: Life of Columcille Compiled by Manus O'Donnell in 1532*, U.I. Bulletin 15, no. 48 (Urbana: University of Illinois, 1918), pp. 176–201 (hereafter referred to as O'Donnell's *Life*). The story of the book and battle told by O'Donnell, chief of the O'Donnells, is also found along with other details of Col-

umcille's life in *Four Masters*, 1:304–5, 178–79, 190–95, 214–15; Keating, *History of Ireland*, pp. 307, 352, 356, 370–88. I quote Keating on the cow and calf (p. 376); it is about the same in O'Donnell's *Life*, pp. 178–79. Columcille's poems, later reworkings of his own verse, or later works ascribed to him to increase their power, are given by Carney, *Medieval Irish Lyrics*, pp. 83–87 (the second poem I quote is taken from Carney's exquisite translation), and Murphy, *Early Irish Lyrics*, pp. 65–71, whose comments on pp. 202–6 are good. Audaciously I have followed neither Carney nor Murphy exactly in the first poem I quote, but merged their translations with that of O'Kelleher and Schoepperle from O'Donnell's *Life*, p. 199. Douglas Hyde discusses Columcille as a bard and translates poems "which may well be genuine" in *The Story of Early Gaelic Literature*, New Irish Library (London: T. Fisher Unwin, 1905), pp. 147–53. Montague, *Book of Irish Verse*, translates one of the Columcille poems (pp. 63–64) and says Columcille, poet, Ireland's lover in exile, is "the typical figure among the Irish saints" (p. 24). The continuing relevance of Columcille's poems, the first Irish songs of exile, has kept them in print: Sharp and Matthay, *Lyra Celtica*, pp. 18–21; Sigerson, *Bards of Gael and Gall*, pp. 35, 44–45, 156–66; Meyer, *Selections from Ancient Irish Poetry*, pp. 83–85, 87; Colum, *Anthology of Irish Verse*, p. 170. His centrality makes Columcille crucial both in the District's system of story and in historical writings on the early church: McNeill, *Celtic Churches*, chap. 6, and pp. 205–7; Ian Finlay, *Columba* (London: Victor Gollancz, 1979), a good biography in which see esp. chap. 5. I follow dates for Niall and Columcille proposed by O'Rahilly, *Early Irish History and Mythology*, pp. 217, 220, 245, 508–9. The tale of Columcille's book and battle appears constantly in popular books that reinforce the oral tradition; typical examples are: Samuel G. Bayne, *On an Irish Jaunting-Car Through Donegal and Connemara* (New York: Harper, 1902), pp. 55, 63–64; and J. M. Flood, *Ireland: Its Saints and Scholars* (Dublin: Talbot Press, [c. 1908]), pp. 21–23.

4. Viking raids and retreat to Ireland: *Four Masters*, 1:406–7, 410–12, 436–37, 456–57, 522–23; Keating, *History of Ireland*, pp. 416, 420, 437–38, 468; Seán MacAirt, ed., *The Annals of Inisfallen* (Dublin: Dublin Institute for Advanced Studies, 1951), pp. 118–19, 166–67; McNeill, *Celtic Churches*, pp. 206–7; Finlay, *Columba*, chap. 14; Rogers, *Prospect of Erne*, pp. 52–53.

5. On the Cathach, its cumdach, and the contention over Columcille's authorship: Margaret Stokes, *Early Christian Art in Ireland*, Victoria and Albert Art Handbook (London: Chapman & Hall, [c. 1890]; 1st pub. 1878), 1:95–96, 100. Françoise Henry, *Irish Art in the Early Christian Period (to 800 A.D.)* (London: Methuen, 1965), pp. 58–67, plates 6 and 12; *Irish Art in the Romanesque Period (1020–1170 A.D.)* (Ithaca: Cornell University Press, 1970), pp. 88–94. Henry, whose superb three-volume survey of early Irish art was first published in 1940 and is now in its third edition, says that nothing in the Cathach prevents it from being dated to Columcille's time. Carl Nordenfalk, *Celtic and Anglo-Saxon Painting: Book Illumination in the British Isles, 600–800* (New York: George Braziller, 1977), pp. 8, 12–14, dates the Cathach circa 625, twenty-eight years after Columcille's death. Douglas Chrétien, *The Battle Book of the O'Donnells* (Berkeley: University of California Press, 1935), concludes that the Cathach is by Columcille's hand (pp. 40–42). In her brief, bright introduction to *Early Irish Art* (Dublin: Department of Foreign Affairs, 1978), pp. 25–26, Máire de Paor says the Cathach is the oldest Irish manuscript and dates it circa 600. Bella Schauman, "Early Irish Manuscripts: The Art of the Scribes," *Expedition* 21, no. 3 (1979): 33–47, says the Cathach is the second oldest manuscript and could be by Columcille. G. Frank Mitchell, writing in the beautiful catalog *Treasures of Early Irish Art:*

1500 B.C. to 1500 A.D. (New York: Metropolitan Museum of Art, 1977), pp. 59–60, says the Cathach is the oldest Irish manuscript and dates from about Columcille's period. J. J. G. Alexander, *Insular Manuscripts: 6th to the 9th Century*, A Survey of Manuscripts Illuminated in the British Isles 1 (London: Harvey Miller, 1978), places the Cathach fourth in his catalog (pp. 28–29), gives its history, and illustrates it (plates 2–5). Gareth W. Dunleavy, *Colum's Other Island: The Irish at Lindisfarne* (Madison: University of Wisconsin Press, 1960), pp. 55–59, describes the Cathach, saying it does not display haste (as O'Curry argued in 1861) but uncertainty in Latin, and though he does not attribute its writing to Columcille, he does say it was "possibly Columba's personal Psalter."

6. Red Hugh O'Donnell, his capture, escape, and election: Paul Walsh and Colm O Lochlainn, eds., *The Life of Aodh Ruadh O Domhnaill, Transcribed from the Book of Lughaidh Ó Clérigh*, Irish Texts Society 42 (Dublin: Educational Company of Ireland for the Irish Texts Society, 1948), pp. 4–33 (hereafter referred to as Ó Clérigh, *Life of Aodh Ruadh*). I quote from pp. 19, 21, 23. *Four Masters*, 6:1894–1905, 1912–33, 2298–99. Twice Standish James O'Grady, historian and novelist, cousin of the scholar Standish Hayes O'Grady, put the story of Red Hugh's captivity and escapes into fiction, second in *The Flight of the Eagle* (Dublin: Talbot Press, n.d. [pub. 1897]). In his preface he says history is both science and art, and he has heightened history's art, dramatizing without altering (as he stresses again in the postscript) the facts. His book is speculative, decorated, patriotic, and true—a written legend. O'Grady's tale popularized and isolated the segment of Red Hugh's biography that Hugh Nolan formed as a story, though Mr. Nolan's story is closer to the seventeenth-century sources than it is to O'Grady's "experiment" in fictional history.

7. Ulster's Nine Years' War, the Siege of Enniskillen, and the Battle at the Ford: Early Accounts: *Four Masters*, 6:1940–45, 1948–55 (I quote from pp. 1948–53, and from 1:lvi, 1); Ó Clérigh, *Life of Aodh Ruadh*, pp. 60–77; Herbert Wood, ed., *The Chronicle of Ireland, 1584–1608, by Sir James Perrott* (Dublin: The Stationery Office for the Irish Manuscripts Commission, 1933), pp. 70–71, 75–81 (I quote from his views on history, pp. 3–13, and his account of the battle, pp. 76–77, 79, 81; hereafter, Perrott's *Chronicle*). Later historians: Richard Bagwell, *Ireland Under the Tudors* (London: Longmans, Green, 1890), 3:220–28, 233–36, 244–45, 252; Lord Ernest Hamilton, *Elizabethan Ulster* (New York: E. P. Dutton, 1919), pp. 95–96, 109, 140–50, 159–66, 171, 174–79; Sean O'Faolain, *The Great O'Neill: A Biography of Hugh O'Neill, Earl of Tyrone* (London: Longmans, Green, 1942), pp. 130–47; Margaret MacCurtain, *Tudor and Stuart Ireland*, Gill History of Ireland 7 (Dublin: Gill & Macmillan, 1972), pp. 83–88. Local histories: Livingstone, *The Fermanagh Story*, chap. 6; Rogers, *Prospect of Erne*, pp. 117, 188; J. E. McKenna, *Lough Erne and Its Shrines* (Dublin: Catholic Truth Society of Ireland, 1909), pp. 62, 64–66; Thomas Maguire, *Fermanagh: Its Native Chiefs and Clans* (Omagh: S. D. Montgomery, 1954), pp. 11–20, 47–48; on p. 19 he writes: "The English army from Dublin arrived on the banks of the river Arney, six miles south of Enniskillen, where Drumane Bridge now stands. . . . Hundreds of the English were slain and drowned. Immense stores of food and military equipment were lost. The place was known afterwards as the Ford of Biscuits." The poem on Enniskillen is translated in full by Eleanor Knott, *The Bardic Poems of Tadhg Dall Ó Huiginn (1550–1591)*, Irish Texts Society 23 (Lúndainn: Simpkins, Marshall, Hamilton, Kent, 1926), 2:49–53. The poem was addressed to Cú Chonnacht Maguire, Hugh's father. Other of Ó Huiginn's poems included in that volume are addressed to Hugh, the father of Red Hugh (pp. 7–18), and to Hugh Maguire, who is courted

by the best poets of Ireland, but Ó Huiginn will not follow, abandoning his "own man, Cú Chonnacht; my strength, my love, my affection" (see above, Chapter 8, note 2). The quote on wooded Fermanagh comes from McCracken, "Woodlands of Ulster," *Ulster Journal of Archaeology* 10 (1947): 17.

8. The Plantation: Hill, *Plantation Papers*, pp. 1, 18–20, 21, 149–78; Harris, *Hibernica*, pp. 105–6, 115–16, 123–30, 139, 162–63, 243. On Davies (1569–1626): "The Life of John Davies," in *Historical Tracts by Sir John Davies* (1787), pp. i–xxxviii. His most important tract is *A Discovery of the True Causes* (see above, Chapter 8, note 1). His letters to the Earl of Salisbury, 1607 and 1610 (pp. 217–86, esp. pp. 219–22, where he tells of Hugh Maguire's rebellion [pp. 243–46] and the survey of Fermanagh [pp. 252–62]), are of great importance, as Davies was one of the surveyors and he writes clearly of his experience, including his encounter in Fermanagh in 1607 with "one O'Bristan, a chronicler and principal brehon of that country," an aged Maguire retainer who was asked to surrender an ancient roll, a historical writing (pp. 253–54). He resisted, saying the roll was burned in the late war, but pressed, "the poor old man, fetching a deep sigh, confessed that he knew where the roll was, but that it was dearer to him than his life" and he would hand it over only if the Lord Chancellor would swear an oath to return it. He, "smiling, gave him his word and his hand," and "the old Brehon drew the roll out of his bosom." That vignette is touching, and Davies reports it well. The old man, having lost his country, had only his history left to him. Then, even that was taken. Later and local writings on the Plantation: Beckett, *Making of Modern Ireland*, chap. 3; James Barkley Woodburn, *The Ulster Scot: His History and Religion* (London: H. R. Allenson, [c. 1914]), chap. 6 (where he recounts the history that led to Fermanagh's high percentage of English, Episcopalian settlers, p. 71); John Johnson, "English Settlement in County Fermanagh, 1610–1640," *Clogher Record* 10, no. 1 (1979): 137–43 (who also stresses English as well as Scottish settlement); Livingstone, *The Fermanagh Story*, chap. 7; Rogers, *Prospect of Erne*, pp. 142–46.

9. Later surveys: Brian Ó Cuív, *Irish Dialects and Irish Speaking Districts* (Dublin: Dublin Institute for Advanced Studies, 1971; 1st pub. 1951), p. 84, reports from the census that in 1851 Clanawley had six of the ten people in Fermanagh who spoke only Irish and 896 people who spoke Irish. By 1891 the number had fallen to 179 (1.9 percent of the population), but that was still more than any other Fermanagh barony. Mogey, *Rural Life in Northern Ireland*, chap. 3; Symons, ed., *Land Use in Northern Ireland*, pp. 238–39.

10. Blennerhassett's Tract and Sir Arthur Chichester quoted from Hill, *Plantation Papers*, pp. 177, 175, 21.

11. Lisgoole and Black Francis: Harris, *Hibernica*, p. 162; Davies, *Historical Tracts*, pp. 245, 261–62; D. A. Chart, *A History of Northern Ireland* (Belfast: Educational Company, 1927), pp. 203–4; Livingstone, *The Fermanagh Story*, pp. 37, 62, 130–32; Rogers, *Prospect of Erne*, pp. 173–76.

12. Through the complex political history of modern Ireland, 1798–1923, I follow: Kee, *The Green Flag*; Beckett, *Making of Modern Ireland*, chaps. 15–23; Curtis, *A History of Ireland*, chaps. 18–20; T. W. Moody, ed., *The Fenian Movement* (Cork: Mercier Press, 1968). Economic background: L. M. Cullen, *An Economic History of Ireland Since 1660* (London: B. T. Batsford, 1972), chaps. 5–6. The crucial events were the Famine and the Agitation. Woodham-Smith narrates the Famine in *The Great Hunger*. W. Stewart Trench, land agent in Monaghan, provides a contemporary account of the Famine in chaps. 3–4 of his book on tensions in the Days of the Landlords:

Realities of Irish Life, the Fitzroy edition by Patrick Kavanagh (London: MacGibbon & Kee, 1966; 1st pub. 1868). Contemporary accounts of the Land League: Sullivan, *Ireland of To-Day* (1881), chaps. 9–11, 15; Robert W. McWade, *The Uncrowned King: The Life and Public Services of Hon. Charles Stewart Parnell* (Philadelphia: Edgewood, 1891), pp. 141–221. Wilfred Scawen Blunt, English supporter of Home Rule and the Land League, friend of Davitt, Dillon, Lady Gregory, and William Morris, gives good contemporary glimpses of the conditions and principal actors of the period of the Agitation in *The Land War in Ireland: Being a Personal Narrative of Events* (London: Stephen Swift, 1912), esp. pp. 40–182, 270–93, 308–32. For the Land League, see above, Chapter 13, note 15. For the Inishmore and Mackan fights: Livingstone, *The Fermanagh Story*, pp. 158–59, 161–66. For Swad Chapel: accounts by Eamon Anderson (Eamon Andrews, Eamonn MacAndrews) of Kinawley in Michael Murphy's notes, IFC 1695 (1965): 74–80, and Anderson's Ulster Notebook, pp. 49, 73–75.

13. *Report of the Irish Boundary Commission, 1925* (Shannon: Irish University Press, 1969), a complete reprint introduced by Geoffrey J. Hand, shows counterclaims entered for the inclusion of all of Fermanagh in the Free State and for the County's inclusion in Northern Ireland (pp. 16, 18, 21). Fermanagh and Tyrone had Catholic majorities by the 1911 census, though not so strong as those of Monaghan and Donegal, which were considered then ceded to the Free State. Fermanagh is surveyed in chap. 3, and the new border is drawn (pp. 142, 149, appendix, pp. 88–90); running about from Kinawley to Derrylin, it would have left Ballymenone in Northern Ireland. According to the 1961 census, Northern Ireland has more people who profess the Roman Catholic faith than any other, though there are more Protestants than Catholics, who comprise about 35 percent. In Northern Ireland, Presbyterians outnumber members of the Church of Ireland, but in Fermanagh Catholics outnumber Protestants, and members of the Church of Ireland outnumber those of other Protestant churches: *Ulster Year Book: 1972*, p. 10; Livingstone, *The Fermanagh Story*, p. 367.

14. Scholarly opinion concerning the accuracy of oral history varies widely. The situation is set forth excellently by Richard Dorson, "The Debate over the Trustworthiness of Oral Traditional History," in *Folklore: Selected Essays*, chap. 8, and outlined by William Lynwood Montell, *The Saga of Coe Ridge: A Study in Oral History* (Knoxville: University of Tennessee Press, 1970), pp. viii–xxi. For two reasons I am not entering the debate, though the conclusions implicit in this chapter have bearing on the issues involved. The minor reason first. Ballymenone's history is authentically "oral" in performance, but it is only primarily "oral" in transmission. It does not come directly from print, and it bears the characteristic marks of dependence on memory and transference by word of mouth. There are minor inaccuracies. Hugh Nolan dated the Inishmore fight at 1822; the date is 1824. Peter Flanagan said Swad Chapel took place in 1860 or 1865; the date is 1868. There is localization. The identity of the landlord who threatened Swad Chapel was shifted by the Flanagans and James Owens from Hamilton to Cole, bringing the villain nearby. There is compression. Mr. Nolan makes the great Red Hugh O'Donnell the leader at the Ford, when the leaders were Hugh Maguire and Cormac, Hugh O'Neill's brother. Further, all of Ballymenone's oral history cannot have come directly from print. Hugh Nolan's account of the courier's escape from Enniskillen, probably taken from McGiveney's song, is not part of the written record. And especially as they near the present, the oral accounts are much more complete and much richer in detail than those of the written record. That is particularly true of Mackan Hill. Still, the local historians are

literate, and they are interested in the truth, not in the maintenance of a purely oral stream of transmission, so some of their sources and many of the sources of their sources are literary. As a result, their accounts cannot be compared easily with those from nonliterate traditions. The second, more important, issue is this. The great concern over the "accuracy" of "oral tradition" springs from the desire to record information that can be connected to our own folk history as it is constructed in the academies by our own historians. But just as the anthropologist does not worry when the social structure of a tribe differs from the Western norm, and just as the folklorist does not worry when the aesthetic of a community does not match that of contemporary high-style art, and just as those scholars have long ago ceased saying that the society and art of other people are inferior to their own, I am not worried when Ballymenone's history differs from mine, I feel no need to think of it as inferior, and what interests me is how the District's people construct their own society, their own art—and their own history. The effort to record information in little communities so as to democratize our own history is of the greatest importance, but it is scientifically anachronistic to make "accuracy" the dominant concern of the study of the histories composed by other people, if by "accuracy" we mean the degree to which those histories agree with, and so can be absorbed into, the history of our society. We should accurately record their historical texts, then accurately link them as they do, seeing their history, just as we see their society or art, as distinct and integral. Then we will have more than a way to make our own history more democratic. We may be able to discover ways to change and improve its basic structure.

29 Culture

1. The Tuatha De Danann brought with them from Scandinavia to Ireland a stone called Lia fail, the fatal stone, from which Ireland took one of her names, Inisfail. Irish monarchs were crowned upon that stone until it was taken to Scotland and kept at the abbey of Scone. Scottish kings were crowned upon it until Edward I took it to England and placed it beneath the coronation chair in Westminster Abbey. That is the story Keating tells in *History of Ireland*, pp. 50–51, 87–89. The stone becomes a symbol of interrupted destiny. The confusions in Peter Flanagan's song are the confusions of recursive Irish history. More than one monarch could be "England's Virgin Queen," though Elizabeth I is intended. More than one Hugh O'Neill rebelled against the English, though the Earl of Tyrone, who surrendered at the end of the Nine Years' War not knowing Elizabeth was dead, is intended. Red Hugh O'Donnell is only the most obvious of the men with names like Donal who sailed to Spain, but he is not intended. This Donal is an early Paddy, an Irish Everyman, akin to the Donal of the popular, often-printed song "The Jacket Green" (Patrick Galvin, *Irish Songs of Resistance* [New York: Folklore Press, (c. 1960)], pp. 97–98), who died fighting William before Sarsfield sailed away. Earls rebel against monarchs, endless Donals die or go into exile. Vagueness and anachronism deepen meaning, forcing similarities to coalesce, raising enduring ideas to the surface, making history cultural.

2. Livingstone, *The Fermanagh Story*, p. 279.

3. Alice Stopford Green, in her history *Irish Nationality* (New York: Henry Holt, 1911), stresses the importance of Keating, the Four Masters, and other historians who kept "the national faith" alive after defeat in the seventeenth century (pp. 144–57), and she stresses the nineteenth-century antiquarians—"nearly all

Protestant; they were all patriots"—whose studies preserved that spirit during the dark and evil days of famine and rackrenting (pp. 242–49). Sheehy, *The Rediscovery of Ireland's Past*, describes the mostly Protestant antiquarians well in her second chapter. Petrie, a Protestant, Irish by heart, not blood, author of major works on ancient architecture, was also the second great early collector of Irish traditional music: Grace J. Calder, *George Petrie and "The Ancient Music of Ireland,"* New Dolmen Chapbooks 19 (Dublin: Dolmen Press, 1968). Petrie was preceded by Edward Bunting, organist of Belfast's only Anglican church, who accurately notated the melodies at the great convocation of harpists in 1792. Wolfe Tone attended, if impatiently. Afterward, Bunting set off to collect in the countryside, the harp gained power as a political symbol, and he produced three monumental compilations of Irish music. Bunting founded an Irish Harp Society in Belfast, within which Protestant and Anglo-Irish men mixed serious interest in artistic tradition with serious interest in the wounded national spirit of 1798: Charlotte Milligan Fox, *Annals of the Irish Harpers* (London: John Murray, 1911), chaps. 1–11; Ita Margaret Hogan, *Anglo-Irish Music, 1780–1830* (Cork: Cork University Press, 1966), pp. 91–100, 214, esp. p. 93; Aiken McClelland, "The Irish Harp Society," *Ulster Folklife* 21 (1975): 15–24. As is natural when powerful ideas guide, the Irish cultural leaders were at once scholars and artists, and they were artists in diverse media. In the early generation, the antiquarian Petrie and the novelist and songwriter Lover were also painters. In the later generation, A.E. painted as well as composing verse, worrying about economic theory, and directing his energies to social organization. All these men are important enough to deserve treatment in Bruce Arnold's *A Concise History of Irish Art* (New York: Oxford University Press, 1977), chaps. 5 and 7. T. Crofton Croker was not a painter, but as Sheehy says (p. 44), he was a friend of Maclise, a fellow Corkman, who gained fame like Barry before him as a painter in England, and he married the daughter of an English watercolorist. His life is sketched by his son, T. F. Dillon Croker, in Wright's edition of *Fairy Legends* (1862), pp. iv–xix. His family came from Devon during the Elizabethan days. In *Researches in the South of Ireland* (1824), Croker displayed wide interest in Irish history, architecture, and folklife. From chap. 5 grew his *Fairy Legends*, published in 1825 and immediately translated by the Grimms, followed by a second edition in 1826 and a second series in 1828. From chap. 18 grew his work of 1839, *Popular Songs of Ireland* (see below, Chapter 31, note 3). On Samuel Ferguson: Robert O'Driscoll, *An Ascendancy of the Heart: Ferguson and the Beginnings of Modern Irish Literature in English* (Toronto: Macmillan, 1976), esp. pp. 22–26, 33–34. On Hyde: Daly, *The Young Douglas Hyde*, presents Hyde's early interest in socialism, nationalism, and folklore (pp. 36, 74–77, 104–6, 142), and Gareth W. Dunleavy provides a clear introduction to Hyde as a writer and folklorist in *Douglas Hyde*, Irish Writers Series (Lewisburg: Bucknell University Press, 1974).

4. Woodham-Smith, *The Great Hunger*, pp. 40–41, 70–77, 88–102, 406–7. Livingstone, *The Fermanagh Story*, pp. 196, 258–65. In 1881, Sullivan, *Ireland of To-Day*, p. 79, wrote that the next agitation after the Land League's will be for the restoration of an Irish Parliament. Clark, *Social Origins of the Irish Land War*, pp. 299–300, discusses increasing nationalism within the Land League.

5. O'Rahilly discusses the sequence of ancient invasions, set in *Lebor Gabála*, the Book of the Conquest of Ireland, a late text of which was compiled at Lisgoole, in *Early Irish History and Mythology*, pp. 15–16, 75–170, 193–208. Hyde, *Literary History of Ireland*, pp. 116, 383–85, 500–512, 608–12, tells of Patrick's problem and of

the adoption of Irish by English settlers. G. B. Adams provides a good account of the history of the language spoken in Ireland, and the ultimate victory of English, in two papers: "Ulster as a Distinct Dialect Area," *Ulster Folklife* 4 (1958): 61–73; and "Language and Man in Ireland," *Ulster Folklife* 15/16 (1970): 140–71, esp. 162–63.

6. Darrell Figgis, *AE (George W. Russell): A Study of a Man and a Nation*, Irishmen of Today (Dublin: Maunsel, 1916), quotes the letter on pp. 38–42. In the days of A.E., Robert Lynd, an Ulster Presbyterian, argued for the oneness of the Irish tradition and mixed good observation (as in his account of ballad-singing, pp. 269–74) with an optimistic opinion of unity in *Home Life in Ireland*, intro. and chaps. 8 and 15. E. Estyn Evans, "The Personality of Ulster," presidential address delivered at the annual conference of the Institute of British Geographers and printed in their *Transactions* 51 (1970): 1–20; I quote from pp. 11–12. Ronald H. Buchanan begins his paper "Tradition and Change in Rural Ulster," *Folk Life* 3 (1965): 39–45, by referring to Evans' life work and saying of the division between Protestants and Catholics that, though "all too real in social and political life," there is culturally "little to distinguish the Protestant small farmer from his Roman Catholic neighbour after three centuries of acculturation." I know only Ballymenone and know only enough about the rest of Ulster to understand the limited applicability of its pattern. Still, Rosemary Harris' "Ballybeg" sounds in many ways familiar, especially when she describes the people of her hill district in *Prejudice and Tolerance in Ulster*. Catholics and Protestants, she writes in chap. 6, share the conditions of farming life and share egalitarian values within the community and hostility to officialdom, yet, as she describes in chap. 7, they are socially divided by church, school, organization, sports, dances, and—to a lesser extent—patronage of shops and pubs. As I did, she heard Unionists express dislike of the English and distrust of urban Protestant leaders (pp. 187–89), and she argues, I think correctly, that people of opposed sides can be good neighbors because their political loyalties are so clear that it is easy to frame appropriate behaviors that make peaceful relations possible (pp. 199–201). The major difference between Ballybeg and Ballymenone seems to be a clearer association of Protestants with wealth and Catholics with tradition in Ballybeg (pp. 149–55). In Ballymenone there are prosperous Catholic farmers and Protestant small farmers who, like their Catholic neighbors, credit the old cures that the Protestants she met disdained. But, shift to Belfast, focus upon children raised amid violence, lacking knowledge of a neighborly past or the maturity to weigh ideology against experience, and the picture is radically different, pathetic, dreadful: Morris Fraser, *Children in Conflict* (New York: Basic Books, 1973). Denis P. Barritt and Charles T. Carter, *The Northern Ireland Problem: A Study in Group Relations* (London: Oxford University Press, 1972; 1st ed. 1962), survey the sociopolitical situation. Numerous problems confuse the attempt to understand similarities and differences among the people of the North. If you follow sensationalistic journalists to the bitter sectors of the cities and generalize from them to all of Ulster, if you concentrate on sectarian differences, setting the Orange Lodges against the IRA, and ignore the way in which differences are exacerbated by British military presence, if you concentrate on social and political separation without considering shared values and culture, then hope fades.

7. Claddagh ring: Mr. and Mrs. Hall, *Ireland*, 3:458; Gibbings, *Lovely Is the Lee*, pp. 15–17; Ward, *God in an Irish Kitchen*, p. 12.

8. I use John Milton as an example because Christopher Hill has done a superb job of treating him both as an individual and as a member of society, a man apart

from and part of his time: *Milton and the English Revolution* (New York: Viking, 1977). On p. 99 he quotes Milton as saying he was making art of "the general murmur"; see esp. also Hill's comments on pp. 77, 248–50.

9. Though appreciating the power of language difference in cultural resistance, I believe it is a tradition of a connection between communication and community—a structure of values more than a particular language—that is necessary to good life, essential to preserve. See Brendan Devlin's essay in Seán Ó Tuama, ed., *The Gaelic League Idea* (Cork: Mercier Press, 1972), chap. 8. Yet, I believe every effort should be made to save and revive Irish and wish to refer you to a brief piece by Flann O'Brien whose great gift for the comic was matched by his good sense: *The Best of Myles* (London: Hart-Davis, MacGibbon, 1975; 1st pub. 1968), pp. 281–84.

30 History

1. Having read the arguments cited in Chapter 28, note 5, I can see no reason to doubt the Cathach as Columcille's, other than a superstitious fear of tradition. Though I was directed by Ballymenone's corpus of story to use the Cathach to illustrate factual difficulties in the lives of the Saints, Saint Patrick provides the great problem and has attracted the great scholarship. See Chapter 28, note 1.

2. Ó Clérigh, *Life of Aodh Ruadh*, pp. 76–77.

3. Claude Lévi-Strauss, *Myth and Meaning* (New York: Schocken Books, 1979), pp. 42–43, says history functions in literate societies as myth does in nonliterate ones: both are social charters, and history is a continuation of myth. He stops there, so I develop his idea, following his own arguments about the nature of myth.

31 The Idea of Place

1. *Mainistir Shligigh: Sligo Abbey: Historical and Descriptive Notes on the Dominican Friary of Sligo* (Dublin: Stationery Office, [c. 1975]), shows the O'Connor monument, as does Homan Potterton, *Irish Church Monuments: 1570–1880* (Belfast: Ulster Architectural Heritage Society, 1975), p. 19. Anne O. Crookshank begins her survey, *Irish Art from 1600 to the Present Day* (Dublin: Department of Foreign Affairs, 1979) with comparable monuments (p. 8).

2. O'Connor and the Battle at Ballyshannon: *Four Masters*, 6:2004–37, 2046–47, 2120–43, 2248–49; Ó Clérigh, *Life of Aodh Ruadh*, pp. 138–61; Perrott's *Chronicle of Ireland*, pp. 137–38; Bagwell, *Ireland Under the Tudors*, 3:284–86, 337–38.

3. Thomas Kinsella's comment comes in his note to *The Tain*, pp. 260–61, moved to the front of the paperback (London: Oxford University Press, 1970), pp. xiii–xiv. Histories of the names of places were a major responsibility of the ancient historians, one of the three types of matter they had to know: Murphy, *Glimpses of Gaelic Ireland*, p. 34. The great collection of artful formulations of early Irish place name legends is Edward Gwynn's *The Metrical Dindsenchas*, Royal Irish Academy, Todd Lecture Series, 5 vols. (Dublin: Hodges, Figgis, 1903, 1903, 1913, 1924, 1935). That concern persisted, flourishing in the Ordnance Survey that claimed scholars as fine as O'Donovan and Petrie, who worked to assemble the land's names and legends. Patrick Weston Joyce, social historian and collector of folk music, student of dialect, also compiled *The Origin and History of Irish Names of Places* (Dublin: McGlashan & Gill, 1875; 4th ed.), a monumental survey. The interest lives in the countryside, as John B. Arthur attests in "The Legends of Place-Names," *Ulster Folklife* 1 (1955):

37–42, and as this excellent study proves: Séamas Ó Catháin and Patrick O'Flanagan, *The Living Landscape: Kilgalligan, Erris, County Mayo*, Folklore Studies 1 (Dublin: Comhairle Bhéaloideas Éireann, 1975). Concern for locality distinguishes Irish folklore. Jeremiah Curtin, with wide experience of folktales to support him, says precise locations typify Irish stories: *Myths and Folk-Lore of Ireland* (Boston: Little, Brown, 1906; 1st pub. 1890), pp. 11–12. Attracted to transnational traditions, professional folklorists undervalue the local, so T. Crofton Croker's early collections of fairy stories, many of them paralleled by tales on the Continent, attracted immediate attention, translation, and comment, while Croker's collection of songs has not received great attention (much as the Grimms' märchen have proved more engaging to scholars than their legends). Croker stressed not old British ballads but "Local Songs" by minor poets, which take up over half the volume *Popular Songs of Ireland* (1839), pp. 122–340. That weighting interestingly represents the Irish song tradition. John Moulden, introducing a vast assemblage of songs from twentieth-century Ulster, *Songs of the People: Selections from the Sam Henry Collection: Part One* (Belfast: Blackstaff Press, 1979), p. 5, remarks that the astonishing thing is that one-third of the collection consists of local songs, and no other folksong collection contains a proportion that high. Closest, he says, is Gavin Greig's from northeastern Scotland. Greig says, "The folk-songist is intensely local. It is pretty much his little district against the world." The tradition Greig discovered did emphasize the local, but it is important that he was willing to see it as it was. "The collector," he says, "must in the first instance take just what he finds. He receives everything with an open mind, and goes ahead, quite prepared for developments." See Gavin Greig, *Folk-Song in Buchan and Folk-Song of the North-East* (Hatboro: Folklore Associates, 1963; reprint of papers of 1906–11), pp. 9, 25. Greig's open, modern attitude, his willingness to accept the tradition in its own terms rather than editing on the spot in accord with scholarly presuppositions, is the attitude in Sam Henry that Moulden connects with the English collector Alfred Williams, who scrupulously recorded the songs he heard. Therefore really useful comparison is possible, and Williams says that of the six hundred songs he collected, not above ten or twelve were local compositions: *Folk Songs of the Upper Thames* (London: Duckworth, 1923), p. 11. My long experience collecting songs along the North Carolina Blue Ridge brought me very few that were locally composed, very few that were attributed to particular poets, but in south Fermanagh many songs are local, many are attributed to local poets. Traditions differ, and the Irish favors the local. A monument to the local muse is Seán P. Ó Cillín, *Ballads of Co. Clare* (Galway: Seán P. Ó Cillín & Patricia F. Brannick, 1976). A century before Alfred Williams and Sam Henry, T. Crofton Croker was right to emphasize the tradition as he did. Concern for place, for the temporal dimension of space and the universal potential of Patrick Kavanagh's parochial (above, Chapter 25, note 3), is found in much of modern Irish art. Kinsella's poem "A Country Walk," in *Selected Poems, 1956–1968* (Dublin: Dolmen Press, 1973), pp. 51–55, provides a magnificent instance, and Maurice Harmon discusses it well in *The Poetry of Thomas Kinsella* (Dublin: Wolfhound Press, 1974), pp. 34–36, 40–42. The dynamic of place is memory, rooted in the specific, branching, enabling the individual to become sited, set in a world neither good nor evil but real, and Kinsella's great poem "Hen Woman" traps the idea of memory with near perfection: *Notes from the Land of the Dead and Other Poems* (New York: Alfred A. Knopf, 1973), pp. 9–12. Seamus Heaney speaks meaningfully of work on the land in several of the poems—"Digging" is first—in *Death of a Naturalist* (London: Faber & Faber, 1966), followed by his thoughts on "Bogland" (see above, Chapter 16, note 3), then by "At the Water's Edge," in *Field Work* (New York: Farrar, Straus & Giroux, 1979), p. 14. And more than that, he has written a superb essay, keying on Kavanagh, "The Sense of Place," in *Preoccupations: Selected Prose, 1968–1978* (New York: Farrar, Straus & Giroux, 1980), pp. 131–49. Richard Murphy, *The Battle of Aughrim and The God Who Eats Corn* (London: Faber & Faber, 1968); I quote from Murphy's fine poem, p. 19. John Montague's *The Rough Field*, which he inscribed to me "this sad song of our native province, Ulster's pain," gets into black and white better than any other book my feelings on Ireland's North today. I quote from "A Lost Tradition" in "A Severed Head," in that volume (pp. 34–35). In "The Errigal Road," *A Slow Dance*, pp. 26–27, he speaks of neighbors of different sides joined by a "shared landscape." Montague's métier is poetic, but his stories "The New Enamel Bucket" and "The Cry," from *Death of a Chieftain and Other Stories* (Dublin: Poolbeg Press, 1978; 1st pub. 1964), also capture important truths about Northern Ireland. Benedict Kiely, like Montague from Tyrone, states perfectly in prose the idea of place in his story "The Night We Rode with Sarsfield," *The State of Ireland*, pp. 263–73. The concept of place that links these fine writers links them as well to the modern painters treated in the first chapter, "A Sense of Place," of *Art in Ulster: 2: A History of Painting, Sculpture and Printmaking, 1957–1977* (Belfast: Blackstaff Press, 1977) by Mike Catto. Terence P. Flanagan of Fermanagh, whose canvases breathe with the atmosphere of Lough Erne and to whom Seamus Heaney dedicated "Bogland," comes first in Catto's essay. Second is Basil Blackshaw of Antrim, who told me once that the intimacy of Ulster, both physical and social, conditions today's painters, turning them from the abstract excesses of their New York peers and back to the feel of their own land. The idea of place, of space in which motion stills, history deepens, and details enlarge, is explored sensitively by Yi-Fu Tuan in *Space and Place: The Perspective of Experience* (Minneapolis: University of Minnesota Press, 1977), esp. pp. 6, 32, 65, 122–23, and chaps. 10–13.

32 The Star's Nature

1. Thinking about especially creative folk artists, I once noted a biographical pattern—many were unmarried, many were unsuccessful as workers: "'Take That Night Train to Selma': An Excursion to the Outskirts of Scholarship," in Glassie, Edward D. Ives, and John F. Szwed, *Folksongs and Their Makers* (Bowling Green: Bowling Green Popular Press, 1970), pp. 1–68. Edward Ives treated the idea seriously, and correctly found fault with it, in the last chapter of *Lawrence Doyle*. Michael Owen Jones interprets my idea differently in his study of a highly creative, idiosyncratic chairmaker, *The Hand Made Object and Its Maker* (Berkeley: University of California Press, 1975), pp. 164–67.

2. Eamon Anderson tells briefly of Charlie Farmer and mentions a few of his songs in these manuscripts: Murphy, IFC 1695 (1965): 85–88; Ulster Notebook, pp. 47, 52 (see above, Chapter 9, note 3).

3. Marvin Harris sets out the anthropological contrast in *The Rise of Anthropological Theory: A History of Theories of Culture* (New York: Thomas Y. Crowell, 1968), esp. chaps. 20–23. To characterize history, I closely follow Fernand Braudel, *On History*, esp. part 2.

4. These modes of explanation—one fundamentally sacred, spatial, and typological, the other fundamentally secular, temporal, and sequential—provide the

internal dynamic that creates the contrast between cool and hot cultures beautifully presented by Claude Lévi-Strauss in *The Scope of Anthropology*, trans. Sherry Ortner Paul and Robert A. Paul (London: Jonathan Cape, 1967), esp. pp. 46–50, and *The Savage Mind*, esp. chap. 8.

5. The ancient Irish roles—*ollamh* (professor, historian), *file* (poet), and *recaire* (bard, reciter, singer)—are not lost in Ballymenone. The *ollamh* might be a *file*, but the *file* always had a *recaire* to present his compositions in public: Osborn Bergin, *Irish Bardic Poetry* (Dublin: Dublin Institute for Advanced Studies, 1970), pp. 6–8; Keating, *History of Ireland*, p. 292; Murphy, *Glimpses of Gaelic Ireland*, p. 44; Dillon and Chadwick, *Celtic Realms*, pp. 96–97, 239; J. E. Caerwyn Williams, *The Court Poet in Medieval Ireland*, Proceedings of the British Academy 57 (London: Oxford University Press), pp. 29–40; Montague, *Book of Irish Verse*, p. 25.

Sources

In this section I list for each chapter the major sources of information I recorded in Fermanagh and used in writing this book. They follow as they occur in the text. For each there is a title in small capital letters. If the title appears within quotation marks, then it is the local name, but if there was no local name, I have invented one to ease reference. Next comes the name of the person who taught me, then the date of the conversation, then a letter. A "t" means that the information was tape-recorded and has been transcribed exactly. A "d" means that the information was dictated; I was writing swiftly while the person spoke. When I took down general comment by hand, the results were satisfactory, but when I wrote down stories, they proved less useful than transcriptions from tape. Before the narrators knew me well, they spoke too rapidly for me to get repetitions and pauses correctly. Once they knew me and had joined my project, they spoke slowly to help me, but thereby produced texts too neatly broken into lines and groups of lines, texts that lacked some of the thickened discursive sections and some of the repetitions that the unhindered teller employs for artful effect. An "r" means that I remembered the information and wrote it down later. My practice is to write key words down immediately and turn the statement over and over in my mind until I can write it all down, always within a few hours. Years of fieldwork have trained me to listen sharply and given me the feeling that I can remember short passages nearly verbatim. I quote only one lengthy text from memory, but it was so powerful and burrowed into my mind with such ferocity that I am not embarrassed to quote it (see Mrs. Timoney's Remarkable Walk in Chapter 18). Though confident of my ability to remember, I know memory is less trustworthy than dictation, dictation less trustworthy than tape-recording. Each is a valid way to gather information, but accuracy decreases as time lapses, so I have marked each statement so you can evaluate it. After the date, I make comment where necessary on texts, variation, and situation. Every text was recorded in its author's home territory—at the hearth, bedside, or familiar public house. Last I provide some annotation. I allow my responsibilities to relax as I move away from Ballymenone. Still, I provide citations enough so that comparative scholars will be able to connect their interests with my data and so that any reader will gain some sense of the connections between Ballymenone and the rest of the world.

1 Silence, Speech, Story, Song

THE EVIL TONGUE: Peter Flanagan, 12/17/79t.

COW, CALF, AND DOUGHAL: Michael Boyle, 10/26/72d. Dochal, duhal, du'ghill are among the other spellings for the west Ulster word for dunghill.

ON THE NATURE OF STORY: Hugh Nolan, 8/30/72t, 10/27/72t (second quote on the composer's gift), 11/24/72t, 11/28/72t (forgetfulness), 6/11/77t (discourse and link), 6/16/77t (first quote on the composer's gift), 6/22/77t (composers, tellers, and brightness), 8/14/78d, 12/18/79t.

WILLIAM QUIGLEY: Michael Boyle, 11/11/72t. This story provides a small but good example of the need for synonyms in the narrator's art. As I say in my brief analysis of the story's sound, Mr. Boyle hit hard consonants ("tidier out of that"). Locally "ass" and "donkey" are used interchangeably. The sonic texture of his tale led Mr. Boyle to use "donkey," with its two hard sounds, rather than "ass," throughout.

TOMMY MARTIN AND CANON PRATT: Hugh Nolan, 12/18/79t.

BIG WIND: Hugh Nolan, 11/28/72t (quoted first), 6/16/77t (quoted third), 12/18/79t (quoted second). A "dass" is a section cut away from a haystack or peck with a hay knife. Reversibly it is also, as here, a section potentially cut away, and so it is the shoulder of the construction. Motif X1611.

TOMMY MARTIN, EX-LUNATIC: Hugh Nolan, 12/18/79t.

MAD DROP: Michael Boyle, 10/28/72t.

MASTER MAGUIRE'S BIDS: Peter Flanagan, 11/20/72d; Michael Boyle, 11/25/72t; Hugh Nolan, 6/11/77t. John Wesley visited Enniskillen in 1762, a century before Master Maguire could have met him.

THE RARE ARTISTIC GENERATION: Peter Flanagan, 12/17/79t.

BIOGRAPHICAL INFORMATION ON THE STARS: Hugh Nolan, 8/14/78d, 12/18/79t. The facts I provide are useful in representing accurately Mr. Nolan's memory. Wishing for corroboration, I wrote Mr. P. J. O'Hare, editor of the *Fermanagh Herald*, in hopes that the stars would have been mentioned, if only in obituaries, in the newspaper. On February 16, 1981, Mr. O'Hare replied generously in a long letter that his "largely fruitless searches in our files, in a busy time stolen from our reportorial activities here, saw the weeks pass without documentary dividend and frustration grow in endless searches. The only single thing I found was a thanks notice from relatives to sympathisers on the death of Michael Boyle." The great stars of Ballymenone were not great enough to gain mention in the newspaper published only four miles from their home. I met that news with sadness, knowing the sensitivity of the *Herald* toward Fermanagh's country people. The obscurity of even the most uncommon of the common people is greater than I had imagined. The task of the scholar who seeks to rescue them from oblivion, the responsibility of the folklorist to the world's people, is even greater than we who indulge in rhetoric concerning forgotten people tend to recognize. Mr. O'Hare did more than search his files, he got in touch with Mary McConnell, who told him that George Armstrong "died in Australia from natural causes and not in a fire. . . . Such a tragedy would be bound to have had publication, but after trying in vain to find something about it, I contacted Mrs. McConnell with the foregoing result." He concluded, "Sorry, again, to be of so little help. The men you list would, I think, have made little impact except in your context."

THE LUCKY SHOT: Hugh Nolan, 11/8/72t (credited to George Armstrong, quoted), 6/16/77t (credited to John Brodison), 8/14/78d (credited to Brodison). Aarne-Thompson type 1894, elaborated into type 1890D. See Chapter 2, note 9. Another Irish text: Murphy, *Now You're Talking*, p. 136.

GEORGE ARMSTRONG'S RETURN: Hugh Nolan, 11/8/72t (quoted), 6/16/77t (coda quoted). I once used this story as an example in class, and Katherine Young made comments that helped in my analysis. Cf. motif X924.

BIG POTATO: Hugh Nolan, 11/22/72t, 11/28/72t, 8/14/78d; Michael Boyle, 11/25/72t. Both men credited the tale to John Brodison. Aarne-Thompson type 1960D; motifs X1435.1, X1401.2(g).

A LIE NO ONE WOULD BELIEVE: Hugh Nolan, 6/16/77t.

TWELFTH OF AUGUST: Ellen Cutler, 8/11/72t. "When I came here" is her way of expressing her marriage to Billy Cutler.

ELDERLY TELLERS: Hugh Nolan, 8/14/78d.

MEN DONE THE STORYTELLIN: Michael Boyle, 11/25/72t.

GHOSTS: Joseph Flanagan, 6/9/77t. Motifs: E281 (haunted house), E434.5 (steel protects against revenants), E426.2 (revenant as rolling cask).

FORTHS: Tommy Lunny, 8/15/72r. Motifs of fairy revenge for trespass: F361.4, F361.12. On forths, their disruption, and the troubles that follow: Croker, *Researches in the South of Ireland*, pp. 80–81; Mr. and Mrs. Hall, *Ireland*, 1:375–76; Kennedy, *Fireside Stories of Ireland*, pp. 141–42; Lady Wilde, *Ancient Legends*, pp. 46–47, 142, 234–35; Lady Gregory, *Visions and Beliefs*, chap. 14; McAnally, *Irish Wonders*, pp. 95–96; G. O'Reilly *Stories from O'Dowda's Country* (Inniscrone: G. MacHale, 1971), pp. 65–66; Diarmuid MacManus, *Irish Earth Folk* (New York: Devin-Adair, 1959), pp. 49–51; Andrews, *Ulster Folklore*, pp. 1–8, 31; Paterson, *Country Cracks*, pp. 22, 63–66, 74–75, 92, 104, 106–7; Paterson (Evans), *Harvest Home*, pp. 203–4; Harris, "Extracts (3)," *Ulster Folklife* 6 (1960): 27. Fermanagh: Harbinson, *Song of Erne*, pp. 144–45; Murphy, IFC 1696 (1965): 49–50, 229. And see Chapter 2, note 20.

BILLY, THE FORTH, AND FAIRIES: Ellen Cutler, 8/4/72d, 8/7/72t, 6/22/77d. See FORTHS, above.

NO GHOST ATALL: Hugh Nolan, 8/30/72t. "Pad" is used interchangeably with "pass" to mean minor road, path.

ON HISTORY AND TRUTH: Hugh Nolan, 8/23/72t, 6/16/77t, 12/18/79t (quoted); Michael Boyle, 10/26/72t; Peter Flanagan, 12/18/79t.

SPECIAL CEILIS: Hugh Nolan, 6/22/77t.

JOINS: Hugh Nolan, 11/22/72t (quoted), 6/22/77t.

"MAXWELL'S BALL": Peter Flanagan (tune but no text), 11/7/72t, 11/12/72t, 12/16/79d; Michael Boyle, 11/11/72t (quoted); Hugh Nolan, 11/15/72t (quoted). Alex McConnell gives a text from Annie Owens of Crockareddy in IFC 1403 (1955): 61–64, and in his Ulster Notebook, pp. 48–52.

WATER HORSES: Hugh Nolan, 10/27/72t. Motifs: B71, F420.1.3.3. Irish examples: Hyde, *Literary History of Ireland*, p. 351; Lady Gregory, *Visions and Beliefs*, pp. 16–18, 21, 26; Gibbings, *Lovely Is the Lee*, pp. 30–31; Padraic O'Farrell, *Folktales of the Irish Coast* (Cork: Mercier Press, 1978), pp. 54–55; Messenger, *Inis Beag*, p. 100; Sean O'Sullivan, *The Folklore of Ireland* (New York: Hastings House, 1974), pp. 113–16. Fermanagh: Harris, "Extracts (3)," *Ulster Folklife* 6 (1960): 28; Tunney, *Stone Fiddle*, pp. 2–3; Murphy, IFC 1697 (1966): 57.

"WILLIE THE WISP": Peter Flanagan, 11/12/72d; Hugh Nolan, 11/15/72d. Neither told the story; both reported it as told to them when they were boys. Aarne-Thompson type 330. See Chapter 20, note 3. This is one of Ireland's most popular märchen: Ó Súilleabháin and Christiansen, *Types of the Irish Folktale*, pp. 81–84. The major source for the tradition is literary, running from Carleton's *Tales and Sketches*, pp. 330–57, into collections like these: Seumas MacManus, *In Chimney Corners: Merry Tales of Irish Folk Lore* (New York: McClure, Phillips, 1904), pp. 83–104; Jeremiah Curtin, *Irish Folk-Tales*, ed. Séamus Ó Duilearga (Dublin: Educational Company of Ireland for Folklore of Ireland Society, 1949), pp. 45–46; Gerard Murphy, *Tales from Ireland* (Dublin: Browne & Nolan, 1947), pp. 139–45; Murphy, *At Slieve Gullion's Foot*, pp. 18–21; Murphy, *Now You're Talking*, pp. 120–23. Both its fictional nature and its existence in print make it unfit for adult conversations in Ballymenone, where fictional tales are used to exemplify the truth about known "composers," so fiction by unknown composers is useful only to amuse children.

"THE DEVIL AND THE FARMER'S WIFE": Peter Flanagan, 11/12/72d; Hugh Nolan, 11/15/72d. Both men recited large sections of this song, which was sung to them when they were children. Child 278.

"HUDDON AND DUDDON AND DONALD O'LEARY": Hugh Nolan, 11/24/72d, 11/28/ 72t, 6/11/77t. Michael Boyle also used to tell this story to children. Aarne-Thompson type 1535. The source is "Donald and His Neighbours," in Yeats' *Fairy and Folk Tales of the Irish Peasantry*, pp. 270–73. Yeats also reprinted Carleton's influential version of "Willie the Wisp" in that volume (pp. 214–33). Yeats took the story from a chapbook entitled *Royal Hibernian Tales*, published in 1825, and that original tale was also reprinted in *Béaloideas* in 1940 and then by Séamus Ó Catháin in *The Bedside Book of Irish Folklore*, pp. 50–55.

"THE FIELD MOUSE'S BIRTHDAY BALL": Peter Flanagan, 7/16/72t. He sang this sweetly for my children and the Coyles' son at John O'Prey's house.

"A DEER THAT ONCE WAS SICK": Peter Flanagan, 11/26/72r, 3/10/76d, 6/12/77t (quoted).

"THE MEN BEHIND THE WIRE": Texts: John C. McGee, *Irish Songs of Love and War* (Bryn Mawr: Irish Book Service, 1976), pp. 23–24; John McDonnell, *Songs of Struggle and Protest* (Dublin: Gilbert Dalton, 1979), p. 104.

"TWENTY-SIX WERE WON": Hugh Collins, 8/13/72t; Martin Kelly, 8/13/72t.

"JAMES CONNOLLY": Texts: *Songs and Recitations of Ireland: The Harp: Book No. 2* (Cork: C.F.N., 1971), p. 21; McGee, *Irish Songs*, pp. 20–21.

"JAMES CROSSAN": Owney McBrien, 11/26/72t. *Songs and Recitations of Ireland: The Flag: Book No. 1* (Cork: C.F.N., 1971), p. 27.

"THE FLAG THAT FLOATS ABOVE US": Peter Flanagan, 8/13/72t (quoted), 6/12/77t. Mr. Flanagan said the song was written by a Michael Collins, but not the rebel Michael Collins.

3 Ceili at Flanagans'

THE CEILI: Peter and Joseph Flanagan, Tommy Love, Tommy Lunny, 8/29/72t. Every ceili is both unique and typical. This ceili is unusual because of its focus on music. Still, it incorporates the principles of all ceilis, so I can use it, without obscuring its particularity, to teach the general idea. I chose this ceili because the musical focus allowed the tape recorder to run without disturbing the evening's flow, so I had a good transcript with which to work. In this chapter, I include

The Flag That Floats Above Us

Sung by Peter Flanagan. Tune transcribed by Lore Silverberg.

The slave may bend in ab-ject fear, ___ And he may hug the chains ___ that bind him, ___ And the cow-ard may run his base ca-reer, No flag of free-dom find him. ___ But while a-bove ___ us floats the flag, Of green and or-ange blen-ded, ___ No tyrant, nor no knave, ___ its folds ___ shall drag While our stout arms ___ de-fend it.

quotations from Peter Flanagan on his father's music (12/17/79t) and on his connection of springtime work and music (11/23/72d).

"I'M LOOKING FOR A BONNIE WEE LASS TO LOVE ME": Peter Flanagan, 8/23/72t, 11/12/72t, 11/18/72t. When he sings this song, Mr. Flanagan imitates Harry Lauder's characteristic chuckling style and his Scottish accent.

"BOLD JACK DONOHUE": Peter Flanagan, 8/29/72t. Laws L22. Laws gives North American references. Australian: Meredith and Anderson, *Folk Songs of Australia*, pp. 63–64; Ron Edwards, *The Big Book of Australian Folk Song* (Melbourne: Rigby, 1976), p. 33. Irish: Maureen Jolliffe, *The Third Book of Irish Ballads* (Cork: Mercier Press, 1970), pp. 40–47, recounts the career of John Donohue—born 1806, transported 1825, killed in Australia 1830—and she describes variations in the ballad. Zimmermann treats the song, its versions, and Donohue's life in *Songs of Irish Rebellion*, pp. 269–71. Other texts: *Six Hundred and Seventeen Irish Songs and Ballads* (New York: Wehman Brothers, [c. 1906]), pp. 74, 111; James N. Healy, *The Mercier Book of Old Irish Street Ballads* (Cork: Mercier Press, 1967), 1:122–23. Morton gives a text from Fermanagh in *Come Day, Go Day*, pp. 48–49.

SAINT FEBOR: Packie Love, 8/6/72r, 11/19/72r; Hugh Nolan, 8/23/72t; Tommy Love, 8/29/72t. John O'Donovan writes from Enniskillen on November 6, 1834: "The Village of Monea is called in Irish, Muine Fhiadh, i.e., Hill of the Deer. The name is accounted for by a story similar to those told to account for the names of old Churches in Derry. The Virgin Saint Feber first attempted to build her church in Kildrum, at the place where the holy well now called Tobar Feber is to be seen, but what had been built in the course of the day was destroyed in the night by some invisible being. At last a deer, blessed beast! was pleased to

Bold Jack Donohue

Sung by Peter Flanagan. Tune transcribed by Lore Silverberg.

♩. = c. 80

In Dub-lin's town __ I was brought up, That ci - ty of great fame. __ My pa-rents __ reared me ten - der - ly, As ma-ny __ has done the same. __ For be - in a bold U - ni - ted boy, They sent me a-cross the main. And for se - ven long years, down New South Wales, To wear __ a con - vict's chain. __

point out a site where Feber might erect her Church without interruption. He carried Feber's books on his horns to Monea and there the Holy Virgin finished the erection of her Church without annoyance. But when the deer was crossing the Sillees River (Abhainn na Sailíse) he slipped on its slippery banks and the books fell off his horns. . . . This was effected by the genius or sheaver (shaver) who presided over the Sillees, who did all in his power to prevent the establishment of the Christian Religion in that neighborhood." Once the Saint understood, she filled with "sanctified fury and heavenly anger" and "cursed the River . . . with sterility of fish and fertility in the destruction of human life, and that it might run against the hill." O'Flanagan, ed., *Letters of the Fermanagh Ordnance Survey*, pp. 54–55. William Parke, *Glimpses of Old Derrygonnelly* (1978), p. 21, cites a half-century-old article from the *Impartial Reporter* in which the Sillees—"Sheelees"—is translated Stream of the Fairies. There Saint Febor raised her staff, causing the river to turn back and thus saving the deer that bore her holy books. The river recoiled and rushed for Lisgoole, but the monks met it and turned it into Lough Erne. Since then it has been unlucky to meddle with the crooked Sillees. Earlier (p. 12) Parke tells of Peter Magennis, a local schoolmaster who wrote the Saint's story. While she was visiting Baron O'Phelan's castle in Boho, her deer was hounded by the Baron's harriers and driven into the river. Her books were destroyed. She cursed the Baron's castle, causing it to sink into the earth, and she put three curses on the river, making it dangerous for bathing, bad for fishing, and forcing it to "flow against the hill." Magennis wrote a poem of three stanzas, two couplets apiece, referring to the event without narrating it. The last couplet is the one Packie Love quoted to me: "But green are thy vales and thy fountains clear / MONEA where the Saint has caught her Deer." Robert Harbinson, author of *Song of Erne*, returned to Fermanagh in 1965, where in the neighborhood of Lisgoole he heard stories that he wove into a book of verse: *Songs Out of Oriel* (London: G. H. and R. Hart, 1974). He mentions the Battle of the Ford of Biscuits (pp. 19, 127) and the raid upon Lisgoole by Black Francis M'Hugh of Grouse Hall (p. 73) and tells Saint Febor's story (pp. 38, 110).

BLACK FRANCIS: Peter Flanagan, 8/29/72t, 8/30/72t, 3/12/76d; Hugh Nolan, 8/30/72t; Michael Boyle and Francis O'Reilly, 10/26/72t. The last time Mr. Flanagan told me the story he ended it saying, "Some man will become rich on that some day." Souple is supple, locally meaning agile. In *The Stone Fiddle*, p. 32, Paddy Tunney remembers his mother telling him of "Supple Corrigan, the famous Fermanagh raparee" who ran, rather than rode, from Enniskillen to the Arney, rather than the Sillees, "hotly pursued by Lord Belmore on one of his fastest chargers" but leapt the fifty-foot river. "Belmore's anger turned to admiration: 'A fine jump, Corrigan, a fine jump!' he shouted across the stretch of water. 'Devil thank me Belmore,' he gave him back, 'I had a long race for it!'" The words of the exchange are nearly the same as in Peter Flanagan's second telling. But differences lie in more than detail. Tunney's telling from north Fermanagh has shifted toward the fabulous. Mr. Flanagan puts the river's breadth at twenty, not fifty, feet, he gives Corrigan a horse with which to outrun his mounted pursuers, he gives him less distance to run (Enniskillen to the Sillees), and he identifies his pursuit as a military contingent, not a rich landlord. The telling from the locality of the event is both more complete and more plausible. Lord Belmore is Baron Belmore of Castle Coole in Fermanagh. Armar Lowry Corry was created first Lord Belmore in 1780, so he was a contemporary of Corrigan's. He is remembered in the District in a saying applied to any bad actor: "He has a devil in him as big as Belmore." See Chapter 28, note 11.

4 The Next Day

"THE WILD RAPPAREE": Teresa Rooney, 8/20/72t. Hugh and Lisa Shields list this song, recorded in Donegal, as number 434 in "Irish Folk-Song Recordings, 1966–1972: An Index of Tapes in the Ulster Folk and Transport Museum," *Ulster Folklife* 21 (1975): 53.

The Wild Rapparee

Sung by Teresa Rooney. Tune transcribed by Lore Silverberg.

WILLY REILLY AND HIS DEAR COOLEEN BAWN: Hugh Nolan, 8/30/72t. A comparison of Mr. Nolan's story and William Carleton's novel follows. I use the first edition of *Willy Reilly* (London, 1855); see Chapter 4, notes 3 and 5. Mr. Nolan begins with a generalization on the rapparees. Carleton generalizes in vol. 2, p. 276: rapparees were robbers, often political in motive, who never murdered, except in defense, and who were "quite gallant to females." To compare the stories, I have assigned a number to each paragraph, often single lines, of Mr. Nolan's tale: H.N.1 is "So the way it twas. . . ." I list them and set next to them an abstract of Carleton's novel: W.C.I,1 is vol. I, chap. 1. The chapters (two are numbered XIII, two XIV, none XV) and volumes of Carleton's novel are about equal in length, so it can be quickly seen what Mr. Nolan changed, where he leapt, where he lingered.

H.N.1–8: W.C.I,1: Squire Folliard and a servant get lost in a wood. The servant gives a whistle to call help, but attracts Parra Ruah, Red Patrick O'Donnel, the Red Rapparee, who is about to execute the Squire because he persecuted his uncle for marrying a Catholic to a Protestant, when a man intrudes and saves them: Willy Reilly. (We do not learn until chap. 3 that Reilly is, as Mr. Nolan says, a man of noble birth.)

H.N.9–18: W.C.I,2: The Squire, saying he hopes Reilly is not a papist, takes him home. Helen, his daughter, the Coleen Bawn, enters the room in a blaze of beauty and swoons at the tale of the Squire's near execution. W.C.I,3: Reilly tells the Squire of the Red Rapparee's plan to rob the house and steal the Coleen. At breakfast the next day, Reilly tells the Coleen of his love; she says she loves him too, and receives the first kiss on her virgin lips. W.C.I,4: Reilly knows religion cuts an impassable gulf between them, but the rapture of his heart conquers every argument. The Squire says it is too bad Reilly is a papist or he would marry the Coleen to him, and he tells the Coleen to convert Reilly. Enter Sir Robert Whitecraft, the Coleen's wealthy suitor. He is told of the love scene between Reilly and the Coleen, and he calls Reilly a rapparee. At dinner, Reilly attacks oppressive laws that deprive Catholics of their civil and religious rights. Reilly and the Coleen embrace and reaffirm their love. W.C.I,5: The Squire and Sir Robert talk religion, saying Ireland would be better were the Catholics banished. Insulted, Reilly leaves. Sir Robert puts the Red Rapparee under his protection to rid him of Reilly, and he tells the Squire that Reilly's rescue was a plot devised to gain him access to the Coleen. W.C.I,6: She writes Reilly, telling him to come to her. He does and is told he will be arrested. She says she will fly with him, but he dissuades her, reminding her of laws preventing marriage between Catholics and Protestants. He flies alone, pursued by the Red Rapparee. Sir Robert burns Reilly's house, calling him a "Popish rebel," and the volume ends, at p. 300, with Reilly on the road.

H.N.19–24. Reilly knocks about through chaps. 9–13A of vol. II. W.C.II, 13B: Reilly goes to a friendly Protestant minister, Brown, and sends the Coleen a letter saying he is disguised. He had planned to go to the Continent but could not leave her to Sir Robert, who plans to marry her in a month. Disguised, Reilly takes a job as a gardener with the Squire. W.C.II,14A: The Squire meets the bearded new gardener, who speaks in a brogue. Sir Robert, who is out persecuting priests, is accused of fathering a love-child upon Miss Herbert, a maid of the Coleen's. W.C.II,14B: The Squire castigates Sir Robert for foisting "one of your cast-off strumpets" upon his household. Sir Robert denies the charge,

Miss Herbert turns out to be Miss Wilson, the child is not his, and Sir Robert is once again the Coleen's intended. The Coleen requests a new maid, Connor, a Catholic, and the Squire agrees. W.C.II,16 (no 15): The Squire shelters a priest of noble blood, "one of the Maguires of Fermanagh," who is being pursued by Mr. Smellpriest, even though the Squire had transported a priest who married a Protestant to a Catholic. W.C.III,17: Sir Robert in the Squire's garden spots Reilly, for "our hero was a man exceedingly remarkable for personal cleanliness, and consequently made a point to wash his hands morning and evening with peculiar care. Be that as it may, the lynx eye of Sir Robert observed their whiteness, and he instantly said to himself, 'This is no common labourer.'" When Sir Robert leaves the garden, Reilly says to the Coleen, "I am discovered." They agree to flee.

H.N.24–31: W.C.III,18: In what Carleton calls an eventful chapter, Sir Robert tells the Squire his gardener is Reilly, while upstairs the Coleen says her pockets are too slight to carry her jewelry. Connor suggests giving it to Reilly. The Coleen gives her father a kiss, meets Reilly, and they head for Holland. W.C.III,19: The Coleen is discovered missing. The Squire follows and finds that the Sheriff has already captured Reilly, "a man of honour," because carrying away an heiress is "contrary to the laws of the land." Says the Coleen to Reilly, "I love you; but it was madness in us to take this step; let me return to my father." Reilly is imprisoned in Sligo Gaol, where the Red Rapparee tells the Sheriff that Reilly has the jewels. He admits having them, but says they were given him by the Coleen. The Sheriff says, if nothing else, Reilly will hang for theft. W.C.III,20: The Coleen agrees to marry Sir Robert. The Squire does not relish the idea of her marrying "such a d——d stork of a man. . . . But then he's a good Protestant" and Reilly is not.

H.N.32–33: W.C.III,24: While Reilly awaits the assizes, great interest in his trial develops, so great that peasants in Connacht and Ulster still sing "the rude but fine old ballad" commemorating his love. "This," Carleton says, "is fame." The charges against Reilly are stealing the family jewels and running away with "a ward of chancery."

H.N.34–57. Here Mr. Nolan consolidates a major subplot, returning to the beginning of the second volume to tell a tale Carleton narrated in fragments. W.C.II,9: The Sheriff is robbed, describes the thief, is told that it is "Reilly the Outlaw." Reilly, on the road with a priest, is arrested, but they are rescued by pike-wielding peasants. W.C.II,10: Reilly and the priest visit a cave. W.C.II,11: The Red Rapparee has become a good Protestant. The Sheriff comes to dinner, says Reilly robbed him. Wealthy gentlemen get drunk at the Squire's while their ladies console the Coleen, who has been prevented by law from fulfilling her love. W.C.II,12: Sir Robert unsuccessfully hunts Reilly, who is protected by good Protestant men, Brown and Hastings. W.C.II,13A: Reilly is arrested, but the Sheriff says it was not he who robbed him. W.C.II,13B: Reilly goes into disguise. W.C.II,16: Fergus O'Reilly, Reilly's man, goes in disguise as a beggar to Mary Mahon's and receives lodgings for the night. The Red Rapparee enters and is told the beggar speaks no English, so he brags of his theft of the Sheriff's money. Fergus informs the Sheriff, then tells a lie to Sir Robert, who sends his men with the Red Rapparee to capture a priest, who turns out to be the Sheriff, dressed in mourning, and who recognizes his true assailant. (Fergus is acting to help Reilly. Still earlier, I,5, Carleton had explained, as Mr. Nolan does [par.

35], that the Executive of Ireland, lacking police, made arrangements with bandits.) W.C.III,17: Reilly is discovered. W.C.III,18: The Sheriff plots the capture of the Red Rapparee. W.C.III,19: Fergus leads the Sheriff's party to a house, from which the Red Rapparee attempts to escape by breaking through the thatch, but he is caught. The Sheriff leads him away, encounters Reilly and the Coleen on the road, arrests Reilly, and sends him and the Red Rapparee to Sligo Gaol.

H.N.58–61: W.C.III,20: Reilly and the Red Rapparee are in prison. On the day of the wedding of Sir Robert to the Coleen, Sir Robert is arrested for arson and murder. The house he had burned, in which Reilly lived, was owned by Hastings, one of Reilly's Protestant friends. The Squire says Sir Robert will hang for his outrages against Catholics. Sir Robert arrives at Sligo Gaol. W.C.III,21: The Squire visits Sir Robert, morose in his cell, and tells him to have some "spunk" and remember all those he sent to places like this. The government's real case against Sir Robert stems from his persecution of a French priest (III,17) and fears that oppressed Irish Catholics will join the cause of the Pretender (the date is 1745), so he, "the great and principal criminal," is to be made an example to appease the Catholics. W.C.III,22: The Squire proclaims Sir Robert lost, and appeals to Reilly to convert and be saved. "I will die like a man of honour and a true Christian and Catholic," Reilly says. "As a true fool, Reilly," the Squire retorts, saying he will come to his execution. The Red Rapparee is tried first and sentenced to hanging on Saturday. W.C.III,23: Sir Robert dresses well for his trial but looks a coward. The prosecution argues that religious freedom is an "inalienable right," that persecution is blasphemy, that Catholics have been oppressed by an "inhuman code." He relates the tale of Willy Reilly's saving the Squire as an example of moral action unaffected by religious difference. The jury debates in Irish comic style, the Judge sentences Sir Robert to death. A deputation to the Viceroy threatens that if Sir Robert is hanged Irish Protestants will never again support England in arms. The Viceroy agrees to a pardon.

H.N.62–75: W.C.III,24: At his trial, Reilly appears handsome and brave: "A more noble or majestic figure never stood at that or any other bar." The Sheriff is the first witness and testifies that Reilly had the jewels. The Squire is next, and during cross examination by Reilly's lawyer, Fox, he admits the jewels were left the Coleen by her mother. The Coleen is the third witness. Lawyer Doldrum had asked her to appear in behalf of Sir Robert, but she says the jewels were her own. She eloped with Reilly to avoid Sir Robert—the alternative was suicide—and she gave Reilly the jewels. She hands a ring to a crier to give to Reilly for him to wear in exile or death. The court melts in tears. Moved, Reilly puts the ring in a locket. The jury returns quickly. The foreman, choked up, says the verdict is guilty. Hastings leaves to tell the Coleen, and the light vanishes from her eyes. The foreman continues, guilty on the second count. The Squire rushes to the court to hear the sentence of transportation for seven years. The Coleen, struck into insanity, does not smile or speak, except to ask for Reilly. After seven and a half years, Reilly returns. She does not believe it is truly he. Reilly shows her the ring. She still doubts, he whispers, she screams, "It is he," and recovers completely. The Squire calls Reilly "my son." They marry and have two children. The Squire dies. They move to the Continent, where their sons become distinguished soldiers.

H.N.76–87. The book climaxed with the gift of the token from the Coleen to Reilly (which Mr. Nolan set at the end of his account of the song), and it ended with their marriage, but Mr. Nolan returns to describe the Red Rapparee's trial and hanging. W.C.III,22: When the verdict is brought in at the end of the Red Rapparee's trial, he growls "a hideous laugh" and exclaims, "To the d——l I pitch you all." The Judge returns: "You were born for the rope. Your life has been an outrage upon civilized society." The Red Rapparee damns him, boasts that he has a pardon from Sir Robert Whitecraft, then spits, "Why, you joulter-headed ould dog, you can't hang me, or if you do, I'll leave them behind me that will put such a half-ounce pill into your guts as will make you turn up the whites of your eyes like a duck in thunder." The Judge silences the laughter in the court, addressing the Red Rapparee as a "public malefactor . . . utterly devoid of all the feelings which belong to man." The Red Rapparee responds that he "robbed like an honest man on the king's highways. . . . I never did what you and your class often did; I never robbed the poor in the name of the blessed laws of the land; I never oppressed the widow or the orphan; and for all that I took from those that did oppress them, the devil a grain of sorrow or repentance I feel for it, nor ever will feel for it." The Judge sentences him. Now the hangman had died, so the Sheriff was left with the task, but a man volunteers to act as hangman to gain pardon for his own crime and because Sir Robert had hanged his brother and he wants revenge.

H.N.88–93: W.C.III,23: Sir Robert is tried. W.C.III,24. Reilly is tried and sentenced. On the day of the hanging, the Red Rapparee says his lone regret is not living to see Sir Robert hanged. The hangman tightens the rope next to Sir Robert's ear and tells him not to be downcast. "You'll have company where you're goin'; for the Red Rapparee tould me to tell you that he'd wait for you." From his lofty position, the executioner sees the white flag of pardon arriving in the distance so, knowing Sir Robert is really guilty, he hangs him quickly, saying, "Remember Willy Reilly."

The comparison above was made between Mr. Nolan's story and the first edition of Carleton's novel, completed in February 1855. The popularity of his book immediately prompted a second edition. In its preface, dated December 1856, Carleton—called by Yeats both historian and storyteller—quotes at length John O'Donovan's history of the O'Reilly family, he tells more about the historical period of his tale, and he mentions again the "utter vulgarity" of the many ballads on the theme. He says he wrote his novel swiftly—he apologized similarly in the preface to the second edition of *Parra Sastha; Or, The History of Paddy Go-Easy and His Wife Nancy* (Dublin: James Duffy, n.d., 1st pub. 1845). Reading over his work, he says, he found defects and made changes. The major change was adding "an underplot of affection between Fergus Reilly . . . and the *Cooleen Bawn's* maid, Ellen Connor." Since Mr. Nolan's tale contained that subplot, we can know that his source was Carleton's second edition. Further, Carleton changed the spelling of his heroine's name from Coleen to Cooleen, and that is how Mr. Nolan pronounced it. Because Mr. Nolan avoided names in his tale, one needs to have read the novel to realize how efficiently he kept events and personalities in order while he told his story.

THE SONG OF WILLY REILLY: Hugh Nolan, 8/30/72t. This is "Willy Reilly's Trial," Laws M10. For references to the song see Chapter 4, note 5.

5 Late Harvest

BLACKSMITH, GENTLEMAN, AND PIPE: Tommy and Peter Lunny, 11/28/72d.

CURES: Peter Flanagan, 8/13/72d, 10/29/72d, 11/28/72d, 3/10/76d, 12/18/79d; Ellen Cutler, 8/25/72d, 8/27/72d, 11/16/72d, 12/17/79d; Hugh Nolan, 8/30/72t, 11/15/72t; Meta Rooney, 11/16/72d. See Chapter 5, note 2.

NEIGHBORS: Hugh Quigley, 12/18/79r.

WHEN MY COUNTRY CALLS I MUST GO: Peter Flanagan and Hugh MacManus, 11/19/72r.

PROTESTANT RHYMES AND TOASTS: Ellen Cutler, 8/25/72d, 11/16/72d. Robert Harbinson remembers "If I Had a Penny" as being "amongst our first nursery rhymes" in Protestant Belfast: *No Surrender: An Ulster Childhood* (London: Faber & Faber, 1960), p. 123. "Up the Long Ladder," Lynd writes, is known to every Protestant child: *Home Life in Ireland* (1909), p. 156. Van Voris, *Violence in Ulster*, p. 127, reports a Catholic reversal of the rhyme shouted at Protestant marchers. And see Heaney, *Preoccupations*, p. 25. Fraser, *Children in Conflict*, pp. 36, 134, reports new rhymes from Protestant Belfast playing on the rhyme of rope and pope.

6 Sacred Beginnings

SAINTLY ISLANDS: Hugh Nolan, 8/23/72t (quoted), 6/11/77t.

SAINT SINELL: Peter Flanagan, 8/27/72t; Michael Boyle, 11/25/72t. See Chapter 28, note 2.

SAINT COLUMBANUS: Hugh Nolan, 6/16/77t. See Chapter 28, note 2.

A TIME OF GIANTS: Peter Flanagan, 8/13/72d, 6/12/77d; Hugh Nolan, 8/15/78d. For giants building causeways, hurling stones that become islands (gargantuan feats that would be grouped under motif F531.3): Laganiensis, *Irish Local Legends* (Dublin: James Duffy, 1896), pp. 51–52; Paterson, *Country Cracks*, p. 34; Hayward, *In Praise of Ulster*, pp. 103–4, 125.

SAINT PATRICK: Hugh Nolan, 8/23/72t; Peter Flanagan, 8/27/72t. See Chapter 28, note 1.

SAINT NAILE: Peter Flanagan, 7/30/72r, 8/27/72t (quoted), 11/26/72r, 12/17/79t. On November 12, 1834, John O'Donovan wrote: "I passed through the Parish of Kinawley and met a very intelligent old man of the name Terence or Torlagh Carran (Tiorr McCerthainn) who is deeply versed in traditionary and legendary lore. . . . He told me . . . a story about the Patron Saint of the Parish that I wish to preserve. Saint Naile (which is the same name as Nathaile and Nathaniel) built the old church of Kill Naile, the ruins of which stand in the Townland of the same name. There is a long and wonderful history of his bell not worth preserving. . . . There is a holy well in the Parish called Tobar Naile, the water of which cured the jaundice after the handle of Naile's bell had been immersed in it. . . ." O'Flanagan, ed., *Letters of the Fermanagh Ordnance Survey*, pp. 63–64. Pauline Brennan writes in Gaffney, *Kinawley Through the Ages*, p. 52: "Nowadays the water of the well is reputed to have the cure of warts. There is nothing now known about the handle of the bell. . . ." Eamon Anderson of Kinawley tells the story of Saint Naile's Well in IFC 891 (1942): 407; IFC 948 (1943): 201–2. See Chapter 28, note 2.

SAINT MOGUE: Tommy Lunny, 8/13/72r; Peter Flanagan, 8/23/72r, 8/27/72t (quoted).

Mogue's clay: Patrick Logan, "Folk Medicine in the Cavan-Leitrim Area, II," *Ulster Folklife* 11 (1965): 52; St. Clair, *Folklore of the Ulster People*, p. 69; Eamon Anderson, IFC 948 (1943): 222–31. Clay from the grave of seven nuns buried by Columcille on Tory Island is also used to calm rough waters: Stephen Gwynn, *Highways and Byways in Donegal and Antrim* (London: Macmillan, 1928; 1st ed. 1898), p. 160; Fox, *Tory Islanders*, p. 6. See Chapter 28, note 2.

SAINT COLUMCILLE: Hugh Nolan, 6/11/77t. The classic source of this story is Manus O'Donnell's *Life* of 1532. See Chapter 28, note 3. Though surely conditioned by oral tradition, the numerous published versions of this tale are generally not reports of the story as spoken, but, as number 88 in his excellent collection of religious tales, Seán Ó Súilleabháin does present a text in Irish collected in Galway in 1935: "Scéalta Cráibhtheacha," *Béaloideas* 21 (1951–52).

7 Saints at War

FAITH WITHOUT GOOD WORKS IS DEAD: Peter Flanagan, 12/17/79t.

8 The Ford

"THE FORD OF BISCUITS BATTLE": Mrs. James Owens, 8/2/72r, 8/16/72d; Joseph Flanagan, 8/3/72d; Peter Flanagan, 8/6/72t (quoted), 12/18/79d; Hugh Patrick Owens, 8/11/72d, 8/17/72d; Hugh Nolan, 8/23/72t (quoted), 6/11/77t (quoted in Chapter 31); Michael Boyle, 10/26/72t; James Owens, 11/14/72t. The name of the ancestor in Hugh Patrick Owens' telling is Maurice (Muiris in Irish), which he pronounced two ways: Morris, Morrissey. On November 12, 1834, O'Donovan wrote, "All the old men agree that Beal Atha na mBrioschadh, where Maguire intercepted the passage of those who were going with provisions to the relief of the Garrison of Enniskillen, is Drumane Bridge on the Arney River." Three days later he commented that the name given by Maguire to the Ford was forgotten, "nor do I believe it was retained in the country for any length of time. The Bridge is now named Drumane from the name of the Townland, and before the erection of the bridge the ford had no name but Drumaneford." O'Flanagan, ed., *Letters of the Fermanagh Ordnance Survey*, pp. 63, 65. Twenty years later, in a footnote to the Four Masters' account of the battle, O'Donovan says, "The site of the battle is still traditionally remembered but the name is obsolete." *Four Masters*, 6:1952. In IFC 1253 (1951): 381, Alex McConnell tells the story: "There is a Ford beside me at Drumane known as 'Beal na Briste,' or the Ford of the Biscuits. Maguire, the Fermanagh Chief, held Enniskillen Castle and a large force of English marched upon it from Belturbet. Maguire met and routed them at Beal na Briste, and the English left them in their flight a large consignment of Biscuits." Michael Boyle pronounces the name "Ballinabriskey." Michael Boyle said Hugh McGiveney's song on the Ford was published in the *Fermanagh Herald*, but Mr. O'Hare, the paper's editor, wrote me, 2/16/81, that he searched his files, found nothing, and "gravely doubted" that it was "published at any time during my 45 years here." Saying that a local composition was published in Enniskillen's much admired newspaper is a way to add luster to the community's arts and artists.

HUGH MCGIVENEY: Michael Boyle, 10/26/72t (quoted), 10/28/72t, 11/11/72t; Joseph Flanagan, 11/7/72d; Hugh Nolan, 11/8/72t, 11/22/72t, 11/24/72r, 6/11/77t (quoted),

8/14/78d; James Boyle, 11/24/72r; Peter Flanagan, 12/18/79t. McGivney is the more orthodox spelling, but I asked Michael Boyle to spell all the old stars' names and I use his spelling, for it comes closer to the pronunciation they use: Magevinyuh.

"THE TAKING OF RED HUGH O'DONNELL": Hugh Nolan, 6/16/77t. The verb form Mr. Nolan uses, "a-watchin," performs doubly in Ballymenone as a durative and a passive. It could mean, he was in the process of watching, or he was being watched. The latter is the case in this text. This story comes ultimately from Ó Clérigh's *Life*; see Chapter 28, note 6. The MacDonnells are associated with Antrim, not Down. Seumas MacManus recalls that the story of Red Hugh's escape was told in his Donegal community, and he remembers re-enacting it as a boy in *Bold Blades of Donegal* (New York: Frederick A. Stokes, 1935), chap. 28.

9 Mackan Hill

MACKAN FIGHT STORY: Hugh Patrick Owens, 8/11/72d; Peter Flanagan, 8/13/72r, 8/23/72d, 8/27/72t (quoted); Joseph Flanagan, 8/23/72d, 8/27/72t (quoted); Hugh Nolan, 8/23/72t; Michael Boyle, 10/26/72t; James Owens, 11/14/72t (quoted in Chapter 31). Michael Boyle provided a tolerably accurate description of a percussion ignition system in his account; flintlock arms—"flint guns" P Flanagan said—would have been used. Peter Flanagan mentions Charlie Farmer; see Chapter 32 for him. Mackan is sometimes spelled Mackin, often Macken. I follow the spelling on the maps. Alex McConnell of Bellanaleck tells the story in IFC 1403 (1955): 85–95. See Chapter 28, note 12.

"MACKAN FIGHT" SONGS: Hugh Patrick Owens, 8/11/72d; Hugh Nolan, 8/23/72t; Peter Flanagan, 8/23/72t; Michael Boyle, 10/26/72t. The ballat Mr. Flanagan lent me to copy was taken down from Mrs. Boyle by her niece. I see no reason to preserve a young girl's spelling, so I changed obvious misspellings, broke the text into lines, and regularized capitalization and punctuation. That song is the one written by one of the Maguires of Kinawley, a section of which Mr. Boyle recited. Mr. Flanagan played the tune on the tin whistle, and it is his tune that is transcribed below. Other texts of that "Mackan Fight" appear in Livingstone, *The Fermanagh Story*, pp. 165–66, and these manuscripts: McConnell, IFC 1403 (1955): 93–95; Murphy, IFC 1695 (1965): 100–101. Story and song incorporate motif E422.1.11.5.1(a): ineradicable bloodstain after tragedy. Comparisons among three texts—Mrs. Boyle's (A), Livingstone's (B), and Michael Boyle's (C)—reveal great variation in the order of stanzas, reinforcing the idea that the song is not so much a narrative of an event as a reference to an event, and that is exactly how Sandy McConnell puts it in his IFC manuscript (1403: 85–95): he tells the whole tale in prose, then quotes the song, attributing it to the Yellow Master. Here is the comparison with the stanzas numbered: A1 is B1; A2 is unique; A3 is B2 and C1; B3 is unique; A4 is unique; A5 is C2; A6 is B4; B5, 7–8 are C3–4; A7 is B7; A8 is B8; A9 is B6; A10 is unique. Michael Murphy recorded yet another "Mackan Fight" in Fermanagh, of which there is no knowledge in the District: IFC 1711 (1966): 207–9, 256–58, 268. It tells the story from the perspective of a participant who is transported. Its style is less schoolmasterly, and it begins, "Come all you loyal heroes I hope you will draw near / Of eighteen

Roman Catholics I mean to let you hear." The narrator tells briefly of the fight, dwells on the trial, and concentrates on the hanging of "bold MacManus," who forgives his prosecutors and laments leaving his "wife and children in woeful misery." In the eighth and last stanza, the narrator laments having to "leave old Erin's shore / Swanlinbar and Monesha I'll never see you more / Likewise you sweet Derrylin I now must part with you / May the Lord protect all Catholics that's always just and true." Thomas Owens' poems, which Hugh Pat generously let me copy, are unique. I did not alter spelling in them, but I broke them into lines, regularized capitalization, and changed the plus sign (+) to "and" throughout the text. "Yeos" are Yeomen. The Yeomanry was a predominantly Protestant military force recruited by the landlords in 1796 that proved important in putting down the Rising of 1798. Locally, the term means any historic Protestant militia, the predecessors of the B men of the twentieth century.

Mackan Fight

Played by Peter Flanagan on the tin whistle. Transcribed by Lore Silverberg.

THE POET, MAGUIRE: Hugh Nolan, 8/23/72t (quoted on song), 11/15/72t, 6/11/77t; Michael Boyle, 10/26/72t, 11/25/72t (quoted story); Peter Flanagan, 11/5/72r, 11/7/72d, 11/19/72r (with Hugh MacManus), 11/28/72t, 12/17/79d. Though Mr. MacManus named Master Anderson "Neddy," Seumas MacManus (see Chapter 9, note 3) said Neddy was his father, which makes sense, as names usually skip a generation. Men generally name their sons after their fathers, not themselves.

LEARNING HISTORY: Hugh Nolan, 8/23/72t, 6/16/77t (quoted); Michael Boyle, 10/26/72t.

SWAD CHAPEL STORY: Peter Flanagan, 8/27/72t; Hugh Nolan, 11/15/72t; James Owens, 11/14/72t (quoted in Chapter 31). Eamon Anderson, Ulster Notebook, pp. 49, 73–75, and in Murphy, IFC 1695 (1965): 74–80.

"THE SWAD CHAPEL SONG": Hugh Nolan, 11/15/72t (no text); Peter Flanagan, 11/26/72t, 12/18/79t (no text); Owney McBrien, Pat McGovern, Swanlinbar, 11/26/72t. Mr. Flanagan said the tune was closely related to "Boolavogue" and Father Prout's "Bells of Shandon" (see Chapter 10, note 6), differing mainly in rhythm. In Murphy, IFC 1695 (1965): 80, Eamon Anderson attributes the song to Mary Byrne. In manuscripts from Cavan and Leitrim, mostly dated 1938, which D. K. Wilgus found in the IFC archive, the song was attributed to Thomas McGoldrick of Cloughogue, Swanlinbar. Wilgus generously shared his findings with me in a letter, 7/18/73. The act of attribution, of crediting songs to particular poets, is significant. Local people so want to celebrate local stars that they often cite authors, even if different people credit songs to different noted poets. I heard "The Swad Chapel Song" attributed to three different Maguires from Kinawley. Anderson's text (IFC 1695: 76–78) is not as full as that sung in Swad in 1972. Some of its wording may lie closer to the original composition, however. "Tradition mentions without contradiction" preserves the alliteration (contradiction: Patrick) lost in "Tradition teaches without consultation." The landlord is an "earthly" not an "ugly" bailiff. And Anderson clears up my major confusion in his notes to the text. I could not understand at all why the poet toasts Montgomery and Bennison. Bennison is the land agent recalled with anger by Hugh Nolan and Hugh Patrick Owens in their accounts of the bad Days of the Landlords, but Anderson tells us that Montgomery and Bennison, though of "the land class," did try "to bring about a settlement, so the poet apparently thought they should be mentioned" (p. 79).

The Swad Chapel Song

Sung by Owney McBrien. Tune transcribed by Julie Górka.

You — gen - tle — mu - ses — pray — ex - cuse —
me for my in - tru - sion on learn - ing's wing. And in -
spire my — gen - ius — you bards — and — sa - ges; — my
coun - try's — prai - ses — I mean to sing. Tra - di - tion
teach - es with - out con - sul - ta - tion, and bless - ed Pa - trick was
first — and all, To — Pope Cel - est - ine — and prune — our —
vi - ne - yard called In - is - ill - gi - e or the Vir - gin — Shore.

"LOUGH ERNE'S LOVELY SHORE": Owney McBrien, 11/12/72t, 11/26/72t (quoted).
"T. F. BOURKE": Peter Flanagan, 11/26/72t (quoted), 12/16/79t. Laws J16 ("Burke's Dream"). Paul Mercer, *Newfoundland Songs and Ballads in Print, 1842–1974: A Title and First-Line Index*, M.U. Folklore and Language Publications, Bibliographical and Special Series 6 (St. John's: Memorial University of Newfoundland, 1979), p. 105. Texts: *617 Irish Songs*, p. 46; James N. Healy, *The Mercier Book of Old Irish Street Ballads* (Cork: Mercier Press, 1969), 2:46–47; Jolliffe, *Third*

Lough Erne's Lovely Shore

Sung by Owney McBrien. Tune transcribed by Julie Górka.

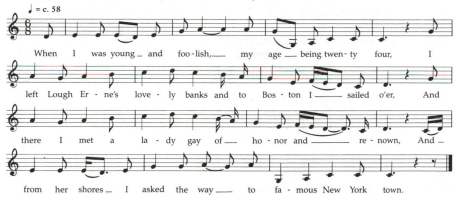

When I was young — and foo-lish,— my age — being twen-ty four, I left Lough Er - ne's love - ly banks and to Bos - ton I — sailed o'er, And there I met a la - dy gay of — ho - nor and — re - nown, And — from her shores — I asked the way — to fa - mous New York town.

Book of Irish Ballads, pp. 96–97; Zimmermann, *Songs of Irish Rebellion*, pp. 262–63. It is easy to find texts of Irish political songs in print, and those texts are useful in suggesting vaguely how the oral tradition is conditioned by publication. But unfortunately most texts are not reports of performances. Song books lift and reprint texts from each other, while some collectors avoid the rich political tradition during their quest for old ballads. So it is useful to find a fragmentary version of this song under the title "McKenna's Dream" (though "McKenna's Dream" is a different song) on the recording *Geordie Hanna Sings*, B3. Mr. Flanagan's tune is "O'Donnell Abu."

"THE TRUE LOVE": Peter Flanagan, 7/23/72t, 8/13/72t. This song, usually called "The Tri-Colored Ribbon," does not mention Thomas Ashe, though Peter Flanagan says it commemorates him (see Chapter 9, note 6). It derives from an earlier song, printed in Joyce, *Old Irish Folk Music and Songs*, p. 47, and was composed by the patriot and great songwriter Peadar Kearney, author of the Irish national anthem, uncle of the playwright Brendan Behan and the songwriter Dominic Behan. Texts: *The Tri-coloured Ribbon* (Dublin: Walton Songs, 1966), p. 8; *Walton's 132 Best Irish Songs and Ballads* (Dublin: Walton Songs, [c. 1966]), p. 5.

"THE STANDARD OF SINN FEIN": Owney McBrien, 11/26/72t. Though not the same song, it is related to "The Green Above the Red," probably a source for its author: *617 Irish Songs*, p. 98; Healy, *Old Irish Street Ballads*, 2:125–26.

THE LAND LEAGUE: Hugh Patrick Owens, 8/11/72d. On April 2, 1878, while eighty-nine tenants were being evicted from his land, Lord Leitrim, driving to Derry, passed an empty cottage from which a widow had been evicted. Men sprang from it and shot him through the heart. His skull was shattered and his body was thrown into a ditch. Men were arrested, but evidence was lacking, and they were acquitted. Sullivan, *Ireland of To-Day* (1881), pp. 238–43. See Chapter 13, note 15.

INISHMORE FIGHT: Hugh Nolan, 8/23/72t. See Chapter 28, note 12.

10 The Band

THE FIRST BAND BATTLE—PRICE VERSUS THE BAND: Michael Boyle, 10/28/72t; Hugh Nolan, 11/22/72t (quoted), 8/14/78d. See below, THE SECOND BAND BATTLE.

BANDS: Peter Flanagan, 8/6/72d; Martin Crudden, 8/6/72r; Hugh Nolan, 8/8/72d; Joseph Flanagan, 8/26/72d (quoted), 12/30/73t. Alex McConnell tells of local march bands in IFC 1403 (1955): 18a–19.

THE SECOND BAND BATTLE—THE SMASHING OF THE BAND: Michael Boyle, 10/26/72t. Art MacMurrough was a king of Leinster who ruled for forty-two years, beginning in 1375. He rebelled against the English and proved victorious in major battles over Richard II. Alex McConnell, IFC 1403 (1955): 18–25, tells the two stories of the band and gives texts of both songs collected from Andrew Boyle, age eighty-eight, of Rossdoney.

FIGHTS OVER RIGHTS-OF-WAY AND PASSES: Hugh Patrick Owens, 8/11/72d.

TALE OF THE CUT TAIL: Peter Flanagan, 10/29/72d. Paterson, *Country Cracks*, p. 78, gives a tale in which people prospered from fairy gifts until they cut the tail of a cow to lay the blame on a neighbor and the fairies withdrew their blessing.

SHINE FINE: Joseph Flanagan, 11/17/72d.

"THE MANCHESTER MARTYRS": Peter Flanagan, 8/13/72t (quoted first), 11/18/72t, 12/17/79t (one stanza quoted later). He learned the song from Patrick Lunny. His renditions were substantially the same, with the exception of the last stanza. Two of the three times he recorded this song, he began it more conventionally: "It was in November." They smashed the van in September and were hanged on November 24, 1867. See Chapter 10, note 9. Mr. Flanagan's is not the most usual of the songs on the Manchester Martyrs. Versions of this song: *617 Irish Songs*, p. 79; Colm O Lochlainn, *More Irish Street Ballads* (Dublin: Three Candles, 1965), pp. 150–51.

The Manchester Martyrs

Sung by Peter Flanagan. Tune transcribed by Lore Silverberg.

FOOTBALL ART: Hugh Nolan 11/8/72d; Peter Flanagan, 12/30/73t.

GOOD NEIGHBOR: Ellen Cutler, 8/13/78d.

"SEAN SOUTH": Gabriel Coyle, 7/13/72t; 8/30/72t (quoted). Mr. Coyle said he attacked some notes "with viciousness" while singing. He especially hated the idea of the Sergeant *spying* them through the door, and he hit that line, he said, with anger and special emphasis, though that does not show up in his lyrically smooth performance. Both times his text was exactly the same, conflating the second and third stanzas of most renditions, such as that on the ballat Mrs. Cutler gave me (8/11/72), which is illustrated in Chapter 2, or that sung by Owney McBrien. Here are Mr. McBrien's second and third stanzas (11/26/72t):

> And as they marched along the street up to the barrack door,
> They scorned the dangers they would meet or the fate that lay in store.
> They were fighting for old Ireland's cause for to free their very own,
> And the foremost of this gallant band was Sean South from Garryowen.

> The Sergeant foiled their daring plans, he spied them through the door.
> From their rifles and stenguns a hail of lead did pour.
> When this awful fight was o'er, two men were as cold as stone:
> There was one brave lad from Monaghan Town, Sean South from Garryowen.

When Peter Flanagan played the tune (7/16/72t) he called it "Rody McCrory." The tune of "Sean South" and some of the ideas in its text were taken from Ethna Carbery's "Rody M'Corley": Seumas MacManus, ed., *The Four Winds of Eirinn: Poems by Ethna Carbery (Anna MacManus)* (Dublin: M. H. Gill, 1905), pp. 82–83. Texts of "Sean South": *Songs of the Irish Republic* (Cork: C.F.N., 1972), p. 4; McGee, *Irish Songs*, pp. 37–38.

Sean South

Sung by Gabriel Coyle. Tune transcribed by Julie Górka.

"BROOKEBOROUGH RAID": Ellen Cutler, 8/14/72d.

CARSON, DE VALERA RHYMES: Ellen Cutler, 8/7/72d. For G. B. Shaw's version see Chapter 10, note 2. From Belfast, Robert Harbinson, *No Surrender*, p. 131, recalls:

> Sir Edward Carson had a cat,
> He sat it by the fender,
> And every time it caught a mouse,
> It shouted, 'No Surrender.'

DUBLIN FUSILIERS: Peter Flanagan, 11/12/72t (quoted), 11/20/72d.

"KEVIN BARRY": Peter Flanagan, 7/16/72r, 7/30/72t, 8/15/72t, 11/12/72t (quoted), 11/28/72t; Joseph Flanagan, 11/28/72t; Hugh Collins, 8/13/72t, 11/26/72t; John Fleming, 8/23/72t. Mr. Flanagan said the same tune was used for a song on the Lord Mayor of Cork dying in prison on a hunger strike. Sean Cronin, *The Story of Kevin Barry* (Cork: National Publications Committee, 1971), tells of Barry and gives several songs on his death, including this, the usual song (pp. 41–42). Lady Gregory printed a text in *The Kiltartan History Book* (1926), p. 146. Others: O Lochlainn, *Irish Street Ballads*, pp. 98–99; Galvin, *Irish Songs of Resistance*, p. 67; *Songs and Recitations: The Harp*, pp. 5–6; *The Guinness Book of Irish Ballads* (Monaghan: R. & S., [c. 1970]), p. 11; *Songs of the Irish Republic*, p. 78; *Down by the Glenside* (Dublin: Walton Songs, 1966), p. 64; McGee, *Irish Songs*, pp. 19–20; *Walton's 132 Best*, p. 58; Mary McGarry, *Best Songs and Ballads of Old Ireland* (London: Wolfe, 1972), pp. 56–57; O'Keeffe, *First Book of Irish Ballads*, p. 103. Though its constant reprinting reinforces tradition, providing singers with texts to refresh the memory, songs like "Kevin Barry" live a strong life outside of books. Collections that reprint texts from other books or that do not report real performances of such songs give little evidence of their vitality. The prayer with which Mr. Flanagan ended the rendition I quote does not appear in print. Further, comparisons of two of his performances show how free the singer is to suit the moment. The text I quote in Chapter 10 was recorded in a crowded bar (11/12/72). When I recorded the song a couple of weeks later in a calm scene at his home (11/28/72), he made the last stanza into a chorus, greatly lengthening the song. He added another stanza between the second and third:

> The night before he faced the hangman in his lonely prison cell,
> The British soldiers tortured Kevin just because he would not tell
> The names of all his brave companions and other things they wished to know.
> Turn informer and we'll free you. But Kevin proudly answered, No.

And minor textual variation is constant. He starts, "In Mountjoy jail," then "But a lad," ". . . that morning, he nobly held his head on high," "Shoot me like an Irish soldier," ". . . to free old Ireland," ". . . where we fought them hand to hand," ". . . fought to free Ireland." The last line of the second stanza, used as a chorus, ran, "For their bravery always has been Ireland's cause to live or die," and it varied the last time to, "Lads like Barry will free Ireland. For her sake they'll live and die."

11 Saints at Work

THE USES OF NATURE: HERBAL CURES AND NATURAL FOODS: Peter Flanagan: 7/23/72t, 8/3/72d, 8/13/72d, 8/20/72d, 8/27/72d, 8/29/72d, 10/25/72d, 10/29/72d, 11/23/72d, 12/29/73d (some cure for everything, quoted), 3/10/76d (even the worm, quoted), 12/18/79d; Ellen Cutler, 7/26/72d, 8/21/72d (nettles, quoted), 8/25/72d, 8/27/72d, 11/16/72d, 12/17/79d; Joseph Flanagan, 8/3/72d, 8/27/72d, 10/29/72d; Tommy Love, 8/23/72d; Hugh Nolan, 8/30/72t, 11/15/72t; James Owens, 11/14/72d; Meta Rooney, 11/16/72d; Mrs. Hugh Patrick Owens, 11/28/72d. Some of these usages have been reported in print: Ó Súilleabháin, *Handbook of Irish Folklore*, pp. 287, 313 (house leek for sore eyes, nettles as blood purifier, nettles for measles); Kavanagh, *Irish Mythology*, pp. 39, 41 (house leek for sore eyes, nettle soup for measles); Murphy, *At Slieve Gullion's Foot*, p. 109 (goats eat herbs, give rich milk); Kavanagh, *Green Fool*, p. 19 (boiled nettles for measles); Maloney, "Cures in County Cavan," *Ulster Folklife* 18 (1972): 72–74, 76 (nettles as blood tonic, garlic water for cold, house leek for sore eyes, house leek for kidney trouble, boiled nettles for measles); St. Clair, *Folklore of the Ulster People*, p. 52 (nettle tea to purify the blood). A. T. Lucas treats "Nettles and Charlock as Famine Food," in *Breifne* 1, no. 2 (1959): 137–46.

CURES AS PROOF OF GOD'S EXISTENCE: Peter Flanagan 12/17/79t.

12 Plans and Snags

PROPHECIES: Ellen Cutler, 8/7/72t; Hugh Patrick Owens, 8/17/72d; William Lunny, 11/23/72d. See Chapter 12, note 2.

13 Home

HOUSE DESIGN AND BUILDING: Rose Murphy, 7/18/72d; Paddy McBrien, 7/28/72d; Bobbie Thornton, 8/22/72r; Ellen Cutler, 8/25/72d; Hugh Nolan, 10/27/72t, 11/8/72t, 11/22/72t; Tommy and Peter Lunny, 11/27/72d; Peter Flanagan, 12/17/79d.

HOME INTERIOR AND DECORATION: Mrs. Andrew Boyle, 7/7/72d; Rose Murphy, 7/10/72r, 7/18/72d; Mr. and Mrs. John O'Prey, 7/17/72r; Doris Crozier, 7/20/72r; Ellen Cutler, 7/20/72r, 7/21/72d, 7/24/72d, 7/31/72d, 8/1/72d, 8/4/72d, 8/14/72d, 8/25/72d, 10/26/72d, 11/21/72d, 6/17/77d, 8/14/78d, 12/17/79d; Mr. and Mrs. Tommy Love, 7/22/72r, 8/1/72r, 8/12/72d; Mr. and Mrs. Bobbie Thornton, 7/27/72d, 8/22/72d; Mr. and Mrs. Paddy McBrien, 7/28/72r, 8/2/72d; Mr. and Mrs. Hugh Patrick Owens, 8/16/72r, 11/28/72r; James and Annie Owens, 8/16/72r; Tommy and Peter Lunny, 11/27/72d. See Chapter 13, note 1.

BAD LUCK TO BUILD ON THE SUNNY SIDE: Bobbie Thornton, 8/22/72r.

THE OLD YEAR, ITS GREAT DAYS AND SET TIMES: Ellen Cutler, 7/26/72t, 8/11/72t, 11/6/72d; Peter Flanagan, 7/30/72t, 8/13/72t, 10/29/72d; 11/5/72d; 11/26/72d, 12/30/73t, 1/1/74d, 8/15/78d; Hugh Patrick Owens, 8/11/72d; Michael Boyle, 10/26/72t, 11/20/72t; Joseph Flanagan, 12/29/73d; Tommy Lunny, 12/29/73r; Hugh Nolan, 1/2/74d. See Chapter 13, note 2; Chapter 20, note 1.

"STICK JACK": Peter Flanagan, 11/28/72t. The rhyme, a riddle (its answer usually a worm or maggot), is known widely in England and North America as well as Ireland: Archer Taylor, *English Riddles from Oral Tradition* (Berkeley: University of California Press, 1951), pp. 651–52. In Ireland it appears in mummers' rhymes: Gailey, "Straw Costume," *Folk Life* 6 (1968): 84. Seán Ó Súilleabháin describes games of this kind in *Irish Wake Amusements* (Cork: Mercier Press, 1967; 1st pub. 1961), p. 32.

COOKING: Ellen Cutler, 7/20/72d, 7/24/72d, 8/1/72d, 8/4/72d, 8/8/72d, 8/25/72d, 10/26/72d; Mrs. James Owens, 8/16/72d; Peter Flanagan, 3/11/76d.

THATCHING: Joseph Murphy, 7/18/72d; Harry Crozier, 7/20/72r; Tommy Love, 7/22/72r, 8/3/72d; John Drumm and Bob Lamb, 8/29/72d, 8/31/72d; Peter Flanagan, 12/29/73d; Hugh Nolan, 6/11/77d. The sod layer is spelled "scraw" and "scragh" in the literature; "scra" seems to get the local pronunciation better. See Chapter 13, note 24.

THINGS GET BETTER AND THEY GET WORSE: Hugh Nolan, 3/11/76d.

14 Clay

COWS AND CROPPING: Paddy McBrien, 7/28/72d, 1/1/74r; Hugh Nolan, 8/1/72d (land gone to grass, quoted), 8/30/72d (runs from father to son, quoted), 11/8/72t, 11/24/72d; Tommy Love, 8/3/72r; Ellen Cutler, 8/4/72d, 11/13/72d (slavery, quoted); Tommy Lunny, 8/13/72d; 8/29/72d, 11/27/72d; Hugh Patrick Owens, 8/17/72d, 11/28/72d; Bobbie Thornton, 8/22/72r; Peter Flanagan, 10/25/72d, 11/17/72d, 11/18/72d, 3/10/76d; Joseph Flanagan, 11/18/72d, 12/29/73d; William Lunny, 11/23/72r; James Boyle, 11/23/72d.

MEASUREMENT: Hugh Nolan, 11/22/72t. For other comparable varieties of measuring land by cattle: Cross, *Tailor and Ansty*, pp. 39–40, 157; Fox, *Tory Islanders*, p. 82; Bryan Hodgson, "Irish Ways Live on in Dingle," *National Geographic* 149, no. 4 (1976): 552.

ERNE DRAINAGE: Joseph Murphy, 7/18/72d; Hugh Nolan, 8/30/72t, 10/27/72d, 11/22/72t, 8/15/78d; Peter Flanagan, 11/19/72d.

TAKE IT THE WAY GOD SENT IT: Hugh Patrick Owens 8/17/72d.

HAY: Hugh Nolan, 7/14/72d, 11/8/72t, 11/22/72t; Peter Flanagan, 7/16/72r, 8/6/72d, 8/29/72d, 11/18/72d, 3/10/76d; Paddy Farmer, Thomas McBrien, Jerry McBrien, Gabriel Dorsey, 7/17/72d; Harry Crozier, 7/20/72r; Paddy McBrien, 7/28/72d; John Gilleece, 8/2/72r; Tommy Love, 8/3/72r; James McGovern, 8/18/72r; Tommy Lunny, 8/29/72d; Joseph Flanagan, 11/18/72d. See Chapter 14, note 5.

SOD-WALL HOUSES: Hugh Nolan, 10/27/72t. See Chapter 14, note 6.

DRAINS: Hugh Nolan, 8/30/72t (quoted), 10/27/72d.

HEDGES: Hugh Nolan and James Boyle, 11/24/72d. See Chapter 14, note 7.

LET A SPIDER WALK ALIVE: Ellen Cutler, 8/18/72d. A version of this rhyme from Clare appears in Ó Catháin, *Bedside Book of Irish Folklore*, p. 114.

"THE FERMANAGH SONG": Martin Crudden, 8/20/72t, 11/20/72t (quoted), 6/12/77t; Peter Flanagan (no texts), 8/20/72r, 12/18/79d.

The Fermanagh Song

Sung by Martin Crudden. Tune transcribed by Lore Silverberg.

Good peo-ple all,— on you — I call, and this song I will sing for you.—— Twas writ-ten with a lo-ving hand,— each word— is fond and true.—— It's all a-bout Fer-managh, and — the first thing I will do — Is— take you to— the Han-gin Rocks— near the vil-lage of Bel-coo.—

IT'S A LOVELY COUNTRY: Hugh Nolan, 7/14/72d.
A VIEW AS LOVELY AS FOOD: Ellen Cutler, 7/26/72r.
LOVELY CABBAGE: Ellen Cutler, 11/13/72d.
WHITEWASH: Ellen Cutler, 7/26/72d; Hugh Nolan, 7/14/72d, 11/22/72t (quoted).
THE WORLD IS NOT A HAPPY PLACE: Hugh Nolan, 6/11/77t.

15 Moss

GARDENING: Peter Flanagan, 7/23/72r, 8/13/72d, 8/20/72d, 10/25/72d, 11/19/72r, 11/20/72d, 11/23/72d, 11/26/72d, 12/29/73t, 3/9/76d, 3/10/76d, 6/12/77r, 8/15/78r; Paddy McBrien, 7/28/72d; Pat McGowan, 7/31/72d; Bob Armstrong, 8/17/72d; Ellen Cutler, 8/25/72d, 11/13/72d; William Lunny, 8/26/72r; Joseph Flanagan, 10/25/72d; Hugh Nolan, 10/27/72t, 11/8/72t; Tommy and Peter Lunny, 11/27/72d. The Champion came from Scotland, as Mr. Lunny said, after a famine, but it was the failure of 1880, not that of 1846. See Chapter 15, note 1.
KEEPING CABBAGE SAFE FROM RABBITS: Michael Boyle, 11/25/72t. Tunney, *Stone Fiddle*, p. 88, gives a different but quite comparable tall tale from north Fermanagh.
CLEANING THE DRAIN: Hugh Nolan, 10/27/72t.
THERE WERE SOME GOOD FIGHTS: Hugh Patrick Owens, 8/11/72d.
ROODS: Hugh Nolan, 11/22/72t.
COURAGE OF THE SINGER: Peter Flanagan, 12/18/79t.
COURAGE OF CONVERSATION: Hugh Nolan, 6/11/77t.
GOOD WORK: Peter Flanagan, 12/17/79t.
WITH EVERY TICK OF THE CLOCK: Hugh Nolan, 3/11/76r.

16 Bog

WORK IN THE BOG: Joseph Murphy, 7/11/72d; Hugh Nolan and James Boyle, 7/14/72d; Peter Flanagan, 7/16/72d, 10/29/72d, 11/19/72d; Paddy McBrien, 7/28/72d; Hugh Patrick Owens, 8/17/72d, 11/28/72d; Hugh Nolan, 8/30/72d, 10/27/72t, 11/22/72t; James Boyle, 10/27/72d; Johnny Boyle, 11/22/72t; William Lunny, 11/23/72r; Tommy Lunny, 12/29/73d. See Chapter 16, note 1.
BOG HISTORY AND DISCOVERIES: Bob Lamb, 8/31/72d; Peter Flanagan, 10/25/72d, 12/16/79d (quoted); Hugh Nolan, 10/27/72t; William Lunny, 10/23/72d. See Chapter 16, note 3.
COLLECTIVE WORK: Hugh Nolan, 8/30/72t, 10/27/72t. See Chapter 20, note 9.
PATIENCE IS A VIRTUE: Ellen Cutler, 7/26/72d.
MODERNIZATION: Paddy McBrien, 7/28/72d; Tommy Love, 8/10/72r; James McGovern, 8/18/72r; Michael Boyle, 10/26/72t; William Lunny, 11/23/72r; Peter Flanagan, 3/11/76d, 8/14/78r; Joseph Flanagan, 6/9/77t; Hugh Nolan, 8/15/78d, 12/18/79t; Ellen Cutler, 12/17/79r.
THE MODERN PUBLIC HOUSE AT ARNEY: Hugh Nolan, 10/27/72t.
BOXTY: Peter Flanagan, 7/23/72d, 10/25/72d; Mary McBrien, 8/10/72d; Ellen Cutler, 8/11/72d, 11/23/72d (quoted); Mrs. Hugh Patrick Owens, 8/17/72r, 11/28/78d; Meta Rooney, 11/16/72d. See Chapter 16, note 6.
THINGS ARE MUCH BETTER NOW: Hugh Patrick Owens, 8/11/72d.

17 The Man Who Would Not Carry Hay

THE LAST SCRA: Bob Lamb, 8/31/72d.

NOBODY WALKS ANY MORE: William Lunny, 11/23/72r.

BLESS THE GOOSE: Hugh Patrick Owens, 8/17/72d. In *Heavy Hangs the Golden Grain*, p. 6, Seumas MacManus says he will "curse the goose that grew the quill" he writes with if his reader gains no feel for "folklore land" from his efforts. Robert Harbinson of Belfast remembers Protestants toasting "the goose that grew the feather" and "the hand that wrote No Surrender": *No Surrender*, p. 127.

THE MAN WHO WOULD NOT CARRY HAY: James Owens, 11/14/72t.

18 The Days of the Landlords

LANDLORDS: Hugh Patrick Owens, 8/11/72d; Peter Flanagan, 10/25/72d (quoted), 3/9/76d, 12/17/79d; Hugh Nolan, 10/27/72t, 11/15/72t; Michael Boyle, 10/28/72t; Ned Cooney, 3/10/76r. I follow Mr. Nolan's first recorded statement exactly, with these exceptions: the seventh paragraph is borrowed from his second statement, and the tenth paragraph is a combination of the two statements without any alteration in individual sentences.

MRS. TIMONEY'S REMARKABLE WALK: Hugh Nolan, 8/12/72r (no story), 11/22/72t (no story), 12/18/79t (quoted); the man from the District I prefer to leave anonymous, 8/12/72r; Michael Boyle, 11/25/72t. Mr. Nolan is not being repetitious when he calls girls children, for "girl" means virgin, so adults can be girls. Mr. Boyle did not know why Mickey the Warrior had his name, but guessed he was pugnacious. The "exploits" of a comparably courageous woman from Kinawley who walked to Dublin to have her eviction canceled are recounted by Patrick T. O'Reilly in Gaffney, *Kinawley Through the Ages*, pp. 122–23.

19 The Famine

FAMINE: Hugh Nolan, 10/27/72t. I spell pratie "prettie" to get the local pronunciation.

"THE IRISH JUBILEE": Peter Flanagan, 7/9/72t. His version is quite like that from Armagh in Robin Morton's *Folksongs Sung in Ulster* (Cork: Mercier Press, 1970), pp. 88–91. "There's some variety in that," Mr. Flanagan said of the song.

FISH SAVE MCBRIEN IN THE FAMINE: Michael Boyle, 10/28/72t. I am fortunate that there was a local correspondent to the Irish Folklore Commission and that it was such a fine man as the late Alex McConnell of Bellanaleck. He frequently volunteered local traditions of importance, so I was able to discover in the archive a few versions of stories and songs—"Mackan Fight" and both the band songs—which he collected from a generation that had passed before I arrived in Ireland. On January 16, 1955, McConnell wrote down this story from Hugh Macken, age seventy-nine, who learned it from his mother: "Many a time I heard her tell the story of a man named Mulhern who lived in Drumbargy at the time of the Famine. He had a wife and four small children. One day they had neither bit nor bite in the house. 'Christie,' said his wife, 'you should go down to the river and fish and maybe you could get a wee fish.' 'Nonsense,' said Christie, 'whoever heard of catching fish in this time of year.' To please her, he went to the river close by and began fishing. To his great surprise, the first time he threw out he caught a darling perch. Again and again he threw out and never quit until he caught six darling perches, but fish as he might he could not get another one. 'Ah well,' he says, 'it's one apiece.' So, Christie went to the river every day and caught six perches. One day his youngest child died and the next day he caught only five, one apiece, and this continued every day until food became plentiful." From IFC 1403 (1955): 26–27. The narrator of that tale was Michael Boyle's uncle, with whom he lived until the old man died. It is the same story with different actors, Mulhern of Drumbargy, rather than McBrien of Rossdoney. McConnell also gives the story in his Ulster Notebook, pp. 82–83.

20 Butter

MUD-WALL HOUSES: Tommy and Peter Lunny, 11/27/72d. See Chapter 14, note 7.
THEY LIVED: Rose Murphy, 7/18/72d.
NEIGHBORS: Ellen Cutler, 11/13/72d.
A FARMER'S THREE SONS: Tommy Lunny, 11/27/72r. McConnell, IFC 1403 (1955): 96.
TWENTY-POUND COW: Hugh Nolan, 7/14/72d.
BUTTER: Ellen Cutler, 11/6/72d. A description of butter-making from Antrim: Avy Dowlin, ed., *Ballycarry in Olden Days* (Belfast: Graham & Heslip, 1963), pp. 110, 116.
THE WEE WOMAN: Hugh Patrick Owens, 8/11/72d (story of discovery), 11/28/72d (subsequent history); James and Annie Owens, 11/14/72t; T. P. Owens, 11/28/72r. Alex McConnell tells the story of the Wee Woman in two manuscripts: IFC 1096 (1947): 337–38, and in his Notebook in the archive of the Ulster Folk and Transport Museum, pp. 61–64. In the first he says, "I can vouch for the truth of this," then recounts how the Owens family of Sessiagh was about to give up the butter-packing business when "Little Maurice" found an oval stone beneath a crab tree in a grazing field. Cleaned, it was revealed to be a "carving of a woman apparently just finished churning." The parents took it for a lucky omen. "Their luck turned and they flourished. . . . I saw the stone a few weeks ago and it is a marvel. This happened about 80 years ago." The second account, that in his Ulster Notebook (1958), is titled, "The Wee Woman that the fairies left for a sign with the Owens family of Sessiagh," and it is credited to Andrew Owens, age eighty-four, who tells of his father and four or five other children playing in the meadow, throwing sods at each other, when one of the boys "pokin' about at the butt of the fairy tree . . . found the quarest looking wee stone." They took it home, and their mother "was astounded at the form of the wee stone and showed it that night to her husband. The figure was of a young woman (girl) sitting dead tired, beside a firkin of butter." They pondered the exquisite carving, then "went to the next market in Enniskillen and bought butter and sold it over again. They prospered at the butter business and were able to buy another piece of land along with what they already had. And then another wee farm and so on till they owned a good big farm that they now own. . . ."
BLACK ART OF BUTTER THEFT: Hugh Nolan, 11/8/72t (quoted), 11/15/72t. Irish butter theft (motifs D2083.3, D2083.3.2, D2084.2: "come all to me," witches drag-

ging rope): Seymour, *Irish Witchcraft*, pp. 225–27, 241–42; Ó Súilleabháin, *Irish Folk Custom and Belief*, pp. 23–25, 61, 65–66; Kennedy, *Legendary Fictions*, pp. 151–53; Yeats, *Fairy and Folk Tales of the Irish Peasantry*, pp. 142–50; Little, *Malachi Horan*, pp. 82–84; Foster, *Ulster Folklore*, pp. 89–41; Evans, *Mourne Country*, pp. 205–6; Paterson (Evans), *Harvest Home*, pp. 206–7; Murphy, *At Slieve Gullion's Foot*, pp. 56–58; Harris, "Schools' Collection," *Ulster Folklife* 3 (1957): 12–13. Fermanagh: McConnell, IFC 1096 (1947): 341; Tunney, *Stone Fiddle*, p. 27. The witch as hare (motifs G211.2.7, G275.12[db]): Croker, *Researches in the South of Ireland* (1824), pp. 94–95, says "numberless variations are in circulation amongst the Irish peasantry." Mr. and Mrs. Hall, *Ireland* (1850), 3: 254–55, report a version. Wilde, *Irish Popular Superstitions* (1852), pp. 56–57, says the story is localized in "almost every county in Ireland." Lady Gregory includes a version in *Visions and Beliefs*, pp. 288–89, and Yeats in his notes says it is the best remembered of all witch stories (p. 302). Fermanagh: McConnell, IFC 1096 (1947): 337; G. W. Saunderson, "Butterwitches and Cow Doctors," *Ulster Folklife* 7 (1961): 73; Tunney, *Stone Fiddle*, pp. 82–83. Elsewhere in Ireland: Lynd, *Home Life in Ireland*, pp. 70–71; Paterson, *Country Cracks*, pp. 28–29; Patrick Byrne, *Witchcraft in Ireland* (Cork: Mercier Press, 1975; 1st pub. 1967), p. 72; Danaher, *Folktales of the Irish Countryside*, pp. 59–61.

WITCHCRAFT: Peter Flanagan, 8/6/72t.

THE DEVIL REFUSES TO MAKE LAWYERS HONEST MEN: Hugh Nolan, 11/8/72t (quoted), 12/18/79t. Samuel Lover was sketching a mill by the Liffey when an old man told him its story, given in full in *Legends and Stories* (1834), "The Devil's Mill," pp. 141–56: A rich man sells his soul, piles up gold, and agrees to go with the Devil, but becomes contrite and, exactly as in Mr. Nolan's story, asks the Devil to do seemingly impossible tasks, such as building the mill in a night and making a rope of sand. The Devil performs them all, but at last the man tricks the Devil and saves himself. Lover's old man presented the tale as "thruth." Lover gives it as an Irish parallel to the famous "German legend." Yeats reprinted the heart out of Lover's sketch in *Irish Fairy Tales* (New York: Macmillan, 1973; 1st pub. 1892), pp. 335–40. Foster, *Ulster Folklore*, pp. 96–97, reports the same story from Antrim and Derry. The trick of Lover's tale (motif K551.9) is used by a lawyer to save his father, who had sold himself to the Devil so his sons could prosper in a tale Michael Murphy collected in Tyrone, 120 years later: *Now You're Talking*, pp. 116–17. The Devil agrees to leave the man alone until a short candle has burned down. The lawyer snuffs the candle, saving his father. A comparable ploy, though more mysterious, is used by a dead priest to save a gentleman from the Devil in story no. 36 in Ó Súilleabháin, "Scéalta Cráibhtheacha," *Béaloideas* 21 (1951–52). The Irish tale, with Lover's as the classic text, is an elaboration of the ancient and widespread tale, Aarne–Thompson type 1187. Its structure—man sells soul, prospers, repents, asks the Devil to build, Devil does, then the Devil is thwarted—was used, but turned to comedy, by the author of Mr. Nolan's story, which he learned from James Quigley.

TRUE ACCOUNT OF THE SALE OF A SOUL: Michael Boyle, 11/11/72t. The key motifs are M211 (man sells soul to Devil), G303.3.4.5 (Devil as barrel), G303.3.4.2.1 (Devil as ball of fire). Alex McConnell in his Ulster Notebook, pp. 35–38, gives a version of this story from Hugh Nolan.

FAIRIES: Peter Flanagan, 7/30/72t (quoted), 8/6/72t, 11/26/72d, 6/9/77t, 6/12/77t; Ellen

Cutler, 8/4/72d, 8/7/72t, 8/11/72t, 6/17/77d, 6/22/77d; Hugh Patrick Owens, 8/11/72r; Tommy Lunny, 8/15/72r; Hugh Nolan, 8/30/72t, 6/22/77t; Joseph Flanagan, 11/26/72d, 6/9/77t. See Chapter 2, notes 18, 19; Chapter 20, notes 4, 5, 6. Tales that compare with the two Peter Flanagan worked into his statement follow. Captured fairy escapes (motif F329.4.3): Croker, *Fairy Legends*, gives three stories like Mr. Flanagan's, in which a fairy who knows where gold is hidden escapes: "Seeing Is Believing," "Turf Cutters," "The Little Shoe" (1834), pp. 94–95, (1862), pp. 85–90, 100–101, 108–9, and in this section, "Treasure Legends"—(1834), pp. 287–310, (1828), 1:221–72, (1862), pp. 303–33—gives texts to support his comment (1834), p. 310, that the human desire for wealth produces similar stories of treasure guarded by dragons (witches in Ballymenone), treasure that is lost if found: "In poor Ireland, the wretched peasant contents himself by soliloquizing—'Money is the devil, they say; and God is good that He keeps it from us." (And those who keep it from us are evil, I would add.) Using Croker's stories, Wilhelm Grimm generalizes that the fairy knows where gold hides, but he will not tell unless captured and pressed, and if caught, tricks his captor and disappears: *Fairy Legends: Second Series* (1828), 2:8. Samuel Lover, in his second series of *Legends and Stories of Ireland* (Plymouth: Popham, Radford, [c. 1875]), builds a humorous story, "The Fairy Finder," pp. 318–40, out of a man making a fool of himself trying to capture a leprechaun. McAnally, *Irish Wonders*, pp. 143–44, and Úna Ní Cathill, *Tales My Father Told* (London: Faber & Faber, 1944), pp. 72–76, give typical stories of fairy escape. Telling of missed treasure, Mr. Flanagan provides a local example of the usual Irish story, but telling of an unsuccessful attempt to retrieve a person from fairyland, Mr. Flanagan counters the more usual tale in which the attempt is successful (motif F322.2; see Chapter 20, note 4). In his tale, the youth abducted by fairies (F324.3) rides by on horseback but is not brought back. He falls and turns to dust. Mr. Flanagan's tale is not alone; Paterson, *Country Cracks*, pp. 90–91, and Foster, *Ulster Folklore*, p. 67, report unsuccessful attempts to retrieve people from fairyland. The difference between Mr. Flanagan's and the usual tales lies in more than actors and outcome. Unlike stories of husbands recapturing wives, Mr. Flanagan's spans generations to emphasize the point he also touches in his comment after the tale—the supernatural lapse of time in fairyland, motif F377. Though his story used a common fairy-story frame, its emphasis on the passage of time causes it to resonate intriguingly with a story from the Fenian Cycle. Oisín visits the Land of Youth, and after what seems a year he returns on horseback to find the country strangely changed. Though warned not to dismount, he does, and he shrivels into an ancient man. Three hundred years had passed. That story, versified by Michael Comyn in the eighteenth century, has often been retold: P. W. Joyce, *Old Celtic Romances: Translated from the Gaelic* (London: C. Kegan Paul, 1879), pp. 385–99; Lady Gregory, *Gods and Fighting Men: The Story of the Tuatha De Danaan and the Fianna of Ireland* (London: John Murray, 1904), pp. 431–42; T. W. Rolleston, *The High Deeds of Finn, and Other Bardic Romances* (New York: Thomas Y. Crowell, 1910), pp. 154–77; Tom Peete Cross and Clark Harris Slover, *Ancient Irish Tales* (New York: Henry Holt, 1936), pp. 439–56. Oisín's story often elaborates into colloquy with Saint Patrick, but as Alan Bruford comments in "Gaelic Folktales and Mediaeval Romances," *Béaloideas* 34 (1966): 10, 73, 235–43, the romances are often compressed and focused in oral tradition, and it is the text Lady Gregory provides, *Kiltartan History Book*, pp. 21–22, pared to forthright narration of the section I sketch above, that compares with Mr. Flanagan's tale.

21 Brick

BRICK-MAKING: Hugh Nolan, 7/14/72d (quoted at end), 8/1/72t (quoted at beginning); Joseph Murphy, 7/18/72d; Paddy McBrien, 7/28/72d; Hugh Patrick Owens, 8/12/72d, 8/15/72r, 8/17/72d; Pat Cooney, 8/17/72d; Michael Boyle, 11/20/72t; Peter Flanagan, 11/18/72d, 11/19/72d, 1/2/74d, 3/11/76d. Alex McConnell, IFC 1403 (1955): 111–15, provides a good account of the process, learned from John McBrien. Michael Murphy heard a comparable account of bricks made on the islands of the Upper Lough, but did not record the details, since they were like those reported by McConnell, IFC 1711 (1966): 181.

22 Humanity

THE RABBIT WAS A VERY NICE WEE ANIMAL: Peter Flanagan, 11/12/72t.

24 Space

FUEL FROM OTHER DISTRICTS: Hugh Nolan, 10/27/72t; Peter Flanagan, 11/19/72d. See Chapter 16, note 1; Chapter 24, note 5.

25 Time

CONACRE: Ellen Cutler, 7/31/72d; Hugh Nolan, 11/18/72d, 11/22/72t (quoted). See Chapter 25, note 1.

POPULATION AND EMIGRATION: Rose Murphy, 7/18/72r; John Gilleece, 8/2/72r; Paddy McBrien, 8/10/72d; Hugh Patrick Owens, 8/11/72d; Bob Lamb, 8/31/72r; Peter Flanagan, 10/25/72d, 3/11/76d; James Owens, 11/14/72d; Hugh Nolan, 11/15/72t, 11/22/72t; Ellen Cutler, 11/21/72d.

THE BRICKIN: GREAT PASTIME AND BLOOD MONEY: Hugh Nolan, 7/14/72d, 8/1/72t; Paddy McBrien, 7/28/72d; Hugh Patrick Owens, 8/12/72r, 8/17/72d (quoted); Peter Flanagan, 11/18/72d.

26 Life

PLACE NAMES: John Gilleece, 8/2/72r; Hugh Patrick Owens, 8/12/72d; Peter Flanagan, 10/25/72d, 11/12/72t (quoted); Michael Boyle, 11/11/72t; Hugh Nolan, 11/12/72t, 11/15/72t (quoted). For Ballymenone, see Chapter 1, note 9. In Irish: druim (hill), druma (drum), margadh (bargain: locally *m* and *b* shift in pronunciation), ros (a point, a wood), Domhnach (Sunday), sé (six). Joyce, *Irish Names of Places*, discusses "ros" and "drum" names, pp. 443–44 (it is hard to know whether ros means wood or peninsula, though generally in the North it means the latter), and pp. 523–24 (Ireland has 2,400 places beginning "Drum," meaning ridge). On p. 252 he says the parish of Donagh in Monaghan took its name from a ruined old church, and on p. 244 he says that sessiagh means the sixth part, a usual form of measure in Ulster and north Connacht, which gave the name to about thirty townlands.

NO PLACE FOR SATAN IN THE HOLY LAND: Hugh Nolan, 11/15/72t.

SAINT PATRICK NEVER CAME TO BALLYMENONE: Michael Boyle, 11/25/72t. There is a story that Saint Patrick did not go to Kerry. He came near, looked, blessed, and hurried on: Mr. and Mrs. Hall, *Ireland*, 1:243; McAnally, *Irish Wonders*, p. 55.

DESPAIR: Peter Flanagan, 3/11/76r.

29 Culture

"GREEN-ROBED INISFAIL": Peter Flanagan, 11/5/72t, 11/28/72t (quoted). See Chapter 29, note 1.

31 The Idea of Place

"THE BATTLE OF THE BISCUIT FORD": Hugh Nolan, 6/11/77t. See Sources for Chapter 8, and Chapter 28, note 7.

MACKAN AND SWAD: James Owens, 11/14/72t. See Sources for Chapter 9, and Chapter 28, notes 12 and 14. General G. Lowry Cole stands atop a column with his saber bared on Forthill at the eastern side of Enniskillen. The monument, 1845–57, is described in Dixon, *Enniskillen*, pp. 40–42.

32 The Star's Nature

CHARLIE FARMER: Peter Flanagan, 8/6/72t (with Joe, quoted first), 8/29/72t, 10/29/72t, 11/5/72r, 11/7/72t, 11/12/72t (quoted second), 11/28/72d (Farmer also wrote a parody of "The Boyne Water"), 12/30/73t, 3/11/76d, 12/17/79t (quoted at end); Hugh MacManus, 11/19/72r (said Farmer also wrote a song on the Men of Easter Week); Michael Boyle, 11/25/72t.

"THE MEN OF NINETY-EIGHT": Peter Flanagan, 8/6/72t, 8/13/72t, 12/18/79t; Tommy Lunny, 8/13/72r (no text). The second time he recorded the song, he was not relaxed at home, but fighting for attention in a loud pub. Then he ordered the song: 1, chorus, 4, chorus, 2. Since feeling, not story, is the song's motive, such reordering did not weaken the performance.

The Men of Ninety-Eight

Sung by Peter Flanagan. Tune transcribed by Lore Silverberg.

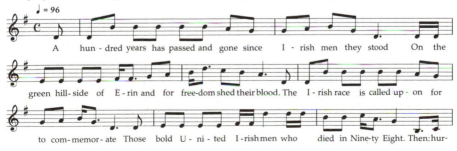

ray for the flag, the dear old flag of green. And hur - ray for the men who be -

neath its folds is seen. Hur - ray for the he - roes — we now com-me-mor-ate: Those

brave U - ni - ted I - rish men who died in Nine-ty Eight.

Kinawley

Sung by Peter Flanagan. Tune transcribed by Lore Silverberg.

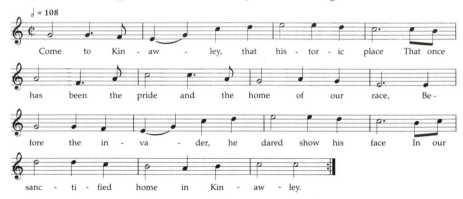

Come to Kin - aw - ley, that his - tor - ic place That once

has been the pride and the home of our race, Be -

fore the in - va - der, he dared show his face In our

sanc - ti - fied home in Kin - aw - ley.

"KINAWLEY": Peter Flanagan, 7/16/72r, 7/23/72t, 8/6/72d, 8/13/72t (introduction quoted), 8/27/72t, 11/26/72t, 12/18/79t (quoted); Ellen Cutler, 8/25/72d; Martin Crudden, 6/12/77r (no text); Hugh Nolan, 8/15/78d. Jimmy Maguire of Kinawley (8/6/72r) credited the song to John Maguire and said the flag was hoisted in a tree during the 1916 Rising so high it could not be brought down. If I number the stanzas of the complete text I quote—1,2,3,2,4,2,5,2,6,2,7,2—then 6/23/72 would appear as 1,2,3,2,5,2,7,2; 8/13/72: 1,2,4,2,5,2,7,2; 11/26/72: 1,2,3,2,4,2,5,2,7,2.

"MOLLY MAGUIRE": Peter Flanagan, 8/6/72t (quoted), 8/11/72t, 11/12/72t, 11/15/72d, 12/30/73t, 12/18/79t. Mr. Flanagan never sang this scrap of song (generally he reserves full performance for full texts), but the tune he said was "Master McGrath." John Maguire of Fermanagh sings his own song on the Molly Maguires and describes the period in Morton's *Come Day, Go Day*, pp. 21–22, 158.

"THE BLOODY CAMPAIGN ON THE BORDER": Peter Flanagan, 8/6/72t, 8/26/72r, 8/27/72t, 11/26/72t, 11/28/72t, 3/11/76d, 6/12/77r. Mr. Flanagan also calls the song "The Great League of Nations." Its tune, he said, was taken from a song describing an old woman sitting by the fire without a tooth in her head, nursing a baby. On 8/27/72: stanzas 1,2,4,5; 11/28/72: 1,3,4, new stanza, 5,6.

"OLIVER'S HARVEST HOME": Peter Flanagan, 8/6/72t, 11/12/72t, 3/11/76d, 12/18/79t. Michael Murphy obtained this song from Eamon Anderson, titled "Willie's Harvest Home," credited to Charlie Farmer; IFC 1695 (1965): 85–88.

"JOHN GREENE": Peter Flanagan, 8/6/72t, 12/18/79t.

The Bloody Campaign on the Border

Sung by Peter Flanagan. Tune transcribed by Lore Silverberg.

The great League of Na-tions is now in des-pair, And war it is loo-ming a-gain in the air, And an or-der has came from Bel-fast to pre-pare For a bloo-dy cam-paign on the Bor-der.

"REILLY": Peter Flanagan, 8/6/72t, 12/18/79t; Michael Boyle, 11/25/72t.

JAMES QUIGLEY: Michael Boyle, 11/25/72t.

"THE STAR OF BALLYMENONE": Michael Boyle, 11/11/72t. As with all the other song texts Mr. Boyle gave me, he recited, did not sing, this. Many Irish songs celebrate a young woman as the star of her locality, many describe places as settings for uneventful, often artful, discussions between lovers. Huntington's unpublished "Sam Henry's 'Songs of the People'" contains several: pp. 219–21 (no. 85), 408–9 (197), 436–37 (555: "The Star of Donegal," which contains some similarities of diction), 475–76 (503), 479–80 (616), 496–97 (102), 521–23 (121), 524–25 (647), 581–83 (500), 607–9 (115), 722–24 (723), 725–26 (170), 731–31c (68), 812–14 (164), 849–50 (752), 855–56 (13), 1206–7 (87). Most similar is "Greenmount Smiling Anne," pp. 470–71 (no. 182), also in Healy, *Old Irish Street Ballads*, 1:273–74, which is certainly related to "The Star of Ballymenone," though it is not the same song.

"IF I WAS A BLACKBIRD": Peter Flanagan, 7/16/72r, 8/13/72r, 8/30/72t. Mr. Flanagan learned this song from a recording by Delia Murphy. Her records were also the source, he said, for other common songs, "The Spinning Wheel," "The Moonshiner" (which he recorded 7/9/72t), and "The Boston Burglar" (Laws L16B, which P said was an Irish song, composed somewhere in the far south). "If I Was a Blackbird": Mercer, *Newfoundland Songs*, p. 135; Shields, "Irish Folk-Song Recordings," *Ulster Folklife* 21 (1975): no. 200; Huntington, ed., "Sam Henry's 'Songs of the People,'": pp. 410–11 (no. 79); O Lochlainn, *Irish Street Ballads*, p. 92; *Reilly's Daughter* (Dublin: Walton Songs, 1966), p. 45; *Walton's 132 Best*, p. 82; O'Keeffe, *First Book of Irish Ballads*, p. 109.

"LOVE SONG": Peter Flanagan, 8/30/72t (quoted), 12/17/79t. He shortened his second recording by following the first two stanzas with one that did the work of stanzas 3, 4, and 5 of the text I quote, then following it with stanzas 6 and 7. That compressed stanza:

> She raised her head from her snow-white pillow,
> And slowly, slowly she let me in.
> It was in our arms we embraced each other
> Until that long night, love, was nearly in.

Mr. Flanagan said the "rocks" of the last stanza are hills of medium size (larger than Drumbargy, smaller than Cuilcagh, the size of Knockninny). There is nothing mysterious in his mind about the song. It is an *aube*. The song is Child

248, "The Grey Cock," and scholars argue that the visiting lover is a revenant, though most of the many recorded texts in Britain and North America do not suggest it. The "burning rocks" of Mr. Flanagan's text, in fact, are stronger evidence of the lover's ghostly nature than anything in Child's eighteenth-century Scottish text (4:390), which set the type. Child 248 merges into a large family of night-visit songs through which it connects—in texts like that in R. H. Cromek's *Remains of Nithside and Galloway Song* (Paisely: Alexander Gardner, 1880; 1st pub. 1810), pp. 178–79—to Laws M4, "The Drowsy Sleeper." Individual texts, then, might be seen as points on a continuous spectrum of night-visiting, stretching from Child 248 (lovers embrace, then part at cock's crow) to Laws M4 (lovers are prevented from loving by parents). In Gale Huntington's unpublished edition of "Sam Henry's 'Songs of the People,'" there is a version of Child 248, pp. 34–35 (no. 699) and there is a song suspended at midpoint, pp. 89–91 (no. 722), for the lovers, having been together, part at cock's crow and then discuss the parental objections that will prevent them from meeting a next time. Huntington classifies it Laws M4, as does Shields, "Irish Folk-Song Recordings," *Ulster Folklife* 21 (1975): no. 86. Henry's song has eleven stanzas, of which 3, 4, 5, and 6 correspond to Mr. Flanagan's 2, 3, 4, and 6. Then subsequent stanzas pull the song toward Laws M4, as the woman describes her parents' objections and sends the man to "court some other." But Mr. Flanagan's song expands the love scene in its fifth stanza (significantly omitted from Henry's version); it contains no suggestion of parental thwarting, and (with its dim hint of ghostliness) shifts positively toward Child 248.

Love Song

Sung by Peter Flanagan. Tune transcribed by Julie Górka.

Here is a health un-to all true lo-vers, A health to my love where e'er he be. This ve-ry night I'll be with my dar-ling For many's a long mile he is from me.

"HOME RULE BILL": Peter Flanagan, 11/28/72t, 12/16/79d, 12/18/79t. The first time P sang it, the song had stanzas 1 and 3. The second and third time, it had stanzas 2 and 3. He learned the song when he was "a Catholic cub" from his neighbor in Kinawley, Johnny Crawford. "I liked Johnny Crawford immensely well," P said, "there's no doubt about that."

"THE RISING OF THE MOON": Joseph Flanagan, 8/30/72t. The author of the song, John Keegan Casey, featured it in his collected verse, *The Rising of the Moon and Other Ballads, Songs and Legends* (Dublin: M. H. Gill, 1933; 1st pub. 1869), pp. 74–75. J. F. Conlon, *Some Irish Poets and Musicians* (Cork: J. F. Conlon, 1974), p. 17, says Casey wrote the song in 1860 at the age of fifteen. It is the favorite patriotic song of the anthologists: Kenedy, *Universal Irish Song Book,* p. 154; *617 Irish Songs,* p. 39; Colum, *Anthology of Irish Verse,* pp. 101–2; Robinson, *Golden Treasury of Irish Verse,* pp. 142–43; O Lochlainn, *More Irish Street Ballads,* pp. 134–35; Galvin, *Irish Songs of Resistance,* p. 35; Zimmermann, *Songs of Irish Rebellion,* pp. 259–60; *Songs of the Irish Republic,* p. 20; *Guinness Book of Irish Ballads,* p. 17; *Tri-coloured Ribbon,* p. 30; McGarry, *Best Songs and Ballads,* pp. 59–60; James N. Healy, *Ballads from the Pubs of Ireland* (Cork: Mercier Press, 1965), pp. 114–15; Healy, *Old Irish Street Ballads,* 2:120–21. With all those texts, it would not seem we need another, yet those are all printings of printings, and Joe's is a real performance; while basically like Casey's composition, his text is exactly like no other. And no other ended with Joe smiling shyly, tipping his cap, and saying, "She was a great moon, that."

"THE DAY WAS GONE, THE BATTLE'S ENDED": Joseph Flanagan, 11/28/72t. He said it was composed on the Easter Rising but referred to no particular rebel. In the books it is titled "The Dying Rebel": *Songs and Recitations: The Harp,* p. 14; *Down by the Glenside,* p. 17.

"AHERLOW": Peter Flanagan, 7/30/72t (quoted), 12/18/79t. This is Laws J11, "Patrick Sheehan." It was composed by Charles Kickham, and his poem can be found in William Murphy, *Charles Joseph Kickham: Patriot, Novelist, and Poet,* Carraig Chapbooks 4 (Dulbin: Carraig Books, 1976; 1st pub. 1903). It has nine stanzas; Mr. Flanagan's five correspond to his 1, 4, 5, 6, and 7. P's editing heightens the song's power. Zimmermann, *Songs of Irish Rebellion,* pp. 245–47, tells how in 1857 Kickham read a news account of Patrick Sheehan, blinded in the Crimea, arrested and imprisoned for begging. Kickham wrote the song to discourage enlistment. Mr. Flanagan did not attribute "Aherlow" to Kickham, but he did attribute a song, "The Beauties of Limerick," which he sang (11/23/72t), to Kickham, and he proclaimed Kickham's great poem to be "She Lived Beside the Anner," which Kickham titled "The Irish Peasant Girl." Laws cites American texts. Australian: Meredith and Anderson, *Folk Songs of Australia,* pp. 88–89. Irish: Kenedy, *Universal Irish Song Book,* pp. 120–22; *617 Irish Songs,* p. 71; Yeats, *Book of Irish Verse,* pp. 176–79; *Songs and Recitations: Tara Brooch,* pp. 18–19; *Down by the Glenside,* pp. 28–29; Healy, *Irish Street Ballads,* 2:115–17; O'Keeffe, *First Book of Irish Ballads,* pp. 50–52. As usual these printings are not reports of performances, so fortunately there is a recording, *Willie McElroy of Brookeborough, Co. Fermanagh: The Fair of Enniskillen* (Belfast: Outlet, 1977), with a fine singing of "Paddy Sheehan," B2. Mr. McElroy's version is longer than Mr. Flanagan's, including Kickham's second and third stanzas, but he ends on the same dramatic stanza Mr. Flanagan does, dropping Kickham's last two, for the point was made and there was no need for the likes of Kickham's last verse:

> Then, Irish youths, dear countrymen,
>   Take heed of what I say;
> For if you join the English ranks,
>   You'll surely rue the day;
> And whenever you are tempted
>   A soldiering to go,
> Remember poor blind Sheehan
>   Of the Glen of Aherlow.

Aherlow

Sung by Peter Flanagan. Tune transcribed by Lore Silverberg.

♩. = c. 84

Ah, my name is Pat-rick Shee-han, and my years are thir-ty four.___ Ti-pper-
ra-ry is ___ my na-tive place,___ not far___ from Gal-ty-more.
I came of hon-est pa-rents,__ but now they're ly-ing low.___ And
___ ma-ny a plea-sant day I spent___ in the Glens__ of A-her-low.

"BALLINAMORE": Peter Flanagan, 7/23/72t (quoted), 8/13/72t, 11/18/72r. The tune is
Rosin the Bow. In the second recording he reversed the order of the second
and third stanzas and changed the second half of stanza 3 to: "God pity those
brave Irish heroes / The steel ring is closing round fast / And there in the midst
of their boyhood / This evening on earth being their last."

"THE SASH": Ellen Cutler, 7/20/72r, 8/7/72t, 8/11/72t (quoted). Both times we recorded she played "The Sash," "We Guard Old Derry's Walls," "Dolly's Brae,"
and "The Enniskillen Dragoon"—as well as "Miss McCloud's Reel" and "We're
Off to Dublin in the Green"—on the harmonica, the "mouth organ" she
bought on a lark in Bundoran, and she sang the chorus of "The Sash." On
8/12/72 she gave me a ballat of "The Sash," written out for her by a young
woman. I quote the ballat without change, except I substitute Mrs. Cutler's
sung chorus for the quite similar chorus of the ballat. She said there are two
versions of "The Sash," and she likes the old one better. The new one is called
"Queen's," she said, because it was made up by college students from Belfast.
Her ballat is the version in the song books: *The Purple Marksman: Book of Orange
Songs* (n.p., [c. 1920]), p. 95; Neil Graham, *The Orange Songster* (Glasgow:
James S. Kerr, [c. 1930]), p. 21; *Orange Songs and Ballads* (London: Toman Music
Publishers, [c. 1970]), pp. 4–5. Samuel B. Charters recorded a version at a pub
in County Down on *The Orangemen of Ulster*, FW3003 (New York: Folkways,
1961), B6. It employs the same chorus and consists of stanzas 1 and 2 of Mrs.
Cutler's ballat with another stanza, more strident, pointed, and political, in-
serted between.

"GLEN SWILLY": Peter Flanagan, 7/7/72r, 7/9/72t, 12/30/73t. He also plays the song's
melody as a "slow air" on the violin. Shields, "Irish Folk-Song Recordings,"
Ulster Folklife 21 (1975): no. 164; *Songs of the Old Turf Fire* (Dublin: Walton Songs,
1966), pp. 62–63; Jolliffe, *Third Book of Irish Ballads*, pp. 60–61.

"CASTLE GARDEN": Peter Flanagan, 7/9/72t. A fragment of this song appears in
Meredith and Anderson, *Folk Songs of Australia*, pp. 149–50.

"SKIBBEREEN": John O'Prey, 7/23/72t. Shields, "Irish Folk-Song Recordings," *Ulster
Folklife* 21 (1975): no. 368; Galvin, *Irish Songs of Resistance*, p. 46; *Songs of the Irish
Republic*, p. 48; *Reilly's Daughter*, p. 24; Healy, *Ballads from the Pubs*, pp. 80–81;

Castle Garden

Sung by Peter Flanagan. Tune transcribed by Lore Silverberg.

Fare - well my old a - cquain - tance,— my friends— both one and all.——— My lot is in A - me - ri - ca ——— to ei - ther rise ——— or fall. ——— From my ca - bin I'm e - vic - ted and like - wise com - pelled to go From that love - ly land called E - rin where— the green sham - rocks grow.

Skibbereen

Sung by John O'Prey. Tune transcribed by Lore Silverberg.

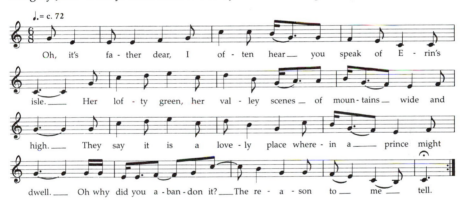

Oh, it's fa - ther dear, I of - ten hear— you speak of E - rin's isle.—— Her lof - ty green, her val - ley scenes — of moun - tains— wide and high. —— They say it is a love - ly place where - in a —— prince might dwell. —— Oh why did you a - ban - don it?——The re - a - son to — me — tell.

Bill Meek, *Songs of the Irish in America* (Dublin: Gilbert Dalton, 1978), pp. 60–61; Robert L. Wright, ed., *Irish Emigrant Ballads and Songs* (Bowling Green: Bowling Green University Popular Press, 1975), pp. 52–63, 682–83; McDonnell, *Songs of Struggle*, p. 61.

"NANCY MORGAN": Peter Flanagan, 7/9/72t.

"THE TURFMAN FROM ARDEE": Peter Flanagan, 8/23/72t. O Lochlainn, *More Irish Street Ballads*, pp. 46–47; *Songs of the Old Turf Fire*, p. 61; McGee, *Irish Songs*, p. 35.

"PAT MOLLOY": Peter Flanagan, 8/23/72r, 8/27/72t. This is not Laws Q24, but apparently it is Shields, "Irish Folk-Song Recordings," *Ulster Folklife* 21 (1975): no. 314.

"THE BATTLE OF LIMERICK": Peter Flanagan, 11/12/72t, 11/18/72r. His song got great response in Swad. Those around him, including Martin Crudden, said they had never heard it. It tells of Sarsfield intercepting a convoy coming from Dublin to the siege of Limerick at two o'clock in the morning, August 12, 1690, near the castle of Ballyneety. Mr. Flanagan explained the third stanza: "Sarsfield" was the password in William's camp. Sarsfield learned that and used his own name to enter and blow up their stores. Mr. Flanagan said he learned the song from a book, though he also heard it "sung around." It contrasts then with "Green-Robed Inisfail" (Chapter 29) which he said he learned from the singing of Mickey Shannon, though he also saw it in a book. P. W. Joyce gives a piece of a song about Sarsfield that is found within the third stanza of Mr. Flanagan's song in *Old Irish Folk Music and Songs*, p. 19. Out of such folksong fragments, his brother, Robert Dwyer Joyce, composed a poem, "Song of Sarsfield's Trooper," included in his works, edited by his brother after his death in 1883, *Ballads of Irish Chivalry* (Dublin: M. H. Gill, 1908), pp. 211–12. O'Hanlon reprinted it in his *Highwaymen in Irish History*, pp. 83–84. It consists of three double stanzas. Mr. Flanagan's text is close to R. D. Joyce's except he omits the first half of Joyce's second stanza to produce a song five, not six, stanzas in length. Other changes are small. In Joyce's first stanza, Sarsfield is "noble," rather than "gallant"; in the second, "Huge guns and tons of powder," rather than "Pontoons and carts of powder"; in the fourth, "Pontoons and carts and powder casks," not, "Pontoons and carts of powder"; in the fifth, "we," not "he" rode away; and consistently Joyce says "Limerick" where Mr. Flanagan says "Limerick town."

The Battle of Limerick

Sung by Peter Flanagan. Tune transcribed by Julie Górka.

"AN IRISHMAN'S TOAST": Peter Flanagan, 8/6/72t, 8/15/72r, 8/20/72r, 8/27/72t (quoted), 8/29/72t.

"ORANGE LILY": Ellen Cutler, 8/7/72t, 8/11/72t.

HUGH MCGIVENEY AND TERRY MAGUIRE: Michael Boyle 11/11/72t; Hugh Nolan 6/22/77t.

HUGH NOLAN, POET: Paddy McBrien, 7/28/72d; Peter Flanagan, 3/11/76d, 12/18/79d; Hugh Nolan, 6/11/77t.

An Irishman's Toast

Sung by Peter Flanagan. Tune transcribed by Lore Silverberg.

♩ = c. 132

Ire - land's the land__ of the harp and the sham - rock. Ire - land's the land __ of the

true and __ the good. Ire - land's the land __ of the true I - rish pa - tri - ots Who

shed for their coun - try, the last drop of blood. Here's · to the lake, to the

vale and the green moss,__ The harp and the sham - rock, the green flag and cross. And

here's to the he - roes that old Ire - land can boast,__ May their names never die;__ it's an

I - rish - man's toast.

Orange Lily

Played by Ellen Cutler on the harmonica. Transcribed by Julie Górka.

♩. = c. 108

JOHN O'PREY: Peter and Joseph Flanagan, 8/23/72d; Hugh Nolan, 8/14/78d.

JOHN O'PREY'S PANTS: Hugh Nolan, 8/23/72t, 8/30/72t, 6/16/77t (quoted), 12/18/79t.
Three of those times Mr. Nolan told both these stories. Once (8/23/72) he separated them with another tale of Mr. O'Prey bicycling violently through the police of Swanlinbar. The other two times (6/16/77, 12/18/79) he linked the stories and told them in the same order.

BOBBY BURNS AND THE LAWYER: Peter Flanagan, 11/12/72t, 11/23/72d, 12/29/73t, 12/17/79t. This is one of four bids of Bobby Burns that Mr. Flanagan learned from two sisters named Farmer for whom he worked for five or six years on a farm near the viaduct in south Fermanagh. He said his father knew some bawdy poems by Burns but would never tell them to him. Kiely, *State of Ireland*, pp. 217–18, tells the story of a comparable improvised couplet and says Burns is as much a part of our place, Ulster, as of his own Scotland. Burns' oeuvre does include brief spontaneous poems, some satirical and comparable to those Mr. Flanagan recites: J. Currie, ed., *The Works of Robert Burns* (London: T. Cadell, W. Davies, W. Creech, 1801), 3:341–42; 4:405; R. H. Cromek, ed., *Reliques of Robert Burns* (London: T. Cadell, W. Davies, 1808), pp. 411, 415–20. None of those poems are Mr. Flanagan's, but his poem is in oral tradition elsewhere in Ireland—Mackie L. Jarrell, "'Jack and the Dane': Swift Traditions in Ireland," *Journal of American Folklore*, 77, no. 304 (1964): 112, and Murphy *Now You're Talking*, p. 60—with Jonathan Swift, rather than Robert Burns, as star.

Index

Aarne-Thompson tale types: (67**),
739–40; (113A), 740, 743; (330), 78,
779, 803–4; (660), 739; (852), 738;
(1187), 538–40, 826; (1350), 761; (1529),
740; (1535), 78, 126, 804; (1889C), 50,
737, 741; (1890D), 51–52, 737, 803;
(1911A), 738–40; (1960D), 55, 568, 738,
803
Abbey Theatre, 73–74
Abrahams, Roger D., xv
Adamnan, 628, 649, 789
A. E. (George W. Russell), 50, 579, 584,
639, 641, 795
Agriculture. *See* Cabbage; Carts; Cattle;
Climate; Conacre; Drainage; Farm
implements; Farm planning; Farm
size; Fields; Gardening; Grass; Hay;
Hedges and ditches; Horses; Land-
scape organization; Measurement;
Outoffices; Pastoral economy; Po-
tatoes; Ridge-and-furrow; Soil; Turf;
Work
Aherlow, 687–88
Anderson, Master Andrew, 234, 698
Anderson, Eamon, 246, 698, 711
Anthropology, 13, 157, 707. *See also*
Culture; Ethnography; Functional-
ism; Structuralism
Architecture. *See* Decor; Framing;
Georgian architecture; Hearth;
House form; Masonry; Outoffices;
Thatching; Whitewash
Argenta, 671
Armstrong, Bob, 365, 367, 390, 397,
452, 528, 716
Armstrong, George, 38, 50–56, 59,
62–63, 179–80, 206, 227–28, 680–99,
706, 802

Armstrong, Jack, 241
Armstrong, Robert Plant, xvi, 371, 769
Arney, 19, 63, 72, 195, 262, 272, 274,
462, 490, 494, 606
Arney River, 5, 15, 106, 187–89, 191,
194–95, 200–201, 214–16, 422, 429, 518,
521, 581, 624, 630, 658, 682
Art and craft (aesthetics), 363–65,
369–71, 441–42, 444–49, 469, 483,
492–93, 520, 531, 567–69, 645, 761
Artifacts, 651–52. *See also* Artifactual
history; Material culture
Artifactual history, 491, 603–6, 608,
624–25. *See also* History
Ashe, Thomas, 251
Assaroe, 661
Attribution, 230–35, 443–44, 752–53,
815–16. *See also* Poet's role
Auchenleck memorial, 505
Aughrim, 377, 663, 690
Australia, 52, 55, 103, 226, 261

Ballads, 54, 126, 212, 275, 684–85,
687–88, 755, 831–32. *See also* Child
ballads; Laws ballads; Songs
Ballats, 57–58, 98, 235, 295, 670–71, 690
Ballinamore, 253, 255, 688
Balls, 74–77, 148, 280, 289
Ballyconnell, 260, 506, 509–11, 660
Ballymenone, 19, 26, 191, 204, 223, 243,
284, 288, 351, 581, 583, 603–4, 610,
612, 633, 682–83, 730–31
Ballyshannon, 659–61
Bands, 74, 97, 143, 222, 272–75, 278–81,
293, 298, 400, 623, 636, 654, 661, 673
Bards, 178
Barrows, 474, 476, 556, 565
Barry, Kevin, 294, 302–3, 686, 820

McCaffrey, John, 697–98, 710
McConnell, Cathal, 104, 670, 745
McConnell, Mary, 745, 802
McCourt, Mickey, 74–77, 698
McGiveney, Hugh, 38, 50–51, 62–63,
  73–74, 76–77, 202, 204–6, 214, 228,
  231–32, 272–76, 278, 285–86, 288, 297,
  429, 444, 510, 612–13, 679–80, 684,
  698–99, 708, 710, 716, 813–14
McGovern, James, 316, 323–25, 367,
  390, 430, 499, 583, 716
McGovern, Pat, 252–57
McGowan, Pat, 452
McGrath, John, 45–47, 49–50, 699
McHugh, Black Francis. See Black
  Francis
McHugh, Father Ned, 225–26, 294
McHugh, Phil, 273, 278
Mackan, 26, 222–23, 235, 239, 256, 286,
  288, 354, 444
Mackan Fight, 223–44, 253, 259–69, 271,
  275, 277–78, 283, 288, 293, 297–98,
  305, 404, 443, 518, 623–25, 635, 637,
  654, 661–64, 704–6, 814–15
Mackan, Hugh, 50, 130, 197, 390
MacManus, Eugene, 226
MacManus, Hugh, 234
MacManus, Hugh Patrick, 288, 591
MacManus, Ignatius, 226, 228, 230, 237,
  239, 243, 261, 268, 293–94, 302, 635
MacManus, John, 443
MacManus, Pat, 241
MacManus, Patrick, 82–83
MacManus, Seumas, 234, 743–45, 753
McMullen, John, 331, 337, 531, 535–36
MacMurrough, Art, 284, 289
McPhillips, Father Patrick, 672–73
MacStiofain, Sean, 250–51
Magh Sleacht, 626
Maguire, Cú Chonnacht, 634
Maguire, Frank, 234
Maguire, Hugh, 212, 376, 629–34
Maguire, James, 50, 273, 279, 293, 706
Maguire, John, 538
Maguire, John Joe, 443
Maguire, Master Mick, 49, 74, 77,
  229–32, 234–35, 238, 263, 679, 680,
  684, 698–99, 708, 710, 752, 815
Maguire, Terry, 279, 288, 698–99

Maguire, Thomas, 234
Maguires, chiefs of Fermanagh, 187,
  192, 197, 199–200, 272, 629, 657–60
Malinowski, Bronislaw, 576
Manchester Martyrs, 102, 286–87, 294,
  298, 303, 635–36, 638, 695, 818
Mangan, James Clarence, 488, 681
Märchen, 78, 126, 803–4. See Aarne-
  Thompson tale types; Fireside tales;
  Stories
Martin, Tommy, 44–45, 48–49
Martyrdom, 296–97, 302–3, 513, 706
Masonry, 189–90, 390, 414, 439, 476,
  502, 549, 562, 571. See also Brick-
  making; Mud construction; Sod
  construction
Material culture. See Art and craft;
  Artifacts; Artifactual history; Boats;
  Carts; Ceramics; Cooperage; Decor;
  Delph; Dresser; Farm implements;
  Farm planning; Firearms; Food;
  Framing; Furniture; Hearth; House
  form; Landscape organization;
  Masonry; Thatching; Transportation
Maxwell's Ball, 74–77, 682–98
May Day, 352, 355, 453, 534, 778. See
  also Calendar
Meaning, 33, 153–54, 520–22, 731, 786.
  See also Context theory
Measurement, 52–53, 205, 228, 232,
  428, 464
Medicine, 139–40, 243, 307. See also
  Cures
Memorat. See Experiences; Personal
  narratives
Memory, 553–55, 558. See also Context
  theory; Meaning; Performance theory
Mercier, Vivian, 50, 468
Metaphor, 276–77, 297. See also
  Proverbs and proverbial phrases
Methal, 293, 304, 485, 581, 775, 782.
  See also Cooperative work;
  Neighborliness
Milesians, 256–58, 753
Milton, John, 643
Mitchel, John, 249
Modernization, 150, 486–91, 614, 704–5,
  716
Mogey, John, 633

O'Clery, Michael, 632, 634, 754
O'Connell, Daniel, 246, 268, 635, 695
O'Connor, Sir Donough, 656, 660
O'Connors, chiefs of Sligo, 660
O'Donnell, Sir Hugh, 630, 656
O'Donnell, Red Hugh, 207–17, 233, 293, 629–33, 648, 656–58, 661, 695, 791, 814
O'Donnells, chiefs of Donegal, 208, 211, 213, 629, 657
O'Faolain, Sean, xix
O'Hanlon, Feargal, 82–83, 294–96. See also South, Sean
Ó hEoghusa, Eochaidh, 212
Ó Huiginn, Tadhg Dall, 630
Oliver, Willie, 676–77, 679, 681, 711
Omagh, 48
O'Neill, Art, 629
O'Neill, Henry, 629
O'Neill, Hugh, 84–85, 629–33, 638–39
O'Neills, chiefs of Tyrone, 209, 211, 213, 629, 657–58
O'Prey, Mr. and Mrs. John, 294, 379, 381, 397, 422, 583, 691–92, 699–706, 715–18
O'Prey, Steve, 700, 718
Oral history, 637, 660–61, 793–94. See also History; Stories of history
Orange Lodge, 19, 218–22, 276, 331, 511, 581, 690
Orange Peggy, 274–76
O'Reilly, Francis, 131–36, 141–42, 153, 163, 639
O'Reillys, chiefs of Cavan, 199–200
Organic order (cultural principle) 361, 379, 384, 391, 460, 468–69, 487, 603, 645. See also Conservative extension; Continuity
Outlaws, 513, 548, 781. See also Black Francis; Rapparees
Outoffices, 344–49, 380, 390, 415, 465, 502. See also Farm planning
Owens, Andy, 194
Owens, Mr. and Mrs. Hugh Patrick, 17, 175–76, 190–94, 200, 212, 259–63, 266, 272, 277, 283, 324, 355, 359, 367, 388, 391, 396, 416, 421, 428, 451, 461–63, 475–77, 492–95, 500, 506–8, 513, 528–29, 552–55, 562, 589, 603, 607, 611, 623–24, 663, 705, 716
Owens, James, 289, 293

Owens, James and Annie, 176, 181, 191, 194–96, 200, 367, 388, 391, 397, 500–501, 532–33, 578, 612, 623, 661–62, 717
Owens, Mr. and Mrs. James of the Ford, 187–89, 191, 196, 664, 717
Owens, John, 187, 192, 211, 260, 533, 607
Owens, Maurice, 192, 813, 825
Owens, Michael, 475, 476–77, 494
Owens, Phil, 194, 347
Owens, Thomas, 175, 260–63, 277, 358–59, 664
Owens, T. P., 494, 532

Palladius, 626
Panofsky, Erwin, 521
Pant: narrative genre, 45–47, 49–56, 59, 69, 227, 458, 565, 568, 700–704; examples of, 45–49, 51–54, 458, 612, 700–704. See also Stories
Parnell, Charles Stewart, 251, 635–36, 639–40, 674
Passing the time (cultural principle), xiii, 462–63, 466–69, 472–73. See also Continuity; Doing the best; Happiness; Time
Pastoral economy, 16, 425–38, 460, 466–67, 532. See also Farm planning; Farm size; Landscape organization
Paterson, T. G. F., 750
Patience, 488, 513. See also Despair; Doing the best; Hope; Passing the time; Time
Patrick, Saint, 162–63, 165, 170–72, 174–76, 179, 183, 211, 249, 252–55, 257–58, 287, 289, 293, 301, 303, 307, 355–56, 372, 378, 444, 464, 489, 612, 623, 626–27, 637–38, 641, 645, 647–48, 654, 660, 696, 706, 788–89
Patrick's Day, 175, 279, 353, 452. See also Calendar
Pearse, Padraic, 294, 636
Penal Tree, 189
Performance theory, xv, 111–12, 118–19, 124–25, 131, 136–47, 148, 155–56, 263, 643. See also Context theory; Hymes, Dell; Structuralism
Perrott, Sir James, 630–32, 634
Personal narratives: genre, 59–62, 236, 240–42, 557–58, 741–42; examples of,